Companies

COMPANIES ACT 2006

A Guide to the New Law

Gary Scanlan, Andrew Harvey, Terence Prime and Tunde Ogowewo

Consultant Editor: *Mark Lewis*

The Law Society

Crown copyright material is reproduced with the permission of the Controller of Her Majesty's Stationery Office

ISBN 978-1-85328-568-4

Published in 2007 by the Law Society
113 Chancery Lane, London WC2A 1PL

Typeset by J&L Composition, Filey, North Yorks
Printed by Antony Rowe Ltd, Chippenham, Wilts

CONTENTS

PREFACE

The writing of this guide upon the Companies Act 2006 proved a somewhat daunting task. The Act seemingly grew without logic or purpose over the summer and autumn of 2006, the decision to produce a codification of the law was taken at the eleventh hour, leaving a considerable amount of material to be introduced after the standing committee had concluded its work, thus requiring frequent last minute re-evaluations of the approach to be taken to this latest codification reform and consolidation of company law. It must be said that although some degree of reform was undertaken by the Act, the Act ultimately proved itself a considerable disappointment in this regard. The Act must therefore be considered a wasted opportunity that will not likely reoccur in a generation. However, there was a view expressed at the time by numerous commentators that the Act offered real achievements, particularly in the areas of deregulation and attention to the needs of private companies; it remains to be seen whether those aspects of the Act described as modernisation and codification of the law will call for interpretation by the courts. We hope that this guide will prove useful for the practitioner who needs to advise clients as to the ramifications of the new Act, and the possible pitfalls that may arise in the day to day application of its provisions.

We would like to thank Simon Blackett the Commissioning Editor who conceived of the need for the book, and who calmly and efficiently managed it through the many difficulties that such projects always give rise to. Marie Gill as Production Editor carried out the thankless task of editing the text with great skill and speed, rendering the reading of proofs, always the most tedious of tasks, the easiest and smoothest part of the production of the book. The manuscripts were up to date as at 20 December 2006.

Gary Scanlan, Andew Harvey,
Terence Prime and Tunde Ogowewo
April 2007

ABOUT THE AUTHORS

Gary Scanlan is a solicitor and Reader In Law at City University, London. His books on the *Law of Limitation* and *Partnership* with Professor Terence Prime have been cited in Law Commission Reports both in England and other common law jurisdictions. His books and articles are frequently cited in the courts, including the House of Lords.

Andrew Harvey is a solicitor with many years' experience in the design and delivery of legal education and training. He currently lectures for Central Law Training on company and commercial law subjects. He was co-author of the textbook *Business Law & Practice* and its companion volume *Business Law & Practice: Legislation Handbook*.

Terence Prime is a solicitor and was formerly Professor of Law at the University of East Anglia. He is the author of many books including *Law of Limitation* and *Partnership* (with Gary Scanlan) and *Law and Practice of Joint Ventures* (with Gary Scanlan and Sarah Gale).

Tunde Ogowewo is a solicitor, barrister (Middle Temple), and senior lecturer in law at King's College, London. He is the author of numerous articles and *The Market for Corporate Control and the Investments and Securities Act 1999*.

Consultant editor

Mark Lewis is a partner in the corporate team at Wright Hassall and has particular experience in mergers and acquisitions, charities and other not for profit organisations, joint ventures, LLPs and partnership law. He has been a contributing editor of *Butterworths Corporate Law Service* for over 15 years and is also a contributing editor of *Butterworths Company Law Guide*.

TABLE OF CASES

TABLE OF STATUTES

TABLE OF STATUTORY INSTRUMENTS AND EUROPEAN LEGISLATION

Statutory instruments

Table of European legislation

1 INTRODUCTION: BACKGROUND TO THE ACT

GENESIS OF THE ACT

1.1 The Companies Act 2006 (the 2006 Act), originally named the Company Law Reform Bill, was born from a plethora of consultations and documents emanating from the Government, the Department of Trade and Industry (DTI) and the Company Law Reform Review Steering Group. The various consultation documents produced by the Company Law Review Steering Group formed the background and impetus for reform of company law (these documents are available at the DTI's website (**www.dti.gov.uk**) – see URN 99/1144 on company general meetings, URN 99/1145 on company formation and capital maintenance and URN 99/1146 on overseas companies). Finally, the Company Law Review produced its Final Report, which in the words of Lord Sainsbury in the House of Lords during the introduction of the Bill on its second reading on 11 January 2006 was a 'thorough and authoritative assessment of the changes that need to be made and is the essential blueprint for the reforms we now propose' (see Hansard Vol.677 No.85 Col.181). The Final Report and the Company Law Review consultations are available on the DTI's website.

The White Papers

1.2 From this thorough examination of the issues which formed the impetus and background to the case for reform of company law, the Government produced two White Papers in 2002 and 2005, with further consultations on specific proposals following their publication. (The 2002 White Paper 'Modernising Company Law' and the 2005 White Paper 'Company Law Reform Bill' are both available from the DTI's website.) The 2005 White Paper set out a draft Bill (which consisted of some 300 clauses) which, together with further clauses made available for public comment in July, September and October 2005, formed the basis for the Bill eventually introduced into the House of Lords early in 2006 as the Company Law Reform Bill (see **para.1.4**). Other useful websites considering company law reform are listed at **para.1.42**.

1.3 Although the documents prepared and published during this review are extensive and cover a period of seven years, the 2005 White Paper constituted an admirable summary of the Government's rationale behind the proposed reform of company law, and was instrumental in determining, as noted above, the ultimate form of the Bill introduced into the House of Lords and to a lesser degree the subsequent Act (whether the Act achieved these laudable aims is however, a moot point: see **para.1.38**). Throughout the opening chapters of this book reference will be made to these documents and in particular to the 2005 White Paper.

The Government's response

1.4 Unlike earlier reviews and proposals for company law reform, the Government responded to the above White Papers by publishing a draft Bill. This was to some extent based on the draft Bill set out in the 2005 White Paper, but with further modifications and additions, based in part on subsequent consultations (see **para.1.2**). As introduced into the House of Lords on 1 November 2005 and on its second reading in the House of Lords on 11 January 2006 (see Hansard Vol.677 No.85 Col.180), the Bill had 885 clauses. Repeated and persistent calls for a rationalisation and consolidation of the legislation governing company law, and a considerable extension of the Bill during its passage through Parliament resulted in a Companies Act which, in the words of Lord Sainsbury constituted:

in effect . . . a complete code of company law. All the company law provisions of the 1985, 1989 and 2004 Acts have been brought into the Bill, other then the self-standing provisions on community enterprise companies and the provisions on investigations which go wider than in companies . . .

(Hansard Vol.686 No.204 Col.431)

1.5 Lord Sainsbury in moving the Bill for its second reading in the House of Lords noted that the Bill as originally drafted repealed about two-thirds of the Companies Acts 1985 and 1989. It is interesting to note the view of the Government as to why the original Bill did not constitute a consolidation where Lord Sainsbury stated:

The legislation has been reordered and redrafted in clearer language to make it much easier for companies of whatever size to understand the requirements on them . . . Noble lords may ask why the Bill is not a complete consolidation of existing company law. That is largely a case of reflecting the views of those whom we consulted. They told us that they wanted to see restatement of the areas which were of day-to-day relevance but not to see provisions reworked for the sake of it.

(Hansard Vol.677 No.85 Cols.181–182)

1.6 Lord Sainsbury also gave another reason for not seeking to consolidate all company law into a single Act. He noted that the law on capital maintenance is the subject of Government pressure for reform in the EU, and that consolidation of all company law legislation would therefore have to await such reform.

1.7 It is submitted that the reasons propounded by the Government against consolidation of company law were unconvincing, albeit that the consolidation 'in effect' that was eventually achieved by the Act may not be without its own problems in view of the nature of the drafting of the provisions of the Act, which may be considered in many instances to lack coherence and structure.

OUTLINE OF THE ORIGINAL BILL

1.8 The Bill as introduced to the House of Lords on 11 January 2006 (and which was subsequently enacted in a modified, albeit an enlarged form), was divided into two volumes. Volume I contained clauses 1–481, and Volume II contained clauses 482–885 and the Schedules to the Bill. The Bill in its original form will be considered briefly below, first because much of this Bill was subsequently enacted, and secondly because it is instructive to note the degree to which the rationale of the Bill as represented by the Bill in its initial form was compromised by the subsequent addition of more than 400 extra clauses.

Anatomy of the Bill

Company formation and constitution

1.9 Clauses 1–111 comprised Parts 1–7 of the Bill and dealt, inter alia, with the definition of companies which were to be subject to the Bill, company formation and registration, the company's constitution, the company's capacity, the selection of its name and the company's registered office, and the re-registration of a company as a means of altering its status. This part of the Bill was enacted with virtually no amendment as Parts 1–7 of the 2006 Act. Chapter 5 relating to the use of company names was supplemented by the enactment of Part 41 of the Act, which re-enacted the essential provisions of the Business Names Act 1985.

Company members and directors' duties and powers

1.10 Clauses 112–238 comprised Parts 8–10 of the Bill which in the case of Parts 8 and 10 were subdivided into Chapters. Part 8 dealt with matters relating to members of the company, the register of members and miscellaneous issues. Part 9 was intended to ensure that companies can enable indirect investors to exercise governance rights. This aspect of the Bill recognised that investors holding their shares in listed companies frequently hold their investment through intermediaries, usually by way of nominee holdings. This results in these kinds of investors relying on contractual arrangements both to obtain information about the company's affairs and to give instructions as to how they wish shares to be voted. The Bill sought to 'enhance the engagement' of these parties in the affairs of their companies.

1.11 Part 10 was and remained a central part of the Bill, and formed a crucial aspect of the Bill in so far as it attempted to bring about significant reforms to company law. Part 10 sought to effect reforms to the law relating to the regulation of the conduct of company directors. The central aspect of this reform related to the codification of the law, which constituted radical reform of the law relating to directors. This last aspect of the Bill was subject to fierce criticism in the press even before the Bill had gone into committee. These clauses were then subject to further trenchant criticism during the passage of the Bill through Parliament (see **Chapter 4**). These provisions with little amendment, but some additional clauses, were enacted as Parts 8–10 of the 2006 Act.

Derivative actions and secretaries

1.12   Clauses 239–257 comprised Parts 11 and 12 of the Bill. Part 11 was divided into two Chapters and sought to effect reforms to the law relating to derivative actions in both England and Wales and Scotland. Part 11 thus dealt with the mechanisms by which members may enforce directors' duties on behalf of the company. It attempted to implement the recommendation of the Law Commission that there should be more modern and flexible and accessible criteria for determining whether a shareholder can pursue such an action (see Hansard Vol.677 No.85 Col.185 and Law Commission Consultation Paper No.142 'Shareholder Remedies').

1.13   Part 12 related to the role of company secretaries, and empowered a private company to operate without the need for a company secretary. These clauses were substantially enacted (albeit in the case of the provisions of Part 12 with some technical amendments) as Parts 11–12 of the 2006 Act. Clauses were subsequently inserted into the Bill during its passage through Parliament relating to authorised signatories but these were then deleted from the Act.

Company meetings and political donations

1.14   Clauses 258–352 originally comprised Parts 13 and 14 of the Bill. Part 13, divided into seven Chapters, effected reforms to the law relating to company meetings. Part 14 concerned the regulation and the control of political donations and expenditure involving companies. These clauses were eventually enacted as Parts 13 and 14 of the 2006 Act.

Company accounts and auditors

1.15   Clauses 353–524 originally comprised Parts 15 and 16 of the Bill. Part 15 and its 13 Chapters dealt with company accounts. The seven Chapters of Part 16 dealt with, inter alia, the appointment and the removal of auditors and the need for audited accounts; however, the exemption from these requirements for small companies was preserved.

1.16   Even during the introduction of the Bill at its second reading Lord Sainsbury, the Under Secretary of State, noted that the Chancellor had announced the Government's intention to repeal the operating and financial review provisions set out in the Bill (see Part 15, Chapter 6 of the original Bill) as they applied to quoted companies, and amending regulations to that effect were laid before Parliament on 15 December 2005. The Parliamentary Under Secretary further informed the House of Lords of the intention of the Government to bring forward appropriate amendments to the relevant parts of the Bill to reflect this change of approach and policy with regard to quoted companies. It was intended to invite comments from the business world before publishing the proposed amendments. At the time of the introduction of the Bill on 11 January 2006 it was envisaged that the process of 'consultation' would be completed by 15 February 2006.

1.17 The repeal of these provisions was criticised from a number of members of the Upper House during the introduction of the Bill to that Chamber on the basis that many quoted companies had already instituted changes in business practice in anticipation of the enactment of the relevant clauses as set out in the Bill. Lord Sainsbury on behalf of the Government justified the removal of the operating and financial review from quoted companies on the basis that '. . . the costs associated with it were . . . disproportionate. It was about £33 million, of which £31 million was extra audit' (see Hansard Vol.677 No.85 Col.246). These clauses, as amended, were enacted as Parts 15–16 of the 2006 Act and were supplemented by Part 42 of the Act.

Private and public companies and share capital and allotments

1.18 Clauses 525–616 originally comprised Parts 17–21 of the Bill. Part 17 was divided into two Chapters which dealt, inter alia, with private and public companies and the prohibition of public offers of securities by public companies, and minimum share capital requirements for public companies. Part 18 dealt with the allotment of shares, and Part 19 was concerned with the share capital requirements of companies. Part 20 provided for the regulation of the transfer of company securities and Part 21 dealt with the legal obligation of companies with regard to the provision of information concerning interests in company shares. Following amendment and considerable additions, these clauses were enacted as Parts 17–24 of the 2006 Act.

Company takeovers and investigations

1.19 Clauses 617–654 comprised Parts 22 and 23 of the Bill. Part 22, which was divided into three Chapters, dealt with company takeovers and the Takeover Panel. These provisions would seek to implement the European Directive on Takeover Bids (Directive 2004/25/EC). Part 23 dealt with company investigations. These clauses with amendments were enacted as Parts 28 and 32 of the 2006 Act. Part 27, concerning mergers and divisions of public companies, was incorporated into the Act at a very late stage, just prior to the Act receiving the Royal Assent.

Companies not formed under the Act and unregistered companies, miscellaneous matters

1.20   Clauses 655–885 comprised Parts 24–37 of the Bill. Part 24, divided into two Chapters, dealt with companies not formed under the 2006 Act and unregistered companies. These provisions were enacted as Part 33 of the Act.

1.21   Overseas companies were dealt with in Part 25 which was enacted as Part 34 of the 2006 Act. Part 26 dealt with the registrar of companies and was enacted as Part 35 of the Act. Part 27 effected amendments to offences prescribed under the Companies Act 1985 (the 1985 Act) and was enacted as Part 36 of the Act.

1.22   Parts 28 and 29 dealt respectively with miscellaneous matters relating to companies, including the requirement to keep certain company records and was enacted as Part 37 of the Act. Part 29 was concerned with the interpretation of provisions in the Bill and with amendment was enacted as Part 38 of the Act. Part 30 sought, inter alia, to repeal certain provisions of the 1985 Act, which were principally concerned with the powers of the Secretary of State with regard to companies. This Part was substantially enacted as Part 39 of the Act.

1.23   Part 31 dealt with the increased power of the Secretary of State to reform company law by a new procedure known as a company law reform order, which would be subject to the affirmative resolution procedure; however this was subsequently lost.

1.24   Part 32, divided into three Chapters, inter alia, sought to regulate the law relating to restrictions on the use of certain business names by companies, including the use of such names by an individual or partnership carrying on a business in the United Kingdom under a business name and was enacted as Part 41 of the Act.

1.25   Part 33 of the Bill, divided into six Chapters, sought to regulate the position of statutory auditors and this became Part 42 of the Act. Part 34 dealt with miscellaneous provisions, which included making amendments to the transparency and corporate governance provisions of Part 6 of the Financial Services and Markets Act 2000 and was enacted as Part 43 of the Act.

1.26   Part 35 of the Bill enabled the Bill on enactment to apply to Northern Ireland. Part 36 dealt with the making of regulations and orders under the Bill on enactment by way of statutory instrument, and also dealt with consequential repeals, and transitional provisions. By Part 37 of the Bill the extent of the Act and the commencement of its provisions on enactment was set out. These provisions were reproduced at the end of the Act. Further provisions were added to the Bill during its passage, and these will be considered in the appropriate chapters of this book. In particular **Chapter 10** will consider these 'miscellaneous' provisions which were tacked on to the end of the 2006 Act without any rationale or logic.

Commencement of the Act

1.27   As in the case of most major legislation, much of the 2006 Act is to come into force by order of the Secretary of State or the Treasury. It is very much to be hoped that the Act will be promptly brought into force, although previous experience of company law legislation suggests that this may not be the case, with consequential confusion and uncertainty. In fact developments during the passage of the Bill suggest that further company legislation may be enacted, and that the 2006 Act will be brought into force piecemeal from 2008 onwards, with the prospect that some of the provisions may be repealed and enacted, perhaps in amended form, in later legislation – hardly an improvement on the previous state of affairs.

ECONOMIC BACKGROUND TO THE BILL

1.28   The Parliamentary Under Secretary of State, Department of Trade and Industry, Lord Sainsbury of Turville in moving the second reading of the Bill in the House of Lords gave the economic grounds for reform of company law in the following terms:

> One Hundred and Fifty years ago, my predecessor Robert Lowe, later First Viscount Sherbrooke, brought forward the Bill that created the joint stock limited liability company. It was the first nationwide codification of company law in the world, and he has recently been described as the 'the father of modern company law'. Our company law continues to have an excellent record. Since 1997 new incorporations have risen by over 60 per cent and the number of foreign firms incorporating in the UK has more than quadrupled. No doubt this is because, according to the World Bank's assessment, it is quicker and cheaper for companies to set up in the UK than in any other EU member state.
>
> We think that improvements can still be made, companies operate internationally and recent legal judgments make cross-border incorporation easier. Overseas owners hold around a third of the stock in listed UK companies – more than twice the level in 1993. If we want these owners to continue to invest in UK companies, we need them to retain their confidence in our system of corporate governance.

> (Hansard Vol.677 No.85 Col.180)

Simplification of operation of companies and saving on costs

1.29   Lord Sainsbury also noted that the reforms to company law were needed to make the operation of the small private company simpler and less expensive, in view of the fact that over 95 per cent of companies in the United Kingdom had five or fewer shareholders. It was expected that the enactment of the Bill would produce savings in the operation of business in the region of £250 million of which £100 million would benefit small private limited companies. As so often in the case of such predications, the Government gave no source or basis for these figures.

AIMS OF THE BILL

Simplifying and modernising company law

1.30   The principal aims of the Bill in its original form could therefore be summarised as simplification and modernisation of company law. It accordingly sought to 'enhance shareholder engagement', and to promote a long-term investment culture, ensuring better regulation of business. By adoption of a policy of, inter alia, further and substantial deregulation of the small company, the Bill also sought to achieve a better climate for the small business man to operate his affairs, unencumbered by excessive and unnecessary regulation and 'red tape'. One of the principal aims of the Bill was to encourage what the Government considered should be a 'think small first' approach to company formation.

1.31   The Bill thus provided, in the Government's view, a regime whereby private companies could be formed and operated with little by way of formality, even permitting 'electronic incorporation'. The rules of formation for private limited companies were thus to be simplified, and the need for a private company to have a company secretary was abolished, as were compulsory annual general meetings. In addition, there would be a move towards the greater use of written resolutions in such companies.

Shareholder engagement – long-term investment culture

1.32   The other policies expounded in the Bill to promote 'shareholder engagement' and thereby a 'long-term investment culture' and better regulation of business were nevertheless stated to be equally as important as the 'think small first' policy. These policies were to be achieved by, inter alia, enhancing the powers available to proxies, and thereby to make it easier for indirect investors to be informed of the company's affairs and consequentially to exercise governance rights in the company, albeit initially on a voluntary basis (see Part 9 of the Bill and **para.1.10**). It was noted that over 40 per cent of investment in quoted companies is held in nominee accounts (see Hansard Vol.677 No.85 Col.217 per Baroness Murphy).

General theme of the Bill

1.33   The Bill had a general theme of modernisation and reform of company law. This aspect of the Bill was most effectively illustrated in respect of the reform of the law relating to director's duties, albeit that these provisions remained controversial. However, reform to the law relating to the auditing of company accounts was also regarded by the Government as radical and not without its difficulties (see **para.1.15–1.16.**).

1.34   Finally the Bill sought to provide for a means by which further company law reform (subject to Parliamentary scrutiny), could be effected faster and more easily than in the past, albeit that this reform was not eventually adopted (see para.1.23).

Conclusion

1.35   In concluding the debate that followed the introduction of the Bill in the House of Lords, Lord Sainbury expressed the hope of the Government as to the effect of the Bill in the following terms:

> This is a long Bill but it will bring significant improvements in many areas of company law. It has the potential to bring significant savings for business, delivers on the 'think small first' principle, and updates the law for the benefit of our largest companies. It also benefits investors. Many people have been involved in the thinking behind this Bill and we are very grateful for all the input we have received. The reason why the Bill has been so widely welcomed is due to the close involvement over a number of years of so many interested parties. I trust that it will attract a similar degree of support from this House, and commend the Bill to the House.
>
> (Hansard Vol.677 No.85 Col.185)

1.36   Only time will tell whether this seemingly self-satisfied approach of the Government, at least with respect to certain provisions of the Bill, was justified.

HISTORY OF THE BILL

1.37   The Bill was introduced into the House of Lords for its second reading on 11 January 2006. It passed through the Committee Stage of the House of Lords by 24 May 2006, when the Bill received its third reading in that House. Following the Report Stage in the House of Commons the Bill reappeared, having been considerably extended to some 47 Parts and over 1,250 clauses. It was printed in that form on 20th July 2006 having passed through the Lords to the Report Stage and passed with indecent haste through the House of Commons Committee D. By the Report Stage in the House of Commons in October–November 2006 the Bill had been further enlarged to some 1,300 clauses. The Act received Royal Assent on 8 November 2006.

Criticism of the Act

1.38   Despite its sheer bulk, as it stands the 2006 Act constitutes a disappointment when the decade of Reviews, White Papers and Reports on company law reform which pre-dated it are considered. The general dissatisfaction with the Bill brought forth calls for the enactment of further company law legislation. The prospect thus beckons of provisions of the 2006 Act never being brought into force, and replaced by later provisions in subsequent legislation, continuing the current state of affairs where company law must be discerned from a number of disparate and piecemeal sources. It is difficult to see how the original philosophy which underpinned the stated aims of the Bill, including accessibility and clarity, are promoted by the Act in its final form.

1.39   Although reform has been achieved, substantial or radical reform such as a minimum share capital requirement for private limited companies was eschewed. The reforms set out in the Act are limited and, for example, even the expansion of the use of electronic means in both forming companies and maintaining company records may give rise to a number of practical difficulties.

1.40   The obsession with the use of plain language in the drafting of the provisions of the Act, and the consequential rejection of the use of recognised terms of art enshrined in previous legislation, in order to make the Act more 'accessible' to directors and those involved in the administration of company affairs may prove an ephemeral and illusory objective. It is difficult to conceive such a large piece of legislation as being 'accessible' to laymen. Furthermore, the use of 'plain' and 'ordinary' language in the Act to prescribe and define concepts in company law and the consequential rejection of 'terms of art' used in previous companies legislation to achieve these ends, despite the fact that such 'terms' were understood by company lawyers on the basis of their constant usage and judicial pronouncements, can it is suggested, only lead to uncertainty of application. In practice, the provisions of the 2006 Act will require considerable future judicial interpretation to give them clarity and form. With this prospect goes the possibility of judicial decisions on the ambit and nature of the provisions of the Act which will defeat the purported intention of the legislature. This can only make the situation for legal advisers more difficult.

1.41   The 'codification' and reform of directors' duties, for example with regard to approval of certain conflicts of interest with respect to a director and the company by the directors as a body, rather than by the members, hardly accords with one of the principal aims of the original Bill, namely the 'enhancing of shareholder engagement'. The future will reveal the degree to which these criticisms are valid, but the omens are not good.

USEFUL WEBSITES

1.42   Further information on aspects of company law and company law reform may be found on the following websites:

- Company Law and Governance (CLG) Consultations – **www.dti.gov.uk/cld-condocs.htm**
- Trade and Industry Select Committee (House of Commons) – **www.parliament.uk/parliamentary_comittees/trade_and_industry.cfm**
- Law Commission – **www.lawcom.gov.uk**
- Companies House – **www.companieshouse.gov.uk**

2 COMPANY FORMATION, CONSTITUTION AND OBJECTS

INTRODUCTION

2.1 One of the principal policies underpinning the 2006 Act is that it should constitute legislation which is accessible to all who operate their business as a company, and therefore the legislation was drafted without needless technical language. Accordingly Parts 1–7 of the Act make little substantive difference to the law relating to company formation and related matters. The major changes made by the Act from the previous provisions relating to company formation contained in the 1985 Act are generally limited to issues of terminology. Where substantive changes have been made, these are considered in some detail in the chapter.

Companies subject to the Act

2.2 The forms of company subject to the 2006 Act, other than those which are registered under the 2006 Act, include companies registered under previous Companies Acts such as those recognised by the 1985 Act. Companies subject to the 2006 Act also include the recently created Community Interest Company (see Part 2 of the Companies (Audit, Investigations and Community Enterprise) Act 2004). Certain unregistered companies are also subject to the Act (see Part 33), as was the case under the 1985 Act (see s.1 of the 2006 Act). 'The Companies Acts' are defined in s.2 as including the 2006 Act, Part 2 of the Companies (Audit, Investigations and Community Enterprise) Act 2004 and the unrepealed provisions of the 1985 Act. The 2006 Act effectively constitutes a consolidation of the law relating to companies (see **Chapter 1** for a consideration of how this state of affairs was achieved). The distinction between a private limited company and a public company is maintained by the Act (see s.4 and Part 20).

COMPANY FORMATION

2.3 In essence, the procedures for forming a company under the 2006 Act are similar to the law and practice prescribed under the 1985 Act, but the requirement of the memorandum of association to state the authorised share capital of a company has been abolished (see Company Law Review, Final Report, para.10.6).

There is now a requirement for the registration documents to state the share-holding of each subscriber (set out in a statement of capital and initial share-holdings) and for the statement of capital to contain, inter alia, a collective statement of the share capital held by the subscribers and the prescribed particulars of the rights attached to the shares (see s.10). Other matters which have previously been included in the memorandum of association such as the name and objects of a company will no longer be included. These are aspects of the Act which generally reduce the importance of the memorandum of association as a constitutional document of the company. This was explained by Lord Sainsbury during the passage of the Bill through the House of Lords, where the Under Secretary of State noted:

> I do not think there is any disagreement that it is important for third parties to be able to find out who forms a company; that is, who its first members are. This information is already required to be included in the memorandum by regulations under the current Act. As noble Lords know, a company's memorandum must be supplied to the registrar on formation and is available to the public once the company is formed. Under the Bill, . . . [and under the Act] . . . the memorandum is in future to perform a more limited purpose and contain significantly less information. Under the new architecture, the information about the shares to be taken will be provided in the company's statement of initial shareholdings instead . . . [subsequently modified in the Act to a combined statement of capital and shareholdings]. It is true that the Bill retains a power to prescribe the form for the new style memorandum, but this is about the prescribing of the form rather than its content.

> (Hansard Vol.678 No.96 Col.GC7)

2.4   It should also be noted that with effect from 1 January 2007, the registrar of companies offers an electronic incorporation facility. This procedure implements a recent amendment to the First Company Law Directive (Directive 68/151/EEC). The provisions in Part 2 of the 2006 Act were thus drafted with the objective of removing any obstacles to the formation of companies online.

Memorandum of association

2.5   The information which is to be set out in the memorandum of association is significantly circumscribed (see s.8 which replaces s.2 of the 1985 Act). Henceforth a memorandum of association is a memorandum which states that the subscribers:

(a) wish to form a company under the 2006 Act; and
(b) agree to become members of the company and to take at least one share each, in the case of a company with a share capital (s.8).

2.6   The policy behind the reduction of the role, function and importance of the memorandum as a constitutional document under the 2006 Act was further explained by the Under Secretary in the following terms:

It may be worth setting out what the memorandum of a company will be under the Bill (and the Act). The Company Law Review looked very carefully at the question of the company's constitution. It was keen to see the company's internal rules as far as possible set out logically in one place and pointed out the potential for over-lap under current arrangements between a company's memorandum and its articles.

In taking forward those valuable suggestions, we wanted to do away with any scope for confusion between the memorandum and the articles, and introduce a clear distinction between the information in the memorandum, which will be in effect an historical snapshot, which, once provided, has no continuing relevance, and the constitution of the company properly-so-called, as contained essentially in its articles, which will be of real significance in the company's life. In making this clear-cut distinction, I believe that the Bill introduces a valuable element of clarity to what can be a confusing picture under existing legislation.

(Hansard Vol.678 No.96 Col.GC3)

Companies registered under earlier Companies Acts

2.7   There is a transitional provision set out in s.28 concerning the status and effect of any provision set out in a memorandum of association of a company registered under any previous Companies Act, but which could only be set out in the company's articles of association under the provisions of the 2006 Act. In these cases provisions set out in a company's memorandum, but which are not provisions that under s.8 are required to be in the memorandum, are to be treated under the 2006 Act as provisions in the company's articles. This is the case whether or not the provisions would be regarded as entrenched provisions under the 2006 Act, s.22 (see **para.2.17** below).

2.8   Unfortunately the section does not provide for any mechanism to deal with the problems that may arise where a provision in the memorandum of such a company is under the terms of the 2006 Act to be regarded as a provision in the company's articles, and is found to be in conflict with a provision in that company's articles. Under case law prior to the enactment of the 2006 Act it was determined that in cases of conflict between provisions in the memorandum and the articles the former were to prevail (see *Guinness v. Land Corporation of Ireland* (1883) LR 22 ChD 349). There was no provision made by the law to deal with the problem where two articles conflict with one another. An amendment to deal with the issue of conflict of provisions in the memorandum and the articles in cases of companies incorporated under previous Companies Acts was promulgated by the Law Society but was rejected in the House of Lords during the passage of the Bill (see Hansard Vol.678 No.96 Col.GC24). This problem therefore remains unresolved and may need to be settled by the courts.

Summary of changes relating to company formation

2.9   The provisions of the 2006 Act thus reflect the Company Law Review proposals. The principal changes to the law on company formation may be summarised as follows:

(a) one person should be able to form any sort of company (see s.7 replacing s.1(1) and (3A) of the 1985 Act and the Company Law Review, Final Report, para.9.2);

(b) the key rules on the internal workings of the company must be in one document, namely the articles (see s.18 which replaces s.7 of the 1985 Act) and the memorandum will contain limited information only by way of 'an historical snapshot' (see **para.2.11** *et seq.* on the articles and **paras.2.5–2.8** on the memorandum);

(c) there should be separate model articles for private companies limited by shares and for public companies (see s.19) (see **para.2.11**).

CONSTITUTION

2.10   The principal documents of the company's constitution consist of the articles and any resolutions or agreements which affect the company's constitution (ss.17 and 29).

Articles for the various companies regulated by the Act (Part 3)

2.11   The 2005 White Paper recommended reform with regard to a company's constitutional documents, and in particular to the articles of association. The White Paper noted that Table A as a constitution governing companies subject to the 1985 Act contained numerous provisions that were irrelevant to many small companies. Table A was also regarded as '. . . user unfriendly, poorly laid out and often unintelligible to non-specialists' (see para.4.3 *et seq.* of the White Paper). The White Paper recommended therefore that the Bill contain a power of the Secretary of State to prescribe, by secondary legislation, stand-alone model articles for public companies, and for private companies limited by shares or by guarantee. This recommendation was adopted in the Bill, and was enacted as s.19 (replacing the 1985 Act, s.8).

Model articles for the small owner-managed company

2.12   The White Paper set out draft model articles for private companies limited by shares. Such articles were defined in the White Paper as 'private company articles' (see Chapter 8 of the White Paper). The White Paper envisaged that (see para.4.3 *et seq.*):

> The private company articles will replace Table A for those private companies limited by shares which are in the future formed under the 2006 Act and will play an important role in the simplification of the law for small companies. Like Table A the private company articles will apply by default where a company does not register its own articles at Companies House (to the extent that the company in question has not specifically excluded or modified the model articles).

This recommendation was enacted as s.20 of the 2006 Act. The old Table A will continue to provide the model articles for companies formed before the new model articles come into force.

2.13   The private company articles set out in the White Paper were drafted in accordance with the principles set out in the Company Law Review's Final Report. Thus what was described by the Company Law Review as 'archaic' and legalistic language has been avoided. It was intended that the new private company articles would be 'leaner', making them more accessible to directors and shareholders, particularly with regard to owner-managed private companies. Thus the draft model articles set out in the White Paper, which it is clearly envisaged will form the basis of the 'private company articles' prescribed by the Secretary of State for private limited companies under s.19, do not deal with issues which are already the subject of regulation under other provisions of the 2006 Act.

2.14   The rationale behind this approach to the private company articles was stated by the authors of the White Paper in the following terms:

> The private company articles contain the minimum number of rules which it is envisaged that a typical private company limited by shares will need and which the shareholders will want to have.
>
> Some or all of these rules may be suitable for less typical private companies, but if they are not, it will be open to any private company limited by shares which is using, or intends to use, the private company articles to add to, amend, or delete rules from the model articles as they see fit (as is the case with Table A), or to adopt completely 'bespoke' articles of their own.

> (White Paper, para.4.3 at p.35)

2.15   The authors of the White Paper gave an example of a lacuna in the private company articles. There are no provisions in the 'private company' articles set out in the White Paper relating to company general meetings. The rational of this lacuna is that procedures are already prescribed under the provisions of the 2006 Act, which the directors/shareholders of an owner-managed company may wish to use to conduct the company's general meetings rather than make provision in their articles. The authors noted:

> The private company articles do not include equivalent articles to the Table A provisions on general meetings. It is envisaged that the majority of private companies will want to take advantage of the new written resolution procedure . . . [see Part 13 Chapter 2] . . . and as such the majority of private companies limited by shares are unlikely to need detailed rules as to the procedure for calling, and the conduct of, meetings of the company's members.

> (White Paper, para.4.3 *et seq.* at p.35)

Alteration of the articles (ss.21–27)

2.16   A company may alter the provisions of its articles by special resolution (see s.21(1)), as was the case under the 1985 Act. However, as the constitutional documents of the company registered under the 2006 Act are constituted principally by the articles (together with any resolutions or agreements of the company: see s.29), the Act deals with the possibility of entrenching provisions of the articles. This was previously effected under the 1985 Act by inserting such provisions into the memorandum of association (in s.17 of the 1985 Act).

2.17   Under s.22(1), a company's articles may provide that specified provisions of the articles may be amended or repealed only if prescribed conditions are met or procedures complied with that are more restrictive than those in the case of a special resolution. These procedures constitute a 'provision for entrenchment'. Such a provision can only be made in the company's articles on formation (s.22(2)(a)), or by an amendment to the company's articles subsequent to formation secured by the unanimous agreement of the members of the company (s.22(2)(b)). Section 22(3) provides that a provision for entrenchment does not prevent amendment of the company's articles by agreement of all the members of the company, or by order of the court or other authority having power to alter the company's articles.

2.18   In all cases where a company's articles contain a provision for entrenchment, whenever created or made, or an entrenched provision is removed, or a court or other authority removes such a provision or removes any other restriction on or any exclusion of the power of the company to amend its articles, notice must be given to the registrar of companies of this fact (s.23). Amendments to the company's articles which relate to entrenchment provisions or to any order of the court or other authority restricting or excluding the company's power to amend the articles require any documents which evidence or make the amendment to be delivered to the registrar, together with a statement of compliance (s.24).

2.19   Section 25 in part reproduces s.16 of the 1985 Act in so far as that provision concerned the articles of association. It restricts the effect of certain amendments to the articles on the member of a company made subsequently to his becoming a member, and renders any provision in these circumstances which seeks to increase his liability ineffective, unless he agrees in writing to the terms of such a provision. Section 26 provides that a copy of any amended articles must be sent to the registrar. The obligation to send any amended articles only arises when the condition is satisfied and the amendment has taken effect (see s.26(1)). This provision ensures that the version of the articles which appears on the public register will be the version of the articles that is in force. Failure to send any documents required to be sent under the Act consequential on the amendment of the company's articles will result in the registrar issuing a notice requiring compliance with the Act. Failure to comply with the terms of the notice may result in civil penalties and criminal sanctions (see s.27(3)–(5)).

Summary of changes with regard to the constitutional documents

2.20   The principal changes to the law relating to the company's constitutional documents may be summarised as follows:

(a) The principal documents of the company's constitution consist of the articles and any resolutions and agreements affecting the company's articles (see ss.17 and 29; for a consideration of the issue of agreements and resolutions see **para 2.21** below).

(b) Members of the company are now able, either at the formation of the company or subsequent to formation, to choose to entrench elements of the company's articles, thus making certain provisions harder to amend subsequently than would otherwise be the case.

Resolutions and agreements

2.21   Section 29 reproduces with amendments s.380 of the 1985 Act. It sets out the resolutions and agreements that are made by a company which affect its constitution and which therefore must be forwarded to the registrar for registration. The view of the Government was that any changes in s.29 from the provisions of s.380 were not intended to be substantive changes. In the words of Lord Sainsbury:

> The clause restates the obligation currently contained in s380 of the Companies Act. The wording has changed somewhat, but only in the interests of clarity. I can confirm that no change is intended or, I believe, is made to the substance of the obligation, namely, that companies must provide the relevant documents within fifteen days.
>
> (Hansard Vol.678 No.96 Col.GC30)

2.22   Section 30 requires that copies of any resolutions and agreements prescribed under the section must be forwarded to and recorded by the registrar.

OBJECTS

2.23   The 2006 Act brings a change in approach to the issue of the company's objects. Instead of companies being required to specify their objects, all companies will under the 2006 Act have unlimited objects unless the objects are specifically restricted by the articles (see s.31(1)). Any change in the company's articles with regard to its objects must be notified to the registrar (see s.31(2)). Any such amendment will not affect any pre-existing rights or obligations of the company or render defective any legal proceedings by or against it (s.31(3)). The issue of capacity and the power of the directors to bind the company will be considered below.

2.24   Section 32 replaces s.19 of the 1985 Act. It gives members the right to receive from the company, free of charge, copies of the company's articles and other resolutions and agreements affecting a company's constitution to which Chapter 3 of Part 3 applies (see also s.29, considered above).

EFFECT OF A COMPANY'S CONSTITUTION

2.25 Section 33(1) of the 2006 Act replaces s.14(1) of the 1985 Act. The Contracts (Rights of Third Parties) Act 1999 does not apply to this provision, and the rights prescribed under the section (as was the case under the 1985 Act) apply only to the company and its members. The new section however refers to the company's constitution as opposed to the reference in the old s.14 to the memorandum and articles. Section 33(2) enacts the 1985 Act, s.14(2).

2.26 A company's constitution may be affected by the passing of legislation which is relevant to that particular class of company, as opposed to the passing of a generally applicable Companies Act. In these circumstances copies of such 'special enactments' (see s.34(4)) should be sent by any company so affected to the registrar.

2.27 Section 35 was a provision originally added to the Bill at the Committee stage. It provides a mechanism for registering alterations to a company's constitution made by an order of the court or other authority, such as the Charity Commissioners. It obliges a company to give notice of such alterations to the registrar unless provision is made by another enactment for the delivery to the registrar of a copy of the order in question.

2.28 Section 36 prescribes the documents (e.g. resolutions or agreements relating to the company to which Chapter 3 of Part 3 applies) that must accompany any copy of the company's articles issued by the company. However, there is no requirement to supply such 'accompanying' documents if the terms of s.36(2) are satisfied, thus there is no requirement if the resolution or agreement has been incorporated into the articles by amendment or is not for the time being in force (s.36(2)).

2.29 Section 37 replaces s.15 of the 1985 Act and provides that in the case of a company limited by guarantee provisions in the company's articles or in any resolution of the company which purport to give a person the right to participate in the profits of the company are void.

Single member companies

2.30 Since under the 2006 Act all types of company may be formed by a single person, s.38 provides that any enactment or rule of law applicable to companies formed by two or more persons or having two or more members applies to companies formed by, or having, a single member, as is the case already in respect of single member private limited companies.

CAPACITY, RELATED AND OTHER MATTERS

2.31 Sections 39 and 40 of the 2006 Act replace ss.35, 35A and 35B of the 1985 Act. By s.39 the validity of a company's acts cannot be contested on the ground of lack of capacity which arises as a consequence of any provision in the company's constitution. In this context the provision is similar to the old s.35(1) of the 1985 Act. However, s.39 does not contain any provisions equivalent to s.35(2) and (3) in the 1985 Act. The view of the drafters of s.39 is that since the 2006 Act provides for a company to have unrestricted objects unless there is an express restriction in the company's constitution (together with a restriction on the consequential power of the directors), when this is combined with the specific duty of the directors to abide by the constitution of the company (see s.171) any further provision with regard to the objects of the company is rendered otiose.

Third parties dealing with a company in good faith

2.32   Section 40 provides safeguards for third parties dealing with a company in good faith. The provision effectively replaces s.35A of the 1985 Act. It thus provides that any power of the directors to bind the company, or to authorise others to do so, is deemed to be unconstrained by the company's constitution. Accordingly, third parties dealing with the company in good faith need not enquire (see s.40(2)(b)(i)) nor concern themselves with the issue as to whether the directors are acting within the terms of the company's constitution.

Transactions involving directors or their associates

2.33   Section 41 preserves the principal aspects of s.322A of the 1985 Act. The provision applies to a transaction involving a company, which is dependent for its validity on s.40. The section determines that where a party to such a transaction is an 'insider', i.e. a director of the company, or a person 'connected' with a director (see s.41(2)(b)(i) and (ii)), then the protection afforded to a party by virtue of s.40 does not apply. Accordingly, the transaction as regards that party will be voidable at the instance of the company.

2.34   Furthermore, irrespective of the fact that such a transaction is voidable at the instance of the company, any director or 'insider' who authorised a transaction which is subject to s.41 is liable to account to the company for any gain made as a result of the transaction and to indemnify the company for any loss or damage incurred by the company (see s.41(3)). However, an 'insider', not being a director of the company, may avoid liability under the section if he can establish that, at the time he entered into the relevant transaction with the company, he was not aware that the directors involved in the transaction were exceeding their powers (see s.41(5)).

2.35   Any transaction will cease to be voidable under s.41 under any of the circumstances prescribed under s.41(4), the most likely event being that restitution of any money or asset the subject of the relevant transaction is no longer possible. Section 42 reproduces s.65 of the Charities Act 1993. It applies, inter alia, and in a modified form, the provisions of ss.39 and 40 of the 2006 Act to companies which are charities. The provision replaces ss.35(4) and 35A(6) of the 1985 Act.

Contracts, execution of documents, common seal and related matters

2.36   Section 43 re-enacts in part s.36 of the 1985 Act. The section provides that a company may enter into a contract in writing, under its common seal or by a person acting on behalf of the company under its authority, be it express or implied.

2.37   Under s.44, which essentially replaces s.36A of the 1985 Act, the ways in which a company may execute documents is prescribed. Apart from by the affixing of the company's common seal, a document may be executed by a company by signature of the company's officers. Under s.44(2) a company may execute a document by the signature of two authorised signatories (which includes directors or company secretaries), or by the signature of a sole director made in the presence of a witness who attests the signature. Such signatures are regarded as the equivalent of execution under the company's common seal (s.44(3)). A company may have, but is not required to have, a company seal (see s.45). If a company has a seal, the seal must include the company's name.

2.38   Section 46 deals with execution of deeds by companies and re-enacts s.36AA of the 1985 Act. Section 47 replaces s.38 of the 1985 Act, and provides that a company may appoint attorneys to execute deeds or other documents on its behalf, and that such execution shall have effect as if the documents were executed by the company. Section 48 applies only in Scotland. Section 49 simply re-enacts s.39 of the 1985 Act, prescribing the circumstances and manner in which a company may use its common seal outside the United Kingdom. Under s.50, which re-enacts s.40 of the 1985 Act, a company which has a common seal may also have an official seal for sealing securities issued by the company, and for sealing documents creating or evidencing securities which it issues.

Pre-incorporation contracts, deeds and obligations

2.39   Section 51 re-enacts s.36C of the 1985 Act. It deals therefore with the problem of contracts or other obligations entered into on behalf of the company by third parties prior to its incorporation. It has been established since *Kelner* v. *Baxter* (1866–67) LR 2 CP 174 that a company is not bound by a contract purportedly made on its behalf by third parties before it was incorporated and therefore came into existence, unless the contractual rights (or other obligations) are subject to a novation. Novation may be express or implied.

2.40   Section 52 re-enacts s.37 of the 1985 Act. By this provision, where a person authorised to act on the company's behalf makes, accepts or endorses a bill of exchange or promissory note in the company's name, or on the company's behalf, the action of that person is treated as the action of the company.

Indications of company type or legal form

2.41   Although not technically part of the formation process, the issue of the legal indicators which indicate the status of a company needs to be addressed. Sections 58 and 59 (which replace ss.25(1)–(2) and 27(4)(a)–(d) of the 1985 Act) therefore reproduce those indicators: s.58 for public limited companies and s.59 for private limited companies, namely whether a company is a private or public company.

2.42   Sections 60–62 replace s.30 of the 1985 Act. These provisions deal with the companies which are exempt from the requirements to conclude their name with the term 'limited'. Section 60 applies this 'exemption' to companies already exempt under previous Companies Acts, but extends the exemption to companies which are charities and to other companies to be exempted by regulations, which will include companies formed under the 2006 Act. Sections 61 and 62, which replace s.30(2) and (3) of the 1985 Act, specify the conditions that must be met for a company currently exempt in order to continue to qualify for exemption under the 2006 Act. Thus the constitution of the company, which should promote objects such as art or science must also, inter alia, continue to preclude distribution of dividends to its members, and in the event of being wound up, require its assets to be passed to a body with similar objects. These conditions are essentially the same whether the company is limited by shares or guarantee.

2.43   Section 63 replaces s.31(1) and (5) of the 1985 Act. It prohibits a company, benefiting from an exemption under the 1985 or previous Companies Acts, from changing its articles in such a way that it no longer meets the requirements for the exemption under s.64 (which replaces s.31(2)–(6) of the 1985 Act). The Secretary of State is given power to withdraw the exemption from a private limited company if it no longer meets the requirements or criteria that applied to the company when the exemption was granted.

2.44   Section 65 replaces s.26(1)(a), (b)–(bbb) of the 1985 Act. This provision restricts the use of various words, expressions and abbreviations as part of a company's name which are indicators of a commercial entity's legal status and are regarded as an inappropriate use of indications in the case of a given commercial entity of company type or legal form.

NAMES

Prohibited names

2.45   Companies, as in the case of all business organisations, are prohibited from using certain names when operating their business. The rationale behind this prohibition includes the need to ensure that the public are not misled as to the nature of the business or are led to believe that the enterprise enjoys an association with e.g. government departments. Although the law relating to passing off and trademarks play a pivotal role in this aspect of the law, company legislation also provides for certain restrictions on the use of names by companies.

2.46   Sections 53–57 of the 2006 Act thus reproduce ss.26 and 29 of the 1985 Act. By these provisions a company cannot register a name which would constitute an offence or be otherwise offensive (see s.53). Nor can a company register a name which suggests association or connection with government or a local or public authority (see s.54), or which uses words that constitute 'sensitive' words or expressions (see s.55), unless there is prior approval from the Secretary of State. Under s.56 the Secretary of State is empowered to specify whose views must be sought when seeking approval of a name, for example a professional regulatory body if the company name proposed suggests association with that body. Section 57, however, unlike the above provisions, is entirely new. It provides that the Secretary of State may by regulations specify what letters, symbols, etc. may be used in a company's registered name. The regulations may also specify a permitted format for a name.

Name already on the index

2.47   Section 66 replaces s.26(1)(c) and (3) of the 1985 Act. The section thus deals with the prohibition of a company adopting a name that is already on the index of company names, and includes for these purposes not only the name of companies but other pre-existing business entities. The section empowers the Secretary of State to make regulations to supplement the powers set out in the section. Under s.66(4) these regulations may in the future permit, in specified circumstances or with specified consent, a company to be registered with a name which because of the previous registration of the name by a pre-existing company would be otherwise prohibited.

2.48   Sections 67 and 68 collectively replace various subsections of s.28 of the 1985 Act. These sections provide power for the Secretary of State in writing to direct a company to change its name if it is the same as or 'too like' an existing company's name within a period of 12 months of registration (as opposed to 15 months as recommended by the Company Law Review) and are supplementary to s.66. In answering criticisms of this power, both as to frequency of use and effectiveness and certainty, Lord McKenzie noted:

> I shall deal with both issues together. Regarding the statistics, less than one per cent of all name changes are as a result of the direction. Between April and November last year, 166 companies were directed to change their names because they were too much like another's.

> The clause, . . . [i.e. now ss.67–68] . . . like its predecessor in the 1985 Act, is there to prevent confusion between very similar names on the registrar's index. We propose to make regulations under Clause 67 . . . [now s.66] . . . to deal with some common, minor differences between names. For example, under the current law, 'Smith Limited' and 'Smith and Co. Limited' are taken as the same and only one can be registered. However, it is impossible to provide for all minor differences in this mechanical way. That is why we need Clause 68 . . . [now ss.67–68] . . . It operates after a

company name has been registered and allows the Secretary of State to direct a change of name.

(Hansard Vol.678 No.96 Col.GC55)

2.49   Section 68 replaces s.28(4) and (5) of the 1985 Act as they apply to s.28(2). It thus provides for deadlines for the Secretary of State's giving the direction under s.67 and for the company's compliance, with failure to comply constituting an offence.

Business names supplementary provisions

2.50   Supplementary provisions were enacted relating to the use of business names by business organisations and are set out in Part 41 of the 2006 Act. In essence these provisions reproduce the provisions of the Business Names Act 1985 save that henceforth they also apply to all overseas companies carrying on business in the United Kingdom. Part 41, covering three Chapters and ss.1192–1208 of the Act, therefore expands upon the provisions considered above. Thus a business is not prevented under the 2006 Act from operating under the name of the persons carrying on that business with permitted additions (see s.1192). The circumstances in which a business name suggests a sensitive connection with government or other bodies or is otherwise sensitive are set out in ss.1193–1194. The Secretary of State when considering an application in respect of a company name which requires the approval of government departments or other relevant bodies may in the future make regulations which are authorised by s.1195, requiring, inter alia, the applicant to follow certain procedures. The grounds upon which the Secretary of State may withdraw approval of a business name are specified in s.1196.

2.51   Regulations may also be made with regard to the power of the Secretary of State to prohibit names which are an inappropriate indication of company type or legal form (see s.1197). Section 1198 prohibits any person from carrying on a business in the United Kingdom under a name which is so misleading about the nature of the activities of the business that it is likely to cause harm to the public. Section 1199 exempts, inter alia, businesses which were operating before Part 41, Chapter 1 came into force from the terms of that Chapter in relation to names which before that date were lawful.

2.52   Chapter 2 of Part 41, ss.1200–1206, essentially governs the disclosure requirements for individuals and partnerships carrying on a business under a business name. These sections mirror provisions prescribed in previous legislation governing partnerships, principally under the Business Names Act 1985 and require no further comment. Chapter 3 is a definition section for the purposes of Part 41.

Similarity to other names in which person has goodwill

2.53   Section 69 is a new provision. It is a response to the Company Law Review's recommendations (see Final Report, para.11.50). It provides for any person, not limited to a company, to object to a company names adjudicator (see s.70) if a company's name is similar to a name in which the objector has prior goodwill. Thus an application can be made to the adjudicator where the applicant can show that the name was chosen by the company with the principal intention of seeking monies from the applicant or preventing the use of the name by the applicant where there is previously acquired goodwill or a reputation. However, s.69(4) sets out the circumstances where a presumption is raised that the name was adopted legitimately by the company. Unless the respondent can show one of these circumstances exists, including that the adoption of the name was otherwise in good faith, or that the applicant's interests have not been significantly affected, the applicant's objection with regard to the company name must be upheld.

2.54   Section 71 provides for the Secretary of State to make procedural rules governing proceedings before a company names adjudicator. Under s.73, upon upholding an objection under s.69, the adjudicator will make an order requiring the offending name to be changed. If the company does not change its name by the date specified in the order, the adjudicator has the power to determine a new name for the company. Any decision of an adjudicator must be made available to the public (s.72). Under s.74 any applicant who has not secured a decision from an adjudicator, or any defendant company that has received a direction from the company names adjudicator, may appeal to a court against the decision. The court may either uphold or reverse the decision of the adjudicator. It was the Government's intention that the powers of the adjudicator were to be complementary and supplementary to the remedies of passing off and in cases of remedies concerning trade mark infringement (see Hansard Vol.678 No.98 Col.GC121).

Provision of misleading information

2.55   Section 75 allows the Secretary of State to direct a change of name by a company in the event of misleading information being given at the time of registration of the name. This decision can be made up to five years from the date of registration of the name. The section replaces s.28(3) of the 1985 Act (and in so far as it supports that subsection), s.28(4)–(6).

2.56   Section 76 replaces s.32 of the 1985 Act. It provides a power for the Secretary of State to direct a company to change its name, no matter how long it has had that name, if the name is so misleading an indication of the nature of its activities as to be likely to cause harm to the public. It is an offence not to comply with a direction given under this section.

Change of name

2.57   Section 77 replaces s.28(1) of the 1985 Act which permits and prescribes the procedures by which a company may change its name. Under the new section a company may change its name by two further procedures, other than those prescribed under the 1985 Act which are preserved. Thus a company may now change its name by any means provided for in the company's articles, or by order of the company names adjudicator. Section 79 supplements s.77(1)(b) whereby a company may change its name by any means provided for in the articles. Section 79(1) requires the company to provide the registrar with both a notice of the name change and a statement that the change has been made in accordance with the company's articles.

2.58   Section 78 is a new provision, requiring a company to inform the registrar of a name change when it is agreed by special resolution. In addition, a company must also do so when a name change is agreed by special resolution but that change is subject to the occurrence of a certain event or events, for example a merger. The latter aspect of the section is not to be regarded, however, as authorising a procedure whereby a company can reserve a name (Hansard Vol.678 No.98 Col.GC124).

New name

2.59   A company may select to carry on business under a new name. Section 80, which partly replaces ss.28(6) and 32(5) of the 1985 Act, prescribes the procedures that the registrar must perform and the conditions that must be satisfied before a company's new name is to be effective. Thus under s.80(2) the new name must comply with all the conditions and requirements for the registration of a company name set out in the applicable provisions considered above, and all relevant documentation must be in the possession of the registrar. Under s.80(3) on the satisfying of these requirements a new certificate of incorporation will be issued. Under s.81 the new name is effective as soon as the altered certificate is issued, but this does not affect the company's obligations or any legal proceedings involving the company under its previous name.

Trading disclosures

2.60   Section 82 replaces ss.348(1), 349(1) and 351(1) and (2) of the 1985 Act, and s.4(1) of the Business Names Act 1985 in so far as it relates to companies. It provides a power for the Secretary of State to make regulations requiring a company, inter alia, to display its name or other specified information at specified locations and on documents and communications, and to disclose its name and other specified information to those who request it in the course of business. This latter requirement is a new provision in so far as it covers companies doing business under their registered names. Sections 83 and 84 provide for civil sanctions and criminal penalties for failure to comply with any requirements prescribed under s.82.

2.61   Section 85 provides that a company's name as used in order to comply with the disclosure requirements does not have to be exactly the same as the registered name. Any differences must be limited, however, to matters such as punctuation and formatting, and must not constitute differences which would give rise to confusion.

REGISTERED OFFICE

2.62   Section 86 requires every company to have a registered office. This section replaces s.287(1) of the 1985 Act. Under s.87 a company may change the location of its registered office. The change of address of the registered office does not take effect until the new address is on the public record, although s.87(2) provides for an overlap between the two addresses for a period of a fortnight, whereby both addresses fulfil the role of a registered office.

Welsh companies

2.63   Section 88 defines the nature of a Welsh company. A Welsh company may deliver its documents to the registrar in Welsh and can end its company name with Welsh versions of the statutory indicators of legal status.

RE-REGISTRATION TO ALTER THE COMPANY'S STATUS

2.64   Part 7 of the Act deals with the re-registration of companies. Although this Part of the Act was subjected to a number of technical amendments during its passage through the House of Lords (Hansard Vol.678 No.98 Col.GC130), these amendments did not effect significant substantive changes. Part 7 replaces equivalent provisions in Part 2 of the 1985 Act. Accordingly, this Part will not be subject to detailed comment in this book. There are, however, a number of substantive changes to the old law and these will be noted below.

2.65   Section 89 is the key provision in Part 7, and provides for the various ways by which a company may alter its status. The amendments to the previous law in Part 2 of the 1985 Act, now contained in Part 7, were principally recommended by the Company Law Review (see Final Report, para.6.11.16). Although Part 7 essentially retains the various possibilities for re-registration of a company's status, the 2006 Act makes one significant change, which is in accordance with the recommendations of the Company Law Review, namely a public company will be able to re-register as an unlimited private company without first having to re-register as a private limited company (see s.109, considered at **para.2.83** below).

2.66   Lord McKenzie in the House of Lords noted the rationale behind Part 7 of the 2006 Act in the following terms:

> Certain transitions of company type are, however, fairly common: for example, those from a private company limited by shares to a public company. Company law has, therefore, provided an express mechanism – re-registration – for dealing with this sort of transition. Necessarily, the re-registration mechanisms need to provide proper safeguards for members of the companies concerned, and for their creditors. The procedures are, therefore, different in different cases. Essentially, the existence of a specific re-registration procedure for any given type of transition recognises that there is a market need for a specific procedure, and that the complexity of the process which would need to be established does not outweigh that need.
>
> (Hansard Vol.678 No.98 Col.131)

Private company becoming public

2.67   Section 90 was amended during the passage of the Bill through the House of Lords (Hansard Vol.678 No.98 Col.GC132), so as to make it clear that any private company may re-register as a public company whether limited or unlimited if it meets the conditions set out in s.90(2)–(4). Perhaps the most important and common condition is the need to make appropriate alterations to the company's articles. Section 90 replaces ss.43(1) and (2) and 48 of the 1985 Act.

2.68   Section 91 also requires a company re-registered as a public company to comply with the requirements of a minimum authorised share capital. Attempts to increase this sum beyond the present minimum of £50,000 were rejected in the House of Lords (ibid., at Col.GC133). Section 91 replaces ss.45 and 47(3) of the 1985 Act.

2.69   Section 92 replaces s.43(3)(b)–(c) and (4) of the 1985 Act. The provision ensures that a newly registered public company has net assets which are not less than the aggregate of its called-up share capital and undistributable reserves. This state of affairs must be confirmed by a written statement from the company's auditor (see s.92(1)(c)).

2.70   Section 93 replaces s.44 of the 1985 Act but makes no substantive change to the law. Section 94 replaces s.43(1)(b), (3)(a)–(d) and (3A) of the 1985 Act. It prescribes the contents of the application for re-registration of a private company to a public company. There is an important change however, to the previous law. This is necessary because of the abolition of the requirement for a private company to have a company secretary. This officer is a requirement however, for a public company. Thus the application under the above provisions must include a statement of the company's proposed secretary.

2.71   Section 95 is a new provision which is required as a consequence of the abolition of the need for a company secretary for private companies. Thus the statement regarding the proposed secretary in cases of re-registration from private to public must record the consent of the person appointed so to act, including (where there are joint secretaries) joint consent.

2.72   Section 96 replaces s.47 of the 1985 Act. It empowers the registrar to issue on re-registration a new certificate of incorporation, which must state it is being issued on re-registration. The certificate is conclusive evidence of the new status of the company.

Public company becoming private

2.73   Section 97 replaces s.53 of the 1985 Act. It enables a public company to re-register as a private limited company if the conditions in s.97(2) are satisfied. The law preserves the law as set out in s.53 of the 1985 Act with two changes. First the new section requires the company to file with the registrar a statement of compliance together with the application to re-register. Secondly, under s.97(2) the registrar may process an application for the re-registration of a company from public to private within the 28-day period during which dissentient members may apply to the court (see s.98 below) for an order cancelling the resolution for re-registration. This power, however, can only be exercised if the registrar is satisfied that such an application cannot be made. This is regarded as incorporating current practice.

2.74   Section 98 (which replaces s.54(1)–(3), (5)–(6) and (8) of the 1985 Act) enables the prescribed minority of shareholders to apply to the court for the cancellation of the resolution to change the status of the company. The application must be made within 28 days of the passing of the resolution.

2.75   Section 99, which replaces s.54(4), (7) and (10) of the 1985 Act, requires the company to give immediate notice to the registrar of any application under s.98 where it has received notice from the applicants. The company must also forward to the registrar a copy of any court order relating to any such application. However, s.99(1), another new provision, requires the dissenting group of shareholders on making an application under s.98 to give direct notice to the registrar. Failure of a company to give notice to the registrar under s.99 constitutes an offence (see s.99(4) which replaces s.54(10) of the 1985 Act).

2.76   Section 100, which replaces s.53(1)(b) of the 1985 Act, prescribes the documents and information which must be supplied with any application for re-registration of a public company as a private company.

2.77   Under s.101 the registrar, being satisfied as to the application under the above provisions, will issue a new certificate of incorporation. The certificate must state the fact that it is being issued on the re-registration of the company. The certificate is conclusive evidence that the company is a private company. Section 101 replaces s.55 of the 1985 Act.

Private limited company becoming unlimited

2.78   Section 102 replaces s.49(1)–(2) and (9) of the 1985 Act. The provision permits a private company limited by shares (or by guarantee) to re-register as an unlimited company, providing the conditions set out in s.102(2) are satisfied, including the unanimous assent of all the members to the change in status. Section 103 sets out the documents and information required to support re-registration, and prescribes the contents of the application for re-registration under s.102. It replaces s.49(4)–(8A) of the 1985 Act. The documents to be forwarded to the registrar must include a statement of compliance. The statement of compliance must also contain a statement by the directors which confirms that all members have assented to the change of status and if a member has not authenticated the assent, that all reasonable steps were taken by the directors that any person who authenticated on behalf of a member was lawfully empowered to do so. This condition is a necessity since the members are accepting unlimited liability in respect of the enterprise.

2.79   Section 104 replaces s.50 of the 1985 Act. The section empowers the registrar to issue a new certificate of incorporation which must state that the certificate is issued on re-registration. The certificate is conclusive evidence that the company is an unlimited company.

Unlimited private company becoming limited

2.80   Section 105 replaces s.51(1)–(3) and (6) of the 1985 Act. The provision enables an unlimited company to re-register as a private limited company if the conditions set out in s.105(2) are satisfied. This includes the passing of a special resolution which must state whether the limitation is to be by way of shares or guarantee.

2.81   Section 106, which replaces s.51(3)–(5) of the 1985 Act, prescribes the contents of the application for re-registration under s.105 and the documents and information that must accompany the application. In the rare case of a company re-registering as a company limited by guarantee, the application must be accompanied by a statement of guarantee (see s.11).

2.82   Under s.107, which replaces s.52 of the 1985 Act, the registrar must issue a certificate of incorporation, which must state that it is being issued on the re-registration of the company. The certificate is conclusive evidence that the company is a private limited company. Section 108 provides, inter alia, that on re-registration under s.107 a company which has allotted share capital must deliver a statement of capital to the registrar. This must be delivered within 15 days after the registration. This provision does not apply if the information that would be contained in such a statement has already been sent to the registrar in a statement of capital and initial shareholdings, or a statement of capital contained in an annual return.

Public company becoming private and unlimited

2.83   Section 109 is a new provision, which was recommended by the Company Law Review (Final Report, para.11.6). The section enables a public company to re-register as a private unlimited company with a share capital without first having to re-register as a private limited company. The application must satisfy the conditions set out in s.109(2), including the assent of all members to the change in status. Assent may be given by the personal representatives or trustee in bankruptcy of any members. However, it should be noted that a public company may not take advantage of s.109 if it has previously been re-registered as limited or unlimited (see s.109(2)).

2.84   Section 110 is another new provision. It prescribes the contents of the application made under s.109 and the documents and information that must be supplied to the registrar to support the application. There must also be a statement of compliance, which in view of the fact that the members are accepting unlimited liability is similar in form to the directors' statement required under s.103(4), namely that the persons by whom or on whose behalf the form of assent is authenticated constitute the whole of the membership of the company, and that the directors have taken all steps to ensure that persons authenticating the assent on behalf of a member were lawfully empowered to do so.

2.85   Under s.111, the registrar must issue a certificate of incorporation, which must state that it is being issued on re-registration. The certificate of incorporation is conclusive evidence that the company is a private unlimited company.

3 COMPANY REGISTRAR

POWERS AND DUTIES OF REGISTRAR

3.1 Part 35 of the 2006 Act, comprising ss.1060–1120, largely replaces Part 24 of the 1985 Act and provides for the continued existence of the registrar of companies. This Part of the Act, inter alia, defines the office and the duties of the registrar and the fees payable to him in respect of the performance of those duties (ss.1060–1063). In particular under s.1064 (replacing s.711(1)(a) of the 1985 Act) the registrar is obliged to cause notice of the issue of any certificate of incorporation to be published in the Gazette, or alternatively to be published by any means as may be determined by the Secretary of State under powers prescribed under s.1116 (see **para.3.31** below for a consideration of this provision which relates to publication of such matters by electronic means).

3.2 Any person may require the registrar to supply a copy of the certificate of incorporation of a company (see s.1065 replacing the 1985 Act, s.710). Under ss.1066–1067 (which replace ss.705 and 705A of the 1985 Act) the registrar must issue all companies with a registered number, including any overseas company whose particulars are registered under Part 34 of the Act (see **para.3.75** *et seq.* below).

DELIVERY OF DOCUMENTS TO THE REGISTRAR

3.3 Under s.1068 the registrar is required to impose requirements as to the form, authentication and manner of delivery of documents to him under the Act (s.1068(1)). Additional requirements are imposed in connection with documents which must be authenticated, with respect to both the class of persons who may authenticate such documents, and the manner of authentication (s.1068(3)). The terms of the requirements that the registrar may impose on documents as to form (s.1068(2)) and manner of delivery (s.1068(4) and (5)) are specified within the section. The registrar is obliged to ensure that all company documents subject to the First Company Law Directive (Directive 68/151/EEC) disclosure requirements (see s.1078 and **para.3.6** below) may be delivered by electronic means from 1 January 2007 (see s.1068(5)). The Secretary of State as part of the process to encourage electronic delivery of documents is empowered to make regulations so as to require documents to be delivered to the registrar by electronic means (s.1069). To further facilitate electronic delivery of documents the registrar may make individual agreements with particular companies for delivery of all documents or a class of documents by electronic means (s.1070). Section 1071 provides that a document is not deemed delivered to the registrar until it is received (s.1071(1)). Section 1071(2) allows provision to be made in the registrar's rules (see s.1117 and para 3.32 below) as to when a document is to be regarded as delivered.

Requirements for proper delivery

3.4   On receipt of documents, the registrar has to decide whether to make the information available to the public for inspection. There is clearly a requirement to ensure that the information registered is accurate, and the following provisions enable the registrar to ensure that such is the case. Sections 1072–1076 clarify his powers and duties in this respect. Under ss.1072 and 1073 the registrar has power to omit from the register any or all of the information contained in a document which does not meet the necessary 'delivery' requirements as to contents, form, authentication and manner of delivery as prescribed in the provisions noted immediately above. The registrar will, however, still be able to accept and register 'defective' documents at his discretion (s.1073). Such 'acceptance' does not exempt the filer from any consequence flowing from the failure to comply with the requirements for delivery. Under s.1074, where a document delivered to the registrar contains 'unnecessary material' (as defined in s.1074(2)), the registrar can regard the document as not meeting the requirements for delivery, and thus refuse to register the document (s.1074(4)). This power can only be exercised when the unnecessary material cannot be readily separated from the rest of the document. If the unnecessary material can be so separated, the document may be registered either with the material deleted, or as it was delivered (s.1074(5)).

Informal correction

3.5   Section 1075 is a new provision, giving the registrar power to use 'informal means' to correct information set out in any documents delivered to him. Nevertheless, the power to correct is limited to the circumstances set out in s.1075(2)–(3), which is restricted to cases where the registrar following an enquiry of the company has instructions so to act, and the company has given its consent (which has not been withdrawn). Section 1076 allows the registrar to accept a replacement document where the original document did not comply with the requirements for proper delivery, or contained unnecessary material.

Public notice

3.6   Sections 1077–1078 replace s.711 of the 1985 Act. The provisions list the documents required to be delivered by a company to the registrar (see s.1078) which must be disclosed by notice in the Gazette or under s.1116 (which provides for an alternative means of giving public notice). The list of documents subject to the public notice requirements set out in s.1078 is derived from the First Company Law Directive (Directive 68/151/EEC) as amended by Directive 2003/58/EC. In effect, s.1079 replaces s.42 of the 1985 Act. It provides that in its dealings with third parties a company may not rely on the consequences of certain events as set out in s.1079(2) unless appropriate notice within the terms of s.1077 has been given. The events listed in s.1079(2) include, for example, amendment of the articles of the company.

THE REGISTER

3.7   Section 1080 imposes an obligation upon the registrar to keep a record of the material received by him relating to registered companies. Although there is a discretion as to the form of the record kept (s.1080(5)), s.1080(3) makes it clear that the discretion is subject to the terms of the First Company Law Directive. Article 3.2 of that Directive requires that any documents and particulars delivered after 1 January 2007 must be retained in electronic form. The register must constitute a source of information on a company that is both useful and transparent. Section 1081 therefore requires the registrar in certain cases (s.1081(1)) to provide an annotation of information on the register with respect to a company, to gloss any information, or to provide supplementary information. This section, which also empowers the Secretary of State to make regulations concerning the obligation of the registrar to annotate information (s.1081(2)), was a specific recommendation of the Company Law Review (see Final Report, para.11.48). Under s.1081(5), in certain circumstances the court can direct that a note should be removed or that no annotation is to be made.

The unique identifier

3.8   Section 1082 is a new provision which supplements the powers set out in Part 10, Chapter 8 of the Act which provides for the home addresses of directors to be kept off the public record. (See **Chapter 4** for a consideration of these provisions.) Part 8, Chapter 2 of the Act, relating to the protection of the private details of individuals from being made available under the right to inspect the register when the application for inspection is for an improper purpose, is considered at **paras.3.62–3.64** below). Section 1082 thus gives the Secretary of State a power to make regulations so that individuals, for example company directors, are allocated a unique identifier. The purpose of the unique identifier is to enable those who search the register to distinguish between different persons of the same name (a common occurrence in family-run private limited companies) while preserving sufficient security for members and directors of companies from the prying of those who may have criminal or malicious intent towards them.

3.9   Section 1083 replaces s.707A(2) of the 1985 Act. However, the registrar is obliged to keep originals of documents received (but see s.1087(3) below) for three years only (reduced from 10 years under the 1985 Act). The obligation does not apply to electronic documents, provided that the information has been recorded in the register. Section 1084 replaces s.707(3)–(4) of the 1985 Act. Under this section, once a company has been dissolved for two years or more, the registrar can direct that records should be removed to the Public Record Office. Equivalent provision applies with respect to certain overseas companies.

Inspection of the register

3.10   Section 1085 makes it clear that any person has the right to inspect the register. Original documents, however, can only be inspected where they are available, and the record kept by the registrar is illegible or unavailable. Under s.1086 a person is entitled to a copy of any material on the register. The fee that can be demanded is regulated by the provisions of the First Company Law Directive, and may not exceed the administrative cost of providing the service.

3.11   Section 1087 prescribes in detail the exceptions to the above provisions whereby certain information is not available for inspection, and these exceptions are set out in s.1087(1)(a)–(k). For example, s.1087(1)(b) relates to what may be defined as protected information relating to directors' home addresses which are subject to protection by virtue of the provisions of Part 10, Chapter 8 of the 2006 Act. However, s.1087(2) makes it clear that information filed with the registrar under one document that is subject to one of the exceptions to public inspection may nevertheless lose its confidentiality if it is also contained in a document which is filed with the registrar within another context which is not subject to s.1087(1). Further, s.1087(3) provides that material to which s.1087 applies need not be retained by the registrar for longer than appears necessary for the purposes for which it was delivered.

3.12   Section 1088 is a new provision. It empowers the Secretary of State to make regulations providing for applications to be made to the registrar to remove addresses from the public record at Companies House. The regulations will determine who can make an application under the section, the grounds of application and any procedure to govern an application.

Applications for inspection and copies of documents

3.13   Sections 1089–1091 empower the registrar to specify the form and manner in which applications for inspection of the register, or for copies of material on it, are to be made. They also allow the registrar to determine the manner and form in which any copies will be supplied. Section 1089(2) determines that applications must be capable of being made in hard copy or in electronic form, as the applicant chooses. Under s.1090(2)–(3) the applicant may insist on receiving the copies in electronic form unless the relevant document was delivered before 1 January 2007 and it is 10 years or more before the receipt of the document and the application, or in any event if the document was delivered before 31 December 1996.

3.14 Section 1091, which incorporates provisions of the amended First Company Law Directive (68/151/EEC), makes it clear that hard copies of documents must be certified as true copies unless the applicant dispenses with this requirement. Electronic copies must not be so certified unless certification is expressly requested by the applicant. The evidential status of certified hard copies in legal proceedings is covered in s.1091(3). The Secretary of State is empowered to prescribe by regulations the way in which copies of documents provided in electronic form will be certified. Finally under s.1091(5) copies of documents provided by the registrar may be sealed as opposed to certified; however this provision does not apply to any documents listed in s.1078, i.e. documents subject to the Directive disclosure requirements.

3.15 Section 1092 (which replaces s.709(5) of the 1985 Act) provides that the permission of the court will be needed before proceedings can be taken against the registrar for production of records.

Correction or removal of material on the register

3.16 Section 1093 allows the registrar to notify a company of any apparent inconsistency or discrepancy in the information held on the register concerning the company. The registrar is empowered to give notice to the company requiring the resolution of the inconsistency or discrepancy within 14 days of the issue of the notice.

3.17 Although not directly an issue as to the accuracy of the information on the register, s.1094 permits the registrar, on giving notice to the company, to remove information from the register which he was empowered to enter on the register but was not duty bound to do so. This provision ensures that the register will not become cluttered with unnecessary detail (see s.1094(2)). Section 1094(3) sets out the material which cannot be removed under the section on the basis that such information has had legal consequences for the company regarding certain key events, for example information regarding the formation of the company or a change of name.

3.18 As an adjunct to the above provisions, s.1095 gives the Secretary of State power to make regulations whereby following an application in the appropriate form, the registrar will be obliged to remove certain prescribed material from the register. The documents and information that may be subject to such regulations are limited to those which are invalid, ineffective or have been placed on the register without the authority of the company (s.1095(1)(a)), or which are inaccurate, or derived from something which is inaccurate or forged (s.1095(1)(b)). Under s.1095(5) a person affected by the removal of any document or information from the register which under s.1094(3) would have legal consequences for the company, may seek an order from the court which may, inter alia, pronounce on the material's legal effect, and thus protect his position with regard to any potential legal liability which follows upon the removal.

3.19   There are similar powers under s.1096, whereby consequential upon a court order the registrar will be obliged to remove material or information from the register. Unlike the power under s.1095, the nature and forms of document subject to s.1096 are unrestricted. The court will thus be able to make an order under s.1096 where the material by its presence on the register has for example caused damage to the company, or may do so in the future, and the company's interests in having the material removed outweigh the interests of others for it to be retained. Furthermore, the court can make any consequential orders as appear just having regard to the period of time in which the material was on the register, and the effect of that material being on the register. Supplementary to s.1096, if the court decides that certain information should be removed from the register, s.1097 enables it to give directions as to the removal from the register of such matters as annotations, including their removal or replacement by new annotations.

3.20   Section 1098 provides for the registrar to give public notice of the receipt of documents subject to the Directive disclosure requirements in the Gazette, or through other means of publication as prescribed under s.1116 (see **para.3.31** below).

Index of company names

3.21   An important record that must be maintained by the registrar is the index of company names. This enables parties, inter alia, when deciding to incorporate to access up-to-date information of pre-existing company names, thus avoiding the expense of seeking to register a company name which the registrar will reject on the grounds that there is a registered company that already bears such a name (see **Chapter 2**). Section 1099 both replaces and updates s.714 of the 1985 Act, and requires the registrar to keep an index of the names of companies incorporated under the Companies Acts. In addition, the index must include names of businesses formed under other legislation, e.g. limited liability partnerships (s.1099(3)(a)), and overseas companies with a UK branch (s.1099(2)(c)). The section also empowers the Secretary of State by regulation to update the categories of business entities to be included in the index. Section 1100 gives the public the right to inspect the index, which may be done free of charge at **www.companieshouse.gov.uk**.

3.22   Section 1101 gives the Secretary of State power to amend the rules concerning the names that can be adopted by business entities which are subject to being placed on the index, other than the forms of company set out in s.1099(2), i.e. bodies other than companies. This power was regarded as necessary in view of the fact that each form of these other business entities has its own rules as to the degree to which they may operate with names similar to those of pre-existing businesses without the risk of confusion to the public. However, they are nevertheless to be subject to the above provisions, and may therefore in certain cases be prevented from being entered on the index. The section is intended to provide in the future a power to remove these anomalies and provide a consistent regime governing the use of business names for all business entities that are subject to being placed on the index.

Language requirements

3.23   Sections 1102–1103 set out the general rule that all documents filed with the registrar should be in English. The exceptions to this rule are considered below. Provisions other than those of the Companies Acts and the Insolvency Act 1986 may require companies to file documents with the registrar. In these circumstances it may or may not be appropriate to impose the language provisions prescribed under the above sections. Section 1102(2) authorises the Secretary of State to make regulations to set out detailed provisions covering non-Companies Act language requirements. The principal exception to the language requirement relates to Welsh companies (see s.1104) and documents that under the terms of s.1105 may be drawn up and delivered in other languages. The documents covered by s.1105 are set out in s.1105(2). Nevertheless such documents must be accompanied by certified translations into English.

3.24   Section 1106 implements elements of the amended First Company Law Directive (Directive 68/151/EEC). It provides that companies may deliver to the registrar certified translations of documents relating to the company. By s.1106(2) the Secretary of State by regulation may determine the languages and documents in relation to which the facility created by the section is available. The languages available must at least be the official languages of the EU, and the documents those covered by the First Company Law Directive (see s.1078). Finally s.1107 defines what constitutes a certified translation for the purposes of the above provisions, which is essentially a translation that has been certified in a manner prescribed by the registrar.

Language requirements: transliteration

3.25   Sections 1108–1110 are new provisions, and cover the situation where the name and address of, for example, a director of an overseas company uses characters such as those in the Japanese language. Section 1108 restricts the letters, characters or symbols that may be used for the above-mentioned purposes to those set out in any future regulations (and see s.1110). Section 1109 provides for the possibility that the regulations made under the aegis of s.1108 may relate to letters that may be used from other alphabets within the EU, for example Greek lettering. The requirement for transliteration of such letters, characters or symbols under s.1108 will not apply to names and/or addresses using letters, characters and symbols covered by any regulations. However, transliteration of the document in these circumstances is nevertheless permitted by s.1108.

3.26   Section 1110 confers power on the Secretary of State to make regulations relating to transliteration of names and addresses. The regulations may distinguish between the circumstances when transliteration is required and those when it is voluntary under ss.1108–1110. Section 1111 authorises the registrar to impose requirements as to the means by which documents that are transliterations or translations are to be certified or verified.

Supplementary provisions

3.27   Section 1112 is a new provision, creating the offence of knowingly or recklessly delivering to the registrar information which is 'misleading, false or deceptive in a material particular'. It was a response to the Company Law Review's recommendation in its Final Report, para.11.48. It is hoped that this offence will make it unnecessary for the authorities to reproduce, or to make future use of, specific offences regarding false information or false statements in cases where false information concerning a company is filed with the registrar.

3.28   Section 1113, which replaces s.713 of the 1985 Act, sets out the means by which obligations to file documents and to give notice to the registrar under the provisions of the Act will be enforced. If a company is in default, the registrar or any member or creditor of the company may serve notice on the company requiring compliance. If following 14 days after the notice has been served the company remains in default, the applicant may apply to court for an order requiring the company or any officer of the company to make good the default. Such an action is in addition to any criminal sanctions.

3.29   Section 1114 replaces s.715A of the 1985 Act and defines terms such as 'document' and 'delivery' for the purposes of Part 35 of the Act.

3.30   Section 1115 replaces s.710A of the 1985 Act. If a company chooses to file documents electronically, this provision allows the registrar to require the company to accept electronic communications from the registrar. It also provides how by rules the registrar can determine how such communications or documents can be 'authenticated' by seal or deemed to be signed, although sent electronically.

3.31   Section 1116 has been referred to above at **para.3.20**. Under the 1985 Act the registrar was obliged to publish documents and information (as noted above) in the Gazette. In recognising a new regime of electronic publication, the section provides (in accordance with the recommendations of the Company Law Review, Final Report, para.11.48) for the Secretary of State to specify alternative means of giving notice, principally electronic, which the registrar may then approve.

3.32   Section 1117 relates to the registrar's rule-making powers and is referred to in **para.3.3** above. Part 35 of the Act enables the registrar in a number of situations to impose requirements with regard to documents and information to be filed by companies. The section simply authorises the registrar to set out these requirements in rules. This will ensure that the best practice can be quickly incorporated and procedures kept up to date.

3.33   Section 1119 essentially reproduces s.704(7)–(8) of the 1985 Act. The Deregulation and Contracting Out Act 1994 recognises that certain of the registrar's functions may be contracted out to private bodies. The section therefore allows for this by determining that where documents subject to Part 35 are to be dealt with by a contractor, the registrar can provide for them to be sent to that party directly. It should be noted that the 1994 Act does not permit the function of making subordinate legislation to be delegated. Section 1119(3) therefore provides that the registrar's rules are not be regarded as subordinate legislation for this purpose, thus enabling contractors to specify, for example, the form and manner in which documents are to be delivered to them.

3.34   Finally s.1120 provides that, except where the context determines otherwise, the provisions of Part 35 apply fully to overseas companies (see paras.3.72–3.74 below).

SUPPLEMENTARY PROVISIONS

Company records

3.35   Part 37 of the Act in so far as it applies to company records is complementary to the provisions set out in Part 35 and relates to the obligations of the company to keep and to make available to the public its own records. Section 1134 is a new provision and defines the nature of company records, albeit principally for the purpose of the provisions of Part 37.

3.36   Section 1135 replaces ss.722(1) and 723 of the 1985 Act. It enables a company to use electronic storage or hard copy for its records, as long as paper printouts of electronic records can be generated. Under s.1136 the Secretary of State by regulation may determine that company records specified in s.1136(2), such as the register of directors, be kept at a place other than the registered office, e.g. the company's principal place of business in the part of the United Kingdom in which the company is registered.

3.37   Section 1137 replaces s.723A of the 1985 Act, and reproduces the existing powers of the Secretary of State to make provisions regarding the obligations of a company to, inter alia, make available for inspection its records and to provide copies of the same.

3.38   Section 1138 replaces s.722(2) and (3) of the 1985 Act. It provides that it is an offence for a company (and every officer who is in default) to fail to take measures to guard against falsification of records or to fail to help to discover any falsification. The section applies to records that are not kept in bound books, irrespective of whether they are kept electronically. However, the section does not apply (s.1138(4)) either to the company's copy of any director's service contract, or to its copy of any qualifying third party indemnity provisions benefiting a director.

Service addresses

3.39   Section 1139 replaces ss.694A, 695 and 725 of the 1985 Act. This section ensures that there is a place at which, or person upon whom, a document may be served in respect of every company registered in the United Kingdom, be it a UK company where service may be effected by forwarding documents to the registered office, or an overseas companies registered under the Companies Acts where service may be upon the persons specified in s.1139(2) or at the company's principal place of business.

3.40 Section 1140 is a new provision, and provides that the address on the public record in respect of any director or secretary is effective for the service of documents on them. By s.1140(3) any such address is to be regarded as effective for the purposes of service, even if the document has no connection with the person's responsibilities as either director or secretary. The section equally applies to the addresses of other persons on the company register, as specified in s.1140(2) and includes, for example, a receiver or manager.

3.41 Section 1141 defines 'service address' and provides a power for the Secretary of State to make regulations to specify conditions with which a service address should comply. Section 1142 is another new provision. It simply provides that an obligation to give a 'service address' as defined in s.1141 is enough to comply with the above provisions relating to service of documents, unless there is a requirement (as may be specified in any future regulations) for a particular address such as the person's usual residential address to be filed with the registrar.

Sending or supplying documents or information

3.42 Section 1143 provides that ss.1144–1148 and Scheds.4 and 5 apply to the sending or receiving of documents and information by and to companies, and their members and shareholders, and where applicable their debenture holders. These provisions apply equally to equivalent 'communications' between the registrar and companies, subject to the provisions of Part 35. The background for these new provisions may be found in the Companies Act 1985 (Electronic Communications) Order 2000, SI 2000/3373 which facilitated the use of electronic and website communications with regard to companies. The above provisions expand upon this piece of delegated legislation and clarify the position with regard to electronic communication in all cases where the 2006 Act prescribes this means of communication. Thus the general principle adopted is that subject to member approval, the company should be able to use electronic communication. However, the right of members to request communication by paper is preserved under s.1145.

3.43 Section 1144 introduces two Schedules which govern communications between companies, persons involved with the company and the registrar. The Schedules must be considered in the context of the above provisions. Section 1146 deals with the requirement of authentication and s.1148 deals with the interpretation of the communication provisions in Part 37 of the Act.

Schedule 4

3.44   Schedule 4 provides for the rules governing communications to a company. Part 1 of Sched.4 makes it clear that the Schedule governs communications from persons including members of the company to the company. Part 2 of Sched.4 sets out the rules governing communication in hard copy. They mirror the rules and practice under the 1985 Act and require no further comment. Part 3 sets out the rules for communication in electronic form, and states that a document or information is validly sent or supplied in electronic form if it is sent in accordance with this part of the Schedule. Part 4 provides that unless the Companies Act specifies a means of communication, then a communication to a company can be sent or supplied in any way agreed by the company.

Schedule 5

3.45   Schedule 5 deals with the rules governing communication from companies to other persons, such as their members and debenture holders. The standard rules for communication in hard copy are covered in Part 2. The addresses to which the company may send or supply either documents or information are set out in para.2(4). In the absence of such an address for the intended recipient, the last known address may be used. Although in general the rules set out in the Schedule apply irrespective of the company's articles, it is possible for the company to provide in its articles that in the absence of a current valid address for a member, there shall be no obligation to send communications such as notices of general meetings or accounts. Part 3 relates to communications in electronic form, and Part 4 governs communications via a company website.

3.46   Paragraph 10 of Part 4 allows the company either by way of member's resolution, or through the articles, to 'default' to communication by a company website, if agreement to this method has been sought and the member has agreed or not responded within 28 days of the request. If the member does not agree to this method of communication the company cannot seek his consent again for a period of 12 months. Part 5, para.15 enables a company and a member to agree to alternative means of communication. For example, this might apply where a company has 'defaulted' to website communications under the above rules, but the member requests another form of communication.

3.47   It should be noted that in any event under s.1145 a member has the right to receive communications by way of hard copy. Part 4, para.11 makes similar provision as to means of communication noted above between the company and its debenture holders. Finally Part 4, para.13 requires the company to give notice to intended recipients when material is to be published on a company website.

Right to hard copy

3.48   Section 1145 provides that individual members or debenture holders have the right to require information to be supplied in hard copy. The company must send a paper copy of the information within 21 days of receiving such a request. It is an offence for the company or any officer to fail to comply with this provision.

3.49   Communications sent by a person to a company may require the authentication of documents. Section 1146 provides that in these cases a signature on any hard copy will constitute sufficient authentication. The section also prescribes the manner of authentication of documents sent by or supplied to the company in electronic form. Where the company has not prescribed a means of authentication, an electronic document is regarded as authenticated if the person sending the document identifies himself or themselves either in the document or by some communication accompanying the document. Where a person sends or supplies a document on another person's behalf, the company can require proof of his authority to do so.

3.50   Section 1147 sets out the circumstances when communications are deemed to have been delivered. The section however, can be excluded by contrary provision in the articles. The deemed delivery within the period of 48 hours of posting or in the case of electronic means within 48 hours of being sent is calculated by reference to normal working hours only. Section 1148 is the definition section for the purposes of the communication provisions considered above, and has already been noted where relevant.

Requirements as to independent valuation

3.51   Sections 1149–1153 were added to the Bill at a late stage, and fall uneasily within Part 37 of the Act. They collectively impose a requirement for any valuation and report made under:

(a) s.93 of the Act concerning re-registration of a company as a public company concerning the recent allotment of shares for non-cash consideration;

(b) s.593 of the Act concerning the allotment of shares of a public company for non-cash consideration; and

(c) s.599 of the Act concerning the transfer of a non-cash asset to a public company,

to be made by an independent and qualified valuer. By s.1150 the valuer must be eligible for appointment as a statutory auditor (see s.1212).

3.52   In addition the valuer must satisfy the condition of independence. Section 1151 sets out the conditions for independence which excludes, inter alia, officers of the company or persons 'associated' with the company from acting as valuer, albeit the company auditor is not excluded from holding the position of valuer for the above purposes. The concept of associate is fully defined in s.1152 so as to include persons who are, for example, the spouse or child of an officer or employee of the company (s.1152(2)).

3.53   Finally, under s.1153 a valuer in making a valuation and report within the terms of the above provisions is entitled to full and frank disclosure from the officers of the company. An offence is committed by an officer of a company who makes a statement with regard to a valuation and report prepared by the valuer knowing or being reckless as to the fact that his statement is false, misleading or deceptive in any material particular.

Notice of appointment of certain officers

3.54   Sections 1154–1155 are new provisions, although s.1154(1)(a) applies only to Scotland. There is a requirement to give notice to the registrar of the appointment of a receiver or manager under the Charities Act or manager under the Companies (Audit, Investigations and Community Enterprise) Act 2004. This includes the requirement to give notice of an address at which service of documents may be effected upon these persons. The notice must be given by the Charity Commissioners in the case of a receiver and manager and the Regulator of Community Interest Companies in the case of the appointment of a manager. The rationale behind the above provisions is that these persons displace the directors as officers of the company.

Meaning of court

3.55   Section 1156 defines the term 'the court' for the purposes of the Companies Acts and would perhaps have been better located in Part 38 of the Act, dealing with definitions. The effect of the section is that claims under the Companies Acts can be heard in the county court or the High Court, except where provided overwise by an enactment or rule of law. Allocation of cases between these courts will be determined in part by the procedural rules, orders made by the Lord Chancellor and by any subordinate legislation. Under s.1157 an officer of the company or a person employed by a company as an auditor may apply to the court for relief from liability for negligence, default, breach of duty or breach of trust (see **Chapters 4** and **7** for a consideration of these matters). A court may grant relief in these circumstances, but only if it appears to the court that the person 'acted honestly and reasonably, and that having regard to all the circumstances of the case . . . he ought fairly to be excused' (s.1157(1)).

3.56   Section 1157(1)–(3) replaces s.727 of the 1985 Act without any substantial amendment.

MEMBERS AND REGISTER OF MEMBERS

3.57   Part 8 of the 2006 Act replaces ss.22–23, and Chapter 2 of Part 11 of the 1985 Act.

3.58   Section 112 replaces s.22 of the 1985 Act. The section makes it clear that the subscribers to the memorandum become members on registration of the company, even if their names are not entered in the register of members. There is therefore no requirement (as was sought in Committee) for a company formally to allot the shares to the subscribers.

Register of members

3.59   Section 113 replaces s.352(1)–(5) of the 1985 Act. However s.113(5) is a new provision. It provides that for the purposes of Part 8, Chapter 1 joint holders of a share will be treated as a single member, albeit that all the names of the holders must be stated in the register.

3.60   Section 114 replaces s.353 of the 1985 Act. However, previous practice is changed in that the register of members is no longer required to be kept at the registered office or at a place within the jurisdiction where it is maintained, but may as an alternative be kept at any place specified in regulations made by the Secretary of State under s.1136 (see **para**. 3.36 above for a consideration of this section). Irrespective of the specified premises chosen by the company to keep the register, it must be kept available for inspection at that location.

3.61   Section 115 replaces s.354 of the 1985 Act. As before, a company with more than 50 members (although in Committee this was sought to be changed to 100 members) must maintain an index of the names of the members, unless the register itself constitutes an index.

Right of inspection of register and copies of entries

3.62   Sections 116–117 deal with the right to inspect and require copies of any entry on the register or index of members. Although reproducing the principal aspects of s.356 of the 1985 Act, the new sections also encompass, in part, the recommendation of the Company Law Review (Final Report, para 11.44), that information concerning members should be made available to an applicant only for specified purposes.

3.63   Section 116 was amended during its passage through Committee. The combined effect of the above provision is that information concerning a member on the register of members can only be inspected and copies provided following a request by the applicant that is supported by information concerning the applicant. The nature and terms of this information are set out in s.116(4). The purpose for which the information concerning the member is sought must also be specified in the application. This requirement was enacted so as to deal with the problem of the applicant seeking details of a member of a company in bad faith, e.g. animal rights activists and terrorists who hope to use the information to pursue a campaign of intimidation and harassment against the member.

3.64   Supplementary to the above provision, s.117 permits the company within five working days following receipt of a request for information and copies concerning a member to apply to court for a direction from the court that the company need not comply with the request, or any future requests from the same source, if the request is not for a 'proper purpose' (see s.117(3)–(4)). Attempts to have the term 'proper purpose' defined in these provisions were rejected by the Government (Hansard Vol.678 No.98 Col.GC149 *et seq.*).

Offences under ss.116–117

3.65   Section 118 provides for sanctions against a company and its officers for failure to comply with a request made under s.116, unless the court has made an order under s.117. Section 119 is a new provision, and creates two new offences. First, it is an offence for a person to provide in a request made under s.116 'a statement that is knowingly or recklessly misleading, false or deceptive in any material particular' (s.119(1)). Secondly, it is an offence to disclose information regarding a company's register of members to another person 'knowing, or having reason to suspect, that person may use the information for a purpose that is not a proper purpose' (s.119((2)).

3.66   Section 120 is a new provision which implements a recommendation of the Company Law Review. When a person exercises his right of inspection, or right to demand a copy of any entry on the register, or the index of members, the company must inform him whether the information on the register or index is up to date, or if not, the date to which the information has been made up (see s.120(1)–(2)). It is an offence to fail to provide this information (s.120(3)).

3.67   Section 121 replaces s.352(6) of the 1985 Act. An entry relating to a past member may be removed from the register after 10 years from the date when he ceased to be a member. This has been reduced from the previous requirement that the entry be kept for 20 years, following a recommendation of the Company Law Review (Final Report, para.11.40).

Shares and securities 'special cases'

3.68   Sections 122–124 deal with 'special cases' concerning securities and single member companies. Section 122 replaces s.355 of the 1985 Act. It implements a recommendation of the Company Law Review (see 'Completing the structure', para.5.41). It provides that shares (in effect with regard to public companies) do not have to be issued first in registered form, but can be issued directly in warrant or bearer form.

3.69   Section 123 replaces s.352A of the 1985 Act, and implements the Twelfth Company Law Directive (Directive 89/667/EEC) on single member private limited companies. In the case of a single member company, this section requires a statement that it only has one member to be entered in a company's register of members. Such an entry must be made on incorporation if that is the case, or at the time this circumstance occurs if it arises subsequently. A corresponding statement must be made if the company ceases to have a single member.

Rectification of register

3.70   Where a company holds treasury shares, s.124 replaces s.352(3A) of the 1985 Act as regards the entries which must be be made in the register of members. Section 125 replaces s.359 of the 1985 Act, and empowers the court to rectify any entry in the register. Section 126 replaces s.360 of the 1985 Act and provides that no notice of any trusts is to be entered on the register of members. The register of members is prima facie evidence of any matters which are entered upon it (s.127).

3.71   Under s.128, the time limit for claims arising from an entry is reduced from 20 years to 10 years. This follows a recommendation of the Company Law Review (Final Report, para.11.40).

Overseas companies

3.72   Sections 129–135 provide for the keeping of an overseas branch register for any company registered in the United Kingdom having a share capital and which conducts business in an overseas territory. The register records the details of members resident in those overseas territories (the territories to which these provisions apply are specified in s.129(2)). The provisions provide for notice to be given of the opening of an overseas branch register to the registrar in England and Wales (s.130).

3.73   The overseas branch register is to be regarded as part of the main register of members kept in the United Kingdom (s.131). The company must therefore keep a duplicate of such a register in the United Kingdom (s.132). Section 133 provides that shares registered in an overseas branch register must be distinguished from those registered in the main register. Overseas courts are provided with jurisdiction with respect to overseas branch registers by virtue of s.134.

3.74   Section 135 provides for the discontinuance of any overseas branch register, and for the transfer of any entries in the register to the main or other overseas branch register.

OVERSEAS COMPANIES OPERATING IN THE UNITED KINGDOM

Introduction

3.75   Part 34 of the Act applies to companies registered outside the United Kingdom, but which operate in the United Kingdom through branches. Part 34, inter alia, regulates the registration, reporting and disclosure requirements imposed on such overseas companies. It is proposed that Part 34 and any regulations made under its aegis will replace Part 23 and Scheds.21A–21D of the 1985 Act.

3.76   The intention of the 2006 Act is that any regulations made under the authority of Part 34 of the Act will continue to implement the provisions of the Eleventh Company Law Directive (Directive 89/666/EEC) which imposes disclosure requirements upon overseas companies operating in the United Kingdom. As a consequence of the 1985 Act and the Directive there were two effective regimes governing the disclosure requirements of overseas companies, depending on whether those companies had either branches or places of business in Great Britain. The Company Law Review provided an outline for reform of this aspect of company law in 'Strategic framework', Chapter 5.6. This was followed by a consultation document published in 1999, 'Reforming the Law Concerning Overseas Companies'. The Company Law Review presented its conclusions in its Final Report, paras.11.21–11.33.

3.77   Section 1044 is deceptively simple. It provides that for the purposes of Part 34 'an "overseas company" means a company incorporated outside the United Kingdom'. Section 744 of the 1985 Act, the precursor to s.1044, contained a narrower definition of an overseas company, which included the requirement that the company establish a place of business in Great Britain. Accordingly, the wider definition contained in s.1044 will permit subsequent regulations to state the precise connection with the United Kingdom that will impose the disclosure requirements under Part 34 upon an overseas company.

3.78   Section 1045 provides that the Secretary of State may make provision by regulations applying ss.43–52 of the 2006 Act (see **Chapter 2** for a consideration of these provisions) to overseas companies, subject to such exceptions, adaptations or modifications as may be specified in the regulations.

3.79   Section 1046 permits the Secretary of State to make regulations to require overseas companies to register with the registrar. The nature of the information that must be registered and the documents supplied, which may form the basis of the regulations, is specified, as is the obligation to inform the registrar of changes in the details and documents supplied. In accordance with the Eleventh Company Law Directive (Directive 89/666/EEC), the regulations may make different disclosure requirements depending on whether overseas companies are registered in an EEA State or not, or depending on the nature of the activities carried on by the overseas company.

3.80   Section 1047 (which together with s.1048 replaces s.694 of the 1985 Act) requires an overseas company subject to the registration regime prescribed under Part 34 to provide a name for registration. This may be the company's corporate name, or an alternative name (see s.1048 below). Section 1047(4)–(5), however, imposes restrictions upon the names that can be registered, and although an EEA registered company may be registered with its corporate name (subject to complying with s.57 (see **para.2.46**)), in all other cases the name sought to be registered by an overseas company must comply with the provisions relating to company names set out in Part 5, Chapter 1, ss.53–56, Chapter 2, s.65, Chapter 3, ss.66–74, and Chapter 4, ss.75–76 (see **Chapter 2** for a consideration of these provisions).

3.81   Section 1048 allows an overseas company to be registered under an alternative name instead of its corporate name, and subsequently to change the name in which it is registered. A statement must be supplied to the registrar to this effect where a name is to be registered. Subject to compliance with s.1047, the new name will be entered on the index of company names in place of the previous name. However, any legal proceedings that are continued or commenced by or against the company will not be affected by the change of name.

Accounts and reports

3.82   Section 1049 empowers the Secretary of State to make regulations requiring overseas companies to prepare accounts, directors' reports and to obtain an auditor's report. These will be similar to the requirements imposed by virtue of Parts 15–16 of the Act on companies registered and formed under the Companies Acts (see **Chapters 6** and **7** for a consideration of these provisions). The regulations may however, modify these requirements where the Secretary of State considers it appropriate.

3.83   Section 1050 applies to credit or financial institutions (such terms are defined in s.1173) which are incorporated or formed outside the United Kingdom and Gibraltar, whose head office is outside the United Kingdom and Gibraltar, but have a branch in the United Kingdom. By this section, the Secretary of State may make regulations regarding the accounts and directors' reports of such companies. Any regulations made under this section will replace those made under s.699A of and Sched.21C to the 1985 Act. Regulations made under s.1050 will implement certain requirements of the Bank Branches Directive (Directive 89/117/EEC). The term 'branch' for the purposes of the section and any regulations made thereunder is based on Directive 2000/12/EC, Art.1.3, which relates to the taking up and pursuit of the business of credit institutions.

3.84   Section 1051 enables the Secretary of State to make regulations requiring overseas companies to display specified information in certain locations, to provide specified information in certain documents and communications, and, on request, to supply specified information to those they deal with in the ordinary course of business. The section replaces any regulations made under s.693 of the 1985 Act. The section has obvious similarities to s.82 and the provisions in Part 5, Chapter 6 of the Act which apply to companies registered under the Companies Acts (see **para.2.59** for a consideration of these provisions and Part 5, Chapter 6 of the Act). As a supplement to the above, s.1053 requires overseas companies which are obliged to register particulars under s.1046 to make further returns. The Secretary of State may make regulations requiring such companies to deliver returns to the registrar if they are being wound up or if they are are subject to insolvency proceedings. The regulations may also provide that the liquidator of such companies should deliver returns to the registrar. The regulations may also determine the circumstances in which returns should be made, the information that should be contained in returns and when the returns should be made. The regulations will replace ss.703P and 703Q of the 1985 Act.

Offences

3.85 Under s.1054, regulations made under Part 34 of the Act will be able to specify the person or persons who will be responsible for complying with any specified requirement. The regulations are able to provide for offences, and to determine in the event of contravention who would be held responsible. They may also provide for any possible defences and for the appropriate penalties.

3.86 If any regulations made under s.1046 require an overseas company to register the usual residential address of an individual (e.g. a director), then s.1055 also requires the regulations to provide for the protection of that information as is provided for in Chapter 8, Part 10 of the Act. (See **Chapter 4** for a consideration of these provisions relating to the protection from disclosure in certain circumstances of a director's residential address.)

3.87 Under s.1056, which replaces s.691(1)(b)(ii) of, and para.3(e) of Sched.21A to, the 1985 Act, every overseas company required by regulations made under s.1046 to register with the registrar must register particulars identifying persons resident in the United Kingdom who are authorised to accept service of documents on the company's behalf. Alternatively, the company must make a statement that there is no such person. Service of a document on such a company will take place by leaving the same or posting it to the registered address of any person resident in the United Kingdom who has been authorised to accept service (s.1139).

3.88 Some overseas companies may be required to, or may have registered, particulars under s.1046 in more than one part of the United Kingdom. Section 1057 allows regulations to be made in respect of such companies.

3.89 If overseas companies which have registered particulars of a branch operating in the United Kingdom subsequently close the branch, s.1058 allows the registrar to make regulations requiring them to give notice of the closure to the registrar. Similar obligations to give notice will arise with respect to particulars registered under s.1046 which subsequently cease to obtain.

3.90 Section 1059 provides that if a branch of an overseas company is relocated from one part of the United Kingdom to another, this is to be treated as the closing of the first branch and the opening of a new branch, with the need, inter alia, to comply with the notice provisions of s.1058 as to the closing of a branch and to inform the registrar of the opening of another branch. This section replaces s.695A(4) of the 1985 Act.

PROHIBITION ON SUBSIDIARY BEING A MEMBER OF ITS HOLDING COMPANY

3.91 Part 8, Chapter 4 of the 2006 Act constitutes a restatement of the provisions of s.23 of the 1985 Act and Part 1 of Sched.2 as it applies for the purposes of that section. There is no change of substance, and accordingly these provisions will be briefly summarised.

3.92   Section 136 prohibits a company from holding shares of its own holding company. The prohibition applies to all corporate bodies irrespective of status or form. Section 137 is a saving provision for certain shares of this kind which were acquired by a subsidiary before the date the prohibition originally came into force under previous Companies Acts. Sections 138–141 provide for exceptions from the prohibition where the subsidiary is acting as personal representative or trustee, or as a dealer in securities.

3.93   Section 142, inter alia, provides for protection of third parties who acquire shares in good faith and without notice and for value in a holding company, and which were acquired from the subsidiary (or a third party dealing with those shares after disposal by the subsidiary), where the subsidiary had purportedly acquired the shares in the holding company in contravention of s.136. This protection however, only applies where the subsidiary is acting as a dealer in securities. If the terms of s.142 are satisfied the acquisition by the third party of the shares is deemed not to be in contravention of the prohibition. Sections 143–144 contain supplementary provisions.

EXERCISE OF MEMBERS' RIGHTS

3.94   Part 9 contains ss.145–153 of the Act, which are new provisions. The rationale behind these provisions was to promote 'shareholder engagement' and thereby a 'long-term investment culture'. The Government had noted that 40 per cent of investment in quoted companies is held in nominee accounts, and the following provisions were in part designed to encourage the continuation of such investment by ensuring that the investors have a more direct involvement in the running of the company (see **para.1.32** for further consideration of the issue of 'shareholder engagement'). This Part of the Act was considerably extended in form and ambit during the passage of the Bill thorough Committee. Under s.145 a member of a company can, under a provision in the company's articles, nominate a person or persons to enjoy or exercise all or specified rights of the member. Anything to be done by or in relation to the member under the Companies Acts shall or may be done in relation to a person nominated by a member so far as is necessary to give effect to the preceding sentence, and in particular the rights conferred by s.145(3). However the rights may not be enforced directly by the nominated person or persons against the company but rather the registered member will need to enforce these rights through the articles.

Information rights

3.95   In addition to the above rights that may be exercised by a nominated person, any person so nominated may also enjoy information rights. The nomination may be made by a member of a company whose shares are traded on regulated markets who holds shares on behalf of another person. Section 146(3) defines 'information rights' as including 'a right to receive a copy of all communications that the company sends to its members generally or to any class of its members that includes the person making the nomination'. It should be noted that by virtue of s.146(5) a company is not required to act on a nomination that purports to relate to certain information only.

3.96   Section 147 determines that the person to be nominated may, within the terms of s.147(2)–(3), seek to have the information in hard copy. This power is subject to the provisions of Parts 3 and 4 of Sched.5 under which a company whose shares are traded on regulated markets may communicate information electronically and via any website (see **para.3.45** above for a consideration of these provisions). Failure of a member making a nomination to have the company notified of a request on the part of the nominated person for information to be supplied in hard copy (or a failure to supply an address for sending the same) may result in the information being supplied via any website (s.147(5)). However, s.147(5) applies only by virtue of a deemed agreement on the part of the nominated person to accept information via a website, and may therefore be 'revoked' by him (s.147(6)). Furthermore the above does not affect the general right to receive information in the form of hard copy prescribed by s.1145 (see **para.3.42** above).

3.97   A nomination to enjoy information rights may be terminated by either the member or the nominated person (s.148(2)) and ceases to have effect in the case of the death, bankruptcy, dissolution or winding up (other than for purposes of reconstruction) of either the member or the nominated person (s.148(3)–(4)). The right to information may also be terminated if after an enquiry by the company to the nominated person as to whether he wishes to continue to receive information, no reply is received within 28 days (s.148(7)).

3.98   Special provision is made with regard to the providing of information concerning company meetings. A nominated person under s.149, who receives from the company a copy of a notice of any company meeting, must be informed by the company, by way of a statement accompanying the copy of the notice, of any right (given by any agreement between the member and nominee) he enjoys with respect to the possible power to appoint a proxy with regard to any company meeting, or a right to give instructions to the member as to the exercise of voting rights. It should be noted that s.325 (see **para.5.52** for a consideration of this provision) does not apply to any copy of the notice of the meeting sent to the nominee.

3.99   Section 150 specifies the rights of the nominee to information regarding the company and the periods when the right is not in operation (see s.150(4)). Section 150(2) provides that enjoyment by a nominated person of the rights to information is enforceable against the company by the member as if they were rights conferred by the articles. However s.150(6) provides that any failure to give effect to the right to information on the part of the company does not affect the validity of anything done by or on behalf of the company (s.150(6)). The powers prescribed by ss.146–150 may be amended by regulation by the Secretary of State under s.151. This includes the power to extend the provisions to any class of company.

3.100   As an adjunct to the above, s.152 permits a member to exercise rights attached to shares held on behalf of others without being obliged to exercise all the rights attached to the shares, or to exercise them all in the same way. The section thus recognises that the shareholder may hold shares on behalf of individuals who may have different interests in how the rights attached to the shares are exercised in given circumstances. In these cases the member is obliged to inform the company of the extent and nature of the exercise of those rights.

3.101   Under s.153, if the conditions set out in s.153(2) are satisfied (the principal condition being a request by at least 100 persons), the company is required to act under certain statutory provisions, namely under:

(a) s.314 (power to require circulation of statement);
(b) s.338 (public companies: power to require circulation of resolution for annual general meeting);
(c) s.342 (power to require independent report on poll); and
(d) s.527 (power to require website publication of audit concerns).

3.102   A request under this section may be made by members of the company or by persons on whose behalf members are holding shares.

4 DIRECTORS AND SECRETARIES

INTRODUCTION

4.1 Part 10 of the 2006 Act prescribes, inter alia, the role and function of the officers of a company and was subjected to considerable debate during its passage through Parliament. Despite the particularly trenchant criticisms of the parts of the Bill which prescribed the duties of directors (set out in Part 10, Chapter 2) this part of the Act, when finally enacted, was a disappointment. Chapter 2 did not constitute a reasoned enactment of such an integral and crucial aspect of company law, following and consequential upon a full and open debate. Part 10 in essence replaced Parts 9, 10 and the confidentiality aspects of Part 25 of the 1985 Act. The consideration of the nature, role and duties and powers of directors (and to a lesser degree secretaries) will, however, be considered briefly, except where the law has been subject to alteration by the 2006 Act, or in the case of directors' duties where the 2006 Act has effected a purported codification.

Definition of director

4.2 For the purposes of Part 10 a director is defined in the same terms as under the 1985 Act. Thus under s.250 a 'director' for the purposes of the 2006 Act includes executive, non-executive and de facto directors. Furthermore the concept of 'shadow director' is retained and defined in s.251 in the same terms as in the 1985 Act, s.741(2). The central functions of the directors of a company are set out in the draft model articles of association for private companies (which at the time of writing are in draft form in a schedule to the 2005 White Paper, see **paras.2.12–2.15**) as:

- managing the company's business; and
- exercising all the powers of the company for any purpose connected with managing the company's business.

The appointment and removal of directors

4.3 Section 154 of the 2006 Act replaces s.282 of the 1985 Act. It continues to distinguish between private and public companies as regards the need for a company to have a minimum number of directors. A private company must have at least one director, and all public companies must have a minimum of two. However s.155 is a new provision. It requires every company to have at least one director who is a natural person; therefore a corporation cannot be a sole director of a private company, unless it is a corporation sole (s.155(2)). Under s.156, if a company does not comply with the provisions of ss.154–155, for example with regard to the minimum number of directors in the case of a public company, the Secretary of State may issue a notice directing it to comply. It is an offence for the company not to comply with any notice issued.

Minimum age of directors

4.4   Section 157 is another new provision. It introduces a minimum age of 16 for an individual to be a director. It was noted during the passage of the Bill (see Hansard Vol.678 No.98 Col.GC168) that there are currently more than 1,000 directors aged 16–17 on the register of directors. However, under the Act a party can be appointed a director below the minimum age, provided the appointment does not take effect until the person attains the age of 16. The age limit applies even if the director's appointment is a consequence of some other appointment made in respect of a company. However, this prohibition on the appointment of under-age directors does not protect a person so appointed from any criminal or civil liability if he acts as a director with respect to the company, in practical terms a highly unlikely event. Section 158 provides for exceptions to be made from the general prohibition of under-age directors. Thus the Secretary of State may by regulation specify the circumstances in which a person under the age of 16 may be appointed a director. Under s.159 a person who is an under-age director when the above provisions come into force will cease to hold office. That fact must be recorded in the register of directors, but there is no requirement imposed on the company to notify the registrar of this change. Under s.159(4) the registrar has power to amend the register of directors if it appears to the registrar that an under-age person has ceased to be a director of the company. This may be done simply on the basis of the record of the date of birth of the director.

Directors and public companies – appointment

4.5   Section 160 of the 2006 Act replaces s.292 of the 1985 Act. Thus the appointment of every director of a public company must be voted on individually unless a block resolution is unanimously agreed. Any appointment of a director that does not comply with the section is void.

Actions of directors

4.6   Section 161 replaces s.285 of the 1985 Act, and provides that the actions of a director with respect to the company are valid even if his appointment is defective or void.

Register of directors

4.7   Section 162 in part replaces s.288 of the 1985 Act. All companies must keep a register of directors, which must be open to inspection at the company's registered office, or at a place specified in regulations made under s.1136 (see **para.3.36**). The company must give notice to the registrar of the current place where the register is kept, unless it has always been kept at the registered office (s.162(4)). Members may inspect the register of directors without the payment of a fee, unlike non-members. It is an offence, inter alia, for the company to refuse inspection of the register to a person making such a request. Default in complying with a notice to inform the registrar of the current location of the register also constitutes an offence.

4.8   Section 163 replaces s.289 of the 1985 Act. It specifies the information that must be entered on the register of directors for every director who is a natural person. The most significant change in the law is that companies are required to provide a service address for a natural director rather than, as under the previous law, the director's usual residential address. This reform is an aspect of the protection from public disclosure of the personal details of a director in certain circumstances (see Chapter 8 of Part 10 which is considered below at **paras.4.73–4.77**). There is no longer a requirement to set out details such as any other directorships held. Another new provision under the section is the requirement to provide in the register any name by which a director is or has been known for business purposes. As was recommended by the Company Law Review in its Final Report (para.11.38), the former name of a married woman who is a director must be recorded.

4.9   Section 165 is another new provision. Under s.165, companies must keep a register of the usual residential address of a director who is a natural person. However, this register is not to be open to public inspection, but is to be used only in accordance with Part 10, Chapter 8 relating to the protection from public disclosure of a director's residential address (see **paras.4.73–4.77** below). Under s.166, another new provision, the Secretary of State is empowered to make regulations amending the particulars that must be entered on the register of directors and the register of directors' residential addresses.

Non-natural directors

4.10   Section 164 of the 2006 Act relates to the names of corporate directors and firms. The section replaces s.289(1)(b) of the 1985 Act. It continues to require a corporate or firm name and the registered or principal office of a non-natural director to be recorded on the register of directors, including those of a firm which is a director, where under the law governing that firm it is regarded as a legal person. The legal form of the non-natural director and the national law by which it is governed should also be recorded. In addition, in accordance with the recommendation of the Company Law Review in its Final Report (para.11.38) there is now a requirement for all EEA companies that are directors of a company registered in the United Kingdom to register their details as prescribed under s.164(c).

4.11   Section 167 replaces s.288(2) of the 1985 Act in so far as it applies to directors. It retains the requirement that the appointment or removal of a director, or his ceasing to hold office, or any change in the particulars of a director, be notified to the registrar within 14 days. The section requires a notice of appointment to be accompanied by a document recording the appointee's consent to the appointment. There is also a requirement to notify the registrar of any change in the particulars in the register of directors' residential addresses.

Removal

4.12   Sections 168–169 replace ss.303–304 of the 1985 Act and make no change in the law save that under s.169(5) the court need only be satisfied that the rights conferred by the section are being abused: under the 1985 Act, s.304(4) the court had to be satisfied that the rights were being abused 'to secure needless publicity for defamatory matter'. A director may therefore be removed on the passing of an ordinary resolution. The presence of a *Bushell* v. *Faith* clause (see [1970] AC 1099) in the articles should however, be noted in these circumstances.

DUTIES OF DIRECTORS

General comment

4.13   Chapter 2 of Part 10 sets out the general duties of directors. In part these provisions were based on the recommendations of the Company Law Review that there should be a statutory statement of directors' duties, which should in general terms be a codification of the common law. It was hoped that the codification would achieve the following aims:

(a) greater clarity on what is expected of directors and to make the law more accessible – in particular the code should clarify the issue of 'in whose interests should companies be run' in accordance with modern business needs and 'responsible business behaviour';

(b) to make development of the law relating to directors and their duties more predictable;

(c) to correct what the Company Law Review saw as defects in the duties relating to conflict of interests. In this case the statutory provisions should effect reform of the law.

4.14   It may be argued with considerable justification that these aims were not achieved by the provisions set out in Chapter 2 of Part 10 of the Act (see **paras.4.15–4.17** below).

Criticism of Chapter 2

4.15 Chapter 2 of Part 10 of the Act was subjected to considerable criticism during the passage of the Bill through Parliament (see for example the scathing criticism of these aspects of the Bill in the *Sunday Telegraph* Business Section, 18 June 2006, entitled 'Labour's Company Law Bill descends into farce'). The rationale of these provisions was first set out by the Government's official spokesman Lord Sainsbury of Turville (see Hansard Vol.677 No.85 Col.184) where his Lordship essentially repeated the aims and objectives of the Company Law Review concerning the codification of directors' duties which has been noted above. The views of Lord Sharman on this aspect of the Act may however, stand as the general nature and form of the criticisms of Chapter 2 that were regularly propounded during the passage of the Bill. His Lordship noted that:

> . . . the clauses in Chapter 2 of Part 10 in particular are flawed and not workable. Commentators such as the Law Society, while supporting the aims of clarification of director's duties – which I also support – does not believe that has been achieved. The new provisions are said by the guidance notes to provide greater clarity on what is expected of directors and make development of the law in this area more predictable. However, it is argued that the provisions are inflexible and will restrict the courts. The code has not adopted common law terminology and introduces new concepts that will make remedies more difficult to apply. For example, clause 156(3) . . . [now s.173(2)] . . . requires directors to fulfil their duties, 'so far as reasonably practicable'
>
> We are advised that that it is both ambiguous and otiose. We question whether it will require senior directors to set up expensive and extensive internal procedures to create audit trails in respect of any authority which they delegate down the management chain.
>
> (Hansard Vol.677 No.85 Col.194)

4.16 Despite these criticisms and other views expressed during the passage of the Bill, to the effect that the code governing directors' duties set out in Chapter 2 would not encourage individuals to undertake the position of non-executive director (see the comparatively full debate on the issues of directors' duties in Hansard Vol.678 No.100 Col.GC237 *et seq.*), the provisions in Chapter 2 concerning director's duties, it is suggested, neither clearly reproduced the previous common law position as regards those duties (where this was the purported intent of the Government) nor, it is suggested, did the provisions produce, as is required in a code, a clarity and certainty of application. The adoption of 'simple straightforward language' in prescribing these duties, rather than well-established 'common law' terms with which company lawyers are familiar and which the courts have honed into terms of art, presumably on the grounds that this approach to drafting will make the provisions more accessible to directors, will it is suggested do no more than create uncertainty for the foreseeable future as to the nature and extent of directors' duties.

4.17 Furthermore, the clauses which constituted Chapter 2 were altered only in the most superficial fashion during the passage of the Bill, despite extensive criticism of these provisions as originally drafted. The amendments to ss.172 and 180 (which were the only provisions in the Chapter subject to substantial amendment) were essentially grammatical except in one respect. Even the eventual removal of the substantive requirement for a director to fulfil his duties 'as far as reasonably practicable' in what was originally s.156(3) and which was to become s.171(2) was not regarded by the Government as substantially changing the nature of the prescribed duties, nor did it alter the view of the Government that the sections in their final form were any less of a codification of the common law duties of a director when compared to the provisions as originally drafted. It is submitted that these provisions, as enacted, will prove to be difficult to apply or enforce (this issue will be examined below). The provisions may also prove exceptionally difficult for practitioners to interpret as regards their nature, ambit and application, rendering the giving of advice to directors by company lawyers as to how they should conduct themselves with regard to their company a hazardous and potentially unfruitful exercise until extensive interpretative case law becomes available.

Fiduciary duties – duties of skill and care

4.18   The Law Commission had recommended that there should be a statutory statement of the fiduciary duties and the duties of care and skill of directors in its report, 'Company Directors: Regulating Conflicts of Interests and Formulating a Statement of Duties'. The recommendations were taken up by the Government in the Bill. However, the provisions in the Act concerning fiduciary duties and conflict of interest, unlike the other provisions of the code governing directors' duties, were intended to effect to some degree reforms in these areas of the law.

The duties and powers of directors

4.19   The statutory duties set out in Chapter 2 of Part 10 do not cover all the duties that a director may owe to the company. Many duties are set out in other legislation, or other Parts of the Act. Section 170 makes it clear, as was the position at common law, that the general duties of directors are owed to the company and can only be enforced by the company. The ability of the members to enforce these duties by derivative claims is preserved by the 2006 Act. These duties are also owed to the company by shadow directors (s.170(5)) and de facto directors. Section 170(3) determines that the statutory duties are based on, and will have effect in place of, the common law rules and equitable principles previously governing the conduct of directors.

Director to act within powers

4.20   Section 171 sets out the principle of law under which a director should exercise his powers in accordance with the terms on which they were granted, and directors must exercise their powers for a proper purpose. This section thus codifies the director's duty to comply with the company's constitution, which includes the articles, or any decisions taken in accordance with the company's articles, and any decisions taken by the members or a class of members if they are to be treated as decisions of the company by virtue of any enactment or rule of law.

To promote the success of the company

4.21   Section 172 was, in the opinion of the Government, designed to ensure that a director would act in the long-term interests of the company whether it was a quasi-partnership company or a listed company. It was intended that the provisions would advance 'enlightened shareholder value'. The section requires a director, in good faith, to act in a way which would be most likely to promote the success of the company for the benefit of its members as a whole, having regard to the factors set out in s.172(1). The list of factors was not, however, intended to be exhaustive (see Hansard Vol.678 No.100 Col.GC243).

4.22   Perhaps the problems of this section may be that the director is to exercise his duty so as to promote the success of the company, but to do so from the viewpoint of any perceived benefit to the members and not, as in the past, the company as a whole (if of course these terms are not subsequently held by the courts to be in practical terms the same thing). There seems, however, no need for a director to have regard to the interests of the future members of the company when acting on behalf of the company. The need also for a director to have regard to the interests of the employees and the company's impact on the environment are clearly factors in the exercise of the duty to ensure the success of the company that may prove to be difficult to reconcile with the duty also to have regard to the benefit of the members of the company as a whole. It will certainly be difficult to ensure these factors are taken into account by directors while acting to ensure the success of the company in the case of most private companies, where the employees for example will not be members of the company. In such a case who will enforce any 'breach' of the duty prescribed under the section?

To exercise independent judgment

4.23   Section 173 was intended to codify the common law principle whereby directors must exercise their powers independently, without subordinating their powers to the will of third parties. This situation could arise through delegating certain powers, which would potentially constitute a breach of the duty to exercise independent judgment, unless for example the articles expressly authorised delegation. A director must not fetter his future exercise of his powers, unless such an action is authorised, for example by virtue of an agreement to that effect which has been entered into by the company, or the company's constitution so provides. The application of this section to directors is subject to the problems that arise with regard to all private limited companies, where the authorisation to fetter such powers may effectively be made by the director on behalf of the company under the guise of a member, who by exercising his voting power may secure an authorisation so to act by way of a provision in the articles.

Reasonable care, skill and diligence

4.24   Section 174 codifies the director's duty to exercise care, skill and diligence. It is clearly based on the level of skill and expertise that was expected of a director of the company acting under and subject to s.214 of the Insolvency Act 1986. Case law had in any event effectively achieved this standard of care and conduct for directors of even private limited companies that were quasi-partnerships and family companies (see *Norman* v. *Theodore Goddard* [1991] BCLC 1028). The standard of competence now expected of all directors will be that currently expected of a director with the expertise and experience of the director in question. The standard therefore is in part objective, but with regard to the limitations and qualities of the director in issue. Nevertheless, in practical terms the consequence of this provision, it is submitted, is that more skill and expertise and competence will generally be expected of a director of a public and particularly a listed company, than a director of a family or quasi-partnership company engaged in a trade.

DUTY TO AVOID CONFLICT OF INTEREST

Introduction

4.25   Unlike the above provisions concerning directors' duties, s.175 does seek to amend the common law and particularly the equitable principles which governed the 'no conflict of interest' rule which was applicable to directors as fiduciaries. Under the law in existence prior to the coming into force of this provision, the rules of equity in particular ensured draconian consequences for directors who placed themselves in a position where their interests conflicted with the interests of the company, or with the exercise of the duties that they owed to the company. Although the section covers all such cases of conflict of interest or duty, actual or potential, that may arise with respect to the director as regards the company (other than those covered by ss.176–177; see also s.175(3) and s.182), the principal reform to this area of the law lies in how such conflicts of interest may be authorised. Under s.175(4)(b) the authorisation of any conflict of duty or interest may be authorised by the directors of the company in a quorate meeting and in accordance with the conditions set out in s.175(5)–(6). Principally these conditions are that authorisation is given by directors who are genuinely independent. Furthermore, in the case of a private company the constitution must not prevent authorisation by the directors, or in the case of public companies authorisation must be expressly permitted by the constitution. The view of Lord Goldsmith in the House of Lords (see Hansard Vol.678 No.100 Col.CG288) was that the section in 'codifying' the law also permitted authorisation by the members of the company, but this is nowhere stated in the section (although s.180(4) provides that any current rule of law enabling the company to authorise conflicts of interest is preserved). In allowing authorisation of a conflict of interest or duty by the directors in the case of a private company, unless there is a prohibition in the company's constitution, the section adopted a recommendation of the

Company Law Review. However, s.175(4) also provides that there is no conflict of interest or duty on the part of a director if the situation the director finds himself in cannot reasonably be regarded as likely to give rise to a conflict of interest (s.175(4)(a)). The purpose of s.175(4)(a) was explained in the following terms by Lord Goldsmith:

> Clause 159(4)(a) ... [now s.175(4)(a)] ... also recognises that unexpected situations can arise where a conflict exists, and you are not in breach because of that. Once you know the conflict is there, that is a different matter. Once you know that you are now in a situation of conflict, you will have to do something about it, but you are not in breach simply because it happened when, as is set out in subsection 4(a), it could not, 'reasonably be regarded as likely to give rise to' the conflict.

(Hansard Vol.678 No.100 Col.GC289)

Duty not to accept benefits from third parties

4.26 Section 176 codifies the law prohibiting exploitation of the position of director for personal benefit. The section thus prohibits the acceptance of benefits (including the receipt of bribes which in accordance with principles of equity should be regarded as the property of the company). The acceptance of a benefit by a director giving rise to an actual or potential conflict under the section could also possibly fall within the provisions of s.175. However, authorisation of any such conflict under the provisions of s.176 can it seems only be undertaken by the members of the company. As in the case of s.175(4)(a), there is no conflict of duty under the section if the acceptance of the benefit cannot reasonably be regarded as likely to give rise to a conflict of interest (s.176(4)). For a consideration of the meaning and effect of this provision see the discussion of s.175(4)(a) at **para.4.25**.

Duty to declare interest in proposed transaction or arrangement

4.27 The rules of equity determined that directors could not enjoy an interest in any proposed transaction or arrangement which involved the company, unless the acquisition of the potential interest had been authorised by the members of the company. Section 177 replaces this particular rule, and requires a director to disclose any proposed interest, be it a direct or indirect interest, that he may enjoy in any proposed transaction or arrangement involving the company. The section applies whether or not the director concerned is a party to the proposed transaction or arrangement. As noted above shareholder approval or authorisation was previously required concerning any such transactions involving a company and a director, albeit that the articles of companies frequently modified this rule. This is no longer a requirement of the law.

4.28 Although the section now requires the director to disclose any proposed interest in any transaction (s.177(4)), there are at present no rules which govern how disclosure may be made. However, s.177(2) allows the disclosure to be made by written notice, general notice, or by disclosure at a meeting of the directors.

The director must declare the full nature and extent of the proposed interest to the other directors, and of any changes in the circumstances of his interest before the company has entered into the transaction or arrangement (s.177(3)). The director is not obliged to make disclosure where he is not aware of any interest as defined in the section, but he is to be regarded as having such knowledge where he ought reasonably to have been aware of the interest.

4.29   A director need not make disclosure under the section if the situation in which he finds himself cannot reasonably be regarded as likely to give rise to a conflict of interest (see s.177(6)(a) and **para.4.25** above for a consideration of the nature of this provision). Neither does a duty to disclose the interest arise if the other directors are already aware or ought reasonably to be aware of the nature of the interest enjoyed by the director (s.177(6)(b)).

4.30   Section 177(6)(c) makes special provision for dealing with potential conflicts of interest with respect to directors' service contracts that are considered at a meeting of the directors or a sub-committee. For practical purposes the company's articles will frequently make provision for dealing with issues of conflict that arise under the terms of s.177. The draft model articles for private limited companies limited by shares (which at the time of writing are in draft form in a schedule to the 2005 White Paper: see **Chapter 2**) provide that the directors in most cases must disregard the views of an interested director when making a majority decision on a matter relating to a proposed transaction involving the company and a fellow director.

Remedies for breach of duty

4.31   Section 178 preserves the common law and equitable remedies available in the case of a breach of any of the duties by a director prescribed under ss.171–177. Section 179 recognises that the conduct of a director may breach more than one of the duties prescribed under the above provisions.

Consent, approval or authorisation

4.32   Section 180 recognises potential conflict between the position of the directors and the members of a company when those parties are different individuals in cases involving the authorisation or approval of a breach of duty on the part of a director by the directors of the company. Thus s.180 provides that in the absence of any provision in the company's articles or any enactment where authorisation has been secured under the provisions of either s.175 or s.177, the relevant transaction or arrangement cannot be set aside by virtue of any common law rule or equitable principle which would have required the consent or approval of the company's members (s.180(1)). This provision may have little practical effect in many companies, however, where the directors are also the shareholders. Nevertheless it may be prudent to consider inserting a provision in the articles protecting and preserving the power of the members to prohibit or veto the powers of the directors in cases where either s.175 or s.177 applies.

4.33   Furthermore, s.180(2) provides that situations which involve a director and which constitute by him a breach of the duties set out in Chapter 2 of Part 10 may also constitute cases which fall within the provisions of Chapter 4 of Part 10 concerning transactions or arrangements involving directors requiring the approval of members, for example where the transaction or arrangement is a substantial one (see **para.4.44** *et seq.*). In these cases if approval is given by the members of the company under Chapter 4 of Part 10, or by virtue of those very provisions approval of the relevant transaction or arrangement is not needed, it is not necessary for the director and company to seek also to comply with s.175 or s.176 (s.180(2)).

4.34   It is also stated that compliance with the provisions for authorisation of any transactions or arrangements giving rise to potential conflicts of interest under the provisions of Chapter 2 does not, however, remove the need for approval of any transaction or arrangement with which a director is involved, and which under the provisions of Chapter 4 requires the approval of the members of the company (s.180(3)). This subsection therefore recognises the ultimate authority of the members of the company in cases where the transaction or arrangement which may give rise to conflict of interest is subject to the provisions of Chapter 4.

4.35   The duties prescribed under Chapter 2 are, however, subject to any rule of law which enables a company to give authority to the directors to act in a way which would otherwise constitute a breach of duty (s.180(4)(a)). The section also recognises that the company's articles may contain provisions that may authorise directors to act in a way which would otherwise constitute a breach of duty (s.180(4)(b)).

Modification of 'no conflict' rules in relation to charitable companies

4.36   Section 181 reverses certain relaxations made to the 'no conflict' rule considered above in respect of the directors of charitable companies in England and Wales. Section 181(2)(a) replaces, in respect of charitable companies, s.175(3) which excludes potential conflict of interest under s.175 in so far as the conflict arises out of transactions or arrangements with the company. It excludes such conflicts of interest from the duty of directors prescribed under s.175, but only in so far as the charitable company's articles permit. The types of transactions or arrangements that are excluded should be set out in the articles.

4.37   Section 181(2)(b) replaces, in respect of charitable companies, s.175(5), allowing authorisation for conflicts of interest to be given by the directors. However they may only do so where the charitable company's constitution expressly permits such authorisation.

4.38   Section 181(3) restricts, in respect of charitable companies, the application of s.180(2)(b), which disapplies s.175 and s.176 regarding matters excepted from the member approval requirements under Chapter 4 of Part 10. Section

180(2)(b) is, as regards charitable companies, restricted so that the duties to avoid conflict or to accept benefits apply to a director only if, or to the extent that, the articles of the charitable company allow the duties under ss.175–176 to be disapplied. The articles of the charitable company must set out the transactions or arrangements which are to be so excluded.

4.39 Section 181(4) amends the Charities Act 1993, and gives the Charity Commission power to authorise acts that would otherwise be in breach of the general duties of directors. This provision was regarded as necessary in order to retain the current power of the Charity Commissioners to authorise such acts, given the statutory statement of the general duties of directors.

DECLARATION OF INTEREST IN EXISTING TRANSACTION OR ARRANGEMENT

4.40 Sections 182–187 (Chapter 3 of Part 10 of the 2006 Act) require a director to declare the nature and extent of any direct or indirect interest that he may have in any transaction or arrangement that the company has entered into. The director in these circumstances is obliged to make a declaration of any matter relating to any transactions or arrangements of which he ought reasonably to have known. The transaction or arrangement must be one already entered into by the company, as opposed to a proposed transaction or arrangement, declarations in respect of which are covered by s.177, considered at **paras.4.27–4.30** above. If the director has made a declaration under s.177 concerning a proposed transaction or arrangement, he is not obliged to make a further declaration under Chapter 3 when the transaction or arrangement becomes an existing one (s.182(1)).

4.41 No declaration need be made under s.182 if the transaction or arrangement 'cannot reasonably be regarded as likely to give rise to a conflict of interest' (for a consideration of this term see **para.4.25** considered in the context of s.175). Neither need a declaration be made if the other directors know of the transaction or arrangement or ought reasonably to know of it, or the matter relates to the terms of the relevant director's service contract, which are to be or have been considered by a meeting of directors or a committee of directors. The section replaces the provisions of s.317 of the 1985 Act. It is an offence not to declare an interest under s.182 (see s.183).

4.42 The declaration under s.182 must be made either:

- at a directors' meeting;
- by notice in writing (see s.184); or
- by general notice (see s.185).

4.43 The notice in writing under s.184 must be sent to all directors, and may if agreed be in electronic form. If delivered within the terms of the section it is a matter to be regarded as forming part of the proceedings of the next directors' meeting. Section 185 permits a director to give a general notice of his interests.

This involves the giving of a notice of interests in other companies or firms, or notice of general connections with another natural person such as a spouse or relative. If the company subsequently enters into a transaction or arrangement with such bodies or persons the director is not obliged to make a fresh declaration. Where a company has a sole director, compliance with s.182 is neither required nor possible. However, where the company should have more than one director, because it is a public company, the sole director must record in writing his interest in any transaction or arrangement that has been entered into by the company (s.186). The provisions of Part 10, Chapter 3 apply also to shadow directors by virtue of s.187, albeit with modifications (see s.187(2)–(4)).

SUBSTANTIAL PROPERTY TRANSACTIONS, LOANS, QUASI-LOANS AND SERVICE CONTRACTS

4.44   Chapters 4 and 5 of Part 10 contain provisions drafted to deal with situations where a director may have a conflict of interest with respect to certain transactions involving the company and which concern, inter alia, substantial property transactions, loans and related matters or the director's service contract. These provisions replace Part 10 of the 1985 Act, but with a number of changes. It is intended to refer briefly to the nature of the provisions in so far as they reproduce the previous law set out in Part 10 of the 1985 Act, and to concentrate on the principal changes to the law made by Chapters 4 and 5.

4.45   The rationale behind the reforms to these aspects of the 'no conflict' rule was to improve accessibility to the law and to make it more consistent with the general rules governing conflicts of interest involving directors and the company. The law as set out in Chapters 4 and 5 seeks to implement the recommendations set out in the Law Commission's joint report 'Company Directors: Regulating Conflicts of Interests and Formulating a Statement of Duties', Annex C of 'Developing the Framework', Chapter 4 of 'Completing the Structure' and Chapter 6 of the Final Report. Chapters 4 and 5 of Part 10 of the 2006 Act maintain the requirement for certain transactions involving directors, as set out in the relevant provisions to be disclosed to members of the company or to be approved by them. The transactions subject to Chapters 4 and 5 are as follows.

Directors' service contracts

4.46   Sections 188–189 replace s.319 of the 1985 Act. Section 188 thus requires member approval of a director's long-term service contract. The principal change to the law is that service contracts of over two years must be approved, rather than the previous requirement for approval of those lasting longer than five years (s.188(1)).

Substantial property transactions

4.47   Sections 190–196 replace ss.320–322 of the 1985 Act. Members must approve property transactions or arrangements where the company buys or sells a substantial non-cash asset (see s.190(1)) to or from a director or a director of its holding company, or a person connected with them.

4.48   An asset will be a substantial non-cash asset if it it exceeds £100,000 in value (s.191(2)(b)) or 10 per cent of the company's net assets, where this is more than £5,000 (s.191(2)(a)).

4.49   As noted in the Explanatory Notes, the principal changes to the law set out in the 1985 Act are:

–   permitting a company to enter into a contract which is conditional on member approval (section 190(1)). This implements a recommendation of the Law Commissions. In cases where the approval of the members of the holding company is also required, the company may enter into arrangements conditional on approval being obtained from the members of the holding company (section 190(2)). The company is not to be liable under the contract if member approval is not forthcoming (section 190(3));

–   providing for the aggregation of non-cash assets forming part of an arrangement or series of arrangements for the purpose of determining whether the financial thresholds have been exceeded so that member approval is required (section 190(5));

–   excluding payments under directors' service contracts and payments for loss of office from the requirements of these sections (section 190(6)). This implements a recommendation of the Law Commissions;

–   raising the minimum value of what may be regarded as a substantial non-cash asset from £2,000 to £5,000 (section 191);

–   expanding the exception for transactions with members to include the acquisition of assets from a person in his character as a member of the company (section 192(a));

–   providing an exception for transactions made by companies in administration (section 193). This implements a recommendation of the Law Commissions;

–   not requiring approval on the part of the members of a company that is in administration or is being wound up (unless it is a members' voluntary winding up) (section 193).

(Explanatory Notes, para 403)

Loans, quasi-loans and credit transactions

4.50   Sections 197–214 require member approval for loans, quasi-loans (see s.199 for a definition of this term), credit transactions (as defined in s.202) and any related guarantees or securities supplied by the company to directors, or directors of holding companies, and in the case of loans and quasi-loans to persons connected with directors. Section 203 prohibits a company taking part in any related arrangements by which another person enters into such transactions as noted above, which if entered into by the company directly would require member approval, unless the approval of the members of the company to that arrangement is secured.

4.51   In the case of a private or public company under s.197, member approval is required for any loans (or guarantees) made to:

(a) a director of the company, or
(b) a director of its holding company.

4.52   In the case of a public company, or a company associated with a public company, under s.198 member approval is required for any quasi-loans transactions (or guarantees) made to:

(a) a director of the company, or
(b) a director of its holding company,

or under s.200 for any loans or quasi-loan transactions (or guarantees) made to:

(a) a person connected with a director, or
(b) a person connected with a director of its holding company.

4.53   In the case of a public company, or a company associated with a public company, under s.201 member approval is required for any credit transaction (or guarantees) made to:

(a) a director of the company or,
(b) a director of its holding company.

4.54   Member approval is not required under the above provisions for:

(a) loans, quasi-loans, credit transactions and related guarantees or security under ss.197, 198, 200 or 201 so as to enable the director of the company or its holding company, or a person connected with any such director, to meet expenditure on company business; however, the total value or aggregate of transactions in order to come within this exception made with respect to a director of the company or its holding company and any person connected with any such director must not exceed £50,000 (s.204(2));
(b) money lent to a director in connection with defence costs incurred in legal proceedings (s.205), or in connection with regulatory action or investigation (s.206);
(c) any small loans and quasi-loans dependent on the total value of such loans and quasi-loans not exceeding £10,000 (s.207(1));
(d) any small credit transactions dependent on the total value of such credit transactions not exceeding £15,000 (s.207(2));
(e) any credit transactions made in the ordinary course of the company's business (s.207(3));
(f) any intra-group transactions (s.208);
(g) any loans and quasi-loans made by a money-lending company in the ordinary course of the company's business, and satisfying the requirements of s.209 of the 2006 Act.

4.55   Sections 197–214 replace ss.330–342 of the 1985 Act. The Explanatory Notes list the principal changes as follows:

- abolishing the prohibition on loans, quasi-loans etc to directors and replacing it with a requirement for member approval. This implements a recommendation of the [Company Law Review];

- abolishing the criminal penalty for breach;

- replacing the concept of relevant company in section 331 of the 1985 Act with associated company, as defined in section 256;

- removing some of the requirements currently imposed by section 337 of the 1985 Act on the exception for expenditure on company business (section 204);

- widening the exception for expenditure on company business to include directors of the company's holding company and connected persons (section 204);

- creating a new exception specifically for expenditure in connection with regulatory action or investigations (section 206);

- restricting the exceptions for expenditure on defending legal or regulatory proceedings to proceedings in connection with any alleged negligence, default, breach of duty or breach of trust by the director in relation to the company or an associated company (sections 205 and 206);

- widening the exception for small loans to include small quasi-loans (section 207(1)) in place of the current exception for short-term small quasi-loans in section 332 of the 1985 Act;

- widening the exception for small loans and quasi-loans to include transactions with connected persons (section 207(1));

- widening the exception for 'home loans' to include those connected persons who are employees (section 209(3));

- raising the maximum amounts permitted under the exception for expenditure on company business (section 204), the exception for small loans and small quasi-loans (section 207(1)) and the exception for small credit transactions (section 207(2));

- widening the exceptions for intra-group transactions (section 208);

- abolishing the maximum amounts permitted under the exception for money-lending companies (section 209); and

- allowing affirmation of loans, quasi-loans and credit transactions entered into by the company in line with the provision in respect of substantial property transactions (section 214).

(Explanatory Notes, para.408)

Payments for loss of office

4.56   Sections 215–222 of the 2006 Act, which replace ss.312–316 of the 1985 Act, require approval of the members for payments for loss of office. These are payments made to a director or former director as compensation for ceasing to hold the office of director, or for the loss of any other office or employment with the company or its subsidiary. Payments to a person connected with the director, or at the direction of the director, may be treated as payments to the director and may therefore, if regarded as sums paid for compensation for loss of office, require member approval. Payments covered by the above provisions include those made in consideration of, or in connection with, the retirement of a director. In the case of payments made regarding retirement or loss of employment, the employment must be in connection with the management of the affairs of the company (s.215).

4.57   Member approval is required under s.217 if the company wishes to make a payment for loss of office to:

(a) a director, or
(b) a director of its holding company, or
(c) a person connected with a director.

4.58   Member approval is also required under the above provisions where any person wishes to make a payment to a director for loss of office in connection with the transfer of the whole or any part of the undertaking or the property of the company (s.218).

4.59   Where a payment for loss of office of a director is to be made in connection with the transfer of shares in the company, or a subsidiary, as a result of a takeover bid, the approval of the holders of the shares to which the bid relates and of any other holders of shares of the same class will required (s.219).

Principal changes to the law

4.60   As noted in the Explanatory Notes, the principal changes to the law set out in the 1985 Act include:

–   extending the requirements to include payments to connected persons (section 215(3));

–   extending the requirements to include payments to directors in respect of the loss of any office, or employment in connection with the management of the affairs of the company, and not merely loss of office as a director as such (section 215). This implements a recommendation of the Law Commissions;

–   extending the requirements to include payments by a company to a director of its holding company (section 217(2));

–   extending the requirements in connection with the transfer of the undertaking or property of the company to include transfers of the undertaking or property of a subsidiary (section 218(2));

–   extending the requirements in connection with share transfers so as to include all transfers of shares in the company or in a subsidiary resulting from a takeover bid (section 219(1));

–   excluding the persons making the offer for shares in the company and any associate of them from voting on any resolution to approve a payment for loss of office in connection with a share transfer (section 219(4)). This implements a recommendation of the Law Commissions;

– setting out the exception for payments in discharge of certain legal obligations (section 220);

– creating a new exception for small payments (section 221);

– clarifying the civil consequences of breach of these sections (section 222(1) to (3)); and

– resolving conflicts between the remedies where more than one requirement of these sections is breached (section 222(4) and (5)). For example, if the payment contravenes both section 217 and section 219 because it was a payment by a company to one of its directors and it was a payment in connection with a takeover bid, and none of the required member approvals have been obtained, then the payment is held on trust for the persons who have sold their shares as a result of the offer and not on trust for the company making the payment.

(Explanatory Notes, para.413)

Supplementary provisions

4.61   Section 223 applies the above provisions to shadow directors. Section 224 provides that where approval is sought under Chapter 4 of Part 10 by written resolution (see **Chapter 5** concerning written resolutions) and a memorandum is also required to be sent to every eligible member before the resolution is passed, then any accidental failure to send or submit the memorandum to one or more members will be disregarded for determining whether the requirement has been met. This saving provision must take effect subject to any provision in the company's articles (s.224(2)). Where approval is required under more than one provision, then s.225 prescribes that approval under each applicable provision must be met, albeit that such multiple approvals can be secured under a single resolution. Section 226 substitutes a new s.66 and also inserts a new s.66A into the Charities Act 1993. These provisions provide that the prior written consent of the Charity Commissioners is required when a charitable company seeks to approve or affirm any transactions under the provisions of Chapter 4 which are set out in s.66(2), or to do any act which does not require approval by virtue of Chapter 4, as prescribed by s.66A(2).

SERVICE CONTRACTS

4.62   Section 227 defines what constitutes a service contract for the purposes of Part 10 of the 2006 Act. The term 'service contract' is used in ss.177, 182, 188 and 190, and in Chapter 5 of Part 10. The contract may relate to services as a director or to any other services, whether as a director or otherwise, which he undertakes personally to perform for the company or any subsidiary. Sections 228–230 replace s.318 of the 1985 Act.

4.63   Section 228 requires a company to keep copies of every service contract entered into by the company or by a subsidiary, and to make these available for inspection at any of the locations set out in s.228(2), namely the company's registered office or a place specified in regulations made under s.1136. The contract must be in writing or its terms recorded in a written memorandum. Section 228(3), however, is a new provision. It requires service contracts to be kept for a year after their expiry. Failure to comply with these requirements is a criminal offence.

4.64   Section 229 gives members the right to inspect, free of charge, any service contract held by the company in accordance with s.228. Section 229(2) is new and gives members a right to request a copy of a service contract on payment of a set fee. Section 230 applies the provisions of Chapter 5 to any service contracts made by the company with any person who is deemed to be a shadow director.

CONTRACTS WITH SOLE MEMBERS WHO ARE DIRECTORS

4.65   Section 231 deals with the situation where contracts are entered into by a company with its only member, where the member is a director (or shadow director), and the contract is not entered into in the ordinary course of the company's business. In these cases the contract must be in writing, or its terms set out in a memorandum or recorded in the minutes of the first meeting of the directors of the company following the making of the contract. The purpose of the section is to ensure that records are kept of such contracts, because of the lack of distinction between the acts of the director acting on behalf of the company with respect to the contract, while also acting in the same transaction in his personal capacity as the other contracting party and sole member of the company. The section is a replacement for s.332B of the 1985 Act, which itself implemented Art.5 of the Twelfth Company Law Directive (Directive 89/667/EEC). As the 2006 Act now permits public companies to have a single member, the section now applies to both private and public limited companies. Any failure to record a contract which is governed by the section cannot affect the validity of the contract (s.231(6)), albeit that other legislation or rules of law might do so. A breach of this section renders every officer of the company who is in default liable to a criminal penalty.

DIRECTORS' LIABILITIES

Introduction

4.66   Chapter 7 of Part 10 principally carries out two functions. The first is to restate, although with minor modifications, ss. 309A–309C of the 1985 Act, which governed the liability of directors. The second function of the Chapter is to introduce a substantive reform of the law on ratification of acts giving rise to liability on the part of a director.

4.67   Section 232 prohibits a company from exempting a director from, or indemnifying him against any liability in connection with any 'negligence, default, breach of duty, or breach of trust' by him in relation to the company. Indemnification is also prohibited by an associated company (s.232(2)). An associated company for these purposes is defined in s.256 as involving companies which are subsidiaries of the relevant company, or where both companies are subsidiaries of a third company. Any provision in the company's articles or in any contract made with the company and the director, usually a service contract, which purports to exempt or indemnify a director from liability who is in breach of the section is void. However, s.232(2) and ss.233–234 permit the purchase by the company of liability insurance relating to any such liability attaching to directors, including directors of any associated company. Similar provision can also be made in respect of third party indemnity insurance under s.234. By this section companies may indemnify directors in respect of proceedings brought by third parties, and in respect of applications for relief from liability made under s.661(3) or (4) or s.1157 (see **para.3.55**). The restrictions on the section set out in s.234(3) should be noted; thus, for example, the indemnity must not cover fines imposed in criminal proceedings, or penalties imposed by regulatory bodies. Section 235 permits companies to make provision to indemnify directors where the directors are trustees of an occupational pension scheme (as defined in s.235(6)). However, as in the previous section the indemnity in these cases may not cover, for example, the liability of the director to pay a fine imposed in criminal proceedings or a penalty imposed by a regulatory body (s.235(3)).

4.68   Under s.236, if either a third party indemnity provision as prescribed by s.234 (known as a qualifying third party indemnity provision), or a pension scheme indemnity provision prescribed by s.235 (also known as a qualifying pension scheme indemnity provision) is in force for the benefit of one or more directors, this must be disclosed by the company in the directors' reports. The company must keep copies of all qualifying third party indemnity provisions (and qualifying pension scheme indemnity provisions) made for its own directors and for any directors of associated companies (s.237).

4.69   Section 237(4) is a new provision. It requires that all third party qualifying indemnity provisions must be retained and be available for inspection for at least one year after they have expired or terminated. Failure to comply with the provisions of the section is a criminal offence (s.237(6)).

4.70   Under s.238 a member of the company has the right to inspect copies of any qualifying third party indemnity provisions (and qualifying pension scheme indemnity provisions) held by the company, free of charge. There is also a new right, on payment of a fee, for members to request a copy of the document recording the qualifying third party indemnity provision (and the qualifying pension scheme indemnity provision) be it set out as a full copy of the relevant document or contained in a memorandum. This fee will be set by regulations.

Ratification

4.71   Section 239 preserves the law which prior to the enactment of the 2006 Act governed the ratification of the acts of directors, but with one important and significant alteration. If the conduct of a director constitutes negligence, default, breach of duty or breach of trust in relation to the company any decision to ratify this conduct must be taken by the members. This must be done without any reliance on the votes in favour of ratification by the director who is at fault (exercising his rights as member) or any connected person (also exercising their rights as a member and including a fellow director: see s.252). The decision to ratify must be made by resolution of the members of the company. If the resolution effecting ratification is by way of written resolution (see Part 14, Chapter 2 and **Chapter 5** for a consideration of the written resolution procedure), neither the director involved (if he is a member of the company) or any person connected with him may take part in the written resolution procedure (s.239(3)). Accordingly, the company is not required to send a copy of the written resolution to any such persons, and they are not counted when the number of votes required for the written resolution to be passed is determined.

4.72   If the ratification decision is to be taken at a meeting, any members whose votes are to be disregarded (such as the relevant director and any person connected with him) are able to attend and take part in the meeting, and count towards the quorum for the meeting, but only if their membership gives them the right to do so. The section makes no change to the law on unanimous consent (s.239(6)). Accordingly, the restrictions imposed by the section as to who may vote on a ratification resolution will not apply when every member votes in favour of the resolution (whether informally or otherwise). Section 239(6) also makes it clear that nothing in this section removes any of the directors' powers to manage the affairs of the company. Finally s.239(7) explains that the requirements imposed by s.239 are in addition to any other limitations or restrictions imposed by law as to what conduct of a director may or may not be ratified and when.

DIRECTOR'S RESIDENTIAL ADDRESS – PROTECTION FROM DISCLOSURE

Introduction

4.73   The requirement under the old law for a director's residential address to be a matter of public record has had to be modified in view of the actions of terrorists and political activists. Under the Criminal Justice and Police Act 2001, ss.723B–723E were inserted into the 1985 Act, and provided for a director to apply for a 'confidentiality order' whereby a service address was placed on the public record and the director's residential address was kept on a secure register. There are in excess of 5,000 orders in force relating to some 1 per cent of directors. The Company Law Review in its Final Report (at para.11.46), while recognising that there should be a record of a director's residential address, which should be made available for persons such as liquidators and creditors, was also of the opinion that confidentiality should be available for all directors who wish it and that they should be able to supply for the public record a service address. These recommendations were enacted by Chapter 8 of Part 10 of the Act, and these provisions replace the confidentiality order regime noted above.

Confidentiality – company's obligations

4.74 Section 240 sets out the information concerning a director's usual residential address (defined as 'protected information') that will be protected under the provisions of Chapter 8 of Part 10. Section 240(3) provides that protected information does not cease to be so on an individual ceasing to be a director. Section 241 prohibits the company from using or disclosing an individual director's usual residential address (as protected information) without his consent, except in order to communicate with him, or to comply with an obligation to send information to the registrar, or when required to do so by a court.

Confidentiality – registrar's obligations

4.75 Section 242 prevents public disclosure of protected information by the registrar. However, the registrar need only protect such information where it has been submitted on a form where the director's usual residential address is required and where it has been entered in the appropriate place. The registrar is not obliged to check all documents submitted to ensure that an address has not been disclosed by mistake. In addition, this protection is not retrospective.

4.76 Section 243 permits certain kinds of protected information to be used or disclosed. Thus the registrar may use the protected information to communicate with a director (s.243(1)). The registrar may also disclose protected information to any public authority specified in regulations and to a credit reference agency (s.243(2)). Under s.243(3)–(6) regulations will determine the conditions under which disclosure under the section may be made. The regulations may also require the registrar on application to refrain from disclosing protected information to a credit reference agency. The regulations may also specify the persons who may make an application concerning disclosure of protected information to a credit reference agency, and the nature and form of the application. The regulations may also provide that a question regarding an application concerning the disclosure of protected information may be referred to a person other than the registrar (s.243(6)(b)).

4.77 Section 244 covers two circumstances in which a court may require the company to disclose protected information concerning a director. The first is where the service address supplied by the director is not proving to be effective. The second is where the usual residential address is needed for the enforcement of an order or decree of the court. If the information cannot be provided by the company, either because the company does not have the address or because the company has been dissolved, then the court can make an order for disclosure by the registrar. An application for an order to require disclosure of protected information may be made by the persons specified under s.244(3). Section 245 provides that if a service address of a director is not effective, then the usual residential address can be placed on the public record. In order to invoke the powers in this section, the registrar must send a warning notice to the director, specifying a period within which representations can be made, before the intended revocation of the protection from disclosure of the protected information takes place. Section 246 provides that if the registrar puts the director's usual residential address on the public record under the provisions of s.245, then the registrar shall update the public record as if he had been notified that the director's usual residential address was the same as the director's service address. The registrar must notify the director of this state of affairs. Any company affected by this provision must put the director's usual residential address on its register of directors as the director's service address. The director may not register a service address other than his usual residential address for five years after the registrar's decision.

SUPPLEMENTARY PROVISIONS

Provision for employees

4.78   Section 247 confers a power on the directors to make provision for the benefit of employees, including former employees of the company or a subsidiary, on the cessation or transfer of the whole or part of the undertaking of the company or subsidiary. This power may be exercised by the directors even if it will not promote the success of the company, and the provisions of s.172 (see **para.4.21** above) need not be observed by the directors if they exercise the power under s.247. The conditions that must be met before the power is exercised are set out in s.247(7). The section replaces s.719 of the 1985 Act with certain changes. Thus the directors can no longer use the power conferred by the new section to make payments to themselves or to former or shadow directors, unless any such payments are authorised by the members. This may prove an illusory restriction in the case of many private limited companies where the directors are also the members.

Minutes

4.79   Sections 248 and 249 replace the provisions of s.382 of the 1985 Act and relate to the records of directors' meetings. The section now requires a company to record minutes of all meetings of the directors. Section 248(2) is a new provision and requires such minutes to be kept by the company for 10 years. Failure to comply with the provisions of s.248 is a criminal offence applying to every officer of the company who is in default. Section 249 covers the evidential value of minutes made in accordance with s.248.

Definitions

4.80   The following provisions provide general definitions of terms used in the Act and generally follow the definitions of such terms in the 1985 Act. Thus 'director' is defined in s.250 as in the same terms as in s.741 of the 1985 Act. Section 251 also defines 'shadow director' in the same terms as in s.741 of the 1985 Act.

Connected persons

4.81   The concept of persons connected with a director for the purposes of determining whether a director is in breach of the 'no conflict' rule has been considered above (see for example s.190 concerning substantial property transactions involving a director or persons connected with a director considered at **para.4.47** *et seq.*). The concept of a 'connected person' is used throughout Part 10 of the Act in relation to the regulation of the conduct of directors and the observance of their duties with respect to the company.

4.82   Sections 252–256 replace s.346 of the 1985 Act and define how individuals and corporations may be connected with a director for the above purposes. Thus s.252 determines that persons connected with a director may include family members of the director (s.252(2)(a) and s.253), companies (s.252(2)(b) and s.254), trustees of a trust under which a director or a relative of the director as set out in s.253 is a beneficiary (s.252(2)(c)), certain partners of the director (s.252(2)(d)), and firms with a legal personality (s.252(2)(e)). The provisions, although broadly following s.346, do effect reforms. In particular the provisions as enacted implement recommendations of the Law Commissions that the definition of connected person be extended so as to include cohabitants, infant children of the cohabitant if they live with the director, adult children of the director and the director's parents.

Corporate bodies

4.83   Section 254 determines whether a company or other body corporate is a person connected with a director for the purposes of Part 10 of the Act. If a company is to be regarded as connected with a director, then the director, along with with any other person connected with him, must be interested in 20 per cent of the equity share capital, or control more than 20 per cent of the voting power exercisable at a general meeting of a company (this may be directly or indirectly through another corporate body controlled by them). Schedule 1 sets out the rules by which it will be determined whether a person is 'interested' in shares for the purposes of s.254.

4.84   Section 255 defines what is meant by the 'control' of a body corporate by a director for the purposes of s.254. The section prescribes a two-stage process. First, the director or any other person connected with him must be interested in the equity share capital or be entitled to exercise (or control the exercise of) some part of the voting power at any general meeting. Secondly, the director, the persons connected to him and his fellow directors must be interested in more than 50 per cent of the equity share capital of the company, or be entitled to exercise (or control the exercise of) more than 50 per cent of the voting power. The rules for determining whether a person is 'interested' in shares for the purposes of s.255 can be found in Sched.1.

4.85 Section 256 defines the concepts of associated bodies corporate and associated companies for the purposes of Part 10 of the Act. The Explanatory Notes (para.477) explain that a 'holding company is associated with all its subsidiaries, and a subsidiary is associated with its holding company and all the other subsidiaries of its holding company'.

The company's constitution

4.86 Section 257 provides that the term the 'company's constitution' for the purposes of Part 10 of the Act includes resolutions and any decision by the members or class of members that is treated by virtue of any enactment or rule of law as equivalent to a decision. This provision is supplementary to s.17 of the 2006 Act which defines the company's constitution for the purposes of the whole of the Act. Section 257 is however particularly pertinent to ss.171 and 173 which have been considered above at **paras.4.20** and **4.23**.

4.87 Section 258 deals with the power of the Secretary of State to increase financial limits in Part 10 of the Act, and simply restates s.345 of the 1985 Act.

4.88 Finally, s.259 restates s.347 of the 1985 Act. The rules concerning the regulation of transactions or arrangements under Part 10 of the Act will apply whether or not the law governing a transaction or arrangement is the law of the United Kingdom, or a part of the United Kingdom. This provision prevents e.g. parties seeking to avoid the application of the rules relating to approval of transactions such as loans and substantial property transactions subject to Part 10, by choosing a foreign law jurisdiction to regulate the relevant transaction.

DERIVATIVE CLAIMS AND PROCEEDINGS BY MEMBERS

Introduction

4.89 Section 170 provides that directors owe their duties to the company. This long-established principle of company law consequently determined and continues to determine that only the company can enforce those duties. The ways in which the company could enforce these duties included, however, the derivative claim, which was brought by a member or class of members, albeit to enforce a right which was vested in and derived from the company under the rule first formulated in the famous case of *Foss* v. *Harbottle* (1843) 2 Hare 461. Part 11 of the 2006 Act seeks to reform this aspect of the law of remedies. The provisions of Part 11 do not prescribe a substantive rule to replace the rule in *Foss* v. *Harbottle*. The provisions do however, reflect the views of the Law Commission that there should be a 'new derivative procedure with more modern, flexible and accessible criteria for determining whether a shareholder can pursue an action' (see 'Shareholder Remedies', Consultation Paper No.142, para.6.15). Thus the new derivative claim will be made available for breach of duty on the part of a director to exercise reasonable care, skill and diligence, and it is not necessary for the applicant to show that the director or directors responsible for the wrongdoing control the majority of the company's shares.

4.90   A two-stage procedure for pursuing a derivative claim is introduced. The applicant must first make a prima facie case for permission to continue a derivative claim. This matter can be considered by the court from evidence filed solely by the applicant. If there is a prima facie case, but before the second stage is heard, the court may hear evidence provided by the company. If the matters set out in Part 11, Chapter 1 and in particular s.263 are established the court may give permission for the derivative claim to be heard.

Chapter 1

4.91   Section 260 sets out the central aspects of a derivative claim. Thus the claim must be brought by a member (which is defined in s.260(5)(c) as including persons in whom shares have been invested by operation of law, such as a personal representative). The claim remains vested in the company, and the relief sought must be on behalf of the company. Section 260(2) provides that the derivative claim in England and Wales may only be brought either under Part 11, Chapter 1 or in pursuance of an order of the court in proceedings under s.994 (see **para.10.3** for a consideration of this provision which replaces s.459 of the Companies Act 1985). By s.260(3) a derivative claim may be brought only in respect of claims arising from 'an actual or proposed act or omission involving negligence, default, breach of duty or breach of trust by a director of the company' (including shadow and former directors: s.260(5)). Thus breach of any of the director's duties under Part 10, Chapter 2 may trigger a derivative claim. Derivative claims against third parties are also permitted by s.260(3), albeit in the rather narrow circumstances in which a director is involved. A member may bring a claim in respect of conduct which occurred before he became a member (s.260(4)).

4.92   Section 261 provides that, once proceedings have been instituted, the member must apply to the court for permission to continue the claim. This merely reflects current civil procedure under the Civil Procedure Rules 1998 (SI 1998/3132), and the procedure in outline has already been considered at **para.4.90** above. A company may institute proceedings against a director in order to thwart the institution of a derivative claim by a member (an abuse of process) and then fail to pursue the claim with diligence. In these circumstances s.262 permits a member to apply to the court to continue the claim as a derivative claim.

4.93   Section 263(3) sets out the criteria that the court must take into account in considering whether to grant permission for the continuance of a derivative claim (these criteria may be amended by future regulations (s.263(5)). The court must address in considering whether to give permission or leave to continue the claim, inter alia, the following questions (s.263(3)):

- Is the claimant acting in good faith in continuing the claim?
- Could the claim be pursued by the member in his own right?
- What importance would a person acting in accordance with s.172 attach to continuing the claim?

4.94   In particular the court should have regard to the views of disinterested members of the company as to the matter which forms the basis of the claim (s.263(4)). However, the court must discontinue the claim if it is of the opinion that a person acting in accordance with the general duties of a director to promote the success of a company under s.172 would not seek to continue the claim (s.263(2)). The court must also discontinue a derivative claim if the relevant conduct of a director has been authorised or ratified by the company. Where a member institutes a derivative claim which constitutes an abuse of process or fails to proceed with due diligence, s.264 permits the claim to be continued by another member.

Derivative claims in Scotland

4.95   Sections 265–269 govern derivative claims in Scotland.

COMPANY SECRETARIES

4.96   The abolition of the requirement for a private limited company to have a secretary has been noted in **Chapter 1**. Substantive effect to this proposal of the Company Law Review in its Final Report, para 4.7 is given by s.270. A private company may however choose to have a secretary. Section 271 replaces s.283(1) of the 1985 Act and retains the requirement for a public company to have a secretary, and s.272 is a new provision which allows the continuing requirement for a public company to have a secretary to be enforced. Where a public company does not appear to have a company secretary the Secretary of State may give a direction to the company to appoint a secretary, and failure to comply with the direction within the specified time is an offence.

4.97   Section 273 replaces s.286 of the 1985 Act. It imposes a duty upon directors of a public company to ensure that any person appointed secretary to the company has the prescribed knowledge, experience and qualifications to perform his duties. The section reproduces the old law except that:

1. The section does not require the secretary to possess the qualification of having held the office of the company's secretary (or assistant or deputy) on 22 December 1980.

2.   The bodies of which the secretary may be a member for the purposes of qualification include the Chartered Institute of Management Accountants. This
body replaces the Institute of Cost and Management Accountants in the
legislation, following its change of name.

There is no requirement that the company secretary must be a natural person.

4.98   Section 274 replaces s.283(3) of the 1985 Act. It covers the situation
where the office of secretary is vacant, or where no secretary is capable of acting.
In this situation the office can be filled by an assistant or deputy, or if there are no
such persons the office can be filled by any person authorised by the directors.
This is a change from the old s.283(3), which only allowed an officer of the
company to act as secretary.

4.99   Section 275 replaces s.288 of the 1985 Act. A public company (or a private
company which has appointed a secretary) must keep a register of its secretaries
containing specified details. The section makes little substantive change to the old
law, and retains for example the right of inspection. The register must be available
for inspection at the company's registered office, or at any place specified in regulations made under s.1136 (s.275(3)). The company must give notice to the registrar of the place where the register is kept for the purposes of inspection, and of
any change in that place (s.275(4)). Under s.276, which replaces s.288(2) of the
1985 Act, the company is obliged to notify the registrar of any change in the
company's secretary, or any change in the particulars contained in the register of
secretaries. This must be done within 14 days.

Supplementary

4.100   Section 277, which applies to public companies (and any private company which appoints a secretary), replaces s.290 of the 1985 Act. It requires a
company to enter the name and address of any individual who is its secretary in
the company's register of secretaries. The section imposes similar requirements as
to details of secretaries to those required to be entered with respect to a company's
directors on the register of directors under s.163 (reference should therefore be
made to that provision at **para.4.8** above). The register must include any name
used by a secretary or in use by him for business purposes. The section retains a
protective provision relating to the former names of peers, but there is no exception relating to any former names of married women (as recommended by the
Company Law Review). The address registered should be a service address (see
the Company Law Review, Final Report, para.11.46).

4.101   Section 278 sets out the details that must be registered where the secretary of a company is either a body corporate or a firm which is a legal person. The
registration requirements involving secretaries that apply in the case of an EEA
company follow the recommendations of the Company Law Review (Final
Report, para.11.39).

4.102   Section 279 is a new provision, and gives power to the Secretary of State to make regulations that amend the particulars that must be entered in a company's register of secretaries. The provision is similar to s.166 relating to the power to make regulations concerning the registration of directors' particulars.

4.103   Section 280 replaces s.284 of the 1985 Act, and relates to acts done by a person when acting in a dual capacity as director and secretary. It determines that a provision requiring or authorising a matter to be done by or to a director and the secretary of a company is not to be regarded as satisfied by its being done by or to the same person acting both as a director and as, or in place of, the secretary.

5 RESOLUTIONS AND MEETINGS

INTRODUCTION

5.1 The changes introduced by the 2006 Act with regard to resolutions and meetings are contained in Part 13 of the legislation. This aims to replace most, but not all, of Chapter 4 of Part 11 of the 1985 Act, which covers the same ground. The changes introduced derive mainly from the Company Law Review's consultation on 'Company General Meetings' and 'Shareholder Communications' and the subsequent recommendations from Chapters 2, 6 and 7 of its Final Report to which have been added the results of two subsequent consultations: the 'Modernising Company Law' White Paper of July 2002, and the 'Company Law Reform Bill' White Paper of March 2005.

5.2 Many of the changes are merely of detail and these will be noted in the course of this discussion. However the new legislation implements two policy changes of general significance. First, the new law changes the current 'elective regime' that is applicable in default of election by private companies. Under the old law an elective resolution had to be passed to dispense with annual general meetings. Now the default positions are reversed and there is no longer any general requirement for a private company to hold an annual general meeting. If one is wanted it will require a resolution to that effect. Conceptually at least this is a radical change, although its real significance is small and, indeed, at a practical level it merely removes a bureaucratic obstacle and a possible trap for the unwary.

5.3 The second major general change is also addressed to private companies. Under the law prior to the 2006 Act the basis of decision making for shareholders has been by formal general meetings, at least in the thrust of the drafting of companies legislation. The new law proceeds on the basis that this legislative norm will cease to be so for many private companies. Instead in the future private companies will have available to them new procedures whereby decisions can be taken by written resolution without the need for formal general meetings. Again the aim is to reduce the burden of administration and bureaucracy on private companies.

5.4 The law is thus changed in favour of increased simplicity and comparative informality for private companies while continuing a higher set of obligations for public companies. The drafting of the Act has tried to articulate this clearly and make the legislation user friendly by stating the law so as to deal first with the informal position relating to private companies and then setting out the additional layers of requirement for public and quoted companies in subsequent provisions which are, necessarily, usually more complex.

RESOLUTIONS GENERALLY

5.5   The 2006 Act contains a provision which is new in being explicit, but which effectively enacts what was previously implicit in companies legislation. Section 281 provides specifically that a resolution of the members (or of a class of members) of a private company must be passed either:

(a) as a written resolution in accordance with Chapter 2 of Part 13; or
(b) at a meeting of the members (to which the provisions of Chapter 3 of Part 13 apply).

5.6   By contrast a resolution of the members (or class of members) of a public company must be passed at a meeting of the members (to which the provisions of Chapter 3 and where relevant Chapter 4 apply). Thus the 2006 Act expressly states that resolutions can only be passed by these prescribed procedures. However, s.281 is quite explicit in subsection (4) that these provisions do not affect any enactment or rule of law as to the following:

(a) things done otherwise than by passing a resolution, so that the validity of any activity not requiring a resolution to be undertaken remains effective;
(b) circumstances in which a resolution is or is not treated as having been passed; or
(c) cases in which a person is precluded from alleging that a resolution has not been duly passed.

5.7   Where a resolution is required by the Act but the kind of resolution is not specified, what is required is an ordinary resolution unless the company's articles require a higher majority (s.281(3)).

5.8   The Act continues the long-established distinction between ordinary and special resolutions in ss.282 and 283 with the former continuing to require a majority of over 50 per cent and the latter one of not less than 75 per cent. The major substantive change is that whereas under the previous companies legislation there is a 21-day period of notice for a special resolution, under the 2006 Act this requirement is abolished. (For notice of meetings, see **para.5.34** *et seq.* below.) It should also be noted that where a resolution is proposed as a special resolution this must be stated in the notice of the meeting or in the written resolution.

5.9   The rules with regard to votes continue under s.284, which is an adaptation of s.370 of the 1985 Act and the default regulations of Table A, enacting the position applicable to most companies. However subsection (4) provides that the general voting rules may be varied by any provisions within the company's articles, so that a company can make alternative arrangements if it wishes. It thus remains possible for weighted voted rights to be given. It should also be observed that on a vote on a show of hands a proxy who has been duly appointed by a member entitled to vote on the resolution has one vote.

5.10   However, the legislation does contain specific requirements with regard to the votes of members which the company's articles are not able to override. Section 285(1) and (2) set out the entitlement to vote where proxies have been appointed to continue the traditional protection to members voting by proxy or proxies, so that on a vote on a show of hands the proxy has the same number of votes as the member who appointed him would have had had he been present, any provision in the articles to the contrary being void. Subsection (3) makes new provision for voting rights on written resolutions reflecting that they will no longer need unanimous support to be valid, so that again a member cannot be disadvantaged when the new procedure is used in terms which parallel those relating to proxy voting. It provides that in relation to a resolution required or authorised by an enactment, if a private company's articles provide that a member has a different number of votes in relation to a resolution when it is passed as a written resolution and when it is passed on a poll taken at meeting:

(a) the provision about how many votes a member has in relation to the resolution passed on a poll is void; and

(b) a member has the same number of votes in relation to the resolution when it is passed on a poll as he has when it is passed on a written resolution.

5.11   Section 286 deals with the issue of votes by the joint holders of shares putting on a statutory footing the default position prescribed under reg.55 of Table A, so that the vote which counts is that of the senior holder who votes. The senior holder is determined simply by the order in which the names of the joint holders appear in the register of members. However with regard to these rules the company may make alternative provisions in its articles if it chooses.

5.12   Finally s.287 deals with the effect of provisions in the articles of a company as to the admissibility of votes by expressly providing that nothing in the clauses affects the operation of provisions in the articles which impose a procedure for objecting to a person's entitlement to vote. Any such procedure is left as a matter for the company to define if it chooses to do so. Commonly companies make express provision in their articles so as to provide certainty of outcome at the meeting itself, such as by the common provision that objections to votes have to be raised with the chairman at the meeting at which the vote is taken and that his decision is final.

WRITTEN RESOLUTIONS

5.13   The rules with regard to written resolutions are contained in Chapter 2 of Part 13 and replace the present rules on the subject contained in ss.381A–381C of the 1985 Act. The major change of principle is that the old regime required unanimity for a valid decision whereas the new rules do not, with a knock-on effect that there is more detail in the new provisions and the procedure which they require.

5.14   For the purposes of the 2006 Act a 'written resolution' means a resolution of a private company proposed and passed in accordance with the Act (s.288). The implications of this as a definition will be discussed later but clearly from this it only embraces resolutions passed by private companies. As with the existing law, s.288(2) provides that the procedure may not be used to remove a director or an auditor. Resolutions may be proposed as a written resolution by either the directors or the members of a private company (s.288(3)). A written resolution of a private company has effect as if passed (as the case may be) by the company in general meeting or by a meeting of a class of members of the company.

5.15   The eligibility of members to vote on a written resolution is fixed on the day the resolution is circulated and, if the persons entitled to vote change during the course of that day, the eligible members are the persons entitled to vote on the resolution at the time that the first copy of the resolution is sent or submitted to a member for his agreement (s.289). This is supported to some extent by the definition of circulation date in s.290 which defines it as the date on which copies of the written resolution are sent or submitted to members in accordance with the requirements of Chapter 2 or, if copies are sent or submitted to members on different days, to the first of those days.

Resolutions proposed by directors

5.16   Where the directors propose a written resolution the rules are prescribed by s.291 which demands that a copy be sent to every eligible member. This may be accomplished in one of two ways. First it may be done by sending copies at the same time (so far as reasonably practicable) to all eligible members in hard copy form, in electronic form or by means of a website. Alternatively if it is possible to do so without undue delay, the same copy can be submitted to each eligible member in turn (or different copies to each of a number of eligible members in turn). It is permissible to combine the two by sending copies to some members in the first manner and copies to others in the second way. In any event the circulated copies must be accompanied by a statement informing the member (a) how to signify agreement to the resolution; and (b) the date by which the resolution must be passed if it is not to lapse.

5.17   If these formal requirements are not met every officer of the company who is in default is guilty of a criminal offence and is liable to a fine, but the validity of the resolution is not affected.

Resolutions proposed by members

5.18   These are dealt with by ss.292–295. The most important provisions are those set out in s.292(1) and (4) which empower the required percentage of the members of a private company to require the company to circulate a resolution that may be properly moved and is proposed to be moved as a written resolution. Any resolution may properly be moved as a written resolution (s.292(2)) unless:

(a) it would, if passed, be ineffective (whether by reason of inconsistency with any enactment or the company's constitution or otherwise);
(b) it is defamatory of any person; or
(c) it is frivolous or vexatious.

5.19   The required percentage is 5 per cent of the company's members or such lower percentage as its articles require. The required percentage may also require a statement of not more than 1,000 words on the subject matter of the resolution to be circulated with it. The request from the required percentage may be in hard copy form or in electronic form and must, inter alia, be authenticated by the person or persons making it (s.292(6)).

5.20   The procedures for circulation are set out in s.293 and are in similar terms to those governing the circulation of resolutions proposed by directors with similar penalties in the event of default. However in the case of the circulation of members' proposals, the members making the request must pay the company's expenses of circulation unless the company resolves otherwise and, further, must deposit with the company a sum reasonably sufficient to meet those expenses before the company is required to act (s.294). A company required to circulate a member's statement may apply to the court to be relieved of its obligations on the grounds that the procedure is being abused (s.295).

Procedure for signifying agreement to written resolutions

5.21   Once the written resolution is in circulation it lapses if it is not passed before the end of either (a) the period specified for the purpose in the company's articles; or (b) if none is specified, 28 days beginning with the circulation date (s.297). To pass, the resolution must gain positive acceptance by the requisite majority of members (the requisite majority depending on whether the proposal is for an ordinary or a special resolution). The procedure for acceptance is contained in s.296 whereby a member may signify agreement to a written resolution in hard copy or, if the company permits electronic form communications, in electronic form. If the company does not permit electronic form communications the member can only use hard copy (see Sched.4, Part 3 which deals with conditions for use of communications in electronic form). Once a member has signified agreement to a written resolution he cannot withdraw his agreement, thus giving company directors and members certainty as to whether and when a resolution has been passed.

Supplementary provisions

5.22   Where a company gives an electronic address in a document containing or accompanying a proposed written resolution it is deemed to have accepted the use of electronic communication to that address (s.298). The use of a website by the company for communication is permissible for the purposes of written resolutions subject to:

(a) the general requirements of Part 4 of Sched.5; and

(b) the resolution being available on the website throughout the period beginning with the circulation date and ending on the date on which the resolution lapses (s.299).

5.23   Finally, provisions in the company's articles cannot remove the ability of a private company and its members to propose and pass a resolution required by statute using the written resolution procedure of the Chapter (s.300).

What is a written resolution?

5.24   There remains for discussion the topic mentioned but passed over earlier, namely what constitutes a written resolution? The Explanatory Notes on the Company Law Reform Bill (HL Bill 34-EN) confidently take the view that a written resolution does not imply the need for a conventional hard copy written document, stating categorically in para.530:

> The use of the expression 'written resolution' does not mean that there is a requirement for 'writing' in the sense of hard copy.

However, is this so?

5.25   As noted the definition of 'written resolution' is a resolution of a private company which has been proposed and passed in accordance with Part 13, Chapter 2. Chapter 2 sets out procedures for passing written resolutions which refer to the circulation of copies of the resolution to members by, inter alia, electronic means (ss.291 and 292) and presumably the argument is that this obviates the need for the existence of a formal written document. This indeed may be the intent, but the outcome is not so clear. What are required to be circulated by electronic means are copies of the proposed resolution and this may be taken as implying the existence of a formal written document which is copied. Alternatively the implication may equally be that a resolution exists as an abstract format of words of which any physical or electronic embodiment is a copy. Either is arguable. To be fair to the Explanatory Notes the present writer prefers the latter view, although viewing the matter as being less clear cut than the Government, whose legislation this is, believes to be the case.

RESOLUTIONS AT MEETINGS

5.26   Chapter 3 of Part 13 deals with the subject of resolutions at general meetings by replacing ss.368–377, 379 and 381 of the 1985 Act with the new provisions similarly applying to both private and public companies. There is, however, change from the old law as the new legislation has to reflect the fact that private companies will no longer need to hold annual general meetings. Thus, for instance, the provisions about circulations of statements in ss.376 and 377 of the 1985 Act are separate in the new legislation from the provisions on circulation of resolutions prior to an annual general meeting which are now in Part 13, Chapter 4, which is devoted to the annual general meetings of public companies. The new legislation also repeals s.367 of the 1985 Act which confers power on the Secretary of State to call a meeting where there is no annual general meeting.

5.27   The provisions on resolutions begin with a general provision in s.301 which provides expressly that a resolution of the members of a company is validly passed at a general meeting if, and only if, the formalities of Chapter 3, the articles of the company, and, where appropriate, Chapter 4 are complied with. It thus emphasises that the passing of a valid resolution at a meeting is a matter not merely of obtaining the requisite majority but also of carrying out the correct procedures in a proper manner. In so providing the 2006 Act extends to all resolutions this express principle (which under the 1985 Act was embodied in s.378(6) but only in respect of extraordinary and special resolutions), thus removing an obvious source of confusion for non-lawyers making reference to the companies legislation in the carrying on of their businesses. This is to be welcomed. So far as possible our legislation should be clear to the diligent laymen who makes reference to it. The 2006 Act also makes it clear that the requirements of both legislation and the company's articles must be complied with and here it must be borne in mind that some of the legislative requirements are mandatory (e.g. proxy rights) and cannot be modified by the company's articles.

Calling meetings

(1)   Directors

5.28   As under the existing law meetings may be called either by directors on their own initiative or at the direction of the members. The power for directors to call meetings is contained in s.302 which puts into statute part of the default regulation of Table A, reg.37 under the 1985 Act. The 2006 Act leaves it to the company's articles to set out how the directors act collectively.

5.29   The members' power to require directors to call a general meeting and the directors' responsibilities in this situation are set out in ss.302–304 and are in terms broadly similar to those of s.368 of the 1985 Act. In particular, for public companies, there is no change in the threshold required for a meeting to be requested which consequently remains at members with voting rights holding at least 10 per cent of the paid-up capital of the company or, in a company with no share capital, members holding 10 per cent of the total voting rights (s.303). However, for private companies, the threshold is now 5 per cent or 10 per cent of the paid-up capital (or of the total voting rights where the company has no share capital) depending on when there was last a meeting in relation to which any members had rights equivalent to the right under s.303 to circulate resolutions. Section 303(5) defines what type of resolution may be properly moved at a meeting in negative terms by providing that a resolution may be properly moved unless it offends one of the three prohibitions of Part 13 of the Act namely:

(a) it would, if passed, be ineffective;
(b) it is defamatory of any person; or
(c) it is frivolous or vexatious.

5.30 There are two changes of detail in relation to the old law. First, s.303(4) now allows a request from the members to include the text of a resolution which might properly be moved and is intended to be moved at the meeting and, secondly, s.303(6) expressly provides that the request may be in hard copy or electronic form.

5.31 The procedures after the directors have been required to call a meeting remain the same as under the 1985 Act. Within 21 days of being so required the directors must summon a meeting to be held within 28 days of the notice convening it (s.304(1)). However, it should be noted that under the new legislation if the request received by the company identifies a resolution intended to be moved at the meeting the notice of meeting issued by the directors must include notice of the specific resolution (s.304(2)).

(2) Members

5.32 If the directors fail to call the meeting which they are obliged to do, s.305 continues the policy of the 1985 legislation of empowering the members who requested the meeting, or any of them representing more than one half of the total voting rights of all of them, themselves to take the initiative and call a general meeting for a date not more than three months after the date on which the directors became subject to the requirement to call a meeting. Again the law is changed by the new legislation so that where the requests received by the company include the text of a resolution intended to be moved at the meeting, the notice of the meeting must include notice of the resolution (s.305(2)). As under the 1985 Act any reasonable expenses incurred by the members requesting the meeting by reason of the failure of the directors duly to call a meeting must be reimbursed by the company (s.305(6)). However, under the 2006 Act for the first time the company is mandatorily required to retain any sum so reimbursed by the company out of any sums due or to become due from the company by way of fees or other remuneration in respect of their services to such of the directors as were in default. No longer will members seeking change have to secure a resolution of the company to this effect, hopefully a significant sanction which will deter directors from obstructing the democratic process of shareholder debate and control.

5.33 Finally if all else fails s.306 reproduces s.371 of the 1985 Act and empowers the court either of its own motion or on the application of a director or a member entitled to vote at the meeting to order a meeting to be called, held and conducted in any manner the court thinks fit.

Notice of meetings

5.34   Section 307 of the 2006 Act sets out the basic requirements by reproducing part of s.369 of the 1985 Act. It retains the existing minimum notice period of 21 days for the annual general meetings of public companies and retains the 14-day period for all other general meetings. In the case of private companies the notice period is 14 days even if a special resolution is proposed. It also continues to allow a general meeting to be called on shorter notice if the requisite majority of members agree. The main change under the new legislation is that the requisite number required to agree a short notice meeting is reduced in the case of private companies from 95 per cent to 90 per cent of voting rights unless the articles of the private company specify a higher percentage (not exceeding 95 per cent). In the case of public companies the requirement of 95 per cent continues.

5.35   Changes are made by the 2006 Act to the manner in which notice may be given. Section 308 continues the policy of the new legislation by allowing notice of a general meeting of a company to be given:

(a) in hard copy form;

(b) in electronic form; or

(c) by means of a website or partly by one such means and partly by another.

5.36   Section 309 adds detail to the permitted publication by website and produces a similar effect to that contained in s.369 of the 1985 Act. To be effective a notice on a website must:

(a) state that it concerns a notice of a company meeting;

(b) specify the place, date and time of the meeting; and

(c) in the case of a public company, state whether the meeting will be an annual general meeting.

5.37   Further, the notice must be available on the website throughout the period beginning with the date of the notification and ending with the conclusion of the meeting. As always the specific provisions concerning electronic and website communication are subject to the general considerations set out in Sched.5 to the Act.

5.38   Notice of a meeting must be given to everyone entitled to receive it and these are set out in s.310 which enacts part of reg.38 of Table A. These are all directors, members, and any person entitled to a share in consequence of the death or bankruptcy of a member if the company has been notified of their entitlement. This is subject to any enactment and any provision in the company's articles so that it is open to a company to modify its obligations by the inclusion of an appropriate provision in its articles such as one allowing the company to cease sending notices of meetings to any member for whom it has ceased to have a valid address.

5.39   The topic of the content of the notice is dealt with by s.311 which enacts a further part of Table A, reg.38, to require notice of a general meeting to state the time and date of the meeting and its venue. It also requires the notice to state the general nature of the business to be dealt with unless this obligation is modified or removed by express provisions in the company's articles.

Resolutions requiring special notice

5.40   The concept of resolutions requiring special notice continues by virtue of s.312 of the 2006 Act which replaces s.379 of the 1985 Act. However, there is necessary modification of the ambit of the special resolution procedure by virtue of the changes to resolution requirements elsewhere. Section 312(1) provides that 'where by any provision of the Companies Acts *special notice is required of a resolution*, the resolution is not effective unless notice of the intention to move it has been given to the company at least 28 days before the meeting at which it is moved'. The words in italic have the effect that the provisions cover only resolutions passed at meetings because such resolutions are either not capable of being passed as written resolutions (such as resolutions to remove directors or auditors) or are written resolutions having their own special procedure such as that arising on failure to re-appoint an auditor within Part 16 (ss.515 and 516). Thus there is no change from the existing law whereby at least 28 days' notice must be given to the company of the intention to move the resolution for the resolution to be valid, subject to the established modifications where this is not practicable.

Accidental failure to give notice

5.41   Accidental failure to give notice of a resolution or meeting to any person entitled does not invalidate the resolution if passed at the meeting by virtue of s.313 which enacts and expands Table A, reg.39. However this is subject to any provision in the company's articles except for:

(a)   notice of meetings required or called by members under ss.304 and 305; and
(b)   notice of resolutions as proposed by members at annual general meetings under s.339.

No doubt the problem for any prejudicially affected member will remain that of establishing that the omission to notify him was not accidental, against the company's assertion of bona fides.

MEMBERS' STATEMENTS

5.42   Sections 314 and 315 continue the legal requirement of a company at the request of the required number of members to circulate to members entitled to receive notice of a general meeting a statement of not more than 1,000 words relating either to a matter referred to in a proposed resolution or to any other business to be dealt with at that meeting. In doing so they replace the 1985 Act, ss.376 and 377, on similar conditions to those prescribed by the old legislation. The request may now be in hard copy or in electronic form and, inter alia, must be received by the company at least one week before the meeting to which it relates (s.314(4)). The company's duty to circulate is continued on traditional terms by s.315.

5.43   There are two changes to the old law over and above the addition of the possibility of electronic means of communication. First, under the 2006 Act the shares relied on to trigger the circulation of a statement must carry with them the right to vote on the relevant resolution and not merely confer a general right to vote at the meeting (s.314(2)). Secondly, where the statement relates to a resolution or other matter to be dealt with at the annual general meeting of a public company and requests sufficient to require the company to circulate the statement are received by the company before its financial year end, the shareholders are no longer required to cover the costs of circulating the statement. In other circumstances the old rules continue whereby the expenses of the company in complying must be paid by the members who requested the circulation of the statement unless the company resolves otherwise. Unless the company has previously so resolved, it is not bound to comply with the request unless a sum reasonably sufficient to meet its expenses in so doing is deposited with the company or tendered to it not later than one week before the meeting (s.316).

5.44   A company or any other person who claims to be aggrieved may apply to the court for an order not to circulate the members' statement, which the court may grant if it is satisfied that the members' right is being abused. If such an order is made the court may order the members who requested the circulation of the statement to pay the whole or part of the company's costs on the application even if the members are not party to the application (s.317 replacing s.377(3) of the 1985 Act).

PROCEDURE AT MEETINGS

5.45   Sections 370(4) and 370A of the 1985 Act which deal with quorum at meetings are replaced by s.318 of the 2006 Act. This sets a quorum for a meeting of one 'qualifying person' in the case of a single member company, and two in all other cases in the absence of a provision to the contrary in the company's articles. The changes introduced by the new legislation are that a member, corporate representative or proxy present at the meeting may all be 'qualifying persons' but two or more corporate representatives or proxies of the same member may not (s.318(2) and (3)). Under the previous provisions proxies and corporate representatives do not count towards the quorum in companies with more than one member.

5.46   Section 319 continues the effect of s.370(5) of the 1985 Act by allowing any member to be chairman of a general meeting unless the company's articles contain restrictions on eligibility for chairmanship. The election or appointment of a chairman remains important because of the substantial powers put into the chairman's hands. In particular s.320 replaces s.378(4) of the 1985 Act and part of Table A, reg.47 to ensure that the chairman's declaration of a vote taken on a show of hands is conclusive evidence of the resolution being passed or lost without further proof unless a poll is demanded on the resolution. The new legislation differs from the old in two important respects, both of which are drawn from old Table A. First, if a demand for a poll is made and then withdrawn, the chairman's declaration of the outcome of the vote stands; and secondly, the minutes of the meeting now provide conclusive evidence of the chairman's declaration (s.320(2) and (3)). This is all in support of the desirable goals of certainty of outcome and preventing old battles from being constantly re-run.

5.47   The right to demand a poll contained in s.373 of the 1985 Act continues in s.321 of the 2006 Act on the same terms. It should be remembered that this is mandatory, and under neither the 1985 Act nor the new legislation may it be restricted by provisions in the articles.

5.48   Section 322 replaces s.374 of the 1985 Act in identical terms. It recognises that a member may hold shares on behalf of third parties and permits a member to cast votes in respect of different shares in different ways according to the interests or instructions of the different people he represents.

Authorised corporate representation

5.49   Section 323 replaces s.375 of the 1985 Act in authorising corporate representation at meetings. It is differently worded because it is intended to clarify a matter which is less than fully clear under the 1985 Act, namely the effect of appointing multiple representatives. The new law is clear and explicit. Any one of the corporate representatives is entitled to vote and exercise its powers on behalf of the member at meetings, but in the event that the vote or other powers are used by the various representatives in a conflicting manner the company is taken to have abstained from exercising its vote or power. The solution at a practical level, of course, is for the company to appoint a competent proxy or proxies with clear and non-conflicting mandates.

PROXIES

5.50   The subject of proxies was dealt with in the 1985 Act by a single section, s.372, supported by Table A. Under the new legislation the law is now set out in ss.324–331. Inevitably the result is an increase in complexity.

5.51   A member of a company is entitled to appoint another person as his proxy to exercise all or any of his rights to attend and speak and vote at a meeting of the company (s.324(1)). Further, in the case of a company having a share capital, a member may appoint more than one proxy in relation to a meeting, provided that each proxy is appointed to exercise the rights attached to a different share or shares held by him, or (as the case may be) to a different £10, or multiple of £10 of stock held by him (s.324(2)). Since more than one proxy can be appointed with both voting and speaking rights this power allows a corporation to use the proxy system where it wishes to appoint people with different voting intentions or with authority to vote in respect of different blocks of shares, a possibility now ineffective under the representation route. Finally s.331 of the 2006 Act expressly provides that none of the statutory provisions with regard to proxies prevents a company's articles relating to proxies from conferring more extensive rights on either members or proxies than are conferred by the statutory provisions.

Proxies – procedural matters

5.52   The extension of rights to appoint proxies contained in s.324 necessarily causes changes to the provisions requiring notices of meetings to contain statements of members' rights to appoint proxies to attend meetings. This is accomplished by s.325 which replaces the old s.372(3) and (4) of the 1985 Act. Section 325 requires every notice calling a meeting to contain a statement informing the member of his rights to appoint one or more proxies together with details of any more extensive rights conferred by the articles of the particular company. Failure to do this constitutes an offence for which each and every officer of the company may be fined. The validity of the meeting is, however, not affected.

5.53   The effect of the 1985 Act, s.372(6) is reproduced by s.326 of the 2006 Act which imposes a general duty on a company to ensure that if it invites members to appoint a particular person or persons as proxy the invitation is extended to all members entitled to vote at the meeting. To this general duty there are two exceptions, namely if either:

(a) there is issued to a member at his request a form of appointment naming the proxy or a list of persons willing to act as proxy; and

(b) the form or list is available on request to all members entitled to vote at the meeting (s.326(2)).

Again the consequence of failure to comply is purely criminal with every officer who is in default being liable to a fine.

5.54   Section 372(5) of the 1985 Act is replaced by s.327 of the 2006 Act in continuing to invalidate any provision of a company's articles which require excessive periods of notice of appointment of proxies. The periods allowed by the legislation remain unchanged (48 hours). The change is in the detail and deals with Christmas Day, Good Friday and weekends which are excluded from inclusion in the time calculation since the 2006 Act now requires that no account be taken of any part of a day which is not a working day. As the Explanatory Notes accompanying the Bill explain:

> This means for example for a meeting to be held at 3 p.m. on Tuesday after a bank holiday Monday, the cut off point for proxy appointment will be 3 p.m. the previous Thursday, not 3 p.m. on Sunday as under the 1985 Act.

Proxies – non-immediate polls

5.55   A second change effected by the new legislation is that polls which are not taken immediately are covered by the rules as well as meetings and adjourned meetings. It thus provides (s.327(2)) that any provision in a company articles is void so far as it would have the effect of requiring any appointment or document relating thereto to be received by the company or another person earlier than:

(a)   in the case of a meeting or an adjourned meeting, 48 hours before the time for holding it;
(b)   in the case of a poll taken more than 48 hours after it was demanded, 24 hours before the time appointed for the taking of the poll;
(c)   in the case of a poll taken not more than 48 hours after it was demanded, the time at which it was demanded.

Proxies – appointment of proxy as chairman and right of proxy to demand a poll

5.56   The 2006 Act, s.328 now allows a proxy to be elected chairman of a general meeting by resolution passed at the meeting subject to any provisions to the contrary in the company's articles. Section 329 is similarly novel. It expressly provides that the appointment of a proxy to vote on a matter at a meeting of the company authorises the proxy to demand, or join in demanding, a poll on that matter. The proxy's demand is treated as a demand of the member concerned in calculating whether sufficient members are requiring a poll for the right to be triggered (s.329(2)).

Effect of termination of proxy's authority

5.57   Section 330 of the 2006 Act reproduces and replaces Table A, reg.63 in providing that, subject to any express provision in the company's articles, an appointed proxy's actions at a meeting are valid unless notice of the termination of his authority is given before the meeting starts. A company's articles may specify a longer advance notice period but this cannot be more than 48 hours in advance of the meeting excluding weekends, Christmas Day, Good Friday, and bank holidays and other non-working days. Again the provisions with regard to notice of termination mirror those with regard to notice of appointment in covering polls which are not immediately taken and adjourned meetings as well as meetings in similar terms.

SUPPLEMENTAL

Resolution passed at an adjourned meeting

5.58   Section 381 of the 1985 Act is replaced by s.332 of the 2006 Act as it applies to members' meetings although the effect is the same, so that a resolution of the members of a company passed at an adjourned meeting is passed at that date and not at any earlier date.

Electronic communications relating to notice of meetings and proxies

5.59   Section 333 of the 2006 Act, taken with the general provisions about electronic communications in Part 3 of Sched.4, allows a member to communicate by electronic means with a company where the company has given an electronic address in a notice calling a meeting or in an instrument of proxy invitation.

Class meetings

5.60   Section 334 applies the provisions of Part 13, Chapter 3 to class meetings with necessary modifications (s.334(1)). However, the members' and the court's powers to require directors to call general meetings do not apply (s.334(2)). Neither do the provisions with regard to quorum nor those relating to the right to demand a poll apply to meetings in connection with the variation of rights attached to a class of shares (s.334(3)). With regard to the quorum for a variation of class rights special provision is made instead. The quorum for a meeting other than an adjourned meeting is two persons present holding at least one-third in nominal value of the issued shares of the class in question (excluding any held as treasury shares), and, in the case of an adjourned meeting one person present holding shares of the class in question (s.334(4)). On the question of quorum where a person is present by proxy or proxies he is treated as holding only those shares in respect of which proxies are authorised to exercise voting rights (s.334(5)). With regard to the right to demand a poll, any holder of shares of the class in question may demand a poll at a variation of class rights meeting (s.334(6)). Variation of class rights remains widely defined: it includes any alteration of a provision contained in a company's articles for the variation of the rights attached to a class of shares, or the insertion of any such provision into the articles. Further, references to the variation of rights attached to a class of shares include references to their abrogation (s.334(7)(b)).

5.61   These provisions require some modification in respect of class meetings of companies without share capital. Section 335 applies the general effect of s.334 to this situation but introduces the necessary variation. It arises with regard to quorum, where the quorum for a meeting other than an adjourned meeting is fixed as two members of the class present (in person or by proxy) who together represent at least one-third of the voting rights of the class.

PUBLIC COMPANIES: ADDITIONAL REQUIREMENTS FOR ANNUAL GENERAL MEETINGS

General

5.62   Whilst the duty to hold annual general meetings is abolished for private companies, it is retained for public corporations, and the obligations of public companies in this respect are set out in Part 13, Chapter 4. The main change to the rules applicable under the 1985 Act is that under the 2006 legislation the annual general meeting of a public company must be held within six months of the financial year end, whereas the 1985 Act, s.366 required an annual general meeting to be held each year and not more than 15 months after the previous annual general meeting. The new requirement is less flexible, and it ensures that investors in public companies have more prompt and regular opportunities to hold to account the directors of companies in which they have invested. If a company fails to comply with this requirement a criminal offence is committed by every officer of the company who is in default, which may be punished by the infliction of a fine on the officer (s.336).

5.63   The parts of s.369 of the 1985 Act which related to the giving of notice of the annual general meeting are now reproduced in the 2006 Act, s.337, the minimum notice remaining at 21 days (by virtue of s.307(2)) or longer if a longer period is specified by the company's articles. The meeting may be called at shorter notice if all members of the company agree.

Members' powers to demand circulation of resolutions

5.64   The 1985 Act provisions set out in ss.376 and 377 containing members' powers to require circulation of resolutions for annual general meetings are replaced by ss.338–340 of the 2006 Act. The rules are changed in some respects by the new legislation. Members holding at least 5 per cent voting rights or at least 100 members holding on average £100 paid-up capital have the right to request a resolution to be proposed at the annual general meeting unless it would offend one of three ongoing restrictions of the 2006 Act, namely it would be:

- ineffective;
- defamatory; or
- frivolous or vexatious (s.338(1) and (2)).

5.65   The company remains obliged to circulate details of the resolution to all members. Unlike the position under the 1985 Act, the shares to be taken into account must carry voting rights in respect of the proposed resolution. Further, under the new legislation, if the members' request is received before the financial year end, the costs of circulation fall on the company and not the proposing members. The time limits on an effective request are slightly amended in that it must be received by the company not later than six weeks before the annual general meeting to which it relates or, if later, the time at which notice is given of the meeting. (Note that under the 1985 Act the later time was not less than a week before the meeting.)

5.66   The request may be in hard copy or electronic form. The obligation of the company when a proper request is made remains as under s.376 of the 1985 Act by virtue of s.339 of the 2006 Act. Non-compliance is a criminal offence rendering any officer of the company in default liable to a fine. Where the expenses of circulation do not fall on the company they fall on the requesting members who are obliged to lodge with the company a sum reasonably sufficient to meet these expenses (s.340).

ADDITIONAL REQUIREMENTS FOR QUOTED COMPANIES

5.67   Part 13, Chapter 5 imposes new requirements in quoted companies relating to the disclosure on a website of the results of polls at general meetings, and an independent report on a poll if a sufficient number of members demand one. This implements recommendations of the Company Law Review (Final Report, para.6.39).

The website publication of poll results

5.68   A key provision with regard to publication of poll results is s.341, which provides that where a poll is taken at a general meeting of a quoted company, the company must ensure that certain information is made available on a website, the information being:

(a)   the date of the meeting;
(b)   the text of the resolution, or as the case may be, a description of the subject matter of the poll;
(c)   the number of votes cast in favour; and
(d)   the number of votes cast against.

5.69   Failure to comply is a criminal offence rendering any officer in default liable to a fine but neither the validity of the poll nor the resolution or other business (if passed or agreed to) to which the poll relates is affected. There are provisions relating to website availability, discussed at **para.5.83**.

Independent report on poll

5.70   Section 342 creates a new right conferred on members to require the directors of a quoted company to obtain an independent report on any poll taken, or to be taken, at a general meeting, of the company. The threshold required for an effective demand is the same as that for the circulation of a resolution and the members' request must be made within one week of the meeting at which the poll is taken, so that members have up to a week after the poll is taken to consider its implications and the circumstances under which it was taken. It appears that the request may be made in advance of the meeting if the requesting members wish but as the Explanatory Notes point out, unless the company's articles already require all votes to be taken on a poll, the requesting members will need to take steps to ensure that one is called. A request may be in either hard copy or electronic form (s.342(4)(a)).

The independent assessor

5.71   Section 343 obliges the directors where a report is validly required to appoint within a week of being so required, a person they consider to be appropriate (an 'independent assessor') to prepare a report for the company on the poll or polls concerned. The directors must not appoint a person who fails to meet the requirements of independence (as defined), or one who has another role in connection with the collecting or counting of votes or with the appointment of proxies (s.343(3)). In the event of default by the company a criminal offence is committed and every officer in default is liable to a fine.

5.72   It has been seen that the demand for a report can be made before a poll is taken with the result that the independent assessor may be appointed prior to the meeting. It may then be that at the meeting no poll is taken. The 2006 Act provides for this situation by specifying that in such circumstances the obligation on the directors comes to an end as does the appointment of the assessor, but this is without prejudice to the latter's right to be paid for work done before the appointment ceased (s.343(6)).

The independence requirement

5.73   The independence requirement is contained in ss.344 and 345 and excludes anyone who is too closely connected with the company or an associated undertaking of the company. The independence requirement corresponds to the provisions relating to auditors. An auditor may be appointed as an assessor. A partnership may also be appointed and the Act makes provision for this, dealing with the consequences of the fact that a partnership is not a legal person (s.346).

The contents of the report

5.74   The report of the independent assessor must state whether, in the assessor's opinion:

(a) the procedures adopted in connection with the poll or polls were adequate;
(b) the votes cast (including proxy votes) were fairly and accurately recorded and counted;
(c) the validity and members' appointments of proxies were fairly assessed;
(d) the notice of meeting complied with the requirement that it contained a proper statement of the rights to appoint a proxy; and

(e) the requirements with regard to the company sponsored invitations to appoint proxies were complied with in relation to the meeting.

5.75   The report must deal with these matters but the assessor is free to deal with other issues if he chooses so to do. In any event the report must contain the assessor's reasons for the opinions stated, and, if the assessor is unable to form an opinion on any of the required matters, the report must record that fact and state the reasons for it. Finally the report must state the name of the assessor (s.347).

Assessor's rights to information

5.76   Clearly an independent assessor cannot function if he is not given rights to access the company and obtain information from it. The relevant rights are conferred by s.348. The independent assessor is given rights to attend the meeting at which the poll or polls are to be taken, and to be provided with information in relation thereto. However, he is to make use of those rights only to the extent that he considers necessary for the preparation of the report (s.348). He also has the right to access company records relating to any poll on which he is to report and also relating to the meeting at which the poll or polls are to be taken (s.349(1)).

5.77   In particular an independent assessor is entitled to require certain persons to provide him with information or explanations for the purpose of preparing his report. The persons covered are:

(a) a director or secretary of the company;
(b) an employee of the company;
(c) a person holding or accountable for any of the company's records;
(d) a member of the company; or
(e) an agent of the company (this includes the company's bankers, solicitors and auditors).

5.78   A person from whom information is sought is not required to breach legal professional privilege or to incriminate himself except in relation to the offences relating to the provision of information discussed immediately below (s.349(4)–(5)).

Offences in relation to the provision of information

5.79   The 2006 Act creates two offences in relation to the provision of information. First, a person who fails to comply with a requirement for information without delay commits an offence unless it was not reasonably practicable for him to provide the information or explanation. This is punishable by the imposition of a fine (s.350(1) and (2)). Secondly, a person commits an offence who knowingly or recklessly makes to an independent assessor a statement, whether oral or written, that:

(a) conveys or purports to convey any information or explanation which an
    independent assessor requires, or is entitled to require under s.349; and
(b) is misleading, false or deceptive in a material particular (s.350(3)).

This is plainly a more serious matter and is punishable by both fines and
imprisonment.

5.80   Finally, the company is required to publish the independent assessor's
report on a website so as to set out certain minimum information, namely the
assessor's identity, the text of the resolution, and a copy of his report (s.351).
In the event of default a criminal offence is committed and every officer in
default is liable to a fine, but failure to publish invalidates neither the poll nor
the resolution or any other business (if passed or agreed to) to which the poll
relates.

General

5.81   The provisions with regard to publication of both polls and independent
assessor's reports apply with necessary amendments and modifications to class
meetings (s.352).

5.82   The Secretary of State is empowered to make regulations to limit or extend
the types of company to which the website publication requirements apply so that
they may be extended to apply beyond quoted companies (s.354).

5.83   The Act prescribes minimum requirements with regard to website availability applicable to the publication of both poll results and independent assessor's reports (s.353). The website on which the information is made available
must be maintained by or on behalf of the quoted company which must be identified by it. Thus, a company is not obliged to maintain the website itself and may
allow the service to be provided by a website provider. Access to the website and
the ability to obtain a hard copy of the information from the website must not be
conditional on payment of a fee or any other term. The information must be made
available as soon as is reasonably practicable and must be kept available for a
period of two years from the date on which it is first made available on the website. However, a failure to keep the information available for the full period is
disregarded if it is available for part to the extent that the failure is wholly attributable to circumstances that it would not be reasonable to have expected the
company to prevent or avoid (s.353(5)).

RECORDS OF RESOLUTIONS AND MEETINGS

5.84   The 2006 Act makes significant changes to the requirements with regard
to records, both substantive and organisational. With regard to the records of resolutions and meetings the law is contained in Part 13, Chapter 6 (ss.355–359
inclusive). Sections 382, 382A, 382B and 383 of the 1985 Act are repealed. The

new law divides record keeping into two separate parts, the provisions relating to meetings of directors being dealt with in Part 10 of the Act.

Keeping of records

5.85   The new legislation requires all companies to keep records comprising copies of all resolutions of members passed otherwise than at general meetings, minutes of the proceedings of general meetings and details of all decisions taken by a sole member (s.355). The main change in this respect is that whereas under the 1985 Act the obligation was to keep the records for an indefinite duration, the 2006 Act imposes a period of 10 years, thus clarifying the obligations of companies and reducing the burden on them. Failure by a company to comply with this duty constitutes a criminal offence rendering all officers in default liable to a fine. By s.359 the duties with regard to the keeping of records apply to class meetings; this alters the law contained in the 1985 Act.

Availability of records for inspection

5.86   Not only must the records be kept for the 10-year period, but they must also be kept available for inspection at the registered office during this period without charge (s.358(1)). Further, on payment of a fee any member is entitled to a copy of any of the records (s.358(2)). Refusal of inspection or failure to send a copy is a criminal offence rendering any officer in default liable to a fine and, if the contravention continues, a daily default fine (s.358(5) and (6)). Further, in the case of such refusal or default the court may compel the inspection or the supply of documents (s.358(7)).

Evidential value of records

5.87   As under the 1985 Act all records of resolutions or written resolutions and minutes of meetings when appropriately signed off are evidence of the passing of the resolution or the proceedings at the meeting, so creating in legal proceedings a rebuttable presumption of the accuracy of the records (s.356).

6 ACCOUNTS AND REPORTS

INTRODUCTION

6.1 The Companies Act 1985, Part 7 deals with both (a) accounts and reports and (b) the auditing requirements. It is replaced under the new Act by two parts, Part 15 dealing with accounts and reports and Part 16 with auditing requirements. The new Part 15 is extensively redrafted to try to make the Act more user friendly. It also contains provisions making substantive changes. As the introductory notes point out, a further development is to allow the Secretary of State to replace the detailed Schedules to the 1985 Act, Part 7, by regulations. About this the Explanatory Notes comment:

> This will give more flexibility to arrange the material currently in Schedules to make it easier to follow for different types of company. It is unnecessary and undesirable to have parallel and duplicative regimes on the detail for different types of company in primary legislation, but this could be done in parallel sets of regulations for different sizes and types of company.
>
> (Explanatory Notes, para.634)

6.2 The main substantive changes are listed as:

- a reduction in the time limit for private companies to file their accounts from ten months to nine months after the year end (section 442);
- a reduction in the time limit for public companies to lay full financial statements before the company in general meeting and file them from 7 months to 6 months after the year end (section 442);
- new requirements for quoted companies to publish their annual accounts and reports and preliminary results on a website (section 430); and
- replacement of the general power of the Secretary of State to alter accounting requirements in section 257 of the 1985 Act by a general power of amendment by regulations (section 468) and more specific powers in relation to specific sections.

> (Explanatory Notes, para.635)

Basic distinction

6.3   The redrafting and reworking of the legislation to make it more easy to follow and therefore user friendly is clear in s.380, which notes that in certain respects different provisions apply to different kinds of company (s.380(2)) and specifies (s.380(3)) that the main distinctions for this purpose are:

(a) between companies subject to the small companies regime (see s.381) and those which are not; and
(b) between quoted companies (see s.385) and those which are not.

Where distinctions have to be made because of provisions which do not apply to all kinds of company then (s.380(4)):

(a) provisions applying to companies subject to the small companies regime appear before the provisions applying to other companies;
(b) provisions applying to private companies appear before the provisions applying to public companies, and
(c) provisions applying to quoted companies appear after the provisions applying to other companies.

Companies subject to the small companies regime

6.4   The specification of the companies subject to the small companies regime is contained in ss.381–384 and these sections set out which companies, parent companies and groups of companies fall within the small companies regime by qualifying in principle for the regime, and not being excluded from the regime for one of the reasons set out in s.384. The regime continues largely unchanged from the regime established by ss.247, 247A and 249 of the 1985 Act. There is one small change in that whereas the 1985 Act, s.247A(2) provides that the group is ineligible if any of its members is a body corporate having power to offer its shares or debentures to the public, the reference in the new s.384(2)(b) is to such a body corporate whose shares are admitted to trading on a regulated market in an EEA state. This is to incorporate changes effected by the Accounts Modernisation Directive (Directive 2003/51/EC).

6.5   The qualifying conditions are also redrafted for simplicity. By s.382(1) a company qualifies as small in relation to its first financial year if the qualifying conditions are met in that year. Thereafter it will only qualify in a subsequent year if either:

(a) the qualifying conditions are met both in that year and in the preceding financial year; or
(b) the qualifying conditions are met in that year and the company qualified as small in relation to the preceding financial year.

6.6   The second possibility clearly allows for a company to qualify as small in relation to a financial year even if it does not meet the qualifying conditions for that year. This is expressly provided for by a third possibility for qualification which allows qualification if the qualifying conditions were met in the preceding financial year and the company qualified as small in relation to that year, thus allowing qualification in a financial year purely because of the position in the previous financial year. This means that one year's departure from the financial or other criteria does not bring to an end the company's classification (see s.382(1) and (2)). The financial and other conditions themselves remain unchanged.

6.7 The provisions dealing with parent companies within groups work in parallel (see s.383).

Quoted and unquoted companies

6.8 The definitions of quoted and unquoted companies are set out in s.385 in terms equivalent to the distinctions made in s.262 of the 1985 Act. A power is included allowing for the amendment of the definition of quoted companies by regulation.

Accounting records

6.9 Part 15, Chapter 2 contains in ss.386–389 similar provisions to those contained in ss.221 and 222 of the 1985 Act as to the keeping of financial records so as to allow the effective financial management of the company complying with the Companies Act and, where appropriate, international accounting standards (IAS). The criminal liabilities for breach with similar consequences are continued.

A company's financial year

6.10 The requirements for this set out in s.223 of the 1985 Act are incorporated into s.390 of the 2006 Act with the company's accounting year being its accounting reference period, subject to the directors being able to alter the last day of the period by plus or minus seven days.

6.11 The accounting reference dates of companies incorporated before 1 April 1996 in the case of companies incorporated in Great Britain and before 22 August 1997 in the case of companies incorporated in Northern Ireland are unchanged. In other cases a company's accounting reference date is the last day of the month in which the anniversary of its incorporation falls. Its first accounting reference period is a period of more than six months but not more than 18 months beginning with the date of incorporation and ending with the accounting reference date unless the company chooses to change that date. Subsequent accounting reference dates are financial years being successive periods of 12 months unless the company changes its accounting reference date. The power to change its accounting reference date thus remains with the company.

6.12   The substantive change is contained in s.392(4) of the 2006 Act. Under the 1985 Act a company could not change its accounting date once the period allowed for laying and delivering accounts had expired, but under the new legislation only public companies are obliged to lay their accounts at general meeting. Consequently s.392(4) provides that a company cannot change its accounting reference date if the period allowed for delivering accounts and reports to the registrar has already expired.

ANNUAL ACCOUNTS

6.13   The duty to prepare the annual accounts remains that of the directors, who are subject to the overall duty only to approve accounts if they give a true and fair view of the financial position of the company. In the case of a company's group accounts the obligation to give a true and fair view extends to the assets, liabilities, financial position and profit and loss of the undertakings included in the consolidation as a whole, so far as concerns members of the company (s.393(1)(b)). The directors are thus now expressly directed by the primary legislation to extract that information in the consolidated accounts relevant to the situation of the individual company. As before, supervision obligations are borne by the auditors (s.393 and Part 16, Chapter 3).

6.14   The rules concerning accounts of individual companies at present contained in ss.226, 226A and 226B of the 1985 Act are repealed but are largely replaced by the 2006 Act, ss.394–397. The individual accounts may either be prepared in accordance with the Act or (unless the company is a charity) in accordance with international accounting standards adopted under the IAS Regulation (the terms 'IAS Regulation' and 'international accounting standards' are both defined in s.474). Once a company has switched to IAS requirements all subsequent individual accounts must be prepared in accordance with IAS unless there is a relevant change of circumstances (see s.395(3) to (5)).

6.15   The complex and detailed provisions concerning the form and content of the Companies Act accounts contained within the Schedules to the 1985 Act have no place in the 2006 Act structure. Instead detailed requirements will in future be contained in regulations to be made by the Secretary of State (s.396(3)).

6.16   The option conferred on small companies which are parent companies by the 1985 Act, s.248 not to prepare group accounts in addition to their individual accounts is continued by the 2006 Act, s.398. On the other hand the exemption from the preparation of group accounts conferred by the same section of the 1985 Act on parent companies at the centre of medium-sized groups has been abolished following the substantial increase in the financial thresholds for medium-sized groups.

Group accounts

6.17   The provisions with regard to group accounts have been reorganised to make them more user friendly. Sections 227(1) and (8), 228, 228A and 229(5) of the 1985 Act are replaced by ss.399–402, which re-enact them. Section 399 enacts the general duty with regard to the preparation of such accounts including a duty on parent companies not subject to the small companies regime to prepare such accounts unless exempt under either s.400 or s.401. Section 400 contains an exemption in respect of companies included in EEA group accounts of a larger group and s.402 contains an exemption when all the company's subsidiary undertakings can be excluded from consolidation in Companies Act group accounts under s.405.

Framework for group accounts

6.18   The applicable accounting framework in respect of group accounts is set out in s.403, replacing s.227(2)–(5) of the 1985 Act. Parent companies whose shares are publicly traded must, under the 2006 Act, prepare group accounts in accordance with the IAS Regulation. With the exception of charitable companies, other parent companies have the option whether to prepare their accounts under the Companies Act or the IAS requirements for group accounts. Again, once a company has switched to the IAS group accounts approach all subsequent accounts must be prepared to these requirements unless there is a relevant change of circumstances.

6.19   The framework for the preparation of group accounts under the Companies Act is also changed with the repealing of the requirements of the 1985 Act, Sched.4A. The required format will be set out in due course in regulations made by the Secretary of State (s.404(3)). A subsidiary undertaking must be included in the accounts subject to specified permitted exclusions (s.405 replacing s.229 of the 1985 Act). Where the IAS formula is used, this must be stated on notes to the accounts (s.406 replacing s.227B of the 1985 Act). Section 227C of the 1985 Act is re-enacted in s.407 of the 2006 Act to ensure consistency of financial reporting within the group by providing that if the parent company prepares both consolidated and individual accounts under IAS it is not required to ensure that all of its subsidiary undertakings use this form. It is sufficient to ensure that all of its individual accounts and those of all of its subsidiary undertakings use the same financial reporting framework, unless there are good reasons for not so doing.

6.20   The 1985 Act, s.230 provides an exemption from the inclusion of a profit and loss account as part of the accounts in certain circumstances and this is continued by s.408 of the 2006 Act which repeals the similar provision in the 1985 Act. The exemption applies where:

(a) a company prepares group accounts;
(b) the notes to the company's individual balance sheet show the company's profit or loss for the financial year,

and the account is approved by the directors. The account also need not in any event contain the information about employee numbers and costs required by s.411. The fact that the exemption is being relied on must be disclosed in the company's annual accounts.

Information to be given in notes to the accounts

6.21   Section 409 continues the obligations imposed by s.231(1)–(4) of the 1985 Act to disclose information about related undertakings in the notes to a company's annual accounts but with changes. The obligation applies whether or not the company has to produce group accounts but the disclosure requirements differ depending on this. The detailed requirements set out in the 1985 Act are repealed and will be replaced by detailed regulations made by the Secretary of State.

6.22   Section 409(3) enables regulations to be made (making provision similar to s.231(3) of the 1985 Act) to authorise the omission from the notes to the accounts of information in respect of undertakings established or carrying on business outside the UK where the directors of the company believe that full disclosure would be seriously prejudicial to the business of the company or any of its subsidiary undertakings. The Secretary of State must agree to the omission. According to the Explanatory Notes the exemption is sought by a very small number of companies each year.

Alternative compliance in relation to related undertakings

6.23   The alternative compliance provisions concerning information about related undertakings contained in s.231(5)–(7) of the 1985 Act are replaced by s.410 which allows the directors, where there are numerous related undertakings and they believe that full disclosure would result in information of excessive length to be included in the accounts, to give more limited information. This must still, however, meet the minimum disclosure requirement set out in s.410(2). However, where advantage is taken of this dispensation the full information (both that which is disclosed in the notes to the accounts and that which is not) must be annexed to the company's next annual return (s.410(3)(b)).

Employee numbers and costs

6.24   The duty to include information about employee numbers and costs is continued by s.411 and the existing provisions in the 1985 Act, including the recently enacted s.231A which imposed the responsibility on companies preparing IAS accounts, are repealed. It will be remembered that the continuing duty is imposed on companies not subject to the small companies regime who have to give the following information with respect to their employees in notes to the annual accounts:

(a) the average number of persons employed during the financial year;
(b) the average number employed within each category of person employed (the categories are selected by the directors having regard to the manner in which the company's activities are organised);
(c) the aggregate amounts of wages and salaries paid or payable in respect of the year to each person;
(d) social security costs incurred by the company on their behalf; and
(e) other pension costs incurred.

Directors' benefits

6.25   Similarly a duty to give information about directors' benefits is continued by ss.412 and 413 although the law is recast from the repealed provisions of the 1985 Act, s.232. Under s.412 the Secretary of State may make provision by regulations requiring information to be given in notes to a company's accounts about directors' remuneration including:

(a) gains made by the exercise of share options;
(b) benefits received or receivable under long-term incentive schemes;
(c) payments for loss of office;
(d) benefits receivable and contributions for the purpose of providing benefits in respect of past services of the individual whether given as director or otherwise; and
(e) consideration paid to or receivable by third parties for making available the services of a person as director or in any other capacity while director.

6.26   Directors and past directors are required to give notice to the company of such matters relating to themselves and any director in default commits a fine-bearing offence. By virtue of s.413 details of advantages and credit granted to a director and guarantees entered into on the director's behalf must be shown in the appropriate individual company or group accounts.

6.27   The wording used by s.413 is much closer than the provisions in the 1985 Act to Arts.43.1(13) and 34.13 of the Fourth and Seventh European Company Law Directives (Directives 78/660/EEC and 83/349/EEC respectively). A substantive change effected by the new law is that companies are no longer required to disclose transactions made between the company and its officers other than directors. A further substantive change is that banks and holding companies of credit institutions need only state:

(a) the amount of an advance or credit; and
(b) in relation to a guarantee, the amount of the maximum liability which may be incurred by the company or its subsidiary.

6.28   The extensive provisions in respect of financial institutions in ss.343 and 344 of the 1985 Act are repealed.

Approval and signing of accounts

6.29   The obligations contained in s.233 of the 1985 Act are replaced in s.414 so that the board of directors must approve the annual accounts, which must be signed, and a balance sheet of accounts prepared in accordance with the small companies regime must carry a statement that this is so. The old provision of the 1985 Act, s.233(4), which required that a director of the company should sign a copy of the balance sheet delivered to the registrar, has been repealed and not replaced as it was felt that it would have hampered developments in the electronic delivery of accounts.

DIRECTORS' REPORT

6.30   The 2006 Act continues the obligation to prepare a directors' report with details of required content, approval and signature in similar terms to that of the 1985 Act. It repeals ss.234, 234ZZA, 234ZZB, 234ZA, 234A, 234AA, 234AB, 246(4)(a), 246A(2A) and 246(8) of the 1985 Act. The new provisions are more logically contained in Part 15, Chapter 5 and, if not elegantly expressed, are considerably more user friendly. The detailed provisions of Sched.7 to the 1985 Act are repealed. Instead s.416(4) gives power to the Secretary of State to make provision by regulations as to other matters which must be disclosed in the directors' report which may include matters formerly embodied in Sched.7.

6.31   The new provisions carry out one tidying up substantive change. Under the old s.234ZA the obligation was imposed that the directors' report should contain a statement to the effect that:

(a) so far as the director is aware, there is no relevant audit information of which the company's auditor is unaware; and

(b) he has taken all of the steps that he ought to have taken as a director in order to make himself aware of any relevant audit information and to establish that the company's auditor is aware of that information.

This obligation is continued by s.418(2). However under the 1985 Act this was disapplied for companies exempt from audit under ss.249A(1) or 249AA(1) but, anomalously, not for charitable companies exempt by virtue of having a report prepared by a reporting accountant under s.249C. This anomaly is rectified under the new legislation.

Obligation of enquiry

6.32   Under s.418 a director remains regarded as having taken all steps that he ought to have taken as director to discharge his obligation if he has both made such enquiries of his fellow directors and of the company's auditor for the purpose and taken such other steps (if any) for that purpose as are required by his duty as a director of the company to exercise reasonable care, skill and diligence (s.418(4)). The sanctions remain the same under the new provisions. Where a directors' report containing the required information is approved but the statement is false, every director of the company who knew that the statement was false, or was reckless as to whether it was false and failed to take reasonable steps to prevent the report from being approved, commits a criminal offence punishable on conviction by imprisonment for up to 12 months or a fine or both (s.418(5) and (6)). By contrast the similar offence for approving and signing a report which does not comply with the provisions of the Act is punishable merely by a fine (s.419(3) and (4)).

The business review

6.33   Sections 234AA and 234AB of the 1985 Act imposed obligations to include a business review in the directors' report. Whilst these provisions are repealed, an obligation to include such matters within the directors' report is continued by s.417 unless the company is subject to the small companies regime. The purpose of the review is declared to be to inform members of the company and help them to assess how the directors have performed their statutory duty under s.172 to promote the success of the company (s.417(2)). The review must contain a fair review of the company's business and a description of the principal risks and uncertainties facing the company. It must constitute a balanced and comprehensive analysis consistent with the size and complexity of the business of:

(a)   the development and performance of the company's business during the financial year; and

(b)   the position of the company's business at the end of the year.

6.34   In relation to a group, the directors' report provisions have effect as if the references to the company were references to the company and those subsidiary undertakings included in the consolidation. The obligations imposed do not require the disclosure of information about impending developments or matters in the course of negotiation, if the disclosure would, in the directors' opinion, be seriously prejudicial to the company's interest (s.417(10)).

6.35   In general the review must include certain information to the extent necessary for an understanding of the development, performance or position of the company's business. The specified information includes analysis using financial key performance indicators and, where appropriate, analysis using other key performance indicators, including information relating to environmental matters and employee matters. Key performance indicators means factors by reference to which the development, performance or position of the company's business can be effectively measured (s.417(6)). However, in relation to medium-sized companies the directors' report need not comply with the requirements of s.417(6) so far as they relate to non-financial information (s.417(7)). Clearly in relation to larger companies non-financial information is required to be dealt with.

6.36 Additional requirements are imposed on quoted companies where the business review must, to the extent necessary for an understanding of the development, performance or position of the company's business, include specific further information. The requirement covers first the main trends and factors likely to affect the future development, performance and position of the company's business. It also includes information about:

(a) environmental matters (including the impact of the company's business on the environment;

(b) the company's employees; and

(c) social and community issues.

6.37 If for any reason, the review does not contain information on each of these three categories, it must state which of those kinds of information it does not contain (s.417(5)).

Quoted companies – directors' remuneration report

6.38 Sections 234B and 234C of the 1985 Act contained provisions requiring the directors of a quoted company to file a directors' remuneration report each year, and this obligation is continued by the 2006 Act, s.420. Failure to do so renders every person who was a director of the company immediately before the end of the period for filing accounts and reports for the financial year and who failed to take all reasonable steps for securing compliance with the requirement, guilty of an offence which on conviction leads to the imposition of a fine. The report must be approved by the board and any director similarly failing to ensure that the report complies with the requirements is guilty of an offence which carries a fine (s.422).

6.39 Under the 1985 Act the matters to be included in the report were set out in Sched.7ZA, which is repealed. It will be replaced by regulations made by the Secretary of State under s.421 which empowers him to make provision by regulation as to the information that must be contained in the report, how the information is to be set out in the report, and what is to be the auditable part of the report. Each director is required to give notice to the company of such matters relating to himself as may be necessary to satisfy the regulatory requirements. A director in default commits an offence which carries a fine.

PUBLICATION OF ACCOUNTS AND REPORTS

6.40 Publication of accounts and reports are dealt with by Part 15, Chapter 7 (ss.423–436) of the 2006 Act. Section 238 of the 1985 Act is replaced by s.423 which imposes the same general duty to send copies of its annual accounts and reports to the same designated persons. However, this general duty is now restricted by s.423(2) which removes the obligation in respect of circulation to persons for whom a company no longer has a current address. This is to avoid the inconvenient, ineffective and wasteful consequences of the previous law, which required companies to send copies of the annual reports and accounts to addresses from which correspondence had previously been returned marked 'not known at this address' or similar electronic communication. A company has a current address for a person if an address has been notified to the company by a person as one at which documents may be sent to him and the company has no reason to believe that documents sent to that person at that address will not reach him (s.423(3)). General provisions about how to supply copies to joint holders are set out in the 2006 Act in Part 6 of Sched.5.

Time for sending out copies

6.41   The time allowed for sending out copies of accounts and reports is now dealt with by s.424 which deals with both private and public companies and makes substantive changes. Under the 1985 Act regime private companies were required to lay their accounts at a general meeting and to send their accounts and reports to members 21 days before that meeting. Since they are no longer required to hold any general meeting they are now required to send out their accounts and reports not later than the earlier of the date of actual delivery to the registrar or the deadline for delivery. Public companies must send out the annual accounts not later than 21 days before the relevant accounts meeting, which is the meeting at which the accounts and reports in question are to be laid (s.424(3) and (6)). Whether the permitted time is that for a private or public company is determined by reference to the company's status immediately before the end of the accounting reference period by reference to which the financial year for the accounts in question was determined (s.424(5)).

6.42   Section 238(5) of the 1985 Act which created offences in respect of default in sending out copies of accounts and reports is repealed but s.425 of the 2006 Act provides for identical offences.

Option to provide summary financial statements

6.43   This was provided for by s.251 of the 1985 Act which is repealed, but the law is substantially restated by ss.426–429 of the 2006 Act. Under s.426 all companies are given the option to provide summary financial statements instead of copies of the full accounts and reports although a member requiring copies of the full accounts and reports must be supplied with them. As under the old law, power is conferred on the Secretary of State to make provision by regulations both as to the circumstances in which a company may send out summary financial statements and as to the manner in which it is to be ascertained whether a person wishes to receive a full set of accounts and reports. If a summary financial statement is used it must be in the appropriate form with s.427 setting out that for unquoted companies and s.428 that for quoted companies. In either case the statement must record certain prescribed matters (see s.427(4) and s.428(4) as appropriate) and comply with detailed regulations to be made by the Secretary of

State (s.427(2) and s.428(2) as appropriate). The option where operative covers both the circulation of accounts and reports under s.423 to members of the company and the copies required to be sent to a person nominated to enjoy information rights under s.146.

6.44   There is a new power for regulations to provide that specified material be sent separately at the same time as the summary financial statements instead of being included in it, thus allowing the requirements of the Takeovers Directive (Directive 2004/25/EC) as to necessary explanatory material to be honoured (ss.427(5) and 428(5)).

6.45   Section 429 creates offences in respect of default in the same terms as those in the repealed s.251(6) of the 1985 Act.

Quoted companies – requirements of website publication

6.46   Section 430 introduces new requirements on quoted companies to publish the annual accounts and reports themselves on a website. This is in addition to the responsibility of such companies to send the full accounts and reports to their members under provisions previously discussed.

6.47   With regard to the annual accounts and reports, the company must ensure that these are made available on a website and remain available until the annual accounts and reports for the company's next financial year are published on the site. Default in complying with either of these requirements is a criminal offence rendering every officer of the company in default liable to a fine (s.430(6) and (7)).

6.48   The provisions with regard to website publications are part of the legislative embodiment of the recommendations made by the Company Law Review in its Final Report, para.8.86.

Right of member or debenture holder to demand copies of the report

6.49   Sections 431 and 432 impose the obligations embodied previously in s.239 of the 1985 Act and entitle a member or debenture holder to receive a copy of the company's last annual accounts and reports without charge (s.431 dealing with unquoted companies and s.432 dealing with quoted companies). The variation rests upon the different documentation which the different categories of company are obliged to prepare. In both cases the documentation includes the company's last accounts, the last directors' report and the auditor's report, including a statement on the last directors' report. In the case of a quoted company it must also include the last directors' remuneration report and the auditor's report in relation to this. Any demand made for these reports must be complied with within seven days and failure so to do is a criminal offence committed by the company and any officer in default, which is punishable by a fine and, in the event of continued contravention, a daily default fine.

Publication of accounts and reports and inclusion of names of signatories

6.50   Under the 1985 Act the procedural requirements with regard to the statement of the name of the signatory are scattered in a series of statutory provisions which, as a result, are far from user friendly. They may be found in Part 7 of the 1985 Act in ss.233(3), 233(6)(a), 234A(2), 234A(4)(a), 234C(2) and 234AB(2). With the 2006 Act they are drawn together in a single section: s.433. In the case of unquoted companies, every copy of the balance sheet and directors' report that is published by or on behalf of the company must be signed and must state the name of the director who signed it on behalf of the board. For quoted companies this also applies to copies of the balance sheet, directors' remuneration report and the directors' report.

6.51   The 1985 Act provision (s.240) concerning requirements in connection with the publication of statutory and non-statutory accounts is repealed but then substantially re-enacted in ss.434 and 435.

Statutory accounts

6.52   By virtue of ss.434 and 435 if a company publishes any of its statutory accounts they must be accompanied by the auditor's report on those accounts unless, of course, the company is exempted from audit and the directors have taken advantage of the exemption. A company's statutory accounts are its accounts for a financial year as required to be delivered to the registrar under s.441 (s.434(1) and (2)). A company that prepares statutory group accounts for a financial year must not publish its statutory individual accounts for that year without also publishing with them its statutory group accounts (s.434(2)). However, the provision does not apply in relation to the provision by a company of a summary financial statement (s.434(6)). Contravention of the requirements constitutes an offence by the company and any director in default, which is punishable by a fine.

Non-statutory accounts

6.53   While s.434 deals with publication of statutory accounts, the publication of non-statutory accounts is the province of s.435. The publication by a company of 'non-statutory accounts' is the publication of either any balance sheet or profit and loss account relating to, or purporting to deal with, a financial year of the company or an account in any form purporting to be a balance sheet or profit and loss account for a group headed by the company relating to, or purporting to deal with, a financial year of the company. In either case publication must be otherwise than as part of the statutory accounts (s.435(3)). For the purpose of the second alternative 'a group headed by the company' means a group consisting of the company and any other undertaking (regardless of whether it is a subsidiary undertaking of the company) other than a parent undertaking of the company (s.435(4)).

6.54   The legislation sets out the regulatory requirements in s.435(1) which provides that if a company publishes non-statutory accounts it must publish with them a statement indicating:

(a) that they are not the company's statutory accounts; and
(b) whether statutory accounts dealing with any financial year with which the non-statutory accounts purport to deal have been delivered to the registrar; and
(c) whether an auditor's report has been made on the company's statutory accounts for any such financial year, and if so whether the report:
  (i)   was qualified or unqualified, or included a reference to any matters to which the auditor drew attention by way of emphasis without qualifying the report, or
  (ii) contained a statement under s.498(2) (accounting records or returns inadequate or accounts or directors' remuneration report not agreeing with records and returns) or s.498(3) (failure to obtain necessary information and explanations).

6.55   Further, the company must not publish with non-statutory accounts the auditor's report on the company's statutory accounts (s.435(2)). However, the requirements do not apply at all in relation to the provision by a company of a summary financial statement (s.435(7)).

6.56   Breach of the requirements constitutes a criminal offence rendering, on conviction, the company and any officer in default liable to a fine.

Publication

6.57   A company is regarded as publishing a document if it publishes, issues or circulates it or otherwise makes it available for public inspection in a manner calculated to invite members of the public generally, or any class of members of the public, to read it (s.436(2)).

Public companies – laying of accounts and reports before general meeting

6.58   Laying accounts before a general meeting is dealt with in Part 15, Chapter 8 (ss.437 and 438). These provisions restate the requirements of the 1985 Act, s.241 with regard to the laying of accounts and reports before the company in general meeting (an 'accounts meeting', meaning a general meeting in accordance with s.437(3)). However, the 2006 Act restricts the application of the requirement to public companies in line with its approach that private companies should be under no statutory obligation to hold an annual general meeting (AGM) or to lay accounts and reports in general meetings. The statutory link between the accounts and AGMs is therefore severed, although such a link may be provided for in the company's articles. An AGM held pursuant to the requirements of a private company's articles will not be an accounts meeting, which by definition must be a statutory meeting (see s.437(3)). Public companies must of course continue to hold AGMs which, it will be remembered, must now be held within six months of the end of the accounting reference period.

Quoted companies – approval of directors' remuneration report

6.59   The obligation imposed by s.241A of the 1985 Act that a quoted company has to seek a resolution approving the directors' remuneration report for the preceding financial year and that a resolution to that effect be circulated to its shareholders prior to the AGM is re-enacted in Part 15, Chapter 9 (ss.439 and 440). The idea behind this is to make the directors more accountable to the shareholders in respect of their remuneration package but it is questionable how effective the provision has been in establishing any real control over directors' rewards. The extent to which the modern quoted company is truly democratic given the position of large institutional shareholders is itself questionable. In any event the vote is advisory so that, as such, it does not require directors to change or give up contractual entitlements or even to amend their remuneration policy. Probably optimistically the Explanatory Notes comment:

> . . . the result of the vote will send a very strong signal to the directors about the level of support among shareholders for the board's remuneration policy. In practice, directors will wish to take notice of the views of the company's members, and to respond appropriately.

(Explanatory Notes, para.686)

6.60   The responsibility for ensuring compliance with this provision is that of the existing directors, who are defined as those persons who are directors of the company immediately before the meeting. The requirement does not apply to past directors even though their remuneration package may be a part of what is to be approved, or they may have served on the board as members of the remuneration committee in the financial year covered by the report. If the resolution is not put to a vote at the accounts meeting an offence is committed by each existing director which can lead to the imposition of a fine. It is, however, a defence for a person charged with an offence to prove that he took all reasonable steps for securing that the resolution was put to the vote at the meeting.

FILING OF ACCOUNTS AND REPORTS

6.61   The detailed requirements with regard to the filing of accounts and reports are set out in Part 15, Chapter 10 (ss.441–453). In general the provisions take those of the 1985 Act and restructure them to make clearer what must be done, but there are also substantive alterations. The provisions begin with the imposition of a general duty to file the appropriate accounts and reports for each financial year (s.441(1)). The reports required are set out by type of company dealt with by individual sections of the Act, namely small companies (s.444), medium-sized companies (s.445), unquoted companies (s.446) and quoted companies (s.447).

Period for filing accounts

6.62   The period for filing accounts is dealt with by s.442, which contains substantive alterations to the regime under the 1985 Act. Under s.442 in respect of private companies the period is reduced from 10 months to nine months and for public companies from seven months to six months. In both cases the periods are calculated from the end of the relevant accounting period (s.442(2)). The Explanatory Notes give useful background information, pointing out that the:

> timetable for delivering accounts to the registrar was last amended in 1976. The periods have been reduced to reflect improvements in technology and the increased rate at which information becomes out of date. Filing time scales in other countries are generally less generous than in the UK.
>
> (Explanatory Notes, para.688)

6.63   The rules for the calculation of the period involved have been altered and are set out in s.443. In general the date is fixed by simply taking the same date the relevant number of months later so that if the end of the accounting reference period is 3 January and the period allowed is nine months, this will make the appropriate date 3 October. However, months are of unequal length and this can lead to confusion. Does nine months from 28 February mean 28 November (the corresponding date) or 30 November (the end of the month)? In *Dodds* v. *Walker* [1981] 1 WLR 1027 the House of Lords ruled that the 'corresponding' date rule should be applied. In the 2006 Act the 'last day of the month' date has been chosen, thus reversing the position achieved by the House of Lords (see s.443(3), (4) and (5)).

Extent of obligation

6.64   The detail of the obligations is dealt with in successive sections for different types of company in ss.444–447 which restructure the provisions of ss.242, 246, 246A and 254 of the 1985 Act, with the intention of making clearer what companies are required to do. The provisions deal first with small companies (previously covered by the 1985 Act, s.246(1) and (5)–(7)). Under s.444 such companies may file abbreviated accounts and the Secretary of State is given power to make regulations with regard to abbreviated accounts in relation to small companies. Medium-sized companies are dealt with by s.445 which restates s.246A of the 1985 Act and allows the company to file abbreviated accounts, and again the Secretary of State is given the power to make regulations concerning abbreviated accounts for such companies. The filing obligations of unquoted companies are dealt with by s.446 and those of quoted companies by s.447. The latter is a restatement of the 1985 Act, s.242, and includes in s.447(3) the requirement that the copies of all accounting documents including the balance sheet must state the name of the person who signed the documents. Finally s.448 replaces s.254 of the 1985 Act in exempting unlimited companies from the obligations to file accounts provided (s.448(2)) that at no time during the relevant accounting reference period:

(a) has the company been, to its knowledge, a subsidiary undertaking of an undertaking which was then limited, or
(b) have there been to, its knowledge, exercised by or on behalf of two or more undertakings which were then limited, rights which if exercised by one of them would have made the company a subsidiary undertaking of it, or
(c) has the company been a parent company of an undertaking which was then limited.

6.65   The references to an undertaking being limited at a particular time are to an undertaking (under whatever law established) the liability of whose members is at that time limited.

Abbreviated accounts

6.66   Where abbreviated accounts are delivered the provisions of s.247B of the 1985 Act are replaced by s.449 of the 2006 Act in requiring a special auditor's report in place of the auditor's report, under which the auditor states that in his opinion: (a) the company is entitled to deliver abbreviated accounts; and (b) the abbreviated accounts to be delivered are properly prepared in accordance with the governing regulations. If this is done, the auditor's report on the company's annual accounts need not be delivered. However, if that report was qualified, the special report must set out the report in full, together with any further material necessary to understand the qualification. Further, if the auditor's report contained a statement that the accounts or returns were inadequate or accounts failed to agree with records and returns or they had failed to obtain necessary information and explanation, the special report must set out the statement in full. On the other hand there is no requirement at all for the special auditor's report where the company is entitled to exemption from audit and has taken advantage of that exemption.

6.67   Section 450 simply replaces ss.246(7) and (8) and 246A(4) of the 1985 Act in setting out the requirements concerning the approval and signing of abbreviated accounts.

Failure to file accounts and reports

6.68   The consequences of failure to file accounts and reports are dealt with in ss.451 and 452 which replace and re-enact the provisions of the 1985 Act, s.242(2)–(5). If the statutory requirements are not complied with every person who immediately before the end of the period for filing the accounts and reports was a director of the company commits an offence and it is no defence to prove that the documents were not filed because they were not in fact prepared. However it is a defence to prove that the person charged with an offence took all reasonable steps for securing that the requirements for filing would be complied with within the permitted period. On conviction an offender is liable to a fine, and for continued contravention a daily default fine. Further, where there is default in the filing of accounts and reports and the directors fail to make good the default within 14 days after the service of a notice on them requiring compliance the court may, on application of any member or creditor of the company or of the registrar of companies, make an order directing the directors (or any of them) to make good the default within a specified time. In making such an order the court may require that all the costs incidental to the application be borne by the directors (s.452(2)).

6.69   Section s.453 repeals and re-enacts s.242A of the 1985 Act and provides a civil penalty for failure to file the accounts and reports as required. In so doing it makes one substantive change to the replaced legislation. The latter has within it a table of penalties. In its place s.453(2) provides for the Secretary of State to make regulations setting out both the relevant periods and the amounts of the penalties.

REVISION OF DEFECTIVE ACCOUNTS AND REPORTS

6.70   Part 15, Chapter 11 of the 2006 Act re-enacts the detailed provisions of ss.245–245G of the 1985 Act. The provisions are detailed and are far from exciting. Only an overview is attempted here as readers familiar with the law under the 1985 Act will already be familiar with the conceptual structure and most of the detail.

6.71   Section 454 of the 2006 Act essentially restates s.245 of the 1985 Act in allowing a company voluntarily to prepare revised accounts and a revised report or statement where it appears to the directors that the original was defective. The existing power of the Secretary of State to make provisions in regulations as to the application of the provisions of the Act to revised accounts and reports is replicated. Section 455 replicates s.245A of the 1985 Act conferring on the Secretary of State power to give notice to the directors that it appears to him that there is, or may be, a question of whether the accounts or reports comply with the statutory requirements and specifying a period of not less than one month for the directors to give an explanation or prepare revised accounts.

Applications to the court in respect of defective accounts and reports

6.72   The provisions of ss.245B and 245C of the 1985 Act concerning applications to the court in respect of defective accounts and reports are re-enacted in ss.456–457 of the 2006 Act. An application may be made by the Secretary of State or anyone authorised by him so to do under s.456(1). The application is for a declaration that the annual accounts and/or directors' reports do not comply with the statutory requirements. In so declaring, the court may make an order that the complying documents be filed and that the directors who were a party to the approval of the defective documents pay the costs of the application and any reasonable expenses incurred by the company in the preparation of the revised documents (s.456(1) and (5)).

6.73   The power of the Secretary of State to authorise persons to make application to the court is contained in s.457, which empowers him to authorise any person appearing to him:

(a) to have an interest in, and to have satisfactory procedures directed to securing, compliance by companies with the statutory requirements;

(b) to have satisfactory procedures for receiving and investigating complaints about annual accounts and directors' reports;

(c) otherwise to be a fit and proper person to be authorised.

6.74   Under the 1985 legislation the only body authorised by the Secretary of State is the Financial Reporting Review Panel (FRRP) authorised under the Companies (Defective Accounts) (Authorised Person) Order 2005, SI 2005/699.

Disclosure of information by tax authorities

6.75   The disclosure provisions in support of applications to the court embodied in ss.245D and 245E of the 1985 Act are re-enacted in s.458 which provides for the disclosure of information by the Commissioner for Her Majesty's Revenue and Customs to a person authorised by the Secretary of State under s.457, despite any statutory or other restriction on the disclosure of information. However, in the case of personal data within the meaning of the Data Protection Act 1998, information is not to be disclosed in contravention of that Act. The disclosure provisions do contain important limitations on its use, and in particular create a criminal offence in respect of the use or disclosure of the information released by authorities other than for the permitted purpose.

Power of authorised persons to require documents, etc.

6.76   The power of an authorised person to require the production of documents and the giving of explanations and information by the company and its officers, employees and auditors embodied in s.245F of the 1985 Act is re-enacted in s.459. If the document, explanation and/or information are not given to the authorised person it may make an application to the court for an order and failure to comply with this would amount to contempt of court and could, and no doubt would, be dealt with as such. A statement obtained from a person cannot be used in evidence against him in any criminal proceedings and no person is compelled to produce any document or give information in respect of which a claim to legal professional privilege exists (s.459(6) and (7)).

Restrictions on use of disclosed information

6.77   Where information is given pursuant to the compulsory powers, s.460 re-enacts the 1985 Act, s.245G to ensure that the authorised person to whom the information is given may not freely disclose it and may only use it for the purposes for which it has been given. In particular, information may not be disclosed by the authorised person without the consent of the individual or business which gave it except for the purpose of the authorised person carrying out its functions or unless it is disclosed to the specific persons or for specified purposes set out in s.461.

Exceptions to the restrictions on use provisions

6.78   Section 461, re-enacting and restating s.245G(3) of and Sched.7B to the 1985 Act, sets out the disclosures of information permitted under s.459. The list of persons to whom disclosure is permitted is set out in s.461(3). It includes the Secretary of State, the Department of Enterprise, Trade and Investment for Northern Ireland, the Treasury, the Bank of England, the Financial Services Authority, and the Commissioners for Her Majesty's Revenue and Customs. Section 461(2) and (4) lists the purposes for which disclosure is permitted. These are disclosure:

(a) for the purpose of carrying out by the authorised person of his functions under s.456;
(b) for the purpose of assisting a body designated by an order under the Companies Act 1989, s.46 to exercise its functions under Part 2 of that Act;
(c) with a view to the institution of, or otherwise for the purposes of disciplinary proceedings relating to the performance by an accountant or auditor of his professional duties;
(d) for the purpose of enabling or assisting the Secretary of State or the Treasury to exercise any of their functions under any of the following:
  (i)   the Companies Acts;
  (ii) the insider dealing legislation;
  (iii) the Insolvency Act 1986 or the Insolvency (Northern Ireland) Order 1989 (SI 1989/2405);
  (iv) the Company Directors Disqualification Act 1986 or the Company Directors Disqualification (Northern Ireland) Order 2002 (SI 2002/3150);
  (v)   the Financial Services and Markets Act 2000;

(e) for the purpose of enabling or assisting the Department of Enterprise, Trade and Investment for Northern Ireland to exercise any of the powers conferred on it by the enactments concerning companies, insolvency or directors' disqualification;

(f) for the purpose of enabling or assisting the Bank of England to exercise its functions;

(g) for the purpose of enabling or assisting the Commissioners for Her Majesty's Revenue and Customs to exercise their functions;

(h) for the purpose of enabling or assisting the Financial Services Authority to exercise its functions under:

(i)   the legislation relating to friendly societies or to industrial and provident societies;

(ii) the Building Societies Act 1986;

(iii) the Companies Act 1989, Part 7;

(iv) the Financial Services and Markets Act 2000;

(i) in pursuance of any European Community obligation.

6.79 The provisions of s.461(5) and (6) should be noted. The restriction on disclosure do not apply to a body exercising functions of a public nature under any legislation in any country or territory outside the UK that appear to the authorised person to be similar to his own functions under s.456 for the purpose of enabling or assisting that body to exercise those functions. However, in determining whether to disclose information to a body in accordance with this provision the authorised person must have regard to two considerations. First, whether the use which the body is likely to make of the information is sufficiently important to justify making the disclosure. Secondly, whether the body has adequate arrangements to prevent the information from being used or disclosed other than either for the purposes of carrying out the functions set out in the section or for other purposes substantially similar to those for which information disclosed to the authorised person could be used or further disclosed.

Power to amend disclosure provisions

6.80 Finally with regard to permitted disclosure, s.462 continues the power previously given by the 1985 Act, s.245G(4) to the Secretary of State to amend the disclosure provisions relating to information obtained by an authorised person.

SUPPLEMENTARY PROVISIONS: ACCOUNTING STANDARDS

6.81 Part 15, Chapter 12 contains the supplementary provisions with regard to the accounts and reports required of companies. It originally began by dealing with accounting standards in ss.464 and 465 respectively. With regard to accounting standards s.464 re-enacts s.256 of the 1985 Act and specifies that 'accounting standards' means statements of standard accounting practice issued by a body or bodies prescribed by regulations made by the Secretary of State. Under the 1985 Act the Accounting Standards Board is the body prescribed (the Accounting Standards (Prescribed Body) Regulations 2005, SI 2005/697), and no doubt this will be continued.

Civil liability of directors

6.82   However, these provisions are now preceded by a provision (s.463) imposing civil liability on a director in respect of false and misleading statements in:

- the directors' report;
- the directors' remuneration report; and
- any summary financial statement so far as it is derived from the directors' report or directors' remuneration report.

6.83   Under s.463 a director of a company is liable to compensate the company for any loss suffered by it as a result of either any untrue or misleading statement in such a report or the omission from such a report of anything required to be included in it (s.463(2)). However, he is only liable if either he knew the statement to be untrue or misleading or was reckless as to whether it was untrue or misleading or he knew the omission to be dishonest concealment of a material fact (s.463(3)). The provision is limited to his liability to the company and does not impose any liability on him with regard to any other person who relies on the report (s.463(4) and (5)). This limitation is significant. At the very least it is difficult to see why a director's liability should be limited in this way when his actions have been deliberate or dishonest and there is no reason why his duty to the company should be seen as embracing a duty to tell deliberate lies or dishonestly conceal material facts. It is hypocritical for a society to weep for perceived declines in personal commercial probity when its very legislation can only encourage this. Even when the duty is breached it may be difficult for the company itself to show a loss or, if it has suffered a loss, that the loss in question was caused by the directors' activities rather than other circumstances which the activities simply sought to cover up. At the level of both basic morality and commercial practicality the provision is a disappointment.

6.84   The provision affects neither the director's liability for a civil penalty nor his liability for a criminal offence (s.463(6)).

Definition of medium-sized company

6.85   There follows a cluster of three sections setting out the definition of and requirements to qualify as a medium-sized company in order to gain the benefits given to such companies in relation to the limitation of accounting and reporting obligations upon them. Sections 465–467 set out which companies or parent companies qualify. The restructuring of the law by the 2006 Act separates the rules as to qualification from those governing qualification as a small company thereby making them easier to find and follow, but makes no substantive difference to the current regime embodied in ss.247, 247A and 249 of the 1985 Act.

General power to amend given to Secretary of State

6.86   A general power is given by s.468 to the Secretary of State to make further provisions about accounts and reports by regulation which may amend the rules relating to accounts and reports by adding, altering or repealing provisions. The regulations may concern the following (s.468(1)):

(a) the accounts and reports that companies are required to prepare;
(b) the categories of companies required to prepare accounts and reports of any description;
(c) the form and content of accounts and reports that companies are required to prepare;
(d) the obligations of companies and others as regards –
    (i)   the approval of accounts and reports,
    (ii) the sending of accounts and reports to members and others,
    (iii) the laying of accounts and reports before the company in general meeting,
    (iv) the delivery of copies of accounts and reports to the registrar, and
    (v)   the publication of accounts and reports.

6.87   Any regulation so made must not amend (other than consequentially) the obligation under s.393 that the accounts must show a true and fair view or the provisions of Part 15, Chapter 11 relating to the revision of defective accounts and reports. The regulations may both provide civil penalties and create criminal offences.

Miscellaneous

6.88   Companies may continue to show the amounts of their annual accounts additionally in euros and to deliver to the registrar an additional copy of their accounts translated into euros by virtue of s.469 which re-enacts s.242B of the 1985 Act.

6.89   With regard to banking partnerships s.470 re-enacts s.255D of the 1985 Act in giving the Secretary of State the power to apply the accounting and reporting provisions of the legislation applicable to banking companies to banking partnerships.

6.90   Section 472 re-enacts s.261 of the 1985 Act in allowing information required to be given in notes to a company's annual accounts to be contained either in the accounts or in a separate document annexed to the accounts.

6.91   Section 473 sets out the parliamentary procedure that must be followed in connection with regulations made under the various enabling provisions of Part 15 of the Act discussed in this Chapter. It follows the 1985 Act, s.257 in its approach by requiring affirmative resolution procedure for regulations which add to the documents to be prepared by companies, restrict the exemptions available to particular classes or types of company, add to the information to be included in any particular document, or otherwise make the requirements more onerous.

Definitions

6.92   Definitions for Part 15 of the Act are contained in ss.471 and 474 respectively, the former dealing with the meaning of 'annual accounts' and related expressions, and the latter with minor definitions.

7 AUDITING AND RELATED MATTERS

AUDIT

Introduction

7.1 Much of the law in the area of auditing reflects the requirements of EU Company Law Directives. The 2006 Act implements the terms of the Audit Directive (Directive 2006/43/EC), which was published, and came into force, in June 2006; this Directive amends the Fourth and Seventh Company Law Directives and replaces the Eighth Company Law Directive.

7.2 Generally there is some restructuring and adjustment. For example, private companies are dealt with separately from public companies. Also, there are to be new provisions on the form and content of accounts, but these will be contained in regulations rather than (as at present) in the Companies Act.

Requirement for audited accounts

7.3 Chapter 1 of Part 16 (ss.475–484) restates s.235 of the 1985 Act as to the requirement for audit of a company's annual accounts and the possible exemptions from that requirement in ss.249A–249E. Sections 482 and 483 contain new provisions in relation to non-profit making companies which are subject to a public sector audit, with the objective that those companies are not required to be audited under the Act.

Appointment and reappointment of auditors – private companies

7.4 Under the 1985 Act, s.385, normally the auditor had to be appointed at the general meeting at which the accounts were laid before the company; such appointment would continue until the end of the next such general meeting. Under s.385A of that Act, there was a different provision for the situation where the company had adopted the option (under the 'elective regime') of dispensing with the annual laying of accounts before the company in general meeting.

7.5   Now that the elective regime becomes the default position for private companies, the period allowed for appointing auditors is 28 days after circulation of the annual accounts and reports for the previous financial year (s.485). The auditor's term of office runs until the end of the corresponding period in the following year (s.487(1)(b)). These changes apply even if the company chooses to lay its accounts before the company in general meeting.

7.6   Under s.386 of the 1985 Act the elective regime offered private companies the option of dispensing with the obligation to appoint auditors annually. This also becomes the default position, such that under s.487(2) the auditor's appointment is deemed to be renewed unless:

- the appointment of the auditor was made by the directors (this might be where the directors were making the appointment as the company's first auditor or where they were filling a casual vacancy);
- the company's articles require actual reappointment; this would be where the company has been set up not to take advantage of the deregulatory default position;
- members holding at least 5 per cent of the voting rights give notice to the company preventing automatic reappointment; the 5 per cent requirement is the level set by the Act, but the company's articles can empower members with less than 5 per cent of the voting rights to give such notice;
- the members have passed an ordinary resolution to the effect that the auditor should not be reappointed;
- the directors decide that the company does not need auditors for the following year; this might arise where, for example, the company has become subject to the 'small companies regime' (see ss.381–384 of the Act) and thus exempt from the audit requirement.

7.7   There is a new power, in s.493, which applies to all companies, for the Secretary of State to make regulations requiring disclosure of the auditor's terms of appointment, including terms as to remuneration. The aim of this is to increase transparency and to enable third parties better to understand the scope of the audit and the terms on which it has been undertaken. The regulations may require that the place and means of such disclosure are stated in a note to the annual accounts, the directors' report or the auditor's report.

Appointment and reappointment of auditors – public companies

7.8   Since the provisions which make the elective regime the default position are only applicable to private companies, it follows that the provisions on public companies are a restatement of the previous position. For example, a public company's auditor will normally be appointed by ordinary resolution at the general meeting at which the accounts are laid before the company (s.489(4)); the auditor will cease to hold office at the end of the next general meeting at which accounts are laid before the company, unless reappointed (s.491(1)(b)).

Signature of the report

7.9   If the auditor is a firm, the auditor's report is to be signed in his own name on behalf of the firm by the 'senior statutory auditor' (s.503). This is a requirement of the EU Audit Directive (Directive 2006/43/EC) and it is expected that this will serve to improve audit standards by encouraging further personal responsibility for the actions taken by the audit team.

7.10   The term 'senior statutory auditor' is explained in s.504 as meaning the individual identified by the firm as senior statutory auditor in relation to the audit in accordance with standards issued by the European Commission (or, in the absence of any such standards, in accordance with relevant guidance issued by, or on behalf of, the Secretary of State).

7.11   Signature of the report by the senior statutory auditor does not lead to any civil liability to which he would not otherwise be exposed (s.504(3)); the consequences of signature therefore relate to the person's reputation rather than being of a 'legal' character.

7.12   The auditor and the senior statutory auditor are to be named in the auditor's report (s.505), subject to exemption from this requirement. This exemption is available where the company passes an ordinary resolution not to reveal the names on the basis that it considers, on reasonable grounds, that revealing them would lead to a serious risk of violence or intimidation. If using the exemption the company must inform the Secretary of State, giving the names of the auditor and the senior statutory auditor (s.506).

Offences in connection with an auditor's report

7.13   There are provisions in s.507 creating a new offence in connection with an auditor's report. The offence is committed by a person who knowingly or recklessly causes a report to include anything that is misleading, false or deceptive in a material particular or who knowingly or recklessly causes a report to omit a statement required by s.498 of the Act as to a problem with the accounts.

7.14   The Secretary of State (or the Lord Advocate in Scotland) may, with the consent of the Attorney General, issue guidance for regulatory authorities on how they should carry out their functions in cases where behaviour occurs which may involve commission of the offence under s.507 or which has been, or may be, investigated under complaints or disciplinary procedures (ss.508–509).

Changing auditor

7.15   Where a company proposes a written resolution for appointment of a replacement auditor for an outgoing auditor (rather than reappointing the same auditor), s.514 introduces a new procedure to be observed. Unless the period allowed for appointment has already expired without any appointment, the company must send a copy of the proposed resolution to both the outgoing auditor and the proposed replacement auditor. This allows for written representations to be submitted to the company by the outgoing auditor and for these to be circulated by the company to its members. The company may be relieved of its obligation to circulate the representations if the court is satisfied that they are being used to secure needless publicity for defamatory matter.

7.16 This procedure is only relevant to private companies since there is no provision in the Act for public companies to pass written resolutions. Also, it only applies to appointment of a replacement auditor rather than removal of the existing auditor because removal of an auditor is one of the two decisions for which a written resolution cannot be used under the Act; the other is removal of a director. Sections 510 *et seq.* contain similar provisions to those in the 1985 Act in relation to a resolution removing an auditor from office and the special notice required for such a resolution at a general meeting, and s.515 contains provisions with regard to the failure to reappoint an auditor and the special notice required for a resolution appointing a replacement auditor at a general meeting.

Departing auditors

7.17 Before the changes introduced by the 2006 Act, the law required an auditor who was (for whatever reason) ceasing to hold office either to state that there were no circumstances connected with his resignation that needed to be brought to the attention of members or creditors of the company or to set out these circumstances in a statement for the company to circulate. Experience suggested that the risk of legal action might have led to a less frank approach to such statements than was desirable. The Government's consultation showed that all concerned were keen to improve transparency.

7.18 The 2006 Act introduces a distinction between, on the one hand, quoted companies and, on the other hand, other public companies and private companies:

1. By s.519(3), an auditor of a quoted company who is ceasing to hold office must prepare a statement explaining the circumstances of his departure. Thus auditors of quoted companies must now always make a statement of the circumstances even where previously they would have simply stated that there were no circumstances that needed to be brought to the attention of members or creditors of the company.
2. If the company is an unquoted public company or a private company, the position under the 1985 Act is maintained, meaning that the outgoing auditor can simply state (if appropriate) that there are no circumstances which should be brought to the attention of shareholders or creditors (s.519(1)).

7.19 Under s.520, the company is obliged to send the auditor's statement of circumstances to those who are entitled under s.423 to copies of the accounts (principally the members of the company). This obligation does not apply where, in the case of an unquoted public company or a private company, the statement says that there are no circumstances which should be brought to the attention of shareholders or creditors. The same section provides for the company to apply to court for relief from the obligation to send out copies of the auditor's statement if it believes that the statement is being used to secure needless publicity for defamatory matter.

7.20   The auditor is obliged to send a copy to the registrar of companies (s.521).

7.21   Sections 522–523 introduce a new obligation on the auditor and the company to send a copy:

(a) to an appropriate audit authority; and
(b) in the case of a 'major audit', to the Secretary of State.

A major audit is the audit of a listed company or of any other company where there is a major public interest (s.525). The appropriate audit authority is obliged to pass on information to the accounting authorities (s.524).

RAISING AUDIT CONCERNS AT THE ACCOUNTS MEETING OF A QUOTED COMPANY

Posting concerns on the company's website before the meeting

7.22   If they have sufficient shareholding, members of a quoted company can notify the company of audit concerns that they propose to raise at the next accounts meeting. This notification can require that the company posts the concerns on a website (maintained by or on behalf of the company) in advance of the meeting (s.527). 'Sufficient shareholding' means 5 per cent of the total voting rights or 100 members with an average per member of £100 paid up on their shares. 'Audit concerns' may relate to the company's accounts to be laid before the meeting or any circumstances connected with an auditor of the company ceasing to hold office since the previous accounts meeting.

7.23   As a safeguard against 'abuse' of this provision, the company or another person who claims to be aggrieved can apply to court for an order relieving the company of its obligation to place on a website a statement under this section (s.527(5)).

7.24   If the company defaults in relation to its obligations, every officer in default (although not the company itself) commits an offence (s.530).

LIMITING THE AUDITOR'S LIABILITY TO THE COMPANY

Liability limitation agreements

7.25   Where a company has failed financially, those who stand to suffer losses are likely to look to the auditors as one avenue for pursuing a claim for compensation. In the event that the auditor is held to have been negligent in the course of an audit it may be that the auditor is then made to bear full responsibility for compensation, even though the auditor's share of the blame (when compared with the other parties involved) may be less than 100 per cent. In practice, however, most claims are settled out of court.

7.26   In December 2003, the Government started a public consultation followed by an invitation to auditors, their clients and investors to suggest ways in which liability might be limited and to identify ways in which audit quality might be improved and competition enhanced. This led to the changes introduced by the 2006 Act, one of which is the set of provisions allowing for liability limitation agreements.

7.27   These provisions start (s.532) by declaring to be void, except as permitted by the Act, any provision in the company's articles or in a contract with the company which seeks to exempt a company's auditor from liability for negligence, default, breach of duty or breach of trust occurring in the course of the audit of the accounts. This wording is very similar to that of s.310 of the 1985 Act except that s.310 did not use the words 'in the course of the audit of the accounts' (as above) but used the less limiting words 'in relation to the company'.

7.28   The previous exception allowing the company to provide an indemnity for the costs of successfully defending proceedings is preserved by s.533 and then the new exception which allows for liability limitation agreements is added by s.534.

7.29   A 'liability limitation agreement' is defined in s.534(1) as an agreement that purports to limit the amount of a liability owed to a company by its auditor in respect of any negligence, default, breach of duty or breach of trust occurring in the course of the audit of accounts.

7.30   There is no restriction on the way in which the agreement is allowed to limit the liability. Examples of possibilities are limits to a specified amount or by a formula such as a multiple of fees; on the other hand, where there is more than one person potentially liable, it might be that the limitation is based on proportionate liability.

7.31   The Secretary of State is given power to prescribe or proscribe specified provisions as to how the limitation should work. At the time of writing, there are reported to be no plans to exercise this power and it seems that it will only be used if it transpires that liability limitation agreements develop in a way which needs to be controlled by legislation. This could be the case if their use were to develop in ways that would have adverse effects on competition; for example, if major firms were to agree very high caps on liability, it might be that medium-sized firms could not compete.

7.32   In order to be valid, a liability limitation agreement can only relate to the audit for one financial year (s.535(1)(a)) and it must be authorised by ordinary resolution or a higher voting threshold that may be prescribed by the company's articles (s.536). The resolution can be passed before or after the company enters into the agreement and can be reversed by another ordinary resolution passed before the company enters into the agreement or before the start of the financial year to which the agreement relates (s.536(5)).

7.33   Under s.537, the agreement can only be effective to limit liability to such amount as is fair and reasonable in all the circumstances of the case having regard (in particular) to:

- the auditor's responsibilities under this Part 16 of the 2006 Act;
- the nature and purpose of the auditor's contractual obligations to the company; and
- the professional standards expected of him.

7.34   It is worth noting that, in two respects, the provisions on liability limitation agreements work differently from the provisions on other contracts contained in the Unfair Contract Terms Act 1977 (UCTA 1977):

1.   Under UCTA 1977, a contractual provision is void if it seeks to limit liability to a degree that is more than reasonable; if a liability limitation agreement purports to provide for excessive limitation of an auditor's liability, the agreement has effect as if liability were limited to such amount as is fair and reasonable as above (s.537(2)).
2.   Under UCTA 1977, the limitation is judged by whether the bargain was reasonable at the time that the agreement was made; in judging whether a liability limitation agreement purports to limit the auditor's liability to less than is fair and reasonable under the Companies Act, the court can take account of circumstances occurring after the agreement was made, although this does not include matters arising after the loss or damage has occurred or matters affecting the possibility of recovery of compensation from other persons liable in respect of the same loss or damage.

The court must, therefore, assess under the Companies Act whether the result of the agreement is fair and reasonable rather than, as under UCTA 1977, whether the terms of the contract were reasonable at the time.

7.35   A company which enters into a liability limitation agreement must make such disclosure in connection with the agreement as the Secretary of State may require by regulations. These may require disclosure in a note to the annual accounts or in the directors' report (s.538).

STATUTORY AUDITORS (PART 42)

Introduction

7.36   The purpose of Part 42 is expressed (in s.1209) as being to secure that only persons properly supervised and appropriately qualified are appointed as statutory auditors and that audits are carried out by such persons properly, with integrity and with a proper degree of independence.

The changes

7.37   The sections restate, extend and adapt provisions of the Companies Act 1989, which regulate only the auditors of companies.

7.38   Many of the provisions in Part 42 relate to implementation of the EU Audit Directive, which as noted above amended the Fourth and Seventh, and replaced the Eighth, Company Law Directives.

7.39   The provisions on Auditors General (Part 42, Chapter 3) implement recommendations contained in the report of Lord Sharman entitled 'Holding to Account'.

7.40   These provisions govern a wider range of audit than those of companies under Part 16 (see **para.7.1**) so that, although statutory auditors include companies' auditors, the definition applies also to audits of building societies, friendly societies, insurers, banks, etc.

7.41   Auditors General are recognised as eligible for appointment as statutory auditors. These are the Comptroller and Auditor General (the head of the National Audit Office), the Auditor General for Scotland, the Auditor General for Wales and the Comptroller and Auditor General for Northern Ireland. A mechanism is provided for the regulation and supervision of their functions as statutory auditors.

7.42   The Secretary of State is required by s.1239 to maintain a register of auditors, identifying those persons eligible for appointment as statutory auditors and this register is now to include 'third country auditors'. A third country auditor is the auditor of the accounts of a traded non-Community company and these are required to be subject to systems of independent monitoring and discipline in the UK (s.1242). The Secretary of State is obliged to make regulations as to the keeping of this register.

8 COMPANY SHARES AND MAINTENANCE OF CAPITAL

A COMPANY'S SHARE CAPITAL

Nominal value of shares to be fixed

8.1 One consequence of the abolition of authorised share capital (see **Chapter 2**) is that a company's memorandum of association will no longer fix the nominal (alternatively described as 'par') value of the company's shares. It is a requirement of Art.8 of the Second EC Company Law Directive (Directive 77/91/EEC) that shares in a public company have a fixed nominal value and so there has to be another provision for their nominal value to be fixed; the 2006 Act makes the same provision applicable to private companies.

8.2 Section 542(1) imposes the requirement that shares in a limited company must each have a fixed nominal value; an allotment of shares which do not have a fixed nominal value is void and every officer in default (not the company itself) is liable to a fine. The nominal value can be in any currency and different classes of shares may be denominated in different currencies, except that under s.765 the initial authorised minimum share capital requirement for a public company has to be met by reference to share capital denominated either in sterling or in euros.

8.3 It is worth remembering in this context that s.10 imposes a requirement as to nominal value when describing the statement of capital and initial shareholdings required on application for registration of a new company (see **Chapter 2**). The statement under s.10 must provide not only the number of shares to be taken on incorporation but also the aggregate nominal value of those shares.

Abolition of reserve capital

8.4 Section 120 of the 1985 Act provided for a limited company to pass a special resolution for the creation of 'reserve capital', whereby a part of the uncalled share capital of the company could be set aside in terms that it was incapable of being called up except in the event of the company being wound up. There was equivalent provision for unlimited companies in s.124 of the 1985 Act.

8.5   These provisions have been repealed by Sched.16 to the 2006 Act with the intended effect that it will no longer be possible to create reserve capital. It is stated that this is not to invalidate any special resolution for the creation of reserve capital before the repeal takes effect.

Subscribers' shares included in allotted share capital

8.6   Where there are references in the Companies Acts to issued or allotted shares or share capital, these references are to include the shares taken by the subscriber(s) on incorporation, whether or not the shares have been formally issued or allotted (s.546(2)).

ALLOTMENT OF SHARES

Allotment of shares and return of allotments

8.7   Where a private company has only one class of shares, the directors are empowered by the 2006 Act to allot those shares unless there is a restriction or prohibition of this power in the company's articles (s.550). The former requirement (contained in s.80 of the 1985 Act) for authorisation by ordinary resolution or by the company's articles no longer applies in this context.

8.8   This is a very significant change and one which derives from the same deregulatory impetus that has led to the abolition of the requirement for authorised share capital. The combination of these two deregulatory changes means that the directors of a private company without separate classes of shares can issue new shares without reference to a vote of the members; previously, before the directors could issue shares, there may well have been a need for ordinary resolutions of the members in general meeting both (a) to increase the authorised share capital; and (b) to authorise the issue under the 1985 Act, s.80. As a result of the changes, it may be that there is only one reason for requiring a members' resolution before the directors issue shares: this would be where the company wishes to disapply (by special resolution under s.569) the statutory pre-emption rights of existing members under s.561 (formerly s.89 of the 1985 Act). As an alternative to this special resolution, it may be appropriate for the shareholders to waive their pre-emption rights, in which case there will be no need for any members' resolution.

8.9   In so far as these changes may appear to be a cause for concern, the directors' duty to exercise their powers for the purpose for which they are conferred (s.171) and to promote the success of the company having regard to the need to act fairly as between the members (s.172) should be some safeguard. Alternatively, consideration may be given to inserting provisions in the company's articles in order to limit the directors' powers in this regard.

8.10   In other cases (i.e. private companies with more than one class of shares or public companies), the previous position is essentially maintained by s.551 in that there must be prior authorisation by ordinary resolution or by the company's articles. The authorisation must state the maximum amount of share capital to which it relates and the expiry date of the authorisation (with a maximum duration of five years).

8.11   A company must register an allotment of shares as soon as is practicable and in any event within two months of the allotment (s.554). Failure to comply with this means that the company and every officer in default commit an offence.

8.12   A return of allotments must be delivered to the registrar within one month of the allotment (s.555) and now this must be accompanied by a statement of capital containing prescribed particulars. The prescribed particulars are:

- the total number of shares of the company;
- their aggregate nominal value;
- the total number (and aggregate nominal value) of shares in each class of shares, together with prescribed particulars of the class rights; and
- the amount paid up on each share.

8.13   This new requirement to provide a statement of capital accompanying the return of allotments will ensure that the public register contains up-to-date information on a company's issued share capital.

8.14   Previously (under s.88 of the 1985 Act), where shares were paid for other than in cash, companies were obliged to deliver to the registrar the contract between the company and the allottee; where the contract was not in writing, a written statement of the particulars prescribed under s.88(3) was required. In response to awareness that the contract might contain commercially sensitive information, this requirement to deliver the contract (or a written statement of its particulars) has been abolished. There are safeguards in that the registrar is given power to prescribe the information which must be included in the return of allotments.

EXISTING SHAREHOLDERS' RIGHTS OF PRE-EMPTION ON ALLOTMENT

8.15   The 2006 Act restates, with little change, the provisions in ss.89–96 of the 1985 Act with regard to existing shareholders' pre-emption rights on allotment of new shares (ss.560–577). Section 90 of the 1985 Act required the offer to existing shareholders to state a period of not less than 21 days during which the offer was required to remain open for acceptance. Section 562(6) gives the Secretary of State a new power, by regulations made by statutory instrument, to increase that period or to reduce it, but not so as to reduce the period to fewer than 14 days.

VARIATION OF RIGHTS ATTACHED TO A CLASS OF SHARES

8.16   The previous provisions on variation of class rights are retained with some simplification and are extended to companies without a share capital, e.g. companies limited by guarantee.

8.17   Section 630 is concerned with the variation of class rights of companies with a share capital; s.631 makes equivalent provision for companies without a share capital. Both sections provide that class rights may only be varied in accordance with provisions on variation in the company's articles or, where the company's articles are silent, with the consent of the members of that class in accordance with the section. The section provides for consent to be established either in writing by three-quarters in nominal value of the class or by special resolution (previously an extraordinary resolution under s.125 of the 1985 Act) of the members of that class.

8.18   The Company Law Review recommended that the consent of three-quarters of the class (as above) should become a statutory minimum percentage which should apply in spite of any less demanding procedure specified in the company's articles, but as a result of a late change to the Bill this recommendation has not been adopted. The company's articles can, therefore, provide for either a less or a more onerous requirement for variation of class rights.

8.19   Under s.125 of the 1985 Act, class rights might be set out in the memorandum of association in order to give them greater protection against variation. Such provisions are not, of course, restated in the 2006 Act because of the changes made by the Act to the role and content of the memorandum of association (see **Chapter 2**). Variation of class rights by a more onerous requirement than three-quarters of the class (as above) could be provided for in the company's articles and such provision would need to be observed (ss.630(3) and 631(3)). This could apply, for example, where s.22 (permitting entrenchment of a company's articles (see **Chapter 2**) had been used to entrench provisions on class rights; alteration of the entrenched article would need an unanimous decision of the members.

8.20   As noted at **para.8.12**, a return of allotments under s.555 must state, inter alia, the rights attached to a class of shares. In the same spirit, the company must notify the registrar of any variation of class rights within one month (ss.637 and 640).

SHARE PREMIUMS

8.21   As previously, the share premium account is required to record the amount by which the issue price of shares exceeds their nominal value and the account is treated as part of the company's paid-up share capital.

8.22   Under s.610, the permitted uses of the share premium account are further restricted. Permitted uses continue to include writing off the expenses of the issue of those shares and any commission paid on their issue, as well as paying up new shares to be allotted to members as fully paid bonus shares. However, the permitted uses no longer include writing-off expenses incurred in connection with the company's formation.

REDENOMINATION OF SHARE CAPITAL

8.23 The expression 'redenomination' is used to describe conversion of the nominal value of shares into a different currency. Previously, there was no easy way of achieving this and so, where a company has wished to redenominate its share capital or any class of its share capital, it has been necessary to cancel the shares in question and issue new shares of the preferred denomination. This has arisen for example in instances where a company has wanted to have different classes of shares denominated in different currencies.

8.24 The new procedure is set out in s.622 and requires an ordinary resolution. The exercise of the power conferred by this section may be restricted or prohibited by the company's articles.

8.25 The new nominal value of each share is calculated by aggregating the nominal values of all the shares of the relevant class, converting that total into the new currency and then dividing the resulting figure by the number of shares. This may result in an awkward figure for the nominal value of each share. Provision is made for the company to adjust the nominal value of the shares within the ensuing three months by passing a special resolution (s.626). This may involve a minor reduction in capital, which must not exceed 10 per cent of the nominal value of the company's allotted share capital immediately after the reduction (s.626(4)).

8.26 The company must give notice to the registrar of the date of the ordinary resolution under s.622 and that of the special resolution under s.626, together with a statement of capital and a statement by the directors as to compliance with the requirements of s.626(4). These requirements are in addition to the need to file copies of the resolutions in accordance with s.30.

8.27 To reflect the amount by which the company's share capital is reduced, the company is required to create a redenomination reserve (s.628). This reserve is required to be treated like a paid-up capital account; it can, for example, be applied in paying up fully paid bonus shares.

REDUCTION OF SHARE CAPITAL

Changes to the rules on maintenance of share capital

8.28 In its 2005 White Paper, the Government stated that the provisions on maintenance of capital in the 1985 Act gave rise to some of the most complex and technically challenging provisions of that Act. These were capable of catching a number of potentially beneficial (or at least innocuous) transactions; as a result, companies and their advisers were liable to spend disproportionate amounts of time and money ensuring that they did not inadvertently fall foul of the rules.

8.29   These rules in the 1985 Act were said to be largely irrelevant to the vast majority of private companies and their creditors. This fact was recognised by that Act, which carved out a number of exceptions to the rules for private companies only. The 2006 Act therefore introduces a number of deregulatory measures targeting requirements that appeared unnecessary and burdensome for private companies.

No need for provision in the company's articles

8.30   There is no longer any requirement for authority to reduce capital to be stated in the company's articles. Since Table A, reg.34 contained such authority, this change is more a shift of emphasis than a change of substance: a company will be taken to have power to reduce its share capital unless there is a restriction or prohibition in the company's articles (s.641(6)).

Established procedure preserved

8.31   The established procedure under the 1985 Act is preserved whereby either a public company or a private company can apply to court for an order confirming the company's special resolution to reduce share capital (ss.641(1)(b) and 645–651).

New procedure introduced

8.32   The established procedure described above can be time-consuming and expensive because of the need for confirmation by court order. The 2006 Act therefore introduces a new, simpler procedure for capital reductions, although this is only available to private companies. The Company Law Review recommended that the new procedure should be available to public companies as well as private companies. However, the Government chose not to adopt this recommendation because it appeared that few such companies would use this procedure; this is because there would have had to be additional safeguards in order to satisfy unavoidable EU requirements. In particular, it would have been necessary to give creditors of a public company a right of objection by application to court and so there was thought not to be much advantage in making the new procedure available.

8.33   The new procedure for a private company to reduce its share capital (the 'solvency statement procedure') requires a special resolution of the members supported by a solvency statement (ss.641–644). As noted in **para.8.30** above, the previous requirement that the reduction of capital must be authorised by the company's articles has not been retained, although in a reversal of emphasis the company's articles can restrict or prohibit the reduction of the company's share capital (s.641(6)). The solvency statement must be made by all of the continuing directors not more than 15 days before the resolution is passed (s.642(1)).

8.34   If the resolution is passed at a general meeting, a copy of the solvency statement must be available for inspection by members at the meeting; if the resolution is passed as a written resolution, a copy of the solvency statement must be sent to every eligible member (s.642(2) and (3)). The validity of the resolution is not affected by a failure to comply with these requirements (s.642(4)).

8.35   The solvency statement must state that each of the directors has formed the opinion, taking account of all liabilities (including contingent or prospective liabilities), that:

• there is no ground on which the company could then be found to be unable to pay its debts; and
• the company will continue to be able to pay its debts for 12 months (or, if winding up commences in that period, that it will be able to pay its debts in full within 12 months of the commencement of winding up).

If any of the current directors is unable or unwilling to make the statement, the solvency statement procedure will not be available to the company unless the director in question resigns.

8.36   A prescribed form of solvency statement is to be set by statutory instrument and the registrar is to make rules as to how the solvency statement is to be authenticated by the directors.

8.37   The sanction for making a solvency statement without reasonable grounds and delivering it to the registrar is that an offence is committed by every director who is in default (s.643(4)).

8.38   Within 15 days after passing the special resolution, the company must file with the registrar a copy of the solvency statement, a statement by the directors that the solvency statement was duly made and a statement of capital (s.644), in addition to the special resolution (s.30).

ACQUISITION BY A LIMITED COMPANY OF ITS OWN SHARES

Financial assistance for purchase of own shares

8.39   The provisions on financial assistance by a private company to persons buying its own shares were designed to protect creditors and shareholders against the misuse and depletion of a company's assets. The Company Law Review concluded that it was inappropriate for private companies to continue to bear the cost of compliance with these rules since abuse could be controlled in other ways. Examples of such control, as given in the 2005 White Paper, included:

- the new statutory statement of directors' duties (see **Chapter 4**);
- the wrongful trading provisions in the Insolvency Act 1986.

8.40   Therefore, the prohibition of a company providing financial assistance to a person who is acquiring, or has acquired, shares in that company no longer applies to private companies; it is now restricted to public companies, including a public company which is a subsidiary of a private company (s.678).

8.41   Since private companies are no longer prohibited from providing such assistance the 'whitewash procedure' provided for by the 1985 Act (under which a private company could, in limited circumstances, provide such financial assistance) no longer has any relevance and the provisions of ss.155–158 of the 1985 Act have been abandoned.

8.42   The Government has stated in the Standing Committee proceedings that it is not intended that a company's own share purchase should be regarded as the provision of financial assistance.

Redeemable shares

8.43   The issue of redeemable shares by a private company no longer needs prior authorisation in the company's articles; the position under the 2006 Act is that the authority exists unless the company's articles restrict or remove this authority (s.684). This is one of numerous instances where the Act provides an authority that was previously required to be in the company's articles (and was provided by Table A).

8.44   Under the 1985 Act, the terms, conditions and manner of redemption had to be set out in the company's articles. Under the 2006 Act, this is no longer necessary. For both private and public companies, the terms, conditions and manner of redemption may be determined by the directors, if they are authorised to do so either by ordinary resolution of the company or by the company's articles (s.685). An ordinary resolution is stated to suffice even though its effect is to amend the company's articles (s.685(2)).

8.45   A further change is that the terms of redemption do not need to provide for payment on redemption; the agreement between the company and the shareholder can provide for payment to be made on a date later than the redemption date (s.686).

8.46   Where directors are authorised to determine the terms, conditions and manner of redemption, they must do so before the shares are allotted and details must be stated in any statement of capital which the company is required to file (s.685(3)).

8.47   When any shares are redeemed, notice must be given to the registrar, accompanied by a statement of capital providing details as to the company's shares immediately after the redemption (s.689).

Purchase by limited company of its own shares

8.48   As in other contexts, authorisation that previously had to be given in the company's articles (for example, Table A, reg.35) is now given by the 2006 Act. Section 690 authorises the company to purchase its own shares, including any redeemable shares. The company's articles may restrict or prohibit the use of this power.

8.49   When planning the financing of such a purchase, the position for a public company remains that it is only allowed to use distributable profits or the proceeds of a fresh issue of shares made for the purpose. Private companies continue to be allowed to redeem or purchase out of capital, but now the 2006 Act (in s.709) provides this power, whereas previously the power had to be provided by the company's articles (for example, Table A, reg.35). Again, a company's articles may restrict or prohibit the use of the power provided by the Act.

8.50   The procedural requirements for a private company to redeem or purchase its own shares out of capital are partly aligned with the new solvency statement procedure on reduction of capital (see **paras.8.32–8.38**). For example, the directors are required to make a 'statement in accordance with this section', whereas under the 1985 Act a statutory declaration of solvency was required.

8.51   More particularly, the following requirements must be observed:

1.   Under s.714, the company's directors must make a statement setting out the permissible capital payment and other prescribed information which is broadly similar to that required for a 'solvency statement' on reduction of capital under s.643 (see **para.8.35**). There are subtle differences between the solvency statement (s.643) and this statement (s.714); for example, s.643 requires that the statement as to the company's ability to pay its debts relates to the date of the statement, whereas s.714 requires the equivalent statement to relate to the date of the capital payment. Directors who make this statement without reasonable grounds commit an offence under s.715.
2.   Annexed to the directors' statement, there must be an auditor's report supporting the contents of the directors' statement (s.714(6)).
3.   The payment out of capital must be approved by special resolution (s.716), in relation to which the holders of the shares in question are not entitled to vote (s.717).
4.   There must be public notice (in the Gazette and in an appropriate national newspaper) of the above and of the right of any creditor to apply to court under s.721 within five weeks of the resolution for an order preventing the payment (s.719).
5.   Returns to the registrar of companies following the purchase (s.708) must include a statement of capital.

CERTIFICATION AND TRANSFER OF SECURITIES

Company's response to an application to register a transfer of shares

8.52   Section 771 makes provision as to the procedure required of the company when a transfer of shares is lodged. The company (i.e. generally the directors) are required either to register the transfer or to notify the transferee of refusal to register the transfer as soon as practicable and in any event within two months after the transfer was lodged. This provision is similar to the requirement in s.554 as to registering an allotment of new shares (see **para.8.11**).

8.53   This provision tightens up on the previous position (1985 Act, s.183(5)) under which the company was only required to notify a refusal to register a transfer within two months, i.e. there was no requirement to notify as soon as practicable.

8.54   If refusing to register a transfer (for which, as previously, there would have to be provision in the articles of the company), the company must provide such further information about the reasons for refusal as the transferee may reasonably request, although this does not extend to requiring copies of minutes of board meetings. Previously, there had been no requirement for the company to give reasons for refusal unless the company's articles imposed such a requirement.

8.55   The consequence of non-compliance by the company with these obligations is that the company and those officers who are in default have committed an offence.

Transfer of securities without a written instrument (s.784)

8.56   Since the introduction of s.207 of the Companies Act 1989, the Secretary of State has had power to make regulations enabling title to securities to be evidenced and transferred without a written instrument. The current regulations are the Uncertificated Securities Regulations 2001, SI 2001/3755. At present all such transfers are made by means of the CREST system.

8.57   An industry working group put forward proposals for it to become compulsory for all transfers of shares in quoted companies to be paperless, thus producing savings on the cost and complexity of transactions; at the time of the Bill's passage through Parliament there were said to be about 10,000 paper-based share transfers per day.

8.58   The power given by s.784 restates and extends the powers under s.207 of the Companies Act 1989, allowing the Treasury and the Secretary of State (jointly or concurrently) to make regulations requiring, as well as permitting, the paper-free holding and transfer of shares in quoted companies.

INFORMATION ABOUT INTERESTS IN PUBLIC COMPANY SHARES

8.59   The material described in this section applies only to public companies.

Automatic disclosure obligations

8.60   Sections 198–211 of the 1985 Act impose automatic disclosure obligations on persons who acquire an interest in shares comprised in a public company's relevant share capital or who cease to be interested in such shares: the obligation is to disclose to the company the person's interest in the shares. These provisions are to be repealed and replaced by regulations under the Financial Services and Markets Act 2000, in implementation of the Transparency Obligations Directive. In the regulations, the interests to which the provisions relate will need to be defined differently from the definitions under the Companies Act 1985 in order to comply with the Transparency Obligations Directive (Directive 2004/109/EC). Also the regulations will make provision as to how interests notified under the automatic disclosure rules will be made public.

The company's right to investigate interests in its shares

8.61   The provisions in Part 22 (ss.791–828) replace equivalent provisions in ss.212–219 of the 1985 Act. They deal with a public company's right to investigate the question of who has an interest in its shares by giving notice to a person requiring information as to his shareholding in the company.

8.62   This applies to shares carrying the right to vote in all circumstances at general meetings. It also applies to shares held by a company 'in treasury'; this means shares which, following a purchase of its own shares out of distributable profits, the company has chosen to hold (as an alternative to cancellation of the shares).

The changes

8.63   It is made clear that the notice given to a person by a company is not required to be in hard copy; it can therefore be given by electronic means of communication (s.793, read with provisions in s.1144).

8.64   Information obtained by the company as a result of a notice under s.793 has to be recorded on a register maintained by the company (s.808). Section 808(3) provides clarification as to how the company is to record information where the identity of the current holder of the shares is unknown; it provides that the information is to be recorded against the name of the person holding the interest.

8.65   Companies are given authority by s.816 to remove entries from the register maintained under s.808 after six years have elapsed since the entry was made. Previously, this was subject to certain limitations.

8.66   Section 817 deals with the situation where, in response to a notice given by the company under s.793, a person provides information relating to a third party. The company is no longer required to verify the information before entering it on the register maintained under s.808. Under s.817(2), the third party can apply to the company for the removal of incorrect information from the register; if necessary, the third party can apply to court for an order requiring removal of the entry in question (s.817(4)).

DISTRIBUTIONS

Transfer of assets at a possible undervalue

8.67   Since the decision in *Aveling Barford Ltd* v. *Perion Ltd* [1989] BCLC 626, there has been uncertainty as to the treatment of an intra-group transfer of an asset at a possible undervalue. The decision concerned the sale of property at an undervalue by one company to another company with which it was associated (by common ownership). The transferring company had no distributable profits. The transaction was held to be void as an unauthorised return of capital.

8.68   Such transfers are often carried out by reference to book value, rather than market value, for business, administrative or tax reasons. The decision in *Aveling Barford* (above) raised the question of whether such a transfer could amount to a transfer at an undervalue and thus constitute a distribution for which the company would need to be able to show distributable profits.

8.69   By s.845, if the company has distributable profits and these would be sufficient to justify a distribution calculated by reference to the book value of the asset, then the book value (not market value) will be used for assessing the amount (if any) of the distribution. Provided that the company has sufficient distributable profits, this means that if the asset is transferred at its book value, the amount of the distribution will be zero; if transferred at a value which is less than the book value, the difference will be treated as a distribution.

8.70   The result of this clarification of treatment is that such transactions can often proceed without any need for the company to carry out a revaluation of the asset, which might have required significant professional advice and fees to advisers.

9 REGULATION OF THE CONDUCT OF TAKEOVERS AND MERGERS

INTRODUCTION

9.1 This chapter is concerned with the provisions of the 2006 Act relevant to the contractual and statutory mechanisms employed to effect those outcomes commonly described (although not as terms of art) as a merger and takeover. The chapter is not concerned with the regulation of the outcomes (such as whether the outcome engages competition law) since such regulation does not fall within the province of company and securities laws.

9.2 This focus on the 2006 Act means that the acquisition mechanism to be found in the Insolvency Act 1986, s.110, falls outside the purview of this chapter. That said, it will suffice for present purposes to note that s.110 can be used to effect a takeover or merger in one of two ways:

(a) the target company is placed in voluntary liquidation and its business is transferred by its liquidator to the offeror company in consideration for shares of the offeror company, which are distributed on a pro rata basis among the shareholders of the liquidated company;

(b) the target and offeror companies both go into voluntary liquidation and their respective businesses are transferred to NewCo in consideration for the issuance of shares of NewCo to the shareholders of the liquidated companies.

9.3 It should be noted, however, that these s.110 transactions can be effected through the statutory mechanism provided in Part 26 of the 2006 Act (the scheme of arrangement), which is dealt with at **para.9.17** *et seq.* Use of the scheme of arrangement for this purpose is allowed so long as the reason for using it is not to avoid the rights that are conferred on dissenting shareholders for their protection under the s.110 procedure. (See *Re Anglo-Continental Supply Co. Ltd* [1922] 2 Ch 723.)

9.4 Specifically, the objective of this chapter is to examine the acquisition route regulating rules (i.e. the rules regulating the transactions that lead to either a merger or a takeover) that are to be found in, or that derive their statutory authority from, the 2006 Act. The provisions introduced by the new Act to this area of company law are arguably the most radical in the statute. The Act assimilates into company law an area of corporate finance practice that had hitherto been largely unregulated by law and the mode of this assimilation makes it impossible to have a full understanding of the new regulatory regime through a perusal of the relevant provision of the 2006 Act, which even though having a statutory basis in the Act is not to be found there. The fundamental and complex nature of these changes therefore calls for a comprehensive examination in this chapter.

9.5   This examination can be approached in at least three different ways. First, it can be approached by considering how each acquisition route is regulated. This will entail a treatment of the issues that arise in asset and share acquisitions and the various routes that can be used. Were this approach to be adopted in respect of one acquisition route (e.g. the takeover bid) the following issues will need to be considered: pre-bid issues, the approach and regulation of share dealings, voluntary, mandatory and partial bids, conduct during the offer, timetable issues, profit forecasts and asset valuations, defensive and frustrating action, and consequences of withdrawn, failed and successful bids. However, space constraints preclude the adoption of this approach in respect of the acquisition routes under consideration.

9.6   A second approach could conceivably entail examining relevant transactions according to the applicable regime (those governed by the EU Takeovers Directive (Directive 2004/25/EC) and those that fall outside the Takeovers Directive) within the UK regulatory framework. But even this would provide an incomplete picture. A more comprehensive categorisation would need to unpack this dual classification by isolating the different regimes that govern the following transactions:

(a) schemes of arrangement (and takeover bids) for entities not subject to the jurisdiction of the Takeover Panel, such as most private companies;

(b) schemes of arrangement (and takeover bids) for non-listed entities (certain private companies and all public companies) – these are subject to the jurisdiction of the Takeover Panel but are not governed by the Takeovers Directive;

(c) takeover bids for listed UK companies – these are governed by the Takeovers Directive and therefore subject to the jurisdiction of the Takeover Panel; and

(d) takeover bids for UK registered companies whose securities are admitted to trading on a regulated market in a Member State of the European Economic Area although not on a regulated market in the UK – here jurisdiction is shared between the UK and the jurisdiction where the securities are admitted to trading. Again, considerations of space preclude the adoption of this approach.

9.7   A third approach is to follow the structure of the relevant statutory framework. Before 20 May 2006 this would have been at best incomplete, if not misleading. This was because the substantial part of regulation was non-statutory. However this is no longer the case. If this approach is adopted in the case of the 2006 Act it will entail a consideration of Part 26 (arrangements and reconstructions), Part 27 (mergers and divisions of public companies) and Part 28 (takeovers – this is dealt with mainly in Chapters 1–3 of Part 28). Yet even this approach will be incomplete if it does not deal with the rules of the Takeover Code and the jurisprudence of the Takeover Panel, since the statutory framework in the Act merely provides the statutory foundation for the work of the Takeover Panel, which continues. Accordingly, in adopting this approach, the chapter makes the necessary link between relevant provisions of the 2006 Act and the Takeover Code, placing emphasis on the fundamental changes introduced by the Act to the regulation of the conduct of transactions leading to takeovers and mergers. The fundamental changes are with respect to the structure of the regulatory framework involving a shift from a non-statutory regulatory framework to a statutory one (see G. Morse, 'Implementing the Thirteenth EC Directive – the end of self-regulation in form only' (2005) *Journal of Business Law* 403). Even when the Takeover Code had no statutory foundation the Takeover Panel was never in doubt that ignorance of the Code was not a valid excuse for its breach, as is evident from its rulings in *Cordiant* (2003/16), *Re Dundee Football Club* (1992/9) and *Knightswood (Property & Investments) Co Ltd/PCT* (1996/16). Now that the Code has statutory effect the consequences of non-compliance are radically different, extending as far as criminal liability.

A framework for conceptual clarity: acquisition outcomes and routes

9.8   When an entity acquires direct or indirect control over the assets of a company the outcome is described as a takeover; on the other hand, when the assets of two or more companies become vested in, or under the control of, one company (which may or may not be one of the original companies), which has as its shareholders all, or substantially all, the shareholders of the companies, the outcome is described as a merger (Rabinowitz (ed.), *Weinberg and Blank on Take-Overs and Mergers* 5th edn (Sweet & Maxwell, looseleaf), para.1–004)). There are various acquisition routes to bring about these outcomes.

9.9   It is important not to confuse outcomes with the acquisition routes used to effect them. In most jurisdictions (including the UK) once either outcome occurs or is about to occur, outcome regulating rules, such as competition law or laws restricting ownership or control of strategic industries, may be triggered. Regardless of how the outcome is classified (a merger or takeover), upon which not much turns, or the acquisition route employed to bring about the outcome (e.g. a scheme of arrangement or a takeover bid) outcome regulating rules will apply if those rules are triggered by the relevant transaction, and the application of the rules will not be dependent on the classification of the outcome or the particular acquisition route used. For instance, a merger or takeover involving a company that provides goods or services to the UK Ministry of Defence may lead to an intervention notice under the Enterprise Act 2002 and this will not depend on the route employed to bring about the outcome or the outcome's classification. On the other hand, acquisition route regulating rules, although not dependent on the classification of the outcome, are dependent on the choice of acquisition route used. For instance, a takeover or merger brought about through use of the statutory scheme of arrangement will be governed by rules (statutory and judge-made) applicable to schemes of arrangement aimed at ensuring the protection of minorities in the affected categories of parties and the disclosure of information by directors and this will not depend on outcome type. Likewise is the case of the contractual takeover bid, which is governed by rules (formerly non-statutory but now statutory) principally aimed at reducing the effects of bargaining asymmetry and protecting minorities and ensuring shareholder sovereignty. (See T.I. Ogowewo, 'The underlying themes of tender offer regulation in the United Kingdom and the United States of America' (1996) *Journal of Business Law* 463 and Y.Z. Stern, 'A general model for corporate acquisition law' (2001) 26 *Journal of Corporation Law* 675). These rules apply because of use of the acquisition route, not because of the outcome type that eventuates.

9.10   This distinction between outcomes and acquisition routes is highlighted to ensure conceptual clarity and to assist in delineating the scope of this chapter. Since the difference in the outcomes entails no regulatory implications, for reasons of brevity the term 'takeover' is used hereafter to denote either outcome.

9.11   As the role of the Takeover Panel, as regulator, is central to the acquisition routes that this chapter examines it is to the origin of this body that we now turn.

The origin of the Takeover Panel

9.12   On 27 March 1968 a Bank of England Press Release announced the constitution of a body to be known as the Panel on Takeovers and Mergers. However, the process leading to the formation of the Panel commenced much earlier. The brief account of the history of the Takeover Panel given here is based on Johnston, *The City Take-Over Code* (OUP, 1980) and Stamp & Marley, *Accounting Principles and the City Code* (Butterworths, 1970). In October 1959, at the behest of the Governor of the Bank of England, six City Associations formed themselves into a City Working Party. This body issued notes under the title 'Notes on Amalgamations of British Businesses'. This was meant to be a general guide to the principles and practices which should be followed by those engaged in the conduct of takeover and merger transactions.

9.13   The Notes were amended in 1963 and published in October as the 'Revised Notes on Company Amalgamations and Mergers'. By July 1967 it was evident, owing to a number of scandals related to the conduct of takeover and merger transactions, that a root and branch reform of the system was necessary. Accordingly, the City Working Party was reconvened and the result was the publication of the Code on Takeovers and Mergers. In view of the fact that the rules in the Code were not legally enforceable, the Governor of the Bank of England put forward a proposal that a Panel with a membership representative of informed City opinion should be established to supervise the Code's operation. This led to its announcement on 20 September 1967 that agreement had been reached on the establishment of an authoritative Panel whose membership was to be comprised of the bodies represented on the City Working Party. A few months later, on 27 March 1968, this Panel was inaugurated. The Panel has since then remained an unincorporated body.

9.14   Until 20 May 2006 it did not have statutory powers. The absence of statutory force however ended at midnight on 19 May 2006, after which the Takeovers Directive (Interim Implementation) Regulations 2006, SI 2006/1183 came into force. The Takeovers Directive (Directive 2004/25/EC), one of the measures adopted under the EU Financial Services Action Plan, is a minimum standards measure concerning the regulation of takeovers of companies whose shares are traded on a regulated market. Article 4.1 of the Takeovers Directive required Member States to designate the authority or authorities competent to supervise bids for the purposes of the rules which they make or introduce pursuant to the Directive. As the designated authority can be a non-statutory body recognised and empowered by national law to carry out the relevant regulatory functions, the Takeover Panel was designated.

9.15   The Takeovers Directive (Interim Implementation) Regulations 2006 provided statutory underpinning to the regulatory activities of the Panel in accordance with the Directive. The Regulations were introduced to ensure compliance with the United Kingdom's obligation under community law to implement the Takeovers Directive, which was adopted on 21 April 2004, by no later than 20 May 2006.

9.16   The implementing Regulations were a stop-gap measure designed for the interim period commencing 20 May 2006 until the time when the 2006 Act is enacted and the relevant provisions (Part 28) are brought into force. These provisions will come into force, according to s.1300(2) of the Act, on such day as may be appointed by the order of the Secretary of State or the Treasury. On 18 December 2006 the Minister for Industry and the Regions issued a written ministerial statement in which it was stated that the provisions implementing the Takeovers Directive will come into force on 6 April 2007 (House of Commons *Hansard* Ministerial Statements for 18 December 2006, Margaret Hodge, col.127WS6). The relevant instrument is the Companies Act 2006 (Commencement No.2, Consequential Amendments, Transitional Provisions and Savings) Order 2007. A consequence of this order is the revocation of the Takeovers Directive (Interim Implementation) Regulations 2006, SI 2006/1183 as of 6 April 2007.

PART 26 SCHEME OF ARRANGEMENT AS AN ACQUISITION ROUTE

An overview

9.17   The Government has announced that Part 26 is to come into force on 6 April 2008 (House of Commons Handsard Ministerial Statements for 28 February 2007. Margaret Hodge, col.90–92ws). Please note the discussion here proceeds on the basis that Part 26 is in force. Although an arrangement under Part

26 includes a reorganisation of share capital by the consolidation of shares of different classes or by the division of shares into shares of different classes, the term is much wider than this. It is judicially recognised as having a very wide scope embracing a multitude of schemes (*Re National Bank Ltd* [1966] 1 All ER 1006), subject to the limitation that it must involve some element of 'give and take' rather than confiscation or total surrender and must not be illegal or ultra vires (*Re Oceanic Steam Navigation Co. Ltd* [1939] Ch 41 and *Re NFU Development Trust Ltd* [1973] 1 All ER 135). Aside from these limitations the courts will not impose a limitation or qualification on the generality of the word 'arrangement'. See for example, Plowman J. in *Re National Bank Ltd* [1966] 1 WLR 819 at 829 and Megarry J. in *Re Calgary and Edmonton Land Co. Ltd (In Liquidation)* [1975] 1 WLR 355 at 363. Beyond the identified limits, the courts have said that it is neither necessary nor desirable to attempt a definition of 'arrangement'. See *Re Savoy Hotel Ltd* [1981] Ch 351.

9.18   A scheme of arrangement under Part 26 is a mechanism for implementing arrangements in any company liable to be wound up under the Insolvency Act 1986, s.895(2)(b) or the Insolvency (Northern Ireland) Order 1989; that is to say, lawful corporate transactions having an element of accommodation that affect members and/or creditors. It is the mechanism that statutory company law provides to bring about any change – regardless of how drastic – that can otherwise be achieved through unanimous consent (see Warrington L.J. in *Re Guardian Assurance Co.* [1917] 1 Ch 431 at 449–450). It is a common feature of companies legislation throughout the Commonwealth. For present purposes, the discussion of a scheme of arrangement will be limited to schemes used to effect a takeover, as opposed to compromises with creditors or other forms of arrangements.

9.19   A scheme of arrangement to effect a takeover falls within Part 26. This is so even if it is a scheme involving a sale of shares to which the company is not a party aside from acting as applicant under Part 26 (see Lord President, Lord Clyde in *Singer Manufacturing Co. v. Robinow* 1971 SC 11 at 13–14). In its commonest form – where it is used to effect a merger or takeover without an amalgamation or reconstruction – the arrangement takes effect when a copy of the court sanctioned member approved scheme (approved in line with the statutory threshold at each different meeting of the relevant classes of members, if more than one class exists) is delivered to the registrar. It is the court's sanctioning of the scheme that enables it to bind all affected parties. In essence, this judicial sanction enables less than all the parties to reach an arrangement that has effect as one produced by their unanimous consent. However, it must be stressed that not even unanimous acquiescence in alterations to the sanctioned scheme can have effect without a further court sanction (*Devi v. Peoples Bank of Northern India Ltd* [1938] 4 All ER 337).

9.20   The use of a scheme of arrangement carries a number of significant advantages over a takeover bid. They include the following. First, the Takeovers Directive is not applicable to schemes. This means that the complex rules on shared jurisdiction, for instance, will not apply to takeover schemes. Secondly, if the scheme is structured as a cancellation scheme there will be no stamp duty liability since no transfer of shares occurs. A takeover bid however attracts stamp duty liability at 0.5 per cent of the value of the acquisition consideration because a transfer of shares occurs (see Finance Act 1999, Sched.13, para.3). The same rate applies where the shares are dematerialised and held in CREST. Thirdly, as will be seen below, a scheme of arrangement makes it easier to acquire 100 per cent ownership and this avoids the problem of minority shareholders. Furthermore, owing to the statutorily required method of determining shareholder approval, a method that is determined by reference to the votes of shareholders present (in person or by proxy), shareholder apathy operates in favour of the scheme since not all shareholders will invariably vote on the scheme. Another advantage is that a scheme guarantees the accrual of relief under s.612 from the requirement to set up a share premium account imposed by s.610. A further advantage relates to the applicability of the statutory prohibition of unlawful financial assistance for the purchase by a company of its own shares in the 2006 Act, Part 18, Chapter 2 (see ss.678–9). Where a target company provides financial assistance for the purchase of its own shares as part of the takeover such assistance will ordinarily fall foul of s.678. However, where the assistance is provided in pursuance of an order of the court sanctioning the scheme for a takeover, then s.681 protects the transaction from invalidity.

The procedure for using a scheme of arrangement to effect a takeover

9.21   The process begins with negotiations between the target company and the would-be acquirer concerning the terms upon which the target company is to be acquired. Once the terms are settled following due diligence the target company (i.e. the company undergoing the arrangement) applies under s.896(1) for a discretionary court ordered meeting of the members of the company (or classes of members) (see *Re Savoy Hotel Ltd* for a discretionary court ordered meeting of the members of the company (or classes of members)). If the court grants the application and the meeting(s) are called, so long as the notice summoning the meeting is accompanied by the statutorily required explanatory circular, as stipulated by s.897(1), and a majority in number representing 75 per cent in value (of the company's issued capital) of the members (or classes of members), present and voting in person or by proxy approve the scheme, a second application can then be made under s.899(1) for the court's discretionary sanction. As mentioned earlier, the court's order, if granted, only has effect when a copy of the order has been delivered to the registrar pursuant to s.899(4).

9.22   According to s.895(1), the provisions of Part 26 apply where the arrangement is proposed between the target company, i.e. through an organ with the appropriate authority, and its members (or any class of them) leading to a takeover of the company by another party, which need not be a company. The role of an organ of the company with appropriate authority is vital, since without it there is nothing to show that the scheme involves the target company. To be sure, a scheme between members falls outside Part 26. On the other hand, a scheme between members and the company even if it involves a party not mentioned in the relevant statutory provisions in Part 26, such as the acquiring party, falls within Part 26 (*Barclays Bank Plc* v. *British and Commonwealth Holdings Plc* [1996] 1 BCLC 1). In *Re Savoy Hotel Ltd*, Nourse J. held that the court has no jurisdiction to sanction an arrangement which does not have the approval of the company either through the board or, if appropriate, by means of a simple majority of the members in general meeting. There is however a strong case for the argument that in a company where the managerial function has been contractually vested in the board (as is often the case), a scheme involving the management of the company's business which does not secure the support of the board requires the approval of the members in general meeting with a 75 per cent majority before the first application to the court under s.896(1) can be made, as opposed to a simple majority. This argument rests on the principle articulated in *Automatic Self-Cleansing Filter Co.* v. *Cuninghame* [1906] 2 Ch 34 and *Quin & Axtens Ltd* v. *Salmon* [1909] AC 442.

9.23   The Takeover Code in para.3(b) of its introduction indicates that a scheme of arrangement leading to a takeover falls within the Takeover Panel's subject matter jurisdiction. Accordingly, where the target company is subject to the Panel's jurisdiction pursuant to para.3(a) of the Takeover Code (such as a public company) the Takeover Panel will have jurisdiction to ensure that the relevant provisions of the Code are complied with.

9.24   The Code may not apply where the target company re-registers as a private company (see para.3(e), Introduction to the Takeover Code) or a Code waiver is obtained pursuant to para.2(c) of the Introduction to the Takeover Code.

The two forms

9.25   A takeover scheme may take one of two forms. The first is a transfer scheme. An example is to be found in *Re Savoy Hotel* (above). As Nourse J. observed in that case:

> The scheme proposed by T.H.F. is what is sometimes known as a transfer scheme. Shortly stated, it provides for the acquisition by T.H.F. of the whole of the issued share capital of the Savoy, other than the shares already beneficially owned by it, on terms that the holder of every 100 A shares should receive a specified number of T.H.F. ordinary shares or at his election £165 in cash, and that the holder of each B share should receive a specified number of T.H.F. ordinary shares or (at the like election) £9.75 in cash, and so in proportion for any greater or lesser number of A shares or B shares as the case may be, with provisions for adjustment.

9.26   This clearly resembles a takeover bid. The difference is that whilst in the case of a bid the target shares are transferred to the bidder by virtue of the contract between the bidder and the target shareholders, in the case of a transfer scheme the transfer occurs by virtue of the effect of the court order sanctioning the scheme.

9.27   The second kind of takeover scheme is a cancellation scheme. An example can be found in *Re BTR Plc* [2000] 1 BCLC 740. In that case, it was described thus:

> The scheme, in the broadest terms, is designed to effect a merger between *BTR* and *Siebe plc* ... The scheme provides for the cancellation of the scheme shares [this is done by a reduction in capital under s.135 of the Companies Act 1985], for the allotment to holders of scheme shares of new fully paid shares in *Siebe* on the basis of 0.533 of a new share for every one scheme share cancelled, and for the capitalisation of the reserve arising on the cancellation of the scheme shares in paying up new shares in *BTR* to be allotted credited as fully paid to *Siebe* or its nominees [the capitalisation occurs by transferring the amount standing in the reserve (created on the cancellation) to the company's share capital account – this is an accounting adjustment that has the effect of treating the new shares issued to offeror as paid for].

9.28   In a cancellation scheme, all the shares in the target company not already owned by the acquirer are cancelled by a reduction of capital of the target. The acquirer pays the consideration to the target shareholders in consideration for the cancellation of their shares, and the reserve created by the cancellation is capitalised and applied in paying up new shares which are issued by the target directly to the acquirer. Since this kind of scheme involves a reduction of capital the provisions of the 2006 Act, Part 17, Chapter 10 on reduction of capital will need to be complied with. In exercising its discretion as to whether to confirm a reduction of capital (a judicial role now applicable only in the case of public companies: s.641(1)(b)) the court will consider whether the shareholders are being treated equitably, whether the cause of the reduction has been properly explained to shareholders and whether the reduction is for a discernible purpose (*Re Waste Recycling Group Plc* [2003] EWHC 2065 (Ch), [2004] 1 BCLC 352). A reduction of capital in a private company no longer requires the approval of the court. In a public company, a reduction of capital requires a general meeting to be held for its approval and the steps required to be taken in connection with it. This meeting is usually convened immediately following the court convened meeting to approve the scheme. In a private company, a reduction of capital does not require a general meeting, as it can be the subject of a written resolution so long as it is supported by a solvency statement as required by s.642.

9.29   One advantage of a cancellation scheme is that it avoids liability to stamp duty since no transfer of shares occurs. For this reason, the vast majority of takeover schemes are structured in this way. An example is the recent ntl/Virgin Mobile takeover.

The three stages in a scheme of arrangement

9.30   Once a decision is made on the type of scheme to be proposed the target company will need to go through the three stages outlined in Part 26 of the 2006

Act. The first stage is an application to the court under s.896(1) for an order that a meeting (or meetings) of members be summoned. As a meeting of members is a different concept from a meeting of the company through its members, it therefore follows that the provisions of the 2006 Act on company meetings (Part 13, Chapters 3 and 4) will not ordinarily apply save for those situations where the scheme proposed involves a matter that requires approval outside the scheme, such as a reduction of capital in a cancellation scheme.

9.31   It is the responsibility of the target company to decide whether to summon a single meeting or more than one meeting where it takes the view that there are different classes of members affected by the scheme. Unlike in the past where a failure to identify the relevant classes at this first stage was fatal to the scheme, the effect of *Practice Statement* [2002] BCC 355 is to enable the court to deal with the question at any stage.

9.32   Where a meeting is summoned every notice summoning the meeting sent to members (or given by advertisement) must be accompanied by an explanatory circular (or in the case of an advertisement state where and how invited members may obtain such a circular) complying with s.897. For an explanatory circular to be s.897 compliant it must:

(a) explain the effect of the arrangement; and
(b) in particular, state:
    (i)   any material interests of the directors of the company (whether as directors or as members or as creditors of the company or otherwise); and
    (ii) the effect on those interests of the arrangement, in so far as it is different from the effect on the like interests of other persons.

9.33   The concept of a 'material interest' will take its meaning from the context. Since the context is the power relationship between the directors and the shareholders, albeit not of a fiduciary character, the concept will be given a wide meaning. *Re Minster Assets Plc* [1985] BCLC 200 demonstrates that if there is a change in the material interests of a director as set out in the explanatory circular the court would not sanction the scheme unless satisfied that no reasonable shareholder would alter his decision with regard to the scheme.

9.34   If a company defaults in complying with this requirement the company and all its officers in default will be subject to criminal liability pursuant to s.897(5), although a person will not be guilty of an offence if he shows that the default was due to the refusal of a director to supply the necessary particulars of his interests as is required by s.898 (see s.897(7)).

9.35   The purpose of the first stage is for the court to direct how the meeting or meetings are to be summoned. It is concerned to ensure that those who are to be affected by the arrangement proposed have a proper opportunity of being present (in person or by proxy) at the meeting or meetings at which the proposals are to be considered and voted upon (see *Re Hawk Insurance Co Ltd* [2001] EWCA Civ 241).

9.36   The second stage is the holding of the meeting or meetings at which the scheme proposals are put to those present in person or by proxy and at which they vote upon them. The purpose of this stage is to ensure that the proposals are acceptable to at least a majority in number, representing three-quarters in value, of those who take the opportunity of being present (in person or by proxy) at the meeting or meetings (*Re Hawk Insurance Co. Ltd* (above)). A favourable resolution (according to the terms of s.899(1)) at the meeting is what gives eligibility to seek court sanction.

9.37   The threshold in s.899(1) has three aspects. First, the approval must be by a majority in number at the meeting (or class). Secondly, there must be approval from 75 per cent in value of the meeting (or class). Thirdly, the first and second requirements are not to be determined based on all the company's shareholders; instead, they will be determined based on those that are present and vote in person or by proxy. Considering that it is necessary to take into account not only the numbers of members who approve the scheme but also the nominal value of their shareholdings, the resolution to approve the scheme must be by way of a poll.

9.38   The final stage involves a further application by the target company or member (s.899(2)(a) and (b)) to the court under s.899(1) to obtain the court's sanction to the scheme of arrangement. The purpose of the third stage is to enable the court to:

(a) ensure that the meeting or meetings have been summoned and held in accordance with its previous order;
(b) ensure that the proposals have been approved by the requisite majority of those present at the meeting or meetings; and
(c) to ensure that the views and interests of those who have not approved the proposals at the meeting or meetings (either because they were not present or, being present, did not vote in favour of the proposals) receive impartial consideration (*Re Hawk Insurance Co. Ltd* (above)).

9.39   A copy of the court order sanctioning the scheme is required to be delivered to the registrar of companies for registration pursuant to s.899(4), after which the scheme becomes binding on the members or class of members (as the case may be) and the company.

Function of the court

9.40   In determining whether the arrangement should be sanctioned the court's first duty is to see that the resolutions are passed by the statutory majority in value and number in accordance with the statutory scheme at a meeting or meetings duly convened and held. Essentially, the court seeks to ensure that the statutory provisions have been complied with. Upon this the jurisdiction of the court to sanction the scheme depends. The problem of class definition is dealt with in the section below.

9.41 Formal compliance with the statutory provisions is no guarantee of the court's sanction, since the court does not function as a rubber stamp or register. Therefore, the court's second duty is in the nature of a discretionary power. The wording of the statutory provisions shows that the court has discretion to discount the majority vote. Such a discount will be applied if the court takes the view that the meeting (or class) was not fairly represented by those who attended because they had such personal or special interests in supporting the proposals that their views cannot be regarded as fairly representative of the meeting, or that the statutory majority were not acting bona fide, or were coercing the minority, or that the scheme when viewed objectively is such that an intelligent and honest man, a holder of those shares acting in respect of his interest, would not approve it. This is based on the test of *Buckley on the Companies Act*, 15th edn (Lexis Nexis) – routinely cited by the courts in a long line of cases (see e.g. *Re Abbey National Plc* [2004] EWHC 2776 (Ch)). Yet the court will be slow to differ from the position of the meeting. Ultimately, the court must, whilst considering all relevant factors, balance two issues: the fairness of the scheme, and the fact that in commercial matters members are much better judges of their own interests than the courts (*Re Telewest Communications Plc* [2004] EWHC 1466 (Ch)).

Class definition

9.42 An important issue for the court is that of class definition. For the purposes of Part 26, the concept of a 'class' is wider than the concept of class for the purposes of protecting class rights under Part 17, Chapter 9 of the Companies Act 2006. The test applied to determine the question of whether more than one class of shares exists is to be found in the words of Lord Justice Bowen in *Sovereign Life Assurance Co. v. Dodd* [1892] 2 QB 573:

> The word 'class' is vague, and to find out what is meant by it we must look at the scope of the section, which is a section enabling the Court to order a meeting of a class of creditors [or members] to be called. It seems plain that we must give such a meaning to the term 'class' as will prevent the section being so worked as to result in confiscation and injustice, and that it must be confined to those persons whose rights are not so dissimilar as to make it impossible for them to consult together with a view to their common interest.

9.43 The key problem that the courts have grappled with ever since is the determination of what constitutes a dissimilarity of rights. The issue is whether separate class meetings should have been summoned or is the scheme of a kind in relation to which only one class of members is identifiable. A failure to summon the appropriate class meetings will be fatal to the scheme even if it secured the requisite statutory majority as it goes to jurisdiction. In the past, this proved to be a serious problem because the courts considered the question not at the first stage but at the third stage (this was because of *Practice Note* [1934] WN 142), even though the decision of the company on the issue would have had to be made at the first stage. As mentioned earlier, the position has now changed somewhat as it is now possible for an application to be made to the court at an earlier stage for directions on the proper constitution of classes (see *Practice Statement* [2002] BCC 355).

9.44 Although considerable judicial ink has been spilled on the question, the decision of Lord Millett NPJ in *Re UDL Holdings Ltd* [2001] HKCFA 54 is now regarded as setting out the appropriate approach (cf. the approach of the Court of Appeal in *Re Hawk Insurance Co. Ltd* [2001] EWCA Civ 241). In its application to the issue in the context of a scheme of arrangement leading to a takeover (in respect of which class constitution issues do not generate the difficulties they do in regard to schemes involving creditors) the 'Millett principles' are set out below.

9.45 The first principle is that persons whose rights are so dissimilar that they cannot sensibly consult together with a view to their common interest must be given separate meetings; persons whose rights are sufficiently similar that they can consult together with a view to their common interest should be summoned to a single meeting. Although the emphasis of Lord Millett NPJ on rights is correct it should be noted that the acquirer who owns substantial shares in the target may have similar rights with the remaining shareholders in the target but will not be able to consult with them with a view to their common interest since there will be no common interest. Accordingly, such a shareholder or its affiliates (such as its subsidiaries (see *Re Hellenic and General Trust Ltd* [1975] 3 All ER 382)) are excluded from the meeting.

9.46 The second Millett principle is that the test is based on similarity or dissimilarity of legal rights against the company, not on similarity or dissimilarity of interests not derived from such legal rights; the fact that individuals may hold divergent views based on their private interests not derived from their legal rights against the company is not a ground for calling separate meetings. This principle appears to underpin the response of the court to arguments for a separate class where some shareholders in the target also hold shares in the acquirer. In some cases the parcel in the acquirer may be larger than their parcel in the target. Lord Millett NPJ's second principle leads to the view that such shareholders are not to be excluded from the class simply because their interests may diverge.

9.47 The final Millett principle is that the question is whether the rights which are to be released or varied under the scheme or the new rights which the scheme gives in their place are so different that the scheme must be treated as an arrangement with more than one class. It follows from this principle that if the scheme deals with different classes of shares or in regard to the same class of shares it contemplates their different treatment, then separate class meetings are required.

Schemes involving a reconstruction or amalgamation and Part 27

9.48 A takeover or merger through a scheme of arrangement rarely involves the amalgamation of both companies, since all that occurs pursuant to the scheme is a change in ownership of the target company's shares, so that it continues its existence as before only that it is now a wholly owned subsidiary of the acquirer and the former shareholders of the target now own a proportionate share interest in the acquirer company.

9.49   Although it is largely unnecessary to amalgamate both companies when the target can be acquired as a wholly owned subsidiary and run as a division within the larger group structure, there may be situations where the scheme of arrangement also has as its purpose the amalgamation of the target with the acquiring company. An example is the so-called 'merger of equals' transaction. This can, although it need not, be structured through a scheme of arrangement plus amalgamation. In this case, both companies undergo an arrangement which provides for the transfer of the undertakings of each company to a newly formed NewCo and the dissolution of both companies. In consideration for the transfers, NewCo will issue shares to the erstwhile shareholders of the two dissolved companies. In such situations – so long as each company undergoing the arrangement is a company within the meaning of the 2006 Act (s.895(2)(a)) – the court may by the order sanctioning the arrangement (or by a subsequent order) facilitate the amalgamation by ordering the transfer of undertaking and of the property or liabilities, the continuation of legal proceedings pending by or against each transferor company and its dissolution, without the need to go through a winding up. The court's facilitating powers extend to the making of incidental, consequential and supplemental matters as are necessary to secure that the amalgamation is fully and effectively carried out.

9.50   Where the relevant transfers of undertaking, property and liabilities for purposes of the amalgamation or absorption involve public companies (as transferee and transferor) or are made from such companies to a new company (whether or not a public company), the requirements of Part 27 should be complied with. This is because ss.895(3) and 903(1) preclude a court from making an order sanctioning the scheme pursuant to Part 26 if Part 27 is not complied with.

9.51   Part 27 implements the Third and Sixth Company Law Directives on mergers and divisions of public limited liability companies. The former, Directive 78/855/EEC of 9 October 1978, whose basis is Art.54.3(g) EEC Treaty, is part of the general programme for the abolition of restrictions on freedom of establishment. It relates to domestic mergers of public companies. The latter, Directive 82/891/EEC of 17 December 1982, whose basis is Art.54.3(g) EEC Treaty, is also part of the general programme for the abolition of restrictions on freedom of establishment. It relates to the division of public companies. Part 27 will apply, according to s.904, if there is a scheme of arrangement involving the transfer of the target company's undertaking, property, and liabilities occurs in consideration of the offeror company's (or NewCo's) shares and the merging companies are public companies. Where Part 27 applies, the directors of the merging companies must draw up and adopt draft terms of the scheme (s.905) and deliver a copy of it to the registrar of companies. The registrar is required to publish in the Gazette notice of receipt by him from the merging companies of a copy of the draft terms at least one month before the meetings of their respective shareholders (s.906) to approve the scheme. The threshold for approval of the scheme is the same as the threshold required by Part 26 (s.907). There is also a requirement for an explanatory statement from the directors of the merging companies (s.908) and an independent expert report to the shareholders on draft terms of the merger (s.909).

9.52   As most merger and takeover schemes in the UK are not structured with an amalgamation in view it is not often the case that the provisions of Part 27 will preclude a court from sanctioning a scheme of arrangement under Part 26.

TAKEOVER BID AS AN ACQUISITION ROUTE

An overview of Part 28

9.53   A takeover bid is a general offer addressed to target shareholders offering to purchase their shares usually made conditional as to acceptances. Buckley J. in *Ridge Nominees Ltd v. Inland Revenue Commissioners* [1961] 2 All ER 354 (overruled on a different ground in [1962] Ch 376) said:

> What then was the nature of the transaction in the present case? The offer was manifestly an offer to buy stock in Gresham. True, it is a conditional offer but it is an offer to buy stock at a price in terms of money. The acceptance is an acceptance of that offer, and I think that, as soon as any stockholder in Gresham accepted the offer, there was a contract between Ridge and that stockholder in Gresham. It was a conditional contract, not in the sense that the assent of either party was subject to some condition precedent, so that he could say that there was no true contract until that condition was satisfied, but only in the sense that it was a binding and completed contract, some of the rights and obligations under which were dependent on certain conditions. At that stage it seems to me that there was a contract of sale between the stockholder who accepted the offer and Ridge who made it. The fact that it was a conditional contract does not in my view make it any the less a contract of sale. One of the terms of the offer was that acceptance should be accompanied by an executed transfer of the stock to which the acceptance related, and that transfer was clearly intended to be used for completing the contract if and when the purchaser was in a position to insist on the sale being carried out.

9.54   Part 28 of the 2006 Act deals with the takeover bid. The legislative history of the provisions in Part 28 can be traced to the consultation document 'Company Law – Implementation of the European Directive on Takeover Bids' (Department of Trade and Industry, January 2005). In addition to this, the provisions following a successful takeover bid allowing the offeror to squeeze out minority non-assenting shareholders and correspondingly, the right of such shareholders to compel the offeror to buy their shares if they wished to sell out, can be traced to the recommendations arising from the independent Company Law Review Steering Group sponsored by the Department of Trade and Industry (see Company Law Review, Final Report (pp.282–300) and 'Completing the Structure' (Annex B, pp.377–390)).

9.55   Part 28 is the statutory basis for the implementation of the Takeovers Directive. But it goes beyond implementing the Directive. It provides the legislative framework for the activities of the Takeover Panel. The Takeovers Directive only extends to takeover bids for the securities of companies governed by the laws of Member States, where all or some of those securities are admitted to trading on a regulated market within the meaning of Directive 93/22/EEC in one or more Member States. There are therefore a number of transactions covered by the Takeover Code but not covered by the Directive. A scheme of arrangement, takeover bids for companies not traded on a regulated market, and dual holding company transactions are all not covered by the Directive, although such are covered by the Code. Through s.943(2)–(3), the 2006 Act gives statutory authority to the rules of the Takeover Panel with respect to its regulatory activities. The result of this is that the regulatory activities of the Panel falling outside the Directive also have statutory backing. Accordingly, the position now is that there is statutory basis for the Code's regulation of all takeover bids and merger transactions of the relevant companies, however effected, including by means of statutory merger or court approved scheme of arrangement and its regulation of other transactions such as offers by a parent company for shares in its subsidiary, dual holding company transactions, new share issues, share capital reorganisations and offers to minority shareholders which have as their objective or potential effect (directly or indirectly) obtaining or consolidating control of the relevant companies. Even the publication of the Panel's Annual Report now has a statutory basis in s.963. There is no longer any need for indirect statutory support through the Financial Services and Markets Act 2000, as s.143 of that statute (the power to make rules endorsing the Takeover Code) has been repealed by the 2006 Act, s.964(2).

9.56   The relevant chapters of Part 28 are as follows: Chapter 1 deals with matters related to the Takeover Panel and its functions; Chapter 2 deals with impediments or barriers to takeovers; Chapter 3 deals with squeeze-out and sell-out rights; and Chapter 4 deals with certain disclosure obligations.

The Takeover Panel

9.57   Chapter 1 of Part 28 confers statutory functions on the Takeover Panel (s.942(1)). The Panel may do anything that it considers necessary or expedient for the purposes of, or in connection with, these statutory functions (s.942(2)). Furthermore, notwithstanding the fact that the Panel is an unincorporated body, s.960 makes it clear that it is capable of bringing proceedings under Chapter 1 in its own name and bringing or defending any other proceedings in its own name. Furthermore, the Panel and any person who is (or is acting as) a member, officer or member of staff of the Panel and any person authorised by the Panel under s.947(5) are given immunity from damages by s.961. This immunity is lost if the act or omission is shown to have been in bad faith. Neither will it apply in respect of an act or omission incompatible with Convention rights (i.e. the act or omission that is unlawful as a result of the Human Rights Act 1998, s.6(1)).

Structure of the Takeover Panel System

9.58   In this discussion, the expression 'the Takeover Panel System' is meant to identify the constituent organs of the Panel even whilst operationally independent of the Panel. Although Part 28 does not whittle the power of the Panel to provide for its own constitution, s.942(3) lays down a minimum constitutional structure. It provides that the Panel may make arrangements for any of its functions to be discharged by:

(a) a committee or sub-committee of the Panel; or
(b) an officer or member of staff of the Panel, or a person acting as such (this is subject to s.943(4) and (5)).

9.59   Within this system there is the Panel. Although the Panel operates through a number of Committees, it is directly responsible for those matters which are not dealt with through its Committees. It has overall responsibility for the policy, financing and administration of the Takeover Panel's functions and for the functioning and operation of the Takeover Code.

9.60   The next organ is the Executive. This organ carries out the day-to-day work of takeover supervision and regulation and in doing so it operates independently of the Panel. The Executive is available for consultation with the Panel's regulated community. One of its functions is to give rulings (any decision, direction, determination, order or other instruction) on the interpretation, application or effect of the Code before, during and, where appropriate, after takeovers or other relevant transactions. The Executive gives rulings on points of interpretation, application or effect of the Code which are based on the particular facts of a case. In addition to giving rulings at the request of a party, the Executive may, on its own initiative, give rulings on the interpretation, application or effect of the Code where it considers it necessary or appropriate to do so. Section 945 of the 2006 Act is the statutory basis of such rulings. To the extent and in the circumstances specified in rules, and subject to any review or appeal, a ruling has binding effect (s.945(2)).

9.61   The Code Committee is the legislative arm of the Takeover Panel. Section 944(2) requires that rules must be made by an instrument in writing. On the promulgation of its rules, they are required to be made available to the public, with or without payment, in whatever way the Panel thinks appropriate (s.944(3)). Section 944(4) provides that:

> [A] person is not to be taken to have contravened a rule if he shows that at the time of the alleged contravention the text of the rule had not been made available as required by subsection (3).

9.62   The Code Committee usually consults publicly on proposed amendments to the Code through the publication of Public Consultation Papers (PCPs). Following the end of the consultation period, the Committee publishes its conclusions and the resultant Code Amendments in a Response Statement (RS). It would not be accurate, however, to view the Code Committee as having plenary legislative competence since it has no competence to legislate on the matters set out in the following sections of the Introduction to the Takeover Code: sections 1 (Overview of Panel and Takeover Code), 2(a) (Nature and purpose of the Code) and (b) (General Principles and Rules of the Code), 4(a) (Panel, a part of the Panel System), 4(b) (Code Committee) and 4(c) (Hearings Committee), 5 (Executive), 7 (Hearings Committee procedural rules), 8 (Takeover Appeal Board) and 13 (Fees and charges). These matters are the responsibility of the Panel although, amendments to those matters set out in section 8 (which deals with the Takeover Appeal Board) will be agreed by the Takeover Appeal Board and will be issued by the Panel.

9.63   A fourth organ is the Hearings Committee. The existence of the Hearings Committee is in compliance with the 2006 Act, s.951(1), which requires rules of the Panel to provide for a decision of the Panel to be subject to review by a committee of the Panel at the instance of such persons affected by the decision as are specified in the rules. A principal function of the Hearings Committee is to review rulings of the Executive. Section 951(3) requires that rules provide for there to be a right of appeal against a decision of the Hearings Committee to an independent tribunal, the Takeover Appeal Board. The Code gives effect to this provision in the following manner:

1.   Although an unconditional ruling of the Executive is binding on those who are made aware of it, it ceases to be binding once it is overturned by the Hearings Committee or the Takeover Appeal Board.
2.   Rulings of the Executive, including any grant or refusal to grant a waiver or derogation from the application of any rules, may be referred to the Hearings Committee for review.
3.   Any party to the hearing before the Hearings Committee (or any person denied permission to be a party to the hearing before the Hearings Committee) may appeal to the Takeover Appeal Board against any ruling of the Hearings Committee or the chairman of the hearing (including in respect of procedural directions). The Board may confirm, vary, set aside, annul or replace the contested ruling of the Hearings Committee. On reaching its decision, the Board remits the matter to the Hearings Committee with such directions (if any) as the Board (or the chairman of the hearing) considers appropriate for giving effect to its (or his) decision. The Hearings Committee will give effect to the Board's decision.

9.64   The provisions of the Code as to matters of procedure, evidence in relation to proceedings before the Hearings Committee (and its powers) and enforcement of decisions of the Hearings Committee (section 7 of the Introduction to the Takeover Code) and the Takeover Appeal Board (section 8 of the Introduction to the Takeover Code) now have a statutory basis in s.951(4).

9.65   Section 4(d) of the Introduction to the Takeover Code contains membership and representation restrictions designed to ensure a separation of legislative and judicial personnel, as required by s.951(5). The Code stipulates that no person who is or has been a member (or an alternate of a member) of the Code

Committee may simultaneously or subsequently be a member (or an alternate of a member) of the Hearings Committee or the Takeover Appeal Board. Section 4(d) also states that when acting in relation to any proceedings before the Hearings Committee or the Takeover Appeal Board, the Panel shall do so only by an officer or member of staff (or a person acting as such).

9.66   Lastly, there is the Nomination Committee, which monitors the size, composition and balance of the Panel and, in particular, it makes recommendations about the appointment (and any renewal of appointment) of the Chairman and Deputy Chairmen of the Panel and of Panel members (and their alternates) who will serve on either the Hearings Committee or the Code Committee (but not those members appointed by the Nominating Bodies). It also makes recommendations about the appointment of the Director General of the Panel.

Funding of the Takeover Panel System

9.67   Prior to the statutory transformation of the system the Takeover Panel had three sources of revenue. First, there were 'document charges': charges payable on offer documents valued at £1m and above. The amount of the charge depended upon the value of the offer according to a sliding scale set out in the Code. The second way was through a levy collected by member firms of the London Stock Exchange (LSE) and OFEX (an unregulated over-the-counter market specialising in small companies – now known as the PLUS Markets Group) set at a flat rate charge of £1 on contract notes on all chargeable transactions with a consideration in excess of £10,000. Finally, the Panel received income from sales of the Code and fees in relation to the granting, and maintenance, of exempt principal trader or exempt fund manager status. The concepts of 'exempt fund managers' and 'exempt principal traders' in the Code are in recognition of the fact that fund management and principal trading may be conducted quite separately within the same multi-service organisation. Accordingly, the status results in certain obligations of the Code which would otherwise arise not applying to those with the status. Although these three revenue sources remain there is now a statutory basis for them in s.957 so that the Panel is able to meet the costs of the Panel System (this includes payments in respect of the expenses of the independent Takeover Appeal Board).

9.68   One notable change to the existing funding arrangement was introduced by s.958. This pertains to the second revenue source mentioned above. Section 958 allows the Secretary of State by regulations to widen the categories of bodies or transactions to which the levy would apply to include other specified persons capable of being directly affected by the exercise of the Panel's functions or otherwise having a substantial interest in those functions or transactions in securities on markets other than the LSE or OFEX. The amount levied by the Secretary of State will be determined by any other income received or expected by the Panel in respect of that period and the estimated and actual expenses of the Panel during the relevant period.

9.69   Section 959 provides that any amount payable by any person or body by virtue of the Code or the regulations of the Secretary of State is a debt due from that person or body to the Panel, and is recoverable accordingly.

Information gathering power of the Panel

9.70   Prior to the statutory transformation of the Panel it did not have formal powers to require those involved in takeover activity to provide it with the information it needed to discharge its duties. The position is now vastly different.

9.71   In regard to documents and information reasonably required in connection with the exercise by the Panel of its functions (s.947(3)), s.947(1) gives the Panel the power to require a person to produce any documents and information that are specified or described in a written notice. Such a requirement must be complied with at a place specified in the notice and before the end of such reasonable period as may be so specified (s.947(2)). The Panel may require any document produced to be authenticated, or any information provided (whether in a document or otherwise) to be verified, in such manner as it may reasonably require. The production of a document in pursuance of s.947 does not affect any lien that a person has on the document (s.947(7)). Neither is a person required to disclose documents or information in respect of which a claim to legal professional privilege could get maintained in legal proceedings (s.947(10). Section 962 gives privilege against self incrimination in that a statement made by a person in response to a s.947(1) notice or an order made by the court under s.955 to secure compliance with such a requirement, may not be used against him in criminal proceedings in which he is charged with any offence other than one under Perjury Act 1911, s.5 (which concerns false statements made otherwise than on oath).

9.72   Such information obtained by the Panel pursuant to s.947 may be shared with other regulators. This is because the Panel now has a statutory duty imposed by s.950 to take such steps as it considers appropriate to co-operate with the Financial Services Authority and any authority designated as a supervisory authority for the purposes of Art.4.1 of the Takeovers Directive and any other body that exercises functions of a public nature, under legislation in any country or territory outside the United Kingdom, that appear to the Panel to be similar to its own functions or those of the Financial Services Authority. Such co-operation may include the sharing of information that the Panel is not prevented from disclosing.

9.73   Section 948 prohibits the disclosure of information provided to the Panel (in connection with the exercise of its functions) relating to the private affairs of an individual during the lifetime of the individual or to any particular business so long as the business continues to be carried on, without the consent of the individual or the person for the time being carrying on that business.

9.74   Section 948(3) makes it clear that the prohibition does not apply to any disclosure of information that is made for the purpose of facilitating the carrying out by the Panel of any of its functions; neither does it apply to any disclosures made to a person specified in Part 1 of Sched.2 (such as a constable), nor is of a description specified in Part 2 of that Schedule (a list of 70 specified disclosures), nor to disclosures made in accordance with Part 3 of that Schedule (related to overseas regulatory bodies). The Secretary of State, subject to certain limitations, may amend Sched.2 by order subject to negative resolution procedure. The prohibition on the disclosure of information does not apply to the disclosure by an authority within s.948(7) (such as the Financial Services Authority or a designated supervisory authority in a Member State) of information disclosed to it by the Panel in reliance on s.948(3). Also, the prohibition does not apply to the disclosure of such information by anyone who has obtained it directly or indirectly from an authority within s.948(7). Neither does the prohibition apply to the disclosure of information if the information is or has been available to the public from any other source. Furthermore, s.948 does not permit a disclosure in contravention of the Data Protection Act 1998.

9.75   Section 949 provides that a criminal offence is committed if there is disclosure in contravention of s.948 unless the person making the disclosure can demonstrate that he did not know, and had no reason to suspect, that the information had been provided as mentioned in s.948(1), or he took all reasonable steps and exercised all due diligence to avoid the commission of the offence.

Statutory power to grant derogations and waivers

9.76   The Panel now has a statutory power in s.944(1) to derogate from takeover rules or grant a waiver from them. Accordingly, the Introduction to the Takeover Code in section 2(c) states that the Panel may derogate or grant a waiver to a person from the application of a rule (provided, in the case of a transaction and rule subject to the requirements of the Directive, that the General Principles are respected). Such a derogation or waiver may be granted either in the circumstances set out in the rule or in other circumstances where the Panel considers that the particular rule would operate unduly harshly or in an unnecessarily restrictive or burdensome or otherwise inappropriate manner (in which case a reasoned decision will be given), as required by s.944(1)(d).

Statutory obligation on the Panel to implement the norms of Takeovers Directive

9.77   The European Union adopted the Takeovers Directive with a view to establishing a framework consisting of uniform general principles and a limited number of general requirements which Member States would be required to implement through more detailed rules in accordance with their national systems and their cultural contexts. The aim of the framework is to protect investors in companies whose securities are admitted to trading on a regulated market in a Member State when those companies are the subject of takeover bids or changes of control. To accomplish this s.943(1) requires the Takeover Panel to make rules giving effect to Arts.3.1, 4.2, 5, 6.1 to 6.3, 7 to 9 and 13 of the Directive.

9.78   The General Principles of the Directive are contained in Art.3.1 and the applicable jurisdictional rules are contained in Art.4.2. The implementation of both represents the starting point for analysis.

Implementing the Article 3.1 General Principles

9.79   For the purpose of implementing the Directive, Member States are required to ensure that the General Principles in Art.3.1 are complied with. These General Principles have been promulgated in section B1 of the Takeover Code. Furthermore, rules giving effect to them are to be found in the Takeover Code. According to the Takeover Code (see Takeover Code, Introduction, section 2(b)), the General Principles, which are expressed in broad general terms, do not define the precise extent of, or the limitations on, their application; instead, the General Principles and the rules of the Takeover Code are to be applied in accordance with their spirit in order to achieve their underlying purpose.

9.80   The idea of regulating through a set of high level general principles, the content of such principles, and the interpretative approach to them have always been key features of the Panel system, upon which these aspects of the Directive are modelled.

9.81   Whilst the Panel now has statutory authority through s.944(1)(d) to dispense with or modify the application of rules in particular cases and by reference to any circumstances, no such derogation can undermine the General Principles in a bid subject to the Directive.

9.82   The first General Principle of the Takeovers Directive states that:

> all holders of securities of an offeree company of the same class must be afforded equivalent treatment; moreover, if a person acquires control of a company, the other holders of securities must be protected;

(Takeovers Directive, Art.3.1(a))

The philosophy behind this General Principle can be found in rules of the Code and the case law of the Panel. The General Principle is given effect by rules 6, 9, 10, 11, 14, 15, 16 and 20 of the Takeover Code. So even in the case of a voluntary bid it will be seen that these rules require certain mandatory terms designed to give effect to this General Principle. For instance, the form and value of the offer consideration is regulated to achieve equality and the over 50 per cent acceptance condition prescribed by rule 10 is designed, as was said by the Panel in *BP/Britoil* 1987/32, to 'secure that, where a person attempts to take over a company, the premium necessary to obtain control must be paid'.

9.83   The second General Principle states that:

> holders of securities of an offeree company must have sufficient time and information to enable them to reach a properly informed decision on the bid; where it advises the holders of securities, the board of the offeree company must give its views on the effects of implementation of the bid on employment, conditions of employment and the locations of the company's places of business;
>
> (Takeovers Directive, Art.3.1(b))

This General Principle is given effect by a number of rules, notably rules 23 and 25 of the Code.

9.84   The third General Principle states that:

> the board of an offeree company is to act in the interests of the company as a whole and must not deny the holders of securities the opportunity to decide on the merits of the bid;
>
> (Takeovers Directive, Art.3.1(c))

Principally, rule 21 of the Code gives effect to this General Principle and we see its application in Panel case law, notably in *Consolidated Gold Fields* 1989/7. (See Barboutis, 'Takeover defence tactics: Part 1: The general legal framework on takeovers' (1999) 20 *Company Lawyer* 14; 'Part II: Specific defensive devices' (1999) 20 *Company Lawyer* 40 and T.I. Ogowewo, 'Rationalising General Principle 7 of the City Code' (1997) *Company, Financial, Insolvency Law Review* 74. (Before 20 May 2006, the neutrality principle was the subject of General Principle 7 and rule 21.)

9.85   The fourth General Principle states:

> false markets must not be created in the securities of the offeree company, of the offeror company or of any other company concerned by the bid in such a way that the rise or fall of the prices of the securities becomes artificial and the normal functioning of the markets is distorted;
>
> (Takeovers Directive, Art.3.1(d))

This is given effect principally by rules 2.2, 8; and 28 (see T.I. Ogowewo, 'Profit forecasts and the City Code' (2003) 24 *Company Lawyer* 11). A reading of the Panel's jurisprudence on the rule 2.2 duty to make a public announcement of a bid under certain circumstances demonstrates the importance the Panel attaches to the prevention of false markets (see *Rentokil/BET* 1996/2, *SPP/Let* 1990/9, *Petrocon* 1992/3, *Applied Distribution* 1997/3, *Morris Ashby* 1997/13 and *Transcomm Plc* 2004/9).

9.86   The fifth General Principle is given effect by rules 2.5 and 24.7 of the Takeover Code. The General Principle states (Art.3.1(e)):

> an offeror must announce a bid only after ensuring that it can fulfil in full any cash consideration, if such is offered, and after taking all reasonable measures to secure the implementation of any other type of consideration;

This Principle can be seen applied by the Panel in *WM Low/Budgens Plc* 1989/14 and *Corporate Resolve/Focus Dynamics* 2001/2.

9.87 Rule 2.5(a) requires the offeror to give careful and responsible consideration to announcing a firm intention to make an offer. The offeror and its financial adviser should have every reason to believe that it can and will be able to implement the offer.

9.88 Rule 24.7 requires a cash offeror to obtain confirmation from an appropriate third party that resources are available to the offeror to implement the offer.

9.89 The final General Principle states:

> an offeree company must not be hindered in the conduct of its affairs for longer than is reasonable by a bid for its securities.

> (Takeovers Directive, Art.3.1(f))

This anti-siege principle is reflected in many aspects of the Code, such as rule 35.1 (which imposes a delay of 12 months on the making of a fresh bid by the bidder or its concert parties following the withdrawal or lapsing of an offer) and the elaborate Takeover Code timetable for offers (prescribed by rules 30–34). A key rule in this regard is rule 31.6, which stipulates the final date for satisfying the acceptance condition.

Implementing Article 4.2 on jurisdictional rules

9.90 Article 4.2 lays down the jurisdictional rules governing the assumption and sharing of jurisdiction by supervisory bodies of Member States. Pursuant to s.943(1), the Takeover Code, in section 3(a) of the Introduction, gives effect to this Article.

9.91 Section 3(a)(i) of the Introduction to the Takeover Code states that an offer will be subject to the jurisdiction of the Takeover Panel where the offeree (the target) has its registered office in the United Kingdom, the Channel Islands or the Isle of Man if any of its securities are admitted to trading on a regulated market in the aforementioned jurisdictions.

9.92 Article 4.2 also deals with the situation where the offeree's registered office and the regulated market where its securities are admitted to trading do not coincide. Here jurisdiction is shared. The division is between, on the one hand, matters relating to the consideration offered in the case of a bid, in particular the price, bid procedure, the information on the offeror's decision to make a bid, the contents of the offer document and the disclosure of the bid and, on the other hand, matters relating to the information to be provided to the employees of the offeree company and in matters relating to company law, in particular the percentage of voting rights which confers control and any derogation from the obligation to launch a bid, as well as the conditions under which the board of the offeree company may undertake any action which might result in the frustration of the bid. The former are therefore broadly consideration and procedural matters, while the latter are broadly employee information and company law matters.

9.93   This division is implemented in section 3(a)(iii) of the Introduction to the Takeover Code. Matters of the first kind will fall to be regulated by the competent authority, as determined by Art.4.2(b) and (c), while the latter matters will fall to be regulated by the competent authority of the Member State in which the offeree company has its registered office (Art.4.2(e)).

9.94   Article 4.2(b) provides that where the offeree's registered office and the regulated market where its securities are admitted to trading do not coincide, the authority competent to supervise the bid shall be that of the Member State on the regulated market of which the company's securities are admitted to trading; and where the offeree's securities are admitted to trading on regulated markets in more than one Member State the competent authority shall be that of the State where it was first admitted to trading. Accordingly, the Takeover Code provides that a company which has its registered office in another Member State of the EEA, whose securities are admitted to trading only on a regulated market in the United Kingdom (or if admitted to trading on more than one such market the securities were first admitted to trading only in the United Kingdom), will be subject to the jurisdiction of the Takeover Panel (Introduction to the Takeover Code, sections 3(a)(iii)(B) and 3(a)(iii)(C)(i)). It will, of course, follow that the employee information and company law matters will fall to be regulated by the competent authority of the Member State in which the offeree company has its registered office.

9.95   Article 4.2(c) stipulates that where the offeree company's securities were first admitted to trading on regulated markets in more than one Member State simultaneously, the issue of jurisdiction will be dependent on the notified choice of the offeree as of the first day of trading. Accordingly, the Takeover Code provides that where a company which has its registered office in another Member State of the EEA, whose securities are admitted to trading on regulated markets in more than one Member State of the European Economic Area including the United Kingdom and the securities of the company are simultaneously admitted to trading on more than one regulated market, but not on a regulated market in the Member State in which it has its registered office, on or after 20 May 2006, the Panel will have jurisdiction if the company notifies the Panel and the relevant regulatory authorities on the first day of trading that it has chosen the Panel to regulate it (see Introduction to the Takeover Code, section 3(a)(iii)(C)(ii)).

9.96   If the offeree company's securities have already been admitted to trading on regulated markets in more than one Member State on 20 May 2006 and were admitted simultaneously, the supervisory authorities of those Member States shall agree which one of them shall be the authority competent to supervise the bid within four weeks of the aforementioned date. Otherwise, the offeree company shall determine which of those authorities shall be the competent authority on the first day of trading following that four-week period (Introduction to the Takeover Code, section 3(a)(iii)(C)(iii)).

Implementing Articles 5, 6.1 to 6.3, 7 to 9 and 13 of the Directive

9.97 Article 5 deals with the protection of minority shareholders, the mandatory bid and the equitable price. These are implemented by the Takeover Code primarily by rule 9, which stipulates the circumstances when a mandatory bid is to be made and its terms, such as the equitable price.

9.98 Articles 6.1–6.3 deal with information concerning bids. These are implemented by the Takeover Code primarily by rule 2.2 (when an announcement is required), rule 2.5 (the terms of the announcement of a firm offer), rule 2.6 (the obligation on the offeror and the offeree to circulate announcements) and rule 24 (offeror documents).

9.99 Article 7, which deals with the time allowed for acceptance, is implemented by rule 31 of the Code (dealing with the timing of the offer). Article 8, which deals with disclosure issues, is implemented by rule 2.6 (obligation on the offeror and the offerree company to circulate announcements), rule 19 (information), rule 23 (general obligation as to information) and rule 24 (offeror documents).

9.100 Article 9 deals with obligations of the board of the offeree company – the duty of neutrality and the duty to publish a response to the offer. These are implemented by rule 21 (restrictions on frustrating action) and rule 25 (offeree board circulars).

9.101 Lastly, Art.13 of the Directive requires Member States to lay down rules which govern the conduct of bids, at least as regards the following:

- the lapsing of bids (this is implemented by rules 31.6 and 31.7 of the Takeover Code);
- the revision of bids (implemented by rule 32);
- competing bids (implemented by rules 20.2 and 32.5);
- the disclosure of the results of bids (implemented by rule 17); and
- the irrevocability of bids and the conditions permitted (implemented by rule 13).

Enforcement and sanctions for contravention of the Code

9.102 Section 946 of the 2006 Act provides that rules may contain provision conferring power on the Panel to give any direction that appears to it to be necessary in order to restrain a person from acting (or continuing to act) in breach of rules or to restrain a person from doing (or continuing to do) a particular thing, pending determination of whether that or any other conduct would be a breach of rules; or otherwise to secure compliance with rules. Sections 10(b)–(c) of the Introduction to the Takeover Code sets out rules pursuant to which the Panel enforces the Takeover Code. The statutory basis of this is s.952, which provides that Code rules may contain provision conferring power on the Panel to impose sanctions on a person who has:

(a) acted in breach of rules; or

(b) failed to comply with a s.946 direction.

9.103   The Panel has the statutory power to issue compliance and compensation rulings. Compliance rulings will be issued if the Panel is satisfied that:

(a) there is a reasonable likelihood that a person will contravene a requirement imposed by or under rules; or

(b) a person has contravened a requirement imposed by or under rules.

9.104   In either case, the Panel may give any direction that appears to it to be necessary in order to restrain a person from acting (or continuing to act) in breach of rules or to restrain a person from doing (or continuing to do) a particular thing, pending determination of whether that or any other conduct of his is or would be a breach of rules or otherwise to secure compliance with rules (Introduction to the Takeover Code, section 10(b)). Compensation rulings will be issued where a person has breached the requirements of any of rules 6, 9, 11, 14, 15, 16 or 35.3 of the Code.

9.105   The statutory authority for this power of the Panel to legislate for compensation rulings, which may include provision for the payment of interest (including compound interest), is s.954. An example of a compensation ruling of the Panel, albeit without statutory support, can be found in the *Guinness* case (*Guinness/Distillers* 1989/13). As in that case, the Panel may make a ruling requiring the person concerned to pay, within such period as is specified, to the holders, or former holders, of securities of the target company such amount as it thinks just and reasonable so as to ensure that such holders receive what they would have been entitled to receive if the relevant rule (rule 11 in the *Guinness* case) had been complied with. Again, as in the *Guinness* case, the Panel may make a ruling requiring simple or compound interest to be paid at a rate and for a period (including in respect of any period prior to the date of the ruling and until payment) to be determined.

9.106   As these enforcement powers are newly conferred statutory powers s.952(3) requires the Panel to publish a policy statement (which it may revise at any time) with respect to the imposition of the sanction in question, and where the sanction is in the nature of a financial penalty, the amount of the penalty that may be imposed. Section 952(4) provides that an element of the policy must be that in making a decision concerning the sanction the Panel has regard to:

(a) the seriousness of the breach or failure in question in relation to the nature of the rule or direction contravened;

(b) the extent to which the breach or failure was deliberate or reckless; and

(c) whether the person on whom the sanction is to be imposed is an individual.

9.107   The Panel must prepare a draft of any proposed policy statement (or revised policy statement) and consult such persons about the draft as the Panel considers appropriate. In exercising, or deciding whether to exercise, its power to impose these newly statutorily created sanctions, the Panel must have regard to any relevant policy statement published and in force at the time when the breach or failure occurred.

9.108   Article 6.2 of the Takeovers Directive requires Member States to ensure that an offeror publishes an offer document containing the information necessary to enable the holders of the offeree company's securities to reach a properly informed decision on the bid. Article 6.3 goes on to lay down the relevant rules applicable to an offer document. It was mentioned above that these offer document rules have been implemented by the Takeover Code in rule 24. What is noteworthy is that s.953 criminalises a breach of these rules. The provision applies where a takeover bid is made for a company that has securities carrying voting rights admitted to trading on a regulated market in the United Kingdom. Where an offer document published in respect of the bid for such a target does not comply with offer document rules, an offence is committed by the offeror if the offeror knew that the offer document did not comply, or was reckless as to whether it complied, and failed to take all reasonable steps to secure that it did comply. Pursuant to s.953(2), the offence is committed by the person making the bid, and where the person making the bid is a body of persons, any director, officer or member of that body who caused the document to be published.

9.109   Criminal liability does not extend only to the offeror. The publication of a response document that is similarly defective may trigger criminal sanctions. Article 9.5 requires Member States to ensure that the board of the offeree company draw up and make public a document setting out its opinion of the bid and the reasons on which it is based, including its views on the effects of implementation of the bid on all the company's interests and specifically employment, and on the offeror's strategic plans for the offeree company and their likely repercussions on employment and the locations of the company's places of business as set out in the offer document in accordance with Art.6.3(i).

9.110   Rule 25 of the Code gives effect to Art.9.5. Such rules are now known as response document rules. (The 'offer document rules' and the 'response document rules' are together known as the bid documentation rules. They are those parts of rules 24 (offeror document) and 25 (response document), set out in Appendix 6 to the Takeover Code and, in each case, rule 27 which deals with documents subsequently sent to shareholders. This requires the inclusion of material changes to, or the updating of, the information in those parts of rules 24 or 25, as the case may be, in relation to the offer documents and offeree board circulars referred to in rules 30.1 and 30.2 respectively and the revised offer documents and subsequent offeree board circulars referred to in rules 32.1 and 32.6(a) respectively.) As in the case with offer documents, s.953 criminalises a breach of these rules. Nothing in s.953 affects any power of the Panel in relation to the enforcement of its rules (s.953(7)).

9.111   Pursuant to s.955, the Panel may under section 10(d) of the Introduction to the Takeover Code seek enforcement by the courts. If the court is satisfied that:

(a)   there is a reasonable likelihood that a person will contravene a requirement imposed by or under rules; or

(b)   a person has contravened a rule-based requirement or a disclosure requirement,

the court may make any order it thinks fit to secure compliance with the requirement. Any failure to comply with a resulting court order may be a contempt of court.

Tackling the risk of tactical litigation

9.112   The Government broadly describes tactical litigation as legal proceedings taken by parties to a bid with a view to frustrating or hampering the bid or the defence of the bid (see 'Company Law Implementation of The European Directive On Takeover Bids: A Consultative Document', January 2005, para.2.32, p.15). Such litigation undermines the General Principles aimed at ensuring shareholder sovereignty through board neutrality and preventing siege. Non-statutory regulation ensured that UK takeover practice was virtually free of tactical litigation. Private law litigation on the basis of a breach of the Takeover Code was non-existent, as the Code could not form the basis of a cause of action. The position was not significantly better in public law. In *R. v. Panel on Takeovers and Mergers, ex parte Datafin* [1987] 3 BCC 10, the Court of Appeal imposed substantial fetters on its supervisory jurisdiction through the eponymous *Datafin* principles. The goal of keeping takeover practice in the United Kingdom free of tactical litigation was a major objective of the Government during the negotiation of the Directive.

9.113   With the Directive in the shape that the UK Government wanted as far as preventing tactical litigation is concerned, Part 28 of the 2006 Act contains a number of provisions aimed at restricting tactical litigation. These provisions are aimed at ensuring that takeover disputes are dealt with within the context of the procedures established under the Panel system, albeit with judicial review as a backup. First, s.955(3)(a) removes the right to seek an injunction to prevent a person from contravening (or continuing to contravene) or failing to comply with a rule-based requirement (a 'rule-based requirement' means a requirement imposed by or under rules) or a disclosure requirement (a requirement imposed under s.947). Secondly, s.956(1) precludes any action for breach of statutory duty in respect of a contravention of a rule-based requirement or a disclosure requirement. Thirdly, s.956(2) provides that a contravention of a rule-based requirement does not make any transaction void or unenforceable or (subject to any provision made by rules) affect the validity of any other thing.

9.114   Parties remain free to make representations in relation to decisions of the Panel and appeal those decisions to the Takeover Appeal Board and ultimately to seek a judicial review of those decisions in appropriate cases.

IMPEDIMENTS TO TAKEOVERS

9.115   It is common knowledge that the negotiation of the Takeovers Directive was a difficult one. A key area of difficulty was the extent to which the Directive should tackle barriers to takeovers within the European Union. This was a matter in respect of which political agreement proved impossible. As a consequence, a compromise solution was reached by making the key Articles of the Directive optional (see B. Clarke, 'Articles 9 and 11 of the Takeover Directive (2004/25) and the market for corporate control' (2006) *Journal of Business Law* 355). Pursuant to Art.12, Member States can choose whether or not to impose Art.9 and/or Art.11 on companies registered within their territories. However, if Member States choose not to so apply both or either of those Articles, the implementing legislation should allow companies to voluntarily decide to opt-in to those regimes. Chapter 2 of Part 28 of the 2006 Act implements this compromise solution.

The duty of neutrality

9.116   The relevant part of Art.9, which establishes the duty of neutrality, provides:

> (2)   During the period referred to in the second subparagraph, the board of the offeree company shall obtain the prior authorisation of the general meeting of shareholders given for this purpose before taking any action, other than seeking alternative bids, which may result in the frustration of the bid and in particular before issuing any shares which may result in a lasting impediment to the offeror's acquiring control of the offeree company.
>
> Such authorisation shall be mandatory at least from the time the board of the offeree company receives the information referred to in the first sentence of Article 6(1) concerning the bid and until the result of the bid is made public or the bid lapses. Member States may require that such authorisation be obtained at an earlier stage, for example as soon as the board of the offeree company becomes aware that the bid is imminent.
>
> (3)   As regards decisions taken before the beginning of the period referred to in the second subparagraph of paragraph 2 and not yet partly or fully implemented, the general meeting of shareholders shall approve or confirm any decision which does not form part of the normal course of the company's business and the implementation of which may result in the frustration of the bid.

9.117   Section 943(1) of the 2006 Act mandates the Panel to make rules giving effect to Art.9, which establishes an agreed but optional board neutrality principle (see J. Winter, 'The good, the bad and the ugly of the European Takeover Directive' in J. Grant (ed.), *European Takeovers – The Art of Acquisition*

(Euromoney Books, 2005), xxv at xxvii). The UK has opted for it to be mandatory. The consequence of this is that the Code requires board neutrality in rule 21. The principle of board neutrality has always been a core feature of the Takeover Code ever since its promulgation.

The breakthrough rule

9.118   Article 11 introduces a rule that allows for a breakthrough of certain takeover pre-bid impediments subject to the optional arrangements in Art.12. These impediments are share transfer restrictions in the articles (or in contractual agreements), voting right restrictions in the articles (or in contractual agreements), including weighted voting rights and special rights to appoint directors. Article 11 relates to both the takeover bid period and following the bid where the bidder has acquired 75 per cent or more of the target company's capital carrying voting rights. Its effect is to override the aforementioned restrictions and it also provides that, in certain circumstances, shares carrying multiple voting rights shall only have one vote.

9.119   The breakthrough rule was designed to increase the number of takeovers in the European Union by eliminating these pre-bid defences which might otherwise impede takeovers. Article 10 requires companies to disclose in their annual accounts all impediments to takeovers. This has been implemented by the 2006 Act, s.992, which deals with disclosures in directors' reports of certain publicly traded companies. The information required by Art.10 must now be set out in the directors' report. The aim is to ensure greater transparency. The provision applies to all companies registered in the UK which have shares traded on a regulated market.

9.120   The breakthrough rule would ordinarily have had limited application to the United Kingdom considering the effect market pressure has had on the capital structure of UK companies. However since the Government considered that there would be few benefits in imposing the breakthrough rule on all UK companies and that such a rule would have certain drawbacks, it took advantage of Art.12, which allows for an opt-out by Member States, whilst giving companies with voting shares traded on a regulated market the right to opt in to these provisions should they wish to do so. Accordingly, pursuant to s.966, a company can opt in by special resolution. (A company may revoke an opting-in resolution by a further special resolution, termed an opting-out resolution: s.966(5)). Such an opt-in would have the effect of rendering the aforementioned pre-bid defences ineffectual in the face of a takeover bid.

9.121   Three conditions must be met, however, before the passing of a s.966 opting-in resolution. First, the company's shares must be admitted to trading on a regulated market. Secondly, the company's articles must not contain restrictions as are mentioned in Art.11 (or other provisions which would be incompatible with the said article) or, if they do contain those restrictions, they will not apply in circumstances related to a takeover bid as described by Art.11. Finally, it is a condition that no shares are held by a Minister of the Crown conferring special rights in the company and no such special rights are provided for in law. Such special rights held by Government are commonly known as 'Golden shares' and the UK Government holds a number of such shares in formerly publicly owned businesses which have been privatised. The rationale for holding such shares is to ensure essential public interest considerations are protected by the Government following a privatisation.

9.122   Section 968(2) deals with the consequences of opting-in. Essentially, opting-in effects a breakthrough of pre-bid defences. The consequences apply to a relevant agreement entered into between a person holding shares in the company and another such person on or after 21 April 2004, or entered into at any time between such a person and the company, and it applies to such an agreement even if the law applicable to the agreement (apart from this section) is not the law of a part of the United Kingdom. Such an agreement is rendered invalid in so far as it places any restriction:

(a) on the transfer to the offeror (or at his direction to another person) of shares in the company during the offer period;

(b) on the transfer to any person of shares in the company at a time during the offer period when the offeror holds shares amounting to not less than 75 per cent in value of all the voting shares in the company;

(c) on rights to vote at a general meeting of the company that decides whether to take any action which might result in the frustration of the bid; and

(d) on the rights to vote at a general meeting of the company that is the first such meeting to be held after the end of the offer period, and is held at a time when the offeror holds shares amounting to not less than 75 per cent in value of all the voting shares in the company. The offeror is given a special right by s.969 to require the directors of the company to call a general meeting of the company at short notice (not less than 14 days) where he holds 75 per cent in value of all the voting shares in the company.

9.123   Where a breakthrough occurs (i.e. contractual restrictions on shares are overridden) and loss is caused, s.968(6) entitles the person suffering such loss to compensation, of such amount as the court considers just and equitable. However, there is no right to compensation if the shares in question do not normally carry rights to vote at the company's general meetings, such as the standard preference shares which have voting rights only where specified pecuniary advantages are not provided because preferential dividends are in arrears.

9.124   Section 967 contains provisions relating to the date that the opting-in and opting-out resolutions will take effect. The effective date of an opting-in resolution may not be earlier than the date on which the resolution is passed, while the effective date of an opting-out resolution may not be earlier than the first anniversary of the date on which a copy of the opting-in resolution was forwarded to the registrar (s.967(6)). This is designed to prevent companies opting-out during, or in contemplation of, a bid process.

9.125   Where a company has passed an opting-in resolution or an opting-out resolution, s.970 requires it to notify the Panel. Such notification must be given within 15 days after the resolution is passed. Section 970(3) makes a failure to comply with this notification obligation a criminal offence on the part of the company and every officer of it who is in default.

CONSEQUENCES OF A SUCCESSFUL BID

9.126   Takeover bids for listed companies that achieve 100 per cent acceptances are a rarity. Shareholders may be untraceable or inert or unable or unwilling to accept a bid for a variety of reasons. A successful bid, in the sense that it has not lapsed or been withdrawn, which has not received 100 per cent acceptances poses problems for the bidder and non-assenting shareholders alike. The bidder might not want to have to contend with minority interests and the complications they generate; the non-assenting shareholders might no longer wish to remain in the target as residual minority shareholders. Chapter 3 of Part 28 accordingly provides squeeze-out rights, to enable the successful bidder to compulsorily purchase the shares of non-assenting shareholders, and sell-out rights, so that the residual minority can compel the successful bidder to purchase their shares. By so doing, Chapter 3 implements Arts.15 and 16 of the Takeovers Directive.

9.127   These rights are not new as far as British company law is concerned. The right to squeeze out on attaining a 90 per cent acceptance in respect of the target's share capital following a takeover bid has been a part of British company law since 1929 and the corresponding right to sell out has been a feature since 1985. Not surprisingly, the right to squeeze out has affected takeover practice, so that although the Takeover Code in rule 10 stipulates a minimum acceptance threshold of over 50 per cent, it is the norm in UK takeover practice to use a 90 per cent acceptance condition in voluntary offers – with the right to waive down to the 'over 50 per cent' level – so as to enable the offeror to take advantage of the statutory scheme for squeezing out minority shareholders.

9.128   Whilst Art.1 of the First Protocol to the European Convention for the Protection of Human Rights and Fundamental Freedoms might theoretically be engaged by a compulsory acquisition of shares, the courts are unanimous that a compulsory acquisition of shares pursuant to the Companies Act does not infringe Art.1 of the First Protocol. This position is not altered even in a case where the shareholder argues that its interest in the target company is not purely financial, as was argued in *Re Waste Recycling Group Plc* [2003] EWHC 2065 (Ch).

Squeeze-out rights

9.129   The starting point is s.979, which gives the offeror the right compulsorily to buy out minority shareholders if a 'takeover offer' is used. For the purposes of Part 28, Chapter 3 a takeover offer must satisfy three conditions.

9.130   First, it must be an offer. This is because the term 'offer' will be construed strictly for purposes of Chapter 3. In *Re Chez Nico (Restaurants) Ltd* [1992] BCLC 192, where the shares of the target shareholders were acquired not by virtue of acceptances of shareholders of any offer made by the bidder but in consequence of the bidder accepting offers made by the shareholders, Browne-Wilkinson VC held that there was no takeover offer for the purposes of activating the compulsory acquisition mechanism. The reason for this strict constructionist approach was that since the bidder is given the right to acquire other people's property, the terms upon which that right is exercisable having been defined by statute ought to be construed strictly.

9.131   The second condition is stipulated by s.974(2). The provision requires the offer to be one to acquire all the allotted shares in the target company other than shares that at the date of the offer (see s.991 for the definition) are already held by the offeror. This condition also applies where there is more than one class of shares in a company: in such a case, the offer must be one to acquire all the shares of one or more classes other than shares that at the date of the offer are already held by the offeror. The condition is treated as satisfied where the offer does not extend to shares that associates of the offeror hold or have contracted to acquire (whether unconditionally or subject to conditions being met) (s.975(4)). Furthermore, the offer need not be made to acquire shares that are allotted after the date of the offer or treasury shares (s.974(4)–(6)).

9.132   In determining the shares that at the date of the offer are already held by the offeror (so that they are excluded from the shares to which the offer relates), shares that the offeror has contracted to acquire, whether unconditionally or conditionally, are treated by s.975(1) as held by the offeror and are therefore excluded. So the position now is that shares which the offeror has conditionally contracted to acquire are excluded from the pool. The exclusion of the shares that the offeror has contracted to acquire does not, however, extend to irrevocable undertakings entered into by deed and for no consideration, or for consideration of negligible value, or for consideration consisting of a promise by the offeror to make the offer (s.975(2)).

9.133   Section 977 also excludes from the pool to which the offer relates shares that the offeror (or its associates) acquire or contract to acquire during the offer period but outside the offer (i.e. not by virtue of acceptance of the offer), if the acquisition consideration outside the offer exceeds the value of the consideration specified in the offer (see s.977(3) and s.979(8) and (9)). If the acquisition consideration does not exceed the value of the consideration specified in the offer, the shares are not excluded by s.977(1) from those to which the offer relates.

9.134   The term 'associate' is defined by s.988 for purposes of Part 28, Chapter 3 to mean:

(a) a nominee of the offeror;
(b) a holding company, subsidiary or fellow subsidiary of the offeror or a nominee of such a holding company, subsidiary or fellow subsidiary;

(c) a body corporate in which the offeror is substantially interested;

(d) a person who is, or is a nominee of, a party to a share acquisition agreement with the offeror; or

(e) (where the offeror is an individual) his spouse or civil partner and any minor child or step-child of his.

9.135   The third condition a takeover offer must satisfy is that the terms of the offer must be the same in relation to all the shares to which the offer relates. As in the case of the first statutorily required condition this parity condition applies where the target's shares include shares of different classes. However, there are two situations (s.976) where the parity condition will be treated as having been satisfied even though there is no parity in fact. First, where the consideration offered by the offeror involves a difference in value that is explicable only by the fact that some target shares carry an entitlement to a particular dividend which other shares of the same class, by reason of being allotted later, do not. Secondly, where foreign law precludes an offer of consideration in the form, or any of the forms, specified in the terms of the offer or precludes it except after compliance by the offeror with conditions with which he is unable to comply or which he regards as unduly onerous and the persons to whom an offer of consideration in the specified form is precluded are able to receive consideration in another form that is of substantially equivalent value. Thus, an offer is to be treated as being on the same terms irrespective of the relative ability or inability of offerees to take it up.

9.136   The parity condition does not extend to provisions as to the mechanics of the offer and of the acceptance of the offer. The practice of keeping the offer outside the jurisdiction of overseas securities laws, endorsed in *Winpar Holdings Ltd* v. *Joseph Holt Group Plc* [2001] EWCA Civ 770, has now been given robust statutory support by s.978, which goes beyond the ambit defined by *Winpar*. Pursuant to that provision, an offer will not cease being a takeover offer for the purposes of Chapter 3 if a shareholder has no registered address in the United Kingdom and the offer is not communicated to him to avoid contravening the law of another country as long as either the offer itself is published in the Gazette or a notice is published in the Gazette stating that a copy of the offer document can be obtained at a place in an EEA State or on a website (s.978(1)). Furthermore, if there are some target shareholders for whom, because of the law of an overseas jurisdiction, it is impossible to accept the offer, or more difficult to do so, that does not prevent the offer from being a takeover offer for the purposes of Chapter 3 (s.978(2), see also s.978(3)).

The squeeze-out process

9.137   Where the aforementioned conditions are satisfied and the offeror has, by virtue of acceptances of the offer, acquired (or unconditionally contracted to acquire) not less than 90 per cent in value of the shares to which the offer relates and in a case where the shares to which the offer relates are voting shares, not less than 90 per cent of the voting rights carried by those shares, he may give notice in the manner prescribed to the non-assenting shareholders that he desires to acquire those shares pursuant to s.979. This squeeze-out right – exercisable by issuing a s.979 notice – also applies in similar terms where the takeover offer relates to shares of different classes (s.979(4)).

9.138   There are three situations where although the 90 per cent requirement is not satisfied the bidder will nevertheless be allowed to proceed to squeeze out the minority shareholders under Chapter 3. It is, of course, possible to squeeze out a minority outside Chapter 3, such as where a scheme of arrangement is used or a squeeze-out procedure is contained in the articles. In regard to the former, even though one consequence of a scheme of arrangement is the elimination of a dis-sentient minority on the achievement of a lower threshold (75 per cent) the courts will not impeach the use of the scheme of arrangement simply because the 90 per cent threshold required for a compulsory acquisition following a takeover bid was not reached.

9.139   The three situations are as follows. First, where the offeror (or its associ-ates) acquires the target's shares (or unconditionally contracts to acquire them) not by virtue of acceptances of the offer – such as where the shares are bought in the market – the shares will be deemed as having been acquired or contracted to be acquired by virtue of acceptances of the offer (s.979(8)), so long as the con-sideration paid for such shares acquired outside the offer does not exceed the value of the consideration specified in the terms of the offer (s.979(10)).

9.140   Secondly, where the court, on an application made by the offeror who has not achieved the 90 per cent requirement, makes an order authorising the offeror to issue the squeeze-out notice. The court must however be satisfied that the offeror has after reasonable enquiry been unable to trace one or more of the per-sons holding shares to which the offer relates and that the 90 per cent acceptance requirement would have been met had such 'untraceables' accepted the offer – that is to say, the value of the shares held by the 'untraceables' when combined with the number of acceptances received by the offeror is not less than the 90 per cent acceptance level – and that the consideration offered is fair and reasonable (s.986(9)). A court order to serve the notice will not automatically follow simply because the court is satisfied with respect to the aforementioned conditions. This is because the court retains a discretion not to make such an order unless it con-siders that making the order is just and equitable having regard, in particular, to the number of shareholders who have been traced but who have not accepted the offer (s.986(10)).

9.141   The third situation arises where the offeror makes an offer not only for all the target company's allotted shares but also for shares subsequently allotted or relevant treasury shares. This is allowed by s.974(5). An offer for treasury shares is likely to be made in cases where the bid is a recommended one, although the Takeover Code in rule 4.5 prevents target management from using such shares to influence the outcome of a bid. Rule 4.5 provides that '[a]n offeree com-pany may not accept an offer in respect of treasury shares until after the offer is unconditional as to acceptances'. In this third situation, if the subsequently allotted shares or treasury shares that ceased to be treasury shares after the date of the offer are taken into account, the offeror may not satisfy the 90 per cent requirement. However, s.979(5) has the effect that in deciding whether the offeror has reached the 90 per cent threshold on any particular date this should be determined as if the shares to which the offer relates did not include any allotted, or ceasing to be held as treasury shares, on or after that date.

9.142   It will be noticed that one feature of Part 28, Chapter 3 is that it requires the bidder to have acquired both 90 per cent in value of the shares (or class of shares) to which the offer relates and 90 per cent of the voting rights in the company (or class of shares) to which the offer relates. This dual threshold, although new, is not expected to matter much because of the capital structure of most UK companies.

9.143   Another area of change concerns the time limit for the service of a squeeze-out notice. Since the Takeovers Directive provides in Art.15.4 that squeeze-out rights must be exercisable within a three-month period following the time allowed for acceptance of the bid, s.980 requires that the notice to the non-assenting shareholders must be given before the end of three months beginning with the day after the last day on which the offer can be accepted. An exception to this exists where the time allowed for acceptance of the offer is not governed by rules of the Takeover Code giving effecting to the Takeovers Directive. An example will be where the offer is made for a private company. In such a case, to ensure that the offeror is not able to continually extend the offer period, s.980(2)(b) requires that the notice must be given within six months of the date of the offer if this is earlier than the period ending three months after the end of the offer.

The section 979 notice to squeeze out

9.144   Where a notice to squeeze out is sent in compliance with s.979 its effect, according to s.981(2), is that the offeror will be entitled and bound to acquire the shares to which the notice relates on the terms of the offer, although this is subject to the shareholder's right to make a court application under s.986 to limit the exercise of this right. The underlying aim of the law, as was stated in *Re Carlton Holdings* [1971] 1 WLR 918, is to ensure that a non-assenting shareholder is not prejudiced for a failure to accept the offer and therefore should receive a consideration equivalent to assenting shareholders. Accordingly, the offeror remains bound if the offer consideration is not cash and the offeror is no longer able to provide it; likewise is the case where the consideration was to have been provided by the underwriter of an underwritten cash alternative who is no longer bound to provide it. In such cases, the consideration is to be taken to consist of an amount of cash, payable by the offeror, which at the date of the notice is equivalent to the consideration offered or (as the case may be) chosen (s.981(5)).

9.145   Where the offer is a 'mix and match' offer, s.981(3) ensures that non-assenting shareholders are treated on the same terms by requiring the offeror to offer those to whom squeeze-out notices are sent a choice of consideration giving the exact same proportions of the various types of consideration as were available to those who participated in the original 'mix and match' offer. In addition to this, the notice is required to state that the shareholder may, within six weeks from the date of the notice, indicate his choice by a written communication sent to the offeror at an address specified in the notice, and which consideration will apply in default if no choice is specified (s.981(3)). Where the shareholder fails to choose within six weeks from the date of the notice, such a shareholder will be allocated the primary consideration provided by the offer.

9.146   Section 980 requires the offeror to send to the target company a copy of the s.979 notice and a statutory declaration (signed by a director where the offeror is a company) in the prescribed form stating that the conditions for the giving of the notice are satisfied (s.980(4) and (5)). A failure to do this or the making of the relevant statutory declaration knowing it to be false or without having reasonable grounds for believing it to be true are criminal offences (s.980(6) – a defence is provided in s.980(7)). Although s.980 requires the target company to be given the documents at or about the same time as the notice to squeeze out is served, it appears that if this provision is breached the courts will, notwithstanding the penal sanction and the element of compulsion in the statutory framework, regard the provision as directory, not mandatory. In *Re Chez Nico (Restaurants) Ltd* (above) Browne-Wilkinson V-C held that there was nothing to suggest that a failure strictly to comply with the requirement was intended to nullify the whole procedure since the purpose of requiring the giving of the documents to the company is that otherwise the company will not know that 90 per cent acceptances have been obtained and that the compulsory acquisition procedure is being activated.

The statutory trust

9.147   In the absence of an application to the court by the offeree shareholder seeking to limit the right of the offeror to proceed with the compulsory acquisition, the offeror must immediately pay or transfer to the target company the consideration for the shares to which the notice relates at the end of six weeks from the date of the notice (s.981(6)). Such consideration is to be held on trust by the offeree company.

9.148   Section 982(2) requires the offeree company to pay into a separate interest bearing bank account that allows for withdrawals any money it receives and any dividend or other sum accruing from any other consideration. If, after reasonable enquiries have been made at reasonable intervals to find the person entitled to the consideration and 12 years have elapsed since the consideration was received (or the company is wound up), the person entitled to the consideration still cannot be found, then the consideration (together with any interest, dividend or other benefit that has accrued from it) is required to be paid into court (s.982(4)).

Sell-out rights

9.149 Article 16 of the Takeovers Directive requires Member States to ensure that, following a bid made to all the holders of the offeree company's securities for all of their securities, a non-assenting minority has the right to request to be bought out. The right to sell out is a statutory put option conferred on a minority shareholder in a target company (s.983(2) and (3)) that is triggered when the offeror in a takeover offer for all the shares (s.983(1)), or a class of shares (s.983(4)), in the target company acquires or unconditionally contracts to acquire shares amounting to not less than 90 per cent in value (or of the class) and not less than 90 per cent of the voting rights (or of the class) in the target company, but not all the shares in the company (or class) so that minority interests exist. In such a case, holders of target voting shares (s.983(2)) and non-voting shares (s.983(3)) who have not accepted the takeover offer may require the offeror to acquire their shares if, at any time before the end of the period within which the offer can be accepted the offeror and its associates (s.983(8)) reach the 90 per cent threshold.

9.150 Within one month of reaching the 90 per cent threshold, save for those situations where the offeror has already served a s.979 notice to squeeze out (s.984(4)), the offeror is under a statutory duty to give non-assenting shareholders notice in the prescribed manner of their sell-out rights and the statutory time limits within which they are to be exercised (s.984(3)). A failure to serve such a notice is a criminal offence under s.984(5). If such a request, in the form of a written communication addressed to the offeror (s.984(1)), is made within the appropriate statutory time limit (s.984(2)), the offeror will become entitled and bound to acquire the shares on the terms of the offer or on such other terms as may be agreed (s.985(2)).

9.151 For the purpose of assessing whether the 90 per cent threshold is reached any shares which the offeror had acquired or contracted to acquire (whether unconditionally or subject to conditions) prior to the posting of the offer and those acquired in the market outside the offer are included (s.983(2) and (3)). In this regard, shares held by the target as treasury shares are to be treated as having been acquired by the offeror for this purpose (s.983(5)).

9.152 As was stated earlier, the consequence of a valid request to sell out is that the offeror will be entitled and bound to acquire those shares on the terms of the offer or on such other terms as may be agreed. Where the terms of the offer are such as to give the shareholder a choice of consideration the offeror's notice to the shareholder should give particulars of the choice, the consideration specified in the offer which will apply by default if the shareholder fails to indicate a choice, and the statutory rights of the shareholder (s.985(3)). With this, the shareholder may indicate his choice when requiring the offeror to buy his shares. If the consideration offered to or (as the case may be) chosen by the shareholder is not cash and the offeror is no longer able to provide it, or it was to have been provided by a third party who is no longer bound or able to provide it, the consideration is to be taken to consist of an amount of cash, payable by the offeror, which at the date when the shareholder requires the offeror to buy his shares is at par to the consideration offered or (as the case may be) chosen (s.985(5)).

Applications to the court under s.986

9.153   A non-assenting shareholder who receives a squeeze-out notice and who objects to either being squeezed out or the terms of the squeeze out can apply to the court to intervene within six weeks from the date on which notice was given. Such an application will be made with a view to securing a ruling that the offeror is not entitled and bound to acquire his shares or that the terms on which the offeror is entitled and bound to acquire his shares shall be such as the court thinks fit (s.986(1)). Also, a non-assenting shareholder who wishes to exercise sell-out rights (or an offeror who is confronted with such an exercise of rights) can apply to the court with a view to the court ordering that the terms on which the offeror is entitled and bound to acquire the shares shall be such as the court thinks fit (s.986(3)).

9.154   The applicant shareholder is required to give notice of the application to the offeror (s.986(6)). (This applies also where the shareholder seeks a sell out and makes an application for the court's intervention.) It is a consequence of this requirement that the offeror is now required at the earliest opportunity to notify shareholders not party to a s.986 application that proceedings have been commenced. The court may grant such an order or order that the terms on which the offeror is entitled and bound to acquire the shares shall be such as the court thinks fit (s.986(1)). The onus is on the non-assenting shareholders to give reasons why their shares should not be acquired. In *Re Hoare & Co Ltd* (1933) 150 LT 374, Maugham J. said at p.375:

> I think, however, the view of the legislature is that where not less than 9/10 of the shareholders in the transferor company approved the scheme, or accept the offer, prima facie at any rate, the offer must be taken to be a proper one, and in default of an application by the dissenting shareholders, which includes those who do not assent, the shares of the dissentients may be acquired on the original terms by the transferee company. Accordingly, I think it is manifest that the reasons for inducing the court to order otherwise are reasons which must be supplied by the dissentients who take the step of making an application to the court and that the onus is on them, giving a reason why their shares should not be acquired by the transferee company.
>
> One conclusion which I draw from that fact is that the mere circumstance that the sale or exchange is compulsory is one which ought not to influence the court. It has been called an expropriation, but I do not regard that phrase as being very apt in the circumstances of the case.

The other conclusion I draw is this that again prima facie the court ought to regard the scheme as a fair one, in as much as it seems to me impossible to suppose that the court, in the absence of very strong grounds, is to be entitled to set up its own view of the fairness of the scheme in opposition to so very large a majority of the shareholders who are concerned.

Accordingly, without expressing a final opinion on the matter, because there may be special circumstances in special cases, I am unable to see that I have any right to order otherwise in such a case as I have before me unless it is affirmatively established that, notwithstanding the views of a very large majority of shareholders the scheme is unfair. There may be other grounds, but I see no other grounds available in the present case for the interference of the court.

9.155   For the non-assenting shareholder to discharge this onus he would have to clearly establish that, notwithstanding the view of the majority, the offer is unfair. In *Re Sussex Brick Co Ltd* [1961] 1 Ch 289, Vaisey J. said at p.293:

It must be affirmatively established that, notwithstanding the view of the majority, the scheme is unfair and that is a different thing from saying that it must be established that the scheme is not a very fair or not a fair one. The scheme has to be shown affirmatively, patently, obviously and convincingly to be unfair.

9.156   In *Fiske Nominees Ltd and others v. Dwyka Diamonds Ltd* [2002] EWHC 770 (Ch), the judge, Peter Lever QC, cautioned that these principles should not be taken too literally since the relevant statutory provision gives no guidance and imposes no limit as regards the grounds on which the discretion is to be exercised. Ultimately, it must be recognised that the court has a discretion whether or not to make an order. This discretion has, however, been affected significantly by Part 28, Chapter 3 in that the court will no longer be able to reduce the consideration from the consideration offered in the bid, although it may require consideration of a higher value where the shareholder shows that the offer value would be unfair (s.986(4)).

9.157   Lastly, where the shareholder's application (with regard to a squeeze out or sell out) is not considered by the court as being unnecessary, improper or vexatious and there has been no unreasonable delay in making the application and the applicant's conduct during proceedings has not been unreasonable, no order for costs or expenses may be made against the applicant by the court (s.986(5)).

10 MISCELLANEOUS

INTRODUCTION

10.1   This chapter considers a number of provisions that were added to the Bill during its passage through Parliament, or which are self-contained aspects of the 2006 Act that have little if any connection with one another or other parts of the Act and have therefore been placed in this chapter as a 'catch all'.

FRAUDULENT TRADING

10.2   Part 29 of the Act consists of one section, namely s.993, which was added to the Bill at a late stage. It simply reproduces the 1985 Act, s.458 and requires no further comment, save that it increases the maximum sentence of imprisonment for the offence of fraudulent trading from seven to 10 years.

PROTECTION OF MEMBERS AGAINST UNFAIR PREJUDICE

10.3   Part 30 principally comprises ss.994–996 of the 2006 Act. These provisions reproduce ss.459–461 of the 1985 Act and give a member of a company or a person in whom shares in a company have been vested by operation of law (s.994(2)) and the Secretary of State (s.995) the power to petition the court for an order (s.996) for the relief of any prejudicial conduct of a company's affairs. These sections require no further comment. Section 997 provides that the power to make rules under s.411 of the Insolvency Act 1986, so far as they relate to a winding-up petition, applies for the purposes of a petition under Part 30 of the Act. Section 998 provides that where an order of the court made under Part 30 alters the company's articles, or gives leave for the company to make any alterations in its articles, then the company must deliver within 14 days from the making of the order (or such longer period as the court may allow), a copy of the order to the registrar. Any copy of the order delivered to the registrar under s.998 must be accompanied by a copy of the company's articles, or the resolution or agreement in question, as amended (s.999(2)).

DISSOLUTION AND RESTORATION TO THE REGISTER

Striking defunct company off the register

10.4 The power of the registrar to strike off the register a defunct company which he believes is not carrying on a business, or is not in operation, is preserved by the 2006 Act, s.1000, as is the power of a company's directors to make an application to have their company struck off the register under s.1003. These sections replace ss.652 and 652A of the 1985 Act, with one principal amendment, namely, whereas the power to seek the voluntary striking off of a company by the directors was limited to private companies under the 1985 Act, under s.1003 the power of voluntarily striking off is now extended to public companies. Under s.1001, the registrar is obliged on giving notice to a company to have the company struck off the register. It should be noted that notice under the section is limited to notice in the Gazette, there being no power to give notice by alternative means under s.1116. This duty of the registrar to strike a company off the register is limited to cases where the company is being wound up and the registrar believes that no liquidator is acting, or that the affairs of the company are fully wound up, and no returns required to be made by the liquidator have been made for a period of six consecutive months. Any notice or letter served under ss.1000 or 1001 may be addressed either to the company's registered office, or to the care of any officer of the company (s.1002).

10.5 Section 1004 prohibits the directors of a company from seeking to strike off their company under s.1003 where for example the company has at any time in the previous three months changed its name (s.1004(1)(a)), or has traded, or otherwise carried on business (s.1004(1)(b)), or has engaged in any disposal of property or activity set out in s.1004(1)(c). Neither can a company be voluntarily struck off the register under s.1003 if other proceedings such as a voluntary arrangement have been proposed in respect of the company, or the company is in administration, or any other proceedings listed in s.1005(1) are being conducted or are in force and these proceedings have not been concluded. The circumstances when the proceedings listed in s.1005(1) are regarded as concluded (so that an application under s.1003 could be made) are prescribed under s.1005(2)–(3).

10.6 Where an application is made by the director(s) under s.1003, he or they must within seven days from the date of application ensure that copies of the same are given to the persons listed in s.1006(1). These persons include the members of the company, any employees, creditors (which includes contingent or prospective creditors (s.1011)), other directors, managers or trustees of any company pension fund, or any person specified by regulations made by the Secretary of State. This duty to supply copies of the application applies by virtue of s.1006 to any person who between the date of an application made under s.1003 and the date the application is finally dealt with becomes one of any of the groups of persons listed above, i.e. a new member or creditor of the company (s.1007(2)).

10.7   For the purposes of either s.1006 or s.1007 a copy or document is to regarded as given to a person if it is delivered to him, left at his proper address or sent by post to him at that address (s.1008(2)). The term 'proper address' for the above purposes is defined in s.1008(3), which prescribes the term, for example in the case of a firm incorporated or formed in the United Kingdom, as either the firm's registered or principal office. In the case of a creditor, the address to which the copy of the application may be sent is the place of business of the creditor with which the company has had dealings, or if there is more than one such address the copy of the application must be sent or posted to all such addresses (s.1008(4)).

10.8   If between the date of an application under s.1003 and the date on which the application is finally dealt with any of the circumstances set out in s.1009(1) arise or occur, a director of the company must ensure that the application to strike off the company is withdrawn (s.1009(2)). The circumstances requiring the withdrawal of the application are essentially those factors, circumstances or proceedings which would prohibit the making of an application under ss.1004–1005, albeit they are set out in s.1009(1). An application is withdrawn by giving notice to the registrar under s.1010.

Bona vacantia

10.9   Under s.1012 all property either legally or beneficially owned by a company which has been dissolved under Part 31, Chapter 1, is deemed to be bona vacantia. However, the Crown may disclaim such property under the terms of s.1013. Unlike the equivalent provision under the 1985 Act (i.e. s.656), s.1013 provides that the notice of disclaimer must be executed within three years of the date of the vesting of the property coming to the notice of the Crown representative. The section also provides that if ownership of the property is not established when the Crown representative first has notice that the property may have vested, the three-year period runs from the end of the period reasonably necessary for the Crown representative to establish ownership (s.1013(3)).

10.10   Under s.1013(4) a disclaimer may be made within 12 months of the Crown representative receiving an application from a person interested in the property. Where a notice of disclaimer is executed under s.1013, s.1014 provides that the relevant property is deemed not to have vested in the Crown. The general effect of a disclaimer is to determine, from that date, the rights, interests and liabilities of the company in or in respect of that property (s.1015). Under s.1016, which concerns disclaimers made in respect of leasehold property, a notice of disclaimer (by way of a copy of the disclaimer) cannot take effect as against underlessees or a mortgagee of a leasehold, unless the notice has been served on these parties (but only in so far as the Crown is aware of their addresses) and no application has been made by such parties within 14 days beginning with the day on which the last notice was served under s.1016, or the court directs that the disclaimer shall take effect (see below).

10.11   Under s.1017 the court on an application of a person claiming an interest in disclaimed property, or of a person who is under a liability in respect of property which has been disclaimed, may make an order in respect of that property. The orders that can be made are set out in s.1017(2) and include an order vesting the property in or delivering the same to a person or trustee who has an entitlement to, or liability in respect of, the property.

10.12   Under s.1018 there is further protection for a person who has a leasehold interest in property the subject of a disclaimer. Thus under s.1018, the court in making an order under s.1017 in respect of leasehold property in favour of an underlessee or mortgagee must, inter alia, on making a vesting order ensure that the person in whose favour the order is made holds the property subject to the same liabilities and obligations as those to which the company was subject under the lease, or subject to the same liabilities and obligations as if the lease had been assigned to that party. However, where in consequence of a disclaimer, land subject to a rentcharge is vested in a person, neither he nor his successors in title are subject to any personal liability in respect of the sums due under the rentcharge, except for such sums which arise after he, or some person claiming through him has possession or control of the land or is in occupation (see s.1019).

Scotland

10.13   Sections 1020–1023 deal with the effect of disclaimers made in respect of companies dissolved in Scotland.

Restoration to the register

10.14   Under the 1985 Act, if a company had been struck off the register, procedures were prescribed under ss.651 and 653 whereby the company could be restored to the register. The Company Law Review (Final Report, pp.227–229) recommended that, in certain circumstances, an alternative administrative procedure for restoration should be available. Sections 1024–1028 implement that recommendation.

10.15   Section 1024 provides that an application may be made to restore a company that has been struck off by the registrar under ss.1000–1001 (see **paras.10.4–10.8**). The application may be made whether or not the company has been dissolved; however the application must be made by a former director or a former member of the company, and where there has been dissolution, it must be made within six years of the date of dissolution.

10.16   Section 1025 sets out the requirements for restoration. This includes the following conditions:

- the company was carrying on business or was in operation at the time of its striking off;
- the Crown representative has given any necessary consent;

- the applicant has delivered any documents required to bring the registrar's records up to date; and
- the applicant has paid any penalties due at the date of dissolution or striking off.

Section 1026 requires that an application for restoration be accompanied by a statement of compliance that the applicant has the necessary standing to make the application and that the requirements for administrative restoration have been met. The statement of compliance can be accepted by the registrar as sufficient evidence of these matters.

10.17   Section 1027 provides that the registrar must give notice of any decision taken on an application made under s.1024. If the registrar decides that the company is to be restored, this restoration will take effect from the date when the notice is sent. Other actions which the registrar must take as a consequence of the decision to restore are also set out in s.1024.

10.18   The effects of restoration of a company under the above provisions are prescribed under s.1028. The company is deemed to have continued to exist, as if it had not been struck off. In addition, within three years of restoration application may be made to the court for such directions as may be needed to place the company, and any other persons, in the same position as they would have been had the striking off not taken place.

Restoration to the register by the court

10.19   Sections 1029–1034 amalgamate what were two separate procedures for a company to be restored to the register by court order under ss.651 and 653 of the 1985 Act. The Company Law Review in its Final Report recommended (at pp.227–229) that the two separate procedures be replaced by a single procedure, which was to be based in essence on the procedures set out in s.653 of the 1985 Act.

10.20   Section 1029 determines that an application may be made for the restoration of companies which have been dissolved, are deemed to have been dissolved, or have been struck off under the provisions set out in s.1029(1). The persons who may make such an application are specified in s.1029(2). Under s.1030(4) an application to the court for the restoration of a company must be made within six years; however, special provision is made in s.1030(5) for an application to be made outside the six-year period in situations where a previous application for administrative restoration has been made and refused. Furthermore under s.1030(1) there is no time limit where the application for restoration is made in order to bring proceedings against the company for damages for personal injury.

10.21   Section 1031 sets out when the court may order restoration, which will include any case in which the court considers it just to do so. Restoration will take effect when the order is delivered to the registrar, and the registrar must give appropriate public notice of the restoration.

10.22   Under s.1032, the effect of restoration is that the company is deemed to have continued in existence as if it had not been struck off. The court may make such directions as are needed to place the company itself, and other persons, in the same position as they would have been if the striking off had not taken place. The court may also make directions as to the issues set out in s.1032(4) relating to delivery of documents to the registrar to bring his records up to date and the payment of costs.

10.23   Under s.1033 when the company is restored to the register it is with the name it had before it was struck off. However, it may be that restoration would mean that two companies with the same or very similar names would appear in the registrar's index. This section thus makes a new provision for the restored company to change its name in these circumstances (see **Chapter 2** where the issue of a company's name is considered).

10.24   Section 1034 replaces s.655 of the 1985 Act. There is new provision under s.1034(3) so that where a company's property has passed to the Crown and been disposed of, when the Crown reimburses the company it may deduct the reasonable costs of sale which were incurred.

COMPANY INVESTIGATIONS

Introduction

10.25   Companies registered under the Companies Acts are subject to having their affairs investigated by the Department of Trade and Industry. In doing so it may use extensive powers to collect evidence and to pass this evidence on to regulatory or prosecuting authorities. There are under the 1985 Act two different forms of investigation, namely by way of an inspection of documents under s.447, and by an investigation by inspectors under ss.431 and 432. Inspection by documents is frequently an informal procedure, and usually carried out by Department of Trade and Industry officials, albeit backed by powers requiring parties to supply information on pain of prosecution. An inspection by an appointed inspector is a substantial matter that may last years, and usually results in a published report.

10.26   Part 32 of the 2006 Act amends Part 14 of the 1985 Act which relates to company investigations. The Secretary of State is given new powers to bring to an end an investigation into a company when it is no longer in the public interest, for example if it is taking too long.

10.27   Section 1035 inserts new ss.446A and 446B into the 1985 Act. These provisions empower the Secretary of State to give directions to inspectors as to the subject matter of an investigation, or to take or not to take a specified step in an investigation (s.446A), or to terminate an investigation (s.446B). Section 1036 inserts new ss.446C and 446D into Part 14 of the 1985 Act. These provisions relate to the resignation and revocation of an appointment of an inspector, and the appointment of replacement inspectors in respect of an investigation.

10.28   Under s.1037 a new s.446E is inserted into Part 14 of the 1985 Act, which empowers the Secretary of State to require a former inspector to produce documents obtained or generated by that person during the course of his investigation, either to the Secretary of State or to an inspector appointed under Part 14 of the 1985 Act.

10.29   Section 1038 amends s.434 of the 1985 Act to permit, inter alia, documents required to be produced to inspectors or the Secretary of State under either s.434 or s.447 of the 1985 Act to be supplied in hard copy form, or in a form from which a hard copy can be readily obtained.

10.30   Section 1039 makes consequential amendments to s.8(1A)(b)(i) of the Company Directors Disqualification Act 1986. Section 8 thus authorises the disqualification of a director under the 1986 Act following an inspection of a company, by making reference to and incorporating ss.437, 446E and 451A (disclosure of information by Secretary of State or inspector) of Part 14 of the 1985 Act within the section. Accordingly, a decision as to whether to take action to disqualify a director can now be taken on the basis of information that was obtained or generated by an inspector as a result of an investigation.

COMPANIES AUTHORISED TO REGISTER UNDER THE ACT (PART 33)

10.31   Section 1040 replaces the 1985 Act, s.680. Companies incorporated within the United Kingdom, but not formed under the Companies Acts, or earlier companies legislation, may apply to register under the provisions of the 2006 Act by virtue of s.1040. The types of company that can use this section are set out in s.1040(1), and include companies formed before 2 November 1862, companies formed by private Act of Parliament and companies formed by Royal Charter. A company under the section may apply to register as a company limited by shares or by guarantee, or as an unlimited company. However, s.1040(4)–(5) restricts the choice of the status of a company registering under the section; for example a limited liability company cannot register under the section as an unlimited company. A company may wish to register under s.1040 to take advantage of legislation which applies to companies registered under the 2006 Act. Section 1040(6) makes it clear that a company can register as a company under the 2006 Act even if this is done in order to take advantage of provisions of the Insolvency Act 1986 which are not otherwise available to unregistered companies.

10.32   Section 1041 defines a joint stock company for the purposes of s.1040, and it is drafted in the same terms as the 1985 Act, s.683. Section 1040 allows certain joint stock companies to register as companies limited by shares.

10.33   Section 1042 confers new powers on the Secretary of State to make regulations in connection with the registration of a company following an application under s.1040. Any such regulations which will cover for example procedural requirements for registration, or the conditions to be satisfied before registration, will replace the provisions made by ss.681–682, 684–690 of and Sched.21 to the 1985 Act.

UNREGISTERED COMPANIES

10.34   Section 1043 replaces s.718 of the 1985 Act. The section empowers the Secretary of State to apply provisions of the Companies Acts to certain unregistered companies. These companies are companies incorporated in the United Kingdom, and having their principal place of business in the United Kingdom, but not formed or registered under the Companies Acts or any other public general Act of Parliament. Examples of such companies are those formed by letters patent, or by private Act of Parliament. Certain other companies are exempted from regulations made under this section (s.1043(1)), including those companies exempted by direction of the Secretary of State.

OFFENCES UNDER THE COMPANIES ACTS

Introduction

10.35   The Company Law Review sought to clarify and to differentiate the basis upon which those breaches of company law under previous companies legislation allocated responsibility between the company and the officers of the company. The Review also considered that a new Companies Act must have its offences underpinned by effective and proportionate sanctions and enforcement. These views were enacted in Part 36 of the Act. Accordingly, the new provisions amend the previous framework regarding 'officers in default' to make it clear which individuals and in what circumstances may be held liable for their conduct in respect of the affairs of the company. Part 36 also removes liability from the company in certain circumstances. The general principle thus adopted by Part 36 as to whether a company should be liable for a breach of any provision contained in the Companies Acts (which includes provisions in the 2006 Act and those provisions in the 1985 Act which remain in force), is that the company should not be liable for the offence where the only victims are the company or its members. However, where other persons are potential victims, then the company may be held liable for a breach of a provision in the Companies Act. All the offences in the Companies Act 1985 (which include those unrepealed parts of the 1985 Act set out in Sched.3 to the 2006 Act), have been reviewed in the light of the above principle.

Liability of officer in default

10.36   Section 1121 specifies the persons who may be liable as an officer of the company for any offence committed under the Companies Acts as defined above. An 'officer' of the company for the purposes of determining liability includes a director, manager or company secretary, together with any person who is treated as an officer of the company. An officer so defined is liable for any offence when he is 'in default'; this means that he has authorised or permitted, participated in, or has failed to take all reasonable steps to prevent the commission of an offence. These terms are well understood in the criminal law.

10.37   Section 1122 provides that where a company is an officer of another company (for example a company secretary), liability for breach of any provision in the Companies Acts can only be attributed to the company as an officer if one of its own officers is in default. Section 1123 provides that s.1121 applies to persons and bodies other than companies where their role or function with regard to a company is equivalent to an officer of the company. It makes specific provision to this effect for bodies corporate, partnerships and unincorporated bodies.

Offences under the Companies Acts

10.38   Section 1124 introduces Sched.3 to the 2006 Act which contains amendments to certain unrepealed provisions of the 1985 Act that relate to offences. Space does not permit consideration of this Schedule in detail and reference should be made to this Schedule in **Appendix 1**. However, the general effect of the Schedule is to effect certain changes in the wording of a number of offences contained in the 1985 Act for the purposes of clarification, and to ensure the offences set out in the Schedule accord with the principles governing criminal liability adopted in Part 36. In addition the system of sanctions is rationalised, with maximum penalties increased.

General provisions

10.39   Section 1125 defines 'daily default fine', replacing provisions set out in the 1985 Act, s.730(4).

10.40   Section 1126 provides that proceedings or prosecutions as prescribed in the section can only be brought with the consent of the Secretary of State, or in some circumstances the Director of Public Prosecutions. This section replaces s.731(1) and (2) of the 1985 Act.

10.41   Section 1127 restates s.731(1) of the 1985 Act, specifying the possible venues for summary proceedings for any offence under the Companies Act. For example, for a body corporate the venue may be any place where it has a place of business.

10.42   Section 1128 restates s.731(2)–(4) of the 1985 Act. It sets out the time limits for instituting summary proceedings under any provisions of the

Companies Acts. Thus a summary prosecution under the Companies Acts must be commenced within three years of the offence, and within one year from when the prosecuting authorities receive enough evidence to justify prosecution.

10.43 Section 1129 restates s.732(3) of the 1985 Act and applies to all offences under the Companies Acts. Companies Acts provisions concerning offences should not to be taken to require any person to disclose information that is protected by legal professional privilege.

10.44 Section 1130 restates s.734(1)–(4) of the 1985 Act. Proceedings for offences under the Companies Acts committed by unincorporated bodies are to be brought against them as if they were corporate bodies.

10.45 Section 1131 is an interim provision, which will operate until s.154(1) of the Criminal Justice Act 2003 comes into force. This latter section makes new provision about the powers of magistrates' courts to impose sentences of imprisonment on summary conviction. In the interim, s.1131 provides that the maximum term of imprisonment for a person convicted of an offence under the Companies Acts on summary conviction is to be six months, as it was under the 1985 Act, rather than 12 months.

10.46 Section 1132 empowers the Secretary of State, the Director of Public Prosecutions or a chief officer of police to make an application to the High Court for an order against any person where there is reasonable cause to believe that while an officer of a company he committed an offence (in connection with the management of the company's affairs), and that evidence of the commission of the offence is to be found in any documents in the possession or control of the company. Such an order may authorise inspection of the documents in question to be carried out for the purposes of securing evidence relating to any such offence (s.1132(2)–(3)). The order may also require an officer of the company, including the company secretary, to produce any documents to a person named in the order at a place so named (s.1132(3)(b)). Section 1133 provides that the provisions of Part 36 of the Act (except for s.1132) do not apply to offences committed before the commencement of the relevant provisions.

INTERPRETATION (PART 38)

10.47 Sections 1158–1174 together with Scheds.6, 7 and 8 define such terms as 'UK-registered company', 'subsidiary', 'undertaking and related matters' and 'parent and subsidiary undertakings' and 'non-cash asset' for the purposes of the 2006 Act. These terms are relevant in particular to the provisions of the 2006 Act dealing with directors' duties (which are considered in **Chapter 4**) and to the accounting provisions of the Companies Act set out in Part 15 of the Act (considered in **Chapter 6**). These accounting provisions derive from the Seventh Company Law Directive (Directive 83/349/EEC) and reflect changes in the definition of subsidiary undertakings for accounting purposes made by the Accounts Modernisation Directive (Directive 2003/51/EEC).

10.48   Section 1160 empowers the Secretary of State by regulation to amend the definition of subsidiary set out in s.1159.

10.49   Sections 1164–1166 define the terms 'banking company' and 'banking group', 'insurance company' and related expressions and 'employees' share scheme'.

10.50   One of the principal reforms effected by the 2006 Act is the considerable extension of the use of electronic means to record and register information relating to company matters. Section 1168 is accordingly a new provision to define the terms 'hard copy', 'electronic form' and related expressions which are used throughout the 2006 Act. Section 1168(5) requires that documents or information sent in electronic form must be capable of being read and retained for future reference. Section 1169 deals with dormant companies and restates the terms of s.249AA(4)–(7) of the 1985 Act. Thus s.1169(1) provides that a company is dormant during any period in which it has no significant accounting transactions. This term is itself defined in s.1169(2)–(3). Subject to certain exceptions a dormant company is exempt from the need to have its accounts audited (see **Chapter 7**).

10.51   The concept of the EEA State and related expressions such as EEA Company is relevant throughout the 2006 Act. It is defined in s.1170, which reproduces s.744 of the 1985 Act without any change of substance. Section 1171 defines the term 'former Companies Acts'.

10.52   Section 1172 is an interpretative provision. It provides that requirements to be imposed under the 2006 Act, by regulations or orders to be made under a power contained in the Act, are also caught by references in the Act to the term 'the requirements of this Act'. Section 1173 provides definitions of a number of other terms used in the Act. Schedule 8 to the Act is introduced by s.1174. This Schedule provides an index setting out where the definitions of terms used in the Companies Acts can be found.

MINOR AMENDMENTS (PART 39)

10.53   Section 1175 amends Part 7 of the 1985 Act in accordance with Sched.9 to the 2006 Act so as to remove the special provisions about accounts and audit of companies that are charities. This is because certain companies are subject to an accountant's report or to audit as charities when, if they were not charities, they would otherwise be exempt as small companies.

10.54   By s.1176, the power of the Secretary of State under s.438 of the 1985 Act to bring civil proceedings on behalf of a company is repealed. Section 1176(2)–(3) makes consequential amendments to ss.439 and 453(1A) of the 1985 Act. Proceedings under s.438 commenced before the coming into force of this section remain unaffected.

10.55   In view of the extensive reform of the law relating to directors' duties in Part 10 of the 2006 Act, s.1177 repeals certain provisions in Part 10 of the 1985 Act set out in the section. The repeal of these provisions had in most part been recommended by the Law Commission.

10.56   Section 1178 repeals s.720 of, and Sched.23 to, the 1985 Act. These provisions related to the requirement for certain insurers, provident and benefit societies to publish a periodical statement in the form set out in the Schedule. The application of these provisions had become very limited as they did not apply to United Kingdom insurance companies which are regulated under the Financial Services and Markets Act 2000 by the Financial Service Authority, with its own requirements as to publication of annual accounts and balance sheet in respect of such entities.

10.57   By s.1179 the Secretary of State is no longer required to cause a 'general annual report on matters within the Companies Acts' to be prepared and laid before Parliament. This repeals the requirement under s.279 of the 1985 Act.

10.58   Section 1180 repeals the provisions of Part 4 of the Companies Act 1989 relating to company charges. These provisions were never brought into force (see Part 25 of the 2006 Act considered at **paras.10.79** *et seq.* where the new provisions relating to company charges are set out).

10.59   Section 1181 gives the Secretary of State power to make an order amending certain provisions of the Commonhold and Leasehold Reform Act 2002 and the Leasehold Reform, Housing and Urban Development Act 1993, so as to make it easier to ascertain the contents of the articles and other constitutional documents of Right To Manage and Right To Enfranchise companies. These are two new types of company provided for in the 2002 Act, and, in the case of Right to Manage companies, by amendment to the 1993 Act. This must be seen in the light of the likely future adjustment to be made to the constitutional documents of these forms of company by amendment of the relevant legislation to reflect the status of the memorandum in company law effected by the 2006 Act.

COMPANY DIRECTORS – FOREIGN DISQUALIFICATION

10.60   Part 40 of the 2006 Act provides that a person who has been disqualified from acting as a director, receiver or otherwise acting in connection with the affairs of a company under the law of another jurisdiction (or who has given undertakings not to act in any of the above capacities) is deemed under the terms of s.1182 to be subject to 'foreign restrictions'. Under ss.1184–1185 the Secretary of State is empowered to make regulations to disqualify a person subject to foreign restrictions from performing the office of director, receiver or in any way being connected with a United Kingdom company. Such disqualification may be either automatic or following upon an order by the court on the application of the Secretary of State under s.1184(1)–(2) (see also s.1183 which defines for the purposes of Part 40 'the court' and a 'UK company'). The regulations should also state the grounds upon which disqualification may be made, and may, inter alia, mirror the grounds for disqualification prescribed under the Company Directors Disqualification Act 1986 (s.1185(3)(a)).

10.61   Under s.1186 the regulations may also provide that it will be an offence for a person disqualified under Part 40 of the Act and any regulations made thereunder to act in breach of any disqualification. There is also power under s.1187 for any regulations made under Part 40 to provide that a person subject to a foreign restriction, who during the period when he is subject to such a restriction is a director of a United Kingdom company, or is involved in the management of such a company, be held personally responsible (jointly and severally with the company, or any other person held so liable) for all debts and liabilities of the company incurred during that time (s.1187(1)–(2)).

10.62   Under s.1188, any regulations made under Part 40 may also empower the Secretary of State to require a person subject to a foreign restriction, but who at the time is not disqualified under Part 40, to send a statement to the registrar if he does anything that if done by a person disqualified under Part 40 would be a breach of the disqualification. Any regulations made under Part 40 may also require that a person disqualified under Part 40, who is seeking to act with regard to a United Kingdom company in any of the ways or capacities specified in s.1189(2), and where a statement or notice to that effect is being sent to the registrar, to provide an additional statement that he has obtained permission from a court under the terms of s.1184(5) to act in a way, with respect to the company, which would otherwise be in breach of the disqualification. The regulations may provide that statements supplied under either s.1188 or s.1189 are to be treated as records relating to the company for the purposes of maintaining the register under s.1080 (see **Chapter 3**).

10.63   Finally the regulations may provide that failure to comply with the provisions of ss.1188–1189 and the relevant requirements prescribed under the regulations will be an offence (s.1191).

TRANSPARENCY OBLIGATIONS AND RELATED MATTERS

10.64   Part 43 of the Act deals with transparency obligations of listed companies. Section 1265 inserts a definition of the 'Transparency Obligations Directive' (Directive 2004/109/EC) into Part 6 of the Financial Services and Markets Act 2000. Section 1266 inserts seven new sections into Part 6 the 2000 Act, namely ss.89A–89G. Part 6 of the 2000 Act deals with the regulation of securities that are traded on markets in the United Kingdom. These new sections will enable the Financial Services Authority as the 'competent authority' to make transparency rules. Transparency rules will require information to be either notified to the Authority or made public by issuers of securities who are trading on a regulated market. Certain aspects of the rules can also be extended to apply to issuers whose shares are traded on other UK markets. One of the main purposes of such rules is to ensure that the markets on which securities are traded have sufficient information about the issuers of securities, and the level of holdings in those securities, to enable the price of those securities to accurately reflect these matters, in so far as such matters affect their value.

10.65 Section 1267 inserts three new sections into Part 6 of the 2000 Act, namely ss.89H–89J. The new sections permit the Financial Services Authority (the 'Authority') to call for information from specified persons. The provisions also set out the requirements connected with the Authority's power to call for information.

10.66 Section 1268 inserts four new sections into Part 6 of the 2000 Act, namely ss.89K–89N. The new sections set out the Authority's powers in cases of infringement of transparency obligations, which include the power for the Authority to make a public statement if an issuer is failing or has failed to comply with its obligations.

CORPORATE GOVERNANCE RULES

10.67 Section 1269 inserts a new s.89O into Part 6 of the 2000 Act. It gives the Authority a power to make rules implementing, or enabling the implementation of, and dealing with matters arising out of Community obligations relating to corporate governance of issuers who have requested or approved admission of their securities to trading on a regulated market. (The rule-making power will enable the Authority to make corporate governance rules covering issuers that have the United Kingdom as their home Member State, and with securities traded on a regulated market in the United Kingdom or elsewhere in the EEA.)

10.68 Section 1270 inserts new ss.90A–90B into Part 6 of the 2000 Act. The sections, inter alia, establish civil liability to third parties in respect of disclosures made as a result of the Transparency Obligations Directive by issuers of securities that are traded on a regulated market.

10.69 Section 1271 inserts a new s.100A into Part 6 of the 2000 Act. This section sets out the Authority's ability to exercise powers where prospectus rules, transparency rules or other related provisions have been infringed and the home State of the issuer is a Member State other than the United Kingdom.

10.70 Section 1272 inserts a new Sched.15 into the 2000 Act, making minor and consequential amendments to other parts of the 2000 Act in so far as they relate to the Authority's new rule-making powers inserted into Part 6 of the 2000 Act by ss.1265–1271. The section also makes amendments to the Companies (Audit, Investigations and Community Enterprise) Act 2004, which allows an authority other than the Financial Services Authority to act as competent authority in examining periodic accounts and reports of issuers as required under the Directive. This role will be carried out by the Financial Reporting and Review Panel.

10.71 Section 1273 provides the Secretary of State with a regulation-making power similar to that given to the relevant competent authority under s.1269.

MISCELLANEOUS PROVISIONS

10.72 Part 44 contains miscellaneous provisions. Sections 1274–1276 amend ss.16–17, and are relevant to s.18, of the Companies (Audit, Investigations and Community Enterprise) Act 2004. The principal purpose of these sections is to take the first steps in implementing the recommendations of the Morris Review of the actuarial profession. The principal recommendation of the review was that the Financial Reporting Council should oversee the actuarial profession in a similar way as it currently does the accountancy and auditors professions.

10.73 Sections 1277–1280 permit the Treasury or the Secretary of State to make provision by way of regulation to require institutions which are prescribed under s.1277 to provide information about the exercise of voting rights (set out in s.1280) which are attached to shares (as specified in s.1279).

10.74 Section 1281 inserts s.241A into Part 9 of the Enterprise Act 2002 so as to enable public authorities, in certain circumstances, to disclose information where the information is to be used in civil proceedings or otherwise in order to establish, enforce or defend legal rights.

10.75 Section 1282 inserts s.176ZA into Chapter 8 of Part 4 of the Insolvency Act 1986. The intended effect of this provision is to reverse the House of Lords judgment in *Buchler and another v. Talbot and others*; *Re Leyland Daf* [2004] UKHL 9. If necessary, the general expenses of winding up can be funded using property subject to a floating charge, in priority to any claims by the floating charge holder and any preferential creditors. It also provides a power to make secondary legislation that will prescribe circumstances in which a liquidator must seek the authorisation or approval of the floating charge holder, or preferential creditors, or the court, in order to recover certain expenses of winding up from property subject to a floating charge.

10.76 Section 1283 amends para.3(1) of Sched.3 to the Commonhold and Leasehold Reform Act 2002. The 2002 Act requires commonhold associations to file with the Land Registry any amended memorandum or articles. Until this action is completed any alterations are to be regarded as having no effect. This requirement had the unintended effect of effectively prohibiting any change in these documents before the land which the commonhold association is established to manage is registered as commonhold land, or after it has stopped being commonhold land. Amending para.3(1) removes this difficulty.

10.77 Part 46 contains supplementary provisions. The way in which regulations and orders made under the Act are to be made is set out in ss.1288–1292. Section 1293 provides that the term 'enactment' used in the Act includes, inter alia, an enactment contained in subordinate legislation within the meaning of the Interpretation Act 1978. Section 1294 gives the Secretary of State and the

Treasury powers to make orders in consequence of any provision in the Act. Section 1295 states that the enactments specified in Sched.16 are repealed in whole or in part. Section 1296 gives the Secretary of State and the Treasury powers to make orders which make transitional provisions and savings in connection with the commencement of any provisions of the 2006 Act. By s.1297, anything done in reliance on provisions in the 1985 Act which have been repealed and replaced by the 2006 Act continue to be legally effective.

10.78   Part 47 contains s.1300, which provides for commencement of provisions contained in Parts 43, 44, 46 and 47 on the day when the 2006 Act is passed.

COMPANY CHARGES

10.79   The Bill originally introduced by Government for company law reform contained no provisions with regard to company charges, leaving these to be governed by the 1985 Act, Part 12, ss.395–424 which would have been replaced by the Companies Act 1989, Part 4 if those provisions had ever been brought into force. Clearly this was always unsatisfactory in that it was one of the many omissions which prevented the Bill from being the proper reforming consolidation measure which English company law urgently needed. By the time that the Bill emerged from Standing Committee D the lack of logic of this position had been perceived as a result of the volume of well-directed criticism, and provisions dealing with the registration of company charges were inserted, so that the 2006 Act (Part 25) does address the subject of company charges.

Duty to register charges

10.80   The new provisions begin by requiring a company that creates a charge to deliver to the registrar for registration the prescribed particulars of the charge, along with any instrument by which the charge is created or evidenced. This must be done before the end of the period allowed for registration (s.860(1)). As an alternative, registration may be effected on the application of a person interested in it (s.860(2)), and where this occurs the person registering is entitled to recover from the company any fees paid by him to the registrar (s.860(3)). Where registration does not occur within the permitted period an offence is committed by the company and every officer who is in default punishable by a fine. These duties are substantially the same as those up to now imposed by the 1985 Act, s.399 although the wording is different. Duties continue also to exist in relation to charges of a registrable nature on property which is acquired already subject to the charge. The company must deliver to the registrar for registration the prescribed particulars of the charge and a certified copy of any instrument by which the charge is created or evidenced, and this must be done within the registration period (ss.860(1) and 870). If there is default the company and any officer in default is guilty of an offence punishable by a fine.

Charges requiring registration

10.81   The list of charges requiring registration is set out in s.860(7) which lists:

(a) a charge on land or any interest in land, other than a charge for any rent or other periodical sum issuing out of land,

(b) a charge created or evidenced by an instrument which, if executed by an individual, would require registration as a bill of sale,

(c) a charge for the purposes of securing any issue of debentures,

(d) a charge on uncalled share capital of the company,

(e) a charge on calls made but not paid,

(f) a charge on book debts of the company,

(g) a floating charge on the company's property or undertaking,

(h) a charge on a ship or aircraft, or any share in a ship,

(i) a charge on goodwill or on any intellectual property.

10.82   This again mirrors s.396 of the 1985 Act, and again the 2006 Act is clear that where a negotiable instrument has been given to secure the payment of any book debt of a company, the deposit of the instrument for the purpose of securing an advance to the company is not for the purpose of registration to be treated as a charge on those book debts (s.861(3)). It also remains clear that in relation to charges on land it does not matter where the land charged is situated (s.861(2)) and that the holding of debentures entitling the holder to a charge on land is not deemed to be an interest in land (s.861(1)). Similarly 'intellectual property' remains defined as (s.861(4)):

(a) any patent, trade mark, registered design, copyright or design right;

(b) any licence under or in respect of any such right.

'Charge' continues to include mortgage (s.861(5)).

Special rules relating to debentures

10.83   The 2006 Act brings together special rules relating to debentures which amplify the previous provisions of the 1985 Act, s.397.

10.84   The first set of provisions address specifically the issue of a series of debentures which create a charge. The 2006 Act, s.863 provides:

> Where a series of debentures containing, or giving by reference to another instrument, any charge to the benefit of which debenture holders of that series are entitled *pari passu* is created by a company, it is for the purposes of section 860(1) sufficient if the required particulars, together with the deed containing the charge (or, if there is no such deed, one of the debentures of the series), are delivered to the registrar before the end of the period allowed for registration.

The 1985 Act simply required the deed and the particulars to be delivered to the registrar within 21 days after execution of the deed. The accompanying particulars required remain unchanged and are under s.863(2):

(a) the total amount secured by the whole series, and
(b) the dates of the resolutions authorising the issue of the series and the date of the covering deed (if any) by which the series is created or defined, and
(c) a general description of the property charged, and
(d) the names of the trustees (if any) for the debenture holders.

10.85 Further, the registrar must be sent particulars of the date and amount of each issue of debentures in a series so that these can be entered into the register of charges (s.863(3)).

10.86 Failure to comply continues to have no effect on the validity of the debentures issued (s.863(4)).

Additional requirement in respect of commissions relating to debentures

10.87 The requirements in respect of commissions relating to debentures contained in s.397(2) of the 1985 Act are continued by s.864(1):

Where any commission, allowance or discount has been paid or made either directly or indirectly by a company to a person in consideration of his –

(a) subscribing or agreeing to subscribe, whether absolutely or conditionally, for debentures in a company, or
(b) procuring or agreeing to procure subscriptions, whether absolute or conditional, for such debentures,

the particulars required to be sent for registration under section 860 shall include particulars as to the amount or rate per cent of the commission, discount or allowance so paid or made.

10.88 The deposit of debentures as security for the debt of a company continues to be treated as not issuing the debentures at a discount (s.864(2)), and failure to comply with the registration does not affect the validity of the debentures (s.864(3)).

Endorsement of certificate on debenture

10.89 The requirement that the company must cause a copy of every certificate of registration to be endorsed on every debenture or certificate of debenture stock affected, which was contained in the 1985 Act, s.402, is continued on identical terms by the 2006 Act, s.865.

Charges in or over property in other jurisdictions

10.90 Charges in or over property in other jurisdictions can fall into two categories. First, the charge may be by a UK company in or over property in a non-UK jurisdiction; secondly, the charge may be that of a UK company (e.g. an English company) in one UK jurisdiction in or over property in another UK jurisdiction (e.g. Scotland). The two situations were treated differently under s.398 of the 1985 Act, and this continues under the new Act.

Charges over property in non-UK jurisdictions

10.91 In respect of charges created in or over property in jurisdictions outside the United Kingdom, s.866(1) provides that:

> Where a charge is created outside the United Kingdom comprising property situated outside the United Kingdom, the delivery to the registrar of a verified copy of the instrument by which the charge is created or evidenced has the same effect for the purposes of this Chapter as the delivery of the instrument itself.

10.92 Section 866 further provides (s.866(2)):

> Where a charge is created in the United Kingdom but comprises property outside the United Kingdom, the instrument creating or purporting to create the charge may be sent for registration under section 860 even if further proceedings may be necessary to make the charge valid or effectual according to the law of the country in which the property is situated.

10.93 This is substantially the same as under the 1985 Act.

Charges over property in other UK jurisdictions

10.94 In respect of charges by a company registered in one part of the UK created by or over property in another jurisdiction in the UK (e.g. an English company and a Scottish or Northern Ireland property) the provisions are the same as under the 1985 Act. The 2006 provision applies where (s.867):

(a) a charge comprises property situated in a part of the UK other than the part in which the company is registered, and
(b) registration in that other part is necessary to make the charge valid or effectual under the law of that part of the United Kingdom.

10.95 In these circumstances, s.867(2) provides:

> The delivery to the registrar of a verified copy of the instrument by which the charge is created or evidenced, together with a certificate stating that the charge was presented for registration in that other part of the United Kingdom on the date on which it was so presented has . . . the same effect as the delivery of the instrument itself.

Northern Ireland

10.96 The provisions of the 2006 Act relating to charges discussed here are substantially the same for both England and Wales and Northern Ireland. However, in the latter jurisdiction this creates special issues in respect of changes affecting land given the system of land registration there and special provisions dealing with this are contained in s.868. This is beyond the scope of this book, and so s.868 is set out in full below with no further discussion.

868 Northern Ireland: registration of certain charges etc. affecting land

(1) Where a charge imposed by an order under Article 46 of the 1981 Order or notice of such a charge is registered in the Land Registry against registered land or any estate in registered land of a company, the Registrar of Titles shall as soon as may be cause two copies of the order made under Article 46 of that Order or of any notice under Article 48 of that Order to be delivered to the registrar.

(2) Where a charge imposed by an order under Article 46 of the 1981 Order is registered in the Registry of Deeds against any unregistered land or estate in land of a company, the Registrar of Deeds shall as soon as may be cause two copies of the order to be delivered to the registrar.

(3) On delivery of copies under this section, the registrar shall –
    (a) register one of them in accordance with section 869, and
    (b) not later than 7 days from that date of delivery, cause the other copy together with a certificate of registration under section 869(5) to be sent to the company against which judgment was given.

(4) Where a charge to which subsection (1) or (2) applies is vacated, the Registrar of Titles or, as the case may be, the Registrar of Deeds shall cause a certified copy of the certificate of satisfaction lodged under Article 132(1) of the 1981 Order to be delivered to the registrar for entry of a memorandum of satisfaction in accordance with section 872.

(5) In this section –

'the 1981 Order' means the Judgments Enforcement (Northern Ireland) Order 1981 (S.I. 1981/226 N.I.6));

'the Registrar of Deeds' means the registrar appointed under the Registration of Deeds Act (Northern Ireland) 1970; (c.25)

'Registry of Deeds' has the same meaning as in the Registration of Deeds Acts;

'Registration of Deeds Acts' means the Registration of Deeds (Northern Ireland) 1970 and every statutory provision for the time being in force amending that Act or otherwise relating to the registry of deeds, or the registration of deeds, orders or other instruments or documents in such registry;

'the Land Registry' and 'the Registrar of Titles' are to be construed in accordance with section 1 of the Land Registration Act (Northern Ireland) 1970 (c.18);

'registered land' and 'unregistered land' have the same meaning as in Part 3 of the Land Registration Act (Northern Ireland) 1970.

Register of charges

10.97   The duties imposed by the 1985 Act, s.401 on the registrar of companies to keep a register of charges are contained in similar language in s.869. On the register as before he must enter the particulars required to be given in the case of a charge to the benefit of which the holders of a series of debentures are entitled. In other cases he must enter (s.869(4)):

(a) if it is a charge created by a company, the date of its creation and, if it is a charge which was existing on property acquired by the company, the date of acquisition,
(b) the amount secured by the charge,

(c)   short particulars of the property charged, and

(d)   the persons entitled to the charge.

10.98   He is also obliged to give a signed or sealed certificate of the registration of any charge registered stating the amount secured by the charge which is conclusive evidence that the registration requirements have been satisfied (s.869(5), (6)). The register of charges continues to be open to inspection by any person (s.869(7)).

Time for registration

10.99   The 2006 Act, s.870 usefully brings together into a single section the provisions relating to the periods allowed for registration previously contained in ss.395 and 400 of the 1985 Act. The general period allowed remains at 21 days beginning, in the case of a charge created by a company, with the day on which the charge is created or, in the case of the registration of a charge to which property acquired by a company is subject, with the day after the date on which the acquisition is completed. However, if the charge is created outside the United Kingdom or if the property charged is situated and the charge created outside the United Kingdom, the period is 21 days beginning with the day after the day on which the instrument by which the charge is created or evidenced (or a copy of it) could, in due course of post (and if despatched with due diligence) have been received in the UK (s.870(1) and (2)).

10.100   In the case of a series of debentures the required particulars must be registered (s.870(3)):

(a)   if there is a deed containing the charge . . ., 21 days beginning with the day after the day on which that deed is executed, or

(b)   if there is no such deed, 21 days beginning with the day after the day on which the first debenture of the series is executed.

Registration of enforcement of security

10.101   The 1985 Act, s.405 contains provisions dealing with the registration of enforcement of security by giving notice of an order for the appointment of a receiver or manager of a company's property, or the appointment of such a receiver or manager under powers contained in an instrument, and these are contained in s.871 on the same terms. The registration period remains seven days.

Entries of satisfaction and release

10.102   Section 872 simplifies the complex provisions relating to entries of satisfaction and release contained in s.403 of the 1985 Act. Under the new simpler provisions the registrar may enter on the register a memorandum of satisfaction in whole or in part, or of the fact that part of the property or undertaking has been released from the charge or has ceased to form part of the company's property or undertaking (as the case may be).

10.103   He can exercise this power if a statement is delivered to him verifying with respect to the registration charge either (s.872(1)):

(a)   that the debt for which the charge was given has been paid or satisfied in whole or in part, or
(b)   that part of the property or undertaking charged has been released from the charge or has ceased to form part of the company's property or undertaking.

10.104   Where the registrar exercises the power to enter a memorandum of satisfaction in whole he must send a copy to the company.

Rectification of register of charges

10.105   The power conferred on the court to rectify the register of charges in respect of failures to register charges in time in appropriate cases (contained in s.404 of the 1985 Act) is continued in s.873 of the 2006 Act. The circumstances in which the power arises remain unchanged. Where it arises, on the application of the company or a person interested, the court can order that the period allowed for registration should be extended or that the omission or mis-statement should be corrected.

Consequences of failure to register

10.106   Subject to the court's power of rectification the consequences of failure to register prescribed by s.395 of the 1985 Act are continued by s.874 so that such a charge is void against a liquidator, administrator and creditor of the company. This however continues to be without prejudice to any contract or obligation for repayment of the money secured; and when a charge becomes void under this section, the money secured by it immediately becomes payable (s.874(3)).

Companies to keep copies of instruments creating charge

10.107   The obligation imposed by s.406 of the 1985 Act on companies to keep copies of instruments creating charges at their registered office is continued by s.875. If there is a series of uniform debentures, it is sufficient to keep a copy of one of the debentures.

Company's register of charges

10.108   The obligation on a company to keep a register of charges currently contained in s.407 of the 1985 Act is continued under s.876 with slightly different wording.

(1) Every limited company shall keep available for inspection a register of charges and enter in it –
    (a) all charges specifically affecting the property of the company, and
    (b) all floating charges on the whole or part of the company's property or undertaking.
(2) The entry shall in each case give a short description of the property charged, the amount of the charge and, except in the cases of securities to bearer, the names of the persons entitled to it.

10.109   The consequences of breach remain criminal rather than civil. An officer of the company who knowingly and wilfully authorises or permits the omission of an entry required to be made commits an offence punishable by a fine (s.876(3) and (4)).

Right to inspect instruments which create charges

10.110   The rights to inspect documents creating charges and registers of charges at present contained in s.408 of the 1985 Act are contained in the same terms by s.877 of the 2006 Act.

Companies registered in Scotland

10.111   Part 25, Chapter 2 of the 2006 Act (like the 1985 Act) makes detailed specific provisions for Scotland. This is beyond the scope of this book, and none of the authors are authorities on Scottish law, but the effect would seem to be to adapt the law of Scotland to a similar regime to that of the rest of the UK.

Powers of the Secretary of State

10.112   Powers are conferred on the Secretary of State by Part 25, Chapter 3 of the Act, one set being specific and the second set general.

Power to make provision for registration in special register

10.113   The specific power is a power to make provision for registration in a special register for the purpose of information sharing, that is, arrangements to share and make use of information on the register. Where satisfactory information sharing arrangements have been made the charge can be registered in a special register and may be exempted from the requirement to be registered on the general register in order to be valid (s.893).

General power to make amendments to the registration of charges requirement

10.114   The Secretary of State is given power by the use of the affirmative resolution procedure to amend the requirements as to registration of charges by altering, adding, or repealing provisions and to make consequential amendments and repeals in the 2006 Act and any other enactment (s.894).

CONTROL OF POLITICAL DONATIONS AND EXPENDITURE

10.115 The issue of the use of corporate funds for funding political parties has been a sensitive one for some years. It was, therefore, no surprise that it was put forward as a matter for consideration to the Committee of Standards in Public Life when it deliberated on the funding of political parties in the UK, and that the Committee included recommendations in the report which it presented to the Prime Minister in October 1998. The Report recommended that any company intending to make a donation (whether in cash or kind, by sponsorship or loans or transactions at a favourable rate) to a particular party or organisation should first obtain the prior authority of its shareholders, thus increasing the democratic control of the membership of the company over the process. The Government accepted the principle and implemented it through the Political Parties, Elections and Referendums Act 2000 (PPERA 2000) which to some extent stands independently but also inserted a new Part 10A into the Companies Act 1985 (see PPERA 2000, s.139 and Sched.19).

10.116 The 2006 Act deals with the topic in Part 14, restating the framework established by PPERA 2000 with necessary stylistic changes to ensure consistency with changes elsewhere within the 2006 Act but with some changes of substance. The broad principle of the legislation remains that a company must not make political donations exceeding £5,000 per annum nor incur political expenditure unless authorised by a resolution of its members (ss.366 and 378). If contributions are made or expenditure incurred without authority, the directors at the time when these were made are liable to reimburse the company with interest as well as compensating the company for any loss or damage sustained by it as a result of the unauthorised donation or expenditure (s.369).

Political donation

10.117 The concept of a political donation continues to be defined by reference to PPERA 2000, ss.50–52. More specifically under the 2006 Act, s.364 'political donation' means anything falling within PPERA 2000, ss.50–52 as constituting 'a donation for the purposes of Chapter 1 of Part 4 of that Act' or 'would constitute such a donation reading references in those sections to a registered party as references to any political party or other organisation'. Thus, as well as referring to PPERA 2000 it is also necessary to take into account the extensive meaning given to political parties or other organisations in s.364.

Political parties and organisations

10.118   Section 363 of the 2006 Act applies the provisions of Part 14 of the 2006 Act to a political party if it is registered under PPERA 2000, Part 2 or if 'it carries on or proposes to carry on activities for the purposes of, or in connection with, the participation of the party in any elections to public office in an EU member State other than the UK'. Part 14 also applies to 'an independent election candidate at any election to public office held in the United Kindom or another member State'. It also applies to any organisation ('political organisation') if it carries on or proposes to carry on, activities which are capable of being reasonably regarded as intended either 'to affect public support for a political party to which, or an independent election candidate to whom [Part 14] applies', or 'to influence voters in relation to any national or regional referendum held under the law of the United Kingdom or another member State' (s.363).

10.119   An 'organisation' includes any body corporate or unincorporated association and any combination of persons (s.379).

Political expenditure

10.120   The political expenditure of a company has a twofold parallel definition. First, it is expenditure on (s.365(1)(a)):

> the preparation, publication or dissemination of advertising or other promotional or publicity material –
>
> (i)   of whatever nature, and
> (ii) however published or otherwise disseminated,
>
> that, at the time of publication or dissemination, is capable of being reasonably regarded as intended to affect public support for a political party or other political organisation, or an independent election candidate . . .

Secondly, s.365(1)(b) provides that it is:

> activities on the part of the company that are capable of being reasonably regarded as intended –
>
> (i)   to affect public support for a political party or other political organisation, or an independent election candidate, or
> (ii) to influence voters in relation to any national or regional referendum held under the law of a member State.

The concepts of 'political donation' and 'political expenditure' are mutually exclusive since s.365(2) provides that a political donation does not count as political expenditure.

Authorisation

10.121   The central provision of the legislation is s.366(1) which provides that a company must not make a political donation or incur any political expenditure unless that donation or expenditure is first authorised in accordance with the Act. In the case of a company which is not the subsidiary of another company authorisation is by a resolution of that company; in the case of a subsidiary authorisation is by resolutions of both the members of the company and those of the holding company (s.366(2)). However, no resolution is required on the part of a company which is the wholly owned subsidiary of a UK company. The detail makes it clear that in respect of holding companies there are two significant changes. First, a holding company must authorise a donation or expenditure by a subsidiary company only if it is a 'relevant holding company' i.e. the ultimate holding company or, where such a company is not a 'UK company' the holding company the highest up the chain which is a 'UK company'. Secondly, a holding company is permitted under the new law to seek authorisation of donations and expenditure in respect of itself and one or more subsidiaries (including wholly owned subsidiaries) through a single approval resolution (s.367(1)(c)). The special rules applicable to the parent company of a non-UK subsidiary undertaking under the 1985 Act, ss.347E and 347G are discontinued.

10.122   An approval resolution may authorise the making of donations and incurring of expenditure for a period of not more than four years starting with the date of the resolution up to a total value authorised by the resolution (s.368). Section 367 requires that in some circumstances donations or expenditure by a subsidiary must be authorised by a resolution of the members of the holding company. Where such authorisation is not duly obtained the directors of the holding company continue to be liable for the unauthorised donations (s.369).

Time of donation or expenditure

10.123   The obligations created by the legislation make it important to be clear as to the time at which the donation or expenditure under review are made or incurred. This is largely a factual matter but the provisions do specify that, except as otherwise provided, any reference to the time at which a donation is made or expenditure incurred is, in a case where the donation is made or expenditure incurred in pursuance of a contract, any earlier time at which that contract is entered into by the company. Consequently where action is taken pursuant to a pre-existing contractual liability it is the date the contractual obligation was entered into which is the relevant date (s.379(2)).

Miscellaneous

10.124   The 2006 Act removes references to the general meeting (a feature of the earlier legislation) so as to make it clear that private companies can authorise donations and expenditure by written resolution. A company may now table separate approval resolutions in respect of donations to political parties and donations to other political organisations (s.367(3)). As noted companies are now required to seek authorisation for donations to independent candidates at any election to public office held in the UK or other EU Member States, and for expenditure by the company relating to independent election candidates.

Exempt donations and expenditure

10.125   Certain donations and expenditure are exempted, namely those to trade unions and all-party political groups which are not classified as political organisations (ss.374 and 376). The provision with regard to trade unions is new. Donations not amounting to more than £5,000 in any 12-month period are exempt (s.378), as are subscriptions paid for membership of trade associations to the extent the payment is made for the purpose of financing any particular activity of the association (s.375). The Explanatory Notes accompanying the Bill explain that it did not seek to introduce a specific exemption in relation to paid leave for local councillors because this is not considered to constitute a political donation under the legislation.

Directors' liability

10.126   Significant changes are made to the liability of directors (including shadow directors) for unauthorised donations or expenditure by s.369. The directors in default are jointly and severally liable both to make good to the company the amount of the unauthorised donation with interest and, further, to compensate the company for any loss or damage sustained by it as a result of the unauthorised payment having been made (s.369(2)). The directors will be both those of the company which made the payment and, where there is a relevant holding company, any directors of that company who fail to take all reasonable steps to prevent the payment being made. Thus where it is a subsidiary which makes the payment both the directors of the subsidiary and the culpable directors of the holding company will be liable.

Enforcement of directors' duties by company

10.127   The directors' duties in this respect are of course enforceable by the company. They are also enforceable by shareholder action by virtue of s.370 which provides that any liability is enforceable in the name of the company by an authorised group of its members. An authorised group means (s.370(3)):

(a)   the holders of not less than 5 per cent in nominal value of the company's issued share capital, or

(b)   if the company is not limited by shares, not less than 5 per cent of its members, or

(c)   not less than 50 of the company's members.

10.128   Prior to bringing shareholder proceedings the group of members must give written notice to the company stating (s.371(1)):

(a) the cause of action and a summary of the facts in which the proceedings are based,
(b) the names and addresses of the members comprising the group, and
(c) the grounds on which it is alleged that these members constitute an authorised group . . .

10.129   They must then allow 28 days to elapse prior to bringing the proceedings (s.371(1)(b)). On receipt of such a notice by the company any director may apply to the court within the 28-day period for an order directing that the proposed proceedings should not be brought on one, or more, of the following grounds (s.371(2)):

(a) that the unauthorised amount has been made good to the company;
(b) that proceedings to enforce the liability have been brought, and are being pursued with due diligence, by the company;
(c) that the members proposing to bring proceedings under this section do not constitute an authorised group.

Group's right to information

10.130   Where proceedings have been brought, the group can require the company to provide it with 'all information relating to the subject matter of the proceedings that is in the company's possession or under its control or which is reasonably obtainable by it'. If the company then refuses to provide the group with that information, the group can apply to the court to order the company and any of its officers and employees specified in the application to provide the group with the information in question (s.373).

Powers of court

10.131   A wide discretion is conferred on the court in dealing with such an application. The members by whom the shareholder action is brought owe the same duties to the company in relation to the proceedings as would be owed by directors to that company if the proceedings were being brought by the company. Shareholder proceedings may not be discontinued or settled by the group without the permission of the court (s.371(4) and (5)).

Costs

10.132   The group may apply to the court for an order that the company indemnify it for the costs incurred, but if no such order is made, the group is not entitled to any of its costs out of the assets of the company (ss.372(2) and (3)).

10.133   If no order for indemnity in favour of the group is made two courses of action are available to the court. The company may be awarded costs in connection with the proceedings, or there may be an agreement that defendant directors should pay the costs of the company. In these cases the costs must be paid to the group (s.372(4)). Equally, defendant directors may be awarded costs or there may be agreement that directors' costs should be paid, in which case the costs are born by the group of shareholders (s.372(4)).

ARRANGEMENTS AND RECONSTRUCTION

10.134   As with company charges, the Bill originally introduced by the Government for company law reform contained no provisions with regard to the subject of arrangements and reconstructions, leaving them to be governed by the 1985 Act, Part 13. Again subsequently it was felt that it would be better if provisions governing this topic were included in the 2006 Act and by the time the Bill emerged from Standing Committee D provisions to this end had been added. Those provisions constitute Part 26 of the 2006 Act, and aim to reproduce the substance of the previous legislation but in clearer language and arrangement.

Application of provisions

10.135   The provisions of the 2006 Act apply where a compromise or arrangement is proposed either between a company and its creditors, or any class of them, or between a company and its members, or any class of them (s.895(1)), mirroring the opening of the 1985 Act, s.425. For the purpose of this Part of the Act 'arrangement' includes a 'reorganisation of the company's share capital by the consolidation of shares of different classes or by the division of shares into shares of different classes, or by both of these methods' (s.895(2)). Apart from in s.900, 'company' means any company liable to be wound up under the Insolvency Act 1986 or the Insolvency (Northern Ireland) Order 1989 (SI 1989/2405)).

Application for court approval

10.136   The possible applicants for a court order sanctioning the proposed compromise or arrangement remain the same as under s.425(1) of the 1985 Act. The possible applicants are (s.899(2)):

(a) the company;
(b) any creditor or member of the company; or
(c) if the company is being wound up or if there is an administration order in force relating to the company, the liquidator or administrator.

Meeting ordered by court

10.137   On receiving an effective application the court is empowered to order a meeting of the creditors or class of creditors, or of the members of the company or class of members (as the case may be), to be summoned in such manner as the court directs (s.896). The holding of such a meeting is a condition precedent to the court's use of its powers.

Notice of meeting

10.138   Section 426 of the 1985 Act required extensive information of the compromise to be circulated prior to the meeting and these requirements are continued by s.897 of the 2006 Act. Where a meeting is summoned every notice summoning the meeting which is sent to a creditor or member must contain a statement explaining the effect of the compromise or arrangement. In addition, every notice given by advertisement must either give this information or state where and how creditors or members entitled to attend the meeting may obtain copies. The statement explaining the effect of the compromise or arrangement must, in particular, state both any material interest of the directors of the company (whether as directors or as members or as creditors of the company or otherwise), and the effect on those interests of the compromise or arrangement, in so far as it is different from the effect on the like interests of other persons (s.897(2)).

10.139   Further, where the compromise or arrangement affects the rights of debenture holders of the company, the statement must 'give the like explanation as respects the trustees of any deed for securing the issue of the debentures as it is required to give as respects the company's directors' (s.897(3)). Finally, where 'a notice given by advertisement states that copies of an explanatory statement can be obtained by creditors or members entitled to attend the meeting, every such creditor or member is entitled, on making application in the manner indicated by the notice, to be provided by the company with a copy of the statement free of charge' (s.897(4)).

10.140   Once again the consequences of breach are criminal. If a company defaults in complying with the requirements to give the required information an offence is committed by the company and every officer in default, and for this purpose both a liquidator or administrator of the company and a trustee of a deed for securing the issue of debentures to the company are treated as officers of the company. The possible punishment is a fine (s.897(8)). However, a person is not guilty of an offence under this section if he shows that the default was due to the refusal of a director or trustee for debenture holders to supply the necessary particulars of his interests.

Duty of directors and trustees to provide information

10.141   The ability of the company and its officers to obtain information necessary to be circulated is assisted by the continuation of the duty of any director of the company and any trustee for its debenture holders to give notice to the company of such matters relating to himself as may be necessary for the requirements to be met. Any person in default commits an offence punishable by a fine. This duty, found in s.426(7) of the 1985 Act, is continued by s.898.

Sanctioning the arrangements

10.142   The rules for the court sanctioning the compromise or arrangement remain unchanged from those contained in s.425 of the 1985 Act. Under s.899(1) the court may sanction a compromise or arrangement only if, at the meeting summoned under s.896, a majority in number representing 75 per cent in value of the creditors or class of creditors or members or class of members (as the case may be), present and voting either in person or by proxy at the meeting, agree to the compromise or arrangement.

10.143   If sanctioned by the court a compromise or arrangement is binding on (s.899(3)):

    (a)   all creditors or the class of creditors or on the members or the class of members (as the case may be), and

    (b)   the company or, in the case of a company in the course of being wound up, the liquidator and contributories of the company.

The court's order has no effect until a copy of it has been delivered to the registrar of companies for registration (1985 Act, s.425(3) and 2006 Act, s.899(4)).

Court powers to facilitate reconstruction and amalgamation

10.144   As well as having power to make an order the court is also empowered to make orders to facilitate the amalgamation or reconstruction of the company once application for an order is made to it. These powers are at present to be found in s.427 of the 1985 Act, and are contained in s.900 of the 2006 Act. In both Acts the definition of the company for these purposes differs from that applied to the earlier sections dealing with amalgamation and reconstruction, applying now simply to a company within the meaning of the Act generally.

Bringing the powers into play

10.145   The court's powers will come into play if on an application for an order for reconstruction and amalgamation it is shown that (s.900(1)):

    (a)   the compromise or arrangement is proposed for the purposes of, or in connection with, a scheme for the reconstruction of any company or companies, or the amalgamation of any two or more companies; and

(b) under the scheme the whole or any part of the undertaking or the property of any company concerned in the scheme ('a transferor company') is to be transferred to another company ('the transferee company').

The powers available

10.146   Either by the order sanctioning the compromise or arrangement or by any subsequent order, the court may make provision for (s.900(2)):

(a) the transfer to the transferee company of the whole or any part of the under-taking and of the property or liabilities of any transferor company;
(b) the allotting or appropriation by the transferee company of any shares, debentures, policies or other like interests in that company which under the compromise or arrangement are to be allotted or appropriated by that company to or for any person;
(c) the continuation by or against the transferee company of any legal proceedings pending by or against any transferor company;
(d) the dissolution, without winding up, of any transferor company;
(e) the provision to be made for any persons who, within such time and in such manner as the court directs, dissent from the compromise or arrangement;
(f) such incidental, consequential and supplemental matters as are necessary to secure that the reconstruction or amalgamation is fully and effectively carried out.

10.147   Section 900(3) provides that:

If such an order provides for the transfer of property or liabilities –

(a) the property is by virtue of the order transferred to, and vests in, the transferee company, and
(b) the liabilities are, by virtue of the order, transferred to and become liabilities of that company.

Further, s.900(4) provides that:

The property (if the order so directs) vests freed from any charge that is by reason of the compromise or arrangement to cease to have effect.

For the purpose of the exercise of these facilitation powers 'property' includes property, rights and powers of every description, and 'liabilities' include duties.

Registration of facilitation orders

10.148   The requirement for registration of facilitation orders at present contained in s.427(5) of the 1985 Act is continued by s.900(6), which requires every company in relation to which the order is made to deliver a copy to the registrar for registration within seven days of its making. Default renders the company and every officer in default guilty of an offence (s.900(7)).

Publication of constitutional changes

10.149   The requirements for publication of an order contained in the 1985 Act, ss.425(3) are continued by the 2006 Act in an amended form and are made applicable to both court orders sanctioning a compromise or arrangement and those facilitating reconstruction or amalgamation. The new provisions will be found in s.901. Section 901(2) provides:

> If the order amends:
>
> (a) the company's articles, or
> (b) any resolution or agreement to which Chapter 3 of Part 3 applies (resolution or agreement affecting a company's constitution),
>
> the copy of the order delivered to the registrar by the company . . . must be accompanied by a copy of the company's articles, or the resolution or agreement in question, as amended.

Unless the effect of the order is incorporated into the articles by amendment, after the order is made any copy of the company's articles issued by the company must also be accompanied by a copy of the order (s.901(3)). Default in complying with these provisions renders the company and any officer who is in default liable, on conviction, to a fine.

DEBENTURES

10.150   There continues to be no requirement for a company to maintain a register of debenture holders but, if a company chooses to maintain such a register, this must be kept available for public inspection in the same way as the company's register of members (s.743).

10.151   There are provisions for the protection of debenture holders from use of the right of public access to this register for an improper purpose; these provisions are similar to the provisions as to access to the register of members (s.116–119), as described in **Chapter 3**.

10.152   Certain changes made by s.610 as to the permitted uses of the company's share premium account were noted in **Chapter 8**. Other changes are that the section does not permit the use of the share premium account for writing off expenses incurred, commission paid or discount allowed in respect of an issue of debentures or for providing for the premium payable on a redemption of debentures.

PRIVATE AND PUBLIC COMPANIES

Introduction

10.153   As described in **Chapter 2**, the definitions of private and public companies remain the same.

Offer of shares to the public

10.154   The rule that a private company may not offer its shares to the public remains (s.755) but, in a change from s.81 of the 1985 Act, a breach of this provision is not a criminal offence.

10.155   There are new provisions for enforcement of the prohibition:

1. If there is a proposed contravention of the prohibition, a restraining order may be made (s.757). An application for such an order may be made by a member, a creditor or the Secretary of State (s.757(3)).
2. If the company has already acted in contravention of the prohibition, the court can order that the company must re-register as a public company unless the company does not meet the requirements for re-registration as a public company and it is impractical or undesirable for the court to order it to do so. As an alternative, the court can make a remedial order under s.759 (see below) and/or an order that the company be compulsorily wound up (s.758(3)). An application for an order under this section may be made by a member, a creditor or the Secretary of State (s.758(4)); those who are eligible to make an application are therefore the same as in relation to a proposed contravention, except that the member or creditor must have been a member or creditor at the time of the offer (or, in the case of a member, have become such as a result of the offer).
3. A remedial order may be made for the restoration of the position of a person affected by anything done in breach of the prohibition (s.759). Such an order may, for example, require that the shares be purchased by the company or any person knowingly concerned in the contravention.
4. It is provided (in s.760) that these provisions do not affect the validity of any allotment of shares or agreement to allot shares.

ANNUAL RETURN

Introduction

10.156   Sections 363–365 of the 1985 Act set out the duty to deliver annual returns and the contents thereof. The contents required under those provisions included the 'usual residential address' of the company secretary and every director and the 'addresses' of members (both current members and those who ceased to be member since the last return).

Contents of the annual return

10.157   The obligation to file annual returns is preserved by ss.854–859 of the 2006 Act and much of the information required in the annual return is unchanged.

10.158   However, there are certain changes:

1.   In relation to the company's directors and its secretary, rather than following the approach in the 1985 Act, s.364 of specifying the information required, s.855 requires 'prescribed particulars'. Thus, the Secretary of State will prescribe the required information by regulations. Presumably this will reflect the changes noted elsewhere in this book designed to protect those involved with a company from threats of intimidation or violence targeted towards them using information publicly available (such as residential addresses).

2.   In relation to members of the company at the date to which the return is made up (and those who have ceased to be members since the date of the last return), s.856 similarly requires 'prescribed particulars' of each person, as well as the number of shares held by each member.

3.   For companies having a share capital, the annual return must contain a statement of capital with the information usually required of a statement of capital under the Act.

Appendix 1
COMPANIES ACT 2006

PART 1

GENERAL INTRODUCTORY PROVISIONS

PART 2

COMPANY FORMATION

PART 3

A COMPANY'S CONSTITUTION

CHAPTER 1

INTRODUCTORY

CHAPTER 2

ARTICLES OF ASSOCIATION

General

Alteration of articles

Supplementary

CHAPTER 3

RESOLUTIONS AND AGREEMENTS AFFECTING A COMPANY'S CONSTITUTION

CHAPTER 4

MISCELLANEOUS AND SUPPLEMENTARY PROVISIONS

Statement of company's objects

PART 4

A COMPANY'S CAPACITY AND RELATED MATTERS

PART 5

A COMPANY'S NAME

CHAPTER 1

GENERAL REQUIREMENTS

Sensitive words and expressions

Permitted characters etc

CHAPTER 2

INDICATIONS OF COMPANY TYPE OR LEGAL FORM

Required indications for limited companies

Inappropriate use of indications of company type or legal form

CHAPTER 3

SIMILARITY TO OTHER NAMES

Similarity to other name on registrar's index

Similarity to other name in which person has goodwill

CHAPTER 4

OTHER POWERS OF THE SECRETARY OF STATE

CHAPTER 5

CHANGE OF NAME

CHAPTER 6

TRADING DISCLOSURES

PART 6

A COMPANY'S REGISTERED OFFICE

General

Welsh companies

PART 7

RE-REGISTRATION AS A MEANS OF ALTERING A COMPANY'S STATUS

Introductory

Private company becoming public

PART 8

A COMPANY'S MEMBERS

CHAPTER 1

THE MEMBERS OF A COMPANY

CHAPTER 2

REGISTER OF MEMBERS

CHAPTER 3

OVERSEAS BRANCH REGISTERS

CHAPTER 4

PROHIBITION ON SUBSIDIARY BEING MEMBER OF ITS HOLDING COMPANY

PART 9

EXERCISE OF MEMBERS' RIGHTS

PART 10

A COMPANY'S DIRECTORS

CHAPTER 1

APPOINTMENT AND REMOVAL OF DIRECTORS

CHAPTER 2

GENERAL DUTIES OF DIRECTORS

CHAPTER 3

DECLARATION OF INTEREST IN EXISTING TRANSACTION OR ARRANGEMENT

CHAPTER 4

TRANSACTIONS WITH DIRECTORS REQUIRING APPROVAL OF MEMBERS

CHAPTER 5

DIRECTORS' SERVICE CONTRACTS

CHAPTER 6

CONTRACTS WITH SOLE MEMBERS WHO ARE DIRECTORS

CHAPTER 7

DIRECTORS' LIABILITIES

Provision protecting directors from liability

Ratification of acts giving rise to liability

CHAPTER 8

DIRECTORS' RESIDENTIAL ADDRESSES: PROTECTION FROM DISCLOSURE

CHAPTER 9

SUPPLEMENTARY PROVISIONS

Provision for employees on cessation or transfer of business

Records of meetings of directors

PART 11

DERIVATIVE CLAIMS AND PROCEEDINGS BY MEMBERS

CHAPTER 1

DERIVATIVE CLAIMS IN ENGLAND AND WALES OR NORTHERN IRELAND

CHAPTER 2

DERIVATIVE PROCEEDINGS IN SCOTLAND

PART 12

COMPANY SECRETARIES

PART 13

RESOLUTIONS AND MEETINGS

CHAPTER 1

GENERAL PROVISIONS ABOUT RESOLUTIONS

CHAPTER 2

WRITTEN RESOLUTIONS

CHAPTER 3

RESOLUTIONS AT MEETINGS

General provisions about resolutions at meetings

Calling meetings

Notice of meetings

Members' statements

Procedure at meetings

CHAPTER 4

PUBLIC COMPANIES: ADDITIONAL REQUIREMENTS FOR AGMS

CHAPTER 5

ADDITIONAL REQUIREMENTS FOR QUOTED COMPANIES

PART 15

ACCOUNTS AND REPORTS

CHAPTER 1

INTRODUCTION

CHAPTER 2

ACCOUNTING RECORDS

CHAPTER 3

A COMPANY'S FINANCIAL YEAR

CHAPTER 4

ANNUAL ACCOUNTS

General

Individual accounts

Group accounts: small companies

Group accounts: other companies

Group accounts: general

Information to be given in notes to the accounts

Approval and signing of accounts

CHAPTER 5

DIRECTORS' REPORT

Directors' report

CHAPTER 6

QUOTED COMPANIES: DIRECTORS' REMUNERATION REPORT

CHAPTER 7

PUBLICATION OF ACCOUNTS AND REPORTS

Duty to circulate copies of accounts and reports

Option to provide summary financial statement

Quoted companies: requirements as to website publication

Right of member or debenture holder to demand copies of accounts and reports

Requirements in connection with publication of accounts and reports

CHAPTER 8

PUBLIC COMPANIES: LAYING OF ACCOUNTS AND REPORTS BEFORE GENERAL MEETING

CHAPTER 9

QUOTED COMPANIES: MEMBERS' APPROVAL OF DIRECTORS' REMUNERATION REPORT

CHAPTER 10

FILING OF ACCOUNTS AND REPORTS

CHAPTER 11

REVISION OF DEFECTIVE ACCOUNTS AND REPORTS

CHAPTER 12

SUPPLEMENTARY PROVISIONS

PART 16

AUDIT

CHAPTER 1

REQUIREMENT FOR AUDITED ACCOUNTS

CHAPTER 2

APPOINTMENT OF AUDITORS

CHAPTER 3

FUNCTIONS OF AUDITOR

CHAPTER 4

REMOVAL, RESIGNATION, ETC OF AUDITORS

CHAPTER 5

QUOTED COMPANIES: RIGHT OF MEMBERS TO RAISE AUDIT CONCERNS AT ACCOUNTS MEETING

CHAPTER 6

AUDITORS' LIABILITY

Voidness of provisions protecting auditors from liability

Indemnity for costs of defending proceedings

Liability limitation agreements

CHAPTER 7

SUPPLEMENTARY PROVISIONS

PART 17

A COMPANY'S SHARE CAPITAL

CHAPTER 1

SHARES AND SHARE CAPITAL OF A COMPANY

Shares

CHAPTER 2

ALLOTMENT OF SHARES: GENERAL PROVISIONS

CHAPTER 3

ALLOTMENT OF EQUITY SECURITIES: EXISTING SHAREHOLDERS' RIGHT OF PRE-EMPTION

CHAPTER 4

PUBLIC COMPANIES: ALLOTMENT WHERE ISSUE NOT FULLY SUBSCRIBED

CHAPTER 5

PAYMENT FOR SHARES

CHAPTER 6

PUBLIC COMPANIES: INDEPENDENT VALUATION OF NON-CASH CONSIDERATION

CHAPTER 7

SHARE PREMIUMS

CHAPTER 10

REDUCTION OF SHARE CAPITAL

CHAPTER 11

MISCELLANEOUS AND SUPPLEMENTARY PROVISIONS

PART 18

ACQUISITION BY LIMITED COMPANY OF ITS OWN SHARES

CHAPTER 1

GENERAL PROVISIONS

CHAPTER 2

FINANCIAL ASSISTANCE FOR PURCHASE OF OWN SHARES

CHAPTER 3

REDEEMABLE SHARES

CHAPTER 4

PURCHASE OF OWN SHARES

General provisions

Authority for purchase of own shares

Authority for off-market purchase

Authority for market purchase

Supplementary provisions

CHAPTER 5

REDEMPTION OR PURCHASE BY PRIVATE COMPANY OUT OF CAPITAL

CHAPTER 6

TREASURY SHARES

CHAPTER 7

SUPPLEMENTARY PROVISIONS

PART 19

DEBENTURES

General provisions

Register of debenture holders

Supplementary provisions

PART 20

PRIVATE AND PUBLIC COMPANIES

CHAPTER 1

PROHIBITION OF PUBLIC OFFERS BY PRIVATE COMPANIES

CHAPTER 2

MINIMUM SHARE CAPITAL REQUIREMENT FOR PUBLIC COMPANIES

PART 21

CERTIFICATION AND TRANSFER OF SECURITIES

CHAPTER 1

CERTIFICATION AND TRANSFER OF SECURITIES: GENERAL

Share certificates

Issue of certificates etc on allotment

Transfer of securities

Issue of certificates etc on transfer

Issue of certificates etc on allotment or transfer to financial institution

PART 23

DISTRIBUTIONS

CHAPTER 1

RESTRICTIONS ON WHEN DISTRIBUTIONS MAY BE MADE

CHAPTER 2

JUSTIFICATION OF DISTRIBUTION BY REFERENCE TO ACCOUNTS

CHAPTER 3

SUPPLEMENTARY PROVISIONS

PART 24

A COMPANY'S ANNUAL RETURN

PART 25

COMPANY CHARGES

CHAPTER 1

COMPANIES REGISTERED IN ENGLAND AND WALES OR IN NORTHERN IRELAND

Requirement to register company charges

Special rules about debentures

Charges in other jurisdictions

Orders charging land: Northern Ireland

The register of charges

Avoidance of certain charges

CHAPTER 2

COMPANIES REGISTERED IN SCOTLAND

CHAPTER 3

POWERS OF THE SECRETARY OF STATE

CHAPTER 3

DIVISION

CHAPTER 4

SUPPLEMENTARY PROVISIONS

Expert's report and related matters

Powers of the court

Liability of transferee companies

Interpretation

PART 28

TAKEOVERS ETC

CHAPTER 1

THE TAKEOVER PANEL

The Panel and its rules

Information

Co-operation

Hearings and appeals

Contravention of rules etc

CHAPTER 2

IMPEDIMENTS TO TAKEOVERS

CHAPTER 3

"SQUEEZE-OUT" AND "SELL-OUT"

CHAPTER 4

AMENDMENTS TO PART 7 OF THE COMPANIES ACT 1985

PART 29

FRAUDULENT TRADING

PART 30

PROTECTION OF MEMBERS AGAINST UNFAIR PREJUDICE

PART 31

DISSOLUTION AND RESTORATION TO THE REGISTER

CHAPTER 1

STRIKING OFF

CHAPTER 2

PROPERTY OF DISSOLVED COMPANY

CHAPTER 3

RESTORATION TO THE REGISTER

PART 32

COMPANY INVESTIGATIONS: AMENDMENTS

PART 33

UK COMPANIES NOT FORMED UNDER COMPANIES LEGISLATION

CHAPTER 1

COMPANIES NOT FORMED UNDER COMPANIES LEGISLATION BUT AUTHORISED TO REGISTER

CHAPTER 2

UNREGISTERED COMPANIES

PART 34

OVERSEAS COMPANIES

PART 35

THE REGISTRAR OF COMPANIES

PART 36

OFFENCES UNDER THE COMPANIES ACTS

PART 39

COMPANIES: MINOR AMENDMENTS

PART 40

COMPANY DIRECTORS: FOREIGN DISQUALIFICATION ETC

PART 41

BUSINESS NAMES

CHAPTER 1

RESTRICTED OR PROHIBITED NAMES

CHAPTER 2

DISCLOSURE REQUIRED IN CASE OF INDIVIDUAL OR PARTNERSHIP

CHAPTER 5

REGISTERED THIRD COUNTRY AUDITORS

CHAPTER 6

SUPPLEMENTARY AND GENERAL

COMPANIES ACT 2006

An Act to reform company law and restate the greater part of the enactments relating to companies; to make other provision relating to companies and other forms of business organisation; to make provision about directors' disqualification, business names, auditors and actuaries; to amend Part 9 of the Enterprise Act 2002; and for connected purposes.

[8th November 2006]

BE IT ENACTED by the Queen's most Excellent Majesty, by and with the advice and consent of the Lords Spiritual and Temporal, and Commons, in this present parliament assembled, and by the authority of the same, as follows: –

PART 1

GENERAL INTRODUCTORY PROVISIONS

Companies and Companies Acts

1 Companies

(1) In the Companies Acts, unless the context otherwise requires –
"company" means a company formed and registered under this Act, that is –

   (a) a company so formed and registered after the commencement of this Part, or
   (b) a company that immediately before the commencement of this Part –

      (i) was formed and registered under the Companies Act 1985 (c. 6) or the Companies (Northern Ireland) Order 1986 (S.I. 1986/1032 (N.I. 6)), or
      (ii) was an existing company for the purposes of that Act or that Order,

   (which is to be treated on commencement as if formed and registered under this Act).

(2) Certain provisions of the Companies Acts apply to –

   (a) companies registered, but not formed, under this Act (see Chapter 1 of Part 33), and
   (b) bodies incorporated in the United Kingdom but not registered under this Act (see Chapter 2 of that Part).

(3) For provisions applying to companies incorporated outside the United Kingdom, see Part 34 (overseas companies).

2 The Companies Acts

(1) In this Act "the Companies Acts" means –

   (a) the company law provisions of this Act,
   (b) Part 2 of the Companies (Audit, Investigations and Community Enterprise) Act 2004 (c. 27) (community interest companies), and
   (c) the provisions of the Companies Act 1985 (c. 6) and the Companies Consolidation (Consequential Provisions) Act 1985 (c. 9) that remain in force.

(2) The company law provisions of this Act are –

   (a) the provisions of Parts 1 to 39 of this Act, and
   (b) the provisions of Parts 45 to 47 of this Act so far as they apply for the purposes of those Parts.

Types of company

3 Limited and unlimited companies

(1) A company is a "limited company" if the liability of its members is limited by its constitution.
It may be limited by shares or limited by guarantee.

(2) If their liability is limited to the amount, if any, unpaid on the shares held by them, the company is "limited by shares".

(3) If their liability is limited to such amount as the members undertake to contribute to the assets of the company in the event of its being wound up, the company is "limited by guarantee".

(4) If there is no limit on the liability of its members, the company is an "unlimited company".

4 Private and public companies

(1) A "private company" is any company that is not a public company.

(2) A "public company" is a company limited by shares or limited by guarantee and having a share capital –

  (a) whose certificate of incorporation states that it is a public company, and

  (b) in relation to which the requirements of this Act, or the former Companies Acts, as to registration or re-registration as a public company have been complied with on or after the relevant date.

(3) For the purposes of subsection (2)(b) the relevant date is –

  (a) in relation to registration or re-registration in Great Britain, 22nd December 1980;

  (b) in relation to registration or re-registration in Northern Ireland, 1st July 1983.

(4) For the two major differences between private and public companies, see Part 20.

5 Companies limited by guarantee and having share capital

(1) A company cannot be formed as, or become, a company limited by guarantee with a share capital.

(2) Provision to this effect has been in force –

  (a) in Great Britain since 22nd December 1980, and

  (b) in Northern Ireland since 1st July 1983.

(3) Any provision in the constitution of a company limited by guarantee that purports to divide the company's undertaking into shares or interests is a provision for a share capital.
This applies whether or not the nominal value or number of the shares or interests is specified by the provision.

6 Community interest companies

(1) In accordance with Part 2 of the Companies (Audit, Investigations and Community Enterprise) Act 2004 (c. 27) –

  (a) a company limited by shares or a company limited by guarantee and not having a share capital may be formed as or become a community interest company, and

  (b) a company limited by guarantee and having a share capital may become a community interest company.

(2) The other provisions of the Companies Acts have effect subject to that Part.

PART 2

COMPANY FORMATION

General

7 Method of forming company

(1) A company is formed under this Act by one or more persons –

    (a) subscribing their names to a memorandum of association (see section 8), and

    (b) complying with the requirements of this Act as to registration (see sections 9 to 13).

(2) A company may not be so formed for an unlawful purpose.

8 Memorandum of association

(1) A memorandum of association is a memorandum stating that the subscribers –

    (a) wish to form a company under this Act, and

    (b) agree to become members of the company and, in the case of a company that is to have a share capital, to take at least one share each.

(2) The memorandum must be in the prescribed form and must be authenticated by each subscriber.

Requirements for registration

9 Registration documents

(1) The memorandum of association must be delivered to the registrar together with an application for registration of the company, the documents required by this section and a statement of compliance.

(2) The application for registration must state –

    (a) the company's proposed name,

    (b) whether the company's registered office is to be situated in England and Wales (or in Wales), in Scotland or in Northern Ireland,

    (c) whether the liability of the members of the company is to be limited, and if so whether it is to be limited by shares or by guarantee, and

    (d) whether the company is to be a private or a public company.

(3) If the application is delivered by a person as agent for the subscribers to the memorandum of association, it must state his name and address.

(4) The application must contain –

    (a) in the case of a company that is to have a share capital, a statement of capital and initial shareholdings (see section 10);

    (b) in the case of a company that is to be limited by guarantee, a statement of guarantee (see section 11);

    (c) a statement of the company's proposed officers (see section 12).

(5) The application must also contain –

    (a) a statement of the intended address of the company's registered office; and

    (b) a copy of any proposed articles of association (to the extent that these are not supplied by the default application of model articles: see section 20).

(6) The application must be delivered –

    (a) to the registrar of companies for England and Wales, if the registered office of the company is to be situated in England and Wales (or in Wales);

(b) to the registrar of companies for Scotland, if the registered office of the company is to be situated in Scotland;

(c) to the registrar of companies for Northern Ireland, if the registered office of the company is to be situated in Northern Ireland.

10 Statement of capital and initial shareholdings

(1) The statement of capital and initial shareholdings required to be delivered in the case of a company that is to have a share capital must comply with this section.

(2) It must state –

(a) the total number of shares of the company to be taken on formation by the subscribers to the memorandum of association,

(b) the aggregate nominal value of those shares,

(c) for each class of shares –

    (i) prescribed particulars of the rights attached to the shares,

    (ii) the total number of shares of that class, and

    (iii) the aggregate nominal value of shares of that class, and

(d) the amount to be paid up and the amount (if any) to be unpaid on each share (whether on account of the nominal value of the share or by way of premium).

(3) It must contain such information as may be prescribed for the purpose of identifying the subscribers to the memorandum of association.

(4) It must state, with respect to each subscriber to the memorandum –

(a) the number, nominal value (of each share) and class of shares to be taken by him on formation, and

(b) the amount to be paid up and the amount (if any) to be unpaid on each share (whether on account of the nominal value of the share or by way of premium).

(5) Where a subscriber to the memorandum is to take shares of more than one class, the information required under subsection (4)(a) is required for each class.

11 Statement of guarantee

(1) The statement of guarantee required to be delivered in the case of a company that is to be limited by guarantee must comply with this section.

(2) It must contain such information as may be prescribed for the purpose of identifying the subscribers to the memorandum of association.

(3) It must state that each member undertakes that, if the company is wound up while he is a member, or within one year after he ceases to be a member, he will contribute to the assets of the company such amount as may be required for –

(a) payment of the debts and liabilities of the company contracted before he ceases to be a member,

(b) payment of the costs, charges and expenses of winding up, and

(c) adjustment of the rights of the contributories among themselves,

not exceeding a specified amount.

12 Statement of proposed officers

(1) The statement of the company's proposed officers required to be delivered to the registrar must contain the required particulars of –

(a) the person who is, or persons who are, to be the first director or directors of the company;

(b) in the case of a company that is to be a private company, any person who is (or any persons who are) to be the first secretary (or joint secretaries) of the company;

(c) in the case of a company that is to be a public company, the person who is (or the persons who are) to be the first secretary (or joint secretaries) of the company.

(2) The required particulars are the particulars that will be required to be stated –

(a) in the case of a director, in the company's register of directors and register of directors' residential addresses (see sections 162 to 166);

(b) in the case of a secretary, in the company's register of secretaries (see sections 277 to 279).

(3) The statement must also contain a consent by each of the persons named as a director, as secretary or as one of joint secretaries, to act in the relevant capacity.
If all the partners in a firm are to be joint secretaries, consent may be given by one partner on behalf of all of them.

13 Statement of compliance

(1) The statement of compliance required to be delivered to the registrar is a statement that the requirements of this Act as to registration have been complied with.

(2) The registrar may accept the statement of compliance as sufficient evidence of compliance.

Registration and its effect

14 Registration

If the registrar is satisfied that the requirements of this Act as to registration are complied with, he shall register the documents delivered to him.

15 Issue of certificate of incorporation

(1) On the registration of a company, the registrar of companies shall give a certificate that the company is incorporated.

(2) The certificate must state –

(a) the name and registered number of the company,

(b) the date of its incorporation,

(c) whether it is a limited or unlimited company, and if it is limited whether it is limited by shares or limited by guarantee,

(d) whether it is a private or a public company, and

(e) whether the company's registered office is situated in England and Wales (or in Wales), in Scotland or in Northern Ireland.

(3) The certificate must be signed by the registrar or authenticated by the registrar's official seal.

(4) The certificate is conclusive evidence that the requirements of this Act as to registration have been complied with and that the company is duly registered under this Act.

16 Effect of registration

(1) The registration of a company has the following effects as from the date of incorporation.

(2) The subscribers to the memorandum, together with such other persons as may from time to time become members of the company, are a body corporate by the name stated in the certificate of incorporation.

(3) That body corporate is capable of exercising all the functions of an incorporated company.

(4) The status and registered office of the company are as stated in, or in connection with, the application for registration.

(5) In the case of a company having a share capital, the subscribers to the memorandum become holders of the shares specified in the statement of capital and initial shareholdings.

(6) The persons named in the statement of proposed officers –

(a) as director, or
(b) as secretary or joint secretary of the company,

are deemed to have been appointed to that office.

PART 3

A COMPANY'S CONSTITUTION

CHAPTER 1

INTRODUCTORY

17 A company's constitution

Unless the context otherwise requires, references in the Companies Acts to a company's constitution include –

(a) the company's articles, and
(b) any resolutions and agreements to which Chapter 3 applies (see section 29).

CHAPTER 2

ARTICLES OF ASSOCIATION

General

18 Articles of association

(1) A company must have articles of association prescribing regulations for the company.
(2) Unless it is a company to which model articles apply by virtue of section 20 (default application of model articles in case of limited company), it must register articles of association.
(3) Articles of association registered by a company must –

(a) be contained in a single document, and
(b) be divided into paragraphs numbered consecutively.

(4) References in the Companies Acts to a company's "articles" are to its articles of association.

19 Power of Secretary of State to prescribe model articles

(1) The Secretary of State may by regulations prescribe model articles of association for companies.
(2) Different model articles may be prescribed for different descriptions of company.
(3) A company may adopt all or any of the provisions of model articles.
(4) Any amendment of model articles by regulations under this section does not affect a company registered before the amendment takes effect.
    "Amendment" here includes addition, alteration or repeal.
(5) Regulations under this section are subject to negative resolution procedure.

20 Default application of model articles

(1) On the formation of a limited company –

(a) if articles are not registered, or

(b) if articles are registered, in so far as they do not exclude or modify the relevant model articles,

the relevant model articles (so far as applicable) form part of the company's articles in the same manner and to the same extent as if articles in the form of those articles had been duly registered.

(2) The "relevant model articles" means the model articles prescribed for a company of that description as in force at the date on which the company is registered.

Alteration of articles

21 Amendment of articles

(1) A company may amend its articles by special resolution.
(2) In the case of a company that is a charity, this is subject to –

(a) in England and Wales, section 64 of the Charities Act 1993 (c. 10);
(b) in Northern Ireland, Article 9 of the Charities (Northern Ireland) Order 1987 (S.I. 1987/2048 (N.I. 19)).

(3) In the case of a company that is registered in the Scottish Charity Register, this is subject to –

(a) section 112 of the Companies Act 1989 (c. 40), and
(b) section 16 of the Charities and Trustee Investment (Scotland) Act 2005 (asp 10).

22 Entrenched provisions of the articles

(1) A company's articles may contain provision ("provision for entrenchment") to the effect that specified provisions of the articles may be amended or repealed only if conditions are met, or procedures are complied with, that are more restrictive than those applicable in the case of a special resolution.
(2) Provision for entrenchment may only be made –

(a) in the company's articles on formation, or
(b) by an amendment of the company's articles agreed to by all the members of the company.

(3) Provision for entrenchment does not prevent amendment of the company's articles –

(a) by agreement of all the members of the company, or
(b) by order of a court or other authority having power to alter the company's articles.

(4) Nothing in this section affects any power of a court or other authority to alter a company's articles.

23 Notice to registrar of existence of restriction on amendment of articles

(1) Where a company's articles –

(a) on formation contain provision for entrenchment,
(b) are amended so as to include such provision, or
(c) are altered by order of a court or other authority so as to restrict or exclude the power of the company to amend its articles,

the company must give notice of that fact to the registrar.
(2) Where a company's articles –

(a) are amended so as to remove provision for entrenchment, or
(b) are altered by order of a court or other authority –

(i) so as to remove such provision, or
(ii) so as to remove any other restriction on, or any exclusion of, the power of the company to amend its articles,

the company must give notice of that fact to the registrar.

24 Statement of compliance where amendment of articles restricted

(1) This section applies where a company's articles are subject –

    (a) to provision for entrenchment, or

    (b) to an order of a court or other authority restricting or excluding the company's power to amend the articles.

(2) If the company –

    (a) amends its articles, and

    (b) is required to send to the registrar a document making or evidencing the amendment,

the company must deliver with that document a statement of compliance.

(3) The statement of compliance required is a statement certifying that the amendment has been made in accordance with the company's articles and, where relevant, any applicable order of a court or other authority.

(4) The registrar may rely on the statement of compliance as sufficient evidence of the matters stated in it.

25 Effect of alteration of articles on company's members

(1) A member of a company is not bound by an alteration to its articles after the date on which he became a member, if and so far as the alteration –

    (a) requires him to take or subscribe for more shares than the number held by him at the date on which the alteration is made, or

    (b) in any way increases his liability as at that date to contribute to the company's share capital or otherwise to pay money to the company.

(2) Subsection (1) does not apply in a case where the member agrees in writing, either before or after the alteration is made, to be bound by the alteration.

26 Registrar to be sent copy of amended articles

(1) Where a company amends its articles it must send to the registrar a copy of the articles as amended not later than 15 days after the amendment takes effect.

(2) This section does not require a company to set out in its articles any provisions of model articles that –

    (a) are applied by the articles, or

    (b) apply by virtue of section 20 (default application of model articles).

(3) If a company fails to comply with this section an offence is committed by –

    (a) the company, and

    (b) every officer of the company who is in default.

(4) A person guilty of an offence under this section is liable on summary conviction to a fine not exceeding level 3 on the standard scale and, for continued contravention, a daily default fine not exceeding one-tenth of level 3 on the standard scale.

27 Registrar's notice to comply in case of failure with respect to amended articles

(1) If it appears to the registrar that a company has failed to comply with any enactment requiring it –

    (a) to send to the registrar a document making or evidencing an alteration in the company's articles, or

    (b) to send to the registrar a copy of the company's articles as amended,

the registrar may give notice to the company requiring it to comply.

(2) The notice must –

    (a) state the date on which it is issued, and

    (b) require the company to comply within 28 days from that date.

(3) If the company complies with the notice within the specified time, no criminal proceedings may be brought in respect of the failure to comply with the enactment mentioned in subsection (1).

(4) If the company does not comply with the notice within the specified time, it is liable to a civil penalty of £200.

This is in addition to any liability to criminal proceedings in respect of the failure mentioned in subsection (1).

(5) The penalty may be recovered by the registrar and is to be paid into the Consolidated Fund.

Supplementary

28 Existing companies: provisions of memorandum treated as provisions of articles

(1) Provisions that immediately before the commencement of this Part were contained in a company's memorandum but are not provisions of the kind mentioned in section 8 (provisions of new-style memorandum) are to be treated after the commencement of this Part as provisions of the company's articles.

(2) This applies not only to substantive provisions but also to provision for entrenchment (as defined in section 22).

(3) The provisions of this Part about provision for entrenchment apply to such provision as they apply to provision made on the company's formation, except that the duty under section 23(1)(a) to give notice to the registrar does not apply.

CHAPTER 3

RESOLUTIONS AND AGREEMENTS AFFECTING A COMPANY'S CONSTITUTION

29 Resolutions and agreements affecting a company's constitution

(1) This Chapter applies to –

   (a) any special resolution;
   (b) any resolution or agreement agreed to by all the members of a company that, if not so agreed to, would not have been effective for its purpose unless passed as a special resolution;
   (c) any resolution or agreement agreed to by all the members of a class of shareholders that, if not so agreed to, would not have been effective for its purpose unless passed by some particular majority or otherwise in some particular manner;
   (d) any resolution or agreement that effectively binds all members of a class of shareholders though not agreed to by all those members;
   (e) any other resolution or agreement to which this Chapter applies by virtue of any enactment.

(2) References in subsection (1) to a member of a company, or of a class of members of a company, do not include the company itself where it is such a member by virtue only of its holding shares as treasury shares.

30 Copies of resolutions or agreements to be forwarded to registrar

(1) A copy of every resolution or agreement to which this Chapter applies, or (in the case of a resolution or agreement that is not in writing) a written memorandum setting out its terms, must be forwarded to the registrar within 15 days after it is passed or made.

(2) If a company fails to comply with this section, an offence is committed by –

(a) the company, and
(b) every officer of it who is in default.

(3) A person guilty of an offence under this section is liable on summary conviction to a fine not exceeding level 3 on the standard scale and, for continued contravention, a daily default fine not exceeding one-tenth of level 3 on the standard scale.

(4) For the purposes of this section, a liquidator of the company is treated as an officer of it.

CHAPTER 4

MISCELLANEOUS AND SUPPLEMENTARY PROVISIONS

Statement of company's objects

31 Statement of company's objects

(1) Unless a company's articles specifically restrict the objects of the company, its objects are unrestricted.

(2) Where a company amends its articles so as to add, remove or alter a statement of the company's objects –

(a) it must give notice to the registrar,
(b) on receipt of the notice, the registrar shall register it, and
(c) the amendment is not effective until entry of that notice on the register.

(3) Any such amendment does not affect any rights or obligations of the company or render defective any legal proceedings by or against it.

(4) In the case of a company that is a charity, the provisions of this section have effect subject to –

(a) in England and Wales, section 64 of the Charities Act 1993 (c. 10);
(b) in Northern Ireland, Article 9 of the Charities (Northern Ireland) Order 1987 (S.I. 1987/2048 (N.I. 19)).

(5) In the case of a company that is entered in the Scottish Charity Register, the provisions of this section have effect subject to the provisions of the Charities and Trustee Investment (Scotland) Act 2005 (asp 10).

Other provisions with respect to a company's constitution

32 Constitutional documents to be provided to members

(1) A company must, on request by any member, send to him the following documents –

(a) an up-to-date copy of the company's articles;
(b) a copy of any resolution or agreement relating to the company to which Chapter 3 applies (resolutions and agreements affecting a company's constitution) and that is for the time being in force;
(c) a copy of any document required to be sent to the registrar under –

(i) section 34(2) (notice where company's constitution altered by enactment), or
(ii) section 35(2)(a) (notice where order of court or other authority alters company's constitution);

(d) a copy of any court order under section 899 (order sanctioning compromise or arrangement) or section 900 (order facilitating reconstruction or amalgamation);
(e) a copy of any court order under section 996 (protection of members against unfair prejudice: powers of the court) that alters the company's constitution;

(f)   a copy of the company's current certificate of incorporation, and of any past certificates of incorporation;

(g)   in the case of a company with a share capital, a current statement of capital;

(h)   in the case of a company limited by guarantee, a copy of the statement of guarantee.

(2)   The statement of capital required by subsection (1)(g) is a statement of –

(a)   the total number of shares of the company,

(b)   the aggregate nominal value of those shares,

(c)   for each class of shares –

(i)   prescribed particulars of the rights attached to the shares,

(ii)   the total number of shares of that class, and

(iii) the aggregate nominal value of shares of that class, and

(d)   the amount paid up and the amount (if any) unpaid on each share (whether on account of the nominal value of the share or by way of premium).

(3)   If a company makes default in complying with this section, an offence is committed by every officer of the company who is in default.

(4)   A person guilty of an offence under this section is liable on summary conviction to a fine not exceeding level 3 on the standard scale.

33 Effect of company's constitution

(1)   The provisions of a company's constitution bind the company and its members to the same extent as if there were covenants on the part of the company and of each member to observe those provisions.

(2)   Money payable by a member to the company under its constitution is a debt due from him to the company.

In England and Wales and Northern Ireland it is of the nature of an ordinary contract debt.

34 Notice to registrar where company's constitution altered by enactment

(1)   This section applies where a company's constitution is altered by an enactment, other than an enactment amending the general law.

(2)   The company must give notice of the alteration to the registrar, specifying the enactment, not later than 15 days after the enactment comes into force.

In the case of a special enactment the notice must be accompanied by a copy of the enactment.

(3)   If the enactment amends –

(a)   the company's articles, or

(b)   a resolution or agreement to which Chapter 3 applies (resolutions and agreements affecting a company's constitution),

the notice must be accompanied by a copy of the company's articles, or the resolution or agreement in question, as amended.

(4)   A "special enactment" means an enactment that is not a public general enactment, and includes –

(a)   an Act for confirming a provisional order,

(b)   any provision of a public general Act in relation to the passing of which any of the standing orders of the House of Lords or the House of Commons relating to Private Business applied, or

(c)   any enactment to the extent that it is incorporated in or applied for the purposes of a special enactment.

(5)   If a company fails to comply with this section an offence is committed by –

(a)   the company, and

(b)   every officer of the company who is in default.

(6) A person guilty of an offence under this section is liable on summary conviction to a fine not exceeding level 3 on the standard scale and, for continued contravention, a daily default fine not exceeding one-tenth of level 3 on the standard scale.

35 Notice to registrar where company's constitution altered by order

(1) Where a company's constitution is altered by an order of a court or other authority, the company must give notice to the registrar of the alteration not later than 15 days after the alteration takes effect.

(2) The notice must be accompanied by –

   (a) a copy of the order, and
   (b) if the order amends –

      (i)   the company's articles, or
      (ii)   a resolution or agreement to which Chapter 3 applies (resolutions and agreements affecting the company's constitution),

      a copy of the company's articles, or the resolution or agreement in question, as amended.

(3) If a company fails to comply with this section an offence is committed by –

   (a) the company, and
   (b) every officer of the company who is in default.

(4) A person guilty of an offence under this section is liable on summary conviction to a fine not exceeding level 3 on the standard scale and, for continued contravention, a daily default fine not exceeding one-tenth of level 3 on the standard scale.

(5) This section does not apply where provision is made by another enactment for the delivery to the registrar of a copy of the order in question.

36 Documents to be incorporated in or accompany copies of articles issued by company

(1) Every copy of a company's articles issued by the company must be accompanied by –

   (a) a copy of any resolution or agreement relating to the company to which Chapter 3 applies (resolutions and agreements affecting a company's constitution),
   (b) where the company has been required to give notice to the registrar under section 34(2) (notice where company's constitution altered by enactment), a statement that the enactment in question alters the effect of the company's constitution,
   (c) where the company's constitution is altered by a special enactment (see section 34(4)), a copy of the enactment, and
   (d) a copy of any order required to be sent to the registrar under section 35(2)(a) (order of court or other authority altering company's constitution).

(2) This does not require the articles to be accompanied by a copy of a document or by a statement if –

   (a) the effect of the resolution, agreement, enactment or order (as the case may be) on the company's constitution has been incorporated into the articles by amendment, or
   (b) the resolution, agreement, enactment or order (as the case may be) is not for the time being in force.

(3) If the company fails to comply with this section, an offence is committed by every officer of the company who is in default.

(4) A person guilty of an offence under this section is liable on summary conviction to a fine not exceeding level 3 on the standard scale for each occasion on which copies are issued, or, as the case may be, requested.

(5) For the purposes of this section, a liquidator of the company is treated as an officer of it.

Supplementary provisions

37 Right to participate in profits otherwise than as member void

In the case of a company limited by guarantee and not having a share capital any provision in the company's articles, or in any resolution of the company, purporting to give a person a right to participate in the divisible profits of the company otherwise than as a member is void.

38 Application to single member companies of enactments and rules of law

Any enactment or rule of law applicable to companies formed by two or more persons or having two or more members applies with any necessary modification in relation to a company formed by one person or having only one person as a member.

PART 4

A COMPANY'S CAPACITY AND RELATED MATTERS

Capacity of company and power of directors to bind it

39 A company's capacity

(1) The validity of an act done by a company shall not be called into question on the ground of lack of capacity by reason of anything in the company's constitution.

(2) This section has effect subject to section 42 (companies that are charities).

40 Power of directors to bind the company

(1) In favour of a person dealing with a company in good faith, the power of the directors to bind the company, or authorise others to do so, is deemed to be free of any limitation under the company's constitution.

(2) For this purpose –

    (a) a person "deals with" a company if he is a party to any transaction or other act to which the company is a party,

    (b) a person dealing with a company –

        (i) is not bound to enquire as to any limitation on the powers of the directors to bind the company or authorise others to do so,

        (ii) is presumed to have acted in good faith unless the contrary is proved, and

        (iii) is not to be regarded as acting in bad faith by reason only of his knowing that an act is beyond the powers of the directors under the company's constitution.

(3) The references above to limitations on the directors' powers under the company's constitution include limitations deriving –

    (a) from a resolution of the company or of any class of shareholders, or

    (b) from any agreement between the members of the company or of any class of shareholders.

(4) This section does not affect any right of a member of the company to bring proceedings to restrain the doing of an action that is beyond the powers of the directors.

But no such proceedings lie in respect of an act to be done in fulfilment of a legal obligation arising from a previous act of the company.

(5) This section does not affect any liability incurred by the directors, or any other person, by reason of the directors' exceeding their powers.

(6) This section has effect subject to –

section 41 (transactions with directors or their associates), and
section 42 (companies that are charities).

41 Constitutional limitations: transactions involving directors or their associates

(1) This section applies to a transaction if or to the extent that its validity depends on section 40 (power of directors deemed to be free of limitations under company's constitution in favour of person dealing with company in good faith).

Nothing in this section shall be read as excluding the operation of any other enactment or rule of law by virtue of which the transaction may be called in question or any liability to the company may arise.

(2) Where –

(a) a company enters into such a transaction, and
(b) the parties to the transaction include –

(i) a director of the company or of its holding company, or
(ii) a person connected with any such director,

the transaction is voidable at the instance of the company.

(3) Whether or not it is avoided, any such party to the transaction as is mentioned in subsection (2)(b)(i) or (ii), and any director of the company who authorised the transaction, is liable –

(a) to account to the company for any gain he has made directly or indirectly by the transaction, and
(b) to indemnify the company for any loss or damage resulting from the transaction.

(4) The transaction ceases to be voidable if –

(a) restitution of any money or other asset which was the subject matter of the transaction is no longer possible, or
(b) the company is indemnified for any loss or damage resulting from the transaction, or
(c) rights acquired bona fide for value and without actual notice of the directors' exceeding their powers by a person who is not party to the transaction would be affected by the avoidance, or
(d) the transaction is affirmed by the company.

(5) A person other than a director of the company is not liable under subsection (3) if he shows that at the time the transaction was entered into he did not know that the directors were exceeding their powers.

(6) Nothing in the preceding provisions of this section affects the rights of any party to the transaction not within subsection (2)(b)(i) or (ii).

But the court may, on the application of the company or any such party, make an order affirming, severing or setting aside the transaction on such terms as appear to the court to be just.

(7) In this section –

(a) "transaction" includes any act; and
(b) the reference to a person connected with a director has the same meaning as in Part 10 (company directors).

42 Constitutional limitations: companies that are charities

(1) Sections 39 and 40 (company's capacity and power of directors to bind company) do not apply to the acts of a company that is a charity except in favour of a person who –

(a) does not know at the time the act is done that the company is a charity, or
(b) gives full consideration in money or money's worth in relation to the act in question and does not know (as the case may be) –

(i)   that the act is not permitted by the company's constitution, or

(ii)   that the act is beyond the powers of the directors.

(2) Where a company that is a charity purports to transfer or grant an interest in property, the fact that (as the case may be) –

(a) the act was not permitted by the company's constitution, or

(b) the directors in connection with the act exceeded any limitation on their powers under the company's constitution,

does not affect the title of a person who subsequently acquires the property or any interest in it for full consideration without actual notice of any such circumstances affecting the validity of the company's act.

(3) In any proceedings arising out of subsection (1) or (2) the burden of proving –

(a) that a person knew that the company was a charity, or

(b) that a person knew that an act was not permitted by the company's constitution or was beyond the powers of the directors,

lies on the person asserting that fact.

(4) In the case of a company that is a charity the affirmation of a transaction to which section 41 applies (transactions with directors or their associates) is ineffective without the prior written consent of –

(a) in England and Wales, the Charity Commission;

(b) in Northern Ireland, the Department for Social Development.

(5) This section does not extend to Scotland (but see section 112 of the Companies Act 1989 (c. 40)).

Formalities of doing business under the law of England and Wales or Northern Ireland

43 Company contracts

(1) Under the law of England and Wales or Northern Ireland a contract may be made –

(a) by a company, by writing under its common seal, or

(b) on behalf of a company, by a person acting under its authority, express or implied.

(2) Any formalities required by law in the case of a contract made by an individual also apply, unless a contrary intention appears, to a contract made by or on behalf of a company.

44 Execution of documents

(1) Under the law of England and Wales or Northern Ireland a document is executed by a company –

(a) by the affixing of its common seal, or

(b) by signature in accordance with the following provisions.

(2) A document is validly executed by a company if it is signed on behalf of the company –

(a) by two authorised signatories, or

(b) by a director of the company in the presence of a witness who attests the signature.

(3) The following are "authorised signatories" for the purposes of subsection (2) –

(a) every director of the company, and

(b) in the case of a private company with a secretary or a public company, the secretary (or any joint secretary) of the company.

(4) A document signed in accordance with subsection (2) and expressed, in whatever

words, to be executed by the company has the same effect as if executed under the common seal of the company.

(5) In favour of a purchaser a document is deemed to have been duly executed by a company if it purports to be signed in accordance with subsection (2).

A "purchaser" means a purchaser in good faith for valuable consideration and includes a lessee, mortgagee or other person who for valuable consideration acquires an interest in property.

(6) Where a document is to be signed by a person on behalf of more than one company, it is not duly signed by that person for the purposes of this section unless he signs it separately in each capacity.

(7) References in this section to a document being (or purporting to be) signed by a director or secretary are to be read, in a case where that office is held by a firm, as references to its being (or purporting to be) signed by an individual authorised by the firm to sign on its behalf.

(8) This section applies to a document that is (or purports to be) executed by a company in the name of or on behalf of another person whether or not that person is also a company.

45 Common seal

(1) A company may have a common seal, but need not have one.

(2) A company which has a common seal shall have its name engraved in legible characters on the seal.

(3) If a company fails to comply with subsection (2) an offence is committed by –

(a) the company, and
(b) every officer of the company who is in default.

(4) An officer of a company, or a person acting on behalf of a company, commits an offence if he uses, or authorises the use of, a seal purporting to be a seal of the company on which its name is not engraved as required by subsection (2).

(5) A person guilty of an offence under this section is liable on summary conviction to a fine not exceeding level 3 on the standard scale.

(6) This section does not form part of the law of Scotland.

46 Execution of deeds

(1) A document is validly executed by a company as a deed for the purposes of section 1(2)(b) of the Law of Property (Miscellaneous Provisions) Act 1989 (c. 34) and for the purposes of the law of Northern Ireland if, and only if –

(a) it is duly executed by the company, and
(b) it is delivered as a deed.

(2) For the purposes of subsection (1)(b) a document is presumed to be delivered upon its being executed, unless a contrary intention is proved.

47 Execution of deeds or other documents by attorney

(1) Under the law of England and Wales or Northern Ireland a company may, by instrument executed as a deed, empower a person, either generally or in respect of specified matters, as its attorney to execute deeds or other documents on its behalf.

(2) A deed or other document so executed, whether in the United Kingdom or elsewhere, has effect as if executed by the company.

Formalities of doing business under the law of Scotland

48 Execution of documents by companies

(1) The following provisions form part of the law of Scotland only.

(2) Notwithstanding the provisions of any enactment, a company need not have a company seal.

(3) For the purposes of any enactment –

    (a) providing for a document to be executed by a company by affixing its common seal, or

    (b) referring (in whatever terms) to a document so executed,

a document signed or subscribed by or on behalf of the company in accordance with the provisions of the Requirements of Writing (Scotland) Act 1995 (c. 7) has effect as if so executed.

Other matters

49 Official seal for use abroad

(1) A company that has a common seal may have an official seal for use outside the United Kingdom.

(2) The official seal must be a facsimile of the company's common seal, with the addition on its face of the place or places where it is to be used.

(3) The official seal when duly affixed to a document has the same effect as the company's common seal.

This subsection does not extend to Scotland.

(4) A company having an official seal for use outside the United Kingdom may –

    (a) by writing under its common seal, or

    (b) as respects Scotland, by writing subscribed in accordance with the Requirements of Writing (Scotland) Act 1995,

authorise any person appointed for the purpose to affix the official seal to any deed or other document to which the company is party.

(5) As between the company and a person dealing with such an agent, the agent's authority continues –

    (a) during the period mentioned in the instrument conferring the authority, or

    (b) if no period is mentioned, until notice of the revocation or termination of the agent's authority has been given to the person dealing with him.

(6) The person affixing the official seal must certify in writing on the deed or other document to which the seal is affixed the date on which, and place at which, it is affixed.

50 Official seal for share certificates etc

(1) A company that has a common seal may have an official seal for use –

    (a) for sealing securities issued by the company, or

    (b) for sealing documents creating or evidencing securities so issued.

(2) The official seal –

    (a) must be a facsimile of the company's common seal, with the addition on its face of the word "Securities", and

    (b) when duly affixed to the document has the same effect as the company's common seal.

51 Pre-incorporation contracts, deeds and obligations

(1) A contract that purports to be made by or on behalf of a company at a time when the company has not been formed has effect, subject to any agreement to the contrary, as

one made with the person purporting to act for the company or as agent for it, and he is personally liable on the contract accordingly.

(2) Subsection (1) applies –

    (a) to the making of a deed under the law of England and Wales or Northern Ireland, and

    (b) to the undertaking of an obligation under the law of Scotland,

as it applies to the making of a contract.

52 Bills of exchange and promissory notes

A bill of exchange or promissory note is deemed to have been made, accepted or endorsed on behalf of a company if made, accepted or endorsed in the name of, or by or on behalf or on account of, the company by a person acting under its authority.

PART 5

A COMPANY'S NAME

CHAPTER 1

GENERAL REQUIREMENTS

Prohibited names

53 Prohibited names

A company must not be registered under this Act by a name if, in the opinion of the Secretary of State –

    (a) its use by the company would constitute an offence, or

    (b) it is offensive.

Sensitive words and expressions

54 Names suggesting connection with government or public authority

(1) The approval of the Secretary of State is required for a company to be registered under this Act by a name that would be likely to give the impression that the company is connected with –

    (a) Her Majesty's Government, any part of the Scottish administration or Her Majesty's Government in Northern Ireland,

    (b) a local authority, or

    (c) any public authority specified for the purposes of this section by regulations made by the Secretary of State.

(2) For the purposes of this section –

"local authority" means –

    (a) a local authority within the meaning of the Local Government Act 1972 (c. 70), the Common Council of the City of London or the Council of the Isles of Scilly,

    (b) a council constituted under section 2 of the Local Government etc. (Scotland) Act 1994 (c. 39), or

    (c) a district council in Northern Ireland;

"public authority" includes any person or body having functions of a public nature.

(3) Regulations under this section are subject to affirmative resolution procedure.

55 Other sensitive words or expressions

(1) The approval of the Secretary of State is required for a company to be registered under this Act by a name that includes a word or expression for the time being specified in regulations made by the Secretary of State under this section.

(2) Regulations under this section are subject to approval after being made.

56 Duty to seek comments of government department or other specified body

(1) The Secretary of State may by regulations under –

   (a) section 54 (name suggesting connection with government or public authority), or

   (b) section 55 (other sensitive words or expressions),

   require that, in connection with an application for the approval of the Secretary of State under that section, the applicant must seek the view of a specified Government department or other body.

(2) Where such a requirement applies, the applicant must request the specified department or other body (in writing) to indicate whether (and if so why) it has any objections to the proposed name.

(3) Where a request under this section is made in connection with an application for the registration of a company under this Act, the application must –

   (a) include a statement that a request under this section has been made, and

   (b) be accompanied by a copy of any response received.

(4) Where a request under this section is made in connection with a change in a company's name, the notice of the change sent to the registrar must be accompanied by –

   (a) a statement by a director or secretary of the company that a request under this section has been made, and

   (b) a copy of any response received.

(5) In this section "specified" means specified in the regulations.

Permitted characters etc

57 Permitted characters etc

(1) The Secretary of State may make provision by regulations –

   (a) as to the letters or other characters, signs or symbols (including accents and other diacritical marks) and punctuation that may be used in the name of a company registered under this Act; and

   (b) specifying a standard style or format for the name of a company for the purposes of registration.

(2) The regulations may prohibit the use of specified characters, signs or symbols when appearing in a specified position (in particular, at the beginning of a name).

(3) A company may not be registered under this Act by a name that consists of or includes anything that is not permitted in accordance with regulations under this section.

(4) Regulations under this section are subject to negative resolution procedure.

(5) In this section "specified" means specified in the regulations.

CHAPTER 2

INDICATIONS OF COMPANY TYPE OR LEGAL FORM

Required indications for limited companies

58 Public limited companies

(1) The name of a limited company that is a public company must end with "public limited company" or "p.l.c.".
(2) In the case of a Welsh company, its name may instead end with "cwmni cyfyngedig cyhoeddus" or "c.c.c.".
(3) This section does not apply to community interest companies (but see section 33(3) and (4) of the Companies (Audit, Investigations and Community Enterprise) Act 2004 (c. 27)).

59 Private limited companies

(1) The name of a limited company that is a private company must end with "limited" or "ltd.".
(2) In the case of a Welsh company, its name may instead end with "cyfyngedig" or "cyf.".
(3) Certain companies are exempt from this requirement (see section 60).
(4) This section does not apply to community interest companies (but see section 33(1) and (2) of the Companies (Audit, Investigations and Community Enterprise) Act 2004).

60 Exemption from requirement as to use of "limited"

(1) A private company is exempt from section 59 (requirement to have name ending with "limited" or permitted alternative) if –
   (a) it is a charity,
   (b) it is exempted from the requirement of that section by regulations made by the Secretary of State, or
   (c) it meets the conditions specified in –

   section 61 (continuation of existing exemption: companies limited by shares), or
   section 62 (continuation of existing exemption: companies limited by guarantee).

(2) The registrar may refuse to register a private limited company by a name that does not include the word "limited" (or a permitted alternative) unless a statement has been delivered to him that the company meets the conditions for exemption.
(3) The registrar may accept the statement as sufficient evidence of the matters stated in it.
(4) Regulations under this section are subject to negative resolution procedure.

61 Continuation of existing exemption: companies limited by shares

(1) This section applies to a private company limited by shares –
   (a) that on 25th February 1982 –
      (i) was registered in Great Britain, and
      (ii) had a name that, by virtue of a licence under section 19 of the Companies Act 1948 (c. 38) (or corresponding earlier legislation), did not include the word "limited" or any of the permitted alternatives, or
   (b) that on 30th June 1983 –
      (i) was registered in Northern Ireland, and
      (ii) had a name that, by virtue of a licence under section 19 of the Companies Act (Northern Ireland) 1960 (c. 22 (N.I.)) (or corresponding earlier

legislation), did not include the word "limited" or any of the permitted alternatives.

(2) A company to which this section applies is exempt from section 59 (requirement to have name ending with "limited" or permitted alternative) so long as –

(a) it continues to meet the following two conditions, and

(b) it does not change its name.

(3) The first condition is that the objects of the company are the promotion of commerce, art, science, education, religion, charity or any profession, and anything incidental or conducive to any of those objects.

(4) The second condition is that the company's articles –

(a) require its income to be applied in promoting its objects,

(b) prohibit the payment of dividends, or any return of capital, to its members, and

(c) require all the assets that would otherwise be available to its members generally to be transferred on its winding up either –

(i)   to another body with objects similar to its own, or

(ii) to another body the objects of which are the promotion of charity and anything incidental or conducive thereto,

(whether or not the body is a member of the company).

62 Continuation of existing exemption: companies limited by guarantee

(1) A private company limited by guarantee that immediately before the commencement of this Part –

(a) was exempt by virtue of section 30 of the Companies Act 1985 (c. 6) or Article 40 of the Companies (Northern Ireland) Order 1986 (S.I. 19861032 (N.I. 6)) from the requirement to have a name including the word "limited" or a permitted alternative, and

(b) had a name that did not include the word "limited" or any of the permitted alternatives,

is exempt from section 59 (requirement to have name ending with "limited" or permitted alternative) so long as it continues to meet the following two conditions and does not change its name.

(2) The first condition is that the objects of the company are the promotion of commerce, art, science, education, religion, charity or any profession, and anything incidental or conducive to any of those objects.

(3) The second condition is that the company's articles –

(a) require its income to be applied in promoting its objects,

(b) prohibit the payment of dividends to its members, and

(c) require all the assets that would otherwise be available to its members generally to be transferred on its winding up either –

(i)   to another body with objects similar to its own, or

(ii) to another body the objects of which are the promotion of charity and anything incidental or conducive thereto,

(whether or not the body is a member of the company).

63 Exempt company: restriction on amendment of articles

(1) A private company –

(a) that is exempt under section 61 or 62 from the requirement to use "limited" (or a permitted alternative) as part of its name, and

(b) whose name does not include "limited" or any of the permitted alternatives, must not amend its articles so that it ceases to comply with the conditions for exemption under that section.

(2) If subsection (1) above is contravened an offence is committed by –

(a) the company, and

(b) every officer of the company who is in default.

For this purpose a shadow director is treated as an officer of the company.

(3) A person guilty of an offence under this section is liable on summary conviction to a fine not exceeding level 5 on the standard scale and, for continued contravention, a daily default fine not exceeding one-tenth of level 5 on the standard scale.

(4) Where immediately before the commencement of this section –

(a) a company was exempt by virtue of section 30 of the Companies Act 1985 (c. 6) or Article 40 of the Companies (Northern Ireland) Order 1986 (S.I. 1986/1032 (N.I. 6)) from the requirement to have a name including the word "limited" (or a permitted alternative), and

(b) the company's memorandum or articles contained provision preventing an alteration of them without the approval of –

(i)   the Board of Trade or a Northern Ireland department (or any other department or Minister), or

(ii)   the Charity Commission,

that provision, and any condition of any such licence as is mentioned in section 61(1)(a)(ii) or (b)(ii) requiring such provision, shall cease to have effect.

This does not apply if, or to the extent that, the provision is required by or under any other enactment.

(5) It is hereby declared that any such provision as is mentioned in subsection (4)(b) formerly contained in a company's memorandum was at all material times capable, with the appropriate approval, of being altered or removed under section 17 of the Companies Act 1985 or Article 28 of the Companies (Northern Ireland) Order 1986 (S.I. 1986/1032 (N.I. 6)) (or corresponding earlier enactments).

64 Power to direct change of name in case of company ceasing to be entitled to exemption

(1) If it appears to the Secretary of State that a company whose name does not include "limited" or any of the permitted alternatives –

(a) has ceased to be entitled to exemption under section 60(1)(a) or (b), or

(b) in the case of a company within section 61 or 62 (which impose conditions as to the objects and articles of the company) –

(i)   has carried on any business other than the promotion of any of the objects mentioned in subsection (3) of section 61 or, as the case may be, subsection (2) of section 62, or

(ii)   has acted inconsistently with the provision required by subsection (4)(a) or (b) of section 61 or, as the case may be, subsection (3)(a) or (b) of section 62,

the Secretary of State may direct the company to change its name so that it ends with "limited" or one of the permitted alternatives.

(2) The direction must be in writing and must specify the period within which the company is to change its name.

(3) A change of name in order to comply with a direction under this section may be made by resolution of the directors.

This is without prejudice to any other method of changing the company's name.

(4) Where a resolution of the directors is passed in accordance with subsection (3), the company must give notice to the registrar of the change.

Sections 80 and 81 apply as regards the registration and effect of the change.

(5) If the company fails to comply with a direction under this section an offence is committed by –

  (a) the company, and
  (b) every officer of the company who is in default.

(6) A person guilty of an offence under this section is liable on summary conviction to a fine not exceeding level 5 on the standard scale and, for continued contravention, a daily default fine not exceeding one-tenth of level 5 on the standard scale.

(7) A company that has been directed to change its name under this section may not, without the approval of the Secretary of State, subsequently change its name so that it does not include "limited" or one of the permitted alternatives.

  This does not apply to a change of name on re-registration or on conversion to a community interest company.

Inappropriate use of indications of company type or legal form

65 Inappropriate use of indications of company type or legal form

(1) The Secretary of State may make provision by regulations prohibiting the use in a company name of specified words, expressions or other indications –

  (a) that are associated with a particular type of company or form of organisation, or
  (b) that are similar to words, expressions or other indications associated with a particular type of company or form of organisation.

(2) The regulations may prohibit the use of words, expressions or other indications –

  (a) in a specified part, or otherwise than in a specified part, of a company's name;
  (b) in conjunction with, or otherwise than in conjunction with, such other words, expressions or indications as may be specified.

(3) A company must not be registered under this Act by a name that consists of or includes anything prohibited by regulations under this section.

(4) In this section "specified" means specified in the regulations.

(5) Regulations under this section are subject to negative resolution procedure.

CHAPTER 3

SIMILARITY TO OTHER NAMES

Similarity to other name on registrar's index

66 Name not to be the same as another in the index

(1) A company must not be registered under this Act by a name that is the same as another name appearing in the registrar's index of company names.

(2) The Secretary of State may make provision by regulations supplementing this section.

(3) The regulations may make provision –

  (a) as to matters that are to be disregarded, and
  (b) as to words, expressions, signs or symbols that are, or are not, to be regarded as the same,

  for the purposes of this section.

(4) The regulations may provide –

  (a) that registration by a name that would otherwise be prohibited under this section is permitted –

        (i)   in specified circumstances, or

        (ii) with specified consent, and

  (b) that if those circumstances obtain or that consent is given at the time a company is registered by a name, a subsequent change of circumstances or withdrawal of consent does not affect the registration.

(5) Regulations under this section are subject to negative resolution procedure.

(6) In this section "specified" means specified in the regulations.

67 Power to direct change of name in case of similarity to existing name

(1) The Secretary of State may direct a company to change its name if it has been registered in a name that is the same as or, in the opinion of the Secretary of State, too like –

  (a) a name appearing at the time of the registration in the registrar's index of company names, or

  (b) a name that should have appeared in that index at that time.

(2) The Secretary of State may make provision by regulations supplementing this section.

(3) The regulations may make provision –

  (a) as to matters that are to be disregarded, and

  (b) as to words, expressions, signs or symbols that are, or are not, to be regarded as the same,

for the purposes of this section.

(4) The regulations may provide –

  (a) that no direction is to be given under this section in respect of a name –

        (i)   in specified circumstances, or

        (ii) if specified consent is given, and

  (b) that a subsequent change of circumstances or withdrawal of consent does not give rise to grounds for a direction under this section.

(5) Regulations under this section are subject to negative resolution procedure.

(6) In this section "specified" means specified in the regulations.

68 Direction to change name: supplementary provisions

(1) The following provisions have effect in relation to a direction under section 67 (power to direct change of name in case of similarity to existing name).

(2) Any such direction –

  (a) must be given within twelve months of the company's registration by the name in question, and

  (b) must specify the period within which the company is to change its name.

(3) The Secretary of State may by a further direction extend that period.

Any such direction must be given before the end of the period for the time being specified.

(4) A direction under section 67 or this section must be in writing.

(5) If a company fails to comply with the direction, an offence is committed by –

  (a) the company, and

  (b) every officer of the company who is in default.

For this purpose a shadow director is treated as an officer of the company.

(6) A person guilty of an offence under this section is liable on summary conviction to a fine not exceeding level 3 on the standard scale and, for continued contravention, a daily default fine not exceeding one-tenth of level 3 on the standard scale.

Similarity to other name in which person has goodwill

69 Objection to company's registered name

(1) A person ("the applicant") may object to a company's registered name on the ground –

(a) that it is the same as a name associated with the applicant in which he has goodwill, or

(b) that it is sufficiently similar to such a name that its use in the United Kingdom would be likely to mislead by suggesting a connection between the company and the applicant.

(2) The objection must be made by application to a company names adjudicator (see section 70).

(3) The company concerned shall be the primary respondent to the application.
Any of its members or directors may be joined as respondents.

(4) If the ground specified in subsection (1)(a) or (b) is established, it is for the respondents to show –

(a) that the name was registered before the commencement of the activities on which the applicant relies to show goodwill; or

(b) that the company –

(i)   is operating under the name, or

(ii)   is proposing to do so and has incurred substantial start-up costs in preparation, or

(iii) was formerly operating under the name and is now dormant; or

(c) that the name was registered in the ordinary course of a company formation business and the company is available for sale to the applicant on the standard terms of that business; or

(d) that the name was adopted in good faith; or

(e) that the interests of the applicant are not adversely affected to any significant extent.

If none of those is shown, the objection shall be upheld.

(5) If the facts mentioned in subsection (4)(a), (b) or (c) are established, the objection shall nevertheless be upheld if the applicant shows that the main purpose of the respondents (or any of them) in registering the name was to obtain money (or other consideration) from the applicant or prevent him from registering the name.

(6) If the objection is not upheld under subsection (4) or (5), it shall be dismissed.

(7) In this section "goodwill" includes reputation of any description.

70 Company names adjudicators

(1) The Secretary of State shall appoint persons to be company names adjudicators.

(2) The persons appointed must have such legal or other experience as, in the Secretary of State's opinion, makes them suitable for appointment.

(3) An adjudicator –

(a) holds office in accordance with the terms of his appointment,

(b) is eligible for re-appointment when his term of office ends,

(c) may resign at any time by notice in writing given to the Secretary of State, and

(d) may be dismissed by the Secretary of State on the ground of incapacity or misconduct.

(4) One of the adjudicators shall be appointed Chief Adjudicator.
He shall perform such functions as the Secretary of State may assign to him.

(5) The other adjudicators shall undertake such duties as the Chief Adjudicator may determine.

(6) The Secretary of State may –

    (a) appoint staff for the adjudicators;

    (b) pay remuneration and expenses to the adjudicators and their staff;

    (c) defray other costs arising in relation to the performance by the adjudicators of their functions;

    (d) compensate persons for ceasing to be adjudicators.

71 Procedural rules

(1) The Secretary of State may make rules about proceedings before a company names adjudicator.

(2) The rules may, in particular, make provision –

    (a) as to how an application is to be made and the form and content of an application or other documents;

    (b) for fees to be charged;

    (c) about the service of documents and the consequences of failure to serve them;

    (d) as to the form and manner in which evidence is to be given;

    (e) for circumstances in which hearings are required and those in which they are not;

    (f) for cases to be heard by more than one adjudicator;

    (g) setting time limits for anything required to be done in connection with the proceedings (and allowing for such limits to be extended, even if they have expired);

    (h) enabling the adjudicator to strike out an application, or any defence, in whole or in part –

        (i) on the ground that it is vexatious, has no reasonable prospect of success or is otherwise misconceived, or

        (ii) for failure to comply with the requirements of the rules;

    (i) conferring power to order security for costs (in Scotland, caution for expenses);

    (j) as to how far proceedings are to be held in public;

    (k) requiring one party to bear the costs (in Scotland, expenses) of another and as to the taxing (or settling) the amount of such costs (or expenses).

(3) The rules may confer on the Chief Adjudicator power to determine any matter that could be the subject of provision in the rules.

(4) Rules under this section shall be made by statutory instrument which shall be subject to annulment in pursuance of a resolution of either House of Parliament.

72 Decision of adjudicator to be made available to public

(1) A company names adjudicator must, within 90 days of determining an application under section 69, make his decision and his reasons for it available to the public.

(2) He may do so by means of a website or by such other means as appear to him to be appropriate.

73 Order requiring name to be changed

(1) If an application under section 69 is upheld, the adjudicator shall make an order –

    (a) requiring the respondent company to change its name to one that is not an offending name, and

    (b) requiring all the respondents –

        (i) to take all such steps as are within their power to make, or facilitate the making, of that change, and

        (ii) not to cause or permit any steps to be taken calculated to result in another company being registered with a name that is an offending name.

(2) An "offending name" means a name that, by reason of its similarity to the name associated with the applicant in which he claims goodwill, would be likely –

(a) to be the subject of a direction under section 67 (power of Secretary of State to direct change of name), or

(b) to give rise to a further application under section 69.

(3) The order must specify a date by which the respondent company's name is to be changed and may be enforced –

    (a) in England and Wales or Northern Ireland, in the same way as an order of the High Court;

    (b) in Scotland, in the same way as a decree of the Court of Session.

(4) If the respondent company's name is not changed in accordance with the order by the specified date, the adjudicator may determine a new name for the company.

(5) If the adjudicator determines a new name for the respondent company he must give notice of his determination –

    (a) to the applicant,

    (b) to the respondents, and

    (c) to the registrar.

(6) For the purposes of this section a company's name is changed when the change takes effect in accordance with section 81(1) (on the issue of the new certification of incorporation).

74 Appeal from adjudicator's decision

(1) An appeal lies to the court from any decision of a company names adjudicator to uphold or dismiss an application under section 69.

(2) Notice of appeal against a decision upholding an application must be given before the date specified in the adjudicator's order by which the respondent company's name is to be changed.

(3) If notice of appeal is given against a decision upholding an application, the effect of the adjudicator's order is suspended.

(4) If on appeal the court –

    (a) affirms the decision of the adjudicator to uphold the application, or

    (b) reverses the decision of the adjudicator to dismiss the application,

the court may (as the case may require) specify the date by which the adjudicator's order is to be complied with, remit the matter to the adjudicator or make any order or determination that the adjudicator might have made.

(5) If the court determines a new name for the company it must give notice of the determination –

    (a) to the parties to the appeal, and

    (b) to the registrar.

CHAPTER 4

OTHER POWERS OF THE SECRETARY OF STATE

75 Provision of misleading information etc

(1) If it appears to the Secretary of State –

    (a) that misleading information has been given for the purposes of a company's registration by a particular name, or

    (b) that an undertaking or assurance has been given for that purpose and has not been fulfilled,

the Secretary of State may direct the company to change its name.

(2) Any such direction –

    (a) must be given within five years of the company's registration by that name, and

    (b) must specify the period within which the company is to change its name.

(3) The Secretary of State may by a further direction extend the period within which the company is to change its name.

    Any such direction must be given before the end of the period for the time being specified.

(4) A direction under this section must be in writing.

(5) If a company fails to comply with a direction under this section, an offence is committed by –

    (a) the company, and

    (b) every officer of the company who is in default.

    For this purpose a shadow director is treated as an officer of the company.

(6) A person guilty of an offence under this section is liable on summary conviction to a fine not exceeding level 3 on the standard scale and, for continued contravention, a daily default fine not exceeding one-tenth of level 3 on the standard scale.

76 Misleading indication of activities

(1) If in the opinion of the Secretary of State the name by which a company is registered gives so misleading an indication of the nature of its activities as to be likely to cause harm to the public, the Secretary of State may direct the company to change its name.

(2) The direction must be in writing.

(3) The direction must be complied with within a period of six weeks from the date of the direction or such longer period as the Secretary of State may think fit to allow.

    This does not apply if an application is duly made to the court under the following provisions.

(4) The company may apply to the court to set the direction aside.

    The application must be made within the period of three weeks from the date of the direction.

(5) The court may set the direction aside or confirm it.

    If the direction is confirmed, the court shall specify the period within which the direction is to be complied with.

(6) If a company fails to comply with a direction under this section, an offence is committed by –

    (a) the company, and

    (b) every officer of the company who is in default.

    For this purpose a shadow director is treated as an officer of the company.

(7) A person guilty of an offence under this section is liable on summary conviction to a fine not exceeding level 3 on the standard scale and, for continued contravention, a daily default fine not exceeding one-tenth of level 3 on the standard scale.

CHAPTER 5

CHANGE OF NAME

77 Change of name

(1) A company may change its name –

    (a) by special resolution (see section 78), or

    (b) by other means provided for by the company's articles (see section 79).

(2) The name of a company may also be changed –

    (a) by resolution of the directors acting under section 64 (change of name to comply with direction of Secretary of State under that section);

    (b) on the determination of a new name by a company names adjudicator under section 73 (powers of adjudicator on upholding objection to company name);

    (c) on the determination of a new name by the court under section 74 (appeal against decision of company names adjudicator);

    (d) under section 1033 (company's name on restoration to the register).

78 Change of name by special resolution

(1) Where a change of name has been agreed to by a company by special resolution, the company must give notice to the registrar.

This is in addition to the obligation to forward a copy of the resolution to the registrar.

(2) Where a change of name by special resolution is conditional on the occurrence of an event, the notice given to the registrar of the change must –

    (a) specify that the change is conditional, and

    (b) state whether the event has occurred.

(3) If the notice states that the event has not occurred –

    (a) the registrar is not required to act under section 80 (registration and issue of new certificate of incorporation) until further notice,

    (b) when the event occurs, the company must give notice to the registrar stating that it has occurred, and

    (c) the registrar may rely on the statement as sufficient evidence of the matters stated in it.

79 Change of name by means provided for in company's articles

(1) Where a change of a company's name has been made by other means provided for by its articles –

    (a) the company must give notice to the registrar, and

    (b) the notice must be accompanied by a statement that the change of name has been made by means provided for by the company's articles.

(2) The registrar may rely on the statement as sufficient evidence of the matters stated in it.

80 Change of name: registration and issue of new certificate of incorporation

(1) This section applies where the registrar receives notice of a change of a company's name.

(2) If the registrar is satisfied –

    (a) that the new name complies with the requirements of this Part, and

    (b) that the requirements of the Companies Acts, and any relevant requirements of the company's articles, with respect to a change of name are complied with,

the registrar must enter the new name on the register in place of the former name.

(3) On the registration of the new name, the registrar must issue a certificate of incorporation altered to meet the circumstances of the case.

81 Change of name: effect

(1) A change of a company's name has effect from the date on which the new certificate of incorporation is issued.

(2) The change does not affect any rights or obligations of the company or render defective any legal proceedings by or against it.

(3) Any legal proceedings that might have been continued or commenced against it by its former name may be continued or commenced against it by its new name.

CHAPTER 6

TRADING DISCLOSURES

82 Requirement to disclose company name etc

(1) The Secretary of State may by regulations make provision requiring companies –

    (a) to display specified information in specified locations,

    (b) to state specified information in specified descriptions of document or communication, and

    (c) to provide specified information on request to those they deal with in the course of their business.

(2) The regulations –

    (a) must in every case require disclosure of the name of the company, and

    (b) may make provision as to the manner in which any specified information is to be displayed, stated or provided.

(3) The regulations may provide that, for the purposes of any requirement to disclose a company's name, any variation between a word or words required to be part of the name and a permitted abbreviation of that word or those words (or vice versa) shall be disregarded.

(4) In this section "specified" means specified in the regulations.

(5) Regulations under this section are subject to affirmative resolution procedure.

83 Civil consequences of failure to make required disclosure

(1) This section applies to any legal proceedings brought by a company to which section 82 applies (requirement to disclose company name etc) to enforce a right arising out of a contract made in the course of a business in respect of which the company was, at the time the contract was made, in breach of regulations under that section.

(2) The proceedings shall be dismissed if the defendant (in Scotland, the defender) to the proceedings shows –

    (a) that he has a claim against the claimant (pursuer) arising out of the contract that he has been unable to pursue by reason of the latter's breach of the regulations, or

    (b) that he has suffered some financial loss in connection with the contract by reason of the claimant's (pursuer's) breach of the regulations,

unless the court before which the proceedings are brought is satisfied that it is just and equitable to permit the proceedings to continue.

(3) This section does not affect the right of any person to enforce such rights as he may have against another person in any proceedings brought by that person.

84 Criminal consequences of failure to make required disclosures

(1) Regulations under section 82 may provide –

    (a) that where a company fails, without reasonable excuse, to comply with any specified requirement of regulations under that section an offence is committed by –

        (i) the company, and

        (ii) every officer of the company who is in default;

    (b) that a person guilty of such an offence is liable on summary conviction to a fine not exceeding level 3 on the standard scale and, for continued contravention, a daily default fine not exceeding one-tenth of level 3 on the standard scale.

(2) The regulations may provide that, for the purposes of any provision made under subsection (1), a shadow director of the company is to be treated as an officer of the company.

(3) In subsection (1)(a) "specified" means specified in the regulations.

85 Minor variations in form of name to be left out of account

(1) For the purposes of this Chapter, in considering a company's name no account is to be taken of –

    (a) whether upper or lower case characters (or a combination of the two) are used,

    (b) whether diacritical marks or punctuation are present or absent,

    (c) whether the name is in the same format or style as is specified under section 57(1)(b) for the purposes of registration, provided there is no real likelihood of names differing only in those respects being taken to be different names.

(2) This does not affect the operation of regulations under section 57(1)(a) permitting only specified characters, diacritical marks or punctuation.

PART 6

A COMPANY'S REGISTERED OFFICE

General

86 A company's registered office

A company must at all times have a registered office to which all communications and notices may be addressed.

87 Change of address of registered office

(1) A company may change the address of its registered office by giving notice to the registrar.

(2) The change takes effect upon the notice being registered by the registrar, but until the end of the period of 14 days beginning with the date on which it is registered a person may validly serve any document on the company at the address previously registered.

(3) For the purposes of any duty of a company –

    (a) to keep available for inspection at its registered office any register, index or other document, or

    (b) to mention the address of its registered office in any document,

a company that has given notice to the registrar of a change in the address of its registered office may act on the change as from such date, not more than 14 days after the notice is given, as it may determine.

(4) Where a company unavoidably ceases to perform at its registered office any such duty as is mentioned in subsection (3)(a) in circumstances in which it was not practicable to give prior notice to the registrar of a change in the address of its registered office, but –

    (a) resumes performance of that duty at other premises as soon as practicable, and

    (b) gives notice accordingly to the registrar of a change in the situation of its registered office within 14 days of doing so,

it is not to be treated as having failed to comply with that duty.

Welsh companies

88 Welsh companies

(1) In the Companies Acts a "Welsh company" means a company as to which it is stated in the register that its registered office is to be situated in Wales.

(2) A company –

(a) whose registered office is in Wales, and

(b) as to which it is stated in the register that its registered office is to be situated in England and Wales,

may by special resolution require the register to be amended so that it states that the company's registered office is to be situated in Wales.

(3) A company –

(a) whose registered office is in Wales, and

(b) as to which it is stated in the register that its registered office is to be situated in Wales,

may by special resolution require the register to be amended so that it states that the company's registered office is to be situated in England and Wales.

(4) Where a company passes a resolution under this section it must give notice to the registrar, who shall –

(a) amend the register accordingly, and

(b) issue a new certificate of incorporation altered to meet the circumstances of the case.

PART 7

RE-REGISTRATION AS A MEANS OF ALTERING A COMPANY'S STATUS

Introductory

89 Alteration of status by re-registration

A company may by re-registration under this Part alter its status –

(a) from a private company to a public company (see sections 90 to 96);

(b) from a public company to a private company (see sections 97 to 101);

(c) from a private limited company to an unlimited company (see sections 102 to 104);

(d) from an unlimited private company to a limited company (see sections 105 to 108);

(e) from a public company to an unlimited private company (see sections 109 to 111).

Private company becoming public

90 Re-registration of private company as public

(1) A private company (whether limited or unlimited) may be re-registered as a public company limited by shares if –

(a) a special resolution that it should be so re-registered is passed,

(b) the conditions specified below are met, and

(c) an application for re-registration is delivered to the registrar in accordance with section 94, together with –

(i)   the other documents required by that section, and

(ii) a statement of compliance.

(2) The conditions are –

(a) that the company has a share capital;

(b) that the requirements of section 91 are met as regards its share capital;

(c) that the requirements of section 92 are met as regards its net assets;

(d) if section 93 applies (recent allotment of shares for non-cash consideration), that the requirements of that section are met; and

(e) that the company has not previously been re-registered as unlimited.

(3) The company must make such changes –

(a) in its name, and

(b) in its articles,

as are necessary in connection with its becoming a public company.

(4) If the company is unlimited it must also make such changes in its articles as are necessary in connection with its becoming a company limited by shares.

91 Requirements as to share capital

(1) The following requirements must be met at the time the special resolution is passed that the company should be re-registered as a public company –

(a) the nominal value of the company's allotted share capital must be not less than the authorised minimum;

(b) each of the company's allotted shares must be paid up at least as to one quarter of the nominal value of that share and the whole of any premium on it;

(c) if any shares in the company or any premium on them have been fully or partly paid up by an undertaking given by any person that he or another should do work or perform services (whether for the company or any other person), the undertaking must have been performed or otherwise discharged;

(d) if shares have been allotted as fully or partly paid up as to their nominal value or any premium on them otherwise than in cash, and the consideration for the allotment consists of or includes an undertaking to the company (other than one to which paragraph (c) applies), then either –

(i)   the undertaking must have been performed or otherwise discharged, or

(ii) there must be a contract between the company and some person pursuant to which the undertaking is to be performed within five years from the time the special resolution is passed.

(2) For the purpose of determining whether the requirements in subsection (1)(b), (c) and (d) are met, the following may be disregarded –

(a) shares allotted –

(i)   before 22nd June 1982 in the case of a company then registered in Great Britain, or

(ii) before 31st December 1984 in the case of a company then registered in Northern Ireland;

(b) shares allotted in pursuance of an employees' share scheme by reason of which the company would, but for this subsection, be precluded under subsection (1)(b) (but not otherwise) from being re-registered as a public company.

(3) No more than one-tenth of the nominal value of the company's allotted share capital is to be disregarded under subsection (2)(a).

For this purpose the allotted share capital is treated as not including shares disregarded under subsection (2)(b).

(4) Shares disregarded under subsection (2) are treated as not forming part of the allotted share capital for the purposes of subsection (1)(a).

(5) A company must not be re-registered as a public company if it appears to the registrar that –

    (a) the company has resolved to reduce its share capital,

    (b) the reduction –

        (i)   is made under section 626 (reduction in connection with redenomination of share capital),

        (ii)   is supported by a solvency statement in accordance with section 643, or

        (iii) has been confirmed by an order of the court under section 648, and

    (c) the effect of the reduction is, or will be, that the nominal value of the company's allotted share capital is below the authorised minimum.

92 Requirements as to net assets

(1) A company applying to re-register as a public company must obtain –

    (a) a balance sheet prepared as at a date not more than seven months before the date on which the application is delivered to the registrar,

    (b) an unqualified report by the company's auditor on that balance sheet, and

    (c) a written statement by the company's auditor that in his opinion at the balance sheet date the amount of the company's net assets was not less than the aggregate of its called-up share capital and undistributable reserves.

(2) Between the balance sheet date and the date on which the application for reregistration is delivered to the registrar, there must be no change in the company's financial position that results in the amount of its net assets becoming less than the aggregate of its called-up share capital and undistributable reserves.

(3) In subsection (1)(b) an "unqualified report" means –

    (a) if the balance sheet was prepared for a financial year of the company, a report stating without material qualification the auditor's opinion that the balance sheet has been properly prepared in accordance with the requirements of this Act;

    (b) if the balance sheet was not prepared for a financial year of the company, a report stating without material qualification the auditor's opinion that the balance sheet has been properly prepared in accordance with the provisions of this Act which would have applied if it had been prepared for a financial year of the company.

(4) For the purposes of an auditor's report on a balance sheet that was not prepared for a financial year of the company, the provisions of this Act apply with such modifications as are necessary by reason of that fact.

(5) For the purposes of subsection (3) a qualification is material unless the auditor states in his report that the matter giving rise to the qualification is not material for the purpose of determining (by reference to the company's balance sheet) whether at the balance sheet date the amount of the company's net assets was not less than the aggregate of its called-up share capital and undistributable reserves.

(6) In this Part "net assets" and "undistributable reserves" have the same meaning as in section 831 (net asset restriction on distributions by public companies).

93 Recent allotment of shares for non-cash consideration

(1) This section applies where –

    (a) shares are allotted by the company in the period between the date as at which the balance sheet required by section 92 is prepared and the passing of the resolution that the company should re-register as a public company, and

    (b) the shares are allotted as fully or partly paid up as to their nominal value or any premium on them otherwise than in cash.

(2) The registrar shall not entertain an application by the company for re-registration as a public company unless –

(a) the requirements of section 593(1)(a) and (b) have been complied with (independent valuation of non-cash consideration; valuer's report to company not more than six months before allotment), or

(b) the allotment is in connection with –

(i) a share exchange (see subsections (3) to (5) below), or

(ii) a proposed merger with another company (see subsection (6) below).

(3) An allotment is in connection with a share exchange if –

(a) the shares are allotted in connection with an arrangement under which the whole or part of the consideration for the shares allotted is provided by –

(i) the transfer to the company allotting the shares of shares (or shares of a particular class) in another company, or

(ii) the cancellation of shares (or shares of a particular class) in another company; and

(b) the allotment is open to all the holders of the shares of the other company in question (or, where the arrangement applies only to shares of a particular class, to all the holders of the company's shares of that class) to take part in the arrangement in connection with which the shares are allotted.

(4) In determining whether a person is a holder of shares for the purposes of subsection (3), there shall be disregarded –

(a) shares held by, or by a nominee of, the company allotting the shares;

(b) shares held by, or by a nominee of –

(i) the holding company of the company allotting the shares,

(ii) a subsidiary of the company allotting the shares, or

(iii) a subsidiary of the holding company of the company allotting the shares.

(5) It is immaterial, for the purposes of deciding whether an allotment is in connection with a share exchange, whether or not the arrangement in connection with which the shares are allotted involves the issue to the company allotting the shares of shares (or shares of a particular class) in the other company.

(6) There is a proposed merger with another company if one of the companies concerned proposes to acquire all the assets and liabilities of the other in exchange for the issue of its shares or other securities to shareholders of the other (whether or not accompanied by a cash payment).

"Another company" includes any body corporate.

(7) For the purposes of this section –

(a) the consideration for an allotment does not include any amount standing to the credit of any of the company's reserve accounts, or of its profit and loss account, that has been applied in paying up (to any extent) any of the shares allotted or any premium on those shares; and

(b) "arrangement" means any agreement, scheme or arrangement, (including an arrangement sanctioned in accordance with –

(i) Part 26 of this Act (arrangements and reconstructions), or

(ii) section 110 of the Insolvency Act 1986 (c. 45) or Article 96 of the Insolvency (Northern Ireland) Order 1989 (S.I. 1989/2405 (N.I. 19)) (liquidator in winding up accepting shares as consideration for sale of company's property)).

94 Application and accompanying documents

(1) An application for re-registration as a public company must contain –

(a) a statement of the company's proposed name on re-registration; and

(b) in the case of a company without a secretary, a statement of the company's proposed secretary (see section 95).

(2) The application must be accompanied by –

    (a) a copy of the special resolution that the company should re-register as a public company (unless a copy has already been forwarded to the registrar under Chapter 3 of Part 3);

    (b) a copy of the company's articles as proposed to be amended;

    (c) a copy of the balance sheet and other documents referred to in section 92(1); and

    (d) if section 93 applies (recent allotment of shares for non-cash consideration), a copy of the valuation report (if any) under subsection (2)(a) of that section.

(3) The statement of compliance required to be delivered together with the application is a statement that the requirements of this Part as to re-registration as a public company have been complied with.

(4) The registrar may accept the statement of compliance as sufficient evidence that the company is entitled to be re-registered as a public company.

95 Statement of proposed secretary

(1) The statement of the company's proposed secretary must contain the required particulars of the person who is or the persons who are to be the secretary or joint secretaries of the company.

(2) The required particulars are the particulars that will be required to be stated in the company's register of secretaries (see sections 277 to 279).

(3) The statement must also contain a consent by the person named as secretary, or each of the persons named as joint secretaries, to act in the relevant capacity.

If all the partners in a firm are to be joint secretaries, consent may be given by one partner on behalf of all of them.

96 Issue of certificate of incorporation on re-registration

(1) If on an application for re-registration as a public company the registrar is satisfied that the company is entitled to be so re-registered, the company shall be re-registered accordingly.

(2) The registrar must issue a certificate of incorporation altered to meet the circumstances of the case.

(3) The certificate must state that it is issued on re-registration and the date on which it is issued.

(4) On the issue of the certificate –

    (a) the company by virtue of the issue of the certificate becomes a public company,

    (b) the changes in the company's name and articles take effect, and

    (c) where the application contained a statement under section 95 (statement of proposed secretary), the person or persons named in the statement as secretary or joint secretary of the company are deemed to have been appointed to that office.

(5) The certificate is conclusive evidence that the requirements of this Act as to reregistration have been complied with.

Public company becoming private

97 Re-registration of public company as private limited company

(1) A public company may be re-registered as a private limited company if –

    (a) a special resolution that it should be so re-registered is passed,

    (b) the conditions specified below are met, and

    (c) an application for re-registration is delivered to the registrar in accordance with section 100, together with –

        (i) the other documents required by that section, and

        (ii) a statement of compliance.

(2) The conditions are that –

    (a) where no application under section 98 for cancellation of the resolution has been made –

        (i) having regard to the number of members who consented to or voted in favour of the resolution, no such application may be made, or

        (ii) the period within which such an application could be made has expired, or

    (b) where such an application has been made –

        (i) the application has been withdrawn, or

        (ii) an order has been made confirming the resolution and a copy of that order has been delivered to the registrar.

(3) The company must make such changes –

    (a) in its name, and

    (b) in its articles,

as are necessary in connection with its becoming a private company limited by shares or, as the case may be, by guarantee.

98 Application to court to cancel resolution

(1) Where a special resolution by a public company to be re-registered as a private limited company has been passed, an application to the court for the cancellation of the resolution may be made –

    (a) by the holders of not less in the aggregate than 5% in nominal value of the company's issued share capital or any class of the company's issued share capital (disregarding any shares held by the company as treasury shares);

    (b) if the company is not limited by shares, by not less than 5% of its members; or

    (c) by not less than 50 of the company's members;

but not by a person who has consented to or voted in favour of the resolution.

(2) The application must be made within 28 days after the passing of the resolution and may be made on behalf of the persons entitled to make it by such one or more of their number as they may appoint for the purpose.

(3) On the hearing of the application the court shall make an order either cancelling or confirming the resolution.

(4) The court may –

    (a) make that order on such terms and conditions as it thinks fit,

    (b) if it thinks fit adjourn the proceedings in order that an arrangement may be made to the satisfaction of the court for the purchase of the interests of dissentient members, and

    (c) give such directions, and make such orders, as it thinks expedient for facilitating or carrying into effect any such arrangement.

(5) The court's order may, if the court thinks fit –

    (a) provide for the purchase by the company of the shares of any of its members and for the reduction accordingly of the company's capital; and

    (b) make such alteration in the company's articles as may be required in consequence of that provision.

(6) The court's order may, if the court thinks fit, require the company not to make any, or any specified, amendments to its articles without the leave of the court.

99 Notice to registrar of court application or order

(1) On making an application under section 98 (application to court to cancel resolution) the applicants, or the person making the application on their behalf, must immediately give notice to the registrar.

This is without prejudice to any provision of rules of court as to service of notice of the application.

(2) On being served with notice of any such application, the company must immediately give notice to the registrar.

(3) Within 15 days of the making of the court's order on the application, or such longer period as the court may at any time direct, the company must deliver to the registrar a copy of the order.

(4) If a company fails to comply with subsection (2) or (3) an offence is committed by –

  (a) the company, and
  (b) every officer of the company who is in default.

(5) A person guilty of an offence under this section is liable on summary conviction to a fine not exceeding level 3 on the standard scale and, for continued contravention, a daily default fine not exceeding one-tenth of level 3 on the standard scale.

100 Application and accompanying documents

(1) An application for re-registration as a private limited company must contain a statement of the company's proposed name on re-registration.

(2) The application must be accompanied by –

  (a) a copy of the resolution that the company should re-register as a private limited company (unless a copy has already been forwarded to the registrar under Chapter 3 of Part 3); and
  (b) a copy of the company's articles as proposed to be amended.

(3) The statement of compliance required to be delivered together with the application is a statement that the requirements of this Part as to re-registration as a private limited company have been complied with.

(4) The registrar may accept the statement of compliance as sufficient evidence that the company is entitled to be re-registered as a private limited company.

101 Issue of certificate of incorporation on re-registration

(1) If on an application for re-registration as a private limited company the registrar is satisfied that the company is entitled to be so re-registered, the company shall be re-registered accordingly.

(2) The registrar must issue a certificate of incorporation altered to meet the circumstances of the case.

(3) The certificate must state that it is issued on re-registration and the date on which it is issued.

(4) On the issue of the certificate –

  (a) the company by virtue of the issue of the certificate becomes a private limited company, and
  (b) the changes in the company's name and articles take effect.

(5) The certificate is conclusive evidence that the requirements of this Act as to reregistration have been complied with.

Private limited company becoming unlimited

102 Re-registration of private limited company as unlimited

(1) A private limited company may be re-registered as an unlimited company if –

  (a) all the members of the company have assented to its being so re-registered,
  (b) the condition specified below is met, and
  (c) an application for re-registration is delivered to the registrar in accordance with section 103, together with –

(i)   the other documents required by that section, and

(ii)   a statement of compliance.

(2)   The condition is that the company has not previously been re-registered as limited.

(3)   The company must make such changes in its name and its articles –

(a)   as are necessary in connection with its becoming an unlimited company; and

(b)   if it is to have a share capital, as are necessary in connection with its becoming an unlimited company having a share capital.

(4)   For the purposes of this section –

(a)   a trustee in bankruptcy of a member of the company is entitled, to the exclusion of the member, to assent to the company's becoming unlimited; and

(b)   the personal representative of a deceased member of the company may assent on behalf of the deceased.

(5)   In subsection (4)(a), "a trustee in bankruptcy of a member of the company" includes –

(a)   a permanent trustee or an interim trustee (within the meaning of the Bankruptcy (Scotland) Act 1985 (c. 66)) on the sequestrated estate of a member of the company;

(b)   a trustee under a protected trustee deed (within the meaning of the Bankruptcy (Scotland) Act 1985) granted by a member of the company.

103 Application and accompanying documents

(1)   An application for re-registration as an unlimited company must contain a statement of the company's proposed name on re-registration.

(2)   The application must be accompanied by –

(a)   the prescribed form of assent to the company's being registered as an unlimited company, authenticated by or on behalf of all the members of the company;

(b)   a copy of the company's articles as proposed to be amended.

(3)   The statement of compliance required to be delivered together with the application is a statement that the requirements of this Part as to re-registration as an unlimited company have been complied with.

(4)   The statement must contain a statement by the directors of the company –

(a)   that the persons by whom or on whose behalf the form of assent is authenticated constitute the whole membership of the company, and

(b)   if any of the members have not authenticated that form themselves, that the directors have taken all reasonable steps to satisfy themselves that each person who authenticated it on behalf of a member was lawfully empowered to do so.

(5)   The registrar may accept the statement of compliance as sufficient evidence that the company is entitled to be re-registered as an unlimited company.

104 Issue of certificate of incorporation on re-registration

(1)   If on an application for re-registration of a private limited company as an unlimited company the registrar is satisfied that the company is entitled to be so re-registered, the company shall be re-registered accordingly.

(2)   The registrar must issue a certificate of incorporation altered to meet the circumstances of the case.

(3)   The certificate must state that it is issued on re-registration and the date on which it is issued.

(4)   On the issue of the certificate –

(a)   the company by virtue of the issue of the certificate becomes an unlimited company, and

(b)   the changes in the company's name and articles take effect.

(5) The certificate is conclusive evidence that the requirements of this Act as to reregistration have been complied with.

Unlimited private company becoming limited

105 Re-registration of unlimited company as limited

(1) An unlimited company may be re-registered as a private limited company if –

    (a) a special resolution that it should be so re-registered is passed,

    (b) the condition specified below is met, and

    (c) an application for re-registration is delivered to the registrar in accordance with section 106, together with –

        (i)   the other documents required by that section, and

        (ii) a statement of compliance.

(2) The condition is that the company has not previously been re-registered as unlimited.

(3) The special resolution must state whether the company is to be limited by shares or by guarantee.

(4) The company must make such changes –

    (a) in its name, and

    (b) in its articles,

as are necessary in connection with its becoming a company limited by shares or, as the case may be, by guarantee.

106 Application and accompanying documents

(1) An application for re-registration as a limited company must contain a statement of the company's proposed name on re-registration.

(2) The application must be accompanied by –

    (a) a copy of the resolution that the company should re-register as a private limited company (unless a copy has already been forwarded to the registrar under Chapter 3 of Part 3);

    (b) if the company is to be limited by guarantee, a statement of guarantee;

    (c) a copy of the company's articles as proposed to be amended.

(3) The statement of guarantee required to be delivered in the case of a company that is to be limited by guarantee must state that each member undertakes that, if the company is wound up while he is a member, or within one year after he ceases to be a member, he will contribute to the assets of the company such amount as may be required for –

    (a) payment of the debts and liabilities of the company contracted before he ceases to be a member,

    (b) payment of the costs, charges and expenses of winding up, and

    (c) adjustment of the rights of the contributories among themselves,

not exceeding a specified amount.

(4) The statement of compliance required to be delivered together with the application is a statement that the requirements of this Part as to re-registration as a limited company have been complied with.

(5) The registrar may accept the statement of compliance as sufficient evidence that the company is entitled to be re-registered as a limited company.

107 Issue of certificate of incorporation on re-registration

(1) If on an application for re-registration of an unlimited company as a limited company the registrar is satisfied that the company is entitled to be so re-registered, the company shall be re-registered accordingly.

(2) The registrar must issue a certificate of incorporation altered to meet the circumstances of the case.

(3) The certificate must state that it is issued on re-registration and the date on which it is so issued.

(4) On the issue of the certificate –

(a) the company by virtue of the issue of the certificate becomes a limited company, and

(b) the changes in the company's name and articles take effect.

(5) The certificate is conclusive evidence that the requirements of this Act as to reregistration have been complied with.

108 Statement of capital required where company already has share capital

(1) A company which on re-registration under section 107 already has allotted share capital must within 15 days after the re-registration deliver a statement of capital to the registrar.

(2) This does not apply if the information which would be included in the statement has already been sent to the registrar in –

(a) a statement of capital and initial shareholdings (see section 10), or

(b) a statement of capital contained in an annual return (see section 856(2)).

(3) The statement of capital must state with respect to the company's share capital on re-registration –

(a) the total number of shares of the company,

(b) the aggregate nominal value of those shares,

(c) for each class of shares –

(i) prescribed particulars of the rights attached to the shares,

(ii) the total number of shares of that class, and

(iii) the aggregate nominal value of shares of that class, and

(d) the amount paid up and the amount (if any) unpaid on each share (whether on account of the nominal value of the share or by way of premium).

(4) If default is made in complying with this section, an offence is committed by –

(a) the company, and

(b) every officer of the company who is in default.

(5) A person guilty of an offence under this section is liable on summary conviction to a fine not exceeding level 3 on the standard scale and, for continued contravention, a daily default fine not exceeding one-tenth of level 3 on the standard scale.

Public company becoming private and unlimited

109 Re-registration of public company as private and unlimited

(1) A public company limited by shares may be re-registered as an unlimited private company with a share capital if –

(a) all the members of the company have assented to its being so re-registered,

(b) the condition specified below is met, and

(c) an application for re-registration is delivered to the registrar in accordance with section 110, together with –

(i) the other documents required by that section, and

(ii) a statement of compliance.

(2) The condition is that the company has not previously been re-registered –

(a) as limited, or

(b) as unlimited.

(3)   The company must make such changes –

(a)   in its name, and
(b)   in its articles,

as are necessary in connection with its becoming an unlimited private company.

(4)   For the purposes of this section –

(a)   a trustee in bankruptcy of a member of the company is entitled, to the exclusion of the member, to assent to the company's re-registration; and
(b)   the personal representative of a deceased member of the company may assent on behalf of the deceased.

(5)   In subsection (4)(a), "a trustee in bankruptcy of a member of the company" includes –

(a)   a permanent trustee or an interim trustee (within the meaning of the Bankruptcy (Scotland) Act 1985 (c. 66)) on the sequestrated estate of a member of the company;
(b)   a trustee under a protected trustee deed (within the meaning of the Bankruptcy (Scotland) Act 1985) granted by a member of the company.

110 Application and accompanying documents

(1)   An application for re-registration of a public company as an unlimited private company must contain a statement of the company's proposed name on re-registration.

(2)   The application must be accompanied by –

(a)   the prescribed form of assent to the company's being registered as an unlimited company, authenticated by or on behalf of all the members of the company, and
(b)   a copy of the company's articles as proposed to be amended.

(3)   The statement of compliance required to be delivered together with the application is a statement that the requirements of this Part as to re-registration as an unlimited private company have been complied with.

(4)   The statement must contain a statement by the directors of the company –

(a)   that the persons by whom or on whose behalf the form of assent is authenticated constitute the whole membership of the company, and
(b)   if any of the members have not authenticated that form themselves, that the directors have taken all reasonable steps to satisfy themselves that each person who authenticated it on behalf of a member was lawfully empowered to do so.

(5)   The registrar may accept the statement of compliance as sufficient evidence that the company is entitled to be re-registered as an unlimited private company.

111 Issue of certificate of incorporation on re-registration

(1)   If on an application for re-registration of a public company as an unlimited private company the registrar is satisfied that the company is entitled to be so re-registered, the company shall be re-registered accordingly.

(2)   The registrar must issue a certificate of incorporation altered to meet the circumstances of the case.

(3)   The certificate must state that it is issued on re-registration and the date on which it is so issued.

(4)   On the issue of the certificate –

(a)   the company by virtue of the issue of the certificate becomes an unlimited private company, and
(b)   the changes in the company's name and articles take effect.

(5)   The certificate is conclusive evidence that the requirements of this Act as to reregistration have been complied with.

PART 8

A COMPANY'S MEMBERS

CHAPTER 1

THE MEMBERS OF A COMPANY

112 The members of a company

(1) The subscribers of a company's memorandum are deemed to have agreed to become members of the company, and on its registration become members and must be entered as such in its register of members.

(2) Every other person who agrees to become a member of a company, and whose name is entered in its register of members, is a member of the company.

CHAPTER 2

REGISTER OF MEMBERS

General

113 Register of members

(1) Every company must keep a register of its members.

(2) There must be entered in the register –

    (a) the names and addresses of the members,

    (b) the date on which each person was registered as a member, and

    (c) the date at which any person ceased to be a member.

(3) In the case of a company having a share capital, there must be entered in the register, with the names and addresses of the members, a statement of –

    (a) the shares held by each member, distinguishing each share –

        (i)   by its number (so long as the share has a number), and

        (ii) where the company has more than one class of issued shares, by its class, and

    (b) the amount paid or agreed to be considered as paid on the shares of each member.

(4) If the company has converted any of its shares into stock, and given notice of the conversion to the registrar, the register of members must show the amount and class of stock held by each member instead of the amount of shares and the particulars relating to shares specified above.

(5) In the case of joint holders of shares or stock in a company, the company's register of members must state the names of each joint holder.

In other respects joint holders are regarded for the purposes of this Chapter as a single member (so that the register must show a single address).

(6) In the case of a company that does not have a share capital but has more than one class of members, there must be entered in the register, with the names and addresses of the members, a statement of the class to which each member belongs.

(7) If a company makes default in complying with this section an offence is committed by –

    (a) the company, and

(b) every officer of the company who is in default.

(8) A person guilty of an offence under this section is liable on summary conviction to a fine not exceeding level 3 on the standard scale and, for continued contravention, a daily default fine not exceeding one-tenth of level 3 on the standard scale.

114 Register to be kept available for inspection

(1) A company's register of members must be kept available for inspection –

(a) at its registered office, or
(b) at a place specified in regulations under section 1136.

(2) A company must give notice to the registrar of the place where its register of members is kept available for inspection and of any change in that place.

(3) No such notice is required if the register has, at all times since it came into existence (or, in the case of a register in existence on the relevant date, at all times since then) been kept available for inspection at the company's registered office.

(4) The relevant date for the purposes of subsection (3) is –

(a) 1st July 1948 in the case of a company registered in Great Britain, and
(b) 1st April 1961 in the case of a company registered in Northern Ireland.

(5) If a company makes default for 14 days in complying with subsection (2), an offence is committed by –

(a) the company, and
(b) every officer of the company who is in default.

(6) A person guilty of an offence under this section is liable on summary conviction to a fine not exceeding level 3 on the standard scale and, for continued contravention, a daily default fine not exceeding one-tenth of level 3 on the standard scale.

115 Index of members

(1) Every company having more than 50 members must keep an index of the names of the members of the company, unless the register of members is in such a form as to constitute in itself an index.

(2) The company must make any necessary alteration in the index within 14 days after the date on which any alteration is made in the register of members.

(3) The index must contain, in respect of each member, a sufficient indication to enable the account of that member in the register to be readily found.

(4) The index must be at all times kept available for inspection at the same place as the register of members.

(5) If default is made in complying with this section, an offence is committed by –

(a) the company, and
(b) every officer of the company who is in default.

(6) A person guilty of an offence under this section is liable on summary conviction to a fine not exceeding level 3 on the standard scale and, for continued contravention, a daily default fine not exceeding one-tenth of level 3 on the standard scale.

116 Rights to inspect and require copies

(1) The register and the index of members' names must be open to the inspection –

(a) of any member of the company without charge, and
(b) of any other person on payment of such fee as may be prescribed.

(2) Any person may require a copy of a company's register of members, or of any part of it, on payment of such fee as may be prescribed.

(3) A person seeking to exercise either of the rights conferred by this section must make a request to the company to that effect.

(4) The request must contain the following information –

(a) in the case of an individual, his name and address;
(b) in the case of an organisation, the name and address of an individual responsible for making the request on behalf of the organisation;
(c) the purpose for which the information is to be used; and
(d) whether the information will be disclosed to any other person, and if so –

    (i) where that person is an individual, his name and address,
    (ii) where that person is an organisation, the name and address of an individual responsible for receiving the information on its behalf, and
    (iii) the purpose for which the information is to be used by that person.

117 Register of members: response to request for inspection or copy

(1) Where a company receives a request under section 116 (register of members: right to inspect and require copy), it must within five working days either –

(a) comply with the request, or
(b) apply to the court.

(2) If it applies to the court it must notify the person making the request.
(3) If on an application under this section the court is satisfied that the inspection or copy is not sought for a proper purpose –

(a) it shall direct the company not to comply with the request, and
(b) it may further order that the company's costs (in Scotland, expenses) on the application be paid in whole or in part by the person who made the request, even if he is not a party to the application.

(4) If the court makes such a direction and it appears to the court that the company is or may be subject to other requests made for a similar purpose (whether made by the same person or different persons), it may direct that the company is not to comply with any such request.
The order must contain such provision as appears to the court appropriate to identify the requests to which it applies.

(5) If on an application under this section the court does not direct the company not to comply with the request, the company must comply with the request immediately upon the court giving its decision or, as the case may be, the proceedings being discontinued.

118 Register of members: refusal of inspection or default in providing copy

(1) If an inspection required under section 116 (register of members: right to inspect and require copy) is refused or default is made in providing a copy required under that section, otherwise than in accordance with an order of the court, an offence is committed by –

(a) the company, and
(b) every officer of the company who is in default.

(2) A person guilty of an offence under this section is liable on summary conviction to a fine not exceeding level 3 on the standard scale and, for continued contravention, a daily default fine not exceeding one-tenth of level 3 on the standard scale.
(3) In the case of any such refusal or default the court may by order compel an immediate inspection or, as the case may be, direct that the copy required be sent to the person requesting it.

119 Register of members: offences in connection with request for or disclosure of information

(1) It is an offence for a person knowingly or recklessly to make in a request under section 116 (register of members: right to inspect or require copy) a statement that is misleading, false or deceptive in a material particular.

(2)   It is an offence for a person in possession of information obtained by exercise of either of the rights conferred by that section –

  (a)   to do anything that results in the information being disclosed to another person, or

  (b)   to fail to do anything with the result that the information is disclosed to another person,

knowing, or having reason to suspect, that person may use the information for a purpose that is not a proper purpose.

(3)   A person guilty of an offence under this section is liable –

  (a)   on conviction on indictment, to imprisonment for a term not exceeding two years or a fine (or both);

  (b)   on summary conviction –

    (i)   in England and Wales, to imprisonment for a term not exceeding twelve months or to a fine not exceeding the statutory maximum (or both);

    (ii)   in Scotland or Northern Ireland, to imprisonment for a term not exceeding six months, or to a fine not exceeding the statutory maximum (or both).

120 Information as to state of register and index

(1)   When a person inspects the register, or the company provides him with a copy of the register or any part of it, the company must inform him of the most recent date (if any) on which alterations were made to the register and there were no further alterations to be made.

(2)   When a person inspects the index of members' names, the company must inform him whether there is any alteration to the register that is not reflected in the index.

(3)   If a company fails to provide the information required under subsection (1) or (2), an offence is committed by –

  (a)   the company, and

  (b)   every officer of the company who is in default.

(4)   A person guilty of an offence under this section is liable on summary conviction to a fine not exceeding level 3 on the standard scale.

121 Removal of entries relating to former members

An entry relating to a former member of the company may be removed from the register after the expiration of ten years from the date on which he ceased to be a member.

Special cases

122 Share warrants

(1)   On the issue of a share warrant the company must –

  (a)   enter in the register of members –

    (i)   the fact of the issue of the warrant,

    (ii)   a statement of the shares included in the warrant, distinguishing each share by its number so long as the share has a number, and

    (iii) the date of the issue of the warrant,

    and

  (b)   amend the register, if necessary, so that no person is named on the register as the holder of the shares specified in the warrant.

(2)   Until the warrant is surrendered, the particulars specified in subsection (1)(a) are deemed to be those required by this Act to be entered in the register of members.

(3)   The bearer of a share warrant may, if the articles of the company so provide, be

deemed a member of the company within the meaning of this Act, either to the full extent or for any purposes defined in the articles.

(4) Subject to the company's articles, the bearer of a share warrant is entitled, on surrendering it for cancellation, to have his name entered as a member in the register of members.

(5) The company is responsible for any loss incurred by any person by reason of the company entering in the register the name of a bearer of a share warrant in respect of the shares specified in it without the warrant being surrendered and cancelled.

(6) On the surrender of a share warrant, the date of the surrender must be entered in the register.

123 Single member companies

(1) If a limited company is formed under this Act with only one member there shall be entered in the company's register of members, with the name and address of the sole member, a statement that the company has only one member.

(2) If the number of members of a limited company falls to one, or if an unlimited company with only one member becomes a limited company on reregistration, there shall upon the occurrence of that event be entered in the company's register of members, with the name and address of the sole member –

   (a) a statement that the company has only one member, and
   (b) the date on which the company became a company having only one member.

(3) If the membership of a limited company increases from one to two or more members, there shall upon the occurrence of that event be entered in the company's register of members, with the name and address of the person who was formerly the sole member –

   (a) a statement that the company has ceased to have only one member, and
   (b) the date on which that event occurred.

(4) If a company makes default in complying with this section, an offence is committed by –

   (a) the company, and
   (b) every officer of the company who is in default.

(5) A person guilty of an offence under this section is liable on summary conviction to a fine not exceeding level 3 on the standard scale and, for continued contravention, a daily default fine not exceeding one-tenth of level 3 on the standard scale.

124 Company holding its own shares as treasury shares

(1) Where a company purchases its own shares in circumstances in which section 724 (treasury shares) applies –

   (a) the requirements of section 113 (register of members) need not be complied with if the company cancels all of the shares forthwith after the purchase, and
   (b) if the company does not cancel all of the shares forthwith after the purchase, any share that is so cancelled shall be disregarded for the purposes of that section.

(2) Subject to subsection (1), where a company holds shares as treasury shares the company must be entered in the register as the member holding those shares.

Supplementary

125 Power of court to rectify register

(1) If –

   (a) the name of any person is, without sufficient cause, entered in or omitted from a company's register of members, or

(b) default is made or unnecessary delay takes place in entering on the register the fact of any person having ceased to be a member,

the person aggrieved, or any member of the company, or the company, may apply to the court for rectification of the register.

(2) The court may either refuse the application or may order rectification of the register and payment by the company of any damages sustained by any party aggrieved.

(3) On such an application the court may decide any question relating to the title of a person who is a party to the application to have his name entered in or omitted from the register, whether the question arises between members or alleged members, or between members or alleged members on the one hand and the company on the other hand, and generally may decide any question necessary or expedient to be decided for rectification of the register.

(4) In the case of a company required by this Act to send a list of its members to the registrar of companies, the court, when making an order for rectification of the register, shall by its order direct notice of the rectification to be given to the registrar.

126 Trusts not to be entered on register

No notice of any trust, expressed, implied or constructive, shall be entered on the register of members of a company registered in England and Wales or Northern Ireland, or be receivable by the registrar.

127 Register to be evidence

The register of members is prima facie evidence of any matters which are by this Act directed or authorised to be inserted in it.

128 Time limit for claims arising from entry in register

(1) Liability incurred by a company –

(a) from the making or deletion of an entry in the register of members, or
(b) from a failure to make or delete any such entry,

is not enforceable more than ten years after the date on which the entry was made or deleted or, as the case may be, the failure first occurred.

(2) This is without prejudice to any lesser period of limitation (and, in Scotland, to any rule that the obligation giving rise to the liability prescribes before the expiry of that period).

CHAPTER 3

OVERSEAS BRANCH REGISTERS

129 Overseas branch registers

(1) A company having a share capital may, if it transacts business in a country or territory to which this Chapter applies, cause to be kept there a branch register of members resident there (an "overseas branch register").

(2) This Chapter applies to –

(a) any part of Her Majesty's dominions outside the United Kingdom, the Channel Islands and the Isle of Man, and
(b) the countries or territories listed below.

Bangladesh	Malaysia
Cyprus	Malta
Dominica	Nigeria
The Gambia	Pakistan

Ghana	Seychelles
Guyana	Sierra Leone
The Hong Kong Special Administrative Region	
of the People's Republic of China	Singapore
India	South Africa
Ireland	Sri Lanka
Kenya	Swaziland
Kiribati	Trinidad and Tobago
Lesotho	Uganda
Malawi	Zimbabwe

(3) The Secretary of State may make provision by regulations as to the circumstances in which a company is to be regarded as keeping a register in a particular country or territory.

(4) Regulations under this section are subject to negative resolution procedure.

(5) References –

(a) in any Act or instrument (including, in particular, a company's articles) to a dominion register, or

(b) in articles registered before 1st November 1929 to a colonial register,

are to be read (unless the context otherwise requires) as a reference to an overseas branch register kept under this section.

130 Notice of opening of overseas branch register

(1) A company that begins to keep an overseas branch register must give notice to the registrar within 14 days of doing so, stating the country or territory in which the register is kept.

(2) If default is made in complying with subsection (1), an offence is committed by –

(a) the company, and

(b) every officer of the company who is in default.

(3) A person guilty of an offence under subsection (2) is liable on summary conviction to a fine not exceeding level 3 on the standard scale and, for continued contravention, a daily default fine not exceeding one-tenth of level 3 on the standard scale.

131 Keeping of overseas branch register

(1) An overseas branch register is regarded as part of the company's register of members ("the main register").

(2) The Secretary of State may make provision by regulations modifying any provision of Chapter 2 (register of members) as it applies in relation to an overseas branch register.

(3) Regulations under this section are subject to negative resolution procedure.

(4) Subject to the provisions of this Act, a company may by its articles make such provision as it thinks fit as to the keeping of overseas branch registers.

132 Register or duplicate to be kept available for inspection in UK

(1) A company that keeps an overseas branch register must keep available for inspection –

(a) the register, or

(b) a duplicate of the register duly entered up from time to time,

at the place in the United Kingdom where the company's main register is kept available for inspection.

(2) Any such duplicate is treated for all purposes of this Act as part of the main register.

(3) If default is made in complying with subsection (1), an offence is committed by –

(a) the company, and

(b) every officer of the company who is in default.

(4)   A person guilty of an offence under subsection (3) is liable on summary conviction to a fine not exceeding level 3 on the standard scale and, for continued contravention, a daily default fine not exceeding one-tenth of level 3 on the standard scale.

133 Transactions in shares registered in overseas branch register

(1)   Shares registered in an overseas branch register must be distinguished from those registered in the main register.
(2)   No transaction with respect to shares registered in an overseas branch register may be registered in any other register.
(3)   An instrument of transfer of a share registered in an overseas branch register –

(a)   is regarded as a transfer of property situated outside the United Kingdom, and
(b)   unless executed in a part of the United Kingdom, is exempt from stamp duty.

134 Jurisdiction of local courts

(1)   A competent court in a country or territory where an overseas branch register is kept may exercise the same jurisdiction as is exercisable by a court in the United Kingdom –

(a)   to rectify the register (see section 125), or
(b)   in relation to a request for inspection or a copy of the register (see section 117).

(2)   The offences –

(a)   of refusing inspection or failing to provide a copy of the register (see section 118), and
(b)   of making a false, misleading or deceptive statement in a request for inspection or a copy (see section 119),

may be prosecuted summarily before any tribunal having summary criminal jurisdiction in the country or territory where the register is kept.
(3)   This section extends only to those countries and territories to which paragraph 3 of Schedule 14 to the Companies Act 1985 (c. 6) (which made similar provision) extended immediately before the coming into force of this Chapter.

135 Discontinuance of overseas branch register

(1)   A company may discontinue an overseas branch register.
(2)   If it does so all the entries in that register must be transferred –

(a)   to some other overseas branch register kept in the same country or territory, or
(b)   to the main register.

(3)   The company must give notice to the registrar within 14 days of the discontinuance.
(4)   If default is made in complying with subsection (3), an offence is committed by –

(a)   the company, and
(b)   every officer of the company who is in default.

(5)   A person guilty of an offence under subsection (4) is liable on summary conviction to a fine not exceeding level 3 on the standard scale and, for continued contravention, a daily default fine not exceeding one-tenth of level 3 on the standard scale.

CHAPTER 4

PROHIBITION ON SUBSIDIARY BEING MEMBER OF ITS HOLDING COMPANY

General prohibition

136 Prohibition on subsidiary being a member of its holding company

(1) Except as provided by this Chapter –
   (a) a body corporate cannot be a member of a company that is its holding company, and
   (b) any allotment or transfer of shares in a company to its subsidiary is void.

(2) The exceptions are provided for in –

   section 138 (subsidiary acting as personal representative or trustee), and
   section 141 (subsidiary acting as authorised dealer in securities).

137 Shares acquired before prohibition became applicable

(1) Where a body corporate became a holder of shares in a company –
   (a) before the relevant date, or
   (b) on or after that date and before the commencement of this Chapter in circumstances in which the prohibition in section 23(1) of the Companies Act 1985 or Article 33(1) of the Companies (Northern Companies Act 2006 (c. 46) Ireland) Order 1986 (S.I. 1986/1032 (N.I. 6)) (or any corresponding earlier enactment), as it then had effect, did not apply, or
   (c) on or after the commencement of this Chapter in circumstances in which the prohibition in section 136 did not apply, it may continue to be a member of the company.

(2) The relevant date for the purposes of subsection (1)(a) is –
   (a) 1st July 1948 in the case of a company registered in Great Britain, and
   (b) 1st April 1961 in the case of a company registered in Northern Ireland.

(3) So long as it is permitted to continue as a member of a company by virtue of this section, an allotment to it of fully paid shares in the company may be validly made by way of capitalisation of reserves of the company.

(4) But, so long as the prohibition in section 136 would (apart from this section) apply, it has no right to vote in respect of the shares mentioned in subsection (1) above, or any shares allotted as mentioned in subsection (3) above, on a written resolution or at meetings of the company or of any class of its members.

Subsidiary acting as personal representative or trustee

138 Subsidiary acting as personal representative or trustee

(1) The prohibition in section 136 (prohibition on subsidiary being a member of its holding company) does not apply where the subsidiary is concerned only –
   (a) as personal representative, or
   (b) as trustee,

   unless, in the latter case, the holding company or a subsidiary of it is beneficially interested under the trust.

(2) For the purpose of ascertaining whether the holding company or a subsidiary is so interested, there shall be disregarded –

(a) any interest held only by way of security for the purposes of a transaction entered into by the holding company or subsidiary in the ordinary course of a business that includes the lending of money;

(b) any interest within –

section 139 (interests to be disregarded: residual interest under pension scheme or employees' share scheme), or

section 140 (interests to be disregarded: employer's rights of recovery under pension scheme or employees' share scheme);

(c) any rights that the company or subsidiary has in its capacity as trustee, including in particular –

  (i) any right to recover its expenses or be remunerated out of the trust property, and

  (ii) any right to be indemnified out of the trust property for any liability incurred by reason of any act or omission in the performance of its duties as trustee.

139 Interests to be disregarded: residual interest under pension scheme or employees' share scheme

(1) Where shares in a company are held on trust for the purposes of a pension scheme or employees' share scheme, there shall be disregarded for the purposes of section 138 any residual interest that has not vested in possession.

(2) A "residual interest" means a right of the company or subsidiary ("the residual beneficiary") to receive any of the trust property in the event of –

(a) all the liabilities arising under the scheme having been satisfied or provided for, or

(b) the residual beneficiary ceasing to participate in the scheme, or

(c) the trust property at any time exceeding what is necessary for satisfying the liabilities arising or expected to arise under the scheme.

(3) In subsection (2) –

(a) the reference to a right includes a right dependent on the exercise of a discretion vested by the scheme in the trustee or another person, and

(b) the reference to liabilities arising under a scheme includes liabilities that have resulted, or may result, from the exercise of any such discretion.

(4) For the purposes of this section a residual interest vests in possession –

(a) in a case within subsection (2)(a), on the occurrence of the event mentioned there (whether or not the amount of the property receivable pursuant to the right is ascertained);

(b) in a case within subsection (2)(b) or (c), when the residual beneficiary becomes entitled to require the trustee to transfer to him any of the property receivable pursuant to the right.

(5) In this section "pension scheme" means a scheme for the provision of benefits consisting of or including relevant benefits for or in respect of employees or former employees.

(6) In subsection (5) –

(a) "relevant benefits" means any pension, lump sum, gratuity or other like benefit given or to be given on retirement or on death or in anticipation of retirement or, in connection with past service, after retirement or death; and

(b) "employee" shall be read as if a director of a company were employed by it.

140 Interests to be disregarded: employer's rights of recovery under pension scheme or employees' share scheme

(1) Where shares in a company are held on trust for the purposes of a pension scheme or employees' share scheme, there shall be disregarded for the purposes of section 138

any charge or lien on, or set-off against, any benefit or other right or interest under the scheme for the purpose of enabling the employer or former employer of a member of the scheme to obtain the discharge of a monetary obligation due to him from the member.

(2) In the case of a trust for the purposes of a pension scheme there shall also be disregarded any right to receive from the trustee of the scheme, or as trustee of the scheme to retain, an amount that can be recovered or retained, under section 61 of the Pension Schemes Act 1993 (c. 48) or section 57 of the Pension Companies Act 2006 (c. 46) Schemes (Northern Ireland) Act 1993 (c. 49) (deduction of contributions equivalent premium from refund of scheme contributions) or otherwise, as reimbursement or partial reimbursement for any contributions equivalent premium paid in connection with the scheme under Part 3 of that Act.

(3) In this section "pension scheme" means a scheme for the provision of benefits consisting of or including relevant benefits for or in respect of employees or former employees.
"Relevant benefits" here means any pension, lump sum, gratuity or other like benefit given or to be given on retirement or on death or in anticipation of retirement or, in connection with past service, after retirement or death.

(4) In this section "employer" and "employee" shall be read as if a director of a company were employed by it.

Subsidiary acting as dealer in securities

141 Subsidiary acting as authorised dealer in securities

(1) The prohibition in section 136 (prohibition on subsidiary being a member of its holding company) does not apply where the shares are held by the subsidiary in the ordinary course of its business as an intermediary.

(2) For this purpose a person is an intermediary if he –

   (a) carries on a bona fide business of dealing in securities,
   (b) is a member of or has access to a regulated market, and
   (c) does not carry on an excluded business.

(3) The following are excluded businesses –

   (a) a business that consists wholly or mainly in the making or managing of investments;
   (b) a business that consists wholly or mainly in, or is carried on wholly or mainly for the purposes of, providing services to persons who are connected with the person carrying on the business;
   (c) a business that consists in insurance business;
   (d) a business that consists in managing or acting as trustee in relation to a pension scheme, or that is carried on by the manager or trustee of such a scheme in connection with or for the purposes of the scheme;
   (e) a business that consists in operating or acting as trustee in relation to a collective investment scheme, or that is carried on by the operator or trustee of such a scheme in connection with and for the purposes of the scheme.

(4) For the purposes of this section –

   (a) the question whether a person is connected with another shall be determined in accordance with section 839 of the Income and Corporation Taxes Act 1988 (c. 1);
   (b) "collective investment scheme" has the meaning given in section 235 of the Financial Services and Markets Act 2000 (c. 8);
   (c) "insurance business" means business that consists in the effecting or carrying out of contracts of insurance;

(d) "securities" includes –

    (i)   options,

    (ii) futures, and

    (iii) contracts for differences,

    and rights or interests in those investments;

(e) "trustee" and "the operator" in relation to a collective investment scheme shall be construed in accordance with section 237(2) of the Financial Services and Markets Act 2000 (c. 8).

(5) Expressions used in this section that are also used in the provisions regulating activities under the Financial Services and Markets Act 2000 have the same meaning here as they do in those provisions.

See section 22 of that Act, orders made under that section and Schedule 2 to that Act.

142 Protection of third parties in other cases where subsidiary acting as dealer in securities

(1) This section applies where –

(a) a subsidiary that is a dealer in securities has purportedly acquired shares in its holding company in contravention of the prohibition in section 136, and

(b) a person acting in good faith has agreed, for value and without notice of the contravention, to acquire shares in the holding company –

    (i) from the subsidiary, or

    (ii) from someone who has purportedly acquired the shares after their disposal by the subsidiary.

(2) A transfer to that person of the shares mentioned in subsection (1)(a) has the same effect as it would have had if their original acquisition by the subsidiary had not been in contravention of the prohibition.

Supplementary

143 Application of provisions to companies not limited by shares

In relation to a company other than a company limited by shares, the references in this Chapter to shares shall be read as references to the interest of its members as such, whatever the form of that interest.

144 Application of provisions to nominees

The provisions of this Chapter apply to a nominee acting on behalf of a subsidiary as to the subsidiary itself.

PART 9

EXERCISE OF MEMBERS' RIGHTS

Effect of provisions in company's articles

145 Effect of provisions of articles as to enjoyment or exercise of members' rights

(1) This section applies where provision is made by a company's articles enabling a member to nominate another person or persons as entitled to enjoy or exercise all or any specified rights of the member in relation to the company.

(2) So far as is necessary to give effect to that provision, anything required or authorised

by any provision of the Companies Acts to be done by or in relation to the member shall instead be done, or (as the case may be) may instead be done, by or in relation to the nominated person (or each of them) as if he were a member of the company.

(3) This applies, in particular, to the rights conferred by –

  (a) sections 291 and 293 (right to be sent proposed written resolution);
  (b) section 292 (right to require circulation of written resolution);
  (c) section 303 (right to require directors to call general meeting);
  (d) section 310 (right to notice of general meetings);
  (e) section 314 (right to require circulation of a statement);
  (f) section 324 (right to appoint proxy to act at meeting);
  (g) section 338 (right to require circulation of resolution for AGM of public company); and
  (h) section 423 (right to be sent a copy of annual accounts and reports).

(4) This section and any such provision as is mentioned in subsection (1) –

  (a) do not confer rights enforceable against the company by anyone other than the member, and
  (b) do not affect the requirements for an effective transfer or other disposition of the whole or part of a member's interest in the company.

Information rights

146 Traded companies: nomination of persons to enjoy information rights

(1) This section applies to a company whose shares are admitted to trading on a regulated market.

(2) A member of such a company who holds shares on behalf of another person may nominate that person to enjoy information rights.

(3) "Information rights" means –

  (a) the right to receive a copy of all communications that the company sends to its members generally or to any class of its members that includes the person making the nomination, and
  (b) the rights conferred by –
    (i) section 431 or 432 (right to require copies of accounts and reports), and
    (ii) section 1145 (right to require hard copy version of document or information provided in another form).

(4) The reference in subsection (3)(a) to communications that a company sends to its members generally includes the company's annual accounts and reports.
For the application of section 426 (option to provide summary financial statement) in relation to a person nominated to enjoy information rights, see subsection (5) of that section.

(5) A company need not act on a nomination purporting to relate to certain information rights only.

147 Information rights: form in which copies to be provided

(1) This section applies as regards the form in which copies are to be provided to a person nominated under section 146 (nomination of person to enjoy information rights).

(2) If the person to be nominated wishes to receive hard copy communications, he must –

  (a) request the person making the nomination to notify the company of that fact, and
  (b) provide an address to which such copies may be sent.

This must be done before the nomination is made.

(3) If having received such a request the person making the nomination –

    (a) notifies the company that the nominated person wishes to receive hard copy communications, and

    (b) provides the company with that address,

the right of the nominated person is to receive hard copy communications accordingly.

(4) This is subject to the provisions of Parts 3 and 4 of Schedule 5 (communications by company) under which the company may take steps to enable it to communicate in electronic form or by means of a website.

(5) If no such notification is given (or no address is provided), the nominated person is taken to have agreed that documents or information may be sent or supplied to him by the company by means of a website.

(6) That agreement –

    (a) may be revoked by the nominated person, and

    (b) does not affect his right under section 1145 to require a hard copy version of a document or information provided in any other form.

148 Termination or suspension of nomination

(1) The following provisions have effect in relation to a nomination under section 146 (nomination of person to enjoy information rights).

(2) The nomination may be terminated at the request of the member or of the nominated person.

(3) The nomination ceases to have effect on the occurrence in relation to the member or the nominated person of any of the following –

    (a) in the case of an individual, death or bankruptcy;

    (b) in the case of a body corporate, dissolution or the making of an order for the winding up of the body otherwise than for the purposes of reconstruction.

(4) In subsection (3) –

    (a) the reference to bankruptcy includes –

        (i) the sequestration of a person's estate, and

        (ii) a person's estate being the subject of a protected trust deed (within the meaning of the Bankruptcy (Scotland) Act 1985 (c. 66)); and

    (b) the reference to the making of an order for winding up is to –

        (i) the making of such an order under the Insolvency Act 1986 (c. 45) or the Insolvency (Northern Ireland) Order 1989 (S.I. 1989/2405 (N.I. 19)), or

        (ii) any corresponding proceeding under the law of a country or territory outside the United Kingdom.

(5) The effect of any nominations made by a member is suspended at any time when there are more nominated persons than the member has shares in the company.

(6) Where –

    (a) the member holds different classes of shares with different information rights, and

    (b) there are more nominated persons than he has shares conferring a particular right,

the effect of any nominations made by him is suspended to the extent that they confer that right.

(7) Where the company –

    (a) enquires of a nominated person whether he wishes to retain information rights, and

    (b) does not receive a response within the period of 28 days beginning with the date on which the company's enquiry was sent, the nomination ceases to have effect at the end of that period.

Such an enquiry is not to be made of a person more than once in any twelve-month period.

(8) The termination or suspension of a nomination means that the company is not required to act on it.

It does not prevent the company from continuing to do so, to such extent or for such period as it thinks fit.

149 Information as to possible rights in relation to voting

(1) This section applies where a company sends a copy of a notice of a meeting to a person nominated under section 146 (nomination of person to enjoy information rights).

(2) The copy of the notice must be accompanied by a statement that –

(a) he may have a right under an agreement between him and the member by whom he was nominated to be appointed, or to have someone else appointed, as a proxy for the meeting, and

(b) if he has no such right or does not wish to exercise it, he may have a right under such an agreement to give instructions to the member as to the exercise of voting rights.

(3) Section 325 (notice of meeting to contain statement of member's rights in relation to appointment of proxy) does not apply to the copy, and the company must either –

(a) omit the notice required by that section, or

(b) include it but state that it does not apply to the nominated person.

150 Information rights: status of rights

(1) This section has effect as regards the rights conferred by a nomination under section 146 (nomination of person to enjoy information rights).

(2) Enjoyment by the nominated person of the rights conferred by the nomination is enforceable against the company by the member as if they were rights conferred by the company's articles.

(3) Any enactment, and any provision of the company's articles, having effect in relation to communications with members has a corresponding effect (subject to any necessary adaptations) in relation to communications with the nominated person.

(4) In particular –

(a) where under any enactment, or any provision of the company's articles, the members of a company entitled to receive a document or information are determined as at a date or time before it is sent or supplied, the company need not send or supply it to a nominated person –

(i) whose nomination was received by the company after that date or time, or

(ii) if that date or time falls in a period of suspension of his nomination; and

(b) where under any enactment, or any provision of the company's articles, the right of a member to receive a document or information depends on the company having a current address for him, the same applies to any person nominated by him.

(5) The rights conferred by the nomination –

(a) are in addition to the rights of the member himself, and

(b) do not affect any rights exercisable by virtue of any such provision as is mentioned in section 145 (provisions of company's articles as to enjoyment or exercise of members' rights).

(6) A failure to give effect to the rights conferred by the nomination does not affect the validity of anything done by or on behalf of the company.

(7) References in this section to the rights conferred by the nomination are to –

(a) the rights referred to in section 146(3) (information rights), and

(b) where applicable, the rights conferred by section 147(3) (right to hard copy communications) and section 149 (information as to possible voting rights).

151 Information rights: power to amend

(1) The Secretary of State may by regulations amend the provisions of sections 146 to 150 (information rights) so as to –

(a) extend or restrict the classes of companies to which section 146 applies,
(b) make other provision as to the circumstances in which a nomination may be made under that section, or
(c) extend or restrict the rights conferred by such a nomination.

(2) The regulations may make such consequential modifications of any other provisions of this Part, or of any other enactment, as appear to the Secretary of State to be necessary.

(3) Regulations under this section are subject to affirmative resolution procedure.

Exercise of rights where shares held on behalf of others

152 Exercise of rights where shares held on behalf of others: exercise in different ways

(1) Where a member holds shares in a company on behalf of more than one person –

(a) rights attached to the shares, and
(b) rights under any enactment exercisable by virtue of holding the shares,

need not all be exercised, and if exercised, need not all be exercised in the same way.

(2) A member who exercises such rights but does not exercise all his rights, must inform the company to what extent he is exercising the rights.

(3) A member who exercises such rights in different ways must inform the company of the ways in which he is exercising them and to what extent they are exercised in each way.

(4) If a member exercises such rights without informing the company –

(a) that he is not exercising all his rights, or
(b) that he is exercising his rights in different ways,

the company is entitled to assume that he is exercising all his rights and is exercising them in the same way.

153 Exercise of rights where shares held on behalf of others: members' requests

(1) This section applies for the purposes of –

(a) section 314 (power to require circulation of statement),
(b) section 338 (public companies: power to require circulation of resolution for AGM),
(c) section 342 (power to require independent report on poll), and
(d) section 527 (power to require website publication of audit concerns).

(2) A company is required to act under any of those sections if it receives a request in relation to which the following conditions are met –

(a) it is made by at least 100 persons;
(b) it is authenticated by all the persons making it;
(c) in the case of any of those persons who is not a member of the company, it is accompanied by a statement –

(i) of the full name and address of a person ("the member") who is a member of the company and holds shares on behalf of that person,
(ii) that the member is holding those shares on behalf of that person in the course of a business,

(iii)   of the number of shares in the company that the member holds on behalf of that person,

(iv)   of the total amount paid up on those shares,

(v)   that those shares are not held on behalf of anyone else or, if they are, that the other person or persons are not among the other persons making the request,

(vi)   that some or all of those shares confer voting rights that are relevant for the purposes of making a request under the section in question, and

(vii)   that the person has the right to instruct the member how to exercise those rights;

(d)   in the case of any of those persons who is a member of the company, it is accompanied by a statement –

(i)   that he holds shares otherwise than on behalf of another person, or

(ii)   that he holds shares on behalf of one or more other persons but those persons are not among the other persons making the request;

(e)   it is accompanied by such evidence as the company may reasonably require of the matters mentioned in paragraph (c) and (d);

(f)   the total amount of the sums paid up on –

(i)   shares held as mentioned in paragraph (c), and

(ii)   shares held as mentioned in paragraph (d),

divided by the number of persons making the request, is not less than £100;

(g)   the request complies with any other requirements of the section in question as to contents, timing and otherwise.

PART 10

A COMPANY'S DIRECTORS

CHAPTER 1

APPOINTMENT AND REMOVAL OF DIRECTORS

Requirement to have directors

154 Companies required to have directors

(1)   A private company must have at least one director.

(2)   A public company must have at least two directors.

155 Companies required to have at least one director who is a natural person

(1)   A company must have at least one director who is a natural person.

(2)   This requirement is met if the office of director is held by a natural person as a corporation sole or otherwise by virtue of an office.

156 Direction requiring company to make appointment

(1)   If it appears to the Secretary of State that a company is in breach of –

section 154 (requirements as to number of directors), or
section 155 (requirement to have at least one director who is a natural person),
the Secretary of State may give the company a direction under this section.

(2)   The direction must specify –

(a)   the statutory requirement the company appears to be in breach of,

(b) what the company must do in order to comply with the direction, and

(c) the period within which it must do so.

That period must be not less than one month or more than three months after the date on which the direction is given.

(3) The direction must also inform the company of the consequences of failing to comply.

(4) Where the company is in breach of section 154 or 155 it must comply with the direction by –

(a) making the necessary appointment or appointments, and

(b) giving notice of them under section 167,

before the end of the period specified in the direction.

(5) If the company has already made the necessary appointment or appointments (or so far as it has done so), it must comply with the direction by giving notice of them under section 167 before the end of the period specified in the direction.

(6) If a company fails to comply with a direction under this section, an offence is committed by –

(a) the company, and

(b) every officer of the company who is in default.

For this purpose a shadow director is treated as an officer of the company.

(7) A person guilty of an offence under this section is liable on summary conviction to a fine not exceeding level 5 on the standard scale and, for continued contravention, a daily default fine not exceeding one-tenth of level 5 on the standard scale.

Appointment

157 Minimum age for appointment as director

(1) A person may not be appointed a director of a company unless he has attained the age of 16 years.

(2) This does not affect the validity of an appointment that is not to take effect until the person appointed attains that age.

(3) Where the office of director of a company is held by a corporation sole, or otherwise by virtue of another office, the appointment to that other office of a person who has not attained the age of 16 years is not effective also to make him a director of the company until he attains the age of 16 years.

(4) An appointment made in contravention of this section is void.

(5) Nothing in this section affects any liability of a person under any provision of the Companies Acts if he –

(a) purports to act as director, or

(b) acts as a shadow director,

although he could not, by virtue of this section, be validly appointed as a director.

(6) This section has effect subject to section 158 (power to provide for exceptions from minimum age requirement).

158 Power to provide for exceptions from minimum age requirement

(1) The Secretary of State may make provision by regulations for cases in which a person who has not attained the age of 16 years may be appointed a director of a company.

(2) The regulations must specify the circumstances in which, and any conditions subject to which, the appointment may be made.

(3) If the specified circumstances cease to obtain, or any specified conditions cease to be met, a person who was appointed by virtue of the regulations and who has not since attained the age of 16 years ceases to hold office.

(4) The regulations may make different provision for different parts of the United Kingdom.

This is without prejudice to the general power to make different provision for different cases.

(5) Regulations under this section are subject to negative resolution procedure.

159 Existing under-age directors

(1) This section applies where –

   (a) a person appointed a director of a company before section 157 (minimum age for appointment as director) comes into force has not attained the age of 16 when that section comes into force, or

   (b) the office of director of a company is held by a corporation sole, or otherwise by virtue of another office, and the person appointed to that other office has not attained the age of 16 years when that section comes into force,

and the case is not one excepted from that section by regulations under section 158.

(2) That person ceases to be a director on section 157 coming into force.

(3) The company must make the necessary consequential alteration in its register of directors but need not give notice to the registrar of the change.

(4) If it appears to the registrar (from other information) that a person has ceased by virtue of this section to be a director of a company, the registrar shall note that fact on the register.

160 Appointment of directors of public company to be voted on individually

(1) At a general meeting of a public company a motion for the appointment of two or more persons as directors of the company by a single resolution must not be made unless a resolution that it should be so made has first been agreed to by the meeting without any vote being given against it.

(2) A resolution moved in contravention of this section is void, whether or not its being so moved was objected to at the time.

But where a resolution so moved is passed, no provision for the automatic reappointment of retiring directors in default of another appointment applies.

(3) For the purposes of this section a motion for approving a person's appointment, or for nominating a person for appointment, is treated as a motion for his appointment.

(4) Nothing in this section applies to a resolution amending the company's articles.

161 Validity of acts of directors

(1) The acts of a person acting as a director are valid notwithstanding that it is afterwards discovered –

   (a) that there was a defect in his appointment;

   (b) that he was disqualified from holding office;

   (c) that he had ceased to hold office;

   (d) that he was not entitled to vote on the matter in question.

(2) This applies even if the resolution for his appointment is void under section 160 (appointment of directors of public company to be voted on individually).

Register of directors, etc

162 Register of directors

(1) Every company must keep a register of its directors.

(2) The register must contain the required particulars (see sections 163, 164 and 166) of each person who is a director of the company.

(3) The register must be kept available for inspection –

   (a) at the company's registered office, or

   (b) at a place specified in regulations under section 1136.

(4)   The company must give notice to the registrar –

(a)   of the place at which the register is kept available for inspection, and
(b)   of any change in that place,

unless it has at all times been kept at the company's registered office.

(5)   The register must be open to the inspection –

(a)   of any member of the company without charge, and
(b)   of any other person on payment of such fee as may be prescribed.

(6)   If default is made in complying with subsection (1), (2) or (3) or if default is made for 14 days in complying with subsection (4), or if an inspection required under subsection (5) is refused, an offence is committed by –

(a)   the company, and
(b)   every officer of the company who is in default.

For this purpose a shadow director is treated as an officer of the company.

(7)   A person guilty of an offence under this section is liable on summary conviction to a fine not exceeding level 5 on the standard scale and, for continued contravention, a daily default fine not exceeding one-tenth of level 5 on the standard scale.

(8)   In the case of a refusal of inspection of the register, the court may by order compel an immediate inspection of it.

163 Particulars of directors to be registered: individuals

(1)   A company's register of directors must contain the following particulars in the case of an individual –

(a)   name and any former name;
(b)   a service address;
(c)   the country or state (or part of the United Kingdom) in which he is usually resident;
(d)   nationality;
(e)   business occupation (if any);
(f)   date of birth.

(2)   For the purposes of this section "name" means a person's Christian name (or other forename) and surname, except that in the case of –

(a)   a peer, or
(b)   an individual usually known by a title,

the title may be stated instead of his Christian name (or other forename) and surname or in addition to either or both of them.

(3)   For the purposes of this section a "former name" means a name by which the individual was formerly known for business purposes.
Where a person is or was formerly known by more than one such name, each of them must be stated.

(4)   It is not necessary for the register to contain particulars of a former name in the following cases –

(a)   in the case of a peer or an individual normally known by a British title, where the name is one by which the person was known previous to the adoption of or succession to the title;
(b)   in the case of any person, where the former name –

(i)   was changed or disused before the person attained the age of 16 years, or
(ii)   has been changed or disused for 20 years or more.

(5)   A person's service address may be stated to be "The company's registered office".

164 Particulars of directors to be registered: corporate directors and firms

A company's register of directors must contain the following particulars in the case of a body corporate, or a firm that is a legal person under the law by which it is governed –

(a) corporate or firm name;

(b) registered or principal office;

(c) in the case of an EEA company to which the First Company Law Directive (68/151/EEC) applies, particulars of –

    (i) the register in which the company file mentioned in Article 3 of that Directive is kept (including details of the relevant state), and

    (ii) the registration number in that register;

(d) in any other case, particulars of –

    (i) the legal form of the company or firm and the law by which it is governed, and

    (ii) if applicable, the register in which it is entered (including details of the state) and its registration number in that register.

165 Register of directors' residential addresses

(1) Every company must keep a register of directors' residential addresses.

(2) The register must state the usual residential address of each of the company's directors.

(3) If a director's usual residential address is the same as his service address (as stated in the company's register of directors), the register of directors' residential addresses need only contain an entry to that effect.

This does not apply if his service address is stated to be "The company's registered office".

(4) If default is made in complying with this section, an offence is committed by –

(a) the company, and

(b) every officer of the company who is in default.

For this purpose a shadow director is treated as an officer of the company.

(5) A person guilty of an offence under this section is liable on summary conviction to a fine not exceeding level 5 on the standard scale and, for continued contravention, a daily default fine not exceeding one-tenth of level 5 on the standard scale.

(6) This section applies only to directors who are individuals, not where the director is a body corporate or a firm that is a legal person under the law by which it is governed.

166 Particulars of directors to be registered: power to make regulations

(1) The Secretary of State may make provision by regulations amending –

section 163 (particulars of directors to be registered: individuals),

section 164 (particulars of directors to be registered: corporate directors and firms), or

section 165 (register of directors' residential addresses),

so as to add to or remove items from the particulars required to be contained in a company's register of directors or register of directors' residential addresses.

(2) Regulations under this section are subject to affirmative resolution procedure.

167 Duty to notify registrar of changes

(1) A company must, within the period of 14 days from –

(a) a person becoming or ceasing to be a director, or

(b) the occurrence of any change in the particulars contained in its register of directors or its register of directors' residential addresses,

give notice to the registrar of the change and of the date on which it occurred.

(2) Notice of a person having become a director of the company must –

    (a) contain a statement of the particulars of the new director that are required to be included in the company's register of directors and its register of directors' residential addresses, and

    (b) be accompanied by a consent, by that person, to act in that capacity.

(3) Where –

    (a) a company gives notice of a change of a director's service address as stated in the company's register of directors, and

    (b) the notice is not accompanied by notice of any resulting change in the particulars contained in the company's register of directors' residential addresses,

the notice must be accompanied by a statement that no such change is required.

(4) If default is made in complying with this section, an offence is committed by –

    (a) the company, and

    (b) every officer of the company who is in default.

For this purpose a shadow director is treated as an officer of the company.

(5) A person guilty of an offence under this section is liable on summary conviction to a fine not exceeding level 5 on the standard scale and, for continued contravention, a daily default fine not exceeding one-tenth of level 5 on the standard scale.

Removal

168 Resolution to remove director

(1) A company may by ordinary resolution at a meeting remove a director before the expiration of his period of office, notwithstanding anything in any agreement between it and him.

(2) Special notice is required of a resolution to remove a director under this section or to appoint somebody instead of a director so removed at the meeting at which he is removed.

(3) A vacancy created by the removal of a director under this section, if not filled at the meeting at which he is removed, may be filled as a casual vacancy.

(4) A person appointed director in place of a person removed under this section is treated, for the purpose of determining the time at which he or any other director is to retire, as if he had become director on the day on which the person in whose place he is appointed was last appointed a director.

(5) This section is not to be taken –

    (a) as depriving a person removed under it of compensation or damages payable to him in respect of the termination of his appointment as director or of any appointment terminating with that as director, or

    (b) as derogating from any power to remove a director that may exist apart from this section.

169 Director's right to protest against removal

(1) On receipt of notice of an intended resolution to remove a director under section 168, the company must forthwith send a copy of the notice to the director concerned.

(2) The director (whether or not a member of the company) is entitled to be heard on the resolution at the meeting.

(3) Where notice is given of an intended resolution to remove a director under that section, and the director concerned makes with respect to it representations in writing to the company (not exceeding a reasonable length) and requests their notification to members of the company, the company shall, unless the representations are received by it too late for it to do so –

(a) in any notice of the resolution given to members of the company state the fact of the representations having been made; and

(b) send a copy of the representations to every member of the company to whom notice of the meeting is sent (whether before or after receipt of the representations by the company).

(4) If a copy of the representations is not sent as required by subsection (3) because received too late or because of the company's default, the director may (without prejudice to his right to be heard orally) require that the representations shall be read out at the meeting.

(5) Copies of the representations need not be sent out and the representations need not be read out at the meeting if, on the application either of the company or of any other person who claims to be aggrieved, the court is satisfied that the rights conferred by this section are being abused.

(6) The court may order the company's costs (in Scotland, expenses) on an application under subsection (5) to be paid in whole or in part by the director, notwithstanding that he is not a party to the application.

CHAPTER 2

GENERAL DUTIES OF DIRECTORS

Introductory

170 Scope and nature of general duties

(1) The general duties specified in sections 171 to 177 are owed by a director of a company to the company.

(2) A person who ceases to be a director continues to be subject –

(a) to the duty in section 175 (duty to avoid conflicts of interest) as regards the exploitation of any property, information or opportunity of which he became aware at a time when he was a director, and

(b) to the duty in section 176 (duty not to accept benefits from third parties) as regards things done or omitted by him before he ceased to be a director.

To that extent those duties apply to a former director as to a director, subject to any necessary adaptations.

(3) The general duties are based on certain common law rules and equitable principles as they apply in relation to directors and have effect in place of those rules and principles as regards the duties owed to a company by a director.

(4) The general duties shall be interpreted and applied in the same way as common law rules or equitable principles, and regard shall be had to the corresponding common law rules and equitable principles in interpreting and applying the general duties.

(5) The general duties apply to shadow directors where, and to the extent that, the corresponding common law rules or equitable principles so apply.

The general duties

171 Duty to act within powers

A director of a company must –

(a) act in accordance with the company's constitution, and

(b) only exercise powers for the purposes for which they are conferred.

172 Duty to promote the success of the company

(1) A director of a company must act in the way he considers, in good faith, would be most likely to promote the success of the company for the benefit of its members as a whole, and in doing so have regard (amongst other matters) to –

 (a) the likely consequences of any decision in the long term,
 (b) the interests of the company's employees,
 (c) the need to foster the company's business relationships with suppliers, customers and others,
 (d) the impact of the company's operations on the community and the environment,
 (e) the desirability of the company maintaining a reputation for high standards of business conduct, and
 (f) the need to act fairly as between members of the company.

(2) Where or to the extent that the purposes of the company consist of or include purposes other than the benefit of its members, subsection (1) has effect as if the reference to promoting the success of the company for the benefit of its members were to achieving those purposes.

(3) The duty imposed by this section has effect subject to any enactment or rule of law requiring directors, in certain circumstances, to consider or act in the interests of creditors of the company.

173 Duty to exercise independent judgment

(1) A director of a company must exercise independent judgment.

(2) This duty is not infringed by his acting –

 (a) in accordance with an agreement duly entered into by the company that restricts the future exercise of discretion by its directors, or
 (b) in a way authorised by the company's constitution.

174 Duty to exercise reasonable care, skill and diligence

(1) A director of a company must exercise reasonable care, skill and diligence.

(2) This means the care, skill and diligence that would be exercised by a reasonably diligent person with –

 (a) the general knowledge, skill and experience that may reasonably be expected of a person carrying out the functions carried out by the director in relation to the company, and
 (b) the general knowledge, skill and experience that the director has.

175 Duty to avoid conflicts of interest

(1) A director of a company must avoid a situation in which he has, or can have, a direct or indirect interest that conflicts, or possibly may conflict, with the interests of the company.

(2) This applies in particular to the exploitation of any property, information or opportunity (and it is immaterial whether the company could take advantage of the property, information or opportunity).

(3) This duty does not apply to a conflict of interest arising in relation to a transaction or arrangement with the company.

(4) This duty is not infringed –

 (a) if the situation cannot reasonably be regarded as likely to give rise to a conflict of interest; or
 (b) if the matter has been authorised by the directors.

(5) Authorisation may be given by the directors –

 (a) where the company is a private company and nothing in the company's constitution invalidates such authorisation, by the matter being proposed to and authorised by the directors; or

(b) where the company is a public company and its constitution includes provision enabling the directors to authorise the matter, by the matter being proposed to and authorised by them in accordance with the constitution.

(6) The authorisation is effective only if –

(a) any requirement as to the quorum at the meeting at which the matter is considered is met without counting the director in question or any other interested director, and

(b) the matter was agreed to without their voting or would have been agreed to if their votes had not been counted.

(7) Any reference in this section to a conflict of interest includes a conflict of interest and duty and a conflict of duties.

176 Duty not to accept benefits from third parties

(1) A director of a company must not accept a benefit from a third party conferred by reason of –

(a) his being a director, or

(b) his doing (or not doing) anything as director.

(2) A "third party" means a person other than the company, an associated body corporate or a person acting on behalf of the company or an associated body corporate.

(3) Benefits received by a director from a person by whom his services (as a director or otherwise) are provided to the company are not regarded as conferred by a third party.

(4) This duty is not infringed if the acceptance of the benefit cannot reasonably be regarded as likely to give rise to a conflict of interest.

(5) Any reference in this section to a conflict of interest includes a conflict of interest and duty and a conflict of duties.

177 Duty to declare interest in proposed transaction or arrangement

(1) If a director of a company is in any way, directly or indirectly, interested in a proposed transaction or arrangement with the company, he must declare the nature and extent of that interest to the other directors.

(2) The declaration may (but need not) be made –

(a) at a meeting of the directors, or

(b) by notice to the directors in accordance with –

(i) section 184 (notice in writing), or

(ii) section 185 (general notice).

(3) If a declaration of interest under this section proves to be, or becomes, inaccurate or incomplete, a further declaration must be made.

(4) Any declaration required by this section must be made before the company enters into the transaction or arrangement.

(5) This section does not require a declaration of an interest of which the director is not aware or where the director is not aware of the transaction or arrangement in question.

For this purpose a director is treated as being aware of matters of which he ought reasonably to be aware.

(6) A director need not declare an interest –

(a) if it cannot reasonably be regarded as likely to give rise to a conflict of interest;

(b) if, or to the extent that, the other directors are already aware of it (and for this purpose the other directors are treated as aware of anything of which they ought reasonably to be aware); or

(c) if, or to the extent that, it concerns terms of his service contract that have been or are to be considered –

    (i) by a meeting of the directors, or

    (ii) by a committee of the directors appointed for the purpose under the company's constitution.

Supplementary provisions

178 Civil consequences of breach of general duties

(1) The consequences of breach (or threatened breach) of sections 171 to 177 are the same as would apply if the corresponding common law rule or equitable principle applied.

(2) The duties in those sections (with the exception of section 174 (duty to exercise reasonable care, skill and diligence)) are, accordingly, enforceable in the same way as any other fiduciary duty owed to a company by its directors.

179 Cases within more than one of the general duties

Except as otherwise provided, more than one of the general duties may apply in any given case.

180 Consent, approval or authorisation by members

(1) In a case where –

    (a) section 175 (duty to avoid conflicts of interest) is complied with by authorisation by the directors, or

    (b) section 177 (duty to declare interest in proposed transaction or arrangement) is complied with,

the transaction or arrangement is not liable to be set aside by virtue of any common law rule or equitable principle requiring the consent or approval of the members of the company.

This is without prejudice to any enactment, or provision of the company's constitution, requiring such consent or approval.

(2) The application of the general duties is not affected by the fact that the case also falls within Chapter 4 (transactions requiring approval of members), except that where that Chapter applies and –

    (a) approval is given under that Chapter, or

    (b) the matter is one as to which it is provided that approval is not needed,

it is not necessary also to comply with section 175 (duty to avoid conflicts of interest) or section 176 (duty not to accept benefits from third parties).

(3) Compliance with the general duties does not remove the need for approval under any applicable provision of Chapter 4 (transactions requiring approval of members).

(4) The general duties –

    (a) have effect subject to any rule of law enabling the company to give authority, specifically or generally, for anything to be done (or omitted) by the directors, or any of them, that would otherwise be a breach of duty, and

    (b) where the company's articles contain provisions for dealing with conflicts of interest, are not infringed by anything done (or omitted) by the directors, or any of them, in accordance with those provisions.

(5) Otherwise, the general duties have effect (except as otherwise provided or the context otherwise requires) notwithstanding any enactment or rule of law.

181 Modification of provisions in relation to charitable companies

(1) In their application to a company that is a charity, the provisions of this Chapter have effect subject to this section.

(2) Section 175 (duty to avoid conflicts of interest) has effect as if –

    (a) for subsection (3) (which disapplies the duty to avoid conflicts of interest in the case of a transaction or arrangement with the company) there were substituted –

        "(3) This duty does not apply to a conflict of interest arising in relation to a transaction or arrangement with the company if or to the extent that the company's articles allow that duty to be so disapplied, which they may do only in relation to descriptions of transaction or arrangement specified in the company's articles.";

    (b) for subsection (5) (which specifies how directors of a company may give authority under that section for a transaction or arrangement) there were substituted –

        "(5) Authorisation may be given by the directors where the company's constitution includes provision enabling them to authorise the matter, by the matter being proposed to and authorised by them in accordance with the constitution.".

(3) Section 180(2)(b) (which disapplies certain duties under this Chapter in relation to cases excepted from requirement to obtain approval by members under Chapter 4) applies only if or to the extent that the company's articles allow those duties to be so disapplied, which they may do only in relation to descriptions of transaction or arrangement specified in the company's articles.

(4) After section 26(5) of the Charities Act 1993 (c. 10) (power of Charity Commission to authorise dealings with charity property etc) insert –

    "(5A) In the case of a charity that is a company, an order under this section may authorise an act notwithstanding that it involves the breach of a duty imposed on a director of the company under Chapter 2 of Part 10 of the Companies Act 2006 (general duties of directors).".

(5) This section does not extend to Scotland.

CHAPTER 3

DECLARATION OF INTEREST IN EXISTING TRANSACTION OR ARRANGEMENT

182 Declaration of interest in existing transaction or arrangement

(1) Where a director of a company is in any way, directly or indirectly, interested in a transaction or arrangement that has been entered into by the company, he must declare the nature and extent of the interest to the other directors in accordance with this section.

This section does not apply if or to the extent that the interest has been declared under section 177 (duty to declare interest in proposed transaction or arrangement).

(2) The declaration must be made –

    (a) at a meeting of the directors, or

    (b) by notice in writing (see section 184), or

    (c) by general notice (see section 185).

(3) If a declaration of interest under this section proves to be, or becomes, inaccurate or incomplete, a further declaration must be made.

(4) Any declaration required by this section must be made as soon as is reasonably practicable.

Failure to comply with this requirement does not affect the underlying duty to make the declaration.

(5) This section does not require a declaration of an interest of which the director is not aware or where the director is not aware of the transaction or arrangement in question. For this purpose a director is treated as being aware of matters of which he ought reasonably to be aware.

(6) A director need not declare an interest under this section –

(a) if it cannot reasonably be regarded as likely to give rise to a conflict of interest;

(b) if, or to the extent that, the other directors are already aware of it (and for this purpose the other directors are treated as aware of anything of which they ought reasonably to be aware); or

(c) if, or to the extent that, it concerns terms of his service contract that have been or are to be considered –

(i) by a meeting of the directors, or

(ii) by a committee of the directors appointed for the purpose under the company's constitution.

183 Offence of failure to declare interest

(1) A director who fails to comply with the requirements of section 182 (declaration of interest in existing transaction or arrangement) commits an offence.

(2) A person guilty of an offence under this section is liable –

(a) on conviction on indictment, to a fine;

(b) on summary conviction, to a fine not exceeding the statutory maximum.

184 Declaration made by notice in writing

(1) This section applies to a declaration of interest made by notice in writing.

(2) The director must send the notice to the other directors.

(3) The notice may be sent in hard copy form or, if the recipient has agreed to receive it in electronic form, in an agreed electronic form.

(4) The notice may be sent –

(a) by hand or by post, or

(b) if the recipient has agreed to receive it by electronic means, by agreed electronic means.

(5) Where a director declares an interest by notice in writing in accordance with this section –

(a) the making of the declaration is deemed to form part of the proceedings at the next meeting of the directors after the notice is given, and

(b) the provisions of section 248 (minutes of meetings of directors) apply as if the declaration had been made at that meeting.

185 General notice treated as sufficient declaration

(1) General notice in accordance with this section is a sufficient declaration of interest in relation to the matters to which it relates.

(2) General notice is notice given to the directors of a company to the effect that the director –

(a) has an interest (as member, officer, employee or otherwise) in a specified body corporate or firm and is to be regarded as interested in any transaction or arrangement that may, after the date of the notice, be made with that body corporate or firm, or

(b) is connected with a specified person (other than a body corporate or firm) and is to be regarded as interested in any transaction or arrangement that may, after the date of the notice, be made with that person.

(3) The notice must state the nature and extent of the director's interest in the body corporate or firm or, as the case may be, the nature of his connection with the person.

(4) General notice is not effective unless –

(a) it is given at a meeting of the directors, or

(b) the director takes reasonable steps to secure that it is brought up and read at the next meeting of the directors after it is given.

186 Declaration of interest in case of company with sole director

(1) Where a declaration of interest under section 182 (duty to declare interest in existing transaction or arrangement) is required of a sole director of a company that is required to have more than one director –

(a) the declaration must be recorded in writing,

(b) the making of the declaration is deemed to form part of the proceedings at the next meeting of the directors after the notice is given, and

(c) the provisions of section 248 (minutes of meetings of directors) apply as if the declaration had been made at that meeting.

(2) Nothing in this section affects the operation of section 231 (contract with sole member who is also a director: terms to be set out in writing or recorded in minutes).

187 Declaration of interest in existing transaction by shadow director

(1) The provisions of this Chapter relating to the duty under section 182 (duty to declare interest in existing transaction or arrangement) apply to a shadow director as to a director, but with the following adaptations.

(2) Subsection (2)(a) of that section (declaration at meeting of directors) does not apply.

(3) In section 185 (general notice treated as sufficient declaration), subsection (4) (notice to be given at or brought up and read at meeting of directors) does not apply.

(4) General notice by a shadow director is not effective unless given by notice in writing in accordance with section 184.

CHAPTER 4

TRANSACTIONS WITH DIRECTORS REQUIRING APPROVAL OF MEMBERS

Service contracts

188 Directors' long-term service contracts: requirement of members' approval

(1) This section applies to provision under which the guaranteed term of a director's employment –

(a) with the company of which he is a director, or

(b) where he is the director of a holding company, within the group consisting of that company and its subsidiaries,

is, or may be, longer than two years.

(2) A company may not agree to such provision unless it has been approved –

(a) by resolution of the members of the company, and

(b) in the case of a director of a holding company, by resolution of the members of that company.

(3) The guaranteed term of a director's employment is –

(a) the period (if any) during which the director's employment –

> (i)   is to continue, or may be continued otherwise than at the instance of the company (whether under the original agreement or under a new agreement entered into in pursuance of it), and
>
> (ii) cannot be terminated by the company by notice, or can be so terminated only in specified circumstances, or

(b) in the case of employment terminable by the company by notice, the period of notice required to be given,

or, in the case of employment having a period within paragraph (a) and a period within paragraph (b), the aggregate of those periods.

(4) If more than six months before the end of the guaranteed term of a director's employment the company enters into a further service contract (otherwise than in pursuance of a right conferred, by or under the original contract, on the other party to it), this section applies as if there were added to the guaranteed term of the new contract the unexpired period of the guaranteed term of the original contract.

(5) A resolution approving provision to which this section applies must not be passed unless a memorandum setting out the proposed contract incorporating the provision is made available to members –

(a) in the case of a written resolution, by being sent or submitted to every eligible member at or before the time at which the proposed resolution is sent or submitted to him;

(b) in the case of a resolution at a meeting, by being made available for inspection by members of the company both –

> (i)   at the company's registered office for not less than 15 days ending with the date of the meeting, and
>
> (ii) at the meeting itself.

(6) No approval is required under this section on the part of the members of a body corporate that –

(a) is not a UK-registered company, or

(b) is a wholly-owned subsidiary of another body corporate.

(7) In this section "employment" means any employment under a director's service contract.

189 Directors' long-term service contracts: civil consequences of contravention

If a company agrees to provision in contravention of section 188 (directors' long-term service contracts: requirement of members' approval) –

(a) the provision is void, to the extent of the contravention, and

(b) the contract is deemed to contain a term entitling the company to terminate it at any time by the giving of reasonable notice.

Substantial property transactions

190 Substantial property transactions: requirement of members' approval

(1) A company may not enter into an arrangement under which –

(a) a director of the company or of its holding company, or a person connected with such a director, acquires or is to acquire from the company (directly or indirectly) a substantial non-cash asset, or

(b) the company acquires or is to acquire a substantial non-cash asset (directly or indirectly) from such a director or a person so connected,

unless the arrangement has been approved by a resolution of the members of the company or is conditional on such approval being obtained.

For the meaning of "substantial non-cash asset" see section 191.

(2) If the director or connected person is a director of the company's holding company or a person connected with such a director, the arrangement must also have been approved by a resolution of the members of the holding company or be conditional on such approval being obtained.

(3) A company shall not be subject to any liability by reason of a failure to obtain approval required by this section.

(4) No approval is required under this section on the part of the members of a body corporate that –

   (a) is not a UK-registered company, or
   (b) is a wholly-owned subsidiary of another body corporate.

(5) For the purposes of this section –

   (a) an arrangement involving more than one non-cash asset, or
   (b) an arrangement that is one of a series involving non-cash assets,

   shall be treated as if they involved a non-cash asset of a value equal to the aggregate value of all the non-cash assets involved in the arrangement or, as the case may be, the series.

(6) This section does not apply to a transaction so far as it relates –

   (a) to anything to which a director of a company is entitled under his service contract, or
   (b) to payment for loss of office as defined in section 215 (payments requiring members' approval).

191 Meaning of "substantial"

(1) This section explains what is meant in section 190 (requirement of approval for substantial property transactions) by a "substantial" non-cash asset.

(2) An asset is a substantial asset in relation to a company if its value –

   (a) exceeds 10% of the company's asset value and is more than £5,000, or
   (b) exceeds £100,000.

(3) For this purpose a company's "asset value" at any time is –

   (a) the value of the company's net assets determined by reference to its most recent statutory accounts, or
   (b) if no statutory accounts have been prepared, the amount of the company's called-up share capital.

(4) A company's "statutory accounts" means its annual accounts prepared in accordance with Part 15, and its "most recent" statutory accounts means those in relation to which the time for sending them out to members (see section 424) is most recent.

(5) Whether an asset is a substantial asset shall be determined as at the time the arrangement is entered into.

192 Exception for transactions with members or other group companies

Approval is not required under section 190 (requirement of members' approval for substantial property transactions) –

   (a) for a transaction between a company and a person in his character as a member of that company, or
   (b) for a transaction between –

      (i)   a holding company and its wholly-owned subsidiary, or
      (ii) two wholly-owned subsidiaries of the same holding company.

193 Exception in case of company in winding up or administration

(1) This section applies to a company –

(a) that is being wound up (unless the winding up is a members' voluntary winding up), or

(b) that is in administration within the meaning of Schedule B1 to the Insolvency Act 1986 (c. 45) or the Insolvency (Northern Ireland) Order 1989 (S.I. 1989/2405 (N.I. 19)).

(2) Approval is not required under section 190 (requirement of members' approval for substantial property transactions) –

(a) on the part of the members of a company to which this section applies, or

(b) for an arrangement entered into by a company to which this section applies.

194 Exception for transactions on recognised investment exchange

(1) Approval is not required under section 190 (requirement of members' approval for substantial property transactions) for a transaction on a recognised investment exchange effected by a director, or a person connected with him, through the agency of a person who in relation to the transaction acts as an independent broker.

(2) For this purpose –

(a) "independent broker" means a person who, independently of the director or any person connected with him, selects the person with whom the transaction is to be effected; and

(b) "recognised investment exchange" has the same meaning as in Part 18 of the Financial Services and Markets Act 2000 (c. 8).

195 Property transactions: civil consequences of contravention

(1) This section applies where a company enters into an arrangement in contravention of section 190 (requirement of members' approval for substantial property transactions).

(2) The arrangement, and any transaction entered into in pursuance of the arrangement (whether by the company or any other person), is voidable at the instance of the company, unless –

(a) restitution of any money or other asset that was the subject matter of the arrangement or transaction is no longer possible,

(b) the company has been indemnified in pursuance of this section by any other persons for the loss or damage suffered by it, or

(c) rights acquired in good faith, for value and without actual notice of the contravention by a person who is not a party to the arrangement or transaction would be affected by the avoidance.

(3) Whether or not the arrangement or any such transaction has been avoided, each of the persons specified in subsection (4) is liable –

(a) to account to the company for any gain that he has made directly or indirectly by the arrangement or transaction, and

(b) (jointly and severally with any other person so liable under this section) to indemnify the company for any loss or damage resulting from the arrangement or transaction.

(4) The persons so liable are –

(a) any director of the company or of its holding company with whom the company entered into the arrangement in contravention of section 190,

(b) any person with whom the company entered into the arrangement in contravention of that section who is connected with a director of the company or of its holding company,

(c) the director of the company or of its holding company with whom any such person is connected, and

(d) any other director of the company who authorised the arrangement or any transaction entered into in pursuance of such an arrangement.

(5) Subsections (3) and (4) are subject to the following two subsections.
(6) In the case of an arrangement entered into by a company in contravention of section 190 with a person connected with a director of the company or of its holding company, that director is not liable by virtue of subsection (4)(c) if he shows that he took all reasonable steps to secure the company's compliance with that section.
(7) In any case –

(a) a person so connected is not liable by virtue of subsection (4)(b), and
(b) a director is not liable by virtue of subsection (4)(d),

if he shows that, at the time the arrangement was entered into, he did not know the relevant circumstances constituting the contravention.
(8) Nothing in this section shall be read as excluding the operation of any other enactment or rule of law by virtue of which the arrangement or transaction may be called in question or any liability to the company may arise.

196 Property transactions: effect of subsequent affirmation

Where a transaction or arrangement is entered into by a company in contravention of section 190 (requirement of members' approval) but, within a reasonable period, it is affirmed –

(a) in the case of a contravention of subsection (1) of that section, by resolution of the members of the company, and
(b) in the case of a contravention of subsection (2) of that section, by resolution of the members of the holding company,

the transaction or arrangement may no longer be avoided under section 195.

Loans, quasi-loans and credit transactions

197 Loans to directors: requirement of members' approval

(1) A company may not –

(a) make a loan to a director of the company or of its holding company, or
(b) give a guarantee or provide security in connection with a loan made by any person to such a director,

unless the transaction has been approved by a resolution of the members of the company.
(2) If the director is a director of the company's holding company, the transaction must also have been approved by a resolution of the members of the holding company.
(3) A resolution approving a transaction to which this section applies must not be passed unless a memorandum setting out the matters mentioned in subsection
(4) is made available to members –

(a) in the case of a written resolution, by being sent or submitted to every eligible member at or before the time at which the proposed resolution is sent or submitted to him;
(b) in the case of a resolution at a meeting, by being made available for inspection by members of the company both –

(i) at the company's registered office for not less than 15 days ending with the date of the meeting, and
(ii) at the meeting itself.

(4) The matters to be disclosed are –

(a) the nature of the transaction,
(b) the amount of the loan and the purpose for which it is required, and
(c) the extent of the company's liability under any transaction connected with the loan.

(5) No approval is required under this section on the part of the members of a body corporate that –

    (a) is not a UK-registered company, or

    (b) is a wholly-owned subsidiary of another body corporate.

198 Quasi-loans to directors: requirement of members' approval

(1) This section applies to a company if it is –

    (a) a public company, or

    (b) a company associated with a public company.

(2) A company to which this section applies may not –

    (a) make a quasi-loan to a director of the company or of its holding company, or

    (b) give a guarantee or provide security in connection with a quasi-loan made by any person to such a director, unless the transaction has been approved by a resolution of the members of the company.

(3) If the director is a director of the company's holding company, the transaction must also have been approved by a resolution of the members of the holding company.

(4) A resolution approving a transaction to which this section applies must not be passed unless a memorandum setting out the matters mentioned in subsection (5) is made available to members –

    (a) in the case of a written resolution, by being sent or submitted to every eligible member at or before the time at which the proposed resolution is sent or submitted to him;

    (b) in the case of a resolution at a meeting, by being made available for inspection by members of the company both –

        (i)   at the company's registered office for not less than 15 days ending with the date of the meeting, and

        (ii) at the meeting itself.

(5) The matters to be disclosed are –

    (a) the nature of the transaction,

    (b) the amount of the quasi-loan and the purpose for which it is required, and

    (c) the extent of the company's liability under any transaction connected with the quasi-loan.

(6) No approval is required under this section on the part of the members of a body corporate that –

    (a) is not a UK-registered company, or

    (b) is a wholly-owned subsidiary of another body corporate.

199 Meaning of "quasi-loan" and related expressions

(1) A "quasi-loan" is a transaction under which one party ("the creditor") agrees to pay, or pays otherwise than in pursuance of an agreement, a sum for another ("the borrower") or agrees to reimburse, or reimburses otherwise than in pursuance of an agreement, expenditure incurred by another party for another ("the borrower") –

    (a) on terms that the borrower (or a person on his behalf) will reimburse the creditor; or

    (b) in circumstances giving rise to a liability on the borrower to reimburse the creditor.

(2) Any reference to the person to whom a quasi-loan is made is a reference to the borrower.

(3) The liabilities of the borrower under a quasi-loan include the liabilities of any person who has agreed to reimburse the creditor on behalf of the borrower.

200 Loans or quasi-loans to persons connected with directors: requirement of members' approval

(1) This section applies to a company if it is –

    (a)   a public company, or

    (b)   a company associated with a public company.

(2) A company to which this section applies may not –

    (a)   make a loan or quasi-loan to a person connected with a director of the company or of its holding company, or

    (b)   give a guarantee or provide security in connection with a loan or quasi-loan made by any person to a person connected with such a director,

unless the transaction has been approved by a resolution of the members of the company.

(3) If the connected person is a person connected with a director of the company's holding company, the transaction must also have been approved by a resolution of the members of the holding company.

(4) A resolution approving a transaction to which this section applies must not be passed unless a memorandum setting out the matters mentioned in subsection (5) is made available to members –

    (a)   in the case of a written resolution, by being sent or submitted to every eligible member at or before the time at which the proposed resolution is sent or submitted to him;

    (b)   in the case of a resolution at a meeting, by being made available for inspection by members of the company both –

        (i)   at the company's registered office for not less than 15 days ending with the date of the meeting, and

        (ii)   at the meeting itself.

(5) The matters to be disclosed are –

    (a)   the nature of the transaction,

    (b)   the amount of the loan or quasi-loan and the purpose for which it is required, and

    (c)   the extent of the company's liability under any transaction connected with the loan or quasi-loan.

(6) No approval is required under this section on the part of the members of a body corporate that –

    (a)   is not a UK-registered company, or

    (b)   is a wholly-owned subsidiary of another body corporate.

201 Credit transactions: requirement of members' approval

(1) This section applies to a company if it is –

    (a)   a public company, or

    (b)   a company associated with a public company.

(2) A company to which this section applies may not –

    (a)   enter into a credit transaction as creditor for the benefit of a director of the company or of its holding company, or a person connected with such a director, or

    (b)   give a guarantee or provide security in connection with a credit transaction entered into by any person for the benefit of such a director, or a person connected with such a director,

unless the transaction (that is, the credit transaction, the giving of the guarantee or the provision of security, as the case may be) has been approved by a resolution of the members of the company.

(3) If the director or connected person is a director of its holding company or a person connected with such a director, the transaction must also have been approved by a resolution of the members of the holding company.

(4) A resolution approving a transaction to which this section applies must not be passed unless a memorandum setting out the matters mentioned in subsection (5) is made available to members –

(a) in the case of a written resolution, by being sent or submitted to every eligible member at or before the time at which the proposed resolution is sent or submitted to him;

(b) in the case of a resolution at a meeting, by being made available for inspection by members of the company both –

(i) at the company's registered office for not less than 15 days ending with the date of the meeting, and

(ii) at the meeting itself.

(5) The matters to be disclosed are –

(a) the nature of the transaction,

(b) the value of the credit transaction and the purpose for which the land, goods or services sold or otherwise disposed of, leased, hired or supplied under the credit transaction are required, and

(c) the extent of the company's liability under any transaction connected with the credit transaction.

(6) No approval is required under this section on the part of the members of a body corporate that –

(a) is not a UK-registered company, or

(b) is a wholly-owned subsidiary of another body corporate.

202 Meaning of "credit transaction"

(1) A "credit transaction" is a transaction under which one party ("the creditor") –

(a) supplies any goods or sells any land under a hire-purchase agreement or a conditional sale agreement,

(b) leases or hires any land or goods in return for periodical payments, or

(c) otherwise disposes of land or supplies goods or services on the understanding that payment (whether in a lump sum or instalments or by way of periodical payments or otherwise) is to be deferred.

(2) Any reference to the person for whose benefit a credit transaction is entered into is to the person to whom goods, land or services are supplied, sold, leased, hired or otherwise disposed of under the transaction.

(3) In this section –

"conditional sale agreement" has the same meaning as in the Consumer Credit Act 1974 (c. 39); and

"services" means anything other than goods or land.

203 Related arrangements: requirement of members' approval

(1) A company may not –

(a) take part in an arrangement under which –

(i) another person enters into a transaction that, if it had been entered into by the company, would have required approval under section 197, 198, 200 or 201, and

(ii) that person, in pursuance of the arrangement, obtains a benefit from the company or a body corporate associated with it, or

   (b) arrange for the assignment to it, or assumption by it, of any rights, obligations or liabilities under a transaction that, if it had been entered into by the company, would have required such approval,

unless the arrangement in question has been approved by a resolution of the members of the company.

(2) If the director or connected person for whom the transaction is entered into is a director of its holding company or a person connected with such a director, the arrangement must also have been approved by a resolution of the members of the holding company.

(3) A resolution approving an arrangement to which this section applies must not be passed unless a memorandum setting out the matters mentioned in subsection (4) is made available to members –

   (a) in the case of a written resolution, by being sent or submitted to every eligible member at or before the time at which the proposed resolution is sent or submitted to him;

   (b) in the case of a resolution at a meeting, by being made available for inspection by members of the company both –

      (i) at the company's registered office for not less than 15 days ending with the date of the meeting, and

      (ii) at the meeting itself.

(4) The matters to be disclosed are –

   (a) the matters that would have to be disclosed if the company were seeking approval of the transaction to which the arrangement relates,

   (b) the nature of the arrangement, and

   (c) the extent of the company's liability under the arrangement or any transaction connected with it.

(5) No approval is required under this section on the part of the members of a body corporate that –

   (a) is not a UK-registered company, or

   (b) is a wholly-owned subsidiary of another body corporate.

(6) In determining for the purposes of this section whether a transaction is one that would have required approval under section 197, 198, 200 or 201 if it had been entered into by the company, the transaction shall be treated as having been entered into on the date of the arrangement.

204 Exception for expenditure on company business

(1) Approval is not required under section 197, 198, 200 or 201 (requirement of members' approval for loans etc) for anything done by a company –

   (a) to provide a director of the company or of its holding company, or a person connected with any such director, with funds to meet expenditure incurred or to be incurred by him –

      (i) for the purposes of the company, or

      (ii) for the purpose of enabling him properly to perform his duties as an officer of the company, or

   (b) to enable any such person to avoid incurring such expenditure.

(2) This section does not authorise a company to enter into a transaction if the aggregate of –

   (a) the value of the transaction in question, and

   (b) the value of any other relevant transactions or arrangements,

exceeds £50,000.

205 Exception for expenditure on defending proceedings etc

(1) Approval is not required under section 197, 198, 200 or 201 (requirement of members' approval for loans etc) for anything done by a company –

    (a) to provide a director of the company or of its holding company with funds to meet expenditure incurred or to be incurred by him –

        (i) in defending any criminal or civil proceedings in connection with any alleged negligence, default, breach of duty or breach of trust by him in relation to the company or an associated company, or

        (ii) in connection with an application for relief (see subsection (5)), or

    (b) to enable any such director to avoid incurring such expenditure,

    if it is done on the following terms.

(2) The terms are –

    (a) that the loan is to be repaid, or (as the case may be) any liability of the company incurred under any transaction connected with the thing done is to be discharged, in the event of –

        (i) the director being convicted in the proceedings,

        (ii) judgment being given against him in the proceedings, or

        (iii) the court refusing to grant him relief on the application; and

    (b) that it is to be so repaid or discharged not later than –

        (i) the date when the conviction becomes final,

        (ii) the date when the judgment becomes final, or

        (iii) the date when the refusal of relief becomes final.

(3) For this purpose a conviction, judgment or refusal of relief becomes final –

    (a) if not appealed against, at the end of the period for bringing an appeal;

    (b) if appealed against, when the appeal (or any further appeal) is disposed of.

(4) An appeal is disposed of –

    (a) if it is determined and the period for bringing any further appeal has ended, or

    (b) if it is abandoned or otherwise ceases to have effect.

(5) The reference in subsection (1)(a)(ii) to an application for relief is to an application for relief under –

    section 661(3) or (4) (power of court to grant relief in case of acquisition of shares by innocent nominee), or

    section 1157 (general power of court to grant relief in case of honest and reasonable conduct).

206 Exception for expenditure in connection with regulatory action or investigation

Approval is not required under section 197, 198, 200 or 201 (requirement of members' approval for loans etc) for anything done by a company –

    (a) to provide a director of the company or of its holding company with funds to meet expenditure incurred or to be incurred by him in defending himself –

        (i) in an investigation by a regulatory authority, or

        (ii) against action proposed to be taken by a regulatory authority,

    in connection with any alleged negligence, default, breach of duty or breach of trust by him in relation to the company or an associated company, or

    (b) to enable any such director to avoid incurring such expenditure.

207 Exceptions for minor and business transactions

(1) Approval is not required under section 197, 198 or 200 for a company to make a loan or quasi-loan, or to give a guarantee or provide security in connection with a loan or quasi-loan, if the aggregate of –

(a) the value of the transaction, and
(b) the value of any other relevant transactions or arrangements,

does not exceed £10,000.

(2) Approval is not required under section 201 for a company to enter into a credit transaction, or to give a guarantee or provide security in connection with a credit transaction, if the aggregate of –

(a) the value of the transaction (that is, of the credit transaction, guarantee or security), and
(b) the value of any other relevant transactions or arrangements,

does not exceed £15,000.

(3) Approval is not required under section 201 for a company to enter into a credit transaction, or to give a guarantee or provide security in connection with a credit transaction, if –

(a) the transaction is entered into by the company in the ordinary course of the company's business, and
(b) the value of the transaction is not greater, and the terms on which it is entered into are not more favourable, than it is reasonable to expect the company would have offered to, or in respect of, a person of the same financial standing but unconnected with the company.

208 Exceptions for intra-group transactions

(1) Approval is not required under section 197, 198 or 200 for –

(a) the making of a loan or quasi-loan to an associated body corporate, or
(b) the giving of a guarantee or provision of security in connection with a loan or quasi-loan made to an associated body corporate.

(2) Approval is not required under section 201 –

(a) to enter into a credit transaction as creditor for the benefit of an associated body corporate, or
(b) to give a guarantee or provide security in connection with a credit transaction entered into by any person for the benefit of an associated body corporate.

209 Exceptions for money-lending companies

(1) Approval is not required under section 197, 198 or 200 for the making of a loan or quasi-loan, or the giving of a guarantee or provision of security in connection with a loan or quasi-loan, by a money-lending company if –

(a) the transaction (that is, the loan, quasi-loan, guarantee or security) is entered into by the company in the ordinary course of the company's business, and
(b) the value of the transaction is not greater, and its terms are not more favourable, than it is reasonable to expect the company would have offered to a person of the same financial standing but unconnected with the company.

(2) A "money-lending company" means a company whose ordinary business includes the making of loans or quasi-loans, or the giving of guarantees or provision of security in connection with loans or quasi-loans.

(3) The condition specified in subsection (1)(b) does not of itself prevent a company from making a home loan –

(a) to a director of the company or of its holding company, or
(b) to an employee of the company,

if loans of that description are ordinarily made by the company to its employees and the terms of the loan in question are no more favourable than those on which such loans are ordinarily made.

(4) For the purposes of subsection (3) a "home loan" means a loan –

(a) for the purpose of facilitating the purchase, for use as the only or main residence of the person to whom the loan is made, of the whole or part of any dwelling-house together with any land to be occupied and enjoyed with it,

(b) for the purpose of improving a dwelling-house or part of a dwelling-house so used or any land occupied and enjoyed with it, or

(c) in substitution for any loan made by any person and falling within paragraph (a) or (b).

210 Other relevant transactions or arrangements

(1) This section has effect for determining what are "other relevant transactions or arrangements" for the purposes of any exception to section 197, 198, 200 or 201.
In the following provisions "the relevant exception" means the exception for the purposes of which that falls to be determined.

(2) Other relevant transactions or arrangements are those previously entered into, or entered into at the same time as the transaction or arrangement in question in relation to which the following conditions are met.

(3) Where the transaction or arrangement in question is entered into –

(a) for a director of the company entering into it, or

(b) for a person connected with such a director,

the conditions are that the transaction or arrangement was (or is) entered into for that director, or a person connected with him, by virtue of the relevant exception by that company or by any of its subsidiaries.

(4) Where the transaction or arrangement in question is entered into –

(a) for a director of the holding company of the company entering into it, or

(b) for a person connected with such a director,

the conditions are that the transaction or arrangement was (or is) entered into for that director, or a person connected with him, by virtue of the relevant exception by the holding company or by any of its subsidiaries.

(5) A transaction or arrangement entered into by a company that at the time it was entered into –

(a) was a subsidiary of the company entering into the transaction or arrangement in question, or

(b) was a subsidiary of that company's holding company,

is not a relevant transaction or arrangement if, at the time the question arises whether the transaction or arrangement in question falls within a relevant exception, it is no longer such a subsidiary.

211 The value of transactions and arrangements

(1) For the purposes of sections 197 to 214 (loans etc) –

(a) the value of a transaction or arrangement is determined as follows, and

(b) the value of any other relevant transaction or arrangement is taken to be the value so determined reduced by any amount by which the liabilities of the person for whom the transaction or arrangement was made have been reduced.

(2) The value of a loan is the amount of its principal.

(3) The value of a quasi-loan is the amount, or maximum amount, that the person to whom the quasi-loan is made is liable to reimburse the creditor.

(4) The value of a credit transaction is the price that it is reasonable to expect could be obtained for the goods, services or land to which the transaction relates if they had

been supplied (at the time the transaction is entered into) in the ordinary course of business and on the same terms (apart from price) as they have been supplied, or are to be supplied, under the transaction in question.

(5) The value of a guarantee or security is the amount guaranteed or secured.

(6) The value of an arrangement to which section 203 (related arrangements) applies is the value of the transaction to which the arrangement relates.

(7) If the value of a transaction or arrangement is not capable of being expressed as a specific sum of money –

    (a) whether because the amount of any liability arising under the transaction or arrangement is unascertainable, or for any other reason, and

    (b) whether or not any liability under the transaction or arrangement has been reduced,

its value is deemed to exceed £50,000.

212 The person for whom a transaction or arrangement is entered into

For the purposes of sections 197 to 214 (loans etc) the person for whom a transaction or arrangement is entered into is –

    (a) in the case of a loan or quasi-loan, the person to whom it is made;

    (b) in the case of a credit transaction, the person to whom goods, land or services are supplied, sold, hired, leased or otherwise disposed of under the transaction;

    (c) in the case of a guarantee or security, the person for whom the transaction is made in connection with which the guarantee or security is entered into;

    (d) in the case of an arrangement within section 203 (related arrangements), the person for whom the transaction is made to which the arrangement relates.

213 Loans etc: civil consequences of contravention

(1) This section applies where a company enters into a transaction or arrangement in contravention of section 197, 198, 200, 201 or 203 (requirement of members' approval for loans etc).

(2) The transaction or arrangement is voidable at the instance of the company, unless –

    (a) restitution of any money or other asset that was the subject matter of the transaction or arrangement is no longer possible,

    (b) the company has been indemnified for any loss or damage resulting from the transaction or arrangement, or

    (c) rights acquired in good faith, for value and without actual notice of the contravention by a person who is not a party to the transaction or arrangement would be affected by the avoidance.

(3) Whether or not the transaction or arrangement has been avoided, each of the persons specified in subsection (4) is liable –

    (a) to account to the company for any gain that he has made directly or indirectly by the transaction or arrangement, and

    (b) (jointly and severally with any other person so liable under this section) to indemnify the company for any loss or damage resulting from the transaction or arrangement.

(4) The persons so liable are –

    (a) any director of the company or of its holding company with whom the company entered into the transaction or arrangement in contravention of section 197, 198, 201 or 203,

    (b) any person with whom the company entered into the transaction or arrangement in contravention of any of those sections who is connected with a director of the company or of its holding company,

(c) the director of the company or of its holding company with whom any such person is connected, and

(d) any other director of the company who authorised the transaction or arrangement.

(5) Subsections (3) and (4) are subject to the following two subsections.

(6) In the case of a transaction or arrangement entered into by a company in contravention of section 200, 201 or 203 with a person connected with a director of the company or of its holding company, that director is not liable by virtue of subsection (4)(c) if he shows that he took all reasonable steps to secure the company's compliance with the section concerned.

(7) In any case –

(a) a person so connected is not liable by virtue of subsection (4)(b), and

(b) a director is not liable by virtue of subsection (4)(d),

if he shows that, at the time the transaction or arrangement was entered into, he did not know the relevant circumstances constituting the contravention.

(8) Nothing in this section shall be read as excluding the operation of any other enactment or rule of law by virtue of which the transaction or arrangement may be called in question or any liability to the company may arise.

214 Loans etc: effect of subsequent affirmation

Where a transaction or arrangement is entered into by a company in contravention of section 197, 198, 200, 201 or 203 (requirement of members' approval for loans etc) but, within a reasonable period, it is affirmed –

(a) in the case of a contravention of the requirement for a resolution of the members of the company, by a resolution of the members of the company, and

(b) in the case of a contravention of the requirement for a resolution of the members of the company's holding company, by a resolution of the members of the holding company,

the transaction or arrangement may no longer be avoided under section 213.

Payments for loss of office

215 Payments for loss of office

(1) In this Chapter a "payment for loss of office" means a payment made to a director or past director of a company –

(a) by way of compensation for loss of office as director of the company,

(b) by way of compensation for loss, while director of the company or in connection with his ceasing to be a director of it, of –

(i) any other office or employment in connection with the management of the affairs of the company, or

(ii) any office (as director or otherwise) or employment in connection with the management of the affairs of any subsidiary undertaking of the company,

(c) as consideration for or in connection with his retirement from his office as director of the company, or

(d) as consideration for or in connection with his retirement, while director of the company or in connection with his ceasing to be a director of it, from –

(i) any other office or employment in connection with the management of the affairs of the company, or

(ii) any office (as director or otherwise) or employment in connection with the management of the affairs of any subsidiary undertaking of the company.

(2) The references to compensation and consideration include benefits otherwise than in cash and references in this Chapter to payment have a corresponding meaning.

(3) For the purposes of sections 217 to 221 (payments requiring members' approval) –

    (a) payment to a person connected with a director, or

    (b) payment to any person at the direction of, or for the benefit of, a director or a person connected with him,

is treated as payment to the director.

(4) References in those sections to payment by a person include payment by another person at the direction of, or on behalf of, the person referred to.

216 Amounts taken to be payments for loss of office

(1) This section applies where in connection with any such transfer as is mentioned in section 218 or 219 (payment in connection with transfer of undertaking, property or shares) a director of the company –

    (a) is to cease to hold office, or

    (b) is to cease to be the holder of –

        (i) any other office or employment in connection with the management of the affairs of the company, or

        (ii) any office (as director or otherwise) or employment in connection with the management of the affairs of any subsidiary undertaking of the company.

(2) If in connection with any such transfer –

    (a) the price to be paid to the director for any shares in the company held by him is in excess of the price which could at the time have been obtained by other holders of like shares, or

    (b) any valuable consideration is given to the director by a person other than the company,

the excess or, as the case may be, the money value of the consideration is taken for the purposes of those sections to have been a payment for loss of office.

217 Payment by company: requirement of members' approval

(1) A company may not make a payment for loss of office to a director of the company unless the payment has been approved by a resolution of the members of the company.

(2) A company may not make a payment for loss of office to a director of its holding company unless the payment has been approved by a resolution of the members of each of those companies.

(3) A resolution approving a payment to which this section applies must not be passed unless a memorandum setting out particulars of the proposed payment (including its amount) is made available to the members of the company whose approval is sought –

    (a) in the case of a written resolution, by being sent or submitted to every eligible member at or before the time at which the proposed resolution is sent or submitted to him;

    (b) in the case of a resolution at a meeting, by being made available for inspection by the members both –

        (i) at the company's registered office for not less than 15 days ending with the date of the meeting, and

        (ii) at the meeting itself.

(4) No approval is required under this section on the part of the members of a body corporate that –

    (a) is not a UK-registered company, or

    (b) is a wholly-owned subsidiary of another body corporate.

218 Payment in connection with transfer of undertaking etc: requirement of members' approval

(1) No payment for loss of office may be made by any person to a director of a company in connection with the transfer of the whole or any part of the undertaking or property of the company unless the payment has been approved by a resolution of the members of the company.

(2) No payment for loss of office may be made by any person to a director of a company in connection with the transfer of the whole or any part of the undertaking or property of a subsidiary of the company unless the payment has been approved by a resolution of the members of each of the companies.

(3) A resolution approving a payment to which this section applies must not be passed unless a memorandum setting out particulars of the proposed payment (including its amount) is made available to the members of the company whose approval is sought –

    (a) in the case of a written resolution, by being sent or submitted to every eligible member at or before the time at which the proposed resolution is sent or submitted to him;

    (b) in the case of a resolution at a meeting, by being made available for inspection by the members both –

        (i) at the company's registered office for not less than 15 days ending with the date of the meeting, and

        (ii) at the meeting itself.

(4) No approval is required under this section on the part of the members of a body corporate that –

    (a) is not a UK-registered company, or

    (b) is a wholly-owned subsidiary of another body corporate.

(5) A payment made in pursuance of an arrangement –

    (a) entered into as part of the agreement for the transfer in question, or within one year before or two years after that agreement, and

    (b) to which the company whose undertaking or property is transferred, or any person to whom the transfer is made, is privy,

is presumed, except in so far as the contrary is shown, to be a payment to which this section applies.

219 Payment in connection with share transfer: requirement of members' approval

(1) No payment for loss of office may be made by any person to a director of a company in connection with a transfer of shares in the company, or in a subsidiary of the company, resulting from a takeover bid unless the payment has been approved by a resolution of the relevant shareholders.

(2) The relevant shareholders are the holders of the shares to which the bid relates and any holders of shares of the same class as any of those shares.

(3) A resolution approving a payment to which this section applies must not be passed unless a memorandum setting out particulars of the proposed payment (including its amount) is made available to the members of the company whose approval is sought –

    (a) in the case of a written resolution, by being sent or submitted to every eligible member at or before the time at which the proposed resolution is sent or submitted to him;

    (b) in the case of a resolution at a meeting, by being made available for inspection by the members both –

        (i)   at the company's registered office for not less than 15 days ending with the date of the meeting, and

        (ii) at the meeting itself.

(4) Neither the person making the offer, nor any associate of his (as defined in section 988), is entitled to vote on the resolution, but –

    (a) where the resolution is proposed as a written resolution, they are entitled (if they would otherwise be so entitled) to be sent a copy of it, and

    (b) at any meeting to consider the resolution they are entitled (if they would otherwise be so entitled) to be given notice of the meeting, to attend and speak and if present (in person or by proxy) to count towards the quorum.

(5) If at a meeting to consider the resolution a quorum is not present, and after the meeting has been adjourned to a later date a quorum is again not present, the payment is (for the purposes of this section) deemed to have been approved.

(6) No approval is required under this section on the part of shareholders in a body corporate that –

    (a) is not a UK-registered company, or

    (b) is a wholly-owned subsidiary of another body corporate.

(7) A payment made in pursuance of an arrangement –

    (a) entered into as part of the agreement for the transfer in question, or within one year before or two years after that agreement, and

    (b) to which the company whose shares are the subject of the bid, or any person to whom the transfer is made, is privy,

is presumed, except in so far as the contrary is shown, to be a payment to which this section applies.

220 Exception for payments in discharge of legal obligations etc

(1) Approval is not required under section 217, 218 or 219 (payments requiring members' approval) for a payment made in good faith –

    (a) in discharge of an existing legal obligation (as defined below),

    (b) by way of damages for breach of such an obligation,

    (c) by way of settlement or compromise of any claim arising in connection with the termination of a person's office or employment, or

    (d) by way of pension in respect of past services.

(2) In relation to a payment within section 217 (payment by company) an existing legal obligation means an obligation of the company, or any body corporate associated with it, that was not entered into in connection with, or in consequence of, the event giving rise to the payment for loss of office.

(3) In relation to a payment within section 218 or 219 (payment in connection with transfer of undertaking, property or shares) an existing legal obligation means an obligation of the person making the payment that was not entered into for the purposes of, in connection with or in consequence of, the transfer in question.

(4) In the case of a payment within both section 217 and section 218, or within both section 217 and section 219, subsection (2) above applies and not subsection (3).

(5) A payment part of which falls within subsection (1) above and part of which does not is treated as if the parts were separate payments.

221 Exception for small payments

(1) Approval is not required under section 217, 218 or 219 (payments requiring members' approval) if –

(a) the payment in question is made by the company or any of its subsidiaries, and

(b) the amount or value of the payment, together with the amount or value of any other relevant payments, does not exceed £200.

(2) For this purpose "other relevant payments" are payments for loss of office in relation to which the following conditions are met.

(3) Where the payment in question is one to which section 217 (payment by company) applies, the conditions are that the other payment was or is paid –

(a) by the company making the payment in question or any of its subsidiaries,

(b) to the director to whom that payment is made, and

(c) in connection with the same event.

(4) Where the payment in question is one to which section 218 or 219 applies (payment in connection with transfer of undertaking, property or shares), the conditions are that the other payment was (or is) paid in connection with the same transfer –

(a) to the director to whom the payment in question was made, and

(b) by the company making the payment or any of its subsidiaries.

222 Payments made without approval: civil consequences

(1) If a payment is made in contravention of section 217 (payment by company) –

(a) it is held by the recipient on trust for the company making the payment, and

(b) any director who authorised the payment is jointly and severally liable to indemnify the company that made the payment for any loss resulting from it.

(2) If a payment is made in contravention of section 218 (payment in connection with transfer of undertaking etc), it is held by the recipient on trust for the company whose undertaking or property is or is proposed to be transferred.

(3) If a payment is made in contravention of section 219 (payment in connection with share transfer) –

(a) it is held by the recipient on trust for persons who have sold their shares as a result of the offer made, and

(b) the expenses incurred by the recipient in distributing that sum amongst those persons shall be borne by him and not retained out of that sum.

(4) If a payment is in contravention of section 217 and section 218, subsection (2) of this section applies rather than subsection (1).

(5) If a payment is in contravention of section 217 and section 219, subsection (3) of this section applies rather than subsection (1), unless the court directs otherwise.

Supplementary

223 Transactions requiring members' approval: application of provisions to shadow directors

(1) For the purposes of –

(a) sections 188 and 189 (directors' service contracts),

(b) sections 190 to 196 (property transactions),

(c) sections 197 to 214 (loans etc), and

(d) sections 215 to 222 (payments for loss of office),

a shadow director is treated as a director.

(2) Any reference in those provisions to loss of office as a director does not apply in relation to loss of a person's status as a shadow director.

224 Approval by written resolution: accidental failure to send memorandum

(1) Where –

    (a) approval under this Chapter is sought by written resolution, and

    (b) a memorandum is required under this Chapter to be sent or submitted to every eligible member before the resolution is passed,

any accidental failure to send or submit the memorandum to one or more members shall be disregarded for the purpose of determining whether the requirement has been met.

(2) Subsection (1) has effect subject to any provision of the company's articles.

225 Cases where approval is required under more than one provision

(1) Approval may be required under more than one provision of this Chapter.

(2) If so, the requirements of each applicable provision must be met.

(3) This does not require a separate resolution for the purposes of each provision.

226 Requirement of consent of Charity Commission: companies that are charities

For section 66 of the Charities Act 1993 (c. 10) substitute –

"**66 Consent of Commission required for approval etc by members of charitable companies**

(1) Where a company is a charity –

    (a) any approval given by the members of the company under any provision of Chapter 4 of Part 10 of the Companies Act 2006 (transactions with directors requiring approval by members) listed in subsection (2) below, and

    (b) any affirmation given by members of the company under section 196 or 214 of that Act (affirmation of unapproved property transactions and loans),

is ineffective without the prior written consent of the Commission.

(2) The provisions are –

    (a) section 188 (directors' long-term service contracts);

    (b) section 190 (substantial property transactions with directors etc);

    (c) section 197, 198 or 200 (loans and quasi-loans to directors etc);

    (d) section 201 (credit transactions for benefit of directors etc);

    (e) section 203 (related arrangements);

    (f) section 217 (payments to directors for loss of office);

    (g) section 218 (payments to directors for loss of office: transfer of undertaking etc).

66A Consent of Commission required for certain acts of charitable company

(1) A company that is a charity may not do an act to which this section applies without the prior written consent of the Commission.

(2) This section applies to an act that –

    (a) does not require approval under a listed provision of Chapter 4 of Part 10 of the Companies Act 2006 (transactions with directors) by the members of the company, but

    (b) would require such approval but for an exemption in the provision in question that disapplies the need for approval on the part of the members of a body corporate which is a whollyowned subsidiary of another body corporate.

(3) The reference to a listed provision is a reference to a provision listed in section 66(2) above.

(4) If a company acts in contravention of this section, the exemption referred to in subsection (2)(b) shall be treated as of no effect in relation to the act.".

CHAPTER 5

DIRECTORS' SERVICE CONTRACTS

227 Directors' service contracts

(1) For the purposes of this Part a director's "service contract", in relation to a company, means a contract under which –

    (a) a director of the company undertakes personally to perform services (as director or otherwise) for the company, or for a subsidiary of the company, or

    (b) services (as director or otherwise) that a director of the company undertakes personally to perform are made available by a third party to the company, or to a subsidiary of the company.

(2) The provisions of this Part relating to directors' service contracts apply to the terms of a person's appointment as a director of a company.

They are not restricted to contracts for the performance of services outside the scope of the ordinary duties of a director.

228 Copy of contract or memorandum of terms to be available for inspection

(1) A company must keep available for inspection –

    (a) a copy of every director's service contract with the company or with a subsidiary of the company, or

    (b) if the contract is not in writing, a written memorandum setting out the terms of the contract.

(2) All the copies and memoranda must be kept available for inspection at –

    (a) the company's registered office, or

    (b) a place specified in regulations under section 1136.

(3) The copies and memoranda must be retained by the company for at least one year from the date of termination or expiry of the contract and must be kept available for inspection during that time.

(4) The company must give notice to the registrar –

    (a) of the place at which the copies and memoranda are kept available for inspection, and

    (b) of any change in that place,

unless they have at all times been kept at the company's registered office.

(5) If default is made in complying with subsection (1), (2) or (3), or default is made for 14 days in complying with subsection (4), an offence is committed by every officer of the company who is in default.

(6) A person guilty of an offence under this section is liable on summary conviction to a fine not exceeding level 3 on the standard scale and, for continued contravention, a daily default fine not exceeding one-tenth of level 3 on the standard scale.

(7) The provisions of this section apply to a variation of a director's service contract as they apply to the original contract.

229 Right of member to inspect and request copy

(1) Every copy or memorandum required to be kept under section 228 must be open to inspection by any member of the company without charge.

(2) Any member of the company is entitled, on request and on payment of such fee as may be prescribed, to be provided with a copy of any such copy or memorandum.

The copy must be provided within seven days after the request is received by the company.

(3) If an inspection required under subsection (1) is refused, or default is made in com-

plying with subsection (2), an offence is committed by every officer of the company who is in default.

(4) A person guilty of an offence under this section is liable on summary conviction to a fine not exceeding level 3 on the standard scale and, for continued contravention, a daily default fine not exceeding one-tenth of level 3 on the standard scale.

(5) In the case of any such refusal or default the court may by order compel an immediate inspection or, as the case may be, direct that the copy required be sent to the person requiring it.

230 Directors' service contracts: application of provisions to shadow directors

A shadow director is treated as a director for the purposes of the provisions of this Chapter.

CHAPTER 6

CONTRACTS WITH SOLE MEMBERS WHO ARE DIRECTORS

231 Contract with sole member who is also a director

(1) This section applies where –
- (a) a limited company having only one member enters into a contract with the sole member,
- (b) the sole member is also a director of the company, and
- (c) the contract is not entered into in the ordinary course of the company's business.

(2) The company must, unless the contract is in writing, ensure that the terms of the contract are either –
- (a) set out in a written memorandum, or
- (b) recorded in the minutes of the first meeting of the directors of the company following the making of the contract.

(3) If a company fails to comply with this section an offence is committed by every officer of the company who is in default.

(4) A person guilty of an offence under this section is liable on summary conviction to a fine not exceeding level 5 on the standard scale.

(5) For the purposes of this section a shadow director is treated as a director.

(6) Failure to comply with this section in relation to a contract does not affect the validity of the contract.

(7) Nothing in this section shall be read as excluding the operation of any other enactment or rule of law applying to contracts between a company and a director of the company.

CHAPTER 7

DIRECTORS' LIABILITIES

Provision protecting directors from liability

232 Provisions protecting directors from liability

(1) Any provision that purports to exempt a director of a company (to any extent) from any liability that would otherwise attach to him in connection with any negligence, default, breach of duty or breach of trust in relation to the company is void.

(2) Any provision by which a company directly or indirectly provides an indemnity (to

any extent) for a director of the company, or of an associated company, against any liability attaching to him in connection with any negligence, default, breach of duty or breach of trust in relation to the company of which he is a director is void, except as permitted by –

(a) section 233 (provision of insurance),
(b) section 234 (qualifying third party indemnity provision), or
(c) section 235 (qualifying pension scheme indemnity provision).

(3) This section applies to any provision, whether contained in a company's articles or in any contract with the company or otherwise.
(4) Nothing in this section prevents a company's articles from making such provision as has previously been lawful for dealing with conflicts of interest.

233 Provision of insurance

Section 232(2) (voidness of provisions for indemnifying directors) does not prevent a company from purchasing and maintaining for a director of the company, or of an associated company, insurance against any such liability as is mentioned in that subsection.

234 Qualifying third party indemnity provision

(1) Section 232(2) (voidness of provisions for indemnifying directors) does not apply to qualifying third party indemnity provision.
(2) Third party indemnity provision means provision for indemnity against liability incurred by the director to a person other than the company or an associated company.
Such provision is qualifying third party indemnity provision if the following requirements are met.
(3) The provision must not provide any indemnity against –
(a) any liability of the director to pay –
(i)   a fine imposed in criminal proceedings, or
(ii) a sum payable to a regulatory authority by way of a penalty in respect of non-compliance with any requirement of a regulatory nature (however arising); or
(b) any liability incurred by the director –
(i)   in defending criminal proceedings in which he is convicted, or
(ii) in defending civil proceedings brought by the company, or an associated company, in which judgment is given against him, or
(iii) in connection with an application for relief (see subsection (6)) in which the court refuses to grant him relief.
(4) The references in subsection (3)(b) to a conviction, judgment or refusal of relief are to the final decision in the proceedings.
(5) For this purpose –
(a) a conviction, judgment or refusal of relief becomes final –
(i)   if not appealed against, at the end of the period for bringing an appeal, or
(ii) if appealed against, at the time when the appeal (or any further appeal) is disposed of; and
(b) an appeal is disposed of –
(i)   if it is determined and the period for bringing any further appeal has ended, or
(ii) if it is abandoned or otherwise ceases to have effect.
(6) The reference in subsection (3)(b)(iii) to an application for relief is to an application for relief under –

section 661(3) or (4) (power of court to grant relief in case of acquisition of shares by innocent nominee), or

section 1157 (general power of court to grant relief in case of honest and reasonable conduct).

235 Qualifying pension scheme indemnity provision

(1) Section 232(2) (voidness of provisions for indemnifying directors) does not apply to qualifying pension scheme indemnity provision.

(2) Pension scheme indemnity provision means provision indemnifying a director of a company that is a trustee of an occupational pension scheme against liability incurred in connection with the company's activities as trustee of the scheme.

Such provision is qualifying pension scheme indemnity provision if the following requirements are met.

(3) The provision must not provide any indemnity against –

   (a) any liability of the director to pay –

      (i) a fine imposed in criminal proceedings, or

      (ii) a sum payable to a regulatory authority by way of a penalty in respect of non-compliance with any requirement of a regulatory nature (however arising); or

   (b) any liability incurred by the director in defending criminal proceedings in which he is convicted.

(4) The reference in subsection (3)(b) to a conviction is to the final decision in the proceedings.

(5) For this purpose –

   (a) a conviction becomes final –

      (i) if not appealed against, at the end of the period for bringing an appeal, or

      (ii) if appealed against, at the time when the appeal (or any further appeal) is disposed of; and

   (b) an appeal is disposed of –

      (i) if it is determined and the period for bringing any further appeal has ended, or

      (ii) if it is abandoned or otherwise ceases to have effect.

(6) In this section "occupational pension scheme" means an occupational pension scheme as defined in section 150(5) of the Finance Act 2004 (c. 12) that is established under a trust.

236 Qualifying indemnity provision to be disclosed in directors' report

(1) This section requires disclosure in the directors' report of –

   (a) qualifying third party indemnity provision, and

   (b) qualifying pension scheme indemnity provision.

Such provision is referred to in this section as "qualifying indemnity provision".

(2) If when a directors' report is approved any qualifying indemnity provision (whether made by the company or otherwise) is in force for the benefit of one or more directors of the company, the report must state that such provision is in force.

(3) If at any time during the financial year to which a directors' report relates any such provision was in force for the benefit of one or more persons who were then directors of the company, the report must state that such provision was in force.

(4) If when a directors' report is approved qualifying indemnity provision made by the company is in force for the benefit of one or more directors of an associated company, the report must state that such provision is in force.

(5) If at any time during the financial year to which a directors' report relates any such

provision was in force for the benefit of one or more persons who were then directors of an associated company, the report must state that such provision was in force.

237 Copy of qualifying indemnity provision to be available for inspection

(1) This section has effect where qualifying indemnity provision is made for a director of a company, and applies –

   (a) to the company of which he is a director (whether the provision is made by that company or an associated company), and
   (b) where the provision is made by an associated company, to that company.

(2) That company or, as the case may be, each of them must keep available for inspection –

   (a) a copy of the qualifying indemnity provision, or
   (b) if the provision is not in writing, a written memorandum setting out its terms.

(3) The copy or memorandum must be kept available for inspection at –

   (a) the company's registered office, or
   (b) a place specified in regulations under section 1136.

(4) The copy or memorandum must be retained by the company for at least one year from the date of termination or expiry of the provision and must be kept available for inspection during that time.

(5) The company must give notice to the registrar –

   (a) of the place at which the copy or memorandum is kept available for inspection, and
   (b) of any change in that place,

   unless it has at all times been kept at the company's registered office.

(6) If default is made in complying with subsection (2), (3) or (4), or default is made for 14 days in complying with subsection (5), an offence is committed by every officer of the company who is in default.

(7) A person guilty of an offence under this section is liable on summary conviction to a fine not exceeding level 3 on the standard scale and, for continued contravention, a daily default fine not exceeding one-tenth of level 3 on the standard scale.

(8) The provisions of this section apply to a variation of a qualifying indemnity provision as they apply to the original provision.

(9) In this section "qualifying indemnity provision" means –

   (a) qualifying third party indemnity provision, and
   (b) qualifying pension scheme indemnity provision.

238 Right of member to inspect and request copy

(1) Every copy or memorandum required to be kept by a company under section 237 must be open to inspection by any member of the company without charge.

(2) Any member of the company is entitled, on request and on payment of such fee as may be prescribed, to be provided with a copy of any such copy or memorandum.
   The copy must be provided within seven days after the request is received by the company.

(3) If an inspection required under subsection (1) is refused, or default is made in complying with subsection (2), an offence is committed by every officer of the company who is in default.

(4) A person guilty of an offence under this section is liable on summary conviction to a fine not exceeding level 3 on the standard scale and, for continued contravention, a daily default fine not exceeding one-tenth of level 3 on the standard scale.

(5) In the case of any such refusal or default the court may by order compel an immediate inspection or, as the case may be, direct that the copy required be sent to the person requiring it.

Ratification of acts giving rise to liability

239 Ratification of acts of directors

(1) This section applies to the ratification by a company of conduct by a director amounting to negligence, default, breach of duty or breach of trust in relation to the company.

(2) The decision of the company to ratify such conduct must be made by resolution of the members of the company.

(3) Where the resolution is proposed as a written resolution neither the director (if a member of the company) nor any member connected with him is an eligible member.

(4) Where the resolution is proposed at a meeting, it is passed only if the necessary majority is obtained disregarding votes in favour of the resolution by the director (if a member of the company) and any member connected with him.

This does not prevent the director or any such member from attending, being counted towards the quorum and taking part in the proceedings at any meeting at which the decision is considered.

(5) For the purposes of this section –

    (a) "conduct" includes acts and omissions;

    (b) "director" includes a former director;

    (c) a shadow director is treated as a director; and

    (d) in section 252 (meaning of "connected person"), subsection (3) does not apply (exclusion of person who is himself a director).

(6) Nothing in this section affects –

    (a) the validity of a decision taken by unanimous consent of the members of the company, or

    (b) any power of the directors to agree not to sue, or to settle or release a claim made by them on behalf of the company.

(7) This section does not affect any other enactment or rule of law imposing additional requirements for valid ratification or any rule of law as to acts that are incapable of being ratified by the company.

CHAPTER 8

DIRECTORS' RESIDENTIAL ADDRESSES: PROTECTION FROM DISCLOSURE

240 Protected information

(1) This Chapter makes provision for protecting, in the case of a company director who is an individual –

    (a) information as to his usual residential address;

    (b) the information that his service address is his usual residential address.

(2) That information is referred to in this Chapter as "protected information".

(3) Information does not cease to be protected information on the individual ceasing to be a director of the company.

References in this Chapter to a director include, to that extent, a former director.

241 Protected information: restriction on use or disclosure by company

(1) A company must not use or disclose protected information about any of its directors, except –

    (a) for communicating with the director concerned,

    (b) in order to comply with any requirement of the Companies Acts as to particulars to be sent to the registrar, or

(c) in accordance with section 244 (disclosure under court order).

(2) Subsection (1) does not prohibit any use or disclosure of protected information with the consent of the director concerned.

242 Protected information: restriction on use or disclosure by registrar

(1) The registrar must omit protected information from the material on the register that is available for inspection where –

    (a) it is contained in a document delivered to him in which such information is required to be stated, and

    (b) in the case of a document having more than one part, it is contained in a part of the document in which such information is required to be stated.

(2) The registrar is not obliged –

    (a) to check other documents or (as the case may be) other parts of the document to ensure the absence of protected information, or

    (b) to omit from the material that is available for public inspection anything registered before this Chapter comes into force.

(3) The registrar must not use or disclose protected information except –

    (a) as permitted by section 243 (permitted use or disclosure by registrar), or

    (b) in accordance with section 244 (disclosure under court order).

243 Permitted use or disclosure by the registrar

(1) The registrar may use protected information for communicating with the director in question.

(2) The registrar may disclose protected information –

    (a) to a public authority specified for the purposes of this section by regulations made by the Secretary of State, or

    (b) to a credit reference agency.

(3) The Secretary of State may make provision by regulations –

    (a) specifying conditions for the disclosure of protected information in accordance with this section, and

    (b) providing for the charging of fees.

(4) The Secretary of State may make provision by regulations requiring the registrar, on application, to refrain from disclosing protected information relating to a director to a credit reference agency.

(5) Regulations under subsection (4) may make provision as to –

    (a) who may make an application,

    (b) the grounds on which an application may be made,

    (c) the information to be included in and documents to accompany an application, and

    (d) how an application is to be determined.

(6) Provision under subsection (5)(d) may in particular –

    (a) confer a discretion on the registrar;

    (b) provide for a question to be referred to a person other than the registrar for the purposes of determining the application.

(7) In this section –

"credit reference agency" means a person carrying on a business comprising the furnishing of information relevant to the financial standing of individuals, being information collected by the agency for that purpose; and

"public authority" includes any person or body having functions of a public nature.

(8) Regulations under this section are subject to negative resolution procedure.

244 Disclosure under court order

(1) The court may make an order for the disclosure of protected information by the company or by the registrar if –

    (a) there is evidence that service of documents at a service address other than the director's usual residential address is not effective to bring them to the notice of the director, or

    (b) it is necessary or expedient for the information to be provided in connection with the enforcement of an order or decree of the court,

and the court is otherwise satisfied that it is appropriate to make the order.

(2) An order for disclosure by the registrar is to be made only if the company –

    (a) does not have the director's usual residential address, or

    (b) has been dissolved.

(3) The order may be made on the application of a liquidator, creditor or member of the company, or any other person appearing to the court to have a sufficient interest.

(4) The order must specify the persons to whom, and purposes for which, disclosure is authorised.

245 Circumstances in which registrar may put address on the public record

(1) The registrar may put a director's usual residential address on the public record if –

    (a) communications sent by the registrar to the director and requiring a response within a specified period remain unanswered, or

    (b) there is evidence that service of documents at a service address provided in place of the director's usual residential address is not effective to bring them to the notice of the director.

(2) The registrar must give notice of the proposal –

    (a) to the director, and

    (b) to every company of which the registrar has been notified that the individual is a director.

(3) The notice must –

    (a) state the grounds on which it is proposed to put the director's usual residential address on the public record, and

    (b) specify a period within which representations may be made before that is done.

(4) It must be sent to the director at his usual residential address, unless it appears to the registrar that service at that address may be ineffective to bring it to the individual's notice, in which case it may be sent to any service address provided in place of that address.

(5) The registrar must take account of any representations received within the specified period.

(6) What is meant by putting the address on the public record is explained in section 246.

246 Putting the address on the public record

(1) The registrar, on deciding in accordance with section 245 that a director's usual residential address is to be put on the public record, shall proceed as if notice of a change of registered particulars had been given –

    (a) stating that address as the director's service address, and

    (b) stating that the director's usual residential address is the same as his service address.

(2) The registrar must give notice of having done so –

    (a) to the director, and

    (b) to the company.

(3) On receipt of the notice the company must –

(a) enter the director's usual residential address in its register of directors as his service address, and

(b) state in its register of directors' residential addresses that his usual residential address is the same as his service address.

(4) If the company has been notified by the director in question of a more recent address as his usual residential address, it must –

(a) enter that address in its register of directors as the director's service address, and

(b) give notice to the registrar as on a change of registered particulars.

(5) If a company fails to comply with subsection (3) or (4), an offence is committed by –

(a) the company, and

(b) every officer of the company who is in default.

(6) A person guilty of an offence under subsection (5) is liable on summary conviction to a fine not exceeding level 5 on the standard scale and, for continued contravention, a daily default fine not exceeding one-tenth of level 5 on the standard scale.

(7) A director whose usual residential address has been put on the public record by the registrar under this section may not register a service address other than his usual residential address for a period of five years from the date of the registrar's decision.

CHAPTER 9

SUPPLEMENTARY PROVISIONS

Provision for employees on cessation or transfer of business

247 Power to make provision for employees on cessation or transfer of business

(1) The powers of the directors of a company include (if they would not otherwise do so) power to make provision for the benefit of persons employed or formerly employed by the company, or any of its subsidiaries, in connection with the cessation or the transfer to any person of the whole or part of the undertaking of the company or that subsidiary.

(2) This power is exercisable notwithstanding the general duty imposed by section 172 (duty to promote the success of the company).

(3) In the case of a company that is a charity it is exercisable notwithstanding any restrictions on the directors' powers (or the company's capacity) flowing from the objects of the company.

(4) The power may only be exercised if sanctioned –

(a) by a resolution of the company, or

(b) by a resolution of the directors,

in accordance with the following provisions.

(5) A resolution of the directors –

(a) must be authorised by the company's articles, and

(b) is not sufficient sanction for payments to or for the benefit of directors, former directors or shadow directors.

(6) Any other requirements of the company's articles as to the exercise of the power conferred by this section must be complied with.

(7) Any payment under this section must be made –

(a) before the commencement of any winding up of the company, and

(b) out of profits of the company that are available for dividend.

Records of meetings of directors

248 Minutes of directors' meetings

(1) Every company must cause minutes of all proceedings at meetings of its directors to be recorded.
(2) The records must be kept for at least ten years from the date of the meeting.
(3) If a company fails to comply with this section, an offence is committed by every officer of the company who is in default.
(4) A person guilty of an offence under this section is liable on summary conviction to a fine not exceeding level 3 on the standard scale and, for continued contravention, a daily default fine not exceeding one-tenth of level 3 on the standard scale.

249 Minutes as evidence

(1) Minutes recorded in accordance with section 248, if purporting to be authenticated by the chairman of the meeting or by the chairman of the next directors' meeting, are evidence (in Scotland, sufficient evidence) of the proceedings at the meeting.
(2) Where minutes have been made in accordance with that section of the proceedings of a meeting of directors, then, until the contrary is proved –
    (a) the meeting is deemed duly held and convened,
    (b) all proceedings at the meeting are deemed to have duly taken place, and
    (c) all appointments at the meeting are deemed valid.

Meaning of "director" and "shadow director"

250 "Director"

In the Companies Acts "director" includes any person occupying the position of director, by whatever name called.

251 "Shadow director"

(1) In the Companies Acts "shadow director", in relation to a company, means a person in accordance with whose directions or instructions the directors of the company are accustomed to act.
(2) A person is not to be regarded as a shadow director by reason only that the directors act on advice given by him in a professional capacity.
(3) A body corporate is not to be regarded as a shadow director of any of its subsidiary companies for the purposes of –

Chapter 2 (general duties of directors),
Chapter 4 (transactions requiring members' approval), or
Chapter 6 (contract with sole member who is also a director),

by reason only that the directors of the subsidiary are accustomed to act in accordance with its directions or instructions.

Other definitions

252 Persons connected with a director

(1) This section defines what is meant by references in this Part to a person being "connected" with a director of a company (or a director being "connected" with a person).
(2) The following persons (and only those persons) are connected with a director of a company –

    (a) members of the director's family (see section 253);

   (b) a body corporate with which the director is connected (as defined in section 254);

   (c) a person acting in his capacity as trustee of a trust –

      (i)   the beneficiaries of which include the director or a person who by virtue of paragraph (a) or (b) is connected with him, or

      (ii) the terms of which confer a power on the trustees that may be exercised for the benefit of the director or any such person,

     other than a trust for the purposes of an employees' share scheme or a pension scheme;

   (d) a person acting in his capacity as partner –

      (i)   of the director, or

      (ii) of a person who, by virtue of paragraph (a), (b) or (c), is connected with that director;

   (e) a firm that is a legal person under the law by which it is governed and in which –

      (i)   the director is a partner,

      (ii) a partner is a person who, by virtue of paragraph (a), (b) or (c) is connected with the director, or

      (iii) a partner is a firm in which the director is a partner or in which there is a partner who, by virtue of paragraph (a), (b) or (c), is connected with the director.

(3) References in this Part to a person connected with a director of a company do not include a person who is himself a director of the company.

253 Members of a director's family

(1) This section defines what is meant by references in this Part to members of a director's family.

(2) For the purposes of this Part the members of a director's family are –

   (a) the director's spouse or civil partner;

   (b) any other person (whether of a different sex or the same sex) with whom the director lives as partner in an enduring family relationship;

   (c) the director's children or step-children;

   (d) any children or step-children of a person within paragraph (b) (and who are not children or step-children of the director) who live with the director and have not attained the age of 18;

   (e) the director's parents.

(3) Subsection (2)(b) does not apply if the other person is the director's grandparent or grandchild, sister, brother, aunt or uncle, or nephew or niece.

254 Director "connected with" a body corporate

(1) This section defines what is meant by references in this Part to a director being "connected with" a body corporate.

(2) A director is connected with a body corporate if, but only if, he and the persons connected with him together –

   (a) are interested in shares comprised in the equity share capital of that body corporate of a nominal value equal to at least 20% of that share capital, or

   (b) are entitled to exercise or control the exercise of more than 20% of the voting power at any general meeting of that body.

(3) The rules set out in Schedule 1 (references to interest in shares or debentures) apply for the purposes of this section.

(4) References in this section to voting power the exercise of which is controlled by a director include voting power whose exercise is controlled by a body corporate controlled by him.

(5) Shares in a company held as treasury shares, and any voting rights attached to such shares, are disregarded for the purposes of this section.

(6) For the avoidance of circularity in the application of section 252 (meaning of "connected person") –

    (a) a body corporate with which a director is connected is not treated for the purposes of this section as connected with him unless it is also connected with him by virtue of subsection (2)(c) or (d) of that section (connection as trustee or partner); and

    (b) a trustee of a trust the beneficiaries of which include (or may include) a body corporate with which a director is connected is not treated for the purposes of this section as connected with a director by reason only of that fact.

255 Director "controlling" a body corporate

(1) This section defines what is meant by references in this Part to a director "controlling" a body corporate.

(2) A director of a company is taken to control a body corporate if, but only if –

    (a) he or any person connected with him –

        (i) is interested in any part of the equity share capital of that body, or

        (ii) is entitled to exercise or control the exercise of any part of the voting power at any general meeting of that body, and

    (b) he, the persons connected with him and the other directors of that company, together –

        (i) are interested in more than 50% of that share capital, or

        (ii) are entitled to exercise or control the exercise of more than 50% of that voting power.

(3) The rules set out in Schedule 1 (references to interest in shares or debentures) apply for the purposes of this section.

(4) References in this section to voting power the exercise of which is controlled by a director include voting power whose exercise is controlled by a body corporate controlled by him.

(5) Shares in a company held as treasury shares, and any voting rights attached to such shares, are disregarded for the purposes of this section.

(6) For the avoidance of circularity in the application of section 252 (meaning of "connected person") –

    (a) a body corporate with which a director is connected is not treated for the purposes of this section as connected with him unless it is also connected with him by virtue of subsection (2)(c) or (d) of that section (connection as trustee or partner); and

    (b) a trustee of a trust the beneficiaries of which include (or may include) a body corporate with which a director is connected is not treated for the purposes of this section as connected with a director by reason only of that fact.

256 Associated bodies corporate

For the purposes of this Part –

    (a) bodies corporate are associated if one is a subsidiary of the other or both are subsidiaries of the same body corporate, and

    (b) companies are associated if one is a subsidiary of the other or both are subsidiaries of the same body corporate.

257 References to company's constitution

(1) References in this Part to a company's constitution include –

   (a) any resolution or other decision come to in accordance with the constitution, and

   (b) any decision by the members of the company, or a class of members, that is treated by virtue of any enactment or rule of law as equivalent to a decision by the company.

(2) This is in addition to the matters mentioned in section 17 (general provision as to matters contained in company's constitution).

General

258 Power to increase financial limits

(1) The Secretary of State may by order substitute for any sum of money specified in this Part a larger sum specified in the order.

(2) An order under this section is subject to negative resolution procedure.

(3) An order does not have effect in relation to anything done or not done before it comes into force.

Accordingly, proceedings in respect of any liability incurred before that time may be continued or instituted as if the order had not been made.

259 Transactions under foreign law

For the purposes of this Part it is immaterial whether the law that (apart from this Act) governs an arrangement or transaction is the law of the United Kingdom, or a part of it, or not.

PART 11

DERIVATIVE CLAIMS AND PROCEEDINGS BY MEMBERS

CHAPTER 1

DERIVATIVE CLAIMS IN ENGLAND AND WALES OR NORTHERN IRELAND

260 Derivative claims

(1) This Chapter applies to proceedings in England and Wales or Northern Ireland by a member of a company –

   (a) in respect of a cause of action vested in the company, and

   (b) seeking relief on behalf of the company.

This is referred to in this Chapter as a "derivative claim".

(2) A derivative claim may only be brought –

   (a) under this Chapter, or

   (b) in pursuance of an order of the court in proceedings under section 994 (proceedings for protection of members against unfair prejudice).

(3) A derivative claim under this Chapter may be brought only in respect of a cause of action arising from an actual or proposed act or omission involving negligence, default, breach of duty or breach of trust by a director of the company.

The cause of action may be against the director or another person (or both).

(4) It is immaterial whether the cause of action arose before or after the person seeking to bring or continue the derivative claim became a member of the company.

(5) For the purposes of this Chapter –

(a) "director" includes a former director;

(b) a shadow director is treated as a director; and

(c) references to a member of a company include a person who is not a member but to whom shares in the company have been transferred or transmitted by operation of law.

261 Application for permission to continue derivative claim

(1) A member of a company who brings a derivative claim under this Chapter must apply to the court for permission (in Northern Ireland, leave) to continue it.

(2) If it appears to the court that the application and the evidence filed by the applicant in support of it do not disclose a prima facie case for giving permission (or leave), the court –

(a) must dismiss the application, and

(b) may make any consequential order it considers appropriate.

(3) If the application is not dismissed under subsection (2), the court –

(a) may give directions as to the evidence to be provided by the company, and

(b) may adjourn the proceedings to enable the evidence to be obtained.

(4) On hearing the application, the court may –

(a) give permission (or leave) to continue the claim on such terms as it thinks fit,

(b) refuse permission (or leave) and dismiss the claim, or

(c) adjourn the proceedings on the application and give such directions as it thinks fit.

262 Application for permission to continue claim as a derivative claim

(1) This section applies where –

(a) a company has brought a claim, and

(b) the cause of action on which the claim is based could be pursued as a derivative claim under this Chapter.

(2) A member of the company may apply to the court for permission (in Northern Ireland, leave) to continue the claim as a derivative claim on the ground that –

(a) the manner in which the company commenced or continued the claim amounts to an abuse of the process of the court,

(b) the company has failed to prosecute the claim diligently, and

(c) it is appropriate for the member to continue the claim as a derivative claim.

(3) If it appears to the court that the application and the evidence filed by the applicant in support of it do not disclose a prima facie case for giving permission (or leave), the court –

(a) must dismiss the application, and

(b) may make any consequential order it considers appropriate.

(4) If the application is not dismissed under subsection (3), the court –

(a) may give directions as to the evidence to be provided by the company, and

(b) may adjourn the proceedings to enable the evidence to be obtained.

(5) On hearing the application, the court may –

(a) give permission (or leave) to continue the claim as a derivative claim on such terms as it thinks fit,

(b) refuse permission (or leave) and dismiss the application, or

(c) adjourn the proceedings on the application and give such directions as it thinks fit.

263 Whether permission to be given

(1) The following provisions have effect where a member of a company applies for permission (in Northern Ireland, leave) under section 261 or 262.

(2) Permission (or leave) must be refused if the court is satisfied –

    (a) that a person acting in accordance with section 172 (duty to promote the success of the company) would not seek to continue the claim, or

    (b) where the cause of action arises from an act or omission that is yet to occur, that the act or omission has been authorised by the company, or

    (c) where the cause of action arises from an act or omission that has already occurred, that the act or omission –

        (i)   was authorised by the company before it occurred, or

        (ii) has been ratified by the company since it occurred.

(3) In considering whether to give permission (or leave) the court must take into account, in particular –

    (a) whether the member is acting in good faith in seeking to continue the claim;

    (b) the importance that a person acting in accordance with section 172 (duty to promote the success of the company) would attach to continuing it;

    (c) where the cause of action results from an act or omission that is yet to occur, whether the act or omission could be, and in the circumstances would be likely to be –

        (i)   authorised by the company before it occurs, or

        (ii) ratified by the company after it occurs;

    (d) where the cause of action arises from an act or omission that has already occurred, whether the act or omission could be, and in the circumstances would be likely to be, ratified by the company;

    (e) whether the company has decided not to pursue the claim;

    (f) whether the act or omission in respect of which the claim is brought gives rise to a cause of action that the member could pursue in his own right rather than on behalf of the company.

(4) In considering whether to give permission (or leave) the court shall have particular regard to any evidence before it as to the views of members of the company who have no personal interest, direct or indirect, in the matter.

(5) The Secretary of State may by regulations –

    (a) amend subsection (2) so as to alter or add to the circumstances in which permission (or leave) is to be refused;

    (b) amend subsection (3) so as to alter or add to the matters that the court is required to take into account in considering whether to give permission (or leave).

(6) Before making any such regulations the Secretary of State shall consult such persons as he considers appropriate.

(7) Regulations under this section are subject to affirmative resolution procedure.

264 Application for permission to continue derivative claim brought by another member

(1) This section applies where a member of a company ("the claimant") –

    (a) has brought a derivative claim,

    (b) has continued as a derivative claim a claim brought by the company, or

    (c) has continued a derivative claim under this section.

(2) Another member of the company ("the applicant") may apply to the court for permission (in Northern Ireland, leave) to continue the claim on the ground that –

(a) the manner in which the proceedings have been commenced or continued by the claimant amounts to an abuse of the process of the court,

(b) the claimant has failed to prosecute the claim diligently, and

(c) it is appropriate for the applicant to continue the claim as a derivative claim.

(3) If it appears to the court that the application and the evidence filed by the applicant in support of it do not disclose a prima facie case for giving permission (or leave), the court –

(a) must dismiss the application, and

(b) may make any consequential order it considers appropriate.

(4) If the application is not dismissed under subsection (3), the court –

(a) may give directions as to the evidence to be provided by the company, and

(b) may adjourn the proceedings to enable the evidence to be obtained.

(5) On hearing the application, the court may –

(a) give permission (or leave) to continue the claim on such terms as it thinks fit,

(b) refuse permission (or leave) and dismiss the application, or

(c) adjourn the proceedings on the application and give such directions as it thinks fit.

CHAPTER 2

DERIVATIVE PROCEEDINGS IN SCOTLAND

265 Derivative proceedings

(1) In Scotland, a member of a company may raise proceedings in respect of an act or omission specified in subsection (3) in order to protect the interests of the company and obtain a remedy on its behalf.

(2) A member of a company may raise such proceedings only under subsection (1).

(3) The act or omission referred to in subsection (1) is any actual or proposed act or omission involving negligence, default, breach of duty or breach of trust by a director of the company.

(4) Proceedings may be raised under subsection (1) against (either or both) –

(a) the director referred to in subsection (3), or

(b) another person.

(5) It is immaterial whether the act or omission in respect of which the proceedings are to be raised or, in the case of continuing proceedings under section 267 or 269, are raised, arose before or after the person seeking to raise or continue them became a member of the company.

(6) This section does not affect –

(a) any right of a member of a company to raise proceedings in respect of an act or omission specified in subsection (3) in order to protect his own interests and obtain a remedy on his own behalf, or

(b) the court's power to make an order under section 996(2)(c) or anything done under such an order.

(7) In this Chapter –

(a) proceedings raised under subsection (1) are referred to as "derivative proceedings",

(b) the act or omission in respect of which they are raised is referred to as the "cause of action",

(c) "director" includes a former director,

(d) references to a director include a shadow director, and

(e) references to a member of a company include a person who is not a member but to whom shares in the company have been transferred or transmitted by operation of law.

266 Requirement for leave and notice

(1) Derivative proceedings may be raised by a member of a company only with the leave of the court.

(2) An application for leave must –

(a) specify the cause of action, and

(b) summarise the facts on which the derivative proceedings are to be based.

(3) If it appears to the court that the application and the evidence produced by the applicant in support of it do not disclose a prima facie case for granting it, the court –

(a) must refuse the application, and

(b) may make any consequential order it considers appropriate.

(4) If the application is not refused under subsection (3) –

(a) the applicant must serve the application on the company,

(b) the court –

(i) may make an order requiring evidence to be produced by the company, and

(ii) may adjourn the proceedings on the application to enable the evidence to be obtained, and

(c) the company is entitled to take part in the further proceedings on the application.

(5) On hearing the application, the court may –

(a) grant the application on such terms as it thinks fit,

(b) refuse the application, or

(c) adjourn the proceedings on the application and make such order as to further procedure as it thinks fit.

267 Application to continue proceedings as derivative proceedings

(1) This section applies where –

(a) a company has raised proceedings, and

(b) the proceedings are in respect of an act or omission which could be the basis for derivative proceedings.

(2) A member of the company may apply to the court to be substituted for the company in the proceedings, and for the proceedings to continue in consequence as derivative proceedings, on the ground that –

(a) the manner in which the company commenced or continued the proceedings amounts to an abuse of the process of the court,

(b) the company has failed to prosecute the proceedings diligently, and

(c) it is appropriate for the member to be substituted for the company in the proceedings.

(3) If it appears to the court that the application and the evidence produced by the applicant in support of it do not disclose a prima facie case for granting it, the court –

(a) must refuse the application, and

(b) may make any consequential order it considers appropriate.

(4) If the application is not refused under subsection (3) –

(a) the applicant must serve the application on the company,

(b) the court –

      (i)   may make an order requiring evidence to be produced by the company, and

      (ii)   may adjourn the proceedings on the application to enable the evidence to be obtained, and

(c)   the company is entitled to take part in the further proceedings on the application.

(5) On hearing the application, the court may –

    (a)   grant the application on such terms as it thinks fit,

    (b)   refuse the application, or

    (c)   adjourn the proceedings on the application and make such order as to further procedure as it thinks fit.

268 Granting of leave

(1) The court must refuse leave to raise derivative proceedings or an application under section 267 if satisfied –

    (a)   that a person acting in accordance with section 172 (duty to promote the success of the company) would not seek to raise or continue the proceedings (as the case may be), or

    (b)   where the cause of action is an act or omission that is yet to occur, that the act or omission has been authorised by the company, or

    (c)   where the cause of action is an act or omission that has already occurred, that the act or omission –

      (i)   was authorised by the company before it occurred, or

      (ii)   has been ratified by the company since it occurred.

(2) In considering whether to grant leave to raise derivative proceedings or an application under section 267, the court must take into account, in particular –

    (a)   whether the member is acting in good faith in seeking to raise or continue the proceedings (as the case may be),

    (b)   the importance that a person acting in accordance with section 172 (duty to promote the success of the company) would attach to raising or continuing them (as the case may be),

    (c)   where the cause of action is an act or omission that is yet to occur, whether the act or omission could be, and in the circumstances would be likely to be –

      (i)   authorised by the company before it occurs, or

      (ii)   ratified by the company after it occurs,

    (d)   where the cause of action is an act or omission that has already occurred, whether the act or omission could be, and in the circumstances would be likely to be, ratified by the company,

    (e)   whether the company has decided not to raise proceedings in respect of the same cause of action or to persist in the proceedings (as the case may be),

    (f)   whether the cause of action is one which the member could pursue in his own right rather than on behalf of the company.

(3) In considering whether to grant leave to raise derivative proceedings or an application under section 267, the court shall have particular regard to any evidence before it as to the views of members of the company who have no personal interest, direct or indirect, in the matter.

(4) The Secretary of State may by regulations –

    (a)   amend subsection (1) so as to alter or add to the circumstances in which leave or an application is to be refused,

    (b)   amend subsection (2) so as to alter or add to the matters that the court is required to take into account in considering whether to grant leave or an application.

(5) Before making any such regulations the Secretary of State shall consult such persons as he considers appropriate.

(6) Regulations under this section are subject to affirmative resolution procedure.

269 Application by member to be substituted for member pursuing derivative proceedings

(1) This section applies where a member of a company ("the claimant") –

    (a) has raised derivative proceedings,

    (b) has continued as derivative proceedings raised by the company, or

    (c) has continued derivative proceedings under this section.

(2) Another member of the company ("the applicant") may apply to the court to be substituted for the claimant in the action on the ground that –

    (a) the manner in which the proceedings have been commenced or continued by the claimant amounts to an abuse of the process of the court,

    (b) the claimant has failed to prosecute the proceedings diligently, and

    (c) it is appropriate for the applicant to be substituted for the claimant in the proceedings.

(3) If it appears to the court that the application and the evidence produced by the applicant in support of it do not disclose a prima facie case for granting it, the court –

    (a) must refuse the application, and

    (b) may make any consequential order it considers appropriate.

(4) If the application is not refused under subsection (3) –

    (a) the applicant must serve the application on the company,

    (b) the court –

        (i)   may make an order requiring evidence to be produced by the company, and

        (ii) may adjourn the proceedings on the application to enable the evidence to be obtained, and

    (c) the company is entitled to take part in the further proceedings on the application.

(5) On hearing the application, the court may –

    (a) grant the application on such terms as it thinks fit,

    (b) refuse the application, or

    (c) adjourn the proceedings on the application and make such order as to further procedure as it thinks fit.

PART 12

COMPANY SECRETARIES

Private companies

270 Private company not required to have secretary

(1) A private company is not required to have a secretary.

(2) References in the Companies Acts to a private company "without a secretary" are to a private company that for the time being is taking advantage of the exemption in subsection (1); and references to a private company "with a secretary" shall be construed accordingly.

(3) In the case of a private company without a secretary –

(a) anything authorised or required to be given or sent to, or served on, the company by being sent to its secretary –

    (i)   may be given or sent to, or served on, the company itself, and

    (ii)   if addressed to the secretary shall be treated as addressed to the company; and

(b) anything else required or authorised to be done by or to the secretary of the company may be done by or to –

    (i)   a director, or

    (ii)   a person authorised generally or specifically in that behalf by the directors.

Public companies

271 Public company required to have secretary

A public company must have a secretary.

272 Direction requiring public company to appoint secretary

(1) If it appears to the Secretary of State that a public company is in breach of section 271 (requirement to have secretary), the Secretary of State may give the company a direction under this section.

(2) The direction must state that the company appears to be in breach of that section and specify –

(a) what the company must do in order to comply with the direction, and

(b) the period within which it must do so.

That period must be not less than one month or more than three months after the date on which the direction is given.

(3) The direction must also inform the company of the consequences of failing to comply.

(4) Where the company is in breach of section 271 it must comply with the direction by –

(a) making the necessary appointment, and

(b) giving notice of it under section 276,

before the end of the period specified in the direction.

(5) If the company has already made the necessary appointment, it must comply with the direction by giving notice of it under section 276 before the end of the period specified in the direction.

(6) If a company fails to comply with a direction under this section, an offence is committed by –

(a) the company, and

(b) every officer of the company who is in default.

For this purpose a shadow director is treated as an officer of the company.

(7) A person guilty of an offence under this section is liable on summary conviction to a fine not exceeding level 5 on the standard scale and, for continued contravention, a daily default fine not exceeding one-tenth of level 5 on the standard scale.

273 Qualifications of secretaries of public companies

(1) It is the duty of the directors of a public company to take all reasonable steps to secure that the secretary (or each joint secretary) of the company –

(a) is a person who appears to them to have the requisite knowledge and experience to discharge the functions of secretary of the company, and

(b) has one or more of the following qualifications.

(2) The qualifications are –

    (a) that he has held the office of secretary of a public company for at least three of the five years immediately preceding his appointment as secretary;

    (b) that he is a member of any of the bodies specified in subsection (3);

    (c) that he is a barrister, advocate or solicitor called or admitted in any part of the United Kingdom;

    (d) that he is a person who, by virtue of his holding or having held any other position or his being a member of any other body, appears to the directors to be capable of discharging the functions of secretary of the company.

(3) The bodies referred to in subsection (2)(b) are –

    (a)   the Institute of Chartered Accountants in England and Wales;

    (b)   the Institute of Chartered Accountants of Scotland;

    (c)   the Association of Chartered Certified Accountants;

    (d)   the Institute of Chartered Accountants in Ireland;

    (e)   the Institute of Chartered Secretaries and Administrators;

    (f)   the Chartered Institute of Management Accountants;

    (g)   the Chartered Institute of Public Finance and Accountancy.

Provisions applying to private companies with a secretary and to public companies

274 Discharge of functions where office vacant or secretary unable to act

Where in the case of any company the office of secretary is vacant, or there is for any other reason no secretary capable of acting, anything required or authorised to be done by or to the secretary may be done –

    (a) by or to an assistant or deputy secretary (if any), or

    (b) if there is no assistant or deputy secretary or none capable of acting, by or to any person authorised generally or specifically in that behalf by the directors.

275 Duty to keep register of secretaries

(1) A company must keep a register of its secretaries.

(2) The register must contain the required particulars (see sections 277 to 279) of the person who is, or persons who are, the secretary or joint secretaries of the company.

(3) The register must be kept available for inspection –

    (a) at the company's registered office, or

    (b) at a place specified in regulations under section 1136.

(4) The company must give notice to the registrar –

    (a) of the place at which the register is kept available for inspection, and

    (b) of any change in that place,

unless it has at all times been kept at the company's registered office.

(5) The register must be open to the inspection –

    (a) of any member of the company without charge, and

    (b) of any other person on payment of such fee as may be prescribed.

(6) If default is made in complying with subsection (1), (2) or (3), or if default is made for 14 days in complying with subsection (4), or if an inspection required under subsection (5) is refused, an offence is committed by –

    (a) the company, and

    (b) every officer of the company who is in default.

For this purpose a shadow director is treated as an officer of the company.

(7) A person guilty of an offence under this section is liable on summary conviction to a fine not exceeding level 5 on the standard scale and, for continued contravention, a daily default fine not exceeding one-tenth of level 5 on the standard scale.

(8) In the case of a refusal of inspection of the register, the court may by order compel an immediate inspection of it.

276 Duty to notify registrar of changes

(1) A company must, within the period of 14 days from –

    (a) a person becoming or ceasing to be its secretary or one of its joint secretaries, or

    (b) the occurrence of any change in the particulars contained in its register of secretaries,

give notice to the registrar of the change and of the date on which it occurred.

(2) Notice of a person having become secretary, or one of joint secretaries, of the company must be accompanied by a consent by that person to act in the relevant capacity.

(3) If default is made in complying with this section, an offence is committed by every officer of the company who is in default.

For this purpose a shadow director is treated as an officer of the company.

(4) A person guilty of an offence under this section is liable on summary conviction to a fine not exceeding level 5 on the standard scale and, for continued contravention, a daily default fine not exceeding one-tenth of level 5 on the standard scale.

277 Particulars of secretaries to be registered: individuals

(1) A company's register of secretaries must contain the following particulars in the case of an individual –

    (a) name and any former name;

    (b) address.

(2) For the purposes of this section "name" means a person's Christian name (or other forename) and surname, except that in the case of –

    (a) a peer, or

    (b) an individual usually known by a title,

the title may be stated instead of his Christian name (or other forename) and surname or in addition to either or both of them.

(3) For the purposes of this section a "former name" means a name by which the individual was formerly known for business purposes.

Where a person is or was formerly known by more than one such name, each of them must be stated.

(4) It is not necessary for the register to contain particulars of a former name in the following cases –

    (a) in the case of a peer or an individual normally known by a British title, where the name is one by which the person was known previous to the adoption of or succession to the title;

    (b) in the case of any person, where the former name –

        (i) was changed or disused before the person attained the age of 16 years, or

        (ii) has been changed or disused for 20 years or more.

(5) The address required to be stated in the register is a service address.

This may be stated to be "The company's registered office".

278 Particulars of secretaries to be registered: corporate secretaries and firms

(1) A company's register of secretaries must contain the following particulars in the case of a body corporate, or a firm that is a legal person under the law by which it is governed –

(a)   corporate or firm name;

(b)   registered or principal office;

(c)   in the case of an EEA company to which the First Company Law Directive (68/151/EEC) applies, particulars of –

  (i)   the register in which the company file mentioned in Article 3 of that Directive is kept (including details of the relevant state), and

  (ii)   the registration number in that register;

(d)   in any other case, particulars of –

  (i)   the legal form of the company or firm and the law by which it is governed, and

  (ii)   if applicable, the register in which it is entered (including details of the state) and its registration number in that register.

(2)   If all the partners in a firm are joint secretaries it is sufficient to state the particulars that would be required if the firm were a legal person and the firm had been appointed secretary.

279 Particulars of secretaries to be registered: power to make regulations

(1)   The Secretary of State may make provision by regulations amending –

section 277 (particulars of secretaries to be registered: individuals), or

section 278 (particulars of secretaries to be registered: corporate secretaries and firms),

so as to add to or remove items from the particulars required to be contained in a company's register of secretaries.

(2)   Regulations under this section are subject to affirmative resolution procedure.

280 Acts done by person in dual capacity

A provision requiring or authorising a thing to be done by or to a director and the secretary of a company is not satisfied by its being done by or to the same person acting both as director and as, or in place of, the secretary.

PART 13

RESOLUTIONS AND MEETINGS

CHAPTER 1

GENERAL PROVISIONS ABOUT RESOLUTIONS

281 Resolutions

(1)   A resolution of the members (or of a class of members) of a private company must be passed –

  (a)   as a written resolution in accordance with Chapter 2, or

  (b)   at a meeting of the members (to which the provisions of Chapter 3 apply).

(2)   A resolution of the members (or of a class of members) of a public company must be passed at a meeting of the members (to which the provisions of Chapter 3 and, where relevant, Chapter 4 apply).

(3)   Where a provision of the Companies Acts –

  (a)   requires a resolution of a company, or of the members (or a class of members) of a company, and

(b) does not specify what kind of resolution is required,

what is required is an ordinary resolution unless the company's articles require a higher majority (or unanimity).

(4) Nothing in this Part affects any enactment or rule of law as to –

(a) things done otherwise than by passing a resolution,

(b) circumstances in which a resolution is or is not treated as having been passed, or

(c) cases in which a person is precluded from alleging that a resolution has not been duly passed.

282 Ordinary resolutions

(1) An ordinary resolution of the members (or of a class of members) of a company means a resolution that is passed by a simple majority.

(2) A written resolution is passed by a simple majority if it is passed by members representing a simple majority of the total voting rights of eligible members (see Chapter 2).

(3) A resolution passed at a meeting on a show of hands is passed by a simple majority if it is passed by a simple majority of –

(a) the members who, being entitled to do so, vote in person on the resolution, and

(b) the persons who vote on the resolution as duly appointed proxies of members entitled to vote on it.

(4) A resolution passed on a poll taken at a meeting is passed by a simple majority if it is passed by members representing a simple majority of the total voting rights of members who (being entitled to do so) vote in person or by proxy on the resolution.

(5) Anything that may be done by ordinary resolution may also be done by special resolution.

283 Special resolutions

(1) A special resolution of the members (or of a class of members) of a company means a resolution passed by a majority of not less than 75%.

(2) A written resolution is passed by a majority of not less than 75% if it is passed by members representing not less than 75% of the total voting rights of eligible members (see Chapter 2).

(3) Where a resolution of a private company is passed as a written resolution –

(a) the resolution is not a special resolution unless it stated that it was proposed as a special resolution, and

(b) if the resolution so stated, it may only be passed as a special resolution.

(4) A resolution passed at a meeting on a show of hands is passed by a majority of not less than 75% if it is passed by not less than 75% of –

(a) the members who, being entitled to do so, vote in person on the resolution, and

(b) the persons who vote on the resolution as duly appointed proxies of members entitled to vote on it.

(5) A resolution passed on a poll taken at a meeting is passed by a majority of not less than 75% if it is passed by members representing not less than 75% of the total voting rights of the members who (being entitled to do so) vote in person or by proxy on the resolution.

(6) Where a resolution is passed at a meeting –

(a) the resolution is not a special resolution unless the notice of the meeting included the text of the resolution and specified the intention to propose the resolution as a special resolution, and

(b) if the notice of the meeting so specified, the resolution may only be passed as a special resolution.

284 Votes: general rules

(1) On a vote on a written resolution –

(a) in the case of a company having a share capital, every member has one vote in respect of each share or each £10 of stock held by him, and

(b) in any other case, every member has one vote.

(2) On a vote on a resolution on a show of hands at a meeting –

(a) every member present in person has one vote, and

(b) every proxy present who has been duly appointed by a member entitled to vote on the resolution has one vote.

(3) On a vote on a resolution on a poll taken at a meeting –

(a) in the case of a company having a share capital, every member has one vote in respect of each share or each £10 of stock held by him, and

(b) in any other case, every member has one vote.

(4) The provisions of this section have effect subject to any provision of the company's articles.

285 Votes: specific requirements

(1) Where a member entitled to vote on a resolution has appointed one proxy only, and the company's articles provide that the proxy has fewer votes in a vote on a resolution on a show of hands taken at a meeting than the member would have if he were present in person –

(a) the provision about how many votes the proxy has on a show of hands is void, and

(b) the proxy has the same number of votes on a show of hands as the member who appointed him would have if he were present at the meeting.

(2) Where a member entitled to vote on a resolution has appointed more than one proxy, subsection (1) applies as if the references to the proxy were references to the proxies taken together.

(3) In relation to a resolution required or authorised by an enactment, if a private company's articles provide that a member has a different number of votes in relation to a resolution when it is passed as a written resolution and when it is passed on a poll taken at a meeting –

(a) the provision about how many votes a member has in relation to the resolution passed on a poll is void, and

(b) a member has the same number of votes in relation to the resolution when it is passed on a poll as he has when it is passed as a written resolution.

286 Votes of joint holders of shares

(1) In the case of joint holders of shares of a company, only the vote of the senior holder who votes (and any proxies duly authorised by him) may be counted by the company.

(2) For the purposes of this section, the senior holder of a share is determined by the order in which the names of the joint holders appear in the register of members.

(3) Subsections (1) and (2) have effect subject to any provision of the company's articles.

287 Saving for provisions of articles as to determination of entitlement to vote

Nothing in this Chapter affects –

(a) any provision of a company's articles –

(i) requiring an objection to a person's entitlement to vote on a resolution to be made in accordance with the articles, and

(ii) for the determination of any such objection to be final and conclusive, or

(b) the grounds on which such a determination may be questioned in legal proceedings.

CHAPTER 2

WRITTEN RESOLUTIONS

General provisions about written resolutions

288 Written resolutions of private companies

(1) In the Companies Acts a "written resolution" means a resolution of a private company proposed and passed in accordance with this Chapter.

(2) The following may not be passed as a written resolution –

    (a) a resolution under section 168 removing a director before the expiration of his period of office;

    (b) a resolution under section 510 removing an auditor before the expiration of his term of office.

(3) A resolution may be proposed as a written resolution –

    (a) by the directors of a private company (see section 291), or

    (b) by the members of a private company (see sections 292 to 295).

(4) References in enactments passed or made before this Chapter comes into force to –

    (a) a resolution of a company in general meeting, or

    (b) a resolution of a meeting of a class of members of the company,

have effect as if they included references to a written resolution of the members, or of a class of members, of a private company (as appropriate).

(5) A written resolution of a private company has effect as if passed (as the case may be) –

    (a) by the company in general meeting, or

    (b) by a meeting of a class of members of the company,

and references in enactments passed or made before this section comes into force to a meeting at which a resolution is passed or to members voting in favour of a resolution shall be construed accordingly.

289 Eligible members

(1) In relation to a resolution proposed as a written resolution of a private company, the eligible members are the members who would have been entitled to vote on the resolution on the circulation date of the resolution (see section 290).

(2) If the persons entitled to vote on a written resolution change during the course of the day that is the circulation date of the resolution, the eligible members are the persons entitled to vote on the resolution at the time that the first copy of the resolution is sent or submitted to a member for his agreement.

Circulation of written resolutions

290 Circulation date

References in this Part to the circulation date of a written resolution are to the date on which copies of it are sent or submitted to members in accordance with this Chapter (or if copies are sent or submitted to members on different days, to the first of those days).

291 Circulation of written resolutions proposed by directors

(1) This section applies to a resolution proposed as a written resolution by the directors of the company.

(2) The company must send or submit a copy of the resolution to every eligible member.

(3) The company must do so –

   (a) by sending copies at the same time (so far as reasonably practicable) to all eligible members in hard copy form, in electronic form or by means of a website, or

   (b) if it is possible to do so without undue delay, by submitting the same copy to each eligible member in turn (or different copies to each of a number of eligible members in turn),

   or by sending copies to some members in accordance with paragraph (a) and submitting a copy or copies to other members in accordance with paragraph (b).

(4) The copy of the resolution must be accompanied by a statement informing the member –

   (a) how to signify agreement to the resolution (see section 296), and

   (b) as to the date by which the resolution must be passed if it is not to lapse (see section 297).

(5) In the event of default in complying with this section, an offence is committed by every officer of the company who is in default.

(6) A person guilty of an offence under this section is liable –

   (a) on conviction on indictment, to a fine;

   (b) on summary conviction, to a fine not exceeding the statutory maximum.

(7) The validity of the resolution, if passed, is not affected by a failure to comply with this section.

292 Members' power to require circulation of written resolution

(1) The members of a private company may require the company to circulate a resolution that may properly be moved and is proposed to be moved as a written resolution.

(2) Any resolution may properly be moved as a written resolution unless –

   (a) it would, if passed, be ineffective (whether by reason of inconsistency with any enactment or the company's constitution or otherwise),

   (b) it is defamatory of any person, or

   (c) it is frivolous or vexatious.

(3) Where the members require a company to circulate a resolution they may require the company to circulate with it a statement of not more than 1,000 words on the subject matter of the resolution.

(4) A company is required to circulate the resolution and any accompanying statement once it has received requests that it do so from members representing not less than the requisite percentage of the total voting rights of all members entitled to vote on the resolution.

(5) The "requisite percentage" is 5% or such lower percentage as is specified for this purpose in the company's articles.

(6) A request –

   (a) may be in hard copy form or in electronic form,

   (b) must identify the resolution and any accompanying statement, and

   (c) must be authenticated by the person or persons making it.

293 Circulation of written resolution proposed by members

(1) A company that is required under section 292 to circulate a resolution must send or submit to every eligible member –

   (a) a copy of the resolution, and

   (b) a copy of any accompanying statement.

   This is subject to section 294(2) (deposit or tender of sum in respect of expenses of circulation) and section 295 (application not to circulate members' statement).

(2) The company must do so –

  (a) by sending copies at the same time (so far as reasonably practicable) to all eligible members in hard copy form, in electronic form or by means of a website, or

  (b) if it is possible to do so without undue delay, by submitting the same copy to each eligible member in turn (or different copies to each of a number of eligible members in turn),

  or by sending copies to some members in accordance with paragraph (a) and submitting a copy or copies to other members in accordance with paragraph (b).

(3) The company must send or submit the copies (or, if copies are sent or submitted to members on different days, the first of those copies) not more than 21 days after it becomes subject to the requirement under section 292 to circulate the resolution.

(4) The copy of the resolution must be accompanied by guidance as to –

  (a) how to signify agreement to the resolution (see section 296), and

  (b) the date by which the resolution must be passed if it is not to lapse (see section 297).

(5) In the event of default in complying with this section, an offence is committed by every officer of the company who is in default.

(6) A person guilty of an offence under this section is liable –

  (a) on conviction on indictment, to a fine;

  (b) on summary conviction, to a fine not exceeding the statutory maximum.

(7) The validity of the resolution, if passed, is not affected by a failure to comply with this section.

294 Expenses of circulation

(1) The expenses of the company in complying with section 293 must be paid by the members who requested the circulation of the resolution unless the company resolves otherwise.

(2) Unless the company has previously so resolved, it is not bound to comply with that section unless there is deposited with or tendered to it a sum reasonably sufficient to meet its expenses in doing so.

295 Application not to circulate members' statement

(1) A company is not required to circulate a members' statement under section 293 if, on an application by the company or another person who claims to be aggrieved, the court is satisfied that the rights conferred by section 292 and that section are being abused.

(2) The court may order the members who requested the circulation of the statement to pay the whole or part of the company's costs (in Scotland, expenses) on such an application, even if they are not parties to the application.

Agreeing to written resolutions

296 Procedure for signifying agreement to written resolution

(1) A member signifies his agreement to a proposed written resolution when the company receives from him (or from someone acting on his behalf) an authenticated document –

  (a) identifying the resolution to which it relates, and

  (b) indicating his agreement to the resolution.

(2) The document must be sent to the company in hard copy form or in electronic form.

(3) A member's agreement to a written resolution, once signified, may not be revoked.

(4) A written resolution is passed when the required majority of eligible members have signified their agreement to it.

297 Period for agreeing to written resolution

(1) A proposed written resolution lapses if it is not passed before the end of –

    (a) the period specified for this purpose in the company's articles, or

    (b) if none is specified, the period of 28 days beginning with the circulation date.

(2) The agreement of a member to a written resolution is ineffective if signified after the expiry of that period.

Supplementary

298 Sending documents relating to written resolutions by electronic means

(1) Where a company has given an electronic address in any document containing or accompanying a proposed written resolution, it is deemed to have agreed that any document or information relating to that resolution may be sent by electronic means to that address (subject to any conditions or limitations specified in the document).

(2) In this section "electronic address" means any address or number used for the purposes of sending or receiving documents or information by electronic means.

299 Publication of written resolution on website

(1) This section applies where a company sends –

    (a) a written resolution, or

    (b) a statement relating to a written resolution,

to a person by means of a website.

(2) The resolution or statement is not validly sent for the purposes of this Chapter unless the resolution is available on the website throughout the period beginning with the circulation date and ending on the date on which the resolution lapses under section 297.

300 Relationship between this Chapter and provisions of company's articles

A provision of the articles of a private company is void in so far as it would have the effect that a resolution that is required by or otherwise provided for in an enactment could not be proposed and passed as a written resolution.

CHAPTER 3

RESOLUTIONS AT MEETINGS

General provisions about resolutions at meetings

301 Resolutions at general meetings

A resolution of the members of a company is validly passed at a general meeting if –

    (a) notice of the meeting and of the resolution is given, and

    (b) the meeting is held and conducted,

in accordance with the provisions of this Chapter (and, where relevant, Chapter 4) and the company's articles.

Calling meetings

302 Directors' power to call general meetings

The directors of a company may call a general meeting of the company.

303 Members' power to require directors to call general meeting

(1)   The members of a company may require the directors to call a general meeting of the company.

(2)   The directors are required to call a general meeting once the company has received requests to do so from –

    (a)   members representing at least the required percentage of such of the paid-up capital of the company as carries the right of voting at general meetings of the company (excluding any paid-up capital held as treasury shares); or

    (b)   in the case of a company not having a share capital, members who represent at least the required percentage of the total voting rights of all the members having a right to vote at general meetings.

(3)   The required percentage is 10% unless, in the case of a private company, more than twelve months has elapsed since the end of the last general meeting –

    (a)   called in pursuance of a requirement under this section, or

    (b)   in relation to which any members of the company had (by virtue of an enactment, the company's articles or otherwise) rights with respect to the circulation of a resolution no less extensive than they would have had if the meeting had been so called at their request,

in which case the required percentage is 5%.

(4)   A request –

    (a)   must state the general nature of the business to be dealt with at the meeting, and

    (b)   may include the text of a resolution that may properly be moved and is intended to be moved at the meeting.

(5)   A resolution may properly be moved at a meeting unless –

    (a)   it would, if passed, be ineffective (whether by reason of inconsistency with any enactment or the company's constitution or otherwise),

    (b)   it is defamatory of any person, or

    (c)   it is frivolous or vexatious.

(6)   A request –

    (a)   may be in hard copy form or in electronic form, and

    (b)   must be authenticated by the person or persons making it.

304 Directors' duty to call meetings required by members

(1)   Directors required under section 303 to call a general meeting of the company must call a meeting –

    (a)   within 21 days from the date on which they become subject to the requirement, and

    (b)   to be held on a date not more than 28 days after the date of the notice convening the meeting.

(2)   If the requests received by the company identify a resolution intended to be moved at the meeting, the notice of the meeting must include notice of the resolution.

(3)   The business that may be dealt with at the meeting includes a resolution of which notice is given in accordance with this section.

(4)   If the resolution is to be proposed as a special resolution, the directors are treated as not having duly called the meeting if they do not give the required notice of the resolution in accordance with section 283.

305 Power of members to call meeting at company's expense

(1)   If the directors –

    (a)   are required under section 303 to call a meeting, and

    (b)   do not do so in accordance with section 304,

the members who requested the meeting, or any of them representing more than one half of the total voting rights of all of them, may themselves call a general meeting.

(2) Where the requests received by the company included the text of a resolution intended to be moved at the meeting, the notice of the meeting must include notice of the resolution.

(3) The meeting must be called for a date not more than three months after the date on which the directors become subject to the requirement to call a meeting.

(4) The meeting must be called in the same manner, as nearly as possible, as that in which meetings are required to be called by directors of the company.

(5) The business which may be dealt with at the meeting includes a resolution of which notice is given in accordance with this section.

(6) Any reasonable expenses incurred by the members requesting the meeting by reason of the failure of the directors duly to call a meeting must be reimbursed by the company.

(7) Any sum so reimbursed shall be retained by the company out of any sums due or to become due from the company by way of fees or other remuneration in respect of the services of such of the directors as were in default.

306 Power of court to order meeting

(1) This section applies if for any reason it is impracticable –

    (a) to call a meeting of a company in any manner in which meetings of that company may be called, or

    (b) to conduct the meeting in the manner prescribed by the company's articles or this Act.

(2) The court may, either of its own motion or on the application –

    (a) of a director of the company, or

    (b) of a member of the company who would be entitled to vote at the meeting,

order a meeting to be called, held and conducted in any manner the court thinks fit.

(3) Where such an order is made, the court may give such ancillary or consequential directions as it thinks expedient.

(4) Such directions may include a direction that one member of the company present at the meeting be deemed to constitute a quorum.

(5) A meeting called, held and conducted in accordance with an order under this section is deemed for all purposes to be a meeting of the company duly called, held and conducted.

Notice of meetings

307 Notice required of general meeting

(1) A general meeting of a private company (other than an adjourned meeting) must be called by notice of at least 14 days.

(2) A general meeting of a public company (other than an adjourned meeting) must be called by notice of –

    (a) in the case of an annual general meeting, at least 21 days, and

    (b) in any other case, at least 14 days.

(3) The company's articles may require a longer period of notice than that specified in subsection (1) or (2).

(4) A general meeting may be called by shorter notice than that otherwise required if shorter notice is agreed by the members.

(5) The shorter notice must be agreed to by a majority in number of the members having a right to attend and vote at the meeting, being a majority who –

(a) together hold not less than the requisite percentage in nominal value of the shares giving a right to attend and vote at the meeting (excluding any shares in the company held as treasury shares), or

(b) in the case of a company not having a share capital, together represent not less than the requisite percentage of the total voting rights at that meeting of all the members.

(6) The requisite percentage is –

(a) in the case of a private company, 90% or such higher percentage (not exceeding 95%) as may be specified in the company's articles;

(b) in the case of a public company, 95%.

(7) Subsections (5) and (6) do not apply to an annual general meeting of a public company (see instead section 337(2)).

308 Manner in which notice to be given

Notice of a general meeting of a company must be given –

(a) in hard copy form,

(b) in electronic form, or

(c) by means of a website (see section 309),

or partly by one such means and partly by another.

309 Publication of notice of meeting on website

(1) Notice of a meeting is not validly given by a company by means of a website unless it is given in accordance with this section.

(2) When the company notifies a member of the presence of the notice on the website the notification must –

(a) state that it concerns a notice of a company meeting,

(b) specify the place, date and time of the meeting, and

(c) in the case of a public company, state whether the meeting will be an annual general meeting.

(3) The notice must be available on the website throughout the period beginning with the date of that notification and ending with the conclusion of the meeting.

310 Persons entitled to receive notice of meetings

(1) Notice of a general meeting of a company must be sent to –

(a) every member of the company, and

(b) every director.

(2) In subsection (1), the reference to members includes any person who is entitled to a share in consequence of the death or bankruptcy of a member, if the company has been notified of their entitlement.

(3) In subsection (2), the reference to the bankruptcy of a member includes –

(a) the sequestration of the estate of a member;

(b) a member's estate being the subject of a protected trust deed (within the meaning of the Bankruptcy (Scotland) Act 1985 (c. 66)).

(4) This section has effect subject to –

(a) any enactment, and

(b) any provision of the company's articles.

311 Contents of notices of meetings

(1) Notice of a general meeting of a company must state –

(a) the time and date of the meeting, and

(b) the place of the meeting.

(2) Notice of a general meeting of a company must state the general nature of the business to be dealt with at the meeting.
This subsection has effect subject to any provision of the company's articles.

312 Resolution requiring special notice

(1) Where by any provision of the Companies Acts special notice is required of a resolution, the resolution is not effective unless notice of the intention to move it has been given to the company at least 28 days before the meeting at which it is moved.
(2) The company must, where practicable, give its members notice of any such resolution in the same manner and at the same time as it gives notice of the meeting.
(3) Where that is not practicable, the company must give its members notice at least 14 days before the meeting –

    (a)   by advertisement in a newspaper having an appropriate circulation, or
    (b)   in any other manner allowed by the company's articles.

(4) If, after notice of the intention to move such a resolution has been given to the company, a meeting is called for a date 28 days or less after the notice has been given, the notice is deemed to have been properly given, though not given within the time required.

313 Accidental failure to give notice of resolution or meeting

(1) Where a company gives notice of –

    (a)   a general meeting, or
    (b)   a resolution intended to be moved at a general meeting,

any accidental failure to give notice to one or more persons shall be disregarded for the purpose of determining whether notice of the meeting or resolution (as the case may be) is duly given.
(2) Except in relation to notice given under –

    (a)   section 304 (notice of meetings required by members),
    (b)   section 305 (notice of meetings called by members), or
    (c)   section 339 (notice of resolutions at AGMs proposed by members),

subsection (1) has effect subject to any provision of the company's articles.

Members' statements

314 Members' power to require circulation of statements

(1) The members of a company may require the company to circulate, to members of the company entitled to receive notice of a general meeting, a statement of not more than 1,000 words with respect to –

    (a)   a matter referred to in a proposed resolution to be dealt with at that meeting, or
    (b)   other business to be dealt with at that meeting.

(2) A company is required to circulate a statement once it has received requests to do so from –

    (a)   members representing at least 5% of the total voting rights of all the members who have a relevant right to vote (excluding any voting rights attached to any shares in the company held as treasury shares), or
    (b)   at least 100 members who have a relevant right to vote and hold shares in the company on which there has been paid up an average sum, per member, of at least £100.

See also section 153 (exercise of rights where shares held on behalf of others).
(3) In subsection (2), a "relevant right to vote" means –

(a) in relation to a statement with respect to a matter referred to in a proposed resolution, a right to vote on that resolution at the meeting to which the requests relate, and

(b) in relation to any other statement, a right to vote at the meeting to which the requests relate.

(4) A request –

    (a) may be in hard copy form or in electronic form,

    (b) must identify the statement to be circulated,

    (c) must be authenticated by the person or persons making it, and

    (d) must be received by the company at least one week before the meeting to which it relates.

315 Company's duty to circulate members' statement

(1) A company that is required under section 314, to circulate a statement must send a copy of it to each member of the company entitled to receive notice of the meeting –

    (a) in the same manner as the notice of the meeting, and

    (b) at the same time as, or as soon as reasonably practicable after, it gives notice of the meeting.

(2) Subsection (1) has effect subject to section 316(2) (deposit or tender of sum in respect of expenses of circulation) and section 317 (application not to circulate members' statement).

(3) In the event of default in complying with this section, an offence is committed by every officer of the company who is in default.

(4) A person guilty of an offence under this section is liable –

    (a) on conviction on indictment, to a fine;

    (b) on summary conviction, to a fine not exceeding the statutory maximum.

316 Expenses of circulating members' statement

(1) The expenses of the company in complying with section 315 need not be paid by the members who requested the circulation of the statement if –

    (a) the meeting to which the requests relate is an annual general meeting of a public company, and

    (b) requests sufficient to require the company to circulate the statement are received before the end of the financial year preceding the meeting.

(2) Otherwise –

    (a) the expenses of the company in complying with that section must be paid by the members who requested the circulation of the statement unless the company resolves otherwise, and

    (b) unless the company has previously so resolved, it is not bound to comply with that section unless there is deposited with or tendered to it, not later than one week before the meeting, a sum reasonably sufficient to meet its expenses in doing so.

317 Application not to circulate members' statement

(1) A company is not required to circulate a members' statement under section 315 if, on an application by the company or another person who claims to be aggrieved, the court is satisfied that the rights conferred by section 314 and that section are being abused.

(2) The court may order the members who requested the circulation of the statement to pay the whole or part of the company's costs (in Scotland, expenses) on such an application, even if they are not parties to the application.

Procedure at meetings

318 Quorum at meetings

(1) In the case of a company limited by shares or guarantee and having only one member, one qualifying person present at a meeting is a quorum.

(2) In any other case, subject to the provisions of the company's articles, two qualifying persons present at a meeting are a quorum, unless –

    (a) each is a qualifying person only because he is authorised under section 323 to act as the representative of a corporation in relation to the meeting, and they are representatives of the same corporation; or

    (b) each is a qualifying person only because he is appointed as proxy of a member in relation to the meeting, and they are proxies of the same member.

(3) For the purposes of this section a "qualifying person" means –

    (a) an individual who is a member of the company,

    (b) a person authorised under section 323 (representation of corporations at meetings) to act as the representative of a corporation in relation to the meeting, or

    (c) a person appointed as proxy of a member in relation to the meeting.

319 Chairman of meeting

(1) A member may be elected to be the chairman of a general meeting by a resolution of the company passed at the meeting.

(2) Subsection (1) is subject to any provision of the company's articles that states who may or may not be chairman.

320 Declaration by chairman on a show of hands

(1) On a vote on a resolution at a meeting on a show of hands, a declaration by the chairman that the resolution –

    (a) has or has not been passed, or

    (b) passed with a particular majority,

is conclusive evidence of that fact without proof of the number or proportion of the votes recorded in favour of or against the resolution.

(2) An entry in respect of such a declaration in minutes of the meeting recorded in accordance with section 355 is also conclusive evidence of that fact without such proof.

(3) This section does not have effect if a poll is demanded in respect of the resolution (and the demand is not subsequently withdrawn).

321 Right to demand a poll

(1) A provision of a company's articles is void in so far as it would have the effect of excluding the right to demand a poll at a general meeting on any question other than –

    (a) the election of the chairman of the meeting, or

    (b) the adjournment of the meeting.

(2) A provision of a company's articles is void in so far as it would have the effect of making ineffective a demand for a poll on any such question which is made –

    (a) by not less than 5 members having the right to vote on the resolution; or

    (b) by a member or members representing not less than 10% of the total voting rights of all the members having the right to vote on the resolution (excluding any voting rights attached to any shares in the company held as treasury shares); or

    (c) by a member or members holding shares in the company conferring a right to vote on the resolution, being shares on which an aggregate sum has been paid up equal to not less than 10% of the total sum paid up on all the shares conferring that right (excluding shares in the company conferring a right to vote on the resolution which are held as treasury shares).

322 Voting on a poll

On a poll taken at a general meeting of a company, a member entitled to more than one vote need not, if he votes, use all his votes or cast all the votes he uses in the same way.

323 Representation of corporations at meetings

(1) If a corporation (whether or not a company within the meaning of this Act) is a member of a company, it may by resolution of its directors or other governing body authorise a person or persons to act as its representative or representatives at any meeting of the company.

(2) Where the corporation authorises only one person, he is entitled to exercise the same powers on behalf of the corporation as the corporation could exercise if it were an individual member of the company.

(3) Where the corporation authorises more than one person, any one of them is entitled to exercise the same powers on behalf of the corporation as the corporation could exercise if it were an individual member of the company.

(4) Where the corporation authorises more than one person and more than one of them purport to exercise a power under subsection (3) –

    (a) if they purport to exercise the power in the same way, the power is treated as exercised in that way,

    (b) if they do not purport to exercise the power in the same way, the power is treated as not exercised.

Proxies

324 Rights to appoint proxies

(1) A member of a company is entitled to appoint another person as his proxy to exercise all or any of his rights to attend and to speak and vote at a meeting of the company.

(2) In the case of a company having a share capital, a member may appoint more than one proxy in relation to a meeting, provided that each proxy is appointed to exercise the rights attached to a different share or shares held by him, or (as the case may be) to a different £10, or multiple of £10, of stock held by him.

325 Notice of meeting to contain statement of rights

(1) In every notice calling a meeting of a company there must appear, with reasonable prominence, a statement informing the member of –

    (a) his rights under section 324, and

    (b) any more extensive rights conferred by the company's articles to appoint more than one proxy.

(2) Failure to comply with this section does not affect the validity of the meeting or of anything done at the meeting.

(3) If this section is not complied with as respects any meeting, an offence is committed by every officer of the company who is in default.

(4) A person guilty of an offence under this section is liable on summary conviction to a fine not exceeding level 3 on the standard scale.

326 Company-sponsored invitations to appoint proxies

(1) If for the purposes of a meeting there are issued at the company's expense invitations to members to appoint as proxy a specified person or a number of specified persons, the invitations must be issued to all members entitled to vote at the meeting.

(2) Subsection (1) is not contravened if –

    (a) there is issued to a member at his request a form of appointment naming the proxy or a list of persons willing to act as proxy, and

    (b) the form or list is available on request to all members entitled to vote at the meeting.

(3) If subsection (1) is contravened as respects a meeting, an offence is committed by every officer of the company who is in default.

(4) A person guilty of an offence under this section is liable on summary conviction to a fine not exceeding level 3 on the standard scale.

327 Notice required of appointment of proxy etc

(1) This section applies to –

    (a) the appointment of a proxy, and

    (b) any document necessary to show the validity of, or otherwise relating to, the appointment of a proxy.

(2) Any provision of the company's articles is void in so far as it would have the effect of requiring any such appointment or document to be received by the company or another person earlier than the following time –

    (a) in the case of a meeting or adjourned meeting, 48 hours before the time for holding the meeting or adjourned meeting;

    (b) in the case of a poll taken more than 48 hours after it was demanded, 24 hours before the time appointed for the taking of the poll;

    (c) in the case of a poll taken not more than 48 hours after it was demanded, the time at which it was demanded.

(3) In calculating the periods mentioned in subsection (2) no account shall be taken of any part of a day that is not a working day.

328 Chairing meetings

(1) A proxy may be elected to be the chairman of a general meeting by a resolution of the company passed at the meeting.

(2) Subsection (1) is subject to any provision of the company's articles that states who may or who may not be chairman.

329 Right of proxy to demand a poll

(1) The appointment of a proxy to vote on a matter at a meeting of a company authorises the proxy to demand, or join in demanding, a poll on that matter.

(2) In applying the provisions of section 321(2) (requirements for effective demand), a demand by a proxy counts –

    (a) for the purposes of paragraph (a), as a demand by the member;

    (b) for the purposes of paragraph (b), as a demand by a member representing the voting rights that the proxy is authorised to exercise;

    (c) for the purposes of paragraph (c), as a demand by a member holding the shares to which those rights are attached.

330 Notice required of termination of proxy's authority

(1) This section applies to notice that the authority of a person to act as proxy is terminated ("notice of termination").

(2) The termination of the authority of a person to act as proxy does not affect –

    (a) whether he counts in deciding whether there is a quorum at a meeting,

    (b) the validity of anything he does as chairman of a meeting, or

    (c) the validity of a poll demanded by him at a meeting,

unless the company receives notice of the termination before the commencement of the meeting.

(3) The termination of the authority of a person to act as proxy does not affect the validity of a vote given by that person unless the company receives notice of the termination –

   (a) before the commencement of the meeting or adjourned meeting at which the vote is given, or

   (b) in the case of a poll taken more than 48 hours after it is demanded, before the time appointed for taking the poll.

(4) If the company's articles require or permit members to give notice of termination to a person other than the company, the references above to the company receiving notice have effect as if they were or (as the case may be) included a reference to that person.

(5) Subsections (2) and (3) have effect subject to any provision of the company's articles which has the effect of requiring notice of termination to be received by the company or another person at a time earlier than that specified in those subsections.

   This is subject to subsection (6).

(6) Any provision of the company's articles is void in so far as it would have the effect of requiring notice of termination to be received by the company or another person earlier than the following time –

   (a) in the case of a meeting or adjourned meeting, 48 hours before the time for holding the meeting or adjourned meeting;

   (b) in the case of a poll taken more than 48 hours after it was demanded, 24 hours before the time appointed for the taking of the poll;

   (c) in the case of a poll taken not more than 48 hours after it was demanded, the time at which it was demanded.

(7) In calculating the periods mentioned in subsections (3)(b) and (6) no account shall be taken of any part of a day that is not a working day.

331 Saving for more extensive rights conferred by articles

Nothing in sections 324 to 330 (proxies) prevents a company's articles from conferring more extensive rights on members or proxies than are conferred by those sections.

Adjourned meetings

332 Resolution passed at adjourned meeting

Where a resolution is passed at an adjourned meeting of a company, the resolution is for all purposes to be treated as having been passed on the date on which it was in fact passed, and is not to be deemed passed on any earlier date.

Electronic communications

333 Sending documents relating to meetings etc in electronic form

(1) Where a company has given an electronic address in a notice calling a meeting, it is deemed to have agreed that any document or information relating to proceedings at the meeting may be sent by electronic means to that address (subject to any conditions or limitations specified in the notice).

(2) Where a company has given an electronic address –

   (a) in an instrument of proxy sent out by the company in relation to the meeting, or

   (b) in an invitation to appoint a proxy issued by the company in relation to the meeting, it is deemed to have agreed that any document or information relating to proxies for that meeting may be sent by electronic means to that address (subject to any conditions or limitations specified in the notice).

(3) In subsection (2), documents relating to proxies include –

    (a) the appointment of a proxy in relation to a meeting,

    (b) any document necessary to show the validity of, or otherwise relating to, the appointment of a proxy, and

    (c) notice of the termination of the authority of a proxy.

(4) In this section "electronic address" means any address or number used for the purposes of sending or receiving documents or information by electronic means.

Application to class meetings

334 Application to class meetings

(1) The provisions of this Chapter apply (with necessary modifications) in relation to a meeting of holders of a class of shares as they apply in relation to a general meeting. This is subject to subsections (2) and (3).

(2) The following provisions of this Chapter do not apply in relation to a meeting of holders of a class of shares –

    (a) sections 303 to 305 (members' power to require directors to call general meeting), and

    (b) section 306 (power of court to order meeting).

(3) The following provisions (in addition to those mentioned in subsection (2)) do not apply in relation to a meeting in connection with the variation of rights attached to a class of shares (a "variation of class rights meeting") –

    (a) section 318 (quorum), and

    (b) section 321 (right to demand a poll).

(4) The quorum for a variation of class rights meeting is –

    (a) for a meeting other than an adjourned meeting, two persons present holding at least one-third in nominal value of the issued shares of the class in question (excluding any shares of that class held as treasury shares);

    (b) for an adjourned meeting, one person present holding shares of the class in question.

(5) For the purposes of subsection (4), where a person is present by proxy or proxies, he is treated as holding only the shares in respect of which those proxies are authorised to exercise voting rights.

(6) At a variation of class rights meeting, any holder of shares of the class in question present may demand a poll.

(7) For the purposes of this section –

    (a) any amendment of a provision contained in a company's articles for the variation of the rights attached to a class of shares, or the insertion of any such provision into the articles, is itself to be treated as a variation of those rights, and

    (b) references to the variation of rights attached to a class of shares include references to their abrogation.

335 Application to class meetings: companies without a share capital

(1) The provisions of this Chapter apply (with necessary modifications) in relation to a meeting of a class of members of a company without a share capital as they apply in relation to a general meeting.

This is subject to subsections (2) and (3).

(2) The following provisions of this Chapter do not apply in relation to a meeting of a class of members –

(a) sections 303 to 305 (members' power to require directors to call general meeting), and

(b) section 306 (power of court to order meeting).

(3) The following provisions (in addition to those mentioned in subsection (2)) do not apply in relation to a meeting in connection with the variation of the rights of a class of members (a "variation of class rights meeting") –

(a) section 318 (quorum), and

(b) section 321 (right to demand a poll).

(4) The quorum for a variation of class rights meeting is –

(a) for a meeting other than an adjourned meeting, two members of the class present (in person or by proxy) who together represent at least one-third of the voting rights of the class;

(b) for an adjourned meeting, one member of the class present (in person or by proxy).

(5) At a variation of class rights meeting, any member present (in person or by proxy) may demand a poll.

(6) For the purposes of this section –

(a) any amendment of a provision contained in a company's articles for the variation of the rights of a class of members, or the insertion of any such provision into the articles, is itself to be treated as a variation of those rights, and

(b) references to the variation of rights of a class of members include references to their abrogation.

CHAPTER 4

PUBLIC COMPANIES: ADDITIONAL REQUIREMENTS FOR AGMS

336 Public companies: annual general meeting

(1) Every public company must hold a general meeting as its annual general meeting in each period of 6 months beginning with the day following its accounting reference date (in addition to any other meetings held during that period).

(2) A company that fails to comply with subsection (1) as a result of giving notice under section 392 (alteration of accounting reference date) –

(a) specifying a new accounting reference date, and

(b) stating that the current accounting reference period or the previous accounting reference period is to be shortened,

shall be treated as if it had complied with subsection (1) if it holds a general meeting as its annual general meeting within 3 months of giving that notice.

(3) If a company fails to comply with subsection (1), an offence is committed by every officer of the company who is in default.

(4) A person guilty of an offence under this section is liable –

(a) on conviction on indictment, to a fine;

(b) on summary conviction, to a fine not exceeding the statutory maximum.

337 Public companies: notice of AGM

(1) A notice calling an annual general meeting of a public company must state that the meeting is an annual general meeting.

(2) An annual general meeting may be called by shorter notice than that required by section 307(2) or by the company's articles (as the case may be), if all the members entitled to attend and vote at the meeting agree to the shorter notice.

338 Public companies: members' power to require circulation of resolutions for AGMs

(1) The members of a public company may require the company to give, to members of the company entitled to receive notice of the next annual general meeting, notice of a resolution which may properly be moved and is intended to be moved at that meeting.

(2) A resolution may properly be moved at an annual general meeting unless –

   (a) it would, if passed, be ineffective (whether by reason of inconsistency with any enactment or the company's constitution or otherwise),
   (b) it is defamatory of any person, or
   (c) it is frivolous or vexatious.

(3) A company is required to give notice of a resolution once it has received requests that it do so from –

   (a) members representing at least 5% of the total voting rights of all the members who have a right to vote on the resolution at the annual general meeting to which the requests relate (excluding any voting rights attached to any shares in the company held as treasury shares), or
   (b) at least 100 members who have a right to vote on the resolution at the annual general meeting to which the requests relate and hold shares in the company on which there has been paid up an average sum, per member, of at least £100.

   See also section 153 (exercise of rights where shares held on behalf of others).

(4) A request –

   (a) may be in hard copy form or in electronic form,
   (b) must identify the resolution of which notice is to be given,
   (c) must be authenticated by the person or persons making it, and
   (d) must be received by the company not later than –

      (i)   6 weeks before the annual general meeting to which the requests relate, or
      (ii) if later, the time at which notice is given of that meeting.

339 Public companies: company's duty to circulate members' resolutions for AGMs

(1) A company that is required under section 338 to give notice of a resolution must send a copy of it to each member of the company entitled to receive notice of the annual general meeting –

   (a) in the same manner as notice of the meeting, and
   (b) at the same time as, or as soon as reasonably practicable after, it gives notice of the meeting.

(2) Subsection (1) has effect subject to section 340(2) (deposit or tender of sum in respect of expenses of circulation).

(3) The business which may be dealt with at an annual general meeting includes a resolution of which notice is given in accordance with this section.

(4) In the event of default in complying with this section, an offence is committed by every officer of the company who is in default.

(5) A person guilty of an offence under this section is liable –

   (a) on conviction on indictment, to a fine;
   (b) on summary conviction, to a fine not exceeding the statutory maximum.

340 Public companies: expenses of circulating members' resolutions for AGM

(1) The expenses of the company in complying with section 339 need not be paid by the members who requested the circulation of the resolution if requests sufficient to

require the company to circulate it are received before the end of the financial year preceding the meeting.

(2) Otherwise –

    (a) the expenses of the company in complying with that section must be paid by the members who requested the circulation of the resolution unless the company resolves otherwise, and

    (b) unless the company has previously so resolved, it is not bound to comply with that section unless there is deposited with or tendered to it, not later than –

        (i) six weeks before the annual general meeting to which the requests relate, or

        (ii) if later, the time at which notice is given of that meeting,

    a sum reasonably sufficient to meet its expenses in complying with that section.

CHAPTER 5

ADDITIONAL REQUIREMENTS FOR QUOTED COMPANIES

Website publication of poll results

341 Results of poll to be made available on website

(1) Where a poll is taken at a general meeting of a quoted company, the company must ensure that the following information is made available on a website –

    (a) the date of the meeting,

    (b) the text of the resolution or, as the case may be, a description of the subject matter of the poll,

    (c) the number of votes cast in favour, and

    (d) the number of votes cast against.

(2) The provisions of section 353 (requirements as to website availability) apply.

(3) In the event of default in complying with this section (or with the requirements of section 353 as it applies for the purposes of this section), an offence is committed by every officer of the company who is in default.

(4) A person guilty of an offence under subsection (3) is liable on summary conviction to a fine not exceeding level 3 on the standard scale.

(5) Failure to comply with this section (or the requirements of section 353) does not affect the validity of –

    (a) the poll, or

    (b) the resolution or other business (if passed or agreed to) to which the poll relates.

(6) This section only applies to polls taken after this section comes into force.

Independent report on poll

342 Members' power to require independent report on poll

(1) The members of a quoted company may require the directors to obtain an independent report on any poll taken, or to be taken, at a general meeting of the company.

(2) The directors are required to obtain an independent report if they receive requests to do so from –

    (a) members representing not less than 5% of the total voting rights of all the members who have a right to vote on the matter to which the poll relates (excluding any voting rights attached to any shares in the company held as treasury shares), or

(b) not less than 100 members who have a right to vote on the matter to which the poll relates and hold shares in the company on which there has been paid up an average sum, per member, of not less than £100.

See also section 153 (exercise of rights where shares held on behalf of others).

(3) Where the requests relate to more than one poll, subsection (2) must be satisfied in relation to each of them.

(4) A request –

(a) may be in hard copy form or in electronic form,

(b) must identify the poll or polls to which it relates,

(c) must be authenticated by the person or persons making it, and

(d) must be received by the company not later than one week after the date on which the poll is taken.

343 Appointment of independent assessor

(1) Directors who are required under section 342 to obtain an independent report on a poll or polls must appoint a person they consider to be appropriate (an "independent assessor") to prepare a report for the company on it or them.

(2) The appointment must be made within one week after the company being required to obtain the report.

(3) The directors must not appoint a person who –

(a) does not meet the independence requirement in section 344, or

(b) has another role in relation to any poll on which he is to report (including, in particular, a role in connection with collecting or counting votes or with the appointment of proxies).

(4) In the event of default in complying with this section, an offence is committed by every officer of the company who is in default.

(5) A person guilty of an offence under this section is liable on summary conviction to a fine not exceeding level 5 on the standard scale.

(6) If at the meeting no poll on which a report is required is taken –

(a) the directors are not required to obtain a report from the independent assessor, and

(b) his appointment ceases (but without prejudice to any right to be paid for work done before the appointment ceased).

344 Independence requirement

(1) A person may not be appointed as an independent assessor –

(a) if he is –

(i) an officer or employee of the company, or

(ii) a partner or employee of such a person, or a partnership of which such a person is a partner;

(b) if he is –

(i) an officer or employee of an associated undertaking of the company, or

(ii) a partner or employee of such a person, or a partnership of which such a person is a partner;

(c) if there exists between –

(i) the person or an associate of his, and

(ii) the company or an associated undertaking of the company, a connection of any such description as may be specified by regulations made by the Secretary of State.

(2) An auditor of the company is not regarded as an officer or employee of the company for this purpose.

(3) In this section –

"associated undertaking" means –

(a) a parent undertaking or subsidiary undertaking of the company, or
(b) a subsidiary undertaking of a parent undertaking of the company; and

"associate" has the meaning given by section 345.

(4) Regulations under this section are subject to negative resolution procedure.

345 Meaning of "associate"

(1) This section defines "associate" for the purposes of section 344 (independence requirement).

(2) In relation to an individual, "associate" means –

(a) that individual's spouse or civil partner or minor child or step-child,
(b) any body corporate of which that individual is a director, and
(c) any employee or partner of that individual.

(3) In relation to a body corporate, "associate" means –

(a) any body corporate of which that body is a director,
(b) any body corporate in the same group as that body, and
(c) any employee or partner of that body or of any body corporate in the same group.

(4) In relation to a partnership that is a legal person under the law by which it is governed, "associate" means –

(a) any body corporate of which that partnership is a director,
(b) any employee of or partner in that partnership, and
(c) any person who is an associate of a partner in that partnership.

(5) In relation to a partnership that is not a legal person under the law by which it is governed, "associate" means any person who is an associate of any of the partners.

(6) In this section, in relation to a limited liability partnership, for "director" read "member".

346 Effect of appointment of a partnership

(1) This section applies where a partnership that is not a legal person under the law by which it is governed is appointed as an independent assessor.

(2) Unless a contrary intention appears, the appointment is of the partnership as such and not of the partners.

(3) Where the partnership ceases, the appointment is to be treated as extending to –

(a) any partnership that succeeds to the practice of that partnership, or
(b) any other person who succeeds to that practice having previously carried it on in partnership.

(4) For the purposes of subsection (3) –

(a) a partnership is regarded as succeeding to the practice of another partnership only if the members of the successor partnership are substantially the same as those of the former partnership, and
(b) a partnership or other person is regarded as succeeding to the practice of a partnership only if it or he succeeds to the whole or substantially the whole of the business of the former partnership.

(5) Where the partnership ceases and the appointment is not treated under subsection (3) as extending to any partnership or other person, the appointment may with the consent of the company be treated as extending to a partnership, or other person, who succeeds to –

(a) the business of the former partnership, or
(b) such part of it as is agreed by the company is to be treated as comprising the appointment.

347 The independent assessor's report

(1) The report of the independent assessor must state his opinion whether –

    (a) the procedures adopted in connection with the poll or polls were adequate;
    (b) the votes cast (including proxy votes) were fairly and accurately recorded and counted;
    (c) the validity of members' appointments of proxies was fairly assessed;
    (d) the notice of the meeting complied with section 325 (notice of meeting to contain statement of rights to appoint proxy);
    (e) section 326 (company-sponsored invitations to appoint proxies) was complied with in relation to the meeting.

(2) The report must give his reasons for the opinions stated.
(3) If he is unable to form an opinion on any of those matters, the report must record that fact and state the reasons for it.
(4) The report must state the name of the independent assessor.

348 Rights of independent assessor: right to attend meeting etc

(1) Where an independent assessor has been appointed to report on a poll, he is entitled to attend –

    (a) the meeting at which the poll may be taken, and
    (b) any subsequent proceedings in connection with the poll.

(2) He is also entitled to be provided by the company with a copy of –

    (a) the notice of the meeting, and
    (b) any other communication provided by the company in connection with the meeting to persons who have a right to vote on the matter to which the poll relates.

(3) The rights conferred by this section are only to be exercised to the extent that the independent assessor considers necessary for the preparation of his report.
(4) If the independent assessor is a firm, the right under subsection (1) to attend the meeting and any subsequent proceedings in connection with the poll is exercisable by an individual authorised by the firm in writing to act as its representative for that purpose.

349 Rights of independent assessor: right to information

(1) The independent assessor is entitled to access to the company's records relating to –

    (a) any poll on which he is to report;
    (b) the meeting at which the poll or polls may be, or were, taken.

(2) The independent assessor may require anyone who at any material time was –

    (a) a director or secretary of the company,
    (b) an employee of the company,
    (c) a person holding or accountable for any of the company's records,
    (d) a member of the company, or
    (e) an agent of the company,

to provide him with information or explanations for the purpose of preparing his report.

(3) For this purpose "agent" includes the company's bankers, solicitors and auditor.

(4) A statement made by a person in response to a requirement under this section may not be used in evidence against him in criminal proceedings except proceedings for an offence under section 350 (offences relating to provision of information).

(5) A person is not required by this section to disclose information in respect of which a claim to legal professional privilege (in Scotland, to confidentiality of communications) could be maintained in legal proceedings.

350 Offences relating to provision of information

(1) A person who fails to comply with a requirement under section 349 without delay commits an offence unless it was not reasonably practicable for him to provide the required information or explanation.

(2) A person guilty of an offence under subsection (1) is liable on summary conviction to a fine not exceeding level 3 on the standard scale.

(3) A person commits an offence who knowingly or recklessly makes to an independent assessor a statement (oral or written) that –

(a) conveys or purports to convey any information or explanations which the independent assessor requires, or is entitled to require, under section 349, and

(b) is misleading, false or deceptive in a material particular.

(4) A person guilty of an offence under subsection (3) is liable –

(a) on conviction on indictment, to imprisonment for a term not exceeding two years or a fine (or both);

(b) on summary conviction –

(i) in England and Wales, to imprisonment for a term not exceeding twelve months or to a fine not exceeding the statutory maximum (or both);

(ii) in Scotland or Northern Ireland, to imprisonment for a term not exceeding six months, or to a fine not exceeding the statutory maximum (or both).

(5) Nothing in this section affects any right of an independent assessor to apply for an injunction (in Scotland, an interdict or an order for specific performance) to enforce any of his rights under section 348 or 349.

351 Information to be made available on website

(1) Where an independent assessor has been appointed to report on a poll, the company must ensure that the following information is made available on a website –

(a) the fact of his appointment,

(b) his identity,

(c) the text of the resolution or, as the case may be, a description of the subject matter of the poll to which his appointment relates, and

(d) a copy of a report by him which complies with section 347.

(2) The provisions of section 353 (requirements as to website availability) apply.

(3) In the event of default in complying with this section (or with the requirements of section 353 as it applies for the purposes of this section), an offence is committed by every officer of the company who is in default.

(4) A person guilty of an offence under subsection (3) is liable on summary conviction to a fine not exceeding level 3 on the standard scale.

(5) Failure to comply with this section (or the requirements of section 353) does not affect the validity of –

(a) the poll, or

(b) the resolution or other business (if passed or agreed to) to which the poll relates.

Supplementary

352 Application of provisions to class meetings

(1) The provisions of –

section 341 (results of poll to be made available on website), and
sections 342 to 351 (independent report on poll),

apply (with any necessary modifications) in relation to a meeting of holders of a class of shares of a quoted company in connection with the variation of the rights attached to such shares as they apply in relation to a general meeting of the company.

(2) For the purposes of this section –

(a) any amendment of a provision contained in a company's articles for the variation of the rights attached to a class of shares, or the insertion of any such provision into the articles, is itself to be treated as a variation of those rights, and

(b) references to the variation of rights attached to a class of shares include references to their abrogation.

353 Requirements as to website availability

(1) The following provisions apply for the purposes of –

section 341 (results of poll to be made available on website), and
section 351 (report of independent observer to be made available on website).

(2) The information must be made available on a website that –

(a) is maintained by or on behalf of the company, and

(b) identifies the company in question.

(3) Access to the information on the website, and the ability to obtain a hard copy of the information from the website, must not be conditional on the payment of a fee or otherwise restricted.

(4) The information –

(a) must be made available as soon as reasonably practicable, and

(b) must be kept available throughout the period of two years beginning with the date on which it is first made available on a website in accordance with this section.

(5) A failure to make information available on a website throughout the period specified in subsection (4)(b) is disregarded if –

(a) the information is made available on the website for part of that period, and

(b) the failure is wholly attributable to circumstances that it would not be reasonable to have expected the company to prevent or avoid.

354 Power to limit or extend the types of company to which provisions of this Chapter apply

(1) The Secretary of State may by regulations –

(a) limit the types of company to which some or all of the provisions of this Chapter apply, or

(b) extend some or all of the provisions of this Chapter to additional types of company.

(2) Regulations under this section extending the application of any provision of this Chapter are subject to affirmative resolution procedure.

(3) Any other regulations under this section are subject to negative resolution procedure.

(4) Regulations under this section may –

(a) amend the provisions of this Chapter (apart from this section);

(b)   repeal and re-enact provisions of this Chapter with modifications of form or arrangement, whether or not they are modified in substance;

(c)   contain such consequential, incidental and supplementary provisions (including provisions amending, repealing or revoking enactments) as the Secretary of State thinks fit.

CHAPTER 6

RECORDS OF RESOLUTIONS AND MEETINGS

355 Records of resolutions and meetings etc

(1)   Every company must keep records comprising –

(a)   copies of all resolutions of members passed otherwise than at general meetings,

(b)   minutes of all proceedings of general meetings, and

(c)   details provided to the company in accordance with section 357 (decisions of sole member).

(2)   The records must be kept for at least ten years from the date of the resolution, meeting or decision (as appropriate).

(3)   If a company fails to comply with this section, an offence is committed by every officer of the company who is in default.

(4)   A person guilty of an offence under this section is liable on summary conviction to a fine not exceeding level 3 on the standard scale and, for continued contravention, a daily default fine not exceeding one-tenth of level 3 on the standard scale.

356 Records as evidence of resolutions etc

(1)   This section applies to the records kept in accordance with section 355.

(2)   The record of a resolution passed otherwise than at a general meeting, if purporting to be signed by a director of the company or by the company secretary, is evidence (in Scotland, sufficient evidence) of the passing of the resolution.

(3)   Where there is a record of a written resolution of a private company, the requirements of this Act with respect to the passing of the resolution are deemed to be complied with unless the contrary is proved.

(4)   The minutes of proceedings of a general meeting, if purporting to be signed by the chairman of that meeting or by the chairman of the next general meeting, are evidence (in Scotland, sufficient evidence) of the proceedings at the meeting.

(5)   Where there is a record of proceedings of a general meeting of a company, then, until the contrary is proved –

(a)   the meeting is deemed duly held and convened,

(b)   all proceedings at the meeting are deemed to have duly taken place, and

(c)   all appointments at the meeting are deemed valid.

357 Records of decisions by sole member

(1)   This section applies to a company limited by shares or by guarantee that has only one member.

(2)   Where the member takes any decision that –

(a)   may be taken by the company in general meeting, and

(b)   has effect as if agreed by the company in general meeting,

he must (unless that decision is taken by way of a written resolution) provide the company with details of that decision.

(3)   If a person fails to comply with this section he commits an offence.

(4) A person guilty of an offence under this section is liable on summary conviction to a fine not exceeding level 2 on the standard scale.

(5) Failure to comply with this section does not affect the validity of any decision referred to in subsection (2).

358 Inspection of records of resolutions and meetings

(1) The records referred to in section 355 (records of resolutions etc) relating to the previous ten years must be kept available for inspection –

  (a) at the company's registered office, or

  (b) at a place specified in regulations under section 1136.

(2) The company must give notice to the registrar –

  (a) of the place at which the records are kept available for inspection, and

  (b) of any change in that place,

  unless they have at all times been kept at the company's registered office.

(3) The records must be open to the inspection of any member of the company without charge.

(4) Any member may require a copy of any of the records on payment of such fee as may be prescribed.

(5) If default is made for 14 days in complying with subsection (2) or an inspection required under subsection (3) is refused, or a copy requested under subsection (4) is not sent, an offence is committed by every officer of the company who is in default.

(6) A person guilty of an offence under this section is liable on summary conviction to a fine not exceeding level 3 on the standard scale and, for continued contravention, a daily default fine not exceeding one-tenth of level 3 on the standard scale.

(7) In a case in which an inspection required under subsection (3) is refused or a copy requested under subsection (4) is not sent, the court may by order compel an immediate inspection of the records or direct that the copies required be sent to the persons who requested them.

359 Records of resolutions and meetings of class of members

The provisions of this Chapter apply (with necessary modifications) in relation to resolutions and meetings of –

  (a) holders of a class of shares, and

  (b) in the case of a company without a share capital, a class of members,

as they apply in relation to resolutions of members generally and to general meetings.

CHAPTER 7

SUPPLEMENTARY PROVISIONS

360 Computation of periods of notice etc: clear day rule

(1) This section applies for the purposes of the following provisions of this Part –

  section 307(1) and (2) (notice required of general meeting),

  section 312(1) and (3) (resolution requiring special notice),

  section 314(4)(d) (request to circulate members' statement),

  section 316(2)(b) (expenses of circulating statement to be deposited or tendered before meeting),

  section 338(4)(d)(i) (request to circulate member's resolution at AGM of public company), and section 340(2)(b)(i) (expenses of circulating statement to be deposited or tendered before meeting).

(2) Any reference in those provisions to a period of notice, or to a period before a meeting by which a request must be received or sum deposited or tendered, is to a period of the specified length excluding –

    (a) the day of the meeting, and

    (b) the day on which the notice is given, the request received or the sum deposited or tendered.

361 Meaning of "quoted company"

In this Part "quoted company" has the same meaning as in Part 15 of this Act.

PART 14

CONTROL OF POLITICAL DONATIONS AND EXPENDITURE

Introductory

362 Introductory

This Part has effect for controlling –

    (a) political donations made by companies to political parties, to other political organisations and to independent election candidates, and

    (b) political expenditure incurred by companies.

Donations and expenditure to which this Part applies

363 Political parties, organisations etc to which this Part applies

(1) This Part applies to a political party if –

    (a) it is registered under Part 2 of the Political Parties, Elections and Referendums Act 2000 (c. 41), or

    (b) it carries on, or proposes to carry on, activities for the purposes of or in connection with the participation of the party in any election or elections to public office held in a member State other than the United Kingdom.

(2) This Part applies to an organisation (a "political organisation") if it carries on, or proposes to carry on, activities that are capable of being reasonably regarded as intended –

    (a) to affect public support for a political party to which, or an independent election candidate to whom, this Part applies, or

    (b) to influence voters in relation to any national or regional referendum held under the law of the United Kingdom or another member State.

(3) This Part applies to an independent election candidate at any election to public office held in the United Kingdom or another member State.

(4) Any reference in the following provisions of this Part to a political party, political organisation or independent election candidate, or to political expenditure, is to a party, organisation, independent candidate or expenditure to which this Part applies.

364 Meaning of "political donation"

(1) The following provisions have effect for the purposes of this Part as regards the meaning of "political donation".

(2) In relation to a political party or other political organisation –

(a) "political donation" means anything that in accordance with sections 50 to 52 of the Political Parties, Elections and Referendums Act 2000 –

    (i) constitutes a donation for the purposes of Chapter 1 of Part 4 of that Act (control of donations to registered parties), or

    (ii) would constitute such a donation reading references in those sections to a registered party as references to any political party or other political organisation,

and

(b) section 53 of that Act applies, in the same way, for the purpose of determining the value of a donation.

(3) In relation to an independent election candidate –

(a) "political donation" means anything that, in accordance with sections 50 to 52 of that Act, would constitute a donation for the purposes of Chapter 1 of Part 4 of that Act (control of donations to registered parties) reading references in those sections to a registered party as references to the independent election candidate, and

(b) section 53 of that Act applies, in the same way, for the purpose of determining the value of a donation.

(4) For the purposes of this section, sections 50 and 53 of the Political Parties, Elections and Referendums Act 2000 (c. 41) (definition of "donation" and value of donations) shall be treated as if the amendments to those sections made by the Electoral Administration Act 2006 (which remove from the definition of "donation" loans made otherwise than on commercial terms) had not been made.

365 Meaning of "political expenditure"

(1) In this Part "political expenditure", in relation to a company, means expenditure incurred by the company on –

(a) the preparation, publication or dissemination of advertising or other promotional or publicity material –

    (i) of whatever nature, and

    (ii) however published or otherwise disseminated,

that, at the time of publication or dissemination, is capable of being reasonably regarded as intended to affect public support for a political party or other political organisation, or an independent election candidate, or

(b) activities on the part of the company that are capable of being reasonably regarded as intended –

    (i) to affect public support for a political party or other political organisation, or an independent election candidate, or

    (ii) to influence voters in relation to any national or regional referendum held under the law of a member State.

(2) For the purposes of this Part a political donation does not count as political expenditure.

Authorisation required for donations or expenditure

366 Authorisation required for donations or expenditure

(1) A company must not –

(a) make a political donation to a political party or other political organisation, or to an independent election candidate, or

(b) incur any political expenditure,

unless the donation or expenditure is authorised in accordance with the following provisions.

(2) The donation or expenditure must be authorised –

    (a) in the case of a company that is not a subsidiary of another company, by a resolution of the members of the company;

    (b) in the case of a company that is a subsidiary of another company by –

        (i) a resolution of the members of the company, and

        (ii) a resolution of the members of any relevant holding company.

(3) No resolution is required on the part of a company that is a wholly-owned subsidiary of a UK-registered company.

(4) For the purposes of subsection (2)(b)(ii) a "relevant holding company" means a company that, at the time the donation was made or the expenditure was incurred –

    (a) was a holding company of the company by which the donation was made or the expenditure was incurred,

    (b) was a UK-registered company, and

    (c) was not a subsidiary of another UK-registered company.

(5) The resolution or resolutions required by this section –

    (a) must comply with section 367 (form of authorising resolution), and

    (b) must be passed before the donation is made or the expenditure incurred.

(6) Nothing in this section enables a company to be authorised to do anything that it could not lawfully do apart from this section.

367 Form of authorising resolution

(1) A resolution conferring authorisation for the purposes of this Part may relate to –

    (a) the company passing the resolution,

    (b) one or more subsidiaries of that company, or

    (c) the company passing the resolution and one or more subsidiaries of that company.

(2) A resolution may be expressed to relate to all companies that are subsidiaries of the company passing the resolution –

    (a) at the time the resolution is passed, or

    (b) at any time during the period for which the resolution has effect,

without identifying them individually.

(3) The resolution may authorise donations or expenditure under one or more of the following heads –

    (a) donations to political parties or independent election candidates;

    (b) donations to political organisations other than political parties;

    (c) political expenditure.

(4) The resolution must specify a head or heads –

    (a) in the case of a resolution under subsection (2), for all of the companies to which it relates taken together;

    (b) in the case of any other resolution, for each company to which it relates.

(5) The resolution must be expressed in general terms conforming with subsection (2) and must not purport to authorise particular donations or expenditure.

(6) For each of the specified heads the resolution must authorise donations or, as the case may be, expenditure up to a specified amount in the period for which the resolution has effect (see section 368).

(7) The resolution must specify such amounts –

    (a) in the case of a resolution under subsection (2), for all of the companies to which it relates taken together;

    (b) in the case of any other resolution, for each company to which it relates.

368 Period for which resolution has effect

(1) A resolution conferring authorisation for the purposes of this Part has effect for a period of four years beginning with the date on which it is passed unless the directors determine, or the articles require, that it is to have effect for a shorter period beginning with that date.

(2) The power of the directors to make a determination under this section is subject to any provision of the articles that operates to prevent them from doing so.

Remedies in case of unauthorised donations or expenditure

369 Liability of directors in case of unauthorised donation or expenditure

(1) This section applies where a company has made a political donation or incurred political expenditure without the authorisation required by this Part.

(2) The directors in default are jointly and severally liable –

  (a) to make good to the company the amount of the unauthorised donation or expenditure, with interest, and

  (b) to compensate the company for any loss or damage sustained by it as a result of the unauthorised donation or expenditure having been made.

(3) The directors in default are –

  (a) those who, at the time the unauthorised donation was made or the unauthorised expenditure was incurred, were directors of the company by which the donation was made or the expenditure was incurred, and

  (b) where –

    (i) that company was a subsidiary of a relevant holding company, and

    (ii) the directors of the relevant holding company failed to take all reasonable steps to prevent the donation being made or the expenditure being incurred,

  the directors of the relevant holding company.

(4) For the purposes of subsection (3)(b) a "relevant holding company" means a company that, at the time the donation was made or the expenditure was incurred –

  (a) was a holding company of the company by which the donation was made or the expenditure was incurred,

  (b) was a UK-registered company, and

  (c) was not a subsidiary of another UK-registered company.

(5) The interest referred to in subsection (2)(a) is interest on the amount of the unauthorised donation or expenditure, so far as not made good to the company –

  (a) in respect of the period beginning with the date when the donation was made or the expenditure was incurred, and

  (b) at such rate as the Secretary of State may prescribe by regulations.

  Section 379(2) (construction of references to date when donation made or expenditure incurred) does not apply for the purposes of this subsection.

(6) Where only part of a donation or expenditure was unauthorised, this section applies only to so much of it as was unauthorised.

370 Enforcement of directors' liabilities by shareholder action

(1) Any liability of a director under section 369 is enforceable –

  (a) in the case of a liability of a director of a company to that company, by proceedings brought under this section in the name of the company by an authorised group of its members;

  (b) in the case of a liability of a director of a holding company to a subsidiary, by proceedings brought under this section in the name of the subsidiary by –

      (i)   an authorised group of members of the subsidiary, or

      (ii)   an authorised group of members of the holding company.

(2) This is in addition to the right of the company to which the liability is owed to bring proceedings itself to enforce the liability.

(3) An "authorised group" of members of a company means –

    (a) the holders of not less than 5% in nominal value of the company's issued share capital,

    (b) if the company is not limited by shares, not less than 5% of its members, or

    (c) not less than 50 of the company's members.

(4) The right to bring proceedings under this section is subject to the provisions of section 371.

(5) Nothing in this section affects any right of a member of a company to bring or continue proceedings under Part 11 (derivative claims or proceedings).

371 Enforcement of directors' liabilities by shareholder action: supplementary

(1) A group of members may not bring proceedings under section 370 in the name of a company unless –

    (a) the group has given written notice to the company stating –

      (i)   the cause of action and a summary of the facts on which the proceedings are to be based,

      (ii)   the names and addresses of the members comprising the group, and

      (iii) the grounds on which it is alleged that those members constitute an authorised group; and

    (b) not less than 28 days have elapsed between the date of the giving of the notice to the company and the bringing of the proceedings.

(2) Where such a notice is given to a company, any director of the company may apply to the court within the period of 28 days beginning with the date of the giving of the notice for an order directing that the proposed proceedings shall not be brought, on one or more of the following grounds –

    (a) that the unauthorised amount has been made good to the company;

    (b) that proceedings to enforce the liability have been brought, and are being pursued with due diligence, by the company;

    (c) that the members proposing to bring proceedings under this section do not constitute an authorised group.

(3) Where an application is made on the ground mentioned in subsection (2)(b), the court may as an alternative to directing that the proposed proceedings under section 370 are not to be brought, direct –

    (a) that such proceedings may be brought on such terms and conditions as the court thinks fit, and

    (b) that the proceedings brought by the company –

      (i)   shall be discontinued, or

      (ii)   may be continued on such terms and conditions as the court thinks fit.

(4) The members by whom proceedings are brought under section 370 owe to the company in whose name they are brought the same duties in relation to the proceedings as would be owed by the company's directors if the proceedings were being brought by the company.

But proceedings to enforce any such duty may be brought by the company only with the permission of the court.

(5) Proceedings brought under section 370 may not be discontinued or settled by the group except with the permission of the court, which may be given on such terms as the court thinks fit.

372 Costs of shareholder action

(1) This section applies in relation to proceedings brought under section 370 in the name of a company ("the company") by an authorised group ("the group").

(2) The group may apply to the court for an order directing the company to indemnify the group in respect of costs incurred or to be incurred by the group in connection with the proceedings.
The court may make such an order on such terms as it thinks fit.

(3) The group is not entitled to be paid any such costs out of the assets of the company except by virtue of such an order.

(4) If no such order has been made with respect to the proceedings, then –

    (a) if the company is awarded costs in connection with the proceedings, or it is agreed that costs incurred by the company in connection with the proceedings should be paid by any defendant, the costs shall be paid to the group; and

    (b) if any defendant is awarded costs in connection with the proceedings, or it is agreed that any defendant should be paid costs incurred by him in connection with the proceedings, the costs shall be paid by the group.

(5) In the application of this section to Scotland for "costs" read "expenses" and for "defendant" read "defender".

373 Information for purposes of shareholder action

(1) Where proceedings have been brought under section 370 in the name of a company by an authorised group, the group is entitled to require the company to provide it with all information relating to the subject matter of the proceedings that is in the company's possession or under its control or which is reasonably obtainable by it.

(2) If the company, having been required by the group to do so, refuses to provide the group with all or any of that information, the court may, on an application made by the group, make an order directing –

    (a) the company, and

    (b) any of its officers or employees specified in the application,

to provide the group with the information in question in such form and by such means as the court may direct.

Exemptions

374 Trade unions

(1) A donation to a trade union, other than a contribution to the union's political fund, is not a political donation for the purposes of this Part.

(2) A trade union is not a political organisation for the purposes of section 365 (meaning of "political expenditure").

(3) In this section –

"trade union" has the meaning given by section 1 of Trade Union and Labour Relations (Consolidation) Act 1992 (c. 52) or Article 3 of the Industrial Relations (Northern Ireland) Order 1992 (S.I. 1992/807 (N.I. 5));

"political fund" means the fund from which payments by a trade union in the furtherance of political objects are required to be made by virtue of section 82(1)(a) of that Act or Article 57(2)(a) of that Order.

375 Subscription for membership of trade association

(1) A subscription paid to a trade association for membership of the association is not a political donation for the purposes of this Part.

(2) For this purpose –

"trade association" means an organisation formed for the purpose of furthering the trade interests of its members, or of persons represented by its members, and

"subscription" does not include a payment to the association to the extent that it is made for the purpose of financing any particular activity of the association.

376 All-party parliamentary groups

(1) An all-party parliamentary group is not a political organisation for the purposes of this Part.

(2) An "all-party parliamentary group" means an all-party group composed of members of one or both of the Houses of Parliament (or of such members and other persons).

377 Political expenditure exempted by order

(1) Authorisation under this Part is not needed for political expenditure that is exempt by virtue of an order of the Secretary of State under this section.

(2) An order may confer an exemption in relation to –

  (a) companies of any description or category specified in the order, or

  (b) expenditure of any description or category so specified (whether framed by reference to goods, services or other matters in respect of which such expenditure is incurred or otherwise),

  or both.

(3) If or to the extent that expenditure is exempt from the requirement of authorisation under this Part by virtue of an order under this section, it shall be disregarded in determining what donations are authorised by any resolution of the company passed for the purposes of this Part.

(4) An order under this section is subject to affirmative resolution procedure.

378 Donations not amounting to more than £5,000 in any twelve month period

(1) Authorisation under this Part is not needed for a donation except to the extent that the total amount of –

  (a) that donation, and

  (b) other relevant donations made in the period of 12 months ending with the date on which that donation is made,

  exceeds £5,000.

(2) In this section –

  "donation" means a donation to a political party or other political organisation or to an independent election candidate; and

  "other relevant donations" means –

  (a) in relation to a donation made by a company that is not a subsidiary, any other donations made by that company or by any of its subsidiaries;

  (b) in relation to a donation made by a company that is a subsidiary, any other donations made by that company, by any holding company of that company or by any other subsidiary of any such holding company.

(3) If or to the extent that a donation is exempt by virtue of this section from the requirement of authorisation under this Part, it shall be disregarded in determining what donations are authorised by any resolution passed for the purposes of this Part.

Supplementary provisions

379 Minor definitions

(1) In this Part –

  "director" includes shadow director; and

"organisation" includes any body corporate or unincorporated association and any combination of persons.

(2) Except as otherwise provided, any reference in this Part to the time at which a donation is made or expenditure is incurred is, in a case where the donation is made or expenditure incurred in pursuance of a contract, any earlier time at which that contract is entered into by the company.

PART 15

ACCOUNTS AND REPORTS

CHAPTER 1

INTRODUCTION

General

380 Scheme of this Part

(1) The requirements of this Part as to accounts and reports apply in relation to each financial year of a company.

(2) In certain respects different provisions apply to different kinds of company.

(3) The main distinctions for this purpose are –

  (a) between companies subject to the small companies regime (see section 381) and companies that are not subject to that regime; and

  (b) between quoted companies (see section 385) and companies that are not quoted.

(4) In this Part, where provisions do not apply to all kinds of company –

  (a) provisions applying to companies subject to the small companies regime appear before the provisions applying to other companies,

  (b) provisions applying to private companies appear before the provisions applying to public companies, and

  (c) provisions applying to quoted companies appear after the provisions applying to other companies.

Companies subject to the small companies regime

381 Companies subject to the small companies regime

The small companies regime for accounts and reports applies to a company for a financial year in relation to which the company –

  (a) qualifies as small (see sections 382 and 383), and

  (b) is not excluded from the regime (see section 384).

382 Companies qualifying as small: general

(1) A company qualifies as small in relation to its first financial year if the qualifying conditions are met in that year.

(2) A company qualifies as small in relation to a subsequent financial year –

  (a) if the qualifying conditions are met in that year and the preceding financial year;

  (b) if the qualifying conditions are met in that year and the company qualified as small in relation to the preceding financial year;

  (c) if the qualifying conditions were met in the preceding financial year and the company qualified as small in relation to that year.

(3) The qualifying conditions are met by a company in a year in which it satisfies two or more of the following requirements –

1.	Turnover	Not more than £5.6 million
2.	Balance sheet total	Not more than £2.8 million
3.	Number of employees	Not more than 50

(4) For a period that is a company's financial year but not in fact a year the maximum figures for turnover must be proportionately adjusted.

(5) The balance sheet total means the aggregate of the amounts shown as assets in the company's balance sheet.

(6) The number of employees means the average number of persons employed by the company in the year, determined as follows –

(a) find for each month in the financial year the number of persons employed under contracts of service by the company in that month (whether throughout the month or not),

(b) add together the monthly totals, and

(c) divide by the number of months in the financial year.

(7) This section is subject to section 383 (companies qualifying as small: parent companies).

383 Companies qualifying as small: parent companies

(1) A parent company qualifies as a small company in relation to a financial year only if the group headed by it qualifies as a small group.

(2) A group qualifies as small in relation to the parent company's first financial year if the qualifying conditions are met in that year.

(3) A group qualifies as small in relation to a subsequent financial year of the parent company –

(a) if the qualifying conditions are met in that year and the preceding financial year;

(b) if the qualifying conditions are met in that year and the group qualified as small in relation to the preceding financial year;

(c) if the qualifying conditions were met in the preceding financial year and the group qualified as small in relation to that year.

(4) The qualifying conditions are met by a group in a year in which it satisfies two or more of the following requirements –

1.	Aggregate turnover	Not more than £5.6 million net (or £6.72 million gross)
2.	Aggregate balance sheet total	Not more than £2.8 million net (or £3.36 million gross)
3.	Aggregate number of employees	Not more than 50

(5) The aggregate figures are ascertained by aggregating the relevant figures determined in accordance with section 382 for each member of the group.

(6) In relation to the aggregate figures for turnover and balance sheet total –

"net" means after any set-offs and other adjustments made to eliminate group transactions –

(a) in the case of Companies Act accounts, in accordance with regulations under section 404,

(b) in the case of IAS accounts, in accordance with international accounting standards; and

"gross" means without those set-offs and other adjustments.

A company may satisfy any relevant requirement on the basis of either the net or the gross figure.

(7) The figures for each subsidiary undertaking shall be those included in its individual accounts for the relevant financial year, that is –

(a) if its financial year ends with that of the parent company, that financial year, and

(b) if not, its financial year ending last before the end of the financial year of the parent company.

If those figures cannot be obtained without disproportionate expense or undue delay, the latest available figures shall be taken.

384 Companies excluded from the small companies regime

(1) The small companies regime does not apply to a company that is, or was at any time within the financial year to which the accounts relate –

    (a) a public company,

    (b) a company that –

        (i) is an authorised insurance company, a banking company, an emoney issuer, an ISD investment firm or a UCITS management company, or

        (ii) carries on insurance market activity, or

    (c) a member of an ineligible group.

(2) A group is ineligible if any of its members is –

    (a) a public company,

    (b) a body corporate (other than a company) whose shares are admitted to trading on a regulated market in an EEA State,

    (c) a person (other than a small company) who has permission under Part 4 of the Financial Services and Markets Act 2000 (c. 8) to carry on a regulated activity,

    (d) a small company that is an authorised insurance company, a banking company, an e-money issuer, an ISD investment firm or a UCITS management company, or

    (e) a person who carries on insurance market activity.

(3) A company is a small company for the purposes of subsection (2) if it qualified as small in relation to its last financial year ending on or before the end of the financial year to which the accounts relate.

Quoted and unquoted companies

385 Quoted and unquoted companies

(1) For the purposes of this Part a company is a quoted company in relation to a financial year if it is a quoted company immediately before the end of the accounting reference period by reference to which that financial year was determined.

(2) A "quoted company" means a company whose equity share capital –

    (a) has been included in the official list in accordance with the provisions of Part 6 of the Financial Services and Markets Act 2000 (c. 8), or

    (b) is officially listed in an EEA State, or

    (c) is admitted to dealing on either the New York Stock Exchange or the exchange known as Nasdaq.

In paragraph (a) "the official list" has the meaning given by section 103(1) of the Financial Services and Markets Act 2000.

(3) An "unquoted company" means a company that is not a quoted company.

(4) The Secretary of State may by regulations amend or replace the provisions of subsections (1) to (2) so as to limit or extend the application of some or all of the provisions of this Part that are expressed to apply to quoted companies.

(5) Regulations under this section extending the application of any such provision of this Part are subject to affirmative resolution procedure.

(6) Any other regulations under this section are subject to negative resolution procedure.

CHAPTER 2

ACCOUNTING RECORDS

386 Duty to keep accounting records

(1) Every company must keep adequate accounting records.

(2) Adequate accounting records means records that are sufficient –

    (a) to show and explain the company's transactions,

    (b) to disclose with reasonable accuracy, at any time, the financial position of the company at that time, and

    (c) to enable the directors to ensure that any accounts required to be prepared comply with the requirements of this Act (and, where applicable, of Article 4 of the IAS Regulation).

(3) Accounting records must, in particular, contain –

    (a) entries from day to day of all sums of money received and expended by the company and the matters in respect of which the receipt and expenditure takes place, and

    (b) a record of the assets and liabilities of the company.

(4) If the company's business involves dealing in goods, the accounting records must contain –

    (a) statements of stock held by the company at the end of each financial year of the company,

    (b) all statements of stocktakings from which any statement of stock as is mentioned in paragraph (a) has been or is to be prepared, and

    (c) except in the case of goods sold by way of ordinary retail trade, statements of all goods sold and purchased, showing the goods and the buyers and sellers in sufficient detail to enable all these to be identified.

(5) A parent company that has a subsidiary undertaking in relation to which the above requirements do not apply must take reasonable steps to secure that the undertaking keeps such accounting records as to enable the directors of the parent company to ensure that any accounts required to be prepared under this Part comply with the requirements of this Act (and, where applicable, of Article 4 of the IAS Regulation).

387 Duty to keep accounting records: offence

(1) If a company fails to comply with any provision of section 386 (duty to keep accounting records), an offence is committed by every officer of the company who is in default.

(2) It is a defence for a person charged with such an offence to show that he acted honestly and that in the circumstances in which the company's business was carried on the default was excusable.

(3) A person guilty of an offence under this section is liable –

    (a) on conviction on indictment, to imprisonment for a term not exceeding two years or a fine (or both);

    (b) on summary conviction –

        (i) in England and Wales, to imprisonment for a term not exceeding twelve months or to a fine not exceeding the statutory maximum (or both);

        (ii) in Scotland or Northern Ireland, to imprisonment for a term not exceeding six months, or to a fine not exceeding the statutory maximum (or both).

388 Where and for how long records to be kept

(1) A company's accounting records –

(a) must be kept at its registered office or such other place as the directors think fit, and

(b) must at all times be open to inspection by the company's officers.

(2) If accounting records are kept at a place outside the United Kingdom, accounts and returns with respect to the business dealt with in the accounting records so kept must be sent to, and kept at, a place in the United Kingdom, and must at all times be open to such inspection.

(3) The accounts and returns to be sent to the United Kingdom must be such as to –

(a) disclose with reasonable accuracy the financial position of the business in question at intervals of not more than six months, and

(b) enable the directors to ensure that the accounts required to be prepared under this Part comply with the requirements of this Act (and, where applicable, of Article 4 of the IAS Regulation).

(4) Accounting records that a company is required by section 386 to keep must be preserved by it –

(a) in the case of a private company, for three years from the date on which they are made;

(b) in the case of a public company, for six years from the date on which they are made.

(5) Subsection (4) is subject to any provision contained in rules made under section 411 of the Insolvency Act 1986 (c. 45) (company insolvency rules) or Article 359 of the Insolvency (Northern Ireland) Order 1989 (S.I. 1989/2405 (N.I. 19)).

389 Where and for how long records to be kept: offences

(1) If a company fails to comply with any provision of subsections (1) to (3) of section 388 (requirements as to keeping of accounting records), an offence is committed by every officer of the company who is in default.

(2) It is a defence for a person charged with such an offence to show that he acted honestly and that in the circumstances in which the company's business was carried on the default was excusable.

(3) An officer of a company commits an offence if he –

(a) fails to take all reasonable steps for securing compliance by the company with subsection (4) of that section (period for which records to be preserved), or

(b) intentionally causes any default by the company under that subsection.

(4) A person guilty of an offence under this section is liable –

(a) on conviction on indictment, to imprisonment for a term not exceeding two years or a fine (or both);

(b) on summary conviction –

(i) in England and Wales, to imprisonment for a term not exceeding twelve months or to a fine not exceeding the statutory maximum (or both);

(ii) in Scotland or Northern Ireland, to imprisonment for a term not exceeding six months, or to a fine not exceeding the statutory maximum (or both).

CHAPTER 3

A COMPANY'S FINANCIAL YEAR

390 A company's financial year

(1) A company's financial year is determined as follows.

(2) Its first financial year –

    (a) begins with the first day of its first accounting reference period, and

    (b) ends with the last day of that period or such other date, not more than seven days before or after the end of that period, as the directors may determine.

(3) Subsequent financial years –

    (a) begin with the day immediately following the end of the company's previous financial year, and

    (b) end with the last day of its next accounting reference period or such other date, not more than seven days before or after the end of that period, as the directors may determine.

(4) In relation to an undertaking that is not a company, references in this Act to its financial year are to any period in respect of which a profit and loss account of the undertaking is required to be made up (by its constitution or by the law under which it is established), whether that period is a year or not.

(5) The directors of a parent company must secure that, except where in their opinion there are good reasons against it, the financial year of each of its subsidiary undertakings coincides with the company's own financial year.

391 Accounting reference periods and accounting reference date

(1) A company's accounting reference periods are determined according to its accounting reference date in each calendar year.

(2) The accounting reference date of a company incorporated in Great Britain before 1st April 1996 is –

    (a) the date specified by notice to the registrar in accordance with section 224(2) of the Companies Act 1985 (c. 6) (notice specifying accounting reference date given within nine months of incorporation), or

    (b) failing such notice –

        (i) in the case of a company incorporated before 1st April 1990, 31st March, and

        (ii) in the case of a company incorporated on or after 1st April 1990, the last day of the month in which the anniversary of its incorporation falls.

(3) The accounting reference date of a company incorporated in Northern Ireland before 22nd August 1997 is –

    (a) the date specified by notice to the registrar in accordance with article 232(2) of the Companies (Northern Ireland) Order 1986 (S.I. 1986/1032 (N.I. 6)) (notice specifying accounting reference date given within nine months of incorporation), or

    (b) failing such notice –

        (i) in the case of a company incorporated before the coming into operation of Article 5 of the Companies (Northern Ireland) Order 1990 (S.I. 1990/593 (N.I. 5)), 31st March, and

        (ii) in the case of a company incorporated after the coming into operation of that Article, the last day of the month in which the anniversary of its incorporation falls.

(4) The accounting reference date of a company incorporated –

(a) in Great Britain on or after 1st April 1996 and before the commencement of this Act,

(b) in Northern Ireland on or after 22nd August 1997 and before the commencement of this Act, or

(c) after the commencement of this Act,

is the last day of the month in which the anniversary of its incorporation falls.

(5) A company's first accounting reference period is the period of more than six months, but not more than 18 months, beginning with the date of its incorporation and ending with its accounting reference date.

(6) Its subsequent accounting reference periods are successive periods of twelve months beginning immediately after the end of the previous accounting reference period and ending with its accounting reference date.

(7) This section has effect subject to the provisions of section 392 (alteration of accounting reference date).

392 Alteration of accounting reference date

(1) A company may by notice given to the registrar specify a new accounting reference date having effect in relation to –

(a) the company's current accounting reference period and subsequent periods, or

(b) the company's previous accounting reference period and subsequent periods.

A company's "previous accounting reference period" means the one immediately preceding its current accounting reference period.

(2) The notice must state whether the current or previous accounting reference period –

(a) is to be shortened, so as to come to an end on the first occasion on which the new accounting reference date falls or fell after the beginning of the period, or

(b) is to be extended, so as to come to an end on the second occasion on which that date falls or fell after the beginning of the period.

(3) A notice extending a company's current or previous accounting reference period is not effective if given less than five years after the end of an earlier accounting reference period of the company that was extended under this section.

This does not apply –

(a) to a notice given by a company that is a subsidiary undertaking or parent undertaking of another EEA undertaking if the new accounting reference date coincides with that of the other EEA undertaking or, where that undertaking is not a company, with the last day of it financial year, or

(b) where the company is in administration under Part 2 of the Insolvency Act 1986 (c. 45) or Part 3 of the Insolvency (Northern Ireland) Order 1989 (S.I. 1989/2405 (N.I. 19)), or

(c) where the Secretary of State directs that it should not apply, which he may do with respect to a notice that has been given or that may be given.

(4) A notice under this section may not be given in respect of a previous accounting reference period if the period for filing accounts and reports for the financial year determined by reference to that accounting reference period has already expired.

(5) An accounting reference period may not be extended so as to exceed 18 months and a notice under this section is ineffective if the current or previous accounting reference period as extended in accordance with the notice would exceed that limit.

This does not apply where the company is in administration under Part 2 of the Insolvency Act 1986 (c. 45) or Part 3 of the Insolvency (Northern Ireland) Order 1989 (S.I. 1989/2405 (N.I. 19)).

(6) In this section "EEA undertaking" means an undertaking established under the law of any part of the United Kingdom or the law of any other EEA State.

CHAPTER 4

ANNUAL ACCOUNTS

General

393 Accounts to give true and fair view

(1) The directors of a company must not approve accounts for the purposes of this Chapter unless they are satisfied that they give a true and fair view of the assets, liabilities, financial position and profit or loss –

    (a) in the case of the company's individual accounts, of the company;

    (b) in the case of the company's group accounts, of the undertakings included in the consolidation as a whole, so far as concerns members of the company.

(2) The auditor of a company in carrying out his functions under this Act in relation to the company's annual accounts must have regard to the directors' duty under subsection (1).

Individual accounts

394 Duty to prepare individual accounts

The directors of every company must prepare accounts for the company for each of its financial years.

Those accounts are referred to as the company's "individual accounts".

395 Individual accounts: applicable accounting framework

(1) A company's individual accounts may be prepared –

    (a) in accordance with section 396 ("Companies Act individual accounts"), or

    (b) in accordance with international accounting standards ("IAS individual accounts").

    This is subject to the following provisions of this section and to section 407 (consistency of financial reporting within group).

(2) The individual accounts of a company that is a charity must be Companies Act individual accounts.

(3) After the first financial year in which the directors of a company prepare IAS individual accounts ("the first IAS year"), all subsequent individual accounts of the company must be prepared in accordance with international accounting standards unless there is a relevant change of circumstance.

(4) There is a relevant change of circumstance if, at any time during or after the first IAS year –

    (a) the company becomes a subsidiary undertaking of another undertaking that does not prepare IAS individual accounts,

    (b) the company ceases to be a company with securities admitted to trading on a regulated market in an EEA State, or

    (c) a parent undertaking of the company ceases to be an undertaking with securities admitted to trading on a regulated market in an EEA State.

(5) If, having changed to preparing Companies Act individual accounts following a relevant change of circumstance, the directors again prepare IAS individual accounts for the company, subsections (3) and (4) apply again as if the first financial year for which such accounts are again prepared were the first IAS year.

396 Companies Act individual accounts

(1) Companies Act individual accounts must comprise –

(a) a balance sheet as at the last day of the financial year, and
(b) a profit and loss account.

(2) The accounts must –

(a) in the case of the balance sheet, give a true and fair view of the state of affairs of the company as at the end of the financial year, and
(b) in the case of the profit and loss account, give a true and fair view of the profit or loss of the company for the financial year.

(3) The accounts must comply with provision made by the Secretary of State by regulations as to –

(a) the form and content of the balance sheet and profit and loss account, and
(b) additional information to be provided by way of notes to the accounts.

(4) If compliance with the regulations, and any other provision made by or under this Act as to the matters to be included in a company's individual accounts or in notes to those accounts, would not be sufficient to give a true and fair view, the necessary additional information must be given in the accounts or in a note to them.

(5) If in special circumstances compliance with any of those provisions is inconsistent with the requirement to give a true and fair view, the directors must depart from that provision to the extent necessary to give a true and fair view.

Particulars of any such departure, the reasons for it and its effect must be given in a note to the accounts.

397 IAS individual accounts

Where the directors of a company prepare IAS individual accounts, they must state in the notes to the accounts that the accounts have been prepared in accordance with international accounting standards.

Group accounts: small companies

398 Option to prepare group accounts

If at the end of a financial year a company subject to the small companies regime is a parent company the directors, as well as preparing individual accounts for the year, may prepare group accounts for the year.

Group accounts: other companies

399 Duty to prepare group accounts

(1) This section applies to companies that are not subject to the small companies regime.
(2) If at the end of a financial year the company is a parent company the directors, as well as preparing individual accounts for the year, must prepare group accounts for the year unless the company is exempt from that requirement.
(3) There are exemptions under –

section 400 (company included in EEA accounts of larger group),
section 401 (company included in non-EEA accounts of larger group), and
section 402 (company none of whose subsidiary undertakings need be included in the consolidation).

(4) A company to which this section applies but which is exempt from the requirement to prepare group accounts, may do so.

400 Exemption for company included in EEA group accounts of larger group

(1) A company is exempt from the requirement to prepare group accounts if it is itself a subsidiary undertaking and its immediate parent undertaking is established under the law of an EEA State, in the following cases –

  (a) where the company is a wholly-owned subsidiary of that parent undertaking;
  (b) where that parent undertaking holds more than 50% of the allotted shares in the company and notice requesting the preparation of group accounts has not been served on the company by shareholders holding in aggregate –

    (i) more than half of the remaining allotted shares in the company, or
    (ii) 5% of the total allotted shares in the company.

  Such notice must be served not later than six months after the end of the financial year before that to which it relates.

(2) Exemption is conditional upon compliance with all of the following conditions –

  (a) the company must be included in consolidated accounts for a larger group drawn up to the same date, or to an earlier date in the same financial year, by a parent undertaking established under the law of an EEA State;
  (b) those accounts must be drawn up and audited, and that parent undertaking's annual report must be drawn up, according to that law –

    (i) in accordance with the provisions of the Seventh Directive (83/349/EEC) (as modified, where relevant, by the provisions of the Bank Accounts Directive (86/635/EEC) or the Insurance Accounts Directive (91/674/EEC)), or
    (ii) in accordance with international accounting standards;

  (c) the company must disclose in its individual accounts that it is exempt from the obligation to prepare and deliver group accounts;
  (d) the company must state in its individual accounts the name of the parent undertaking that draws up the group accounts referred to above and –

    (i) if it is incorporated outside the United Kingdom, the country in which it is incorporated, or
    (ii) if it is unincorporated, the address of its principal place of business;

  (e) the company must deliver to the registrar, within the period for filing its accounts and reports for the financial year in question, copies of –

    (i) those group accounts, and
    (ii) the parent undertaking's annual report,

    together with the auditor's report on them;

  (f) any requirement of Part 35 of this Act as to the delivery to the registrar of a certified translation into English must be met in relation to any document comprised in the accounts and reports delivered in accordance with paragraph (e).

(3) For the purposes of subsection (1)(b) shares held by a wholly-owned subsidiary of the parent undertaking, or held on behalf of the parent undertaking or a wholly-owned subsidiary, shall be attributed to the parent undertaking.

(4) The exemption does not apply to a company any of whose securities are admitted to trading on a regulated market in an EEA State.

(5) Shares held by directors of a company for the purpose of complying with any share qualification requirement shall be disregarded in determining for the purposes of this section whether the company is a wholly-owned subsidiary.

(6) In subsection (4) "securities" includes –

  (a) shares and stock,
  (b) debentures, including debenture stock, loan stock, bonds, certificates of deposit and other instruments creating or acknowledging indebtedness,
  (c) warrants or other instruments entitling the holder to subscribe for securities falling within paragraph (a) or (b), and

(d) certificates or other instruments that confer –

    (i)   property rights in respect of a security falling within paragraph (a), (b) or (c),

    (ii) any right to acquire, dispose of, underwrite or convert a security, being a right to which the holder would be entitled if he held any such security to which the certificate or other instrument relates, or

    (iii) a contractual right (other than an option) to acquire any such security therwise than by subscription.

401 Exemption for company included in non-EEA group accounts of larger group

(1) A company is exempt from the requirement to prepare group accounts if it is itself a subsidiary undertaking and its parent undertaking is not established under the law of an EEA State, in the following cases –

(a) where the company is a wholly-owned subsidiary of that parent undertaking;

(b) where that parent undertaking holds more than 50% of the allotted shares in the company and notice requesting the preparation of group accounts has not been served on the company by shareholders holding in aggregate –

    (i)   more than half of the remaining allotted shares in the company, or

    (ii) 5% of the total allotted shares in the company.

Such notice must be served not later than six months after the end of the financial year before that to which it relates.

(2) Exemption is conditional upon compliance with all of the following conditions –

(a) the company and all of its subsidiary undertakings must be included in consolidated accounts for a larger group drawn up to the same date, or to an earlier date in the same financial year, by a parent undertaking;

(b) those accounts and, where appropriate, the group's annual report, must be drawn up –

    (i)   in accordance with the provisions of the Seventh Directive (83/349/EEC) (as modified, where relevant, by the provisions of the Bank Accounts Directive (86/635/EEC) or the Insurance Accounts Directive (91/674/EEC)), or

    (ii) in a manner equivalent to consolidated accounts and consolidated annual reports so drawn up;

(c) the group accounts must be audited by one or more persons authorised to audit accounts under the law under which the parent undertaking which draws them up is established;

(d) the company must disclose in its individual accounts that it is exempt from the obligation to prepare and deliver group accounts;

(e) the company must state in its individual accounts the name of the parent undertaking which draws up the group accounts referred to above and –

    (i)   if it is incorporated outside the United Kingdom, the country in which it is incorporated, or

    (ii) if it is unincorporated, the address of its principal place of business;

(f) the company must deliver to the registrar, within the period for filing its accounts and reports for the financial year in question, copies of –

    (i)   the group accounts, and

    (ii) where appropriate, the consolidated annual report, together with the auditor's report on them;

(g) any requirement of Part 35 of this Act as to the delivery to the registrar of a certified translation into English must be met in relation to any document comprised in the accounts and reports delivered in accordance with paragraph (f).

(3) For the purposes of subsection (1)(b), shares held by a wholly-owned subsidiary of the parent undertaking, or held on behalf of the parent undertaking or a wholly-owned subsidiary, are attributed to the parent undertaking.

(4) The exemption does not apply to a company any of whose securities are admitted to trading on a regulated market in an EEA State.

(5) Shares held by directors of a company for the purpose of complying with any share qualification requirement shall be disregarded in determining for the purposes of this section whether the company is a wholly-owned subsidiary.

(6) In subsection (4) "securities" includes –

    (a) shares and stock,

    (b) debentures, including debenture stock, loan stock, bonds, certificates of deposit and other instruments creating or acknowledging indebtedness,

    (c) warrants or other instruments entitling the holder to subscribe for securities falling within paragraph (a) or (b), and

    (d) certificates or other instruments that confer –

        (i) property rights in respect of a security falling within paragraph (a), (b) or (c),

        (ii) any right to acquire, dispose of, underwrite or convert a security, being a right to which the holder would be entitled if he held any such security to which the certificate or other instrument relates, or

        (iii) a contractual right (other than an option) to acquire any such security otherwise than by subscription.

402 Exemption if no subsidiary undertakings need be included in the consolidation

A parent company is exempt from the requirement to prepare group accounts if under section 405 all of its subsidiary undertakings could be excluded from consolidation in Companies Act group accounts.

Group accounts: general

403 Group accounts: applicable accounting framework

(1) The group accounts of certain parent companies are required by Article 4 of the IAS Regulation to be prepared in accordance with international accounting standards ("IAS group accounts").

(2) The group accounts of other companies may be prepared –

    (a) in accordance with section 404 ("Companies Act group accounts"), or

    (b) in accordance with international accounting standards ("IAS group accounts").

This is subject to the following provisions of this section.

(3) The group accounts of a parent company that is a charity must be Companies Act group accounts.

(4) After the first financial year in which the directors of a parent company prepare IAS group accounts ("the first IAS year"), all subsequent group accounts of the company must be prepared in accordance with international accounting standards unless there is a relevant change of circumstance.

(5) There is a relevant change of circumstance if, at any time during or after the first IAS year –

    (a) the company becomes a subsidiary undertaking of another undertaking that does not prepare IAS group accounts,

    (b) the company ceases to be a company with securities admitted to trading on a regulated market in an EEA State, or

    (c) a parent undertaking of the company ceases to be an undertaking with securities admitted to trading on a regulated market in an EEA State.

(6) If, having changed to preparing Companies Act group accounts following a relevant change of circumstance, the directors again prepare IAS group accounts for the

company, subsections (4) and (5) apply again as if the first financial year for which such accounts are again prepared were the first IAS year.

404 Companies Act group accounts

(1) Companies Act group accounts must comprise –

    (a) a consolidated balance sheet dealing with the state of affairs of the parent company and its subsidiary undertakings, and

    (b) a consolidated profit and loss account dealing with the profit or loss of the parent company and its subsidiary undertakings.

(2) The accounts must give a true and fair view of the state of affairs as at the end of the financial year, and the profit or loss for the financial year, of the undertakings included in the consolidation as a whole, so far as concerns members of the company.

(3) The accounts must comply with provision made by the Secretary of State by regulations as to –

    (a) the form and content of the consolidated balance sheet and consolidated profit and loss account, and

    (b) additional information to be provided by way of notes to the accounts.

(4) If compliance with the regulations, and any other provision made by or under this Act as to the matters to be included in a company's group accounts or in notes to those accounts, would not be sufficient to give a true and fair view, the necessary additional information must be given in the accounts or in a note to them.

(5) If in special circumstances compliance with any of those provisions is inconsistent with the requirement to give a true and fair view, the directors must depart from that provision to the extent necessary to give a true and fair view.
Particulars of any such departure, the reasons for it and its effect must be given in a note to the accounts.

405 Companies Act group accounts: subsidiary undertakings included in the consolidation

(1) Where a parent company prepares Companies Act group accounts, all the subsidiary undertakings of the company must be included in the consolidation, subject to the following exceptions.

(2) A subsidiary undertaking may be excluded from consolidation if its inclusion is not material for the purpose of giving a true and fair view (but two or more undertakings may be excluded only if they are not material taken together).

(3) A subsidiary undertaking may be excluded from consolidation where –

    (a) severe long-term restrictions substantially hinder the exercise of the rights of the parent company over the assets or management of that undertaking, or

    (b) the information necessary for the preparation of group accounts cannot be obtained without disproportionate expense or undue delay, or

    (c) the interest of the parent company is held exclusively with a view to subsequent resale.

(4) The reference in subsection (3)(a) to the rights of the parent company and the reference in subsection (3)(c) to the interest of the parent company are, respectively, to rights and interests held by or attributed to the company for the purposes of the definition of "parent undertaking" (see section 1162) in the absence of which it would not be the parent company.

406 IAS group accounts

Where the directors of a company prepare IAS group accounts, they must state in the notes to those accounts that the accounts have been prepared in accordance with international accounting standards.

407 Consistency of financial reporting within group

(1) The directors of a parent company must secure that the individual accounts of –

    (a) the parent company, and

    (b) each of its subsidiary undertakings,

    are all prepared using the same financial reporting framework, except to the extent that in their opinion there are good reasons for not doing so.

(2) Subsection (1) does not apply if the directors do not prepare group accounts for the parent company.

(3) Subsection (1) only applies to accounts of subsidiary undertakings that are required to be prepared under this Part.

(4) Subsection (1) does not require accounts of undertakings that are charities to be prepared using the same financial reporting framework as accounts of undertakings which are not charities.

(5) Subsection (1)(a) does not apply where the directors of a parent company prepare IAS group accounts and IAS individual accounts.

408 Individual profit and loss account where group accounts prepared

(1) This section applies where –

    (a) a company prepares group accounts in accordance with this Act, and

    (b) the notes to the company's individual balance sheet show the company's profit or loss for the financial year determined in accordance with this Act.

(2) The profit and loss account need not contain the information specified in section 411 (information about employee numbers and costs).

(3) The company's individual profit and loss account must be approved in accordance with section 414(1) (approval by directors) but may be omitted from the company's annual accounts for the purposes of the other provisions of the Companies Acts.

(4) The exemption conferred by this section is conditional upon its being disclosed in the company's annual accounts that the exemption applies.

Information to be given in notes to the accounts

409 Information about related undertakings

(1) The Secretary of State may make provision by regulations requiring information about related undertakings to be given in notes to a company's annual accounts.

(2) The regulations –

    (a) may make different provision according to whether or not the company prepares group accounts, and

    (b) may specify the descriptions of undertaking in relation to which they apply, and make different provision in relation to different descriptions of related undertaking.

(3) The regulations may provide that information need not be disclosed with respect to an undertaking that –

    (a) is established under the law of a country outside the United Kingdom, or

    (b) carries on business outside the United Kingdom,

    if the following conditions are met.

(4) The conditions are –

    (a) that in the opinion of the directors of the company the disclosure would be seriously prejudicial to the business of –

        (i) that undertaking,

        (ii) the company,

(iii) any of the company's subsidiary undertakings, or

(iv) any other undertaking which is included in the consolidation;

(b) that the Secretary of State agrees that the information need not be disclosed.

(5) Where advantage is taken of any such exemption, that fact must be stated in a note to the company's annual accounts.

410 Information about related undertakings: alternative compliance

(1) This section applies where the directors of a company are of the opinion that the number of undertakings in respect of which the company is required to disclose information under any provision of regulations under section 409 (related undertakings) is such that compliance with that provision would result in information of excessive length being given in notes to the company's annual accounts.

(2) The information need only be given in respect of –

(a) the undertakings whose results or financial position, in the opinion of the directors, principally affected the figures shown in the company's annual accounts, and

(b) where the company prepares group accounts, undertakings excluded from consolidation under section 405(3) (undertakings excluded on grounds other than materiality).

(3) If advantage is taken of subsection (2) –

(a) there must be included in the notes to the company's annual accounts a statement that the information is given only with respect to such undertakings as are mentioned in that subsection, and

(b) the full information (both that which is disclosed in the notes to the accounts and that which is not) must be annexed to the company's next annual return.

For this purpose the "next annual return" means that next delivered to the registrar after the accounts in question have been approved under section 414.

(4) If a company fails to comply with subsection (3)(b), an offence is committed by –

(a) the company, and

(b) every officer of the company who is in default.

(5) A person guilty of an offence under subsection (4) is liable on summary conviction to a fine not exceeding level 3 on the standard scale and, for continued contravention, a daily default fine not exceeding one-tenth of level 3 on the standard scale.

411 Information about employee numbers and costs

(1) In the case of a company not subject to the small companies regime, the following information with respect to the employees of the company must be given in notes to the company's annual accounts –

(a) the average number of persons employed by the company in the financial year, and

(b) the average number of persons so employed within each category of persons employed by the company.

(2) The categories by reference to which the number required to be disclosed by subsection (1)(b) is to be determined must be such as the directors may select having regard to the manner in which the company's activities are organised.

(3) The average number required by subsection (1)(a) or (b) is determined by dividing the relevant annual number by the number of months in the financial year.

(4) The relevant annual number is determined by ascertaining for each month in the financial year –

(a) for the purposes of subsection (1)(a), the number of persons employed under contracts of service by the company in that month (whether throughout the month or not);

(b) for the purposes of subsection (1)(b), the number of persons in the category in question of persons so employed;

and adding together all the monthly numbers.

(5) In respect of all persons employed by the company during the financial year who are taken into account in determining the relevant annual number for the purposes of subsection (1)(a) there must also be stated the aggregate amounts respectively of –

(a) wages and salaries paid or payable in respect of that year to those persons;

(b) social security costs incurred by the company on their behalf; and

(c) other pension costs so incurred.

This does not apply in so far as those amounts, or any of them, are stated elsewhere in the company's accounts.

(6) In subsection (5) –

"pension costs" includes any costs incurred by the company in respect of –

(a) any pension scheme established for the purpose of providing pensions for persons currently or formerly employed by the company,

(b) any sums set aside for the future payment of pensions directly by the company to current or former employees, and

(c) any pensions paid directly to such persons without having first been set aside;

"social security costs" means any contributions by the company to any state social security or pension scheme, fund or arrangement.

(7) Where the company prepares group accounts, this section applies as if the undertakings included in the consolidation were a single company.

412 Information about directors' benefits: remuneration

(1) The Secretary of State may make provision by regulations requiring information to be given in notes to a company's annual accounts about directors' remuneration.

(2) The matters about which information may be required include –

(a) gains made by directors on the exercise of share options;

(b) benefits received or receivable by directors under long-term incentive schemes;

(c) payments for loss of office (as defined in section 215);

(d) benefits receivable, and contributions for the purpose of providing benefits, in respect of past services of a person as director or in any other capacity while director;

(e) consideration paid to or receivable by third parties for making available the services of a person as director or in any other capacity while director.

(3) Without prejudice to the generality of subsection (1), regulations under this section may make any such provision as was made immediately before the commencement of this Part by Part 1 of Schedule 6 to the Companies Act 1985 (c. 6).

(4) For the purposes of this section, and regulations made under it, amounts paid to or receivable by –

(a) a person connected with a director, or

(b) a body corporate controlled by a director,

are treated as paid to or receivable by the director.

The expressions "connected with" and "controlled by" in this subsection have the same meaning as in Part 10 (company directors).

(5) It is the duty of –

(a) any director of a company, and

(b) any person who is or has at any time in the preceding five years been a director of the company,

to give notice to the company of such matters relating to himself as may be necessary for the purposes of regulations under this section.

(6) A person who makes default in complying with subsection (5) commits an offence and is liable on summary conviction to a fine not exceeding level 3 on the standard scale.

413 Information about directors' benefits: advances, credit and guarantees

(1) In the case of a company that does not prepare group accounts, details of –

    (a)   advances and credits granted by the company to its directors, and
    (b)   guarantees of any kind entered into by the company on behalf of its directors,

    must be shown in the notes to its individual accounts.

(2) In the case of a parent company that prepares group accounts, details of –

    (a)   advances and credits granted to the directors of the parent company, by that company or by any of its subsidiary undertakings, and
    (b)   guarantees of any kind entered into on behalf of the directors of the parent company, by that company or by any of its subsidiary undertakings,

    must be shown in the notes to the group accounts.

(3) The details required of an advance or credit are –

    (a)   its amount,
    (b)   an indication of the interest rate,
    (c)   its main conditions, and
    (d)   any amounts repaid.

(4) The details required of a guarantee are –

    (a)   its main terms,
    (b)   the amount of the maximum liability that may be incurred by the company (or its subsidiary), and
    (c)   any amount paid and any liability incurred by the company (or its subsidiary) for the purpose of fulfilling the guarantee (including any loss incurred by reason of enforcement of the guarantee).

(5) There must also be stated in the notes to the accounts the totals –

    (a)   of amounts stated under subsection (3)(a),
    (b)   of amounts stated under subsection (3)(d),
    (c)   of amounts stated under subsection (4)(b), and
    (d)   of amounts stated under subsection (4)(c).

(6) References in this section to the directors of a company are to the persons who were a director at any time in the financial year to which the accounts relate.

(7) The requirements of this section apply in relation to every advance, credit or guarantee subsisting at any time in the financial year to which the accounts relate –

    (a)   whenever it was entered into,
    (b)   whether or not the person concerned was a director of the company in question at the time it was entered into, and
    (c)   in the case of an advance, credit or guarantee involving a subsidiary undertaking of that company, whether or not that undertaking was such a subsidiary undertaking at the time it was entered into.

(8) Banking companies and the holding companies of credit institutions need only state the details required by subsections (3)(a) and (4)(b).

Approval and signing of accounts

414 Approval and signing of accounts

(1) A company's annual accounts must be approved by the board of directors and signed on behalf of the board by a director of the company.

(2) The signature must be on the company's balance sheet.

(3) If the accounts are prepared in accordance with the provisions applicable to companies subject to the small companies regime, the balance sheet must contain a statement to that effect in a prominent position above the signature.

(4) If annual accounts are approved that do not comply with the requirements of this Act (and, where applicable, of Article 4 of the IAS Regulation), every director of the company who –

    (a) knew that they did not comply, or was reckless as to whether they complied, and

    (b) failed to take reasonable steps to secure compliance with those requirements or, as the case may be, to prevent the accounts from being approved,

commits an offence.

(5) A person guilty of an offence under this section is liable –

    (a) on conviction on indictment, to a fine;

    (b) on summary conviction, to a fine not exceeding the statutory maximum.

CHAPTER 5

DIRECTORS' REPORT

Directors' report

415 Duty to prepare directors' report

(1) The directors of a company must prepare a directors' report for each financial year of the company.

(2) For a financial year in which –

    (a) the company is a parent company, and

    (b) the directors of the company prepare group accounts,

the directors' report must be a consolidated report (a "group directors' report") relating to the undertakings included in the consolidation.

(3) A group directors' report may, where appropriate, give greater emphasis to the matters that are significant to the undertakings included in the consolidation, taken as a whole.

(4) In the case of failure to comply with the requirement to prepare a directors' report, an offence is committed by every person who –

    (a) was a director of the company immediately before the end of the period for filing accounts and reports for the financial year in question, and

    (b) failed to take all reasonable steps for securing compliance with that requirement.

(5) A person guilty of an offence under this section is liable –

    (a) on conviction on indictment, to a fine;

    (b) on summary conviction, to a fine not exceeding the statutory maximum.

416 Contents of directors' report: general

(1) The directors' report for a financial year must state –

    (a) the names of the persons who, at any time during the financial year, were directors of the company, and

    (b) the principal activities of the company in the course of the year.

(2) In relation to a group directors' report subsection (1)(b) has effect as if the reference to the company was to the undertakings included in the consolidation.

(3) Except in the case of a company subject to the small companies regime, the report must state the amount (if any) that the directors recommend should be paid by way of dividend.

(4) The Secretary of State may make provision by regulations as to other matters that must be disclosed in a directors' report.

Without prejudice to the generality of this power, the regulations may make any such provision as was formerly made by Schedule 7 to the Companies Act 1985.

417 Contents of directors' report: business review

(1) Unless the company is subject to the small companies' regime, the directors' report must contain a business review.

(2) The purpose of the business review is to inform members of the company and help them assess how the directors have performed their duty under section 172 (duty to promote the success of the company).

(3) The business review must contain –

(a) a fair review of the company's business, and

(b) a description of the principal risks and uncertainties facing the company.

(4) The review required is a balanced and comprehensive analysis of –

(a) the development and performance of the company's business during the financial year, and

(b) the position of the company's business at the end of that year,

consistent with the size and complexity of the business.

(5) In the case of a quoted company the business review must, to the extent necessary for an understanding of the development, performance or position of the company's business, include –

(a) the main trends and factors likely to affect the future development, performance and position of the company's business; and

(b) information about –

(i) environmental matters (including the impact of the company's business on the environment),

(ii) the company's employees, and

(iii) social and community issues,

including information about any policies of the company in relation to those matters and the effectiveness of those policies; and

(c) subject to subsection (11), information about persons with whom the company has contractual or other arrangements which are essential to the business of the company.

If the review does not contain information of each kind mentioned in paragraphs (b)(i), (ii) and (iii) and (c), it must state which of those kinds of information it does not contain.

(6) The review must, to the extent necessary for an understanding of the development, performance or position of the company's business, include –

(a) analysis using financial key performance indicators, and

(b) where appropriate, analysis using other key performance indicators, including information relating to environmental matters and employee matters.

"Key performance indicators" means factors by reference to which the development, performance or position of the company's business can be measured effectively.

(7) Where a company qualifies as medium-sized in relation to a financial year (see sections 465 to 467), the directors' report for the year need not comply with the requirements of subsection (6) so far as they relate to non-financial information.

(8) The review must, where appropriate, include references to, and additional explanations of, amounts included in the company's annual accounts.

(9) In relation to a group directors' report this section has effect as if the references to the company were references to the undertakings included in the consolidation.

(10) Nothing in this section requires the disclosure of information about impending developments or matters in the course of negotiation if the disclosure would, in the opinion of the directors, be seriously prejudicial to the interests of the company.

(11) Nothing in subsection (5)(c) requires the disclosure of information about a person if the disclosure would, in the opinion of the directors, be seriously prejudicial to that person and contrary to the public interest.

418 Contents of directors' report: statement as to disclosure to auditors

(1) This section applies to a company unless –

    (a) it is exempt for the financial year in question from the requirements of Part 16 as to audit of accounts, and

    (b) the directors take advantage of that exemption.

(2) The directors' report must contain a statement to the effect that, in the case of each of the persons who are directors at the time the report is approved –

    (a) so far as the director is aware, there is no relevant audit information of which the company's auditor is unaware, and

    (b) he has taken all the steps that he ought to have taken as a director in order to make himself aware of any relevant audit information and to establish that the company's auditor is aware of that information.

(3) "Relevant audit information" means information needed by the company's auditor in connection with preparing his report.

(4) A director is regarded as having taken all the steps that he ought to have taken as a director in order to do the things mentioned in subsection (2)(b) if he has –

    (a) made such enquiries of his fellow directors and of the company's auditors for that purpose, and

    (b) taken such other steps (if any) for that purpose,

as are required by his duty as a director of the company to exercise reasonable care, skill and diligence.

(5) Where a directors' report containing the statement required by this section is approved but the statement is false, every director of the company who –

    (a) knew that the statement was false, or was reckless as to whether it was false, and

    (b) failed to take reasonable steps to prevent the report from being approved,

commits an offence.

(6) A person guilty of an offence under subsection (5) is liable –

    (a) on conviction on indictment, to imprisonment for a term not exceeding two years or a fine (or both);

    (b) on summary conviction –

        (i) in England and Wales, to imprisonment for a term not exceeding twelve months or to a fine not exceeding the statutory maximum (or both);

        (ii) in Scotland or Northern Ireland, to imprisonment for a term not exceeding six months, or to a fine not exceeding the statutory maximum (or both).

419 Approval and signing of directors' report

(1) The directors' report must be approved by the board of directors and signed on behalf of the board by a director or the secretary of the company.

(2) If the report is prepared in accordance with the small companies regime, it must contain a statement to that effect in a prominent position above the signature.

(3) If a directors' report is approved that does not comply with the requirements of this Act, every director of the company who –

    (a) knew that it did not comply, or was reckless as to whether it complied, and

    (b) failed to take reasonable steps to secure compliance with those requirements or, as the case may be, to prevent the report from being approved,

commits an offence.

(4) A person guilty of an offence under this section is liable –

    (a) on conviction on indictment, to a fine;

    (b) on summary conviction, to a fine not exceeding the statutory maximum.

CHAPTER 6

QUOTED COMPANIES: DIRECTORS' REMUNERATION REPORT

420 Duty to prepare directors' remuneration report

(1) The directors of a quoted company must prepare a directors' remuneration report for each financial year of the company.

(2) In the case of failure to comply with the requirement to prepare a directors' remuneration report, every person who –

    (a) was a director of the company immediately before the end of the period for filing accounts and reports for the financial year in question, and

    (b) failed to take all reasonable steps for securing compliance with that requirement,

commits an offence.

(3) A person guilty of an offence under this section is liable –

    (a) on conviction on indictment, to a fine;

    (b) on summary conviction, to a fine not exceeding the statutory maximum.

421 Contents of directors' remuneration report

(1) The Secretary of State may make provision by regulations as to –

    (a) the information that must be contained in a directors' remuneration report,

    (b) how information is to be set out in the report, and

    (c) what is to be the auditable part of the report.

(2) Without prejudice to the generality of this power, the regulations may make any such provision as was made, immediately before the commencement of this Part, by Schedule 7A to the Companies Act 1985 (c. 6).

(3) It is the duty of –

    (a) any director of a company, and

    (b) any person who is or has at any time in the preceding five years been a director of the company,

to give notice to the company of such matters relating to himself as may be necessary for the purposes of regulations under this section.

(4) A person who makes default in complying with subsection (3) commits an offence and is liable on summary conviction to a fine not exceeding level 3 on the standard scale.

422 Approval and signing of directors' remuneration report

(1) The directors' remuneration report must be approved by the board of directors and signed on behalf of the board by a director or the secretary of the company.

(2) If a directors' remuneration report is approved that does not comply with the requirements of this Act, every director of the company who –

    (a) knew that it did not comply, or was reckless as to whether it complied, and

    (b) failed to take reasonable steps to secure compliance with those requirements or, as the case may be, to prevent the report from being approved,

commits an offence.

(3) A person guilty of an offence under this section is liable –

    (a) on conviction on indictment, to a fine;

    (b) on summary conviction, to a fine not exceeding the statutory maximum.

CHAPTER 7

PUBLICATION OF ACCOUNTS AND REPORTS

Duty to circulate copies of accounts and reports

423 Duty to circulate copies of annual accounts and reports

(1) Every company must send a copy of its annual accounts and reports for each financial year to –

    (a) every member of the company,

    (b) every holder of the company's debentures, and

    (c) every person who is entitled to receive notice of general meetings.

(2) Copies need not be sent to a person for whom the company does not have a current address.

(3) A company has a "current address" for a person if –

    (a) an address has been notified to the company by the person as one at which documents may be sent to him, and

    (b) the company has no reason to believe that documents sent to him at that address will not reach him.

(4) In the case of a company not having a share capital, copies need not be sent to anyone who is not entitled to receive notices of general meetings of the company.

(5) Where copies are sent out over a period of days, references in the Companies Acts to the day on which copies are sent out shall be read as references to the last day of that period.

(6) This section has effect subject to section 426 (option to provide summary financial statement).

424 Time allowed for sending out copies of accounts and reports

(1) The time allowed for sending out copies of the company's annual accounts and reports is as follows.

(2) A private company must comply with section 423 not later than –

    (a) the end of the period for filing accounts and reports, or

    (b) if earlier, the date on which it actually delivers its accounts and reports to the registrar.

(3) A public company must comply with section 423 at least 21 days before the date of the relevant accounts meeting.

(4) If in the case of a public company copies are sent out later than is required by subsection (3), they shall, despite that, be deemed to have been duly sent if it is so agreed by all the members entitled to attend and vote at the relevant accounts meeting.

(5) Whether the time allowed is that for a private company or a public company is determined by reference to the company's status immediately before the end of the accounting reference period by reference to which the financial year for the accounts in question was determined.

(6) In this section the "relevant accounts meeting" means the accounts meeting of the company at which the accounts and reports in question are to be laid.

425 Default in sending out copies of accounts and reports: offences

(1) If default is made in complying with section 423 or 424, an offence is committed by –

    (a) the company, and

    (b) every officer of the company who is in default.

(2) A person guilty of an offence under this section is liable –

  (a) on conviction on indictment, to a fine;
  (b) on summary conviction, to a fine not exceeding the statutory maximum.

Option to provide summary financial statement

426 Option to provide summary financial statement

(1) A company may –

  (a) in such cases as may be specified by regulations made by the Secretary of State, and
  (b) provided any conditions so specified are complied with,

  provide a summary financial statement instead of copies of the accounts and reports required to be sent out in accordance with section 423.
(2) Copies of those accounts and reports must, however, be sent to any person entitled to be sent them in accordance with that section and who wishes to receive them.
(3) The Secretary of State may make provision by regulations as to the manner in which it is to be ascertained, whether before or after a person becomes entitled to be sent a copy of those accounts and reports, whether he wishes to receive them.
(4) A summary financial statement must comply with the requirements of –

  section 427 (form and contents of summary financial statement: unquoted companies), or
  section 428 (form and contents of summary financial statement: quoted companies).

(5) This section applies to copies of accounts and reports required to be sent out by virtue of section 146 to a person nominated to enjoy information rights as it applies to copies of accounts and reports required to be sent out in accordance with section 423 to a member of the company.
(6) Regulations under this section are subject to negative resolution procedure.

427 Form and contents of summary financial statement: unquoted companies

(1) A summary financial statement by a company that is not a quoted company must –

  (a) be derived from the company's annual accounts, and
  (b) be prepared in accordance with this section and regulations made under it.

(2) The summary financial statement must be in such form, and contain such information, as the Secretary of State may specify by regulations.
  The regulations may require the statement to include information derived from the directors' report.
(3) Nothing in this section or regulations made under it prevents a company from including in a summary financial statement additional information derived from the company's annual accounts or the directors' report.
(4) The summary financial statement must –

  (a) state that it is only a summary of information derived from the company's annual accounts;
  (b) state whether it contains additional information derived from the directors' report and, if so, that it does not contain the full text of that report;
  (c) state how a person entitled to them can obtain a full copy of the company's annual accounts and the directors' report;
  (d) contain a statement by the company's auditor of his opinion as to whether the summary financial statement –

    (i)   is consistent with the company's annual accounts and, where information derived from the directors' report is included in the statement, with that report, and

      (ii)   complies with the requirements of this section and regulations made under it;

(e)   state whether the auditor's report on the annual accounts was unqualified or qualified and, if it was qualified, set out the report in full together with any further material needed to understand the qualification;

(f)   state whether, in that report, the auditor's statement under section 496 (whether directors' report consistent with accounts) was qualified or unqualified and, if it was qualified, set out the qualified statement in full together with any further material needed to understand the qualification;

(g) state whether that auditor's report contained a statement under –

      (i)   section 498(2)(a) or (b) (accounting records or returns inadequate or accounts not agreeing with records and returns), or

      (ii)   section 498(3) (failure to obtain necessary information and explanations),

  and if so, set out the statement in full.

(5) Regulations under this section may provide that any specified material may, instead of being included in the summary financial statement, be sent separately at the same time as the statement.

(6) Regulations under this section are subject to negative resolution procedure.

428 Form and contents of summary financial statement: quoted companies

(1) A summary financial statement by a quoted company must –

(a) be derived from the company's annual accounts and the directors' remuneration report, and

(b) be prepared in accordance with this section and regulations made under it.

(2) The summary financial statement must be in such form, and contain such information, as the Secretary of State may specify by regulations.

The regulations may require the statement to include information derived from the directors' report.

(3) Nothing in this section or regulations made under it prevents a company from including in a summary financial statement additional information derived from the company's annual accounts, the directors' remuneration report or the directors' report.

(4) The summary financial statement must –

(a) state that it is only a summary of information derived from the company's annual accounts and the directors' remuneration report;

(b) state whether it contains additional information derived from the directors' report and, if so, that it does not contain the full text of that report;

(c) state how a person entitled to them can obtain a full copy of the company's annual accounts, the directors' remuneration report or the directors' report;

(d) contain a statement by the company's auditor of his opinion as to whether the summary financial statement –

      (i)   is consistent with the company's annual accounts and the directors' remuneration report and, where information derived from the directors' report is included in the statement, with that report, and

      (ii)   complies with the requirements of this section and regulations made under it;

(e) state whether the auditor's report on the annual accounts and the auditable part of the directors' remuneration report was unqualified or qualified and, if it was qualified, set out the report in full together with any further material needed to understand the qualification;

(f)   state whether that auditor's report contained a statement under –

> (i)   section 498(2) (accounting records or returns inadequate or accounts or directors' remuneration report not agreeing with records and returns), or
>
> (ii) section 498(3) (failure to obtain necessary information and explanations), and if so, set out the statement in full;
>
> (g) state whether, in that report, the auditor's statement under section 496 (whether directors' report consistent with accounts) was qualified or unqualified and, if it was qualified, set out the qualified statement in full together with any further material needed to understand the qualification.

(5) Regulations under this section may provide that any specified material may, instead of being included in the summary financial statement, be sent separately at the same time as the statement.

(6) Regulations under this section are subject to negative resolution procedure.

429 Summary financial statements: offences

(1) If default is made in complying with any provision of section 426, 427 or 428, or of regulations under any of those sections, an offence is committed by –

>   (a) the company, and
>   (b) every officer of the company who is in default.

(2) A person guilty of an offence under this section is liable on summary conviction to a fine not exceeding level 3 on the standard scale.

Quoted companies: requirements as to website publication

430 Quoted companies: annual accounts and reports to be made available on website

(1) A quoted company must ensure that its annual accounts and reports –

>   (a) are made available on a website, and
>   (b) remain so available until the annual accounts and reports for the company's next financial year are made available in accordance with this section.

(2) The annual accounts and reports must be made available on a website that –

>   (a) is maintained by or on behalf of the company, and
>   (b) identifies the company in question.

(3) Access to the annual accounts and reports on the website, and the ability to obtain a hard copy of the annual accounts and reports from the website, must not be –

>   (a) conditional on the payment of a fee, or
>   (b) otherwise restricted, except so far as necessary to comply with any enactment or regulatory requirement (in the United Kingdom or elsewhere).

(4) The annual accounts and reports –

>   (a) must be made available as soon as reasonably practicable, and
>   (b) must be kept available throughout the period specified in subsection (1)(b).

(5) A failure to make the annual accounts and reports available on a website throughout that period is disregarded if –

>   (a) the annual accounts and reports are made available on the website for part of that period, and
>   (b) the failure is wholly attributable to circumstances that it would not be reasonable to have expected the company to prevent or avoid.

(6) In the event of default in complying with this section, an offence is committed by every officer of the company who is in default.

(7) A person guilty of an offence under subsection (6) is liable on summary conviction to a fine not exceeding level 3 on the standard scale.

Right of member or debenture holder to demand copies of accounts and reports

431 Right of member or debenture holder to copies of accounts and reports: unquoted companies

(1) A member of, or holder of debentures of, an unquoted company is entitled to be provided, on demand and without charge, with a copy of –

    (a) the company's last annual accounts,

    (b) the last directors' report, and

    (c) the auditor's report on those accounts (including the statement on that report).

(2) The entitlement under this section is to a single copy of those documents, but that is in addition to any copy to which a person may be entitled under section 423.

(3) If a demand made under this section is not complied with within seven days of receipt by the company, an offence is committed by –

    (a) the company, and

    (b) every officer of the company who is in default.

(4) A person guilty of an offence under this section is liable on summary conviction to a fine not exceeding level 3 on the standard scale and, for continued contravention, a daily default fine not exceeding one-tenth of level 3 on the standard scale.

432 Right of member or debenture holder to copies of accounts and reports: quoted companies

(1) A member of, or holder of debentures of, a quoted company is entitled to be provided, on demand and without charge, with a copy of –

    (a) the company's last annual accounts,

    (b) the last directors' remuneration report,

    (c) the last directors' report, and

    (d) the auditor's report on those accounts (including the report on the directors' remuneration report and on the directors' report).

(2) The entitlement under this section is to a single copy of those documents, but that is in addition to any copy to which a person may be entitled under section 423.

(3) If a demand made under this section is not complied with within seven days of receipt by the company, an offence is committed by –

    (a) the company, and

    (b) every officer of the company who is in default.

(4) A person guilty of an offence under this section is liable on summary conviction to a fine not exceeding level 3 on the standard scale and, for continued contravention, a daily default fine not exceeding one-tenth of level 3 on the standard scale.

Requirements in connection with publication of accounts and reports

433 Name of signatory to be stated in published copies of accounts and reports

(1) Every copy of a document to which this section applies that is published by or on behalf of the company must state the name of the person who signed it on behalf of the board.

(2) In the case of an unquoted company, this section applies to copies of –

    (a) the company's balance sheet, and

    (b) the directors' report.

(3) In the case of a quoted company, this section applies to copies of –

     (a)   the company's balance sheet,

     (b)   the directors' remuneration report, and

     (c)   the directors' report.

(4)   If a copy is published without the required statement of the signatory's name, an offence is committed by –

     (a)   the company, and

     (b)   every officer of the company who is in default.

(5)   A person guilty of an offence under this section is liable on summary conviction to a fine not exceeding level 3 on the standard scale.

434 Requirements in connection with publication of statutory accounts

(1)   If a company publishes any of its statutory accounts, they must be accompanied by the auditor's report on those accounts (unless the company is exempt from audit and the directors have taken advantage of that exemption).

(2)   A company that prepares statutory group accounts for a financial year must not publish its statutory individual accounts for that year without also publishing with them its statutory group accounts.

(3)   A company's "statutory accounts" are its accounts for a financial year as required to be delivered to the registrar under section 441.

(4)   If a company contravenes any provision of this section, an offence is committed by –

     (a)   the company, and

     (b)   every officer of the company who is in default.

(5)   A person guilty of an offence under this section is liable on summary conviction to a fine not exceeding level 3 on the standard scale.

(6)   This section does not apply in relation to the provision by a company of a summary financial statement (see section 426).

435 Requirements in connection with publication of non-statutory accounts

(1)   If a company publishes non-statutory accounts, it must publish with them a statement indicating –

     (a)   that they are not the company's statutory accounts,

     (b)   whether statutory accounts dealing with any financial year with which the non-statutory accounts purport to deal have been delivered to the registrar, and

     (c)   whether an auditor's report has been made on the company's statutory accounts for any such financial year, and if so whether the report –

          (i)   was qualified or unqualified, or included a reference to any matters to which the auditor drew attention by way of emphasis without qualifying the report, or

          (ii)   contained a statement under section 498(2) (accounting records or returns inadequate or accounts or directors' remuneration report not agreeing with records and returns), or section 498(3) (failure to obtain necessary information and explanations).

(2)   The company must not publish with non-statutory accounts the auditor's report on the company's statutory accounts.

(3)   References in this section to the publication by a company of "non-statutory accounts" are to the publication of –

     (a)   any balance sheet or profit and loss account relating to, or purporting to deal with, a financial year of the company, or

     (b)   an account in any form purporting to be a balance sheet or profit and loss account for a group headed by the company relating to, or purporting to deal with, a financial year of the company, otherwise than as part of the company's statutory accounts.

(4) In subsection (3)(b) "a group headed by the company" means a group consisting of the company and any other undertaking (regardless of whether it is a subsidiary undertaking of the company) other than a parent undertaking of the company.

(5) If a company contravenes any provision of this section, an offence is committed by –

(a) the company, and

(b) every officer of the company who is in default.

(6) A person guilty of an offence under this section is liable on summary conviction to a fine not exceeding level 3 on the standard scale.

(7) This section does not apply in relation to the provision by a company of a summary financial statement (see section 426).

436 Meaning of "publication" in relation to accounts and reports

(1) This section has effect for the purposes of –

section 433 (name of signatory to be stated in published copies of accounts and reports),

section 434 (requirements in connection with publication of statutory accounts), and

section 435 (requirements in connection with publication of non-statutory accounts).

(2) For the purposes of those sections a company is regarded as publishing a document if it publishes, issues or circulates it or otherwise makes it available for public inspection in a manner calculated to invite members of the public generally, or any class of members of the public, to read it.

CHAPTER 8

PUBLIC COMPANIES: LAYING OF ACCOUNTS AND REPORTS BEFORE GENERAL MEETING

437 Public companies: laying of accounts and reports before general meeting

(1) The directors of a public company must lay before the company in general meeting copies of its annual accounts and reports.

(2) This section must be complied with not later than the end of the period for filing the accounts and reports in question.

(3) In the Companies Acts "accounts meeting", in relation to a public company, means a general meeting of the company at which the company's annual accounts and reports are (or are to be) laid in accordance with this section.

438 Public companies: offence of failure to lay accounts and reports

(1) If the requirements of section 437 (public companies: laying of accounts and reports before general meeting) are not complied with before the end of the period allowed, every person who immediately before the end of that period was a director of the company commits an offence.

(2) It is a defence for a person charged with such an offence to prove that he took all reasonable steps for securing that those requirements would be complied with before the end of that period.

(3) It is not a defence to prove that the documents in question were not in fact prepared as required by this Part.

(4) A person guilty of an offence under this section is liable on summary conviction to a fine not exceeding level 5 on the standard scale and, for continued contravention, a daily default fine not exceeding one-tenth of level 5 on the standard scale.

CHAPTER 9

QUOTED COMPANIES: MEMBERS' APPROVAL OF DIRECTORS' REMUNERATION REPORT

439 Quoted companies: members' approval of directors' remuneration report

(1) A quoted company must, prior to the accounts meeting, give to the members of the company entitled to be sent notice of the meeting notice of the intention to move at the meeting, as an ordinary resolution, a resolution approving the directors' remuneration report for the financial year.

(2) The notice may be given in any manner permitted for the service on the member of notice of the meeting.

(3) The business that may be dealt with at the accounts meeting includes the resolution. This is so notwithstanding any default in complying with subsection (1) or (2).

(4) The existing directors must ensure that the resolution is put to the vote of the meeting.

(5) No entitlement of a person to remuneration is made conditional on the resolution being passed by reason only of the provision made by this section.

(6) In this section –

"the accounts meeting" means the general meeting of the company before which the company's annual accounts for the financial year are to be laid; and

"existing director" means a person who is a director of the company immediately before that meeting.

440 Quoted companies: offences in connection with procedure for approval

(1) In the event of default in complying with section 439(1) (notice to be given of resolution for approval of directors' remuneration report), an offence is committed by every officer of the company who is in default.

(2) If the resolution is not put to the vote of the accounts meeting, an offence is committed by each existing director.

(3) It is a defence for a person charged with an offence under subsection (2) to prove that he took all reasonable steps for securing that the resolution was put to the vote of the meeting.

(4) A person guilty of an offence under this section is liable on summary conviction to a fine not exceeding level 3 on the standard scale.

(5) In this section –

"the accounts meeting" means the general meeting of the company before which the company's annual accounts for the financial year are to be laid; and

"existing director" means a person who is a director of the company immediately before that meeting.

CHAPTER 10

FILING OF ACCOUNTS AND REPORTS

Duty to file accounts and reports

441 Duty to file accounts and reports with the registrar

(1) The directors of a company must deliver to the registrar for each financial year the accounts and reports required by –

section 444 (filing obligations of companies subject to small companies regime),

section 445 (filing obligations of medium-sized companies),
section 446 (filing obligations of unquoted companies), or
section 447 (filing obligations of quoted companies).

(2) This is subject to section 448 (unlimited companies exempt from filing obligations).

442 Period allowed for filing accounts

(1) This section specifies the period allowed for the directors of a company to comply with their obligation under section 441 to deliver accounts and reports for a financial year to the registrar.

This is referred to in the Companies Acts as the "period for filing" those accounts and reports.

(2) The period is –

    (a) for a private company, nine months after the end of the relevant accounting reference period, and

    (b) for a public company, six months after the end of that period.

This is subject to the following provisions of this section.

(3) If the relevant accounting reference period is the company's first and is a period of more than twelve months, the period is –

    (a) nine months or six months, as the case may be, from the first anniversary of the incorporation of the company, or

    (b) three months after the end of the accounting reference period,

whichever last expires.

(4) If the relevant accounting reference period is treated as shortened by virtue of a notice given by the company under section 392 (alteration of accounting reference date), the period is –

    (a) that applicable in accordance with the above provisions, or

    (b) three months from the date of the notice under that section,

whichever last expires.

(5) If for any special reason the Secretary of State thinks fit he may, on an application made before the expiry of the period otherwise allowed, by notice in writing to a company extend that period by such further period as may be specified in the notice.

(6) Whether the period allowed is that for a private company or a public company is determined by reference to the company's status immediately before the end of the relevant accounting reference period.

(7) In this section "the relevant accounting reference period" means the accounting reference period by reference to which the financial year for the accounts in question was determined.

443 Calculation of period allowed

(1) This section applies for the purposes of calculating the period for filing a company's accounts and reports which is expressed as a specified number of months from a specified date or after the end of a specified previous period.

(2) Subject to the following provisions, the period ends with the date in the appropriate month corresponding to the specified date or the last day of the specified previous period.

(3) If the specified date, or the last day of the specified previous period, is the last day of a month, the period ends with the last day of the appropriate month (whether or not that is the corresponding date).

(4) If –

    (a) the specified date, or the last day of the specified previous period, is not the last day of a month but is the 29th or 30th, and

    (b) the appropriate month is February,

the period ends with the last day of February.

(5) "The appropriate month" means the month that is the specified number of months after the month in which the specified date, or the end of the specified previous period, falls.

Filing obligations of different descriptions of company

444 Filing obligations of companies subject to small companies regime

(1) The directors of a company subject to the small companies regime –

    (a) must deliver to the registrar for each financial year a copy of a balance sheet drawn up as at the last day of that year, and

    (b) may also deliver to the registrar –

        (i)   a copy of the company's profit and loss account for that year, and

        (ii) a copy of the directors' report for that year.

(2) The directors must also deliver to the registrar a copy of the auditor's report on those accounts (and on the directors' report).
This does not apply if the company is exempt from audit and the directors have taken advantage of that exemption.

(3) The copies of accounts and reports delivered to the registrar must be copies of the company's annual accounts and reports, except that where the company prepares Companies Act accounts –

    (a) the directors may deliver to the registrar a copy of a balance sheet drawn up in accordance with regulations made by the Secretary of State, and

    (b) there may be omitted from the copy profit and loss account delivered to the registrar such items as may be specified by the regulations.

These are referred to in this Part as "abbreviated accounts".

(4) If abbreviated accounts are delivered to the registrar the obligation to deliver a copy of the auditor's report on the accounts is to deliver a copy of the special auditor's report required by section 449.

(5) Where the directors of a company subject to the small companies regime deliver to the registrar IAS accounts, or Companies Act accounts that are not abbreviated accounts, and in accordance with this section –

    (a) do not deliver to the registrar a copy of the company's profit and loss account, or

    (b) do not deliver to the registrar a copy of the directors' report,

the copy of the balance sheet delivered to the registrar must contain in a prominent position a statement that the company's annual accounts and reports have been delivered in accordance with the provisions applicable to companies subject to the small companies regime.

(6) The copies of the balance sheet and any directors' report delivered to the registrar under this section must state the name of the person who signed it on behalf of the board.

(7) The copy of the auditor's report delivered to the registrar under this section must –

    (a) state the name of the auditor and (where the auditor is a firm) the name of the person who signed it as senior statutory auditor, or

    (b) if the conditions in section 506 (circumstances in which names may be omitted) are met, state that a resolution has been passed and notified to the Secretary of State in accordance with that section.

445 Filing obligations of medium-sized companies

(1) The directors of a company that qualifies as a medium-sized company in relation to a financial year (see sections 465 to 467) must deliver to the registrar a copy of –

(a)   the company's annual accounts, and

(b)   the directors' report.

(2)   They must also deliver to the registrar a copy of the auditor's report on those accounts (and on the directors' report).
This does not apply if the company is exempt from audit and the directors have taken advantage of that exemption.

(3)   Where the company prepares Companies Act accounts, the directors may deliver to the registrar a copy of the company's annual accounts for the financial year –

(a)   that includes a profit and loss account in which items are combined in accordance with regulations made by the Secretary of State, and

(b)   that does not contain items whose omission is authorised by the regulations.

These are referred to in this Part as "abbreviated accounts".

(4)   If abbreviated accounts are delivered to the registrar the obligation to deliver a copy of the auditor's report on the accounts is to deliver a copy of the special auditor's report required by section 449.

(5)   The copies of the balance sheet and directors' report delivered to the registrar under this section must state the name of the person who signed it on behalf of the board.

(6)   The copy of the auditor's report delivered to the registrar under this section must –

(a)   state the name of the auditor and (where the auditor is a firm) the name of the person who signed it as senior statutory auditor, or

(b)   if the conditions in section 506 (circumstances in which names may be omitted) are met, state that a resolution has been passed and notified to the Secretary of State in accordance with that section.

(7)   This section does not apply to companies within section 444 (filing obligations of companies subject to the small companies regime).

446 Filing obligations of unquoted companies

(1)   The directors of an unquoted company must deliver to the registrar for each financial year of the company a copy of –

(a)   the company's annual accounts, and

(b)   the directors' report.

(2)   The directors must also deliver to the registrar a copy of the auditor's report on those accounts (and the directors' report).
This does not apply if the company is exempt from audit and the directors have taken advantage of that exemption.

(3)   The copies of the balance sheet and directors' report delivered to the registrar under this section must state the name of the person who signed it on behalf of the board.

(4)   The copy of the auditor's report delivered to the registrar under this section must –

(a)   state the name of the auditor and (where the auditor is a firm) the name of the person who signed it as senior statutory auditor, or

(b)   if the conditions in section 506 (circumstances in which names may be omitted) are met, state that a resolution has been passed and notified to the Secretary of State in accordance with that section.

(5)   This section does not apply to companies within –

(a)   section 444 (filing obligations of companies subject to the small companies regime), or

(b)   section 445 (filing obligations of medium-sized companies).

447 Filing obligations of quoted companies

(1)   The directors of a quoted company must deliver to the registrar for each financial year of the company a copy of –

(a) the company's annual accounts,

(b) the directors' remuneration report, and

(c) the directors' report.

(2) They must also deliver a copy of the auditor's report on those accounts (and on the directors' remuneration report and the directors' report).

(3) The copies of the balance sheet, the directors' remuneration report and the directors' report delivered to the registrar under this section must state the name of the person who signed it on behalf of the board.

(4) The copy of the auditor's report delivered to the registrar under this section must –

(a) state the name of the auditor and (where the auditor is a firm) the name of the person who signed it as senior statutory auditor, or

(b) if the conditions in section 506 (circumstances in which names may be omitted) are met, state that a resolution has been passed and notified to the Secretary of State in accordance with that section.

448 Unlimited companies exempt from obligation to file accounts

(1) The directors of an unlimited company are not required to deliver accounts and reports to the registrar in respect of a financial year if the following conditions are met.

(2) The conditions are that at no time during the relevant accounting reference period –

(a) has the company been, to its knowledge, a subsidiary undertaking of an undertaking which was then limited, or

(b) have there been, to its knowledge, exercisable by or on behalf of two or more undertakings which were then limited, rights which if exercisable by one of them would have made the company a subsidiary undertaking of it, or

(c) has the company been a parent company of an undertaking which was then limited.

The references above to an undertaking being limited at a particular time are to an undertaking (under whatever law established) the liability of whose members is at that time limited.

(3) The exemption conferred by this section does not apply if –

(a) the company is a banking or insurance company or the parent company of a banking or insurance group, or

(b) the company is a qualifying company within the meaning of the Partnerships and Unlimited Companies (Accounts) Regulations 1993 (S.I. 1993/1820).

(4) Where a company is exempt by virtue of this section from the obligation to deliver accounts –

(a) section 434(3) (requirements in connection with publication of statutory accounts: meaning of "statutory accounts") has effect with the substitution for the words "as required to be delivered to the registrar under section 441" of the words "as prepared in accordance with this Part and approved by the board of directors"; and

(b) section 435(1)(b) (requirements in connection with publication of nonstatutory accounts: statement whether statutory accounts delivered) has effect with the substitution for the words from "whether statutory accounts" to "have been delivered to the registrar" of the words "that the company is exempt from the requirement to deliver statutory accounts".

(5) In this section the "relevant accounting reference period", in relation to a financial year, means the accounting reference period by reference to which that financial year was determined.

Requirements where abbreviated accounts delivered

449 Special auditor's report where abbreviated accounts delivered

(1) This section applies where –

    (a) the directors of a company deliver abbreviated accounts to the registrar, and

    (b) the company is not exempt from audit (or the directors have not taken advantage of any such exemption).

(2) The directors must also deliver to the registrar a copy of a special report of the company's auditor stating that in his opinion –

    (a) the company is entitled to deliver abbreviated accounts in accordance with the section in question, and

    (b) the abbreviated accounts to be delivered are properly prepared in accordance with regulations under that section.

(3) The auditor's report on the company's annual accounts need not be delivered, but –

    (a) if that report was qualified, the special report must set out that report in full together with any further material necessary to understand the qualification, and

    (b) if that report contained a statement under –

        (i) section 498(2)(a) or (b) (accounts, records or returns inadequate or accounts not agreeing with records and returns), or

        (ii) section 498(3) (failure to obtain necessary information and explanations),

    the special report must set out that statement in full.

(4) The provisions of –

sections 503 to 506 (signature of auditor's report), and
sections 507 to 509 (offences in connection with auditor's report),

apply to a special report under this section as they apply to an auditor's report on the company's annual accounts prepared under Part 16.

(5) If abbreviated accounts are delivered to the registrar, the references in section 434 or 435 (requirements in connection with publication of accounts) to the auditor's report on the company's annual accounts shall be read as references to the special auditor's report required by this section.

450 Approval and signing of abbreviated accounts

(1) Abbreviated accounts must be approved by the board of directors and signed on behalf of the board by a director of the company.

(2) The signature must be on the balance sheet.

(3) The balance sheet must contain in a prominent position above the signature a statement to the effect that it is prepared in accordance with the special provisions of this Act relating (as the case may be) to companies subject to the small companies regime or to medium-sized companies.

(4) If abbreviated accounts are approved that do not comply with the requirements of regulations under the relevant section, every director of the company who –

    (a) knew that they did not comply, or was reckless as to whether they complied, and

    (b) failed to take reasonable steps to prevent them from being approved,

commits an offence.

(5) A person guilty of an offence under subsection (4) is liable –

    (a) on conviction on indictment, to a fine;

    (b) on summary conviction, to a fine not exceeding the statutory maximum.

Failure to file accounts and reports

451 Default in filing accounts and reports: offences

(1) If the requirements of section 441 (duty to file accounts and reports) are not complied with in relation to a company's accounts and reports for a financial year before the end of the period for filing those accounts and reports, every person who immediately before the end of that period was a director of the company commits an offence.

(2) It is a defence for a person charged with such an offence to prove that he took all reasonable steps for securing that those requirements would be complied with before the end of that period.

(3) It is not a defence to prove that the documents in question were not in fact prepared as required by this Part.

(4) A person guilty of an offence under this section is liable on summary conviction to a fine not exceeding level 5 on the standard scale and, for continued contravention, a daily default fine not exceeding one-tenth of level 5 on the standard scale.

452 Default in filing accounts and reports: court order

(1) If –

    (a) the requirements of section 441 (duty to file accounts and reports) are not complied with in relation to a company's accounts and reports for a financial year before the end of the period for filing those accounts and reports, and

    (b) the directors of the company fail to make good the default within 14 days after the service of a notice on them requiring compliance,

the court may, on the application of any member or creditor of the company or of the registrar, make an order directing the directors (or any of them) to make good the default within such time as may be specified in the order.

(2) The court's order may provide that all costs (in Scotland, expenses) of and incidental to the application are to be borne by the directors.

453 Civil penalty for failure to file accounts and reports

(1) Where the requirements of section 441 are not complied with in relation to a company's accounts and reports for a financial year before the end of the period for filing those accounts and reports, the company is liable to a civil penalty.
This is in addition to any liability of the directors under section 451.

(2) The amount of the penalty shall be determined in accordance with regulations made by the Secretary of State by reference to –

    (a) the length of the period between the end of the period for filing the accounts and reports in question and the day on which the requirements are complied with, and

    (b) whether the company is a private or public company.

(3) The penalty may be recovered by the registrar and is to be paid into the Consolidated Fund.

(4) It is not a defence in proceedings under this section to prove that the documents in question were not in fact prepared as required by this Part.

(5) Regulations under this section having the effect of increasing the penalty payable in any case are subject to affirmative resolution procedure.
Otherwise, the regulations are subject to negative resolution procedure.

CHAPTER 11

REVISION OF DEFECTIVE ACCOUNTS AND REPORTS

Voluntary revision

454 Voluntary revision of accounts etc

(1) If it appears to the directors of a company that –

    (a) the company's annual accounts,

    (b) the directors' remuneration report or the directors' report, or

    (c) a summary financial statement of the company,

    did not comply with the requirements of this Act (or, where applicable, of Article 4 of the IAS Regulation), they may prepare revised accounts or a revised report or statement.

(2) Where copies of the previous accounts or report have been sent out to members, delivered to the registrar or (in the case of a public company) laid before the company in general meeting, the revisions must be confined to –

    (a) the correction of those respects in which the previous accounts or report did not comply with the requirements of this Act (or, where applicable, of Article 4 of the IAS Regulation), and

    (b) the making of any necessary consequential alterations.

(3) The Secretary of State may make provision by regulations as to the application of the provisions of this Act in relation to –

    (a) revised annual accounts,

    (b) a revised directors' remuneration report or directors' report, or

    (c) a revised summary financial statement.

(4) The regulations may, in particular –

    (a) make different provision according to whether the previous accounts, report or statement are replaced or are supplemented by a document indicating the corrections to be made;

    (b) make provision with respect to the functions of the company's auditor in relation to the revised accounts, report or statement;

    (c) require the directors to take such steps as may be specified in the regulations where the previous accounts or report have been –

        (i)   sent out to members and others under section 423,

        (ii) laid before the company in general meeting, or

        (iii) delivered to the registrar,

    or where a summary financial statement containing information derived from the previous accounts or report has been sent to members under section 426;

    (d) apply the provisions of this Act (including those creating criminal offences) subject to such additions, exceptions and modifications as are specified in the regulations.

(5) Regulations under this section are subject to negative resolution procedure.

Secretary of State's notice

455 Secretary of State's notice in respect of accounts or reports

(1) This section applies where –

    (a)   copies of a company's annual accounts or directors' report have been sent out under section 423, or

    (b)   a copy of a company's annual accounts or directors' report has been delivered to the registrar or (in the case of a public company) laid before the company in general meeting,

and it appears to the Secretary of State that there is, or may be, a question whether the accounts or report comply with the requirements of this Act (or, where applicable, of Article 4 of the IAS Regulation).

(2)   The Secretary of State may give notice to the directors of the company indicating the respects in which it appears that such a question arises or may arise.

(3)   The notice must specify a period of not less than one month for the directors to give an explanation of the accounts or report or prepare revised accounts or a revised report.

(4)   If at the end of the specified period, or such longer period as the Secretary of State may allow, it appears to the Secretary of State that the directors have not –

    (a)   given a satisfactory explanation of the accounts or report, or

    (b)   revised the accounts or report so as to comply with the requirements of this Act (or, where applicable, of Article 4 of the IAS Regulation),

the Secretary of State may apply to the court.

(5)   The provisions of this section apply equally to revised annual accounts and revised directors' reports, in which case they have effect as if the references to revised accounts or reports were references to further revised accounts or reports.

Application to court

456 Application to court in respect of defective accounts or reports

(1)   An application may be made to the court –

    (a)   by the Secretary of State, after having complied with section 455, or

    (b)   by a person authorised by the Secretary of State for the purposes of this section,

for a declaration (in Scotland, a declarator) that the annual accounts of a company do not comply, or a directors' report does not comply, with the requirements of this Act (or, where applicable, of Article 4 of the IAS Regulation) and for an order requiring the directors of the company to prepare revised accounts or a revised report.

(2)   Notice of the application, together with a general statement of the matters at issue in the proceedings, shall be given by the applicant to the registrar for registration.

(3)   If the court orders the preparation of revised accounts, it may give directions as to –

    (a)   the auditing of the accounts,

    (b)   the revision of any directors' remuneration report, directors' report or summary financial statement, and

    (c)   the taking of steps by the directors to bring the making of the order to the notice of persons likely to rely on the previous accounts,

and such other matters as the court thinks fit.

(4)   If the court orders the preparation of a revised directors' report it may give directions as to –

    (a)   the review of the report by the auditors,

    (b)   the revision of any summary financial statement,

    (c)   the taking of steps by the directors to bring the making of the order to the notice of persons likely to rely on the previous report, and

    (d)   such other matters as the court thinks fit.

(5)   If the court finds that the accounts or report did not comply with the requirements of this Act (or, where applicable, of Article 4 of the IAS Regulation) it may order that all or part of –

(a)   the costs (in Scotland, expenses) of and incidental to the application, and

(b)   any reasonable expenses incurred by the company in connection with or in consequence of the preparation of revised accounts or a revised report,

are to be borne by such of the directors as were party to the approval of the defective accounts or report.

For this purpose every director of the company at the time of the approval of the accounts or report shall be taken to have been a party to the approval unless he shows that he took all reasonable steps to prevent that approval.

(6)   Where the court makes an order under subsection (5) it shall have regard to whether the directors party to the approval of the defective accounts or report knew or ought to have known that the accounts or report did not comply with the requirements of this Act (or, where applicable, of Article 4 of the IAS Regulation), and it may exclude one or more directors from the order or order the payment of different amounts by different directors.

(7)   On the conclusion of proceedings on an application under this section, the applicant must send to the registrar for registration a copy of the court order or, as the case may be, give notice to the registrar that the application has failed or been withdrawn.

(8)   The provisions of this section apply equally to revised annual accounts and revised directors' reports, in which case they have effect as if the references to revised accounts or reports were references to further revised accounts or reports.

457 Other persons authorised to apply to the court

(1)   The Secretary of State may by order (an "authorisation order") authorise for the purposes of section 456 any person appearing to him –

(a)   to have an interest in, and to have satisfactory procedures directed to securing, compliance by companies with the requirements of this Act (or, where applicable, of Article 4 of the IAS Regulation) relating to accounts and directors' reports,

(b)   to have satisfactory procedures for receiving and investigating complaints about companies' annual accounts and directors' reports, and

(c)   otherwise to be a fit and proper person to be authorised.

(2)   A person may be authorised generally or in respect of particular classes of case, and different persons may be authorised in respect of different classes of case.

(3)   The Secretary of State may refuse to authorise a person if he considers that his authorisation is unnecessary having regard to the fact that there are one or more other persons who have been or are likely to be authorised.

(4)   If the authorised person is an unincorporated association, proceedings brought in, or in connection with, the exercise of any function by the association as an authorised person may be brought by or against the association in the name of a body corporate whose constitution provides for the establishment of the association.

(5)   An authorisation order may contain such requirements or other provisions relating to the exercise of functions by the authorised person as appear to the Secretary of State to be appropriate.

No such order is to be made unless it appears to the Secretary of State that the person would, if authorised, exercise his functions as an authorised person in accordance with the provisions proposed.

(6)   Where authorisation is revoked, the revoking order may make such provision as the Secretary of State thinks fit with respect to pending proceedings.

(7)   An order under this section is subject to negative resolution procedure.

458 Disclosure of information by tax authorities

(1)   The Commissioners for Her Majesty's Revenue and Customs may disclose information to a person authorised under section 457 for the purpose of facilitating –

(a)   the taking of steps by that person to discover whether there are grounds for an application to the court under section 456 (application in respect of defective accounts etc), or

(b)   a decision by the authorised person whether to make such an application.

(2)   This section applies despite any statutory or other restriction on the disclosure of information.

Provided that, in the case of personal data within the meaning of the Data Protection Act 1998 (c. 29), information is not to be disclosed in contravention of that Act.

(3)   Information disclosed to an authorised person under this section –

(a)   may not be used except in or in connection with –

(i)   taking steps to discover whether there are grounds for an application to the court under section 456, or

(ii)   deciding whether or not to make such an application,

or in, or in connection with, proceedings on such an application; and

(b)   must not be further disclosed except –

(i)   to the person to whom the information relates, or

(ii)   in, or in connection with, proceedings on any such application to the court.

(4)   A person who contravenes subsection (3) commits an offence unless –

(a)   he did not know, and had no reason to suspect, that the information had been disclosed under this section, or

(b)   he took all reasonable steps and exercised all due diligence to avoid the commission of the offence.

(5)   A person guilty of an offence under subsection (4) is liable –

(a)   on conviction on indictment, to imprisonment for a term not exceeding two years or a fine (or both);

(b)   on summary conviction –

(i)   in England and Wales, to imprisonment for a term not exceeding twelve months or to a fine not exceeding the statutory maximum (or both);

(ii)   in Scotland or Northern Ireland, to imprisonment for a term not exceeding six months, or to a fine not exceeding the statutory maximum (or both).

Power of authorised person to require documents etc

459 Power of authorised person to require documents, information and explanations

(1)   This section applies where it appears to a person who is authorised under section 457 that there is, or may be, a question whether a company's annual accounts or directors' report comply with the requirements of this Act (or, where applicable, of Article 4 of the IAS Regulation).

(2)   The authorised person may require any of the persons mentioned in subsection (3) to produce any document, or to provide him with any information or explanations, that he may reasonably require for the purpose of –

(a)   discovering whether there are grounds for an application to the court under section 456, or

(b)   deciding whether to make such an application.

(3)   Those persons are –

(a)   the company;

(b)   any officer, employee, or auditor of the company;

(c)   any persons who fell within paragraph (b) at a time to which the document or information required by the authorised person relates.

(4) If a person fails to comply with such a requirement, the authorised person may apply to the court.

(5) If it appears to the court that the person has failed to comply with a requirement under subsection (2), it may order the person to take such steps as it directs for securing that the documents are produced or the information or explanations are provided.

(6) A statement made by a person in response to a requirement under subsection (2) or an order under subsection (5) may not be used in evidence against him in any criminal proceedings.

(7) Nothing in this section compels any person to disclose documents or information in respect of which a claim to legal professional privilege (in Scotland, to confidentiality of communications) could be maintained in legal proceedings.

(8) In this section "document" includes information recorded in any form.

460 Restrictions on disclosure of information obtained under compulsory powers

(1) This section applies to information (in whatever form) obtained in pursuance of a requirement or order under section 459 (power of authorised person to require documents etc) that relates to the private affairs of an individual or to any particular business.

(2) No such information may, during the lifetime of that individual or so long as that business continues to be carried on, be disclosed without the consent of that individual or the person for the time being carrying on that business.

(3) This does not apply –

   (a) to disclosure permitted by section 461 (permitted disclosure of information obtained under compulsory powers), or

   (b) to the disclosure of information that is or has been available to the public from another source.

(4) A person who discloses information in contravention of this section commits an offence, unless –

   (a) he did not know, and had no reason to suspect, that the information had been disclosed under section 459, or

   (b) he took all reasonable steps and exercised all due diligence to avoid the commission of the offence.

(5) A person guilty of an offence under this section is liable –

   (a) on conviction on indictment, to imprisonment for a term not exceeding two years or a fine (or both);

   (b) on summary conviction –

      (i) in England and Wales, to imprisonment for a term not exceeding twelve months or to a fine not exceeding the statutory maximum (or both);

      (ii) in Scotland or Northern Ireland, to imprisonment for a term not exceeding six months, or to a fine not exceeding the statutory maximum (or both).

461 Permitted disclosure of information obtained under compulsory powers

(1) The prohibition in section 460 of the disclosure of information obtained in pursuance of a requirement or order under section 459 (power of authorised person to require documents etc) that relates to the private affairs of an individual or to any particular business has effect subject to the following exceptions.

(2) It does not apply to the disclosure of information for the purpose of facilitating the carrying out by the authorised person of his functions under section 456.

(3) It does not apply to disclosure to –

   (a) the Secretary of State,

   (b) the Department of Enterprise, Trade and Investment for Northern Ireland,

   (c) the Treasury,

    (d) the Bank of England,

    (e) the Financial Services Authority, or

    (f) the Commissioners for Her Majesty's Revenue and Customs.

(4) It does not apply to disclosure –

    (a) for the purpose of assisting a body designated by an order under section 46 of the Companies Act 1989 (c. 40) (delegation of functions of the Secretary of State) to exercise its functions under Part 2 of that Act;

    (b) with a view to the institution of, or otherwise for the purposes of, disciplinary proceedings relating to the performance by an accountant or auditor of his professional duties;

    (c) for the purpose of enabling or assisting the Secretary of State or the Treasury to exercise any of their functions under any of the following –

        (i)   the Companies Acts,

        (ii) Part 5 of the Criminal Justice Act 1993 (c. 36) (insider dealing),

        (iii) the Insolvency Act 1986 (c. 45) or the Insolvency (Northern Ireland) Order 1989 (S.I. 1989/2405 (N.I. 19)),

        (iv) the Company Directors Disqualification Act 1986 (c. 46) or the Company Directors Disqualification (Northern Ireland) Order 2002 (S.I. 2002/3150 (N.I. 4)),

        (v) the Financial Services and Markets Act 2000 (c. 8);

    (d) for the purpose of enabling or assisting the Department of Enterprise, Trade and Investment for Northern Ireland to exercise any powers conferred on it by the enactments relating to companies, directors' disqualification or insolvency;

    (e) for the purpose of enabling or assisting the Bank of England to exercise its functions;

    (f) for the purpose of enabling or assisting the Commissioners for Her Majesty's Revenue and Customs to exercise their functions;

    (g) for the purpose of enabling or assisting the Financial Services Authority to exercise its functions under any of the following –

        (i)   the legislation relating to friendly societies or to industrial and provident societies,

        (ii) the Building Societies Act 1986 (c. 53),

        (iii) Part 7 of the Companies Act 1989 (c. 40),

        (iv) the Financial Services and Markets Act 2000; or

    (h) in pursuance of any Community obligation.

(5) It does not apply to disclosure to a body exercising functions of a public nature under legislation in any country or territory outside the United Kingdom that appear to the authorised person to be similar to his functions under section 456 for the purpose of enabling or assisting that body to exercise those functions.

(6) In determining whether to disclose information to a body in accordance with subsection (5), the authorised person must have regard to the following considerations –

    (a) whether the use which the body is likely to make of the information is sufficiently important to justify making the disclosure;

    (b) whether the body has adequate arrangements to prevent the information from being used or further disclosed other than –

        (i)   for the purposes of carrying out the functions mentioned in that subsection, or

        (ii) for other purposes substantially similar to those for which information disclosed to the authorised person could be used or further disclosed.

(7) Nothing in this section authorises the making of a disclosure in contravention of the Data Protection Act 1998 (c. 29).

462 Power to amend categories of permitted disclosure

(1) The Secretary of State may by order amend section 461(3), (4) and (5).

(2) An order under this section must not –

(a) amend subsection (3) of that section (UK public authorities) by specifying a person unless the person exercises functions of a public nature (whether or not he exercises any other function);

(b) amend subsection (4) of that section (purposes for which disclosure permitted) by adding or modifying a description of disclosure unless the purpose for which the disclosure is permitted is likely to facilitate the exercise of a function of a public nature;

(c) amend subsection (5) of that section (overseas regulatory authorities) so as to have the effect of permitting disclosures to be made to a body other than one that exercises functions of a public nature in a country or territory outside the United Kingdom.

(3) An order under this section is subject to negative resolution procedure.

CHAPTER 12

SUPPLEMENTARY PROVISIONS

Liability for false or misleading statements in reports

463 Liability for false or misleading statements in reports

(1) The reports to which this section applies are –

(a) the directors' report,

(b) the directors' remuneration report, and

(c) a summary financial statement so far as it is derived from either of those reports.

(2) A director of a company is liable to compensate the company for any loss suffered by it as a result of –

(a) any untrue or misleading statement in a report to which this section applies, or

(b) the omission from a report to which this section applies of anything required to be included in it.

(3) He is so liable only if –

(a) he knew the statement to be untrue or misleading or was reckless as to whether it was untrue or misleading, or

(b) he knew the omission to be dishonest concealment of a material fact.

(4) No person shall be subject to any liability to a person other than the company resulting from reliance, by that person or another, on information in a report to which this section applies.

(5) The reference in subsection (4) to a person being subject to a liability includes a reference to another person being entitled as against him to be granted any civil remedy or to rescind or repudiate an agreement.

(6) This section does not affect –

(a) liability for a civil penalty, or

(b) liability for a criminal offence.

Accounting and reporting standards

464 Accounting standards

(1) In this Part "accounting standards" means statements of standard accounting practice issued by such body or bodies as may be prescribed by regulations.

(2) References in this Part to accounting standards applicable to a company's annual accounts are to such standards as are, in accordance with their terms, relevant to the company's circumstances and to the accounts.

(3) Regulations under this section may contain such transitional and other supplementary and incidental provisions as appear to the Secretary of State to be appropriate.

Companies qualifying as medium-sized

465 Companies qualifying as medium-sized: general

(1) A company qualifies as medium-sized in relation to its first financial year if the qualifying conditions are met in that year.

(2) A company qualifies as medium-sized in relation to a subsequent financial year –

    (a) if the qualifying conditions are met in that year and the preceding financial year;

    (b) if the qualifying conditions are met in that year and the company qualified as medium-sized in relation to the preceding financial year;

    (c) if the qualifying conditions were met in the preceding financial year and the company qualified as medium-sized in relation to that year.

(3) The qualifying conditions are met by a company in a year in which it satisfies two or more of the following requirements –

1.	Turnover	Not more than £22.8 million
2.	Balance sheet total	Not more than £11.4 million
3.	Number of employees	Not more than 250

(4) For a period that is a company's financial year but not in fact a year the maximum figures for turnover must be proportionately adjusted.

(5) The balance sheet total means the aggregate of the amounts shown as assets in the company's balance sheet.

(6) The number of employees means the average number of persons employed by the company in the year, determined as follows –

    (a) find for each month in the financial year the number of persons employed under contracts of service by the company in that month (whether throughout the month or not),

    (b) add together the monthly totals, and

    (c) divide by the number of months in the financial year.

(7) This section is subject to section 466 (companies qualifying as medium-sized: parent companies).

466 Companies qualifying as medium-sized: parent companies

(1) A parent company qualifies as a medium-sized company in relation to a financial year only if the group headed by it qualifies as a medium-sized group.

(2) A group qualifies as medium-sized in relation to the parent company's first financial year if the qualifying conditions are met in that year.

(3) A group qualifies as medium-sized in relation to a subsequent financial year of the parent company –

    (a) if the qualifying conditions are met in that year and the preceding financial year;

    (b) if the qualifying conditions are met in that year and the group qualified as medium-sized in relation to the preceding financial year;

(c) if the qualifying conditions were met in the preceding financial year and the group qualified as medium-sized in relation to that year.

(4) The qualifying conditions are met by a group in a year in which it satisfies two or more of the following requirements –

1.	Aggregate turnover	Not more than £22.8 million net (or £27.36 million gross)
2.	Aggregate balance sheet total	Not more than £11.4 million net (or £13.68 million gross)
3.	Aggregate number of employees	Not more than 250

(5) The aggregate figures are ascertained by aggregating the relevant figures determined in accordance with section 465 for each member of the group.

(6) In relation to the aggregate figures for turnover and balance sheet total –

"net" means after any set-offs and other adjustments made to eliminate group transactions –

(a) in the case of Companies Act accounts, in accordance with regulations under section 404,

(b) in the case of IAS accounts, in accordance with international accounting standards; and

"gross" means without those set-offs and other adjustments.

A company may satisfy any relevant requirement on the basis of either the net or the gross figure.

(7) The figures for each subsidiary undertaking shall be those included in its individual accounts for the relevant financial year, that is –

(a) if its financial year ends with that of the parent company, that financial year, and

(b) if not, its financial year ending last before the end of the financial year of the parent company.

If those figures cannot be obtained without disproportionate expense or undue delay, the latest available figures shall be taken.

467 Companies excluded from being treated as medium-sized

(1) A company is not entitled to take advantage of any of the provisions of this Part relating to companies qualifying as medium-sized if it was at any time within the financial year in question –

(a) a public company,

(b) a company that –

(i)   has permission under Part 4 of the Financial Services and Markets Act 2000 (c. 8) to carry on a regulated activity, or

(ii) carries on insurance market activity, or

(c) a member of an ineligible group.

(2) A group is ineligible if any of its members is –

(a) a public company,

(b) a body corporate (other than a company) whose shares are admitted to trading on a regulated market,

(c) a person (other than a small company) who has permission under Part 4 of the Financial Services and Markets Act 2000 to carry on a regulated activity,

(d) a small company that is an authorised insurance company, a banking company, an e-money issuer, an ISD investment firm or a UCITS management company, or

(e) a person who carries on insurance market activity.

(3) A company is a small company for the purposes of subsection (2) if it qualified as small in relation to its last financial year ending on or before the end of the financial year in question.

General power to make further provision about accounts and reports

468 General power to make further provision about accounts and reports

(1) The Secretary of State may make provision by regulations about –

   (a) the accounts and reports that companies are required to prepare;
   (b) the categories of companies required to prepare accounts and reports of any description;
   (c) the form and content of the accounts and reports that companies are required to prepare;
   (d) the obligations of companies and others as regards –

      (i)   the approval of accounts and reports,
      (ii) the sending of accounts and reports to members and others,
      (iii) the laying of accounts and reports before the company in general meeting,
      (iv) the delivery of copies of accounts and reports to the registrar, and
      (v)   the publication of accounts and reports.

(2) The regulations may amend this Part by adding, altering or repealing provisions.
(3) But they must not amend (other than consequentially) –

   (a) section 393 (accounts to give true and fair view), or
   (b) the provisions of Chapter 11 (revision of defective accounts and reports).

(4) The regulations may create criminal offences in cases corresponding to those in which an offence is created by an existing provision of this Part.
   The maximum penalty for any such offence may not be greater than is provided in relation to an offence under the existing provision.
(5) The regulations may provide for civil penalties in circumstances corresponding to those within section 453(1) (civil penalty for failure to file accounts and reports).
   The provisions of section 453(2) to (5) apply in relation to any such penalty.

Other supplementary provisions

469 Preparation and filing of accounts in euros

(1) The amounts set out in the annual accounts of a company may also be shown in the same accounts translated into euros.
(2) When complying with section 441 (duty to file accounts and reports), the directors of a company may deliver to the registrar an additional copy of the company's annual accounts in which the amounts have been translated into euros.
(3) In both cases –

   (a) the amounts must have been translated at the exchange rate prevailing on the date to which the balance sheet is made up, and
   (b) that rate must be disclosed in the notes to the accounts.

(4) For the purposes of sections 434 and 435 (requirements in connection with published accounts) any additional copy of the company's annual accounts delivered to the registrar under subsection (2) above shall be treated as statutory accounts of the company.
   In the case of such a copy, references in those sections to the auditor's report on the company's annual accounts shall be read as references to the auditor's report on the annual accounts of which it is a copy.

470 Power to apply provisions to banking partnerships

(1) The Secretary of State may by regulations apply to banking partnerships, subject to such exceptions, adaptations and modifications as he considers appropriate, the provisions of this Part (and of regulations made under this Part) applying to banking companies.

(2) A "banking partnership" means a partnership which has permission under Part 4 of the Financial Services and Markets Act 2000 (c. 8).

But a partnership is not a banking partnership if it has permission to accept deposits only for the purpose of carrying on another regulated activity in accordance with that permission.

(3) Expressions used in this section that are also used in the provisions regulating activities under the Financial Services and Markets Act 2000 have the same meaning here as they do in those provisions.

See section 22 of that Act, orders made under that section and Schedule 2 to that Act.

(4) Regulations under this section are subject to affirmative resolution procedure.

471 Meaning of "annual accounts" and related expressions

(1) In this Part a company's "annual accounts", in relation to a financial year, means –

    (a) the company's individual accounts for that year (see section 394), and

    (b) any group accounts prepared by the company for that year (see sections 398 and 399).

This is subject to section 408 (option to omit individual profit and loss account from annual accounts where information given in group accounts).

(2) In the case of an unquoted company, its "annual accounts and reports" for a financial year are –

    (a) its annual accounts,

    (b) the directors' report, and

    (c) the auditor's report on those accounts and the directors' report (unless the company is exempt from audit).

(3) In the case of a quoted company, its "annual accounts and reports" for a financial year are –

    (a) its annual accounts,

    (b) the directors' remuneration report,

    (c) the directors' report, and

    (d) the auditor's report on those accounts, on the auditable part of the directors' remuneration report and on the directors' report.

472 Notes to the accounts

(1) Information required by this Part to be given in notes to a company's annual accounts may be contained in the accounts or in a separate document annexed to the accounts.

(2) References in this Part to a company's annual accounts, or to a balance sheet or profit and loss account, include notes to the accounts giving information which is required by any provision of this Act or international accounting standards, and required or allowed by any such provision to be given in a note to company accounts.

473 Parliamentary procedure for certain regulations under this Part

(1) This section applies to regulations under the following provisions of this Part –

    section 396 (Companies Act individual accounts),

    section 404 (Companies Act group accounts),

    section 409 (information about related undertakings),

    section 412 (information about directors' benefits: remuneration, pensions and compensation for loss of office),

    section 416 (contents of directors' report: general),

    section 421 (contents of directors' remuneration report),

    section 444 (filing obligations of companies subject to small companies regime),

    section 445 (filing obligations of medium-sized companies),

    section 468 (general power to make further provision about accounts and reports).

(2) Any such regulations may make consequential amendments or repeals in other provisions of this Act, or in other enactments.

(3) Regulations that –

    (a) restrict the classes of company which have the benefit of any exemption, exception or special provision,

    (b) require additional matter to be included in a document of any class, or

    (c) otherwise render the requirements of this Part more onerous,

    are subject to affirmative resolution procedure.

(4) Otherwise, the regulations are subject to negative resolution procedure.

474 Minor definitions

(1) In this Part –

    "e-money issuer" means a person who has permission under Part 4 of the Financial Services and Markets Act 2000 (c. 8) to carry on the activity of issuing electronic money within the meaning of article 9B of the Financial Services and Markets Act 2000 (Regulated Activities) Order 2001 (S.I. 2001/544);

    "group" means a parent undertaking and its subsidiary undertakings;

    "IAS Regulation" means EC Regulation No. 1606/2002 of the European Parliament and of the Council of 19 July 2002 on the application of international accounting standards;

    "included in the consolidation", in relation to group accounts, or

    "included in consolidated group accounts", means that the undertaking is included in the accounts by the method of full (and not proportional) consolidation, and references to an undertaking excluded from consolidation shall be construed accordingly;

    "international accounting standards" means the international accounting standards, within the meaning of the IAS Regulation, adopted from time to time by the European Commission in accordance with that Regulation;

    "ISD investment firm" has the meaning given by the Glossary forming part of the Handbook made by the Financial Services Authority under the Financial Services and Markets Act 2000;

    "profit and loss account", in relation to a company that prepares IAS accounts, includes an income statement or other equivalent financial statement required to be prepared by international accounting standards;

    "regulated activity" has the meaning given in section 22 of the Financial Services and Markets Act 2000, except that it does not include activities of the kind specified in any of the following provisions of the Financial Services and Markets Act 2000 (Regulated Activities) Order 2001 (S.I. 2001/544) –

        (a) article 25A (arranging regulated mortgage contracts),

        (b) article 25B (arranging regulated home reversion plans),

        (c) article 25C (arranging regulated home purchase plans),

        (d) article 39A (assisting administration and performance of a contract of insurance),

        (e) article 53A (advising on regulated mortgage contracts),

        (f) article 53B (advising on regulated home reversion plans),

        (g) article 53C (advising on regulated home purchase plans),

        (h) article 21 (dealing as agent), article 25 (arranging deals in investments) or article 53 (advising on investments) where the activity concerns relevant investments that are not contractually based investments (within the meaning of article 3 of that Order), or

        (i) article 64 (agreeing to carry on a regulated activity of the kind mentioned in paragraphs (a) to (h));

"turnover", in relation to a company, means the amounts derived from the provision of goods and services falling within the company's ordinary activities, after deduction of –

    (a)   trade discounts,

    (b)   value added tax, and

    (c)   any other taxes based on the amounts so derived;

"UCITS management company" has the meaning given by the Glossary forming part of the Handbook made by the Financial Services Authority under the Financial Services and Markets Act 2000 (c. 8).

(2)   In the case of an undertaking not trading for profit, any reference in this Part to a profit and loss account is to an income and expenditure account.

References to profit and loss and, in relation to group accounts, to a consolidated profit and loss account shall be construed accordingly.

PART 16

AUDIT

CHAPTER 1

REQUIREMENT FOR AUDITED ACCOUNTS

Requirement for audited accounts

475 Requirement for audited accounts

(1)   A company's annual accounts for a financial year must be audited in accordance with this Part unless the company –

    (a)   is exempt from audit under –

        section 477 (small companies), or
        section 480 (dormant companies);

        or

    (b)   is exempt from the requirements of this Part under section 482 (non-profit-making companies subject to public sector audit).

(2)   A company is not entitled to any such exemption unless its balance sheet contains a statement by the directors to that effect.

(3)   A company is not entitled to exemption under any of the provisions mentioned in subsection (1)(a) unless its balance sheet contains a statement by the directors to the effect that –

    (a)   the members have not required the company to obtain an audit of its accounts for the year in question in accordance with section 476, and

    (b)   the directors acknowledge their responsibilities for complying with the requirements of this Act with respect to accounting records and the preparation of accounts.

(4)   The statement required by subsection (2) or (3) must appear on the balance sheet above the signature required by section 414.

476 Right of members to require audit

(1)   The members of a company that would otherwise be entitled to exemption from audit under any of the provisions mentioned in section 475(1)(a) may by notice under this section require it to obtain an audit of its accounts for a financial year.

(2) The notice must be given by –

    (a) members representing not less in total than 10% in nominal value of the company's issued share capital, or any class of it, or

    (b) if the company does not have a share capital, not less than 10% in number of the members of the company.

(3) The notice may not be given before the financial year to which it relates and must be given not later than one month before the end of that year.

Exemption from audit: small companies

477 Small companies: conditions for exemption from audit

(1) A company that meets the following conditions in respect of a financial year is exempt from the requirements of this Act relating to the audit of accounts for that year.

(2) The conditions are –

    (a) that the company qualifies as a small company in relation to that year,

    (b) that its turnover in that year is not more than £5.6 million, and

    (c) that its balance sheet total for that year is not more than £2.8 million.

(3) For a period which is a company's financial year but not in fact a year the maximum figure for turnover shall be proportionately adjusted.

(4) For the purposes of this section –

    (a) whether a company qualifies as a small company shall be determined in accordance with section 382(1) to (6), and

    (b) "balance sheet total" has the same meaning as in that section.

(5) This section has effect subject to –

    section 475(2) and (3) (requirements as to statements to be contained in balance sheet),

    section 476 (right of members to require audit),

    section 478 (companies excluded from small companies exemption), and

    section 479 (availability of small companies exemption in case of group company).

478 Companies excluded from small companies exemption

A company is not entitled to the exemption conferred by section 477 (small companies) if it was at any time within the financial year in question –

    (a) a public company,

    (b) a company that –

        (i)   is an authorised insurance company, a banking company, an emoney issuer, an ISD investment firm or a UCITS management company, or

        (ii) carries on insurance market activity, or

    (c) a special register body as defined in section 117(1) of the Trade Union and Labour Relations (Consolidation) Act 1992 (c. 52) or an employers' association as defined in section 122 of that Act or Article 4 of the Industrial Relations (Northern Ireland) Order 1992 (S.I. 1992/807 (N.I. 5)).

479 Availability of small companies exemption in case of group company

(1) A company is not entitled to the exemption conferred by section 477 (small companies) in respect of a financial year during any part of which it was a group company unless –

    (a) the conditions specified in subsection (2) below are met, or

    (b) subsection (3) applies.

(2) The conditions are –

(a) that the group –

  (i)   qualifies as a small group in relation to that financial year, and
  (ii)   was not at any time in that year an ineligible group;

(b) that the group's aggregate turnover in that year is not more than £5.6 million net (or £6.72 million gross);

(c) that the group's aggregate balance sheet total for that year is not more than £2.8 million net (or £3.36 million gross).

(3) A company is not excluded by subsection (1) if, throughout the whole of the period or periods during the financial year when it was a group company, it was both a subsidiary undertaking and dormant.

(4) In this section –

(a) "group company" means a company that is a parent company or a subsidiary undertaking, and

(b) "the group", in relation to a group company, means that company together with all its associated undertakings.

  For this purpose undertakings are associated if one is a subsidiary undertaking of the other or both are subsidiary undertakings of a third undertaking.

(5) For the purposes of this section –

(a) whether a group qualifies as small shall be determined in accordance with section 383 (companies qualifying as small: parent companies);

(b) "ineligible group" has the meaning given by section 384(2) and (3);

(c) a group's aggregate turnover and aggregate balance sheet total shall be determined as for the purposes of section 383;

(d) "net" and "gross" have the same meaning as in that section;

(e) a company may meet any relevant requirement on the basis of either the gross or the net figure.

(6) The provisions mentioned in subsection (5) apply for the purposes of this section as if all the bodies corporate in the group were companies.

Exemption from audit: dormant companies

480 Dormant companies: conditions for exemption from audit

(1) A company is exempt from the requirements of this Act relating to the audit of accounts in respect of a financial year if –

(a) it has been dormant since its formation, or

(b) it has been dormant since the end of the previous financial year and the following conditions are met.

(2) The conditions are that the company –

(a) as regards its individual accounts for the financial year in question –

  (i)   is entitled to prepare accounts in accordance with the small companies regime (see sections 381 to 384), or

  (ii)   would be so entitled but for having been a public company or a member of an ineligible group, and

(b) is not required to prepare group accounts for that year.

(3) This section has effect subject to –

  section 475(2) and (3) (requirements as to statements to be contained in balance sheet),

  section 476 (right of members to require audit), and

  section 481 (companies excluded from dormant companies exemption).

481 Companies excluded from dormant companies exemption

A company is not entitled to the exemption conferred by section 480 (dormant companies) if it was at any time within the financial year in question a company that –

(a) is an authorised insurance company, a banking company, an e-money issuer, an ISD investment firm or a UCITS management company, or

(b) carries on insurance market activity.

Companies subject to public sector audit

482 Non-profit-making companies subject to public sector audit

(1) The requirements of this Part as to audit of accounts do not apply to a company for a financial year if it is non-profit-making and its accounts –

(a) are subject to audit –

(i) by the Comptroller and Auditor General by virtue of an order under section 25(6) of the Government Resources and Accounts Act 2000 (c. 20), or

(ii) by the Auditor General for Wales by virtue of section 96, or an order under section 144, of the Government of Wales Act 1998 (c. 38);

(b) are accounts –

(i) in relation to which section 21 of the Public Finance and Accountability (Scotland) Act 2000 (asp 1) (audit of accounts: Auditor General for Scotland) applies, or

(ii) that are subject to audit by the Auditor General for Scotland by virtue of an order under section 483 (Scottish public sector companies: audit by Auditor General for Scotland); or

(c) are subject to audit by the Comptroller and Auditor General for Northern Ireland by virtue of an order under Article 5(3) of the Audit and Accountability (Northern Ireland) Order 2003 (S.I. 2003/418 (N.I. 5)).

(2) In the case of a company that is a parent company or a subsidiary undertaking, subsection (1) applies only if every group undertaking is non-profit-making.

(3) In this section "non-profit-making" has the same meaning as in Article 48 of the Treaty establishing the European Community.

(4) This section has effect subject to section 475(2) (balance sheet to contain statement that company entitled to exemption under this section).

483 Scottish public sector companies: audit by Auditor General for Scotland

(1) The Scottish Ministers may by order provide for the accounts of a company having its registered office in Scotland to be audited by the Auditor General for Scotland.

(2) An order under subsection (1) may be made in relation to a company only if it appears to the Scottish Ministers that the company –

(a) exercises in or as regards Scotland functions of a public nature none of which relate to reserved matters (within the meaning of the Scotland Act 1998 (c. 46)), or

(b) is entirely or substantially funded from a body having accounts falling within paragraph (a) or (b) of subsection (3).

(3) Those accounts are –

(a) accounts in relation to which section 21 of the Public Finance and Accountability (Scotland) Act 2000 (asp 1) (audit of accounts: Auditor General for Scotland) applies,

(b) accounts which are subject to audit by the Auditor General for Scotland by virtue of an order under this section.

(4) An order under subsection (1) may make such supplementary or consequential provision (including provision amending an enactment) as the Scottish Ministers think expedient.

(5) An order under subsection (1) shall not be made unless a draft of the statutory instrument containing it has been laid before, and approved by resolution of, the Scottish Parliament.

General power of amendment by regulations

484 General power of amendment by regulations

(1) The Secretary of State may by regulations amend this Chapter or section 539 (minor definitions) so far as applying to this Chapter by adding, altering or repealing provisions.

(2) The regulations may make consequential amendments or repeals in other provisions of this Act, or in other enactments.

(3) Regulations under this section imposing new requirements, or rendering existing requirements more onerous, are subject to affirmative resolution procedure.

(4) Other regulations under this section are subject to negative resolution procedure.

CHAPTER 2

APPOINTMENT OF AUDITORS

Private companies

485 Appointment of auditors of private company: general

(1) An auditor or auditors of a private company must be appointed for each financial year of the company, unless the directors reasonably resolve otherwise on the ground that audited accounts are unlikely to be required.

(2) For each financial year for which an auditor or auditors is or are to be appointed (other than the company's first financial year), the appointment must be made before the end of the period of 28 days beginning with –

    (a) the end of the time allowed for sending out copies of the company's annual accounts and reports for the previous financial year (see section 424), or

    (b) if earlier, the day on which copies of the company's annual accounts and reports for the previous financial year are sent out under section 423.

This is the "period for appointing auditors".

(3) The directors may appoint an auditor or auditors of the company –

    (a) at any time before the company's first period for appointing auditors,

    (b) following a period during which the company (being exempt from audit) did not have any auditor, at any time before the company's next period for appointing auditors, or

    (c) to fill a casual vacancy in the office of auditor.

(4) The members may appoint an auditor or auditors by ordinary resolution –

    (a) during a period for appointing auditors,

    (b) if the company should have appointed an auditor or auditors during a period for appointing auditors but failed to do so, or

    (c) where the directors had power to appoint under subsection (3) but have failed to make an appointment.

(5) An auditor or auditors of a private company may only be appointed –

(a)   in accordance with this section, or

(b)   in accordance with section 486 (default power of Secretary of State).

This is without prejudice to any deemed re-appointment under section 487.

486 Appointment of auditors of private company: default power of Secretary of State

(1)   If a private company fails to appoint an auditor or auditors in accordance with section 485, the Secretary of State may appoint one or more persons to fill the vacancy.

(2)   Where subsection (2) of that section applies and the company fails to make the necessary appointment before the end of the period for appointing auditors, the company must within one week of the end of that period give notice to the Secretary of State of his power having become exercisable.

(3)   If a company fails to give the notice required by this section, an offence is committed by –

(a)   the company, and

(b)   every officer of the company who is in default.

(4)   A person guilty of an offence under this section is liable on summary conviction to a fine not exceeding level 3 on the standard scale and, for continued contravention, a daily default fine not exceeding one-tenth of level 3 on the standard scale.

487 Term of office of auditors of private company

(1)   An auditor or auditors of a private company hold office in accordance with the terms of their appointment, subject to the requirements that –

(a)   they do not take office until any previous auditor or auditors cease to hold office, and

(b)   they cease to hold office at the end of the next period for appointing auditors unless re-appointed.

(2)   Where no auditor has been appointed by the end of the next period for appointing auditors, any auditor in office immediately before that time is deemed to be re-appointed at that time, unless –

(a)   he was appointed by the directors, or

(b)   the company's articles require actual re-appointment, or

(c)   the deemed re-appointment is prevented by the members under section 488, or

(d)   the members have resolved that he should not be re-appointed, or

(e)   the directors have resolved that no auditor or auditors should be appointed for the financial year in question.

(3)   This is without prejudice to the provisions of this Part as to removal and resignation of auditors.

(4)   No account shall be taken of any loss of the opportunity of deemed reappointment under this section in ascertaining the amount of any compensation or damages payable to an auditor on his ceasing to hold office for any reason.

488 Prevention by members of deemed re-appointment of auditor

(1)   An auditor of a private company is not deemed to be re-appointed under section 487(2) if the company has received notices under this section from members representing at least the requisite percentage of the total voting rights of all members who would be entitled to vote on a resolution that the auditor should not be re-appointed.

(2)   The "requisite percentage" is 5%, or such lower percentage as is specified for this purpose in the company's articles.

(3)   A notice under this section –

(a)   may be in hard copy or electronic form,

(b)   must be authenticated by the person or persons giving it, and

(c) must be received by the company before the end of the accounting reference period immediately preceding the time when the deemed re-appointment would have effect.

Public companies

489 Appointment of auditors of public company: general

(1) An auditor or auditors of a public company must be appointed for each financial year of the company, unless the directors reasonably resolve otherwise on the ground that audited accounts are unlikely to be required.

(2) For each financial year for which an auditor or auditors is or are to be appointed (other than the company's first financial year), the appointment must be made before the end of the accounts meeting of the company at which the company's annual accounts and reports for the previous financial year are laid.

(3) The directors may appoint an auditor or auditors of the company –

(a) at any time before the company's first accounts meeting;

(b) following a period during which the company (being exempt from audit) did not have any auditor, at any time before the company's next accounts meeting;

(c) to fill a casual vacancy in the office of auditor.

(4) The members may appoint an auditor or auditors by ordinary resolution –

(a) at an accounts meeting;

(b) if the company should have appointed an auditor or auditors at an accounts meeting but failed to do so;

(c) where the directors had power to appoint under subsection (3) but have failed to make an appointment.

(5) An auditor or auditors of a public company may only be appointed –

(a) in accordance with this section, or

(b) in accordance with section 490 (default power of Secretary of State).

490 Appointment of auditors of public company: default power of Secretary of State

(1) If a public company fails to appoint an auditor or auditors in accordance with section 489, the Secretary of State may appoint one or more persons to fill the vacancy.

(2) Where subsection (2) of that section applies and the company fails to make the necessary appointment before the end of the accounts meeting, the company must within one week of the end of that meeting give notice to the Secretary of State of his power having become exercisable.

(3) If a company fails to give the notice required by this section, an offence is committed by –

(a) the company, and

(b) every officer of the company who is in default.

(4) A person guilty of an offence under this section is liable on summary conviction to a fine not exceeding level 3 on the standard scale and, for continued contravention, a daily default fine not exceeding one-tenth of level 3 on the standard scale.

491 Term of office of auditors of public company

(1) The auditor or auditors of a public company hold office in accordance with the terms of their appointment, subject to the requirements that –

(a) they do not take office until the previous auditor or auditors have ceased to hold office, and

(b) they cease to hold office at the conclusion of the accounts meeting next following their appointment, unless re-appointed.

(2) This is without prejudice to the provisions of this Part as to removal and resignation of auditors.

General provisions

492 Fixing of auditor's remuneration

(1) The remuneration of an auditor appointed by the members of a company must be fixed by the members by ordinary resolution or in such manner as the members may by ordinary resolution determine.

(2) The remuneration of an auditor appointed by the directors of a company must be fixed by the directors.

(3) The remuneration of an auditor appointed by the Secretary of State must be fixed by the Secretary of State.

(4) For the purposes of this section "remuneration" includes sums paid in respect of expenses.

(5) This section applies in relation to benefits in kind as to payments of money.

493 Disclosure of terms of audit appointment

(1) The Secretary of State may make provision by regulations for securing the disclosure of the terms on which a company's auditor is appointed, remunerated or performs his duties.

Nothing in the following provisions of this section affects the generality of this power.

(2) The regulations may –

(a) require disclosure of –

(i) a copy of any terms that are in writing, and

(ii) a written memorandum setting out any terms that are not in writing;

(b) require disclosure to be at such times, in such places and by such means as are specified in the regulations;

(c) require the place and means of disclosure to be stated –

(i) in a note to the company's annual accounts (in the case of its individual accounts) or in such manner as is specified in the regulations (in the case of group accounts),

(ii) in the directors' report, or

(iii) in the auditor's report on the company's annual accounts.

(3) The provisions of this section apply to a variation of the terms mentioned in subsection (1) as they apply to the original terms.

(4) Regulations under this section are subject to affirmative resolution procedure.

494 Disclosure of services provided by auditor or associates and related remuneration

(1) The Secretary of State may make provision by regulations for securing the disclosure of –

(a) the nature of any services provided for a company by the company's auditor (whether in his capacity as auditor or otherwise) or by his associates;

(b) the amount of any remuneration received or receivable by a company's auditor, or his associates, in respect of any such services.

Nothing in the following provisions of this section affects the generality of this power.

(2) The regulations may provide –

(a) for disclosure of the nature of any services provided to be made by reference to any class or description of services specified in the regulations (or any combination of services, however described);

(b) for the disclosure of amounts of remuneration received or receivable in respect of services of any class or description specified in the regulations (or any combination of services, however described);

(c) for the disclosure of separate amounts so received or receivable by the company's auditor or any of his associates, or of aggregate amounts so received or receivable by all or any of those persons.

(3) The regulations may –

(a) provide that "remuneration" includes sums paid in respect of expenses;

(b) apply to benefits in kind as well as to payments of money, and require the disclosure of the nature of any such benefits and their estimated money value;

(c) apply to services provided for associates of a company as well as to those provided for a company;

(d) define "associate" in relation to an auditor and a company respectively.

(4) The regulations may provide that any disclosure required by the regulations is to be made –

(a) in a note to the company's annual accounts (in the case of its individual accounts) or in such manner as is specified in the regulations (in the case of group accounts),

(b) in the directors' report, or

(c) in the auditor's report on the company's annual accounts.

(5) If the regulations provide that any such disclosure is to be made as mentioned in subsection (4)(a) or (b), the regulations may require the auditor to supply the directors of the company with any information necessary to enable the disclosure to be made.

(6) Regulations under this section are subject to negative resolution procedure.

CHAPTER 3

FUNCTIONS OF AUDITOR

Auditor's report

495 Auditor's report on company's annual accounts

(1) A company's auditor must make a report to the company's members on all annual accounts of the company of which copies are, during his tenure of office –

(a) in the case of a private company, to be sent out to members under section 423;

(b) in the case of a public company, to be laid before the company in general meeting under section 437.

(2) The auditor's report must include –

(a) an introduction identifying the annual accounts that are the subject of the audit and the financial reporting framework that has been applied in their preparation, and

(b) a description of the scope of the audit identifying the auditing standards in accordance with which the audit was conducted.

(3) The report must state clearly whether, in the auditor's opinion, the annual accounts –

(a) give a true and fair view –

(i) in the case of an individual balance sheet, of the state of affairs of the company as at the end of the financial year,

(ii) in the case of an individual profit and loss account, of the profit or loss of the company for the financial year,

(iii) in the case of group accounts, of the state of affairs as at the end of the financial year and of the profit or loss for the financial year of the undertakings included in the consolidation as a whole, so far as concerns members of the company;

(b) have been properly prepared in accordance with the relevant financial reporting framework; and

(c) have been prepared in accordance with the requirements of this Act (and, where applicable, Article 4 of the IAS Regulation).

Expressions used in this subsection that are defined for the purposes of Part 15 (see section 474) have the same meaning as in that Part.

(4) The auditor's report –

(a) must be either unqualified or qualified, and

(b) must include a reference to any matters to which the auditor wishes to draw attention by way of emphasis without qualifying the report.

496 Auditor's report on directors' report

The auditor must state in his report on the company's annual accounts whether in his opinion the information given in the directors' report for the financial year for which the accounts are prepared is consistent with those accounts.

497 Auditor's report on auditable part of directors' remuneration report

(1) If the company is a quoted company, the auditor, in his report on the company's annual accounts for the financial year, must –

(a) report to the company's members on the auditable part of the directors' remuneration report, and

(b) state whether in his opinion that part of the directors' remuneration report has been properly prepared in accordance with this Act.

(2) For the purposes of this Part, "the auditable part" of a directors' remuneration report is the part identified as such by regulations under section 421.

Duties and rights of auditors

498 Duties of auditor

(1) A company's auditor, in preparing his report, must carry out such investigations as will enable him to form an opinion as to –

(a) whether adequate accounting records have been kept by the company and returns adequate for their audit have been received from branches not visited by him, and

(b) whether the company's individual accounts are in agreement with the accounting records and returns, and

(c) in the case of a quoted company, whether the auditable part of the company's directors' remuneration report is in agreement with the accounting records and returns.

(2) If the auditor is of the opinion –

(a) that adequate accounting records have not been kept, or that returns adequate for their audit have not been received from branches not visited by him, or

(b) that the company's individual accounts are not in agreement with the accounting records and returns, or

(c) in the case of a quoted company, that the auditable part of its directors' remuneration report is not in agreement with the accounting records and returns, the auditor shall state that fact in his report.

(3) If the auditor fails to obtain all the information and explanations which, to the best of his knowledge and belief, are necessary for the purposes of his audit, he shall state that fact in his report.

(4) If –

(a) the requirements of regulations under section 412 (disclosure of directors' benefits: remuneration, pensions and compensation for loss of office) are not complied with in the annual accounts, or

(b) in the case of a quoted company, the requirements of regulations under section 421 as to information forming the auditable part of the directors' remuneration report are not complied with in that report,

the auditor must include in his report, so far as he is reasonably able to do so, a statement giving the required particulars.

(5) If the directors of the company have prepared accounts and reports in accordance with the small companies regime and in the auditor's opinion they were not entitled so to do, the auditor shall state that fact in his report.

499 Auditor's general right to information

(1) An auditor of a company –

(a) has a right of access at all times to the company's books, accounts and vouchers (in whatever form they are held), and

(b) may require any of the following persons to provide him with such information or explanations as he thinks necessary for the performance of his duties as auditor.

(2) Those persons are –

(a) any officer or employee of the company;

(b) any person holding or accountable for any of the company's books, accounts or vouchers;

(c) any subsidiary undertaking of the company which is a body corporate incorporated in the United Kingdom;

(d) any officer, employee or auditor of any such subsidiary undertaking or any person holding or accountable for any books, accounts or vouchers of any such subsidiary undertaking;

(e) any person who fell within any of paragraphs (a) to (d) at a time to which the information or explanations required by the auditor relates or relate.

(3) A statement made by a person in response to a requirement under this section may not be used in evidence against him in criminal proceedings except proceedings for an offence under section 501.

(4) Nothing in this section compels a person to disclose information in respect of which a claim to legal professional privilege (in Scotland, to confidentiality of communications) could be maintained in legal proceedings.

500 Auditor's right to information from overseas subsidiaries

(1) Where a parent company has a subsidiary undertaking that is not a body corporate incorporated in the United Kingdom, the auditor of the parent company may require it to obtain from any of the following persons such information or explanations as he may reasonably require for the purposes of his duties as auditor.

(2) Those persons are –

(a) the undertaking;

(b) any officer, employee or auditor of the undertaking;

(c) any person holding or accountable for any of the undertaking's books, accounts or vouchers;

(d) any person who fell within paragraph (b) or (c) at a time to which the information or explanations relates or relate.

(3) If so required, the parent company must take all such steps as are reasonably open to it to obtain the information or explanations from the person concerned.

(4) A statement made by a person in response to a requirement under this section may not be used in evidence against him in criminal proceedings except proceedings for an offence under section 501.

(5) Nothing in this section compels a person to disclose information in respect of which a claim to legal professional privilege (in Scotland, to confidentiality of communications) could be maintained in legal proceedings.

501 Auditor's rights to information: offences

(1) A person commits an offence who knowingly or recklessly makes to an auditor of a company a statement (oral or written) that –

   (a) conveys or purports to convey any information or explanations which the auditor requires, or is entitled to require, under section 499, and
   (b) is misleading, false or deceptive in a material particular.

(2) A person guilty of an offence under subsection (1) is liable –

   (a) on conviction on indictment, to imprisonment for a term not exceeding two years or a fine (or both);
   (b) on summary conviction –

      (i) in England and Wales, to imprisonment for a term not exceeding twelve months or to a fine not exceeding the statutory maximum (or both);
      (ii) in Scotland or Northern Ireland, to imprisonment for a term not exceeding six months or to a fine not exceeding the statutory maximum (or both).

(3) A person who fails to comply with a requirement under section 499 without delay commits an offence unless it was not reasonably practicable for him to provide the required information or explanations.

(4) If a parent company fails to comply with section 500, an offence is committed by –

   (a) the company, and
   (b) every officer of the company who is in default.

(5) A person guilty of an offence under subsection (3) or (4) is liable on summary conviction to a fine not exceeding level 3 on the standard scale.

(6) Nothing in this section affects any right of an auditor to apply for an injunction (in Scotland, an interdict or an order for specific performance) to enforce any of his rights under section 499 or 500.

502 Auditor's rights in relation to resolutions and meetings

(1) In relation to a written resolution proposed to be agreed to by a private company, the company's auditor is entitled to receive all such communications relating to the resolution as, by virtue of any provision of Chapter 2 of Part 13 of this Act, are required to be supplied to a member of the company.

(2) A company's auditor is entitled –

   (a) to receive all notices of, and other communications relating to, any general meeting which a member of the company is entitled to receive,
   (b) to attend any general meeting of the company, and
   (c) to be heard at any general meeting which he attends on any part of the business of the meeting which concerns him as auditor.

(3) Where the auditor is a firm, the right to attend or be heard at a meeting is exercisable by an individual authorised by the firm in writing to act as its representative at the meeting.

Signature of auditor's report

503 Signature of auditor's report

(1) The auditor's report must state the name of the auditor and be signed and dated.

(2) Where the auditor is an individual, the report must be signed by him.

(3) Where the auditor is a firm, the report must be signed by the senior statutory auditor in his own name, for and on behalf of the auditor.

504 Senior statutory auditor

(1) The senior statutory auditor means the individual identified by the firm as senior statutory auditor in relation to the audit in accordance with –

   (a) standards issued by the European Commission, or

   (b) if there is no applicable standard so issued, any relevant guidance issued by –

      (i) the Secretary of State, or

      (ii) a body appointed by order of the Secretary of State.

(2) The person identified as senior statutory auditor must be eligible for appointment as auditor of the company in question (see Chapter 2 of Part 42 of this Act).

(3) The senior statutory auditor is not, by reason of being named or identified as senior statutory auditor or by reason of his having signed the auditor's report, subject to any civil liability to which he would not otherwise be subject.

(4) An order appointing a body for the purpose of subsection (1)(b)(ii) is subject to negative resolution procedure.

505 Names to be stated in published copies of auditor's report

(1) Every copy of the auditor's report that is published by or on behalf of the company must –

   (a) state the name of the auditor and (where the auditor is a firm) the name of the person who signed it as senior statutory auditor, or

   (b) if the conditions in section 506 (circumstances in which names may be omitted) are met, state that a resolution has been passed and notified to the Secretary of State in accordance with that section.

(2) For the purposes of this section a company is regarded as publishing the report if it publishes, issues or circulates it or otherwise makes it available for public inspection in a manner calculated to invite members of the public generally, or any class of members of the public, to read it.

(3) If a copy of the auditor's report is published without the statement required by this section, an offence is committed by –

   (a) the company, and

   (b) every officer of the company who is in default.

(4) A person guilty of an offence under this section is liable on summary conviction to a fine not exceeding level 3 on the standard scale.

506 Circumstances in which names may be omitted

(1) The auditor's name and, where the auditor is a firm, the name of the person who signed the report as senior statutory auditor, may be omitted from –

   (a) published copies of the report, and

   (b) the copy of the report delivered to the registrar under Chapter 10 of Part 15 (filing of accounts and reports),

   if the following conditions are met.

(2) The conditions are that the company –

(a) considering on reasonable grounds that statement of the name would create or be likely to create a serious risk that the auditor or senior statutory auditor, or any other person, would be subject to violence or intimidation, has resolved that the name should not be stated, and

(b) has given notice of the resolution to the Secretary of State, stating –

(i) the name and registered number of the company,

(ii) the financial year of the company to which the report relates, and

(iii) the name of the auditor and (where the auditor is a firm) the name of the person who signed the report as senior statutory auditor.

Offences in connection with auditor's report

507 Offences in connection with auditor's report

(1) A person to whom this section applies commits an offence if he knowingly or recklessly causes a report under section 495 (auditor's report on company's annual accounts) to include any matter that is misleading, false or deceptive in a material particular.

(2) A person to whom this section applies commits an offence if he knowingly or recklessly causes such a report to omit a statement required by –

(a) section 498(2)(b) (statement that company's accounts do not agree with accounting records and returns),

(b) section 498(3) (statement that necessary information and explanations not obtained), or

(c) section 498(5) (statement that directors wrongly took advantage of exemption from obligation to prepare group accounts).

(3) This section applies to –

(a) where the auditor is an individual, that individual and any employee or agent of his who is eligible for appointment as auditor of the company;

(b) where the auditor is a firm, any director, member, employee or agent of the firm who is eligible for appointment as auditor of the company.

(4) A person guilty of an offence under this section is liable –

(a) on conviction on indictment, to a fine;

(b) on summary conviction, to a fine not exceeding the statutory maximum.

508 Guidance for regulatory and prosecuting authorities: England, Wales and Northern Ireland

(1) The Secretary of State may issue guidance for the purpose of helping relevant regulatory and prosecuting authorities to determine how they should carry out their functions in cases where behaviour occurs that –

(a) appears to involve the commission of an offence under section 507 (offences in connection with auditor's report), and

(b) has been, is being or may be investigated pursuant to arrangements –

(i) under paragraph 15 of Schedule 10 (investigation of complaints against auditors and supervisory bodies), or

(ii) of a kind mentioned in paragraph 24 of that Schedule (independent investigation for disciplinary purposes of public interest cases).

(2) The Secretary of State must obtain the consent of the Attorney General before issuing any such guidance.

(3) In this section "relevant regulatory and prosecuting authorities" means –

(a) supervisory bodies within the meaning of Part 42 of this Act,

    (b) bodies to which the Secretary of State may make grants under section 16(1) of the Companies (Audit, Investigations and Community Enterprise) Act 2004 (c. 27) (bodies concerned with accounting standards etc),

    (c) the Director of the Serious Fraud Office,

    (d) the Director of Public Prosecutions or the Director of Public Prosecutions for Northern Ireland, and

    (e) the Secretary of State.

(4) This section does not apply to Scotland.

509 Guidance for regulatory authorities: Scotland

(1) The Lord Advocate may issue guidance for the purpose of helping relevant regulatory authorities to determine how they should carry out their functions in cases where behaviour occurs that –

    (a) appears to involve the commission of an offence under section 507 (offences in connection with auditor's report), and

    (b) has been, is being or may be investigated pursuant to arrangements –

        (i) under paragraph 15 of Schedule 10 (investigation of complaints against auditors and supervisory bodies), or

        (ii) of a kind mentioned in paragraph 24 of that Schedule (independent investigation for disciplinary purposes of public interest cases).

(2) The Lord Advocate must consult the Secretary of State before issuing any such guidance.

(3) In this section "relevant regulatory authorities" means –

    (a) supervisory bodies within the meaning of Part 42 of this Act,

    (b) bodies to which the Secretary of State may make grants under section 16(1) of the Companies (Audit, Investigations and Community Enterprise) Act 2004 (c. 27) (bodies concerned with accounting standards etc), and

    (c) the Secretary of State.

(4) This section applies only to Scotland.

CHAPTER 4

REMOVAL, RESIGNATION, ETC OF AUDITORS

Removal of auditor

510 Resolution removing auditor from office

(1) The members of a company may remove an auditor from office at any time.

(2) This power is exercisable only –

    (a) by ordinary resolution at a meeting, and

    (b) in accordance with section 511 (special notice of resolution to remove auditor).

(3) Nothing in this section is to be taken as depriving the person removed of compensation or damages payable to him in respect of the termination –

    (a) of his appointment as auditor, or

    (b) of any appointment terminating with that as auditor.

(4) An auditor may not be removed from office before the expiration of his term of office except by resolution under this section.

511 Special notice required for resolution removing auditor from office

(1) Special notice is required for a resolution at a general meeting of a company removing an auditor from office.

(2) On receipt of notice of such an intended resolution the company must immediately send a copy of it to the auditor proposed to be removed.

(3) The auditor proposed to be removed may make with respect to the intended resolution representations in writing to the company (not exceeding a reasonable length) and request their notification to members of the company.

(4) The company must (unless the representations are received by it too late for it to do so) –

(a) in any notice of the resolution given to members of the company, state the fact of the representations having been made, and

(b) send a copy of the representations to every member of the company to whom notice of the meeting is or has been sent.

(5) If a copy of any such representations is not sent out as required because received too late or because of the company's default, the auditor may (without prejudice to his right to be heard orally) require that the representations be read out at the meeting.

(6) Copies of the representations need not be sent out and the representations need not be read at the meeting if, on the application either of the company or of any other person claiming to be aggrieved, the court is satisfied that the auditor is using the provisions of this section to secure needless publicity for defamatory matter.

The court may order the company's costs (in Scotland, expenses) on the application to be paid in whole or in part by the auditor, notwithstanding that he is not a party to the application.

512 Notice to registrar of resolution removing auditor from office

(1) Where a resolution is passed under section 510 (resolution removing auditor from office), the company must give notice of that fact to the registrar within 14 days.

(2) If a company fails to give the notice required by this section, an offence is committed by –

(a) the company, and

(b) every officer of it who is in default.

(3) A person guilty of an offence under this section is liable on summary conviction to a fine not exceeding level 3 on the standard scale and, for continued contravention, a daily default fine not exceeding one-tenth of level 3 on the standard scale.

513 Rights of auditor who has been removed from office

(1) An auditor who has been removed by resolution under section 510 has, notwithstanding his removal, the rights conferred by section 502(2) in relation to any general meeting of the company –

(a) at which his term of office would otherwise have expired, or

(b) at which it is proposed to fill the vacancy caused by his removal.

(2) In such a case the references in that section to matters concerning the auditor as auditor shall be construed as references to matters concerning him as a former auditor.

Failure to re-appoint auditor

514 Failure to re-appoint auditor: special procedure required for written resolution

(1) This section applies where a resolution is proposed as a written resolution of a private company whose effect would be to appoint a person as auditor in place of a person

(the "outgoing auditor") whose term of office has expired, or is to expire, at the end of the period for appointing auditors.

(2) The following provisions apply if –

(a) no period for appointing auditors has ended since the outgoing auditor ceased to hold office, or

(b) such a period has ended and an auditor or auditors should have been appointed but were not.

(3) The company must send a copy of the proposed resolution to the person proposed to be appointed and to the outgoing auditor.

(4) The outgoing auditor may, within 14 days after receiving the notice, make with respect to the proposed resolution representations in writing to the company (not exceeding a reasonable length) and request their circulation to members of the company.

(5) The company must circulate the representations together with the copy or copies of the resolution circulated in accordance with section 291 (resolution proposed by directors) or section 293 (resolution proposed by members).

(6) Where subsection (5) applies –

(a) the period allowed under section 293(3) for service of copies of the proposed resolution is 28 days instead of 21 days, and

(b) the provisions of section 293(5) and (6) (offences) apply in relation to a failure to comply with that subsection as in relation to a default in complying with that section.

(7) Copies of the representations need not be circulated if, on the application either of the company or of any other person claiming to be aggrieved, the court is satisfied that the auditor is using the provisions of this section to secure needless publicity for defamatory matter.

The court may order the company's costs (in Scotland, expenses) on the application to be paid in whole or in part by the auditor, notwithstanding that he is not a party to the application.

(8) If any requirement of this section is not complied with, the resolution is ineffective.

515 Failure to re-appoint auditor: special notice required for resolution at general meeting

(1) This section applies to a resolution at a general meeting of a company whose effect would be to appoint a person as auditor in place of a person (the "outgoing auditor") whose term of office has ended, or is to end –

(a) in the case of a private company, at the end of the period for appointing auditors;

(b) in the case of a public company, at the end of the next accounts meeting.

(2) Special notice is required of such a resolution if –

(a) in the case of a private company –

(i) no period for appointing auditors has ended since the outgoing auditor ceased to hold office, or

(ii) such a period has ended and an auditor or auditors should have been appointed but were not;

(b) in the case of a public company –

(i) there has been no accounts meeting of the company since the outgoing auditor ceased to hold office, or

(ii) there has been an accounts meeting at which an auditor or auditors should have been appointed but were not.

(3) On receipt of notice of such an intended resolution the company shall forthwith send a copy of it to the person proposed to be appointed and to the outgoing auditor.

(4) The outgoing auditor may make with respect to the intended resolution representations in writing to the company (not exceeding a reasonable length) and request their notification to members of the company.

(5) The company must (unless the representations are received by it too late for it to do so) –

(a) in any notice of the resolution given to members of the company, state the fact of the representations having been made, and

(b) send a copy of the representations to every member of the company to whom notice of the meeting is or has been sent.

(6) If a copy of any such representations is not sent out as required because received too late or because of the company's default, the outgoing auditor may (without prejudice to his right to be heard orally) require that the representations be read out at the meeting.

(7) Copies of the representations need not be sent out and the representations need not be read at the meeting if, on the application either of the company or of any other person claiming to be aggrieved, the court is satisfied that the auditor is using the provisions of this section to secure needless publicity for defamatory matter.

The court may order the company's costs (in Scotland, expenses) on the application to be paid in whole or in part by the outgoing auditor, notwithstanding that he is not a party to the application.

Resignation of auditor

516 Resignation of auditor

(1) An auditor of a company may resign his office by depositing a notice in writing to that effect at the company's registered office.

(2) The notice is not effective unless it is accompanied by the statement required by section 519.

(3) An effective notice of resignation operates to bring the auditor's term of office to an end as of the date on which the notice is deposited or on such later date as may be specified in it.

517 Notice to registrar of resignation of auditor

(1) Where an auditor resigns the company must within 14 days of the deposit of a notice of resignation send a copy of the notice to the registrar of companies.

(2) If default is made in complying with this section, an offence is committed by –

(a) the company, and

(b) every officer of the company who is in default.

(3) A person guilty of an offence under this section is liable –

(a) on conviction on indictment, to a fine;

(b) on summary conviction, to a fine not exceeding the statutory maximum and, for continued contravention, a daily default fine not exceeding one-tenth of the statutory maximum.

518 Rights of resigning auditor

(1) This section applies where an auditor's notice of resignation is accompanied by a statement of the circumstances connected with his resignation (see section 519).

(2) He may deposit with the notice a signed requisition calling on the directors of the company forthwith duly to convene a general meeting of the company for the purpose of receiving and considering such explanation of the circumstances connected with his resignation as he may wish to place before the meeting.

(3) He may request the company to circulate to its members –

(a) before the meeting convened on his requisition, or

(b) before any general meeting at which his term of office would otherwise have expired or at which it is proposed to fill the vacancy caused by his resignation,

a statement in writing (not exceeding a reasonable length) of the circumstances connected with his resignation.

(4) The company must (unless the statement is received too late for it to comply) –

    (a) in any notice of the meeting given to members of the company, state the fact of the statement having been made, and

    (b) send a copy of the statement to every member of the company to whom notice of the meeting is or has been sent.

(5) The directors must within 21 days from the date of the deposit of a requisition under this section proceed duly to convene a meeting for a day not more than 28 days after the date on which the notice convening the meeting is given.

(6) If default is made in complying with subsection (5), every director who failed to take all reasonable steps to secure that a meeting was convened commits an offence.

(7) A person guilty of an offence under this section is liable –

    (a) on conviction on indictment, to a fine;

    (b) on summary conviction to a fine not exceeding the statutory maximum.

(8) If a copy of the statement mentioned above is not sent out as required because received too late or because of the company's default, the auditor may (without prejudice to his right to be heard orally) require that the statement be read out at the meeting.

(9) Copies of a statement need not be sent out and the statement need not be read out at the meeting if, on the application either of the company or of any other person who claims to be aggrieved, the court is satisfied that the auditor is using the provisions of this section to secure needless publicity for defamatory matter.

The court may order the company's costs (in Scotland, expenses) on such an application to be paid in whole or in part by the auditor, notwithstanding that he is not a party to the application.

(10) An auditor who has resigned has, notwithstanding his resignation, the rights conferred by section 502(2) in relation to any such general meeting of the company as is mentioned in subsection (3)(a) or (b) above.

In such a case the references in that section to matters concerning the auditor as auditor shall be construed as references to matters concerning him as a former auditor.

Statement by auditor on ceasing to hold office

519 Statement by auditor to be deposited with company

(1) Where an auditor of an unquoted company ceases for any reason to hold office, he must deposit at the company's registered office a statement of the circumstances connected with his ceasing to hold office, unless he considers that there are no circumstances in connection with his ceasing to hold office that need to be brought to the attention of members or creditors of the company.

(2) If he considers that there are no circumstances in connection with his ceasing to hold office that need to be brought to the attention of members or creditors of the company, he must deposit at the company's registered office a statement to that effect.

(3) Where an auditor of a quoted company ceases for any reason to hold office, he must deposit at the company's registered office a statement of the circumstances connected with his ceasing to hold office.

(4) The statement required by this section must be deposited –

    (a) in the case of resignation, along with the notice of resignation;

(b) in the case of failure to seek re-appointment, not less than 14 days before the end of the time allowed for next appointing an auditor;

(c) in any other case, not later than the end of the period of 14 days beginning with the date on which he ceases to hold office.

(5) A person ceasing to hold office as auditor who fails to comply with this section commits an offence.

(6) In proceedings for such an offence it is a defence for the person charged to show that he took all reasonable steps and exercised all due diligence to avoid the commission of the offence.

(7) A person guilty of an offence under this section is liable –

(a) on conviction on indictment, to a fine;

(b) on summary conviction, to a fine not exceeding the statutory maximum.

520 Company's duties in relation to statement

(1) This section applies where the statement deposited under section 519 states the circumstances connected with the auditor's ceasing to hold office.

(2) The company must within 14 days of the deposit of the statement either –

(a) send a copy of it to every person who under section 423 is entitled to be sent copies of the accounts, or

(b) apply to the court.

(3) If it applies to the court, the company must notify the auditor of the application.

(4) If the court is satisfied that the auditor is using the provisions of section 519 to secure needless publicity for defamatory matter –

(a) it shall direct that copies of the statement need not be sent out, and

(b) it may further order the company's costs (in Scotland, expenses) on the application to be paid in whole or in part by the auditor, even if he is not a party to the application.

The company must within 14 days of the court's decision send to the persons mentioned in subsection (2)(a) a statement setting out the effect of the order.

(5) If no such direction is made the company must send copies of the statement to the persons mentioned in subsection (2)(a) within 14 days of the court's decision or, as the case may be, of the discontinuance of the proceedings.

(6) In the event of default in complying with this section an offence is committed by every officer of the company who is in default.

(7) In proceedings for such an offence it is a defence for the person charged to show that he took all reasonable steps and exercised all due diligence to avoid the commission of the offence.

(8) A person guilty of an offence under this section is liable –

(a) on conviction on indictment, to a fine;

(b) on summary conviction, to a fine not exceeding the statutory maximum.

521 Copy of statement to be sent to registrar

(1) Unless within 21 days beginning with the day on which he deposited the statement under section 519 the auditor receives notice of an application to the court under section 520, he must within a further seven days send a copy of the statement to the registrar.

(2) If an application to the court is made under section 520 and the auditor subsequently receives notice under subsection (5) of that section, he must within seven days of receiving the notice send a copy of the statement to the registrar.

(3) An auditor who fails to comply with subsection (1) or (2) commits an offence.

(4) In proceedings for such an offence it is a defence for the person charged to show that

he took all reasonable steps and exercised all due diligence to avoid the commission of the offence.

(5) A person guilty of an offence under this section is liable –

(a) on conviction on indictment, to a fine;

(b) on summary conviction, to a fine not exceeding the statutory maximum.

522 Duty of auditor to notify appropriate audit authority

(1) Where –

(a) in the case of a major audit, an auditor ceases for any reason to hold office, or

(b) in the case of an audit that is not a major audit, an auditor ceases to hold office before the end of his term of office,

the auditor ceasing to hold office must notify the appropriate audit authority.

(2) The notice must –

(a) inform the appropriate audit authority that he has ceased to hold office, and

(b) be accompanied by a copy of the statement deposited by him at the company's registered office in accordance with section 519.

(3) If the statement so deposited is to the effect that he considers that there are no circumstances in connection with his ceasing to hold office that need to be brought to the attention of members or creditors of the company, the notice must also be accompanied by a statement of the reasons for his ceasing to hold office.

(4) The auditor must comply with this section –

(a) in the case of a major audit, at the same time as he deposits a statement at the company's registered office in accordance with section 519;

(b) in the case of an audit that is not a major audit, at such time (not being earlier than the time mentioned in paragraph (a)) as the appropriate audit authority may require.

(5) A person ceasing to hold office as auditor who fails to comply with this section commits an offence.

(6) If that person is a firm an offence is committed by –

(a) the firm, and

(b) every officer of the firm who is in default.

(7) In proceedings for an offence under this section it is a defence for the person charged to show that he took all reasonable steps and exercised all due diligence to avoid the commission of the offence.

(8) A person guilty of an offence under this section is liable –

(a) on conviction on indictment, to a fine;

(b) on summary conviction, to a fine not exceeding the statutory maximum.

523 Duty of company to notify appropriate audit authority

(1) Where an auditor ceases to hold office before the end of his term of office, the company must notify the appropriate audit authority.

(2) The notice must –

(a) inform the appropriate audit authority that the auditor has ceased to hold office, and

(b) be accompanied by –

(i) a statement by the company of the reasons for his ceasing to hold office, or

(ii) if the copy of the statement deposited by the auditor at the company's registered office in accordance with section 519 contains a statement of circumstances in connection with his ceasing to hold office that need to be brought to the attention of members or creditors of the company, a copy of that statement.

(3) The company must give notice under this section not later than 14 days after the date on which the auditor's statement is deposited at the company's registered office in accordance with section 519.

(4) If a company fails to comply with this section, an offence is committed by –

(a) the company, and
(b) every officer of the company who is in default.

(5) In proceedings for such an offence it is a defence for the person charged to show that he took all reasonable steps and exercised all due diligence to avoid the commission of the offence.

(6) A person guilty of an offence under this section is liable –

(a) on conviction on indictment, to a fine;
(b) on summary conviction, to a fine not exceeding the statutory maximum.

524 Information to be given to accounting authorities

(1) The appropriate audit authority on receiving notice under section 522 or 523 of an auditor's ceasing to hold office –

(a) must inform the accounting authorities, and
(b) may if it thinks fit forward to those authorities a copy of the statement or statements accompanying the notice.

(2) The accounting authorities are –

(a) the Secretary of State, and
(b) any person authorised by the Secretary of State for the purposes of section 456 (revision of defective accounts: persons authorised to apply to court).

(3) If either of the accounting authorities is also the appropriate audit authority it is only necessary to comply with this section as regards any other accounting authority.

(4) If the court has made an order under section 520(4) directing that copies of the statement need not be sent out by the company, sections 460 and 461 (restriction on further disclosure) apply in relation to the copies sent to the accounting authorities as they apply to information obtained under section 459 (power to require documents etc).

525 Meaning of "appropriate audit authority" and "major audit"

(1) In sections 522, 523 and 524 "appropriate audit authority" means –

(a) in the case of a major audit –

(i)   the Secretary of State, or
(ii) if the Secretary of State has delegated functions under section 1252 to a body whose functions include receiving the notice in question, that body;

(b) in the case of an audit that is not a major audit, the relevant supervisory body.

"Supervisory body" has the same meaning as in Part 42 (statutory auditors) (see section 1217).

(2) In sections 522 and this section "major audit" means a statutory audit conducted in respect of –

(a) a company any of whose securities have been admitted to the official list (within the meaning of Part 6 of the Financial Services and Markets Act 2000 (c. 8)), or
(b) any other person in whose financial condition there is a major public interest.

(3) In determining whether an audit is a major audit within subsection (2)(b), regard shall be had to any guidance issued by any of the authorities mentioned in subsection (1).

Supplementary

526 Effect of casual vacancies

If an auditor ceases to hold office for any reason, any surviving or continuing auditor or auditors may continue to act.

CHAPTER 5

QUOTED COMPANIES: RIGHT OF MEMBERS TO RAISE AUDIT CONCERNS AT ACCOUNTS MEETING

527 Members' power to require website publication of audit concerns

(1) The members of a quoted company may require the company to publish on a website a statement setting out any matter relating to –

    (a) the audit of the company's accounts (including the auditor's report and the conduct of the audit) that are to be laid before the next accounts meeting, or

    (b) any circumstances connected with an auditor of the company ceasing to hold office since the previous accounts meeting,

that the members propose to raise at the next accounts meeting of the company.

(2) A company is required to do so once it has received requests to that effect from –

    (a) members representing at least 5% of the total voting rights of all the members who have a relevant right to vote (excluding any voting rights attached to any shares in the company held as treasury shares), or

    (b) at least 100 members who have a relevant right to vote and hold shares in the company on which there has been paid up an average sum, per member, of at least £100.

See also section 153 (exercise of rights where shares held on behalf of others).

(3) In subsection (2) a "relevant right to vote" means a right to vote at the accounts meeting.

(4) A request –

    (a) may be sent to the company in hard copy or electronic form,

    (b) must identify the statement to which it relates,

    (c) must be authenticated by the person or persons making it, and

    (d) must be received by the company at least one week before the meeting to which it relates.

(5) A quoted company is not required to place on a website a statement under this section if, on an application by the company or another person who claims to be aggrieved, the court is satisfied that the rights conferred by this section are being abused.

(6) The court may order the members requesting website publication to pay the whole or part of the company's costs (in Scotland, expenses) on such an application, even if they are not parties to the application.

528 Requirements as to website availability

(1) The following provisions apply for the purposes of section 527 (website publication of members' statement of audit concerns).

(2) The information must be made available on a website that –

    (a) is maintained by or on behalf of the company, and

    (b) identifies the company in question.

(3) Access to the information on the website, and the ability to obtain a hard copy of the information from the website, must not be conditional on the payment of a fee or otherwise restricted.

(4) The statement –

    (a) must be made available within three working days of the company being required to publish it on a website, and

    (b) must be kept available until after the meeting to which it relates.

(5) A failure to make information available on a website throughout the period specified in subsection (4)(b) is disregarded if –

    (a) the information is made available on the website for part of that period, and

    (b) the failure is wholly attributable to circumstances that it would not be reasonable to have expected the company to prevent or avoid.

529 Website publication: company's supplementary duties

(1) A quoted company must in the notice it gives of the accounts meeting draw attention to –

    (a) the possibility of a statement being placed on a website in pursuance of members' requests under section 527, and

    (b) the effect of the following provisions of this section.

(2) A company may not require the members requesting website publication to pay its expenses in complying with that section or section 528 (requirements in connection with website publication).

(3) Where a company is required to place a statement on a website under section 527 it must forward the statement to the company's auditor not later than the time when it makes the statement available on the website.

(4) The business which may be dealt with at the accounts meeting includes any statement that the company has been required under section 527 to publish on a website.

530 Website publication: offences

(1) In the event of default in complying with –

    (a) section 528 (requirements as to website publication), or

    (b) section 529 (companies' supplementary duties in relation to request for website publication),

an offence is committed by every officer of the company who is in default.

(2) A person guilty of an offence under this section is liable –

    (a) on conviction on indictment, to a fine;

    (b) on summary conviction, to a fine not exceeding the statutory maximum.

531 Meaning of "quoted company"

(1) For the purposes of this Chapter a company is a quoted company if it is a quoted company in accordance with section 385 (quoted and unquoted companies for the purposes of Part 15) in relation to the financial year to which the accounts to be laid at the next accounts meeting relate.

(2) The provisions of subsections (4) to (6) of that section (power to amend definition by regulations) apply in relation to the provisions of this Chapter as in relation to the provisions of that Part.

CHAPTER 6

AUDITORS' LIABILITY

Voidness of provisions protecting auditors from liability

532 Voidness of provisions protecting auditors from liability

(1) This section applies to any provision –

   (a) for exempting an auditor of a company (to any extent) from any liability that would otherwise attach to him in connection with any negligence, default, breach of duty or breach of trust in relation to the company occurring in the course of the audit of accounts, or

   (b) by which a company directly or indirectly provides an indemnity (to any extent) for an auditor of the company, or of an associated company, against any liability attaching to him in connection with any negligence, default, breach of duty or breach of trust in relation to the company of which he is auditor occurring in the course of the audit of accounts.

(2) Any such provision is void, except as permitted by –

   (a) section 533 (indemnity for costs of successfully defending proceedings), or

   (b) sections 534 to 536 (liability limitation agreements).

(3) This section applies to any provision, whether contained in a company's articles or in any contract with the company or otherwise.

(4) For the purposes of this section companies are associated if one is a subsidiary of the other or both are subsidiaries of the same body corporate.

Indemnity for costs of defending proceedings

533 Indemnity for costs of successfully defending proceedings

Section 532 (general voidness of provisions protecting auditors from liability) does not prevent a company from indemnifying an auditor against any liability incurred by him –

   (a) in defending proceedings (whether civil or criminal) in which judgment is given in his favour or he is acquitted, or

   (b) in connection with an application under section 1157 (power of court to grant relief in case of honest and reasonable conduct) in which relief is granted to him by the court.

Liability limitation agreements

534 Liability limitation agreements

(1) A "liability limitation agreement" is an agreement that purports to limit the amount of a liability owed to a company by its auditor in respect of any negligence, default, breach of duty or breach of trust, occurring in the course of the audit of accounts, of which the auditor may be guilty in relation to the company.

(2) Section 532 (general voidness of provisions protecting auditors from liability) does not affect the validity of a liability limitation agreement that –

   (a) complies with section 535 (terms of liability limitation agreement) and of any regulations under that section, and

   (b) is authorised by the members of the company (see section 536).

(3) Such an agreement –

    (a) is effective to the extent provided by section 537, and

    (b) is not subject –

        (i)   in England and Wales or Northern Ireland, to section 2(2) or 3(2)(a) of the Unfair Contract Terms Act 1977 (c. 50);

        (ii) in Scotland, to section 16(1)(b) or 17(1)(a) of that Act.

535 Terms of liability limitation agreement

(1) A liability limitation agreement –

    (a) must not apply in respect of acts or omissions occurring in the course of the audit of accounts for more than one financial year, and

    (b) must specify the financial year in relation to which it applies.

(2) The Secretary of State may by regulations –

    (a) require liability limitation agreements to contain specified provisions or provisions of a specified description;

    (b) prohibit liability limitation agreements from containing specified provisions or provisions of a specified description.

    "Specified" here means specified in the regulations.

(3) Without prejudice to the generality of the power conferred by subsection (2), that power may be exercised with a view to preventing adverse effects on competition.

(4) Subject to the preceding provisions of this section, it is immaterial how a liability limitation agreement is framed.

    In particular, the limit on the amount of the auditor's liability need not be a sum of money, or a formula, specified in the agreement.

(5) Regulations under this section are subject to negative resolution procedure.

536 Authorisation of agreement by members of the company

(1) A liability limitation agreement is authorised by the members of the company if it has been authorised under this section and that authorisation has not been withdrawn.

(2) A liability limitation agreement between a private company and its auditor may be authorised –

    (a) by the company passing a resolution, before it enters into the agreement, waiving the need for approval,

    (b) by the company passing a resolution, before it enters into the agreement, approving the agreement's principal terms, or

    (c) by the company passing a resolution, after it enters into the agreement, approving the agreement.

(3) A liability limitation agreement between a public company and its auditor may be authorised –

    (a) by the company passing a resolution in general meeting, before it enters into the agreement, approving the agreement's principal terms, or

    (b) by the company passing a resolution in general meeting, after it enters into the agreement, approving the agreement.

(4) The "principal terms" of an agreement are terms specifying, or relevant to the determination of –

    (a) the kind (or kinds) of acts or omissions covered,

    (b) the financial year to which the agreement relates, or

    (c) the limit to which the auditor's liability is subject.

(5) Authorisation under this section may be withdrawn by the company passing an ordinary resolution to that effect –

    (a) at any time before the company enters into the agreement, or

(b) if the company has already entered into the agreement, before the beginning of the financial year to which the agreement relates.

Paragraph (b) has effect notwithstanding anything in the agreement.

537 Effect of liability limitation agreement

(1) A liability limitation agreement is not effective to limit the auditor's liability to less than such amount as is fair and reasonable in all the circumstances of the case having regard (in particular) to –

(a) the auditor's responsibilities under this Part,

(b) the nature and purpose of the auditor's contractual obligations to the company, and

(c) the professional standards expected of him.

(2) A liability limitation agreement that purports to limit the auditor's liability to less than the amount mentioned in subsection (1) shall have effect as if it limited his liability to that amount.

(3) In determining what is fair and reasonable in all the circumstances of the case no account is to be taken of –

(a) matters arising after the loss or damage in question has been incurred, or

(b) matters (whenever arising) affecting the possibility of recovering compensation from other persons liable in respect of the same loss or damage.

538 Disclosure of agreement by company

(1) A company which has entered into a liability limitation agreement must make such disclosure in connection with the agreement as the Secretary of State may require by regulations.

(2) The regulations may provide, in particular, that any disclosure required by the regulations shall be made –

(a) in a note to the company's annual accounts (in the case of its individual accounts) or in such manner as is specified in the regulations (in the case of group accounts), or

(b) in the directors' report.

(3) Regulations under this section are subject to negative resolution procedure.

CHAPTER 7

SUPPLEMENTARY PROVISIONS

539 Minor definitions

In this Part –

"e-money issuer" means a person who has permission under Part 4 of the Financial Services and Markets Act 2000 (c. 8) to carry on the activity of issuing electronic money within the meaning of article 9B of the Financial Services and Markets Act 2000 (Regulated Activities) Order 2001 (S.I. 2001/544);

"ISD investment firm" has the meaning given by the Glossary forming part of the Handbook made by the Financial Services Authority under the Financial Services and Markets Act 2000;

"qualified", in relation to an auditor's report (or a statement contained in an auditor's report), means that the report or statement does not state the auditor's unqualified opinion that the accounts have been properly prepared in accordance with this Act or, in the case of an undertaking not required to prepare accounts in accordance with this Act, under any corresponding legislation under which it is required to prepare accounts;

"turnover", in relation to a company, means the amounts derived from the provision of goods and services falling within the company's ordinary activities, after deduction of –

(a)   trade discounts,
(b)   value added tax, and
(c)   any other taxes based on the amounts so derived;

"UCITS management company" has the meaning given by the Glossary forming part of the Handbook made by the Financial Services Authority under the Financial Services and Markets Act 2000.

PART 17

A COMPANY'S SHARE CAPITAL

CHAPTER 1
SHARES AND SHARE CAPITAL OF A COMPANY

Shares

540 Shares

(1) In the Companies Acts "share", in relation to a company, means share in the company's share capital.
(2) A company's shares may no longer be converted into stock.
(3) Stock created before the commencement of this Part may be reconverted into shares in accordance with section 620.
(4) In the Companies Acts –

(a) references to shares include stock except where a distinction between share and stock is express or implied, and
(b) references to a number of shares include an amount of stock where the context admits of the reference to shares being read as including stock.

541 Nature of shares

The shares or other interest of a member in a company are personal property (or, in Scotland, moveable property) and are not in the nature of real estate (or heritage).

542 Nominal value of shares

(1) Shares in a limited company having a share capital must each have a fixed nominal value.
(2) An allotment of a share that does not have a fixed nominal value is void.
(3) Shares in a limited company having a share capital may be denominated in any currency, and different classes of shares may be denominated in different currencies. But see section 765 (initial authorised minimum share capital requirement for public company to be met by reference to share capital denominated in sterling or euros).
(4) If a company purports to allot shares in contravention of this section, an offence is committed by every officer of the company who is in default.
(5) A person guilty of an offence under this section is liable –

(a) on conviction on indictment, to a fine;
(b) on summary conviction, to a fine not exceeding the statutory maximum.

543 Numbering of shares

(1) Each share in a company having a share capital must be distinguished by its appropriate number, except in the following circumstances.

(2) If at any time –

    (a) all the issued shares in a company are fully paid up and rank *pari passu* for all purposes, or

    (b) all the issued shares of a particular class in a company are fully paid up and rank *pari passu* for all purposes,

none of those shares need thereafter have a distinguishing number so long as it remains fully paid up and ranks *pari passu* for all purposes with all shares of the same class for the time being issued and fully paid up.

544 Transferability of shares

(1) The shares or other interest of any member in a company are transferable in accordance with the company's articles.

(2) This is subject to –

    (a) the Stock Transfer Act 1963 (c. 18) or the Stock Transfer Act (Northern Ireland) 1963 (c.24 (N.I.)) (which enables securities of certain descriptions to be transferred by a simplified process), and

    (b) regulations under Chapter 2 of Part 21 of this Act (which enable title to securities to be evidenced and transferred without a written instrument).

(3) See Part 21 of this Act generally as regards share transfers.

545 Companies having a share capital

References in the Companies Acts to a company having a share capital are to a company that has power under its constitution to issue shares.

546 Issued and allotted share capital

(1) References in the Companies Acts –

    (a) to "issued share capital" are to shares of a company that have been issued;

    (b) to "allotted share capital" are to shares of a company that have been allotted.

(2) References in the Companies Acts to issued or allotted shares, or to issued or allotted share capital, include shares taken on the formation of the company by the subscribers to the company's memorandum.

Share capital

547 Called-up share capital

In the Companies Acts –

    "called-up share capital", in relation to a company, means so much of its share capital as equals the aggregate amount of the calls made on its shares (whether or not those calls have been paid), together with –

        (a) any share capital paid up without being called, and

        (b) any share capital to be paid on a specified future date under the articles, the terms of allotment of the relevant shares or any other arrangements for payment of those shares; and

    "uncalled share capital" is to be construed accordingly.

548 Equity share capital

In the Companies Acts "equity share capital", in relation to a company, means its issued share capital excluding any part of that capital that, neither as respects dividends nor as respects capital, carries any right to participate beyond a specified amount in a distribution.

CHAPTER 2

ALLOTMENT OF SHARES: GENERAL PROVISIONS

Power of directors to allot shares

549 Exercise by directors of power to allot shares etc

(1) The directors of a company must not exercise any power of the company –

(a) to allot shares in the company, or

(b) to grant rights to subscribe for, or to convert any security into, shares in the company,

except in accordance with section 550 (private company with single class of shares) or section 551 (authorisation by company).

(2) Subsection (1) does not apply –

(a) to the allotment of shares in pursuance of an employees' share scheme, or

(b) to the grant of a right to subscribe for, or to convert any security into, shares so allotted.

(3) If this section applies in relation to the grant of a right to subscribe for, or to convert any security into, shares, it does not apply in relation to the allotment of shares pursuant to that right.

(4) A director who knowingly contravenes, or permits or authorises a contravention of, this section commits an offence.

(5) A person guilty of an offence under this section is liable –

(a) on conviction on indictment, to a fine;

(b) on summary conviction, to a fine not exceeding the statutory maximum.

(6) Nothing in this section affects the validity of an allotment or other transaction.

550 Power of directors to allot shares etc: private company with only one class of shares

Where a private company has only one class of shares, the directors may exercise any power of the company –

(a) to allot shares of that class, or

(b) to grant rights to subscribe for or to convert any security into such shares,

except to the extent that they are prohibited from doing so by the company's articles.

551 Power of directors to allot shares etc: authorisation by company

(1) The directors of a company may exercise a power of the company –

(a) to allot shares in the company, or

(b) to grant rights to subscribe for or to convert any security into shares in the company,

if they are authorised to do so by the company's articles or by resolution of the company.

(2) Authorisation may be given for a particular exercise of the power or for its exercise generally, and may be unconditional or subject to conditions.

(3) Authorisation must –

(a) state the maximum amount of shares that may be allotted under it, and

(b) specify the date on which it will expire, which must be not more than five years from –

   (i) in the case of authorisation contained in the company's articles at the time of its original incorporation, the date of that incorporation;

   (ii) in any other case, the date on which the resolution is passed by virtue of which the authorisation is given.

(4) Authorisation may –

(a) be renewed or further renewed by resolution of the company for a further period not exceeding five years, and

(b) be revoked or varied at any time by resolution of the company.

(5) A resolution renewing authorisation must –

(a) state (or restate) the maximum amount of shares that may be allotted under the authorisation or, as the case may be, the amount remaining to be allotted under it, and

(b) specify the date on which the renewed authorisation will expire.

(6) In relation to rights to subscribe for or to convert any security into shares in the company, references in this section to the maximum amount of shares that may be allotted under the authorisation are to the maximum amount of shares that may be allotted pursuant to the rights.

(7) The directors may allot shares, or grant rights to subscribe for or to convert any security into shares, after authorisation has expired if –

(a) the shares are allotted, or the rights are granted, in pursuance of an offer or agreement made by the company before the authorisation expired, and

(b) the authorisation allowed the company to make an offer or agreement which would or might require shares to be allotted, or rights to be granted, after the authorisation had expired.

(8) A resolution of a company to give, vary, revoke or renew authorisation under this section may be an ordinary resolution, even though it amends the company's articles.

(9) Chapter 3 of Part 3 (resolutions affecting a company's constitution) applies to a resolution under this section.

Prohibition of commissions, discounts and allowances

552 General prohibition of commissions, discounts and allowances

(1) Except as permitted by section 553 (permitted commission), a company must not apply any of its shares or capital money, either directly or indirectly, in payment of any commission, discount or allowance to any person in consideration of his –

(a) subscribing or agreeing to subscribe (whether absolutely or conditionally) for shares in the company, or

(b) procuring or agreeing to procure subscriptions (whether absolute or conditional) for shares in the company.

(2) It is immaterial how the shares or money are so applied, whether by being added to the purchase money of property acquired by the company or to the contract price of work to be executed for the company, or being paid out of the nominal purchase money or contract price, or otherwise.

(3) Nothing in this section affects the payment of such brokerage as has previously been lawful.

553 Permitted commission

(1) A company may, if the following conditions are satisfied, pay a commission to a person in consideration of his subscribing or agreeing to subscribe (whether absolutely or conditionally) for shares in the company, or procuring or agreeing to procure subscriptions (whether absolute or conditional) for shares in the company.

(2) The conditions are that –

    (a) the payment of the commission is authorised by the company's articles; and

    (b) the commission paid or agreed to be paid does not exceed –

        (i)   10% of the price at which the shares are issued, or

        (ii)   the amount or rate authorised by the articles,

    whichever is the less.

(3) A vendor to, or promoter of, or other person who receives payment in money or shares from, a company may apply any part of the money or shares so received in payment of any commission the payment of which directly by the company would be permitted by this section.

Registration of allotment

554 Registration of allotment

(1) A company must register an allotment of shares as soon as practicable and in any event within two months after the date of the allotment.

(2) This does not apply if the company has issued a share warrant in respect of the shares (see section 779).

(3) If a company fails to comply with this section, an offence is committed by –

    (a) the company, and

    (b) every officer of the company who is in default.

(4) A person guilty of an offence under this section is liable on summary conviction to a fine not exceeding level 3 on the standard scale and, for continued contravention, a daily default fine not exceeding one-tenth of level 3 on the standard scale.

(5) For the company's duties as to the issue of share certificates etc, see Part 21 (certification and transfer of securities).

Return of allotment

555 Return of allotment by limited company

(1) This section applies to a company limited by shares and to a company limited by guarantee and having a share capital.

(2) The company must, within one month of making an allotment of shares, deliver to the registrar for registration a return of the allotment.

(3) The return must –

    (a) contain the prescribed information, and

    (b) be accompanied by a statement of capital.

(4) The statement of capital must state with respect to the company's share capital at the date to which the return is made up –

    (a) the total number of shares of the company,

    (b) the aggregate nominal value of those shares,

    (c) for each class of shares –

        (i)   prescribed particulars of the rights attached to the shares,

        (ii)   the total number of shares of that class, and

        (iii) the aggregate nominal value of shares of that class, and

(d) the amount paid up and the amount (if any) unpaid on each share (whether on account of the nominal value of the share or by way of premium).

556 Return of allotment by unlimited company allotting new class of shares

(1) This section applies to an unlimited company that allots shares of a class with rights that are not in all respects uniform with shares previously allotted.

(2) The company must, within one month of making such an allotment, deliver to the registrar for registration a return of the allotment.

(3) The return must contain the prescribed particulars of the rights attached to the shares.

(4) For the purposes of this section shares are not to be treated as different from shares previously allotted by reason only that the former do not carry the same rights to dividends as the latter during the twelve months immediately following the former's allotment.

557 Offence of failure to make return

(1) If a company makes default in complying with –

section 555 (return of allotment of shares by limited company), or
section 556 (return of allotment of new class of shares by unlimited company),

an offence is committed by every officer of the company who is in default.

(2) A person guilty of an offence under this section is liable –

(a) on conviction on indictment, to a fine;

(b) on summary conviction, to a fine not exceeding the statutory maximum and, for continued contravention, a daily default fine not exceeding one-tenth of the statutory maximum.

(3) In the case of default in delivering to the registrar within one month after the allotment the return required by section 555 or 556 –

(a) any person liable for the default may apply to the court for relief, and

(b) the court, if satisfied –

(i)   that the omission to deliver the document was accidental or due to inadvertence, or

(ii) that it is just and equitable to grant relief,

may make an order extending the time for delivery of the document for such period as the court thinks proper.

Supplementary provisions

558 When shares are allotted

For the purposes of the Companies Acts shares in a company are taken to be allotted when a person acquires the unconditional right to be included in the company's register of members in respect of the shares.

559 Provisions about allotment not applicable to shares taken on formation

The provisions of this Chapter have no application in relation to the taking of shares by the subscribers to the memorandum on the formation of the company.

CHAPTER 3

ALLOTMENT OF EQUITY SECURITIES: EXISTING SHAREHOLDERS' RIGHT OF PRE-EMPTION

Introductory

560 Meaning of "equity securities" and related expressions

(1) In this Chapter –

"equity securities" means –

(a) ordinary shares in the company, or
(b) rights to subscribe for, or to convert securities into, ordinary shares in the company;

"ordinary shares" means shares other than shares that as respects dividends and capital carry a right to participate only up to a specified amount in a distribution.

(2) References in this Chapter to the allotment of equity securities include –

(a) the grant of a right to subscribe for, or to convert any securities into, ordinary shares in the company, and
(b) the sale of ordinary shares in the company that immediately before the sale are held by the company as treasury shares.

Existing shareholders' right of pre-emption

561 Existing shareholders' right of pre-emption

(1) A company must not allot equity securities to a person on any terms unless –

(a) it has made an offer to each person who holds ordinary shares in the company to allot to him on the same or more favourable terms a proportion of those securities that is as nearly as practicable equal to the proportion in nominal value held by him of the ordinary share capital of the company, and
(b) the period during which any such offer may be accepted has expired or the company has received notice of the acceptance or refusal of every offer so made.

(2) Securities that a company has offered to allot to a holder of ordinary shares may be allotted to him, or anyone in whose favour he has renounced his right to their allotment, without contravening subsection (1)(b).

(3) If subsection (1) applies in relation to the grant of such a right, it does not apply in relation to the allotment of shares in pursuance of that right.

(4) Shares held by the company as treasury shares are disregarded for the purposes of this section, so that –

(a) the company is not treated as a person who holds ordinary shares, and
(b) the shares are not treated as forming part of the ordinary share capital of the company.

(5) This section is subject to –

(a) sections 564 to 566 (exceptions to pre-emption right),
(b) sections 567 and 568 (exclusion of rights of pre-emption),
(c) sections 569 to 573 (disapplication of pre-emption rights), and
(d) section 576 (saving for certain older pre-emption procedures).

562 Communication of pre-emption offers to shareholders

(1) This section has effect as to the manner in which offers required by section 561 are to be made to holders of a company's shares.

(2) The offer may be made in hard copy or electronic form.

(3) If the holder –

(a) has no registered address in an EEA State and has not given to the company an address in an EEA State for the service of notices on him, or

(b) is the holder of a share warrant,

the offer may be made by causing it, or a notice specifying where a copy of it can be obtained or inspected, to be published in the Gazette.

(4) The offer must state a period during which it may be accepted and the offer shall not be withdrawn before the end of that period.

(5) The period must be a period of at least 21 days beginning –

(a) in the case of an offer made in hard copy form, with the date on which the offer is sent or supplied;

(b) in the case of an offer made in electronic form, with the date on which the offer is sent;

(c) in the case of an offer made by publication in the Gazette, with the date of publication.

(6) The Secretary of State may by regulations made by statutory instrument –

(a) reduce the period specified in subsection (5) (but not to less than 14 days), or

(b) increase that period.

(7) A statutory instrument containing regulations made under subsection (6) is subject to affirmative resolution procedure.

563 Liability of company and officers in case of contravention

(1) This section applies where there is a contravention of –

section 561 (existing shareholders' right of pre-emption), or
section 562 (communication of pre-emption offers to shareholders).

(2) The company and every officer of it who knowingly authorised or permitted the contravention are jointly and severally liable to compensate any person to whom an offer should have been made in accordance with those provisions for any loss, damage, costs or expenses which the person has sustained or incurred by reason of the contravention.

(3) No proceedings to recover any such loss, damage, costs or expenses shall be commenced after the expiration of two years –

(a) from the delivery to the registrar of companies of the return of allotment, or

(b) where equity securities other than shares are granted, from the date of the grant.

Exceptions to right of pre-emption

564 Exception to pre-emption right: bonus shares

Section 561(1) (existing shareholders' right of pre-emption) does not apply in relation to the allotment of bonus shares.

565 Exception to pre-emption right: issue for non-cash consideration

Section 561(1) (existing shareholders' right of pre-emption) does not apply to a particular allotment of equity securities if these are, or are to be, wholly or partly paid up otherwise than in cash.

566 Exception to pre-emption right: securities held under employees' share scheme

Section 561 (existing shareholders' right of pre-emption) does not apply to the allotment of securities that would, apart from any renunciation or assignment of the right to their allotment, be held under an employees' share scheme.

Exclusion of right of pre-emption

567 Exclusion of requirements by private companies

(1) All or any of the requirements of –

    (a)   section 561 (existing shareholders' right of pre-emption), or

    (b)   section 562 (communication of pre-emption offers to shareholders)

may be excluded by provision contained in the articles of a private company.

(2) They may be excluded –

    (a)   generally in relation to the allotment by the company of equity securities, or

    (b)   in relation to allotments of a particular description.

(3) Any requirement or authorisation contained in the articles of a private company that is inconsistent with either of those sections is treated for the purposes of this section as a provision excluding that section.

(4) A provision to which section 568 applies (exclusion of pre-emption right: corresponding right conferred by articles) is not to be treated as inconsistent with section 561.

568 Exclusion of pre-emption right: articles conferring corresponding right

(1) The provisions of this section apply where, in a case in which section 561 (existing shareholders' right of pre-emption) would otherwise apply –

    (a)   a company's articles contain provision ("pre-emption provision") prohibiting the company from allotting ordinary shares of a particular class unless it has complied with the condition that it makes such an offer as is described in section 561(1) to each person who holds ordinary shares of that class, and

    (b)   in accordance with that provision –

        (i)   the company makes an offer to allot shares to such a holder, and

        (ii) he or anyone in whose favour he has renounced his right to their allotment accepts the offer.

(2) In that case, section 561 does not apply to the allotment of those shares and the company may allot them accordingly.

(3) The provisions of section 562 (communication of pre-emption offers to shareholders) apply in relation to offers made in pursuance of the pre-emption provision of the company's articles.

This is subject to section 567 (exclusion of requirements by private companies).

(4) If there is a contravention of the pre-emption provision of the company's articles, the company, and every officer of it who knowingly authorised or permitted the contravention, are jointly and severally liable to compensate any person to whom an offer should have been made under the provision for any loss, damage, costs or expenses which the person has sustained or incurred by reason of the contravention.

(5) No proceedings to recover any such loss, damage, costs or expenses may be commenced after the expiration of two years –

    (a)   from the delivery to the registrar of companies of the return of allotment, or

    (b)   where equity securities other than shares are granted, from the date of the grant.

Disapplication of pre-emption rights

569 Disapplication of pre-emption rights: private company with only one class of shares

(1) The directors of a private company that has only one class of shares may be given power by the articles, or by a special resolution of the company, to allot equity securities of that class as if section 561 (existing shareholders' right of pre-emption) –

(a)   did not apply to the allotment, or

(b)   applied to the allotment with such modifications as the directors may determine.

(2)   Where the directors make an allotment under this section, the provisions of this Chapter have effect accordingly.

570 Disapplication of pre-emption rights: directors acting under general authorisation

(1)   Where the directors of a company are generally authorised for the purposes of section 551 (power of directors to allot shares etc: authorisation by company), they may be given power by the articles, or by a special resolution of the company, to allot equity securities pursuant to that authorisation as if section 561 (existing shareholders' right of pre-emption) –

(a)   did not apply to the allotment, or

(b)   applied to the allotment with such modifications as the directors may determine.

(2)   Where the directors make an allotment under this section, the provisions of this Chapter have effect accordingly.

(3)   The power conferred by this section ceases to have effect when the authorisation to which it relates –

(a)   is revoked, or

(b)   would (if not renewed) expire.

But if the authorisation is renewed the power may also be renewed, for a period not longer than that for which the authorisation is renewed, by a special resolution of the company.

(4)   Notwithstanding that the power conferred by this section has expired, the directors may allot equity securities in pursuance of an offer or agreement previously made by the company if the power enabled the company to make an offer or agreement that would or might require equity securities to be allotted after it expired.

571 Disapplication of pre-emption rights by special resolution

(1)   Where the directors of a company are authorised for the purposes of section 551 (power of directors to allot shares etc: authorisation by company), whether generally or otherwise, the company may by special resolution resolve that section 561 (existing shareholders' right of pre-emption) –

(a)   does not apply to a specified allotment of equity securities to be made pursuant to that authorisation, or

(b)   applies to such an allotment with such modifications as may be specified in the resolution.

(2)   Where such a resolution is passed the provisions of this Chapter have effect accordingly.

(3)   A special resolution under this section ceases to have effect when the authorisation to which it relates –

(a)   is revoked, or

(b)   would (if not renewed) expire.

But if the authorisation is renewed the resolution may also be renewed, for a period not longer than that for which the authorisation is renewed, by a special resolution of the company.

(4)   Notwithstanding that any such resolution has expired, the directors may allot equity securities in pursuance of an offer or agreement previously made by the company if the resolution enabled the company to make an offer or agreement that would or might require equity securities to be allotted after it expired.

(5)   A special resolution under this section, or a special resolution to renew such a resolution, must not be proposed unless –

(a) it is recommended by the directors, and

(b) the directors have complied with the following provisions.

(6) Before such a resolution is proposed, the directors must make a written statement setting out –

(a) their reasons for making the recommendation,

(b) the amount to be paid to the company in respect of the equity securities to be allotted, and

(c) the directors' justification of that amount.

(7) The directors' statement must –

(a) if the resolution is proposed as a written resolution, be sent or submitted to every eligible member at or before the time at which the proposed resolution is sent or submitted to him;

(b) if the resolution is proposed at a general meeting, be circulated to the members entitled to notice of the meeting with that notice.

572 Liability for false statement in directors' statement

(1) This section applies in relation to a directors' statement under section 571 (special resolution disapplying pre-emption rights) that is sent, submitted or circulated under subsection (7) of that section.

(2) A person who knowingly or recklessly authorises or permits the inclusion of any matter that is misleading, false or deceptive in a material particular in such a statement commits an offence.

(3) A person guilty of an offence under this section is liable –

(a) on conviction on indictment, to imprisonment for a term not exceeding two years or a fine (or both);

(b) on summary conviction –

(i) in England and Wales, to imprisonment for a term not exceeding twelve months or to a fine not exceeding the statutory maximum (or both);

(ii) in Scotland or Northern Ireland, to imprisonment for a term not exceeding six months, or to a fine not exceeding the statutory maximum (or both).

573 Disapplication of pre-emption rights: sale of treasury shares

(1) This section applies in relation to a sale of shares that is an allotment of equity securities by virtue of section 560(2)(b) (sale of shares held by company as treasury shares).

(2) The directors of a company may be given power by the articles, or by a special resolution of the company, to allot equity securities as if section 561 (existing shareholders' right of pre-emption) –

(a) did not apply to the allotment, or

(b) applied to the allotment with such modifications as the directors may determine.

(3) The provisions of section 570(2) and (4) apply in that case as they apply to a case within subsection (1) of that section.

(4) The company may by special resolution resolve that section 561 –

(a) shall not apply to a specified allotment of securities, or

(b) shall apply to the allotment with such modifications as may be specified in the resolution.

(5) The provisions of section 571(2) and (4) to (7) apply in that case as they apply to a case within subsection (1) of that section.

Supplementary

574 References to holder of shares in relation to offer

(1) In this Chapter, in relation to an offer to allot securities required by –

    (a)   section 561 (existing shareholders' right of pre-emption), or

    (b)   any provision to which section 568 applies (articles conferring corresponding right),

a reference (however expressed) to the holder of shares of any description is to whoever was the holder of shares of that description at the close of business on a date to be specified in the offer.

(2) The specified date must fall within the period of 28 days immediately before the date of the offer.

575 Saving for other restrictions on offer or allotment

(1) The provisions of this Chapter are without prejudice to any other enactment by virtue of which a company is prohibited (whether generally or in specified circumstances) from offering or allotting equity securities to any person.

(2) Where a company cannot by virtue of such an enactment offer or allot equity securities to a holder of ordinary shares of the company, those shares are disregarded for the purposes of section 561 (existing shareholders' right of preemption), so that –

    (a)   the person is not treated as a person who holds ordinary shares, and

    (b)   the shares are not treated as forming part of the ordinary share capital of the company.

576 Saving for certain older pre-emption requirements

(1) In the case of a public company the provisions of this Chapter do not apply to an allotment of equity securities that are subject to a pre-emption requirement in relation to which section 96(1) of the Companies Act 1985 (c. 6) or Article 106(1) of the Companies (Northern Ireland) Order 1986 (S.I. 1986/1032 (N.I. 6)) applied immediately before the commencement of this Chapter.

(2) In the case of a private company a pre-emption requirement to which section 96(3) of the Companies Act 1985 or Article 106(3) of the Companies (Northern Ireland) Order 1986 applied immediately before the commencement of this Chapter shall have effect, so long as the company remains a private company, as if it were contained in the company's articles.

(3) A pre-emption requirement to which section 96(4) of the Companies Act 1985 or Article 106(4) of the Companies (Northern Ireland) Order 1986 applied immediately before the commencement of this section shall be treated for the purposes of this Chapter as if it were contained in the company's articles.

577 Provisions about pre-emption not applicable to shares taken on formation

The provisions of this Chapter have no application in relation to the taking of shares by the subscribers to the memorandum on the formation of the company.

CHAPTER 4

PUBLIC COMPANIES: ALLOTMENT WHERE ISSUE NOT FULLY SUBSCRIBED

578 Public companies: allotment where issue not fully subscribed

(1) No allotment shall be made of shares of a public company offered for subscription unless –

    (a) the issue is subscribed for in full, or

    (b) the offer is made on terms that the shares subscribed for may be allotted –

        (i)   in any event, or

        (ii) if specified conditions are met (and those conditions are met).

(2) If shares are prohibited from being allotted by subsection (1) and 40 days have elapsed after the first making of the offer, all money received from applicants for shares must be repaid to them forthwith, without interest.

(3) If any of the money is not repaid within 48 days after the first making of the offer, the directors of the company are jointly and severally liable to repay it, with interest at the rate for the time being specified under section 17 of the Judgments Act 1838 (c. 110) from the expiration of the 48th day.

A director is not so liable if he proves that the default in the repayment of the money was not due to any misconduct or negligence on his part.

(4) This section applies in the case of shares offered as wholly or partly payable otherwise than in cash as it applies in the case of shares offered for subscription.

(5) In that case –

    (a) the references in subsection (1) to subscription shall be construed accordingly;

    (b) references in subsections (2) and (3) to the repayment of money received from applicants for shares include –

        (i)   the return of any other consideration so received (including, if the case so requires, the release of the applicant from any undertaking), or

        (ii) if it is not reasonably practicable to return the consideration, the payment of money equal to its value at the time it was so received;

    (c) references to interest apply accordingly.

(6) Any condition requiring or binding an applicant for shares to waive compliance with any requirement of this section is void.

579 Public companies: effect of irregular allotment where issue not fully subscribed

(1) An allotment made by a public company to an applicant in contravention of section 578 (public companies: allotment where issue not fully subscribed) is voidable at the instance of the applicant within one month after the date of the allotment, and not later.

(2) It is so voidable even if the company is in the course of being wound up.

(3) A director of a public company who knowingly contravenes, or permits or authorises the contravention of, any provision of section 578 with respect to allotment is liable to compensate the company and the allottee respectively for any loss, damages, costs or expenses that the company or allottee may have sustained or incurred by the contravention.

(4) Proceedings to recover any such loss, damages, costs or expenses may not be brought more than two years after the date of the allotment.

CHAPTER 5

PAYMENT FOR SHARES

General rules

580 Shares not to be allotted at a discount

(1) A company's shares must not be allotted at a discount.

(2) If shares are allotted in contravention of this section, the allottee is liable to pay the company an amount equal to the amount of the discount, with interest at the appropriate rate.

581 Provision for different amounts to be paid on shares

A company, if so authorised by its articles, may –

    (a) make arrangements on the issue of shares for a difference between the shareholders in the amounts and times of payment of calls on their shares;

    (b) accept from any member the whole or part of the amount remaining unpaid on any shares held by him, although no part of that amount has been called up;

    (c) pay a dividend in proportion to the amount paid up on each share where a larger amount is paid up on some shares than on others.

582 General rule as to means of payment

(1) Shares allotted by a company, and any premium on them, may be paid up in money or money's worth (including goodwill and know-how).

(2) This section does not prevent a company –

    (a) from allotting bonus shares to its members, or

    (b) from paying up, with sums available for the purpose, any amounts for the time being unpaid on any of its shares (whether on account of the nominal value of the shares or by way of premium).

(3) This section has effect subject to the following provisions of this Chapter (additional rules for public companies).

583 Meaning of payment in cash

(1) The following provisions have effect for the purposes of the Companies Acts.

(2) A share in a company is deemed paid up (as to its nominal value or any premium on it) in cash, or allotted for cash, if the consideration received for the allotment or payment up is a cash consideration.

(3) A "cash consideration" means –

    (a) cash received by the company,

    (b) a cheque received by the company in good faith that the directors have no reason for suspecting will not be paid,

    (c) a release of a liability of the company for a liquidated sum,

    (d) an undertaking to pay cash to the company at a future date, or

    (e) payment by any other means giving rise to a present or future entitlement (of the company or a person acting on the company's behalf) to a payment, or credit equivalent to payment, in cash.

(4) The Secretary of State may by order provide that particular means of payment specified in the order are to be regarded as falling within subsection (3)(e).

(5) In relation to the allotment or payment up of shares in a company –

    (a) the payment of cash to a person other than the company, or

    (b) an undertaking to pay cash to a person other than the company, counts as consideration other than cash.

This does not apply for the purposes of Chapter 3 (allotment of equity securities: existing shareholders' right of pre-emption).

(6) For the purpose of determining whether a share is or is to be allotted for cash, or paid up in cash, "cash" includes foreign currency.

(7) An order under this section is subject to negative resolution procedure.

Additional rules for public companies

584 Public companies: shares taken by subscribers of memorandum

Shares taken by a subscriber to the memorandum of a public company in pursuance of an undertaking of his in the memorandum, and any premium on the shares, must be paid up in cash.

585 Public companies: must not accept undertaking to do work or perform services

(1) A public company must not accept at any time, in payment up of its shares or any premium on them, an undertaking given by any person that he or another should do work or perform services for the company or any other person.

(2) If a public company accepts such an undertaking in payment up of its shares or any premium on them, the holder of the shares when they or the premium are treated as paid up (in whole or in part) by the undertaking is liable –

  (a) to pay the company in respect of those shares an amount equal to their nominal value, together with the whole of any premium or, if the case so requires, such proportion of that amount as is treated as paid up by the undertaking; and

  (b) to pay interest at the appropriate rate on the amount payable under paragraph (a).

(3) The reference in subsection (2) to the holder of shares includes a person who has an unconditional right –

  (a) to be included in the company's register of members in respect of those shares, or

  (b) to have an instrument of transfer of them executed in his favour.

586 Public companies: shares must be at least one-quarter paid up

(1) A public company must not allot a share except as paid up at least as to one-quarter of its nominal value and the whole of any premium on it.

(2) This does not apply to shares allotted in pursuance of an employees' share scheme.

(3) If a company allots a share in contravention of this section –

  (a) the share is to be treated as if one-quarter of its nominal value, together with the whole of any premium on it, had been received, and

  (b) the allottee is liable to pay the company the minimum amount which should have been received in respect of the share under subsection (1) (less the value of any consideration actually applied in payment up, to any extent, of the share and any premium on it), with interest at the appropriate rate.

(4) Subsection (3) does not apply to the allotment of bonus shares, unless the allottee knew or ought to have known the shares were allotted in contravention of this section.

587 Public companies: payment by long-term undertaking

(1) A public company must not allot shares as fully or partly paid up (as to their nominal value or any premium on them) otherwise than in cash if the consideration for the allotment is or includes an undertaking which is to be, or may be, performed more than five years after the date of the allotment.

(2) If a company allots shares in contravention of subsection (1), the allottee is liable to pay the company an amount equal to the aggregate of their nominal value and the whole of any premium (or, if the case so requires, so much of that aggregate as is treated as paid up by the undertaking), with interest at the appropriate rate.

(3) Where a contract for the allotment of shares does not contravene subsection (1), any variation of the contract that has the effect that the contract would have contravened the subsection, if the terms of the contract as varied had been its original terms, is void.

This applies also to the variation by a public company of the terms of a contract entered into before the company was re-registered as a public company.

(4) Where –

(a) a public company allots shares for a consideration which consists of or includes (in accordance with subsection (1)) an undertaking that is to be performed within five years of the allotment, and

(b) the undertaking is not performed within the period allowed by the contract for the allotment of the shares,

the allottee is liable to pay the company, at the end of the period so allowed, an amount equal to the aggregate of the nominal value of the shares and the whole of any premium (or, if the case so requires, so much of that aggregate as is treated as paid up by the undertaking), with interest at the appropriate rate.

(5) References in this section to a contract for the allotment of shares include an ancillary contract relating to payment in respect of them.

Supplementary provisions

588 Liability of subsequent holders of shares

(1) If a person becomes a holder of shares in respect of which –

(a) there has been a contravention of any provision of this Chapter, and

(b) by virtue of that contravention another is liable to pay any amount under the provision contravened,

that person is also liable to pay that amount (jointly and severally with any other person so liable), subject as follows.

(2) A person otherwise liable under subsection (1) is exempted from that liability if either –

(a) he is a purchaser for value and, at the time of the purchase, he did not have actual notice of the contravention concerned, or

(b) he derived title to the shares (directly or indirectly) from a person who became a holder of them after the contravention and was not liable under subsection (1).

(3) References in this section to a holder, in relation to shares in a company, include any person who has an unconditional right –

(a) to be included in the company's register of members in respect of those shares, or

(b) to have an instrument of transfer of the shares executed in his favour.

(4) This section applies in relation to a failure to carry out a term of a contract as mentioned in section 587(4) (public companies: payment by long-term undertaking) as it applies in relation to a contravention of a provision of this Chapter.

589 Power of court to grant relief

(1) This section applies in relation to liability under –

section 585(2) (liability of allottee in case of breach by public company of prohibition on accepting undertaking to do work or perform services),

section 587(2) or (4) (liability of allottee in case of breach by public company of prohibition on payment by long-term undertaking), or

section 588 (liability of subsequent holders of shares),

as it applies in relation to a contravention of those sections.

(2) A person who –

(a) is subject to any such liability to a company in relation to payment in respect of shares in the company, or

(b) is subject to any such liability to a company by virtue of an undertaking given to it in, or in connection with, payment for shares in the company,

may apply to the court to be exempted in whole or in part from the liability.

(3) In the case of a liability within subsection (2)(a), the court may exempt the applicant from the liability only if and to the extent that it appears to the court just and equitable to do so having regard to –

(a) whether the applicant has paid, or is liable to pay, any amount in respect of –

(i) any other liability arising in relation to those shares under any provision of this Chapter or Chapter 6, or

(ii) any liability arising by virtue of any undertaking given in or in connection with payment for those shares;

(b) whether any person other than the applicant has paid or is likely to pay, whether in pursuance of any order of the court or otherwise, any such amount;

(c) whether the applicant or any other person –

(i) has performed in whole or in part, or is likely so to perform any such undertaking, or

(ii) has done or is likely to do any other thing in payment or part payment for the shares.

(4) In the case of a liability within subsection (2)(b), the court may exempt the applicant from the liability only if and to the extent that it appears to the court just and equitable to do so having regard to –

(a) whether the applicant has paid or is liable to pay any amount in respect of liability arising in relation to the shares under any provision of this Chapter or Chapter 6;

(b) whether any person other than the applicant has paid or is likely to pay, whether in pursuance of any order of the court or otherwise, any such amount.

(5) In determining whether it should exempt the applicant in whole or in part from any liability, the court must have regard to the following overriding principles –

(a) a company that has allotted shares should receive money or money's worth at least equal in value to the aggregate of the nominal value of those shares and the whole of any premium or, if the case so requires, so much of that aggregate as is treated as paid up;

(b) subject to that, where a company would, if the court did not grant the exemption, have more than one remedy against a particular person, it should be for the company to decide which remedy it should remain entitled to pursue.

(6) If a person brings proceedings against another ("the contributor") for a contribution in respect of liability to a company arising under any provision of this Chapter or Chapter 6 and it appears to the court that the contributor is liable to make such a contribution, the court may, if and to the extent that it appears to it just and equitable to do so having regard to the respective culpability (in respect of the liability to the company) of the contributor and the person bringing the proceedings –

(a) exempt the contributor in whole or in part from his liability to make such a contribution, or

(b) order the contributor to make a larger contribution than, but for this subsection, he would be liable to make.

590 Penalty for contravention of this Chapter

(1) If a company contravenes any of the provisions of this Chapter, an offence is committed by –

(a) the company, and

(b) every officer of the company who is in default.

(2) A person guilty of an offence under this section is liable –

(a) on conviction on indictment, to a fine;

(b) on summary conviction, to a fine not exceeding the statutory maximum.

591 Enforceability of undertakings to do work etc

(1) An undertaking given by any person, in or in connection with payment for shares in a company, to do work or perform services or to do any other thing, if it is enforceable by the company apart from this Chapter, is so enforceable notwithstanding that there has been a contravention in relation to it of a provision of this Chapter or Chapter 6.

(2) This is without prejudice to section 589 (power of court to grant relief etc in respect of liabilities).

592 The appropriate rate of interest

(1) For the purposes of this Chapter the "appropriate rate" of interest is 5% per annum or such other rate as may be specified by order made by the Secretary of State.

(2) An order under this section is subject to negative resolution procedure.

CHAPTER 6

PUBLIC COMPANIES: INDEPENDENT VALUATION OF NON-CASH CONSIDERATION

Non-cash consideration for shares

593 Public company: valuation of non-cash consideration for shares

(1) A public company must not allot shares as fully or partly paid up (as to their nominal value or any premium on them) otherwise than in cash unless –

(a) the consideration for the allotment has been independently valued in accordance with the provisions of this Chapter,

(b) the valuer's report has been made to the company during the six months immediately preceding the allotment of the shares, and

(c) a copy of the report has been sent to the proposed allottee.

(2) For this purpose the application of an amount standing to the credit of –

(a) any of a company's reserve accounts, or

(b) its profit and loss account,

in paying up (to any extent) shares allotted to members of the company, or premiums on shares so allotted, does not count as consideration for the allotment.
Accordingly, subsection (1) does not apply in that case.

(3) If a company allots shares in contravention of subsection (1) and either –

    (a) the allottee has not received the valuer's report required to be sent to him, or

    (b) there has been some other contravention of the requirements of this section or section 596 that the allottee knew or ought to have known amounted to a contravention,

the allottee is liable to pay the company an amount equal to the aggregate of the nominal value of the shares and the whole of any premium (or, if the case so requires, so much of that aggregate as is treated as paid up by the consideration), with interest at the appropriate rate.

(4) This section has effect subject to –

section 594 (exception to valuation requirement: arrangement with another company), and

section 595 (exception to valuation requirement: merger).

594 Exception to valuation requirement: arrangement with another company

(1) Section 593 (valuation of non-cash consideration) does not apply to the allotment of shares by a company ("company A") in connection with an arrangement to which this section applies.

(2) This section applies to an arrangement for the allotment of shares in company A on terms that the whole or part of the consideration for the shares allotted is to be provided by –

    (a) the transfer to that company, or

    (b) the cancellation,

of all or some of the shares, or of all or some of the shares of a particular class, in another company ("company B").

(3) It is immaterial whether the arrangement provides for the issue to company A of shares, or shares of any particular class, in company B.

(4) This section applies to an arrangement only if under the arrangement it is open to all the holders of the shares in company B (or, where the arrangement applies only to shares of a particular class, to all the holders of shares of that class) to take part in the arrangement.

(5) In determining whether that is the case, the following shall be disregarded –

    (a) shares held by or by a nominee of company A;

    (b) shares held by or by a nominee of a company which is –

        (i) the holding company, or a subsidiary, of company A, or

        (ii) a subsidiary of such a holding company;

    (c) shares held as treasury shares by company B.

(6) In this section –

    (a) "arrangement" means any agreement, scheme or arrangement (including an arrangement sanctioned in accordance with –

        (i) Part 26 (arrangements and reconstructions), or

        (ii) section 110 of the Insolvency Act 1986 (c. 45) or Article 96 of the Insolvency (Northern Ireland) Order 1989 (S.I. 1989/2405 (N.I. 19)) (liquidator in winding up accepting shares as (consideration for sale of company property)), and

    (b) "company", except in reference to company A, includes any body corporate.

595 Exception to valuation requirement: merger

(1) Section 593 (valuation of non-cash consideration) does not apply to the allotment of shares by a company in connection with a proposed merger with another company.

(2)   A proposed merger is where one of the companies proposes to acquire all the assets and liabilities of the other in exchange for the issue of shares or other securities of that one to shareholders of the other, with or without any cash payment to shareholders.

(3)   In this section "company", in reference to the other company, includes any body corporate.

596 Non-cash consideration for shares: requirements as to valuation and report

(1)   The provisions of sections 1150 to 1153 (general provisions as to independent valuation and report) apply to the valuation and report required by section 593 (public company: valuation of non-cash consideration for shares).

(2)   The valuer's report must state –

(a)   the nominal value of the shares to be wholly or partly paid for by the consideration in question;

(b)   the amount of any premium payable on the shares;

(c)   the description of the consideration and, as respects so much of the consideration as he himself has valued, a description of that part of the consideration, the method used to value it and the date of the valuation;

(d)   the extent to which the nominal value of the shares and any premium are to be treated as paid up –

(i)   by the consideration;

(ii)   in cash.

(3)   The valuer's report must contain or be accompanied by a note by him –

(a)   in the case of a valuation made by a person other than himself, that it appeared to himself reasonable to arrange for it to be so made or to accept a valuation so made,

(b)   whoever made the valuation, that the method of valuation was reasonable in all the circumstances,

(c)   that it appears to the valuer that there has been no material change in the value of the consideration in question since the valuation, and

(d)   that, on the basis of the valuation, the value of the consideration, together with any cash by which the nominal value of the shares or any premium payable on them is to be paid up, is not less than so much of the aggregate of the nominal value and the whole of any such premium as is treated as paid up by the consideration and any such cash.

(4)   Where the consideration to be valued is accepted partly in payment up of the nominal value of the shares and any premium and partly for some other consideration given by the company, section 593 and the preceding provisions of this section apply as if references to the consideration accepted by the company included the proportion of that consideration that is properly attributable to the payment up of that value and any premium.

(5)   In such a case –

(a)   the valuer must carry out, or arrange for, such other valuations as will enable him to determine that proportion, and

(b)   his report must state what valuations have been made under this subsection and also the reason for, and method and date of, any such valuation and any other matters which may be relevant to that determination.

597 Copy of report to be delivered to registrar

(1)   A company to which a report is made under section 593 as to the value of any consideration for which, or partly for which, it proposes to allot shares must deliver a copy of the report to the registrar for registration.

(2) The copy must be delivered at the same time that the company files the return of the allotment of those shares under section 555 (return of allotment by limited company).

(3) If default is made in complying with subsection (1) or (2), an offence is committed by every officer of the company who is in default.

(4) A person guilty of an offence under this section is liable –

    (a) on conviction on indictment, to a fine;

    (b) on summary conviction, to a fine not exceeding the statutory maximum and, for continued contravention, a daily default fine not exceeding one-tenth of the statutory maximum.

(5) In the case of default in delivering to the registrar any document as required by this section, any person liable for the default may apply to the court for relief.

(6) The court, if satisfied –

    (a) that the omission to deliver the document was accidental or due to inadvertence, or

    (b) that it is just and equitable to grant relief,

may make an order extending the time for delivery of the document for such period as the court thinks proper.

Transfer of non-cash asset in initial period

598 Public company: agreement for transfer of non-cash asset in initial period

(1) A public company formed as such must not enter into an agreement –

    (a) with a person who is a subscriber to the company's memorandum,

    (b) for the transfer by him to the company, or another, before the end of the company's initial period of one or more non-cash assets, and

    (c) under which the consideration for the transfer to be given by the company is at the time of the agreement equal in value to one-tenth or more of the company's issued share capital,

unless the conditions referred to below have been complied with.

(2) The company's "initial period" means the period of two years beginning with the date of the company being issued with a certificate under section 761 (trading certificate).

(3) The conditions are those specified in –

section 599 (requirement of independent valuation), and
section 601 (requirement of approval by members).

(4) This section does not apply where –

    (a) it is part of the company's ordinary business to acquire, or arrange for other persons to acquire, assets of a particular description, and

    (b) the agreement is entered into by the company in the ordinary course of that business.

(5) This section does not apply to an agreement entered into by the company under the supervision of the court or of an officer authorised by the court for the purpose.

599 Agreement for transfer of non-cash asset: requirement of independent valuation

(1) The following conditions must have been complied with –

    (a) the consideration to be received by the company, and any consideration other than cash to be given by the company, must have been independently valued in accordance with the provisions of this Chapter,

    (b) the valuer's report must have been made to the company during the six months immediately preceding the date of the agreement, and

    (c) a copy of the report must have been sent to the other party to the proposed agreement not later than the date on which copies have to be circulated to members under section 601(3).

(2) The reference in subsection (1)(a) to the consideration to be received by the company is to the asset to be transferred to it or, as the case may be, to the advantage to the company of the asset's transfer to another person.

(3) The reference in subsection (1)(c) to the other party to the proposed agreement is to the person referred to in section 598(1)(a).

If he has received a copy of the report under section 601 in his capacity as a member of the company, it is not necessary to send another copy under this section.

(4) This section does not affect any requirement to value any consideration for purposes of section 593 (valuation of non-cash consideration for shares).

600 Agreement for transfer of non-cash asset: requirements as to valuation and report

(1) The provisions of sections 1150 to 1153 (general provisions as to independent valuation and report) apply to the valuation and report required by section 599 (public company: transfer of non-cash asset).

(2) The valuer's report must state –

(a) the consideration to be received by the company, describing the asset in question (specifying the amount to be received in cash) and the consideration to be given by the company (specifying the amount to be given in cash), and

(b) the method and date of valuation.

(3) The valuer's report must contain or be accompanied by a note by him –

(a) in the case of a valuation made by a person other than himself, that it appeared to himself reasonable to arrange for it to be so made or to accept a valuation so made,

(b) whoever made the valuation, that the method of valuation was reasonable in all the circumstances,

(c) that it appears to the valuer that there has been no material change in the value of the consideration in question since the valuation, and

(d) that, on the basis of the valuation, the value of the consideration to be received by the company is not less than the value of the consideration to be given by it.

(4) Any reference in section 599 or this section to consideration given for the transfer of an asset includes consideration given partly for its transfer.

(5) In such a case –

(a) the value of any consideration partly so given is to be taken as the proportion of the consideration properly attributable to its transfer,

(b) the valuer must carry out or arrange for such valuations of anything else as will enable him to determine that proportion, and

(c) his report must state what valuations have been made for that purpose and also the reason for and method and date of any such valuation and any other matters which may be relevant to that determination.

601 Agreement for transfer of non-cash asset: requirement of approval by members

(1) The following conditions must have been complied with –

(a) the terms of the agreement must have been approved by an ordinary resolution of the company,

(b) the requirements of this section must have been complied with as respects the circulation to members of copies of the valuer's report under section 599, and

(c) a copy of the proposed resolution must have been sent to the other party to the proposed agreement.

(2) The reference in subsection (1)(c) to the other party to the proposed agreement is to the person referred to in section 598(1)(a).

(3) The requirements of this section as to circulation of copies of the valuer's report are as follows –

    (a) if the resolution is proposed as a written resolution, copies of the valuer's report must be sent or submitted to every eligible member at or before the time at which the proposed resolution is sent or submitted to him;

    (b) if the resolution is proposed at a general meeting, copies of the valuer's report must be circulated to the members entitled to notice of the meeting not later than the date on which notice of the meeting is given.

602 Copy of resolution to be delivered to registrar

(1) A company that has passed a resolution under section 601 with respect to the transfer of an asset must, within 15 days of doing so, deliver to the registrar a copy of the resolution together with the valuer's report required by that section.

(2) If a company fails to comply with subsection (1), an offence is committed by –

    (a) the company, and

    (b) every officer of the company who is in default.

(3) A person guilty of an offence under this section is liable on summary conviction to a fine not exceeding level 3 on the standard scale and, for continued contravention, to a daily default fine not exceeding one-tenth of level 3 on the standard scale.

603 Adaptation of provisions in relation to company re-registering as public

The provisions of sections 598 to 602 (public companies: transfer of non-cash assets) apply with the following adaptations in relation to a company re-registered as a public company –

    (a) the reference in section 598(1)(a) to a person who is a subscriber to the company's memorandum shall be read as a reference to a person who is a member of the company on the date of re-registration;

    (b) the reference in section 598(2) to the date of the company being issued with a certificate under section 761 (trading certificate) shall be read as a reference to the date of re-registration.

604 Agreement for transfer of non-cash asset: effect of contravention

(1) This section applies where a public company enters into an agreement in contravention of section 598 and either –

    (a) the other party to the agreement has not received the valuer's report required to be sent to him, or

    (b) there has been some other contravention of the requirements of this Chapter that the other party to the agreement knew or ought to have known amounted to a contravention.

(2) In those circumstances –

    (a) the company is entitled to recover from that person any consideration given by it under the agreement, or an amount equal to the value of the consideration at the time of the agreement, and

    (b) the agreement, so far as not carried out, is void.

(3) If the agreement is or includes an agreement for the allotment of shares in the company, then –

    (a) whether or not the agreement also contravenes section 593 (valuation of non-cash consideration for shares), this section does not apply to it in so far as it is for the allotment of shares, and

    (b) the allottee is liable to pay the company an amount equal to the aggregate of the nominal value of the shares and the whole of any premium (or, if the case so requires, so much of that aggregate as is treated as paid up by the consideration), with interest at the appropriate rate.

Supplementary provisions

605 Liability of subsequent holders of shares

(1) If a person becomes a holder of shares in respect of which –

(a) there has been a contravention of section 593 (public company: valuation of non-cash consideration for shares), and

(b) by virtue of that contravention another is liable to pay any amount under the provision contravened,

that person is also liable to pay that amount (jointly and severally with any other person so liable), unless he is exempted from liability under subsection (3) below.

(2) If a company enters into an agreement in contravention of section 598 (public company: agreement for transfer of non-cash asset in initial period) and –

(a) the agreement is or includes an agreement for the allotment of shares in the company,

(b) a person becomes a holder of shares allotted under the agreement, and

(c) by virtue of the agreement and allotment under it another person is liable to pay an amount under section 604,

the person who becomes the holder of the shares is also liable to pay that amount (jointly and severally with any other person so liable), unless he is exempted from liability under subsection (3) below.

This applies whether or not the agreement also contravenes section 593.

(3) A person otherwise liable under subsection (1) or (2) is exempted from that liability if either –

(a) he is a purchaser for value and, at the time of the purchase, he did not have actual notice of the contravention concerned, or

(b) he derived title to the shares (directly or indirectly) from a person who became a holder of them after the contravention and was not liable under subsection (1) or (2).

(4) References in this section to a holder, in relation to shares in a company, include any person who has an unconditional right –

(a) to be included in the company's register of members in respect of those shares, or

(b) to have an instrument of transfer of the shares executed in his favour.

606 Power of court to grant relief

(1) A person who –

(a) is liable to a company under any provision of this Chapter in relation to payment in respect of any shares in the company, or

(b) is liable to a company by virtue of an undertaking given to it in, or in connection with, payment for any shares in the company,

may apply to the court to be exempted in whole or in part from the liability.

(2) In the case of a liability within subsection (1)(a), the court may exempt the applicant from the liability only if and to the extent that it appears to the court just and equitable to do so having regard to –

(a) whether the applicant has paid, or is liable to pay, any amount in respect of –

(i) any other liability arising in relation to those shares under any provision of this Chapter or Chapter 5, or

      (ii)   any liability arising by virtue of any undertaking given in or in connection with payment for those shares;

  (b) whether any person other than the applicant has paid or is likely to pay, whether in pursuance of any order of the court or otherwise, any such amount;

  (c) whether the applicant or any other person –

      (i)   has performed in whole or in part, or is likely so to perform any such undertaking, or

      (ii)   has done or is likely to do any other thing in payment or part payment for the shares.

(3) In the case of a liability within subsection (1)(b), the court may exempt the applicant from the liability only if and to the extent that it appears to the court just and equitable to do so having regard to –

  (a) whether the applicant has paid or is liable to pay any amount in respect of liability arising in relation to the shares under any provision of this Chapter or Chapter 5;

  (b) whether any person other than the applicant has paid or is likely to pay, whether in pursuance of any order of the court or otherwise, any such amount.

(4) In determining whether it should exempt the applicant in whole or in part from any liability, the court must have regard to the following overriding principles –

  (a) that a company that has allotted shares should receive money or money's worth at least equal in value to the aggregate of the nominal value of those shares and the whole of any premium or, if the case so requires, so much of that aggregate as is treated as paid up;

  (b) subject to this, that where such a company would, if the court did not grant the exemption, have more than one remedy against a particular person, it should be for the company to decide which remedy it should remain entitled to pursue.

(5) If a person brings proceedings against another ("the contributor") for a contribution in respect of liability to a company arising under any provision of this Chapter or Chapter 5 and it appears to the court that the contributor is liable to make such a contribution, the court may, if and to the extent that it appears to it, just and equitable to do so having regard to the respective culpability (in respect of the liability to the company) of the contributor and the person bringing the proceedings –

  (a) exempt the contributor in whole or in part from his liability to make such a contribution, or

  (b) order the contributor to make a larger contribution than, but for this subsection, he would be liable to make.

(6) Where a person is liable to a company under section 604(2) (agreement for transfer of non-cash asset: effect of contravention), the court may, on application, exempt him in whole or in part from that liability if and to the extent that it appears to the court to be just and equitable to do so having regard to any benefit accruing to the company by virtue of anything done by him towards the carrying out of the agreement mentioned in that subsection.

607 Penalty for contravention of this Chapter

(1) This section applies where a company contravenes –

section 593 (public company allotting shares for non-cash consideration), or
section 598 (public company entering into agreement for transfer of non-cash asset).

(2) An offence is committed by –

  (a) the company, and

  (b) every officer of the company who is in default.

(3) A person guilty of an offence under this section is liable –

(a)   on conviction on indictment, to a fine;

(b)   on summary conviction, to a fine not exceeding the statutory maximum.

608 Enforceability of undertakings to do work etc

(1)   An undertaking given by any person, in or in connection with payment for shares in a company, to do work or perform services or to do any other thing, if it is enforceable by the company apart from this Chapter, is so enforceable notwithstanding that there has been a contravention in relation to it of a provision of this Chapter or Chapter 5.

(2)   This is without prejudice to section 606 (power of court to grant relief etc in respect of liabilities).

609 The appropriate rate of interest

(1)   For the purposes of this Chapter the "appropriate rate" of interest is 5% per annum or such other rate as may be specified by order made by the Secretary of State.

(2)   An order under this section is subject to negative resolution procedure.

CHAPTER 7

SHARE PREMIUMS

The share premium account

610 Application of share premiums

(1)   If a company issues shares at a premium, whether for cash or otherwise, a sum equal to the aggregate amount or value of the premiums on those shares must be transferred to an account called "the share premium account".

(2)   Where, on issuing shares, a company has transferred a sum to the share premium account, it may use that sum to write off –

(a)   the expenses of the issue of those shares;

(b)   any commission paid on the issue of those shares.

(3)   The company may use the share premium account to pay up new shares to be allotted to members as fully paid bonus shares.

(4)   Subject to subsections (2) and (3), the provisions of the Companies Acts relating to the reduction of a company's share capital apply as if the share premium account were part of its paid up share capital.

(5)   This section has effect subject to –

section 611 (group reconstruction relief);
section 612 (merger relief);
section 614 (power to make further provisions by regulations).

(6)   In this Chapter "the issuing company" means the company issuing shares as mentioned in subsection (1) above.

Relief from requirements as to share premiums

611 Group reconstruction relief

(1)   This section applies where the issuing company –

(a)   is a wholly-owned subsidiary of another company ("the holding company"), and
(b)   allots shares –

(i)   to the holding company, or

(ii)　to another wholly-owned subsidiary of the holding company,

in consideration for the transfer to the issuing company of non-cash assets of a company ("the transferor company") that is a member of the group of companies that comprises the holding company and all its wholly-owned subsidiaries.

(2)　Where the shares in the issuing company allotted in consideration for the transfer are issued at a premium, the issuing company is not required by section 610 to transfer any amount in excess of the minimum premium value to the share premium account.

(3)　The minimum premium value means the amount (if any) by which the base value of the consideration for the shares allotted exceeds the aggregate nominal value of the shares.

(4)　The base value of the consideration for the shares allotted is the amount by which the base value of the assets transferred exceeds the base value of any liabilities of the transferor company assumed by the issuing company as part of the consideration for the assets transferred.

(5)　For the purposes of this section –

(a)　the base value of assets transferred is taken as –

(i)　the cost of those assets to the transferor company, or

(ii)　if less, the amount at which those assets are stated in the transferor company's accounting records immediately before the transfer;

(b)　the base value of the liabilities assumed is taken as the amount at which they are stated in the transferor company's accounting records immediately before the transfer.

612 Merger relief

(1)　This section applies where the issuing company has secured at least a 90% equity holding in another company in pursuance of an arrangement providing for the allotment of equity shares in the issuing company on terms that the consideration for the shares allotted is to be provided –

(a)　by the issue or transfer to the issuing company of equity shares in the other company, or

(b)　by the cancellation of any such shares not held by the issuing company.

(2)　If the equity shares in the issuing company allotted in pursuance of the arrangement in consideration for the acquisition or cancellation of equity shares in the other company are issued at a premium, section 610 does not apply to the premiums on those shares.

(3)　Where the arrangement also provides for the allotment of any shares in the issuing company on terms that the consideration for those shares is to be provided –

(a)　by the issue or transfer to the issuing company of non-equity shares in the other company, or

(b)　by the cancellation of any such shares in that company not held by the issuing company,

relief under subsection (2) extends to any shares in the issuing company allotted on those terms in pursuance of the arrangement.

(4)　This section does not apply in a case falling within section 611 (group reconstruction relief).

613 Merger relief: meaning of 90% equity holding

(1)　The following provisions have effect to determine for the purposes of section 612 (merger relief) whether a company ("company A") has secured at least a 90% equity holding in another company ("company B") in pursuance of such an arrangement as is mentioned in subsection (1) of that section.

(2)　Company A has secured at least a 90% equity holding in company B if in consequence of an acquisition or cancellation of equity shares in company B (in pursuance of that arrangement) it holds equity shares in company B of an aggregate amount equal to 90% or more of the nominal value of that company's equity share capital.

(3) For this purpose –

    (a) it is immaterial whether any of those shares were acquired in pursuance of the arrangement; and

    (b) shares in company B held by the company as treasury shares are excluded in determining the nominal value of company B's share capital.

(4) Where the equity share capital of company B is divided into different classes of shares, company A is not regarded as having secured at least a 90% equity holding in company B unless the requirements of subsection (2) are met in relation to each of those classes of shares taken separately.

(5) For the purposes of this section shares held by –

    (a) a company that is company A's holding company or subsidiary, or

    (b) a subsidiary of company A's holding company, or

    (c) its or their nominees,

are treated as held by company A.

614 Power to make further provision by regulations

(1) The Secretary of State may by regulations make such provision as he thinks appropriate –

    (a) for relieving companies from the requirements of section 610 (application of share premiums) in relation to premiums other than cash premiums;

    (b) for restricting or otherwise modifying any relief from those requirements provided by this Chapter.

(2) Regulations under this section are subject to affirmative resolution procedure.

615 Relief may be reflected in company's balance sheet

An amount corresponding to the amount representing the premiums, or part of the premiums, on shares issued by a company that by virtue of any relief under this Chapter is not included in the company's share premium account may also be disregarded in determining the amount at which any shares or other consideration provided for the shares issued is to be included in the company's balance sheet.

Supplementary provisions

616 Interpretation of this Chapter

(1) In this Chapter –

"arrangement" means any agreement, scheme or arrangement (including an arrangement sanctioned in accordance with –

    (a) Part 26 (arrangements and reconstructions), or

    (b) section 110 of the Insolvency Act 1986 (c. 45) or Article 96 of the Insolvency (Northern Ireland) Order 1989 (S.I. 1989/2405 (N.I. 19)) (liquidator in winding up accepting shares as consideration for sale of company property));

"company", except in reference to the issuing company, includes any body corporate;

"equity shares" means shares comprised in a company's equity share capital, and "non-equity shares" means shares (of any class) that are not so comprised;

"the issuing company" has the meaning given by section 610(6).

(2) References in this Chapter (however expressed) to –

(a)   the acquisition by a company of shares in another company, and
(b)   the issue or allotment of shares to, or the transfer of shares to or by, a company,

include (respectively) the acquisition of shares by, and the issue or allotment or transfer of shares to or by, a nominee of that company.

The reference in section 611 to the transferor company shall be read accordingly.

(3)   References in this Chapter to the transfer of shares in a company include the transfer of a right to be included in the company's register of members in respect of those shares.

CHAPTER 8

ALTERATION OF SHARE CAPITAL

How share capital may be altered

617 Alteration of share capital of limited company

(1)   A limited company having a share capital may not alter its share capital except in the following ways.

(2)   The company may –

(a)   increase its share capital by allotting new shares in accordance with this Part, or
(b)   reduce its share capital in accordance with Chapter 10.

(3)   The company may –

(a)   sub-divide or consolidate all or any of its share capital in accordance with section 618, or
(b)   reconvert stock into shares in accordance with section 620.

(4)   The company may redenominate all or any of its shares in accordance with section 622, and may reduce its share capital in accordance with section 626 in connection with such a redenomination.

(5)   Nothing in this section affects –

(a)   the power of a company to purchase its own shares, or to redeem shares, in accordance with Part 18;
(b)   the power of a company to purchase its own shares in pursuance of an order of the court under –

(i)   section 98 (application to court to cancel resolution for reregistration as a private company),
(ii)   section 721(6) (powers of court on objection to redemption or purchase of shares out of capital),
(iii) section 759 (remedial order in case of breach of prohibition of public offers by private company), or
(iv)   Part 30 (protection of members against unfair prejudice);

(c)   the forfeiture of shares, or the acceptance of shares surrendered in lieu, in pursuance of the company's articles, for failure to pay any sum payable in respect of the shares;
(d)   the cancellation of shares under section 662 (duty to cancel shares held by or for a public company);
(e)   the power of a company –

(i)   to enter into a compromise or arrangement in accordance with Part 26 (arrangements and reconstructions), or
(ii)   to do anything required to comply with an order of the court on an application under that Part.

Sub-division or consolidation of shares

618 Sub-division or consolidation of shares

(1) A limited company having a share capital may –

    (a) sub-divide its shares, or any of them, into shares of a smaller nominal amount than its existing shares, or

    (b) consolidate and divide all or any of its share capital into shares of a larger nominal amount than its existing shares.

(2) In any sub-division, consolidation or division of shares under this section, the proportion between the amount paid and the amount (if any) unpaid on each resulting share must be the same as it was in the case of the share from which that share is derived.

(3) A company may exercise a power conferred by this section only if its members have passed a resolution authorising it to do so.

(4) A resolution under subsection (3) may authorise a company –

    (a) to exercise more than one of the powers conferred by this section;

    (b) to exercise a power on more than one occasion;

    (c) to exercise a power at a specified time or in specified circumstances.

(5) The company's articles may exclude or restrict the exercise of any power conferred by this section.

619 Notice to registrar of sub-division or consolidation

(1) If a company exercises the power conferred by section 618 (sub-division or consolidation of shares) it must within one month after doing so give notice to the registrar, specifying the shares affected.

(2) The notice must be accompanied by a statement of capital.

(3) The statement of capital must state with respect to the company's share capital immediately following the exercise of the power –

    (a) the total number of shares of the company,

    (b) the aggregate nominal value of those shares,

    (c) for each class of shares –

        (i) prescribed particulars of the rights attached to the shares,

        (ii) the total number of shares of that class, and

        (iii) the aggregate nominal value of shares of that class, and

    (d) the amount paid up and the amount (if any) unpaid on each share (whether on account of the nominal value of the share or by way of premium).

(4) If default is made in complying with this section, an offence is committed by –

    (a) the company, and

    (b) every officer of the company who is in default.

(5) A person guilty of an offence under this section is liable on summary conviction to a fine not exceeding level 3 on the standard scale and, for continued contravention, a daily default fine not exceeding one-tenth of level 3 on the standard scale.

Reconversion of stock into shares

620 Reconversion of stock into shares

(1) A limited company that has converted paid-up shares into stock (before the repeal by this Act of the power to do so) may reconvert that stock into paid-up shares of any nominal value.

(2) A company may exercise the power conferred by this section only if its members have passed an ordinary resolution authorising it to do so.

(3) A resolution under subsection (2) may authorise a company to exercise the power conferred by this section –

   (a) on more than one occasion;
   (b) at a specified time or in specified circumstances.

621 Notice to registrar of reconversion of stock into shares

(1) If a company exercises a power conferred by section 620 (reconversion of stock into shares) it must within one month after doing so give notice to the registrar, specifying the stock affected.
(2) The notice must be accompanied by a statement of capital.
(3) The statement of capital must state with respect to the company's share capital immediately following the exercise of the power –

   (a) the total number of shares of the company,
   (b) the aggregate nominal value of those shares,
   (c) for each class of shares –

      (i) prescribed particulars of the rights attached to the shares,
      (ii) the total number of shares of that class, and
      (iii) the aggregate nominal value of shares of that class, and

   (d) the amount paid up and the amount (if any) unpaid on each share (whether on account of the nominal value of the share or by way of premium).

(4) If default is made in complying with this section, an offence is committed by –

   (a) the company, and
   (b) every officer of the company who is in default.

(5) A person guilty of an offence under this section is liable on summary conviction to a fine not exceeding level 3 on the standard scale and, for continued contravention, a daily default fine not exceeding one-tenth of level 3 on the standard scale.

Redenomination of share capital

622 Redenomination of share capital

(1) A limited company having a share capital may by resolution redenominate its share capital or any class of its share capital.
   "Redenominate" means convert shares from having a fixed nominal value in one currency to having a fixed nominal value in another currency.
(2) The conversion must be made at an appropriate spot rate of exchange specified in the resolution.
(3) The rate must be either –

   (a) a rate prevailing on a day specified in the resolution, or
   (b) a rate determined by taking the average of rates prevailing on each consecutive day of a period specified in the resolution.

   The day or period specified for the purposes of paragraph (a) or (b) must be within the period of 28 days ending on the day before the resolution is passed.

(4) A resolution under this section may specify conditions which must be met before the redenomination takes effect.
(5) Redenomination in accordance with a resolution under this section takes effect –

   (a) on the day on which the resolution is passed, or
   (b) on such later day as may be determined in accordance with the resolution.

(6) A resolution under this section lapses if the redenomination for which it provides has not taken effect at the end of the period of 28 days beginning on the date on which it is passed.

(7) A company's articles may prohibit or restrict the exercise of the power conferred by this section.

(8) Chapter 3 of Part 3 (resolutions affecting a company's constitution) applies to a resolution under this section.

623 Calculation of new nominal values

For each class of share the new nominal value of each share is calculated as follows:
Step One
Take the aggregate of the old nominal values of all the shares of that class.
Step Two
Translate that amount into the new currency at the rate of exchange specified in the resolution.
Step Three
Divide that amount by the number of shares in the class.

624 Effect of redenomination

(1) The redenomination of shares does not affect any rights or obligations of members under the company's constitution, or any restrictions affecting members under the company's constitution.
In particular, it does not affect entitlement to dividends (including entitlement to dividends in a particular currency), voting rights or any liability in respect of amounts unpaid on shares.

(2) For this purpose the company's constitution includes the terms on which any shares of the company are allotted or held.

(3) Subject to subsection (1), references to the old nominal value of the shares in any agreement or statement, or in any deed, instrument or document, shall (unless the context otherwise requires) be read after the resolution takes effect as references to the new nominal value of the shares.

625 Notice to registrar of redenomination

(1) If a limited company having a share capital redenominates any of its share capital, it must within one month after doing so give notice to the registrar, specifying the shares redenominated.

(2) The notice must –
  (a) state the date on which the resolution was passed, and
  (b) be accompanied by a statement of capital.

(3) The statement of capital must state with respect to the company's share capital as redenominated by the resolution –
  (a) the total number of shares of the company,
  (b) the aggregate nominal value of those shares,
  (c) for each class of shares –
    (i) prescribed particulars of the rights attached to the shares,
    (ii) the total number of shares of that class, and
    (iii) the aggregate nominal value of shares of that class, and
  (d) the amount paid up and the amount (if any) unpaid on each share (whether on account of the nominal value of the share or by way of premium).

(4) If default is made in complying with this section, an offence is committed by –
  (a) the company, and
  (b) every officer of the company who is in default.

(5) A person guilty of an offence under this section is liable on summary conviction to a fine not exceeding level 3 on the standard scale and, for continued contravention, a daily default fine not exceeding one-tenth of level 3 on the standard scale.

626 Reduction of capital in connection with redenomination

(1) A limited company that passes a resolution redenominating some or all of its shares may, for the purpose of adjusting the nominal values of the redenominated shares to obtain values that are, in the opinion of the company, more suitable, reduce its share capital under this section.

(2) A reduction of capital under this section requires a special resolution of the company.

(3) Any such resolution must be passed within three months of the resolution effecting the redenomination.

(4) The amount by which a company's share capital is reduced under this section must not exceed 10% of the nominal value of the company's allotted share capital immediately after the reduction.

(5) A reduction of capital under this section does not extinguish or reduce any liability in respect of share capital not paid up.

(6) Nothing in Chapter 10 applies to a reduction of capital under this section.

627 Notice to registrar of reduction of capital in connection with redenomination

(1) A company that passes a resolution under section 626 (reduction of capital in connection with redenomination) must within 15 days after the resolution is passed give notice to the registrar stating –

(a) the date of the resolution, and

(b) the date of the resolution under section 622 in connection with which it was passed.

This is in addition to the copies of the resolutions themselves that are required to be delivered to the registrar under Chapter 3 of Part 3.

(2) The notice must be accompanied by a statement of capital.

(3) The statement of capital must state with respect to the company's share capital as reduced by the resolution –

(a) the total number of shares of the company,

(b) the aggregate nominal value of those shares,

(c) for each class of shares –

(i) prescribed particulars of the rights attached to the shares,

(ii) the total number of shares of that class, and

(iii) the aggregate nominal value of shares of that class, and

(d) the amount paid up and the amount (if any) unpaid on each share (whether on account of the nominal value of the share or by way of premium).

(4) The registrar must register the notice and the statement on receipt.

(5) The reduction of capital is not effective until those documents are registered.

(6) The company must also deliver to the registrar, within 15 days after the resolution is passed, a statement by the directors confirming that the reduction in share capital is in accordance with section 626(4) (reduction of capital not to exceed 10% of nominal value of allotted shares immediately after reduction).

(7) If default is made in complying with this section, an offence is committed by –

(a) the company, and

(b) every officer of the company who is in default.

(8) A person guilty of an offence under this section is liable –

(a) on conviction on indictment to a fine, and

(b) on summary conviction to a fine not exceeding the statutory maximum.

628 Redenomination reserve

(1) The amount by which a company's share capital is reduced under section 626 (reduction of capital in connection with redenomination) must be transferred to a reserve, called "the redenomination reserve".

(2) The redenomination reserve may be applied by the company in paying up shares to be allotted to members as fully paid bonus shares.

(3) Subject to that, the provisions of the Companies Acts relating to the reduction of a company's share capital apply as if the redenomination reserve were paid-up share capital of the company.

CHAPTER 9

CLASSES OF SHARE AND CLASS RIGHTS

Introductory

629 Classes of shares

(1) For the purposes of the Companies Acts shares are of one class if the rights attached to them are in all respects uniform.

(2) For this purpose the rights attached to shares are not regarded as different from those attached to other shares by reason only that they do not carry the same rights to dividends in the twelve months immediately following their allotment.

Variation of class rights

630 Variation of class rights: companies having a share capital

(1) This section is concerned with the variation of the rights attached to a class of shares in a company having a share capital.

(2) Rights attached to a class of a company's shares may only be varied –

  (a) in accordance with provision in the company's articles for the variation of those rights, or

  (b) where the company's articles contain no such provision, if the holders of shares of that class consent to the variation in accordance with this section.

(3) This is without prejudice to any other restrictions on the variation of the rights.

(4) The consent required for the purposes of this section on the part of the holders of a class of a company's shares is –

  (a) consent in writing from the holders of at least three-quarters in nominal value of the issued shares of that class (excluding any shares held as treasury shares), or

  (b) a special resolution passed at a separate general meeting of the holders of that class sanctioning the variation.

(5) Any amendment of a provision contained in a company's articles for the variation of the rights attached to a class of shares, or the insertion of any such provision into the articles, is itself to be treated as a variation of those rights.

(6) In this section, and (except where the context otherwise requires) in any provision in a company's articles for the variation of the rights attached to a class of shares, references to the variation of those rights include references to their abrogation.

631 Variation of class rights: companies without a share capital

(1) This section is concerned with the variation of the rights of a class of members of a company where the company does not have a share capital.

(2) Rights of a class of members may only be varied –

  (a) in accordance with provision in the company's articles for the variation of those rights, or
  (b) where the company's articles contain no such provision, if the members of that class consent to the variation in accordance with this section.

(3) This is without prejudice to any other restrictions on the variation of the rights.

(4) The consent required for the purposes of this section on the part of the members of a class is –

  (a) consent in writing from at least three-quarters of the members of the class, or
  (b) a special resolution passed at a separate general meeting of the members of that class sanctioning the variation.

(5) Any amendment of a provision contained in a company's articles for the variation of the rights of a class of members, or the insertion of any such provision into the articles, is itself to be treated as a variation of those rights.

(6) In this section, and (except where the context otherwise requires) in any provision in a company's articles for the variation of the rights of a class of members, references to the variation of those rights include references to their abrogation.

632 Variation of class rights: saving for court's powers under other provisions

Nothing in section 630 or 631 (variation of class rights) affects the power of the court under –

  section 98 (application to cancel resolution for public company to be re-registered as private),
  Part 26 (arrangements and reconstructions), or
  Part 30 (protection of members against unfair prejudice).

633 Right to object to variation: companies having a share capital

(1) This section applies where the rights attached to any class of shares in a company are varied under section 630 (variation of class rights: companies having a share capital).

(2) The holders of not less in the aggregate than 15% of the issued shares of the class in question (being persons who did not consent to or vote in favour of the resolution for the variation) may apply to the court to have the variation cancelled.
    For this purpose any of the company's share capital held as treasury shares is disregarded.

(3) If such an application is made, the variation has no effect unless and until it is confirmed by the court.

(4) Application to the court –

  (a) must be made within 21 days after the date on which the consent was given or the resolution was passed (as the case may be), and
  (b) may be made on behalf of the shareholders entitled to make the application by such one or more of their number as they may appoint in writing for the purpose.

(5) The court, after hearing the applicant and any other persons who apply to the court to be heard and appear to the court to be interested in the application, may, if satisfied having regard to all the circumstances of the case that the variation would unfairly prejudice the shareholders of the class represented by the applicant, disallow the variation, and shall if not so satisfied confirm it.
    The decision of the court on any such application is final.

(6) References in this section to the variation of the rights of holders of a class of shares include references to their abrogation.

634 Right to object to variation: companies without a share capital

(1) This section applies where the rights of any class of members of a company are varied under section 631 (variation of class rights: companies without a share capital).

(2) Members amounting to not less than 15% of the members of the class in question (being persons who did not consent to or vote in favour of the resolution for the variation) may apply to the court to have the variation cancelled.

(3) If such an application is made, the variation has no effect unless and until it is confirmed by the court.

(4) Application to the court must be made within 21 days after the date on which the consent was given or the resolution was passed (as the case may be) and may be made on behalf of the members entitled to make the application by such one or more of their number as they may appoint in writing for the purpose.

(5) The court, after hearing the applicant and any other persons who apply to the court to be heard and appear to the court to be interested in the application, may, if satisfied having regard to all the circumstances of the case that the variation would unfairly prejudice the members of the class represented by the applicant, disallow the variation, and shall if not so satisfied confirm it.

The decision of the court on any such application is final.

(6) References in this section to the variation of the rights of a class of members include references to their abrogation.

635 Copy of court order to be forwarded to the registrar

(1) The company must within 15 days after the making of an order by the court on an application under section 633 or 634 (objection to variation of class rights) forward a copy of the order to the registrar.

(2) If default is made in complying with this section an offence is committed by –

    (a) the company, and

    (b) every officer of the company who is in default.

(3) A person guilty of an offence under this section is liable on summary conviction to a fine not exceeding level 3 on the standard scale and, for continued contravention, a daily default fine not exceeding one-tenth of level 3 on the standard scale.

Matters to be notified to the registrar

636 Notice of name or other designation of class of shares

(1) Where a company assigns a name or other designation, or a new name or other designation, to any class or description of its shares, it must within one month from doing so deliver to the registrar a notice giving particulars of the name or designation so assigned.

(2) If default is made in complying with this section, an offence is committed by –

    (a) the company, and

    (b) every officer of the company who is in default.

(3) A person guilty of an offence under this section is liable on summary conviction to a fine not exceeding level 3 on the standard scale and, for continued contravention, a daily default fine not exceeding one-tenth of level 3 on the standard scale.

637 Notice of particulars of variation of rights attached to shares

(1) Where the rights attached to any shares of a company are varied, the company must within one month from the date on which the variation is made deliver to the registrar a notice giving particulars of the variation.

(2) If default is made in complying with this section, an offence is committed by –

(a) the company, and
(b) every officer of the company who is in default.

(3) A person guilty of an offence under this section is liable on summary conviction to a fine not exceeding level 3 on the standard scale and, for continued contravention, a daily default fine not exceeding one-tenth of level 3 on the standard scale.

638 Notice of new class of members

(1) If a company not having a share capital creates a new class of members, the company must within one month from the date on which the new class is created deliver to the registrar a notice containing particulars of the rights attached to that class.

(2) If default is made in complying with this section, an offence is committed by –

(a) the company, and
(b) every officer of the company who is in default.

(3) A person guilty of an offence under this section is liable on summary conviction to a fine not exceeding level 3 on the standard scale and, for continued contravention, a daily default fine not exceeding one-tenth of level 3 on the standard scale.

639 Notice of name or other designation of class of members

(1) Where a company not having a share capital assigns a name or other designation, or a new name or other designation, to any class of its members, it must within one month from doing so deliver to the registrar a notice giving particulars of the name or designation so assigned.

(2) If default is made in complying with this section, an offence is committed by –

(a) the company, and
(b) every officer of the company who is in default.

(3) A person guilty of an offence under this section is liable on summary conviction to a fine not exceeding level 3 on the standard scale and, for continued contravention, a daily default fine not exceeding one-tenth of level 3 on the standard scale.

640 Notice of particulars of variation of class rights

(1) If the rights of any class of members of a company not having a share capital are varied, the company must within one month from the date on which the variation is made deliver to the registrar a notice containing particulars of the variation.

(2) If default is made in complying with this section, an offence is committed by –

(a) the company, and
(b) every officer of the company who is in default.

(3) A person guilty of an offence under this section is liable on summary conviction to a fine not exceeding level 3 on the standard scale and, for continued contravention, a daily default fine not exceeding one-tenth of level 3 on the standard scale.

CHAPTER 10

REDUCTION OF SHARE CAPITAL

Introductory

641 Circumstances in which a company may reduce its share capital

(1) A limited company having a share capital may reduce its share capital –

(a) in the case of a private company limited by shares, by special resolution supported by a solvency statement (see sections 642 to 644);

(b) in any case, by special resolution confirmed by the court (see sections 645 to 651).

(2) A company may not reduce its capital under subsection (1)(a) if as a result of the reduction there would no longer be any member of the company holding shares other than redeemable shares.

(3) Subject to that, a company may reduce its share capital under this section in any way.

(4) In particular, a company may –

(a) extinguish or reduce the liability on any of its shares in respect of share capital not paid up, or

(b) either with or without extinguishing or reducing liability on any of its shares –

(i) cancel any paid-up share capital that is lost or unrepresented by available assets, or

(ii) repay any paid-up share capital in excess of the company's wants.

(5) A special resolution under this section may not provide for a reduction of share capital to take effect later than the date on which the resolution has effect in accordance with this Chapter.

(6) This Chapter (apart from subsection (5) above) has effect subject to any provision of the company's articles restricting or prohibiting the reduction of the company's share capital.

Private companies: reduction of capital supported by solvency statement

642 Reduction of capital supported by solvency statement

(1) A resolution for reducing share capital of a private company limited by shares is supported by a solvency statement if –

(a) the directors of the company make a statement of the solvency of the company in accordance with section 643 (a "solvency statement") not more than 15 days before the date on which the resolution is passed, and

(b) the resolution and solvency statement are registered in accordance with section 644.

(2) Where the resolution is proposed as a written resolution, a copy of the solvency statement must be sent or submitted to every eligible member at or before the time at which the proposed resolution is sent or submitted to him.

(3) Where the resolution is proposed at a general meeting, a copy of the solvency statement must be made available for inspection by members of the company throughout that meeting.

(4) The validity of a resolution is not affected by a failure to comply with subsection (2) or (3).

643 Solvency statement

(1) A solvency statement is a statement that each of the directors –

(a) has formed the opinion, as regards the company's situation at the date of the statement, that there is no ground on which the company could then be found to be unable to pay (or otherwise discharge) its debts; and

(b) has also formed the opinion –

(i) if it is intended to commence the winding up of the company within twelve months of that date, that the company will be able to pay (or otherwise discharge) its debts in full within twelve months of the commencement of the winding up; or

(ii)   in any other case, that the company will be able to pay (or otherwise discharge) its debts as they fall due during the year immediately following that date.

(2)   In forming those opinions, the directors must take into account all of the company's liabilities (including any contingent or prospective liabilities).

(3)   The solvency statement must be in the prescribed form and must state –

(a)   the date on which it is made, and

(b)   the name of each director of the company.

(4)   If the directors make a solvency statement without having reasonable grounds for the opinions expressed in it, and the statement is delivered to the registrar, an offence is committed by every director who is in default.

(5)   A person guilty of an offence under subsection (4) is liable –

(a)   on conviction on indictment, to imprisonment for a term not exceeding two years or a fine (or both);

(b)   on summary conviction –

(i)   in England and Wales, to imprisonment for a term not exceeding twelve months or to a fine not exceeding the statutory maximum (or both);

(ii)   in Scotland or Northern Ireland, to imprisonment for a term not exceeding six months, or to a fine not exceeding the statutory maximum (or both).

644 Registration of resolution and supporting documents

(1)   Within 15 days after the resolution for reducing share capital is passed the company must deliver to the registrar –

(a)   a copy of the solvency statement, and

(b)   a statement of capital.

This is in addition to the copy of the resolution itself that is required to be delivered to the registrar under Chapter 3 of Part 3.

(2)   The statement of capital must state with respect to the company's share capital as reduced by the resolution –

(a)   the total number of shares of the company,

(b)   the aggregate nominal value of those shares,

(c)   for each class of shares –

(i)   prescribed particulars of the rights attached to the shares,

(ii)   the total number of shares of that class, and

(iii)   the aggregate nominal value of shares of that class, and

(d)   the amount paid up and the amount (if any) unpaid on each share (whether on account of the nominal value of the share or by way of premium).

(3)   The registrar must register the documents delivered to him under subsection (1) on receipt.

(4)   The resolution does not take effect until those documents are registered.

(5)   The company must also deliver to the registrar, within 15 days after the resolution is passed, a statement by the directors confirming that the solvency statement was –

(a)   made not more than 15 days before the date on which the resolution was passed, and

(b)   provided to members in accordance with section 642(2) or (3).

(6)   The validity of a resolution is not affected by –

(a)   a failure to deliver the documents required to be delivered to the registrar under subsection (1) within the time specified in that subsection, or

(b)   a failure to comply with subsection (5).

(7)   If the company delivers to the registrar a solvency statement that was not provided to

members in accordance with section 642(2) or (3), an offence is committed by every officer of the company who is in default.

(8) If default is made in complying with this section, an offence is committed by –

(a) the company, and

(b) every officer of the company who is in default.

(9) A person guilty of an offence under subsection (7) or (8) is liable –

(a) on conviction on indictment, to a fine;

(b) on summary conviction, to a fine not exceeding the statutory maximum.

Reduction of capital confirmed by the court

645 Application to court for order of confirmation

(1) Where a company has passed a resolution for reducing share capital, it may apply to the court for an order confirming the reduction.

(2) If the proposed reduction of capital involves either –

(a) diminution of liability in respect of unpaid share capital, or

(b) the payment to a shareholder of any paid-up share capital,

section 646 (creditors entitled to object to reduction) applies unless the court directs otherwise.

(3) The court may, if having regard to any special circumstances of the case it thinks proper to do so, direct that section 646 is not to apply as regards any class or classes of creditors.

(4) The court may direct that section 646 is to apply in any other case.

646 Creditors entitled to object to reduction

(1) Where this section applies (see section 645(2) and (4)), every creditor of the company who at the date fixed by the court is entitled to any debt or claim that, if that date were the commencement of the winding up of the company would be admissible in proof against the company, is entitled to object to the reduction of capital.

(2) The court shall settle a list of creditors entitled to object.

(3) For that purpose the court –

(a) shall ascertain, as far as possible without requiring an application from any creditor, the names of those creditors and the nature and amount of their debts or claims, and

(b) may publish notices fixing a day or days within which creditors not entered on the list are to claim to be so entered or are to be excluded from the right of objecting to the reduction of capital.

(4) If a creditor entered on the list whose debt or claim is not discharged or has not determined does not consent to the reduction, the court may, if it thinks fit, dispense with the consent of that creditor on the company securing payment of his debt or claim.

(5) For this purpose the debt or claim must be secured by appropriating (as the court may direct) the following amount –

(a) if the company admits the full amount of the debt or claim or, though not admitting it, is willing to provide for it, the full amount of the debt or claim;

(b) if the company does not admit, and is not willing to provide for, the full amount of the debt or claim, or if the amount is contingent or not ascertained, an amount fixed by the court after the like enquiry and adjudication as if the company were being wound up by the court.

647 Offences in connection with list of creditors

(1) If an officer of the company –

    (a) intentionally or recklessly –

        (i) conceals the name of a creditor entitled to object to the reduction of capital, or

        (ii) misrepresents the nature or amount of the debt or claim of a creditor, or

    (b) is knowingly concerned in any such concealment or misrepresentation,

    he commits an offence.

(2) A person guilty of an offence under this section is liable –

    (a) on conviction on indictment, to a fine;

    (b) on summary conviction, to a fine not exceeding the statutory maximum.

648 Court order confirming reduction

(1) The court may make an order confirming the reduction of capital on such terms and conditions as it thinks fit.

(2) The court must not confirm the reduction unless it is satisfied, with respect to every creditor of the company who is entitled to object to the reduction of capital that either –

    (a) his consent to the reduction has been obtained, or

    (b) his debt or claim has been discharged, or has determined or has been secured.

(3) Where the court confirms the reduction, it may order the company to publish (as the court directs) the reasons for reduction of capital, or such other information in regard to it as the court thinks expedient with a view to giving proper information to the public, and (if the court thinks fit) the causes that led to the reduction.

(4) The court may, if for any special reason it thinks proper to do so, make an order directing that the company must, during such period (commencing on or at any time after the date of the order) as is specified in the order, add to its name as its last words the words "and reduced".

    If such an order is made, those words are, until the end of the period specified in the order, deemed to be part of the company's name.

649 Registration of order and statement of capital

(1) The registrar, on production of an order of the court confirming the reduction of a company's share capital and the delivery of a copy of the order and of a statement of capital (approved by the court), shall register the order and statement.

    This is subject to section 650 (public company reducing capital below authorised minimum).

(2) The statement of capital must state with respect to the company's share capital as altered by the order –

    (a) the total number of shares of the company,

    (b) the aggregate nominal value of those shares,

    (c) for each class of shares –

        (i) prescribed particulars of the rights attached to the shares,

        (ii) the total number of shares of that class, and

        (iii) the aggregate nominal value of shares of that class, and

    (d) the amount paid up and the amount (if any) unpaid on each share (whether on account of the nominal value of the share or by way of premium).

(3) The resolution for reducing share capital, as confirmed by the court's order, takes effect –

    (a) in the case of a reduction of share capital that forms part of a compromise or arrangement sanctioned by the court under Part 26 (arrangements and reconstructions) –

      (i)   on delivery of the order and statement of capital to the registrar, or

      (ii)   if the court so orders, on the registration of the order and statement of capital;

  (b) in any other case, on the registration of the order and statement of capital.

(4) Notice of the registration of the order and statement of capital must be published in such manner as the court may direct.

(5) The registrar must certify the registration of the order and statement of capital.

(6) The certificate –

  (a) must be signed by the registrar or authenticated by the registrar's official seal, and

  (b) is conclusive evidence –

      (i)   that the requirements of this Act with respect to the reduction of share capital have been complied with, and

      (ii)   that the company's share capital is as stated in the statement of capital.

Public company reducing capital below authorised minimum

650 Public company reducing capital below authorised minimum

(1) This section applies where the court makes an order confirming a reduction of a public company's capital that has the effect of bringing the nominal value of its allotted share capital below the authorised minimum.

(2) The registrar must not register the order unless either –

  (a) the court so directs, or

  (b) the company is first re-registered as a private company.

(3) Section 651 provides an expedited procedure for re-registration in these circumstances.

651 Expedited procedure for re-registration as a private company

(1) The court may authorise the company to be re-registered as a private company without its having passed the special resolution required by section 97.

(2) If it does so, the court must specify in the order the changes to the company's name and articles to be made in connection with the re-registration.

(3) The company may then be re-registered as a private company if an application to that effect is delivered to the registrar together with –

  (a) a copy of the court's order, and

  (b) notice of the company's name, and a copy of the company's articles, as altered by the court's order.

(4) On receipt of such an application the registrar must issue a certificate of incorporation altered to meet the circumstances of the case.

(5) The certificate must state that it is issued on re-registration and the date on which it is issued.

(6) On the issue of the certificate –

  (a) the company by virtue of the issue of the certificate becomes a private company, and

  (b) the changes in the company's name and articles take effect.

(7) The certificate is conclusive evidence that the requirements of this Act as to re-registration have been complied with.

Effect of reduction of capital

652 Liability of members following reduction of capital

(1) Where a company's share capital is reduced a member of the company (past or present) is not liable in respect of any share to any call or contribution exceeding in amount the difference (if any) between –

    (a) the nominal amount of the share as notified to the registrar in the statement of capital delivered under section 644 or 649, and

    (b) the amount paid on the share or the reduced amount (if any) which is deemed to have been paid on it, as the case may be.

(2) This is subject to section 653 (liability to creditor in case of omission from list).

(3) Nothing in this section affects the rights of the contributories among themselves.

653 Liability to creditor in case of omission from list of creditors

(1) This section applies where, in the case of a reduction of capital confirmed by the court –

    (a) a creditor entitled to object to the reduction of share capital is by reason of his ignorance –

        (i) of the proceedings for reduction of share capital, or

        (ii) of their nature and effect with respect to his debt or claim,

    not entered on the list of creditors, and

    (b) after the reduction of capital the company is unable to pay the amount of his debt or claim.

(2) Every person who was a member of the company at the date on which the resolution for reducing capital took effect under section 649(3) is liable to contribute for the payment of the debt or claim an amount not exceeding that which he would have been liable to contribute if the company had commenced to be wound up on the day before that date.

(3) If the company is wound up, the court on the application of the creditor in question, and proof of ignorance as mentioned in subsection (1)(a), may if it thinks fit –

    (a) settle accordingly a list of persons liable to contribute under this section, and

    (b) make and enforce calls and orders on them as if they were ordinary contributories in a winding up.

(4) The reference in subsection (1)(b) to a company being unable to pay the amount of a debt or claim has the same meaning as in section 123 of the Insolvency Act 1986 (c. 45) or Article 103 of the Insolvency (Northern Ireland) Order 1989 (S.I. 1989/2405 (N.I. 19)).

CHAPTER 11

MISCELLANEOUS AND SUPPLEMENTARY PROVISIONS

654 Treatment of reserve arising from reduction of capital

(1) A reserve arising from the reduction of a company's share capital is not distributable, subject to any provision made by order under this section.

(2) The Secretary of State may by order specify cases in which –

    (a) the prohibition in subsection (1) does not apply, and

    (b) the reserve is to be treated for the purposes of Part 23 (distributions) as a realised profit.

(3) An order under this section is subject to affirmative resolution procedure.

655 Shares no bar to damages against company

A person is not debarred from obtaining damages or other compensation from a company by reason only of his holding or having held shares in the company or any right to apply or subscribe for shares or to be included in the company's register of members in respect of shares.

656 Public companies: duty of directors to call meeting on serious loss of capital

(1) Where the net assets of a public company are half or less of its called-up share capital, the directors must call a general meeting of the company to consider whether any, and if so what, steps should be taken to deal with the situation.

(2) They must do so not later than 28 days from the earliest day on which that fact is known to a director of the company.

(3) The meeting must be convened for a date not later than 56 days from that day.

(4) If there is a failure to convene a meeting as required by this section, each of the directors of the company who –

(a) knowingly authorises or permits the failure, or

(b) after the period during which the meeting should have been convened, knowingly authorises or permits the failure to continue,

commits an offence.

(5) A person guilty of an offence under this section is liable –

(a) on conviction on indictment, to a fine;

(b) on summary conviction, to a fine not exceeding the statutory maximum.

(6) Nothing in this section authorises the consideration at a meeting convened in pursuance of subsection (1) of any matter that could not have been considered at that meeting apart from this section.

657 General power to make further provision by regulations

(1) The Secretary of State may by regulations modify the following provisions of this Part –

sections 552 and 553 (prohibited commissions, discounts and allowances),
Chapter 5 (payment for shares),
Chapter 6 (public companies: independent valuation of non-cash consideration),
Chapter 7 (share premiums),
sections 622 to 628 (redenomination of share capital),
Chapter 10 (reduction of capital), and
section 656 (public companies: duty of directors to call meeting on serious loss of capital).

(2) The regulations may –

(a) amend or repeal any of those provisions, or

(b) make such other provision as appears to the Secretary of State appropriate in place of any of those provisions.

(3) Regulations under this section may make consequential amendments or repeals in other provisions of this Act, or in other enactments.

(4) Regulations under this section are subject to affirmative resolution procedure.

PART 18

ACQUISITION BY LIMITED COMPANY OF ITS OWN SHARES

CHAPTER 1

GENERAL PROVISIONS

Introductory

658 General rule against limited company acquiring its own shares

(1) A limited company must not acquire its own shares, whether by purchase, subscription or otherwise, except in accordance with the provisions of this Part.

(2) If a company purports to act in contravention of this section –

    (a) an offence is committed by –

        (i)   the company, and

        (ii) every officer of the company who is in default, and

    (b) the purported acquisition is void.

(3) A person guilty of an offence under this section is liable –

    (a) on conviction on indictment, to imprisonment for a term not exceeding two years or a fine (or both);

    (b) on summary conviction –

        (i)   in England and Wales, to imprisonment for a term not exceeding twelve months or a fine not exceeding the statutory maximum (or both);

        (ii) in Scotland or Northern Ireland, to imprisonment for a term not exceeding six months or a fine not exceeding the statutory maximum (or both).

659 Exceptions to general rule

(1) A limited company may acquire any of its own fully paid shares otherwise than for valuable consideration.

(2) Section 658 does not prohibit –

    (a) the acquisition of shares in a reduction of capital duly made;

    (b) the purchase of shares in pursuance of an order of the court under –

        (i)   section 98 (application to court to cancel resolution for re-registration as a private company),

        (ii) section 721(6) (powers of court on objection to redemption or purchase of shares out of capital),

        (iii) section 759 (remedial order in case of breach of prohibition of public offers by private company), or

        (iv) Part 30 (protection of members against unfair prejudice);

    (c) the forfeiture of shares, or the acceptance of shares surrendered in lieu, in pursuance of the company's articles, for failure to pay any sum payable in respect of the shares.

Shares held by company's nominee

660 Treatment of shares held by nominee

(1) This section applies where shares in a limited company –

    (a) are taken by a subscriber to the memorandum as nominee of the company,

(b)   are issued to a nominee of the company, or

(c)   are acquired by a nominee of the company, partly paid up, from a third person.

(2) For all purposes –

    (a)   the shares are to be treated as held by the nominee on his own account, and

    (b)   the company is to be regarded as having no beneficial interest in them.

(3) This section does not apply –

    (a)   to shares acquired otherwise than by subscription by a nominee of a public company, where –

        (i)   a person acquires shares in the company with financial assistance given to him, directly or indirectly, by the company for the purpose of or in connection with the acquisition, and

        (ii)   the company has a beneficial interest in the shares;

    (b)   to shares acquired by a nominee of the company when the company has no beneficial interest in the shares.

661 Liability of others where nominee fails to make payment in respect of shares

(1) This section applies where shares in a limited company –

    (a)   are taken by a subscriber to the memorandum as nominee of the company,

    (b)   are issued to a nominee of the company, or

    (c)   are acquired by a nominee of the company, partly paid up, from a third person.

(2) If the nominee, having been called on to pay any amount for the purposes of paying up, or paying any premium on, the shares, fails to pay that amount within 21 days from being called on to do so, then –

    (a)   in the case of shares that he agreed to take as subscriber to the memorandum, the other subscribers to the memorandum, and

    (b)   in any other case, the directors of the company when the shares were issued to or acquired by him,

are jointly and severally liable with him to pay that amount.

(3) If in proceedings for the recovery of an amount under subsection (2) it appears to the court that the subscriber or director –

    (a)   has acted honestly and reasonably, and

    (b)   having regard to all the circumstances of the case, ought fairly to be relieved from liability,

the court may relieve him, either wholly or in part, from his liability on such terms as the court thinks fit.

(4) If a subscriber to a company's memorandum or a director of a company has reason to apprehend that a claim will or might be made for the recovery of any such amount from him –

    (a)   he may apply to the court for relief, and

    (b)   the court has the same power to relieve him as it would have had in proceedings for recovery of that amount.

(5) This section does not apply to shares acquired by a nominee of the company when the company has no beneficial interest in the shares.

Shares held by or for public company

662 Duty to cancel shares in public company held by or for the company

(1) This section applies in the case of a public company –

(a) where shares in the company are forfeited, or surrendered to the company in lieu of forfeiture, in pursuance of the articles, for failure to pay any sum payable in respect of the shares;

(b) where shares in the company are surrendered to the company in pursuance of section 102C(1)(b) of the Building Societies Act 1986 (c. 53);

(c) where shares in the company are acquired by it (otherwise than in accordance with this Part or Part 30 (protection of members against unfair prejudice)) and the company has a beneficial interest in the shares;

(d) where a nominee of the company acquires shares in the company from a third party without financial assistance being given directly or indirectly by the company and the company has a beneficial interest in the shares; or

(e) where a person acquires shares in the company, with financial assistance given to him, directly or indirectly, by the company for the purpose of or in connection with the acquisition, and the company has a beneficial interest in the shares.

(2) Unless the shares or any interest of the company in them are previously disposed of, the company must –

(a) cancel the shares and diminish the amount of the company's share capital by the nominal value of the shares cancelled, and

(b) where the effect is that the nominal value of the company's allotted share capital is brought below the authorised minimum, apply for re-registration as a private company, stating the effect of the cancellation.

(3) It must do so no later than –

(a) in a case within subsection (1)(a) or (b), three years from the date of the forfeiture or surrender;

(b) in a case within subsection (1)(c) or (d), three years from the date of the acquisition;

(c) in a case within subsection (1)(e), one year from the date of the acquisition.

(4) The directors of the company may take any steps necessary to enable the company to comply with this section, and may do so without complying with the provisions of Chapter 10 of Part 17 (reduction of capital).
See also section 664 (re-registration as private company in consequence of cancellation).

(5) Neither the company nor, in a case within subsection (1)(d) or (e), the nominee or other shareholder may exercise any voting rights in respect of the shares.

(6) Any purported exercise of those rights is void.

663 Notice of cancellation of shares

(1) Where a company cancels shares in order to comply with section 662, it must within one month after the shares are cancelled give notice to the registrar, specifying the shares cancelled.

(2) The notice must be accompanied by a statement of capital.

(3) The statement of capital must state with respect to the company's share capital immediately following the cancellation –

(a) the total number of shares of the company,

(b) the aggregate nominal value of those shares,

(c) for each class of shares –

(i)   prescribed particulars of the rights attached to the shares,

(ii) the total number of shares of that class, and

(iii) the aggregate nominal value of shares of that class, and

(d) the amount paid up and the amount (if any) unpaid on each share (whether on account of the nominal value of the share or by way of premium).

(4) If default is made in complying with this section, an offence is committed by –

(a) the company, and

(b) every officer of the company who is in default.

(5) A person guilty of an offence under this section is liable on summary conviction to a fine not exceeding level 3 on the standard scale and, for continued contravention, a daily default fine not exceeding one-tenth of level 3 on the standard scale.

664 Re-registration as private company in consequence of cancellation

(1) Where a company is obliged to re-register as a private company to comply with section 662, the directors may resolve that the company should be so re-registered. Chapter 3 of Part 3 (resolutions affecting a company's constitution) applies to any such resolution.

(2) The resolution may make such changes –

(a) in the company's name, and

(b) in the company's articles,

as are necessary in connection with its becoming a private company.

(3) The application for re-registration must contain a statement of the company's proposed name on re-registration.

(4) The application must be accompanied by –

(a) a copy of the resolution (unless a copy has already been forwarded under Chapter 3 of Part 3),

(b) a copy of the company's articles as amended by the resolution, and

(c) a statement of compliance.

(5) The statement of compliance required is a statement that the requirements of this section as to re-registration as a private company have been complied with.

(6) The registrar may accept the statement of compliance as sufficient evidence that the company is entitled to be re-registered as a private company.

665 Issue of certificate of incorporation on re-registration

(1) If on an application under section 664 the registrar is satisfied that the company is entitled to be re-registered as a private company, the company shall be re-registered accordingly.

(2) The registrar must issue a certificate of incorporation altered to meet the circumstances of the case.

(3) The certificate must state that it is issued on re-registration and the date on which it is issued.

(4) On the issue of the certificate –

(a) the company by virtue of the issue of the certificate becomes a private company, and

(b) the changes in the company's name and articles take effect.

(5) The certificate is conclusive evidence that the requirements of this Act as to re-registration have been complied with.

666 Effect of failure to re-register

(1) If a public company that is required by section 662 to apply to be re-registered as a private company fails to do so before the end of the period specified in subsection (3) of that section, Chapter 1 of Part 20 (prohibition of public offers by private company) applies to it as if it were a private company.

(2) Subject to that, the company continues to be treated as a public company until it is so re-registered.

667 Offence in case of failure to cancel shares or re-register

(1) This section applies where a company, when required to do by section 662 –

    (a) fails to cancel any shares, or

    (b) fails to make an application for re-registration as a private company,

within the time specified in subsection (3) of that section.

(2) An offence is committed by –

    (a) the company, and

    (b) every officer of the company who is in default.

(3) A person guilty of an offence under this section is liable on summary conviction to a fine not exceeding level 3 on the standard scale and, for continued contravention, a daily default fine not exceeding one-tenth of level 3 on the standard scale.

668 Application of provisions to company re-registering as public company

(1) This section applies where, after shares in a private company –

    (a) are forfeited in pursuance of the company's articles or are surrendered to the company in lieu of forfeiture,

    (b) are acquired by the company (otherwise than by any of the methods permitted by this Part or Part 30 (protection of members against unfair prejudice)), the company having a beneficial interest in the shares,

    (c) are acquired by a nominee of the company from a third party without financial assistance being given directly or indirectly by the company, the company having a beneficial interest in the shares, or

    (d) are acquired by a person with financial assistance given to him, directly or indirectly, by the company for the purpose of or in connection with the acquisition, the company having a beneficial interest in the shares,

the company is re-registered as a public company.

(2) In that case the provisions of sections 662 to 667 apply to the company as if it had been a public company at the time of the forfeiture, surrender or acquisition, subject to the following modification.

(3) The modification is that the period specified in section 662(3)(a), (b) or (c) (period for complying with obligations under that section) runs from the date of the re-registration of the company as a public company.

669 Transfer to reserve on acquisition of shares by public company or nominee

(1) Where –

    (a) a public company, or a nominee of a public company, acquires shares in the company, and

    (b) those shares are shown in a balance sheet of the company as an asset, an amount equal to the value of the shares must be transferred out of profits available for dividend to a reserve fund and is not then available for distribution.

(2) Subsection (1) applies to an interest in shares as it applies to shares.

As it so applies the reference to the value of the shares shall be read as a reference to the value to the company of its interest in the shares.

Charges of public company on own shares

670 Public companies: general rule against lien or charge on own shares

(1) A lien or other charge of a public company on its own shares (whether taken expressly or otherwise) is void, except as permitted by this section.

(2) In the case of any description of company, a charge is permitted if the shares are not fully paid up and the charge is for an amount payable in respect of the shares.

(3) In the case of a company whose ordinary business –

    (a) includes the lending of money, or

    (b) consists of the provision of credit or the bailment (in Scotland, hiring) of goods under a hire-purchase agreement, or both,

a charge is permitted (whether the shares are fully paid or not) if it arises in connection with a transaction entered into by the company in the ordinary course of that business.

(4) In the case of a company that has been re-registered as a public company, a charge is permitted if it was in existence immediately before the application for re-registration.

Supplementary provisions

671 Interests to be disregarded in determining whether company has beneficial interest

In determining for the purposes of this Chapter whether a company has a beneficial interest in shares, there shall be disregarded any such interest as is mentioned in –

    section 672 (residual interest under pension scheme or employees' share scheme),
    section 673 (employer's charges and other rights of recovery), or
    section 674 (rights as personal representative or trustee).

672 Residual interest under pension scheme or employees' share scheme

(1) Where the shares are held on trust for the purposes of a pension scheme or employees' share scheme, there shall be disregarded any residual interest of the company that has not vested in possession.

(2) A "residual interest" means a right of the company to receive any of the trust property in the event of –

    (a) all the liabilities arising under the scheme having been satisfied or provided for, or

    (b) the company ceasing to participate in the scheme, or

    (c) the trust property at any time exceeding what is necessary for satisfying the liabilities arising or expected to arise under the scheme.

(3) In subsection (2) –

    (a) the reference to a right includes a right dependent on the exercise of a discretion vested by the scheme in the trustee or another person, and

    (b) the reference to liabilities arising under a scheme includes liabilities that have resulted, or may result, from the exercise of any such discretion.

(4) For the purposes of this section a residual interest vests in possession –

    (a) in a case within subsection (2)(a), on the occurrence of the event mentioned there (whether or not the amount of the property receivable pursuant to the right is ascertained);

    (b) in a case within subsection (2)(b) or (c), when the company becomes entitled to require the trustee to transfer to it any of the property receivable pursuant to that right.

(5) Where by virtue of this section shares are exempt from section 660 or 661 (shares held by company's nominee) at the time they are taken, issued or acquired but the residual interest in question vests in possession before they are disposed of or fully paid up, those sections apply to the shares as if they had been taken, issued or acquired on the date on which that interest vests in possession.

(6) Where by virtue of this section shares are exempt from sections 662 to 668 (shares held by or for public company) at the time they are acquired but the residual interest in question vests in possession before they are disposed of, those sections apply to the

shares as if they had been acquired on the date on which the interest vests in possession.

673 Employer's charges and other rights of recovery

(1) Where the shares are held on trust for the purposes of a pension scheme there shall be disregarded –

    (a) any charge or lien on, or set-off against, any benefit or other right or interest under the scheme for the purpose of enabling the employer or former employer of a member of the scheme to obtain the discharge of a monetary obligation due to him from the member;

    (b) any right to receive from the trustee of the scheme, or as trustee of the scheme to retain, an amount that can be recovered or retained –

        (i) under section 61 of the Pension Schemes Act 1993 (c. 48), or otherwise, as reimbursement or partial reimbursement for any contributions equivalent premium paid in connection with the scheme under Part 3 of that Act, or

        (ii) under section 57 of the Pension Schemes (Northern Ireland) Act 1993 (c. 49), or otherwise, as reimbursement or partial reimbursement for any contributions equivalent premium paid in connection with the scheme under Part 3 of that Act.

(2) Where the shares are held on trust for the purposes of an employees' share scheme, there shall be disregarded any charge or lien on, or set-off against, any benefit or other right or interest under the scheme for the purpose of enabling the employer or former employer of a member of the scheme to obtain the discharge of a monetary obligation due to him from the member.

674 Rights as personal representative or trustee

Where the company is a personal representative or trustee, there shall be disregarded any rights that the company has in that capacity including, in particular –

    (a) any right to recover its expenses or be remunerated out of the estate or trust property, and

    (b) any right to be indemnified out of that property for any liability incurred by reason of any act or omission of the company in the performance of its duties as personal representative or trustee.

675 Meaning of "pension scheme"

(1) In this Chapter "pension scheme" means a scheme for the provision of benefits consisting of or including relevant benefits for or in respect of employees or former employees.

(2) In subsection (1) "relevant benefits" means any pension, lump sum, gratuity or other like benefit given or to be given on retirement or on death or in anticipation of retirement or, in connection with past service, after retirement or death.

676 Application of provisions to directors

For the purposes of this Chapter references to "employer" and "employee", in the context of a pension scheme or employees' share scheme, shall be read as if a director of a company were employed by it.

CHAPTER 2

FINANCIAL ASSISTANCE FOR PURCHASE OF OWN SHARES

Introductory

677 Meaning of "financial assistance"

(1) In this Chapter "financial assistance" means –

    (a) financial assistance given by way of gift,

    (b) financial assistance given –

        (i) by way of guarantee, security or indemnity (other than an indemnity in respect of the indemnifier's own neglect or default), or

        (ii) by way of release or waiver,

    (c) financial assistance given –

        (i) by way of a loan or any other agreement under which any of the obligations of the person giving the assistance are to be fulfilled at a time when in accordance with the agreement any obligation of another party to the agreement remains unfulfilled, or

        (ii) by way of the novation of, or the assignment (in Scotland, assignation) of rights arising under, a loan or such other agreement, or

    (d) any other financial assistance given by a company where –

        (i) the net assets of the company are reduced to a material extent by the giving of the assistance, or

        (ii) the company has no net assets.

(2) "Net assets" here means the aggregate amount of the company's assets less the aggregate amount of its liabilities.

(3) For this purpose a company's liabilities include –

    (a) where the company draws up Companies Act individual accounts, any provision of a kind specified for the purposes of this subsection by regulations under section 396, and

    (b) where the company draws up IAS individual accounts, any provision made in those accounts.

Circumstances in which financial assistance prohibited

678 Assistance for acquisition of shares in public company

(1) Where a person is acquiring or proposing to acquire shares in a public company, it is not lawful for that company, or a company that is a subsidiary of that company, to give financial assistance directly or indirectly for the purpose of the acquisition before or at the same time as the acquisition takes place.

(2) Subsection (1) does not prohibit a company from giving financial assistance for the acquisition of shares in it or its holding company if –

    (a) the company's principal purpose in giving the assistance is not to give it for the purpose of any such acquisition, or

    (b) the giving of the assistance for that purpose is only an incidental part of some larger purpose of the company,

and the assistance is given in good faith in the interests of the company.

(3) Where –

    (a) a person has acquired shares in a company, and

(b) a liability has been incurred (by that or another person) for the purpose of the acquisition,

it is not lawful for that company, or a company that is a subsidiary of that company, to give financial assistance directly or indirectly for the purpose of reducing or discharging the liability if, at the time the assistance is given, the company in which the shares were acquired is a public company.

(4) Subsection (3) does not prohibit a company from giving financial assistance if –

(a) the company's principal purpose in giving the assistance is not to reduce or discharge any liability incurred by a person for the purpose of the acquisition of shares in the company or its holding company, or

(b) the reduction or discharge of any such liability is only an incidental part of some larger purpose of the company,

and the assistance is given in good faith in the interests of the company.

(5) This section has effect subject to sections 681 and 682 (unconditional and conditional exceptions to prohibition).

679 Assistance by public company for acquisition of shares in its private holding company

(1) Where a person is acquiring or proposing to acquire shares in a private company, it is not lawful for a public company that is a subsidiary of that company to give financial assistance directly or indirectly for the purpose of the acquisition before or at the same time as the acquisition takes place.

(2) Subsection (1) does not prohibit a company from giving financial assistance for the acquisition of shares in its holding company if –

(a) the company's principal purpose in giving the assistance is not to give it for the purpose of any such acquisition, or

(b) the giving of the assistance for that purpose is only an incidental part of some larger purpose of the company,

and the assistance is given in good faith in the interests of the company.

(3) Where –

(a) a person has acquired shares in a private company, and

(b) a liability has been incurred (by that or another person) for the purpose of the acquisition,

it is not lawful for a public company that is a subsidiary of that company to give financial assistance directly or indirectly for the purpose of reducing or discharging the liability.

(4) Subsection (3) does not prohibit a company from giving financial assistance if –

(a) the company's principal purpose in giving the assistance is not to reduce or discharge any liability incurred by a person for the purpose of the acquisition of shares in its holding company, or

(b) the reduction or discharge of any such liability is only an incidental part of some larger purpose of the company,

and the assistance is given in good faith in the interests of the company.

(5) This section has effect subject to sections 681 and 682 (unconditional and conditional exceptions to prohibition).

680 Prohibited financial assistance an offence

(1) If a company contravenes section 678(1) or (3) or section 679(1) or (3) (prohibited financial assistance) an offence is committed by –

(a) the company, and

(b) every officer of the company who is in default.

(2) A person guilty of an offence under this section is liable –

    (a) on conviction on indictment, to imprisonment for a term not exceeding two years or a fine (or both);

    (b) on summary conviction –

        (i) in England and Wales, to imprisonment for a term not exceeding twelve months or to a fine not exceeding the statutory maximum (or both);

        (ii) in Scotland or Northern Ireland, to imprisonment for a term not exceeding six months, or to a fine not exceeding the statutory maximum (or both).

Exceptions from prohibition

681 Unconditional exceptions

(1) Neither section 678 nor section 679 prohibits a transaction to which this section applies.

(2) Those transactions are –

    (a) a distribution of the company's assets by way of –

        (i) dividend lawfully made, or

        (ii) distribution in the course of a company's winding up;

    (b) an allotment of bonus shares;

    (c) a reduction of capital under Chapter 10 of Part 17;

    (d) a redemption of shares under Chapter 3 or a purchase of shares under Chapter 4 of this Part;

    (e) anything done in pursuance of an order of the court under Part 26 (order sanctioning compromise or arrangement with members or creditors);

    (f) anything done under an arrangement made in pursuance of section 110 of the Insolvency Act 1986 (c. 45) or Article 96 of the Insolvency (Northern Ireland) Order 1989 (S.I. 1989/2405 (N.I. 19)) (liquidator in winding up accepting shares as consideration for sale of company's property);

    (g) anything done under an arrangement made between a company and its creditors that is binding on the creditors by virtue of Part 1 of the Insolvency Act 1986 or Part 2 of the Insolvency (Northern Ireland) Order 1989 (S.I. 1989/2405 (N.I. 19)).

682 Conditional exceptions

(1) Neither section 678 nor section 679 prohibits a transaction to which this section applies –

    (a) if the company giving the assistance is a private company, or

    (b) if the company giving the assistance is a public company and –

        (i) the company has net assets that are not reduced by the giving of the assistance, or

        (ii) to the extent that those assets are so reduced, the assistance is provided out of distributable profits.

(2) The transactions to which this section applies are –

    (a) where the lending of money is part of the ordinary business of the company, the lending of money in the ordinary course of the company's business;

    (b) the provision by the company, in good faith in the interests of the company or its holding company, of financial assistance for the purposes of an employees' share scheme;

    (c) the provision of financial assistance by the company for the purposes of or in connection with anything done by the company (or another company in the same group) for the purpose of enabling or facilitating transactions in shares in the first-mentioned company or its holding company between, and involving the acquisition of beneficial ownership of those shares by –

    (i)   bona fide employees or former employees of that company (or another company in the same group), or

    (ii)   spouses or civil partners, widows, widowers or surviving civil partners, or minor children or step-children of any such employees or former employees;

  (d)   the making by the company of loans to persons (other than directors) employed in good faith by the company with a view to enabling those persons to acquire fully paid shares in the company or its holding company to be held by them by way of beneficial ownership.

(3) The references in this section to "net assets" are to the amount by which the aggregate of the company's assets exceeds the aggregate of its liabilities.

(4) For this purpose –

  (a) the amount of both assets and liabilities shall be taken to be as stated in the company's accounting records immediately before the financial assistance is given, and

  (b) "liabilities" includes any amount retained as reasonably necessary for the purpose of providing for a liability the nature of which is clearly defined and that is either likely to be incurred or certain to be incurred but uncertain as to amount or as to the date on which it will arise.

(5) For the purposes of subsection (2)(c) a company is in the same group as another company if it is a holding company or subsidiary of that company or a subsidiary of a holding company of that company.

Supplementary

683 Definitions for this Chapter

(1) In this Chapter –

"distributable profits", in relation to the giving of any financial assistance –

  (a) means those profits out of which the company could lawfully make a distribution equal in value to that assistance, and

  (b) includes, in a case where the financial assistance consists of or includes, or is treated as arising in consequence of, the sale, transfer or other disposition of a non-cash asset, any profit that, if the company were to make a distribution of that character would be available for that purpose (see section 846); and

"distribution" has the same meaning as in Part 23 (distributions) (see section 829).

(2) In this Chapter –

  (a) a reference to a person incurring a liability includes his changing his financial position by making an agreement or arrangement (whether enforceable or unenforceable, and whether made on his own account or with any other person) or by any other means, and

  (b) a reference to a company giving financial assistance for the purposes of reducing or discharging a liability incurred by a person for the purpose of the acquisition of shares includes its giving such assistance for the purpose of wholly or partly restoring his financial position to what it was before the acquisition took place.

CHAPTER 3

REDEEMABLE SHARES

684 Power of limited company to issue redeemable shares

(1) A limited company having a share capital may issue shares that are to be redeemed or are liable to be redeemed at the option of the company or the shareholder ("redeemable shares"), subject to the following provisions.

(2) The articles of a private limited company may exclude or restrict the issue of redeemable shares.

(3) A public limited company may only issue redeemable shares if it is authorised to do so by its articles.

(4) No redeemable shares may be issued at a time when there are no issued shares of the company that are not redeemable.

685 Terms and manner of redemption

(1) The directors of a limited company may determine the terms, conditions and manner of redemption of shares if they are authorised to do so –

    (a) by the company's articles, or

    (b) by a resolution of the company.

(2) A resolution under subsection (1)(b) may be an ordinary resolution, even though it amends the company's articles.

(3) Where the directors are authorised under subsection (1) to determine the terms, conditions and manner of redemption of shares –

    (a) they must do so before the shares are allotted, and

    (b) any obligation of the company to state in a statement of capital the rights attached to the shares extends to the terms, conditions and manner of redemption.

(4) Where the directors are not so authorised, the terms, conditions and manner of redemption of any redeemable shares must be stated in the company's articles.

686 Payment for redeemable shares

(1) Redeemable shares in a limited company may not be redeemed unless they are fully paid.

(2) The terms of redemption of shares in a limited company may provide that the amount payable on redemption may, by agreement between the company and the holder of the shares, be paid on a date later than the redemption date.

(3) Unless redeemed in accordance with a provision authorised by subsection (2), the shares must be paid for on redemption.

687 Financing of redemption

(1) A private limited company may redeem redeemable shares out of capital in accordance with Chapter 5.

(2) Subject to that, redeemable shares in a limited company may only be redeemed out of –

    (a) distributable profits of the company, or

    (b) the proceeds of a fresh issue of shares made for the purposes of the redemption.

(3) Any premium payable on redemption of shares in a limited company must be paid out of distributable profits of the company, subject to the following provision.

(4) If the redeemable shares were issued at a premium, any premium payable on their redemption may be paid out of the proceeds of a fresh issue of shares made for the purposes of the redemption, up to an amount equal to –

   (a) the aggregate of the premiums received by the company on the issue of the shares redeemed, or

   (b) the current amount of the company's share premium account (including any sum transferred to that account in respect of premiums on the new shares),

   whichever is the less.

(5) The amount of the company's share premium account is reduced by a sum corresponding (or by sums in the aggregate corresponding) to the amount of any payment made under subsection (4).

(6) This section is subject to section 735(4) (terms of redemption enforceable in a winding up).

688 Redeemed shares treated as cancelled

Where shares in a limited company are redeemed –

   (a) the shares are treated as cancelled, and

   (b) the amount of the company's issued share capital is diminished accordingly by the nominal value of the shares redeemed.

689 Notice to registrar of redemption

(1) If a limited company redeems any redeemable shares it must within one month after doing so give notice to the registrar, specifying the shares redeemed.

(2) The notice must be accompanied by a statement of capital.

(3) The statement of capital must state with respect to the company's share capital immediately following the redemption –

   (a) the total number of shares of the company,

   (b) the aggregate nominal value of those shares,

   (c) for each class of shares –

      (i)   prescribed particulars of the rights attached to the shares,

      (ii) the total number of shares of that class, and

      (iii) the aggregate nominal value of shares of that class, and

   (d) the amount paid up and the amount (if any) unpaid on each share (whether on account of the nominal value of the share or by way of premium).

(4) If default is made in complying with this section, an offence is committed by –

   (a) the company, and

   (b) every officer of the company who is in default.

(5) A person guilty of an offence under this section is liable on summary conviction to a fine not exceeding level 3 on the standard scale and, for continued contravention, a daily default fine not exceeding one-tenth of level 3 on the standard scale.

CHAPTER 4

PURCHASE OF OWN SHARES

General provisions

690 Power of limited company to purchase own shares

(1) A limited company having a share capital may purchase its own shares (including any redeemable shares), subject to –

   (a) the following provisions of this Chapter, and

   (b) any restriction or prohibition in the company's articles.

(2) A limited company may not purchase its own shares if as a result of the purchase there would no longer be any issued shares of the company other than redeemable shares or shares held as treasury shares.

691 Payment for purchase of own shares

(1) A limited company may not purchase its own shares unless they are fully paid.
(2) Where a limited company purchases its own shares, the shares must be paid for on purchase.

692 Financing of purchase of own shares

(1) A private limited company may purchase its own shares out of capital in accordance with Chapter 5.
(2) Subject to that –
  (a) a limited company may only purchase its own shares out of –
    (i)   distributable profits of the company, or
    (ii) the proceeds of a fresh issue of shares made for the purpose of financing the purchase, and
  (b) any premium payable on the purchase by a limited company of its own shares must be paid out of distributable profits of the company, subject to subsection (3).
(3) If the shares to be purchased were issued at a premium, any premium payable on their purchase by the company may be paid out of the proceeds of a fresh issue of shares made for the purpose of financing the purchase, up to an amount equal to –
  (a) the aggregate of the premiums received by the company on the issue of the shares purchased, or
  (b) the current amount of the company's share premium account (including any sum transferred to that account in respect of premiums on the new shares),
  whichever is the less.
(4) The amount of the company's share premium account is reduced by a sum corresponding (or by sums in the aggregate corresponding) to the amount of any payment made under subsection (3).
(5) This section has effect subject to section 735(4) (terms of purchase enforceable in a winding up).

Authority for purchase of own shares

693 Authority for purchase of own shares

(1) A limited company may only purchase its own shares –
  (a) by an off-market purchase, in pursuance of a contract approved in advance in accordance with section 694;
  (b) by a market purchase, authorised in accordance with section 701.
(2) A purchase is "off-market" if the shares either –
  (a) are purchased otherwise than on a recognised investment exchange, or
  (b) are purchased on a recognised investment exchange but are not subject to a marketing arrangement on the exchange.
(3) For this purpose a company's shares are subject to a marketing arrangement on a recognised investment exchange if –
  (a) they are listed under Part 6 of the Financial Services and Markets Act 2000 (c. 8), or

(b) the company has been afforded facilities for dealings in the shares to take place on the exchange –

    (i)   without prior permission for individual transactions from the authority governing that investment exchange, and

    (ii) without limit as to the time during which those facilities are to be available.

(4) A purchase is a "market purchase" if it is made on a recognised investment exchange and is not an off-market purchase by virtue of subsection (2)(b).

(5) In this section "recognised investment exchange" means a recognised investment exchange (within the meaning of Part 18 of the Financial Services and Markets Act 2000) other than an overseas exchange (within the meaning of that Part).

Authority for off-market purchase

694 Authority for off-market purchase

(1) A company may only make an off-market purchase of its own shares in pursuance of a contract approved prior to the purchase in accordance with this section.

(2) Either –

    (a) the terms of the contract must be authorised by a special resolution of the company before the contract is entered into, or

    (b) the contract must provide that no shares may be purchased in pursuance of the contract until its terms have been authorised by a special resolution of the company.

(3) The contract may be a contract, entered into by the company and relating to shares in the company, that does not amount to a contract to purchase the shares but under which the company may (subject to any conditions) become entitled or obliged to purchase the shares.

(4) The authority conferred by a resolution under this section may be varied, revoked or from time to time renewed by a special resolution of the company.

(5) In the case of a public company a resolution conferring, varying or renewing authority must specify a date on which the authority is to expire, which must not be later than 18 months after the date on which the resolution is passed.

(6) A resolution conferring, varying, revoking or renewing authority under this section is subject to –

section 695 (exercise of voting rights), and
section 696 (disclosure of details of contract).

695 Resolution authorising off-market purchase: exercise of voting rights

(1) This section applies to a resolution to confer, vary, revoke or renew authority for the purposes of section 694 (authority for off-market purchase of own shares).

(2) Where the resolution is proposed as a written resolution, a member who holds shares to which the resolution relates is not an eligible member.

(3) Where the resolution is proposed at a meeting of the company, it is not effective if –

    (a) any member of the company holding shares to which the resolution relates exercises the voting rights carried by any of those shares in voting on the resolution, and

    (b) the resolution would not have been passed if he had not done so.

(4) For this purpose –

    (a) a member who holds shares to which the resolution relates is regarded as exercising the voting rights carried by those shares not only if he votes in respect of them on a poll on the question whether the resolution shall be passed, but also if he votes on the resolution otherwise than on a poll;

    (b) any member of the company may demand a poll on that question;

(c)   a vote and a demand for a poll by a person as proxy for a member are the same respectively as a vote and a demand by the member.

696 Resolution authorising off-market purchase: disclosure of details of contract

(1)   This section applies in relation to a resolution to confer, vary, revoke or renew authority for the purposes of section 694 (authority for off-market purchase of own shares).

(2)   A copy of the contract (if it is in writing) or a memorandum setting out its terms (if it is not) must be made available to members –

    (a)   in the case of a written resolution, by being sent or submitted to every eligible member at or before the time at which the proposed resolution is sent or submitted to him;

    (b)   in the case of a resolution at a meeting, by being made available for inspection by members of the company both –

        (i)   at the company's registered office for not less than 15 days ending with the date of the meeting, and

        (ii)   at the meeting itself.

(3)   A memorandum of contract terms so made available must include the names of the members holding shares to which the contract relates.

(4)   A copy of the contract so made available must have annexed to it a written memorandum specifying such of those names as do not appear in the contract itself.

(5)   The resolution is not validly passed if the requirements of this section are not complied with.

697 Variation of contract for off-market purchase

(1)   A company may only agree to a variation of a contract authorised under section 694 (authority for off-market purchase) if the variation is approved in advance in accordance with this section.

(2)   The terms of the variation must be authorised by a special resolution of the company before it is agreed to.

(3)   That authority may be varied, revoked or from time to time renewed by a special resolution of the company.

(4)   In the case of a public company a resolution conferring, varying or renewing authority must specify a date on which the authority is to expire, which must not be later than 18 months after the date on which the resolution is passed.

(5)   A resolution conferring, varying, revoking or renewing authority under this section is subject to –

section 698 (exercise of voting rights), and
section 699 (disclosure of details of variation).

698 Resolution authorising variation: exercise of voting rights

(1)   This section applies to a resolution to confer, vary, revoke or renew authority for the purposes of section 697 (variation of contract for off-market purchase of own shares).

(2)   Where the resolution is proposed as a written resolution, a member who holds shares to which the resolution relates is not an eligible member.

(3)   Where the resolution is proposed at a meeting of the company, it is not effective if –

    (a)   any member of the company holding shares to which the resolution relates exercises the voting rights carried by any of those shares in voting on the resolution, and

    (b)   the resolution would not have been passed if he had not done so.

(4)   For this purpose –

    (a)   a member who holds shares to which the resolution relates is regarded as exercising the voting rights carried by those shares not only if he votes in respect of them on a poll on the question whether the resolution shall be passed, but also if he votes on the resolution otherwise than on a poll;

(b) any member of the company may demand a poll on that question;

(c) a vote and a demand for a poll by a person as proxy for a member are the same respectively as a vote and a demand by the member.

699 Resolution authorising variation: disclosure of details of variation

(1) This section applies in relation to a resolution under section 697 (variation of contract for off-market purchase of own shares).

(2) A copy of the proposed variation (if it is in writing) or a written memorandum giving details of the proposed variation (if it is not) must be made available to members –

(a) in the case of a written resolution, by being sent or submitted to every eligible member at or before the time at which the proposed resolution is sent or submitted to him;

(b) in the case of a resolution at a meeting, by being made available for inspection by members of the company both –

(i) at the company's registered office for not less than 15 days ending with the date of the meeting, and

(ii) at the meeting itself.

(3) There must also be made available as mentioned in subsection (2) a copy of the original contract or, as the case may be, a memorandum of its terms, together with any variations previously made.

(4) A memorandum of the proposed variation so made available must include the names of the members holding shares to which the variation relates.

(5) A copy of the proposed variation so made available must have annexed to it a written memorandum specifying such of those names as do not appear in the variation itself.

(6) The resolution is not validly passed if the requirements of this section are not complied with.

700 Release of company's rights under contract for off-market purchase

(1) An agreement by a company to release its rights under a contract approved under section 694 (authorisation of off-market purchase) is void unless the terms of the release agreement are approved in advance in accordance with this section.

(2) The terms of the proposed agreement must be authorised by a special resolution of the company before the agreement is entered into.

(3) That authority may be varied, revoked or from time to time renewed by a special resolution of the company.

(4) In the case of a public company a resolution conferring, varying or renewing authority must specify a date on which the authority is to expire, which must not be later than 18 months after the date on which the resolution is passed.

(5) The provisions of –

section 698 (exercise of voting rights), and

section 699 (disclosure of details of variation),

apply to a resolution authorising a proposed release agreement as they apply to a resolution authorising a proposed variation.

Authority for market purchase

701 Authority for market purchase

(1) A company may only make a market purchase of its own shares if the purchase has first been authorised by a resolution of the company.

(2) That authority –

(a) may be general or limited to the purchase of shares of a particular class or description, and

(b) may be unconditional or subject to conditions.

(3) The authority must –

(a) specify the maximum number of shares authorised to be acquired, and

(b) determine both the maximum and minimum prices that may be paid for the shares.

(4) The authority may be varied, revoked or from time to time renewed by a resolution of the company.

(5) A resolution conferring, varying or renewing authority must specify a date on which it is to expire, which must not be later than 18 months after the date on which the resolution is passed.

(6) A company may make a purchase of its own shares after the expiry of the time limit specified if –

(a) the contract of purchase was concluded before the authority expired, and

(b) the terms of the authority permitted the company to make a contract of purchase that would or might be executed wholly or partly after its expiration.

(7) A resolution to confer or vary authority under this section may determine either or both the maximum and minimum price for purchase by –

(a) specifying a particular sum, or

(b) providing a basis or formula for calculating the amount of the price (but without reference to any person's discretion or opinion).

(8) Chapter 3 of Part 3 (resolutions affecting a company's constitution) applies to a resolution under this section.

Supplementary provisions

702 Copy of contract or memorandum to be available for inspection

(1) This section applies where a company has entered into –

(a) a contract approved under section 694 (authorisation of contract for off-market purchase), or

(b) a contract for a purchase authorised under section 701 (authorisation of market purchase).

(2) The company must keep available for inspection –

(a) a copy of the contract, or

(b) if the contract is not in writing, a written memorandum setting out its terms.

(3) The copy or memorandum must be kept available for inspection from the conclusion of the contract until the end of the period of ten years beginning with –

(a) the date on which the purchase of all the shares in pursuance of the contract is completed, or

(b) the date on which the contract otherwise determines.

(4) The copy or memorandum must be kept available for inspection –

(a) at the company's registered office, or

(b) at a place specified in regulations under section 1136.

(5) The company must give notice to the registrar –

(a) of the place at which the copy or memorandum is kept available for inspection, and

(b) of any change in that place,

unless it has at all times been kept at the company's registered office.

(6) Every copy or memorandum required to be kept under this section must be kept open
to inspection without charge –

(a) by any member of the company, and
(b) in the case of a public company, by any other person.

(7) The provisions of this section apply to a variation of a contract as they apply to the
original contract.

703 Enforcement of right to inspect copy or memorandum

(1) If default is made in complying with section 702(2), (3) or (4) or default is made for
14 days in complying with section 702(5), or an inspection required under section
702(6) is refused, an offence is committed by –

(a) the company, and
(b) every officer of the company who is in default.

(2) A person guilty of an offence under this section is liable on summary conviction to a
fine not exceeding level 3 on the standard scale and, for continued contravention, a
daily default fine not exceeding one-tenth of level 3 on the standard scale.

(3) In the case of refusal of an inspection required under section 702(6) the court may by
order compel an immediate inspection.

704 No assignment of company's right to purchase own shares

The rights of a company under a contract authorised under –

(a) section 694 (authority for off-market purchase), or
(b) section 701 (authority for market purchase)

are not capable of being assigned.

705 Payments apart from purchase price to be made out of distributable profits

(1) A payment made by a company in consideration of –

(a) acquiring any right with respect to the purchase of its own shares in pursuance
of a contingent purchase contract approved under section 694 (authorisation of
off-market purchase),
(b) the variation of any contract approved under that section, or
(c) the release of any of the company's obligations with respect to the purchase of
any of its own shares under a contract –

(i)   approved under section 694, or
(ii) authorised under section 701 (authorisation of market purchase),

must be made out of the company's distributable profits.

(2) If this requirement is not met in relation to a contract, then –

(a) in a case within subsection (1)(a), no purchase by the company of its own shares
in pursuance of that contract may be made under this Chapter;
(b) in a case within subsection (1)(b), no such purchase following the variation may
be made under this Chapter;
(c) in a case within subsection (1)(c), the purported release is void.

706 Treatment of shares purchased

Where a limited company makes a purchase of its own shares in accordance with this
Chapter, then –

(a) if section 724 (treasury shares) applies, the shares may be held and deal with in
accordance with Chapter 6;
(b) if that section does not apply –

(i)   the shares are treated as cancelled, and

(ii)   the amount of the company's issued share capital is diminished accordingly by the nominal value of the shares cancelled.

707 Return to registrar of purchase of own shares

(1)   Where a company purchases shares under this Chapter, it must deliver a return to the registrar within the period of 28 days beginning with the date on which the shares are delivered to it.

(2)   The return must distinguish –

(a)   shares in relation to which section 724 (treasury shares) applies and shares in relation to which that section does not apply, and

(b)   shares in relation to which that section applies –

(i)   that are cancelled forthwith (under section 729 (cancellation of treasury shares)), and

(ii)   that are not so cancelled.

(3)   The return must state, with respect to shares of each class purchased –

(a)   the number and nominal value of the shares, and

(b)   the date on which they were delivered to the company.

(4)   In the case of a public company the return must also state –

(a)   the aggregate amount paid by the company for the shares, and

(b)   the maximum and minimum prices paid in respect of shares of each class purchased.

(5)   Particulars of shares delivered to the company on different dates and under different contracts may be included in a single return.
In such a case the amount required to be stated under subsection (4)(a) is the aggregate amount paid by the company for all the shares to which the return relates.

(6)   If default is made in complying with this section an offence is committed by every officer of the company who is in default.

(7)   A person guilty of an offence under this section is liable –

(a)   on conviction on indictment, to a fine;

(b)   on summary conviction to a fine not exceeding the statutory maximum and, for continued contravention, a daily default fine not exceeding one-tenth of the statutory maximum.

708 Notice to registrar of cancellation of shares

(1)   If on the purchase by a company of any of its own shares in accordance with this Part –

(a)   section 724 (treasury shares) does not apply (so that the shares are treated as cancelled), or

(b)   that section applies but the shares are cancelled forthwith (under section 729 (cancellation of treasury shares)),

the company must give notice of cancellation to the registrar, within the period of 28 days beginning with the date on which the shares are delivered to it, specifying the shares cancelled.

(2)   The notice must be accompanied by a statement of capital.

(3)   The statement of capital must state with respect to the company's share capital immediately following the cancellation –

(a)   the total number of shares of the company,

(b)   the aggregate nominal value of those shares,

(c)   for each class of shares –

(i)   prescribed particulars of the rights attached to the shares,

(ii)   the total number of shares of that class, and

(iii)   the aggregate nominal value of shares of that class, and

(d) the amount paid up and the amount (if any) unpaid on each share (whether on account of the nominal value of the share or by way of premium).

(4) If default is made in complying with this section, an offence is committed by –

(a) the company, and

(b) every officer of the company who is in default.

(5) A person guilty of an offence under this section is liable on summary conviction to a fine not exceeding level 3 on the standard scale and, for continued contravention, a daily default fine not exceeding one-tenth of level 3 on the standard scale.

CHAPTER 5

REDEMPTION OR PURCHASE BY PRIVATE COMPANY OUT OF CAPITAL

Introductory

709 Power of private limited company to redeem or purchase own shares out of capital

(1) A private limited company may in accordance with this Chapter, but subject to any restriction or prohibition in the company's articles, make a payment in respect of the redemption or purchase of its own shares otherwise than out of distributable profits or the proceeds of a fresh issue of shares.

(2) References below in this Chapter to payment out of capital are to any payment so made, whether or not it would be regarded apart from this section as a payment out of capital.

The permissible capital payment

710 The permissible capital payment

(1) The payment that may, in accordance with this Chapter, be made by a company out of capital in respect of the redemption or purchase of its own shares is such amount as, after applying for that purpose –

(a) any available profits of the company, and

(b) the proceeds of any fresh issue of shares made for the purposes of the redemption or purchase,

is required to meet the price of redemption or purchase.

(2) That is referred to below in this Chapter as "the permissible capital payment" for the shares.

711 Available profits

(1) For the purposes of this Chapter the available profits of the company, in relation to the redemption or purchase of any shares, are the profits of the company that are available for distribution (within the meaning of Part 23).

(2) But the question whether a company has any profits so available, and the amount of any such profits, shall be determined in accordance with section 712 instead of in accordance with sections 836 to 842 in that Part.

712 Determination of available profits

(1) The available profits of the company are determined as follows.

(2) First, determine the profits of the company by reference to the following items as stated in the relevant accounts –

    (a) profits, losses, assets and liabilities,

    (b) provisions of the following kinds –

        (i) where the relevant accounts are Companies Act accounts, provisions of a kind specified for the purposes of this subsection by regulations under section 396;

        (ii) where the relevant accounts are IAS accounts, provisions of any kind;

    (c) share capital and reserves (including undistributable reserves).

(3) Second, reduce the amount so determined by the amount of –

    (a) any distribution lawfully made by the company, and

    (b) any other relevant payment lawfully made by the company out of distributable profits,

after the date of the relevant accounts and before the end of the relevant period.

(4) For this purpose "other relevant payment lawfully made" includes –

    (a) financial assistance lawfully given out of distributable profits in accordance with Chapter 2,

    (b) payments lawfully made out of distributable profits in respect of the purchase by the company of any shares in the company, and

    (c) payments of any description specified in section 705 (payments other than purchase price to be made out of distributable profits) lawfully made by the company.

(5) The resulting figure is the amount of available profits.

(6) For the purposes of this section "the relevant accounts" are any accounts that –

    (a) are prepared as at a date within the relevant period, and

    (b) are such as to enable a reasonable judgment to be made as to the amounts of the items mentioned in subsection (2).

(7) In this section "the relevant period" means the period of three months ending with the date on which the directors' statement is made in accordance with section 714.

Requirements for payment out of capital

713 Requirements for payment out of capital

(1) A payment out of capital by a private company for the redemption or purchase of its own shares is not lawful unless the requirements of the following sections are met –

section 714 (directors' statement and auditor's report);
section 716 (approval by special resolution);
section 719 (public notice of proposed payment);
section 720 (directors' statement and auditor's report to be available for inspection).

(2) This is subject to any order of the court under section 721 (power of court to extend period for compliance on application by persons objecting to payment).

714 Directors' statement and auditor's report

(1) The company's directors must make a statement in accordance with this section.

(2) The statement must specify the amount of the permissible capital payment for the shares in question.

(3) It must state that, having made full inquiry into the affairs and prospects of the company, the directors have formed the opinion –

    (a) as regards its initial situation immediately following the date on which the payment out of capital is proposed to be made, that there will be no grounds on which the company could then be found unable to pay its debts, and

    (b) as regards its prospects for the year immediately following that date, that having regard to –

(i)   their intentions with respect to the management of the company's business during that year, and

(ii)   the amount and character of the financial resources that will in their view be available to the company during that year,

the company will be able to continue to carry on business as a going concern (and will accordingly be able to pay its debts as they fall due) throughout that year.

(4)   In forming their opinion for the purposes of subsection (3)(a), the directors must take into account all of the company's liabilities (including any contingent or prospective liabilities).

(5)   The directors' statement must be in the prescribed form and must contain such information with respect to the nature of the company's business as may be prescribed.

(6)   It must in addition have annexed to it a report addressed to the directors by the company's auditor stating that –

(a)   he has inquired into the company's state of affairs,

(b)   the amount specified in the statement as the permissible capital payment for the shares in question is in his view properly determined in accordance with sections 710 to 712, and

(c)   he is not aware of anything to indicate that the opinion expressed by the directors in their statement as to any of the matters mentioned in subsection (3) above is unreasonable in all the circumstances.

715 Directors' statement: offence if no reasonable grounds for opinion

(1)   If the directors make a statement under section 714 without having reasonable grounds for the opinion expressed in it, an offence is committed by every director who is in default.

(2)   A person guilty of an offence under this section is liable –

(a)   on conviction on indictment, to imprisonment for a term not exceeding two years or a fine (or both);

(b)   on summary conviction –

(i)   in England and Wales, to imprisonment for a term not exceeding twelve months or a fine not exceeding the statutory maximum (or both);

(ii)   in Scotland or Northern Ireland, to imprisonment for a term not exceeding six months or a fine not exceeding the statutory maximum (or both).

716 Payment to be approved by special resolution

(1)   The payment out of capital must be approved by a special resolution of the company.

(2)   The resolution must be passed on, or within the week immediately following, the date on which the directors make the statement required by section 714.

(3)   A resolution under this section is subject to –

section 717 (exercise of voting rights), and

section 718 (disclosure of directors' statement and auditors' report).

717 Resolution authorising payment: exercise of voting rights

(1)   This section applies to a resolution under section 716 (authority for payment out of capital for redemption or purchase of own shares).

(2)   Where the resolution is proposed as a written resolution, a member who holds shares to which the resolution relates is not an eligible member.

(3)   Where the resolution is proposed at a meeting of the company, it is not effective if –

(a)   any member of the company holding shares to which the resolution relates exercises the voting rights carried by any of those shares in voting on the resolution, and

(b)   the resolution would not have been passed if he had not done so.

(4) For this purpose –

    (a) a member who holds shares to which the resolution relates is regarded as exercising the voting rights carried by those shares not only if he votes in respect of them on a poll on the question whether the resolution shall be passed, but also if he votes on the resolution otherwise than on a poll;

    (b) any member of the company may demand a poll on that question;

    (c) a vote and a demand for a poll by a person as proxy for a member are the same respectively as a vote and a demand by the member.

718 Resolution authorising payment: disclosure of directors' statement and auditor's report

(1) This section applies to a resolution under section 716 (resolution authorising payment out of capital for redemption or purchase of own shares).

(2) A copy of the directors' statement and auditor's report under section 714 must be made available to members –

    (a) in the case of a written resolution, by being sent or submitted to every eligible member at or before the time at which the proposed resolution is sent or submitted to him;

    (b) in the case of a resolution at a meeting, by being made available for inspection by members of the company at the meeting.

(3) The resolution is ineffective if this requirement is not complied with.

719 Public notice of proposed payment

(1) Within the week immediately following the date of the resolution under section 716 the company must cause to be published in the Gazette a notice –

    (a) stating that the company has approved a payment out of capital for the purpose of acquiring its own shares by redemption or purchase or both (as the case may be),

    (b) specifying –

        (i) the amount of the permissible capital payment for the shares in question, and

        (ii) the date of the resolution,

    (c) stating where the directors' statement and auditor's report required by section 714 are available for inspection, and

    (d) stating that any creditor of the company may at any time within the five weeks immediately following the date of the resolution apply to the court under section 721 for an order preventing the payment.

(2) Within the week immediately following the date of the resolution the company must also either –

    (a) cause a notice to the same effect as that required by subsection (1) to be published in an appropriate national newspaper, or

    (b) give notice in writing to that effect to each of its creditors.

(3) "An appropriate national newspaper" means a newspaper circulating throughout the part of the United Kingdom in which the company is registered.

(4) Not later than the day on which the company –

    (a) first publishes the notice required by subsection (1), or

    (b) if earlier, first publishes or gives the notice required by subsection (2),

the company must deliver to the registrar a copy of the directors' statement and auditor's report required by section 714.

720 Directors' statement and auditor's report to be available for inspection

(1) The directors' statement and auditor's report must be kept available for inspection throughout the period –

  (a) beginning with the day on which the company –

    (i)   first publishes the notice required by section 719(1), or

    (ii) if earlier, first publishes or gives the notice required by section 719(2), and

  (b) ending five weeks after the date of the resolution for payment out of capital.

(2) They must be kept available for inspection –

  (a) at the company's registered office, or

  (b) at a place specified in regulations under section 1136.

(3) The company must give notice to the registrar –

  (a) of the place at which the statement and report are kept available for inspection, and

  (b) of any change in that place,

unless they have at all times been kept at the company's registered office.

(4) They must be open to the inspection of any member or creditor of the company without charge.

(5) If default is made for 14 days in complying with subsection (3), or an inspection under subsection (4) is refused, an offence is committed by –

  (a) the company, and

  (b) every officer of the company who is in default.

(6) A person guilty of an offence under this section is liable on summary conviction to a fine not exceeding level 3 on the standard scale and, for continued contravention, a daily default fine not exceeding one-tenth of level 3 on the standard scale.

(7) In the case of a refusal of an inspection required by subsection (4), the court may by order compel an immediate inspection.

Objection to payment by members or creditors

721 Application to court to cancel resolution

(1) Where a private company passes a special resolution approving a payment out of capital for the redemption or purchase of any of its shares –

  (a) any member of the company (other than one who consented to or voted in favour of the resolution), and

  (b) any creditor of the company,

may apply to the court for the cancellation of the resolution.

(2) The application –

  (a) must be made within five weeks after the passing of the resolution, and

  (b) may be made on behalf of the persons entitled to make it by such one or more of their number as they may appoint in writing for the purpose.

(3) On an application under this section the court may if it thinks fit –

  (a) adjourn the proceedings in order that an arrangement may be made to the satisfaction of the court –

    (i)   for the purchase of the interests of dissentient members, or

    (ii) for the protection of dissentient creditors, and

  (b) give such directions and make such orders as it thinks expedient for facilitating or carrying into effect any such arrangement.

(4) Subject to that, the court must make an order either cancelling or confirming the resolution, and may do so on such terms and conditions as it thinks fit.

(5) If the court confirms the resolution, it may by order alter or extend any date or period of time specified –

   (a) in the resolution, or

   (b) in any provision of this Chapter applying to the redemption or purchase to which the resolution relates.

(6) The court's order may, if the court thinks fit –

   (a) provide for the purchase by the company of the shares of any of its members and for the reduction accordingly of the company's capital, and

   (b) make any alteration in the company's articles that may be required in consequence of that provision.

(7) The court's order may, if the court thinks fit, require the company not to make any, or any specified, amendments of its articles without the leave of the court.

722 Notice to registrar of court application or order

(1) On making an application under section 721 (application to court to cancel resolution) the applicants, or the person making the application on their behalf, must immediately give notice to the registrar.
This is without prejudice to any provision of rules of court as to service of notice of the application.

(2) On being served with notice of any such application, the company must immediately give notice to the registrar.

(3) Within 15 days of the making of the court's order on the application, or such longer period as the court may at any time direct, the company must deliver to the registrar a copy of the order.

(4) If a company fails to comply with subsection (2) or (3) an offence is committed by –

   (a) the company, and

   (b) every officer of the company who is in default.

(5) A person guilty of an offence under this section is liable on summary conviction to a fine not exceeding level 3 on the standard scale and, for continued contravention, a daily default fine not exceeding one-tenth of level 3 on the standard scale.

Supplementary provisions

723 When payment out of capital to be made

(1) The payment out of capital must be made –

   (a) no earlier than five weeks after the date on which the resolution under section 716 is passed, and

   (b) no more than seven weeks after that date.

(2) This is subject to any exercise of the court's powers under section 721(5) (power to alter or extend time where resolution confirmed after objection).

CHAPTER 6

TREASURY SHARES

724 Treasury shares

(1) This section applies where –

    (a) a limited company makes a purchase of its own shares in accordance with Chapter 4,

    (b) the purchase is made out of distributable profits, and

    (c) the shares are qualifying shares.

(2) For this purpose "qualifying shares" means shares that –

    (a) are included in the official list in accordance with the provisions of Part 6 of the Financial Services and Markets Act 2000 (c. 8),

    (b) are traded on the market known as the Alternative Investment Market established under the rules of London Stock Exchange plc,

    (c) are officially listed in an EEA State, or

    (d) are traded on a regulated market.

In paragraph (a) "the official list" has the meaning given in section 103(1) of the Financial Services and Markets Act 2000.

(3) Where this section applies the company may –

    (a) hold the shares (or any of them), or

    (b) deal with any of them, at any time, in accordance with section 727 or 729.

(4) Where shares are held by the company, the company must be entered in its register of members as the member holding the shares.

(5) In the Companies Acts references to a company holding shares as treasury shares are to the company holding shares that –

    (a) were (or are treated as having been) purchased by it in circumstances in which this section applies, and

    (b) have been held by the company continuously since they were so purchased (or treated as purchased).

725 Treasury shares: maximum holdings

(1) Where a company has shares of only one class, the aggregate nominal value of shares held as treasury shares must not at any time exceed 10% of the nominal value of the issued share capital of the company at that time.

(2) Where the share capital of a company is divided into shares of different classes, the aggregate nominal value of the shares of any class held as treasury shares must not at any time exceed 10% of the nominal value of the issued share capital of the shares of that class at that time.

(3) If subsection (1) or (2) is contravened by a company, the company must dispose of or cancel the excess shares, in accordance with section 727 or 729, before the end of the period of twelve months beginning with the date on which that contravention occurs. The "excess shares" means such number of the shares held by the company as treasury shares at the time in question as resulted in the limit being exceeded.

(4) Where a company purchases qualifying shares out of distributable profits in accordance with section 724, a contravention by the company of subsection (1) or (2) above does not render the acquisition void under section 658 (general rule against limited company acquiring its own shares).

726 Treasury shares: exercise of rights

(1) This section applies where shares are held by a company as treasury shares.

(2) The company must not exercise any right in respect of the treasury shares, and any purported exercise of such a right is void.
This applies, in particular, to any right to attend or vote at meetings.

(3) No dividend may be paid, and no other distribution (whether in cash or otherwise) of the company's assets (including any distribution of assets to members on a winding up) may be made to the company, in respect of the treasury shares.

(4) Nothing in this section prevents –

(a) an allotment of shares as fully paid bonus shares in respect of the treasury shares, or

(b) the payment of any amount payable on the redemption of the treasury shares (if they are redeemable shares).

(5) Shares allotted as fully paid bonus shares in respect of the treasury shares are treated as if purchased by the company, at the time they were allotted, in circumstances in which section 724(1) (treasury shares) applied.

727 Treasury shares: disposal

(1) Where shares are held as treasury shares, the company may at any time –

(a) sell the shares (or any of them) for a cash consideration, or

(b) transfer the shares (or any of them) for the purposes of or pursuant to an employees' share scheme.

(2) In subsection (1)(a) "cash consideration" means –

(a) cash received by the company, or

(b) a cheque received by the company in good faith that the directors have no reason for suspecting will not be paid, or

(c) a release of a liability of the company for a liquidated sum, or

(d) an undertaking to pay cash to the company on or before a date not more than 90 days after the date on which the company agrees to sell the shares, or

(e) payment by any other means giving rise to a present or future entitlement (of the company or a person acting on the company's behalf) to a payment, or credit equivalent to payment, in cash.

For this purpose "cash" includes foreign currency.

(3) The Secretary of State may by order provide that particular means of payment specified in the order are to be regarded as falling within subsection (2)(e).

(4) If the company receives a notice under section 979 (takeover offers: right of offeror to buy out minority shareholders) that a person desires to acquire shares held by the company as treasury shares, the company must not sell or transfer the shares to which the notice relates except to that person.

(5) An order under this section is subject to negative resolution procedure.

728 Treasury shares: notice of disposal

(1) Where shares held by a company as treasury shares –

(a) are sold, or

(b) are transferred for the purposes of an employees' share scheme,

the company must deliver a return to the registrar not later than 28 days after the shares are disposed of.

(2) The return must state with respect to shares of each class disposed of –

(a) the number and nominal value of the shares, and

(b) the date on which they were disposed of.

(3) Particulars of shares disposed of on different dates may be included in a single return.

(4) If default is made in complying with this section an offence is committed by every officer of the company who is in default.

(5) A person guilty of an offence under this section is liable –

    (a) on conviction on indictment, to a fine;

    (b) on summary conviction, to a fine not exceeding the statutory maximum and, for continued contravention, a daily default fine not exceeding one-tenth of the statutory maximum.

729 Treasury shares: cancellation

(1) Where shares are held as treasury shares, the company may at any time cancel the shares (or any of them).

(2) If shares held as treasury shares cease to be qualifying shares, the company must forthwith cancel the shares.

(3) For this purpose shares are not to be regarded as ceasing to be qualifying shares by virtue only of –

    (a) the suspension of their listing in accordance with the applicable rules in the EEA State in which the shares are officially listed, or

    (b) the suspension of their trading in accordance with –

        (i) in the case of shares traded on the market known as the Alternative Investment Market, the rules of London Stock Exchange plc, and

        (ii) in any other case, the rules of the regulated market on which they are traded.

(4) If company cancels shares held as treasury shares, the amount of the company's share capital is reduced accordingly by the nominal amount of the shares cancelled.

(5) The directors may take any steps required to enable the company to cancel its shares under this section without complying with the provisions of Chapter 10 of Part 17 (reduction of share capital).

730 Treasury shares: notice of cancellation

(1) Where shares held by a company as treasury shares are cancelled, the company must deliver a return to the registrar not later than 28 days after the shares are cancelled. This does not apply to shares that are cancelled forthwith on their acquisition by the company (see section 708).

(2) The return must state with respect to shares of each class cancelled –

    (a) the number and nominal value of the shares, and

    (b) the date on which they were cancelled.

(3) Particulars of shares cancelled on different dates may be included in a single return.

(4) The notice must be accompanied by a statement of capital.

(5) The statement of capital must state with respect to the company's share capital immediately following the cancellation –

    (a) the total number of shares of the company,

    (b) the aggregate nominal value of those shares,

    (c) for each class of shares –

        (i) prescribed particulars of the rights attached to the shares,

        (ii) the total number of shares of that class, and

        (iii) the aggregate nominal value of shares of that class, and

    (d) the amount paid up and the amount (if any) unpaid on each share (whether on account of the nominal value of the share or by way of premium).

(6) If default is made in complying with this section, an offence is committed by –

    (a) the company, and

    (b) every officer of the company who is in default.

(7) A person guilty of an offence under this section is liable on summary conviction to a

fine not exceeding level 3 on the standard scale and, for continued contravention, a daily default fine not exceeding one-tenth of level 3 on the standard scale.

731 Treasury shares: treatment of proceeds of sale

(1) Where shares held as treasury shares are sold, the proceeds of sale must be dealt with in accordance with this section.

(2) If the proceeds of sale are equal to or less than the purchase price paid by the company for the shares, the proceeds are treated for the purposes of Part 23 (distributions) as a realised profit of the company.

(3) If the proceeds of sale exceed the purchase price paid by the company –

   (a) an amount equal to the purchase price paid is treated as a realised profit of the company for the purposes of that Part, and

   (b) the excess must be transferred to the company's share premium account.

(4) For the purposes of this section –

   (a) the purchase price paid by the company must be determined by the application of a weighted average price method, and

   (b) if the shares were allotted to the company as fully paid bonus shares, the purchase price paid for them is treated as nil.

732 Treasury shares: offences

(1) If a company contravenes any of the provisions of this Chapter (except section 730 (notice of cancellation)), an offence is committed by –

   (a) the company, and

   (b) every officer of the company who is in default.

(2) A person guilty of an offence under this section is liable –

   (a) on conviction on indictment, to a fine;

   (b) on summary conviction to a fine not exceeding the statutory maximum.

CHAPTER 7

SUPPLEMENTARY PROVISIONS

733 The capital redemption reserve

(1) In the following circumstances a company must transfer amounts to a reserve, called the "capital redemption reserve".

(2) Where under this Part shares of a limited company are redeemed or purchased wholly out of the company's profits, the amount by which the company's issued share capital is diminished in accordance with –

   (a) section 688(b) (on the cancellation of shares redeemed), or

   (b) section 706(b)(ii) (on the cancellation of shares purchased),

   must be transferred to the capital redemption reserve.

(3) If –

   (a) the shares are redeemed or purchased wholly or partly out of the proceeds of a fresh issue, and

   (b) the aggregate amount of the proceeds is less than the aggregate nominal value of the shares redeemed or purchased,

   the amount of the difference must be transferred to the capital redemption reserve.

   This does not apply in the case of a private company if, in addition to the proceeds of the fresh issue, the company applies a payment out of capital under Chapter 5 in making the redemption or purchase.

(4) The amount by which a company's share capital is diminished in accordance with section 729(4) (on the cancellation of shares held as treasury shares) must be transferred to the capital redemption reserve.

(5) The company may use the capital redemption reserve to pay up new shares to be allotted to members as fully paid bonus shares.

(6) Subject to that, the provisions of the Companies Acts relating to the reduction of a company's share capital apply as if the capital redemption reserve were part of its paid up share capital.

734 Accounting consequences of payment out of capital

(1) This section applies where a payment out of capital is made in accordance with Chapter 5 (redemption or purchase of own shares by private company out of capital).

(2) If the permissible capital payment is less than the nominal amount of the shares redeemed or purchased, the amount of the difference must be transferred to the company's capital redemption reserve.

(3) If the permissible capital payment is greater than the nominal amount of the shares redeemed or purchased –

(a) the amount of any capital redemption reserve, share premium account or fully paid share capital of the company, and

(b) any amount representing unrealised profits of the company for the time being standing to the credit of any revaluation reserve maintained by the company,

may be reduced by a sum not exceeding (or by sums not in total exceeding) the amount by which the permissible capital payment exceeds the nominal amount of the shares.

(4) Where the proceeds of a fresh issue are applied by the company in making a redemption or purchase of its own shares in addition to a payment out of capital under this Chapter, the references in subsections (2) and (3) to the permissible capital payment are to be read as referring to the aggregate of that payment and those proceeds.

735 Effect of company's failure to redeem or purchase

(1) This section applies where a company –

(a) issues shares on terms that they are or are liable to be redeemed, or

(b) agrees to purchase any of its shares.

(2) The company is not liable in damages in respect of any failure on its part to redeem or purchase any of the shares.

This is without prejudice to any right of the holder of the shares other than his right to sue the company for damages in respect of its failure.

(3) The court shall not grant an order for specific performance of the terms of redemption or purchase if the company shows that it is unable to meet the costs of redeeming or purchasing the shares in question out of distributable profits.

(4) If the company is wound up and at the commencement of the winding up any of the shares have not been redeemed or purchased, the terms of redemption or purchase may be enforced against the company.

When shares are redeemed or purchased under this subsection, they are treated as cancelled.

(5) Subsection (4) does not apply if –

(a) the terms provided for the redemption or purchase to take place at a date later than that of the commencement of the winding up, or

(b) during the period –

(i) beginning with the date on which the redemption or purchase was to have taken place, and

   (ii) ending with the commencement of the winding up,

the company could not at any time have lawfully made a distribution equal in value to the price at which the shares were to have been redeemed or purchased.

(6) There shall be paid in priority to any amount that the company is liable under subsection (4) to pay in respect of any shares –

  (a) all other debts and liabilities of the company (other than any due to members in their character as such), and

  (b) if other shares carry rights (whether as to capital or as to income) that are preferred to the rights as to capital attaching to the first-mentioned shares, any amount due in satisfaction of those preferred rights.

Subject to that, any such amount shall be paid in priority to any amounts due to members in satisfaction of their rights (whether as to capital or income) as members.

736 Meaning of "distributable profits"

In this Part (except in Chapter 2 (financial assistance): see section 683) "distributable profits", in relation to the making of any payment by a company, means profits out of which the company could lawfully make a distribution (within the meaning given by section 830) equal in value to the payment.

737 General power to make further provision by regulations

(1) The Secretary of State may by regulations modify the provisions of this Part.

(2) The regulations may –

  (a) amend or repeal any of the provisions of this Part, or

  (b) make such other provision as appears to the Secretary of State appropriate in place of any of the provisions of this Part.

(3) Regulations under this section may make consequential amendments or repeals in other provisions of this Act, or in other enactments.

(4) Regulations under this section are subject to affirmative resolution procedure.

PART 19

DEBENTURES

General provisions

738 Meaning of "debenture"

In the Companies Acts "debenture" includes debenture stock, bonds and any other securities of a company, whether or not constituting a charge on the assets of the company.

739 Perpetual debentures

(1) A condition contained in debentures, or in a deed for securing debentures, is not invalid by reason only that the debentures are made –

  (a) irredeemable, or

  (b) redeemable only –

   (i) on the happening of a contingency (however remote), or

   (ii) on the expiration of a period (however long),

any rule of equity to the contrary notwithstanding.

(2) Subsection (1) applies to debentures whenever issued and to deeds whenever executed.

740 Enforcement of contract to subscribe for debentures

A contract with a company to take up and pay for debentures of the company may be enforced by an order for specific performance.

741 Registration of allotment of debentures

(1) A company must register an allotment of debentures as soon as practicable and in any event within two months after the date of the allotment.

(2) If a company fails to comply with this section, an offence is committed by –

    (a) the company, and

    (b) every officer of the company who is in default.

(3) A person guilty of an offence under this section is liable on summary conviction to a fine not exceeding level 3 on the standard scale and, for continued contravention, a daily default fine not exceeding one-tenth of level 3 on the standard scale.

(4) For the duties of the company as to the issue of the debentures, or certificates of debenture stock, see Part 21 (certification and transfer of securities)

742 Debentures to bearer (Scotland)

Notwithstanding anything in the statute of the Scots Parliament of 1696, chapter 25, debentures to bearer issued in Scotland are valid and binding according to their terms.

Register of debenture holders

743 Register of debenture holders

(1) Any register of debenture holders of a company that is kept by the company must be kept available for inspection –

    (a) at the company's registered office, or

    (b) at a place specified in regulations under section 1136.

(2) A company must give notice to the registrar of the place where any such register is kept available for inspection and of any change in that place.

(3) No such notice is required if the register has, at all times since it came into existence, been kept available for inspection at the company's registered office.

(4) If a company makes default for 14 days in complying with subsection (2), an offence is committed by –

    (a) the company, and

    (b) every officer of the company who is in default.

(5) A person guilty of an offence under this section is liable on summary conviction to a fine not exceeding level 3 on the standard scale and, for continued contravention, a daily default fine not exceeding one-tenth of level 3 on the standard scale.

(6) References in this section to a register of debenture holders include a duplicate –

    (a) of a register of debenture holders that is kept outside the United Kingdom, or

    (b) of any part of such a register.

744 Register of debenture holders: right to inspect and require copy

(1) Every register of debenture holders of a company must, except when duly closed, be open to the inspection –

    (a) of the registered holder of any such debentures, or any holder of shares in the company, without charge, and

    (b) of any other person on payment of such fee as may be prescribed.

(2) Any person may require a copy of the register, or any part of it, on payment of such fee as may be prescribed.

(3) A person seeking to exercise either of the rights conferred by this section must make a request to the company to that effect.

(4) The request must contain the following information –

    (a) in the case of an individual, his name and address;

    (b) in the case of an organisation, the name and address of an individual responsible for making the request on behalf of the organisation;

    (c) the purpose for which the information is to be used; and

    (d) whether the information will be disclosed to any other person, and if so –

        (i) where that person is an individual, his name and address,

        (ii) where that person is an organisation, the name and address of an individual responsible for receiving the information on its behalf, and

        (iii) the purpose for which the information is to be used by that person.

(5) For the purposes of this section a register is "duly closed" if it is closed in accordance with provision contained –

    (a) in the articles or in the debentures,

    (b) in the case of debenture stock in the stock certificates, or

    (c) in the trust deed or other document securing the debentures or debenture stock.

The total period for which a register is closed in any year must not exceed 30 days.

(6) References in this section to a register of debenture holders include a duplicate –

    (a) of a register of debenture holders that is kept outside the United Kingdom, or

    (b) of any part of such a register.

745 Register of debenture holders: response to request for inspection or copy

(1) Where a company receives a request under section 744 (register of debenture holders: right to inspect and require copy), it must within five working days either –

    (a) comply with the request, or

    (b) apply to the court.

(2) If it applies to the court it must notify the person making the request.

(3) If on an application under this section the court is satisfied that the inspection or copy is not sought for a proper purpose –

    (a) it shall direct the company not to comply with the request, and

    (b) it may further order that the company's costs (in Scotland, expenses) on the application be paid in whole or in part by the person who made the request, even if he is not a party to the application.

(4) If the court makes such a direction and it appears to the court that the company is or may be subject to other requests made for a similar purpose (whether made by the same person or different persons), it may direct that the company is not to comply with any such request.

The order must contain such provision as appears to the court appropriate to identify the requests to which it applies.

(5) If on an application under this section the court does not direct the company not to comply with the request, the company must comply with the request immediately upon the court giving its decision or, as the case may be, the proceedings being discontinued.

746 Register of debenture holders: refusal of inspection or default in providing copy

(1) If an inspection required under section 744 (register of debenture holders: right to inspect and require copy) is refused or default is made in providing a copy required under that section, otherwise than in accordance with an order of the court, an offence is committed by –

    (a) the company, and

(b) every officer of the company who is in default.

(2) A person guilty of an offence under this section is liable on summary conviction to a fine not exceeding level 3 on the standard scale and, for continued contravention, a daily default fine not exceeding one-tenth of level 3 on the standard scale.

(3) In the case of any such refusal or default the court may by order compel an immediate inspection or, as the case may be, direct that the copy required be sent to the person requesting it.

747 Register of debenture holders: offences in connection with request for or disclosure of information

(1) It is an offence for a person knowingly or recklessly to make in a request under section 744 (register of debenture holders: right to inspect and require copy) a statement that is misleading, false or deceptive in a material particular.

(2) It is an offence for a person in possession of information obtained by exercise of either of the rights conferred by that section –

(a) to do anything that results in the information being disclosed to another person, or

(b) to fail to do anything with the result that the information is disclosed to another person,

knowing, or having reason to suspect, that person may use the information for a purpose that is not a proper purpose.

(3) A person guilty of an offence under this section is liable –

(a) on conviction on indictment, to imprisonment for a term not exceeding two years or a fine (or both);

(b) on summary conviction –

(i) in England and Wales, to imprisonment for a term not exceeding twelve months or to a fine not exceeding the statutory maximum (or both);

(ii) in Scotland or Northern Ireland, to imprisonment for a term not exceeding six months, or to a fine not exceeding the statutory maximum (or both).

748 Time limit for claims arising from entry in register

(1) Liability incurred by a company –

(a) from the making or deletion of an entry in the register of debenture holders, or

(b) from a failure to make or delete any such entry,

is not enforceable more than ten years after the date on which the entry was made or deleted or, as the case may be, the failure first occurred.

(2) This is without prejudice to any lesser period of limitation (and, in Scotland, to any rule that the obligation giving rise to the liability prescribes before the expiry of that period).

Supplementary provisions

749 Right of debenture holder to copy of deed

(1) Any holder of debentures of a company is entitled, on request and on payment of such fee as may be prescribed, to be provided with a copy of any trust deed for securing the debentures.

(2) If default is made in complying with this section, an offence is committed by every officer of the company who is in default.

(3) A person guilty of an offence under this section is liable on summary conviction to a fine not exceeding level 3 on the standard scale and, for continued contravention, a daily default fine not exceeding one-tenth of level 3 on the standard scale.

(4) In the case of any such default the court may direct that the copy required be sent to the person requiring it.

750 Liability of trustees of debentures

(1) Any provision contained in –

  (a) a trust deed for securing an issue of debentures, or
  (b) any contract with the holders of debentures secured by a trust deed,

is void in so far as it would have the effect of exempting a trustee of the deed from, or indemnifying him against, liability for breach of trust where he fails to show the degree of care and diligence required of him as trustee, having regard to the provisions of the trust deed conferring on him any powers, authorities or discretions.

(2) Subsection (1) does not invalidate –

  (a) a release otherwise validly given in respect of anything done or omitted to be done by a trustee before the giving of the release;
  (b) any provision enabling such a release to be given –

    (i) on being agreed to by a majority of not less than 75% in value of the debenture holders present and voting in person or, where proxies are permitted, by proxy at a meeting summoned for the purpose, and
    (ii) either with respect to specific acts or omissions or on the trustee dying or ceasing to act.

(3) This section is subject to section 751 (saving for certain older provisions).

751 Liability of trustees of debentures: saving for certain older provisions

(1) Section 750 (liability of trustees of debentures) does not operate –

  (a) to invalidate any provision in force on the relevant date so long as any person –

    (i) then entitled to the benefit of the provision, or
    (ii) afterwards given the benefit of the provision under subsection (3) below,

    remains a trustee of the deed in question, or
  (b) to deprive any person of any exemption or right to be indemnified in respect of anything done or omitted to be done by him while any such provision was in force.

(2) The relevant date for this purpose is –

  (a) 1st July 1948 in a case where section 192 of the Companies Act 1985 (c. 6) applied immediately before the commencement of this section;
  (b) 1st July 1961 in a case where Article 201 of the Companies (Northern Ireland) Order 1986 (S.I. 1986/1032 (N.I. 6)) then applied.

(3) While any trustee of a trust deed remains entitled to the benefit of a provision saved by subsection (1) above the benefit of that provision may be given either –

  (a) to all trustees of the deed, present and future, or
  (b) to any named trustees or proposed trustees of it,

by a resolution passed by a majority of not less than 75% in value of the debenture holders present in person or, where proxies are permitted, by proxy at a meeting summoned for the purpose.

(4) A meeting for that purpose must be summoned in accordance with the provisions of the deed or, if the deed makes no provision for summoning meetings, in a manner approved by the court.

752 Power to re-issue redeemed debentures

(1) Where a company has redeemed debentures previously issued, then unless –

(a) provision to the contrary (express or implied) is contained in the company's articles or in any contract made by the company, or

(b) the company has, by passing a resolution to that effect or by some other act, manifested its intention that the debentures shall be cancelled,

the company may re-issue the debentures, either by re-issuing the same debentures or by issuing new debentures in their place.

This subsection is deemed always to have had effect.

(2) On a re-issue of redeemed debentures the person entitled to the debentures has (and is deemed always to have had) the same priorities as if the debentures had never been redeemed.

(3) The re-issue of a debenture or the issue of another debenture in its place under this section is treated as the issue of a new debenture for the purposes of stamp duty.

It is not so treated for the purposes of any provision limiting the amount or number of debentures to be issued.

(4) A person lending money on the security of a debenture re-issued under this section which appears to be duly stamped may give the debenture in evidence in any proceedings for enforcing his security without payment of the stamp duty or any penalty in respect of it, unless he had notice (or, but for his negligence, might have discovered) that the debenture was not duly stamped.

In that case the company is liable to pay the proper stamp duty and penalty.

753 Deposit of debentures to secure advances

Where a company has deposited any of its debentures to secure advances from time to time on current account or otherwise, the debentures are not treated as redeemed by reason only of the company's account having ceased to be in debit while the debentures remained so deposited.

754 Priorities where debentures secured by floating charge

(1) This section applies where debentures of a company registered in England and Wales or Northern Ireland are secured by a charge that, as created, was a floating charge.

(2) If possession is taken, by or on behalf of the holders of the debentures, of any property comprised in or subject to the charge, and the company is not at that time in the course of being wound up, the company's preferential debts shall be paid out of assets coming to the hands of the persons taking possession in priority to any claims for principal or interest in respect of the debentures.

(3) "Preferential debts" means the categories of debts listed in Schedule 6 to the Insolvency Act 1986 (c. 45) or Schedule 4 to the Insolvency (Northern Ireland) Order 1989 (S.I. 1989/2405 (N.I. 19)).

For the purposes of those Schedules "the relevant date" is the date of possession being taken as mentioned in subsection (2).

(4) Payments under this section shall be recouped, as far as may be, out of the assets of the company available for payment of general creditors.

PART 20

PRIVATE AND PUBLIC COMPANIES

CHAPTER 1

PROHIBITION OF PUBLIC OFFERS BY PRIVATE COMPANIES

755 Prohibition of public offers by private company

(1) A private company limited by shares or limited by guarantee and having a share capital must not –

    (a) offer to the public any securities of the company, or

    (b) allot or agree to allot any securities of the company with a view to their being offered to the public.

(2) Unless the contrary is proved, an allotment or agreement to allot securities is presumed to be made with a view to their being offered to the public if an offer of the securities (or any of them) to the public is made –

    (a) within six months after the allotment or agreement to allot, or

    (b) before the receipt by the company of the whole of the consideration to be received by it in respect of the securities.

(3) A company does not contravene this section if –

    (a) it acts in good faith in pursuance of arrangements under which it is to re-register as a public company before the securities are allotted, or

    (b) as part of the terms of the offer it undertakes to re-register as a public company within a specified period, and that undertaking is complied with.

(4) The specified period for the purposes of subsection (3)(b) must be a period ending not later than six months after the day on which the offer is made (or, in the case of an offer made on different days, first made).

(5) In this Chapter "securities" means shares or debentures.

756 Meaning of "offer to the public"

(1) This section explains what is meant in this Chapter by an offer of securities to the public.

(2) An offer to the public includes an offer to any section of the public, however selected.

(3) An offer is not regarded as an offer to the public if it can properly be regarded, in all the circumstances, as –

    (a) not being calculated to result, directly or indirectly, in securities of the company becoming available to persons other than those receiving the offer, or

    (b) otherwise being a private concern of the person receiving it and the person making it.

(4) An offer is to be regarded (unless the contrary is proved) as being a private concern of the person receiving it and the person making it if –

    (a) it is made to a person already connected with the company and, where it is made on terms allowing that person to renounce his rights, the rights may only be renounced in favour of another person already connected with the company; or

    (b) it is an offer to subscribe for securities to be held under an employees' share scheme and, where it is made on terms allowing that person to renounce his rights, the rights may only be renounced in favour of –

        (i) another person entitled to hold securities under the scheme, or

        (ii) a person already connected with the company.

(5) For the purposes of this section "person already connected with the company" means –

    (a) an existing member or employee of the company,

    (b) a member of the family of a person who is or was a member or employee of the company,

    (c) the widow or widower, or surviving civil partner, of a person who was a member or employee of the company,

    (d) an existing debenture holder of the company, or

    (e) a trustee (acting in his capacity as such) of a trust of which the principal beneficiary is a person within any of paragraphs (a) to (d).

(6) For the purposes of subsection (5)(b) the members of a person's family are the person's spouse or civil partner and children (including step-children) and their descendants.

757 Enforcement of prohibition: order restraining proposed contravention

(1) If it appears to the court –

    (a) on an application under this section, or

    (b) in proceedings under Part 30 (protection of members against unfair prejudice),

    that a company is proposing to act in contravention of section 755 (prohibition of public offers by private companies), the court shall make an order under this section.

(2) An order under this section is an order restraining the company from contravening that section.

(3) An application for an order under this section may be made by –

    (a) a member or creditor of the company, or

    (b) the Secretary of State.

758 Enforcement of prohibition: orders available to the court after contravention

(1) This section applies if it appears to the court –

    (a) on an application under this section, or

    (b) in proceedings under Part 30 (protection of members against unfair prejudice),

    that a company has acted in contravention of section 755 (prohibition of public offers by private companies).

(2) The court must make an order requiring the company to re-register as a public company unless it appears to the court –

    (a) that the company does not meet the requirements for re-registration as a public company, and

    (b) that it is impractical or undesirable to require it to take steps to do so.

(3) If it does not make an order for re-registration, the court may make either or both of the following –

    (a) a remedial order (see section 759), or

    (b) an order for the compulsory winding up of the company.

(4) An application under this section may be made by –

    (a) a member of the company who –

        (i) was a member at the time the offer was made (or, if the offer was made over a period, at any time during that period), or

        (ii) became a member as a result of the offer,

    (b) a creditor of the company who was a creditor at the time the offer was made (or, if the offer was made over a period, at any time during that period), or

    (c) the Secretary of State.

759 Enforcement of prohibition: remedial order

(1) A "remedial order" is an order for the purpose of putting a person affected by any-thing done in contravention of section 755 (prohibition of public offers by private company) in the position he would have been in if it had not been done.

(2) The following provisions are without prejudice to the generality of the power to make such an order.

(3) Where a private company has –

   (a) allotted securities pursuant to an offer to the public, or

   (b) allotted or agreed to allot securities with a view to their being offered to the public,

   a remedial order may require any person knowingly concerned in the contravention of section 755 to offer to purchase any of those securities at such price and on such other terms as the court thinks fit.

(4) A remedial order may be made –

   (a) against any person knowingly concerned in the contravention, whether or not an officer of the company;

   (b) notwithstanding anything in the company's constitution (which includes, for this purpose, the terms on which any securities of the company are allotted or held);

   (c) whether or not the holder of the securities subject to the order is the person to whom the company allotted or agreed to allot them.

(5) Where a remedial order is made against the company itself, the court may provide for the reduction of the company's capital accordingly.

760 Validity of allotment etc not affected

Nothing in this Chapter affects the validity of any allotment or sale of securities or of any agreement to allot or sell securities.

CHAPTER 2

MINIMUM SHARE CAPITAL REQUIREMENT FOR PUBLIC COMPANIES

761 Public company: requirement as to minimum share capital

(1) A company that is a public company (otherwise than by virtue of re-registration as a public company) must not do business or exercise any borrowing powers unless the registrar has issued it with a certificate under this section (a "trading certificate").

(2) The registrar shall issue a trading certificate if, on an application made in accordance with section 762, he is satisfied that the nominal value of the company's allotted share capital is not less than the authorised minimum.

(3) For this purpose a share allotted in pursuance of an employees' share scheme shall not be taken into account unless paid up as to –

   (a) at least one-quarter of the nominal value of the share, and

   (b) the whole of any premium on the share.

(4) A trading certificate has effect from the date on which it is issued and is conclusive evidence that the company is entitled to do business and exercise any borrowing powers.

762 Procedure for obtaining certificate

(1) An application for a certificate under section 761 must –

    (a) state that the nominal value of the company's allotted share capital is not less than the authorised minimum,

    (b) specify the amount, or estimated amount, of the company's preliminary expenses,

    (c) specify any amount or benefit paid or given, or intended to be paid or given, to any promoter of the company, and the consideration for the payment or benefit, and

    (d) be accompanied by a statement of compliance.

(2) The statement of compliance is a statement that the company meets the requirements for the issue of a certificate under section 761.

(3) The registrar may accept the statement of compliance as sufficient evidence of the matters stated in it.

763 The authorised minimum

(1) "The authorised minimum", in relation to the nominal value of a public company's allotted share capital is –

    (a) £50,000, or

    (b) the prescribed euro equivalent.

(2) The Secretary of State may by order prescribe the amount in euros that is for the time being to be treated as equivalent to the sterling amount of the authorised minimum.

(3) This power may be exercised from time to time as appears to the Secretary of State to be appropriate.

(4) The amount prescribed shall be determined by applying an appropriate spot rate of exchange to the sterling amount and rounding to the nearest 100 euros.

(5) An order under this section is subject to negative resolution procedure.

(6) This section has effect subject to any exercise of the power conferred by section 764 (power to alter authorised minimum).

764 Power to alter authorised minimum

(1) The Secretary of State may by order –

    (a) alter the sterling amount of the authorised minimum, and

    (b) make a corresponding alteration of the prescribed euro equivalent.

(2) The amount of the prescribed euro equivalent shall be determined by applying an appropriate spot rate of exchange to the sterling amount and rounding to the nearest 100 euros.

(3) An order under this section that increases the authorised minimum may –

    (a) require a public company having an allotted share capital of which the nominal value is less than the amount specified in the order to –

        (i) increase that value to not less than that amount, or

        (ii) re-register as a private company;

    (b) make provision in connection with any such requirement for any of the matters for which provision is made by this Act relating to –

        (i) a company's registration, re-registration or change of name,

        (ii) payment for shares comprised in a company's share capital, and

        (iii) offers to the public of shares in or debentures of a company,

    including provision as to the consequences (in criminal law or otherwise) of a failure to comply with any requirement of the order;

    (c) provide for any provision of the order to come into force on different days for different purposes.

(4) An order under this section is subject to affirmative resolution procedure.

765 Authorised minimum: application of initial requirement

(1)   The initial requirement for a public company to have allotted share capital of a nominal value not less than the authorised minimum, that is –

(a)   the requirement in section 761(2) for the issue of a trading certificate, or

(b)   the requirement in section 91(1)(a) for re-registration as a public company,

must be met either by reference to allotted share capital denominated in sterling or by reference to allotted share capital denominated in euros (but not partly in one and partly in the other).

(2)   Whether the requirement is met is determined in the first case by reference to the sterling amount and in the second case by reference to the prescribed euro equivalent.

(3)   No account is to be taken of any allotted share capital of the company denominated in a currency other than sterling or, as the case may be, euros.

(4)   If the company could meet the requirement either by reference to share capital denominated in sterling or by reference to share capital denominated in euros, it must elect in its application for a trading certificate or, as the case may be, for re-registration as a public company which is to be the currency by reference to which the matter is determined.

766 Authorised minimum: application where shares denominated in different currencies etc

(1)   The Secretary of State may make provision by regulations as to the application of the authorised minimum in relation to a public company that –

(a)   has shares denominated in more than one currency,

(b)   redenominates the whole or part of its allotted share capital, or

(c)   allots new shares.

(2)   The regulations may make provision as to the currencies, exchange rates and dates by reference to which it is to be determined whether the nominal value of the company's allotted share capital is less than the authorised minimum.

(3)   The regulations may provide that where –

(a)   a company has redenominated the whole or part of its allotted share capital, and

(b)   the effect of the redenomination is that the nominal value of the company's allotted share capital is less than the authorised minimum,

the company must re-register as a private company.

(4)   Regulations under subsection (3) may make provision corresponding to any provision made by sections 664 to 667 (re-registration as private company in consequence of cancellation of shares).

(5)   Any regulations under this section have effect subject to section 765 (authorised minimum: application of initial requirement).

(6)   Regulations under this section are subject to negative resolution procedure.

767 Consequences of doing business etc without a trading certificate

(1)   If a company does business or exercises any borrowing powers in contravention of section 761, an offence is committed by –

(a)   the company, and

(b)   every officer of the company who is in default.

(2)   A person guilty of an offence under subsection (1) is liable –

(a)   on conviction on indictment, to a fine;

(b)   on summary conviction, to a fine not exceeding the statutory maximum.

(3)   A contravention of section 761 does not affect the validity of a transaction entered into by the company, but if a company –

(a)   enters into a transaction in contravention of that section, and

(b)   fails to comply with its obligations in connection with the transaction within 21 days from being called on to do so,

the directors of the company are jointly and severally liable to indemnify any other party to the transaction in respect of any loss or damage suffered by him by reason of the company's failure to comply with its obligations.

(4)   The directors who are so liable are those who were directors at the time the company entered into the transaction.

PART 21

CERTIFICATION AND TRANSFER OF SECURITIES

CHAPTER 1

CERTIFICATION AND TRANSFER OF SECURITIES: GENERAL

Share certificates

768 Share certificate to be evidence of title

(1)   In the case of a company registered in England and Wales or Northern Ireland, a certificate under the common seal of the company specifying any shares held by a member is prima facie evidence of his title to the shares.

(2)   In the case of a company registered in Scotland –

(a)   a certificate under the common seal of the company specifying any shares held by a member, or

(b)   a certificate specifying any shares held by a member and subscribed by the company in accordance with the Requirements of Writing (Scotland) Act 1995 (c. 7),

is sufficient evidence, unless the contrary is shown, of his title to the shares.

Issue of certificates etc on allotment

769 Duty of company as to issue of certificates etc on allotment

(1)   A company must, within two months after the allotment of any of its shares, debentures or debenture stock, complete and have ready for delivery –

(a)   the certificates of the shares allotted,

(b)   the debentures allotted, or

(c)   the certificates of the debenture stock allotted.

(2)   Subsection (1) does not apply –

(a)   if the conditions of issue of the shares, debentures or debenture stock provide otherwise,

(b)   in the case of allotment to a financial institution (see section 778), or

(c)   in the case of an allotment of shares if, following the allotment, the company has issued a share warrant in respect of the shares (see section 779).

(3)   If default is made in complying with subsection (1) an offence is committed by every officer of the company who is in default.

(4)   A person guilty of an offence under subsection (3) is liable on summary conviction to a fine not exceeding level 3 on the standard scale and, for continued contravention, a daily default fine not exceeding one-tenth of level 3 on the standard scale.

Transfer of securities

770 Registration of transfer

(1) A company may not register a transfer of shares in or debentures of the company unless –

    (a) a proper instrument of transfer has been delivered to it, or

    (b) the transfer –

        (i)   is an exempt transfer within the Stock Transfer Act 1982 (c. 41), or

        (ii) is in accordance with regulations under Chapter 2 of this Part.

(2) Subsection (1) does not affect any power of the company to register as shareholder or debenture holder a person to whom the right to any shares in or debentures of the company has been transmitted by operation of law.

771 Procedure on transfer being lodged

(1) When a transfer of shares in or debentures of a company has been lodged with the company, the company must either –

    (a) register the transfer, or

    (b) give the transferee notice of refusal to register the transfer, together with its reasons for the refusal,

as soon as practicable and in any event within two months after the date on which the transfer is lodged with it.

(2) If the company refuses to register the transfer, it must provide the transferee with such further information about the reasons for the refusal as the transferee may reasonably request.

This does not include copies of minutes of meetings of directors.

(3) If a company fails to comply with this section, an offence is committed by –

    (a) the company, and

    (b) every officer of the company who is in default.

(4) A person guilty of an offence under this section is liable on summary conviction to a fine not exceeding level 3 on the standard scale and, for continued contravention, a daily default fine not exceeding one-tenth of level 3 on the standard scale.

(5) This section does not apply –

    (a) in relation to a transfer of shares if the company has issued a share warrant in respect of the shares (see section 779);

    (b) in relation to the transmission of shares or debentures by operation of law.

772 Transfer of shares on application of transferor

On the application of the transferor of any share or interest in a company, the company shall enter in its register of members the name of the transferee in the same manner and subject to the same conditions as if the application for the entry were made by the transferee.

773 Execution of share transfer by personal representative

An instrument of transfer of the share or other interest of a deceased member of a company –

    (a) may be made by his personal representative although the personal representative is not himself a member of the company, and

    (b) is as effective as if the personal representative had been such a member at the time of the execution of the instrument.

774 Evidence of grant of probate etc

The production to a company of any document that is by law sufficient evidence of the grant of –

- (a) probate of the will of a deceased person,
- (b) letters of administration of the estate of a deceased person, or
- (c) confirmation as executor of a deceased person,

shall be accepted by the company as sufficient evidence of the grant.

775 Certification of instrument of transfer

(1) The certification by a company of an instrument of transfer of any shares in, or debentures of, the company is to be taken as a representation by the company to any person acting on the faith of the certification that there have been produced to the company such documents as on their face show a prima facie title to the shares or debentures in the transferor named in the instrument.

(2) The certification is not to be taken as a representation that the transferor has any title to the shares or debentures.

(3) Where a person acts on the faith of a false certification by a company made negligently, the company is under the same liability to him as if the certification had been made fraudulently.

(4) For the purposes of this section –

- (a) an instrument of transfer is certificated if it bears the words "certificate lodged" (or words to the like effect);
- (b) the certification of an instrument of transfer is made by a company if –
  - (i) the person issuing the instrument is a person authorised to issue certificated instruments of transfer on the company's behalf, and
  - (ii) the certification is signed by a person authorised to certificate transfers on the company's behalf or by an officer or employee either of the company or of a body corporate so authorised;
- (c) a certification is treated as signed by a person if –
  - (i) it purports to be authenticated by his signature or initials (whether handwritten or not), and
  - (ii) it is not shown that the signature or initials was or were placed there neither by himself nor by a person authorised to use the signature or initials for the purpose of certificating transfers on the company's behalf.

Issue of certificates etc on transfer

776 Duty of company as to issue of certificates etc on transfer

(1) A company must, within two months after the date on which a transfer of any of its shares, debentures or debenture stock is lodged with the company, complete and have ready for delivery –

- (a) the certificates of the shares transferred,
- (b) the debentures transferred, or
- (c) the certificates of the debenture stock transferred.

(2) For this purpose a "transfer" means –

- (a) a transfer duly stamped and otherwise valid, or
- (b) an exempt transfer within the Stock Transfer Act 1982 (c. 41),

but does not include a transfer that the company is for any reason entitled to refuse to register and does not register.

(3) Subsection (1) does not apply –

    (a) if the conditions of issue of the shares, debentures or debenture stock provide otherwise,

    (b) in the case of a transfer to a financial institution (see section 778), or

    (c) in the case of a transfer of shares if, following the transfer, the company has issued a share warrant in respect of the shares (see section 779).

(4) Subsection (1) has effect subject to section 777 (cases where the Stock Transfer Act 1982 applies).

(5) If default is made in complying with subsection (1) an offence is committed by every officer of the company who is in default.

(6) A person guilty of an offence under this section is liable on summary conviction to a fine not exceeding level 3 on the standard scale and, for continued contravention, a daily default fine not exceeding one-tenth of level 3 on the standard scale.

777 Issue of certificates etc: cases within the Stock Transfer Act 1982

(1) Section 776(1) (duty of company as to issue of certificates etc on transfer) does not apply in the case of a transfer to a person where, by virtue of regulations under section 3 of the Stock Transfer Act 1982, he is not entitled to a certificate or other document of or evidencing title in respect of the securities transferred.

(2) But if in such a case the transferee –

    (a) subsequently becomes entitled to such a certificate or other document by virtue of any provision of those regulations, and

    (b) gives notice in writing of that fact to the company,

section 776 (duty to company as to issue of certificates etc) has effect as if the reference in subsection (1) of that section to the date of the lodging of the transfer were a reference to the date of the notice.

Issue of certificates etc on allotment or transfer to financial institution

778 Issue of certificates etc: allotment or transfer to financial institution

(1) A company –

    (a) of which shares or debentures are allotted to a financial institution,

    (b) of which debenture stock is allotted to a financial institution, or

    (c) with which a transfer for transferring shares, debentures or debenture stock to a financial institution is lodged,

is not required in consequence of that allotment or transfer to comply with section 769(1) or 776(1) (duty of company as to issue of certificates etc).

(2) A "financial institution" means –

    (a) a recognised clearing house acting in relation to a recognised investment exchange, or

    (b) a nominee of –

        (i) a recognised clearing house acting in that way, or

        (ii) a recognised investment exchange,

designated for the purposes of this section in the rules of the recognised investment exchange in question.

(3) Expressions used in subsection (2) have the same meaning as in Part 18 of the Financial Services and Markets Act 2000 (c. 8).

Share warrants

779 Issue and effect of share warrant to bearer

(1) A company limited by shares may, if so authorised by its articles, issue with respect to any fully paid shares a warrant (a "share warrant") stating that the bearer of the warrant is entitled to the shares specified in it.

(2) A share warrant issued under the company's common seal or (in the case of a company registered in Scotland) subscribed in accordance with the Requirements of Writing (Scotland) Act 1995 (c. 7) entitles the bearer to the shares specified in it and the shares may be transferred by delivery of the warrant.

(3) A company that issues a share warrant may, if so authorised by its articles, provide (by coupons or otherwise) for the payment of the future dividends on the shares included in the warrant.

780 Duty of company as to issue of certificates on surrender of share warrant

(1) A company must, within two months of the surrender of a share warrant for cancellation, complete and have ready for delivery the certificates of the shares specified in the warrant.

(2) Subsection (1) does not apply if the company's articles provide otherwise.

(3) If default is made in complying with subsection (1) an offence is committed by every officer of the company who is in default.

(4) A person guilty of an offence under subsection (3) is liable on summary conviction to a fine not exceeding level 3 on the standard scale and, for continued contravention, a daily default fine not exceeding one-tenth of level 3 on the standard scale.

781 Offences in connection with share warrants (Scotland)

(1) If in Scotland a person –

(a) with intent to defraud, forges or alters, or offers, utters, disposes of, or puts off, knowing the same to be forged or altered, any share warrant or coupon, or any document purporting to be a share warrant or coupon issued in pursuance of this Act, or

(b) by means of any such forged or altered share warrant, coupon or document –

(i) demands or endeavours to obtain or receive any share or interest in a company under this Act, or

(ii) demands or endeavours to receive any dividend or money payment in respect of any such share or interest,

knowing the warrant, coupon or document to be forged or altered,

he commits an offence.

(2) If in Scotland a person without lawful authority or excuse (of which proof lies on him) –

(a) engraves or makes on any plate, wood, stone, or other material, any share warrant or coupon purporting to be –

(i) a share warrant or coupon issued or made by any particular company in pursuance of this Act, or

(ii) a blank share warrant or coupon so issued or made, or

(iii) a part of such a share warrant or coupon, or

(b) uses any such plate, wood, stone, or other material, for the making or printing of any such share warrant or coupon, or of any such blank share warrant or coupon or of any part of such a share warrant or coupon, or

(c) knowingly has in his custody or possession any such plate, wood, stone, or other material,

he commits an offence.

(3) A person guilty of an offence under subsection (1) is liable on summary conviction to imprisonment for a term not exceeding six months or to a fine not exceeding level 5 on the standard scale (or both).

(4) A person guilty of an offence under subsection (2) is liable –

   (a) on conviction on indictment, to imprisonment for a term not exceeding seven years or a fine (or both);

   (b) on summary conviction, to imprisonment for a term not exceeding six months or a fine not exceeding the statutory maximum (or both).

Supplementary provisions

782 Issue of certificates etc: court order to make good default

(1) If a company on which a notice has been served requiring it to make good any default in complying with –

   (a) section 769(1) (duty of company as to issue of certificates etc on allotment),

   (b) section 776(1) (duty of company as to issue of certificates etc on transfer), or

   (c) section 780(1) (duty of company as to issue of certificates etc on surrender of share warrant),

   fails to make good the default within ten days after service of the notice, the person entitled to have the certificates or the debentures delivered to him may apply to the court.

(2) The court may on such an application make an order directing the company and any officer of it to make good the default within such time as may be specified in the order.

(3) The order may provide that all costs (in Scotland, expenses) of and incidental to the application are to be borne by the company or by an officer of it responsible for the default.

CHAPTER 2

EVIDENCING AND TRANSFER OF TITLE TO SECURITIES WITHOUT WRITTEN INSTRUMENT

Introductory

783 Scope of this Chapter

In this Chapter –

   (a) "securities" means shares, debentures, debenture stock, loan stock, bonds, units of a collective investment scheme within the meaning of the Financial Services and Markets Act 2000 (c. 8) and other securities of any description;

   (b) references to title to securities include any legal or equitable interest in securities;

   (c) references to a transfer of title include a transfer by way of security;

   (d) references to transfer without a written instrument include, in relation to bearer securities, transfer without delivery.

784 Power to make regulations

(1) The power to make regulations under this Chapter is exercisable by the Treasury and the Secretary of State, either jointly or concurrently.

(2) References in this Chapter to the authority having power to make regulations shall accordingly be read as references to both or either of them, as the case may require.

(3) Regulations under this Chapter are subject to affirmative resolution procedure.

Powers exercisable

785 Provision enabling procedures for evidencing and transferring title

(1) Provision may be made by regulations for enabling title to securities to be evidenced and transferred without a written instrument.

(2) The regulations may make provision –

    (a) for procedures for recording and transferring title to securities, and

    (b) for the regulation of those procedures and the persons responsible for or involved in their operation.

(3) The regulations must contain such safeguards as appear to the authority making the regulations appropriate for the protection of investors and for ensuring that competition is not restricted, distorted or prevented.

(4) The regulations may, for the purpose of enabling or facilitating the operation of the procedures provided for by the regulations, make provision with respect to the rights and obligations of persons in relation to securities dealt with under the procedures.

(5) The regulations may include provision for the purpose of giving effect to –

    (a) the transmission of title to securities by operation of law;

    (b) any restriction on the transfer of title to securities arising by virtue of the provisions of any enactment or instrument, court order or agreement;

    (c) any power conferred by any such provision on a person to deal with securities on behalf of the person entitled.

(6) The regulations may make provision with respect to the persons responsible for the operation of the procedures provided for by the regulations –

    (a) as to the consequences of their insolvency or incapacity, or

    (b) as to the transfer from them to other persons of their functions in relation to those procedures.

786 Provision enabling or requiring arrangements to be adopted

(1) Regulations under this Chapter may make provision –

    (a) enabling the members of a company or of any designated class of companies to adopt, by ordinary resolution, arrangements under which title to securities is required to be evidenced or transferred (or both) without a written instrument; or

    (b) requiring companies, or any designated class of companies, to adopt such arrangements.

(2) The regulations may make such provision –

    (a) in respect of all securities issued by a company, or

    (b) in respect of all securities of a specified description.

(3) The arrangements provided for by regulations making such provision as is mentioned in subsection (1) –

    (a) must not be such that a person who but for the arrangements would be entitled to have his name entered in the company's register of members ceases to be so entitled, and

    (b) must be such that a person who but for the arrangements would be entitled to exercise any rights in respect of the securities continues to be able effectively to control the exercise of those rights.

(4) The regulations may –

    (a) prohibit the issue of any certificate by the company in respect of the issue or transfer of securities,

    (b) require the provision by the company to holders of securities of statements (at specified intervals or on specified occasions) of the securities held in their name, and

(c) make provision as to the matters of which any such certificate or statement is, or is not, evidence.

(5) In this section –

    (a) references to a designated class of companies are to a class designated in the regulations or by order under section 787; and

    (b) "specified" means specified in the regulations.

787 Provision enabling or requiring arrangements to be adopted: order-making powers

(1) The authority having power to make regulations under this Chapter may by order –

    (a) designate classes of companies for the purposes of section 786 (provision enabling or requiring arrangements to be adopted);

    (b) provide that, in relation to securities of a specified description –

        (i) in a designated class of companies, or

        (ii) in a specified company or class of companies,

    specified provisions of regulations made under this Chapter by virtue of that section either do not apply or apply subject to specified modifications.

(2) In subsection (1) "specified" means specified in the order.

(3) An order under this section is subject to negative resolution procedure.

Supplementary

788 Provision that may be included in regulations

Regulations under this Chapter may –

    (a) modify or exclude any provision of any enactment or instrument, or any rule of law;

    (b) apply, with such modifications as may be appropriate, the provisions of any enactment or instrument (including provisions creating criminal offences);

    (c) require the payment of fees, or enable persons to require the payment of fees, of such amounts as may be specified in the regulations or determined in accordance with them;

    (d) empower the authority making the regulations to delegate to any person willing and able to discharge them any functions of the authority under the regulations.

789 Duty to consult

Before making –

    (a) regulations under this Chapter, or

    (b) any order under section 787,

the authority having power to make regulations under this Chapter must carry out such consultation as appears to it to be appropriate.

790 Resolutions to be forwarded to registrar

Chapter 3 of Part 3 (resolutions affecting a company's constitution) applies to a resolution passed by virtue of regulations under this Chapter.

PART 22

INFORMATION ABOUT INTERESTS IN A COMPANY'S SHARES

Introductory

791 Companies to which this Part applies

This Part applies only to public companies.

792 Shares to which this Part applies

(1) References in this Part to a company's shares are to the company's issued shares of a class carrying rights to vote in all circumstances at general meetings of the company (including any shares held as treasury shares).

(2) The temporary suspension of voting rights in respect of any shares does not affect the application of this Part in relation to interests in those or any other shares.

Notice requiring information about interests in shares

793 Notice by company requiring information about interests in its shares

(1) A public company may give notice under this section to any person whom the company knows or has reasonable cause to believe –

    (a) to be interested in the company's shares, or

    (b) to have been so interested at any time during the three years immediately preceding the date on which the notice is issued.

(2) The notice may require the person –

    (a) to confirm that fact or (as the case may be) to state whether or not it is the case, and

    (b) if he holds, or has during that time held, any such interest, to give such further information as may be required in accordance with the following provisions of this section.

(3) The notice may require the person to whom it is addressed to give particulars of his own present or past interest in the company's shares (held by him at any time during the three year period mentioned in subsection (1)(b)).

(4) The notice may require the person to whom it is addressed, where –

    (a) his interest is a present interest and another interest in the shares subsists, or

    (b) another interest in the shares subsisted during that three year period at a time when his interest subsisted,

to give, so far as lies within his knowledge, such particulars with respect to that other interest as may be required by the notice.

(5) The particulars referred to in subsections (3) and (4) include –

    (a) the identity of persons interested in the shares in question, and

    (b) whether persons interested in the same shares are or were parties to –

        (i) an agreement to which section 824 applies (certain share acquisition agreements), or

        (ii) an agreement or arrangement relating to the exercise of any rights conferred by the holding of the shares.

(6) The notice may require the person to whom it is addressed, where his interest is a past interest, to give (so far as lies within his knowledge) particulars of the identity of the person who held that interest immediately upon his ceasing to hold it.

(7)   The information required by the notice must be given within such reasonable time as may be specified in the notice.

794 Notice requiring information: order imposing restrictions on shares

(1)   Where –

    (a)   a notice under section 793 (notice requiring information about interests in company's shares) is served by a company on a person who is or was interested in shares in the company, and

    (b)   that person fails to give the company the information required by the notice within the time specified in it,

the company may apply to the court for an order directing that the shares in question be subject to restrictions.

For the effect of such an order see section 797.

(2)   If the court is satisfied that such an order may unfairly affect the rights of third parties in respect of the shares, the court may, for the purpose of protecting those rights and subject to such terms as it thinks fit, direct that such acts by such persons or descriptions of persons and for such purposes as may be set out in the order shall not constitute a breach of the restrictions.

(3)   On an application under this section the court may make an interim order.

Any such order may be made unconditionally or on such terms as the court thinks fit.

(4)   Sections 798 to 802 make further provision about orders under this section.

795 Notice requiring information: offences

(1)   A person who –

    (a)   fails to comply with a notice under section 793 (notice requiring information about interests in company's shares), or

    (b)   in purported compliance with such a notice –

        (i)   makes a statement that he knows to be false in a material particular, or

        (ii)   recklessly makes a statement that is false in a material particular,

commits an offence.

(2)   A person does not commit an offence under subsection (1)(a) if he proves that the requirement to give information was frivolous or vexatious.

(3)   A person guilty of an offence under this section is liable –

    (a)   on conviction on indictment, to imprisonment for a term not exceeding two years or a fine (or both);

    (b)   on summary conviction –

        (i)   in England and Wales, to imprisonment for a term not exceeding twelve months or to a fine not exceeding the statutory maximum (or both);

        (ii)   in Scotland or Northern Ireland, to imprisonment for a term not exceeding six months, or to a fine not exceeding the statutory maximum (or both).

796 Notice requiring information: persons exempted from obligation to comply

(1)   A person is not obliged to comply with a notice under section 793 (notice requiring information about interests in company's shares) if he is for the time being exempted by the Secretary of State from the operation of that section.

(2)   The Secretary of State must not grant any such exemption unless –

    (a)   he has consulted the Governor of the Bank of England, and

    (b)   he (the Secretary of State) is satisfied that, having regard to any undertaking given by the person in question with respect to any interest held or to be held by him in any shares, there are special reasons why that person should not be subject to the obligations imposed by that section.

Orders imposing restrictions on shares

797 Consequences of order imposing restrictions

(1) The effect of an order under section 794 that shares are subject to restrictions is as follows –

    (a) any transfer of the shares is void;

    (b) no voting rights are exercisable in respect of the shares;

    (c) no further shares may be issued in right of the shares or in pursuance of an offer made to their holder;

    (d) except in a liquidation, no payment may be made of sums due from the company on the shares, whether in respect of capital or otherwise.

(2) Where shares are subject to the restriction in subsection (1)(a), an agreement to transfer the shares is void.

This does not apply to an agreement to transfer the shares on the making of an order under section 800 made by virtue of subsection (3)(b) (removal of restrictions in case of court-approved transfer).

(3) Where shares are subject to the restriction in subsection (1)(c) or (d), an agreement to transfer any right to be issued with other shares in right of those shares, or to receive any payment on them (otherwise than in a liquidation), is void.

This does not apply to an agreement to transfer any such right on the making of an order under section 800 made by virtue of subsection (3)(b) (removal of restrictions in case of court-approved transfer).

(4) The provisions of this section are subject –

    (a) to any directions under section 794(2) or section 799(3) (directions for protection of third parties), and

    (b) in the case of an interim order under section 794(3), to the terms of the order.

798 Penalty for attempted evasion of restrictions

(1) This section applies where shares are subject to restrictions by virtue of an order under section 794.

(2) A person commits an offence if he –

    (a) exercises or purports to exercise any right –

        (i) to dispose of shares that to his knowledge, are for the time being subject to restrictions, or

        (ii) to dispose of any right to be issued with any such shares, or

    (b) votes in respect of any such shares (whether as holder or proxy), or appoints a proxy to vote in respect of them, or

    (c) being the holder of any such shares, fails to notify of their being subject to those restrictions a person whom he does not know to be aware of that fact but does know to be entitled (apart from the restrictions) to vote in respect of those shares whether as holder or as proxy, or

    (d) being the holder of any such shares, or being entitled to a right to be issued with other shares in right of them, or to receive any payment on them (otherwise than in a liquidation), enters into an agreement which is void under section 797(2) or (3).

(3) If shares in a company are issued in contravention of the restrictions, an offence is committed by –

    (a) the company, and

    (b) every officer of the company who is in default.

(4) A person guilty of an offence under this section is liable –

    (a) on conviction on indictment, to a fine;

    (b) on summary conviction, to a fine not exceeding the statutory maximum.

(5) The provisions of this section are subject –

    (a) to any directions under –

        section 794(2) (directions for protection of third parties), or
        section 799 or 800 (relaxation or removal of restrictions), and

    (b) in the case of an interim order under section 794(3), to the terms of the order.

799 Relaxation of restrictions

(1) An application may be made to the court on the ground that an order directing that shares shall be subject to restrictions unfairly affects the rights of third parties in respect of the shares.

(2) An application for an order under this section may be made by the company or by any person aggrieved.

(3) If the court is satisfied that the application is well-founded, it may, for the purpose of protecting the rights of third parties in respect of the shares, and subject to such terms as it thinks fit, direct that such acts by such persons or descriptions of persons and for such purposes as may be set out in the order do not constitute a breach of the restrictions.

800 Removal of restrictions

(1) An application may be made to the court for an order directing that the shares shall cease to be subject to restrictions.

(2) An application for an order under this section may be made by the company or by any person aggrieved.

(3) The court must not make an order under this section unless –

    (a) it is satisfied that the relevant facts about the shares have been disclosed to the company and no unfair advantage has accrued to any person as a result of the earlier failure to make that disclosure, or

    (b) the shares are to be transferred for valuable consideration and the court approves the transfer.

(4) An order under this section made by virtue of subsection (3)(b) may continue, in whole or in part, the restrictions mentioned in section 797(1)(c) and (d) (restrictions on issue of further shares or making of payments) so far as they relate to a right acquired or offer made before the transfer.

(5) Where any restrictions continue in force under subsection (4) –

    (a) an application may be made under this section for an order directing that the shares shall cease to be subject to those restrictions, and

    (b) subsection (3) does not apply in relation to the making of such an order.

801 Order for sale of shares

(1) The court may order that the shares subject to restrictions be sold, subject to the court's approval as to the sale.

(2) An application for an order under subsection (1) may only be made by the company.

(3) Where the court has made an order under this section, it may make such further order relating to the sale or transfer of the shares as it thinks fit.

(4) An application for an order under subsection (3) may be made –

    (a) by the company,

    (b) by the person appointed by or in pursuance of the order to effect the sale, or

    (c) by any person interested in the shares.

(5) On making an order under subsection (1) or (3) the court may order that the applicant's costs (in Scotland, expenses) be paid out of the proceeds of sale.

802 Application of proceeds of sale under court order

(1) Where shares are sold in pursuance of an order of the court under section 801, the proceeds of the sale, less the costs of the sale, must be paid into court for the benefit of the persons who are beneficially interested in the shares.

(2) A person who is beneficially interested in the shares may apply to the court for the whole or part of those proceeds to be paid to him.

(3) On such an application the court shall order the payment to the applicant of –

(a) the whole of the proceeds of sale together with any interest on them, or

(b) if another person had a beneficial interest in the shares at the time of their sale, such proportion of the proceeds and interest as the value of the applicant's interest in the shares bears to the total value of the shares.

This is subject to the following qualification.

(4) If the court has ordered under section 801(5) that the costs (in Scotland, expenses) of an applicant under that section are to be paid out of the proceeds of sale, the applicant is entitled to payment of his costs (or expenses) out of those proceeds before any person interested in the shares receives any part of those proceeds.

Power of members to require company to act

803 Power of members to require company to act

(1) The members of a company may require it to exercise its powers under section 793 (notice requiring information about interests in shares).

(2) A company is required to do so once it has received requests (to the same effect) from members of the company holding at least 10% of such of the paid-up capital of the company as carries a right to vote at general meetings of the company (excluding any voting rights attached to any shares in the company held as treasury shares).

(3) A request –

(a) may be in hard copy form or in electronic form,

(b) must –

(i)   state that the company is requested to exercise its powers under section 793,

(ii) specify the manner in which the company is requested to act, and

(iii) give reasonable grounds for requiring the company to exercise those powers in the manner specified, and

(c) must be authenticated by the person or persons making it.

804 Duty of company to comply with requirement

(1) A company that is required under section 803 to exercise its powers under section 793 (notice requiring information about interests in company's shares) must exercise those powers in the manner specified in the requests.

(2) If default is made in complying with subsection (1) an offence is committed by every officer of the company who is in default.

(3) A person guilty of an offence under this section is liable –

(a) on conviction on indictment, to a fine;

(b) on summary conviction, to a fine not exceeding the statutory maximum.

805 Report to members on outcome of investigation

(1) On the conclusion of an investigation carried out by a company in pursuance of a requirement under section 803 the company must cause a report of the information received in pursuance of the investigation to be prepared.

The report must be made available for inspection within a reasonable period (not more than 15 days) after the conclusion of the investigation.

(2) Where –

    (a) a company undertakes an investigation in pursuance of a requirement under section 803, and

    (b) the investigation is not concluded within three months after the date on which the company became subject to the requirement,

the company must cause to be prepared in respect of that period, and in respect of each succeeding period of three months ending before the conclusion of the investigation, an interim report of the information received during that period in pursuance of the investigation.

(3) Each such report must be made available for inspection within a reasonable period (not more than 15 days) after the end of the period to which it relates.

(4) The reports must be retained by the company for at least six years from the date on which they are first made available for inspection and must be kept available for inspection during that time –

    (a) at the company's registered office, or

    (b) at a place specified in regulations under section 1136.

(5) The company must give notice to the registrar –

    (a) of the place at which the reports are kept available for inspection, and

    (b) of any change in that place,

unless they have at all times been kept at the company's registered office.

(6) The company must within three days of making any report prepared under this section available for inspection, notify the members who made the requests under section 803 where the report is so available.

(7) For the purposes of this section an investigation carried out by a company in pursuance of a requirement under section 803 is concluded when –

    (a) the company has made all such inquiries as are necessary or expedient for the purposes of the requirement, and

    (b) in the case of each such inquiry –

        (i) a response has been received by the company, or

        (ii) the time allowed for a response has elapsed.

806 Report to members: offences

(1) If default is made for 14 days in complying with section 805(5) (notice to registrar of place at which reports made available for inspection) an offence is committed by –

    (a) the company, and

    (b) every officer of the company who is in default.

(2) A person guilty of an offence under subsection (1) is liable on summary conviction to a fine not exceeding level 3 on the standard scale and, for continued contravention, a daily default fine not exceeding one-tenth of level 3 on the standard scale.

(3) If default is made in complying with any other provision of section 805 (report to members on outcome of investigation), an offence is committed by every officer of the company who is in default.

(4) A person guilty of an offence under subsection (3) is liable –

    (a) on conviction on indictment, to a fine;

    (b) on summary conviction, to a fine not exceeding the statutory maximum.

807 Right to inspect and request copy of reports

(1) Any report prepared under section 805 must be open to inspection by any person without charge.

(2) Any person is entitled, on request and on payment of such fee as may be prescribed, to be provided with a copy of any such report or any part of it.

The copy must be provided within ten days after the request is received by the company.

(3) If an inspection required under subsection (1) is refused, or default is made in complying with subsection (2), an offence is committed by –

(a) the company, and

(b) every officer of the company who is in default.

(4) A person guilty of an offence under this section is liable on summary conviction to a fine not exceeding level 3 on the standard scale and, for continued contravention, a daily default fine not exceeding one-tenth of level 3 on the standard scale.

(5) In the case of any such refusal or default the court may by order compel an immediate inspection or, as the case may be, direct that the copy required be sent to the person requiring it.

Register of interests disclosed

808 Register of interests disclosed

(1) The company must keep a register of information received by it in pursuance of a requirement imposed under section 793 (notice requiring information about interests in company's shares).

(2) A company which receives any such information must, within three days of the receipt, enter in the register –

(a) the fact that the requirement was imposed and the date on which it was imposed, and

(b) the information received in pursuance of the requirement.

(3) The information must be entered against the name of the present holder of the shares in question or, if there is no present holder or the present holder is not known, against the name of the person holding the interest.

(4) The register must be made up so that the entries against the names entered in it appear in chronological order.

(5) If default is made in complying with this section an offence is committed by –

(a) the company, and

(b) every officer of the company who is in default.

(6) A person guilty of an offence under this section is liable on summary conviction to a fine not exceeding level 3 on the standard scale and, for continued contravention, a daily default fine not exceeding one-tenth of level 3 on the standard scale.

(7) The company is not by virtue of anything done for the purposes of this section affected with notice of, or put upon inquiry as to, the rights of any person in relation to any shares.

809 Register to be kept available for inspection

(1) The register kept under section 808 (register of interests disclosed) must be kept available for inspection –

(a) at the company's registered office, or

(b) at a place specified in regulations under section 1136.

(2) A company must give notice to the registrar of companies of the place where the register is kept available for inspection and of any change in that place.

(3) No such notice is required if the register has at all times been kept available for inspection at the company's registered office.

(4) If default is made in complying with subsection (1), or a company makes default for 14 days in complying with subsection (2), an offence is committed by –

(a) the company, and

(b) every officer of the company who is in default.

(5) A person guilty of an offence under this section is liable on summary conviction to a fine not exceeding level 3 on the standard scale and, for continued contravention, a daily default fine not exceeding one-tenth of level 3 on the standard scale.

810 Associated index

(1) Unless the register kept under section 808 (register of interests disclosed) is kept in such a form as itself to constitute an index, the company must keep an index of the names entered in it.

(2) The company must make any necessary entry or alteration in the index within ten days after the date on which any entry or alteration is made in the register.

(3) The index must contain, in respect of each name, a sufficient indication to enable the information entered against it to be readily found.

(4) The index must be at all times kept available for inspection at the same place as the register.

(5) If default is made in complying with this section, an offence is committed by –

(a) the company, and
(b) every officer of the company who is in default.

(6) A person guilty of an offence under this section is liable on summary conviction to a fine not exceeding level 3 on the standard scale and, for continued contravention, a daily default fine not exceeding one-tenth of level 3 on the standard scale.

811 Rights to inspect and require copy of entries

(1) The register required to be kept under section 808 (register of interests disclosed), and any associated index, must be open to inspection by any person without charge.

(2) Any person is entitled, on request and on payment of such fee as may be prescribed, to be provided with a copy of any entry in the register.

(3) A person seeking to exercise either of the rights conferred by this section must make a request to the company to that effect.

(4) The request must contain the following information –

(a) in the case of an individual, his name and address;
(b) in the case of an organisation, the name and address of an individual responsible for making the request on behalf of the organisation;
(c) the purpose for which the information is to be used; and
(d) whether the information will be disclosed to any other person, and if so –

(i)   where that person is an individual, his name and address,
(ii) where that person is an organisation, the name and address of an individual responsible for receiving the information on its behalf, and
(iii) the purpose for which the information is to be used by that person.

812 Court supervision of purpose for which rights may be exercised

(1) Where a company receives a request under section 811 (register of interests disclosed: right to inspect and require copy), it must –

(a) comply with the request if it is satisfied that it is made for a proper purpose, and
(b) refuse the request if it is not so satisfied.

(2) If the company refuses the request, it must inform the person making the request, stating the reason why it is not satisfied.

(3) A person whose request is refused may apply to the court.

(4) If an application is made to the court –

(a) the person who made the request must notify the company, and

(b)   the company must use its best endeavours to notify any persons whose details would be disclosed if the company were required to comply with the request.

(5)   If the court is not satisfied that the inspection or copy is sought for a proper purpose, it shall direct the company not to comply with the request.

(6)   If the court makes such a direction and it appears to the court that the company is or may be subject to other requests made for a similar purpose (whether made by the same person or different persons), it may direct that the company is not to comply with any such request.
The order must contain such provision as appears to the court appropriate to identify the requests to which it applies.

(7)   If the court does not direct the company not to comply with the request, the company must comply with the request immediately upon the court giving its decision or, as the case may be, the proceedings being discontinued.

813 Register of interests disclosed: refusal of inspection or default in providing copy

(1)   If an inspection required under section 811 (register of interests disclosed: right to inspect and require copy) is refused or default is made in providing a copy required under that section, otherwise than in accordance with an order of the court, an offence is committed by –
(a)   the company, and
(b)   every officer of the company who is in default.

(2)   A person guilty of an offence under this section is liable on summary conviction to a fine not exceeding level 3 on the standard scale and, for continued contravention, a daily default fine not exceeding one-tenth of level 3 on the standard scale.

(3)   In the case of any such refusal or default the court may by order compel an immediate inspection or, as the case may be, direct that the copy required be sent to the person requesting it.

814 Register of interests disclosed: offences in connection with request for or disclosure of information

(1)   It is an offence for a person knowingly or recklessly to make in a request under section 811 (register of interests disclosed: right to inspect or require copy) a statement that is misleading, false or deceptive in a material particular.

(2)   It is an offence for a person in possession of information obtained by exercise of either of the rights conferred by that section –
(a)   to do anything that results in the information being disclosed to another person, or
(b)   to fail to do anything with the result that the information is disclosed to another person,
knowing, or having reason to suspect, that person may use the information for a purpose that is not a proper purpose.

(3)   A person guilty of an offence under this section is liable –
(a)   on conviction on indictment, to imprisonment for a term not exceeding two years or a fine (or both);
(b)   on summary conviction –
(i)   in England and Wales, to imprisonment for a term not exceeding twelve months or to a fine not exceeding the statutory maximum (or both);
(ii)   in Scotland or Northern Ireland, to imprisonment for a term not exceeding six months, or to a fine not exceeding the statutory maximum (or both).

815 Entries not to be removed from register

(1)   Entries in the register kept under section 808 (register of interests disclosed) must not be deleted except in accordance with –

section 816 (old entries), or

section 817 (incorrect entry relating to third party).

(2) If an entry is deleted in contravention of subsection (1), the company must restore it as soon as reasonably practicable.

(3) If default is made in complying with subsection (1) or (2), an offence is committed by –

(a) the company, and

(b) every officer of the company who is in default.

(4) A person guilty of an offence under this section is liable on summary conviction to a fine not exceeding level 3 on the standard scale and, for continued contravention of subsection (2), a daily default fine not exceeding one-tenth of level 3 on the standard scale.

816 Removal of entries from register: old entries

A company may remove an entry from the register kept under section 808 (register of interests disclosed) if more than six years have elapsed since the entry was made.

817 Removal of entries from register: incorrect entry relating to third party

(1) This section applies where in pursuance of an obligation imposed by a notice under section 793 (notice requiring information about interests in company's shares) a person gives to a company the name and address of another person as being interested in shares in the company.

(2) That other person may apply to the company for the removal of the entry from the register.

(3) If the company is satisfied that the information in pursuance of which the entry was made is incorrect, it shall remove the entry.

(4) If an application under subsection (3) is refused, the applicant may apply to the court for an order directing the company to remove the entry in question from the register. The court may make such an order if it thinks fit.

818 Adjustment of entry relating to share acquisition agreement

(1) If a person who is identified in the register kept by a company under section 808 (register of interests disclosed) as being a party to an agreement to which section 824 applies (certain share acquisition agreements) ceases to be a party to the agreement, he may apply to the company for the inclusion of that information in the register.

(2) If the company is satisfied that he has ceased to be a party to the agreement, it shall record that information (if not already recorded) in every place where his name appears in the register as a party to the agreement.

(3) If an application under this section is refused (otherwise than on the ground that the information has already been recorded), the applicant may apply to the court for an order directing the company to include the information in question in the register. The court may make such an order if it thinks fit.

819 Duty of company ceasing to be public company

(1) If a company ceases to be a public company, it must continue to keep any register kept under section 808 (register of interests disclosed), and any associated index, until the end of the period of six years after it ceased to be such a company.

(2) If default is made in complying with this section, an offence is committed by –

(a) the company, and

(b) every officer of the company who is in default.

(3) A person guilty of an offence under this section is liable on summary conviction to a fine not exceeding level 3 on the standard scale and, for continued contravention, a daily default fine not exceeding one-tenth of level 3 on the standard scale.

Meaning of interest in shares

820 Interest in shares: general

(1) This section applies to determine for the purposes of this Part whether a person has an interest in shares.

(2) In this Part –

  (a) a reference to an interest in shares includes an interest of any kind whatsoever in the shares, and

  (b) any restraints or restrictions to which the exercise of any right attached to the interest is or may be subject shall be disregarded.

(3) Where an interest in shares is comprised in property held on trust, every beneficiary of the trust is treated as having an interest in the shares.

(4) A person is treated as having an interest in shares if –

  (a) he enters into a contract to acquire them, or

  (b) not being the registered holder, he is entitled –

    (i)   to exercise any right conferred by the holding of the shares, or

    (ii) to control the exercise of any such right.

(5) For the purposes of subsection (4)(b) a person is entitled to exercise or control the exercise of a right conferred by the holding of shares if he –

  (a) has a right (whether subject to conditions or not) the exercise of which would make him so entitled, or

  (b) is under an obligation (whether subject to conditions or not) the fulfilment of which would make him so entitled.

(6) A person is treated as having an interest in shares if –

  (a) he has a right to call for delivery of the shares to himself or to his order, or

  (b) he has a right to acquire an interest in shares or is under an obligation to take an interest in shares.

  This applies whether the right or obligation is conditional or absolute.

(7) Persons having a joint interest are treated as each having that interest.

(8) It is immaterial that shares in which a person has an interest are unidentifiable.

821 Interest in shares: right to subscribe for shares

(1) Section 793 (notice by company requiring information about interests in its shares) applies in relation to a person who has, or previously had, or is or was entitled to acquire, a right to subscribe for shares in the company as it applies in relation to a person who is or was interested in shares in that company.

(2) References in that section to an interest in shares shall be read accordingly.

822 Interest in shares: family interests

(1) For the purposes of this Part a person is taken to be interested in shares in which –

  (a) his spouse or civil partner, or

  (b) any infant child or step-child of his,

  is interested.

(2) In relation to Scotland "infant" means a person under the age of 18 years.

823 Interest in shares: corporate interests

(1) For the purposes of this Part a person is taken to be interested in shares if a body corporate is interested in them and –

  (a) the body or its directors are accustomed to act in accordance with his directions or instructions, or

(b) he is entitled to exercise or control the exercise of one-third or more of the voting power at general meetings of the body.

(2) For the purposes of this section a person is treated as entitled to exercise or control the exercise of voting power if –

(a) another body corporate is entitled to exercise or control the exercise of that voting power, and

(b) he is entitled to exercise or control the exercise of one-third or more of the voting power at general meetings of that body corporate.

(3) For the purposes of this section a person is treated as entitled to exercise or control the exercise of voting power if –

(a) he has a right (whether or not subject to conditions) the exercise of which would make him so entitled, or

(b) he is under an obligation (whether or not subject to conditions) the fulfilment of which would make him so entitled.

824 Interest in shares: agreement to acquire interests in a particular company

(1) For the purposes of this Part an interest in shares may arise from an agreement between two or more persons that includes provision for the acquisition by any one or more of them of interests in shares of a particular public company (the "target company" for that agreement).

(2) This section applies to such an agreement if –

(a) the agreement includes provision imposing obligations or restrictions on any one or more of the parties to it with respect to their use, retention or disposal of their interests in the shares of the target company acquired in pursuance of the agreement (whether or not together with any other interests of theirs in the company's shares to which the agreement relates), and

(b) an interest in the target company's shares is in fact acquired by any of the parties in pursuance of the agreement.

(3) The reference in subsection (2) to the use of interests in shares in the target company is to the exercise of any rights or of any control or influence arising from those interests (including the right to enter into an agreement for the exercise, or for control of the exercise, of any of those rights by another person).

(4) Once an interest in shares in the target company has been acquired in pursuance of the agreement, this section continues to apply to the agreement so long as the agreement continues to include provisions of any description mentioned in subsection (2). This applies irrespective of –

(a) whether or not any further acquisitions of interests in the company's shares take place in pursuance of the agreement;

(b) any change in the persons who are for the time being parties to it;

(c) any variation of the agreement.

References in this subsection to the agreement include any agreement having effect (whether directly or indirectly) in substitution for the original agreement.

(5) In this section –

(a) "agreement" includes any agreement or arrangement, and

(b) references to provisions of an agreement include –

(i) undertakings, expectations or understandings operative under an arrangement, and

(ii) any provision whether express or implied and whether absolute or not.

References elsewhere in this Part to an agreement to which this section applies have a corresponding meaning.

(6) This section does not apply –

(a) to an agreement that is not legally binding unless it involves mutuality in the undertakings, expectations or understandings of the parties to it; or

(b) to an agreement to underwrite or sub-underwrite an offer of shares in a company, provided the agreement is confined to that purpose and any matters incidental to it.

825 Extent of obligation in case of share acquisition agreement

(1) For the purposes of this Part each party to an agreement to which section 824 applies is treated as interested in all shares in the target company in which any other party to the agreement is interested apart from the agreement (whether or not the interest of the other party was acquired, or includes any interest that was acquired, in pursuance of the agreement).

(2) For those purposes an interest of a party to such an agreement in shares in the target company is an interest apart from the agreement if he is interested in those shares otherwise than by virtue of the application of section 824 (and this section) in relation to the agreement.

(3) Accordingly, any such interest of the person (apart from the agreement) includes for those purposes any interest treated as his under section 822 or 823 (family or corporate interests) or by the application of section 824 (and this section) in relation to any other agreement with respect to shares in the target company to which he is a party.

(4) A notification with respect to his interest in shares in the target company made to the company under this Part by a person who is for the time being a party to an agreement to which section 824 applies must –

(a) state that the person making the notification is a party to such an agreement,

(b) include the names and (so far as known to him) the addresses of the other parties to the agreement, identifying them as such, and

(c) state whether or not any of the shares to which the notification relates are shares in which he is interested by virtue of section 824 (and this section) and, if so, the number of those shares.

Other supplementary provisions

826 Information protected from wider disclosure

(1) Information in respect of which a company is for the time being entitled to any exemption conferred by regulations under section 409(3) (information about related undertakings to be given in notes to accounts: exemption where disclosure harmful to company's business) –

(a) must not be included in a report under section 805 (report to members on outcome of investigation), and

(b) must not be made available under section 811 (right to inspect and request copy of entries).

(2) Where any such information is omitted from a report under section 805, that fact must be stated in the report.

827 Reckoning of periods for fulfilling obligations

Where the period allowed by any provision of this Part for fulfilling an obligation is expressed as a number of days, any day that is not a working day shall be disregarded in reckoning that period.

828 Power to make further provision by regulations

(1) The Secretary of State may by regulations amend –

(a) the definition of shares to which this Part applies (section 792),

(b) the provisions as to notice by a company requiring information about interests in its shares (section 793), and

(c) the provisions as to what is taken to be an interest in shares (sections 820 and 821).

(2) The regulations may amend, repeal or replace those provisions and make such other consequential amendments or repeals of provisions of this Part as appear to the Secretary of State to be appropriate.

(3) Regulations under this section are subject to affirmative resolution procedure.

PART 23

DISTRIBUTIONS

CHAPTER 1

RESTRICTIONS ON WHEN DISTRIBUTIONS MAY BE MADE

Introductory

829 Meaning of "distribution"

(1) In this Part "distribution" means every description of distribution of a company's assets to its members, whether in cash or otherwise, subject to the following exceptions.

(2) The following are not distributions for the purposes of this Part –

(a) an issue of shares as fully or partly paid bonus shares;

(b) the reduction of share capital –

(i) by extinguishing or reducing the liability of any of the members on any of the company's shares in respect of share capital not paid up, or

(ii) by repaying paid-up share capital;

(c) the redemption or purchase of any of the company's own shares out of capital (including the proceeds of any fresh issue of shares) or out of unrealised profits in accordance with Chapter 3, 4 or 5 of Part 18;

(d) a distribution of assets to members of the company on its winding up.

General rules

830 Distributions to be made only out of profits available for the purpose

(1) A company may only make a distribution out of profits available for the purpose.

(2) A company's profits available for distribution are its accumulated, realised profits, so far as not previously utilised by distribution or capitalisation, less its accumulated, realised losses, so far as not previously written off in a reduction or reorganisation of capital duly made.

(3) Subsection (2) has effect subject to sections 832 and 835 (investment companies etc: distributions out of accumulated revenue profits).

831 Net asset restriction on distributions by public companies

(1) A public company may only make a distribution –

(a) if the amount of its net assets is not less than the aggregate of its called-up share capital and undistributable reserves, and

(b) if, and to the extent that, the distribution does not reduce the amount of those assets to less than that aggregate.

(2) For this purpose a company's "net assets" means the aggregate of the company's assets less the aggregate of its liabilities.

(3) "Liabilities" here includes –

(a) where the relevant accounts are Companies Act accounts, provisions of a kind specified for the purposes of this subsection by regulations under section 396;

(b) where the relevant accounts are IAS accounts, provisions of any kind.

(4) A company's undistributable reserves are –

(a) its share premium account;

(b) its capital redemption reserve;

(c) the amount by which its accumulated, unrealised profits (so far as not previously utilised by capitalisation) exceed its accumulated, unrealised losses (so far as not previously written off in a reduction or reorganisation of capital duly made);

(d) any other reserve that the company is prohibited from distributing –

(i) by any enactment (other than one contained in this Part), or

(ii) by its articles.

The reference in paragraph (c) to capitalisation does not include a transfer of profits of the company to its capital redemption reserve.

(5) A public company must not include any uncalled share capital as an asset in any accounts relevant for purposes of this section.

(6) Subsection (1) has effect subject to sections 832 and 835 (investment companies etc: distributions out of accumulated revenue profits).

Distributions by investment companies

832 Distributions by investment companies out of accumulated revenue profits

(1) An investment company may make a distribution out of its accumulated, realised revenue profits if the following conditions are met.

(2) It may make such a distribution only if, and to the extent that, its accumulated, realised revenue profits, so far as not previously utilised by a distribution or capitalisation, exceed its accumulated revenue losses (whether realised or unrealised), so far as not previously written off in a reduction or reorganisation of capital duly made.

(3) It may make such a distribution only –

(a) if the amount of its assets is at least equal to one and a half times the aggregate of its liabilities to creditors, and

(b) if, and to the extent that, the distribution does not reduce that amount to less than one and a half times that aggregate.

(4) For this purpose a company's liabilities to creditors include –

(a) in the case of Companies Act accounts, provisions of a kind specified for the purposes of this subsection by regulations under section 396;

(b) in the case of IAS accounts, provisions for liabilities to creditors.

(5) The following conditions must also be met –

(a) the company's shares must be listed on a recognised UK investment exchange;

(b) during the relevant period it must not have –

(i) distributed any capital profits otherwise than by way of the redemption or purchase of any of the company's own shares in accordance with Chapter 3 or 4 of Part 18, or

(ii) applied any unrealised profits or any capital profits (realised or unrealised) in paying up debentures or amounts unpaid on its issued shares;

    (c) it must have given notice to the registrar under section 833(1) (notice of intention to carry on business as an investment company) –

        (i)   before the beginning of the relevant period, or

        (ii) as soon as reasonably practicable after the date of its incorporation.

(6) For the purposes of this section –

    (a) "recognised UK investment exchange" means a recognised investment exchange within the meaning of Part 18 of the Financial Services and Markets Act 2000 (c. 8), other than an overseas investment exchange within the meaning of that Part; and

    (b) the "relevant period" is the period beginning with –

        (i)   the first day of the accounting reference period immediately preceding that in which the proposed distribution is to be made, or

        (ii) where the distribution is to be made in the company's first accounting reference period, the first day of that period,

    and ending with the date of the distribution.

(7) The company must not include any uncalled share capital as an asset in any accounts relevant for purposes of this section.

833 Meaning of "investment company"

(1) In this Part an "investment company" means a public company that –

    (a) has given notice (which has not been revoked) to the registrar of its intention to carry on business as an investment company, and

    (b) since the date of that notice has complied with the following requirements.

(2) Those requirements are –

    (a) that the business of the company consists of investing its funds mainly in securities, with the aim of spreading investment risk and giving members of the company the benefit of the results of the management of its funds;

    (b) that the condition in section 834 is met as regards holdings in other companies;

    (c) that distribution of the company's capital profits is prohibited by its articles;

    (d) that the company has not retained, otherwise than in compliance with this Part, in respect of any accounting reference period more than 15% of the income it derives from securities.

(3) Subsection (2)(c) does not require an investment company to be prohibited by its articles from redeeming or purchasing its own shares in accordance with Chapter 3 or 4 of Part 18 out of its capital profits.

(4) Notice to the registrar under this section may be revoked at any time by the company on giving notice to the registrar that it no longer wishes to be an investment company within the meaning of this section.

(5) On giving such a notice, the company ceases to be such a company.

834 Investment company: condition as to holdings in other companies

(1) The condition referred to in section 833(2)(b) (requirements to be complied with by investment company) is that none of the company's holdings in companies (other than those that are for the time being investment companies) represents more than 15% by value of the company's investments.

(2) For this purpose –

    (a) holdings in companies that –

        (i)   are members of a group (whether or not including the investing company), and

        (ii) are not for the time being investment companies,

    are treated as holdings in a single company; and

(b) where the investing company is a member of a group, money owed to it by another member of the group –

  (i) is treated as a security of the latter held by the investing company, and

  (ii) is accordingly treated as, or as part of, the holding of the investing company in the company owing the money.

(3) The condition does not apply –

  (a) to a holding in a company acquired before 6th April 1965 that on that date represented not more than 25% by value of the investing company's investments, or

  (b) to a holding in a company that, when it was acquired, represented not more than 15% by value of the investing company's investments,

so long as no addition is made to the holding.

(4) For the purposes of subsection (3) –

  (a) "holding" means the shares or securities (whether or one class or more than one class) held in any one company;

  (b) an addition is made to a holding whenever the investing company acquires shares or securities of that one company, otherwise than by being allotted shares or securities without becoming liable to give any consideration, and if an addition is made to a holding that holding is acquired when the addition or latest addition is made to the holding; and

  (c) where in connection with a scheme of reconstruction a company issues shares or securities to persons holding shares or securities in a second company in respect of and in proportion to (or as nearly as may be in proportion to) their holdings in the second company, without those persons becoming liable to give any consideration, a holding of the shares or securities in the second company and a corresponding holding of the shares or securities so issued shall be regarded as the same holding.

(5) In this section –

"company" and "shares" shall be construed in accordance with sections 99 and 288 of the Taxation of Chargeable Gains Act 1992 (c. 12);

"group" means a company and all companies that are its 51% subsidiaries (within the meaning of section 838 of the Income and Corporation Taxes Act 1988 (c. 1)); and

"scheme of reconstruction" has the same meaning as in section 136 of the Taxation of Chargeable Gains Act 1992.

835 Power to extend provisions relating to investment companies

(1) The Secretary of State may by regulations extend the provisions of sections 832 to 834 (distributions by investment companies out of accumulated profits), with or without modifications, to other companies whose principal business consists of investing their funds in securities, land or other assets with the aim of spreading investment risk and giving their members the benefit of the results of the management of the assets.

(2) Regulations under this section are subject to affirmative resolution procedure.

CHAPTER 2

JUSTIFICATION OF DISTRIBUTION BY REFERENCE TO ACCOUNTS

Justification of distribution by reference to accounts

836 Justification of distribution by reference to relevant accounts

(1) Whether a distribution may be made by a company without contravening this Part is determined by reference to the following items as stated in the relevant accounts –

    (a) profits, losses, assets and liabilities;

    (b) provisions of the following kinds –

        (i) where the relevant accounts are Companies Act accounts, provisions of a kind specified for the purposes of this subsection by regulations under section 396;

        (ii) where the relevant accounts are IAS accounts, provisions of any kind;

    (c) share capital and reserves (including undistributable reserves).

(2) The relevant accounts are the company's last annual accounts, except that –

    (a) where the distribution would be found to contravene this Part by reference to the company's last annual accounts, it may be justified by reference to interim accounts, and

    (b) where the distribution is proposed to be declared during the company's first accounting reference period, or before any accounts have been circulated in respect of that period, it may be justified by reference to initial accounts.

(3) The requirements of –

    section 837 (as regards the company's last annual accounts),
    section 838 (as regards interim accounts), and
    section 839 (as regards initial accounts),

    must be complied with, as and where applicable.

(4) If any applicable requirement of those sections is not complied with, the accounts may not be relied on for the purposes of this Part and the distribution is accordingly treated as contravening this Part.

Requirements applicable in relation to relevant accounts

837 Requirements where last annual accounts used

(1) The company's last annual accounts means the company's individual accounts –

    (a) that were last circulated to members in accordance with section 423 (duty to circulate copies of annual accounts and reports), or

    (b) if in accordance with section 426 the company provided a summary financial statement instead, that formed the basis of that statement.

(2) The accounts must have been properly prepared in accordance with this Act, or have been so prepared subject only to matters that are not material for determining (by reference to the items mentioned in section 836(1)) whether the distribution would contravene this Part.

(3) Unless the company is exempt from audit and the directors take advantage of that exemption, the auditor must have made his report on the accounts.

(4) If that report was qualified –

    (a) the auditor must have stated in writing (either at the time of his report or subsequently) whether in his opinion the matters in respect of which his report is qualified are material for determining whether a distribution would contravene this Part, and

(b) a copy of that statement must –

    (i)   in the case of a private company, have been circulated to members in accordance with section 423, or

    (ii) in the case of a public company, have been laid before the company in general meeting.

(5) An auditor's statement is sufficient for the purposes of a distribution if it relates to distributions of a description that includes the distribution in question, even if at the time of the statement it had not been proposed.

838 Requirements where interim accounts used

(1) Interim accounts must be accounts that enable a reasonable judgment to be made as to the amounts of the items mentioned in section 836(1).

(2) Where interim accounts are prepared for a proposed distribution by a public company, the following requirements apply.

(3) The accounts must have been properly prepared, or have been so prepared subject to matters that are not material for determining (by reference to the items mentioned in section 836(1)) whether the distribution would contravene this Part.

(4) "Properly prepared" means prepared in accordance with sections 395 to 397 (requirements for company individual accounts), applying those requirements with such modifications as are necessary because the accounts are prepared otherwise than in respect of an accounting reference period.

(5) The balance sheet comprised in the accounts must have been signed in accordance with section 414.

(6) A copy of the accounts must have been delivered to the registrar.

Any requirement of Part 35 of this Act as to the delivery of a certified translation into English of any document forming part of the accounts must also have been met.

839 Requirements where initial accounts used

(1) Initial accounts must be accounts that enable a reasonable judgment to be made as to the amounts of the items mentioned in section 836(1).

(2) Where initial accounts are prepared for a proposed distribution by a public company, the following requirements apply.

(3) The accounts must have been properly prepared, or have been so prepared subject to matters that are not material for determining (by reference to the items mentioned in section 836(1)) whether the distribution would contravene this Part.

(4) "Properly prepared" means prepared in accordance with sections 395 to 397 (requirements for company individual accounts), applying those requirements with such modifications as are necessary because the accounts are prepared otherwise than in respect of an accounting reference period.

(5) The company's auditor must have made a report stating whether, in his opinion, the accounts have been properly prepared.

(6) If that report was qualified –

(a) the auditor must have stated in writing (either at the time of his report or subsequently) whether in his opinion the matters in respect of which his report is qualified are material for determining whether a distribution would contravene this Part, and

(b) a copy of that statement must –

    (i)   in the case of a private company, have been circulated to members in accordance with section 423, or

    (ii) in the case of a public company, have been laid before the company in general meeting.

(7) A copy of the accounts, of the auditor's report and of any auditor's statement must have been delivered to the registrar.

Any requirement of Part 35 of this Act as to the delivery of a certified translation into English of any of those documents must also have been met.

Application of provisions to successive distributions etc

840 Successive distributions etc by reference to the same accounts

(1) In determining whether a proposed distribution may be made by a company in a case where –

   (a) one or more previous distributions have been made in pursuance of a determination made by reference to the same relevant accounts, or

   (b) relevant financial assistance has been given, or other relevant payments have been made, since those accounts were prepared,

   the provisions of this Part apply as if the amount of the proposed distribution was increased by the amount of the previous distributions, financial assistance and other payments.

(2) The financial assistance and other payments that are relevant for this purpose are –

   (a) financial assistance lawfully given by the company out of its distributable profits;

   (b) financial assistance given by the company in contravention of section 678 or 679 (prohibited financial assistance) in a case where the giving of that assistance reduces the company's net assets or increases its net liabilities;

   (c) payments made by the company in respect of the purchase by it of shares in the company, except a payment lawfully made otherwise than out of distributable profits;

   (d) payments of any description specified in section 705 (payments apart from purchase price of shares to be made out of distributable profits).

(3) In this section "financial assistance" has the same meaning as in Chapter 2 of Part 18 (see section 677).

(4) For the purpose of applying subsection (2)(b) in relation to any financial assistance –

   (a) "net assets" means the amount by which the aggregate amount of the company's assets exceeds the aggregate amount of its liabilities, and

   (b) "net liabilities" means the amount by which the aggregate amount of the company's liabilities exceeds the aggregate amount of its assets,

   taking the amount of the assets and liabilities to be as stated in the company's accounting records immediately before the financial assistance is given.

(5) For this purpose a company's liabilities include any amount retained as reasonably necessary for the purposes of providing for any liability –

   (a) the nature of which is clearly defined, and

   (b) which is either likely to be incurred or certain to be incurred but uncertain as to amount or as to the date on which it will arise.

CHAPTER 3

SUPPLEMENTARY PROVISIONS

Accounting matters

841 Realised losses and profits and revaluation of fixed assets

(1) The following provisions have effect for the purposes of this Part.

(2) The following are treated as realised losses –

    (a) in the case of Companies Act accounts, provisions of a kind specified for the purposes of this paragraph by regulations under section 396 (except revaluation provisions);

    (b) in the case of IAS accounts, provisions of any kind (except revaluation provisions).

(3) A "revaluation provision" means a provision in respect of a diminution in value of a fixed asset appearing on a revaluation of all the fixed assets of the company, or of all of its fixed assets other than goodwill.

(4) For the purpose of subsections (2) and (3) any consideration by the directors of the value at a particular time of a fixed asset is treated as a revaluation provided –

    (a) the directors are satisfied that the aggregate value at that time of the fixed assets of the company that have not actually been revalued is not less than the aggregate amount at which they are then stated in the company's accounts, and

    (b) it is stated in a note to the accounts –

        (i)   that the directors have considered the value of some or all of the fixed assets of the company without actually revaluing them,

        (ii)   that they are satisfied that the aggregate value of those assets at the time of their consideration was not less than the aggregate amount at which they were then stated in the company's accounts, and

        (iii) that accordingly, by virtue of this subsection, amounts are stated in the accounts on the basis that a revaluation of fixed assets of the company is treated as having taken place at that time.

(5) Where –

    (a) on the revaluation of a fixed asset, an unrealised profit is shown to have been made, and

    (b) on or after the revaluation, a sum is written off or retained for depreciation of that asset over a period,

an amount equal to the amount by which that sum exceeds the sum which would have been so written off or retained for the depreciation of that asset over that period, if that profit had not been made, is treated as a realised profit made over that period.

842 Determination of profit or loss in respect of asset where records incomplete

In determining for the purposes of this Part whether a company has made a profit or loss in respect of an asset where –

    (a) there is no record of the original cost of the asset, or

    (b) a record cannot be obtained without unreasonable expense or delay,

its cost is taken to be the value ascribed to it in the earliest available record of its value made on or after its acquisition by the company.

843 Realised profits and losses of long-term insurance business

(1) The provisions of this section have effect for the purposes of this Part as it applies in relation to an authorised insurance company carrying on long-term business.

(2) An amount included in the relevant part of the company's balance sheet that –

    (a) represents a surplus in the fund or funds maintained by it in respect of its long-term business, and

    (b) has not been allocated to policy holders or, as the case may be, carried forward unappropriated in accordance with asset identification rules made under section 142(2) of the Financial Services and Markets Act 2000 (c. 8),

is treated as a realised profit.

(3) For the purposes of subsection (2) –

    (a) the relevant part of the balance sheet is that part of the balance sheet that represents accumulated profit or loss;

    (b) a surplus in the fund or funds maintained by the company in respect of its long-term business means an excess of the assets representing that fund or those funds over the liabilities of the company attributable to its long-term business, as shown by an actuarial investigation.

(4) A deficit in the fund or funds maintained by the company in respect of its long-term business is treated as a realised loss.

For this purpose a deficit in any such fund or funds means an excess of the liabilities of the company attributable to its long-term business over the assets representing that fund or those funds, as shown by an actuarial investigation.

(5) Subject to subsections (2) and (4), any profit or loss arising in the company's long-term business is to be left out of account.

(6) For the purposes of this section an "actuarial investigation" means an investigation made into the financial condition of an authorised insurance company in respect of its long-term business –

    (a) carried out once in every period of twelve months in accordance with rules made under Part 10 of the Financial Services and Markets Act 2000, or

    (b) carried out in accordance with a requirement imposed under section 166 of that Act,

by an actuary appointed as actuary to the company.

(7) In this section "long-term business" means business that consists of effecting or carrying out contracts of long-term insurance.

This definition must be read with section 22 of the Financial Services and Markets Act 2000, any relevant order under that section and Schedule 2 to that Act.

844 Treatment of development costs

(1) Where development costs are shown or included as an asset in a company's accounts, any amount shown or included in respect of those costs is treated –

    (a) for the purposes of section 830 (distributions to be made out of profits available for the purpose) as a realised loss, and

    (b) for the purposes of section 832 (distributions by investment companies out of accumulated revenue profits) as a realised revenue loss.

This is subject to the following exceptions.

(2) Subsection (1) does not apply to any part of that amount representing an unrealised profit made on revaluation of those costs.

(3) Subsection (1) does not apply if –

    (a) there are special circumstances in the company's case justifying the directors in deciding that the amount there mentioned is not to be treated as required by subsection (1),

    (b) it is stated –

(i) in the case of Companies Act accounts, in the note required by regulations under section 396 as to the reasons for showing development costs as an asset, or

(ii) in the case of IAS accounts, in any note to the accounts, that the amount is not to be so treated, and

(c) the note explains the circumstances relied upon to justify the decision of the directors to that effect.

Distributions in kind

845 Distributions in kind: determination of amount

(1) This section applies for determining the amount of a distribution consisting of or including, or treated as arising in consequence of, the sale, transfer or other disposition by a company of a non-cash asset where –

(a) at the time of the distribution the company has profits available for distribution, and

(b) if the amount of the distribution were to be determined in accordance with this section, the company could make the distribution without contravening this Part.

(2) The amount of the distribution (or the relevant part of it) is taken to be –

(a) in a case where the amount or value of the consideration for the disposition is not less than the book value of the asset, zero;

(b) in any other case, the amount by which the book value of the asset exceeds the amount or value of any consideration for the disposition.

(3) For the purposes of subsection (1)(a) the company's profits available for distribution are treated as increased by the amount (if any) by which the amount or value of any consideration for the disposition exceeds the book value of the asset.

(4) In this section "book value", in relation to an asset, means –

(a) the amount at which the asset is stated in the relevant accounts, or

(b) where the asset is not stated in those accounts at any amount, zero.

(5) The provisions of Chapter 2 (justification of distribution by reference to accounts) have effect subject to this section.

846 Distributions in kind: treatment of unrealised profits

(1) This section applies where –

(a) a company makes a distribution consisting of or including, or treated as arising in consequence of, the sale, transfer or other disposition by the company of a non-cash asset, and

(b) any part of the amount at which that asset is stated in the relevant accounts represents an unrealised profit.

(2) That profit is treated as a realised profit –

(a) for the purpose of determining the lawfulness of the distribution in accordance with this Part (whether before or after the distribution takes place), and

(b) for the purpose of the application, in relation to anything done with a view to or in connection with the making of the distribution, of any provision of regulations under section 396 under which only realised profits are to be included in or transferred to the profit and loss account.

Consequences of unlawful distribution

847 Consequences of unlawful distribution

(1) This section applies where a distribution, or part of one, made by a company to one of its members is made in contravention of this Part.

(2) If at the time of the distribution the member knows or has reasonable grounds for believing that it is so made, he is liable –

    (a) to repay it (or that part of it, as the case may be) to the company, or

    (b) in the case of a distribution made otherwise than in cash, to pay the company a sum equal to the value of the distribution (or part) at that time.

(3) This is without prejudice to any obligation imposed apart from this section on a member of a company to repay a distribution unlawfully made to him.

(4) This section does not apply in relation to –

    (a) financial assistance given by a company in contravention of section 678 or 679, or

    (b) any payment made by a company in respect of the redemption or purchase by the company of shares in itself.

Other matters

848 Saving for certain older provisions in articles

(1) Where immediately before the relevant date a company was authorised by a provision of its articles to apply its unrealised profits in paying up in full or inpart unissued shares to be allotted to members of the company as fully or partly paid bonus shares, that provision continues (subject to any alteration of the articles) as authority for those profits to be so applied after that date.

(2) For this purpose the relevant date is –

    (a) for companies registered in Great Britain, 22nd December 1980;

    (b) for companies registered in Northern Ireland, 1st July 1983.

849 Restriction on application of unrealised profits

A company must not apply an unrealised profit in paying up debentures or any amounts unpaid on its issued shares.

850 Treatment of certain older profits or losses

(1) Where the directors of a company are, after making all reasonable enquiries, unable to determine whether a particular profit made before the relevant date is realised or unrealised, they may treat the profit as realised.

(2) Where the directors of a company, after making all reasonable enquiries, are unable to determine whether a particular loss made before the relevant date is realised or unrealised, they may treat the loss as unrealised.

(3) For the purposes of this section the relevant date is –

    (a) for companies registered in Great Britain, 22nd December 1980;

    (b) for companies registered in Northern Ireland, 1st July 1983.

851 Application of rules of law restricting distributions

(1) Except as provided in this section, the provisions of this Part are without prejudice to any rule of law restricting the sums out of which, or the cases in which, a distribution may be made.

(2) For the purposes of any rule of law requiring distributions to be paid out of profits or restricting the return of capital to members –

(a) section 845 (distributions in kind: determination of amount) applies to determine the amount of any distribution or return of capital consisting of or including, or treated as arising in consequence of the sale, transfer or other disposition by a company of a non-cash asset; and

(b) section 846 (distributions in kind: treatment of unrealised profits) applies as it applies for the purposes of this Part.

(3) In this section references to distributions are to amounts regarded as distributions for the purposes of any such rule of law as is referred to in subsection (1).

852 Saving for other restrictions on distributions

The provisions of this Part are without prejudice to any enactment, or any provision of a company's articles, restricting the sums out of which, or the cases in which, a distribution may be made.

853 Minor definitions

(1) The following provisions apply for the purposes of this Part.

(2) References to profit or losses of any description –

(a) are to profits or losses of that description made at any time, and

(b) except where the context otherwise requires, are to profits or losses of a revenue or capital character.

(3) "Capitalisation", in relation to a company's profits, means any of the following operations (whenever carried out) –

(a) applying the profits in wholly or partly paying up unissued shares in the company to be allotted to members of the company as fully or partly paid bonus shares, or

(b) transferring the profits to capital redemption reserve.

(4) References to "realised profits" and "realised losses", in relation to a company's accounts, are to such profits or losses of the company as fall to be treated as realised in accordance with principles generally accepted at the time when the accounts are prepared, with respect to the determination for accounting purposes of realised profits or losses.

(5) Subsection (4) is without prejudice to –

(a) the construction of any other expression (where appropriate) by reference to accepted accounting principles or practice, or

(b) any specific provision for the treatment of profits or losses of any description as realised.

(6) "Fixed assets" means assets of a company which are intended for use on a continuing basis in the company's activities.

PART 24

A COMPANY'S ANNUAL RETURN

854 Duty to deliver annual returns

(1) Every company must deliver to the registrar successive annual returns each of which is made up to a date not later than the date that is from time to time the company's return date.

(2) The company's return date is –

(a) the anniversary of the company's incorporation, or

(b) if the company's last return delivered in accordance with this Part was made up to a different date, the anniversary of that date.

(3) Each return must –

    (a) contain the information required by or under the following provisions of this Part, and

    (b) be delivered to the registrar within 28 days after the date to which it is made up.

855 Contents of annual return: general

(1) Every annual return must state the date to which it is made up and contain the following information –

    (a) the address of the company's registered office;

    (b) the type of company it is and its principal business activities;

    (c) the prescribed particulars of –

        (i)   the directors of the company, and

        (ii) in the case of a private company with a secretary or a public company, the secretary or joint secretaries;

    (d) if the register of members is not kept available for inspection at the company's registered office, the address of the place where it is kept available for inspection;

    (e) if any register of debenture holders (or a duplicate of any such register or a part of it) is not kept available for inspection at the company's registered office, the address of the place where it is kept available for inspection.

(2) The information as to the company's type must be given by reference to the classification scheme prescribed for the purposes of this section.

(3) The information as to the company's principal business activities may be given by reference to one or more categories of any prescribed system of classifying business activities.

856 Contents of annual return: information about share capital and shareholders

(1) The annual return of a company having a share capital must also contain –

    (a) a statement of capital, and

    (b) the particulars required by subsections (3) to (6) about the members of the company.

(2) The statement of capital must state with respect to the company's share capital at the date to which the return is made up –

    (a) the total number of shares of the company,

    (b) the aggregate nominal value of those shares,

    (c) for each class of shares –

        (i)   prescribed particulars of the rights attached to the shares,

        (ii)   the total number of shares of that class, and

        (iii) the aggregate nominal value of shares of that class, and

    (d) the amount paid up and the amount (if any) unpaid on each share (whether on account of the nominal value of the share or by way of premium).

(3) The return must contain the prescribed particulars of every person who –

    (a) is a member of the company on the date to which the return is made up, or

    (b) has ceased to be a member of the company since the date to which the last return was made up (or, in the case of the first return, since the incorporation of the company).

The return must conform to such requirements as may be prescribed for the purpose of enabling the entries relating to any given person to be easily found.

(4) The return must also state –

    (a) the number of shares of each class held by each member of the company at the date to which the return is made up,

(b) the number of shares of each class transferred –

   (i)   since the date to which the last return was made up, or
   (ii) in the case of the first return, since the incorporation of the company,

   by each member or person who has ceased to be a member, and
(c) the dates of registration of the transfers.

(5) If either of the two immediately preceding returns has given the full particulars required by subsections (3) and (4), the return need only give such particulars as relate –

(a) to persons ceasing to be or becoming members since the date of the last return, and
(b) to shares transferred since that date.

(6) Where the company has converted any of its shares into stock, the return must give the corresponding information in relation to that stock, stating the amount of stock instead of the number or nominal value of shares.

857 Contents of annual return: power to make further provision by regulations

(1) The Secretary of State may by regulations make further provision as to the information to be given in a company's annual return.
(2) The regulations may –

(a) amend or repeal the provisions of sections 855 and 856, and
(b) provide for exceptions from the requirements of those sections as they have effect from time to time.

(3) Regulations under this section are subject to negative resolution procedure.

858 Failure to deliver annual return

(1) If a company fails to deliver an annual return before the end of the period of 28 days after a return date, an offence is committed by –

(a) the company,
(b) subject to subsection (4) –

   (i)   every director of the company, and
   (ii) in the case of a private company with a secretary or a public company, every secretary of the company, and

(c) every other officer of the company who is in default.

(2) A person guilty of an offence under subsection (1) is liable on summary conviction to a fine not exceeding level 5 on the standard scale and, for continued contravention, a daily default fine not exceeding one-tenth of level 5 on the standard scale.
(3) The contravention continues until such time as an annual return made up to that return date is delivered by the company to the registrar.
(4) It is a defence for a director or secretary charged with an offence under subsection (1)(b) to prove that he took all reasonable steps to avoid the commission or continuation of the offence.
(5) In the case of continued contravention, an offence is also committed by every officer of the company who did not commit an offence under subsection (1) in relation to the initial contravention but is in default in relation to the continued contravention. A person guilty of an offence under this subsection is liable on summary conviction to a fine not exceeding one-tenth of level 5 on the standard scale for each day on which the contravention continues and he is in default.

859 Application of provisions to shadow directors

For the purposes of this Part a shadow director is treated as a director.

PART 25

COMPANY CHARGES

CHAPTER 1

COMPANIES REGISTERED IN ENGLAND AND WALES OR IN NORTHERN IRELAND

Requirement to register company charges

860 Charges created by a company

(1) A company that creates a charge to which this section applies must deliver the prescribed particulars of the charge, together with the instrument (if any) by which the charge is created or evidenced, to the registrar for registration before the end of the period allowed for registration.

(2) Registration of a charge to which this section applies may instead be effected on the application of a person interested in it.

(3) Where registration is effected on the application of some person other than the company, that person is entitled to recover from the company the amount of any fees properly paid by him to the registrar on registration.

(4) If a company fails to comply with subsection (1), an offence is committed by –

   (a) the company, and
   (b) every officer of it who is in default.

(5) A person guilty of an offence under this section is liable –

   (a) on conviction on indictment, to a fine;
   (b) on summary conviction, to a fine not exceeding the statutory maximum.

(6) Subsection (4) does not apply if registration of the charge has been effected on the application of some other person.

(7) This section applies to the following charges –

   (a) a charge on land or any interest in land, other than a charge for any rent or other periodical sum issuing out of land,
   (b) a charge created or evidenced by an instrument which, if executed by an individual, would require registration as a bill of sale,
   (c) a charge for the purposes of securing any issue of debentures,
   (d) a charge on uncalled share capital of the company,
   (e) a charge on calls made but not paid,
   (f) a charge on book debts of the company,
   (g) a floating charge on the company's property or undertaking,
   (h) a charge on a ship or aircraft, or any share in a ship,
   (i) a charge on goodwill or on any intellectual property.

861 Charges which have to be registered: supplementary

(1) The holding of debentures entitling the holder to a charge on land is not, for the purposes of section 860(7)(a), an interest in the land.

(2) It is immaterial for the purposes of this Chapter where land subject to a charge is situated.

(3) The deposit by way of security of a negotiable instrument given to secure the payment of book debts is not, for the purposes of section 860(7)(f), a charge on those book debts.

(4) For the purposes of section 860(7)(i), "intellectual property" means –

(a) any patent, trade mark, registered design, copyright or design right;
(b) any licence under or in respect of any such right.

(5) In this Chapter –

"charge" includes mortgage, and

"company" means a company registered in England and Wales or in Northern Ireland.

862 Charges existing on property acquired

(1) This section applies where a company acquires property which is subject to a charge of a kind which would, if it had been created by the company after the acquisition of the property, have been required to be registered under this Chapter.

(2) The company must deliver the prescribed particulars of the charge, together with a certified copy of the instrument (if any) by which the charge is created or evidenced, to the registrar for registration.

(3) Subsection (2) must be complied with before the end of the period allowed for registration.

(4) If default is made in complying with this section, an offence is committed by –

   (a) the company, and
   (b) every officer of it who is in default.

(5) A person guilty of an offence under this section is liable –

   (a) on conviction on indictment, to a fine;
   (b) on summary conviction, to a fine not exceeding the statutory maximum.

Special rules about debentures

863 Charge in series of debentures

(1) Where a series of debentures containing, or giving by reference to another instrument, any charge to the benefit of which debenture holders of that series are entitled *pari passu* is created by a company, it is for the purposes of section 860(1) sufficient if the required particulars, together with the deed containing the charge (or, if there is no such deed, one of the debentures of the series), are delivered to the registrar before the end of the period allowed for registration.

(2) The following are the required particulars –

   (a) the total amount secured by the whole series, and
   (b) the dates of the resolutions authorising the issue of the series and the date of the covering deed (if any) by which the series is created or defined, and
   (c) a general description of the property charged, and
   (d) the names of the trustees (if any) for the debenture holders.

(3) Particulars of the date and amount of each issue of debentures of a series of the kind mentioned in subsection (1) must be sent to the registrar for entry in the register of charges.

(4) Failure to comply with subsection (3) does not affect the validity of the debentures issued.

(5) Subsections (2) to (6) of section 860 apply for the purposes of this section as they apply for the purposes of that section, but as if references to the registration of a charge were references to the registration of a series of debentures.

864 Additional registration requirement for commission etc in relation to debentures

(1) Where any commission, allowance or discount has been paid or made either directly or indirectly by a company to a person in consideration of his –

   (a) subscribing or agreeing to subscribe, whether absolutely or conditionally, for debentures in a company, or

(b) procuring or agreeing to procure subscriptions, whether absolute or conditional, for such debentures,

the particulars required to be sent for registration under section 860 shall include particulars as to the amount or rate per cent. of the commission, discount or allowance so paid or made.

(2) The deposit of debentures as security for a debt of the company is not, for the purposes of this section, treated as the issue of debentures at a discount.

(3) Failure to comply with this section does not affect the validity of the debentures issued.

865 Endorsement of certificate on debentures

(1) The company shall cause a copy of every certificate of registration given under section 869 to be endorsed on every debenture or certificate of debenture stock which is issued by the company, and the payment of which is secured by the charge so registered.

(2) But this does not require a company to cause a certificate of registration of any charge so given to be endorsed on any debenture or certificate of debenture stock issued by the company before the charge was created.

(3) If a person knowingly and wilfully authorises or permits the delivery of a debenture or certificate of debenture stock which under this section is required to have endorsed on it a copy of a certificate of registration, without the copy being so endorsed upon it, he commits an offence.

(4) A person guilty of an offence under this section is liable on summary conviction to a fine not exceeding level 3 on the standard scale.

Charges in other jurisdictions

866 Charges created in, or over property in, jurisdictions outside the United Kingdom

(1) Where a charge is created outside the United Kingdom comprising property situated outside the United Kingdom, the delivery to the registrar of a verified copy of the instrument by which the charge is created or evidenced has the same effect for the purposes of this Chapter as the delivery of the instrument itself.

(2) Where a charge is created in the United Kingdom but comprises property outside the United Kingdom, the instrument creating or purporting to create the charge may be sent for registration under section 860 even if further proceedings may be necessary to make the charge valid or effectual according to the law of the country in which the property is situated.

867 Charges created in, or over property in, another United Kingdom jurisdiction

(1) Subsection (2) applies where –

(a) a charge comprises property situated in a part of the United Kingdom other than the part in which the company is registered, and

(b) registration in that other part is necessary to make the charge valid or effectual under the law of that part of the United Kingdom.

(2) The delivery to the registrar of a verified copy of the instrument by which the charge is created or evidenced, together with a certificate stating that the charge was presented for registration in that other part of the United Kingdom on the date on which it was so presented has, for the purposes of this Chapter, the same effect as the delivery of the instrument itself.

Orders charging land: Northern Ireland

868 Northern Ireland: registration of certain charges etc. affecting land

(1) Where a charge imposed by an order under Article 46 of the 1981 Order or notice of such a charge is registered in the Land Registry against registered land or any estate in registered land of a company, the Registrar of Titles shall as soon as may be cause two copies of the order made under Article 46 of that Order or of any notice under Article 48 of that Order to be delivered to the registrar.

(2) Where a charge imposed by an order under Article 46 of the 1981 Order is registered in the Registry of Deeds against any unregistered land or estate in land of a company, the Registrar of Deeds shall as soon as may be cause two copies of the order to be delivered to the registrar.

(3) On delivery of copies under this section, the registrar shall –

    (a) register one of them in accordance with section 869, and

    (b) not later than 7 days from that date of delivery, cause the other copy together with a certificate of registration under section 869(5) to be sent to the company against which judgment was given.

(4) Where a charge to which subsection (1) or (2) applies is vacated, the Registrar of Titles or, as the case may be, the Registrar of Deeds shall cause a certified copy of the certificate of satisfaction lodged under Article 132(1) of the 1981 Order to be delivered to the registrar for entry of a memorandum of satisfaction in accordance with section 872.

(5) In this section –

    "the 1981 Order" means the Judgments Enforcement (Northern Ireland) Order 1981 (S.I. 1981/226 (N.I. 6));

    "the Registrar of Deeds" means the registrar appointed under the Registration of Deeds Act (Northern Ireland) 1970 (c. 25);

    "Registry of Deeds" has the same meaning as in the Registration of Deeds Acts;

    "Registration of Deeds Acts" means the Registration of Deeds Act (Northern Ireland) 1970 and every statutory provision for the time being in force amending that Act or otherwise relating to the registry of deeds, or the registration of deeds, orders or other instruments or documents in such registry;

    "the Land Registry" and "the Registrar of Titles" are to be construed in accordance with section 1 of the Land Registration Act (Northern Ireland) 1970 (c. 18);

    "registered land" and "unregistered land" have the same meaning as in Part 3 of the Land Registration Act (Northern Ireland) 1970.

The register of charges

869 Register of charges to be kept by registrar

(1) The registrar shall keep, with respect to each company, a register of all the charges requiring registration under this Chapter.

(2) In the case of a charge to the benefit of which holders of a series of debentures are entitled, the registrar shall enter in the register the required particulars specified in section 863(2).

(3) In the case of a charge imposed by the Enforcement of Judgments Office under Article 46 of the Judgments Enforcement (Northern Ireland) Order 1981, the registrar shall enter in the register the date on which the charge became effective.

(4) In the case of any other charge, the registrar shall enter in the register the following particulars –

    (a) if it is a charge created by a company, the date of its creation and, if it is a charge which was existing on property acquired by the company, the date of the acquisition,

(b) the amount secured by the charge,

(c) short particulars of the property charged, and

(d) the persons entitled to the charge.

(5) The registrar shall give a certificate of the registration of any charge registered in pursuance of this Chapter, stating the amount secured by the charge.

(6) The certificate –

(a) shall be signed by the registrar or authenticated by the registrar's official seal, and

(b) is conclusive evidence that the requirements of this Chapter as to registration have been satisfied.

(7) The register kept in pursuance of this section shall be open to inspection by any person.

870 The period allowed for registration

(1) The period allowed for registration of a charge created by a company is –

(a) 21 days beginning with the day after the day on which the charge is created, or

(b) if the charge is created outside the United Kingdom, 21 days beginning with the day after the day on which the instrument by which the charge is created or evidenced (or a copy of it) could, in due course of post (and if despatched with due diligence) have been received in the United Kingdom.

(2) The period allowed for registration of a charge to which property acquired by a company is subject is –

(a) 21 days beginning with the day after the day on which the acquisition is completed, or

(b) if the property is situated and the charge was created outside the United Kingdom, 21 days beginning with the day after the day on which the instrument by which the charge is created or evidenced (or a copy of it) could, in due course of post (and if despatched with due diligence) have been received in the United Kingdom.

(3) The period allowed for registration of particulars of a series of debentures as a result of section 863 is –

(a) if there is a deed containing the charge mentioned in section 863(1), 21 days beginning with the day after the day on which that deed is executed, or

(b) if there is no such deed, 21 days beginning with the day after the day on which the first debenture of the series is executed.

871 Registration of enforcement of security

(1) If a person obtains an order for the appointment of a receiver or manager of a company's property, or appoints such a receiver or manager under powers contained in an instrument, he shall within 7 days of the order or of the appointment under those powers, give notice of the fact to the registrar.

(2) Where a person appointed receiver or manager of a company's property under powers contained in an instrument ceases to act as such receiver or manager, he shall, on so ceasing, give the registrar notice to that effect.

(3) The registrar must enter a fact of which he is given notice under this section in the register of charges.

(4) A person who makes default in complying with the requirements of this section commits an offence.

(5) A person guilty of an offence under this section is liable on summary conviction to a fine not exceeding level 3 on the standard scale and, for continued contravention, a daily default fine not exceeding one-tenth of level 3 on the standard scale.

872 Entries of satisfaction and release

(1) Subsection (2) applies if a statement is delivered to the registrar verifying with respect to a registered charge –

  (a) that the debt for which the charge was given has been paid or satisfied in whole or in part, or

  (b) that part of the property or undertaking charged has been released from the charge or has ceased to form part of the company's property or undertaking.

(2) The registrar may enter on the register a memorandum of satisfaction in whole or in part, or of the fact part of the property or undertaking has been released from the charge or has ceased to form part of the company's property or undertaking (as the case may be).

(3) Where the registrar enters a memorandum of satisfaction in whole, the registrar shall if required send the company a copy of it.

873 Rectification of register of charges

(1) Subsection (2) applies if the court is satisfied –

  (a) that the failure to register a charge before the end of the period allowed for registration, or the omission or mis-statement of any particular with respect to any such charge or in a memorandum of satisfaction –

    (i) was accidental or due to inadvertence or to some other sufficient cause, or

    (ii) is not of a nature to prejudice the position of creditors or shareholders of the company, or

  (b) that on other grounds it is just and equitable to grant relief.

(2) The court may, on the application of the company or a person interested, and on such terms and conditions as seem to the court just and expedient, order that the period allowed for registration shall be extended or, as the case may be, that the omission or mis-statement shall be rectified.

Avoidance of certain charges

874 Consequence of failure to register charges created by a company

(1) If a company creates a charge to which section 860 applies, the charge is void (so far as any security on the company's property or undertaking is conferred by it) against –

  (a) a liquidator of the company,

  (b) an administrator of the company, and

  (c) a creditor of the company,

  unless that section is complied with.

(2) Subsection (1) is subject to the provisions of this Chapter.

(3) Subsection (1) is without prejudice to any contract or obligation for repayment of the money secured by the charge; and when a charge becomes void under this section, the money secured by it immediately becomes payable.

Companies' records and registers

875 Companies to keep copies of instruments creating charges

(1) A company must keep available for inspection a copy of every instrument creating a charge requiring registration under this Chapter, including any document delivered to the company under section 868(3)(b) (Northern Ireland: orders imposing charges affecting land).

(2) In the case of a series of uniform debentures, a copy of one of the debentures of the series is sufficient.

876 Company's register of charges

(1) Every limited company shall keep available for inspection a register of charges and enter in it –

    (a) all charges specifically affecting property of the company, and

    (b) all floating charges on the whole or part of the company's property or undertaking.

(2) The entry shall in each case give a short description of the property charged, the amount of the charge and, except in the cases of securities to bearer, the names of the persons entitled to it.

(3) If an officer of the company knowingly and wilfully authorises or permits the omission of an entry required to be made in pursuance of this section, he commits an offence.

(4) A person guilty of an offence under this section is liable –

    (a) on conviction on indictment, to a fine;

    (b) on summary conviction, to a fine not exceeding the statutory maximum.

877 Instruments creating charges and register of charges to be available for inspection

(1) This section applies to –

    (a) documents required to be kept available for inspection under section 875 (copies of instruments creating charges), and

    (b) a company's register of charges kept in pursuance of section 876.

(2) The documents and register must be kept available for inspection –

    (a) at the company's registered office, or

    (b) at a place specified in regulations under section 1136.

(3) The company must give notice to the registrar –

    (a) of the place at which the documents and register are kept available for inspection, and

    (b) of any change in that place,

unless they have at all times been kept at the company's registered office.

(4) The documents and register shall be open to the inspection –

    (a) of any creditor or member of the company without charge, and

    (b) of any other person on payment of such fee as may be prescribed.

(5) If default is made for 14 days in complying with subsection (3) or an inspection required under subsection (4) is refused, an offence is committed by –

    (a) the company, and

    (b) every officer of the company who is in default.

(6) A person guilty of an offence under this section is liable on summary conviction to a fine not exceeding level 3 on the standard scale and, for continued contravention, a daily default fine not exceeding one-tenth of level 3 on the standard scale.

(7) If an inspection required under subsection (4) is refused the court may by order compel an immediate inspection.

CHAPTER 2

COMPANIES REGISTERED IN SCOTLAND

Charges requiring registration

878 Charges created by a company

(1) A company that creates a charge to which this section applies must deliver the prescribed particulars of the charge, together with a copy certified as a correct copy of the instrument (if any) by which the charge is created or evidenced, to the registrar for registration before the end of the period allowed for registration.

(2) Registration of a charge to which this section applies may instead be effected on the application of a person interested in it.

(3) Where registration is effected on the application of some person other than the company, that person is entitled to recover from the company the amount of any fees properly paid by him to the registrar on the registration.

(4) If a company fails to comply with subsection (1), an offence is committed by –

    (a) the company, and

    (b) every officer of the company who is in default.

(5) A person guilty of an offence under this section is liable –

    (a) on conviction on indictment, to a fine;

    (b) on summary conviction, to a fine not exceeding the statutory maximum.

(6) Subsection (4) does not apply if registration of the charge has been effected on the application of some other person.

(7) This section applies to the following charges –

    (a) a charge on land or any interest in such land, other than a charge for any rent or other periodical sum payable in respect of the land,

    (b) a security over incorporeal moveable property of any of the following categories –

        (i) goodwill,

        (ii) a patent or a licence under a patent,

        (iii) a trademark,

        (iv) a copyright or a licence under a copyright,

        (v) a registered design or a licence in respect of such a design,

        (vi) a design right or a licence under a design right,

        (vii) the book debts (whether book debts of the company or assigned to it), and

        (viii) uncalled share capital of the company or calls made but not paid,

    (c) a security over a ship or aircraft or any share in a ship,

    (d) a floating charge.

879 Charges which have to be registered: supplementary

(1) A charge on land, for the purposes of section 878(7)(a), includes a charge created by a heritable security within the meaning of section 9(8) of the Conveyancing and Feudal Reform (Scotland) Act 1970 (c. 35).

(2) The holding of debentures entitling the holder to a charge on land is not, for the purposes of section 878(7)(a), deemed to be an interest in land.

(3) It is immaterial for the purposes of this Chapter where land subject to a charge is situated.

(4) The deposit by way of security of a negotiable instrument given to secure the payment of book debts is not, for the purposes of section 878(7)(b)(vii), to be treated as a charge on those book debts.

(5) References in this Chapter to the date of the creation of a charge are –

(a) in the case of a floating charge, the date on which the instrument creating the floating charge was executed by the company creating the charge, and

(b) in any other case, the date on which the right of the person entitled to the benefit of the charge was constituted as a real right.

(6) In this Chapter "company" means an incorporated company registered in Scotland.

880 Duty to register charges existing on property acquired

(1) Subsection (2) applies where a company acquires any property which is subject to a charge of any kind as would, if it had been created by the company after the acquisition of the property, have been required to be registered under this Chapter.

(2) The company must deliver the prescribed particulars of the charge, together with a copy (certified to be a correct copy) of the instrument (if any) by which the charge was created or is evidenced, to the registrar for registration before the end of the period allowed for registration.

(3) If default is made in complying with this section, an offence is committed by –

(a) the company, and

(b) every officer of it who is in default.

(4) A person guilty of an offence under this section is liable –

(a) on conviction on indictment, to a fine;

(b) on summary conviction, to a fine not exceeding the statutory maximum.

881 Charge by way of ex facie absolute disposition, etc

(1) For the avoidance of doubt, it is hereby declared that, in the case of a charge created by way of an ex facie absolute disposition or assignation qualified by a back letter or other agreement, or by a standard security qualified by an agreement, compliance with section 878(1) does not of itself render the charge unavailable as security for indebtedness incurred after the date of compliance.

(2) Where the amount secured by a charge so created is purported to be increased by a further back letter or agreement, a further charge is held to have been created by the ex facie absolute disposition or assignation or (as the case may be) by the standard security, as qualified by the further back letter or agreement.

(3) In that case, the provisions of this Chapter apply to the further charge as if –

(a) references in this Chapter (other than in this section) to a charge were references to the further charge, and

(b) references to the date of the creation of a charge were references to the date on which the further back letter or agreement was executed.

Special rules about debentures

882 Charge in series of debentures

(1) Where a series of debentures containing, or giving by reference to any other instrument, any charge to the benefit of which the debenture-holders of that series are entitled *pari passu*, is created by a company, it is sufficient for purposes of section 878 if the required particulars, together with a copy of the deed containing the charge (or, if there is no such deed, of one of the debentures of the series) are delivered to the registrar before the end of the period allowed for registration.

(2) The following are the required particulars –

(a) the total amount secured by the whole series,

(b) the dates of the resolutions authorising the issue of the series and the date of the covering deed (if any) by which the security is created or defined,

(c) a general description of the property charged,

(d) the names of the trustees (if any) for the debenture-holders, and

(e) in the case of a floating charge, a statement of any provisions of the charge and of any instrument relating to it which prohibit or restrict or regulate the power of the company to grant further securities ranking in priority to, or *pari passu* with, the floating charge, or which vary or otherwise regulate the order of ranking of the floating charge in relation to subsisting securities.

(3) Where more than one issue is made of debentures in the series, particulars of the date and amount of each issue of debentures of the series must be sent to the registrar for entry in the register of charges.

(4) Failure to comply with subsection (3) does not affect the validity of any of those debentures.

(5) Subsections (2) to (6) of section 878 apply for the purposes of this section as they apply for the purposes of that section but as if for the reference to the registration of the charge there was substituted a reference to the registration of the series of debentures.

883 Additional registration requirement for commission etc in relation to debentures

(1) Where any commission, allowance or discount has been paid or made either directly or indirectly by a company to a person in consideration of his –

(a) subscribing or agreeing to subscribe, whether absolutely or conditionally, for debentures in a company, or

(b) procuring or agreeing to procure subscriptions, whether absolute or conditional, for such debentures,

the particulars required to be sent for registration under section 878 shall include particulars as to the amount or rate per cent. of the commission, discount or allowance so paid or made.

(2) The deposit of debentures as security for a debt of the company is not, for the purposes of this section, treated as the issue of debentures at a discount.

(3) Failure to comply with this section does not affect the validity of the debentures issued.

Charges on property outside the United Kingdom

884 Charges on property outside United Kingdom

Where a charge is created in the United Kingdom but comprises property outside the United Kingdom, the copy of the instrument creating or purporting to create the charge may be sent for registration under section 878 even if further proceedings may be necessary to make the charge valid or effectual according to the law of the country in which the property is situated.

The register of charges

885 Register of charges to be kept by registrar

(1) The registrar shall keep, with respect to each company, a register of all the charges requiring registration under this Chapter.

(2) In the case of a charge to the benefit of which holders of a series of debentures are entitled, the registrar shall enter in the register the required particulars specified in section 882(2).

(3) In the case of any other charge, the registrar shall enter in the register the following particulars –

(a) if it is a charge created by a company, the date of its creation and, if it is a charge which was existing on property acquired by the company, the date of the acquisition,

(b) the amount secured by the charge,

(c) short particulars of the property charged,

(d) the persons entitled to the charge, and

(e) in the case of a floating charge, a statement of any of the provisions of the charge and of any instrument relating to it which prohibit or restrict or regulate the company's power to grant further securities ranking in priority to, or *pari passu* with, the floating charge, or which vary or otherwise regulate the order of ranking of the floating charge in relation to subsisting securities.

(4) The registrar shall give a certificate of the registration of any charge registered in pursuance of this Chapter, stating –

(a) the name of the company and the person first-named in the charge among those entitled to the benefit of the charge (or, in the case of a series of debentures, the name of the holder of the first such debenture issued), and

(b) the amount secured by the charge.

(5) The certificate –

(a) shall be signed by the registrar or authenticated by the registrar's official seal, and

(b) is conclusive evidence that the requirements of this Chapter as to registration have been satisfied.

(6) The register kept in pursuance of this section shall be open to inspection by any person.

886 The period allowed for registration

(1) The period allowed for registration of a charge created by a company is –

(a) 21 days beginning with the day after the day on which the charge is created, or

(b) if the charge is created outside the United Kingdom, 21 days beginning with the day after the day on which a copy of the instrument by which the charge is created or evidenced could, in due course of post (and if despatched with due diligence) have been received in the United Kingdom.

(2) The period allowed for registration of a charge to which property acquired by a company is subject is –

(a) 21 days beginning with the day after the day on which the transaction is settled, or

(b) if the property is situated and the charge was created outside the United Kingdom, 21 days beginning with the day after the day on which a copy of the instrument by which the charge is created or evidenced could, in due course of post (and if despatched with due diligence) have been received in the United Kingdom.

(3) The period allowed for registration of particulars of a series of debentures as a result of section 882 is –

(a) if there is a deed containing the charge mentioned in section 882(1), 21 days beginning with the day after the day on which that deed is executed, or

(b) if there is no such deed, 21 days beginning with the day after the day on which the first debenture of the series is executed.

887 Entries of satisfaction and relief

(1) Subsection (2) applies if a statement is delivered to the registrar verifying with respect to any registered charge –

(a) that the debt for which the charge was given has been paid or satisfied in whole or in part, or

(b) that part of the property charged has been released from the charge or has ceased to form part of the company's property.

(2) If the charge is a floating charge, the statement must be accompanied by either –

(a) a statement by the creditor entitled to the benefit of the charge, or a person authorised by him for the purpose, verifying that the statement mentioned in subsection (1) is correct, or

(b) a direction obtained from the court, on the ground that the statement by the creditor mentioned in paragraph (a) could not be readily obtained, dispensing with the need for that statement.

(3) The registrar may enter on the register a memorandum of satisfaction (in whole or in part) regarding the fact contained in the statement mentioned in subsection (1).

(4) Where the registrar enters a memorandum of satisfaction in whole, he shall, if required, furnish the company with a copy of the memorandum.

(5) Nothing in this section requires the company to submit particulars with respect to the entry in the register of a memorandum of satisfaction where the company, having created a floating charge over all or any part of its property, disposes of part of the property subject to the floating charge.

888 Rectification of register of charges

(1) Subsection (2) applies if the court is satisfied –

(a) that the failure to register a charge before the end of the period allowed for registration, or the omission or mis-statement of any particular with respect to any such charge or in a memorandum of satisfaction –

(i) was accidental or due to inadvertence or to some other sufficient cause, or

(ii) is not of a nature to prejudice the position of creditors or shareholders of the company, or

(b) that on other grounds it is just and equitable to grant relief.

(2) The court may, on the application of the company or a person interested, and on such terms and conditions as seem to the court just and expedient, order that the period allowed for registration shall be extended or, as the case may be, that the omission or mis-statement shall be rectified.

Avoidance of certain charges

889 Charges void unless registered

(1) If a company creates a charge to which section 878 applies, the charge is void (so far as any security on the company's property or any part of it is conferred by the charge) against –

(a) the liquidator of the company,

(b) an administrator of the company, and

(c) any creditor of the company

unless that section is complied with.

(2) Subsection (1) is without prejudice to any contract or obligation for repayment of the money secured by the charge; and when a charge becomes void under this section the money secured by it immediately becomes payable.

Companies' records and registers

890 Copies of instruments creating charges to be kept by company

(1) Every company shall cause a copy of every instrument creating a charge requiring registration under this Chapter to be kept available for inspection.

(2) In the case of a series of uniform debentures, a copy of one debenture of the series is sufficient.

891 Company's register of charges

(1) Every company shall keep available for inspection a register of charges and enter in it all charges specifically affecting property of the company, and all floating charges on any property of the company.

(2) There shall be given in each case a short description of the property charged, the amount of the charge and, except in the case of securities to bearer, the names of the persons entitled to it.

(3) If an officer of the company knowingly and wilfully authorises or permits the omission of an entry required to be made in pursuance of this section, he commits an offence.

(4) A person guilty of an offence under this section is liable –

  (a) on conviction on indictment, to a fine;
  (b) on summary conviction, to a fine not exceeding the statutory maximum.

892 Instruments creating charges and register of charges to be available for inspection

(1) This section applies to –

  (a) documents required to be kept available for inspection under section 890 (copies of instruments creating charges), and
  (b) a company's register of charges kept in pursuance of section 891.

(2) The documents and register must be kept available for inspection –

  (a) at the company's registered office, or
  (b) at a place specified in regulations under section 1136.

(3) The company must give notice to the registrar –

  (a) of the place at which the documents and register are kept available for inspection, and
  (b) of any change in that place,

  unless they have at all times been kept at the company's registered office.

(4) The documents and register shall be open to the inspection –

  (a) of any creditor or member of the company without charge, and
  (b) of any other person on payment of such fee as may be prescribed.

(5) If default is made for 14 days in complying with subsection (3) or an inspection required under subsection (4) is refused, an offence is committed by –

  (a) the company, and
  (b) every officer of the company who is in default.

(6) A person guilty of an offence under this section is liable on summary conviction to a fine not exceeding level 3 on the standard scale and, for continued contravention, a daily default fine not exceeding one-tenth of level 3 on the standard scale.

(7) If an inspection required under subsection (4) is refused the court may by order compel an immediate inspection.

CHAPTER 3

POWERS OF THE SECRETARY OF STATE

893 Power to make provision for effect of registration in special register

(1) In this section a "special register" means a register, other than the register of charges kept under this Part, in which a charge to which Chapter 1 or Chapter 2 applies is required or authorised to be registered.

(2) The Secretary of State may by order make provision for facilitating the making of information-sharing arrangements between the person responsible for maintaining a special register ("the responsible person") and the registrar that meet the requirement in subsection (4).

"Information-sharing arrangements" are arrangements to share and make use of information held by the registrar or by the responsible person.

(3) If the Secretary of State is satisfied that appropriate information-sharing arrangements have been made, he may by order provide that –

    (a) the registrar is authorised not to register a charge of a specified description under Chapter 1 or Chapter 2,

    (b) a charge of a specified description that is registered in the special register within a specified period is to be treated as if it had been registered (and certified by the registrar as registered) in accordance with the requirements of Chapter 1 or, as the case may be, Chapter 2, and

    (c) the other provisions of Chapter 1 or, as the case may be, Chapter 2 apply to a charge so treated with specified modifications.

(4) The information-sharing arrangements must ensure that persons inspecting the register of charges –

    (a) are made aware, in a manner appropriate to the inspection, of the existence of charges in the special register which are treated in accordance with provision so made, and

    (b) are able to obtain information from the special register about any such charge.

(5) An order under this section may –

    (a) modify any enactment or rule of law which would otherwise restrict or prevent the responsible person from entering into or giving effect to information-sharing arrangements,

    (b) authorise the responsible person to require information to be provided to him for the purposes of the arrangements,

    (c) make provision about –

        (i) the charging by the responsible person of fees in connection with the arrangements and the destination of such fees (including provision modifying any enactment which would otherwise apply in relation to fees payable to the responsible person), and

        (ii) the making of payments under the arrangements by the registrar to the responsible person,

    (d) require the registrar to make copies of the arrangements available to the public (in hard copy or electronic form).

(6) In this section "specified" means specified in an order under this section.

(7) A description of charge may be specified, in particular, by reference to one or more of the following –

    (a) the type of company by which it is created,

    (b) the form of charge which it is,

    (c) the description of assets over which it is granted,

(d) the length of the period between the date of its registration in the special register and the date of its creation.

(8) Provision may be made under this section relating to registers maintained under the law of a country or territory outside the United Kingdom.

(9) An order under this section is subject to negative resolution procedure.

894 General power to make amendments to this Part

(1) The Secretary of State may by regulations under this section –

    (a) amend this Part by altering, adding or repealing provisions,

    (b) make consequential amendments or repeals in this Act or any other enactment (whether passed or made before or after this Act).

(2) Regulations under this section are subject to affirmative resolution procedure.

PART 26

ARRANGEMENTS AND RECONSTRUCTIONS

Application of this Part

895 Application of this Part

(1) The provisions of this Part apply where a compromise or arrangement is proposed between a company and –

    (a) its creditors, or any class of them, or

    (b) its members, or any class of them.

(2) In this Part –

"arrangement" includes a reorganisation of the company's share capital by the consolidation of shares of different classes or by the division of shares into shares of different classes, or by both of those methods; and

"company" –

    (a) in section 900 (powers of court to facilitate reconstruction or amalgamation) means a company within the meaning of this Act, and

    (b) elsewhere in this Part means any company liable to be wound up under the Insolvency Act 1986 (c. 45) or the Insolvency (Northern Ireland) Order 1989 (S.I. 1989/2405 (N.I. 19)).

(3) The provisions of this Part have effect subject to Part 27 (mergers and divisions of public companies) where that Part applies (see sections 902 and 903).

Meeting of creditors or members

896 Court order for holding of meeting

(1) The court may, on an application under this section, order a meeting of the creditors or class of creditors, or of the members of the company or class of members (as the case may be), to be summoned in such manner as the court directs.

(2) An application under this section may be made by –

    (a) the company,

    (b) any creditor or member of the company, or

    (c) if the company is being wound up or an administration order is in force in relation to it, the liquidator or administrator.

897 Statement to be circulated or made available

(1) Where a meeting is summoned under section 896 –

    (a) every notice summoning the meeting that is sent to a creditor or member must be accompanied by a statement complying with this section, and

    (b) every notice summoning the meeting that is given by advertisement must either –

        (i)   include such a statement, or

        (ii) state where and how creditors or members entitled to attend the meeting may obtain copies of such a statement.

(2) The statement must –

    (a) explain the effect of the compromise or arrangement, and

    (b) in particular, state –

        (i)   any material interests of the directors of the company (whether as directors or as members or as creditors of the company or otherwise), and

        (ii) the effect on those interests of the compromise or arrangement, in so far as it is different from the effect on the like interests of other persons.

(3) Where the compromise or arrangement affects the rights of debenture holders of the company, the statement must give the like explanation as respects the trustees of any deed for securing the issue of the debentures as it is required to give as respects the company's directors.

(4) Where a notice given by advertisement states that copies of an explanatory statement can be obtained by creditors or members entitled to attend the meeting, every such creditor or member is entitled, on making application in the manner indicated by the notice, to be provided by the company with a copy of the statement free of charge.

(5) If a company makes default in complying with any requirement of this section, an offence is committed by –

    (a) the company, and

    (b) every officer of the company who is in default.

This is subject to subsection (7) below.

(6) For this purpose the following are treated as officers of the company –

    (a) a liquidator or administrator of the company, and

    (b) a trustee of a deed for securing the issue of debentures of the company.

(7) A person is not guilty of an offence under this section if he shows that the default was due to the refusal of a director or trustee for debenture holders to supply the necessary particulars of his interests.

(8) A person guilty of an offence under this section is liable –

    (a) on conviction on indictment, to a fine;

    (b) on summary conviction, to a fine not exceeding the statutory maximum.

898 Duty of directors and trustees to provide information

(1) It is the duty of –

    (a) any director of the company, and

    (b) any trustee for its debenture holders,

to give notice to the company of such matters relating to himself as may be necessary for the purposes of section 897 (explanatory statement to be circulated or made available).

(2) Any person who makes default in complying with this section commits an offence.

(3) A person guilty of an offence under this section is liable on summary conviction to a fine not exceeding level 3 on the standard scale.

Court sanction for compromise or arrangement

899 Court sanction for compromise or arrangement

(1) If a majority in number representing 75% in value of the creditors or class of creditors or members or class of members (as the case may be), present and voting either in person or by proxy at the meeting summoned under section 896, agree a compromise or arrangement, the court may, on an application under this section, sanction the compromise or arrangement.

(2) An application under this section may be made by –

   (a) the company,

   (b) any creditor or member of the company, or

   (c) if the company is being wound up or an administration order is in force in relation it, the liquidator or administrator.

(3) A compromise or agreement sanctioned by the court is binding on –

   (a) all creditors or the class of creditors or on the members or class of members (as the case may be), and

   (b) the company or, in the case of a company in the course of being wound up, the liquidator and contributories of the company.

(4) The court's order has no effect until a copy of it has been delivered to the registrar.

Reconstructions and amalgamations

900 Powers of court to facilitate reconstruction or amalgamation

(1) This section applies where application is made to the court under section 899 to sanction a compromise or arrangement and it is shown that –

   (a) the compromise or arrangement is proposed for the purposes of, or in connection with, a scheme for the reconstruction of any company or companies, or the amalgamation of any two or more companies, and

   (b) under the scheme the whole or any part of the undertaking or the property of any company concerned in the scheme ("a transferor company") is to be transferred to another company ("the transferee company").

(2) The court may, either by the order sanctioning the compromise or arrangement or by a subsequent order, make provision for all or any of the following matters –

   (a) the transfer to the transferee company of the whole or any part of the undertaking and of the property or liabilities of any transferor company;

   (b) the allotting or appropriation by the transferee company of any shares, debentures, policies or other like interests in that company which under the compromise or arrangement are to be allotted or appropriated by that company to or for any person;

   (c) the continuation by or against the transferee company of any legal proceedings pending by or against any transferor company;

   (d) the dissolution, without winding up, of any transferor company;

   (e) the provision to be made for any persons who, within such time and in such manner as the court directs, dissent from the compromise or arrangement;

   (f) such incidental, consequential and supplemental matters as are necessary to secure that the reconstruction or amalgamation is fully and effectively carried out.

(3) If an order under this section provides for the transfer of property or liabilities –

   (a) the property is by virtue of the order transferred to, and vests in, the transferee company, and

   (b) the liabilities are, by virtue of the order, transferred to and become liabilities of that company.

(4) The property (if the order so directs) vests freed from any charge that is by virtue of the compromise or arrangement to cease to have effect.

(5) In this section –

"property" includes property, rights and powers of every description; and "liabilities" includes duties.

(6) Every company in relation to which an order is made under this section must cause a copy of the order to be delivered to the registrar within seven days after its making.

(7) If default is made in complying with subsection (6) an offence is committed by –

(a) the company, and

(b) every officer of the company who is in default.

(8) A person guilty of an offence under subsection (7) is liable on summary conviction to a fine not exceeding level 3 on the standard scale and, for continued contravention, a daily default fine not exceeding one-tenth of level 3 on the standard scale.

Obligations of company with respect to articles etc

901 Obligations of company with respect to articles etc

(1) This section applies –

(a) to any order under section 899 (order sanctioning compromise or arrangement), and

(b) to any order under section 900 (order facilitating reconstruction or amalgamation) that alters the company's constitution.

(2) If the order amends –

(a) the company's articles, or

(b) any resolution or agreement to which Chapter 3 of Part 3 applies (resolution or agreement affecting a company's constitution),

the copy of the order delivered to the registrar by the company under section 899(4) or section 900(6) must be accompanied by a copy of the company's articles, or the resolution or agreement in question, as amended.

(3) Every copy of the company's articles issued by the company after the order is made must be accompanied by a copy of the order, unless the effect of the order has been incorporated into the articles by amendment.

(4) In this section –

(a) references to the effect of the order include the effect of the compromise or arrangement to which the order relates; and

(b) in the case of a company not having articles, references to its articles shall be read as references to the instrument constituting the company or defining its constitution.

(5) If a company makes default in complying with this section an offence is committed by –

(a) the company, and

(b) every officer of the company who is in default.

(6) A person guilty of an offence under this section is liable on summary conviction to a fine not exceeding level 3 on the standard scale.

PART 27

MERGERS AND DIVISIONS OF PUBLIC COMPANIES

CHAPTER 1

INTRODUCTORY

902 Application of this Part

(1) This Part applies where –

    (a) a compromise or arrangement is proposed between a public company and –

        (i) its creditors or any class of them, or
        (ii) its members or any class of them,

        for the purposes of, or in connection with, a scheme for the reconstruction of any company or companies or the amalgamation of any two or more companies,

    (b) the scheme involves –

        (i) a merger (as defined in section 904), or
        (ii) a division (as defined in section 919), and

    (c) the consideration for the transfer (or each of the transfers) envisaged is to be shares in the transferee company (or one or more of the transferee companies) receivable by members of the transferor company (or transferor companies), with or without any cash payment to members.

(2) In this Part –

    (a) a "new company" means a company formed for the purposes of, or in connection with, the scheme, and

    (b) an "existing company" means a company other than one formed for the purposes of, or in connection with, the scheme.

(3) This Part does not apply where the company in respect of which the compromise or arrangement is proposed is being wound up.

903 Relationship of this Part to Part 26

(1) The court must not sanction the compromise or arrangement under Part 26 (arrangements and reconstructions) unless the relevant requirements of this Part have been complied with.

(2) The requirements applicable to a merger are specified in sections 905 to 914.
Certain of those requirements, and certain general requirements of Part 26, are modified or excluded by the provisions of sections 915 to 918.

(3) The requirements applicable to a division are specified in sections 920 to 930.
Certain of those requirements, and certain general requirements of Part 26, are modified or excluded by the provisions of sections 931 to 934.

CHAPTER 2

MERGER

Introductory

904 Mergers and merging companies

(1) The scheme involves a merger where under the scheme –

   (a) the undertaking, property and liabilities of one or more public companies, including the company in respect of which the compromise or arrangement is proposed, are to be transferred to another existing public company (a "merger by absorption"), or

   (b) the undertaking, property and liabilities of two or more public companies, including the company in respect of which the compromise or arrangement is proposed, are to be transferred to a new company, whether or not a public company, (a "merger by formation of a new company").

(2) References in this Part to "the merging companies" are –

   (a) in relation to a merger by absorption, to the transferor and transferee companies;

   (b) in relation to a merger by formation of a new company, to the transferor companies.

Requirements applicable to merger

905 Draft terms of scheme (merger)

(1) A draft of the proposed terms of the scheme must be drawn up and adopted by the directors of the merging companies.

(2) The draft terms must give particulars of at least the following matters –

   (a) in respect of each transferor company and the transferee company –

      (i)   its name,
      (ii) the address of its registered office, and
      (iii) whether it is a company limited by shares or a company limited by guarantee and having a share capital;

   (b) the number of shares in the transferee company to be allotted to members of a transferor company for a given number of their shares (the "share exchange ratio") and the amount of any cash payment;

   (c) the terms relating to the allotment of shares in the transferee company;

   (d) the date from which the holding of shares in the transferee company will entitle the holders to participate in profits, and any special conditions affecting that entitlement;

   (e) the date from which the transactions of a transferor company are to be treated for accounting purposes as being those of the transferee company;

   (f) any rights or restrictions attaching to shares or other securities in the transferee company to be allotted under the scheme to the holders of shares or other securities in a transferor company to which any special rights or restrictions attach, or the measures proposed concerning them;

   (g) any amount of benefit paid or given or intended to be paid or given –

      (i)   to any of the experts referred to in section 909 (expert's report), or
      (ii) to any director of a merging company,

      and the consideration for the payment of benefit.

(3) The requirements in subsection (2)(b), (c) and (d) are subject to section 915 (circumstances in which certain particulars not required).

906 Publication of draft terms (merger)

(1) The directors of each of the merging companies must deliver a copy of the draft terms to the registrar.

(2) The registrar must publish in the Gazette notice of receipt by him from that company of a copy of the draft terms.

(3) That notice must be published at least one month before the date of any meeting of that company summoned for the purpose of approving the scheme.

907 Approval of members of merging companies

(1) The scheme must be approved by a majority in number, representing 75% in value, of each class of members of each of the merging companies, present and voting either in person or by proxy at a meeting.

(2) This requirement is subject to sections 916, 917 and 918 (circumstances in which meetings of members not required).

908 Directors' explanatory report (merger)

(1) The directors of each of the merging companies must draw up and adopt a report.

(2) The report must consist of –

    (a) the statement required by section 897 (statement explaining effect of compromise or arrangement), and

    (b) insofar as that statement does not deal with the following matters, a further statement –

        (i) setting out the legal and economic grounds for the draft terms, and in particular for the share exchange ratio, and

        (ii) specifying any special valuation difficulties.

(3) The requirement in this section is subject to section 915 (circumstances in which reports not required).

909 Expert's report (merger)

(1) An expert's report must be drawn up on behalf of each of the merging companies.

(2) The report required is a written report on the draft terms to the members of the company.

(3) The court may on the joint application of all the merging companies approve the appointment of a joint expert to draw up a single report on behalf of all those companies.

If no such appointment is made, there must be a separate expert's report to the members of each merging company drawn up by a separate expert appointed on behalf of that company.

(4) The expert must be a person who –

    (a) is eligible for appointment as a statutory auditor (see section 1212), and

    (b) meets the independence requirement in section 936.

(5) The expert's report must –

    (a) indicate the method or methods used to arrive at the share exchange ratio;

    (b) give an opinion as to whether the method or methods used are reasonable in all the circumstances of the case, indicate the values arrived at using each such method and (if there is more than one method) give an opinion on the relative importance attributed to such methods in arriving at the value decided on;

    (c) describe any special valuation difficulties that have arisen;

    (d) state whether in the expert's opinion the share exchange ratio is reasonable; and

    (e) in the case of a valuation made by a person other than himself (see section 935), state that it appeared to him reasonable to arrange for it to be so made or to accept a valuation so made.

(6) The expert (or each of them) has –

(a) the right of access to all such documents of all the merging companies, and
(b) the right to require from the companies' officers all such information, as he thinks necessary for the purposes of making his report.

(7) The requirement in this section is subject to section 915 (circumstances in which reports not required).

910 Supplementary accounting statement (merger)

(1) If the last annual accounts of any of the merging companies relate to a financial year ending more than seven months before the first meeting of the company summoned for the purposes of approving the scheme, the directors of that company must prepare a supplementary accounting statement.
(2) That statement must consist of –

(a) a balance sheet dealing with the state of affairs of the company as at a date not more than three months before the draft terms were adopted by the directors, and
(b) where the company would be required under section 399 to prepare group accounts if that date were the last day of a financial year, a consolidated balance sheet dealing with the state of affairs of the company and the undertakings that would be included in such a consolidation.

(3) The requirements of this Act (and where relevant Article 4 of the IAS Regulation) as to the balance sheet forming part of a company's annual accounts, and the matters to be included in notes to it, apply to the balance sheet required for an accounting state-ment under this section, with such modifications as are necessary by reason of its being prepared otherwise than as at the last day of a financial year.
(4) The provisions of section 414 as to the approval and signing of accounts apply to the balance sheet required for an accounting statement under this section.

911 Inspection of documents (merger)

(1) The members of each of the merging companies must be able, during the period specified below –

(a) to inspect at the registered office of that company copies of the documents listed below relating to that company and every other merging company, and
(b) to obtain copies of those documents or any part of them on request free of charge.

(2) The period referred to above is the period –

(a) beginning one month before, and
(b) ending on the date of,

the first meeting of the members, or any class of members, of the company for the purposes of approving the scheme.
(3) The documents referred to above are –

(a) the draft terms;
(b) the directors' explanatory report;
(c) the expert's report;
(d) the company's annual accounts and reports for the last three financial years end-ing on or before the first meeting of the members, or any class of members, of the company summoned for the purposes of approving the scheme; and
(e) any supplementary accounting statement required by section 910.

(4) The requirements of subsection (3)(b) and (c) are subject to section 915 (circum-stances in which reports not required).

912 Approval of articles of new transferee company (merger)

In the case of a merger by formation of a new company, the articles of the transferee company, or a draft of them, must be approved by ordinary resolution of the transferor company or, as the case may be, each of the transferor companies.

913 Protection of holders of securities to which special rights attached (merger)

(1) The scheme must provide that where any securities of a transferor company (other than shares) to which special rights are attached are held by a person otherwise than as a member or creditor of the company, that person is to receive rights in the transferee company of equivalent value.

(2) Subsection (1) does not apply if –

   (a) the holder has agreed otherwise, or
   (b) the holder is, or under the scheme is to be, entitled to have the securities purchased by the transferee company on terms that the court considers reasonable.

914 No allotment of shares to transferor company or its nominee (merger)

The scheme must not provide for shares in the transferee company to be allotted to a transferor company (or its nominee) in respect of shares in the transferor company held by it (or its nominee).

Exceptions where shares of transferor company held by transferee company

915 Circumstances in which certain particulars and reports not required (merger)

(1) This section applies in the case of a merger by absorption where all of the relevant securities of the transferor company (or, if there is more than one transferor company, of each of them) are held by or on behalf of the transferee company.

(2) The draft terms of the scheme need not give the particulars mentioned in section 905(2)(b), (c) or (d) (particulars relating to allotment of shares to members of transferor company).

(3) Section 897 (explanatory statement to be circulated or made available) does not apply.

(4) The requirements of the following sections do not apply –

   section 908 (directors' explanatory report),
   section 909 (expert's report).

(5) The requirements of section 911 (inspection of documents) so far as relating to any document required to be drawn up under the provisions mentioned in subsection (3) above do not apply.

(6) In this section "relevant securities", in relation to a company, means shares or other securities carrying the right to vote at general meetings of the company.

916 Circumstances in which meeting of members of transferee company not required (merger)

(1) This section applies in the case of a merger by absorption where 90% or more (but not all) of the relevant securities of the transferor company (or, if there is more than one transferor company, of each of them) are held by or on behalf of the transferee company.

(2) It is not necessary for the scheme to be approved at a meeting of the members, or any class of members, of the transferee company if the court is satisfied that the following conditions have been complied with.

(3) The first condition is that publication of notice of receipt of the draft terms by the registrar took place in respect of the transferee company at least one month before the date of the first meeting of members, or any class of members, of the transferor company summoned for the purpose of agreeing to the scheme.

(4) The second condition is that the members of the transferee company were able during the period beginning one month before, and ending on, that date –

    (a) to inspect at the registered office of the transferee company copies of the documents listed in section 911(3)(a), (d) and (e) relating to that company and the transferor company (or, if there is more than one transferor company, each of them), and

    (b) to obtain copies of those documents or any part of them on request free of charge.

(5) The third condition is that –

    (a) one or more members of the transferee company, who together held not less than 5% of the paid-up capital of the company which carried the right to vote at general meetings of the company (excluding any shares in the company held as treasury shares) would have been able, during that period, to require a meeting of each class of members to be called for the purpose of deciding whether or not to agree to the scheme, and

    (b) no such requirement was made.

(6) In this section "relevant securities", in relation to a company, means shares or other securities carrying the right to vote at general meetings of the company.

917 Circumstances in which no meetings required (merger)

(1) This section applies in the case of a merger by absorption where all of the relevant securities of the transferor company (or, if there is more than one transferor company, of each of them) are held by or on behalf of the transferee company.

(2) It is not necessary for the scheme to be approved at a meeting of the members, or any class of members, of any of the merging companies if the court is satisfied that the following conditions have been complied with.

(3) The first condition is that publication of notice of receipt of the draft terms by the registrar took place in respect of all the merging companies at least one month before the date of the court's order.

(4) The second condition is that the members of the transferee company were able during the period beginning one month before, and ending on, that date –

    (a) to inspect at the registered office of that company copies of the documents listed in section 911(3) relating to that company and the transferor company (or, if there is more than one transferor company, each of them), and

    (b) to obtain copies of those documents or any part of them on request free of charge.

(5) The third condition is that –

    (a) one or more members of the transferee company, who together held not less than 5% of the paid-up capital of the company which carried the right to vote at general meetings of the company (excluding any shares in the company held as treasury shares) would have been able, during that period, to require a meeting of each class of members to be called for the purpose of deciding whether or not to agree to the scheme, and

    (b) no such requirement was made.

(6) In this section "relevant securities", in relation to a company, means shares or other securities carrying the right to vote at general meetings of the company.

Other exceptions

918 Other circumstances in which meeting of members of transferee company not required (merger)

(1) In the case of any merger by absorption, it is not necessary for the scheme to be approved by the members of the transferee company if the court is satisfied that the following conditions have been complied with.

(2) The first condition is that publication of notice of receipt of the draft terms by the registrar took place in respect of that company at least one month before the date of the first meeting of members, or any class of members, of the transferor company (or, if there is more than one transferor company, any of them) summoned for the purposes of agreeing to the scheme.

(3) The second condition is that the members of that company were able during the period beginning one month before, and ending on, the date of any such meeting –

   (a) to inspect at the registered office of that company copies of the documents specified in section 911(3) relating to that company and the transferor company (or, if there is more than one transferor company, each of them), and

   (b) to obtain copies of those documents or any part of them on request free of charge.

(4) The third condition is that –

   (a) one or more members of that company, who together held not less than 5% of the paid-up capital of the company which carried the right to vote at general meetings of the company (excluding any shares in the company held as treasury shares) would have been able, during that period, to require a meeting of each class of members to be called for the purpose of deciding whether or not to agree to the scheme, and

   (b) no such requirement was made.

CHAPTER 3

DIVISION

Introductory

919 Divisions and companies involved in a division

(1) The scheme involves a division where under the scheme the undertaking, property and liabilities of the company in respect of which the compromise or arrangement is proposed are to be divided among and transferred to two or more companies each of which is either –

   (a) an existing public company, or

   (b) a new company (whether or not a public company).

(2) References in this Part to the companies involved in the division are to the transferor company and any existing transferee companies.

Requirements to be complied with in case of division

920 Draft terms of scheme (division)

(1) A draft of the proposed terms of the scheme must be drawn up and adopted by the directors of each of the companies involved in the division.

(2) The draft terms must give particulars of at least the following matters –

    (a) in respect of the transferor company and each transferee company –

        (i)   its name,
        (ii)   the address of its registered office, and
        (iii) whether it is a company limited by shares or a company limited by guarantee and having a share capital;

    (b) the number of shares in a transferee company to be allotted to members of the transferor company for a given number of their shares (the "share exchange ratio") and the amount of any cash payment;

    (c) the terms relating to the allotment of shares in a transferee company;

    (d) the date from which the holding of shares in a transferee company will entitle the holders to participate in profits, and any special conditions affecting that entitlement;

    (e) the date from which the transactions of the transferor company are to be treated for accounting purposes as being those of a transferee company;

    (f) any rights or restrictions attaching to shares or other securities in a transferee company to be allotted under the scheme to the holders of shares or other securities in the transferor company to which any special rights or restrictions attach, or the measures proposed concerning them;

    (g) any amount of benefit paid or given or intended to be paid or given –

        (i)   to any of the experts referred to in section 924 (expert's report), or
        (ii)   to any director of a company involved in the division,

    and the consideration for the payment of benefit.

(3) The draft terms must also –

    (a) give particulars of the property and liabilities to be transferred (to the extent that these are known to the transferor company) and their allocation among the transferee companies;

    (b) make provision for the allocation among and transfer to the transferee companies of any other property and liabilities that the transferor company has acquired or may subsequently acquire; and

    (c) specify the allocation to members of the transferor company of shares in the transferee companies and the criteria upon which that allocation is based.

921 Publication of draft terms (division)

(1) The directors of each company involved in the division must deliver a copy of the draft terms to the registrar.

(2) The registrar must publish in the Gazette notice of receipt by him from that company of a copy of the draft terms.

(3) That notice must be published at least one month before the date of any meeting of that company summoned for the purposes of approving the scheme.

(4) The requirements in this section are subject to section 934 (power of court to exclude certain requirements).

922 Approval of members of companies involved in the division

(1) The compromise or arrangement must be approved by a majority in number, representing 75% in value, of each class of members of each of the companies involved in the division, present and voting either in person or by proxy at a meeting.

(2) This requirement is subject to sections 931 and 932 (circumstances in which meeting of members not required).

923 Directors' explanatory report (division)

(1) The directors of the transferor and each existing transferee company must draw up and adopt a report.

(2) The report must consist of –

(a) the statement required by section 897 (statement explaining effect of compromise or arrangement), and

(b) insofar as that statement does not deal with the following matters, a further statement –

    (i) setting out the legal and economic grounds for the draft terms, and in particular for the share exchange ratio and for the criteria on which the allocation to the members of the transferor company of shares in the transferee companies was based, and

    (ii) specifying any special valuation difficulties.

(3) The report must also state –

(a) whether a report has been made to any transferee company under section 593 (valuation of non-cash consideration for shares), and

(b) if so, whether that report has been delivered to the registrar of companies.

(4) The requirement in this section is subject to section 933 (agreement to dispense with reports etc).

924 Expert's report (division)

(1) An expert's report must be drawn up on behalf of each company involved in the division.

(2) The report required is a written report on the draft terms to the members of the company.

(3) The court may on the joint application of the companies involved in the division approve the appointment of a joint expert to draw up a single report on behalf of all those companies.

If no such appointment is made, there must be a separate expert's report to the members of each company involved in the division drawn up by a separate expert appointed on behalf of that company.

(4) The expert must be a person who –

(a) is eligible for appointment as a statutory auditor (see section 1212), and

(b) meets the independence requirement in section 936.

(5) The expert's report must –

(a) indicate the method or methods used to arrive at the share exchange ratio;

(b) give an opinion as to whether the method or methods used are reasonable in all the circumstances of the case, indicate the values arrived at using each such method and (if there is more than one method) give an opinion on the relative importance attributed to such methods in arriving at the value decided on;

(c) describe any special valuation difficulties that have arisen;

(d) state whether in the expert's opinion the share exchange ratio is reasonable; and

(e) in the case of a valuation made by a person other than himself (see section 935), state that it appeared to him reasonable to arrange for it to be so made or to accept a valuation so made.

(6) The expert (or each of them) has –

(a) the right of access to all such documents of the companies involved in the division, and

(b) the right to require from the companies' officers all such information,

as he thinks necessary for the purposes of making his report.

(7) The requirement in this section is subject to section 933 (agreement to dispense with reports etc).

925 Supplementary accounting statement (division)

(1) If the last annual accounts of a company involved in the division relate to a financial year ending more than seven months before the first meeting of the company

summoned for the purposes of approving the scheme, the directors of that company must prepare a supplementary accounting statement.

(2) That statement must consist of –

(a) a balance sheet dealing with the state of affairs of the company as at a date not more than three months before the draft terms were adopted by the directors, and

(b) where the company would be required under section 399 to prepare group accounts if that date were the last day of a financial year, a consolidated balance sheet dealing with the state of affairs of the company and the undertakings that would be included in such a consolidation.

(3) The requirements of this Act (and where relevant Article 4 of the IAS Regulation) as to the balance sheet forming part of a company's annual accounts, and the matters to be included in notes to it, apply to the balance sheet required for an accounting statement under this section, with such modifications as are necessary by reason of its being prepared otherwise than as at the last day of a financial year.

(4) The provisions of section 414 as to the approval and signing of accounts apply to the balance sheet required for an accounting statement under this section.

(5) The requirement in this section is subject to section 933 (agreement to dispense with reports etc).

926 Inspection of documents (division)

(1) The members of each company involved in the division must be able, during the period specified below –

(a) to inspect at the registered office of that company copies of the documents listed below relating to that company and every other company involved in the division, and

(b) to obtain copies of those documents or any part of them on request free of charge.

(2) The period referred to above is the period –

(a) beginning one month before, and

(b) ending on the date of,

the first meeting of the members, or any class of members, of the company for the purposes of approving the scheme.

(3) The documents referred to above are –

(a) the draft terms;

(b) the directors' explanatory report;

(c) the expert's report;

(d) the company's annual accounts and reports for the last three financial years ending on or before the first meeting of the members, or any class of members, of the company summoned for the purposes of approving the scheme; and

(e) any supplementary accounting statement required by section 925.

(4) The requirements in subsection (3)(b), (c) and (e) are subject to section 933 (agreement to dispense with reports etc) and section 934 (power of court to exclude certain requirements).

927 Report on material changes of assets of transferor company (division)

(1) The directors of the transferor company must report –

(a) to every meeting of the members, or any class of members, of that company summoned for the purpose of agreeing to the scheme, and

(b) to the directors of each existing transferee company,

any material changes in the property and liabilities of the transferor company between the date when the draft terms were adopted and the date of the meeting in question.

(2) The directors of each existing transferee company must in turn –

    (a) report those matters to every meeting of the members, or any class of members, of that company summoned for the purpose of agreeing to the scheme, or

    (b) send a report of those matters to every member entitled to receive notice of such a meeting.

(3) The requirement in this section is subject to section 933 (agreement to dispense with reports etc).

928 Approval of articles of new transferee company (division)

The articles of every new transferee company, or a draft of them, must be approved by ordinary resolution of the transferor company.

929 Protection of holders of securities to which special rights attached (division)

(1) The scheme must provide that where any securities of the transferor company (other than shares) to which special rights are attached are held by a person otherwise than as a member or creditor of the company, that person is to receive rights in a transferee company of equivalent value.

(2) Subsection (1) does not apply if –

    (a) the holder has agreed otherwise, or

    (b) the holder is, or under the scheme is to be, entitled to have the securities purchased by a transferee company on terms that the court considers reasonable.

930 No allotment of shares to transferor company or its nominee (division)

The scheme must not provide for shares in a transferee company to be allotted to the transferor company (or its nominee) in respect of shares in the transferor company held by it (or its nominee).

Exceptions where shares of transferor company held by transferee company

931 Circumstances in which meeting of members of transferor company not required (division)

(1) This section applies in the case of a division where all of the shares or other securities of the transferor company carrying the right to vote at general meetings of the company are held by or on behalf of one or more existing transferee companies.

(2) It is not necessary for the scheme to be approved by a meeting of the members, or any class of members, of the transferor company if the court is satisfied that the following conditions have been complied with.

(3) The first condition is that publication of notice of receipt of the draft terms by the registrar took place in respect of all the companies involved in the division at least one month before the date of the court's order.

(4) The second condition is that the members of every company involved in the division were able during the period beginning one month before, and ending on, that date –

    (a) to inspect at the registered office of their company copies of the documents listed in section 926(3) relating to every company involved in the division, and

    (b) to obtain copies of those documents or any part of them on request free of charge.

(5) The third condition is that –

    (a) one or more members of the transferor company, who together held not less than 5% of the paid-up capital of the company (excluding any shares in the company held as treasury shares) would have been able, during that period, to require a meeting of each class of members to be called for the purpose of deciding whether or not to agree to the scheme, and

    (b)   no such requirement was made.

(6) The fourth condition is that the directors of the transferor company have sent –

    (a)   to every member who would have been entitled to receive notice of a meeting to agree to the scheme (had any such meeting been called), and

    (b)   to the directors of every existing transferee company,

a report of any material change in the property and liabilities of the transferor company between the date when the terms were adopted by the directors and the date one month before the date of the court's order.

Other exceptions

932 Circumstances in which meeting of members of transferee company not required (division)

(1) In the case of a division, it is not necessary for the scheme to be approved by the members of a transferee company if the court is satisfied that the following conditions have been complied with in relation to that company.

(2) The first condition is that publication of notice of receipt of the draft terms by the registrar took place in respect of that company at least one month before the date of the first meeting of members of the transferor company summoned for the purposes of agreeing to the scheme.

(3) The second condition is that the members of that company were able during the period beginning one month before, and ending on, that date –

    (a)   to inspect at the registered office of that company copies of the documents specified in section 926(3) relating to that company and every other company involved in the division, and

    (b)   to obtain copies of those documents or any part of them on request free of charge.

(4) The third condition is that –

    (a)   one or more members of that company, who together held not less than 5% of the paid-up capital of the company which carried the right to vote at general meetings of the company (excluding any shares in the company held as treasury shares) would have been able, during that period, to require a meeting of each class of members to be called for the purpose of deciding whether or not to agree to the scheme, and

    (b)   no such requirement was made.

(5) The first and second conditions above are subject to section 934 (power of court to exclude certain requirements).

933 Agreement to dispense with reports etc (division)

(1) If all members holding shares in, and all persons holding other securities of, the companies involved in the division, being shares or securities that carry a right to vote in general meetings of the company in question, so agree, the following requirements do not apply.

(2) The requirements that may be dispensed with under this section are –

    (a)   the requirements of –

        (i)   section 923 (directors' explanatory report),

        (ii)   section 924 (expert's report),

        (iii) section 925 (supplementary accounting statement), and

      (iv)   section 927 (report on material changes in assets of transferor company); and

    (b) the requirements of section 926 (inspection of documents) so far as relating to any document required to be drawn up under the provisions mentioned in paragraph (a)(i), (ii) or (iii) above.

(3) For the purposes of this section –

    (a) the members, or holders of other securities, of a company, and

    (b) whether shares or other securities carry a right to vote in general meetings of the company,

are determined as at the date of the application to the court under section 896.

934 Power of court to exclude certain requirements (division)

(1) In the case of a division, the court may by order direct that –

    (a) in relation to any company involved in the division, the requirements of –

       (i)   section 921 (publication of draft terms), and

      (ii) section 926 (inspection of documents),

    do not apply, and

    (b) in relation to an existing transferee company, section 932 (circumstances in which meeting of members of transferee company not required) has effect with the omission of the first and second conditions specified in that section,

if the court is satisfied that the following conditions will be fulfilled in relation to that company.

(2) The first condition is that the members of that company will have received, or will have been able to obtain free of charge, copies of the documents listed in section 926 –

    (a) in time to examine them before the date of the first meeting of the members, or any class of members, of that company summoned for the purposes of agreeing to the scheme, or

    (b) in the case of an existing transferee company where in the circumstances described in section 932 no meeting is held, in time to require a meeting as mentioned in subsection (4) of that section.

(3) The second condition is that the creditors of that company will have received or will have been able to obtain free of charge copies of the draft terms in time to examine them –

    (a) before the date of the first meeting of the members, or any class of members, of the company summoned for the purposes of agreeing to the scheme, or

    (b) in the circumstances mentioned in subsection (2)(b) above, at the same time as the members of the company.

(4) The third condition is that no prejudice would be caused to the members or creditors of the transferor company or any transferee company by making the order in question.

CHAPTER 4

SUPPLEMENTARY PROVISIONS

Expert's report and related matters

935 Expert's report: valuation by another person

(1) Where it appears to an expert –

  (a) that a valuation is reasonably necessary to enable him to draw up his report, and
  (b) that it is reasonable for that valuation, or part of it, to be made by (or for him to accept a valuation made by) another person who –

    (i) appears to him to have the requisite knowledge and experience to make the valuation or that part of it, and
    (ii) meets the independence requirement in section 936,

  he may arrange for or accept such a valuation, together with a report which will enable him to make his own report under section 909 or 924.

(2) Where any valuation is made by a person other than the expert himself, the latter's report must state that fact and must also –

  (a) state the former's name and what knowledge and experience he has to carry out the valuation, and
  (b) describe so much of the undertaking, property and liabilities as was valued by the other person, and the method used to value them, and specify the date of the valuation.

936 Experts and valuers: independence requirement

(1) A person meets the independence requirement for the purposes of section 909 or 924 (expert's report) or section 935 (valuation by another person) only if –

  (a) he is not –

    (i) an officer or employee of any of the companies concerned in the scheme, or
    (ii) a partner or employee of such a person, or a partnership of which such a person is a partner;

  (b) he is not –

    (i) an officer or employee of an associated undertaking of any of the companies concerned in the scheme, or
    (ii) a partner or employee of such a person, or a partnership of which such a person is a partner; and

  (c) there does not exist between –

    (i) the person or an associate of his, and
    (ii) any of the companies concerned in the scheme or an associated undertaking of such a company,

  a connection of any such description as may be specified by regulations made by the Secretary of State.

(2) An auditor of a company is not regarded as an officer or employee of the company for this purpose.

(3) For the purposes of this section –

  (a) the "companies concerned in the scheme" means every transferor and existing transferee company;
  (b) "associated undertaking", in relation to a company, means –

    (i) a parent undertaking or subsidiary undertaking of the company, or

(ii)   a subsidiary undertaking of a parent undertaking of the company; and

(c) "associate" has the meaning given by section 937.

(4) Regulations under this section are subject to negative resolution procedure.

937 Experts and valuers: meaning of "associate"

(1) This section defines "associate" for the purposes of section 936 (experts and valuers: independence requirement).

(2) In relation to an individual, "associate" means –

(a)   that individual's spouse or civil partner or minor child or step-child,

(b)   any body corporate of which that individual is a director, and

(c)   any employee or partner of that individual.

(3) In relation to a body corporate, "associate" means –

(a)   any body corporate of which that body is a director,

(b)   any body corporate in the same group as that body, and

(c)   any employee or partner of that body or of any body corporate in the same group.

(4) In relation to a partnership that is a legal person under the law by which it is governed, "associate" means –

(a)   any body corporate of which that partnership is a director,

(b)   any employee of or partner in that partnership, and

(c)   any person who is an associate of a partner in that partnership.

(5) In relation to a partnership that is not a legal person under the law by which it is governed, "associate" means any person who is an associate of any of the partners.

(6) In this section, in relation to a limited liability partnership, for "director" read "member".

Powers of the court

938 Power of court to summon meeting of members or creditors of existing transferee company

(1) The court may order a meeting of –

(a)   the members of an existing transferee company, or any class of them, or

(b)   the creditors of an existing transferee company, or any class of them,

to be summoned in such manner as the court directs.

(2) An application for such an order may be made by –

(a)   the company concerned,

(b)   a member or creditor of the company, or

(c)   if an administration order is in force in relation to the company, the administrator.

939 Court to fix date for transfer of undertaking etc of transferor company

(1) Where the court sanctions the compromise or arrangement, it must –

(a)   in the order sanctioning the compromise or arrangement, or

(b)   in a subsequent order under section 900 (powers of court to facilitate reconstruction or amalgamation),

fix a date on which the transfer (or transfers) to the transferee company (or transferee companies) of the undertaking, property and liabilities of the transferor company is (or are) to take place.

(2) Any such order that provides for the dissolution of the transferor company must fix the same date for the dissolution.

(3) If it is necessary for the transferor company to take steps to ensure that the under-taking, property and liabilities are fully transferred, the court must fix a date, not later

than six months after the date fixed under subsection (1), by which such steps must be taken.

(4) In that case, the court may postpone the dissolution of the transferor company until that date.

(5) The court may postpone or further postpone the date fixed under subsection (3) if it is satisfied that the steps mentioned cannot be completed by the date (or latest date) fixed under that subsection.

Liability of transferee companies

940 Liability of transferee companies for each other's defaults

(1) In the case of a division, each transferee company is jointly and severally liable for any liability transferred to any other transferee company under the scheme to the extent that the other company has made default in satisfying that liability.
This is subject to the following provisions.

(2) If a majority in number representing 75% in value of the creditors or any class of creditors of the transferor company, present and voting either in person or by proxy at a meeting summoned for the purposes of agreeing to the scheme, so agree, subsection (1) does not apply in relation to the liabilities owed to the creditors or that class of creditors.

(3) A transferee company is not liable under this section for an amount greater than the net value transferred to it under the scheme.
The "net value transferred" is the value at the time of the transfer of the property transferred to it under the scheme less the amount at that date of the liabilities so transferred.

Interpretation

941 Meaning of "liabilities" and "property"

In this Part –

"liabilities" includes duties;
"property" includes property, rights and powers of every description.

PART 28

TAKEOVERS ETC

CHAPTER 1

THE TAKEOVER PANEL

The Panel and its rules

942 The Panel

(1) The body known as the Panel on Takeovers and Mergers ("the Panel") is to have the functions conferred on it by or under this Chapter.

(2) The Panel may do anything that it considers necessary or expedient for the purposes of, or in connection with, its functions.

(3) The Panel may make arrangements for any of its functions to be discharged by –

(a) a committee or sub-committee of the Panel, or

(b) an officer or member of staff of the Panel, or a person acting as such.

This is subject to section 943(4) and (5).

943 Rules

(1) The Panel must make rules giving effect to Articles 3.1, 4.2, 5, 6.1 to 6.3, 7 to 9 and 13 of the Takeovers Directive.

(2) Rules made by the Panel may also make other provision –

    (a) for or in connection with the regulation of –

        (i) takeover bids,

        (ii) merger transactions, and

        (iii) transactions (not falling within sub-paragraph (i) or (ii)) that have or may have, directly or indirectly, an effect on the ownership or control of companies;

    (b) for or in connection with the regulation of things done in consequence of, or otherwise in relation to, any such bid or transaction;

    (c) about cases where –

        (i) any such bid or transaction is, or has been, contemplated or apprehended, or

        (ii) an announcement is made denying that any such bid or transaction is intended.

(3) The provision that may be made under subsection (2) includes, in particular, provision for a matter that is, or is similar to, a matter provided for by the Panel in the City Code on Takeovers and Mergers as it had effect immediately before the passing of this Act.

(4) In relation to rules made by virtue of section 957 (fees and charges), functions under this section may be discharged either by the Panel itself or by a committee of the Panel (but not otherwise).

(5) In relation to rules of any other description, the Panel must discharge its functions under this section by a committee of the Panel.

(6) Section 1 (meaning of "company") does not apply for the purposes of this section.

(7) In this section "takeover bid" includes a takeover bid within the meaning of the Takeovers Directive.

(8) In this Chapter "the Takeovers Directive" means Directive 2004/25/EC of the European Parliament and of the Council.

(9) A reference to rules in the following provisions of this Chapter is to rules under this section.

944 Further provisions about rules

(1) Rules may –

    (a) make different provision for different purposes;

    (b) make provision subject to exceptions or exemptions;

    (c) contain incidental, supplemental, consequential or transitional provision;

    (d) authorise the Panel to dispense with or modify the application of rules in particular cases and by reference to any circumstances.

Rules made by virtue of paragraph (d) must require the Panel to give reasons for acting as mentioned in that paragraph.

(2) Rules must be made by an instrument in writing.

(3) Immediately after an instrument containing rules is made, the text must be made available to the public, with or without payment, in whatever way the Panel thinks appropriate.

(4) A person is not to be taken to have contravened a rule if he shows that at the time of the alleged contravention the text of the rule had not been made available as required by subsection (3).

(5) The production of a printed copy of an instrument purporting to be made by the Panel on which is endorsed a certificate signed by an officer of the Panel authorised by it for that purpose and stating –

(a) that the instrument was made by the Panel,

(b) that the copy is a true copy of the instrument, and

(c) that on a specified date the text of the instrument was made available to the public as required by subsection (3),

is evidence (or in Scotland sufficient evidence) of the facts stated in the certificate.

(6) A certificate purporting to be signed as mentioned in subsection (5) is to be treated as having been properly signed unless the contrary is shown.

(7) A person who wishes in any legal proceedings to rely on an instrument by which rules are made may require the Panel to endorse a copy of the instrument with a certificate of the kind mentioned in subsection (5).

945 Rulings

(1) The Panel may give rulings on the interpretation, application or effect of rules.

(2) To the extent and in the circumstances specified in rules, and subject to any review or appeal, a ruling has binding effect.

946 Directions

Rules may contain provision conferring power on the Panel to give any direction that appears to the Panel to be necessary in order –

(a) to restrain a person from acting (or continuing to act) in breach of rules;

(b) to restrain a person from doing (or continuing to do) a particular thing, pending determination of whether that or any other conduct of his is or would be a breach of rules;

(c) otherwise to secure compliance with rules.

Information

947 Power to require documents and information

(1) The Panel may by notice in writing require a person –

(a) to produce any documents that are specified or described in the notice;

(b) to provide, in the form and manner specified in the notice, such information as may be specified or described in the notice.

(2) A requirement under subsection (1) must be complied with –

(a) at a place specified in the notice, and

(b) before the end of such reasonable period as may be so specified.

(3) This section applies only to documents and information reasonably required in connection with the exercise by the Panel of its functions.

(4) The Panel may require –

(a) any document produced to be authenticated, or

(b) any information provided (whether in a document or otherwise) to be verified,

in such manner as it may reasonably require.

(5) The Panel may authorise a person to exercise any of its powers under this section.

(6) A person exercising a power by virtue of subsection (5) must, if required to do so, produce evidence of his authority to exercise the power.

(7) The production of a document in pursuance of this section does not affect any lien that a person has on the document.

(8) The Panel may take copies of or extracts from a document produced in pursuance of this section.

(9) A reference in this section to the production of a document includes a reference to the production of –

(a) a hard copy of information recorded otherwise than in hard copy form, or

(b) information in a form from which a hard copy can be readily obtained.

(10) A person is not required by this section to disclose documents or information in respect of which a claim to legal professional privilege (in Scotland, to confidentiality of communications) could be maintained in legal proceedings.

948 Restrictions on disclosure

(1) This section applies to information (in whatever form) –

(a) relating to the private affairs of an individual, or

(b) relating to any particular business,

that is provided to the Panel in connection with the exercise of its functions.

(2) No such information may, during the lifetime of the individual or so long as the business continues to be carried on, be disclosed without the consent of that individual or (as the case may be) the person for the time being carrying on that business.

(3) Subsection (2) does not apply to any disclosure of information that –

(a) is made for the purpose of facilitating the carrying out by the Panel of any of its functions,

(b) is made to a person specified in Part 1 of Schedule 2,

(c) is of a description specified in Part 2 of that Schedule, or

(d) is made in accordance with Part 3 of that Schedule.

(4) The Secretary of State may amend Schedule 2 by order subject to negative resolution procedure.

(5) An order under subsection (4) must not –

(a) amend Part 1 of Schedule 2 by specifying a person unless the person exercises functions of a public nature (whether or not he exercises any other function);

(b) amend Part 2 of Schedule 2 by adding or modifying a description of disclosure unless the purpose for which the disclosure is permitted is likely to facilitate the exercise of a function of a public nature;

(c) amend Part 3 of Schedule 2 so as to have the effect of permitting disclosures to be made to a body other than one that exercises functions of a public nature in a country or territory outside the United Kingdom.

(6) Subsection (2) does not apply to –

(a) the disclosure by an authority within subsection (7) of information disclosed to it by the Panel in reliance on subsection (3);

(b) the disclosure of such information by anyone who has obtained it directly or indirectly from an authority within subsection (7).

(7) The authorities within this subsection are –

(a) the Financial Services Authority;

(b) an authority designated as a supervisory authority for the purposes of Article 4.1 of the Takeovers Directive;

(c) any other person or body that exercises functions of a public nature, under legislation in an EEA State other than the United Kingdom, that are similar to the Panel's functions or those of the Financial Services Authority.

(8) This section does not prohibit the disclosure of information if the information is or has been available to the public from any other source.

(9) Nothing in this section authorises the making of a disclosure in contravention of the Data Protection Act 1998 (c. 29).

949 Offence of disclosure in contravention of section 948

(1) A person who discloses information in contravention of section 948 is guilty of an offence, unless –

    (a) he did not know, and had no reason to suspect, that the information had been provided as mentioned in section 948(1), or

    (b) he took all reasonable steps and exercised all due diligence to avoid the commission of the offence.

(2) A person guilty of an offence under this section is liable –

    (a) on conviction on indictment, to imprisonment for a term not exceeding two years or a fine (or both);

    (b) on summary conviction –

        (i) in England and Wales, to imprisonment for a term not exceeding twelve months or to a fine not exceeding the statutory maximum (or both);

        (ii) in Scotland or Northern Ireland, to imprisonment for a term not exceeding six months, or to a fine not exceeding the statutory maximum (or both).

(3) Where a company or other body corporate commits an offence under this section, an offence is also committed by every officer of the company or other body corporate who is in default.

Co-operation

950 Panel's duty of co-operation

(1) The Panel must take such steps as it considers appropriate to co-operate with –

    (a) the Financial Services Authority;

    (b) an authority designated as a supervisory authority for the purposes of Article 4.1 of the Takeovers Directive;

    (c) any other person or body that exercises functions of a public nature, under legislation in any country or territory outside the United Kingdom, that appear to the Panel to be similar to its own functions or those of the Financial Services Authority.

(2) Co-operation may include the sharing of information that the Panel is not prevented from disclosing.

Hearings and appeals

951 Hearings and appeals

(1) Rules must provide for a decision of the Panel to be subject to review by a committee of the Panel (the "Hearings Committee") at the instance of such persons affected by the decision as are specified in the rules.

(2) Rules may also confer other functions on the Hearings Committee.

(3) Rules must provide for there to be a right of appeal against a decision of the Hearings Committee to an independent tribunal (the "Takeover Appeal Board") in such circumstances and subject to such conditions as are specified in the rules.

(4) Rules may contain –

    (a) provision as to matters of procedure in relation to proceedings before the Hearings Committee (including provision imposing time limits);

    (b) provision about evidence in such proceedings;

(c) provision as to the powers of the Hearings Committee dealing with a matter referred to it;

(d) provision about enforcement of decisions of the Hearings Committee and the Takeover Appeal Board.

(5) Rules must contain provision –

(a) requiring the Panel, when acting in relation to any proceedings before the Hearings Committee or the Takeover Appeal Board, to do so by an officer or member of staff of the Panel (or a person acting as such);

(b) preventing a person who is or has been a member of the committee mentioned in section 943(5) from being a member of the Hearings Committee or the Takeover Appeal Board;

(c) preventing a person who is a member of the committee mentioned in section 943(5), of the Hearings Committee or of the Takeover Appeal Board from acting as mentioned in paragraph (a).

Contravention of rules etc

952 Sanctions

(1) Rules may contain provision conferring power on the Panel to impose sanctions on a person who has –

(a) acted in breach of rules, or

(b) failed to comply with a direction given by virtue of section 946.

(2) Subsection (3) applies where rules made by virtue of subsection (1) confer power on the Panel to impose a sanction of a kind not provided for by the City Code on Takeovers and Mergers as it had effect immediately before the passing of this Act.

(3) The Panel must prepare a statement (a "policy statement") of its policy with respect to –

(a) the imposition of the sanction in question, and

(b) where the sanction is in the nature of a financial penalty, the amount of the penalty that may be imposed.

An element of the policy must be that, in making a decision about any such matter, the Panel has regard to the factors mentioned in subsection (4).

(4) The factors are –

(a) the seriousness of the breach or failure in question in relation to the nature of the rule or direction contravened;

(b) the extent to which the breach or failure was deliberate or reckless;

(c) whether the person on whom the sanction is to be imposed is an individual.

(5) The Panel may at any time revise a policy statement.

(6) The Panel must prepare a draft of any proposed policy statement (or revised policy statement) and consult such persons about the draft as the Panel considers appropriate.

(7) The Panel must publish, in whatever way it considers appropriate, any policy statement (or revised policy statement) that it prepares.

(8) In exercising, or deciding whether to exercise, its power to impose a sanction within subsection (2) in the case of any particular breach or failure, the Panel must have regard to any relevant policy statement published and in force at the time when the breach or failure occurred.

953 Failure to comply with rules about bid documentation

(1) This section applies where a takeover bid is made for a company that has securities carrying voting rights admitted to trading on a regulated market in the United Kingdom.

(2) Where an offer document published in respect of the bid does not comply with offer document rules, an offence is committed by –

    (a) the person making the bid, and

    (b) where the person making the bid is a body of persons, any director, officer or member of that body who caused the document to be published.

(3) A person commits an offence under subsection (2) only if –

    (a) he knew that the offer document did not comply, or was reckless as to whether it complied, and

    (b) he failed to take all reasonable steps to secure that it did comply.

(4) Where a response document published in respect of the bid does not comply with response document rules, an offence is committed by any director or other officer of the company referred to in subsection (1) who –

    (a) knew that the response document did not comply, or was reckless as to whether it complied, and

    (b) failed to take all reasonable steps to secure that it did comply.

(5) Where an offence is committed under subsection (2)(b) or (4) by a company or other body corporate ("the relevant body") –

    (a) subsection (2)(b) has effect as if the reference to a director, officer or member of the person making the bid included a reference to a director, officer or member of the relevant body;

    (b) subsection (4) has effect as if the reference to a director or other officer of the company referred to in subsection (1) included a reference to a director, officer or member of the relevant body.

(6) A person guilty of an offence under this section is liable –

    (a) on conviction on indictment, to a fine;

    (b) on summary conviction, to a fine not exceeding the statutory maximum.

(7) Nothing in this section affects any power of the Panel in relation to the enforcement of its rules.

(8) Section 1 (meaning of "company") does not apply for the purposes of this section.

(9) In this section –

    "designated" means designated in rules;

    "offer document" means a document required to be published by rules giving effect to Article 6.2 of the Takeovers Directive;

    "offer document rules" means rules designated as rules that give effect to Article 6.3 of that Directive;

    "response document" means a document required to be published by rules giving effect to Article 9.5 of that Directive;

    "response document rules" means rules designated as rules that give effect to the first sentence of Article 9.5 of that Directive;

    "securities" means shares or debentures;

    "takeover bid" has the same meaning as in that Directive;

    "voting rights" means rights to vote at general meetings of the company in question, including rights that arise only in certain circumstances.

954 Compensation

(1) Rules may confer power on the Panel to order a person to pay such compensation as it thinks just and reasonable if he is in breach of a rule the effect of which is to require the payment of money.

(2) Rules made by virtue of this section may include provision for the payment of interest (including compound interest).

955 Enforcement by the court

(1) If, on the application of the Panel, the court is satisfied –

    (a) that there is a reasonable likelihood that a person will contravene a rule-based requirement, or

    (b) that a person has contravened a rule-based requirement or a disclosure requirement,

the court may make any order it thinks fit to secure compliance with the requirement.

(2) In subsection (1) "the court" means the High Court or, in Scotland, the Court of Session.

(3) Except as provided by subsection (1), no person –

    (a) has a right to seek an injunction, or

    (b) in Scotland, has title or interest to seek an interdict or an order for specific performance,

to prevent a person from contravening (or continuing to contravene) a rule based requirement or a disclosure requirement.

(4) In this section –

"contravene" includes fail to comply;

"disclosure requirement" means a requirement imposed under section 947;

"rule-based requirement" means a requirement imposed by or under rules.

956 No action for breach of statutory duty etc

(1) Contravention of a rule-based requirement or a disclosure requirement does not give rise to any right of action for breach of statutory duty.

(2) Contravention of a rule-based requirement does not make any transaction void or unenforceable or (subject to any provision made by rules) affect the validity of any other thing.

(3) In this section –

    (a) "contravention" includes failure to comply;

    (b) "disclosure requirement" and "rule-based requirement" have the same meaning as in section 955.

Funding

957 Fees and charges

(1) Rules may provide for fees or charges to be payable to the Panel for the purpose of meeting any part of its expenses.

(2) A reference in this section or section 958 to expenses of the Panel is to any expenses that have been or are to be incurred by the Panel in, or in connection with, the discharge of its functions, including in particular –

    (a) payments in respect of the expenses of the Takeover Appeal Board;

    (b) the cost of repaying the principal of, and of paying any interest on, any money borrowed by the Panel;

    (c) the cost of maintaining adequate reserves.

958 Levy

(1) For the purpose of meeting any part of the expenses of the Panel, the Secretary of State may by regulations provide for a levy to be payable to the Panel –

    (a) by specified persons or bodies, or persons or bodies of a specified description, or

    (b) on transactions, of a specified description, in securities on specified markets.

In this subsection "specified" means specified in the regulations.

(2) The power to specify (or to specify descriptions of) persons or bodies must be exercised in such a way that the levy is payable only by persons or bodies that appear to the Secretary of State –

    (a) to be capable of being directly affected by the exercise of any of the functions of the Panel, or

    (b) otherwise to have a substantial interest in the exercise of any of those functions.

(3) Regulations under this section may in particular –

    (a) specify the rate of the levy and the period in respect of which it is payable at that rate;

    (b) make provision as to the times when, and the manner in which, payments are to be made in respect of the levy.

(4) In determining the rate of the levy payable in respect of a particular period, the Secretary of State –

    (a) must take into account any other income received or expected by the Panel in respect of that period;

    (b) may take into account estimated as well as actual expenses of the Panel in respect of that period.

(5) The Panel must –

    (a) keep proper accounts in respect of any amounts of levy received by virtue of this section;

    (b) prepare, in relation to each period in respect of which any such amounts are received, a statement of account relating to those amounts in such form and manner as is specified in the regulations.

Those accounts must be audited, and the statement certified, by persons appointed by the Secretary of State.

(6) Regulations under this section –

    (a) are subject to affirmative resolution procedure if subsection (7) applies to them;

    (b) otherwise, are subject to negative resolution procedure.

(7) This subsection applies to –

    (a) the first regulations under this section;

    (b) any other regulations under this section that would result in a change in the persons or bodies by whom, or the transactions on which, the levy is payable.

(8) If a draft of an instrument containing regulations under this section would, apart from this subsection, be treated for the purposes of the Standing Orders of either House of Parliament as a hybrid instrument, it is to proceed in that House as if it were not such an instrument.

959 Recovery of fees, charges or levy

An amount payable by any person or body by virtue of section 957 or 958 is a debt due from that person or body to the Panel, and is recoverable accordingly.

Miscellaneous and supplementary

960 Panel as party to proceedings

The Panel is capable (despite being an unincorporated body) of –

    (a) bringing proceedings under this Chapter in its own name;

    (b) bringing or defending any other proceedings in its own name.

961 Exemption from liability in damages

(1) Neither the Panel, nor any person within subsection (2), is to be liable in damages for anything done (or omitted to be done) in, or in connection with, the discharge or purported discharge of the Panel's functions.

(2) A person is within this subsection if –

    (a) he is (or is acting as) a member, officer or member of staff of the Panel, or

    (b) he is a person authorised under section 947(5).

(3) Subsection (1) does not apply –

    (a) if the act or omission is shown to have been in bad faith, or

    (b) so as to prevent an award of damages in respect of the act or omission on the ground that it was unlawful as a result of section 6(1) of the Human Rights Act 1998 (c. 42) (acts of public authorities incompatible with Convention rights).

962 Privilege against self-incrimination

(1) A statement made by a person in response to –

    (a) a requirement under section 947(1), or

    (b) an order made by the court under section 955 to secure compliance with such a requirement,

may not be used against him in criminal proceedings in which he is charged with an offence to which this subsection applies.

(2) Subsection (1) applies to any offence other than an offence under one of the following provisions (which concern false statements made otherwise than on oath) –

    (a) section 5 of the Perjury Act 1911 (c. 6);

    (b) section 44(2) of the Criminal Law (Consolidation) (Scotland) Act 1995 (c. 39);

    (c) Article 10 of the Perjury (Northern Ireland) Order 1979 (S.I. 1979/1714 (N.I. 19)).

963 Annual reports

(1) After the end of each financial year the Panel must publish a report.

(2) The report must –

    (a) set out how the Panel's functions were discharged in the year in question;

    (b) include the Panel's accounts for that year;

    (c) mention any matters the Panel considers to be of relevance to the discharge of its functions.

964 Amendments to Financial Services and Markets Act 2000

(1) The Financial Services and Markets Act 2000 (c. 8) is amended as follows.

(2) Section 143 (power to make rules endorsing the City Code on Takeovers and Mergers etc) is repealed.

(3) In section 144 (power to make price stabilising rules), for subsection (7) substitute –

    "(7) "Consultation procedures" means procedures designed to provide an opportunity for persons likely to be affected by alterations to those provisions to make representations about proposed alterations to any of those provisions.".

(4) In section 349 (exceptions from restrictions on disclosure of confidential information), after subsection (3) insert –

    "(3A)   Section 348 does not apply to –

        (a) the disclosure by a recipient to which subsection (3B) applies of confidential information disclosed to it by the Authority in reliance on subsection (1);

        (b) the disclosure of such information by a person obtaining it directly or indirectly from a recipient to which subsection (3B) applies.

(3B)   This subsection applies to –

(a)   the Panel on Takeovers and Mergers;

(b)   an authority designated as a supervisory authority for the purposes of Article 4.1 of the Takeovers Directive;

(c)   any other person or body that exercises public functions, under legislation in an EEA State other than the United Kingdom, that are similar to the Authority's functions or those of the Panel on Takeovers and Mergers.".

(5)   In section 354 (Financial Services Authority's duty to co-operate with others), after subsection (1) insert –

"(1A)   The Authority must take such steps as it considers appropriate to cooperate with –

(a)   the Panel on Takeovers and Mergers;

(b)   an authority designated as a supervisory authority for the purposes of Article 4.1 of the Takeovers Directive;

(c)   any other person or body that exercises functions of a public nature, under legislation in any country or territory outside the United Kingdom, that appear to the Authority to be similar to those of the Panel on Takeovers and Mergers.".

(6)   In section 417(1) (definitions), insert at the appropriate place –

""Takeovers Directive" means Directive 2004/25/EC of the European Parliament and of the Council;".

965 Power to extend to Isle of Man and Channel Islands

Her Majesty may by Order in Council direct that any of the provisions of this Chapter extend, with such modifications as may be specified in the Order, to the Isle of Man or any of the Channel Islands.

CHAPTER 2

IMPEDIMENTS TO TAKEOVERS

Opting in and opting out

966 Opting in and opting out

(1)   A company may by special resolution (an "opting-in resolution") opt in for the purposes of this Chapter if the following three conditions are met in relation to the company.

(2)   The first condition is that the company has voting shares admitted to trading on a regulated market.

(3)   The second condition is that –

(a)   the company's articles of association –

(i)   do not contain any such restrictions as are mentioned in Article 11 of the Takeovers Directive, or

(ii)   if they do contain any such restrictions, provide for the restrictions not to apply at a time when, or in circumstances in which, they would be disapplied by that Article,

and

(b)   those articles do not contain any other provision which would be incompatible with that Article.

(4)   The third condition is that –

(a) no shares conferring special rights in the company are held by –

    (i)   a minister,

    (ii)   a nominee of, or any other person acting on behalf of, a minister, or

    (iii) a company directly or indirectly controlled by a minister,

and

(b) no such rights are exercisable by or on behalf of a minister under any enactment.

(5) A company may revoke an opting-in resolution by a further special resolution (an "opting-out resolution").

(6) For the purposes of subsection (3), a reference in Article 11 of the Takeovers Directive to Article 7.1 or 9 of that Directive is to be read as referring to rules under section 943(1) giving effect to the relevant Article.

(7) In subsection (4) "minister" means –

(a) the holder of an office in Her Majesty's Government in the United Kingdom;

(b) the Scottish Ministers;

(c) a Minister within the meaning given by section 7(3) of the Northern Ireland Act 1998 (c. 47);

and for the purposes of that subsection "minister" also includes the Treasury, the Board of Trade, the Defence Council and the National Assembly for Wales.

(8) The Secretary of State may by order subject to negative resolution procedure provide that subsection (4) applies in relation to a specified person or body that exercises functions of a public nature as it applies in relation to a minister.
"Specified" means specified in the order.

967 Further provision about opting-in and opting-out resolutions

(1) An opting-in resolution or an opting-out resolution must specify the date from which it is to have effect (the "effective date").

(2) The effective date of an opting-in resolution may not be earlier than the date on which the resolution is passed.

(3) The second and third conditions in section 966 must be met at the time when an opting-in resolution is passed, but the first one does not need to be met until the effective date.

(4) An opting-in resolution passed before the time when voting shares of the company are admitted to trading on a regulated market complies with the requirement in subsection (1) if, instead of specifying a particular date, it provides for the resolution to have effect from that time.

(5) An opting-in resolution passed before the commencement of this section complies with the requirement in subsection (1) if, instead of specifying a particular date, it provides for the resolution to have effect from that commencement.

(6) The effective date of an opting-out resolution may not be earlier than the first anniversary of the date on which a copy of the opting-in resolution was forwarded to the registrar.

(7) Where a company has passed an opting-in resolution, any alteration of its articles of association that would prevent the second condition in section 966 from being met is of no effect until the effective date of an opting-out resolution passed by the company.

Consequences of opting in

968 Effect on contractual restrictions

(1) The following provisions have effect where a takeover bid is made for an opted-in company.

(2) An agreement to which this section applies is invalid in so far as it places any restriction –

(a) on the transfer to the offeror, or at his direction to another person, of shares in the company during the offer period;

(b) on the transfer to any person of shares in the company at a time during the offer period when the offeror holds shares amounting to not less than 75% in value of all the voting shares in the company;

(c) on rights to vote at a general meeting of the company that decides whether to take any action which might result in the frustration of the bid;

(d) on rights to vote at a general meeting of the company that –

(i)   is the first such meeting to be held after the end of the offer period, and

(ii) is held at a time when the offeror holds shares amounting to not less than 75% in value of all the voting shares in the company.

(3) This section applies to an agreement –

(a) entered into between a person holding shares in the company and another such person on or after 21st April 2004, or

(b) entered into at any time between such a person and the company,

and it applies to such an agreement even if the law applicable to the agreement (apart from this section) is not the law of a part of the United Kingdom.

(4) The reference in subsection (2)(c) to rights to vote at a general meeting of the company that decides whether to take any action which might result in the frustration of the bid includes a reference to rights to vote on a written resolution concerned with that question.

(5) For the purposes of subsection (2)(c), action which might result in the frustration of a bid is any action of that kind specified in rules under section 943(1) giving effect to Article 9 of the Takeovers Directive.

(6) If a person suffers loss as a result of any act or omission that would (but for this section) be a breach of an agreement to which this section applies, he is entitled to compensation, of such amount as the court considers just and equitable, from any person who would (but for this section) be liable to him for committing or inducing the breach.

(7) In subsection (6) "the court" means the High Court or, in Scotland, the Court of Session.

(8) A reference in this section to voting shares in the company does not include –

(a) debentures, or

(b) shares that, under the company's articles of association, do not normally carry rights to vote at its general meetings (for example, shares carrying rights to vote that, under those articles, arise only where specified pecuniary advantages are not provided).

969 Power of offeror to require general meeting to be called

(1) Where a takeover bid is made for an opted-in company, the offeror may by making a request to the directors of the company require them to call a general meeting of the company if, at the date at which the request is made, he holds shares amounting to not less than 75% in value of all the voting shares in the company.

(2) The reference in subsection (1) to voting shares in the company does not include –

(a) debentures, or

(b) shares that, under the company's articles of association, do not normally carry rights to vote at its general meetings (for example, shares carrying rights to vote that, under those articles, arise only where specified pecuniary advantages are not provided).

(3) Sections 303 to 305 (members' power to require general meetings to be called) apply as they would do if subsection (1) above were substituted for subsections (1) to (3) of section 303, and with any other necessary modifications.

Supplementary

970 Communication of decisions

(1) A company that has passed an opting-in resolution or an opting-out resolution must notify –

    (a) the Panel, and

    (b) where the company –

        (i) has voting shares admitted to trading on a regulated market in an EEA State other than the United Kingdom, or

        (ii) has requested such admission,

    the authority designated by that state as the supervisory authority for the purposes of Article 4.1 of the Takeovers Directive.

(2) Notification must be given within 15 days after the resolution is passed and, if any admission or request such as is mentioned in subsection (1)(b) occurs at a later time, within 15 days after that time.

(3) If a company fails to comply with this section, an offence is committed by –

    (a) the company, and

    (b) every officer of it who is in default.

(4) A person guilty of an offence under this section is liable on summary conviction to a fine not exceeding level 3 on the standard scale and, for continued contravention, a daily default fine not exceeding one-tenth of level 3 on the standard scale.

971 Interpretation of this Chapter

(1) In this Chapter –

    "offeror" and "takeover bid" have the same meaning as in the Takeovers Directive;

    "offer period", in relation to a takeover bid, means the time allowed for acceptance of the bid by –

        (a) rules under section 943(1) giving effect to Article 7.1 of the Takeovers Directive, or

        (b) where the rules giving effect to that Article which apply to the bid are those of an EEA State other than the United Kingdom, those rules;

    "opted-in company" means a company in relation to which –

        (a) an opting-in resolution has effect, and

        (b) the conditions in section 966(2) and (4) continue to be met;

    "opting-in resolution" has the meaning given by section 966(1);

    "opting-out resolution" has the meaning given by section 966(5);

    "the Takeovers Directive" means Directive 2004/25/EC of the European Parliament and of the Council;

    "voting rights" means rights to vote at general meetings of the company in question, including rights that arise only in certain circumstances;

    "voting shares" means shares carrying voting rights.

(2) For the purposes of this Chapter –

    (a) securities of a company are treated as shares in the company if they are convertible into or entitle the holder to subscribe for such shares;

    (b) debentures issued by a company are treated as shares in the company if they carry voting rights.

972 Transitory provision

(1) Where a takeover bid is made for an opted-in company, section 368 of the Companies Act 1985 (c. 6) (extraordinary general meeting on members' requisition) and section

378 of that Act (extraordinary and special resolutions) have effect as follows until
their repeal by this Act.
(2) Section 368 has effect as if a members' requisition included a requisition of a person
who –

(a) is the offeror in relation to the takeover bid, and
(b) holds at the date of the deposit of the requisition shares amounting to not less
than 75% in value of all the voting shares in the company.

(3) In relation to a general meeting of the company that –

(a) is the first such meeting to be held after the end of the offer period, and
(b) is held at a time when the offeror holds shares amounting to not less than 75%
in value of all the voting shares in the company,

section 378(2) (meaning of "special resolution") has effect as if "14 days' notice" were
substituted for "21 days' notice".
(4) A reference in this section to voting shares in the company does not include –

(a) debentures, or
(b) shares that, under the company's articles of association, do not normally carry
rights to vote at its general meetings (for example, shares carrying rights to vote
that, under those articles, arise only where specified pecuniary advantages are
not provided).

973 Power to extend to Isle of Man and Channel Islands

Her Majesty may by Order in Council direct that any of the provisions of this Chapter
extend, with such modifications as may be specified in the Order, to the Isle of Man or any
of the Channel Islands.

CHAPTER 3

"SQUEEZE-OUT" AND "SELL-OUT"

Takeover offers

974 Meaning of "takeover offer"

(1) For the purposes of this Chapter an offer to acquire shares in a company is a "takeover
offer" if the following two conditions are satisfied in relation to the offer.
(2) The first condition is that it is an offer to acquire –

(a) all the shares in a company, or
(b) where there is more than one class of shares in a company, all the shares of one
or more classes,

other than shares that at the date of the offer are already held by the offeror.
Section 975 contains provision supplementing this subsection.
(3) The second condition is that the terms of the offer are the same –

(a) in relation to all the shares to which the offer relates, or
(b) where the shares to which the offer relates include shares of different classes, in
relation to all the shares of each class.

Section 976 contains provision treating this condition as satisfied in certain
circumstances.
(4) In subsections (1) to (3) "shares" means shares, other than relevant treasury shares,
that have been allotted on the date of the offer (but see subsection (5)).
(5) A takeover offer may include among the shares to which it relates –

(a) all or any shares that are allotted after the date of the offer but before a specified date;

(b) all or any relevant treasury shares that cease to be held as treasury shares before a specified date;

(c) all or any other relevant treasury shares.

(6) In this section –

"relevant treasury shares" means shares that –

(a) are held by the company as treasury shares on the date of the offer, or

(b) become shares held by the company as treasury shares after that date but before a specified date;

"specified date" means a date specified in or determined in accordance with the terms of the offer.

(7) Where the terms of an offer make provision for their revision and for acceptances on the previous terms to be treated as acceptances on the revised terms, then, if the terms of the offer are revised in accordance with that provision –

(a) the revision is not to be regarded for the purposes of this Chapter as the making of a fresh offer, and

(b) references in this Chapter to the date of the offer are accordingly to be read as references to the date of the original offer.

975 Shares already held by the offeror etc

(1) The reference in section 974(2) to shares already held by the offeror includes a reference to shares that he has contracted to acquire, whether unconditionally or subject to conditions being met.
This is subject to subsection (2).

(2) The reference in section 974(2) to shares already held by the offeror does not include a reference to shares that are the subject of a contract –

(a) intended to secure that the holder of the shares will accept the offer when it is made, and

(b) entered into –

(i)   by deed and for no consideration,

(ii) for consideration of negligible value, or

(iii) for consideration consisting of a promise by the offeror to make the offer.

(3) In relation to Scotland, this section applies as if the words "by deed and" in subsection (2)(b)(i) were omitted.

(4) The condition in section 974(2) is treated as satisfied where –

(a) the offer does not extend to shares that associates of the offeror hold or have contracted to acquire (whether unconditionally or subject to conditions being met), and

(b) the condition would be satisfied if the offer did extend to those shares.

(For further provision about such shares, see section 977(2)).

976 Cases where offer treated as being on same terms

(1) The condition in section 974(3) (terms of offer to be the same for all shares or all shares of particular classes) is treated as satisfied where subsection (2) or (3) below applies.

(2) This subsection applies where –

(a) shares carry an entitlement to a particular dividend which other shares of the same class, by reason of being allotted later, do not carry,

(b) there is a difference in the value of consideration offered for the shares allotted earlier as against that offered for those allotted later,

    (c) that difference merely reflects the difference in entitlement to the dividend, and

    (d) the condition in section 974(3) would be satisfied but for that difference.

(3) This subsection applies where –

    (a) the law of a country or territory outside the United Kingdom –

        (i) precludes an offer of consideration in the form, or any of the forms, specified in the terms of the offer ("the specified form"), or

        (ii) precludes it except after compliance by the offeror with conditions with which he is unable to comply or which he regards as unduly onerous,

    (b) the persons to whom an offer of consideration in the specified form is precluded are able to receive consideration in another form that is of substantially equivalent value, and

    (c) the condition in section 974(3) would be satisfied but for the fact that an offer of consideration in the specified form to those persons is precluded.

977 Shares to which an offer relates

(1) Where a takeover offer is made and, during the period beginning with the date of the offer and ending when the offer can no longer be accepted, the offeror –

    (a) acquires or unconditionally contracts to acquire any of the shares to which the offer relates, but

    (b) does not do so by virtue of acceptances of the offer,

those shares are treated for the purposes of this Chapter as excluded from those to which the offer relates.

(2) For the purposes of this Chapter shares that an associate of the offeror holds or has contracted to acquire, whether at the date of the offer or subsequently, are not treated as shares to which the offer relates, even if the offer extends to such shares.

In this subsection "contracted" means contracted unconditionally or subject to conditions being met.

(3) This section is subject to section 979(8) and (9).

978 Effect of impossibility etc of communicating or accepting offer

(1) Where there are holders of shares in a company to whom an offer to acquire shares in the company is not communicated, that does not prevent the offer from being a takeover offer for the purposes of this Chapter if –

    (a) those shareholders have no registered address in the United Kingdom,

    (b) the offer was not communicated to those shareholders in order not to contravene the law of a country or territory outside the United Kingdom, and

    (c) either –

        (i) the offer is published in the Gazette, or

        (ii) the offer can be inspected, or a copy of it obtained, at a place in an EEA State or on a website, and a notice is published in the Gazette specifying the address of that place or website.

(2) Where an offer is made to acquire shares in a company and there are persons for whom, by reason of the law of a country or territory outside the United Kingdom, it is impossible to accept the offer, or more difficult to do so, that does not prevent the offer from being a takeover offer for the purposes of this Chapter.

(3) It is not to be inferred –

    (a) that an offer which is not communicated to every holder of shares in the company cannot be a takeover offer for the purposes of this Chapter unless the requirements of paragraphs (a) to (c) of subsection (1) are met, or

    (b) that an offer which is impossible, or more difficult, for certain persons to accept cannot be a takeover offer for those purposes unless the reason for the impossibility or difficulty is the one mentioned in subsection (2).

"Squeeze-out"

979 Right of offeror to buy out minority shareholder

(1) Subsection (2) applies in a case where a takeover offer does not relate to shares of different classes.

(2) If the offeror has, by virtue of acceptances of the offer, acquired or unconditionally contracted to acquire –

    (a) not less than 90% in value of the shares to which the offer relates, and

    (b) in a case where the shares to which the offer relates are voting shares, not less than 90% of the voting rights carried by those shares,

he may give notice to the holder of any shares to which the offer relates which the offeror has not acquired or unconditionally contracted to acquire that he desires to acquire those shares.

(3) Subsection (4) applies in a case where a takeover offer relates to shares of different classes.

(4) If the offeror has, by virtue of acceptances of the offer, acquired or unconditionally contracted to acquire –

    (a) not less than 90% in value of the shares of any class to which the offer relates, and

    (b) in a case where the shares of that class are voting shares, not less than 90% of the voting rights carried by those shares,

he may give notice to the holder of any shares of that class to which the offer relates which the offeror has not acquired or unconditionally contracted to acquire that he desires to acquire those shares.

(5) In the case of a takeover offer which includes among the shares to which it relates –

    (a) shares that are allotted after the date of the offer, or

    (b) relevant treasury shares (within the meaning of section 974) that cease to be held as treasury shares after the date of the offer,

the offeror's entitlement to give a notice under subsection (2) or (4) on any particular date shall be determined as if the shares to which the offer relates did not include any allotted, or ceasing to be held as treasury shares, on or after that date.

(6) Subsection (7) applies where –

    (a) the requirements for the giving of a notice under subsection (2) or (4) are satisfied, and

    (b) there are shares in the company which the offeror, or an associate of his, has contracted to acquire subject to conditions being met, and in relation to which the contract has not become unconditional.

(7) The offeror's entitlement to give a notice under subsection (2) or (4) shall be determined as if –

    (a) the shares to which the offer relates included shares falling within paragraph (b) of subsection (6), and

    (b) in relation to shares falling within that paragraph, the words "by virtue of acceptances of the offer" in subsection (2) or (4) were omitted.

(8) Where –

    (a) a takeover offer is made,

    (b) during the period beginning with the date of the offer and ending when the offer can no longer be accepted, the offeror –

        (i) acquires or unconditionally contracts to acquire any of the shares to which the offer relates, but

        (ii) does not do so by virtue of acceptances of the offer, and

    (c) subsection (10) applies,

then for the purposes of this section those shares are not excluded by section 977(1) from those to which the offer relates, and the offeror is treated as having acquired or contracted to acquire them by virtue of acceptances of the offer.

(9) Where –

(a) a takeover offer is made,

(b) during the period beginning with the date of the offer and ending when the offer can no longer be accepted, an associate of the offeror acquires or unconditionally contracts to acquire any of the shares to which the offer relates, and

(c) subsection (10) applies,

then for the purposes of this section those shares are not excluded by section 977(2) from those to which the offer relates.

(10) This subsection applies if –

(a) at the time the shares are acquired or contracted to be acquired as mentioned in subsection (8) or (9) (as the case may be), the value of the consideration for which they are acquired or contracted to be acquired ("the acquisition consideration") does not exceed the value of the consideration specified in the terms of the offer, or

(b) those terms are subsequently revised so that when the revision is announced the value of the acquisition consideration, at the time mentioned in paragraph (a), no longer exceeds the value of the consideration specified in those terms.

980 Further provision about notices given under section 979

(1) A notice under section 979 must be given in the prescribed manner.

(2) No notice may be given under section 979(2) or (4) after the end of –

(a) the period of three months beginning with the day after the last day on which the offer can be accepted, or

(b) the period of six months beginning with the date of the offer, where that period ends earlier and the offer is one to which subsection (3) below applies.

(3) This subsection applies to an offer if the time allowed for acceptance of the offer is not governed by rules under section 943(1) that give effect to Article 7 of the Takeovers Directive.

In this subsection "the Takeovers Directive" has the same meaning as in section 943.

(4) At the time when the offeror first gives a notice under section 979 in relation to an offer, he must send to the company –

(a) a copy of the notice, and

(b) a statutory declaration by him in the prescribed form, stating that the conditions for the giving of the notice are satisfied.

(5) Where the offeror is a company (whether or not a company within the meaning of this Act) the statutory declaration must be signed by a director.

(6) A person commits an offence if –

(a) he fails to send a copy of a notice or a statutory declaration as required by subsection (4), or

(b) he makes such a declaration for the purposes of that subsection knowing it to be false or without having reasonable grounds for believing it to be true.

(7) It is a defence for a person charged with an offence for failing to send a copy of a notice as required by subsection (4) to prove that he took reasonable steps for securing compliance with that subsection.

(8) A person guilty of an offence under this section is liable –

(a) on conviction on indictment, to imprisonment for a term not exceeding two years or a fine (or both);

(b) on summary conviction –

    (i)   in England and Wales, to imprisonment for a term not exceeding twelve months or to a fine not exceeding the statutory maximum (or both) and, for continued contravention, a daily default fine not exceeding one-fiftieth of the statutory maximum;

    (ii)   in Scotland or Northern Ireland, to imprisonment for a term not exceeding six months, or to a fine not exceeding the statutory maximum (or both) and, for continued contravention, a daily default fine not exceeding one-fiftieth of the statutory maximum.

981 Effect of notice under section 979

(1) Subject to section 986 (applications to the court), this section applies where the offeror gives a shareholder a notice under section 979.

(2) The offeror is entitled and bound to acquire the shares to which the notice relates on the terms of the offer.

(3) Where the terms of an offer are such as to give the shareholder a choice of consideration, the notice must give particulars of the choice and state –

    (a)   that the shareholder may, within six weeks from the date of the notice, indicate his choice by a written communication sent to the offeror at an address specified in the notice, and

    (b)   which consideration specified in the offer will apply if he does not indicate a choice.

The reference in subsection (2) to the terms of the offer is to be read accordingly.

(4) Subsection (3) applies whether or not any time-limit or other conditions applicable to the choice under the terms of the offer can still be complied with.

(5) If the consideration offered to or (as the case may be) chosen by the shareholder –

    (a)   is not cash and the offeror is no longer able to provide it, or

    (b)   was to have been provided by a third party who is no longer bound or able to provide it,

the consideration is to be taken to consist of an amount of cash, payable by the offeror, which at the date of the notice is equivalent to the consideration offered or (as the case may be) chosen.

(6) At the end of six weeks from the date of the notice the offeror must immediately –

    (a)   send a copy of the notice to the company, and

    (b)   pay or transfer to the company the consideration for the shares to which the notice relates.

Where the consideration consists of shares or securities to be allotted by the offeror, the reference in paragraph (b) to the transfer of the consideration is to be read as a reference to the allotment of the shares or securities to the company.

(7) If the shares to which the notice relates are registered, the copy of the notice sent to the company under subsection (6)(a) must be accompanied by an instrument of transfer executed on behalf of the holder of the shares by a person appointed by the offeror.

On receipt of that instrument the company must register the offeror as the holder of those shares.

(8) If the shares to which the notice relates are transferable by the delivery of warrants or other instruments, the copy of the notice sent to the company under subsection (6)(a) must be accompanied by a statement to that effect.

On receipt of that statement the company must issue the offeror with warrants or other instruments in respect of the shares, and those already in issue in respect of the shares become void.

(9) The company must hold any money or other consideration received by it under subsection (6)(b) on trust for the person who, before the offeror acquired them, was entitled to the shares in respect of which the money or other consideration was received.

Section 982 contains further provision about how the company should deal with such money or other consideration.

982 Further provision about consideration held on trust under section 981(9)

(1) This section applies where an offeror pays or transfers consideration to the company under section 981(6).

(2) The company must pay into a separate bank account that complies with subsection (3) –

(a) any money it receives under paragraph (b) of section 981(6), and

(b) any dividend or other sum accruing from any other consideration it receives under that paragraph.

(3) A bank account complies with this subsection if the balance on the account –

(a) bears interest at an appropriate rate, and

(b) can be withdrawn by such notice (if any) as is appropriate.

(4) If –

(a) the person entitled to the consideration held on trust by virtue of section 981(9) cannot be found, and

(b) subsection (5) applies,

the consideration (together with any interest, dividend or other benefit that has accrued from it) must be paid into court.

(5) This subsection applies where –

(a) reasonable enquiries have been made at reasonable intervals to find the person, and

(b) twelve years have elapsed since the consideration was received, or the company is wound up.

(6) In relation to a company registered in Scotland, subsections (7) and (8) apply instead of subsection (4).

(7) If the person entitled to the consideration held on trust by virtue of section 981(9) cannot be found and subsection (5) applies –

(a) the trust terminates,

(b) the company or (if the company is wound up) the liquidator must sell any consideration other than cash and any benefit other than cash that has accrued from the consideration, and

(c) a sum representing –

(i) the consideration so far as it is cash,

(ii) the proceeds of any sale under paragraph (b), and

(iii) any interest, dividend or other benefit that has accrued from the consideration,

must be deposited in the name of the Accountant of Court in a separate bank account complying with subsection (3) and the receipt for the deposit must be transmitted to the Accountant of Court.

(8) Section 58 of the Bankruptcy (Scotland) Act 1985 (c. 66) (so far as consistent with this Act) applies (with any necessary modifications) to sums deposited Companies Act 2006 (c. 46) under subsection (7) as it applies to sums deposited under section 57(1)(a) of that Act.

(9) The expenses of any such enquiries as are mentioned in subsection (5) may be paid out of the money or other property held on trust for the person to whom the enquiry relates.

"Sell-out"

983 Right of minority shareholder to be bought out by offeror

(1) Subsections (2) and (3) apply in a case where a takeover offer relates to all the shares in a company.

For this purpose a takeover offer relates to all the shares in a company if it is an offer to acquire all the shares in the company within the meaning of section 974.

(2) The holder of any voting shares to which the offer relates who has not accepted the offer may require the offeror to acquire those shares if, at any time before the end of the period within which the offer can be accepted –

    (a) the offeror has by virtue of acceptances of the offer acquired or unconditionally contracted to acquire some (but not all) of the shares to which the offer relates, and

    (b) those shares, with or without any other shares in the company which he has acquired or contracted to acquire (whether unconditionally or subject to conditions being met) –

        (i) amount to not less than 90% in value of all the voting shares in the company (or would do so but for section 990(1)), and

        (ii) carry not less than 90% of the voting rights in the company (or would do so but for section 990(1)).

(3) The holder of any non-voting shares to which the offer relates who has not accepted the offer may require the offeror to acquire those shares if, at any time before the end of the period within which the offer can be accepted –

    (a) the offeror has by virtue of acceptances of the offer acquired or unconditionally contracted to acquire some (but not all) of the shares to which the offer relates, and

    (b) those shares, with or without any other shares in the company which he has acquired or contracted to acquire (whether unconditionally or subject to conditions being met), amount to not less than 90% in value of all the shares in the company (or would do so but for section 990(1)).

(4) If a takeover offer relates to shares of one or more classes and at any time before the end of the period within which the offer can be accepted –

    (a) the offeror has by virtue of acceptances of the offer acquired or unconditionally contracted to acquire some (but not all) of the shares of any class to which the offer relates, and

    (b) those shares, with or without any other shares of that class which he has acquired or contracted to acquire (whether unconditionally or subject to conditions being met) –

        (i) amount to not less than 90% in value of all the shares of that class, and

        (ii) in a case where the shares of that class are voting shares, carry not less than 90% of the voting rights carried by the shares of that class,

the holder of any shares of that class to which the offer relates who has not accepted the offer may require the offeror to acquire those shares.

(5) For the purposes of subsections (2) to (4), in calculating 90% of the value of any shares, shares held by the company as treasury shares are to be treated as having been acquired by the offeror.

(6) Subsection (7) applies where –

    (a) a shareholder exercises rights conferred on him by subsection (2), (3) or (4),

    (b) at the time when he does so, there are shares in the company which the offeror has contracted to acquire subject to conditions being met, and in relation to which the contract has not become unconditional, and

(c) the requirement imposed by subsection (2)(b), (3)(b) or (4)(b) (as the case may be) would not be satisfied if those shares were not taken into account.

(7) The shareholder is treated for the purposes of section 985 as not having exercised his rights under this section unless the requirement imposed by paragraph (b) of subsection (2), (3) or (4) (as the case may be) would be satisfied if –

(a) the reference in that paragraph to other shares in the company which the offeror has contracted to acquire unconditionally or subject to conditions being met were a reference to such shares which he has unconditionally contracted to acquire, and

(b) the reference in that subsection to the period within which the offer can be accepted were a reference to the period referred to in section 984(2).

(8) A reference in subsection (2)(b), (3)(b), (4)(b), (6) or (7) to shares which the offeror has acquired or contracted to acquire includes a reference to shares which an associate of his has acquired or contracted to acquire.

984 Further provision about rights conferred by section 983

(1) Rights conferred on a shareholder by subsection (2), (3) or (4) of section 983 are exercisable by a written communication addressed to the offeror.

(2) Rights conferred on a shareholder by subsection (2), (3) or (4) of that section are not exercisable after the end of the period of three months from –

(a) the end of the period within which the offer can be accepted, or

(b) if later, the date of the notice that must be given under subsection (3) below.

(3) Within one month of the time specified in subsection (2), (3) or (4) (as the case may be) of that section, the offeror must give any shareholder who has not accepted the offer notice in the prescribed manner of –

(a) the rights that are exercisable by the shareholder under that subsection, and

(b) the period within which the rights are exercisable.

If the notice is given before the end of the period within which the offer can be accepted, it must state that the offer is still open for acceptance.

(4) Subsection (3) does not apply if the offeror has given the shareholder a notice in respect of the shares in question under section 979.

(5) An offeror who fails to comply with subsection (3) commits an offence.
If the offeror is a company, every officer of that company who is in default or to whose neglect the failure is attributable also commits an offence.

(6) If an offeror other than a company is charged with an offence for failing to comply with subsection (3), it is a defence for him to prove that he took all reasonable steps for securing compliance with that subsection.

(7) A person guilty of an offence under this section is liable –

(a) on conviction on indictment, to a fine;

(b) on summary conviction, to a fine not exceeding the statutory maximum and, for continued contravention, a daily default fine not exceeding one-fiftieth of the statutory maximum.

985 Effect of requirement under section 983

(1) Subject to section 986, this section applies where a shareholder exercises his rights under section 983 in respect of any shares held by him.

(2) The offeror is entitled and bound to acquire those shares on the terms of the offer or on such other terms as may be agreed.

(3) Where the terms of an offer are such as to give the shareholder a choice of consideration –

(a) the shareholder may indicate his choice when requiring the offeror to acquire the shares, and

   (b) the notice given to the shareholder under section 984(3) –

      (i)   must give particulars of the choice and of the rights conferred by this subsection, and

      (ii) may state which consideration specified in the offer will apply if he does not indicate a choice.

The reference in subsection (2) to the terms of the offer is to be read accordingly.

(4) Subsection (3) applies whether or not any time-limit or other conditions applicable to the choice under the terms of the offer can still be complied with.

(5) If the consideration offered to or (as the case may be) chosen by the shareholder –

   (a) is not cash and the offeror is no longer able to provide it, or

   (b) was to have been provided by a third party who is no longer bound or able to provide it,

the consideration is to be taken to consist of an amount of cash, payable by the offeror, which at the date when the shareholder requires the offeror to acquire the shares is equivalent to the consideration offered or (as the case may be) chosen.

Supplementary

986 Applications to the court

(1) Where a notice is given under section 979 to a shareholder the court may, on an application made by him, order –

   (a) that the offeror is not entitled and bound to acquire the shares to which the notice relates, or

   (b) that the terms on which the offeror is entitled and bound to acquire the shares shall be such as the court thinks fit.

(2) An application under subsection (1) must be made within six weeks from the date on which the notice referred to in that subsection was given.

If an application to the court under subsection (1) is pending at the end of that period, section 981(6) does not have effect until the application has been disposed of.

(3) Where a shareholder exercises his rights under section 983 in respect of any shares held by him, the court may, on an application made by him or the offeror, order that the terms on which the offeror is entitled and bound to acquire the shares shall be such as the court thinks fit.

(4) On an application under subsection (1) or (3) –

   (a) the court may not require consideration of a higher value than that specified in the terms of the offer ("the offer value") to be given for the shares to which the application relates unless the holder of the shares shows that the offer value would be unfair;

   (b) the court may not require consideration of a lower value than the offer value to be given for the shares.

(5) No order for costs or expenses may be made against a shareholder making an application under subsection (1) or (3) unless the court considers that –

   (a) the application was unnecessary, improper or vexatious,

   (b) there has been unreasonable delay in making the application, or

   (c) there has been unreasonable conduct on the shareholder's part in conducting the proceedings on the application.

(6) A shareholder who has made an application under subsection (1) or (3) must give notice of the application to the offeror.

(7) An offeror who is given notice of an application under subsection (1) or (3) must give a copy of the notice to –

(a) any person (other than the applicant) to whom a notice has been given under section 979;

(b) any person who has exercised his rights under section 983.

(8) An offeror who makes an application under subsection (3) must give notice of the application to –

(a) any person to whom a notice has been given under section 979;

(b) any person who has exercised his rights under section 983.

(9) Where a takeover offer has not been accepted to the extent necessary for entitling the offeror to give notices under subsection (2) or (4) of section 979 the court may, on an application made by him, make an order authorising him to give notices under that subsection if it is satisfied that –

(a) the offeror has after reasonable enquiry been unable to trace one or more of the persons holding shares to which the offer relates,

(b) the requirements of that subsection would have been met if the person, or all the persons, mentioned in paragraph (a) above had accepted the offer, and

(c) the consideration offered is fair and reasonable.

This is subject to subsection (10).

(10) The court may not make an order under subsection (9) unless it considers that it is just and equitable to do so having regard, in particular, to the number of shareholders who have been traced but who have not accepted the offer.

987 Joint offers

(1) In the case of a takeover offer made by two or more persons jointly, this Chapter has effect as follows.

(2) The conditions for the exercise of the rights conferred by section 979 are satisfied –

(a) in the case of acquisitions by virtue of acceptances of the offer, by the joint offerors acquiring or unconditionally contracting to acquire the necessary shares jointly;

(b) in other cases, by the joint offerors acquiring or unconditionally contracting to acquire the necessary shares either jointly or separately.

(3) The conditions for the exercise of the rights conferred by section 983 are satisfied –

(a) in the case of acquisitions by virtue of acceptances of the offer, by the joint offerors acquiring or unconditionally contracting to acquire the necessary shares jointly;

(b) in other cases, by the joint offerors acquiring or contracting (whether unconditionally or subject to conditions being met) to acquire the necessary shares either jointly or separately.

(4) Subject to the following provisions, the rights and obligations of the offeror under sections 979 to 985 are respectively joint rights and joint and several obligations of the joint offerors.

(5) A provision of sections 979 to 986 that requires or authorises a notice or other document to be given or sent by or to the joint offerors is complied with if the notice or document is given or sent by or to any of them (but see subsection (6)).

(6) The statutory declaration required by section 980(4) must be made by all of the joint offerors and, where one or more of them is a company, signed by a director of that company.

(7) In sections 974 to 977, 979(9), 981(6), 983(8) and 988 references to the offeror are to be read as references to the joint offerors or any of them.

(8) In section 981(7) and (8) references to the offeror are to be read as references to the joint offerors or such of them as they may determine.

(9) In sections 981(5)(a) and 985(5)(a) references to the offeror being no longer able to provide the relevant consideration are to be read as references to none of the joint offerors being able to do so.

(10) In section 986 references to the offeror are to be read as references to the joint offerors, except that –

  (a) an application under subsection (3) or (9) may be made by any of them, and
  (b) the reference in subsection (9)(a) to the offeror having been unable to trace one or more of the persons holding shares is to be read as a reference to none of the offerors having been able to do so.

Interpretation

988 Associates

(1) In this Chapter "associate", in relation to an offeror, means –

  (a) a nominee of the offeror,
  (b) a holding company, subsidiary or fellow subsidiary of the offeror or a nominee of such a holding company, subsidiary or fellow subsidiary,
  (c) a body corporate in which the offeror is substantially interested,
  (d) a person who is, or is a nominee of, a party to a share acquisition agreement with the offeror, or
  (e) (where the offeror is an individual) his spouse or civil partner and any minor child or step-child of his.

(2) For the purposes of subsection (1)(b) a company is a fellow subsidiary of another body corporate if both are subsidiaries of the same body corporate but neither is a subsidiary of the other.

(3) For the purposes of subsection (1)(c) an offeror has a substantial interest in a body corporate if –

  (a) the body or its directors are accustomed to act in accordance with his directions or instructions, or
  (b) he is entitled to exercise or control the exercise of one-third or more of the voting power at general meetings of the body.

  Subsections (2) and (3) of section 823 (which contain provision about when a person is treated as entitled to exercise or control the exercise of voting power) apply for the purposes of this subsection as they apply for the purposes of that section.

(4) For the purposes of subsection (1)(d) an agreement is a share acquisition agreement if –

  (a) it is an agreement for the acquisition of, or of an interest in, shares to which the offer relates,
  (b) it includes provisions imposing obligations or restrictions on any one or more of the parties to it with respect to their use, retention or disposal of such shares, or their interests in such shares, acquired in pursuance of the agreement (whether or not together with any other shares to which the offer relates or any other interests of theirs in such shares), and
  (c) it is not an excluded agreement (see subsection (5)).

(5) An agreement is an "excluded agreement" –

  (a) if it is not legally binding, unless it involves mutuality in the undertakings, expectations or understandings of the parties to it, or
  (b) if it is an agreement to underwrite or sub-underwrite an offer of shares in a company, provided the agreement is confined to that purpose and any matters incidental to it.

(6) The reference in subsection (4)(b) to the use of interests in shares is to the exercise of any rights or of any control or influence arising from those interests (including the right to enter into an agreement for the exercise, or for control of the exercise, of any of those rights by another person).

(7) In this section –

(a) "agreement" includes any agreement or arrangement;

(b) references to provisions of an agreement include –

(i) undertakings, expectations or understandings operative under an arrangement, and

(ii) any provision whether express or implied and whether absolute or not.

989 Convertible securities

(1) For the purposes of this Chapter securities of a company are treated as shares in the company if they are convertible into or entitle the holder to subscribe for such shares. References to the holder of shares or a shareholder are to be read accordingly.

(2) Subsection (1) is not to be read as requiring any securities to be treated –

(a) as shares of the same class as those into which they are convertible or for which the holder is entitled to subscribe, or

(b) as shares of the same class as other securities by reason only that the shares into which they are convertible or for which the holder is entitled to subscribe are of the same class.

990 Debentures carrying voting rights

(1) For the purposes of this Chapter debentures issued by a company to which subsection (2) applies are treated as shares in the company if they carry voting rights.

(2) This subsection applies to a company that has voting shares, or debentures carrying voting rights, which are admitted to trading on a regulated market.

(3) In this Chapter, in relation to debentures treated as shares by virtue of subsection (1) –

(a) references to the holder of shares or a shareholder are to be read accordingly;

(b) references to shares being allotted are to be read as references to debentures being issued.

991 Interpretation

(1) In this Chapter –

"the company" means the company whose shares are the subject of a takeover offer;

"date of the offer" means –

(a) where the offer is published, the date of publication;

(b) where the offer is not published, or where any notices of the offer are given before the date of publication, the date when notices of the offer (or the first such notices) are given;

and references to the date of the offer are to be read in accordance with section 974(7) (revision of offer terms) where that applies;

"non-voting shares" means shares that are not voting shares;

"offeror" means (subject to section 987) the person making a takeover offer;

"voting rights" means rights to vote at general meetings of the company, including rights that arise only in certain circumstances;

"voting shares" means shares carrying voting rights.

(2) For the purposes of this Chapter a person contracts unconditionally to acquire shares if his entitlement under the contract to acquire them is not (or is no longer) subject to conditions or if all conditions to which it was subject have been met.

A reference to a contract becoming unconditional is to be read accordingly.

CHAPTER 4

AMENDMENTS TO PART 7 OF THE COMPANIES ACT 1985

992 Matters to be dealt with in directors' report

(1) Part 7 of the Companies Act 1985 (c. 6) (accounts and audit) is amended as follows.

(2) In Schedule 7 (matters to be dealt with in directors' report), after Part 6 insert –

"PART 7

DISCLOSURE REQUIRED BY CERTAIN PUBLICLY-TRADED COMPANIES

13 (1) This Part of this Schedule applies to the directors' report for a financial year if the company had securities carrying voting rights admitted to trading on a regulated market at the end of that year.

(2) The report shall contain detailed information, by reference to the end of that year, on the following matters –

(a) the structure of the company's capital, including in particular –

(i) the rights and obligations attaching to the shares or, as the case may be, to each class of shares in the company, and

(ii) where there are two or more such classes, the percentage of the total share capital represented by each class;

(b) any restrictions on the transfer of securities in the company, including in particular –

(i) limitations on the holding of securities, and

(ii) requirements to obtain the approval of the company, or of other holders of securities in the company, for a transfer of securities;

(c) in the case of each person with a significant direct or indirect holding of securities in the company, such details as are known to the company of –

(i) the identity of the person,

(ii) the size of the holding, and

(iii) the nature of the holding;

(d) in the case of each person who holds securities carrying special rights with regard to control of the company –

(i) the identity of the person, and

(ii) the nature of the rights;

(e) where –

(i) the company has an employees' share scheme, and

(ii) shares to which the scheme relates have rights with regard to control of the company that are not exercisable directly by the employees,

how those rights are exercisable;

(f) any restrictions on voting rights, including in particular –

(i) limitations on voting rights of holders of a given percentage or number of votes,

(ii) deadlines for exercising voting rights, and

(iii)   arrangements by which, with the company's cooperation, financial rights carried by securities are held by a person other than the holder of the securities;

(g)   any agreements between holders of securities that are known to the company and may result in restrictions on the transfer of securities or on voting rights;

(h)   any rules that the company has about –

(i)   appointment and replacement of directors, or
(ii)   amendment of the company's articles of association;

(i)   the powers of the company's directors, including in particular any powers in relation to the issuing or buying back by the company of its shares;

(j)   any significant agreements to which the company is a party that take effect, alter or terminate upon a change of control of the company following a takeover bid, and the effects of any such agreements;

(k)   any agreements between the company and its directors or employees providing for compensation for loss of office or employment (whether through resignation, purported redundancy or otherwise) that occurs because of a takeover bid.

(3)   For the purposes of sub-paragraph (2)(a) a company's capital includes any securities in the company that are not admitted to trading on a regulated market.

(4)   For the purposes of sub-paragraph (2)(c) a person has an indirect holding of securities if –

(a)   they are held on his behalf, or
(b)   he is able to secure that rights carried by the securities are exercised in accordance with his wishes.

(5)   Sub-paragraph (2)(j) does not apply to an agreement if –

(a)   disclosure of the agreement would be seriously prejudicial to the company, and
(b)   the company is not under any other obligation to disclose it.

(6)   In this paragraph –

"securities" means shares or debentures;
"takeover bid" has the same meaning as in the Takeovers Directive;
"the Takeovers Directive" means Directive 2004/25/EC of the European Parliament and of the Council;
"voting rights" means rights to vote at general meetings of the company in question, including rights that arise only in certain circumstances.".

(3)   In section 234ZZA (requirements of directors' reports), at the end of subsection (4) (contents of Schedule 7) insert –

"Part 7 specifies information to be disclosed by certain publicly traded companies.".

(4)   After that subsection insert –

"(5) A directors' report shall also contain any necessary explanatory material with regard to information that is required to be included in the report by Part 7 of Schedule 7.".

(5)   In section 251 (summary financial statements), after subsection (2ZA) insert –

"(2ZB)   A company that sends to an entitled person a summary financial statement instead of a copy of its directors' report shall –

(a)   include in the statement the explanatory material required to be included in the directors' report by section 234ZZA(5), or

(b) send that material to the entitled person at the same time as it sends the statement.

For the purposes of paragraph (b), subsections (2A) to (2E) apply in relation to the material referred to in that paragraph as they apply in relation to a summary financial statement.".

(6) The amendments made by this section apply in relation to directors' reports for financial years beginning on or after 20th May 2006.

PART 29

FRAUDULENT TRADING

993 Offence of fraudulent trading

(1) If any business of a company is carried on with intent to defraud creditors of the company or creditors of any other person, or for any fraudulent purpose, every person who is knowingly a party to the carrying on of the business in that manner commits an offence.

(2) This applies whether or not the company has been, or is in the course of being, wound up.

(3) A person guilty of an offence under this section is liable –

(a) on conviction on indictment, to imprisonment for a term not exceeding ten years or a fine (or both);

(b) on summary conviction –

(i) in England and Wales, to imprisonment for a term not exceeding twelve months or a fine not exceeding the statutory maximum (or both);

(ii) in Scotland or Northern Ireland, to imprisonment for a term not exceeding six months or a fine not exceeding the statutory maximum (or both).

PART 30

PROTECTION OF MEMBERS AGAINST UNFAIR PREJUDICE

Main provisions

994 Petition by company member

(1) A member of a company may apply to the court by petition for an order under this Part on the ground –

(a) that the company's affairs are being or have been conducted in a manner that is unfairly prejudicial to the interests of members generally or of some part of its members (including at least himself), or

(b) that an actual or proposed act or omission of the company (including an act or omission on its behalf) is or would be so prejudicial.

(2) The provisions of this Part apply to a person who is not a member of a company but to whom shares in the company have been transferred or transmitted by operation of law as they apply to a member of a company.

(3) In this section, and so far as applicable for the purposes of this section in the other provisions of this Part, "company" means –

(a) a company within the meaning of this Act, or

(b)   a company that is not such a company but is a statutory water company within the meaning of the Statutory Water Companies Act 1991 (c. 58).

995 Petition by Secretary of State

(1)   This section applies to a company in respect of which –

(a)   the Secretary of State has received a report under section 437 of the Companies Act 1985 (c. 6) (inspector's report);

(b)   the Secretary of State has exercised his powers under section 447 or 448 of that Act (powers to require documents and information or to enter and search premises);

(c)   the Secretary of State or the Financial Services Authority has exercised his or its powers under Part 11 of the Financial Services and Markets Act 2000 (c. 8) (information gathering and investigations); or

(d)   the Secretary of State has received a report from an investigator appointed by him or the Financial Services Authority under that Part.

(2)   If it appears to the Secretary of State that in the case of such a company –

(a)   the company's affairs are being or have been conducted in a manner that is unfairly prejudicial to the interests of members generally or of some part of its members, or

(b)   an actual or proposed act or omission of the company (including an act or omission on its behalf) is or would be so prejudicial,

he may apply to the court by petition for an order under this Part.

(3)   The Secretary of State may do this in addition to, or instead of, presenting a petition for the winding up of the company.

(4)   In this section, and so far as applicable for the purposes of this section in the other provisions of this Part, "company" means any body corporate that is liable to be wound up under the Insolvency Act 1986 (c. 45) or the Insolvency (Northern Ireland) Order 1989 (S.I. 1989/2405 (N.I. 19)).

996 Powers of the court under this Part

(1)   If the court is satisfied that a petition under this Part is well founded, it may make such order as it thinks fit for giving relief in respect of the matters complained of.

(2)   Without prejudice to the generality of subsection (1), the court's order may –

(a)   regulate the conduct of the company's affairs in the future;

(b)   require the company –

(i)   to refrain from doing or continuing an act complained of, or

(ii)   to do an act that the petitioner has complained it has omitted to do;

(c)   authorise civil proceedings to be brought in the name and on behalf of the company by such person or persons and on such terms as the court may direct;

(d)   require the company not to make any, or any specified, alterations in its articles without the leave of the court;

(e)   provide for the purchase of the shares of any members of the company by other members or by the company itself and, in the case of a purchase by the company itself, the reduction of the company's capital accordingly.

Supplementary provisions

997 Application of general rule-making powers

The power to make rules under section 411 of the Insolvency Act 1986 (c. 45) or Article 359 of the Insolvency (Northern Ireland) Order 1989 (S.I. 1989/2405 (N.I. 19)), so far as relating to a winding-up petition, applies for the purposes of a petition under this Part.

998 Copy of order affecting company's constitution to be delivered to registrar

(1) Where an order of the court under this Part –

  (a) alters the company's constitution, or

  (b) gives leave for the company to make any, or any specified, alterations to its constitution,

the company must deliver a copy of the order to the registrar.

(2) It must do so within 14 days from the making of the order or such longer period as the court may allow.

(3) If a company makes default in complying with this section, an offence is committed by –

  (a) the company, and

  (b) every officer of the company who is in default.

(4) A person guilty of an offence under this section is liable on summary conviction to a fine not exceeding level 3 on the standard scale and, for continued contravention, a daily default fine not exceeding one-tenth of level 3 on the standard scale.

999 Supplementary provisions where company's constitution altered

(1) This section applies where an order under this Part alters a company's constitution.

(2) If the order amends –

  (a) a company's articles, or

  (b) any resolution or agreement to which Chapter 3 of Part 3 applies (resolution or agreement affecting a company's constitution),

the copy of the order delivered to the registrar by the company under section 998 must be accompanied by a copy of the company's articles, or the resolution or agreement in question, as amended.

(3) Every copy of a company's articles issued by the company after the order is made must be accompanied by a copy of the order, unless the effect of the order has been incorporated into the articles by amendment.

(4) If a company makes default in complying with this section an offence is committed by –

  (a) the company, and

  (b) every officer of the company who is in default.

(5) A person guilty of an offence under this section is liable on summary conviction to a fine not exceeding level 3 on the standard scale.

PART 31

DISSOLUTION AND RESTORATION TO THE REGISTER

CHAPTER 1

STRIKING OFF

Registrar's power to strike off defunct company

1000 Power to strike off company not carrying on business or in operation

(1) If the registrar has reasonable cause to believe that a company is not carrying on business or in operation, the registrar may send to the company by post a letter inquiring whether the company is carrying on business or in operation.

(2)   If the registrar does not within one month of sending the letter receive any answer to it, the registrar must within 14 days after the expiration of that month send to the company by post a registered letter referring to the first letter, and stating –

 (a)   that no answer to it has been received, and

 (b)   that if an answer is not received to the second letter within one month from its date, a notice will be published in the Gazette with a view to striking the company's name off the register.

(3)   If the registrar –

 (a)   receives an answer to the effect that the company is not carrying on business or in operation, or

 (b)   does not within one month after sending the second letter receive any answer,

 the registrar may publish in the Gazette, and send to the company by post, a notice that at the expiration of three months from the date of the notice the name of the company mentioned in it will, unless cause is shown to the contrary, be struck off the register and the company will be dissolved.

(4)   At the expiration of the time mentioned in the notice the registrar may, unless cause to the contrary is previously shown by the company, strike its name off the register.

(5)   The registrar must publish notice in the Gazette of the company's name having been struck off the register.

(6)   On the publication of the notice in the Gazette the company is dissolved.

(7)   However –

 (a)   the liability (if any) of every director, managing officer and member of the company continues and may be enforced as if the company had not been dissolved, and

 (b)   nothing in this section affects the power of the court to wind up a company the name of which has been struck off the register.

1001 Duty to act in case of company being wound up

(1)   If, in a case where a company is being wound up –

 (a)   the registrar has reasonable cause to believe –

  (i)   that no liquidator is acting, or

  (ii)   that the affairs of the company are fully wound up, and

 (b)   the returns required to be made by the liquidator have not been made for a period of six consecutive months,

 the registrar must publish in the Gazette and send to the company or the liquidator (if any) a notice that at the expiration of three months from the date of the notice the name of the company mentioned in it will, unless cause is shown to the contrary, be struck off the register and the company will be dissolved.

(2)   At the expiration of the time mentioned in the notice the registrar may, unless cause to the contrary is previously shown by the company, strike its name off the register.

(3)   The registrar must publish notice in the Gazette of the company's name having been struck off the register.

(4)   On the publication of the notice in the Gazette the company is dissolved.

(5)   However –

 (a)   the liability (if any) of every director, managing officer and member of the company continues and may be enforced as if the company had not been dissolved, and

 (b)   nothing in this section affects the power of the court to wind up a company the name of which has been struck off the register.

1002 Supplementary provisions as to service of letter or notice

(1) A letter or notice to be sent under section 1000 or 1001 to a company may be addressed to the company at its registered office or, if no office has been registered, to the care of some officer of the company.

(2) If there is no officer of the company whose name and address are known to the registrar, the letter or notice may be sent to each of the persons who subscribed the memorandum (if their addresses are known to the registrar).

(3) A notice to be sent to a liquidator under section 1001 may be addressed to him at his last known place of business.

Voluntary striking off

1003 Striking off on application by company

(1) On application by a company, the registrar of companies may strike the company's name off the register.

(2) The application –

    (a) must be made on the company's behalf by its directors or by a majority of them, and

    (b) must contain the prescribed information.

(3) The registrar may not strike a company off under this section until after the expiration of three months from the publication by the registrar in the Gazette of a notice –

    (a) stating that the registrar may exercise the power under this section in relation to the company, and

    (b) inviting any person to show cause why that should not be done.

(4) The registrar must publish notice in the Gazette of the company's name having been struck off.

(5) On the publication of the notice in the Gazette the company is dissolved.

(6) However –

    (a) the liability (if any) of every director, managing officer and member of the company continues and may be enforced as if the company had not been dissolved, and

    (b) nothing in this section affects the power of the court to wind up a company the name of which has been struck off the register.

1004 Circumstances in which application not to be made: activities of company

(1) An application under section 1003 (application for voluntary striking off) on behalf of a company must not be made if, at any time in the previous three months, the company has –

    (a) changed its name,

    (b) traded or otherwise carried on business,

    (c) made a disposal for value of property or rights that, immediately before ceasing to trade or otherwise carry on business, it held for the purpose of disposal for gain in the normal course of trading or otherwise carrying on business, or

    (d) engaged in any other activity, except one which is –

        (i) necessary or expedient for the purpose of making an application under that section, or deciding whether to do so,

        (ii) necessary or expedient for the purpose of concluding the affairs of the company,

        (iii) necessary or expedient for the purpose of complying with any statutory requirement, or

       (iv) specified by the Secretary of State by order for the purposes of this sub-paragraph.

(2) For the purposes of this section, a company is not to be treated as trading or otherwise carrying on business by virtue only of the fact that it makes a payment in respect of a liability incurred in the course of trading or otherwise carrying on business.

(3) The Secretary of State may by order amend subsection (1) for the purpose of altering the period in relation to which the doing of the things mentioned in paragraphs (a) to (d) of that subsection is relevant.

(4) An order under this section is subject to negative resolution procedure.

(5) It is an offence for a person to make an application in contravention of this section.

(6) In proceedings for such an offence it is a defence for the accused to prove that he did not know, and could not reasonably have known, of the existence of the facts that led to the contravention.

(7) A person guilty of an offence under this section is liable –

    (a) on conviction on indictment, to a fine;

    (b) on summary conviction, to a fine not exceeding the statutory maximum.

1005 Circumstances in which application not to be made: other proceedings not concluded

(1) An application under section 1003 (application for voluntary striking off) on behalf of a company must not be made at a time when –

    (a) an application to the court under Part 26 has been made on behalf of the company for the sanctioning of a compromise or arrangement and the matter has not been finally concluded;

    (b) a voluntary arrangement in relation to the company has been proposed under Part 1 of the Insolvency Act 1986 (c. 45) or Part 2 of the Insolvency (Northern Ireland) Order 1989 (S.I. 1989/2405 (N.I. 19)) and the matter has not been finally concluded;

    (c) the company is in administration under Part 2 of that Act or Part 3 of that Order;

    (d) paragraph 44 of Schedule B1 to that Act or paragraph 45 of Schedule B1 to that Order applies (interim moratorium on proceedings where application to the court for an administration order has been made or notice of intention to appoint administrator has been filed);

    (e) the company is being wound up under Part 4 of that Act or Part 5 of that Order, whether voluntarily or by the court, or a petition under that Part for winding up of the company by the court has been presented and not finally dealt with or withdrawn;

    (f) there is a receiver or manager of the company's property;

    (g) the company's estate is being administered by a judicial factor.

(2) For the purposes of subsection (1)(a), the matter is finally concluded if –

    (a) the application has been withdrawn,

    (b) the application has been finally dealt with without a compromise or arrangement being sanctioned by the court, or

    (c) a compromise or arrangement has been sanctioned by the court and has, together with anything required to be done under any provision made in relation to the matter by order of the court, been fully carried out.

(3) For the purposes of subsection (1)(b), the matter is finally concluded if –

    (a) no meetings are to be summoned under section 3 of the Insolvency Act 1986 (c. 45) or Article 16 of the Insolvency (Northern Ireland) Order 1989,

    (b) meetings summoned under that section or Article fail to approve the arrangement with no, or the same, modifications,

(c) an arrangement approved by meetings summoned under that section, or in consequence of a direction under section 6(4)(b) of that Act or Article 19(4)(b) of that Order, has been fully implemented, or

(d) the court makes an order under section 6(5) of that Act or Article 19(5) of that Order revoking approval given at previous meetings and, if the court gives any directions under section 6(6) of that Act or Article 19(6) of that Order, the company has done whatever it is required to do under those directions.

(4) It is an offence for a person to make an application in contravention of this section.

(5) In proceedings for such an offence it is a defence for the accused to prove that he did not know, and could not reasonably have known, of the existence of the facts that led to the contravention.

(6) A person guilty of an offence under this section is liable –

   (a) on conviction on indictment, to a fine;
   (b) on summary conviction, to a fine not exceeding the statutory maximum.

1006 Copy of application to be given to members, employees, etc

(1) A person who makes an application under section 1003 (application for voluntary striking off) on behalf of a company must secure that, within seven days from the day on which the application is made, a copy of it is given to every person who at any time on that day is –

   (a) a member of the company,
   (b) an employee of the company,
   (c) a creditor of the company,
   (d) a director of the company,
   (e) a manager or trustee of any pension fund established for the benefit of employees of the company, or
   (f) a person of a description specified for the purposes of this paragraph by regulations made by the Secretary of State.

   Regulations under paragraph (f) are subject to negative resolution procedure.

(2) Subsection (1) does not require a copy of the application to be given to a director who is a party to the application.

(3) The duty imposed by this section ceases to apply if the application is withdrawn before the end of the period for giving the copy application.

(4) A person who fails to perform the duty imposed on him by this section commits an offence.
   If he does so with the intention of concealing the making of the application from the person concerned, he commits an aggravated offence.

(5) In proceedings for an offence under this section it is a defence for the accused to prove that he took all reasonable steps to perform the duty.

(6) A person guilty of an offence under this section (other than an aggravated offence) is liable –

   (a) on conviction on indictment, to a fine;
   (b) on summary conviction, to a fine not exceeding the statutory maximum.

(7) A person guilty of an aggravated offence under this section is liable –

   (a) on conviction on indictment, to imprisonment for a term not exceeding seven years or a fine (or both);
   (b) on summary conviction –
      (i) in England and Wales, to imprisonment for a term not exceeding twelve months or to a fine not exceeding the statutory maximum (or both);
      (ii) in Scotland or Northern Ireland, to imprisonment for a term not exceeding six months, or to a fine not exceeding the statutory maximum (or both).

1007 Copy of application to be given to new members, employees, etc

(1) This section applies in relation to any time after the day on which a company makes an application under section 1003 (application for voluntary striking off) and before the day on which the application is finally dealt with or withdrawn.

(2) A person who is a director of the company at the end of a day on which a person (other than himself) becomes –

  (a) a member of the company,
  (b) an employee of the company,
  (c) a creditor of the company,
  (d) a director of the company,
  (e) a manager or trustee of any pension fund established for the benefit of employees of the company, or
  (f) a person of a description specified for the purposes of this paragraph by regulations made by the Secretary of State,

must secure that a copy of the application is given to that person within seven days from that day.

Regulations under paragraph (f) are subject to negative resolution procedure.

(3) The duty imposed by this section ceases to apply if the application is finally dealt with or withdrawn before the end of the period for giving the copy application.

(4) A person who fails to perform the duty imposed on him by this section commits an offence.

If he does so with the intention of concealing the making of the application from the person concerned, he commits an aggravated offence.

(5) In proceedings for an offence under this section it is a defence for the accused to prove –

  (a) that at the time of the failure he was not aware of the fact that the company had made an application under section 1003, or
  (b) that he took all reasonable steps to perform the duty.

(6) A person guilty of an offence under this section (other than an aggravated offence) is liable –

  (a) on conviction on indictment, to a fine;
  (b) on summary conviction, to a fine not exceeding the statutory maximum.

(7) A person guilty of an aggravated offence under this section is liable –

  (a) on conviction on indictment, to imprisonment for a term not exceeding seven years or a fine (or both);
  (b) on summary conviction –

    (i)   in England and Wales, to imprisonment for a term not exceeding twelve months or to a fine not exceeding the statutory maximum (or both);
    (ii) in Scotland or Northern Ireland, to imprisonment for a term not exceeding six months, or to a fine not exceeding the statutory maximum (or both).

1008 Copy of application: provisions as to service of documents

(1) The following provisions have effect for the purposes of –

section 1006 (copy of application to be given to members, employees, etc), and

section 1007 (copy of application to be given to new members, employees, etc).

(2) A document is treated as given to a person if it is –

  (a) delivered to him, or
  (b) left at his proper address, or
  (c) sent by post to him at that address.

(3) For the purposes of subsection (2) and section 7 of the Interpretation Act 1978 (c. 30) (service of documents by post) as it applies in relation to that subsection, the proper address of a person is –

   (a) in the case of a firm incorporated or formed in the United Kingdom, its registered or principal office;

   (b) in the case of a firm incorporated or formed outside the United Kingdom –

       (i)   if it has a place of business in the United Kingdom, its principal office in the United Kingdom, or

      (ii)   if it does not have a place of business in the United Kingdom, its registered or principal office;

   (c) in the case of an individual, his last known address.

(4) In the case of a creditor of the company a document is treated as given to him if it is left or sent by post to him –

   (a) at the place of business of his with which the company has had dealings by virtue of which he is a creditor of the company, or

   (b) if there is more than one such place of business, at each of them.

1009 Circumstances in which application to be withdrawn

(1) This section applies where, at any time on or after the day on which a company makes an application under section 1003 (application for voluntary striking off) and before the day on which the application is finally dealt with or withdrawn –

   (a) the company –

       (i)   changes its name,

      (ii)   trades or otherwise carries on business,

     (iii)   makes a disposal for value of any property or rights other than those which it was necessary or expedient for it to hold for the purpose of making, or proceeding with, an application under that section, or

     (iv)   engages in any activity, except one to which subsection (4) applies;

   (b) an application is made to the court under Part 26 on behalf of the company for the sanctioning of a compromise or arrangement;

   (c) a voluntary arrangement in relation to the company is proposed under Part 1 of the Insolvency Act 1986 (c. 45) or Part 2 of the Insolvency (Northern Ireland) Order 1989 (S.I. 1989/2405 (N.I. 19));

   (d) an application to the court for an administration order in respect of the company is made under paragraph 12 of Schedule B1 to that Act or paragraph 13 of Schedule B1 to that Order;

   (e) an administrator is appointed in respect of the company under paragraph 14 or 22 of Schedule B1 to that Act or paragraph 15 or 23 of Schedule B1 to that Order, or a copy of notice of intention to appoint an administrator of the company under any of those provisions is filed with the court;

   (f) there arise any of the circumstances in which, under section 84(1) of that Act or Article 70 of that Order, the company may be voluntarily wound up;

   (g) a petition is presented for the winding up of the company by the court under Part 4 of that Act or Part 5 of that Order;

   (h) a receiver or manager of the company's property is appointed; or

   (i) a judicial factor is appointed to administer the company's estate.

(2) A person who, at the end of a day on which any of the events mentioned in subsection (1) occurs, is a director of the company must secure that the company's application is withdrawn forthwith.

(3) For the purposes of subsection (1)(a), a company is not treated as trading or otherwise carrying on business by virtue only of the fact that it makes a payment in respect of a liability incurred in the course of trading or otherwise carrying on business.

(4) The excepted activities referred to in subsection (1)(a)(iv) are –

   (a) any activity necessary or expedient for the purposes of –

      (i)   making, or proceeding with, an application under section 1003 (application for voluntary striking off),

      (ii)   concluding affairs of the company that are outstanding because of what has been necessary or expedient for the purpose of making, or proceeding with, such an application, or

      (iii) complying with any statutory requirement;

  (b) any activity specified by the Secretary of State by order for the purposes of this subsection.

An order under paragraph (b) is subject to negative resolution procedure.

(5) A person who fails to perform the duty imposed on him by this section commits an offence.

(6) In proceedings for an offence under this section it is a defence for the accused to prove –

  (a) that at the time of the failure he was not aware of the fact that the company had made an application under section 1003, or

  (b) that he took all reasonable steps to perform the duty.

(7) A person guilty of an offence under this section is liable –

  (a) on conviction on indictment, to a fine;

  (b) on summary conviction, to a fine not exceeding the statutory maximum.

1010 Withdrawal of application

An application under section 1003 is withdrawn by notice to the registrar.

1011 Meaning of "creditor"

In this Chapter "creditor" includes a contingent or prospective creditor.

CHAPTER 2

PROPERTY OF DISSOLVED COMPANY

Property vesting as bona vacantia

1012 Property of dissolved company to be bona vacantia

(1) When a company is dissolved, all property and rights whatsoever vested in or held on trust for the company immediately before its dissolution (including leasehold property, but not including property held by the company on trust for another person) are deemed to be bona vacantia and –

  (a) accordingly belong to the Crown, or to the Duchy of Lancaster or to the Duke of Cornwall for the time being (as the case may be), and

  (b) vest and may be dealt with in the same manner as other bona vacantia accruing to the Crown, to the Duchy of Lancaster or to the Duke of Cornwall.

(2) Subsection (1) has effect subject to the possible restoration of the company to the register under Chapter 3 (see section 1034).

1013 Crown disclaimer of property vesting as bona vacantia

(1) Where property vests in the Crown under section 1012, the Crown's title to it under that section may be disclaimed by a notice signed by the Crown representative, that is to say the Treasury Solicitor, or, in relation to property in Scotland, the Queen's and Lord Treasurer's Remembrancer.

(2) The right to execute a notice of disclaimer under this section may be waived by or on behalf of the Crown either expressly or by taking possession.

(3) A notice of disclaimer must be executed within three years after –

(a) the date on which the fact that the property may have vested in the Crown under section 1012 first comes to the notice of the Crown representative, or

(b) if ownership of the property is not established at that date, the end of the period reasonably necessary for the Crown representative to establish the ownership of the property.

(4) If an application in writing is made to the Crown representative by a person interested in the property requiring him to decide whether he will or will not disclaim, any notice of disclaimer must be executed within twelve months after the making of the application or such further period as may be allowed by the court.

(5) A notice of disclaimer under this section is of no effect if it is shown to have been executed after the end of the period specified by subsection (3) or (4).

(6) A notice of disclaimer under this section must be delivered to the registrar and retained and registered by him.

(7) Copies of it must be published in the Gazette and sent to any persons who have given the Crown representative notice that they claim to be interested in the property.

(8) This section applies to property vested in the Duchy of Lancaster or the Duke of Cornwall under section 1012 as if for references to the Crown and the Crown representative there were respectively substituted references to the Duchy of Lancaster and to the Solicitor to that Duchy, or to the Duke of Cornwall and to the Solicitor to the Duchy of Cornwall, as the case may be.

1014 Effect of Crown disclaimer

(1) Where notice of disclaimer is executed under section 1013 as respects any property, that property is deemed not to have vested in the Crown under section 1012.

(2) The following sections contain provisions as to the effect of the Crown disclaimer –

sections 1015 to 1019 apply in relation to property in England and Wales or Northern Ireland;

sections 1020 to 1022 apply in relation to property in Scotland.

Effect of Crown disclaimer: England and Wales and Northern Ireland

1015 General effect of disclaimer

(1) The Crown's disclaimer operates so as to terminate, as from the date of the disclaimer, the rights, interests and liabilities of the company in or in respect of the property disclaimed.

(2) It does not, except so far as is necessary for the purpose of releasing the company from any liability, affect the rights or liabilities of any other person.

1016 Disclaimer of leaseholds

(1) The disclaimer of any property of a leasehold character does not take effect unless a copy of the disclaimer has been served (so far as the Crown representative is aware of their addresses) on every person claiming under the company as underlessee or mortgagee, and either –

(a) no application under section 1017 (power of court to make vesting order) is made with respect to that property before the end of the period of 14 days beginning with the day on which the last notice under this paragraph was served, or

(b) where such an application has been made, the court directs that the disclaimer shall take effect.

(2) Where the court gives a direction under subsection (1)(b) it may also, instead of or in addition to any order it makes under section 1017, make such order as it thinks fit with respect to fixtures, tenant's improvements and other matters arising out of the lease.

(3) In this section the "Crown representative" means –

  (a) in relation to property vested in the Duchy of Lancaster, the Solicitor to that Duchy;

  (b) in relation to property vested in the Duke of Cornwall, the Solicitor to the Duchy of Cornwall;

  (c) in relation to property in Scotland, the Queen's and Lord Treasurer's Remembrancer;

  (d) in relation to other property, the Treasury Solicitor.

1017 Power of court to make vesting order

(1) The court may on application by a person who –

  (a) claims an interest in the disclaimed property, or

  (b) is under a liability in respect of the disclaimed property that is not discharged by the disclaimer,

make an order under this section in respect of the property.

(2) An order under this section is an order for the vesting of the disclaimed property in, or its delivery to –

  (a) a person entitled to it (or a trustee for such a person), or

  (b) a person subject to such a liability as is mentioned in subsection (1)(b) (or a trustee for such a person).

(3) An order under subsection (2)(b) may only be made where it appears to the court that it would be just to do so for the purpose of compensating the person subject to the liability in respect of the disclaimer.

(4) An order under this section may be made on such terms as the court thinks fit.

(5) On a vesting order being made under this section, the property comprised in it vests in the person named in that behalf in the order without conveyance, assignment or transfer.

1018 Protection of persons holding under a lease

(1) The court must not make an order under section 1017 vesting property of a leasehold nature in a person claiming under the company as underlessee or mortgagee except on terms making that person –

  (a) subject to the same liabilities and obligations as those to which the company was subject under the lease, or

  (b) if the court thinks fit, subject to the same liabilities and obligations as if the lease had been assigned to him.

(2) Where the order relates to only part of the property comprised in the lease, subsection (1) applies as if the lease had comprised only the property comprised in the vesting order.

(3) A person claiming under the company as underlessee or mortgagee who declines to accept a vesting order on such terms is excluded from all interest in the property.

(4) If there is no person claiming under the company who is willing to accept an order on such terms, the court has power to vest the company's estate and interest in the property in any person who is liable (whether personally or in a representative character, and whether alone or jointly with the company) to perform the lessee's covenants in the lease.

(5) The court may vest that estate and interest in such a person freed and discharged from all estates, incumbrances and interests created by the company.

1019 Land subject to rentcharge

Where in consequence of the disclaimer land that is subject to a rentcharge vests in any person, neither he nor his successors in title are subject to any personal liability in respect of sums becoming due under the rentcharge, except sums becoming due after he, or some person claiming under or through him, has taken possession or control of the land or has entered into occupation of it.

Effect of Crown disclaimer: Scotland

1020 General effect of disclaimer

(1) The Crown's disclaimer operates to determine, as from the date of the disclaimer, the rights, interests and liabilities of the company, and the property of the company, in or in respect of the property disclaimed.

(2) It does not (except so far as is necessary for the purpose of releasing the company and its property from liability) affect the rights or liabilities of any other person.

1021 Power of court to make vesting order

(1) The court may –

   (a) on application by a person who either claims an interest in disclaimed property or is under a liability not discharged by this Act in respect of disclaimed property, and

   (b) on hearing such persons as it thinks fit,

   make an order for the vesting of the property in or its delivery to any persons entitled to it, or to whom it may seem just that the property should be delivered by way of compensation for such liability, or a trustee for him.

(2) The order may be made on such terms as the court thinks fit.

(3) On a vesting order being made under this section, the property comprised in it vests accordingly in the person named in that behalf in the order, without conveyance or assignation for that purpose.

1022 Protection of persons holding under a lease

(1) Where the property disclaimed is held under a lease the court must not make a vesting order in favour of a person claiming under the company, whether –

   (a) as sub-lessee, or

   (b) as creditor in a duly registered or (as the case may be) recorded heritable security over a lease,

   except on the following terms.

(2) The person must by the order be made subject –

   (a) to the same liabilities and obligations as those to which the company was subject under the lease in respect of the property, or

   (b) if the court thinks fit, only to the same liabilities and obligations as if the lease had been assigned to him.

   In either event (if the case so requires) the liabilities and obligations must be as if the lease had comprised only the property comprised in the vesting order.

(3) A sub-lessee or creditor declining to accept a vesting order on such terms is excluded from all interest in and security over the property.

(4) If there is no person claiming under the company who is willing to accept an order on such terms, the court has power to vest the company's estate and interest in the property in any person liable (either personally or in a representative character, and either alone or jointly with the company) to perform the lessee's obligations under the lease.

(5) The court may vest that estate and interest in such a person freed and discharged from all interests, rights and obligations created by the company in the lease or in relation to the lease.

(6) For the purposes of this section a heritable security –

(a) is duly recorded if it is recorded in the Register of Sasines, and

(b) is duly registered if registered in accordance with the Land Registration (Scotland) Act 1979 (c. 33).

Supplementary provisions

1023 Liability for rentcharge on company's land after dissolution

(1) This section applies where on the dissolution of a company land in England and Wales or Northern Ireland that is subject to a rentcharge vests by operation of law in the Crown or any other person ("the proprietor").

(2) Neither the proprietor nor his successors in title are subject to any personal liability in respect of sums becoming due under the rentcharge, except sums becoming due after the proprietor, or some person claiming under or through him, has taken possession or control of the land or has entered into occupation of it.

(3) In this section "company" includes any body corporate.

CHAPTER 3

RESTORATION TO THE REGISTER

Administrative restoration to the register

1024 Application for administrative restoration to the register

(1) An application may be made to the registrar to restore to the register a company that has been struck off the register under section 1000 or 1001 (power of registrar to strike off defunct company).

(2) An application under this section may be made whether or not the company has in consequence been dissolved.

(3) An application under this section may only be made by a former director or former member of the company.

(4) An application under this section may not be made after the end of the period of six years from the date of the dissolution of the company.

For this purpose an application is made when it is received by the registrar.

1025 Requirements for administrative restoration

(1) On an application under section 1024 the registrar shall restore the company to the register if, and only if, the following conditions are met.

(2) The first condition is that the company was carrying on business or in operation at the time of its striking off.

(3) The second condition is that, if any property or right previously vested in or held on trust for the company has vested as bona vacantia, the Crown representative has signified to the registrar in writing consent to the company's restoration to the register.

(4) It is the applicant's responsibility to obtain that consent and to pay any costs (in Scotland, expenses) of the Crown representative –

(a) in dealing with the property during the period of dissolution, or

(b) in connection with the proceedings on the application,

that may be demanded as a condition of giving consent.

(5) The third condition is that the applicant has –

    (a) delivered to the registrar such documents relating to the company as are necessary to bring up to date the records kept by the registrar, and

    (b) paid any penalties under section 453 or corresponding earlier provisions (civil penalty for failure to deliver accounts) that were outstanding at the date of dissolution or striking off.

(6) In this section the "Crown representative" means –

    (a) in relation to property vested in the Duchy of Lancaster, the Solicitor to that Duchy;

    (b) in relation to property vested in the Duke of Cornwall, the Solicitor to the Duchy of Cornwall;

    (c) in relation to property in Scotland, the Queen's and Lord Treasurer's Remembrancer;

    (d) in relation to other property, the Treasury Solicitor.

1026 Application to be accompanied by statement of compliance

(1) An application under section 1024 (application for administrative restoration to the register) must be accompanied by a statement of compliance.

(2) The statement of compliance required is a statement –

    (a) that the person making the application has standing to apply (see subsection (3) of that section), and

    (b) that the requirements for administrative restoration (see section 1025) are met.

(3) The registrar may accept the statement of compliance as sufficient evidence of those matters.

1027 Registrar's decision on application for administrative restoration

(1) The registrar must give notice to the applicant of the decision on an application under section 1024 (application for administrative restoration to the register).

(2) If the decision is that the company should be restored to the register, the restoration takes effect as from the date that notice is sent.

(3) In the case of such a decision, the registrar must –

    (a) enter on the register a note of the date as from which the company's restoration to the register takes effect, and

    (b) cause notice of the restoration to be published in the Gazette.

(4) The notice under subsection (3)(b) must state –

    (a) the name of the company or, if the company is restored to the register under a different name (see section 1033), that name and its former name,

    (b) the company's registered number, and

    (c) the date as from which the restoration of the company to the register takes effect.

1028 Effect of administrative restoration

(1) The general effect of administrative restoration to the register is that the company is deemed to have continued in existence as if it had not been dissolved or struck off the register.

(2) The company is not liable to a penalty under section 453 or any corresponding earlier provision (civil penalty for failure to deliver accounts) for a financial year in relation to which the period for filing accounts and reports ended –

    (a) after the date of dissolution or striking off, and

    (b) before the restoration of the company to the register.

(3) The court may give such directions and make such provision as seems just for placing the company and all other persons in the same position (as nearly as may be) as if the company had not been dissolved or struck off the register.

(4) An application to the court for such directions or provision may be made any time within three years after the date of restoration of the company to the register.

Restoration to the register by the court

1029 Application to court for restoration to the register

(1) An application may be made to the court to restore to the register a company –

  (a) that has been dissolved under Chapter 9 of Part 4 of the Insolvency Act 1986 (c. 45) or Chapter 9 of Part 5 of the Insolvency (Northern Ireland) Order 1989 (S.I. 1989/2405 (N.I. 19)) (dissolution of company after winding up),

  (b) that is deemed to have been dissolved under paragraph 84(6) of Schedule B1 to that Act or paragraph 85(6) of Schedule B1 to that Order (dissolution of company following administration), or

  (c) that has been struck off the register –

     (i)   under section 1000 or 1001 (power of registrar to strike off defunct company), or

     (ii) under section 1003 (voluntary striking off),

  whether or not the company has in consequence been dissolved.

(2) An application under this section may be made by –

  (a) the Secretary of State,

  (b) any former director of the company,

  (c) any person having an interest in land in which the company had a superior or derivative interest,

  (d) any person having an interest in land or other property –

     (i)   that was subject to rights vested in the company, or

     (ii) that was benefited by obligations owed by the company,

  (e) any person who but for the company's dissolution would have been in a contractual relationship with it,

  (f) any person with a potential legal claim against the company,

  (g) any manager or trustee of a pension fund established for the benefit of employees of the company,

  (h) any former member of the company (or the personal representatives of such a person),

  (i) any person who was a creditor of the company at the time of its striking off or dissolution,

  (j) any former liquidator of the company,

  (k) where the company was struck off the register under section 1003 (voluntary striking off), any person of a description specified by regulations under section 1006(1)(f) or 1007(2)(f) (persons entitled to notice of application for voluntary striking off),

  or by any other person appearing to the court to have an interest in the matter.

1030 When application to the court may be made

(1) An application to the court for restoration of a company to the register may be made at any time for the purpose of bringing proceedings against the company for damages for personal injury.

(2) No order shall be made on such an application if it appears to the court that the proceedings would fail by virtue of any enactment as to the time within which proceedings must be brought.

(3) In making that decision the court must have regard to its power under section 1032(3) (power to give consequential directions etc) to direct that the period between

the dissolution (or striking off) of the company and the making of the order is not to count for the purposes of any such enactment.

(4) In any other case an application to the court for restoration of a company to the register may not be made after the end of the period of six years from the date of the dissolution of the company, subject as follows.

(5) In a case where –

    (a) the company has been struck off the register under section 1000 or 1001 (power of registrar to strike off defunct company),

    (b) an application to the registrar has been made under section 1024 (application for administrative restoration to the register) within the time allowed for making such an application, and

    (c) the registrar has refused the application,

an application to the court under this section may be made within 28 days of notice of the registrar's decision being issued by the registrar, even if the period of six years mentioned in subsection (4) above has expired.

(6) For the purposes of this section –

    (a) "personal injury" includes any disease and any impairment of a person's physical or mental condition; and

    (b) references to damages for personal injury include –

        (i) any sum claimed by virtue of section 1(2)(c) of the Law Reform (Miscellaneous Provisions) Act 1934 (c. 41) or section 14(2)(c) of the Law Reform (Miscellaneous Provisions) Act (Northern Ireland) 1937 (1937 c. 9 (N.I.)) (funeral expenses)), and

        (ii) damages under the Fatal Accidents Act 1976 (c. 30), the Damages (Scotland) Act 1976 (c. 13) or the Fatal Accidents (Northern Ireland) Order 1977 (S.I. 1977/1251 (N.I. 18)).

1031 Decision on application for restoration by the court

(1) On an application under section 1029 the court may order the restoration of the company to the register –

    (a) if the company was struck off the register under section 1000 or 1001 (power of registrar to strike off defunct companies) and the company was, at the time of the striking off, carrying on business or in operation;

    (b) if the company was struck off the register under section 1003 (voluntary striking off) and any of the requirements of sections 1004 to 1009 was not complied with;

    (c) if in any other case the court considers it just to do so.

(2) If the court orders restoration of the company to the register, the restoration takes effect on a copy of the court's order being delivered to the registrar.

(3) The registrar must cause to be published in the Gazette notice of the restoration of the company to the register.

(4) The notice must state –

    (a) the name of the company or, if the company is restored to the register under a different name (see section 1033), that name and its former name,

    (b) the company's registered number, and

    (c) the date on which the restoration took effect.

1032 Effect of court order for restoration to the register

(1) The general effect of an order by the court for restoration to the register is that the company is deemed to have continued in existence as if it had not been dissolved or struck off the register.

(2) The company is not liable to a penalty under section 453 or any corresponding earlier

provision (civil penalty for failure to deliver accounts) for a financial year in relation to which the period for filing accounts and reports ended –

    (a) after the date of dissolution or striking off, and

    (b) before the restoration of the company to the register.

(3) The court may give such directions and make such provision as seems just for placing the company and all other persons in the same position (as nearly as may be) as if the company had not been dissolved or struck off the register.

(4) The court may also give directions as to –

    (a) the delivery to the registrar of such documents relating to the company as are necessary to bring up to date the records kept by the registrar,

    (b) the payment of the costs (in Scotland, expenses) of the registrar in connection with the proceedings for the restoration of the company to the register,

    (c) where any property or right previously vested in or held on trust for the company has vested as bona vacantia, the payment of the costs (in Scotland, expenses) of the Crown representative –

        (i) in dealing with the property during the period of dissolution, or

        (ii) in connection with the proceedings on the application.

(5) In this section the "Crown representative" means –

    (a) in relation to property vested in the Duchy of Lancaster, the Solicitor to that Duchy;

    (b) in relation to property vested in the Duke of Cornwall, the Solicitor to the Duchy of Cornwall;

    (c) in relation to property in Scotland, the Queen's and Lord Treasurer's Remembrancer;

    (d) in relation to other property, the Treasury Solicitor.

Supplementary provisions

1033 Company's name on restoration

(1) A company is restored to the register with the name it had before it was dissolved or struck off the register, subject to the following provisions.

(2) If at the date of restoration the company could not be registered under its former name without contravening section 66 (name not to be the same as another in the registrar's index of company names), it must be restored to the register –

    (a) under another name specified –

        (i) in the case of administrative restoration, in the application to the registrar, or

        (ii) in the case of restoration under a court order, in the court's order, or

    (b) as if its registered number was also its name.

References to a company's being registered in a name, and to registration in that context, shall be read as including the company's being restored to the register.

(3) If a company is restored to the register under a name specified in the application to the registrar, the provisions of –

section 80 (change of name: registration and issue of new certificate of incorporation), and

section 81 (change of name: effect),

apply as if the application to the registrar were notice of a change of name.

(4) If a company is restored to the register under a name specified in the court's order, the provisions of –

section 80 (change of name: registration and issue of new certificate of incorporation), and

section 81 (change of name: effect),

apply as if the copy of the court order delivered to the registrar were notice of a change a name.

(5) If the company is restored to the register as if its registered number was also its name –

(a) the company must change its name within 14 days after the date of the restoration,

(b) the change may be made by resolution of the directors (without prejudice to any other method of changing the company's name),

(c) the company must give notice to the registrar of the change, and

(d) sections 80 and 81 apply as regards the registration and effect of the change.

(6) If the company fails to comply with subsection (5)(a) or (c) an offence is committed by –

(a) the company, and

(b) every officer of the company who is in default.

(7) A person guilty of an offence under subsection (6) is liable on summary conviction to a fine not exceeding level 5 on the standard scale and, for continued contravention, a daily default fine not exceeding one-tenth of level 5 on the standard scale.

1034 Effect of restoration to the register where property has vested as bona vacantia

(1) The person in whom any property or right is vested by section 1012 (property of dissolved company to be bona vacantia) may dispose of, or of an interest in, that property or right despite the fact that the company may be restored to the register under this Chapter.

(2) If the company is restored to the register –

(a) the restoration does not affect the disposition (but without prejudice to its effect in relation to any other property or right previously vested in or held on trust for the company), and

(b) the Crown or, as the case may be, the Duke of Cornwall shall pay to the company an amount equal to –

(i) the amount of any consideration received for the property or right or, as the case may be, the interest in it, or

(ii) the value of any such consideration at the time of the disposition,

or, if no consideration was received an amount equal to the value of the property, right or interest disposed of, as at the date of the disposition.

(3) There may be deducted from the amount payable under subsection (2)(b) the reasonable costs of the Crown representative in connection with the disposition (to the extent that they have not been paid as a condition of administrative restoration or pursuant to a court order for restoration).

(4) Where a liability accrues under subsection (2) in respect of any property or right which before the restoration of the company to the register had accrued as bona vacantia to the Duchy of Lancaster, the Attorney General of that Duchy shall represent Her Majesty in any proceedings arising in connection with that liability.

(5) Where a liability accrues under subsection (2) in respect of any property or right which before the restoration of the company to the register had accrued as bona vacantia to the Duchy of Cornwall, such persons as the Duke of Cornwall (or other possessor for the time being of the Duchy) may appoint shall represent the Duke (or other possessor) in any proceedings arising out of that liability.

(6) In this section the "Crown representative" means –

(a) in relation to property vested in the Duchy of Lancaster, the Solicitor to that Duchy;

    (b) in relation to property vested in the Duke of Cornwall, the Solicitor to the Duchy of Cornwall;

    (c) in relation to property in Scotland, the Queen's and Lord Treasurer's Remembrancer;

    (d) in relation to other property, the Treasury Solicitor.

PART 32

COMPANY INVESTIGATIONS: AMENDMENTS

1035 Powers of Secretary of State to give directions to inspectors

(1) In Part 14 of the Companies Act 1985 (c. 6) (investigation of companies and their affairs), after section 446 insert –

"Powers of Secretary of State to give directions to inspectors

446A General powers to give directions

(1) In exercising his functions an inspector shall comply with any direction given to him by the Secretary of State under this section.

(2) The Secretary of State may give an inspector appointed under section 431, 432(2) or 442(1) a direction –

    (a) as to the subject matter of his investigation (whether by reference to a specified area of a company's operation, a specified transaction, a period of time or otherwise), or

    (b) which requires the inspector to take or not to take a specified step in his investigation.

(3) The Secretary of State may give an inspector appointed under any provision of this Part a direction requiring him to secure that a specified report under section 437 –

    (a) includes the inspector's views on a specified matter,

    (b) does not include any reference to a specified matter,

    (c) is made in a specified form or manner, or

    (d) is made by a specified date.

(4) A direction under this section –

    (a) may be given on an inspector's appointment,

    (b) may vary or revoke a direction previously given, and

    (c) may be given at the request of an inspector.

(5) In this section –

    (a) a reference to an inspector's investigation includes any investigation he undertakes, or could undertake, under section 433(1) (power to investigate affairs of holding company or subsidiary);

    (b) "specified" means specified in a direction under this section.

446B Direction to terminate investigation

(1) The Secretary of State may direct an inspector to take no further steps in his investigation.

(2) The Secretary of State may give a direction under this section to an inspector appointed under section 432(1) or 442(3) only on the grounds that it appears to him that –

(a) matters have come to light in the course of the inspector's investigation which suggest that a criminal offence has been committed, and

(b) those matters have been referred to the appropriate prosecuting authority.

(3) Where the Secretary of State gives a direction under this section, any direction already given to the inspector under section 437(1) to produce an interim report, and any direction given to him under section 446A(3) in relation to such a report, shall cease to have effect.

(4) Where the Secretary of State gives a direction under this section, the inspector shall not make a final report to the Secretary of State unless –

(a) the direction was made on the grounds mentioned in subsection (2) and the Secretary of State directs the inspector to make a final report to him, or

(b) the inspector was appointed under section 432(1) (appointment in pursuance of order of the court).

(5) An inspector shall comply with any direction given to him under this section.

(6) In this section, a reference to an inspector's investigation includes any investigation he undertakes, or could undertake, under section 433(1) (power to investigate affairs of holding company or subsidiary).".

(2) In section 431 of that Act (inspectors' powers during investigation) in subsection (1) for "report on them in such manner as he may direct" substitute "report the result of their investigations to him".

(3) In section 432 of that Act (other company investigations) in subsection (1) for "report on them in such manner as he directs" substitute "report the result of their investigations to him".

(4) In section 437 of that Act (inspectors' reports) –

(a) in subsection (1) omit the second sentence, and

(b) subsections (1B) and (1C) shall cease to have effect.

(5) In section 442 of that Act (power to investigate company ownership), omit subsection (2).

1036 Resignation, removal and replacement of inspectors

After section 446B of the Companies Act 1985 (c. 6) (inserted by section 1035 above) insert –

"Resignation, removal and replacement of inspectors

446C Resignation and revocation of appointment

(1) An inspector may resign by notice in writing to the Secretary of State.

(2) The Secretary of State may revoke the appointment of an inspector by notice in writing to the inspector.

446D Appointment of replacement inspectors

(1) Where –

(a) an inspector resigns,

(b) an inspector's appointment is revoked, or

(c) an inspector dies,

the Secretary of State may appoint one or more competent inspectors to continue the investigation.

(2) An appointment under subsection (1) shall be treated for the purposes of this Part (apart from this section) as an appointment under the provision of this Part under which the former inspector was appointed.

(3) The Secretary of State must exercise his power under subsection (1) so as to secure that at least one inspector continues the investigation.

(4) Subsection (3) does not apply if –

    (a) the Secretary of State could give any replacement inspector a direction under section 446B (termination of investigation), and

    (b) such a direction would (under subsection (4) of that section) result in a final report not being made.

(5) In this section, references to an investigation include any investigation the former inspector conducted under section 433(1) (power to investigate affairs of holding company or subsidiary).".

1037 Power to obtain information from former inspectors etc

(1) After section 446D of the Companies Act 1985 (c. 6) (inserted by section 1036 above) insert –

"*Power to obtain information from former inspectors etc*

446E Obtaining information from former inspectors etc

(1) This section applies to a person who was appointed as an inspector under this Part –

    (a) who has resigned, or

    (b) whose appointment has been revoked.

(2) This section also applies to an inspector to whom the Secretary of State has given a direction under section 446B (termination of investigation).

(3) The Secretary of State may direct a person to whom this section applies to produce documents obtained or generated by that person during the course of his investigation to –

    (a) the Secretary of State, or

    (b) an inspector appointed under this Part.

(4) The power under subsection (3) to require production of a document includes power, in the case of a document not in hard copy form, to require the production of a copy of the document –

    (a) in hard copy form, or

    (b) in a form from which a hard copy can be readily obtained.

(5) The Secretary of State may take copies of or extracts from a document produced in pursuance of this section.

(6) The Secretary of State may direct a person to whom this section applies to inform him of any matters that came to that person's knowledge as a result of his investigation.

(7) A person shall comply with any direction given to him under this section.

(8) In this section –

    (a) references to the investigation of a former inspector or inspector include any investigation he conducted under section 433(1) (power to investigate affairs of holding company or subsidiary), and

    (b) "document" includes information recorded in any form.".

(2) In section 451A of that Act (disclosure of information by Secretary of State or inspector), in subsection (1)(a) for "446" substitute "446E".

(3) In section 452(1) of that Act (privileged information) for "446" substitute "446E".

1038 Power to require production of documents

(1) In section 434 of the Companies Act 1985 (c. 6) (production of documents and evidence to inspectors), for subsection (6) substitute –

"(6) In this section "document" includes information recorded in any form.

(7) The power under this section to require production of a document includes power, in the case of a document not in hard copy form, to require the production of a copy of the document –

(a) in hard copy form, or
(b) in a form from which a hard copy can be readily obtained.

(8) An inspector may take copies of or extracts from a document produced in pursuance of this section.".

(2) In section 447 of the Companies Act 1985 (power of Secretary of State to require documents and information), for subsection (9) substitute –

"(9) The power under this section to require production of a document includes power, in the case of a document not in hard copy form, to require the production of a copy of the document –

(a) in hard copy form, or
(b) in a form from which a hard copy can be readily obtained.".

1039 Disqualification orders: consequential amendments

In section 8(1A)(b)(i) of the Company Directors Disqualification Act 1986 (c. 46) (disqualification after investigation of company: meaning of "investigative material") –

(a) after "section" insert "437, 446E,", and
(b) after "448" insert ", 451A".

PART 33

UK COMPANIES NOT FORMED UNDER COMPANIES LEGISLATION

CHAPTER 1

COMPANIES NOT FORMED UNDER COMPANIES LEGISLATION BUT AUTHORISED TO REGISTER

1040 Companies authorised to register under this Act

(1) This section applies to –

(a) any company that was in existence on 2nd November 1862 (including any company registered under the Joint Stock Companies Acts), and
(b) any company formed after that date (whether before or after the commencement of this Act) –

(i)   in pursuance of an Act of Parliament other than this Act or any of the former Companies Acts,
(ii) in pursuance of letters patent, or
(iii) that is otherwise duly constituted according to law.

(2) Any such company may on making application register under this Act.

(3) Subject to the following provisions, it may register as an unlimited company, as a company limited by shares or as a company limited by guarantee.

(4) A company having the liability of its members limited by Act of Parliament or letters patent –

    (a) may not register under this section unless it is a joint stock company, and

    (b) may not register under this section as an unlimited company or a company limited by guarantee.

(5) A company that is not a joint stock company may not register under this section as a company limited by shares.

(6) The registration of a company under this section is not invalid by reason that it has taken place with a view to the company's being wound up.

1041 Definition of "joint stock company"

(1) For the purposes of section 1040 (companies authorised to register under this Act) "joint stock company" means a company –

    (a) having a permanent paid-up or nominal share capital of fixed amount divided into shares, also of fixed amount, or held and transferable as stock, or divided and held partly in one way and partly in the other, and

    (b) formed on the principle of having for its members the holders of those shares or that stock, and no other persons.

(2) Such a company when registered with limited liability under this Act is deemed a company limited by shares.

1042 Power to make provision by regulations

(1) The Secretary of State may make provision by regulations –

    (a) for and in connection with registration under section 1040 (companies authorised to register under this Act), and

    (b) as to the application to companies so registered of the provisions of the Companies Acts.

(2) Without prejudice to the generality of that power, regulations under this section may make provision corresponding to any provision formerly made by Chapter 2 of Part 22 of the Companies Act 1985 (c. 6).

(3) Regulations under this section are subject to negative resolution procedure.

CHAPTER 2

UNREGISTERED COMPANIES

1043 Unregistered companies

(1) This section applies to bodies corporate incorporated in and having a principal place of business in the United Kingdom, other than –

    (a) bodies incorporated by, or registered under, a public general Act of Parliament;

    (b) bodies not formed for the purpose of carrying on a business that has for its object the acquisition of gain by the body or its individual members;

    (c) bodies for the time being exempted from this section by direction of the Secretary of State;

    (d) open-ended investment companies.

(2) The Secretary of State may make provision by regulations applying specified provisions of the Companies Acts to all, or any specified description of, the bodies to which this section applies.

(3) The regulations may provide that the specified provisions of the Companies Acts

apply subject to any specified limitations and to such adaptations and modifications (if any) as may be specified.

(4) This section does not –

   (a) repeal or revoke in whole or in part any enactment, royal charter or other instrument constituting or regulating any body in relation to which provisions of the Companies Acts are applied by regulations under this section, or

   (b) restrict the power of Her Majesty to grant a charter in lieu or supplementary to any such charter.

But in relation to any such body the operation of any such enactment, charter or instrument is suspended in so far as it is inconsistent with any of those provisions as they apply for the time being to that body.

(5) In this section "specified" means specified in the regulations.

(6) Regulations under this section are subject to negative resolution procedure.

PART 34

OVERSEAS COMPANIES

Introductory

1044 Overseas companies

In the Companies Acts an "overseas company" means a company incorporated outside the United Kingdom.

1045 Company contracts and execution of documents by companies

(1) The Secretary of State may make provision by regulations applying sections 43 to 52 (formalities of doing business and other matters) to overseas companies, subject to such exceptions, adaptations or modifications as may be specified in the regulations.

(2) Regulations under this section are subject to negative resolution procedure.

Registration of particulars

1046 Duty to register particulars

(1) The Secretary of State may make provision by regulations requiring an overseas company –

   (a) to deliver to the registrar for registration a return containing specified particulars, and

   (b) to deliver to the registrar with the return specified documents.

(2) The regulations –

   (a) must, in the case of a company other than a Gibraltar company, require the company to register particulars if the company opens a branch in the United Kingdom, and

   (b) may, in the case of a Gibraltar company, require the company to register particulars if the company opens a branch in the United Kingdom, and

   (c) may, in any case, require the registration of particulars in such other circumstances as may be specified.

(3) In subsection (2) –

   "branch" means a branch within the meaning of the Eleventh Company Law Directive (89/666/EEC);

   "Gibraltar company" means a company incorporated in Gibraltar.

(4)   The regulations may provide that where a company has registered particulars under this section and any alteration is made –

(a)   in the specified particulars, or

(b)   in any document delivered with the return,

the company must deliver to the registrar for registration a return containing specified particulars of the alteration.

(5)   The regulations may make provision –

(a)   requiring the return under this section to be delivered for registration to the registrar for a specified part of the United Kingdom, and

(b)   requiring it to be so delivered before the end of a specified period.

(6)   The regulations may make different provision according to –

(a)   the place where the company is incorporated, and

(b)   the activities carried on (or proposed to be carried on) by it.

This is without prejudice to the general power to make different provision for different cases.

(7)   In this section "specified" means specified in the regulations.

(8)   Regulations under this section are subject to affirmative resolution procedure.

1047 Registered name of overseas company

(1)   Regulations under section 1046 (duty to register particulars) must require an overseas company that is required to register particulars to register its name.

(2)   This may be –

(a)   the company's corporate name (that is, its name under the law of the country or territory in which it is incorporated) or

(b)   an alternative name specified in accordance with section 1048.

(3)   Subject only to subsection (5), an EEA company may always register its corporate name.

(4)   In any other case, the following provisions of Part 5 (a company's name) apply in relation to the registration of the name of an overseas company –

(a)   section 53 (prohibited names);

(b)   sections 54 to 56 (sensitive words and expressions);

(c)   section 65 (inappropriate use of indications of company type or legal form);

(d)   sections 66 to 74 (similarity to other names);

(e)   section 75 (provision of misleading information etc);

(f)   section 76 (misleading indication of activities).

(5)   The provisions of section 57 (permitted characters etc) apply in every case.

(6)   Any reference in the provisions mentioned in subsection (4) or (5) to a change of name shall be read as a reference to registration of a different name under section 1048.

1048 Registration under alternative name

(1)   An overseas company that is required to register particulars under section 1046 may at any time deliver to the registrar for registration a statement specifying a name, other than its corporate name, under which it proposes to carry on business in the United Kingdom.

(2)   An overseas company that has registered an alternative name may at any time deliver to the registrar of companies for registration a statement specifying a different name under which it proposes to carry on business in the United Kingdom (which may be its corporate name or a further alternative) in substitution for the name previously registered.

(3)   The alternative name for the time being registered under this section is treated for all purposes of the law applying in the United Kingdom as the company's corporate name.

(4) This does not –

(a) affect the references in this section or section 1047 to the company's corporate name,

(b) affect any rights or obligation of the company, or

(c) render defective any legal proceedings by or against the company.

(5) Any legal proceedings that might have been continued or commenced against the company by its corporate name, or any name previously registered under this section, may be continued or commenced against it by its name for the time being so registered.

Other requirements

1049 Accounts and reports: general

(1) The Secretary of State may make provision by regulations requiring an overseas company that is required to register particulars under section 1046 –

(a) to prepare the like accounts and directors' report, and

(b) to cause to be prepared such an auditor's report,

as would be required if the company were formed and registered under this Act.

(2) The regulations may for this purpose apply, with or without modifications, all or any of the provisions of –

Part 15 (accounts and reports), and

Part 16 (audit).

(3) The Secretary of State may make provision by regulations requiring an overseas company to deliver to the registrar copies of –

(a) the accounts and reports prepared in accordance with the regulations, or

(b) the accounts and reports that it is required to prepare and have audited under the law of the country in which it is incorporated.

(4) Regulations under this section are subject to negative resolution procedure.

1050 Accounts and reports: credit or financial institutions

(1) This section applies to a credit or financial institution –

(a) that is incorporated or otherwise formed outside the United Kingdom and Gibraltar,

(b) whose head office is outside the United Kingdom and Gibraltar, and

(c) that has a branch in the United Kingdom.

(2) In subsection (1) "branch" means a place of business that forms a legally dependent part of the institution and conducts directly all or some of the operations inherent in its business.

(3) The Secretary of State may make provision by regulations requiring an institution to which this section applies –

(a) to prepare the like accounts and directors' report, and

(b) to cause to be prepared such an auditor's report,

as would be required if the institution were a company formed and registered under this Act.

(4) The regulations may for this purpose apply, with or without modifications, all or any of the provisions of –

Part 15 (accounts and reports), and

Part 16 (audit).

(5) The Secretary of State may make provision by regulations requiring an institution to which this section applies to deliver to the registrar copies of –

(a)   accounts and reports prepared in accordance with the regulations, or

(b)   accounts and reports that it is required to prepare and have audited under the law of the country in which the institution has its head office.

(6)   Regulations under this section are subject to negative resolution procedure.

1051 Trading disclosures

(1)   The Secretary of State may by regulations make provision requiring overseas companies carrying on business in the United Kingdom –

    (a)   to display specified information in specified locations,

    (b)   to state specified information in specified descriptions of document or communication, and

    (c)   to provide specified information on request to those they deal with in the course of their business.

(2)   The regulations –

    (a)   shall in every case require a company that has registered particulars under section 1046 to disclose the name registered by it under section 1047, and

    (b)   may make provision as to the manner in which any specified information is to be displayed, stated or provided.

(3)   The regulations may make provision corresponding to that made by –

section 83 (civil consequences of failure to make required disclosure), and

section 84 (criminal consequences of failure to make required disclosure).

(4)   In this section "specified" means specified in the regulations.

(5)   Regulations under this section are subject to affirmative resolution procedure.

1052 Company charges

(1)   The Secretary of State may by regulations make provision about the registration of specified charges over property in the United Kingdom of a registered overseas company.

(2)   The power in subsection (1) includes power to make provision about –

    (a)   a registered overseas company that –

        (i)   has particulars registered in more than one part of the United Kingdom;

        (ii)   has property in more than one part of the United Kingdom;

    (b)   the circumstances in which property is to be regarded, for the purposes of the regulations, as being, or not being, in the United Kingdom or in a particular part of the United Kingdom;

    (c)   the keeping by a registered overseas company of records and registers about specified charges and their inspection;

    (d)   the consequences of a failure to register a charge in accordance with the regulations;

    (e)   the circumstances in which a registered overseas company ceases to be subject to the regulations.

(3)   The regulations may for this purpose apply, with or without modifications, any of the provisions of Part 25 (company charges).

(4)   The regulations may modify any reference in an enactment to Part 25, or to a particular provision of that Part, so as to include a reference to the regulations or to a specified provision of the regulations.

(5)   Regulations under this section are subject to negative resolution procedure.

(6)   In this section –

"registered overseas company" means an overseas company that has registered particulars under section 1046(1), and

"specified" means specified in the regulations.

1053 Other returns etc

(1) This section applies to overseas companies that are required to register particulars under section 1046.
(2) The Secretary of State may make provision by regulations requiring the delivery to the registrar of returns –
    (a) by a company to which this section applies that –
        (i) is being wound up, or
        (ii) becomes or ceases to be subject to insolvency proceedings, or an arrangement or composition or any analogous proceedings;
    (b) by the liquidator of a company to which this section applies.
(3) The regulations may specify –
    (a) the circumstances in which a return is to be made,
    (b) the particulars to be given in it, and
    (c) the period within which it is to be made.
(4) The Secretary of State may make provision by regulations requiring notice to be given to the registrar of the appointment in relation to a company to which this section applies of a judicial factor (in Scotland).
(5) The regulations may include provision corresponding to any provision made by section 1154 of this Act (duty to notify registrar of certain appointments).
(6) Regulations under this section are subject to affirmative resolution procedure.

Supplementary

1054 Offences

(1) Regulations under this Part may specify the person or persons responsible for complying with any specified requirement of the regulations.
(2) Regulations under this Part may make provision for offences, including provision as to –
    (a) the person or persons liable in the case of any specified contravention of the regulations, and
    (b) circumstances that are, or are not, to be a defence on a charge of such an offence.
(3) The regulations must not provide –
    (a) for imprisonment, or
    (b) for the imposition on summary conviction of a fine exceeding level 5 on the standard scale and, for continued contravention, a daily default fine not exceeding one-tenth of level 5 on the standard scale.
(4) In this section "specified" means specified in the regulations.

1055 Disclosure of individual's residential address: protection from disclosure

Where regulations under section 1046 (overseas companies: duty to register particulars) require an overseas company to register particulars of an individual's usual residential address, they must contain provision corresponding to that made by Chapter 8 of Part 10 (directors' residential addresses: protection from disclosure).

1056 Requirement to identify persons authorised to accept service of documents

Regulations under section 1046 (overseas companies: duty to register particulars) must require an overseas company to register –
    (a) particulars identifying every person resident in the United Kingdom authorised to accept service of documents on behalf of the company, or
    (b) a statement that there is no such person.

1057 Registrar to whom returns, notices etc to be delivered

(1) This section applies to an overseas company that is required to register or has registered particulars under section 1046 in more than one part of the United Kingdom.

(2) The Secretary of State may provide by regulations that, in the case of such a company, anything authorised or required to be delivered to the registrar under this Part is to be delivered –

    (a) to the registrar for each part of the United Kingdom in which the company is required to register or has registered particulars, or

    (b) to the registrar for such part or parts of the United Kingdom as may be specified in or determined in accordance with the regulations.

(3) Regulations under this section are subject to negative resolution procedure.

1058 Duty to give notice of ceasing to have registrable presence

(1) The Secretary of State may make provision by regulations requiring an overseas company –

    (a) if it has registered particulars following the opening of a branch, in accordance with regulations under section 1046(2)(a) or (b), to give notice to the registrar if it closes that branch;

    (b) if it has registered particulars in other circumstances, in accordance with regulations under section 1046(2)(c), to give notice to the registrar if the circumstances that gave rise to the obligation to register particulars cease to obtain.

(2) The regulations must provide for the notice to be given to the registrar for the part of the United Kingdom to which the original return of particulars was delivered.

(3) The regulations may specify the period within which notice must be given.

(4) Regulations under this section are subject to negative resolution procedure.

1059 Application of provisions in case of relocation of branch

For the purposes of this Part –

    (a) the relocation of a branch from one part of the United Kingdom to another counts as the closing of one branch and the opening of another;

    (b) the relocation of a branch within the same part of the United Kingdom does not.

PART 35

THE REGISTRAR OF COMPANIES

The registrar

1060 The registrar

(1) There shall continue to be –

    (a) a registrar of companies for England and Wales,

    (b) a registrar of companies for Scotland, and

    (c) a registrar of companies for Northern Ireland.

(2) The registrars shall be appointed by the Secretary of State.

(3) In the Companies Acts "the registrar of companies" and "the registrar" mean the registrar of companies for England and Wales, Scotland or Northern Ireland, as the case may require.

(4) References in the Companies Acts to registration in a particular part of the United Kingdom are to registration by the registrar for that part of the United Kingdom.

1061 The registrar's functions

(1) The registrar shall continue –

(a) to perform the functions conferred on the registrar –

(i)   under the Companies Acts, and
(ii) under the enactments listed in subsection (2), and

(b) to perform such functions on behalf of the Secretary of State, in relation to the registration of companies or other matters, as the Secretary of State may from time to time direct.

(2) The enactments are –

the Joint Stock Companies Acts;
the Newspaper Libel and Registration Act 1881 (c. 60);
the Limited Partnerships Act 1907 (c. 24);
section 53 of the Industrial and Provident Societies Act 1965 (c. 12) or, for Northern Ireland, section 62 of the Industrial and Provident Societies Act (Northern Ireland) 1969 (c. 24 (N.I.));
the Insolvency Act 1986 (c. 45) or, for Northern Ireland, the Insolvency (Northern Ireland) Order 1989 (S.I. 1989/2405 (N.I. 19));
section 12 of the Statutory Water Companies Act 1991 (c. 58);
sections 3, 4, 6, 63 and 64 of, and Schedule 1 to, the Housing Act 1996 (c. 52) or, for Northern Ireland, Articles 3 and 16 to 32 of the Housing (Northern Ireland) Order 1992 (S.I. 1992/1725 (N.I. 15));
sections 2, 4 and 26 of the Commonwealth Development Corporation Act 1999 (c. 20);
Part 6 and section 366 of the Financial Services and Markets Act 2000 (c. 8);
the Limited Liability Partnerships Act 2000 (c. 12);
section 14 of the Insolvency Act 2000 (c. 39) or, for Northern Ireland, Article 11 of the Insolvency (Northern Ireland) Order 2002 (S.I. 2002/3152 (N.I. 6));
section 121 of the Land Registration Act 2002 (c. 9);
section 1248 of this Act.

(3) References in this Act to the functions of the registrar are to functions within subsection (1)(a) or (b).

1062 The registrar's official seal

The registrar shall have an official seal for the authentication of documents in connection with the performance of the registrar's functions.

1063 Fees payable to registrar

(1) The Secretary of State may make provision by regulations requiring the payment to the registrar of fees in respect of –

(a) the performance of any of the registrar's functions, or
(b) the provision by the registrar of services or facilities for purposes incidental to, or otherwise connected with, the performance of any of the registrar's functions.

(2) The matters for which fees may be charged include –

(a) the performance of a duty imposed on the registrar or the Secretary of State,
(b) the receipt of documents delivered to the registrar, and
(c) the inspection, or provision of copies, of documents kept by the registrar.

(3) The regulations may –

(a) provide for the amount of the fees to be fixed by or determined under the regulations;
(b) provide for different fees to be payable in respect of the same matter in different circumstances;

(c) specify the person by whom any fee payable under the regulations is to be paid;
(d) specify when and how fees are to be paid.

(4) Regulations under this section are subject to negative resolution procedure.
(5) In respect of the performance of functions or the provision of services or facilities –

(a) for which fees are not provided for by regulations, or
(b) in circumstances other than those for which fees are provided for by regulations,

the registrar may determine from time to time what fees (if any) are chargeable.

(6) Fees received by the registrar are to be paid into the Consolidated Fund.
(7) The Limited Partnerships Act 1907 (c. 24) is amended as follows –

(a) in section 16(1) (inspection of statements registered) –

(i) omit the words ", and there shall be paid for such inspection such fees as may be appointed by the Board of Trade, not exceeding 5p for each inspection", and
(ii) omit the words from "and there shall be paid for such certificate" to the end;

(b) in section 17 (power to make rules) –

(i) omit the words "(but as to fees with the concurrence of the Treasury)", and
(ii) omit paragraph (a).

Certificates of incorporation

1064 Public notice of issue of certificate of incorporation

(1) The registrar must cause to be published –

(a) in the Gazette, or
(b) in accordance with section 1116 (alternative means of giving public notice),

notice of the issue by the registrar of any certificate of incorporation of a company.

(2) The notice must state the name and registered number of the company and the date of issue of the certificate.
(3) This section applies to a certificate of incorporation issued under –

(a) section 80 (change of name),
(b) section 88 (Welsh companies), or
(c) any provision of Part 7 (re-registration),

as well as to the certificate issued on a company's formation.

1065 Right to certificate of incorporation

Any person may require the registrar to provide him with a copy of any certificate of incorporation of a company, signed by the registrar or authenticated by the registrar's seal.

Registered numbers

1066 Company's registered numbers

(1) The registrar shall allocate to every company a number, which shall be known as the company's registered number.
(2) Companies' registered numbers shall be in such form, consisting of one or more sequences of figures or letters, as the registrar may determine.
(3) The registrar may on adopting a new form of registered number make such changes of existing registered numbers as appear necessary.
(4) A change of a company's registered number has effect from the date on which the company is notified by the registrar of the change.

(5) For a period of three years beginning with that date any requirement to disclose the company's registered number imposed by regulations under section 82 or section 1051 (trading disclosures) is satisfied by the use of either the old number or the new.

(6) In this section "company" includes an overseas company whose particulars have been registered under section 1046, other than a company that appears to the registrar not to be required to register particulars under that section.

1067 Registered numbers of branches of overseas company

(1) The registrar shall allocate to every branch of an overseas company whose particulars are registered under section 1046 a number, which shall be known as the branch's registered number.

(2) Branches' registered numbers shall be in such form, consisting of one or more sequences of figures or letters, as the registrar may determine.

(3) The registrar may on adopting a new form of registered number make such changes of existing registered numbers as appear necessary.

(4) A change of a branch's registered number has effect from the date on which the company is notified by the registrar of the change.

(5) For a period of three years beginning with that date any requirement to disclose the branch's registered number imposed by regulations under section 1051 (trading disclosures) is satisfied by the use of either the old number or the new.

Delivery of documents to the registrar

1068 Registrar's requirements as to form, authentication and manner of delivery

(1) The registrar may impose requirements as to the form, authentication and manner of delivery of documents required or authorised to be delivered to the registrar under any enactment.

(2) As regards the form of the document, the registrar may –

  (a) require the contents of the document to be in a standard form;
  (b) impose requirements for the purpose of enabling the document to be scanned or copied.

(3) As regards authentication, the registrar may –

  (a) require the document to be authenticated by a particular person or a person of a particular description;
  (b) specify the means of authentication;
  (c) require the document to contain or be accompanied by the name or registered number of the company to which it relates (or both).

(4) As regards the manner of delivery, the registrar may specify requirements as to –

  (a) the physical form of the document (for example, hard copy or electronic form);
  (b) the means to be used for delivering the document (for example, by post or electronic means);
  (c) the address to which the document is to be sent;
  (d) in the case of a document to be delivered by electronic means, the hardware and software to be used, and technical specifications (for example, matters relating to protocol, security, anti-virus protection or encryption).

(5) The registrar must secure that as from 1st January 2007 all documents subject to the Directive disclosure requirements (see section 1078) may be delivered to the registrar by electronic means.

(6) The power conferred by this section does not authorise the registrar to require documents to be delivered by electronic means (see section 1069).

(7) Requirements imposed under this section must not be inconsistent with requirements

imposed by any enactment with respect to the form, authentication or manner of delivery of the document concerned.

1069 Power to require delivery by electronic means

(1) The Secretary of State may make regulations requiring documents that are authorised or required to be delivered to the registrar to be delivered by electronic means.

(2) Any such requirement to deliver documents by electronic means is effective only if registrar's rules have been published with respect to the detailed requirements for such delivery.

(3) Regulations under this section are subject to affirmative resolution procedure.

1070 Agreement for delivery by electronic means

(1) The registrar may agree with a company that documents relating to the company that are required or authorised to be delivered to the registrar –

(a) will be delivered by electronic means, except as provided for in the agreement, and

(b) will conform to such requirements as may be specified in the agreement or specified by the registrar in accordance with the agreement.

(2) An agreement under this section may relate to all or any description of documents to be delivered to the registrar.

(3) Documents in relation to which an agreement is in force under this section must be delivered in accordance with the agreement.

1071 Document not delivered until received

(1) A document is not delivered to the registrar until it is received by the registrar.

(2) Provision may be made by registrar's rules as to when a document is to be regarded as received.

Requirements for proper delivery

1072 Requirements for proper delivery

(1) A document delivered to the registrar is not properly delivered unless all the following requirements are met –

(a) the requirements of the provision under which the document is to be delivered to the registrar as regards –

(i)   the contents of the document, and
(ii) form, authentication and manner of delivery;

(b) any applicable requirements under –

section 1068 (registrar's requirements as to form, authentication and manner of delivery),
section 1069 (power to require delivery by electronic means), or
section 1070 (agreement for delivery by electronic means);

(c) any requirements of this Part as to the language in which the document is drawn up and delivered or as to its being accompanied on delivery by a certified translation into English;

(d) in so far as it consists of or includes names and addresses, any requirements of this Part as to permitted characters, letters or symbols or as to its being accompanied on delivery by a certificate as to the transliteration of any element;

(e) any applicable requirements under section 1111 (registrar's requirements as to certification or verification);

(f) any requirement of regulations under section 1082 (use of unique identifiers);

(g) any requirements as regards payment of a fee in respect of its receipt by the registrar.

(2) A document that is not properly delivered is treated for the purposes of the provision requiring or authorising it to be delivered as not having been delivered, subject to the provisions of section 1073 (power to accept documents not meeting requirements for proper delivery).

1073 Power to accept documents not meeting requirements for proper delivery

(1) The registrar may accept (and register) a document that does not comply with the requirements for proper delivery.

(2) A document accepted by the registrar under this section is treated as received by the registrar for the purposes of section 1077 (public notice of receipt of certain documents).

(3) No objection may be taken to the legal consequences of a document's being accepted (or registered) by the registrar under this section on the ground that the requirements for proper delivery were not met.

(4) The acceptance of a document by the registrar under this section does not affect –

(a) the continuing obligation to comply with the requirements for proper delivery, or

(b) subject as follows, any liability for failure to comply with those requirements.

(5) For the purposes of –

(a) section 453 (civil penalty for failure to file accounts and reports), and

(b) any enactment imposing a daily default fine for failure to deliver the document,

the period after the document is accepted does not count as a period during which there is default in complying with the requirements for proper delivery.

(6) But if, subsequently –

(a) the registrar issues a notice under section 1094(4) in respect of the document (notice of administrative removal from the register), and

(b) the requirements for proper delivery are not complied with before the end of the period of 14 days after the issue of that notice,

any subsequent period of default does count for the purposes of those provisions.

1074 Documents containing unnecessary material

(1) This section applies where a document delivered to the registrar contains unnecessary material.

(2) "Unnecessary material" means material that –

(a) is not necessary in order to comply with an obligation under any enactment, and

(b) is not specifically authorised to be delivered to the registrar.

(3) For this purpose an obligation to deliver a document of a particular description, or conforming to certain requirements, is regarded as not extending to anything that is not needed for a document of that description or, as the case may be, conforming to those requirements.

(4) If the unnecessary material cannot readily be separated from the rest of the document, the document is treated as not meeting the requirements for proper delivery.

(5) If the unnecessary material can readily be separated from the rest of the document, the registrar may register the document either –

(a) with the omission of the unnecessary material, or

(b) as delivered.

1075 Informal correction of document

(1) A document delivered to the registrar may be corrected by the registrar if it appears to the registrar to be incomplete or internally inconsistent.

(2) This power is exercisable only –

    (a) on instructions, and

    (b) if the company has given (and has not withdrawn) its consent to instructions being given under this section.

(3) The following requirements must be met as regards the instructions –

    (a) the instructions must be given in response to an enquiry by the registrar;

    (b) the registrar must be satisfied that the person giving the instructions is authorised to do so –

        (i) by the person by whom the document was delivered, or

        (ii) by the company to which the document relates;

    (c) the instructions must meet any requirements of registrar's rules as to –

        (i) the form and manner in which they are given, and

        (ii) authentication.

(4) The company's consent to instructions being given under this section (and any withdrawal of such consent) –

    (a) may be in hard copy or electronic form, and

    (b) must be notified to the registrar.

(5) This section applies in relation to documents delivered under Part 25 (company charges) by a person other than the company as if the references to the company were to the company or the person by whom the document was delivered.

(6) A document that is corrected under this section is treated, for the purposes of any enactment relating to its delivery, as having been delivered when the correction is made.

(7) The power conferred by this section is not exercisable if the document has been registered under section 1073 (power to accept documents not meeting requirements for proper delivery).

1076 Replacement of document not meeting requirements for proper delivery

(1) The registrar may accept a replacement for a document previously delivered that –

    (a) did not comply with the requirements for proper delivery, or

    (b) contained unnecessary material (within the meaning of section 1074).

(2) A replacement document must not be accepted unless the registrar is satisfied that it is delivered by –

    (a) the person by whom the original document was delivered, or

    (b) the company to which the original document relates,

and that it complies with the requirements for proper delivery.

(3) The power of the registrar to impose requirements as to the form and manner of delivery includes power to impose requirements as to the identification of the original document and the delivery of the replacement in a form and manner enabling it to be associated with the original.

(4) This section does not apply where the original document was delivered under Part 25 (company charges) (but see sections 873 and 888 (rectification of register of charges)).

Public notice of receipt of certain documents

1077 Public notice of receipt of certain documents

(1) The registrar must cause to be published –

    (a) in the Gazette, or

    (b) in accordance with section 1116 (alternative means of giving public notice),

notice of the receipt by the registrar of any document that, on receipt, is subject to the Directive disclosure requirements (see section 1078).

(2) The notice must state the name and registered number of the company, the description of document and the date of receipt.

(3) The registrar is not required to cause notice of the receipt of a document to be published before the date of incorporation of the company to which the document relates.

1078 Documents subject to Directive disclosure requirements

(1) The documents subject to the "Directive disclosure requirements" are as follows.
The requirements referred to are those of Article 3 of the First Company Law Directive (68/151/EEC), as amended, extended and applied.

(2) In the case of every company –

Constitutional documents

    1. The company's memorandum and articles.

    2. Any amendment of the company's articles (including every resolution or agreement required to be embodied in or annexed to copies of the company's articles issued by the company).

    3. After any amendment of the company's articles, the text of the articles as amended.

    4. Any notice of a change of the company's name.

Directors

    1. The statement of proposed officers required on formation of the company.

    2. Notification of any change among the company's directors.

    3. Notification of any change in the particulars of directors required to be delivered to the registrar.

Accounts, reports and returns

    1. All documents required to be delivered to the registrar under section 441 (annual accounts and reports).

    2. The company's annual return.

Registered office

Notification of any change of the company's registered office.

Winding up

    1. Copy of any winding-up order in respect of the company.

    2. Notice of the appointment of liquidators.

    3. Order for the dissolution of a company on a winding up.

    4. Return by a liquidator of the final meeting of a company on a winding up.

(3) In the case of a public company –

Share capital

    1. Any statement of capital and initial shareholdings.

    2. Any return of allotment and the statement of capital accompanying it.

    3. Copy of any resolution under section 570 or 571 (disapplication of pre-emption rights).

    4. Copy of any report under section 593 or 599 as to the value of a non-cash asset.

    5. Statement of capital accompanying notice given under section 625 (notice by company of redenomination of shares).

6. Statement of capital accompanying notice given under section 627 (notice by company of reduction of capital in connection with redenomination of shares).
7. Notice delivered under section 636 (notice of new name of class of shares) or 637 (notice of variation of rights attached to shares).
8. Statement of capital accompanying order delivered under section 649 (order of court confirming reduction of capital).
9. Notification (under section 689) of the redemption of shares and the statement of capital accompanying it.
10. Statement of capital accompanying return delivered under section 708 (notice of cancellation of shares on purchase of own shares) or 730 (notice of cancellation of shares held as treasury shares).
11. Any statement of compliance delivered under section 762 (statement that company meets conditions for issue of trading certificate).

Mergers and divisions
1. Copy of any draft of the terms of a scheme required to be delivered to the registrar under section 906 or 921.
2. Copy of any order under section 899 or 900 in respect of a compromise or arrangement to which Part 27 (mergers and divisions of public companies) applies.

(4) Where a private company re-registers as a public company (see section 96) –

    (a) the last statement of capital relating to the company received by the registrar under any provision of the Companies Acts becomes subject to the Directive disclosure requirements, and

    (b) section 1077 (public notice of receipt of certain documents) applies as if the statement had been received by the registrar when the reregistration takes effect.

(5) In the case of an overseas company, such particulars, returns and other documents required to be delivered under Part 34 as may be specified by the Secretary of State by regulations.

(6) Regulations under subsection (5) are subject to negative resolution procedure.

1079 Effect of failure to give public notice

(1) A company is not entitled to rely against other persons on the happening of any event to which this section applies unless –

    (a) the event has been officially notified at the material time, or

    (b) the company shows that the person concerned knew of the event at the material time.

(2) The events to which this section applies are –

    (a) an amendment of the company's articles,

    (b) a change among the company's directors,

    (c) (as regards service of any document on the company) a change of the company's registered office,

    (d) the making of a winding-up order in respect of the company, or

    (e) the appointment of a liquidator in a voluntary winding up of the company.

(3) If the material time falls –

    (a) on or before the 15th day after the date of official notification, or

    (b) where the 15th day was not a working day, on or before the next day that was,

the company is not entitled to rely on the happening of the event as against a person who shows that he was unavoidably prevented from knowing of the event at that time.

(4) "Official notification" means –

(a) in relation to an amendment of the company's articles, notification in accordance with section 1077 (public notice of receipt by registrar of certain documents) of the amendment and the amended text of the articles;

(b) in relation to anything else stated in a document subject to the Directive disclosure requirements, notification of that document in accordance with that section;

(c) in relation to the appointment of a liquidator in a voluntary winding up, notification of that event in accordance with section 109 of the Insolvency Act 1986 (c. 45) or Article 95 of the Insolvency (Northern Ireland) Order 1989 (S.I.1989/2405 (N.I. 19)).

The register

1080 The register

(1) The registrar shall continue to keep records of –

(a) the information contained in documents delivered to the registrar under any enactment,

(b) certificates of incorporation issued by the registrar, and

(c) certificates issued by the registrar under section 869(5) or 885(4) (certificates of registration of charge).

(2) The records relating to companies are referred to collectively in the Companies Acts as "the register".

(3) Information deriving from documents subject to the Directive disclosure requirements (see section 1078) that are delivered to the registrar on or after 1st January 2007 must be kept by the registrar in electronic form.

(4) Subject to that, information contained in documents delivered to the registrar may be recorded and kept in any form the registrar thinks fit, provided it is possible to inspect it and produce a copy of it.
This is sufficient compliance with any duty of the registrar to keep, file or register the document or to record the information contained in it.

(5) The records kept by the registrar must be such that information relating to a company is associated with that company, in such manner as the registrar may determine, so as to enable all the information relating to the company to be retrieved.

1081 Annotation of the register

(1) The registrar must place a note in the register recording –

(a) the date on which a document is delivered to the registrar;

(b) if a document is corrected under section 1075, the nature and date of the correction;

(c) if a document is replaced (whether or not material derived from it is removed), the fact that it has been replaced and the date of delivery of the replacement;

(d) if material is removed –

(i) what was removed (giving a general description of its contents),

(ii) under what power, and

(iii) the date on which that was done.

(2) The Secretary of State may make provision by regulations –

(a) authorising or requiring the registrar to annotate the register in such other circumstances as may be specified in the regulations, and

(b) as to the contents of any such annotation.

(3) No annotation is required in the case of a document that by virtue of section 1072(2) (documents not meeting requirements for proper delivery) is treated as not having been delivered.

(4) A note may be removed if it no longer serves any useful purpose.

(5) Any duty or power of the registrar with respect to annotation of the register is subject to the court's power under section 1097 (powers of court on ordering removal of material from the register) to direct –

    (a) that a note be removed from the register, or

    (b) that no note shall be made of the removal of material that is the subject of the court's order.

(6) Notes placed in the register in accordance with subsection (1), or in pursuance of regulations under subsection (2), are part of the register for all purposes of the Companies Acts.

(7) Regulations under this section are subject to negative resolution procedure.

1082 Allocation of unique identifiers

(1) The Secretary of State may make provision for the use, in connection with the register, of reference numbers ("unique identifiers") to identify each person who –

    (a) is a director of a company,

    (b) is secretary (or a joint secretary) of a company, or

    (c) in the case of an overseas company whose particulars are registered under section 1046, holds any such position as may be specified for the purposes of this section by regulations under that section.

(2) The regulations may –

    (a) provide that a unique identifier may be in such form, consisting of one or more sequences of letters or numbers, as the registrar may from time to time determine;

    (b) make provision for the allocation of unique identifiers by the registrar;

    (c) require there to be included, in any specified description of documents delivered to the registrar, as well as a statement of the person's name –

        (i) a statement of the person's unique identifier, or

        (ii) a statement that the person has not been allocated a unique identifier;

    (d) enable the registrar to take steps where a person appears to have more than one unique identifier to discontinue the use of all but one of them.

(3) The regulations may contain provision for the application of the scheme in relation to persons appointed, and documents registered, before the commencement of this Act.

(4) The regulations may make different provision for different descriptions of person and different descriptions of document.

(5) Regulations under this section are subject to affirmative resolution procedure.

1083 Preservation of original documents

(1) The originals of documents delivered to the registrar in hard copy form must be kept for three years after they are received by the registrar, after which they may be destroyed provided the information contained in them has been recorded in the register.

This is subject to section 1087(3) (extent of obligation to retain material not available for public inspection).

(2) The registrar is under no obligation to keep the originals of documents delivered in electronic form, provided the information contained in them has been recorded in the register.

(3) This section applies to documents held by the registrar when this section comes into force as well as to documents subsequently received.

1084 Records relating to companies that have been dissolved etc

(1) This section applies where –

    (a) a company is dissolved,

    (b) an overseas company ceases to have any connection with the United Kingdom by virtue of which it is required to register particulars under section 1046, or

    (c) a credit or financial institution ceases to be within section 1050 (overseas institutions required to file accounts with the registrar).

(2) At any time after two years from the date on which it appears to the registrar that –

    (a) the company has been dissolved,

    (b) the overseas company has ceased to have any connection with the United Kingdom by virtue of which it is required to register particulars under section 1046, or

    (c) the credit or financial institution has ceased to be within section 1050 (overseas institutions required to file accounts with the registrar),

the registrar may direct that records relating to the company or institution may be removed to the Public Record Office or, as the case may be, the Public Record Office of Northern Ireland.

(3) Records in respect of which such a direction is given shall be disposed of under the enactments relating to that Office and the rules made under them.

(4) In subsection (1)(a) "company" includes a company provisionally or completely registered under the Joint Stock Companies Act 1844 (c. 110).

(5) This section does not extend to Scotland.

Inspection etc of the register

1085 Inspection of the register

(1) Any person may inspect the register.

(2) The right of inspection extends to the originals of documents delivered to the registrar in hard copy form if, and only if, the record kept by the registrar of the contents of the document is illegible or unavailable.

The period for which such originals are to be kept is limited by section 1083(1).

(3) This section has effect subject to section 1087 (material not available for public inspection).

1086 Right to copy of material on the register

(1) Any person may require a copy of any material on the register.

(2) The fee for any such copy of material derived from a document subject to the Directive disclosure requirements (see section 1078), whether in hard copy or electronic form, must not exceed the administrative cost of providing it.

(3) This section has effect subject to section 1087 (material not available for public inspection).

1087 Material not available for public inspection

(1) The following material must not be made available by the registrar for public inspection –

    (a) the contents of any document sent to the registrar containing views expressed pursuant to section 56 (comments on proposal by company to use certain words or expressions in company name);

    (b) protected information within section 242(1) (directors' residential addresses: restriction on disclosure by registrar) or any corresponding provision of regulations under section 1046 (overseas companies);

(c) any application to the registrar under section 1024 (application for administrative restoration to the register) that has not yet been determined or was not successful;

(d) any document received by the registrar in connection with the giving or withdrawal of consent under section 1075 (informal correction of documents);

(e) any application or other document delivered to the registrar under section 1088 (application to make address unavailable for public inspection) and any address in respect of which such an application is successful;

(f) any application or other document delivered to the registrar under section 1095 (application for rectification of register);

(g) any court order under section 1096 (rectification of the register under court order) that the court has directed under section 1097 (powers of court on ordering removal of material from the register) is not to be made available for public inspection;

(h) the contents of –

    (i) any instrument creating or evidencing a charge and delivered to the registrar under section 860 (registration of company charges: England and Wales or Northern Ireland), or

    (ii) any certified copy of an instrument creating or evidencing a charge and delivered to the registrar under section 878 (registration of company charges: Scotland);

(i) any e-mail address, identification code or password deriving from a document delivered for the purpose of authorising or facilitating electronic filing procedures or providing information by telephone;

(j) the contents of any documents held by the registrar pending a decision of the Regulator of Community Interest Companies under section 36 or 38 of the Companies (Audit, Investigations and Community Enterprise) Act 2004 (c. 27) (decision on eligibility for registration as community interest company) and that the registrar is not later required to record;

(k) any other material excluded from public inspection by or under any other enactment.

(2) A restriction applying by reference to material deriving from a particular description of document does not affect the availability for public inspection of the same information contained in material derived from another description of document in relation to which no such restriction applies.

(3) Material to which this section applies need not be retained by the registrar for longer than appears to the registrar reasonably necessary for the purposes for which the material was delivered to the registrar.

1088 Application to registrar to make address unavailable for public inspection

(1) The Secretary of State may make provision by regulations requiring the registrar, on application, to make an address on the register unavailable for public inspection.

(2) The regulations may make provision as to –

(a) who may make an application,

(b) the grounds on which an application may be made,

(c) the information to be included in and documents to accompany an application,

(d) the notice to be given of an application and of its outcome, and

(e) how an application is to be determined.

(3) Provision under subsection (2)(e) may in particular –

(a) confer a discretion on the registrar;

(b) provide for a question to be referred to a person other than the registrar for the purposes of determining the application.

(4) An application must specify the address to be removed from the register and indicate where on the register it is.

(5) The regulations may provide –

(a) that an address is not to be made unavailable for public inspection under this section unless replaced by a service address, and

(b) that in such a case the application must specify a service address.

(6) Regulations under this section are subject to affirmative resolution procedure.

1089 Form of application for inspection or copy

(1) The registrar may specify the form and manner in which application is to be made for –

(a) inspection under section 1085, or

(b) a copy under section 1086.

(2) As from 1st January 2007, applications in respect of documents subject to the Directive disclosure requirements may be submitted to the registrar in hard copy or electronic form, as the applicant chooses.

This does not affect the registrar's power under subsection (1) above to impose requirements in respect of other matters.

1090 Form and manner in which copies to be provided

(1) The following provisions apply as regards the form and manner in which copies are to be provided under section 1086.

(2) As from 1st January 2007, copies of documents subject to the Directive disclosure requirements must be provided in hard copy or electronic form, as the applicant chooses.

This is subject to the following proviso.

(3) The registrar is not obliged by subsection (2) to provide copies in electronic form of a document that was delivered to the registrar in hard copy form if –

(a) the document was delivered to the registrar on or before 31st December 1996, or

(b) the document was delivered to the registrar on or before 31st December 2006 and ten years or more elapsed between the date of delivery and the date of receipt of the first application for a copy on or after 1st January 2007.

(4) Subject to the preceding provisions of this section, the registrar may determine the form and manner in which copies are to be provided.

1091 Certification of copies as accurate

(1) Copies provided under section 1086 in hard copy form must be certified as true copies unless the applicant dispenses with such certification.

(2) Copies so provided in electronic form must not be certified as true copies unless the applicant expressly requests such certification.

(3) A copy provided under section 1086, certified by the registrar (whose official position it is unnecessary to prove) to be an accurate record of the contents of the original document, is in all legal proceedings admissible in evidence –

(a) as of equal validity with the original document, and

(b) as evidence (in Scotland, sufficient evidence) of any fact stated in the original document of which direct oral evidence would be admissible.

(4) The Secretary of State may make provision by regulations as to the manner in which such a certificate is to be provided in a case where the copy is provided in electronic form.

(5) Except in the case of documents that are subject to the Directive disclosure requirements (see section 1078), copies provided by the registrar may, instead of being certified in writing to be an accurate record, be sealed with the registrar's official seal.

1092 Issue of process for production of records kept by the registrar

(1) No process for compelling the production of a record kept by the registrar shall issue from any court except with the permission of the court.

(2) Any such process shall bear on it a statement that it is issued with the permission of the court.

Correction or removal of material on the register

1093 Registrar's notice to resolve inconsistency on the register

(1) Where it appears to the registrar that the information contained in a document delivered to the registrar is inconsistent with other information on the register, the registrar may give notice to the company to which the document relates –

    (a) stating in what respects the information contained in it appears to be inconsistent with other information on the register, and

    (b) requiring the company to take steps to resolve the inconsistency.

(2) The notice must –

    (a) state the date on which it is issued, and

    (b) require the delivery to the registrar, within 14 days after that date, of such replacement or additional documents as may be required to resolve the inconsistency.

(3) If the necessary documents are not delivered within the period specified, an offence is committed by –

    (a) the company, and

    (b) every officer of the company who is in default.

(4) A person guilty of an offence under subsection (3) is liable on summary conviction to a fine not exceeding level 5 on the standard scale and, for continued contravention, a daily default fine not exceeding one-tenth of level 5 on the standard scale.

1094 Administrative removal of material from the register

(1) The registrar may remove from the register anything that there was power, but no duty, to include.

(2) This power is exercisable, in particular, so as to remove –

    (a) unnecessary material within the meaning of section 1074, and

    (b) material derived from a document that has been replaced under –

        section 1076 (replacement of document not meeting requirements for proper delivery), or

        section 1093 (notice to remedy inconsistency on the register).

(3) This section does not authorise the removal from the register of –

    (a) anything whose registration has had legal consequences in relation to the company as regards –

        (i) its formation,

        (ii) a change of name,

        (iii) its re-registration,

        (iv) its becoming or ceasing to be a community interest company,

        (v) a reduction of capital,

        (vi) a change of registered office,

        (vii) the registration of a charge, or

        (viii) its dissolution;

    (b) an address that is a person's registered address for the purposes of section 1140 (service of documents on directors, secretaries and others).

(4)   On or before removing any material under this section (otherwise than at the request
of the company) the registrar must give notice –

    (a)   to the person by whom the material was delivered (if the identity, and name and
address of that person are known), or

    (b)   to the company to which the material relates (if notice cannot be given under
paragraph (a) and the identity of that company is known).

(5)   The notice must –

    (a)   state what material the registrar proposes to remove, or has removed, and on
what grounds, and

    (b)   state the date on which it is issued.

1095 Rectification of register on application to registrar

(1)   The Secretary of State may make provision by regulations requiring the registrar, on
application, to remove from the register material of a description specified in the
regulations that –

    (a)   derives from anything invalid or ineffective or that was done without the
authority of the company, or

    (b)   is factually inaccurate, or is derived from something that is factually inaccurate
or forged.

(2)   The regulations may make provision as to –

    (a)   who may make an application,

    (b)   the information to be included in and documents to accompany an application,

    (c)   the notice to be given of an application and of its outcome,

    (d)   a period in which objections to an application may be made, and

    (e)   how an application is to be determined.

(3)   An application must –

    (a)   specify what is to be removed from the register and indicate where on the register
it is, and

    (b)   be accompanied by a statement that the material specified in the application
complies with this section and the regulations.

(4)   If no objections are made to the application, the registrar may accept the statement as
sufficient evidence that the material specified in the application should be removed
from the register.

(5)   Where anything is removed from the register under this section the registration of
which had legal consequences as mentioned in section 1094(3), any person appearing to the court to have a sufficient interest may apply to the court for such consequential orders as appear just with respect to the legal effect (if any) to be accorded
to the material by virtue of its having appeared on the register.

(6)   Regulations under this section are subject to affirmative resolution procedure.

1096 Rectification of the register under court order

(1)   The registrar shall remove from the register any material –

    (a)   that derives from anything that the court has declared to be invalid or ineffective,
or to have been done without the authority of the company, or

    (b)   that a court declares to be factually inaccurate, or to be derived from something
that is factually inaccurate, or forged,

and that the court directs should be removed from the register.

(2)   The court order must specify what is to be removed from the register and indicate
where on the register it is.

(3)   The court must not make an order for the removal from the register of anything the
registration of which had legal consequences as mentioned in section 1094(3) unless
satisfied –

(a) that the presence of the material on the register has caused, or may cause, damage to the company, and

(b) that the company's interest in removing the material outweighs any interest of other persons in the material continuing to appear on the register.

(4) Where in such a case the court does make an order for removal, it may make such consequential orders as appear just with respect to the legal effect (if any) to be accorded to the material by virtue of its having appeared on the register.

(5) A copy of the court's order must be sent to the registrar for registration.

(6) This section does not apply where the court has other, specific, powers to deal with the matter, for example under –

(a) the provisions of Part 15 relating to the revision of defective accounts and reports, or

(b) section 873 or 888 (rectification of the register of charges).

1097 Powers of court on ordering removal of material from the register

(1) Where the court makes an order for the removal of anything from the register under section 1096 (rectification of the register), it may give directions under this section.

(2) It may direct that any note on the register that is related to the material that is the subject of the court's order shall be removed from the register.

(3) It may direct that its order shall not be available for public inspection as part of the register.

(4) It may direct –

(a) that no note shall be made on the register as a result of its order, or

(b) that any such note shall be restricted to such matters as may be specified by the court.

(5) The court shall not give any direction under this section unless it is satisfied –

(a) that –

(i) the presence on the register of the note or, as the case may be, of an unrestricted note, or

(ii) the availability for public inspection of the court's order,

may cause damage to the company, and

(b) that the company's interest in non-disclosure outweighs any interest of other persons in disclosure.

1098 Public notice of removal of certain material from the register

(1) The registrar must cause to be published –

(a) in the Gazette, or

(b) in accordance with section 1116 (alternative means of giving public notice),

notice of the removal from the register of any document subject to the Directive disclosure requirements (see section 1078) or of any material derived from such a document.

(2) The notice must state the name and registered number of the company, the description of document and the date of receipt.

The registrar's index of company names

1099 The registrar's index of company names

(1) The registrar of companies must keep an index of the names of the companies and other bodies to which this section applies.

This is "the registrar's index of company names".

(2) This section applies to –

(a) UK-registered companies;

(b) any body to which any provision of the Companies Acts applies by virtue of regulations under section 1043 (unregistered companies); and

(c) overseas companies that have registered particulars with the registrar under section 1046, other than companies that appear to the registrar not to be required to do so.

(3) This section also applies to –

(a) limited partnerships registered in the United Kingdom;

(b) limited liability partnerships incorporated in the United Kingdom;

(c) European Economic Interest Groupings registered in the United Kingdom;

(d) open-ended investment companies authorised in the United Kingdom;

(e) societies registered under the Industrial and Provident Societies Act 1965 (c. 12) or the Industrial and Provident Societies Act (Northern Ireland) 1969 (c. 24 (N.I.)).

(4) The Secretary of State may by order amend subsection (3) –

(a) by the addition of any description of body;

(b) by the deletion of any description of body.

(5) Any such order is subject to negative resolution procedure.

1100 Right to inspect index

Any person may inspect the registrar's index of company names.

1101 Power to amend enactments relating to bodies other than companies

(1) The Secretary of State may by regulations amend the enactments relating to any description of body for the time being within section 1099(3) (bodies other than companies whose names are to be entered in the registrar's index), so as to –

(a) require the registrar to be provided with information as to the names of bodies registered, incorporated, authorised or otherwise regulated under those enactments, and

(b) make provision in relation to such bodies corresponding to that made by –

section 66 (company name not to be the same as another in the index), and

sections 67 and 68 (power to direct change of company name in case of similarity to existing name).

(2) Regulations under this section are subject to affirmative resolution procedure.

Language requirements: translation

1102 Application of language requirements

(1) The provisions listed below apply to all documents required to be delivered to the registrar under any provision of –

(a) the Companies Acts, or

(b) the Insolvency Act 1986 (c. 45) or the Insolvency (Northern Ireland) Order 1989 (S.I. 1989/2405 (N.I. 19)).

(2) The Secretary of State may make provision by regulations applying all or any of the listed provisions, with or without modifications, in relation to documents delivered to the registrar under any other enactment.

(3) The provisions are –

section 1103 (documents to be drawn up and delivered in English),

section 1104 (documents relating to Welsh companies),

section 1105 (documents that may be drawn up and delivered in other languages),

section 1107 (certified translations).

(4) Regulations under this section are subject to negative resolution procedure.

1103 Documents to be drawn up and delivered in English

(1) The general rule is that all documents required to be delivered to the registrar must be drawn up and delivered in English.
(2) This is subject to –

section 1104 (documents relating to Welsh companies) and
section 1105 (documents that may be drawn up and delivered in other languages).

1104 Documents relating to Welsh companies

(1) Documents relating to a Welsh company may be drawn up and delivered to the registrar in Welsh.
(2) On delivery to the registrar any such document must be accompanied by a certified translation into English, unless it is –

(a) of a description excepted from that requirement by regulations made by the Secretary of State, or
(b) in a form prescribed in Welsh (or partly in Welsh and partly in English) by virtue of section 26 of the Welsh Language Act 1993 (c. 38).

(3) Where a document is properly delivered to the registrar in Welsh without a certified translation into English, the registrar must obtain such a translation if the document is to be available for public inspection.
The translation is treated as if delivered to the registrar in accordance with the same provision as the original.
(4) A Welsh company may deliver to the registrar a certified translation into Welsh of any document in English that relates to the company and is or has been delivered to the registrar.
(5) Section 1105 (which requires certified translations into English of documents delivered to the registrar in another language) does not apply to a document relating to a Welsh company that is drawn up and delivered in Welsh.

1105 Documents that may be drawn up and delivered in other languages

(1) Documents to which this section applies may be drawn up and delivered to the registrar in a language other than English, but when delivered to the registrar they must be accompanied by a certified translation into English.
(2) This section applies to –

(a) agreements required to be forwarded to the registrar under Chapter 3 of Part 3 (agreements affecting the company's constitution);
(b) documents required to be delivered under section 400(2)(e) or section 401(2)(f) (company included in accounts of larger group: required to deliver copy of group accounts);
(c) instruments or copy instruments required to be delivered under Part 25 (company charges);
(d) documents of any other description specified in regulations made by the Secretary of State.

(3) Regulations under this section are subject to negative resolution procedure.

1106 Voluntary filing of translations

(1) A company may deliver to the registrar one or more certified translations of any document relating to the company that is or has been delivered to the registrar.
(2) The Secretary of State may by regulations specify –

(a) the languages, and
(b) the descriptions of document,

in relation to which this facility is available.

(3) The regulations must provide that it is available as from 1st January 2007 –

    (a) in relation to all the official languages of the European Union, and

    (b) in relation to all documents subject to the Directive disclosure requirements (see section 1078).

(4) The power of the registrar to impose requirements as to the form and manner of delivery includes power to impose requirements as to the identification of the original document and the delivery of the translation in a form and manner enabling it to be associated with the original.

(5) Regulations under this section are subject to negative resolution procedure.

(6) This section does not apply where the original document was delivered to the registrar before this section came into force.

1107 Certified translations

(1) In this Part a "certified translation" means a translation certified to be a correct translation.

(2) In the case of any discrepancy between the original language version of a document and a certified translation –

    (a) the company may not rely on the translation as against a third party, but

    (b) a third party may rely on the translation unless the company shows that the third party had knowledge of the original.

(3) A "third party" means a person other than the company or the registrar.

Language requirements: transliteration

1108 Transliteration of names and addresses: permitted characters

(1) Names and addresses in a document delivered to the registrar must contain only letters, characters and symbols (including accents and other diacritical marks) that are permitted.

(2) The Secretary of State may make provision by regulations –

    (a) as to the letters, characters and symbols (including accents and other diacritical marks) that are permitted, and

    (b) permitting or requiring the delivery of documents in which names and addresses have not been transliterated into a permitted form.

(3) Regulations under this section are subject to negative resolution procedure.

1109 Transliteration of names and addresses: voluntary transliteration into Roman characters

(1) Where a name or address is or has been delivered to the registrar in a permitted form using other than Roman characters, the company may deliver to the registrar a transliteration into Roman characters.

(2) The power of the registrar to impose requirements as to the form and manner of delivery includes power to impose requirements as to the identification of the original document and the delivery of the transliteration in a form and manner enabling it to be associated with the original.

1110 Transliteration of names and addresses: certification

(1) The Secretary of State may make provision by regulations requiring the certification of transliterations and prescribing the form of certification.

(2) Different provision may be made for compulsory and voluntary transliterations.

(3) Regulations under this section are subject to negative resolution procedure.

Supplementary provisions

1111 Registrar's requirements as to certification or verification

(1) Where a document required or authorised to be delivered to the registrar under any enactment is required –

    (a) to be certified as an accurate translation or transliteration, or

    (b) to be certified as a correct copy or verified,

the registrar may impose requirements as to the person, or description of person, by whom the certificate or verification is to be given.

(2) The power conferred by section 1068 (registrar's requirements as to form, authentication and manner of delivery) is exercisable in relation to the certificate or verification as if it were a separate document.

(3) Requirements imposed under this section must not be inconsistent with requirements imposed by any enactment with respect to the certification or verification of the document concerned.

1112 General false statement offence

(1) It is an offence for a person knowingly or recklessly –

    (a) to deliver or cause to be delivered to the registrar, for any purpose of the Companies Acts, a document, or

    (b) to make to the registrar, for any such purpose, a statement,

that is misleading, false or deceptive in a material particular.

(2) A person guilty of an offence under this section is liable –

    (a) on conviction on indictment, to imprisonment for a term not exceeding two years or a fine (or both);

    (b) on summary conviction –

        (i)   in England and Wales, to imprisonment for a term not exceeding twelve months or to a fine not exceeding the statutory maximum (or both);

        (ii) in Scotland or Northern Ireland, to imprisonment for a term not exceeding six months, or to a fine not exceeding the statutory maximum (or both).

1113 Enforcement of company's filing obligations

(1) This section applies where a company has made default in complying with any obligation under the Companies Acts –

    (a) to deliver a document to the registrar, or

    (b) to give notice to the registrar of any matter.

(2) The registrar, or any member or creditor of the company, may give notice to the company requiring it to comply with the obligation.

(3) If the company fails to make good the default within 14 days after service of the notice, the registrar, or any member or creditor of the company, may apply to the court for an order directing the company, and any specified officer of it, to make good the default within a specified time.

(4) The court's order may provide that all costs (in Scotland, expenses) of or incidental to the application are to be borne by the company or by any officers of it responsible for the default.

(5) This section does not affect the operation of any enactment making it an offence, or imposing a civil penalty, for the default.

1114 Application of provisions about documents and delivery

(1) In this Part –

    (a) "document" means information recorded in any form, and

(b) references to delivering a document include forwarding, lodging, registering, sending, producing or submitting it or (in the case of a notice) giving it.

(2) Except as otherwise provided, this Part applies in relation to the supply to the registrar of information otherwise than in documentary form as it applies in relation to the delivery of a document.

1115 Supplementary provisions relating to electronic communications

(1) Registrar's rules may require a company to give any necessary consents to the use of electronic means for communications by the registrar to the company as a condition of making use of any facility to deliver material to the registrar by electronic means.

(2) A document that is required to be signed by the registrar or authenticated by the registrar's seal shall, if sent by electronic means, be authenticated in such manner as may be specified by registrar's rules.

1116 Alternative to publication in the Gazette

(1) Notices that would otherwise need to be published by the registrar in the Gazette may instead be published by such means as may from time to time be approved by the registrar in accordance with regulations made by the Secretary of State.

(2) The Secretary of State may make provision by regulations as to what alternative means may be approved.

(3) The regulations may, in particular –

(a) require the use of electronic means;

(b) require the same means to be used –

(i) for all notices or for all notices of specified descriptions, and

(ii) whether the company is registered in England and Wales, Scotland or Northern Ireland;

(c) impose conditions as to the manner in which access to the notices is to be made available.

(4) Regulations under this section are subject to negative resolution procedure.

(5) Before starting to publish notices by means approved under this section the registrar must publish at least one notice to that effect in the Gazette.

(6) Nothing in this section prevents the registrar from giving public notice both in the Gazette and by means approved under this section.

In that case, the requirement of public notice is met when notice is first given by either means.

1117 Registrar's rules

(1) Where any provision of this Part enables the registrar to make provision, or impose requirements, as to any matter, the registrar may make such provision or impose such requirements by means of rules under this section.

This is without prejudice to the making of such provision or the imposing of such requirements by other means.

(2) Registrar's rules –

(a) may make different provision for different cases, and

(b) may allow the registrar to disapply or modify any of the rules.

(3) The registrar must –

(a) publicise the rules in a manner appropriate to bring them to the notice of persons affected by them, and

(b) make copies of the rules available to the public (in hard copy or electronic form).

1118 Payments into the Consolidated Fund

Nothing in the Companies Acts or any other enactment as to the payment of receipts into the Consolidated Fund shall be read as affecting the operation in relation to the registrar of section 3(1) of the Government Trading Funds Act 1973 (c. 63).

1119 Contracting out of registrar's functions

(1) Where by virtue of an order made under section 69 of the Deregulation and Contracting Out Act 1994 (c. 40) a person is authorised by the registrar to accept delivery of any class of documents that are under any enactment to be delivered to the registrar, the registrar may direct that documents of that class shall be delivered to a specified address of the authorised person.
Any such direction must be printed and made available to the public (with or without payment).

(2) A document of that class that is delivered to an address other than the specified address is treated as not having been delivered.

(3) Registrar's rules are not subordinate legislation for the purposes of section 71 of the Deregulation and Contracting Out Act 1994 (functions excluded from contracting out).

1120 Application of this Part to overseas companies

Unless the context otherwise requires, the provisions of this Part apply to an overseas company as they apply to a company as defined in section 1.

PART 36

OFFENCES UNDER THE COMPANIES ACTS

Liability of officer in default

1121 Liability of officer in default

(1) This section has effect for the purposes of any provision of the Companies Acts to the effect that, in the event of contravention of an enactment in relation to a company, an offence is committed by every officer of the company who is in default.

(2) For this purpose "officer" includes –

    (a) any director, manager or secretary, and

    (b) any person who is to be treated as an officer of the company for the purposes of the provision in question.

(3) An officer is "in default" for the purposes of the provision if he authorises or permits, participates in, or fails to take all reasonable steps to prevent, the contravention.

1122 Liability of company as officer in default

(1) Where a company is an officer of another company, it does not commit an offence as an officer in default unless one of its officers is in default.

(2) Where any such offence is committed by a company the officer in question also commits the offence and is liable to be proceeded against and punished accordingly.

(3) In this section "officer" and "in default" have the meanings given by section 1121.

1123 Application to bodies other than companies

(1) Section 1121 (liability of officers in default) applies to a body other than a company as it applies to a company.

(2) As it applies in relation to a body corporate other than a company –

(a) the reference to a director of the company shall be read as referring –

    (i) where the body's affairs are managed by its members, to a member of the body,

    (ii) in any other case, to any corresponding officer of the body, and

(b) the reference to a manager or secretary of the company shall be read as referring to any manager, secretary or similar officer of the body.

(3) As it applies in relation to a partnership –

(a) the reference to a director of the company shall be read as referring to a member of the partnership, and

(b) the reference to a manager or secretary of the company shall be read as referring to any manager, secretary or similar officer of the partnership.

(4) As it applies in relation to an unincorporated body other than a partnership –

(a) the reference to a director of the company shall be read as referring –

    (i) where the body's affairs are managed by its members, to a member of the body,

    (ii) in any other case, to a member of the governing body, and

(b) the reference to a manager or secretary of the company shall be read as referring to any manager, secretary or similar officer of the body.

Offences under the Companies Act 1985

1124 Amendments of the Companies Act 1985

Schedule 3 contains amendments of the Companies Act 1985 (c. 6) relating to offences.

General provisions

1125 Meaning of "daily default fine"

(1) This section defines what is meant in the Companies Acts where it is provided that a person guilty of an offence is liable on summary conviction to a fine not exceeding a specified amount "and, for continued contravention, a daily default fine" not exceeding a specified amount.

(2) This means that the person is liable on a second or subsequent summary conviction of the offence to a fine not exceeding the latter amount for each day on which the contravention is continued (instead of being liable to a fine not exceeding the former amount).

1126 Consents required for certain prosecutions

(1) This section applies to proceedings for an offence under any of the following provisions –

section 458, 460 or 949 of this Act (offences of unauthorised disclosure of information);

section 953 of this Act (failure to comply with rules about takeover bid documents);

section 448, 449, 450, 451 or 453A of the Companies Act 1985 (c. 6) (offences in connection with company investigations);

section 798 of this Act or section 455 of the Companies Act 1985 (offence of attempting to evade restrictions on shares).

(2) No such proceedings are to be brought in England and Wales except by or with the consent of –

(a) in the case of an offence under –

    (i) section 458, 460 or 949 of this Act,

   (ii)   section 953 of this Act, or
   (iii) section 448, 449, 450, 451 or 453A of the Companies Act 1985,
   the Secretary of State or the Director of Public Prosecutions;
   (b) in the case of an offence under section 798 of this Act or section 455 of
        the Companies Act 1985, the Secretary of State.
(3) No such proceedings are to be brought in Northern Ireland except by or with the
     consent of –
     (a) in the case of an offence under –
          (i)   section 458, 460 or 949 of this Act,
          (ii)   section 953 of this Act, or
          (iii) section 448, 449, 450, 451 or 453A of the Companies Act 1985,
          the Secretary of State or the Director of Public Prosecutions for Northern Ireland;
     (b) in the case of an offence under section 798 of this Act or section 455 of the
          Companies Act 1985, the Secretary of State.

1127 Summary proceedings: venue

(1) Summary proceedings for any offence under the Companies Acts may be taken –
     (a) against a body corporate, at any place at which the body has a place of business,
          and
     (b) against any other person, at any place at which he is for the time being.
(2) This is without prejudice to any jurisdiction exercisable apart from this section.

1128 Summary proceedings: time limit for proceedings

(1) An information relating to an offence under the Companies Acts that is triable by a
     magistrates' court in England and Wales may be so tried if it is laid –
     (a) at any time within three years after the commission of the offence, and
     (b) within twelve months after the date on which evidence sufficient in the opinion
          of the Director of Public Prosecutions or the Secretary of State (as the case may
          be) to justify the proceedings comes to his knowledge.
(2) Summary proceedings in Scotland for an offence under the Companies Acts –
     (a) must not be commenced after the expiration of three years from the commission
          of the offence;
     (b) subject to that, may be commenced at any time –
          (i)   within twelve months after the date on which evidence sufficient in the
                 Lord Advocate's opinion to justify the proceedings came to his knowledge,
                 or
          (ii)   where such evidence was reported to him by the Secretary of State, within
                 twelve months after the date on which it came to the knowledge of the latter.
     Section 136(3) of the Criminal Procedure (Scotland) Act 1995 (c. 46) (date when pro-
     ceedings deemed to be commenced) applies for the purposes of this subsection as for
     the purposes of that section.
(3) A magistrates' court in Northern Ireland has jurisdiction to hear and determine a
     complaint charging the commission of a summary offence under the Companies Acts
     provided that the complaint is made –
     (a) within three years from the time when the offence was committed, and
     (b) within twelve months from the date on which evidence sufficient in the opinion
          of the Director of Public Prosecutions for Northern Ireland or the Secretary of
          State (as the case may be) to justify the proceedings comes to his knowledge.
(4) For the purposes of this section a certificate of the Director of Public Prosecutions,
     the Lord Advocate, the Director of Public Prosecutions for Northern Ireland or the

Secretary of State (as the case may be) as to the date on which such evidence as is referred to above came to his notice is conclusive evidence.

1129 Legal professional privilege

In proceedings against a person for an offence under the Companies Acts, nothing in those Acts is to be taken to require any person to disclose any information that he is entitled to refuse to disclose on grounds of legal professional privilege (in Scotland, confidentiality of communications).

1130 Proceedings against unincorporated bodies

(1) Proceedings for an offence under the Companies Acts alleged to have been committed by an unincorporated body must be brought in the name of the body (and not in that of any of its members).

(2) For the purposes of such proceedings –

    (a) any rules of court relating to the service of documents have effect as if the body were a body corporate, and

    (b) the following provisions apply as they apply in relation to a body corporate –

        (i) in England and Wales, section 33 of the Criminal Justice Act 1925 (c. 86) and Schedule 3 to the Magistrates' Courts Act 1980 (c. 43),

        (ii) in Scotland, sections 70 and 143 of the Criminal Procedure (Scotland) Act 1995 (c. 46),

        (iii) in Northern Ireland, section 18 of the Criminal Justice Act (Northern Ireland) 1945 (c. 15 (N.I.)) and Article 166 of and Schedule 4 to the Magistrates' Courts (Northern Ireland) Order 1981 (S.I. 1981/1675 (N.I. 26)).

(3) A fine imposed on an unincorporated body on its conviction of an offence under the Companies Acts must be paid out of the funds of the body.

1131 Imprisonment on summary conviction in England and Wales: transitory provision

(1) This section applies to any provision of the Companies Acts that provides that a person guilty of an offence is liable on summary conviction in England and Wales to imprisonment for a term not exceeding twelve months.

(2) In relation to an offence committed before the commencement of section 154(1) of the Criminal Justice Act 2003 (c. 44), for "twelve months" substitute "six months".

Production and inspection of documents

1132 Production and inspection of documents where offence suspected

(1) An application under this section may be made –

    (a) in England and Wales, to a judge of the High Court by the Director of Public Prosecutions, the Secretary of State or a chief officer of police;

    (b) in Scotland, to one of the Lords Commissioners of Justiciary by the Lord Advocate;

    (c) in Northern Ireland, to the High Court by the Director of Public Prosecutions for Northern Ireland, the Department of Enterprise, Trade and Investment or a chief superintendent of the Police Service of Northern Ireland.

(2) If on an application under this section there is shown to be reasonable cause to believe –

    (a) that any person has, while an officer of a company, committed an offence in connection with the management of the company's affairs, and

    (b)   that evidence of the commission of the offence is to be found in any documents in the possession or control of the company,

an order under this section may be made.

(3) The order may –

    (a)   authorise any person named in it to inspect the documents in question, or any of them, for the purpose of investigating and obtaining evidence of the offence, or

    (b)   require the secretary of the company, or such other officer of it as may be named in the order, to produce the documents (or any of them) to a person named in the order at a place so named.

(4) This section applies also in relation to documents in the possession or control of a person carrying on the business of banking, so far as they relate to the company's affairs, as it applies to documents in the possession or control of the company, except that no such order as is referred to in subsection (3)(b) may be made by virtue of this subsection.

(5) The decision under this section of a judge of the High Court, any of the Lords Commissioners of Justiciary or the High Court is not appealable.

(6) In this section "document" includes information recorded in any form.

Supplementary

1133 Transitional provision

The provisions of this Part except section 1132 do not apply to offences committed before the commencement of the relevant provision.

PART 37

COMPANIES: SUPPLEMENTARY PROVISIONS

Company records

1134 Meaning of "company records"

In this Part "company records" means –

    (a)   any register, index, accounting records, agreement, memorandum, minutes or other document required by the Companies Acts to be kept by a company, and

    (b)   any register kept by a company of its debenture holders.

1135 Form of company records

(1) Company records –

    (a)   may be kept in hard copy or electronic form, and

    (b)   may be arranged in such manner as the directors of the company think fit,

provided the information in question is adequately recorded for future reference.

(2) Where the records are kept in electronic form, they must be capable of being reproduced in hard copy form.

(3) If a company fails to comply with this section, an offence is committed by every officer of the company who is in default.

(4) A person guilty of an offence under this section is liable on summary conviction to a fine not exceeding level 3 on the standard scale and, for continued contravention, a daily default fine not exceeding one-tenth of level 3 on the standard scale.

(5) Any provision of an instrument made by a company before 12th February 1979 that

requires a register of holders of the company's debentures to be kept in hard copy form is to be read as requiring it to be kept in hard copy or electronic form.

1136 Regulations about where certain company records to be kept available for inspection

(1) The Secretary of State may make provision by regulations specifying places other than a company's registered office at which company records required to be kept available for inspection under a relevant provision may be so kept in compliance with that provision.

(2) The "relevant provisions" are –

section 114 (register of members);
section 162 (register of directors);
section 228 (directors' service contracts);
section 237 (directors' indemnities);
section 275 (register of secretaries);
section 358 (records of resolutions etc);
section 702 (contracts relating to purchase of own shares);
section 720 (documents relating to redemption or purchase of own shares out of capital by private company);
section 743 (register of debenture holders);
section 805 (report to members of outcome of investigation by public company into interests in its shares);
section 809 (register of interests in shares disclosed to public company);
section 877 (instruments creating charges and register of charges: England and Wales);
section 892 (instruments creating charges and register of charges: Scotland).

(3) The regulations may specify a place by reference to the company's principal place of business, the part of the United Kingdom in which the company is registered, the place at which the company keeps any other records available for inspection or in any other way.

(4) The regulations may provide that a company does not comply with a relevant provision by keeping company records available for inspection at a place specified in the regulations unless conditions specified in the regulations are met.

(5) The regulations –

(a) need not specify a place in relation to each relevant provision;
(b) may specify more than one place in relation to a relevant provision.

(6) A requirement under a relevant provision to keep company records available for inspection is not complied with by keeping them available for inspection at a place specified in the regulations unless all the company's records subject to the requirement are kept there.

(7) Regulations under this section are subject to negative resolution procedure.

1137 Regulations about inspection of records and provision of copies

(1) The Secretary of State may make provision by regulations as to the obligations of a company that is required by any provision of the Companies Acts –

(a) to keep available for inspection any company records, or
(b) to provide copies of any company records.

(2) A company that fails to comply with the regulations is treated as having refused inspection or, as the case may be, having failed to provide a copy.

(3) The regulations may –

(a) make provision as to the time, duration and manner of inspection, including the circumstances in which and extent to which the copying of information is permitted in the course of inspection, and

(b) define what may be required of the company as regards the nature, extent and manner of extracting or presenting any information for the purposes of inspection or the provision of copies.

(4) Where there is power to charge a fee, the regulations may make provision as to the amount of the fee and the basis of its calculation.

(5) Nothing in any provision of this Act or in the regulations shall be read as preventing a company –

(a) from affording more extensive facilities than are required by the regulations, or

(b) where a fee may be charged, from charging a lesser fee than that prescribed or none at all.

(6) Regulations under this section are subject to negative resolution procedure.

1138 Duty to take precautions against falsification

(1) Where company records are kept otherwise than in bound books, adequate precautions must be taken –

(a) to guard against falsification, and

(b) to facilitate the discovery of falsification.

(2) If a company fails to comply with this section, an offence is committed by every officer of the company who is in default.

(3) A person guilty of an offence under this section is liable on summary conviction to a fine not exceeding level 3 on the standard scale and, for continued contravention, a daily default fine not exceeding one-tenth of level 3 on the standard scale.

(4) This section does not apply to the documents required to be kept under –

(a) section 228 (copy of director's service contract or memorandum of its terms); or

(b) section 237 (qualifying indemnity provision).

Service addresses

1139 Service of documents on company

(1) A document may be served on a company registered under this Act by leaving it at, or sending it by post to, the company's registered office.

(2) A document may be served on an overseas company whose particulars are registered under section 1046 –

(a) by leaving it at, or sending it by post to, the registered address of any person resident in the United Kingdom who is authorised to accept service of documents on the company's behalf, or

(b) if there is no such person, or if any such person refuses service or service cannot for any other reason be effected, by leaving it at or sending by post to any place of business of the company in the United Kingdom.

(3) For the purposes of this section a person's "registered address" means any address for the time being shown as a current address in relation to that person in the part of the register available for public inspection.

(4) Where a company registered in Scotland or Northern Ireland carries on business in England and Wales, the process of any court in England and Wales may be served on the company by leaving it at, or sending it by post to, the company's principal place of business in England and Wales, addressed to the manager or other head officer in England and Wales of the company.

Where process is served on a company under this subsection, the person issuing out the process must send a copy of it by post to the company's registered office.

(5) Further provision as to service and other matters is made in the company communications provisions (see section 1143).

1140 Service of documents on directors, secretaries and others

(1) A document may be served on a person to whom this section applies by leaving it at, or sending it by post to, the person's registered address.

(2) This section applies to –

    (a) a director or secretary of a company;

    (b) in the case of an overseas company whose particulars are registered under section 1046, a person holding any such position as may be specified for the purposes of this section by regulations under that section;

    (c) a person appointed in relation to a company as –

        (i) a judicial factor (in Scotland),

        (ii) a receiver and manager appointed under section 18 of the Charities Act 1993 (c. 10), or

        (iii) a manager appointed under section 47 of the Companies (Audit, Investigations and Community Enterprise) Act 2004 (c. 27).

(3) This section applies whatever the purpose of the document in question.
It is not restricted to service for purposes arising out of or in connection with the appointment or position mentioned in subsection (2) or in connection with the company concerned.

(4) For the purposes of this section a person's "registered address" means any address for the time being shown as a current address in relation to that person in the part of the register available for public inspection.

(5) If notice of a change of that address is given to the registrar, a person may validly serve a document at the address previously registered until the end of the period of 14 days beginning with the date on which notice of the change is registered.

(6) Service may not be effected by virtue of this section at an address –

    (a) if notice has been registered of the termination of the appointment in relation to which the address was registered and the address is not a registered address of the person concerned in relation to any other appointment;

    (b) in the case of a person holding any such position as is mentioned in subsection (2)(b), if the overseas company has ceased to have any connection with the United Kingdom by virtue of which it is required to register particulars under section 1046.

(7) Further provision as to service and other matters is made in the company communications provisions (see section 1143).

(8) Nothing in this section shall be read as affecting any enactment or rule of law under which permission is required for service out of the jurisdiction.

1141 Service addresses

(1) In the Companies Acts a "service address", in relation to a person, means an address at which documents may be effectively served on that person.

(2) The Secretary of State may by regulations specify conditions with which a service address must comply.

(3) Regulations under this section are subject to negative resolution procedure.

1142 Requirement to give service address

Any obligation under the Companies Acts to give a person's address is, unless otherwise expressly provided, to give a service address for that person.

Sending or supplying documents or information

1143 The company communications provisions

(1) The provisions of sections 1144 to 1148 and Schedules 4 and 5 ("the company communications provisions") have effect for the purposes of any provision of the Companies Acts that authorises or requires documents or information to be sent or supplied by or to a company.

(2) The company communications provisions have effect subject to any requirements imposed, or contrary provision made, by or under any enactment.

(3) In particular, in their application in relation to documents or information to be sent or supplied to the registrar, they have effect subject to the provisions of Part 35.

(4) For the purposes of subsection (2), provision is not to be regarded as contrary to the company communications provisions by reason only of the fact that it expressly authorises a document or information to be sent or supplied in hard copy form, in electronic form or by means of a website.

1144 Sending or supplying documents or information

(1) Documents or information to be sent or supplied to a company must be sent or supplied in accordance with the provisions of Schedule 4.

(2) Documents or information to be sent or supplied by a company must be sent or supplied in accordance with the provisions of Schedule 5.

(3) The provisions referred to in subsection (2) apply (and those referred to in subsection (1) do not apply) in relation to documents or information that are to be sent or supplied by one company to another.

1145 Right to hard copy version

(1) Where a member of a company or a holder of a company's debentures has received a document or information from the company otherwise than in hard copy form, he is entitled to require the company to send him a version of the document or information in hard copy form.

(2) The company must send the document or information in hard copy form within 21 days of receipt of the request from the member or debenture holder.

(3) The company may not make a charge for providing the document or information in that form.

(4) If a company fails to comply with this section, an offence is committed by the company and every officer of it who is in default.

(5) A person guilty of an offence under this section is liable on summary conviction to a fine not exceeding level 3 on the standard scale and, for continued contravention, a daily default fine not exceeding one-tenth of level 3 on the standard scale.

1146 Requirement of authentication

(1) This section applies in relation to the authentication of a document or information sent or supplied by a person to a company.

(2) A document or information sent or supplied in hard copy form is sufficiently authenticated if it is signed by the person sending or supplying it.

(3) A document or information sent or supplied in electronic form is sufficiently authenticated –

    (a) if the identity of the sender is confirmed in a manner specified by the company, or

    (b) where no such manner has been specified by the company, if the communication contains or is accompanied by a statement of the identity of the sender and the company has no reason to doubt the truth of that statement.

(4) Where a document or information is sent or supplied by one person on behalf of another, nothing in this section affects any provision of the company's articles under

which the company may require reasonable evidence of the authority of the former to act on behalf of the latter.

1147 Deemed delivery of documents and information

(1) This section applies in relation to documents and information sent or supplied by a company.

(2) Where –

    (a) the document or information is sent by post (whether in hard copy or electronic form) to an address in the United Kingdom, and

    (b) the company is able to show that it was properly addressed, prepaid and posted,

it is deemed to have been received by the intended recipient 48 hours after it was posted.

(3) Where –

    (a) the document or information is sent or supplied by electronic means, and

    (b) the company is able to show that it was properly addressed,

it is deemed to have been received by the intended recipient 48 hours after it was sent.

(4) Where the document or information is sent or supplied by means of a website, it is deemed to have been received by the intended recipient –

    (a) when the material was first made available on the website, or

    (b) if later, when the recipient received (or is deemed to have received) notice of the fact that the material was available on the website.

(5) In calculating a period of hours for the purposes of this section, no account shall be taken of any part of a day that is not a working day.

(6) This section has effect subject to –

    (a) in its application to documents or information sent or supplied by a company to its members, any contrary provision of the company's articles;

    (b) in its application to documents or information sent or supplied by a company to its debentures holders, any contrary provision in the instrument constituting the debentures;

    (c) in its application to documents or information sent or supplied by a company to a person otherwise than in his capacity as a member or debenture holder, any contrary provision in an agreement between the company and that person.

1148 Interpretation of company communications provisions

(1) In the company communications provisions –

"address" includes a number or address used for the purposes of sending or receiving documents or information by electronic means;

"company" includes any body corporate;

"document" includes summons, notice, order or other legal process and registers.

(2) References in the company communications provisions to provisions of the Companies Acts authorising or requiring a document or information to be sent or supplied include all such provisions, whatever expression is used, and references to documents or information being sent or supplied shall be construed accordingly.

(3) References in the company communications provisions to documents or information being sent or supplied by or to a company include references to documents or information being sent or supplied by or to the directors of a company acting on behalf of the company.

Requirements as to independent valuation

1149 Application of valuation requirements

The provisions of sections 1150 to 1153 apply to the valuation and report required by –

> section 93 (re-registration as public company: recent allotment of shares for non-cash consideration);
>
> section 593 (allotment of shares of public company in consideration of non-cash asset);
>
> section 599 (transfer of non-cash asset to public company).

1150 Valuation by qualified independent person

(1) The valuation and report must be made by a person ("the valuer") who –

    (a) is eligible for appointment as a statutory auditor (see section 1212), and

    (b) meets the independence requirement in section 1151.

(2) However, where it appears to the valuer to be reasonable for the valuation of the consideration, or part of it, to be made by (or for him to accept a valuation made by) another person who –

    (a) appears to him to have the requisite knowledge and experience to value the consideration or that part of it, and

    (b) is not an officer or employee of –

        (i) the company, or

        (ii) any other body corporate that is that company's subsidiary or holding company or a subsidiary of that company's holding company,

    or a partner of or employed by any such officer or employee,

he may arrange for or accept such a valuation, together with a report which will enable him to make his own report under this section.

(3) The references in subsection (2)(b) to an officer or employee do not include an auditor.

(4) Where the consideration or part of it is valued by a person other than the valuer himself, the latter's report must state that fact and shall also –

    (a) state the former's name and what knowledge and experience he has to carry out the valuation, and

    (b) describe so much of the consideration as was valued by the other person, and the method used to value it, and specify the date of that valuation.

1151 The independence requirement

(1) A person meets the independence requirement for the purposes of section 1150 only if –

    (a) he is not –

        (i) an officer or employee of the company, or

        (ii) a partner or employee of such a person, or a partnership of which such a person is a partner;

    (b) he is not –

        (i) an officer or employee of an associated undertaking of the company, or

        (ii) a partner or employee of such a person, or a partnership of which such a person is a partner; and

    (c) there does not exist between –

        (i) the person or an associate of his, and

        (ii) the company or an associated undertaking of the company, a connection of any such description as may be specified by regulations made by the Secretary of State.

(2) An auditor of the company is not regarded as an officer or employee of the company for this purpose.

(3) In this section –

"associated undertaking" means –

(a)   a parent undertaking or subsidiary undertaking of the company, or

(b)   a subsidiary undertaking of a parent undertaking of the company; and

"associate" has the meaning given by section 1152.

(4) Regulations under this section are subject to negative resolution procedure.

1152 Meaning of "associate"

(1) This section defines "associate" for the purposes of section 1151 (valuation: independence requirement).

(2) In relation to an individual, "associate" means –

(a)   that individual's spouse or civil partner or minor child or step-child,

(b)   any body corporate of which that individual is a director, and

(c)   any employee or partner of that individual.

(3) In relation to a body corporate, "associate" means –

(a)   any body corporate of which that body is a director,

(b)   any body corporate in the same group as that body, and

(c)   any employee or partner of that body or of any body corporate in the same group.

(4) In relation to a partnership that is a legal person under the law by which it is governed, "associate" means –

(a)   any body corporate of which that partnership is a director,

(b)   any employee of or partner in that partnership, and

(c)   any person who is an associate of a partner in that partnership.

(5) In relation to a partnership that is not a legal person under the law by which it is governed, "associate" means any person who is an associate of any of the partners.

(6) In this section, in relation to a limited liability partnership, for "director" read "member".

1153 Valuer entitled to full disclosure

(1) A person carrying out a valuation or making a report with respect to any consideration proposed to be accepted or given by a company, is entitled to require from the officers of the company such information and explanation as he thinks necessary to enable him to –

(a)   carry out the valuation or make the report, and

(b)   provide any note required by section 596(3) or 600(3) (note required where valuation carried out by another person).

(2) A person who knowingly or recklessly makes a statement to which this subsection applies that is misleading, false or deceptive in a material particular commits an offence.

(3) Subsection (2) applies to a statement –

(a)   made (whether orally or in writing) to a person carrying out a valuation or making a report, and

(b)   conveying or purporting to convey any information or explanation which that person requires, or is entitled to require, under subsection (1).

(4) A person guilty of an offence under subsection (2) is liable –

(a) on conviction on indictment, to imprisonment for a term not exceeding two years or a fine (or both);

(b) on summary conviction –

    (i) in England and Wales, to imprisonment for a term not exceeding twelve months or to a fine not exceeding the statutory maximum (or both);

    (ii) in Scotland or Northern Ireland, to imprisonment for a term not exceeding six months, or to a fine not exceeding the statutory maximum (or both).

Notice of appointment of certain officers

1154 Duty to notify registrar of certain appointments etc

(1) Notice must be given to the registrar of the appointment in relation to a company of –

(a) a judicial factor (in Scotland),

(b) a receiver and manager appointed under section 18 of the Charities Act 1993 (c. 10), or

(c) a manager appointed under section 47 of the Companies (Audit, Investigations and Community Enterprise) Act 2004 (c. 27).

(2) The notice must be given –

(a) in the case of appointment of a judicial factor, by the judicial factor;

(b) in the case of appointment of a receiver and manager under section 18 of the Charities Act 1993 (c. 10), by the Charity Commission;

(c) in the case of appointment of a manager under section 47 of the Companies (Audit, Investigations and Community Enterprise) Act 2004, by the Regulator of Community Interest Companies.

(3) The notice must specify an address at which service of documents (including legal process) may be effected on the person appointed.

Notice of a change in the address for service may be given to the registrar by the person appointed.

(4) Where notice has been given under this section of the appointment of a person, notice must also be given to the registrar of the termination of the appointment.

This notice must be given by the person specified in subsection (2).

1155 Offence of failure to give notice

(1) If a judicial factor fails to give notice of his appointment in accordance with section 1154 within the period of 14 days after the appointment he commits an offence.

(2) A person guilty of an offence under this section is liable on summary conviction to a fine not exceeding level 5 on the standard scale and, for continued contravention, a daily default fine not exceeding one-tenth of level 5 on the standard scale.

Courts and legal proceedings

1156 Meaning of "the court"

(1) Except as otherwise provided, in the Companies Acts "the court" means –

(a) in England and Wales, the High Court or (subject to subsection (3)) a county court;

(b) in Scotland, the Court of Session or the sheriff court;

(c) in Northern Ireland, the High Court.

(2) The provisions of the Companies Acts conferring jurisdiction on "the court" as defined above have effect subject to any enactment or rule of law relating to the

allocation of jurisdiction or distribution of business between courts in any part of the United Kingdom.

(3) The Lord Chancellor may, with the concurrence of the Lord Chief Justice, by order –

    (a) exclude a county court from having jurisdiction under the Companies Acts, and

    (b) for the purposes of that jurisdiction attach that court's district, or any part of it, to another county court.

(4) The Lord Chief Justice may nominate a judicial office holder (as defined in section 109(4) of the Constitutional Reform Act 2005 (c. 4)) to exercise his functions under subsection (3).

1157 Power of court to grant relief in certain cases

(1) If in proceedings for negligence, default, breach of duty or breach of trust against –

    (a) an officer of a company, or

    (b) a person employed by a company as auditor (whether he is or is not an officer of the company),

it appears to the court hearing the case that the officer or person is or may be liable but that he acted honestly and reasonably, and that having regard to all the circumstances of the case (including those connected with his appointment) he ought fairly to be excused, the court may relieve him, either wholly or in part, from his liability on such terms as it thinks fit.

(2) If any such officer or person has reason to apprehend that a claim will or might be made against him in respect of negligence, default, breach of duty or breach of trust –

    (a) he may apply to the court for relief, and

    (b) the court has the same power to relieve him as it would have had if it had been a court before which proceedings against him for negligence, default, breach of duty or breach of trust had been brought.

(3) Where a case to which subsection (1) applies is being tried by a judge with a jury, the judge, after hearing the evidence, may, if he is satisfied that the defendant (in Scotland, the defender) ought in pursuance of that subsection to be relieved either in whole or in part from the liability sought to be enforced against him, withdraw the case from the jury and forthwith direct judgment to be entered for the defendant (in Scotland, grant decree of absolvitor) on such terms as to costs (in Scotland, expenses) or otherwise as the judge may think proper.

PART 38

COMPANIES: INTERPRETATION

Meaning of "UK-registered company"

1158 Meaning of "UK-registered company"

In the Companies Acts "UK-registered company" means a company registered under this Act.

The expression does not include an overseas company that has registered particulars under section 1046.

Meaning of "subsidiary" and related expressions

1159 Meaning of "subsidiary" etc

(1) A company is a "subsidiary" of another company, its "holding company", if that other company –

    (a) holds a majority of the voting rights in it, or

    (b) is a member of it and has the right to appoint or remove a majority of its board of directors, or

    (c) is a member of it and controls alone, pursuant to an agreement with other members, a majority of the voting rights in it,

    or if it is a subsidiary of a company that is itself a subsidiary of that other company.

(2) A company is a "wholly-owned subsidiary" of another company if it has no members except that other and that other's wholly-owned subsidiaries or persons acting on behalf of that other or its wholly-owned subsidiaries.

(3) Schedule 6 contains provisions explaining expressions used in this section and otherwise supplementing this section.

(4) In this section and that Schedule "company" includes any body corporate.

1160 Meaning of "subsidiary" etc: power to amend

(1) The Secretary of State may by regulations amend the provisions of section 1159 (meaning of "subsidiary" etc) and Schedule 6 (meaning of "subsidiary" etc: supplementary provisions) so as to alter the meaning of the expressions "subsidiary", "holding company" or "wholly-owned subsidiary".

(2) Regulations under this section are subject to negative resolution procedure.

(3) Any amendment made by regulations under this section does not apply for the purposes of enactments outside the Companies Acts unless the regulations so provide.

(4) So much of section 23(3) of the Interpretation Act 1978 (c. 30) as applies section 17(2)(a) of that Act (effect of repeal and re-enactment) to deeds, instruments and documents other than enactments does not apply in relation to any repeal and re-enactment effected by regulations under this section.

Meaning of "undertaking" and related expressions

1161 Meaning of "undertaking" and related expressions

(1) In the Companies Acts "undertaking" means –

    (a) a body corporate or partnership, or

    (b) an unincorporated association carrying on a trade or business, with or without a view to profit.

(2) In the Companies Acts references to shares –

    (a) in relation to an undertaking with capital but no share capital, are to rights to share in the capital of the undertaking; and

    (b) in relation to an undertaking without capital, are to interests –

        (i) conferring any right to share in the profits or liability to contribute to the losses of the undertaking, or

        (ii) giving rise to an obligation to contribute to the debts or expenses of the undertaking in the event of a winding up.

(3) Other expressions appropriate to companies shall be construed, in relation to an undertaking which is not a company, as references to the corresponding persons, officers, documents or organs, as the case may be, appropriate to undertakings of that description.

    This is subject to provision in any specific context providing for the translation of such expressions.

(4) References in the Companies Acts to "fellow subsidiary undertakings" are to undertakings which are subsidiary undertakings of the same parent undertaking but are not parent undertakings or subsidiary undertakings of each other.

(5) In the Companies Acts "group undertaking", in relation to an undertaking, means an undertaking which is –

(a) a parent undertaking or subsidiary undertaking of that undertaking, or

(b) a subsidiary undertaking of any parent undertaking of that undertaking.

1162 Parent and subsidiary undertakings

(1) This section (together with Schedule 7) defines "parent undertaking" and "subsidiary undertaking" for the purposes of the Companies Acts.

(2) An undertaking is a parent undertaking in relation to another undertaking, a subsidiary undertaking, if –

(a) it holds a majority of the voting rights in the undertaking, or

(b) it is a member of the undertaking and has the right to appoint or remove a majority of its board of directors, or

(c) it has the right to exercise a dominant influence over the undertaking –

(i) by virtue of provisions contained in the undertaking's articles, or

(ii) by virtue of a control contract, or

(d) it is a member of the undertaking and controls alone, pursuant to an agreement with other shareholders or members, a majority of the voting rights in the undertaking.

(3) For the purposes of subsection (2) an undertaking shall be treated as a member of another undertaking –

(a) if any of its subsidiary undertakings is a member of that undertaking, or

(b) if any shares in that other undertaking are held by a person acting on behalf of the undertaking or any of its subsidiary undertakings.

(4) An undertaking is also a parent undertaking in relation to another undertaking, a subsidiary undertaking, if –

(a) it has the power to exercise, or actually exercises, dominant influence or control over it, or

(b) it and the subsidiary undertaking are managed on a unified basis.

(5) A parent undertaking shall be treated as the parent undertaking of undertakings in relation to which any of its subsidiary undertakings are, or are to be treated as, parent undertakings; and references to its subsidiary undertakings shall be construed accordingly.

(6) Schedule 7 contains provisions explaining expressions used in this section and otherwise supplementing this section.

(7) In this section and that Schedule references to shares, in relation to an undertaking, are to allotted shares.

Other definitions

1163 "Non-cash asset"

(1) In the Companies Acts "non-cash asset" means any property or interest in property, other than cash.

For this purpose "cash" includes foreign currency.

(2) A reference to the transfer or acquisition of a non-cash asset includes –

(a) the creation or extinction of an estate or interest in, or a right over, any property, and

(b) the discharge of a liability of any person, other than a liability for a liquidated sum.

1164 Meaning of "banking company" and "banking group"

(1) This section defines "banking company" and "banking group" for the purposes of the Companies Acts.
(2) "Banking company" means a person who has permission under Part 4 of the Financial Services and Markets Act 2000 (c. 8) to accept deposits, other than –

(a) a person who is not a company, and
(b) a person who has such permission only for the purpose of carrying on another regulated activity in accordance with permission under that Part.

(3) The definition in subsection (2) must be read with section 22 of that Act, any relevant order under that section and Schedule 2 to that Act.
(4) References to a banking group are to a group where the parent company is a banking company or where –

(a) the parent company's principal subsidiary undertakings are wholly or mainly credit institutions, and
(b) the parent company does not itself carry on any material business apart from the acquisition, management and disposal of interests in subsidiary undertakings.

"Group" here means a parent undertaking and its subsidiary undertakings.
(5) For the purposes of subsection (4) –

(a) a parent company's principal subsidiary undertakings are the subsidiary undertakings of the company whose results or financial position would principally affect the figures shown in the group accounts, and
(b) the management of interests in subsidiary undertakings includes the provision of services to such undertakings.

1165 Meaning of "insurance company" and related expressions

(1) This section defines "insurance company", "authorised insurance company", "insurance group" and "insurance market activity" for the purposes of the Companies Acts.
(2) An "authorised insurance company" means a person (whether incorporated or not) who has permission under Part 4 of the Financial Services and Markets Act 2000 (c. 8) to effect or carry out contracts of insurance.
(3) An "insurance company" means –

(a) an authorised insurance company, or
(b) any other person (whether incorporated or not) who –

(i)   carries on insurance market activity, or
(ii) may effect or carry out contracts of insurance under which the benefits provided by that person are exclusively or primarily benefits in kind in the event of accident to or breakdown of a vehicle.

(4) Neither expression includes a friendly society within the meaning of the Friendly Societies Act 1992 (c. 40).
(5) References to an insurance group are to a group where the parent company is an insurance company or where –

(a) the parent company's principal subsidiary undertakings are wholly or mainly insurance companies, and
(b) the parent company does not itself carry on any material business apart from the acquisition, management and disposal of interests in subsidiary undertakings.

"Group" here means a parent undertaking and its subsidiary undertakings.
(6) For the purposes of subsection (5) –

(a) a parent company's principal subsidiary undertakings are the subsidiary under-
     takings of the company whose results or financial position would principally
     affect the figures shown in the group accounts, and

(b) the management of interests in subsidiary undertakings includes the provision of
     services to such undertakings.

(7) "Insurance market activity" has the meaning given in section 316(3) of the Financial
     Services and Markets Act 2000.

(8) References in this section to contracts of insurance and to the effecting or carrying out
     of such contracts must be read with section 22 of that Act, any relevant order under
     that section and Schedule 2 to that Act.

1166 "Employees' share scheme"

For the purposes of the Companies Acts an employees' share scheme is a scheme for
encouraging or facilitating the holding of shares in or debentures of a company by or for
the benefit of –

(a) the bona fide employees or former employees of –

   (i)   the company,
   (ii)   any subsidiary of the company, or
   (iii) the company's holding company or any subsidiary of the company's holding
          company, or

(b) the spouses, civil partners, surviving spouses, surviving civil partners, or minor
     children or step-children of such employees or former employees.

1167 Meaning of "prescribed"

In the Companies Acts "prescribed" means prescribed (by order or by regulations) by the
Secretary of State.

1168 Hard copy and electronic form and related expressions

(1) The following provisions apply for the purposes of the Companies Acts.

(2) A document or information is sent or supplied in hard copy form if it is sent or
     supplied in a paper copy or similar form capable of being read.
     References to hard copy have a corresponding meaning.

(3) A document or information is sent or supplied in electronic form if it is sent or
     supplied –

(a) by electronic means (for example, by e-mail or fax), or

(b) by any other means while in an electronic form (for example, sending a disk by
     post).

     References to electronic copy have a corresponding meaning.

(4) A document or information is sent or supplied by electronic means if it is –

(a) sent initially and received at its destination by means of electronic equipment for
     the processing (which expression includes digital compression) or storage of
     data, and

(b) entirely transmitted, conveyed and received by wire, by radio, by optical means
     or by other electromagnetic means.

     References to electronic means have a corresponding meaning.

(5) A document or information authorised or required to be sent or supplied in electronic
     form must be sent or supplied in a form, and by a means, that the sender or supplier
     reasonably considers will enable the recipient –

(a) to read it, and

(b) to retain a copy of it.

(6) For the purposes of this section, a document or information can be read only if –

(a)   it can be read with the naked eye, or

(b)   to the extent that it consists of images (for example photographs, pictures, maps, plans or drawings), it can be seen with the naked eye.

(7)   The provisions of this section apply whether the provision of the Companies Acts in question uses the words "sent" or "supplied" or uses other words (such as "deliver", "provide", "produce" or, in the case of a notice, "give") to refer to the sending or supplying of a document or information.

1169 Dormant companies

(1)   For the purposes of the Companies Acts a company is "dormant" during any period in which it has no significant accounting transaction.

(2)   A "significant accounting transaction" means a transaction that is required by section 386 to be entered in the company's accounting records.

(3)   In determining whether or when a company is dormant, there shall be disregarded –

(a)   any transaction arising from the taking of shares in the company by a subscriber to the memorandum as a result of an undertaking of his in connection with the formation of the company;

(b)   any transaction consisting of the payment of –

(i)   a fee to the registrar on a change of the company's name,

(ii)   a fee to the registrar on the re-registration of the company,

(iii)   a penalty under section 453 (penalty for failure to file accounts), or

(iv)   a fee to the registrar for the registration of an annual return.

(4)   Any reference in the Companies Acts to a body corporate other than a company being dormant has a corresponding meaning.

1170 Meaning of "EEA State" and related expressions

In the Companies Acts –

"EEA State" means a state which is a Contracting Party to the Agreement on the European Economic Area signed at Oporto on 2nd May 1992 (as it has effect from time to time);

"EEA company" and "EEA undertaking" mean a company or undertaking governed by the law of an EEA State.

1171 The former Companies Acts

In the Companies Acts –

"the former Companies Acts" means –

(a)   the Joint Stock Companies Acts, the Companies Act 1862 (c. 89), the Companies (Consolidation) Act 1908 (c. 69), the Companies Act 1929 (c. 23), the Companies Act (Northern Ireland) 1932 (c. 7 (N.I.)), the Companies Acts 1948 to 1983, the Companies Act (Northern Ireland) 1960 (c. 22 (N.I.)), the Companies (Northern Ireland) Order 1986 (S.I. 1986/1032 (N.I. 6)) and the Companies Consolidation (Consequential Provisions) (Northern Ireland) Order 1986 (S.I. 1986/1035 (N.I. 9)), and

(b)   the provisions of the Companies Act 1985 (c. 6) and the Companies Consolidation (Consequential Provisions) Act 1985 (c. 9) that are no longer in force;

"the Joint Stock Companies Acts" means the Joint Stock Companies Act 1856 (c. 47), the Joint Stock Companies Acts 1856, 1857 (20 & 21 Vict. c. 14), the Joint Stock Banking Companies Act 1857 (c. 49), and the Act to enable Joint Stock Banking Companies to be formed on the principle of limited liability (1858 c. 91), but does not include the Joint Stock Companies Act 1844 (c. 110).

General

1172 References to requirements of this Act

References in the company law provisions of this Act to the requirements of this Act include the requirements of regulations and orders made under it.

1173 Minor definitions: general

(1) In the Companies Acts –

"body corporate" and "corporation" include a body incorporated outside the United Kingdom, but do not include –

(a)   a corporation sole, or

(b)   a partnership that, whether or not a legal person, is not regarded as a body corporate under the law by which it is governed;

"credit institution" means a credit institution as defined in Article 4.1(a) of Directive 2006/48/EC of the European Parliament and of the Council relating to the taking up and pursuit of the business of credit institutions;

"financial institution" means a financial institution within the meaning of Article 1.1 of the Council Directive on the obligations of branches established in a Member State of credit and financial institutions having their head offices outside that Member State regarding the publication of annual accounting documents (the Bank Branches Directive, 89/117/EEC);

"firm" means any entity, whether or not a legal person, that is not an individual and includes a body corporate, a corporation sole and a partnership or other unincorporated association;

"the Gazette" means –

(a)   as respects companies registered in England and Wales, the London Gazette,

(b)   as respects companies registered in Scotland, the Edinburgh Gazette, and

(c)   as respects companies registered in Northern Ireland, the Belfast Gazette;

"hire-purchase agreement" has the same meaning as in the Consumer Credit Act 1974 (c. 39);

"officer", in relation to a body corporate, includes a director, manager or secretary;

"parent company" means a company that is a parent undertaking (see section 1162 and Schedule 7);

"regulated activity" has the meaning given in section 22 of the Financial Services and Markets Act 2000 (c. 8);

"regulated market" has the same meaning as in Directive 2004/39/EC of the European Parliament and of the Council on markets in financial instruments (see Article 4.1(14));

"working day", in relation to a company, means a day that is not a Saturday or Sunday, Christmas Day, Good Friday or any day that is a bank holiday under the Banking and Financial Dealings Act 1971 (c. 80) in the part of the United Kingdom where the company is registered.

(2) In relation to an EEA State that has not implemented Directive 2004/39/EC of the European Parliament and of the Council on markets in financial instruments, the following definition of "regulated market" has effect in place of that in subsection (1) –

"regulated market" has the same meaning as it has in Council Directive 93/22/EEC on investment services in the securities field.

1174 Index of defined expressions

Schedule 8 contains an index of provisions defining or otherwise explaining expressions used in the Companies Acts.

PART 39

COMPANIES: MINOR AMENDMENTS

1175 Removal of special provisions about accounts and audit of charitable companies

(1) Part 7 of the Companies Act 1985 (c. 6) and Part 8 of the Companies (Northern Ireland) Order 1986 (accounts and audit) are amended in accordance with Schedule 9 to this Act so as to remove the special provisions about companies that are charities.

(2) In that Schedule –

Part 1 contains repeals and consequential amendments of provisions of the Companies Act 1985;

Part 2 contains repeals and consequential amendments of provisions of the Companies (Northern Ireland) Order 1986.

1176 Power of Secretary of State to bring civil proceedings on company's behalf

(1) Section 438 of the Companies Act 1985 (power of Secretary of State to bring civil proceedings on company's behalf) shall cease to have effect.

(2) In section 439 of that Act (expenses of investigating company's affairs) –

(a) in subsection (2) omit ", or is ordered to pay the whole or any part of the costs of proceedings brought under section 438,";

(b) omit subsections (3) and (7) (which relate to section 438);

(c) in subsection (8) –

(i) for "subsections (2) and (3)" substitute "subsection (2)", and

(ii) omit "; and any such liability imposed by subsection (2) is (subject as mentioned above) a liability also to indemnify all persons against liability under subsection (3)".

(3) In section 453(1A) of that Act (investigation of overseas companies: provisions not applicable), omit paragraph (b) (which relates to section 438).

(4) Nothing in this section affects proceedings brought under section 438 before the commencement of this section.

1177 Repeal of certain provisions about company directors

The following provisions of Part 10 of the Companies Act 1985 shall cease to have effect –

section 311 (prohibition on tax-free payments to directors);

sections 323 and 327 (prohibition on directors dealing in share options);

sections 324 to 326 and 328 to 329, and Parts 2 to 4 of Schedule 13 (register of directors' interests);

sections 343 and 344 (special procedure for disclosure by banks).

1178 Repeal of requirement that certain companies publish periodical statement

The following provisions shall cease to have effect –

section 720 of the Companies Act 1985 (c. 6) (certain companies to publish periodical statement), and

Schedule 23 to that Act (form of statement under section 720).

1179 Repeal of requirement that Secretary of State prepare annual report

Section 729 of the Companies Act 1985 (annual report to Parliament by Secretary of State on matters within the Companies Acts) shall cease to have effect.

1180 Repeal of certain provisions about company charges

Part 4 of the Companies Act 1989 (c. 40) (registration of company charges), which has not been brought into force, is repealed.

1181 Access to constitutional documents of RTE and RTM companies

(1) The Secretary of State may by order –

    (a) amend Chapter 1 of Part 1 of the Leasehold Reform, Housing and Urban Development Act 1993 (c. 28) for the purpose of facilitating access to the provisions of the articles or any other constitutional document of RTE companies;

    (b) amend Chapter 1 of Part 2 of the Commonhold and Leasehold Reform Act 2002 (c. 15) (leasehold reform) for the purpose of facilitating access to the provisions of the articles or any other constitutional document of RTM companies.

(2) References in subsection (1) to provisions of a company's articles or any other constitutional document include any provisions included in those documents by virtue of any enactment.

(3) An order under this section is subject to negative resolution procedure.

(4) In this section –

    "RTE companies" has the same meaning as in Chapter 1 of Part 1 of the Leasehold Reform, Housing and Urban Development Act 1993;

    "RTM companies" has the same meaning as in Chapter 1 of Part 2 of the Commonhold and Leasehold Reform Act 2002.

PART 40

COMPANY DIRECTORS: FOREIGN DISQUALIFICATION ETC

Introductory

1182 Persons subject to foreign restrictions

(1) This section defines what is meant by references in this Part to a person being subject to foreign restrictions.

(2) A person is subject to foreign restrictions if under the law of a country or territory outside the United Kingdom –

    (a) he is, by reason of misconduct or unfitness, disqualified to any extent from acting in connection with the affairs of a company,

    (b) he is, by reason of misconduct or unfitness, required –

        (i) to obtain permission from a court or other authority, or

        (ii) to meet any other condition,

    before acting in connection with the affairs of a company, or

    (c) he has, by reason of misconduct or unfitness, given undertakings to a court or other authority of a country or territory outside the United Kingdom –

        (i) not to act in connection with the affairs of a company, or

        (ii) restricting the extent to which, or the way in which, he may do so.

(3) The references in subsection (2) to acting in connection with the affairs of a company are to doing any of the following –

    (a) being a director of a company,

    (b) acting as receiver of a company's property, or

    (c) being concerned or taking part in the promotion, formation or management of a company.

(4) In this section –

    (a) "company" means a company incorporated or formed under the law of the country or territory in question, and

    (b) in relation to such a company –

        "director" means the holder of an office corresponding to that of director of a UK company; and

        "receiver" includes any corresponding officer under the law of that country or territory.

1183 Meaning of "the court" and "UK company"

In this Part –

    "the court" means –

        (a)   in England and Wales, the High Court or a county court;

        (b)   in Scotland, the Court of Session or the sheriff court;

        (c)   in Northern Ireland, the High Court;

    "UK company" means a company registered under this Act.

Power to disqualify

1184 Disqualification of persons subject to foreign restrictions

(1) The Secretary of State may make provision by regulations disqualifying a person subject to foreign restrictions from –

    (a) being a director of a UK company,

    (b) acting as receiver of a UK company's property, or

    (c) in any way, whether directly or indirectly, being concerned or taking part in the promotion, formation or management of a UK company.

(2) The regulations may provide that a person subject to foreign restrictions –

    (a) is disqualified automatically by virtue of the regulations, or

    (b) may be disqualified by order of the court on the application of the Secretary of State.

(3) The regulations may provide that the Secretary of State may accept an undertaking (a "disqualification undertaking") from a person subject to foreign restrictions that he will not do anything which would be in breach of a disqualification under subsection (1).

(4) In this Part –

    (a) a "person disqualified under this Part" is a person –

        (i)   disqualified as mentioned in subsection (2)(a) or (b), or

        (ii) who has given and is subject to a disqualification undertaking;

    (b) references to a breach of a disqualification include a breach of a disqualification undertaking.

(5) The regulations may provide for applications to the court by persons disqualified under this Part for permission to act in a way which would otherwise be in breach of the disqualification.

(6) The regulations must provide that a person ceases to be disqualified under this Part on his ceasing to be subject to foreign restrictions.

(7) Regulations under this section are subject to affirmative resolution procedure.

1185 Disqualification regulations: supplementary

(1) Regulations under section 1184 may make different provision for different cases and may in particular distinguish between cases by reference to –

    (a) the conduct on the basis of which the person became subject to foreign restrictions;

    (b) the nature of the foreign restrictions;

    (c) the country or territory under whose law the foreign restrictions were imposed.

(2) Regulations under section 1184(2)(b) or (5) (provision for applications to the court) –

    (a) must specify the grounds on which an application may be made;

    (b) may specify factors to which the court shall have regard in determining an application.

(3) The regulations may, in particular, require the court to have regard to the following factors –

    (a) whether the conduct on the basis of which the person became subject to foreign restrictions would, if done in relation to a UK company, have led a court to make a disqualification order on an application under the Company Directors Disqualification Act 1986 (c. 46) or the Company Directors Disqualification (Northern Ireland) Order 2002 (S.I. 2002/3150 (N.I. 4));

    (b) in a case in which the conduct on the basis of which the person became subject to foreign restrictions would not be unlawful if done in relation to a UK company, the fact that the person acted unlawfully under foreign law;

    (c) whether the person's activities in relation to UK companies began after he became subject to foreign restrictions;

    (d) whether the person's activities (or proposed activities) in relation to UK companies are undertaken (or are proposed to be undertaken) outside the United Kingdom.

(4) Regulations under section 1184(3) (provision as to undertakings given to the Secretary of State) may include provision allowing the Secretary of State, in determining whether to accept an undertaking, to take into account matters other than criminal convictions notwithstanding that the person may be criminally liable in respect of those matters.

(5) Regulations under section 1184(5) (provision for application to court for permission to act) may include provision –

    (a) entitling the Secretary of State to be represented at the hearing of the application, and

    (b) as to the giving of evidence or the calling of witnesses by the Secretary of State at the hearing of the application.

1186 Offence of breach of disqualification

(1) Regulations under section 1184 may provide that a person disqualified under this Part who acts in breach of the disqualification commits an offence.

(2) The regulations may provide that a person guilty of such an offence is liable –

    (a) on conviction on indictment, to imprisonment for a term not exceeding two years or a fine (or both);

    (b) on summary conviction –

        (i) in England and Wales, to imprisonment for a term not exceeding twelve months or to a fine not exceeding the statutory maximum (or both);

        (ii) in Scotland or Northern Ireland, to imprisonment for a term not exceeding six months, or to a fine not exceeding the statutory maximum (or both).

(3) In relation to an offence committed before the commencement of section 154(1) of the Criminal Justice Act 2003 (c. 44), for "twelve months" in subsection (2)(b)(i) substitute "six months".

Power to make persons liable for company's debts

1187 Personal liability for debts of company

(1) The Secretary of State may provide by regulations that a person who, at a time when he is subject to foreign restrictions –

(a) is a director of a UK company, or
(b) is involved in the management of a UK company,

is personally responsible for all debts and other liabilities of the company incurred during that time.

(2) A person who is personally responsible by virtue of this section for debts and other liabilities of a company is jointly and severally liable in respect of those debts and liabilities with –

(a) the company, and
(b) any other person who (whether by virtue of this section or otherwise) is so liable.

(3) For the purposes of this section a person is involved in the management of a company if he is concerned, whether directly or indirectly, or takes part, in the management of the company.

(4) The regulations may make different provision for different cases and may in particular distinguish between cases by reference to –

(a) the conduct on the basis of which the person became subject to foreign restrictions;
(b) the nature of the foreign restrictions;
(c) the country or territory under whose law the foreign restrictions were imposed.

(5) Regulations under this section are subject to affirmative resolution procedure.

Power to require statements to be sent to the registrar of companies

1188 Statements from persons subject to foreign restrictions

(1) The Secretary of State may make provision by regulations requiring a person who –

(a) is subject to foreign restrictions, and
(b) is not disqualified under this Part,

to send a statement to the registrar if he does anything that, if done by a person disqualified under this Part, would be in breach of the disqualification.

(2) The statement must include such information as may be specified in the regulations relating to –

(a) the person's activities in relation to UK companies, and
(b) the foreign restrictions to which the person is subject.

(3) The statement must be sent to the registrar within such period as may be specified in the regulations.

(4) The regulations may make different provision for different cases and may in particular distinguish between cases by reference to –

(a) the conduct on the basis of which the person became subject to foreign restrictions;
(b) the nature of the foreign restrictions;
(c) the country or territory under whose law the foreign restrictions were imposed.

(5) Regulations under this section are subject to affirmative resolution procedure.

1189 Statements from persons disqualified

(1) The Secretary of State may make provision by regulations requiring a statement or notice sent to the registrar of companies under any of the provisions listed below that relates (wholly or partly) to a person who –

   (a) is a person disqualified under this Part, or

   (b) is subject to a disqualification order or disqualification undertaking under the Company Directors Disqualification Act 1986 (c. 46) or the Company Directors Disqualification (Northern Ireland) Order 2002 (S.I. 2002/3150 (N.I. 4)),

to be accompanied by an additional statement.

(2) The provisions referred to above are –

   (a) section 12 (statement of a company's proposed officers),

   (b) section 167(2) (notice of person having become director), and

   (c) section 276 (notice of a person having become secretary or one of joint secretaries).

(3) The additional statement is a statement that the person has obtained permission from a court, on an application under section 1184(5) or (as the case may be) for the purposes of section 1(1)(a) of the Company Directors Disqualification Act 1986 (c. 46) or Article 3(1) of the Company Directors Disqualification (Northern Ireland) Order 2002 (S.I. 2002/3150 (N.I. 4)), to act in the capacity in question.

(4) Regulations under this section are subject to affirmative resolution procedure.

1190 Statements: whether to be made public

(1) Regulations under section 1188 or 1189 (statements required to be sent to registrar) may provide that a statement sent to the registrar of companies under the regulations is to be treated as a record relating to a company for the purposes of section 1080 (the companies register).

(2) The regulations may make provision as to the circumstances in which such a statement is to be, or may be –

   (a) withheld from public inspection, or

   (b) removed from the register.

(3) The regulations may, in particular, provide that a statement is not to be withheld from public inspection or removed from the register unless the person to whom it relates provides such information, and satisfies such other conditions, as may be specified.

(4) The regulations may provide that section 1081 (note of removal of material from the register) does not apply, or applies with such modifications as may be specified, in the case of material removed from the register under the regulations.

(5) In this section "specified" means specified in the regulations.

1191 Offences

(1) Regulations under section 1188 or 1189 may provide that it is an offence for a person –

   (a) to fail to comply with a requirement under the regulations to send a statement to the registrar;

   (b) knowingly or recklessly to send a statement under the regulations to the registrar that is misleading, false or deceptive in a material particular.

(2) The regulations may provide that a person guilty of such an offence is liable –

   (a) on conviction on indictment, to imprisonment for a term not exceeding two years or a fine (or both);

   (b) on summary conviction –

      (i) in England and Wales, to imprisonment for a term not exceeding twelve months or to a fine not exceeding the statutory maximum (or both);

      (ii) in Scotland or Northern Ireland, to imprisonment for a term not exceeding six months, or to a fine not exceeding the statutory maximum (or both).

(3) In relation to an offence committed before the commencement of section 154(1) of the Criminal Justice Act 2003 (c. 44), for "twelve months" in subsection (2)(b)(i) substitute "six months".

PART 41

BUSINESS NAMES

CHAPTER 1

RESTRICTED OR PROHIBITED NAMES

Introductory

1192 Application of this Chapter

(1) This Chapter applies to any person carrying on business in the United Kingdom.

(2) The provisions of this Chapter do not prevent –

    (a) an individual carrying on business under a name consisting of his surname without any addition other than a permitted addition, or

    (b) individuals carrying on business in partnership under a name consisting of the surnames of all the partners without any addition other than a permitted addition.

(3) The following are the permitted additions –

    (a) in the case of an individual, his forename or initial;

    (b) in the case of a partnership –

        (i) the forenames of individual partners or the initials of those forenames, or

        (ii) where two or more individual partners have the same surname, the addition of "s" at the end of that surname;

    (c) in either case, an addition merely indicating that the business is carried on in succession to a former owner of the business.

Sensitive words or expressions

1193 Name suggesting connection with government or public authority

(1) A person must not, without the approval of the Secretary of State, carry on business in the United Kingdom under a name that would be likely to give the impression that the business is connected with –

    (a) Her Majesty's Government, any part of the Scottish administration or Her Majesty's Government in Northern Ireland,

    (b) any local authority, or

    (c) any public authority specified for the purposes of this section by regulations made by the Secretary of State.

(2) For the purposes of this section –

"local authority" means –

    (a) a local authority within the meaning of the Local Government Act 1972 (c. 70), the Common Council of the City of London or the Council of the Isles of Scilly,

    (b) a council constituted under section 2 of the Local Government etc. (Scotland) Act 1994 (c. 39), or

    (c) a district council in Northern Ireland;

"public authority" includes any person or body having functions of a public nature.

(3) Regulations under this section are subject to affirmative resolution procedure.

(4) A person who contravenes this section commits an offence.

(5) Where an offence under this section is committed by a body corporate, an offence is also committed by every officer of the body who is in default.

(6) A person guilty of an offence under this section is liable on summary conviction to a fine not exceeding level 3 on the standard scale and, for continued contravention, a daily default fine not exceeding one-tenth of level 3 on the standard scale.

1194 Other sensitive words or expressions

(1) A person must not, without the approval of the Secretary of State, carry on business in the United Kingdom under a name that includes a word or expression for the time being specified in regulations made by the Secretary of State under this section.

(2) Regulations under this section are subject to approval after being made.

(3) A person who contravenes this section commits an offence.

(4) Where an offence under this section is committed by a body corporate, an offence is also committed by every officer of the body who is in default.

(5) A person guilty of an offence under this section is liable on summary conviction to a fine not exceeding level 3 on the standard scale and, for continued contravention, a daily default fine not exceeding one-tenth of level 3 on the standard scale.

1195 Requirement to seek comments of government department or other relevant body

(1) The Secretary of State may by regulations under –

    (a) section 1193 (name suggesting connection with government or public authority), or

    (b) section 1194 (other sensitive words or expressions),

require that, in connection with an application for the approval of the Secretary of State under that section, the applicant must seek the view of a specified Government department or other body.

(2) Where such a requirement applies, the applicant must request the specified department or other body (in writing) to indicate whether (and if so why) it has any objections to the proposed name.

(3) He must submit to the Secretary of State a statement that such a request has been made and a copy of any response received from the specified body.

(4) If these requirements are not complied with, the Secretary of State may refuse to consider the application for approval.

(5) In this section "specified" means specified in the regulations.

1196 Withdrawal of Secretary of State's approval

(1) This section applies to approval given for the purposes of –

section 1193 (name suggesting connection with government or public authority), or section 1194 (other sensitive words or expressions).

(2) If it appears to the Secretary of State that there are overriding considerations of public policy that require such approval to be withdrawn, the approval may be withdrawn by notice in writing given to the person concerned.

(3) The notice must state the date as from which approval is withdrawn.

Misleading names

1197 Name containing inappropriate indication of company type or legal form

(1) The Secretary of State may make provision by regulations prohibiting a person from carrying on business in the United Kingdom under a name consisting of or containing specified words, expressions or other indications –

    (a) that are associated with a particular type of company or form of organisation, or

(b) that are similar to words, expressions or other indications associated with a particular type of company or form of organisation.

(2) The regulations may prohibit the use of words, expressions or other indications –

(a) in a specified part, or otherwise than in a specified part, of a name;

(b) in conjunction with, or otherwise than in conjunction with, such other words, expressions or indications as may be specified.

(3) In this section "specified" means specified in the regulations.

(4) Regulations under this section are subject to negative resolution procedure.

(5) A person who uses a name in contravention of regulations under this section commits an offence.

(6) Where an offence under this section is committed by a body corporate, an offence is also committed by every officer of the body who is in default.

(7) A person guilty of an offence under this section is liable on summary conviction to a fine not exceeding level 3 on the standard scale and, for continued contravention, a daily default fine not exceeding one-tenth of level 3 on the standard scale.

1198 Name giving misleading indication of activities

(1) A person must not carry on business in the United Kingdom under a name that gives so misleading an indication of the nature of the activities of the business as to be likely to cause harm to the public.

(2) A person who uses a name in contravention of this section commits an offence.

(3) Where an offence under this section is committed by a body corporate, an offence is also committed by every officer of the body who is in default.

(4) A person guilty of an offence under this section is liable on summary conviction to a fine not exceeding level 3 on the standard scale and, for continued contravention, a daily default fine not exceeding one-tenth of level 3 on the standard scale.

Supplementary

1199 Savings for existing lawful business names

(1) This section has effect in relation to –

sections 1192 to 1196 (sensitive words or expressions), and
section 1197 (inappropriate indication of company type or legal form).

(2) Those sections do not apply to the carrying on of a business by a person who –

(a) carried on the business immediately before the date on which this Chapter came into force, and

(b) continues to carry it on under the name that immediately before that date was its lawful business name.

(3) Where –

(a) a business is transferred to a person on or after the date on which this Chapter came into force, and

(b) that person carries on the business under the name that was its lawful business name immediately before the transfer,

those sections do not apply in relation to the carrying on of the business under that name during the period of twelve months beginning with the date of the transfer.

(4) In this section "lawful business name", in relation to a business, means a name under which the business was carried on without contravening –

(a) section 2(1) of the Business Names Act 1985 (c. 7) or Article 4(1) of the Business Names (Northern Ireland) Order 1986 (S.I. 1986/1033 N.I. 7)), or

(b) after this Chapter has come into force, the provisions of this Chapter.

CHAPTER 2

DISCLOSURE REQUIRED IN CASE OF INDIVIDUAL OR PARTNERSHIP

Introductory

1200 Application of this Chapter

(1) This Chapter applies to an individual or partnership carrying on business in the United Kingdom under a business name.
References in this Chapter to "a person to whom this Chapter applies" are to such an individual or partnership.
(2) For the purposes of this Chapter a "business name" means a name other than –

(a) in the case of an individual, his surname without any addition other than a permitted addition;
(b) in the case of a partnership –

(i) the surnames of all partners who are individuals, and
(ii) the corporate names of all partners who are bodies corporate,

without any addition other than a permitted addition.
(3) The following are the permitted additions –

(a) in the case of an individual, his forename or initial;
(b) in the case of a partnership –

(i) the forenames of individual partners or the initials of those forenames, or
(ii) where two or more individual partners have the same surname, the addition of "s" at the end of that surname;

(c) in either case, an addition merely indicating that the business is carried on in succession to a former owner of the business.

1201 Information required to be disclosed

The "information required by this Chapter" is –

(a) in the case of an individual, his name;
(b) in the case of a partnership, the name of each member of the partnership;

and in relation to each person so named, an address in the United Kingdom at which service of any document relating in any way to the business will be effective.

Disclosure requirements

1202 Disclosure required: business documents etc

(1) A person to whom this Chapter applies must state the information required by this Chapter, in legible characters, on all –

(a) business letters,
(b) written orders for goods or services to be supplied to the business,
(c) invoices and receipts issued in the course of the business, an
(d) written demands for payment of debts arising in the course of the business.

This subsection has effect subject to section 1203 (exemption for large partnerships if certain conditions met).
(2) A person to whom this Chapter applies must secure that the information required by this Chapter is immediately given, by written notice, to any person with whom anything is done or discussed in the course of the business and who asks for that information.

(3) The Secretary of State may by regulations require that such notices be given in a specified form.

(4) Regulations under this section are subject to negative resolution procedure.

1203 Exemption for large partnerships if certain conditions met

(1) Section 1202(1) (disclosure required in business documents) does not apply in relation to a document issued by a partnership of more than 20 persons if the following conditions are met.

(2) The conditions are that –

    (a) the partnership maintains at its principal place of business a list of the names of all the partners,

    (b) no partner's name appears in the document, except in the text or as a signatory, and

    (c) the document states in legible characters the address of the partnership's principal place of business and that the list of the partners' names is open to inspection there.

(3) Where a partnership maintains a list of the partners' names for the purposes of this section, any person may inspect the list during office hours.

(4) Where an inspection required by a person in accordance with this section is refused, an offence is committed by any member of the partnership concerned who without reasonable excuse refused the inspection or permitted it to be refused.

(5) A person guilty of an offence under subsection (4) is liable on summary conviction to a fine not exceeding level 3 on the standard scale and, for continued contravention, a daily default fine not exceeding one-tenth of level 3 on the standard scale.

1204 Disclosure required: business premises

(1) A person to whom this Chapter applies must, in any premises –

    (a) where the business is carried on, and

    (b) to which customers of the business or suppliers of goods or services to the business have access,

display in a prominent position, so that it may easily be read by such customers or suppliers, a notice containing the information required by this Chapter.

(2) The Secretary of State may by regulations require that such notices be displayed in a specified form.

(3) Regulations under this section are subject to negative resolution procedure.

Consequences of failure to make required disclosure

1205 Criminal consequences of failure to make required disclosure

(1) A person who without reasonable excuse fails to comply with the requirements of –

section 1202 (disclosure required: business documents etc), or
section 1204 (disclosure required: business premises),

commits an offence.

(2) Where an offence under this section is committed by a body corporate, an offence is also committed by every officer of the body who is in default.

(3) A person guilty of an offence under this section is liable on summary conviction to a fine not exceeding level 3 on the standard scale and, for continued contravention, a daily default fine not exceeding one-tenth of level 3 on the standard scale.

(4) References in this section to the requirements of section 1202 or 1204 include the requirements of regulations under that section.

1206 Civil consequences of failure to make required disclosure

(1) This section applies to any legal proceedings brought by a person to whom this Chapter applies to enforce a right arising out of a contract made in the course of a business in respect of which he was, at the time the contract was made, in breach of section 1202(1) or (2) (disclosure in business documents etc) or section 1204(1) (disclosure at business premises).

(2) The proceedings shall be dismissed if the defendant (in Scotland, the defender) to the proceedings shows –

    (a) that he has a claim against the claimant (pursuer) arising out of the contract that he has been unable to pursue by reason of the latter's breach of the requirements of this Chapter, or

    (b) that he has suffered some financial loss in connection with the contract by reason of the claimant's (pursuer's) breach of those requirements,

    unless the court before which the proceedings are brought is satisfied that it is just and equitable to permit the proceedings to continue.

(3) References in this section to the requirements of this Chapter include the requirements of regulations under this Chapter.

(4) This section does not affect the right of any person to enforce such rights as he may have against another person in any proceedings brought by that person.

CHAPTER 3

SUPPLEMENTARY

1207 Application of general provisions about offences

The provisions of sections 1121 to 1123 (liability of officer in default) and 1125 to 1131 (general provisions about offences) apply in relation to offences under this Part as in relation to offences under the Companies Acts.

1208 Interpretation

In this Part –

    "business" includes a profession;
    "initial" includes any recognised abbreviation of a name;
    "partnership" means –

        (a) a partnership within the Partnership Act 1890 (c. 39), or

        (b) a limited partnership registered under the Limited Partnerships Act 1907 (c. 24),

    or a firm or entity of a similar character formed under the law of a country or territory outside the United Kingdom;

    "surname", in relation to a peer or person usually known by a British title different from his surname, means the title by which he is known.

PART 42

STATUTORY AUDITORS

CHAPTER 1

INTRODUCTORY

1209 Main purposes of Part

The main purposes of this Part are –

(a) to secure that only persons who are properly supervised and appropriately qualified are appointed as statutory auditors, and

(b) to secure that audits by persons so appointed are carried out properly, with integrity and with a proper degree of independence.

1210 Meaning of "statutory auditor" etc

(1) In this Part "statutory auditor" means –

(a) a person appointed as auditor under Part 16 of this Act,

(b) a person appointed as auditor under section 77 of or Schedule 11 to the Building Societies Act 1986 (c. 53),

(c) a person appointed as auditor of an insurer that is a friendly society under section 72 of or Schedule 14 to the Friendly Societies Act 1992 (c. 40),

(d) a person appointed as auditor of an insurer that is an industrial and provident society under section 4 of the Friendly and Industrial and Provident Societies Act 1968 (c. 55) or under section 38 of the Industrial and Provident Societies Act (Northern Ireland) 1969 (c. 24 (N.I.)),

(e) a person appointed as auditor for the purposes of regulation 3 of the Insurance Accounts Directive (Lloyd's Syndicate and Aggregate Accounts) Regulations 2004 (S.I. 2004/3219) or appointed to report on the "aggregate accounts" within the meaning of those Regulations,

(f) a person appointed as auditor of an insurer for the purposes of regulation 3 of the Insurance Accounts Directive (Miscellaneous Insurance Undertakings) Regulations 1993 (S.I. 1993/3245),

(g) a person appointed as auditor of a bank for the purposes of regulation 4 of the Bank Accounts Directive (Miscellaneous Banks) Regulations 1991 (S.I. 1991/2704), and

(h) a person appointed as auditor of a prescribed person under a prescribed enactment authorising or requiring the appointment;

and the expressions "statutory audit" and "statutory audit work" are to be construed accordingly.

(2) In this Part "audited person" means the person in respect of whom a statutory audit is conducted.

(3) In subsection (1) –

"bank" means a person who –

(a) is a credit institution within the meaning given by Article 4.1(a) of Directive 2006/48/EC of the European Parliament and of the Council relating to the taking up and pursuit of the business of credit institutions, and

(b) is a company or a firm as defined in Article 48 of the Treaty establishing the European Community;

"friendly society" means a friendly society within the meaning of the Friendly Societies Act 1992 (c. 40);

"industrial and provident society" means –

    (a) a society registered under the Industrial and Provident Societies Act 1965 (c. 12) or a society deemed by virtue of section 4 of that Act to be so registered, or

    (b) a society registered under the Industrial and Provident Societies Act (Northern Ireland) 1969 or a society deemed by virtue of section 4 of that Act to be so registered;

"insurer" means a person who is an insurance undertaking within the meaning given by Article 2.1 of Council Directive 1991/674/EEC on the annual accounts and consolidated accounts of insurance undertakings;

"prescribed" means prescribed, or of a description prescribed, by order made by the Secretary of State for the purposes of subsection (1)(h).

(4) An order under this section is subject to negative resolution procedure.

1211 Eligibility for appointment as a statutory auditor: overview

A person is eligible for appointment as a statutory auditor only if the person is so eligible –

    (a) by virtue of Chapter 2 (individuals and firms), or

    (b) by virtue of Chapter 3 (Comptroller and Auditor General, etc).

CHAPTER 2

INDIVIDUALS AND FIRMS

Eligibility for appointment

1212 Individuals and firms: eligibility for appointment as a statutory auditor

(1) An individual or firm is eligible for appointment as a statutory auditor if the individual or firm –

    (a) is a member of a recognised supervisory body, and

    (b) is eligible for appointment under the rules of that body.

(2) In the cases to which section 1222 applies (individuals retaining only 1967 Act authorisation) a person's eligibility for appointment as a statutory auditor is restricted as mentioned in that section.

1213 Effect of ineligibility

(1) No person may act as statutory auditor of an audited person if he is ineligible for appointment as a statutory auditor.

(2) If at any time during his term of office a statutory auditor becomes ineligible for appointment as a statutory auditor, he must immediately –

    (a) resign his office (with immediate effect), and

    (b) give notice in writing to the audited person that he has resigned by reason of his becoming ineligible for appointment.

(3) A person is guilty of an offence if –

    (a) he acts as a statutory auditor in contravention of subsection (1), or

    (b) he fails to give the notice mentioned in paragraph (b) of subsection (2) in accordance with that subsection.

(4) A person guilty of an offence under subsection (3) is liable –

    (a) on conviction on indictment, to a fine;

(b) on summary conviction, to a fine not exceeding the statutory maximum.

(5) A person is guilty of an offence if –

    (a) he has been convicted of an offence under subsection (3)(a) or this subsection, and

    (b) he continues to act as a statutory auditor in contravention of subsection (1) after the conviction.

(6) A person is guilty of an offence if –

    (a) he has been convicted of an offence under subsection (3)(b) or this subsection, and

    (b) he continues, after the conviction, to fail to give the notice mentioned in subsection (2)(b).

(7) A person guilty of an offence under subsection (5) or (6) is liable –

    (a) on conviction on indictment, to a fine;

    (b) on summary conviction, to a fine not exceeding one-tenth of the statutory maximum for each day on which the act or the failure continues.

(8) In proceedings against a person for an offence under this section it is a defence for him to show that he did not know and had no reason to believe that he was, or had become, ineligible for appointment as a statutory auditor.

Independence requirement

1214 Independence requirement

(1) A person may not act as statutory auditor of an audited person if one or more of subsections (2), (3) and (4) apply to him.

(2) This subsection applies if the person is –

    (a) an officer or employee of the audited person, or

    (b) a partner or employee of such a person, or a partnership of which such a person is a partner.

(3) This subsection applies if the person is –

    (a) an officer or employee of an associated undertaking of the audited person, or

    (b) a partner or employee of such a person, or a partnership of which such a person is a partner.

(4) This subsection applies if there exists, between –

    (a) the person or an associate of his, and

    (b) the audited person or an associated undertaking of the audited person,

a connection of any such description as may be specified by regulations made by the Secretary of State.

(5) An auditor of an audited person is not to be regarded as an officer or employee of the person for the purposes of subsections (2) and (3).

(6) In this section "associated undertaking", in relation to an audited person, means –

    (a) a parent undertaking or subsidiary undertaking of the audited person, or

    (b) a subsidiary undertaking of a parent undertaking of the audited person.

(7) Regulations under subsection (4) are subject to negative resolution procedure.

1215 Effect of lack of independence

(1) If at any time during his term of office a statutory auditor becomes prohibited from acting by section 1214(1), he must immediately –

    (a) resign his office (with immediate effect), and

    (b)   give notice in writing to the audited person that he has resigned by reason of his lack of independence.

(2)   A person is guilty of an offence if –

    (a)   he acts as a statutory auditor in contravention of section 1214(1), or

    (b)   he fails to give the notice mentioned in paragraph (b) of subsection (1) in accordance with that subsection.

(3)   A person guilty of an offence under subsection (2) is liable –

    (a)   on conviction on indictment, to a fine;

    (b)   on summary conviction, to a fine not exceeding the statutory maximum.

(4)   A person is guilty of an offence if –

    (a)   he has been convicted of an offence under subsection (2)(a) or this subsection, and

    (b)   he continues to act as a statutory auditor in contravention of section 1214(1) after the conviction.

(5)   A person is guilty of an offence if –

    (a)   he has been convicted of an offence under subsection (2)(b) or this subsection, and

    (b)   after the conviction, he continues to fail to give the notice mentioned in subsection (1)(b).

(6)   A person guilty of an offence under subsection (4) or (5) is liable –

    (a)   on conviction on indictment, to a fine;

    (b)   on summary conviction, to a fine not exceeding one-tenth of the statutory maximum for each day on which the act or the failure continues.

(7)   In proceedings against a person for an offence under this section it is a defence for him to show that he did not know and had no reason to believe that he was, or had become, prohibited from acting as statutory auditor of the audited person by section 1214(1).

Effect of appointment of a partnership

1216 Effect of appointment of a partnership

(1)   This section applies where a partnership constituted under the law of –

    (a)   England and Wales,

    (b)   Northern Ireland, or

    (c)   any other country or territory in which a partnership is not a legal person,

is by virtue of this Chapter appointed as statutory auditor of an audited person.

(2)   Unless a contrary intention appears, the appointment is an appointment of the partnership as such and not of the partners.

(3)   Where the partnership ceases, the appointment is to be treated as extending to –

    (a)   any appropriate partnership which succeeds to the practice of that partnership, or

    (b)   any other appropriate person who succeeds to that practice having previously carried it on in partnership.

(4)   For the purposes of subsection (3) –

    (a)   a partnership is to be regarded as succeeding to the practice of another partnership only if the members of the successor partnership are substantially the same as those of the former partnership, and

    (b)   a partnership or other person is to be regarded as succeeding to the practice of a partnership only if it or he succeeds to the whole or substantially the whole of the business of the former partnership.

(5) Where the partnership ceases and the appointment is not treated under subsection (3) as extending to any partnership or other person, the appointment may with the consent of the audited person be treated as extending to an appropriate partnership, or other appropriate person, who succeeds to –

(a) the business of the former partnership, or
(b) such part of it as is agreed by the audited person is to be treated as comprising the appointment.

(6) For the purposes of this section, a partnership or other person is "appropriate" if it or he –

(a) is eligible for appointment as a statutory auditor by virtue of this Chapter, and
(b) is not prohibited by section 1214(1) from acting as statutory auditor of the audited person.

Supervisory bodies

1217 Supervisory bodies

(1) In this Part a "supervisory body" means a body established in the United Kingdom (whether a body corporate or an unincorporated association) which maintains and enforces rules as to –

(a) the eligibility of persons for appointment as a statutory auditor, and
(b) the conduct of statutory audit work,

which are binding on persons seeking appointment or acting as a statutory auditor either because they are members of that body or because they are otherwise subject to its control.

(2) In this Part references to the members of a supervisory body are to the persons who, whether or not members of the body, are subject to its rules in seeking appointment or acting as a statutory auditor.

(3) In this Part references to the rules of a supervisory body are to the rules (whether or not laid down by the body itself) which the body has power to enforce and which are relevant for the purposes of this Part.
This includes rules relating to the admission or expulsion of members of the body, so far as relevant for the purposes of this Part.

(4) Schedule 10 has effect with respect to the recognition of supervisory bodies for the purposes of this Part.

1218 Exemption from liability for damages

(1) No person within subsection (2) is to be liable in damages for anything done or omitted in the discharge or purported discharge of functions to which this subsection applies.

(2) The persons within this subsection are –

(a) any recognised supervisory body,
(b) any officer or employee of a recognised supervisory body, and
(c) any member of the governing body of a recognised supervisory body.

(3) Subsection (1) applies to the functions of a recognised supervisory body so far as relating to, or to matters arising out of, any of the following –

(a) rules, practices, powers and arrangements of the body to which the requirements of Part 2 of Schedule 10 apply;
(b) the obligations with which paragraph 20 of that Schedule requires the body to comply;
(c) any guidance issued by the body;
(d) the obligations imposed on the body by or by virtue of this Part.

(4) The reference in subsection (3)(c) to guidance issued by a recognised supervisory body is a reference to any guidance or recommendation which is –

    (a) issued or made by it to all or any class of its members or persons seeking to become members, and

    (b) relevant for the purposes of this Part,

including any guidance or recommendation relating to the admission or expulsion of members of the body, so far as relevant for the purposes of this Part.

(5) Subsection (1) does not apply –

    (a) if the act or omission is shown to have been in bad faith, or

    (b) so as to prevent an award of damages in respect of the act or omission on the ground that it was unlawful as a result of section 6(1) of the Human Rights Act 1998 (c. 42) (acts of public authorities incompatible with Convention rights).

Professional qualifications

1219 Appropriate qualifications

(1) A person holds an appropriate qualification for the purposes of this Chapter if and only if –

    (a) he holds a recognised professional qualification obtained in the United Kingdom,

    (b) immediately before the commencement of this Chapter, he –

        (i) held an appropriate qualification for the purposes of Part 2 of the Companies Act 1989 (c. 40) (eligibility for appointment as company auditor) by virtue of section 31(1)(a) or (c) of that Act, or

        (ii) was treated as holding an appropriate qualification for those purposes by virtue of section 31(2), (3) or (4) of that Act,

    (c) immediately before the commencement of this Chapter, he –

        (i) held an appropriate qualification for the purposes of Part III of the Companies (Northern Ireland) Order 1990 (S.I. 1990/593 (N.I. 5)) by virtue of Article 34(1)(a) or (c) of that Order, or

        (ii) was treated as holding an appropriate qualification for those purposes by virtue of Article 34(2), (3) or (4) of that Order,

    (d) he is within subsection (2),

    (e) he has been authorised to practise the profession of statutory auditor pursuant to the European Communities (Recognition of Professional Qualifications) (First General System) Regulations 2005 (S.I. 2005/18) and has fulfilled any requirements imposed pursuant to regulation 6 of those Regulations, or

    (f) subject to any direction under section 1221(5), he is regarded for the purposes of this Chapter as holding an approved overseas qualification.

(2) A person is within this subsection if –

    (a) before 1st January 1990, he began a course of study or practical training leading to a professional qualification in accountancy offered by a body established in the United Kingdom,

    (b) he obtained that qualification on or after 1st January 1990 and before 1st January 1996, and

    (c) the Secretary of State approves his qualification as an appropriate qualification for the purposes of this Chapter.

(3) The Secretary of State may approve a qualification under subsection (2)(c) only if he is satisfied that, at the time the qualification was awarded, the body concerned had adequate arrangements to ensure that the qualification was awarded only to persons educated and trained to a standard equivalent to that required, at that time, in the case

of a recognised professional qualification under Part 2 of the Companies Act 1989 (c. 40) (eligibility for appointment as company auditor).

1220 Qualifying bodies and recognised professional qualifications

(1) In this Part a "qualifying body" means a body established in the United Kingdom (whether a body corporate or an unincorporated association) which offers a professional qualification in accountancy.

(2) In this Part references to the rules of a qualifying body are to the rules (whether or not laid down by the body itself) which the body has power to enforce and which are relevant for the purposes of this Part.

This includes, so far as so relevant, rules relating to –

    (a) admission to or expulsion from a course of study leading to a qualification,

    (b) the award or deprivation of a qualification, or

    (c) the approval of a person for the purposes of giving practical training or the withdrawal of such approval.

(3) Schedule 11 has effect with respect to the recognition for the purposes of this Part of a professional qualification offered by a qualifying body.

1221 Approval of overseas qualifications

(1) The Secretary of State may declare that the following are to be regarded for the purposes of this Chapter as holding an approved overseas qualification –

    (a) persons who are qualified to audit accounts under the law of a specified foreign country, or

    (b) persons who hold a specified professional qualification in accountancy obtained in a specified foreign country.

(2) A declaration under subsection (1)(b) may be expressed to be subject to the satisfaction of any specified requirement or requirements.

(3) The Secretary of State may make a declaration under subsection (1) only if he is satisfied that –

    (a) in the case of a declaration under subsection (1)(a), the fact that the persons in question are qualified to audit accounts under the law of the specified foreign country, or

    (b) in the case of a declaration under subsection (1)(b), the specified professional qualification taken with any requirement or requirements to be specified under subsection (2),

affords an assurance of professional competence equivalent to that afforded by a recognised professional qualification.

(4) The Secretary of State may make a declaration under subsection (1) only if he is satisfied that the treatment that the persons who are the subject of the declaration will receive as a result of it is comparable to the treatment which is, or is likely to be, afforded in the specified foreign country or a part of it to –

    (a) in the case of a declaration under subsection (1)(a), some or all persons who are eligible to be appointed as a statutory auditor, and

    (b) in the case of a declaration under subsection (1)(b), some or all persons who hold a corresponding recognised professional qualification.

(5) The Secretary of State may direct that persons holding an approved overseas qualification are not to be treated as holding an appropriate qualification for the purposes of this Chapter unless they hold such additional educational qualifications as the Secretary of State may specify for the purpose of ensuring that such persons have an adequate knowledge of the law and practice in the United Kingdom relevant to the audit of accounts.

(6) The Secretary of State may give different directions in relation to different approved overseas qualifications.

(7) The Secretary of State may, if he thinks fit, having regard to the considerations mentioned in subsections (3) and (4), withdraw a declaration under subsection (1) in relation to –

    (a) persons becoming qualified to audit accounts under the law of the specified foreign country after such date as he may specify, or

    (b) persons obtaining the specified professional qualification after such date as he may specify.

(8) The Secretary of State may, if he thinks fit, having regard to the considerations mentioned in subsections (3) and (4), vary or revoke a requirement specified under subsection (2) from such date as he may specify.

(9) In this section "foreign country", in relation to any time, means a country or territory that, at that time, is not a "relevant State" within the meaning of the European Communities (Recognition of Professional Qualifications) (First General System) Regulations 2005 (S.I. 2005/18) or part of such a State.

1222 Eligibility of individuals retaining only 1967 Act authorisation

(1) A person whose only appropriate qualification is based on his retention of an authorisation originally granted by the Board of Trade or the Secretary of State under section 13(1) of the Companies Act 1967 (c. 81) is eligible only for appointment as auditor of an unquoted company.

(2) A company is "unquoted" if, at the time of the person's appointment, neither the company, nor any parent undertaking of which it is a subsidiary undertaking, is a quoted company within the meaning of section 385(2).

(3) References to a person eligible for appointment as a statutory auditor by virtue of this Part in enactments relating to eligibility for appointment as auditor of a person other than a company do not include a person to whom this section applies.

Information

1223 Matters to be notified to the Secretary of State

(1) The Secretary of State may require a recognised supervisory body or a recognised qualifying body –

    (a) to notify him immediately of the occurrence of such events as he may specify in writing and to give him such information in respect of those events as is so specified;

    (b) to give him, at such times or in respect of such periods as he may specify in writing, such information as is so specified.

(2) The notices and information required to be given must be such as the Secretary of State may reasonably require for the exercise of his functions under this Part.

(3) The Secretary of State may require information given under this section to be given in a specified form or verified in a specified manner.

(4) Any notice or information required to be given under this section must be given in writing unless the Secretary of State specifies or approves some other manner.

1224 The Secretary of State's power to call for information

(1) The Secretary of State may by notice in writing require a person within subsection (2) to give him such information as he may reasonably require for the exercise of his functions under this Part.

(2) The persons within this subsection are –

    (a) any recognised supervisory body,

(b) any recognised qualifying body, and
(c) any person eligible for appointment as a statutory auditor by virtue of this Chapter.

(3) The Secretary of State may require that any information which he requires under this section is to be given within such reasonable time and verified in such manner as he may specify.

Enforcement

1225 Compliance orders

(1) If at any time it appears to the Secretary of State –

(a) in the case of a recognised supervisory body, that any requirement of Schedule 10 is not satisfied,
(b) in the case of a recognised professional qualification, that any requirement of Schedule 11 is not satisfied, or
(c) that a recognised supervisory body or a recognised qualifying body has failed to comply with an obligation to which it is subject under or by virtue of this Part,

he may, instead of revoking the relevant recognition order, make an application to the court under this section.

(2) If on an application under this section the court decides that the requirement in question is not satisfied or, as the case may be, that the body has failed to comply with the obligation in question, it may order the body to take such steps as the court directs for securing that the requirement is satisfied or that the obligation is complied with.

(3) In this section "the court" means the High Court or, in Scotland, the Court of Session.

CHAPTER 3

AUDITORS GENERAL

Eligibility for appointment

1226 Auditors General: eligibility for appointment as a statutory auditor

(1) In this Part "Auditor General" means –

(a) the Comptroller and Auditor General,
(b) the Auditor General for Scotland,
(c) the Auditor General for Wales, or
(d) the Comptroller and Auditor General for Northern Ireland.

(2) An Auditor General is eligible for appointment as a statutory auditor.

(3) Subsection (2) is subject to any suspension notice having effect under section 1234 (notices suspending eligibility for appointment as a statutory auditor).

Conduct of audits

1227 Individuals responsible for audit work on behalf of Auditors General

An Auditor General must secure that each individual responsible for statutory audit work on behalf of that Auditor General is eligible for appointment as a statutory auditor by virtue of Chapter 2.

The Independent Supervisor

1228 Appointment of the Independent Supervisor

(1) The Secretary of State must appoint a body ("the Independent Supervisor") to discharge the function mentioned in section 1229(1) ("the supervision function").

(2) An appointment under this section must be made by order.

(3) The order has the effect of making the body appointed under subsection (1) designated under section 5 of the Freedom of Information Act 2000 (c. 36) (further powers to designate public authorities).

(4) A body may be appointed under this section only if it is a body corporate or an unincorporated association which appears to the Secretary of State –

  (a) to be willing and able to discharge the supervision function, and

  (b) to have arrangements in place relating to the discharge of that function which are such as to be likely to ensure that the conditions in subsection (5) are met.

(5) The conditions are –

  (a) that the supervision function will be exercised effectively, and

  (b) where the order is to contain any requirements or other provisions specified under subsection (6), that that function will be exercised in accordance with any such requirements or provisions.

(6) An order under this section may contain such requirements or other provisions relating to the exercise of the supervision function by the Independent Supervisor as appear to the Secretary of State to be appropriate.

(7) An order under this section is subject to negative resolution procedure.

Supervision of Auditors General

1229 Supervision of Auditors General by the Independent Supervisor

(1) The Independent Supervisor must supervise the performance by each Auditor General of his functions as a statutory auditor.

(2) The Independent Supervisor must discharge that duty by –

  (a) entering into supervision arrangements with one or more bodies, and

  (b) overseeing the effective operation of any supervision arrangements entered into by it.

(3) For this purpose "supervision arrangements" are arrangements entered into by the Independent Supervisor with a body, for the purposes of this section, in accordance with which the body does one or more of the following –

  (a) determines standards relating to professional integrity and independence which must be applied by an Auditor General in statutory audit work;

  (b) determines technical standards which must be applied by an Auditor General in statutory audit work and the manner in which those standards are to be applied in practice;

  (c) monitors the performance of statutory audits carried out by an Auditor General;

  (d) investigates any matter arising from the performance by an Auditor General of a statutory audit;

  (e) holds disciplinary hearings in respect of an Auditor General which appear to be desirable following the conclusion of such investigations;

  (f) decides whether (and, if so, what) disciplinary action should be taken against an Auditor General to whom such a hearing related.

(4) The Independent Supervisor may enter into supervision arrangements with a body despite any relationship that may exist between the Independent Supervisor and that body.

(5) The Independent Supervisor must notify each Auditor General in writing of any supervision arrangements that it enters into under this section.

(6) Supervision arrangements within subsection (3)(f) may, in particular, provide for the payment by an Auditor General of a fine to any person.

(7) Any fine received by the Independent Supervisor under supervision arrangements is to be paid into the Consolidated Fund.

1230 Duties of Auditors General in relation to supervision arrangements

(1) Each Auditor General must –

    (a) comply with any standards of the kind mentioned in subsection (3)(a) or (b) of section 1229 determined under the supervision arrangements,

    (b) take such steps as may be reasonably required of that Auditor General to enable his performance of statutory audits to be monitored by means of inspections carried out under the supervision arrangements, and

    (c) comply with any decision of the kind mentioned in subsection (3)(f) of that section made under the supervision arrangements.

(2) Each Auditor General must pay to the body or bodies with which the Independent Supervisor enters into the supervision arrangements such proportion of the costs incurred by the body or bodies for the purposes of the arrangements as the Independent Supervisor may notify to him in writing.

(3) Expenditure under subsection (2) is –

    (a) in the case of expenditure of the Comptroller and Auditor General, to be regarded as expenditure of the National Audit Office for the purposes of section 4(1) of the National Audit Act 1983 (c. 44);

    (b) in the case of expenditure of the Comptroller and Auditor General for Northern Ireland, to be regarded as expenditure of the Northern Ireland Audit Office for the purposes of Article 6(1) of the Audit (Northern Ireland) Order 1987 (S.I. 1987/460 (N.I. 5)).

(4) In this section "the supervision arrangements" means the arrangements entered into under section 1229.

Reporting requirement

1231 Reports by the Independent Supervisor

(1) The Independent Supervisor must, at least once in each calendar year, prepare a report on the discharge of its functions.

(2) The Independent Supervisor must give a copy of each report prepared under subsection (1) to –

    (a) the Secretary of State;

    (b) the First Minister in Scotland;

    (c) the First Minister and the deputy First Minister in Northern Ireland;

    (d) the Assembly First Secretary in Wales.

(3) The Secretary of State must lay before each House of Parliament a copy of each report received by him under subsection (2)(a).

(4) In relation to a calendar year during which an appointment of a body as the Independent Supervisor is made or revoked by an order under section 1228, this section applies with such modifications as may be specified in the order.

Information

1232 Matters to be notified to the Independent Supervisor

(1) The Independent Supervisor may require an Auditor General –

   (a) to notify the Independent Supervisor immediately of the occurrence of such events as it may specify in writing and to give it such information in respect of those events as is so specified;

   (b) to give the Independent Supervisor, at such times or in respect of such periods as it may specify in writing, such information as is so specified.

(2) The notices and information required to be given must be such as the Independent Supervisor may reasonably require for the exercise of the functions conferred on it by or by virtue of this Part.

(3) The Independent Supervisor may require information given under this section to be given in a specified form or verified in a specified manner.

(4) Any notice or information required to be given under this section must be given in writing unless the Independent Supervisor specifies or approves some other manner.

1233 The Independent Supervisor's power to call for information

(1) The Independent Supervisor may by notice in writing require an Auditor General to give it such information as it may reasonably require for the exercise of the functions conferred on it by or by virtue of this Part.

(2) The Independent Supervisor may require that any information which it requires under this section is to be given within such reasonable time and verified in such manner as it may specify.

Enforcement

1234 Suspension notices

(1) The Independent Supervisor may issue –

   (a) a notice (a "suspension notice") suspending an Auditor General's eligibility for appointment as a statutory auditor in relation to all persons, or any specified person or persons, indefinitely or until a date specified in the notice;

   (b) a notice amending or revoking a suspension notice previously issued to an Auditor General.

(2) In determining whether it is appropriate to issue a notice under subsection (1), the Independent Supervisor must have regard to –

   (a) the Auditor General's performance of the obligations imposed on him by or by virtue of this Part, and

   (b) the Auditor General's performance of his functions as a statutory auditor.

(3) A notice under subsection (1) must –

   (a) be in writing, and

   (b) state the date on which it takes effect (which must be after the period of three months beginning with the date on which it is issued).

(4) Before issuing a notice under subsection (1), the Independent Supervisor must –

   (a) give written notice of its intention to do so to the Auditor General, and

   (b) publish the notice mentioned in paragraph (a) in such manner as it thinks appropriate for bringing it to the attention of any other persons who are likely to be affected.

(5) A notice under subsection (4) must –

   (a) state the reasons for which the Independent Supervisor proposes to act, and

(b) give particulars of the rights conferred by subsection (6).

(6) A person within subsection (7) may, within the period of three months beginning with the date of service or publication of the notice under subsection (4) or such longer period as the Independent Supervisor may allow, make written representations to the Independent Supervisor and, if desired, oral representations to a person appointed for that purpose by the Independent Supervisor.

(7) The persons within this subsection are –

(a) the Auditor General, and
(b) any other person who appears to the Independent Supervisor to be affected.

(8) The Independent Supervisor must have regard to any representations made in accordance with subsection (6) in determining –

(a) whether to issue a notice under subsection (1), and
(b) the terms of any such notice.

(9) If in any case the Independent Supervisor considers it appropriate to do so in the public interest it may issue a notice under subsection (1), without regard to the restriction in subsection (3)(b), even if –

(a) no notice has been given or published under subsection (4), or
(b) the period of time for making representations in pursuance of such a notice has not expired.

(10) On issuing a notice under subsection (1), the Independent Supervisor must –

(a) give a copy of the notice to the Auditor General, and
(b) publish the notice in such manner as it thinks appropriate for bringing it to the attention of persons likely to be affected.

(11) In this section "specified" means specified in, or of a description specified in, the suspension notice in question.

1235 Effect of suspension notices

(1) An Auditor General must not act as a statutory auditor at any time when a suspension notice issued to him in respect of the audited person has effect.

(2) If at any time during an Auditor General's term of office as a statutory auditor a suspension notice issued to him in respect of the audited person takes effect, he must immediately –

(a) resign his office (with immediate effect), and
(b) give notice in writing to the audited person that he has resigned by reason of his becoming ineligible for appointment.

(3) A suspension notice does not make an Auditor General ineligible for appointment as a statutory auditor for the purposes of section 1213 (effect of ineligibility: criminal offences).

1236 Compliance orders

(1) If at any time it appears to the Independent Supervisor that an Auditor General has failed to comply with an obligation imposed on him by or by virtue of this Part, the Independent Supervisor may make an application to the court under this section.

(2) If on an application under this section the court decides that the Auditor General has failed to comply with the obligation in question, it may order the Auditor General to take such steps as the court directs for securing that the obligation is complied with.

(3) In this section "the court" means the High Court or, in Scotland, the Court of Session.

Proceedings

1237 Proceedings involving the Independent Supervisor

(1) If the Independent Supervisor is an unincorporated association, any relevant proceedings may be brought by or against it in the name of any body corporate whose constitution provides for the establishment of the body.

(2) For this purpose "relevant proceedings" means proceedings brought in or in connection with the exercise of any function by the body as the Independent Supervisor.

(3) Where an appointment under section 1228 is revoked, the revoking order may make such provision as the Secretary of State thinks fit with respect to pending proceedings.

Grants

1238 Grants to the Independent Supervisor

In section 16 of the Companies (Audit, Investigations and Community Enterprise) Act 2004 (c. 27) (grants to bodies concerned with accounting standards etc), after subsection (2)(k) insert –

"(ka)   exercising functions of the Independent Supervisor appointed under Chapter 3 of Part 42 of the Companies Act 2006;".

CHAPTER 4

THE REGISTER OF AUDITORS ETC

1239 The register of auditors

(1) The Secretary of State must make regulations requiring the keeping of a register of –

(a)   the persons eligible for appointment as a statutory auditor, and

(b)   third country auditors (see Chapter 5) who apply to be registered in the specified manner and in relation to whom specified requirements are met.

(2) The regulations must require each person's entry in the register to contain –

(a)   his name and address,

(b)   in the case of an individual eligible for appointment as a statutory auditor, the specified information relating to any firm on whose behalf he is responsible for statutory audit work,

(c)   in the case of a firm eligible for appointment as a statutory auditor, the specified information relating to the individuals responsible for statutory audit work on its behalf,

(d)   in the case of an individual or firm eligible for appointment as a statutory auditor by virtue of Chapter 2, the name of the relevant supervisory body, and

(e)   in the case of a firm eligible for appointment as a statutory auditor by virtue of Chapter 2 or a third country auditor, the information mentioned in subsection (3),

and may require each person's entry to contain other specified information.

(3) The information referred to in subsection (2)(e) is –

(a)   in relation to a body corporate, except where paragraph (b) applies, the name and address of each person who is a director of the body or holds any shares in it;

(b)   in relation to a limited liability partnership, the name and address of each member of the partnership;

(c)   in relation to a corporation sole, the name and address of the individual for the time being holding the office by the name of which he is the corporation sole;

      (d) in relation to a partnership, the name and address of each partner.

(4) The regulations may provide that different parts of the register are to be kept by different persons.

(5) The regulations may impose such obligations as the Secretary of State thinks fit on –

      (a) recognised supervisory bodies,

      (b) any body designated by order under section 1252 (delegation of Secretary of State's functions),

      (c) persons eligible for appointment as a statutory auditor,

      (d) third country auditors,

      (e) any person with whom arrangements are made by one or more recognised supervisory bodies, or by any body designated by order under section 1252, with respect to the keeping of the register, or

      (f) the Independent Supervisor appointed under section 1228.

(6) The regulations may include –

      (a) provision requiring that specified entries in the register be open to inspection at times and places specified or determined in accordance with the regulations;

      (b) provision enabling a person to require a certified copy of specified entries in the register;

      (c) provision authorising the charging of fees for inspection, or the provision of copies, of such reasonable amount as may be specified or determined in accordance with the regulations.

(7) The Secretary of State may direct in writing that the requirements imposed by the regulations in accordance with subsections (2)(e) and (3), or such of those requirements as are specified in the direction, are not to apply, in whole or in part, in relation to a particular registered third country auditor or class of registered third country auditors.

(8) The obligations imposed by regulations under this section on such persons as are mentioned in subsection (5)(b) or (e) are enforceable on the application of the Secretary of State by injunction or, in Scotland, by an order under section 45 of the Court of Session Act 1988 (c. 36).

(9) In this section "specified" means specified by regulations under this section.

(10) Regulations under this section are subject to negative resolution procedure.

1240 Information to be made available to public

(1) The Secretary of State may make regulations requiring a person eligible for appointment as a statutory auditor, or a member of a specified class of such persons, to keep and make available to the public specified information, including information regarding –

      (a) the person's ownership and governance,

      (b) the person's internal controls with respect to the quality and independence of its audit work,

      (c) the person's turnover, and

      (d) the audited persons of whom the person has acted as statutory auditor.

(2) Regulations under this section may –

      (a) impose such obligations as the Secretary of State thinks fit on persons eligible for appointment as a statutory auditor;

      (b) require the information to be made available to the public in a specified manner.

(3) In this section "specified" means specified by regulations under this section.

(4) Regulations under this section are subject to negative resolution procedure.

CHAPTER 5

REGISTERED THIRD COUNTRY AUDITORS

Introductory

1241 Meaning of "third country auditor", "registered third country auditor" etc

(1) In this Part –

"third country auditor" means the auditor of the accounts of a traded non-Community company, and the expressions "third country audit" and "third country audit work" are to be construed accordingly;

"registered third country auditor" means a third country auditor who is entered in the register kept in accordance with regulations under section 1239(1).

(2) In subsection (1) "traded non-Community company" means a body corporate –

(a) which is incorporated or formed under the law of a country or territory which is not a member State or part of a member State,

(b) whose transferable securities are admitted to trading on a regulated market situated or operating in the United Kingdom, and

(c) which has not been excluded, or is not of a description of bodies corporate which has been excluded, from this definition by an order made by the Secretary of State.

(3) For this purpose –

"regulated market" has the meaning given by Article 4.1(14) of Directive 2004/39/EC of the European Parliament and of the Council on markets in financial instruments;

"transferable securities" has the meaning given by Article 4.1(18) of that Directive.

(4) An order under this section is subject to negative resolution procedure.

Duties

1242 Duties of registered third country auditors

(1) A registered third country auditor must participate in –

(a) arrangements within paragraph 1 of Schedule 12 (arrangements for independent monitoring of audits of traded non-Community companies), and

(b) arrangements within paragraph 2 of that Schedule (arrangements for independent investigation for disciplinary purposes of public interest cases).

(2) A registered third country auditor must –

(a) take such steps as may be reasonably required of it to enable its performance of third country audits to be monitored by means of inspections carried out under the arrangements mentioned in subsection (1)(a), and

(b) comply with any decision as to disciplinary action to be taken against it made under the arrangements mentioned in subsection (1)(b).

(3) Schedule 12 makes further provision with respect to the arrangements in which registered third country auditors are required to participate.

(4) The Secretary of State may direct in writing that subsections (1) to (3) are not to apply, in whole or in part, in relation to a particular registered third country auditor or class of registered third country auditors.

Information

1243 Matters to be notified to the Secretary of State

(1) The Secretary of State may require a registered third country auditor –

    (a) to notify him immediately of the occurrence of such events as he may specify in writing and to give him such information in respect of those events as is so specified;

    (b) to give him, at such times or in respect of such periods as he may specify in writing, such information as is so specified.

(2) The notices and information required to be given must be such as the Secretary of State may reasonably require for the exercise of his functions under this Part.

(3) The Secretary of State may require information given under this section to be given in a specified form or verified in a specified manner.

(4) Any notice or information required to be given under this section must be given in writing unless the Secretary of State specifies or approves some other manner.

1244 The Secretary of State's power to call for information

(1) The Secretary of State may by notice in writing require a registered third country auditor to give him such information as he may reasonably require for the exercise of his functions under this Part.

(2) The Secretary of State may require that any information which he requires under this section is to be given within such reasonable time and verified in such manner as he may specify.

Enforcement

1245 Compliance orders

(1) If at any time it appears to the Secretary of State that a registered third country auditor has failed to comply with an obligation imposed on him by or by virtue of this Part, the Secretary of State may make an application to the court under this section.

(2) If on an application under this section the court decides that the auditor has failed to comply with the obligation in question, it may order the auditor to take such steps as the court directs for securing that the obligation is complied with.

(3) In this section "the court" means the High Court or, in Scotland, the Court of Session.

1246 Removal of third country auditors from the register of auditors

(1) The Secretary of State may, by regulations, confer on the person keeping the register in accordance with regulations under section 1239(1) power to remove a third country auditor from the register.

(2) Regulations under this section must require the person keeping the register, in determining whether to remove a third country auditor from the register, to have regard to the auditor's compliance with obligations imposed on him by or by virtue of this Part.

(3) Where provision is made under section 1239(4) (different parts of the register to be kept by different persons), references in this section to the person keeping the register are to the person keeping that part of the register which relates to third country auditors.

(4) Regulations under this section are subject to negative resolution procedure.

1247 Grants to bodies concerned with arrangements under Schedule 12

In section 16 of the Companies (Audit, Investigations and Community Enterprise) Act 2004 (c. 27) (grants to bodies concerned with accounting standards etc), after subsection (2)(ka) (inserted by section 1238) insert –

"(kb)   establishing, maintaining or carrying out arrangements within paragraph 1 or 2 of Schedule 12 to the Companies Act 2006;".

CHAPTER 6

SUPPLEMENTARY AND GENERAL

Power to require second company audit

1248 Secretary of State's power to require second audit of a company

(1) This section applies where a person appointed as statutory auditor of a company was not an appropriate person for any part of the period during which the audit was conducted.

(2) The Secretary of State may direct the company concerned to retain an appropriate person –

(a) to conduct a second audit of the relevant accounts, or

(b) to review the first audit and to report (giving his reasons) whether a second audit is needed.

(3) For the purposes of subsections (1) and (2) a person is "appropriate" if he –

(a) is eligible for appointment as a statutory auditor or, if the person is an Auditor General, for appointment as statutory auditor of the company, and

(b) is not prohibited by section 1214(1) (independence requirement) from acting as statutory auditor of the company.

(4) The Secretary of State must send a copy of a direction under subsection (2) to the registrar of companies.

(5) The company is guilty of an offence if –

(a) it fails to comply with a direction under subsection (2) within the period of 21 days beginning with the date on which it is given, or

(b) it has been convicted of a previous offence under this subsection and the failure to comply with the direction which led to the conviction continues after the conviction.

(6) The company must –

(a) send a copy of a report under subsection (2)(b) to the registrar of companies, and

(b) if the report states that a second audit is needed, take such steps as are necessary for the carrying out of that audit.

(7) The company is guilty of an offence if –

(a) it fails to send a copy of a report under subsection (2)(b) to the registrar within the period of 21 days beginning with the date on which it receives it,

(b) in a case within subsection (6)(b), it fails to take the steps mentioned immediately it receives the report, or

(c) it has been convicted of a previous offence under this subsection and the failure to send a copy of the report, or take the steps, which led to the conviction continues after the conviction.

(8) A company guilty of an offence under this section is liable on summary conviction –

(a) in a case within subsection (5)(a) or (7)(a) or (b), to a fine not exceeding level 5 on the standard scale, and

(b) in a case within subsection (5)(b) or (7)(c), to a fine not exceeding one tenth of level 5 on the standard scale for each day on which the failure continues.

(9) In this section "registrar of companies" has the meaning given by section 1060.

1249 Supplementary provision about second audits

(1) If a person accepts an appointment, or continues to act, as statutory auditor of a company at a time when he knows he is not an appropriate person, the company may recover from him any costs incurred by it in complying with the requirements of section 1248.

For this purpose "appropriate" is to be construed in accordance with subsection (3) of that section.

(2) Where a second audit is carried out under section 1248, any statutory or other provision applying in relation to the first audit applies also, in so far as practicable, in relation to the second audit.

(3) A direction under section 1248(2) is, on the application of the Secretary of State, enforceable by injunction or, in Scotland, by an order under section 45 of the Court of Session Act 1988 (c. 36).

False and misleading statements

1250 Misleading, false and deceptive statements

(1) A person is guilty of an offence if –

(a) for the purposes of or in connection with any application under this Part, or

(b) in purported compliance with any requirement imposed on him by or by virtue of this Part,

he knowingly or recklessly furnishes information which is misleading, false or deceptive in a material particular.

(2) It is an offence for a person whose name does not appear on the register of auditors kept under regulations under section 1239 in an entry made under subsection (1)(a) of that section to describe himself as a registered auditor or so to hold himself out as to indicate, or be reasonably understood to indicate, that he is a registered auditor.

(3) It is an offence for a person whose name does not appear on the register of auditors kept under regulations under that section in an entry made under subsection (1)(b) of that section to describe himself as a registered third country auditor or so to hold himself out as to indicate, or be reasonably understood to indicate, that he is a registered third country auditor.

(4) It is an offence for a body which is not a recognised supervisory body or a recognised qualifying body to describe itself as so recognised or so to describe itself or hold itself out as to indicate, or be reasonably understood to indicate, that it is so recognised.

(5) A person guilty of an offence under subsection (1) is liable –

(a) on conviction on indictment, to imprisonment for a term not exceeding two years or to a fine (or both);

(b) on summary conviction –

(i) in England and Wales, to imprisonment for a term not exceeding twelve months or to a fine not exceeding the statutory maximum (or both),

(ii) in Scotland or Northern Ireland, to imprisonment for a term not exceeding six months or to a fine not exceeding the statutory maximum (or both).

In relation to an offence committed before the commencement of section 154(1) of the Criminal Justice Act 2003 (c. 44), for "twelve months" in paragraph (b)(i) substitute "six months".

(6) Subject to subsection (7), a person guilty of an offence under subsection (2), (3) or (4) is liable on summary conviction –

(a) in England and Wales, to imprisonment for a term not exceeding 51 weeks or to a fine not exceeding level 5 on the standard scale (or both),

(b) in Scotland or Northern Ireland, to imprisonment for a term not exceeding six months or to a fine not exceeding level 5 on the standard scale (or both).

In relation to an offence committed before the commencement of section 281(5) of the Criminal Justice Act 2003, for "51 weeks" in paragraph (a) substitute "six months".

(7) Where a contravention of subsection (2), (3) or (4) involves a public display of the offending description, the maximum fine that may be imposed is an amount equal to level 5 on the standard scale multiplied by the number of days for which the display has continued.

(8) It is a defence for a person charged with an offence under subsection (2), (3) or (4) to show that he took all reasonable precautions and exercised all due diligence to avoid the commission of the offence.

Fees

1251 Fees

(1) An applicant for a recognition order under this Part must pay such fee in respect of his application as the Secretary of State may by regulations prescribe; and no application is to be regarded as duly made unless this subsection is complied with.

(2) The Secretary of State may by regulations prescribe periodical fees to be paid by –

    (a) every recognised supervisory body,

    (b) every recognised qualifying body,

    (c) every Auditor General, and

    (d) every registered third country auditor.

(3) Fees received by the Secretary of State by virtue of this Part are to be paid into the Consolidated Fund.

(4) Regulations under this section are subject to negative resolution procedure.

Delegation of Secretary of State's functions

1252 Delegation of the Secretary of State's functions

(1) The Secretary of State may make an order under this section (a "delegation order") for the purpose of enabling functions of the Secretary of State under this Part to be exercised by a body designated by the order.

(2) The body designated by a delegation order may be either –

    (a) a body corporate which is established by the order, or

    (b) subject to section 1253, a body (whether a body corporate or an unincorporated association) which is already in existence ("an existing body").

(3) A delegation order has the effect of making the body designated by the order designated under section 5 of the Freedom of Information Act 2000 (c. 36) (further powers to designate public authorities).

(4) A delegation order has the effect of transferring to the body designated by it all functions of the Secretary of State under this Part –

    (a) subject to such exceptions and reservations as may be specified in the order, and

    (b) except –

        (i) his functions in relation to the body itself, and

        (ii) his functions under section 1228 (appointment of Independent Supervisor).

(5) A delegation order may confer on the body designated by it such other functions supplementary or incidental to those transferred as appear to the Secretary of State to be appropriate.

(6) Any transfer of functions under the following provisions must be subject to the reservation that the functions remain exercisable concurrently by the Secretary of State –

(a) section 1224 (power to call for information from recognised bodies etc);

(b) section 1244 (power to call for information from registered third country auditors);

(c) section 1254 (directions to comply with international obligations).

(7) Any transfer of –

(a) the function of refusing to make a declaration under section 1221(1) (approval of overseas qualifications) on the grounds referred to in section 1221(4) (lack of comparable treatment), or

(b) the function of withdrawing such a declaration under section 1221(7) on those grounds,

must be subject to the reservation that the function is exercisable only with the consent of the Secretary of State.

(8) A delegation order may be amended or, if it appears to the Secretary of State that it is no longer in the public interest that the order should remain in force, revoked by a further order under this section.

(9) Where functions are transferred or resumed, the Secretary of State may by order confer or, as the case may be, take away such other functions supplementary or incidental to those transferred or resumed as appear to him to be appropriate.

(10) Where a delegation order is made, Schedule 13 has effect with respect to –

(a) the status of the body designated by the order in exercising functions of the Secretary of State under this Part,

(b) the constitution and proceedings of the body where it is established by the order,

(c) the exercise by the body of certain functions transferred to it, and

(d) other supplementary matters.

(11) An order under this section which has the effect of transferring or resuming any functions is subject to affirmative resolution procedure.

(12) Any other order under this section is subject to negative resolution procedure.

1253 Delegation of functions to an existing body

(1) The Secretary of State's power to make a delegation order under section 1252 which designates an existing body is exercisable in accordance with this section.

(2) The Secretary of State may make such a delegation order if it appears to him that –

(a) the body is able and willing to exercise the functions that would be transferred by the order, and

(b) the body has arrangements in place relating to the exercise of those functions which are such as to be likely to ensure that the conditions in subsection (3) are met.

(3) The conditions are –

(a) that the functions in question will be exercised effectively, and

(b) where the delegation order is to contain any requirements or other provisions specified under subsection (4), that those functions will be exercised in accordance with any such requirements or provisions.

(4) The delegation order may contain such requirements or other provision relating to the exercise of the functions by the designated body as appear to the Secretary of State to be appropriate.

(5) An existing body –

(a) may be designated by a delegation order under section 1252, and

(b) may accordingly exercise functions of the Secretary of State in pursuance of the order,

despite any involvement of the body in the exercise of any functions under arrangements within paragraph 21, 22, 23(1) or 24(1) of Schedule 10 or paragraph 1 or 2 of Schedule 12.

International obligations

1254 Directions to comply with international obligations

(1) If it appears to the Secretary of State –

    (a) that any action proposed to be taken by a recognised supervisory body or a recognised qualifying body, or a body designated by order under section 1252, would be incompatible with Community obligations or any other international obligations of the United Kingdom, or

    (b) that any action which that body has power to take is required for the purpose of implementing any such obligations,

he may direct the body not to take or, as the case may be, to take the action in question.

(2) A direction may include such supplementary or incidental requirements as the Secretary of State thinks necessary or expedient.

(3) A direction under this section given to a body designated by order under section 1252 is enforceable on the application of the Secretary of State by injunction or, in Scotland, by an order under section 45 of the Court of Session Act 1988 (c. 36).

General provision relating to offences

1255 Offences by bodies corporate, partnerships and unincorporated associations

(1) Where an offence under this Part committed by a body corporate is proved to have been committed with the consent or connivance of, or to be attributable to any neglect on the part of, an officer of the body, or a person purporting to act in any such capacity, he as well as the body corporate is guilty of the offence and liable to be proceeded against and punished accordingly.

(2) Where an offence under this Part committed by a partnership is proved to have been committed with the consent or connivance of, or to be attributable to any neglect on the part of, a partner, he as well as the partnership is guilty of the offence and liable to be proceeded against and punished accordingly.

(3) Where an offence under this Part committed by an unincorporated association (other than a partnership) is proved to have been committed with the consent or connivance of, or to be attributable to any neglect on the part of, any officer of the association or any member of its governing body, he as well as the association is guilty of the offence and liable to be proceeded against and punished accordingly.

1256 Time limits for prosecution of offences

(1) An information relating to an offence under this Part which is triable by a magistrates' court in England and Wales may be so tried if it is laid at any time within the period of twelve months beginning with the date on which evidence sufficient in the opinion of the Director of Public Prosecutions or the Secretary of State to justify the proceedings comes to his knowledge.

(2) Proceedings in Scotland for an offence under this Part may be commenced at any time within the period of twelve months beginning with the date on which evidence sufficient in the Lord Advocate's opinion to justify proceedings came to his knowledge or, where such evidence was reported to him by the Secretary of State, within the period of twelve months beginning with the date on which it came to the knowledge of the Secretary of State.

(3) For the purposes of subsection (2) proceedings are to be deemed to be commenced on the date on which a warrant to apprehend or cite the accused is granted, if the warrant is executed without undue delay.

(4) A complaint charging an offence under this Part which is triable by a magistrates' court in Northern Ireland may be so tried if it is made at any time within the period

of twelve months beginning with the date on which evidence sufficient in the opinion of the Director of Public Prosecutions for Northern Ireland or the Secretary of State to justify the proceedings comes to his knowledge.

(5) This section does not authorise –

(a) in the case of proceedings in England and Wales, the trial of an information laid,

(b) in the case of proceedings in Scotland, the commencement of proceedings, or

(c) in the case of proceedings in Northern Ireland, the trial of a complaint made,

more than three years after the commission of the offence.

(6) For the purposes of this section a certificate of the Director of Public Prosecutions, the Lord Advocate, the Director of Public Prosecutions for Northern Ireland or the Secretary of State as to the date on which such evidence as is referred to above came to his knowledge is conclusive evidence.

(7) Nothing in this section affects proceedings within the time limits prescribed by section 127(1) of the Magistrates' Courts Act 1980 (c. 43), section 331 of the Criminal Procedure (Scotland) Act 1975 or Article 19 of the Magistrates' Courts (Northern Ireland) Order 1981 (S.I. 1981/1675 (N.I. 26)) (the usual time limits for criminal proceedings).

1257 Jurisdiction and procedure in respect of offences

(1) Summary proceedings for an offence under this Part may, without prejudice to any jurisdiction exercisable apart from this section, be taken –

(a) against a body corporate or unincorporated association at any place at which it has a place of business, and

(b) against an individual at any place where he is for the time being.

(2) Proceedings for an offence alleged to have been committed under this Part by an unincorporated association must be brought in the name of the association (and not in that of any of its members), and for the purposes of any such proceedings any rules of court relating to the service of documents apply as in relation to a body corporate.

(3) Section 33 of the Criminal Justice Act 1925 (c. 86) and Schedule 3 to the Magistrates' Courts Act 1980 (c. 43) (procedure on charge of offence against a corporation) apply in a case in which an unincorporated association is charged in England and Wales with an offence under this Part as they apply in the case of a corporation.

(4) Section 18 of the Criminal Justice Act (Northern Ireland) 1945 (c. 15 (N.I.)) and Article 166 and Schedule 4 to the Magistrates' Courts (Northern Ireland) Order 1981 (S.I. 1981/1675 (N.I. 26)) (procedure on charge of offence against a corporation) apply in a case in which an unincorporated association is charged in Northern Ireland with an offence under this Part as they apply in the case of a corporation.

(5) In relation to proceedings on indictment in Scotland for an offence alleged to have been committed under this Part by an unincorporated association, section 70 of the Criminal Procedure (Scotland) Act 1995 (proceedings on indictment against bodies corporate) applies as if the association were a body corporate.

(6) A fine imposed on an unincorporated association on its conviction of such an offence must be paid out of the funds of the association.

Notices etc

1258 Service of notices

(1) This section has effect in relation to any notice, direction or other document required or authorised by or by virtue of this Part to be given to or served on any person other than the Secretary of State.

(2) Any such document may be given to or served on the person in question –

(a) by delivering it to him,

(b) by leaving it at his proper address, or

(c) by sending it by post to him at that address.

(3) Any such document may –

   (a) in the case of a body corporate, be given to or served on an officer of that body;

   (b) in the case of a partnership, be given to or served on any partner;

   (c) in the case of an unincorporated association other than a partnership, be given to or served on any member of the governing body of that association.

(4) For the purposes of this section and section 7 of the Interpretation Act 1978 (c. 30) (service of documents by post) in its application to this section, the proper address of any person is his last known address (whether of his residence or of a place where he carries on business or is employed) and also –

   (a) in the case of a person who is eligible under the rules of a recognised supervisory body for appointment as a statutory auditor and who does not have a place of business in the United Kingdom, the address of that body;

   (b) in the case of a body corporate or an officer of that body, the address of the registered or principal office of that body in the United Kingdom;

   (c) in the case of an unincorporated association other than a partnership or a member of its governing body, its principal office in the United Kingdom.

1259 Documents in electronic form

(1) This section applies where –

   (a) section 1258 authorises the giving or sending of a notice, direction or other document by its delivery to a particular person ("the recipient"), and

   (b) the notice, direction or other document is transmitted to the recipient –

      (i) by means of an electronic communications network, or

      (ii) by other means but in a form that requires the use of apparatus by the recipient to render it intelligible.

(2) The transmission has effect for the purposes of this Part as a delivery of the notice, direction or other document to the recipient, but only if the recipient has indicated to the person making the transmission his willingness to receive the notice, direction or other document in the form and manner used.

(3) An indication to a person for the purposes of subsection (2) –

   (a) must be given to the person in such manner as he may require,

   (b) may be a general indication or an indication that is limited to notices, directions or other documents of a particular description,

   (c) must state the address to be used,

   (d) must be accompanied by such other information as the person requires for the making of the transmission, and

   (e) may be modified or withdrawn at any time by a notice given to the person in such manner as he may require.

(4) In this section "electronic communications network" has the same meaning as in the Communications Act 2003 (c. 21).

Interpretation

1260 Meaning of "associate"

(1) In this Part "associate", in relation to a person, is to be construed as follows.

(2) In relation to an individual, "associate" means –

   (a) that individual's spouse, civil partner or minor child or step-child,

   (b) any body corporate of which that individual is a director, and

   (c) any employee or partner of that individual.

(3) In relation to a body corporate, "associate" means –

    (a) any body corporate of which that body is a director,

    (b) any body corporate in the same group as that body, and

    (c) any employee or partner of that body or of any body corporate in the same group.

(4) In relation to a partnership constituted under the law of Scotland, or any other country or territory in which a partnership is a legal person, "associate" means –

    (a) any body corporate of which that partnership is a director,

    (b) any employee of or partner in that partnership, and

    (c) any person who is an associate of a partner in that partnership.

(5) In relation to a partnership constituted under the law of England and Wales or Northern Ireland, or the law of any other country or territory in which a partnership is not a legal person, "associate" means any person who is an associate of any of the partners.

(6) In subsections (2)(b), (3)(a) and (4)(a), in the case of a body corporate which is a limited liability partnership, "director" is to be read as "member".

1261 Minor definitions

(1) In this Part, unless a contrary intention appears –

"address" means –

    (a) in relation to an individual, his usual residential or business address;

    (b) in relation to a firm, its registered or principal office in the United Kingdom;

"company" means any company or other body the accounts of which must be audited in accordance with Part 16;

"director", in relation to a body corporate, includes any person occupying in relation to it the position of a director (by whatever name called) and any person in accordance with whose directions or instructions (not being advice given in a professional capacity) the directors of the body are accustomed to act;

"firm" means any entity, whether or not a legal person, which is not an individual and includes a body corporate, a corporation sole and a partnership or other unincorporated association;

"group", in relation to a body corporate, means the body corporate, any other body corporate which is its holding company or subsidiary and any other body corporate which is a subsidiary of that holding company;

"holding company" and "subsidiary" are to be read in accordance with section 1159 and Schedule 6;

"officer", in relation to a body corporate, includes a director, a manager, a secretary or, where the affairs of the body are managed by its members, a member;

"parent undertaking" and "subsidiary undertaking" are to be read in accordance with section 1162 and Schedule 7.

(2) For the purposes of this Part a body is to be regarded as "established in the United Kingdom" if and only if –

    (a) it is incorporated or formed under the law of the United Kingdom or a part of the United Kingdom, or

    (b) its central management and control are exercised in the United Kingdom;

and any reference to a qualification "obtained in the United Kingdom" is to a qualification obtained from such a body.

(3) The Secretary of State may by regulations make such modifications of this Part as appear to him to be necessary or appropriate for the purposes of its application in relation to any firm, or description of firm, which is not a body corporate or a partnership.

(4) Regulations under subsection (3) are subject to negative resolution procedure.

1262 Index of defined expressions

The following Table shows provisions defining or otherwise explaining expressions used in this Part (other than provisions defining or explaining an expression used only in the same section) –

Expression	Provision
address	section 1261(1)
appropriate qualification	section 1219
associate	section 1260
audited person	section 1210(2)
Auditor General	section 1226(1)
company	section 1261(1)
delegation order	section 1252(1)
director (of a body corporate)	section 1261(1)
enactment	section 1293
established in the United Kingdom	section 1261(2)
firm	section 1261(1)
group (in relation to a body corporate)	section 1261(1)
holding company	section 1261(1)
main purposes of this Part	section 1209
member (of a supervisory body)	section 1217(2)
obtained in the United Kingdom	section 1261(2)
officer	section 1261(1)
parent undertaking	section 1261(1)
qualifying body	section 1220(1)
recognised, in relation to a professional qualification	section 1220(3) and Schedule 11
recognised, in relation to a qualifying body	paragraph 1(2) of Schedule 11
recognised, in relation to a supervisory body	section 1217(4) and Schedule 10
registered third country auditor	section 1241(1)
rules of a qualifying body	section 1220(2)
rules of a supervisory body	section 1217(3)
statutory auditor, statutory audit and statutory audit work	section 1210(1)
subsidiary	section 1261(1)
supervisory body	section 1217(1)
subsidiary undertaking	section 1261(1)
third country auditor, third country audit and third country audit work	section 1241(1)

Miscellaneous and general

1263 Power to make provision in consequence of changes affecting accountancy bodies

(1) The Secretary of State may by regulations make such amendments of enactments as appear to him to be necessary or expedient in consequence of any change of name, merger or transfer of engagements affecting –

(a) a recognised supervisory body or recognised qualifying body, or

(b) a body of accountants referred to in, or approved, authorised or otherwise recognised for the purposes of, any other enactment.

(2) Regulations under this section are subject to negative resolution procedure.

1264 Consequential amendments

Schedule 14 contains consequential amendments relating to this Part.

PART 43

TRANSPARENCY OBLIGATIONS AND RELATED MATTERS

Introductory

1265 The transparency obligations directive

In Part 6 of the Financial Services and Markets Act 2000 (c. 8) (which makes provision about official listing, prospectus requirements for transferable securities, etc), in section 103(1) (interpretation), at the appropriate place insert –

> ""the transparency obligations directive" means Directive 2004/109/EC of the European Parliament and of the Council relating to the harmonisation of transparency requirements in relation to information about issuers whose securities are admitted to trading on a regulated market;".

Transparency obligations

1266 Transparency rules

(1) After section 89 of the Financial Services and Markets Act 2000 insert –

"Transparency obligations

89A Transparency rules

(1) The competent authority may make rules for the purposes of the transparency obligations directive.

(2) The rules may include provision for dealing with any matters arising out of or related to any provision of the transparency obligations directive.

(3) The competent authority may also make rules –

    (a) for the purpose of ensuring that voteholder information in respect of voting shares traded on a UK market other than a regulated market is made public or notified to the competent authority;

    (b) providing for persons who hold comparable instruments (see section 89F(1)(c)) in respect of voting shares to be treated, in the circumstances specified in the rules, as holding some or all of the voting rights in respect of those shares.

(4) Rules under this section may, in particular, make provision –

    (a) specifying how the proportion of –

        (i)   the total voting rights in respect of shares in an issuer, or

        (ii) the total voting rights in respect of a particular class of shares in an issuer,

    held by a person is to be determined;

    (b) specifying the circumstances in which, for the purposes of any determination of the voting rights held by a person ("P") in respect of voting shares in an issuer, any voting rights held, or treated by virtue of subsection (3)(b) as held, by another person in respect of voting shares in the issuer are to be regarded as held by P;

    (c) specifying the nature of the information which must be included in any notification;

    (d) about the form of any notification;

    (e) requiring any notification to be given within a specified period;

(f)   specifying the manner in which any information is to be made public and the period within which it must be made public;

(g)   specifying circumstances in which any of the requirements imposed by rules under this section does not apply.

(5)   Rules under this section are referred to in this Part as "transparency rules".

(6)   Nothing in sections 89B to 89G affects the generality of the power to make rules under this section.

89B Provision of voteholder information

(1)   Transparency rules may make provision for voteholder information in respect of voting shares to be notified, in circumstances specified in the rules –

(a)   to the issuer, or

(b)   to the public,

or to both.

(2)   Transparency rules may make provision for voteholder information notified to the issuer to be notified at the same time to the competent authority.

(3)   In this Part "voteholder information" in respect of voting shares means information relating to the proportion of voting rights held by a person in respect of the shares.

(4)   Transparency rules may require notification of voteholder information relating to a person –

(a)   initially, not later than such date as may be specified in the rules for the purposes of the first indent of Article 30.2 of the transparency obligations directive, and

(b)   subsequently, in accordance with the following provisions.

(5)   Transparency rules under subsection (4)(b) may require notification of voteholder information relating to a person only where there is a notifiable change in the proportion of –

(a)   the total voting rights in respect of shares in the issuer, or

(b)   the total voting rights in respect of a particular class of share in the issuer,

held by the person.

(6)   For this purpose there is a "notifiable change" in the proportion of voting rights held by a person when the proportion changes –

(a)   from being a proportion less than a designated proportion to a proportion equal to or greater than that designated proportion,

(b)   from being a proportion equal to a designated proportion to a proportion greater or less than that designated proportion, or

(c)   from being a proportion greater than a designated proportion to a proportion equal to or less than that designated proportion.

(7)   In subsection (6) "designated" means designated by the rules.

89C Provision of information by issuers of transferable securities

(1)   Transparency rules may make provision requiring the issuer of transferable securities, in circumstances specified in the rules –

(a)   to make public information to which this section applies, or

(b)   to notify to the competent authority information to which this section applies,

or to do both.

(2)   In the case of every issuer, this section applies to –

(a)   information required by Article 4 of the transparency obligations directive;

(b)   information relating to the rights attached to the transferable securities, including information about the terms and conditions of those securities which could indirectly affect those rights; and

(c)   information about new loan issues and about any guarantee or security in connection with any such issue.

(3)   In the case of an issuer of debt securities, this section also applies to information required by Article 5 of the transparency obligations directive.

(4)   In the case of an issuer of shares, this section also applies to –

(a)   information required by Article 5 of the transparency obligations directive;

(b)   information required by Article 6 of that directive;

(c)   voteholder information –

(i)   notified to the issuer, or

(ii)   relating to the proportion of voting rights held by the issuer in respect of shares in the issuer;

(d)   information relating to the issuer's capital; and

(e)   information relating to the total number of voting rights in respect of shares or shares of a particular class.

89D Notification of voting rights held by issuer

(1)   Transparency rules may require notification of voteholder information relating to the proportion of voting rights held by an issuer in respect of voting shares in the issuer –

(a)   initially, not later than such date as may be specified in the rules for the purposes of the second indent of Article 30.2 of the transparency obligations directive, and

(b)   subsequently, in accordance with the following provisions.

(2)   Transparency rules under subsection (1)(b) may require notification of voteholder information relating to the proportion of voting rights held by an issuer in respect of voting shares in the issuer only where there is a notifiable change in the proportion of –

(a)   the total voting rights in respect of shares in the issuer, or

(b)   the total voting rights in respect of a particular class of share in the issuer,

held by the issuer.

(3)   For this purpose there is a "notifiable change" in the proportion of voting rights held by a person when the proportion changes –

(a)   from being a proportion less than a designated proportion to a proportion equal to or greater than that designated proportion,

(b)   from being a proportion equal to a designated proportion to a proportion greater or less than that designated proportion, or

(c)   from being a proportion greater than a designated proportion to a proportion equal to or less than that designated proportion.

(4)   In subsection (3) "designated" means designated by the rules.

89E Notification of proposed amendment of issuer's constitution

Transparency rules may make provision requiring an issuer of transferable securities that are admitted to trading on a regulated market to notify a proposed amendment to its constitution –

(a)   to the competent authority, and

(b)   to the market on which the issuer's securities are admitted,

at times and in circumstances specified in the rules.

89F Transparency rules: interpretation etc

(1) For the purposes of sections 89A to 89G –

    (a) the voting rights in respect of any voting shares are the voting rights attached to those shares,

    (b) a person is to be regarded as holding the voting rights in respect of the shares –

        (i) if, by virtue of those shares, he is a shareholder within the meaning of Article 2.1(e) of the transparency obligations directive;

        (ii) if, and to the extent that, he is entitled to acquire, dispose of or exercise those voting rights in one or more of the cases mentioned in Article 10(a) to (h) of the transparency obligations directive;

        (iii) if he holds, directly or indirectly, a financial instrument which results in an entitlement to acquire the shares and is an Article 13 instrument, and

    (c) a person holds a "comparable instrument" in respect of voting shares if he holds, directly or indirectly, a financial instrument in relation to the shares which has similar economic effects to an Article 13 instrument (whether or not the financial instrument results in an entitlement to acquire the shares).

(2) Transparency rules under section 89A(3)(b) may make different provision for different descriptions of comparable instrument.

(3) For the purposes of sections 89A to 89G two or more persons may, at the same time, each be regarded as holding the same voting rights.

(4) In those sections –

"Article 13 instrument" means a financial instrument of a type determined by the European Commission under Article 13.2 of the transparency obligations directive;

"UK market" means a market that is situated or operating in the United Kingdom;

"voting shares" means shares of an issuer to which voting rights are attached.

89G Transparency rules: other supplementary provisions

(1) Transparency rules may impose the same obligations on a person who has applied for the admission of transferable securities to trading on a regulated market without the issuer's consent as they impose on an issuer of transferable securities.

(2) Transparency rules that require a person to make information public may include provision authorising the competent authority to make the information public in the event that the person fails to do so.

(3) The competent authority may make public any information notified to the authority in accordance with transparency rules.

(4) Transparency rules may make provision by reference to any provision of any rules made by the Panel on Takeovers and Mergers under Part 28 of the Companies Act 2006.

(5) Sections 89A to 89F and this section are without prejudice to any other power conferred by this Part to make Part 6 rules.".

(2) The effectiveness for the purposes of section 155 of the Financial Services and Markets Act 2000 (c. 8) (consultation on proposed rules) of things done by the Financial Services Authority before this section comes into force with a view to making transparency rules (as defined in the provisions to be inserted in that Act by subsection (1) above) is not affected by the fact that those provisions were not then in force.

1267 Competent authority's power to call for information

In Part 6 of the Financial Services and Markets Act 2000 after the sections inserted by section 1266 above insert –

"Power of competent authority to call for information

89H Competent authority's power to call for information

(1)   The competent authority may by notice in writing given to a person to whom this section applies require him –

    (a)   to provide specified information or information of a specified description, or

    (b)   to produce specified documents or documents of a specified description.

(2)   This section applies to –

    (a)   an issuer in respect of whom transparency rules have effect;

    (b)   a voteholder;

    (c)   an auditor of –

        (i)   an issuer to whom this section applies, or

        (ii)   a voteholder;

    (d)   a person who controls a voteholder;

    (e)   a person controlled by a voteholder;

    (f)   a director or other similar officer of an issuer to whom this section applies;

    (g)   a director or other similar officer of a voteholder or, where the affairs of a voteholder are managed by its members, a member of the voteholder.

(3)   This section applies only to information and documents reasonably required in connection with the exercise by the competent authority of functions conferred on it by or under sections 89A to 89G (transparency rules).

(4)   Information or documents required under this section must be provided or produced –

    (a)   before the end of such reasonable period as may be specified, and

    (b)   at such place as may be specified.

(5)   If a person claims a lien on a document, its production under this section does not affect the lien.

89I Requirements in connection with call for information

(1)   The competent authority may require any information provided under section 89H to be provided in such form as it may reasonably require.

(2)   The competent authority may require –

    (a)   any information provided, whether in a document or otherwise, to be verified in such manner as it may reasonably require;

    (b)   any document produced to be authenticated in such manner as it may reasonably require.

(3)   If a document is produced in response to a requirement imposed under section 89H, the competent authority may –

    (a)   take copies of or extracts from the document; or

    (b)   require the person producing the document, or any relevant person, to provide an explanation of the document.

(4)   In subsection (3)(b) "relevant person", in relation to a person who is required to produce a document, means a person who –

    (a)   has been or is a director or controller of that person;

    (b)   has been or is an auditor of that person;

      (c)   has been or is an actuary, accountant or lawyer appointed or instructed by that person; or

      (d)   has been or is an employee of that person.

(5) If a person who is required under section 89H to produce a document fails to do so, the competent authority may require him to state, to the best of his knowledge and belief, where the document is.

89J Power to call for information: supplementary provisions

(1) The competent authority may require an issuer to make public any information provided to the authority under section 89H.

(2) If the issuer fails to comply with a requirement under subsection (1), the competent authority may, after seeking representations from the issuer, make the information public.

(3) In sections 89H and 89I (power of competent authority to call for information) –

"control" and "controlled" have the meaning given by subsection (4) below;
"specified" means specified in the notice;
"voteholder" means a person who –

      (a)   holds voting rights in respect of any voting shares for the purposes of sections 89A to 89G (transparency rules), or

      (b)   is treated as holding such rights by virtue of rules under section 89A(3)(b).

(4) For the purposes of those sections a person ("A") controls another person ("B") if –

      (a)   A holds a majority of the voting rights in B,

      (b)   A is a member of B and has the right to appoint or remove a majority of the members of the board of directors (or, if there is no such board, the equivalent management body) of B,

      (c)   A is a member of B and controls alone, pursuant to an agreement with other shareholders or members, a majority of the voting rights in B, or

      (d)   A has the right to exercise, or actually exercises, dominant influence or control over B.

(5) For the purposes of subsection (4)(b) –

      (a)   any rights of a person controlled by A, and

      (b)   any rights of a person acting on behalf of A or a person controlled by A,

are treated as held by A.".

1268 Powers exercisable in case of infringement of transparency obligation

In Part 6 of the Financial Services and Markets Act 2000 (c. 8), after the sections inserted by section 1267 above insert –

"Powers exercisable in case of infringement of transparency obligation

89K Public censure of issuer

(1) If the competent authority finds that an issuer of securities admitted to trading on a regulated market is failing or has failed to comply with an applicable transparency obligation, it may publish a statement to that effect.

(2) If the competent authority proposes to publish a statement, it must give the issuer a warning notice setting out the terms of the proposed statement.

(3) If, after considering any representations made in response to the warning notice, the competent authority decides to make the proposed statement, it must give the issuer a decision notice setting out the terms of the statement.

(4) A notice under this section must inform the issuer of his right to refer the matter to the Tribunal (see section 89N) and give an indication of the procedure on such a reference.

(5) In this section "transparency obligation" means an obligation under –

(a) a provision of transparency rules, or

(b) any other provision made in accordance with the transparency obligations directive.

(6) In relation to an issuer whose home State is a member State other than the United Kingdom, any reference to an applicable transparency obligation must be read subject to section 100A(2).

89L Power to suspend or prohibit trading of securities

(1) This section applies to securities admitted to trading on a regulated market.

(2) If the competent authority has reasonable grounds for suspecting that an applicable transparency obligation has been infringed by an issuer, it may –

(a) suspend trading in the securities for a period not exceeding 10 days,

(b) prohibit trading in the securities, or

(c) make a request to the operator of the market on which the issuer's securities are traded –

(i) to suspend trading in the securities for a period not exceeding 10 days, or

(ii) to prohibit trading in the securities.

(3) If the competent authority has reasonable grounds for suspecting that a provision required by the transparency obligations directive has been infringed by a voteholder of an issuer, it may –

(a) prohibit trading in the securities, or

(b) make a request to the operator of the market on which the issuer's securities are traded to prohibit trading in the securities.

(4) If the competent authority finds that an applicable transparency obligation has been infringed, it may require the market operator to prohibit trading in the securities.

(5) In this section "transparency obligation" means an obligation under –

(a) a provision contained in transparency rules, or

(b) any other provision made in accordance with the transparency obligations directive.

(6) In relation to an issuer whose home State is a member State other than the United Kingdom, any reference to an applicable transparency obligation must be read subject to section 100A(2).

89M Procedure under section 89L

(1) A requirement under section 89L takes effect –

(a) immediately, if the notice under subsection (2) states that that is the case;

(b) in any other case, on such date as may be specified in the notice.

(2) If the competent authority –

(a) proposes to exercise the powers in section 89L in relation to a person, or

(b) exercises any of those powers in relation to a person with immediate effect,

it must give that person written notice.

(3) The notice must –

(a)   give details of the competent authority's action or proposed action;

(b)   state the competent authority's reasons for taking the action in question and choosing the date on which it took effect or takes effect;

(c)   inform the recipient that he may make representations to the competent authority within such period as may be specified by the notice (whether or not he had referred the matter to the Tribunal);

(d)   inform him of the date on which the action took effect or takes effect;

(e)   inform him of his right to refer the matter to the Tribunal (see section 89N) and give an indication of the procedure on such a reference.

(4)   The competent authority may extend the period within which representations may be made to it.

(5)   If, having considered any representations made to it, the competent authority decides to maintain, vary or revoke its earlier decision, it must give written notice to that effect to the person mentioned in subsection (2).

89N Right to refer matters to the Tribunal

A person –

(a)   to whom a decision notice is given under section 89K (public censure), or

(b)   to whom a notice is given under section 89M (procedure in connection with suspension or prohibition of trading),

may refer the matter to the Tribunal.".

Other matters

1269 Corporate governance rules

In Part 6 of the Financial Services and Markets Act 2000 (c. 8), after the sections inserted by section 1268 above insert –

"Corporate governance

89O Corporate governance rules

(1)   The competent authority may make rules ("corporate governance rules") –

(a)   for the purpose of implementing, enabling the implementation of or dealing with matters arising out of or related to, any Community obligation relating to the corporate governance of issuers who have requested or approved admission of their securities to trading on a regulated market;

(b)   about corporate governance in relation to such issuers for the purpose of implementing, or dealing with matters arising out of or related to, any Community obligation.

(2)   "Corporate governance", in relation to an issuer, includes –

(a)   the nature, constitution or functions of the organs of the issuer;

(b)   the manner in which organs of the issuer conduct themselves;

(c)   the requirements imposed on organs of the issuer;

(d)   the relationship between the different organs of the issuer;

(e)   the relationship between the organs of the issuer and the members of the issuer or holders of the issuer's securities.

(3)   The burdens and restrictions imposed by rules under this section on foreign-traded issuers must not be greater than the burdens and restrictions imposed on UK-traded issuers by –

(a)   rules under this section, and

(b)   listing rules.

(4)   For this purpose –

"foreign-traded issuer" means an issuer who has requested or approved admission of the issuer's securities to trading on a regulated market situated or operating outside the United Kingdom;

"UK-traded issuer" means an issuer who has requested or approved admission of the issuer's securities to trading on a regulated market situated or operating in the United Kingdom.

(5)   This section is without prejudice to any other power conferred by this Part to make Part 6 rules.".

1270 Liability for false or misleading statements in certain publications

In Part 6 of the Financial Services and Markets Act 2000 (c. 8), after section 90 insert –

"90A Compensation for statements in certain publications

(1)   The publications to which this section applies are –

(a)   any reports and statements published in response to a requirement imposed by a provision implementing Article 4, 5 or 6 of the transparency obligations directive, and

(b)   any preliminary statement made in advance of a report or statement to be published in response to a requirement imposed by a provision implementing Article 4 of that directive, to the extent that it contains information that it is intended –

(i)   will appear in the report or statement, and

(ii)   will be presented in the report or statement in substantially the same form as that in which it is presented in the preliminary statement.

(2)   The securities to which this section applies are –

(a)   securities that are traded on a regulated market situated or operating in the United Kingdom, and

(b)   securities that –

(i)   are traded on a regulated market situated or operating outside the United Kingdom, and

(ii)   are issued by an issuer for which the United Kingdom is the home Member State within the meaning of Article 2.1(i) of the transparency obligations directive.

(3)   The issuer of securities to which this section applies is liable to pay compensation to a person who has –

(a)   acquired such securities issued by it, and

(b)   suffered loss in respect of them as a result of –

(i)   any untrue or misleading statement in a publication to which this section applies, or

(ii)   the omission from any such publication of any matter required to be included in it.

(4)   The issuer is so liable only if a person discharging managerial responsibilities within the issuer in relation to the publication –

(a)   knew the statement to be untrue or misleading or was reckless as to whether it was untrue or misleading, or

(b)   knew the omission to be dishonest concealment of a material fact.

(5)   A loss is not regarded as suffered as a result of the statement or omission in the publication unless the person suffering it acquired the relevant securities –

(a)   in reliance on the information in the publication, and

(b)   at a time when, and in circumstances in which, it was reasonable for him to rely on that information.

(6)   Except as mentioned in subsection (8) –

(a)   the issuer is not subject to any other liability than that provided for by this section in respect of loss suffered as a result of reliance by any person on –

(i)   an untrue or misleading statement in a publication to which this section applies, or

(ii)   the omission from any such publication of any matter required to be included in it, and

(b)   a person other than the issuer is not subject to any liability, other than to the issuer, in respect of any such loss.

(7)   Any reference in subsection (6) to a person being subject to a liability includes a reference to another person being entitled as against him to be granted any civil remedy or to rescind or repudiate an agreement.

(8)   This section does not affect –

(a)   the powers conferred by section 382 and 384 (powers of the court to make a restitution order and of the Authority to require restitution);

(b)   liability for a civil penalty;

(c)   liability for a criminal offence.

(9)   For the purposes of this section –

(a)   the following are persons "discharging managerial responsibilities" in relation to a publication –

(i)   any director of the issuer (or person occupying the position of director, by whatever name called),

(ii)   in the case of an issuer whose affairs are managed by its members, any member of the issuer,

(iii)   in the case of an issuer that has no persons within sub-paragraph (i) or (ii), any senior executive of the issuer having responsibilities in relation to the publication;

(b)   references to the acquisition by a person of securities include his contracting to acquire them or any interest in them.

90B Power to make further provision about liability for published information

(1)   The Treasury may by regulations make provision about the liability of issuers of securities traded on a regulated market, and other persons, in respect of information published to holders of securities, to the market or to the public generally.

(2)   Regulations under this section may amend any primary or subordinate legislation, including any provision of, or made under, this Act.".

1271 Exercise of powers where UK is host member State

In Part 6 of the Financial Services and Markets Act 2000 (c. 8), after section 100 insert –

"100A Exercise of powers where UK is host member state

(1)   This section applies to the exercise by the competent authority of any power under this Part exercisable in case of infringement of –

(a)   a provision of prospectus rules or any other provision made in accordance with the prospectus directive, or

(b)   a provision of transparency rules or any other provision made in accordance with the transparency obligations directive, in relation to an issuer whose home State is a member State other than the United Kingdom.

(2) The competent authority may act in such a case only in respect of the infringement of a provision required by the relevant directive.

Any reference to an applicable provision or applicable transparency obligation shall be read accordingly.

(3) If the authority finds that there has been such an infringement, it must give a notice to that effect to the competent authority of the person's home State requesting it –

(a) to take all appropriate measures for the purpose of ensuring that the person remedies the situation that has given rise to the notice, and

(b) to inform the authority of the measures it proposes to take or has taken or the reasons for not taking such measures.

(4) The authority may not act further unless satisfied –

(a) that the competent authority of the person's home State has failed or refused to take measures for the purpose mentioned in subsection (3)(a), or

(b) that the measures taken by that authority have proved inadequate for that purpose.

This does not affect exercise of the powers under section 87K(2), 87L(2) or (3) or 89L(2) or (3) (powers to protect market).

(5) If the authority is so satisfied, it must, after informing the competent authority of the person's home State, take all appropriate measures to protect investors.

(6) In such a case the authority must inform the Commission of the measures at the earliest opportunity.".

1272 Transparency obligations and related matters: minor and consequential amendments

(1) Schedule 15 to this Act makes minor and consequential amendments in connection with the provision made by this Part.

(2) In that Schedule –

Part 1 contains amendments of the Financial Services and Markets Act 2000 (c. 8);

Part 2 contains amendments of the Companies (Audit, Investigations and Community Enterprise) Act 2004 (c. 27).

1273 Corporate governance regulations

(1) The Secretary of State may make regulations –

(a) for the purpose of implementing, enabling the implementation of or dealing with matters arising out of or related to, any Community obligation relating to the corporate governance of issuers who have requested or approved admission of their securities to trading on a regulated market;

(b) about corporate governance in relation to such issuers for the purpose of implementing, or dealing with matters arising out of or related to, any Community obligation.

(2) "Corporate governance", in relation to an issuer, includes –

(a) the nature, constitution or functions of the organs of the issuer;

(b) the manner in which organs of the issuer conduct themselves;

(c) the requirements imposed on organs of the issuer;

(d) the relationship between different organs of the issuer;

(e) the relationship between the organs of the issuer and the members of the issuer or holders of the issuer's securities.

(3) The regulations may –

(a) make provision by reference to any specified code on corporate governance that may be issued from time to time by a specified body;

(b) create new criminal offences (subject to subsection (4));

(c) make provision excluding liability in damages in respect of things done or omitted for the purposes of, or in connection with, the carrying on, or purported carrying on, of any specified activities.

"Specified" here means specified in the regulations.

(4) The regulations may not create a criminal offence punishable by a greater penalty than –

(a) on indictment, a fine;

(b) on summary conviction, a fine not exceeding the statutory maximum or (if calculated on a daily basis) £100 a day.

(5) Regulations under this section are subject to negative resolution procedure.

(6) In this section "issuer", "securities" and "regulated market" have the same meaning as in Part 6 of the Financial Services and Markets Act 2000 (c. 8).

PART 44

MISCELLANEOUS PROVISIONS

Regulation of actuaries etc

1274 Grants to bodies concerned with actuarial standards etc

(1) Section 16 of the Companies (Audit, Investigations and Community Enterprise) Act 2004 (c. 27) (grants to bodies concerned with accounting standards etc) is amended as follows.

(2) In subsection (2) (matters carried on by bodies eligible for grants) for paragraph (l) substitute –

"(l) issuing standards to be applied in actuarial work;

(m) issuing standards in respect of matters to be contained in reports or other communications required to be produced or made by actuaries or in accordance with standards within paragraph (l);

(n) investigating departures from standards within paragraph (l) or (m);

(o) taking steps to secure compliance with standards within paragraph (l) or (m);

(p) carrying out investigations into public interest cases arising in connection with the performance of actuarial functions by members of professional actuarial bodies;

(q) holding disciplinary hearings relating to members of professional actuarial bodies following the conclusion of investigations within paragraph (p);

(r) deciding whether (and, if so, what) disciplinary action should be taken against members of professional actuarial bodies to whom hearings within paragraph (q) related;

(s) supervising the exercise by professional actuarial bodies of regulatory functions in relation to their members;

(t) overseeing or directing any of the matters mentioned above.".

(3) In subsection (5) (definitions) at the appropriate places insert –

""professional actuarial body" means –

(a) the Institute of Actuaries, or

(b) the Faculty of Actuaries in Scotland,

and the "members" of a professional actuarial body include persons who, although not members of the body, are subject to its rules in performing actuarial functions;"

""regulatory functions", in relation to professional actuarial bodies, means any of the following –

(a) investigatory or disciplinary functions exercised by such bodies in relation to the performance by their members of actuarial functions,

(b) the setting by such bodies of standards in relation to the performance by their members of actuarial functions, and

(c) the determining by such bodies of requirements in relation to the education and training of their members;".

1275 Levy to pay expenses of bodies concerned with actuarial standards etc

(1) Section 17 of the Companies (Audit, Investigations and Community Enterprise) Act 2004 (c. 27) (levy to pay expenses of bodies concerned with accounting standards etc) is amended in accordance with subsections (2) to (5).

(2) In subsection (3)(a) after "to which" insert ", or persons within subsection (3A) to whom,".

(3) After subsection (3) insert –

"(3A)   The following persons are within this subsection –

(a) the administrators of a public service pension scheme (within the meaning of section 1 of the Pension Schemes Act 1993);

(b) the trustees or managers of an occupational or personal pension scheme (within the meaning of that section).".

(4) After subsection (4)(b) insert –

"(c) make different provision for different cases.".

(5) After subsection (12) insert –

"(13)   If a draft of any regulations to which subsection (10) applies would, apart from this subsection, be treated for the purposes of the standing orders of either House of Parliament as a hybrid instrument, it is to proceed in that House as if it were not such an instrument.".

(6) The above amendments have effect in relation to any exercise of the power to make regulations under section 17 of the Companies (Audit, Investigations and Community Enterprise) Act 2004 after this section comes into force, regardless of when the expenses to be met by the levy in respect of which the regulations are made were incurred.

(7) In Schedule 3 to the Pensions Act 2004 (c. 35) (disclosure of information held by the Pensions Regulator), in the entry relating to the Secretary of State, in the second column, for "or" at the end of paragraph (g) substitute –

"(ga)   Section 17 of the Companies (Audit, Investigations and Community Enterprise) Act 2004 (levy to pay expenses of bodies concerned with accounting standards, actuarial standards etc), or".

1276 Application of provisions to Scotland and Northern Ireland

(1) Section 16 of the Companies (Audit, Investigations and Community Enterprise) Act 2004 (grants to bodies concerned with accounting standards etc) is amended as follows.

(2) For subsection (6) (application of section to Scotland) substitute –

"(6)   In their application to Scotland, subsection (2)(a) to (t) are to be read as referring only to matters provision relating to which would be outside the legislative competence of the Scottish Parliament.".

(3) In subsection (2) in paragraph (c), after "1985 (c. 6)" insert "or the 1986 Order".

(4) In subsection (5) –

   (a) in the definition of "company" after "1985 (c. 6)" insert "or the 1986 Order",
   (b) in the definition of "subsidiary" after "1985" insert "or Article 4 of the 1986 Order", and
   (c) after that definition insert –

      ""the 1986 Order" means the Companies (Northern Ireland) Order 1986 (S.I. 1986/1032 (N.I. 6)).".

(5) In section 66 of that Act (extent), in subsection (2) (provisions extending to Northern Ireland, as well as England and Wales and Scotland) for "17" substitute "16 to 18".

Information as to exercise of voting rights by institutional investors

1277 Power to require information about exercise of voting rights

(1) The Treasury or the Secretary of State may make provision by regulations requiring institutions to which this section applies to provide information about the exercise of voting rights attached to shares to which this section applies.

(2) This power is exercisable in accordance with –

   section 1278 (institutions to which information provisions apply),
   section 1279 (shares to which information provisions apply), and
   section 1280 (obligations with respect to provision of information).

(3) In this section and the sections mentioned above –

   (a) references to a person acting on behalf of an institution include –

      (i) any person to whom authority has been delegated by the institution to take decisions as to any matter relevant to the subject matter of the regulations, and
      (ii) such other persons as may be specified; and

   (b) "specified" means specified in the regulations.

(4) The obligation imposed by regulations under this section is enforceable by civil proceedings brought by –

   (a) any person to whom the information should have been provided, or
   (b) a specified regulatory authority.

(5) Regulations under this section may make different provision for different descriptions of institution, different descriptions of shares and for other different circumstances.

(6) Regulations under this section are subject to affirmative resolution procedure.

1278 Institutions to which information provisions apply

(1) The institutions to which section 1277 applies are –

   (a) unit trust schemes within the meaning of the Financial Services and Markets Act 2000 (c. 8) in respect of which an order is in force under section 243 of that Act;
   (b) open-ended investment companies incorporated by virtue of regulations under section 262 of that Act;
   (c) companies approved for the purposes of section 842 of the Income and Corporation Taxes Act 1988 (c. 1) (investment trusts);
   (d) pension schemes as defined in section 1(5) of the Pension Schemes Act 1993 (c. 48) or the Pension Schemes (Northern Ireland) Act 1993 (c. 49);
   (e) undertakings authorised under the Financial Services and Markets Act 2000 to carry on long-term insurance business (that is, the activity of effecting or carrying out contracts of long-term insurance within the meaning of the Financial Services and Markets (Regulated Activities) Order 2001 (S.I. 2001/544);

(f)   collective investment schemes that are recognised by virtue of section 270 of that Act (schemes authorised in designated countries or territories).

(2)   Regulations under that section may –

(a)   provide that the section applies to other descriptions of institution;
(b)   provide that the section does not apply to a specified description of institution.

(3)   The regulations must specify by whom, in the case of any description of institution, the duty imposed by the regulations is to be fulfilled.

1279 Shares to which information provisions apply

(1)   The shares to which section 1277 applies are shares –

(a)   of a description traded on a specified market, and
(b)   in which the institution has, or is taken to have, an interest.

Regulations under that section may provide that the section does not apply to shares of a specified description.

(2)   For this purpose an institution has an interest in shares if the shares, or a depositary certificate in respect of them, are held by it, or on its behalf.

A "depositary certificate" means an instrument conferring rights (other than options) –

(a)   in respect of shares held by another person, and
(b)   the transfer of which may be effected without the consent of that person.

(3)   Where an institution has an interest –

(a)   in a specified description of collective investment scheme (within the meaning of the Financial Services and Markets Act 2000 (c. 8)), or
(b)   in any other specified description of scheme or collective investment vehicle,

it is taken to have an interest in any shares in which that scheme or vehicle has or is taken to have an interest.

(4)   For this purpose a scheme or vehicle is taken to have an interest in shares if it would be regarded as having such an interest in accordance with subsection (2) if it was an institution to which section 1277 applied.

1280 Obligations with respect to provision of information

(1)   Regulations under section 1277 may require the provision of specified information about –

(a)   the exercise or non-exercise of voting rights by the institution or any person acting on its behalf,
(b)   any instructions given by the institution or any person acting on its behalf as to the exercise or non-exercise of voting rights, and
(c)   any delegation by the institution or any person acting on its behalf of any functions in relation to the exercise or non-exercise of voting rights or the giving of such instructions.

(2)   The regulations may require information to be provided in respect of specified occasions or specified periods.

(3)   Where instructions are given to act on the recommendations or advice of another person, the regulations may require the provision of information about what recommendations or advice were given.

(4)   The regulations may require information to be provided –

(a)   in such manner as may be specified, and
(b)   to such persons as may be specified, or to the public, or both.

(5)   The regulations may provide –

(a)   that an institution may discharge its obligations under the regulations by referring to information disclosed by a person acting on its behalf, and

    (b) that in such a case it is sufficient, where that other person acts on behalf of more than one institution, that the reference is to information given in aggregated form, that is –

        (i) relating to the exercise or non-exercise by that person of voting rights on behalf of more than one institution, or

        (ii) relating to the instructions given by that person in respect of the exercise or non-exercise of voting rights on behalf of more than one institution, or

        (iii) relating to the delegation by that person of functions in relation to the exercise or non-exercise of voting rights, or the giving of instructions in respect of the exercise or non-exercise of voting rights, on behalf of more than one institution.

(6) References in this section to instructions are to instructions of any description, whether general or specific, whether binding or not and whether or not acted upon.

Disclosure of information under the Enterprise Act 2002

1281 Disclosure of information under the Enterprise Act 2002

In Part 9 of the Enterprise Act 2002 (c. 40) (information), after section 241 insert –

"241A Civil proceedings

(1) A public authority which holds prescribed information to which section 237 applies may disclose that information to any person –

    (a) for the purposes of, or in connection with, prescribed civil proceedings (including prospective proceedings) in the United Kingdom or elsewhere, or

    (b) for the purposes of obtaining legal advice in relation to such proceedings, or

    (c) otherwise for the purposes of establishing, enforcing or defending legal rights that are or may be the subject of such proceedings.

(2) Subsection (1) does not apply to –

    (a) information which comes to a public authority in connection with an investigation under Part 4, 5 or 6 of the 1973 Act or under section 11 of the Competition Act 1980;

    (b) competition information within the meaning of section 351 of the Financial Services and Markets Act 2000;

    (c) information which comes to a public authority in connection with an investigation under Part 3 or 4 or section 174 of this Act;

    (d) information which comes to a public authority in connection with an investigation under the Competition Act 1998 (c. 41).

(3) In subsection (1) "prescribed" means prescribed by order of the Secretary of State.

(4) An order under this section –

    (a) may prescribe information, or civil proceedings, for the purposes of this section by reference to such factors as appear to the Secretary of State to be appropriate;

    (b) may prescribe for the purposes of this section all information, or civil proceedings, or all information or civil proceedings not falling within one or more specified exceptions;

    (c) must be made by statutory instrument subject to annulment in pursuance of a resolution of either House of Parliament.

(5) Information disclosed under this section must not be used by the person to whom it is disclosed for any purpose other than those specified in subsection (1).".

Expenses of winding up

1282 Payment of expenses of winding up

(1) In Chapter 8 of Part 4 of the Insolvency Act 1986 (c. 45) (winding up of companies: provisions of general application), before section 176A (under the heading "Property subject to floating charge") insert –

"176ZA Payment of expenses of winding up (England and Wales)

(1) The expenses of winding up in England and Wales, so far as the assets of the company available for payment of general creditors are insufficient to meet them, have priority over any claims to property comprised in or subject to any floating charge created by the company and shall be paid out of any such property accordingly.

(2) In subsection (1) –

    (a)   the reference to assets of the company available for payment of general creditors does not include any amount made available under section 176A(2)(a);

    (b)   the reference to claims to property comprised in or subject to a floating charge is to the claims of –

        (i)   the holders of debentures secured by, or holders of, the floating charge, and

        (ii)   any preferential creditors entitled to be paid out of that property in priority to them.

(3) Provision may be made by rules restricting the application of subsection (1), in such circumstances as may be prescribed, to expenses authorised or approved –

    (a)   by the holders of debentures secured by, or holders of, the floating charge and by any preferential creditors entitled to be paid in priority to them, or

    (b)   by the court.

(4) References in this section to the expenses of the winding up are to all expenses properly incurred in the winding up, including the remuneration of the liquidator.".

(2) In Chapter 8 of Part 5 of the Insolvency (Northern Ireland) Order 1989 (S.I. 1989/2405 (N.I. 19)) (winding up of companies: provisions of general application), before Article 150A (under the heading "Property subject to floating charge") insert –

"150ZA Payment of expenses of winding up

(1) The expenses of winding up, so far as the assets of the company available for payment of general creditors are insufficient to meet them, have priority over any claims to property comprised in or subject to any floating charge created by the company and shall be paid out of any such property accordingly.

(2) In paragraph (1) –

    (a)   the reference to assets of the company available for payment of general creditors does not include any amount made available under Article 150A(2)(a);

    (b)   the reference to claims to property comprised in or subject to a floating charge is to the claims of –

        (i)   the holders of debentures secured by, or holders of, the floating charge, and

        (ii)   any preferential creditors entitled to be paid out of that property in priority to them.

(3) Provision may be made by rules restricting the application of paragraph (1), in such circumstances as may be prescribed, to expenses authorised or approved –

    (a) by the holders of debentures secured by, or holders of, the floating charge and by any preferential creditors entitled to be paid in priority to them, or

    (b) by the Court.

(4) References in this Article to the expenses of the winding up are to all expenses properly incurred in the winding up, including the remuneration of the liquidator.".

Commonhold associations

1283 Amendment of memorandum or articles of commonhold association

In paragraph 3(1) of Schedule 3 to the Commonhold and Leasehold Reform Act 2002 (c. 15) (alteration of memorandum or articles by commonhold association to be of no effect until altered version registered with Land Registry) for "An alteration of the memorandum or articles of association" substitute "Where a commonhold association alters its memorandum or articles at a time when the land specified in its memorandum is commonhold land, the alteration".

PART 45

NORTHERN IRELAND

1284 Extension of Companies Acts to Northern Ireland

(1) The Companies Acts as defined by this Act (see section 2) extend to Northern Ireland.

(2) The Companies (Northern Ireland) Order 1986 (S.I. 1986/1032 (N.I. 6)), the Companies Consolidation (Consequential Provisions) (Northern Ireland) Order 1986 (S.I. 1986/1035 (N.I. 9)) and Part 3 of the Companies (Audit, Investigations and Community Enterprise) Order 2005 (S.I. 2005/1967 (N.I. 17)) shall cease to have effect accordingly.

1285 Extension of GB enactments relating to SEs

(1) The enactments in force in Great Britain relating to SEs extend to Northern Ireland.

(2) The following enactments shall cease to have effect accordingly –

    (a) the European Public Limited-Liability Company Regulations (Northern Ireland) 2004 (SR 2004/417), and

    (b) the European Public Limited-Liability Company (Fees) Regulations (Northern Ireland) 2004 (SR 2004/418).

(3) In this section "SE" means a European Public Limited-Liability Company (or Societas Europaea) within the meaning of Council Regulation 2157/2001/EC of 8 October 2001 on the Statute for a European Company.

1286 Extension of GB enactments relating to certain other forms of business organisation

(1) The enactments in force in Great Britain relating to –

    (a) limited liability partnerships,

    (b) limited partnerships,

    (c) open-ended investment companies, and

    (d) European Economic Interest Groupings,

extend to Northern Ireland.

(2) The following enactments shall cease to have effect accordingly –

    (a) the Limited Liability Partnerships Act (Northern Ireland) 2002 (c. 12 (N.I.));

    (b) the Limited Partnerships Act 1907 (c. 24) as it formerly had effect in Northern Ireland;

    (c) the Open-Ended Investment Companies Act (Northern Ireland) 2002 (c. 13 (N.I.));

    (d) the European Economic Interest Groupings Regulations (Northern Ireland) 1989 (SR 1989/216).

1287 Extension of enactments relating to business names

(1) The provisions of Part 41 of this Act (business names) extend to Northern Ireland.

(2) The Business Names (Northern Ireland) Order 1986 (S.I. 1986/1033 (N.I. 7)) shall cease to have effect accordingly.

PART 46

GENERAL SUPPLEMENTARY PROVISIONS

Regulations and orders

1288 Regulations and orders: statutory instrument

Except as otherwise provided, regulations and orders under this Act shall be made by statutory instrument.

1289 Regulations and orders: negative resolution procedure

Where regulations or orders under this Act are subject to "negative resolution procedure" the statutory instrument containing the regulations or order shall be subject to annulment in pursuance of a resolution of either House of Parliament.

1290 Regulations and orders: affirmative resolution procedure

Where regulations or orders under this Act are subject to "affirmative resolution procedure" the regulations or order must not be made unless a draft of the statutory instrument containing them has been laid before Parliament and approved by a resolution of each House of Parliament.

1291 Regulations and orders: approval after being made

(1) Regulations or orders under this Act that are subject to "approval after being made" –

    (a) must be laid before Parliament after being made, and

    (b) cease to have effect at the end of 28 days beginning with the day on which they were made unless during that period they are approved by resolution of each House.

(2) In reckoning the period of 28 days no account shall be taken of any time during which Parliament is dissolved or prorogued or during which both Houses are adjourned for more than four days.

(3) The regulations or order ceasing to have effect does not affect –

    (a) anything previously done under them or it, or

    (b) the making of new regulations or a new order.

1292 Regulations and orders: supplementary

(1) Regulations or orders under this Act may –

    (a) make different provision for different cases or circumstances,

    (b) include supplementary, incidental and consequential provision, and

    (c) make transitional provision and savings.

(2) Any provision that may be made by regulations under this Act may be made by order; and any provision that may be made by order under this Act may be made by regulations.

(3) Any provision that may be made by regulations or order under this Act for which no Parliamentary procedure is prescribed may be made by regulations or order subject to negative or affirmative resolution procedure.

(4) Any provision that may be made by regulations or order under this Act subject to negative resolution procedure may be made by regulations or order subject to affirmative resolution procedure.

Meaning of "enactment"

1293 Meaning of "enactment"

In this Act, unless the context otherwise requires, "enactment" includes –

    (a) an enactment contained in subordinate legislation within the meaning of the Interpretation Act 1978 (c. 30),

    (b) an enactment contained in, or in an instrument made under, an Act of the Scottish Parliament, and

    (c) an enactment contained in, or in an instrument made under, Northern Ireland legislation within the meaning of the Interpretation Act 1978.

Consequential and transitional provisions

1294 Power to make consequential amendments etc

(1) The Secretary of State or the Treasury may by order make such provision amending, repealing or revoking any enactment to which this section applies as they consider necessary or expedient in consequence of any provision made by or under this Act.

(2) This section applies to –

    (a) any enactment passed or made before the passing of this Act,

    (b) any enactment contained in this Act or in subordinate legislation made under it, and

    (c) any enactment passed or made before the end of the session after that in which this Act is passed.

(3) Without prejudice to the generality of the power conferred by subsection (1), orders under this section may –

    (a) make provision extending to other forms of organisation any provision made by or under this Act in relation to companies, or

    (b) make provision corresponding to that made by or under this Act in relation to companies,

in either case with such adaptations or other modifications as appear to the Secretary of State or the Treasury to be necessary or expedient.

(4) The references in subsection (3) to provision made by this Act include provision conferring power to make provision by regulations, orders or other subordinate legislation.

(5) Amendments and repeals made under this section are additional, and without prejudice, to those made by or under any other provision of this Act.

(6) Orders under this section are subject to affirmative resolution procedure.

1295 Repeals

The enactments specified in Schedule 16, which include enactments that are no longer of practical utility, are repealed to the extent specified.

1296 Power to make transitional provision and savings

(1) The Secretary of State or the Treasury may by order make such transitional provision and savings as they consider necessary or expedient in connection with the commencement of any provision made by or under this Act.
(2) An order may, in particular, make such adaptations of provisions brought into force as appear to be necessary or expedient in consequence of other provisions of this Act not yet having come into force.
(3) Transitional provision and savings made under this section are additional, and without prejudice, to those made by or under any other provision of this Act.
(4) Orders under this section are subject to negative resolution procedure.

1297 Continuity of the law

(1) This section applies where any provision of this Act re-enacts (with or without modification) an enactment repealed by this Act.
(2) The repeal and re-enactment does not affect the continuity of the law.
(3) Anything done (including subordinate legislation made), or having effect as if done, under or for the purposes of the repealed provision that could have been done under or for the purposes of the corresponding provision of this Act, if in force or effective immediately before the commencement of that corresponding provision, has effect thereafter as if done under or for the purposes of that corresponding provision.
(4) Any reference (express or implied) in this Act or any other enactment, instrument or document to a provision of this Act shall be construed (so far as the context permits) as including, as respects times, circumstances or purposes in relation to which the corresponding repealed provision had effect, a reference to that corresponding provision.
(5) Any reference (express or implied) in any enactment, instrument or document to a repealed provision shall be construed (so far as the context permits), as respects times, circumstances and purposes in relation to which the corresponding provision of this Act has effect, as being or (according to the context) including a reference to the corresponding provision of this Act.
(6) This section has effect subject to any specific transitional provision or saving contained in this Act.
(7) References in this section to this Act include subordinate legislation made under this Act.
(8) In this section "subordinate legislation" has the same meaning as in the Interpretation Act 1978 (c. 30).

PART 47

FINAL PROVISIONS

1298 Short title

The short title of this Act is the Companies Act 2006.

1299 Extent

Except as otherwise provided (or the context otherwise requires), the provisions of this Act extend to the whole of the United Kingdom.

1300 Commencement

(1) The following provisions come into force on the day this Act is passed –

(a) Part 43 (transparency obligations and related matters), except the amendment in paragraph 11(2) of Schedule 15 of the definition of "regulated market" in Part 6 of the Financial Services and Markets Act 2000 (c. 8),

(b) in Part 44 (miscellaneous provisions) –

section 1274 (grants to bodies concerned with actuarial standards etc), and section 1276 (application of provisions to Scotland and Northern Ireland),

(c) Part 46 (general supplementary provisions), except section 1295 and Schedule 16 (repeals), and

(d) this Part.

(2) The other provisions of this Act come into force on such day as may be appointed by order of the Secretary of State or the Treasury.

SCHEDULES

SCHEDULE 1

Sections 254 and 255

CONNECTED PERSONS: REFERENCES TO AN INTEREST IN SHARES OR DEBENTURES

Introduction

1   (1)   The provisions of this Schedule have effect for the interpretation of references in sections 254 and 255 (directors connected with or controlling a body corporate) to an interest in shares or debentures.
   (2)   The provisions are expressed in relation to shares but apply to debentures as they apply to shares.

General provisions

2   (1)   A reference to an interest in shares includes any interest of any kind whatsoever in shares.
   (2)   Any restraints or restrictions to which the exercise of any right attached to the interest is or may be subject shall be disregarded.
   (3)   It is immaterial that the shares in which a person has an interest are not identifiable.
   (4)   Persons having a joint interest in shares are deemed each of them to have that interest.

Rights to acquire shares

3   (1)   A person is taken to have an interest in shares if he enters into a contract to acquire them.
   (2)   A person is taken to have an interest in shares if –

   (a)   he has a right to call for delivery of the shares to himself or to his order, or
   (b)   he has a right to acquire an interest in shares or is under an obligation to take an interest in shares,

   whether the right or obligation is conditional or absolute.
   (3)   Rights or obligations to subscribe for shares are not to be taken for the purposes of sub-paragraph (2) to be rights to acquire or obligations to take an interest in shares.
   (4)   A person ceases to have an interest in shares by virtue of this paragraph –

   (a)   on the shares being delivered to another person at his order –

   (i)   in fulfilment of a contract for their acquisition by him, or
   (ii)   in satisfaction of a right of his to call for their delivery;

   (b)   on a failure to deliver the shares in accordance with the terms of such a contract or on which such a right falls to be satisfied;
   (c)   on the lapse of his right to call for the delivery of shares.

Right to exercise or control exercise of rights

4   (1) A person is taken to have an interest in shares if, not being the registered holder, he is entitled –

   (a) to exercise any right conferred by the holding of the shares, or

   (b) to control the exercise of any such right.

   (2) For this purpose a person is taken to be entitled to exercise or control the exercise of a right conferred by the holding of shares if he –

   (a) has a right (whether subject to conditions or not) the exercise of which would make him so entitled, or

   (b) is under an obligation (whether or not so subject) the fulfilment of which would make him so entitled.

   (3) A person is not by virtue of this paragraph taken to be interested in shares by reason only that –

   (a) he has been appointed a proxy to exercise any of the rights attached to the shares, or

   (b) he has been appointed by a body corporate to act as its representative at any meeting of a company or of any class of its members.

Bodies corporate

5   (1) A person is taken to be interested in shares if a body corporate is interested in them and –

   (a) the body corporate or its directors are accustomed to act in accordance with his directions or instructions, or

   (b) he is entitled to exercise or control the exercise of more than one-half of the voting power at general meetings of the body corporate.

   (2) For the purposes of sub-paragraph (1)(b) where –

   (a) a person is entitled to exercise or control the exercise of more than one-half of the voting power at general meetings of a body corporate, and

   (b) that body corporate is entitled to exercise or control the exercise of any of the voting power at general meetings of another body corporate,

   the voting power mentioned in paragraph (b) above is taken to be exercisable by that person.

Trusts

6   (1) Where an interest in shares is comprised in property held on trust, every beneficiary of the trust is taken to have an interest in shares, subject as follows.

   (2) So long as a person is entitled to receive, during the lifetime of himself or another, income from trust property comprising shares, an interest in the shares in reversion or remainder or (as regards Scotland) in fee shall be disregarded.

   (3) A person is treated as not interested in shares if and so long as he holds them –

   (a) under the law in force in any part of the United Kingdom, as a bare trustee or as a custodian trustee, or

   (b) under the law in force in Scotland, as a simple trustee.

   (4) There shall be disregarded any interest of a person subsisting by virtue of –

   (a) an authorised unit trust scheme (within the meaning of section 237 of the Financial Services and Markets Act 2000 (c. 8));

   (b) a scheme made under section 22 or 22A of the Charities Act 1960 (c. 58), section 25 of the Charities Act (Northern Ireland) 1964 (c. 33 (N.I.)) or section 24 or 25 of the Charities Act 1993 (c. 10), section 11 of the Trustee Investments Act 1961 (c. 62) or section 42 of the Administration of Justice Act 1982 (c. 53); or

(c)   the scheme set out in the Schedule to the Church Funds Investment Measure 1958 (1958 No. 1).

(5)   There shall be disregarded any interest –

(a)   of the Church of Scotland General Trustees or of the Church of Scotland Trust in shares held by them;

(b)   of any other person in shares held by those Trustees or that Trust otherwise than as simple trustees.

"The Church of Scotland General Trustees" are the body incorporated by the order confirmed by the Church of Scotland (General Trustees) Order Confirmation Act 1921 (1921 c. xxv), and "the Church of Scotland Trust" is the body incorporated by the order confirmed by the Church of Scotland Trust Order Confirmation Act 1932 (1932 c. xxi).

SCHEDULE 2

Section 948

SPECIFIED PERSONS, DESCRIPTIONS OF DISCLOSURES ETC FOR THE PURPOSES OF SECTION 948

PART 1

SPECIFIED PERSONS

1   The Secretary of State.
2   The Department of Enterprise, Trade and Investment for Northern Ireland.
3   The Treasury.
4   The Bank of England.
5   The Financial Services Authority.
6   The Commissioners for Her Majesty's Revenue and Customs.
7   The Lord Advocate.
8   The Director of Public Prosecutions.
9   The Director of Public Prosecutions for Northern Ireland.
10   A constable.
11   A procurator fiscal.
12   The Scottish Ministers.

PART 2

SPECIFIED DESCRIPTIONS OF DISCLOSURES

13   A disclosure for the purpose of enabling or assisting a person authorised under section 457 of this Act (persons authorised to apply to court) to exercise his functions. Until the coming into force of section 457, the reference to that section is to be read as a reference to section 245C of the Companies Act 1985 (c. 6).

14   A disclosure for the purpose of enabling or assisting an inspector appointed under Part 14 of the Companies Act 1985 (investigation of companies and their affairs, etc) to exercise his functions.

15   A disclosure for the purpose of enabling or assisting a person authorised under section 447 of the Companies Act 1985 (power to require production of documents) or section 84 of the Companies Act 1989 (c. 40) (exercise of powers by officer etc) to exercise his functions.

16   A disclosure for the purpose of enabling or assisting a person appointed under section 167 of the Financial Services and Markets Act 2000 (c. 8) (general investigations) to conduct an investigation to exercise his functions.

17   A disclosure for the purpose of enabling or assisting a person appointed under section 168 of the Financial Services and Markets Act 2000 (investigations in particular cases) to conduct an investigation to exercise his functions.

18   A disclosure for the purpose of enabling or assisting a person appointed under section 169(1)(b) of the Financial Services and Markets Act 2000 (investigation in support of overseas regulator) to conduct an investigation to exercise his functions.

19   A disclosure for the purpose of enabling or assisting the body corporate responsible for administering the scheme referred to in section 225 of the Financial Services and Markets Act 2000 (the ombudsman scheme) to exercise its functions.

20   A disclosure for the purpose of enabling or assisting a person appointed under paragraph 4 (the panel of ombudsmen) or 5 (the Chief Ombudsman) of Schedule 17 to the Financial Services and Markets Act 2000 to exercise his functions.

21   A disclosure for the purpose of enabling or assisting a person appointed under regulations made under section 262(1) and (2)(k) of the Financial Services and Markets Act 2000 (investigations into open-ended investment companies) to conduct an investigation to exercise his functions.

22   A disclosure for the purpose of enabling or assisting a person appointed under section 284 of the Financial Services and Markets Act 2000 (investigations into affairs of certain collective investment schemes) to conduct an investigation to exercise his functions.

23   A disclosure for the purpose of enabling or assisting the investigator appointed under paragraph 7 of Schedule 1 to the Financial Services and Markets Act 2000 (arrangements for investigation of complaints) to exercise his functions.

24   A disclosure for the purpose of enabling or assisting a person appointed by the Treasury to hold an inquiry into matters relating to financial services (including an inquiry under section 15 of the Financial Services and Markets Act 2000 (c. 8)) to exercise his functions.

25   A disclosure for the purpose of enabling or assisting the Secretary of State or the Treasury to exercise any of their functions under any of the following –

   (a)   the Companies Acts;
   (b)   Part 5 of the Criminal Justice Act 1993 (c. 36) (insider dealing);
   (c)   the Insolvency Act 1986 (c. 45);
   (d)   the Company Directors Disqualification Act 1986 (c. 46);
   (e)   Part 42 of this Act (statutory auditors);
   (f)   Part 3 (investigations and powers to obtain information) or 7 (financial markets and insolvency) of the Companies Act 1989 (c. 40);
   (g)   the Financial Services and Markets Act 2000.

   Until the coming into force of Part 42 of this Act, the reference to it in paragraph (e) is to be read as a reference to Part 2 of the Companies Act 1989.

26   A disclosure for the purpose of enabling or assisting the Scottish Ministers to exercise their functions under the enactments relating to insolvency.

27   A disclosure for the purpose of enabling or assisting the Department of Enterprise, Trade and Investment for Northern Ireland to exercise any powers conferred on it by the enactments relating to companies or insolvency.

28 A disclosure for the purpose of enabling or assisting a person appointed or authorised by the Department of Enterprise, Trade and Investment for Northern Ireland under the enactments relating to companies or insolvency to exercise his functions.

29 A disclosure for the purpose of enabling or assisting the Pensions Regulator to exercise the functions conferred on it by or by virtue of any of the following –

(a) the Pension Schemes Act 1993 (c. 48);
(b) the Pensions Act 1995 (c. 26);
(c) the Welfare Reform and Pensions Act 1999 (c. 30);
(d) the Pensions Act 2004 (c. 35);
(e) any enactment in force in Northern Ireland corresponding to any of those enactments.

30 A disclosure for the purpose of enabling or assisting the Board of the Pension Protection Fund to exercise the functions conferred on it by or by virtue of Part 2 of the Pensions Act 2004 or any enactment in force in Northern Ireland corresponding to that Part.

31 A disclosure for the purpose of enabling or assisting –

(a) the Bank of England,
(b) the European Central Bank, or
(c) the central bank of any country or territory outside the United Kingdom,

to exercise its functions.

32 A disclosure for the purpose of enabling or assisting the Commissioners for Her Majesty's Revenue and Customs to exercise their functions.

33 A disclosure for the purpose of enabling or assisting organs of the Society of Lloyd's (being organs constituted by or under the Lloyd's Act 1982 (c. xiv)) to exercise their functions under or by virtue of the Lloyd's Acts 1871 to 1982.

34 A disclosure for the purpose of enabling or assisting the Office of Fair Trading to exercise its functions under any of the following –

(a) the Fair Trading Act 1973 (c. 41);
(b) the Consumer Credit Act 1974 (c. 39);
(c) the Estate Agents Act 1979 (c. 38);
(d) the Competition Act 1980 (c. 21);
(e) the Competition Act 1998 (c. 41);
(f) the Financial Services and Markets Act 2000 (c. 8);
(g) the Enterprise Act 2002 (c. 40);
(h) the Control of Misleading Advertisements Regulations 1988 (S.I. 1988/915);
(i) the Unfair Terms in Consumer Contracts Regulations 1999 (S.I. 1999/2083).

35 A disclosure for the purpose of enabling or assisting the Competition Commission to exercise its functions under any of the following –

(a) the Fair Trading Act 1973;
(b) the Competition Act 1980;
(c) the Competition Act 1998;
(d) the Enterprise Act 2002.

36 A disclosure with a view to the institution of, or otherwise for the purposes of, proceedings before the Competition Appeal Tribunal.

37 A disclosure for the purpose of enabling or assisting an enforcer under Part 8 of the Enterprise Act 2002 (enforcement of consumer legislation) to exercise its functions under that Part.

38 A disclosure for the purpose of enabling or assisting the Charity Commission to exercise its functions.

39 A disclosure for the purpose of enabling or assisting the Attorney General to exercise his functions in connection with charities.

40 A disclosure for the purpose of enabling or assisting the National Lottery Commission to exercise its functions under sections 5 to 10 (licensing) and 15

(power of Secretary of State to require information) of the National Lottery etc. Act 1993 (c. 39).

41   A disclosure by the National Lottery Commission to the National Audit Office for the purpose of enabling or assisting the Comptroller and Auditor General to carry out an examination under Part 2 of the National Audit Act 1983 (c. 44) into the economy, effectiveness and efficiency with which the National Lottery Commission has used its resources in discharging its functions under sections 5 to 10 of the National Lottery etc. Act 1993.

42   A disclosure for the purpose of enabling or assisting a qualifying body under the Unfair Terms in Consumer Contracts Regulations 1999 (S.I. 1999/2083) to exercise its functions under those Regulations.

43   A disclosure for the purpose of enabling or assisting an enforcement authority under the Consumer Protection (Distance Selling) Regulations 2000 (S.I. 2000/2334) to exercise its functions under those Regulations.

44   A disclosure for the purpose of enabling or assisting an enforcement authority under the Financial Services (Distance Marketing) Regulations 2004 (S.I. 2004/2095) to exercise its functions under those Regulations.

45   A disclosure for the purpose of enabling or assisting a local weights and measures authority in England and Wales to exercise its functions under section 230(2) of the Enterprise Act 2002 (c. 40) (notice of intention to prosecute, etc).

46   A disclosure for the purpose of enabling or assisting the Financial Services Authority to exercise its functions under any of the following –

(a)   the legislation relating to friendly societies or to industrial and provident societies;

(b)   the Building Societies Act 1986 (c. 53);

(c)   Part 7 of the Companies Act 1989 (c. 40) (financial markets and insolvency);

(d)   the Financial Services and Markets Act 2000 (c. 8).

47   A disclosure for the purpose of enabling or assisting the competent authority for the purposes of Part 6 of the Financial Services and Markets Act 2000 (official listing) to exercise its functions under that Part.

48   A disclosure for the purpose of enabling or assisting a body corporate established in accordance with section 212(1) of the Financial Services and Markets Act 2000 (compensation scheme manager) to exercise its functions.

49   A disclosure for the purpose of enabling or assisting a recognised investment exchange or a recognised clearing house to exercise its functions as such.
"Recognised investment exchange" and "recognised clearing house" have the same meaning as in section 285 of the Financial Services and Markets Act 2000.

50   A disclosure for the purpose of enabling or assisting a person approved under the Uncertificated Securities Regulations 2001 (S.I. 2001/3755) as an operator of a relevant system (within the meaning of those regulations) to exercise his functions.

51   A disclosure for the purpose of enabling or assisting a body designated under section 326(1) of the Financial Services and Markets Act 2000 (designated professional bodies) to exercise its functions in its capacity as a body designated under that section.

52   A disclosure with a view to the institution of, or otherwise for the purposes of, civil proceedings arising under or by virtue of the Financial Services and Markets Act 2000.

53   A disclosure for the purpose of enabling or assisting a body designated by order under section 1252 of this Act (delegation of functions of Secretary of State) to exercise its functions under Part 42 of this Act (statutory auditors).
Until the coming into force of that Part, the references to section 1252 and Part 42 are to be read as references to section 46 of the Companies Act 1989 (c. 40) and Part 2 of that Act respectively.

54   A disclosure for the purpose of enabling or assisting a recognised supervisory or qualifying body, within the meaning of Part 42 of this Act, to exercise its functions as such.

Until the coming into force of that Part, the reference to it is to be read as a reference to Part 2 of the Companies Act 1989.

55 A disclosure for the purpose of enabling or assisting an official receiver (including the Accountant in Bankruptcy in Scotland and the Official Assignee in Northern Ireland) to exercise his functions under the enactments relating to insolvency.

56 A disclosure for the purpose of enabling or assisting the Insolvency Practitioners Tribunal to exercise its functions under the Insolvency Act 1986 (c. 45).

57 A disclosure for the purpose of enabling or assisting a body that is for the time being a recognised professional body for the purposes of section 391 of the Insolvency Act 1986 (recognised professional bodies) to exercise its functions as such.

58 A disclosure for the purpose of enabling or assisting an overseas regulatory authority to exercise its regulatory functions.
    "Overseas regulatory authority" and "regulatory functions" have the same meaning as in section 82 of the Companies Act 1989.

59 A disclosure for the purpose of enabling or assisting the Regulator of Community Interest Companies to exercise functions under the Companies (Audit, Investigations and Community Enterprise) Act 2004 (c. 27).

60 A disclosure with a view to the institution of, or otherwise for the purposes of, criminal proceedings.

61 A disclosure for the purpose of enabling or assisting a person authorised by the Secretary of State under Part 2, 3 or 4 of the Proceeds of Crime Act 2002 (c. 29) to exercise his functions.

62 A disclosure with a view to the institution of, or otherwise for the purposes of, proceedings on an application under section 6, 7 or 8 of the Company Directors Disqualification Act 1986 (c. 46) (disqualification for unfitness).

63 A disclosure with a view to the institution of, or otherwise for the purposes of, proceedings before the Financial Services and Markets Tribunal.

64 A disclosure for the purposes of proceedings before the Financial Services Tribunal by virtue of the Financial Services and Markets Act 2000 (Transitional Provisions) (Partly Completed Procedures) Order 2001 (S.I. 2001/3592).

65 A disclosure for the purposes of proceedings before the Pensions Regulator Tribunal.

66 A disclosure for the purpose of enabling or assisting a body appointed under section 14 of the Companies (Audit, Investigations and Community Enterprise) Act 2004 (supervision of periodic accounts and reports of issuers of listed securities) to exercise functions mentioned in subsection (2) of that section.

67 A disclosure with a view to the institution of, or otherwise for the purposes of, disciplinary proceedings relating to the performance by a solicitor, barrister, advocate, foreign lawyer, auditor, accountant, valuer or actuary of his professional duties.
    "Foreign lawyer" has the meaning given by section 89(9) of the Courts and Legal Services Act 1990 (c. 41).

68 A disclosure with a view to the institution of, or otherwise for the purposes of, disciplinary proceedings relating to the performance by a public servant of his duties.
    "Public servant" means an officer or employee of the Crown or of any public or other authority for the time being designated for the purposes of this paragraph by the Secretary of State by order subject to negative resolution procedure.

69 A disclosure for the purpose of the provision of a summary or collection of information framed in such a way as not to enable the identity of any person to whom the information relates to be ascertained.

70 A disclosure in pursuance of any Community obligation.

PART 3

OVERSEAS REGULATORY BODIES

71   A disclosure is made in accordance with this Part of this Schedule if –

   (a)   it is made to a person or body within paragraph 72, and

   (b)   it is made for the purpose of enabling or assisting that person or body to exercise the functions mentioned in that paragraph.

72   The persons or bodies that are within this paragraph are those exercising functions of a public nature, under legislation in any country or territory outside the United Kingdom, that appear to the Panel to be similar to its own functions or those of the Financial Services Authority.

73   In determining whether to disclose information to a person or body in accordance with this Part of this Schedule, the Panel must have regard to the following considerations –

   (a)   whether the use that the person or body is likely to make of the information is sufficiently important to justify making the disclosure;

   (b)   whether the person or body has adequate arrangements to prevent the information from being used or further disclosed otherwise than for the purposes of carrying out the functions mentioned in paragraph 72 or any other purposes substantially similar to those for which information disclosed to the Panel could be used or further disclosed.

SCHEDULE 3

Section 1124

AMENDMENTS OF REMAINING PROVISIONS OF THE COMPANIES ACT 1985 RELATING TO OFFENCES

Failure to give information about interests in shares etc

1   (1)   In subsection (3) of section 444 of the Companies Act 1985 (c. 6) (failure to give information requested by Secretary of State relating to interests in shares etc) for "is liable to imprisonment or a fine, or both" substitute "commits an offence".

   (2)   At the end of that section add –

      "(4)   A person guilty of an offence under this section is liable –

         (a)   on conviction on indictment, to imprisonment for a term not exceeding two years or a fine (or both);

         (b)   on summary conviction –

            (i)   in England and Wales, to imprisonment for a term not exceeding twelve months or to a fine not exceeding the statutory maximum (or both) and, for continued contravention, a daily default fine not exceeding one-fiftieth of the statutory maximum;

            (ii)   in Scotland or Northern Ireland, to imprisonment for a term not exceeding six months, or to a fine not exceeding the statutory maximum (or both) and, for continued contravention, a daily default fine not exceeding one-fiftieth of the statutory maximum.".

Obstruction of rights conferred by a warrant or failure to comply with requirement under section 448

2   (1)   In section 448(7) of the Companies Act 1985 (obstruction of rights conferred by or by virtue of warrant for entry and search of premises) omit the words "and liable to a fine." to the end.

(2)   After that provision insert –

"(7A)   A person guilty of an offence under this section is liable –

(a)   on conviction on indictment, to a fine;

(b)   on summary conviction, to a fine not exceeding the statutory maximum.".

Wrongful disclosure of information to which section 449 applies

3   (1)   Section 449 of the Companies Act 1985 (wrongful disclosure of information obtained in course of company investigation) is amended as follows.

(2)   For subsection (6)(a) and (b) substitute "is guilty of an offence."

(3)   After subsection (6) insert –

"(6A)   A person guilty of an offence under this section is liable –

(a)   on conviction on indictment, to imprisonment for a term not exceeding two years or a fine (or both);

(b)   on summary conviction –

(i)   in England and Wales, to imprisonment for a term not exceeding twelve months or to a fine not exceeding the statutory maximum (or both);

(ii)   in Scotland or Northern Ireland, to imprisonment for a term not exceeding six months, or to a fine not exceeding the statutory maximum (or both).".

(4)   Omit subsection (7).

Destruction, mutilation etc of company documents

4   (1)   For subsection (3) of section 450 of the Companies Act 1985 (offence of destroying, etc company documents) substitute –

"(3)   A person guilty of an offence under this section is liable –

(a)   on conviction on indictment, to imprisonment for a term not exceeding seven years or a fine (or both);

(b)   on summary conviction –

(i)   in England and Wales, to imprisonment for a term not exceeding twelve months or to a fine not exceeding the statutory maximum (or both);

(ii)   in Scotland or Northern Ireland, to imprisonment for a term not exceeding six months, or to a fine not exceeding the statutory maximum (or both).".

(2)   Omit subsection (4) of that section.

Provision of false information in purported compliance with section 447

5   (1)   For subsection (2) of section 451 of the Companies Act 1985 (c. 6) (provision of false information in response to requirement under section 447) substitute –

"(2)   A person guilty of an offence under this section is liable –

(a)   on conviction on indictment, to imprisonment for a term not exceeding two years or a fine (or both);

(b)   on summary conviction –

(i)   in England and Wales, to imprisonment for a term not exceeding twelve months or to a fine not exceeding the statutory maximum (or both);

(ii)   in Scotland or Northern Ireland, to imprisonment for a term not exceeding six months, or to a fine not exceeding the statutory maximum (or both).".

(2)   Omit subsection (3) of that section.

Obstruction of inspector, etc exercising power to enter and remain on premises

6   (1)   Section 453A of the Companies Act 1985 (obstruction of inspector etc exercising power to enter and remain on premises) is amended as follows.

(2)   For subsection (5)(a) and (b) substitute "is guilty of an offence."

(3)   After subsection (5) insert –

"(5A)   A person guilty of an offence under this section is liable –

(a)   on conviction on indictment, to a fine;

(b)   on summary conviction, to a fine not exceeding the statutory maximum.".

(4)   Omit subsection (6).

Attempted evasion of restrictions under Part 15

7   (1)   In subsection (1) of section 455 of the Companies Act 1985 (attempted evasion of restrictions under Part 15) for "is liable to a fine if he" substitute "commits an offence if he".

(2)   In subsection (2) of that section for the words "the company" to the end substitute "an offence is committed by –

(a)   the company, and

(b)   every officer of the company who is in default."

(3)   After that subsection insert –

"(2A)   A person guilty of an offence under this section is liable –

(a)   on conviction on indictment, to a fine;

(b)   on summary conviction, to a fine not exceeding the statutory maximum.".

SCHEDULE 4

Section 1144(1)

DOCUMENTS AND INFORMATION SENT OR SUPPLIED TO A COMPANY

PART 1

INTRODUCTION

Application of Schedule

1   (1) This Schedule applies to documents or information sent or supplied to a company.

(2) It does not apply to documents or information sent or supplied by another company (see section 1144(3) and Schedule 5).

PART 2

COMMUNICATIONS IN HARD COPY FORM

Introduction

2   A document or information is validly sent or supplied to a company if it is sent or supplied in hard copy form in accordance with this Part of this Schedule.

Method of communication in hard copy form

3   (1) A document or information in hard copy form may be sent or supplied by hand or by post to an address (in accordance with paragraph 4).

(2) For the purposes of this Schedule, a person sends a document or information by post if he posts a prepaid envelope containing the document or information.

Address for communications in hard copy form

4   A document or information in hard copy form may be sent or supplied –

(a) to an address specified by the company for the purpose;

(b) to the company's registered office;

(c) to an address to which any provision of the Companies Acts authorises the document or information to be sent or supplied.

PART 3

COMMUNICATIONS IN ELECTRONIC FORM

Introduction

5   A document or information is validly sent or supplied to a company if it is sent or supplied in electronic form in accordance with this Part of this Schedule.

Conditions for use of communications in electronic form

6   A document or information may only be sent or supplied to a company in electronic form if –

(a)   the company has agreed (generally or specifically) that the document or information may be sent or supplied in that form (and has not revoked that agreement), or

(b)   the company is deemed to have so agreed by a provision in the Companies Acts.

Address for communications in electronic form

7   (1)   Where the document or information is sent or supplied by electronic means, it may only be sent or supplied to an address –

(a)   specified for the purpose by the company (generally or specifically), or

(b)   deemed by a provision in the Companies Acts to have been so specified.

(2)   Where the document or information is sent or supplied in electronic form by hand or by post, it must be sent or supplied to an address to which it could be validly sent if it were in hard copy form.

PART 4

OTHER AGREED FORMS OF COMMUNICATION

8   A document or information that is sent or supplied to a company otherwise than in hard copy form or electronic form is validly sent or supplied if it is sent or supplied in a form or manner that has been agreed by the company.

SCHEDULE 5

Section 1144(2)

COMMUNICATIONS BY A COMPANY

PART 1

INTRODUCTION

Application of this Schedule

1   This Schedule applies to documents or information sent or supplied by a company.

PART 2

COMMUNICATIONS IN HARD COPY FORM

Introduction

2   A document or information is validly sent or supplied by a company if it is sent or supplied in hard copy form in accordance with this Part of this Schedule.

Method of communication in hard copy form

3   (1) A document or information in hard copy form must be –

   (a) handed to the intended recipient, or
   (b) sent or supplied by hand or by post to an address (in accordance with paragraph 4).

   (2) For the purposes of this Schedule, a person sends a document or information by post if he posts a prepaid envelope containing the document or information.

Address for communications in hard copy form

4   (1) A document or information in hard copy form may be sent or supplied by the company –

   (a) to an address specified for the purpose by the intended recipient;
   (b) to a company at its registered office;
   (c) to a person in his capacity as a member of the company at his address as shown in the company's register of members;
   (d) to a person in his capacity as a director of the company at his address as shown in the company's register of directors;
   (e) to an address to which any provision of the Companies Acts authorises the document or information to be sent or supplied.

   (2) Where the company is unable to obtain an address falling within sub-paragraph (1), the document or information may be sent or supplied to the intended recipient's last address known to the company.

PART 3

COMMUNICATIONS IN ELECTRONIC FORM

Introduction

5   A document or information is validly sent or supplied by a company if it is sent in electronic form in accordance with this Part of this Schedule.

Agreement to communications in electronic form

6   A document or information may only be sent or supplied by a company in electronic form –
   (a) to a person who has agreed (generally or specifically) that the document or information may be sent or supplied in that form (and has not revoked that agreement), or
   (b) to a company that is deemed to have so agreed by a provision in the Companies Acts.

Address for communications in electronic form

7   (1) Where the document or information is sent or supplied by electronic means, it may only be sent or supplied to an address –
      (a) specified for the purpose by the intended recipient (generally or specifically), or
      (b) where the intended recipient is a company, deemed by a provision of the Companies Acts to have been so specified.
   (2) Where the document or information is sent or supplied in electronic form by hand or by post, it must be –
      (a) handed to the intended recipient, or
      (b) sent or supplied to an address to which it could be validly sent if it were in hard copy form.

PART 4

COMMUNICATIONS BY MEANS OF A WEBSITE

Use of website

8   A document or information is validly sent or supplied by a company if it is made available on a website in accordance with this Part of this Schedule.

Agreement to use of website

9   A document or information may only be sent or supplied by the company to a person by being made available on a website if the person –
   (a) has agreed (generally or specifically) that the document or information may be sent or supplied to him in that manner, or
   (b) is taken to have so agreed under –

(i)   paragraph 10 (members of the company etc), or

(ii)   paragraph 11 (debenture holders),

and has not revoked that agreement.

Deemed agreement of members of company etc to use of website

10   (1)   This paragraph applies to a document or information to be sent or supplied to a person –

(a)   as a member of the company, or

(b)   as a person nominated by a member in accordance with the company's articles to enjoy or exercise all or any specified rights of the member in relation to the company, or

(c)   as a person nominated by a member under section 146 to enjoy information rights.

(2)   To the extent that –

(a)   the members of the company have resolved that the company may send or supply documents or information to members by making them available on a website, or

(b)   the company's articles contain provision to that effect,

a person in relation to whom the following conditions are met is taken to have agreed that the company may send or supply documents or information to him in that manner.

(3)   The conditions are that –

(a)   the person has been asked individually by the company to agree that the company may send or supply documents or information generally, or the documents or information in question, to him by means of a website, and

(b)   the company has not received a response within the period of 28 days beginning with the date on which the company's request was sent.

(4)   A person is not taken to have so agreed if the company's request –

(a)   did not state clearly what the effect of a failure to respond would be, or

(b)   was sent less than twelve months after a previous request made to him for the purposes of this paragraph in respect of the same or a similar class of documents or information.

(5)   Chapter 3 of Part 3 (resolutions affecting a company's constitution) applies to a resolution under this paragraph.

Deemed agreement of debenture holders to use of website

11   (1)   This paragraph applies to a document or information to be sent or supplied to a person as holder of a company's debentures.

(2)   To the extent that –

(a)   the relevant debenture holders have duly resolved that the company may send or supply documents or information to them by making them available on a website, or

(b)   the instrument creating the debenture in question contains provision to that effect,

a debenture holder in relation to whom the following conditions are met is taken to have agreed that the company may send or supply documents or information to him in that manner.

(3)   The conditions are that –

(a) the debenture holder has been asked individually by the company to agree that the company may send or supply documents or information generally, or the documents or information in question, to him by means of a website, and

(b) the company has not received a response within the period of 28 days beginning with the date on which the company's request was sent.

(4) A person is not taken to have so agreed if the company's request –

(a) did not state clearly what the effect of a failure to respond would be, or

(b) was sent less than twelve months after a previous request made to him for the purposes of this paragraph in respect of the same or a similar class of documents or information.

(5) For the purposes of this paragraph –

(a) the relevant debenture holders are the holders of debentures of the company ranking *pari passu* for all purposes with the intended recipient, and

(b) a resolution of the relevant debenture holders is duly passed if they agree in accordance with the provisions of the instruments creating the debentures.

Availability of document or information

12 (1) A document or information authorised or required to be sent or supplied by means of a website must be made available in a form, and by a means, that the company reasonably considers will enable the recipient –

(a) to read it, and

(b) to retain a copy of it.

(2) For this purpose a document or information can be read only if –

(a) it can be read with the naked eye, or

(b) to the extent that it consists of images (for example photographs, pictures, maps, plans or drawings), it can be seen with the naked eye.

Notification of availability

13 (1) The company must notify the intended recipient of –

(a) the presence of the document or information on the website,

(b) the address of the website,

(c) the place on the website where it may be accessed, and

(d) how to access the document or information.

(2) The document or information is taken to be sent –

(a) on the date on which the notification required by this paragraph is sent, or

(b) if later, the date on which the document or information first appears on the website after that notification is sent.

Period of availability on website

14 (1) The company must make the document or information available on the website throughout –

(a) the period specified by any applicable provision of the Companies Acts, or

(b) if no such period is specified, the period of 28 days beginning with the date on which the notification required under paragraph 13 is sent to the person in question.

(2) For the purposes of this paragraph, a failure to make a document or information available on a website throughout the period mentioned in sub-paragraph (1) shall be disregarded if –

(a)   it is made available on the website for part of that period, and

(b)   the failure to make it available throughout that period is wholly attributable to circumstances that it would not be reasonable to have expected the company to prevent or avoid.

PART 5

OTHER AGREED FORMS OF COMMUNICATION

15   A document or information that is sent or supplied otherwise than in hard copy or electronic form or by means of a website is validly sent or supplied if it is sent or supplied in a form or manner that has been agreed by the intended recipient.

PART 6

SUPPLEMENTARY PROVISIONS

Joint holders of shares or debentures

16 (1)   This paragraph applies in relation to documents or information to be sent or supplied to joint holders of shares or debentures of a company.

(2)   Anything to be agreed or specified by the holder must be agreed or specified by all the joint holders.

(3)   Anything authorised or required to be sent or supplied to the holder may be sent or supplied either –

(a)   to each of the joint holders, or

(b)   to the holder whose name appears first in the register of members or the relevant register of debenture holders.

(4)   This paragraph has effect subject to anything in the company's articles.

Death or bankruptcy of holder of shares

17 (1)   This paragraph has effect in the case of the death or bankruptcy of a holder of a company's shares.

(2)   Documents or information required or authorised to be sent or supplied to the member may be sent or supplied to the persons claiming to be entitled to the shares in consequence of the death or bankruptcy –

(a)   by name, or

(b)   by the title of representatives of the deceased, or trustee of the bankrupt, or by any like description,

at the address in the United Kingdom supplied for the purpose by those so claiming.

(3)   Until such an address has been so supplied, a document or information may be

sent or supplied in any manner in which it might have been sent or supplied if the death or bankruptcy had not occurred.

(4) This paragraph has effect subject to anything in the company's articles.

(5) References in this paragraph to the bankruptcy of a person include –

(a) the sequestration of the estate of a person;

(b) a person's estate being the subject of a protected trust deed (within the meaning of the Bankruptcy (Scotland) Act 1985 (c. 66)).

In such a case the reference in sub-paragraph (2)(b) to the trustee of the bankrupt is to be read as the permanent or interim trustee (within the meaning of that Act) on the sequestrated estate or, as the case may be, the trustee under the protected deed.

SCHEDULE 6

Section 1159

MEANING OF "SUBSIDIARY" ETC: SUPPLEMENTARY PROVISIONS

Introduction

1   The provisions of this Part of this Schedule explain expressions used in section 1159 (meaning of "subsidiary" etc) and otherwise supplement that section.

Voting rights in a company

2   In section 1159(1)(a) and (c) the references to the voting rights in a company are to the rights conferred on shareholders in respect of their shares or, in the case of a company not having a share capital, on members, to vote at general meetings of the company on all, or substantially all, matters.

Right to appoint or remove a majority of the directors

3   (1) In section 1159(1)(b) the reference to the right to appoint or remove a majority of the board of directors is to the right to appoint or remove directors holding a majority of the voting rights at meetings of the board on all, or substantially all, matters.

(2) A company shall be treated as having the right to appoint to a directorship if –

(a) a person's appointment to it follows necessarily from his appointment as director of the company, or

(b) the directorship is held by the company itself.

(3) A right to appoint or remove which is exercisable only with the consent or concurrence of another person shall be left out of account unless no other person has a right to appoint or, as the case may be, remove in relation to that directorship.

Rights exercisable only in certain circumstances or temporarily incapable of exercise

4   (1) Rights which are exercisable only in certain circumstances shall be taken into account only –

(a) when the circumstances have arisen, and for so long as they continue to obtain, or

(b) when the circumstances are within the control of the person having the rights.

(2) Rights which are normally exercisable but are temporarily incapable of exercise shall continue to be taken into account.

Rights held by one person on behalf of another

5   Rights held by a person in a fiduciary capacity shall be treated as not held by him.

6   (1) Rights held by a person as nominee for another shall be treated as held by the other.

(2) Rights shall be regarded as held as nominee for another if they are exercisable only on his instructions or with his consent or concurrence.

Rights attached to shares held by way of security

7   Rights attached to shares held by way of security shall be treated as held by the person providing the security –

(a) where apart from the right to exercise them for the purpose of preserving the value of the security, or of realising it, the rights are exercisable only in accordance with his instructions, and

(b) where the shares are held in connection with the granting of loans as part of normal business activities and apart from the right to exercise them for the purpose of preserving the value of the security, or of realising it, the rights are exercisable only in his interests.

Rights attributed to holding company

8   (1) Rights shall be treated as held by a holding company if they are held by any of its subsidiary companies.

(2) Nothing in paragraph 6 or 7 shall be construed as requiring rights held by a holding company to be treated as held by any of its subsidiaries.

(3) For the purposes of paragraph 7 rights shall be treated as being exercisable in accordance with the instructions or in the interests of a company if they are exercisable in accordance with the instructions of or, as the case may be, in the interests of –

(a) any subsidiary or holding company of that company, or

(b) any subsidiary of a holding company of that company.

Disregard of certain rights

9   The voting rights in a company shall be reduced by any rights held by the company itself.

Supplementary

10   References in any provision of paragraphs 5 to 9 to rights held by a person include rights falling to be treated as held by him by virtue of any other provision of those paragraphs but not rights which by virtue of any such provision are to be treated as not held by him.

SCHEDULE 7

Section 1162

PARENT AND SUBSIDIARY UNDERTAKINGS: SUPPLEMENTARY PROVISIONS

Introduction

1   The provisions of this Schedule explain expressions used in section 1162 (parent and subsidiary undertakings) and otherwise supplement that section.

Voting rights in an undertaking

2   (1)   In section 1162(2)(a) and (d) the references to the voting rights in an undertaking are to the rights conferred on shareholders in respect of their shares or, in the case of an undertaking not having a share capital, on members, to vote at general meetings of the undertaking on all, or substantially all, matters.

(2)   In relation to an undertaking which does not have general meetings at which matters are decided by the exercise of voting rights the references to holding a majority of the voting rights in the undertaking shall be construed as references to having the right under the constitution of the undertaking to direct the overall policy of the undertaking or to alter the terms of its constitution.

Right to appoint or remove a majority of the directors

3   (1)   In section 1162(2)(b) the reference to the right to appoint or remove a majority of the board of directors is to the right to appoint or remove directors holding a majority of the voting rights at meetings of the board on all, or substantially all, matters.

(2)   An undertaking shall be treated as having the right to appoint to a directorship if –

(a)   a person's appointment to it follows necessarily from his appointment as director of the undertaking, or

(b)   the directorship is held by the undertaking itself.

(3)   A right to appoint or remove which is exercisable only with the consent or concurrence of another person shall be left out of account unless no other person has a right to appoint or, as the case may be, remove in relation to that directorship.

Right to exercise dominant influence

4   (1)   For the purposes of section 1162(2)(c) an undertaking shall not be regarded as having the right to exercise a dominant influence over another undertaking unless it has a right to give directions with respect to the operating and financial policies of that other undertaking which its directors are obliged to comply with whether or not they are for the benefit of that other undertaking.

(2)   A "control contract" means a contract in writing conferring such a right which –

(a)   is of a kind authorised by the articles of the undertaking in relation to which the right is exercisable, and

(b)   is permitted by the law under which that undertaking is established.

(3) This paragraph shall not be read as affecting the construction of section 1162(4)(a).

Rights exercisable only in certain circumstances or temporarily incapable of exercise

5   (1) Rights which are exercisable only in certain circumstances shall be taken into account only –

    (a) when the circumstances have arisen, and for so long as they continue to obtain, or

    (b) when the circumstances are within the control of the person having the rights.

    (2) Rights which are normally exercisable but are temporarily incapable of exercise shall continue to be taken into account.

Rights held by one person on behalf of another

6   Rights held by a person in a fiduciary capacity shall be treated as not held by him.

7   (1) Rights held by a person as nominee for another shall be treated as held by the other.

    (2) Rights shall be regarded as held as nominee for another if they are exercisable only on his instructions or with his consent or concurrence.

Rights attached to shares held by way of security

8   Rights attached to shares held by way of security shall be treated as held by the person providing the security –

    (a) where apart from the right to exercise them for the purpose of preserving the value of the security, or of realising it, the rights are exercisable only in accordance with his instructions, and

    (b) where the shares are held in connection with the granting of loans as part of normal business activities and apart from the right to exercise them for the purpose of preserving the value of the security, or of realising it, the rights are exercisable only in his interests.

Rights attributed to parent undertaking

9   (1) Rights shall be treated as held by a parent undertaking if they are held by any of its subsidiary undertakings.

    (2) Nothing in paragraph 7 or 8 shall be construed as requiring rights held by a parent undertaking to be treated as held by any of its subsidiary undertakings.

    (3) For the purposes of paragraph 8 rights shall be treated as being exercisable in accordance with the instructions or in the interests of an undertaking if they are exercisable in accordance with the instructions of or, as the case may be, in the interests of any group undertaking.

Disregard of certain rights

10   The voting rights in an undertaking shall be reduced by any rights held by the undertaking itself.

Supplementary

11 References in any provision of paragraphs 6 to 10 to rights held by a person include rights falling to be treated as held by him by virtue of any other provision of those paragraphs but not rights which by virtue of any such provision are to be treated as not held by him.

SCHEDULE 8

Section 1174

INDEX OF DEFINED EXPRESSIONS

abbreviated accounts (in Part 15)	sections 444(4) and 445(3)
accounting reference date and accounting reference period	section 391
accounting standards (in Part 15)	section 464
accounts meeting	section 437(3)
acquisition, in relation to a non-cash asset	section 1163(2)
address	
– generally in the Companies Acts	section 1142
– in the company communications provisions	section 1148(1)
affirmative resolution procedure, in relation to regulations and orders	section 1290
allotment (time of)	section 558
allotment of equity securities (in Chapter 3 of Part 17)	section 560(2)
allotted share capital and allotted shares	section 546(1)(b) and (2)
annual accounts (in Part 15)	section 471
annual accounts and reports (in Part 15)	section 471
annual general meeting	section 336
annual return	section 854
appropriate audit authority (in sections 522, 523 and 524)	section 525(1)
appropriate rate of interest	
– in Chapter 5 of Part 17	section 592
– in Chapter 6 of Part 17	section 609
approval after being made, in relation to regulations and orders	section 1291
arrangement	
– in Chapter 7 of Part 17	section 616(1)
– in Part 26	section 895(2)
articles	section 18
associate (in Chapter 3 of Part 28)	section 988
associated bodies corporate and associated company (in Part 10)	section 256
authenticated, in relation to a document or information sent or supplied to a company	section 1146
authorised group, of members of a company (in Part 14)	section 370(3)
authorised insurance company	section 1165(2)
authorised minimum (in relation to share capital of public company)	section 763
available profits (in Chapter 5 of Part 18)	sections 711 and 712
banking company and banking group	section 1164
body corporate	section 1173(1)
called-up share capital	section 547
capital redemption reserve	section 733

capitalisation in relation to a company's profits (in Part 23)	section 853(3)
cash (in relation to paying up or allotting shares)	section 583
cause of action, in relation to derivative proceedings (in Chapter 2 of Part 11)	section 265(7)
certified translation (in Part 35)	section 1107
charge (in Chapter 1 of Part 25)	section 861(5)
circulation date, in relation to a written resolution (in Part 13)	section 290
class of shares	section 629
the Companies Acts	section 2
Companies Act accounts	sections 395(1)(a) and 403(2)(a)
Companies Act group accounts	section 403(2)(a)
Companies Act individual accounts	section 395(1)(a)
companies involved in the division (in Part 27)	section 919(2)
company	
– generally in the Companies Acts	section 1
– in Chapter 7 of Part 17	section 616(1)
– in Chapter 1 of Part 25	section 861(5)
– in Chapter 2 of Part 25	section 879(6)
– in Part 26	section 895(2)
– in Chapter 3 of Part 28	section 991(1)
– in the company communications provisions	section 1148(1)
the company communications provisions	section 1143
the company law provisions of this Act	section 2(2)
company records (in Part 37)	section 1134
connected with, in relation to a director (in Part 10)	sections 252 to 254
constitution, of a company	
– generally in the Companies Acts	section 17
– in Part 10	section 257
controlling, of a body corporate by a director (in Part 10)	section 255
corporation	section 1173(1)
the court	section 1156
credit institution	section 1173(1)
credit transaction (in Chapter 4 of Part 10)	section 202
creditor (in Chapter 1 of Part 31)	section 1011
daily default fine	section 1125
date of the offer (in Chapter 3 of Part 28)	section 991(1)
debenture	section 738
derivative claim (in Chapter 1 of Part 11)	section 260
derivative proceedings (in Chapter 2 of Part 11)	section 265
Directive disclosure requirements	section 1078
director	
– generally in the Companies Acts	section 250
– in Chapter 8 of Part 10	section 240(3)
– in Chapter 1 of Part 11	section 260(5)
– in Chapter 2 of Part 11	section 265(7)
– in Part 14	section 379(1)
directors' remuneration report	section 420
directors' report	section 415
distributable profits	
– in Chapter 2 of Part 18	section 683(1)
– elsewhere in Part 18	section 736
distribution	
– in Chapter 2 of Part 18	section 683(1)
– in Part 23	section 829

overseas branch register	section 129(1)
paid up	section 583
the Panel (in Part 28)	section 942
parent company	section 1173(1)
parent undertaking	section 1162 (and see Schedule 7)
payment for loss of office (in Chapter 4 of Part 10)	section 215
pension scheme (in Chapter 1 of Part 18)	section 675
period for appointing auditors, in relation to a private company	section 485(2)
period for filing, in relation to accounts and reports for a financial year	section 442
permissible capital payment (in Chapter 5 of Part 18)	section 710
political donation (in Part 14)	section 364
political expenditure (in Part 14)	section 365
political organisation (in Part 14)	section 363(2)
prescribed	section 1167
private company	section 4
profit and loss account (in Part 15)	section 474(1) and (2)
profits and losses (in Part 23)	section 853(2)
profits available for distribution (for the purposes of Part 23)	section 830(2)
property (in Part 27)	section 941
protected information (in Chapter 8 of Part 10)	section 240
provision for entrenchment, in relation to a company's articles	section 22
public company	section 4
publication, in relation to accounts and reports (in sections 433 to 435)	section 436
qualified, in relation to an auditor's report etc (in Part 16)	section 539
qualifying shares (in Chapter 6 of Part 18)	section 724(2)
qualifying third party indemnity provision (in Chapter 7 of Part 10)	section 234
qualifying pension scheme indemnity provision (in Chapter 7 of Part 10)	section 235
quasi-loan (in Chapter 4 of Part 10)	section 199
quoted company	
– in Part 13	section 361
– in Part 15	section 385
– in Chapter 5 of Part 16	section 531 (and section 385)
realised profits and losses (in Part 23)	section 853(4)
redeemable shares	section 684(1)
redenominate	section 622(1)
redenomination reserve	section 628
the register	section 1080
register of charges, kept by registrar	
– in England and Wales and Northern Ireland	section 869
– in Scotland	section 885
register of directors	section 162
register of directors' residential addresses	section 165
register of members	section 113
register of secretaries	section 275
registered number, of a branch of an overseas company	section 1067
registered number, of a company	section 1066
registered office, of a company	section 86
registrar and registrar of companies	section 1060

SCHEDULE 9

Section 1175

REMOVAL OF SPECIAL PROVISIONS ABOUT ACCOUNTS AND AUDIT OF CHARITABLE COMPANIES

PART 1

THE COMPANIES ACT 1985 (C. 6)

1   In section 240 (requirements in connection with publication of accounts) –

    (a)   in subsection (1) omit from "or, as the case may be," to "section 249A(2)";

    (b)   in subsection (3)(c) omit from "and, if no such report" to "any financial year";

    (c)   after subsection (3)(c) insert ", and";

    (d)   omit subsection (3)(e) and the ", and" preceding it;

    (e)   in the closing words of subsection (3) omit from "or any report" to "section 249A(2)".

2   In section 245 (voluntary revision of annual accounts or directors' report), in subsection (4)(b) omit "or reporting accountant".

3   In section 249A (exemptions from audit) –

    (a)   omit subsections (2), (3A) and (4);

(b) in subsection (6) for "figures for turnover or gross income" substitute "figure for turnover";

(c) in subsection (6A) omit "or (2)";

(d) in subsection (7) omit the definition of "gross income" and the ", and" preceding it.

4   In section 249B (cases where exemptions not available) –

(a) in the opening words of subsection (1) omit "or (2)";

(b) in subsection (1C)(b) omit from "where the company referred to" to "is not a charity";

(c) in subsection (3) omit "or (2)";

(d) in subsection (4), in the opening words and in paragraph (a), omit "or (2)".

5   Omit section 249C (report required for purposes of section 249A(2)).

6   Omit section 249D (the reporting accountant).

7   In section 249E (effect of exemptions) omit subsection (2).

8   In section 262A (index of defined expressions) omit the entry for "reporting accountant".

PART 2

THE COMPANIES (NORTHERN IRELAND) ORDER 1986 (S.I. 1986/1032 (N.I. 6)

9   In Article 248 (requirements in connection with publication of accounts) –

(a) in paragraph (1) omit from "or, as the case may be," to "Article 257A(2)";

(b) in paragraph (3)(c) omit from "and, if no such report" to "any such financial year";

(c) after paragraph (3)(c) insert ", and";

(d) omit paragraph (3)(e) and the word ", and" preceding it;

(e) in the closing words of paragraph (3) omit from "or any report" to "Article 257A(2)".

10   In Article 253 (voluntary revision of annual accounts or directors' report), in paragraph (4)(b) omit "or reporting accountant".

11   In Article 257A (exemptions from audit) –

(a) omit paragraphs (2), (3A) and (4);

(b) in paragraph (6) for "figures for turnover or gross income" substitute "figure for turnover";

(c) in paragraph (6A) omit "or (2)";

(d) in paragraph (7) omit the definition of "gross income" and the ", and" preceding it.

12   In Article 257B (cases where exemptions not available) –

(a) in the opening words of paragraph (1) omit "or (2)";

(b) in paragraph (1C)(b) omit from "where the company referred to" to "is not a charity";

(c) in paragraph (3) omit "or (2)";

(d) in paragraph (4), in the opening words and in sub-paragraph (a), omit "or (2)".

13   Omit Article 257C (report required for purposes of Article 257A(2)).

14   Omit Article 257D (the reporting accountant).

15   In Article 257E (effect of exemptions) omit paragraph (2).

16   In Article 270A (index of defined expressions) omit the entry for "reporting accountant".

SCHEDULE 10

Section 1217

RECOGNISED SUPERVISORY BODIES

PART 1

GRANT AND REVOCATION OF RECOGNITION OF A SUPERVISORY BODY

Application for recognition of supervisory body

1   (1)   A supervisory body may apply to the Secretary of State for an order declaring it to be a recognised supervisory body for the purposes of this Part of this Act ("a recognition order").

   (2)   Any such application must be –

      (a)   made in such manner as the Secretary of State may direct, and

      (b)   accompanied by such information as the Secretary of State may reasonably require for the purpose of determining the application.

   (3)   At any time after receiving an application and before determining it the Secretary of State may require the applicant to furnish additional information.

   (4)   The directions and requirements given or imposed under sub-paragraphs (2) and (3) may differ as between different applications.

   (5)   The Secretary of State may require any information to be furnished under this paragraph to be in such form or verified in such manner as he may specify.

   (6)   Every application must be accompanied by –

      (a)   a copy of the applicant's rules, and

      (b)   a copy of any guidance issued by the applicant in writing.

   (7)   The reference in sub-paragraph (6)(b) to guidance issued by the applicant is a reference to any guidance or recommendation –

      (a)   issued or made by it to all or any class of its members or persons seeking to become members,

      (b)   relevant for the purposes of this Part, and

      (c)   intended to have continuing effect,

   including any guidance or recommendation relating to the admission or expulsion of members of the body, so far as relevant for the purposes of this Part.

Grant and refusal of recognition

2   (1)   The Secretary of State may, on an application duly made in accordance with paragraph 1 and after being furnished with all such information as he may require under that paragraph, make or refuse to make a recognition order in respect of the applicant.

   (2)   The Secretary of State may make a recognition order only if it appears to him, from the information furnished by the body and having regard to any other information in his possession, that the requirements of Part 2 of this Schedule are satisfied in the case of that body.

   (3)   The Secretary of State may refuse to make a recognition order in respect of a body if he considers that its recognition is unnecessary having regard to the existence of one or more other bodies which –

    (a)   maintain and enforce rules as to the appointment and conduct of statutory auditors, and

    (b)   have been or are likely to be recognised.

(4)   Where the Secretary of State refuses an application for a recognition order he must give the applicant a written notice to that effect –

    (a)   specifying which requirements, in the opinion of the Secretary of State, are not satisfied, or

    (b)   stating that the application is refused on the ground mentioned in sub-paragraph (3).

(5)   A recognition order must state the date on which it takes effect.

Revocation of recognition

3   (1)   A recognition order may be revoked by a further order made by the Secretary of State if at any time it appears to him –

    (a)   that any requirement of Part 2 of this Schedule is not satisfied in the case of the body to which the recognition order relates ("the recognised body"),

    (b)   that the body has failed to comply with any obligation imposed on it by or by virtue of this Part of this Act, or

    (c)   that the continued recognition of the body is undesirable having regard to the existence of one or more other bodies which have been or are to be recognised.

(2)   An order revoking a recognition order must state the date on which it takes effect, which must be after the period of three months beginning with the date on which the revocation order is made.

(3)   Before revoking a recognition order the Secretary of State must –

    (a)   give written notice of his intention to do so to the recognised body,

    (b)   take such steps as he considers reasonably practicable for bringing the notice to the attention of the members of the body, and

    (c)   publish the notice in such manner as he thinks appropriate for bringing it to the attention of any other persons who are in his opinion likely to be affected.

(4)   A notice under sub-paragraph (3) must –

    (a)   state the reasons for which the Secretary of State proposes to act, and

    (b)   give particulars of the rights conferred by sub-paragraph (5).

(5)   A person within sub-paragraph (6) may, within the period of three months beginning with the date of service or publication of the notice under sub-paragraph (3) or such longer period as the Secretary of State may allow, make written representations to the Secretary of State and, if desired, oral representations to a person appointed for that purpose by the Secretary of State.

(6)   The persons within this sub-paragraph are –

    (a)   the recognised body on which a notice is served under sub-paragraph (3),

    (b)   any member of the body, and

    (c)   any other person who appears to the Secretary of State to be affected.

(7)   The Secretary of State must have regard to any representations made in accordance with sub-paragraph (5) in determining whether to revoke the recognition order.

(8)   If in any case the Secretary of State considers it essential to do so in the public interest he may revoke a recognition order without regard to the restriction imposed by sub-paragraph (2), even if –

    (a)   no notice has been given or published under sub-paragraph (3), or

(b)   the period of time for making representations in pursuance of such a notice has not expired.

(9)   An order revoking a recognition order may contain such transitional provision as the Secretary of State thinks necessary or expedient.

(10) A recognition order may be revoked at the request or with the consent of the recognised body and any such revocation is not subject to –

(a)   the restrictions imposed by sub-paragraphs (1) and (2), or

(b)   the requirements of sub-paragraphs (3) to (5) and (7).

(11) On making an order revoking a recognition order in respect of a body the Secretary of State must –

(a)   give written notice of the making of the order to the body,

(b)   take such steps as he considers reasonably practicable for bringing the making of the order to the attention of the members of the body, and

(c)   publish a notice of the making of the order in such manner as he thinks appropriate for bringing it to the attention of any other persons who are in his opinion likely to be affected.

Transitional provision

4   A recognition order made and not revoked under –

(a) paragraph 2(1) of Schedule 11 to the Companies Act 1989 (c. 40), or

(b) paragraph 2(1) of Schedule 11 to the Companies (Northern Ireland) Order 1990 (S.I. 1990/593 (N.I. 5)),

before the commencement of this Chapter of this Part of this Act is to have effect after the commencement of this Chapter as a recognition order made under paragraph 2(1) of this Schedule.

Orders not statutory instruments

5   Orders under this Part of this Schedule shall not be made by statutory instrument.

PART 2

REQUIREMENTS FOR RECOGNITION OF A SUPERVISORY BODY

Holding of appropriate qualification

6   (1)   The body must have rules to the effect that a person is not eligible for appointment as a statutory auditor unless –

(a)   in the case of an individual, he holds an appropriate qualification,

(b)   in the case of a firm –

(i)   each individual responsible for statutory audit work on behalf of the firm is eligible for appointment as a statutory auditor, and

(ii)   the firm is controlled by qualified persons (see paragraph 7 below).

(2)   Sub-paragraph (1) does not prevent the body from imposing more stringent requirements.

(3)   A firm which has ceased to comply with the conditions mentioned in sub-paragraph (1)(b) may be permitted to remain eligible for appointment as a statutory auditor for a period of not more than three months.

7   (1) This paragraph explains what is meant in paragraph 6(1)(b) by a firm being "controlled by qualified persons".

    (2) In this paragraph references to a person being qualified are –

        (a) in relation to an individual, to his holding –

            (i)   an appropriate qualification, or
            (ii) a corresponding qualification to audit accounts under the law of a member State, or part of a member State, other than the United Kingdom;

        (b) in relation to a firm, to its –

            (i)   being eligible for appointment as a statutory auditor, or
            (ii) being eligible for a corresponding appointment as an auditor under the law of a member State, or part of a member State, other than the United Kingdom.

    (3) A firm is to be treated as controlled by qualified persons if, and only if –

        (a) a majority of the members of the firm are qualified persons, and
        (b) where the firm's affairs are managed by a board of directors, committee or other management body, a majority of that body are qualified persons or, if the body consists of two persons only, at least one of them is a qualified person.

    (4) A majority of the members of a firm means –

        (a) where under the firm's constitution matters are decided upon by the exercise of voting rights, members holding a majority of the rights to vote on all, or substantially all, matters;
        (b) in any other case, members having such rights under the constitution of the firm as enable them to direct its overall policy or alter its constitution.

    (5) A majority of the members of the management body of a firm means –

        (a) where matters are decided at meetings of the management body by the exercise of voting rights, members holding a majority of the rights to vote on all, or substantially all, matters at such meetings;
        (b) in any other case, members having such rights under the constitution of the firm as enable them to direct its overall policy or alter its constitution.

    (6) Paragraphs 5 to 11 of Schedule 7 to this Act (rights to be taken into account and attribution of rights) apply for the purposes of this paragraph.

Auditors to be fit and proper persons

8   (1) The body must have adequate rules and practices designed to ensure that the persons eligible under its rules for appointment as a statutory auditor are fit and proper persons to be so appointed.

    (2) The matters which the body may take into account for this purpose in relation to a person must include –

        (a) any matter relating to any person who is or will be employed by or associated with him for the purposes of or in connection with statutory audit work;

        (b) in the case of a body corporate, any matter relating to –

            (i)   any director or controller of the body,
            (ii)   any other body corporate in the same group, or
            (iii) any director or controller of any such other body; and

        (c) in the case of a partnership, any matter relating to –

      (i)   any of the partners,

      (ii)   any director or controller of any of the partners,

      (iii) any body corporate in the same group as any of the partners, or

      (iv) any director or controller of any such other body.

(3) Where the person is a limited liability partnership, in sub-paragraph (2)(b) "director" is to be read as "member".

(4) In sub-paragraph (2)(b) and (c) "controller", in relation to a body corporate, means a person who either alone or with an associate or associates is entitled to exercise or control the exercise of 15% or more of the rights to vote on all, or substantially all, matters at general meetings of the body or another body corporate of which it is a subsidiary.

Professional integrity and independence

9   (1) The body must have adequate rules and practices designed to ensure that –

      (a)   statutory audit work is conducted properly and with integrity, and

      (b)   persons are not appointed as statutory auditors in circumstances in which they have an interest likely to conflict with the proper conduct of the audit.

(2) The body must participate in arrangements within paragraph 21, and the rules and practices mentioned in sub-paragraph (1) must include provision requiring compliance with any standards for the time being determined under such arrangements.

(3) The body must also have adequate rules and practices designed to ensure that no firm is eligible under its rules for appointment as a statutory auditor unless the firm has arrangements to prevent a person to whom sub-paragraph (4) applies from being able to exert any influence over the way in which a statutory audit is conducted in circumstances in which that influence would be likely to affect the independence or integrity of the audit.

(4) This sub-paragraph applies to –

      (a)   any individual who is not a qualified person within the meaning of paragraph 7, and

      (b)   any person who is not a member of the firm.

Technical standards

10 (1) The body must have rules and practices as to –

      (a)   the technical standards to be applied in statutory audit work, and

      (b)   the manner in which those standards are to be applied in practice.

(2) The body must participate in arrangements within paragraph 22, and the rules and practices mentioned in sub-paragraph (1) must include provision requiring compliance with any standards for the time being determined under such arrangements.

Procedures for maintaining competence

11   The body must have rules and practices designed to ensure that persons eligible under its rules for appointment as a statutory auditor continue to maintain an appropriate level of competence in the conduct of statutory audits.

Monitoring and enforcement

12 (1) The body must have adequate arrangements and resources for the effective monitoring and enforcement of compliance with its rules.

(2) The arrangements for monitoring may make provision for that function to be performed on behalf of the body (and without affecting its responsibility) by any other body or person who is able and willing to perform it.

Independent monitoring of audits of listed companies and other major bodies

13 (1) The body must –

(a) participate in arrangements within paragraph 23(1), and

(b) have rules designed to ensure that members of the body who perform any statutory audit functions in respect of major audits take such steps as may be reasonably required of them to enable their performance of any such functions to be monitored by means of inspections carried out under the arrangements.

(2) Any monitoring of such persons under the arrangements is to be regarded (so far as their performance of statutory audit functions in respect of major audits is concerned) as monitoring of compliance with the body's rules for the purposes of paragraph 12(1).

(3) In this paragraph –

"major audit" means a statutory audit conducted in respect of –

(a) a company any of whose securities have been admitted to the official list (within the meaning of Part 6 of the Financial Services and Markets Act 2000 (c. 8)), or

(b) any other person in whose financial condition there is a major public interest;

"statutory audit function" means any function performed as a statutory auditor.

Membership, eligibility and discipline

14 The rules and practices of the body relating to –

(a) the admission and expulsion of members,

(b) the grant and withdrawal of eligibility for appointment as a statutory auditor, and

(c) the discipline it exercises over its members,

must be fair and reasonable and include adequate provision for appeals.

Investigation of complaints

15 (1) The body must have effective arrangements for the investigation of complaints against –

(a) persons who are eligible under its rules for appointment as a statutory auditor, and

(b) the body in respect of matters arising out of its functions as a supervisory body.

(2) The arrangements mentioned in sub-paragraph (1) may make provision for the whole or part of that function to be performed by and to be the responsibility of a body or person independent of the body itself.

Independent investigation for disciplinary purposes of public interest cases

16 (1) The body must –

   (a) participate in arrangements within paragraph 24(1), and

   (b) have rules and practices designed to ensure that, where the designated persons have decided that any particular disciplinary action should be taken against a member of the body following the conclusion of an investigation under such arrangements, that decision is to be treated as if it were a decision made by the body in disciplinary proceedings against the member.

   (2) In sub-paragraph (1) "the designated persons" means the persons who, under the arrangements, have the function of deciding whether (and if so, what) disciplinary action should be taken against a member of the body in the light of an investigation carried out under the arrangements.

Meeting of claims arising out of audit work

17 (1) The body must have adequate rules or arrangements designed to ensure that persons eligible under its rules for appointment as a statutory auditor take such steps as may reasonably be expected of them to secure that they are able to meet claims against them arising out of statutory audit work.

   (2) This may be achieved by professional indemnity insurance or other appropriate arrangements.

Register of auditors and other information to be made available

18 The body must have rules requiring persons eligible under its rules for appointment as a statutory auditor to comply with any obligations imposed on them by –

   (a) requirements under section 1224 (Secretary of State's power to call for information);

   (b) regulations under section 1239 (the register of auditors);

   (c) regulations under section 1240 (information to be made available to the public).

Taking account of costs of compliance

19 The body must have satisfactory arrangements for taking account, in framing its rules, of the cost to those to whom the rules would apply of complying with those rules and any other controls to which they are subject.

Promotion and maintenance of standards

20 The body must be able and willing –

   (a) to promote and maintain high standards of integrity in the conduct of statutory audit work, and

   (b) to co-operate, by the sharing of information and otherwise, with the Secretary of State and any other authority, body or person having responsibility in the United Kingdom for the qualification, supervision or regulation of auditors.

PART 3

ARRANGEMENTS IN WHICH RECOGNISED SUPERVISORY BODIES ARE REQUIRED TO PARTICIPATE

Arrangements for setting standards relating to professional integrity and independence

21   The arrangements referred to in paragraph 9(2) are appropriate arrangements –

    (a) for the determining of standards for the purposes of the rules and practices mentioned in paragraph 9(1), and

    (b) for ensuring that the determination of those standards is done independently of the body.

Arrangements for setting technical standards

22   The arrangements referred to in paragraph 10(2) are appropriate arrangements –

    (a) for the determining of standards for the purposes of the rules and practices mentioned in paragraph 10(1), and

    (b) for ensuring that the determination of those standards is done independently of the body.

Arrangements for independent monitoring of audits of listed companies and other major bodies

23   (1)   The arrangements referred to in paragraph 13(1) are appropriate arrangements –

    (a) for enabling the performance by members of the body of statutory audit functions in respect of major audits to be monitored by means of inspections carried out under the arrangements, and

    (b) for ensuring that the carrying out of such monitoring and inspections is done independently of the body.

    (2)   In this paragraph "major audit" and "statutory audit function" have the same meaning as in paragraph 13.

Arrangements for independent investigation for disciplinary purposes of public interest cases

24   (1)   The arrangements referred to in paragraph 16(1) are appropriate arrangements –

    (a) for the carrying out of investigations into public interest cases arising in connection with the performance of statutory audit functions by members of the body,

    (b) for the holding of disciplinary hearings relating to members of the body which appear to be desirable following the conclusion of such investigations,

    (c) for requiring such hearings to be held in public except where the interests of justice otherwise require,

    (d) for the persons before whom such hearings have taken place to decide whether (and, if so, what) disciplinary action should be taken against the members to whom the hearings related, and

(e)   for ensuring that the carrying out of those investigations, the holding of those hearings and the taking of those decisions are done independently of the body.

(2)   In this paragraph –

"public interest cases" means matters which raise or appear to raise important issues affecting the public interest;

"statutory audit function" means any function performed as a statutory auditor.

Supplementary: arrangements to operate independently of body

25   (1)   This paragraph applies for the purposes of –

(a)   paragraph 21(b),

(b)   paragraph 22(b),

(c)   paragraph 23(1)(b), or

(d)   paragraph 24(1)(e).

(2)   Arrangements are not to be regarded as appropriate for the purpose of ensuring that a thing is done independently of the body unless they are designed to ensure that the body –

(a)   will have no involvement in the appointment or selection of any of the persons who are to be responsible for doing that thing, and

(b)   will not otherwise be involved in the doing of that thing.

(3)   Sub-paragraph (2) imposes a minimum requirement and does not preclude the possibility that additional criteria may need to be satisfied in order for the arrangements to be regarded as appropriate for the purpose in question.

Supplementary: funding of arrangements

26   The body must pay any of the costs of maintaining any arrangements within paragraph 21, 22, 23 or 24 which the arrangements provide are to be paid by it.

Supplementary: scope of arrangement

27   Arrangements may qualify as arrangements within any of paragraphs 21, 22, 23 and 24 even though the matters for which they provide are more extensive in any respect than those mentioned in the applicable paragraph.

SCHEDULE 11

Section 1220

RECOGNISED PROFESSIONAL QUALIFICATIONS

PART 1

GRANT AND REVOCATION OF RECOGNITION OF A PROFESSIONAL QUALIFICATION

Application for recognition of professional qualification

1   (1) A qualifying body may apply to the Secretary of State for an order declaring a qualification offered by it to be a recognised professional qualification for the purposes of this Part of this Act ("a recognition order").

(2) In this Part of this Act "a recognised qualifying body" means a qualifying body offering a recognised professional qualification.

(3) Any application must be –

    (a)   made in such manner as the Secretary of State may direct, and

    (b)   accompanied by such information as the Secretary of State may reasonably require for the purpose of determining the application.

(4) At any time after receiving an application and before determining it the Secretary of State may require the applicant to furnish additional information.

(5) The directions and requirements given or imposed under sub-paragraphs (3) and (4) may differ as between different applications.

(6) The Secretary of State may require any information to be furnished under this paragraph to be in such form or verified in such manner as he may specify.

(7) In the case of examination standards, the verification required may include independent moderation of the examinations over such a period as the Secretary of State considers necessary.

(8) Every application must be accompanied by –

    (a)   a copy of the applicant's rules, and

    (b)   a copy of any guidance issued by the applicant in writing.

(9) The reference in sub-paragraph (8)(b) to guidance issued by the applicant is a reference to any guidance or recommendation –

    (a)   issued or made by it to all or any class of persons holding or seeking to hold a qualification, or approved or seeking to be approved by the body for the purposes of giving practical training,

    (b)   relevant for the purposes of this Part of this Act, and

    (c)   intended to have continuing effect,

including any guidance or recommendation relating to a matter within sub-paragraph (10).

(10) The matters within this sub-paragraph are –

    (a)   admission to or expulsion from a course of study leading to a qualification,

    (b)   the award or deprivation of a qualification, and

    (c)   the approval of a person for the purposes of giving practical training or the withdrawal of such an approval,

so far as relevant for the purposes of this Part of this Act.

Grant and refusal of recognition

2   (1)   The Secretary of State may, on an application duly made in accordance with paragraph 1 and after being furnished with all such information as he may require under that paragraph, make or refuse to make a recognition order in respect of the qualification in relation to which the application was made.

(2)   The Secretary of State may make a recognition order only if it appears to him, from the information furnished by the applicant and having regard to any other information in his possession, that the requirements of Part 2 of this Schedule are satisfied in relation to the qualification.

(3)   Where the Secretary of State refuses an application for a recognition order he must give the applicant a written notice to that effect specifying which requirements, in his opinion, are not satisfied.

(4)   A recognition order must state the date on which it takes effect.

Revocation of recognition

3   (1)   A recognition order may be revoked by a further order made by the Secretary of State if at any time it appears to him –

(a)   that any requirement of Part 2 of this Schedule is not satisfied in relation to the qualification to which the recognition order relates, or

(b)   that the qualifying body has failed to comply with any obligation imposed on it by or by virtue of this Part of this Act.

(2)   An order revoking a recognition order must state the date on which it takes effect, which must be after the period of three months beginning with the date on which the revocation order is made.

(3)   Before revoking a recognition order the Secretary of State must –

(a)   give written notice of his intention to do so to the qualifying body,

(b)   take such steps as he considers reasonably practicable for bringing the notice to the attention of persons holding the qualification or in the course of studying for it, and

(c)   publish the notice in such manner as he thinks appropriate for bringing it to the attention of any other persons who are in his opinion likely to be affected.

(4)   A notice under sub-paragraph (3) must –

(a)   state the reasons for which the Secretary of State proposes to act, and

(b)   give particulars of the rights conferred by sub-paragraph (5).

(5)   A person within sub-paragraph (6) may, within the period of three months beginning with the date of service or publication or such longer period as the Secretary of State may allow, make written representations to the Secretary of State and, if desired, oral representations to a person appointed for that purpose by the Secretary of State.

(6)   The persons within this sub-paragraph are –

(a)   the qualifying body on which a notice is served under sub-paragraph (3),

(b)   any person holding the qualification or in the course of studying for it, and

(c)   any other person who appears to the Secretary of State to be affected.

(7)   The Secretary of State must have regard to any representations made in accordance with sub-paragraph (5) in determining whether to revoke the recognition order.

(8)   If in any case the Secretary of State considers it essential to do so in the public interest he may revoke a recognition order without regard to the restriction imposed by sub-paragraph (2), even if –

(a)   no notice has been given or published under sub-paragraph (3), or

(b)   the period of time for making representations in pursuance of such a notice has not expired.

(9) An order revoking a recognition order may contain such transitional provision as the Secretary of State thinks necessary or expedient.

(10) A recognition order may be revoked at the request or with the consent of the qualifying body and any such revocation is not subject to –

(a)   the restrictions imposed by sub-paragraphs (1) and (2), or

(b)   the requirements of sub-paragraphs (3) to (5) and (7).

(11) On making an order revoking a recognition order the Secretary of State must –

(a)   give written notice of the making of the order to the qualifying body,

(b)   take such steps as he considers reasonably practicable for bringing the making of the order to the attention of persons holding the qualification or in the course of studying for it, and

(c)   publish a notice of the making of the order in such manner as he thinks appropriate for bringing it to the attention of any other persons who are in his opinion likely to be affected.

Transitional provision

4   A recognition order made and not revoked under –

(a) paragraph 2(1) of Schedule 12 to the Companies Act 1989 (c. 40), or

(b) paragraph 2(1) of Schedule 12 to the Companies (Northern Ireland) Order 1990 (S.I. 1990/593 (N.I. 5)),

before the commencement of this Chapter of this Part of this Act is to have effect after the commencement of this Chapter as a recognition order made under paragraph 2(1) of this Schedule.

Orders not statutory instruments

5   Orders under this Part of this Schedule shall not be made by statutory instrument.

PART 2

REQUIREMENTS FOR RECOGNITION OF A PROFESSIONAL QUALIFICATION

Entry requirements

6   (1) The qualification must only be open to persons who –

(a)   have attained university entrance level, or

(b)   have a sufficient period of professional experience.

(2) In relation to a person who has not been admitted to a university or other similar establishment in the United Kingdom, "attaining university entrance level" means –

(a)   being educated to such a standard as would entitle him to be considered for such admission on the basis of –

(i)   academic or professional qualifications obtained in the United

Kingdom and recognised by the Secretary of State to be of an appropriate standard, or

(ii)   academic or professional qualifications obtained outside the United Kingdom which the Secretary of State considers to be of an equivalent standard, or

(b)   being assessed, on the basis of written tests of a kind appearing to the Secretary of State to be adequate for the purpose (with or without oral examination), as of such a standard of ability as would entitle him to be considered for such admission.

(3)   The assessment, tests and oral examination referred to in sub-paragraph (2)(b) may be conducted by –

(a)   the qualifying body, or

(b)   some other body approved by the Secretary of State.

(4)   The reference in sub-paragraph (1)(b) to "a sufficient period of professional experience" is to not less than seven years' experience in a professional capacity in the fields of finance, law and accountancy.

Requirement for theoretical instruction or professional experience

7   (1)   The qualification must be restricted to persons who –

(a)   have completed a course of theoretical instruction in the subjects prescribed for the purposes of paragraph 8, or

(b)   have a sufficient period of professional experience.

(2)   The reference in sub-paragraph (1)(b) to "a sufficient period of professional experience" is to not less than seven years' experience in a professional capacity in the fields of finance, law and accountancy.

Examination

8   (1)   The qualification must be restricted to persons who have passed an examination (at least part of which is in writing) testing –

(a)   theoretical knowledge of the subjects prescribed for the purposes of this paragraph by regulations made by the Secretary of State, and

(b)   ability to apply that knowledge in practice,

and requiring a standard of attainment at least equivalent to that required to obtain a degree from a university or similar establishment in the United Kingdom.

(2)   The qualification may be awarded to a person without his theoretical knowledge of a subject being tested by examination if he has passed a university or other examination of equivalent standard in that subject or holds a university degree or equivalent qualification in it.

(3)   The qualification may be awarded to a person without his ability to apply his theoretical knowledge of a subject in practice being tested by examination if he has received practical training in that subject which is attested by an examination or diploma recognised by the Secretary of State for the purposes of this paragraph.

(4)   Regulations under this paragraph are subject to negative resolution procedure.

Practical training

9   (1) The qualification must be restricted to persons who have completed at least three years' practical training of which –

    (a) part was spent being trained in statutory audit work, and

    (b) a substantial part was spent being trained in statutory audit work or other audit work of a description approved by the Secretary of State as being similar to statutory audit work.

  (2) For the purpose of sub-paragraph (1) "statutory audit work" includes the work of a person appointed as the auditor of a person under the law of a country or territory outside the United Kingdom where it appears to the Secretary of State that the law and practice with respect to the audit of accounts is similar to that in the United Kingdom.

  (3) The training must be given by persons approved by the body offering the qualification as persons whom the body is satisfied, in the light of undertakings given by them and the supervision to which they are subject (whether by the body itself or some other body or organisation), will provide adequate training.

  (4) At least two-thirds of the training must be given by a person –

    (a) eligible for appointment as a statutory auditor, or

    (b) eligible for a corresponding appointment as an auditor under the law of a member State, or part of a member State, other than the United Kingdom.

Supplementary provision with respect to a sufficient period of professional experience

10   (1) Periods of theoretical instruction in the fields of finance, law and accountancy may be deducted from the required period of professional experience, provided the instruction –

    (a) lasted at least one year, and

    (b) is attested by an examination recognised by the Secretary of State for the purposes of this paragraph;

but the period of professional experience may not be so reduced by more than four years.

  (2) The period of professional experience together with the practical training required in the case of persons satisfying the requirement in paragraph 7 by virtue of having a sufficient period of professional experience must not be shorter than the course of theoretical instruction referred to in that paragraph and the practical training required in the case of persons satisfying the requirement of that paragraph by virtue of having completed such a course.

The body offering the qualification

11   (1) The body offering the qualification must have –

    (a) rules and arrangements adequate to ensure compliance with the requirements of paragraphs 6 to 10, and

    (b) adequate arrangements for the effective monitoring of its continued compliance with those requirements.

  (2) The arrangements must include arrangements for monitoring –

    (a) the standard of the body's examinations, and

    (b) the adequacy of the practical training given by the persons approved by it for that purpose.

SCHEDULE 12

Section 1242

ARRANGEMENTS IN WHICH REGISTERED THIRD COUNTRY AUDITORS ARE REQUIRED TO PARTICIPATE

Arrangements for independent monitoring of audits of traded non-Community companies

1   (1)   The arrangements referred to in section 1242(1)(a) are appropriate arrangements –

    (a)   for enabling the performance by the registered third country auditor of third country audit functions to be monitored by means of inspections carried out under the arrangements, and

    (b)   for ensuring that the carrying out of such monitoring and inspections is done independently of the registered third country auditor.

    (2)   In this paragraph "third country audit function" means any function performed as a third country auditor.

Arrangements for independent investigations for disciplinary purposes

2   (1)   The arrangements referred to in section 1242(1)(b) are appropriate arrangements –

    (a)   for the carrying out of investigations into matters arising in connection with the performance of third country audit functions by the registered third country auditor,

    (b)   for the holding of disciplinary hearings relating to the registered third country auditor which appear to be desirable following the conclusion of such investigations,

    (c)   for requiring such hearings to be held in public except where the interests of justice otherwise require,

    (d)   for the persons before whom such hearings have taken place to decide whether (and, if so, what) disciplinary action should be taken against the registered third country auditor, and

    (e)   for ensuring that the carrying out of those investigations, the holding of those hearings and the taking of those decisions are done independently of the registered third country auditor.

    (2)   In this paragraph –

"disciplinary action" includes the imposition of a fine; and
"third country audit function" means any function performed as a third country auditor.

Supplementary: arrangements to operate independently of third country auditor

3   (1)   This paragraph applies for the purposes of –

    (a)   paragraph 1(1)(b), or

    (b)   paragraph 2(1)(e).

(2) Arrangements are not to be regarded as appropriate for the purpose of ensuring that a thing is done independently of the registered third country auditor unless they are designed to ensure that the registered third country auditor –

(a)   will have no involvement in the appointment or selection of any of the persons who are to be responsible for doing that thing, and

(b)   will not otherwise be involved in the doing of that thing.

(3) Sub-paragraph (2) imposes a minimum requirement and does not preclude the possibility that additional criteria may need to be satisfied in order for the arrangements to be regarded as appropriate for the purpose in question.

Supplementary: funding of arrangements

4   (1)   The registered third country auditor must pay any of the costs of maintaining any relevant arrangements which the arrangements provide are to be paid by it.

(2)   For this purpose "relevant arrangements" are arrangements within paragraph 1 or 2 in which the registered third country auditor is obliged to participate.

Supplementary: scope of arrangements

5   Arrangements may qualify as arrangements within either of paragraphs 1 and 2 even though the matters for which they provide are more extensive in any respect than those mentioned in the applicable paragraph.

Specification of particular arrangements by the Secretary of State

6   (1)   If there exist two or more sets of arrangements within paragraph 1 or within paragraph 2, the obligation of a registered third country auditor under section 1242(1)(a) or (b), as the case may be, is to participate in such set of arrangements as the Secretary of State may by order specify.

(2)   An order under sub-paragraph (1) is subject to negative resolution procedure.

SCHEDULE 13

Section 1252

SUPPLEMENTARY PROVISIONS WITH RESPECT TO DELEGATION ORDER

Operation of this Schedule

1   (1)   This Schedule has effect in relation to a body designated by a delegation order under section 1252 as follows –

(a)   paragraphs 2 to 12 have effect in relation to the body where it is established by the order;

(b)   paragraphs 2 and 6 to 11 have effect in relation to the body where it is an existing body;

(c)   paragraph 13 has effect in relation to the body where it is an existing body that is an unincorporated association.

(2)   In their operation in accordance with sub-paragraph (1)(b), paragraphs 2 and 6 apply only in relation to –

(a)   things done by or in relation to the body in or in connection with the exercise of functions transferred to it by the delegation order, and

(b)   functions of the body which are functions so transferred.

(3)   Any power conferred by this Schedule to make provision by order is a power to make provision by an order under section 1252.

Status

2   The body is not to be regarded as acting on behalf of the Crown and its members, officers and employees are not to be regarded as Crown servants.

Name, members and chairman

3   (1)   The body is to be known by such name as may be specified in the delegation order.

(2)   The body is to consist of such persons (not being less than eight) as the Secretary of State may appoint after such consultation as he thinks appropriate.

(3)   The chairman of the body is to be such person as the Secretary of State may appoint from among its members.

(4)   The Secretary of State may make provision by order as to –

(a)   the terms on which the members of the body are to hold and vacate office;

(b)   the terms on which a person appointed as chairman is to hold and vacate the office of chairman.

Financial provisions

4   (1)   The body must pay to its chairman and members such remuneration, and such allowances in respect of expenses properly incurred by them in the performance of their duties, as the Secretary of State may determine.

(2)   As regards any chairman or member in whose case the Secretary of State so determines, the body must pay or make provision for the payment of –

(a)   such pension, allowance or gratuity to or in respect of that person on his retirement or death, or

(b)   such contributions or other payment towards the provision of such a pension, allowance or gratuity,

as the Secretary of State may determine.

(3)   Where –

(a)   a person ceases to be a member of the body otherwise than on the expiry of his term of office, and

(b)   it appears to the Secretary of State that there are special circumstances which make it right for that person to receive compensation,

the body must make a payment to him by way of compensation of such amount as the Secretary of State may determine.

Proceedings

5   (1)   The delegation order may contain such provision as the Secretary of State considers appropriate with respect to the proceedings of the body.

(2)   The delegation order may, in particular –

(a)   authorise the body to discharge any functions by means of committees consisting wholly or partly of members of the body;

(b)   provide that the validity of proceedings of the body, or of any such committee, is not affected by any vacancy among the members or any defect in the appointment of any member.

Fees

6   (1)   The body may retain fees payable to it.

(2)   The fees must be applied for –

(a)   meeting the expenses of the body in discharging its functions, and

(b)   any purposes incidental to those functions.

(3)   Those expenses include any expenses incurred by the body on such staff, accommodation, services and other facilities as appear to it to be necessary or expedient for the proper performance of its functions.

(4)   In prescribing the amount of fees in the exercise of the functions transferred to it the body must prescribe such fees as appear to it sufficient to defray those expenses, taking one year with another.

(5)   Any exercise by the body of the power to prescribe fees requires the approval of the Secretary of State.

(6)   The Secretary of State may, after consultation with the body, by order vary or revoke any regulations prescribing fees made by the body.

Legislative functions

7   (1)   Regulations or an order made by the body in the exercise of the functions transferred to it must be made by instrument in writing, but not by statutory instrument.

(2)   The instrument must specify the provision of this Part of this Act under which it is made.

(3)   The Secretary of State may by order impose such requirements as he thinks necessary or expedient as to the circumstances and manner in which the body must consult on any regulations or order it proposes to make.

(4)   Nothing in this Part applies to make regulations or an order made by the body subject to negative resolution procedure or affirmative resolution procedure.

8   (1)   Immediately after an instrument is made it must be printed and made available to the public with or without payment.

(2)   A person is not to be taken to have contravened any regulation or order if he shows that at the time of the alleged contravention the instrument containing the regulation or order had not been made available as required by this paragraph.

9   (1)   The production of a printed copy of an instrument purporting to be made by the body on which is endorsed a certificate signed by an officer of the body authorised by it for the purpose and stating –

(a)   that the instrument was made by the body,

(b)   that the copy is a true copy of the instrument, and

(c)   that on a specified date the instrument was made available to the public as required by paragraph 8,

is evidence (or, in Scotland, sufficient evidence) of the facts stated in the certificate.

(2)   A certificate purporting to be signed as mentioned in sub-paragraph (1) is to be deemed to have been duly signed unless the contrary is shown.

(3)   Any person wishing in any legal proceedings to cite an instrument made by the body may require the body to cause a copy of it to be endorsed with such a certificate as is mentioned in this paragraph.

Report and accounts

10   (1)   The body must, at least once in each calendar year for which the delegation order is in force, make a report to the Secretary of State on –

(a)   the discharge of the functions transferred to it, and

(b)   such other matters as the Secretary of State may by order require.

(2)   The delegation order may modify sub-paragraph (1) as it has effect in relation to the calendar year in which the order comes into force or is revoked.

(3)   The Secretary of State must lay before Parliament copies of each report received by him under this paragraph.

(4)   The following provisions of this paragraph apply as follows –

(a)   sub-paragraphs (5) and (6) apply only where the body is established by the order, and

(b)   sub-paragraphs (7) and (8) apply only where the body is an existing body.

(5)   The Secretary of State may, with the consent of the Treasury, give directions to the body with respect to its accounts and the audit of its accounts.

(6)   A person may only be appointed as auditor of the body if he is eligible for appointment as a statutory auditor.

(7)   Unless the body is a company to which section 394 (duty to prepare individual company accounts) applies, the Secretary of State may, with the consent of the Treasury, give directions to the body with respect to its accounts and the audit of its accounts.

(8)   Whether or not the body is a company to which section 394 applies, the Secretary of State may direct that any provisions of this Act specified in the directions are to apply to the body, with or without any modifications so specified.

Other supplementary provisions

11   (1)   The transfer of a function to a body designated by a delegation order does not affect anything previously done in the exercise of the function transferred; and the resumption of a function so transferred does not affect anything previously done in exercise of the function resumed.

(2)   The Secretary of State may by order make such transitional and other supplementary provision as he thinks necessary or expedient in relation to the transfer or resumption of a function.

(3)   The provision that may be made in connection with the transfer of a function includes, in particular, provision –

(a)   for modifying or excluding any provision of this Part of this Act in its application to the function transferred;

(b)   for applying to the body designated by the delegation order, in connection with the function transferred, any provision applying to the Secretary of State which is contained in or made under any other enactment;

(c)   for the transfer of any property, rights or liabilities from the Secretary of State to that body;

(d)   for the carrying on and completion by that body of anything in the process of being done by the Secretary of State when the order takes effect;

(e)   for the substitution of that body for the Secretary of State in any instrument, contract or legal proceedings.

(4)   The provision that may be made in connection with the resumption of a function includes, in particular, provision –

(a)   for the transfer of any property, rights or liabilities from that body to the Secretary of State;

(b)   for the carrying on and completion by the Secretary of State of anything in the process of being done by that body when the order takes effect;

(c)   for the substitution of the Secretary of State for that body in any instrument, contract or legal proceedings.

12   Where a delegation order is revoked, the Secretary of State may by order make provision –

(a)   for the payment of compensation to persons ceasing to be employed by the body established by the delegation order;

(b)   as to the winding up and dissolution of the body.

13   (1)   This paragraph applies where the body is an unincorporated association.

(2)   Any relevant proceedings may be brought by or against the body in the name of any body corporate whose constitution provides for the establishment of the body.

(3)   In sub-paragraph (2) "relevant proceedings" means proceedings brought in or in connection with the exercise of any transferred function.

(4)   In relation to proceedings brought as mentioned in sub-paragraph (2), any reference in paragraph 11(3)(e) or (4)(c) to the body replacing or being replaced by the Secretary of State in any legal proceedings is to be read with the appropriate modifications.

SCHEDULE 14

Section 1264

STATUTORY AUDITORS: CONSEQUENTIAL AMENDMENTS

Companies (Audit, Investigations and Community Enterprise) Act 2004 (c. 27)

1   (1)   Section 16 of the Companies (Audit, Investigations and Community Enterprise) Act 2004 (c. 27) (grants to bodies concerned with accounting standards etc) is amended as follows.

(2)   In subsection (2) –

(a)   in paragraph (f) for "paragraph 17" to the end substitute "paragraph 21, 22, 23(1) or 24(1) of Schedule 10 to the Companies Act 2006;",

(b)   in paragraph (g) for "Part 2 of that Act" substitute "Part 42 of that Act".

(3)   In subsection (5), in the definition of "professional accountancy body" –

(a)   in paragraph (a) for "Part 2 of the Companies Act 1989 (c. 40)" substitute "Part 42 of the Companies Act 2006", and

(b)   in paragraph (b) for "section 32" substitute "section 1220".

SCHEDULE 15

Section 1272

TRANSPARENCY OBLIGATIONS AND RELATED MATTERS: MINOR AND CONSEQUENTIAL AMENDMENTS

PART 1

AMENDMENTS OF THE FINANCIAL SERVICES AND MARKETS ACT 2000

1   Part 6 of the Financial Services and Markets Act 2000 (listing and other matters) is amended as follows.

2   In section 73 (general duty of competent authority), after subsection (1) insert –

"(1A)   To the extent that those general functions are functions under or relating to transparency rules, subsection (1)(c) and (f) have effect as if the references to a regulated market were references to a market."

3   In section 73A (Part 6 Rules), after subsection (5) insert –

"(6)   Transparency rules and corporate governance rules are not listing rules, disclosure rules or prospectus rules, but are Part 6 rules."

4   For the cross-heading before section 90 substitute "*Compensation for false or misleading statements etc*".

5   For the heading to section 90 substitute "**Compensation for statements in listing particulars or prospectus**".

6   (1)   Section 91 (penalties for breach of Part 6 rules) is amended as follows.

      (2)   For subsection (1) substitute –

"(1)   If the competent authority considers that –

        (a)   an issuer of listed securities, or

        (b)   an applicant for listing,

has contravened any provision of listing rules, it may impose on him a penalty of such amount as it considers appropriate.

(1ZA)   If the competent authority considers that –

        (a)   an issuer who has requested or approved the admission of a financial instrument to trading on a regulated market,

        (b)   a person discharging managerial responsibilities within such an issuer, or

        (c)   a person connected with such a person discharging managerial responsibilities,

has contravened any provision of disclosure rules, it may impose on him a penalty of such amount as it considers appropriate.".

      (3)   After subsection (1A) insert –

"(1B)   If the competent authority considers –

        (a)   that a person has contravened –

            (i)   a provision of transparency rules or a provision otherwise made in accordance with the transparency obligations directive, or

            (ii)   a provision of corporate governance rules, or

        (b)   that a person on whom a requirement has been imposed

under section 89L (power to suspend or prohibit trading of securities in case of infringement of applicable transparency obligation), has contravened that requirement, it may impose on the person a penalty of such amount as it considers appropriate.".

(4) In subsection (2) for "(1)(a), (1)(b)(i) or (1A)" substitute "(1), (1ZA)(a), (1A) or (1B)".

7   In section 96B (persons discharging managerial responsibilities and connected persons) –

   (a) for the heading substitute "**Disclosure rules: persons responsible for compliance**";
   (b) in subsection (1) for "For the purposes of this Part" substitute "for the purposes of the provisions of this Part relating to disclosure rules".

8   In section 97(1) (appointment by the competent authority of persons to carry out investigations), for paragraphs (a) and (b) substitute –

"(a) there may have been a contravention of –

   (i)   a provision of this Part or of Part 6 rules, or
   (ii)   a provision otherwise made in accordance with the prospectus directive or the transparency obligations directive;

(b) a person who was at the material time a director of a person mentioned in section 91(1), (1ZA)(a), (1A) or (1B) has been knowingly concerned in a contravention by that person of –

   (i)   a provision of this Part or of Part 6 rules, or
   (ii)   a provision otherwise made in accordance with the prospectus directive or the transparency obligations directive;".

9   In section 99 (fees) after subsection (1B) insert –

"(1C)   Transparency rules may require the payment of fees to the competent authority in respect of the continued admission of financial instruments to trading on a regulated market.".

10   (1) Section 102A (meaning of "securities" etc) is amended as follows.
     (2) After subsection (3) insert –

     "(3A)   "Debt securities" has the meaning given in Article 2.1(b) of the transparency obligations directive.".

     (3) In subsection (3) (meaning of "transferable securities") for "the investment services directive" substitute "Directive 2004/39/EC of the European Parliament and of the Council on markets in financial instruments".
     (4) In subsection (6) (meaning of "issuer"), after paragraph (a) insert –

     "(aa)   in relation to transparency rules, means a legal person whose securities are admitted to trading on a regulated market or whose voting shares are admitted to trading on a UK market other than a regulated market, and in the case of depository receipts representing securities, the issuer is the issuer of the securities represented;".

11   (1) Section 103(1) (interpretation of Part 6) is amended as follows.
     (2) In the definition of "regulated market" for "Article 1.13 of the investment services directive" substitute "Article 4.1(14) of Directive 2004/39/EC of the European Parliament and of the Council on markets in financial instruments".
     (3) At the appropriate place insert –

     ""transparency rules" has the meaning given by section 89A(5);
     "voteholder information" has the meaning given by section 89B(3);".

12   In section 429(2) (Parliamentary control of statutory instruments: affirmative procedure) of the Financial Services and Markets Act 2000 (c. 8) after "section" insert "90B or".

PART 2

AMENDMENTS OF THE COMPANIES (AUDIT, INVESTIGATIONS AND COMMUNITY ENTERPRISE) ACT 2004

13   Chapter 2 of Part 1 of the Companies (Audit, Investigations and Community Enterprise) Act 2004 (accounts and reports) is amended as follows.

14   (1)   Section 14 (supervision of periodic accounts and reports of issuers of listed securities) is amended as follows.

    (2)   In subsection (2)(a) –

        (a)   for "listed" substitute "transferable";

        (b)   for "listing" substitute "Part 6".

    (3)   In subsection (3)(a) –

        (a)   for "listed" substitute "transferable";

        (b)   for "listing" substitute "Part 6".

    (4)   In subsection (7)(b) for "listed" substitute "transferable".

    (5)   In subsection (12) –

        (a)   for ""listed securities" and "listing rules" have" substitute ""Part 6 rules" has";

        (b)   for the definition of "issuer" substitute –

            ""issuer" has the meaning given by section 102A(6) of that Act;";

        (c)   in the definition of "periodic" for "listing" substitute "Part 6";

        (d)   at the end add –

            ""transferable securities" has the meaning given by section 102A(3) of that Act.".

15   (1)   Section 15 (application of certain company law provisions to bodies appointed under section 14) is amended as follows.

    (2)   In subsection (5)(a) –

        (a)   for "listed" substitute "transferable";

        (b)   for "listing" substitute "Part 6".

    (3)   In subsection (5B)(a) –

        (a)   for "listed" substitute "transferable";

        (b)   for "listing" substitute "Part 6".

    (4)   In subsection (6)(b) for ""listing rules" and "security"" substitute ""Part 6 rules" and "transferable securities"".

SCHEDULE 16

Section 1295

REPEALS

COMPANY LAW REPEALS (GREAT BRITAIN)

Short title and chapter	Extent of repeal

Companies Act 1985 (c. 6)	Sections 1 to 430F.
	In section 437 –
	  (a) in subsection (1), the second
	     sentence, and
	  (b) subsections (1B) and (1C).
	Section 438.
	In section 439 –
	  (a) in subsection (2), ", or is ordered
	     to pay the whole or any part of the
	     costs of proceedings brought under
	     section 438",
	  (b) subsections (3) and (7), and
	  (c) in subsection (8), "; and any such
	     liability imposed by subsection (2)
	     is (subject as mentioned above) a
	     liability also to indemnify all
	     persons against liability under
	     subsection (3)".
	Section 442(2).
	Section 446.
	In section 448(7), the words "and liable
	  to a fine." to the end.
	Section 449(7).
	Section 450(4).
	Section 451(3).
	In section 453(1A) –
	  (a) paragraph (b), and
	  (b) paragraph (d) and the word "and"
	     preceding it.
	Section 453A(6).
	Sections 458 to 461.
	Sections 651 to 746.
	Schedules 1 to 15B.
	Schedules 20 to 25.

Insolvency Act 1985 (c. 65)	Schedule 6.

Insolvency Act 1986 (c. 45)	In Schedule 13, in Part 1, the entries
	  relating to the following provisions of
	  the Companies Act 1985 –
	  (a) section 13(4),
	  (b) section 44(7),
	  (c) section 103(7),
	  (d) section 131(7),
	  (e) section 140(2),

	(f) section 156(3), (g) section 173(4), (h) section 196, (i) section 380(4), (j) section 461(6), (k) section 462(5), (l) section 463(2), (m) section 463(3), (n) section 464(6), (o) section 657(2), (p) section 658(1), and (q) section 711(2).
Building Societies Act 1986 (c. 53)	Section 102C(5).
Finance Act 1988 (c. 39)	In section 117(3), from the beginning to "that section";". In section 117(4), the words "and (3)".
Water Act 1989 (c. 15)	In Schedule 25, paragraph 71(3).
Companies Act 1989 (c. 40)	Sections 1 to 22. Section 56(5). Sections 57 and 58. Section 64(2). Section 66(3). Section 71. Sections 92 to 110. Sections 113 to 138. Section 139(1) to (3). Sections 141 to 143. Section 144(1) to (3) and (6). Section 207. Schedules 1 to 9. In Schedule 10, paragraphs 1 to 24. Schedules 15 to 17. In Schedule 18, paragraphs 32 to 38. In Schedule 19, paragraphs 1 to 9 and 11 to 21.
Age of Legal Capacity (Scotland) Act 1991 (c. 50)	In Schedule 1, paragraph 39.
Water Consolidation (Consequential Provisions) Act 1991 (c. 60)	In Schedule 1, paragraph 40(2).
Charities Act 1992 (c. 41)	In Schedule 6, paragraph 11.
Charities Act 1993 (c. 10)	In Schedule 6, paragraph 20.
Criminal Justice Act 1993 (c. 36)	In Schedule 5, paragraph 4.
Welsh Language Act 1993 (c. 38)	Section 30.
Pension Schemes Act 1993 (c. 48)	In Schedule 8, paragraph 16.
Trade Marks Act 1994 (c. 26)	In Schedule 4, in paragraph 1(2), the reference to the Companies Act 1985.

Deregulation and Contracting Out Act 1994 (c. 40)	Section 13(1). Schedule 5. In Schedule 16, paragraphs 8 to 10.
Requirements of Writing (Scotland) Act 1995 (c. 7)	In Schedule 4, paragraphs 51 to 56.
Criminal Procedure (Consequential Provisions) Scotland) Act 1995 (c. 40)	In Schedule 4, paragraph 56(3) and (4).
Disability Discrimination Act 1995 (c. 50)	In Schedule 6, paragraph 4.
Financial Services and Markets Act 2000 (c. 8)	Section 143. Section 263.
Limited Liability Partnerships Act 2000 (c. 12)	In the Schedule, paragraph 1.
Political Parties, Elections and Referendums Act 2000 (c. 41)	Sections 139 and 140. Schedule 19. In Schedule 23, paragraphs 12 and 13.
Criminal Justice and Police Act 2001 (c. 16)	Section 45. In Schedule 2, paragraph 17.
Enterprise Act 2002 (c. 40)	In Schedule 17, paragraphs 3 to 8.
Companies (Audit, Investigations and Community Enterprise) Act 2004 (c. 27)	Sections 7 to 10. Section 11(1). Sections 12 and 13. Sections 19 and 20. Schedule 1. In Schedule 2, paragraphs 5 to 10, 22 to 24 and 26. In Schedule 6, paragraphs 1 to 9.
Civil Partnership Act 2004 (c. 33)	In Schedule 27, paragraphs 99 to 105.
Constitutional Reform Act 2005 (c. 4)	In Schedule 11, in paragraph 4(3), the reference to the Companies Act 1985.

REPEALS AND REVOCATIONS RELATING TO NORTHERN IRELAND

Short title and chapter	Extent of repeal or revocation
Companies (Northern Ireland) Order 1986 (S.I. 1986/1032 (N.I. 6))	The whole Order.
Companies Consolidation (Consequential Provisions) (Northern Ireland) Order 1986 (S.I. 1986/1035 (N.I. 9))	The whole Order.
Business Names (Northern Ireland) Order 1986 (S.I. 1986/1033 (N.I. 7))	The whole Order.
Industrial Relations (Northern Ireland) Order 1987 (S.I. 1987/936 N.I. 9))	Article 3.

Finance Act 1988 (c. 39)	In section 117(3), the words from "and for" to the end.
Companies (Northern Ireland) Order 1989 (S.I. 1989/2404 (N.I. 18))	The whole Order.
Insolvency (Northern Ireland) Order 1989 (S.I. 1989/2405 (N.I. 19))	In Schedule 7, in the entry relating to Article 166(4), the word "office". In Schedule 9, Part I.
European Economic Interest Groupings Regulations (Northern Ireland) 1989 (S.R. 1989/216)	The whole Regulations.
Companies (Northern Ireland) Order 1990 (S.I. 1990/593 (N.I. 5))	The whole Order.
Companies (No. 2) (Northern Ireland) Order 1990 (S.I. 1990/1504 (N.I. 10))	Parts II to IV. Part VI. Schedules 1 to 6.
Criminal Justice Act 1993 (c. 36)	In Schedule 5, Part 2. Schedule 6.
Financial Provisions (Northern Ireland) Order 1993 (S.I. 1993/1252 (N.I. 5))	Article 15.
Deregulation and Contracting Out Act 1994 (c. 40)	Section 13(2). Schedule 6.
Pensions (Northern Ireland) Order 1995 (S.I. 1995/3213 (N.I. 22))	In Schedule 3, paragraph 7.
Deregulation and Contracting Out (Northern Ireland) Order 1996 (S.I. 1996/1632 (N.I. 11))	Article 11. Schedule 2. In Schedule 5, paragraph 4.
Youth Justice and Criminal Evidence Act 1999 (c. 23)	In Schedule 4, paragraph 18.
Limited Liability Partnerships Act (Northern Ireland) 2002 (c. 12 (N.I.))	The whole Act.
Open-Ended Investment Companies Act (Northern Ireland) 2002 (c. 13)	The whole Act.
Company Directors Disqualification (Northern Ireland) Order 2002 (S.I. 2002/3150 (N.I. 4))	In Schedule 3, paragraphs 3 to 5.
Companies (Audit, Investigations and Community Enterprise) Act 2004 (c. 27)	Section 11(2). In Schedule 2, paragraphs 11 to 15.
Law Reform (Miscellaneous Provisions) (Northern Ireland) Order 2005 (S.I. 2005/1452 (N.I. 7))	Article 4(2).
Companies (Audit, Investigations and Community Enterprise) (Northern Ireland) Order 2005 (S.I. 2005/1967 (N.I. 17))	The whole Order.

OTHER REPEALS

Limited Partnerships Act 1907 (c. 24)	In section 16(1) – (a) the words ", and there shall be paid for such inspection such fees as may be appointed by the Board of Trade, not exceeding 5p for each inspection", and (b) the words from "and there shall be paid for such certificate" to the end. In section 17 – (a) the words "(but as to fees with the concurrence of the Treasury)", and (b) paragraph (a).
Business Names Act 1985 (c. 7)	The whole Act.
Companies Act 1989 (c. 40)	Sections 24 to 54. Schedules 11 to 13.
Criminal Procedure (Consequential Provisions) (Scotland) Act 1995 (c. 40)	In Schedule 4, paragraph 74(2).
Companies (Audit, Investigations and Community Enterprise) Act 2004 (c. 27)	Sections 1 to 6. In Schedule 2, Part 1.
Civil Partnership Act 2004 (c. 33)	In Schedule 27, paragraph 128.

Appendix 2
TABLE OF DESTINATIONS

Notes

1. The table identifies the provisions of the Companies Act 1985 (c.6) that are repealed and re-enacted (with or without changes) by the Companies Act 2006 and identifies the corresponding provisions in that Act.
2. The table is based on the table of origins. So it only shows a provision of the Companies Act 2006 as a destination of a provision of the Companies Act 1985 if the latter is cited in that table as an origin for the new provision.
3. A repealed provision of the Companies Act 1985 may not be listed in this table because the provision is spent or it is otherwise unnecessary to re-enact it, because the new provision is fundamentally different from the existing provision or because as a matter of policy it has been decided to repeal the existing provision without replacing it.
4. There is no entry for Schedule 24 to the Companies Act 1985 (punishment of offences) in the table. This is cited in the table of origins for a large number of provisions in the Companies Act 2006.
5. A section at the end of the table identifies the substantive provisions of the Companies Act 1989 (c.40) that are repealed and re-enacted by the Companies Act 2006.

Provision of Companies Act 1985	*Destination in Companies Act 2006*
s.1 Mode of forming incorporated company	
(1)	s.7(1) and (2) (changed)
(2)	s.3(1) to (4)
(3)	s.4(1) to (3)
(4)	s.5(1) and (2)
s.2 Requirements with respect to memorandum	
(1)	s.9(2)
(2)	ss.9(2), 88(2)
(3)	s.9(2) (changed)
(4)	s.11(3) (changed)
s.3 Forms of memorandum	
(1)	s.8(2)
s.7 Articles prescribing regulations for companies	
(1)	s.18(2) (changed)
(3)	s.18(3) (changed)
s.8 Tables A, C, D and E	
(1)	s.19(1) to (3) (changed)
(2)	s.20(1) and (2) (changed)
(3)	s.19(4)
(4)	s.19(1) to (3) (changed)
(5)	s.19(5)

Provision of Companies Act 1985	Destination in Companies Act 2006
s.9 Alteration of articles by special resolution	
(1) and (2)	s.21(1)
s.10 Documents to be sent to registrar	
(1)	s.9(1), (5) and (6) (changed)
(2)	s.12(1) (changed)
(3)	s.12(3)
(4)	s.9(3)
(6)	s.9(5)
s.12 Duty of registrar	
(1) and (2)	s.14
(3) and (3A)	s.13(1) and (2) (changed)
s.13 Effect of registration	
(1)	s.15(1)
(2)	s.15(3)
(3)	s.16(2) (changed)
(4)	s.16(3)
(5)	s.16(6)
(7)	s.15(4)
s.14 Effect of memorandum and articles	
(1)	s.33(1) (changed)
(2)	s.33(2) (changed)
s.15 Memorandum and articles of company limited by guarantee	
(1)	s.37
(2)	s.5(3)
s.16 Effect of alteration on company's members	
(1)	s.25(1)
(2)	s.25(2)
s.18 Amendments of memorandum or articles to be registered	
(1)	s.34(2) (changed)
(2)	ss.26(1), 34(3) (changed)
(3)	ss.26(3) and (4), 34(5) and (6)
s.19 Copies of memorandum and articles to be given to members	
(1)	s.32(1) (changed)
(2)	s.32(3) and (4) (changed)
s.22 Definition of "member"	
(1)	s.112(1) (changed)
(2)	s.112(2)
s.23 Membership of holding company	
(1)	s.136(1)
(2)	s.138(1) and (2)
(3)	s.141(1) and (2)
(3A)	s.141(3)
(3B)	s.141(4)
(3BA)	s.141(5)
(3C)	s.142(1) and (2)
(4) and (5)	s.137(1) and (2)
(6)	s.137(3) and (4)
(7)	s.144
(8)	s.143

Provision of Companies Act 1985	Destination in Companies Act 2006
s.25 Name as stated in memorandum	
(1)	s.58(1) and (2)
(2)	s.59(1), (2) and (3)
s.26 Prohibition on registration of certain names	
(1)	ss.53, 65(1) to (5), 66(1) (changed)
(2)	ss.54(1) to (3) and 55(1) (changed)
(3)	s.66(2) and (3) (changed)
s.27 Alternatives of statutory designations	
(4)	ss.58(1) and (2), 59(1) and (2)
s.28 Change of name	
(1)	s.77(1)
(2)	ss.67(1), 68(2) and (3)
(3)	s.75(1), (2) and (4)
(4)	ss.68(3), 75(3)
(5)	ss.68(5) and (6), 75(5) and (6)
(6)	ss.80(1) to (3), 81(1)
(7)	s.81(2) and (3)
s.29 Regulations about names	
(1)	ss.55(1), 56(1)
(2)	s.56(2)
(3)	s.56(3) and (4) (changed)
(6)	s.55(2)
s.30 Exemption from requirement of "limited" as part of the name	
(2) and (3)	ss.61(1) to (4), 62(1) to (3) (changed)
(4)	s.60(3)
(5B)	s.60(2)
s.31 Provisions applying to company exempt under s.30	
(1)	s.63(1)
(2)	s.64(1) to (4) (changed)
(3)	s.64(7)
(5)	s.63(2) and (3)
(6)	s.64(5) and (6)
s.32 Power to require company to abandon misleading name	
(1)	s.76(1)
(2)	s.76(3)
(3)	s.76(4) and (5)
(4)	s.76(6) and (7) (changed)
(5)	ss.80(1) to (3), 81(1)
(6)	s.81(2) and (3)
s.35 A company's capacity not limited by its memorandum	
(1)	s.39(1) (changed)
(4)	s.39(2)
s.35A Power of directors to bind the company	
(1)	s.40(1)
(2)	s.40(2)
(3)	s.40(3)
(4)	s.40(4)

Provision of Companies Act 1985	Destination in Companies Act 2006
(5)	s.40(5)
(6)	s.40(6)
s.35B No duty to enquire as to capacity of company or authority of directors	
	s.40(2)
s.36 Company contracts: England and Wales	
(1) and (2)	s.43(1) and (2)
s.36A Execution of documents: England and Wales	
(2)	s.44(1)
(3)	s.45(1)
(4)	s.44(2), (3) and (4)
(4A)	s.44(6)
(6)	s.44(5)
(7)	s.44(8)
(8)	s.44(7)
s.36AA Execution of deeds: England and Wales	
(1)	s.46(1)
(2)	s.46(2)
s.36B Execution of documents by companies	
(1)	s.48(2)
(2)	s.48(3)
s.36C Pre-incorporation contracts, deeds and obligations	
(1)	s.51(1)
(2)	s.51(2)
s.37 Bills of exchange and promissory notes	
	s.52
s.38 Execution of deeds abroad	
(1)	s.47(1) (changed)
(2)	s.47(2)
(3)	s.47(1)
s.39 Power of company to have official seal for use abroad	
(1)	s.49(1) and (2) (changed)
(2) and (2A)	s.49(3)
(3)	s.49(4)
(4)	s.49(5)
(5)	s.49(6)
s.40 Official seal for share certificates, etc	
(1)	s.50(1) and (2)
s.42 Events affecting a company's status	
(1)	s.1079(1) to (3)
s.43 Re-registration of private company as public	
(1)	s.90(1) and (2) (changed)
(2)	s.90(3)
(3)	ss.92(1) and (2), 94(2) and (3)
(4)	s.92(1)

Provision of Companies Act 1985	Destination in Companies Act 2006
s.44 Consideration for shares recently allotted to be valued	
(1)	s.93(1)
(2)	s.93(2) and (7)
(4) and (5)	s.93(3) to (5)
(6)	s.93(6)
(7)	s.93(6) and (7)
s.45 Additional requirements relating to share capital	
(1) to (4)	s.91(1)
s.46 Meaning of "unqualified report" in s.43(3)	
(2)	s.92(3)
(3)	s.92(4)
(4)	s.92(5) and (6)
s.47 Certificate of re-registration under s.43	
(1)	s.96(1) and (2)
(2)	s.94(4)
(3)	s.91(5) (changed)
(4)	s.96(4)
(5)	s.96(5)
s.48 Modification for unlimited company re-registering	
(1) and (2)	s.90(4)
(5)	s.91(2)
(6)	s.91(3)
(7)	s.91(4)
s.49 Re-registration of limited company as unlimited	
(1)	s.102(1)
(2)	s.102(2)
(4)	s.102(1)
(5) to (7)	s.102(3)
(8)	ss.102(1), 103(2) to (4) (changed)
(8A)	s.103(3) and (4) (changed)
(9)	s.102(4)
s.50 Certificate of re-registration under s.49	
(1)	s.104(1) and (2)
(2)	s.104(4)
(3)	s.104(5)
s.51 Re-registration of unlimited company as limited	
(1)	s.105(1) (changed)
(2)	s.105(2)
(3)	s.105(3) and (4)
(5)	s.106(2)
s.52 Certificate of re-registration under s.51	
(1)	s.107(1) and (2)
(2)	s.107(4)
(3)	s.107(5)

Provision of Companies Act 1985	Destination in Companies Act 2006
s.53 Re-registration of public company as private	
(1)	ss.97(1), 100(2) (changed)
(2)	s.97(3)
s.54 Litigated objection to resolution under s.53	
(1)	s.98(1)
(2)	ss.98(1), 370(3) (changed)
(3)	s.98(2)
(4)	s.99(1) and (2) (changed)
(5)	s.98(3) and (4)
(6)	s.98(5) and (6)
(7)	s.99(3)
(8)	s.98(6)
(10)	s.99(4) and (5)
s.55 Certificate of re-registration under s.53	
(1)	s.101(1) and (2)
(2)	s.101(4)
(3)	s.101(5)
s.58 Document offering shares etc for sale deemed a prospectus	
(3)	s.755(2)
s.80 Authority of company required for certain allotments	
(1)	s.549(1), s.551(1) (changed)
(2)	ss.549(1) to (3), 551(1), 559
(3)	s.551(2)
(4)	s.551(3) and (4)
(5)	s.551(5)
(6)	s.551(6)
(7)	s.551(7)
(8)	s.551(8)
(9)	s.549(4) and (5)
(10)	s.549(6) (changed)
s.81 Restriction on public offers by private company	
(1)	s.755(1)
(3)	s.760
s.84 Allotment where issue not fully subscribed	
(1)	s.578(1)
(2)	s.578(2)
(3)	s.578(3) (changed)
(4)	s.578(4) and (5)
(5)	s.578(5)
(6)	s.578(6)
s.85 Effect of irregular allotment	
(1)	s.579(1) and (2)
(2)	s.579(3)
(3)	s.579(4)
s.88 Return as to allotments, etc	
(1)	s.555(1)

Provision of Companies Act 1985	Destination in Companies Act 2006
(2)	s.555(2) (changed)
(5)	s.557(1) and (2)
(6)	ss.557(3), 597(5) and (6)
s.89 Offers to shareholders to be on pre-emptive basis	
(1)	s.561(1)
(2)	s.568(1)
(3)	s.568(1) and (2)
(4)	ss.561(2), 565
(5)	s.566
(6)	s.561(4)
s.90 Communication of pre-emption offers to shareholders	
(1)	s.562(1)
(2)	s.568(3)
(5)	s.562(3) (changed)
(6)	s.562(4) and (5) (changed)
s.91 Exclusion of ss.89, 90 by private company	
(1)	s.567(1) and (2)
(2)	s.567(3) and (4)
s.92 Consequences of contravening ss.89, 90	
(1)	ss.563(1) and (2), 568(4)
(2)	ss.563(3), 568(5)
s.93 Saving for other restrictions as to offers	
(1)	s.575(1)
(2)	s.575(2)
s.94 Definitions for ss.89–96	
(2)	ss.560(1), 564, 577
(3)	ss.560(2), 561(3)
(3A)	s.560(2)
(5)	s.560(1)
(7)	s.574(1) and (2)
s.95 Disapplication of pre-emption rights	
(1)	ss.570(1) and (2), 573(2), (3) and (5)
(2)	ss.571(1) and (2), 573(4)
(2A)	s.573(1) to (5)
(3)	ss.570(3), 571(3)
(4)	ss.570(4), 571(4), 573(3) and (5)
(5)	ss.571(5) to (7), 573(5) (changed)
(6)	s.572(1) to (3)
s.96 Saving for company's pre-emption procedure operative before 1982	
(1) and (2)	s.576(1)
(3)	s.576(2)
(4)	s.576(3)
s.97 Power of company to pay commission	
(1)	s.553(1)
(2)	s.553(2)

Provision of Companies Act 1985	Destination in Companies Act 2006
s.98 Apart from s.97, commissions and discounts barred	
(1)	s.552(1)
(2)	s.552(2)
(3)	s.552(3)
(4)	s.553(3)
s.99 General rules as to payment for shares on allotment	
(1)	s.582(1) and (3)
(2)	s.585(1)
(3)	s.585(2)
(4)	s.582(2)
(5)	s.585(3)
s.100 Prohibition on allotment of shares at a discount	
(1)	s.580(1)
(2)	s.580(2)
s.101 Shares to be allotted as at least one-quarter paid-up	
(1)	s.586(1)
(2)	s.586(2)
(3) and (4)	s.586(3)
(5)	s.586(4)
s.102 Restriction on payment by long-term undertaking	
(1)	s.587(1)
(2)	s.587(2)
(3) and (4)	s.587(3)
(5) and (6)	s.587(4)
(7)	s.587(5)
s.103 Non-cash consideration to be valued before allotment	
(1)	s.593(1)
(2)	s.593(2)
(3)	s.594(1) to (3)
(4)	s.594(4) and (5)
(5)	s.595(1) and (2)
(6)	s.593(3)
(7)	ss.594(6), 595(3)
s.104 Transfer to public company of non-cash asset in initial period	
(1)	s.598(1)
(2)	s.598(2)
(3)	s.603
(4)	ss.599(1) and (3), 601(1) to (3) (changed)
(5)	s.599(2) and (4)
(6)	s.598(4) and (5)
s.105 Agreements contravening s.104	
(1)	s.604(1)
(2)	s.604(2)
(3)	s.604(3)

Provision of Companies Act 1985	Destination in Companies Act 2006
s.106 Shares issued to subscribers of memorandum	
	s.584
s.107 Meaning of "the appropriate rate"	
	ss.592(1) and (2), 609(1) and (2)
s.108 Valuation and report (s.103)	
(1)	s.1150(1) (changed)
(2)	s.1150(2)
(3)	s.1150(3)
(4)	s.596(2)
(5)	s.1150(4)
(6)	ss.596(3), 600(3)
(7)	s.596(4) and (5)
s.109 Valuation and report (s.104)	
(2)	s.600(2) and (3)
(3)	s.600(4) and (5)
s.110 Entitlement of valuer to full disclosure	
(1)	s.1153(1)
(2)	s.1153(2) and (4)
(3)	s.1153(3)
s.111 Matters to be communicated to registrar	
(1)	s.597(1) and (2)
(2)	s.602(1)
(3)	s.597(3) to (6)
(4)	s.602(2) and (3)
s.111A Rights to damages, &c not affected	
	s.655
s.112 Liability of subsequent holders of shares allotted	
(1)	ss.588(1), 605(1)
(2)	s.605(2)
(3)	ss.588(2), 605(3)
(4)	ss.588(3), 605(4)
(5)	s.588(1) and (4)
s.113 Relief in respect of certain liabilities under ss.99 ff	
(1)	ss.589(1) and (2), 606(1)
(2)	ss.589(3), 606(2) (changed)
(3)	ss.589(3), 606(2)
(4)	ss.589(4), 606(3)
(5)	ss.589(5), 606(4)
(6) and (7)	ss.589(6), 606(5)
(8)	s.606(6)
s.114 Penalty for contravention	
	ss.590(1) and (2), 607(2) and (3)
s.115 Undertakings to do work, etc	
(1)	ss.591(1) and (2), 608(1) and (2)
s.117 Public company share capital requirements	
(1)	s.761(1)

Provision of Companies Act 1985	Destination in Companies Act 2006
(2)	s.761(2) (changed)
(3)	s.762(1) (changed)
(4)	s.761(3)
(5)	s.762(3)
(6)	s.761(4) (changed)
(7)	s.767(1) and (2)
(8)	s.767(3)
s.118 The authorised minimum	
(1)	ss.763(1), 764(1) (changed)
(2)	s.764(3)
(3)	s.764(4)
s.119 Provision for different amounts to be paid on shares	
	s.581
s.121 Alteration of share capital (limited companies)	
(1)	s.617(1) (changed)
(2)	ss.617(2) and (3), 618(1), 620(1) (changed)
(3)	s.618(2)
(4)	ss.618(3), 620(2) (changed)
s.122 Notice to registrar of alteration	
(1)	ss.619(1) to (3), 621(1), 663(1), 689(1) (changed)
(2)	ss.619(4) and (5), 621(4) and (5), 663(4) and (5), 689(4) and (5)
s.125 Variation of class rights	
(1)	s.630(1)
(2)	s.630(2) to (4) (changed)
(6)	s.334(1) to (4) and (6) (changed)
(7)	ss.334(7), 630(5)
(8)	s.630(6)
s.126 Saving for court's powers under other provisions	
	s.632
s.127 Shareholders' right to object to variation	
(1)	s.633(1)
(2)	s.633(2) and (3)
(2A)	s.633(2)
(3)	s.633(4)
(4)	s.633(5)
(5)	s.635(1) to (3)
(6)	s.633(6)
s.128 Registration of particulars of special rights	
(1)	s.556(1) to (3) (changed)
(2)	ss.556(1) and (4), 629(2)
(3)	s.637(1) (changed)
(4)	s.636(1) (changed)
(5)	ss.557(1) and (2), 636(2) and (3), 637(2) and (3) (changed)

Provision of Companies Act 1985	Destination in Companies Act 2006
s.129 Registration of newly created class rights	
(1)	s.638(1) (changed)
(2)	s.640(1) (changed)
(3)	s.639(1) (changed)
(4)	ss.638(2) and (3), 639(2) and (3), 640(2) and (3)
s.130 Application of share premiums	
(1)	s.610(1)
(2)	s.610(2) and (2) (changed)
(3)	s.610(4)
(4)	s.610(5) and (6)
s.131 Merger relief	
(1)	s.612(1) and (4)
(2)	s.612(2)
(3)	s.612(3)
(4)	s.613(2) and (3)
(5)	s.613(4)
(6)	s.613(5)
(7)	s.616(1)
s.132 Relief in respect of group reconstructions	
(1)	s.611(1)
(2)	s.611(2)
(3)	s.611(3)
(4)	s.611(4)
(5)	s.611(5)
(8)	s.612(4)
s.133 Provisions supplementing ss.131, 132	
(1)	s.615
(2)	s.616(2)
(3)	s.616(3)
(4)	s.616(1)
s.134 Provision for extending or restricting relief from s.130	
(1)	s.614(1)
(3)	s.614(2)
s.135 Special resolution for reduction of share capital	
(1)	s.641(1) to (3) (changed)
(2)	s.641(4)
s.136 Application to court for order of confirmation	
(1)	s.645(1)
(2)	ss.645(2) and (4), 646(4)
(3)	s.646(1)
(4)	s.646(2) and (3)
(5)	s.646(4) and (5)
(6)	s.645(2) and (3)
s.137 Court order confirming reduction	
(1)	s.648(1) and (2)
(2)	s.648(3) and (4)
(3)	s.648(4)

Provision of Companies Act 1985	Destination in Companies Act 2006
s.138 Registration of order and minute of reduction	
(1)	s.649(1) (changed)
(2)	s.649(3) (changed)
(3)	s.649(4) (changed)
(4)	s.649(5) and (6) (changed)
s.139 Public company reducing capital below authorised minimum	
(1)	s.650(1)
(2)	s.650(2)
(3)	s.651(1) and (2)
(4)	s.651(3) (changed)
(5)	s.651(4), (6) and (7)
s.140 Liability of members on reduced shares	
(1)	s.652(1) (changed)
(2)	s.653(1)
(3)	s.653(2)
(4)	s.653(3)
(5)	s.653(3)
s.141 Penalty for concealing name of creditor, etc	
	s.647(1), (2) (changed)
s.142 Duty of directors on serious loss of capital	
(1)	s.656(1) to (3)
(2)	s.656(4) and (5) (changed)
(3)	s.656(6)
s.143 General rule against company acquiring own shares	
(1)	s.658(1)
(2)	s.658(2) and (3)
(2A)	s.725(4)
(3)	s.659(1) and (2)
s.144 Acquisition of shares by company's nominee	
(1)	s.660(1) and (2) (changed)
(2)	s.661(1) and (2) (changed)
(3)	s.661(3)
(4)	s.661(4)
s.145 Exceptions from s.144	
(1)	s.660(3)
(2)	ss.660(3), 661(5)
(3)	s.671
s.146 Treatment of shares held by or for public company	
(1)	ss.662(1), 671
(2)	s.662(2) and (3)
(3)	s.662(3)
(4)	s.662(5) and (6)
s.147 Matters arising out of compliance with s.146(2)	
(2)	s.664(1) and (2)

Provision of Companies Act 1985	Destination in Companies Act 2006
(3)	s.664(4) (changed)
(4)	s.665(1), (2), (4) and (5) (changed)
s.148 Further provisions supplementing ss.146, 147	
(1)	s.668(1) and (2)
(2)	s.668(3)
(3)	s.671
(4)	s.669(1) and (2)
s.149 Sanctions for non-compliance	
(1)	s.666(1) and (2)
(2)	s.667(1) to (3)
s.150 Charges of public companies on own shares	
(1)	s.670(1)
(2)	s.670(2)
(3)	s.670(3)
(4)	s.670(4)
s.151 Financial assistance generally prohibited	
(1)	ss.678(1), 679(1) (changed)
(2)	ss.678(3), 679(3) (changed)
(3)	s.680(1) and (2)
s.152 Definitions for this Chapter	
(1)	ss.677(1), 683(1)
(2)	s.677(2) and (3)
(3)	s.683(2)
s.153 Transactions not prohibited by s.151	
(1)	ss.678(2), 679(2) (changed)
(2)	ss.678(4), 679(4)
(3)	s.681(1) and (2)
(4)	s.682(1) and (2)
(5)	s.682(5)
s.154 Special restriction for public companies	
(1)	s.682(1)
(2)	ss.682(3) and (4), 840(4) and (5)
s.159 Power to issue redeemable shares	
(1)	s.684(1) and (3) (changed)
(2)	s.684(4)
(3)	ss.686(1) to (3) (changed), 691(1) and (2)
s.160 Financing etc of redemption	
(1)	ss.687(1) to (3) and (6), 692(1), (2) and (5)
(2)	ss.687(4) and (5), 692(3) and (4)
(4)	ss.688, 706 (changed)
s.162 Power of company to purchase own shares	
(1)	s.690(1) (changed)
(2)	ss.691(1) and (2), 692(1) to (5)
(2A)	s.706
(2B)	ss.706, 724(1)
(3)	s.690(2)
(4)	s.724(2)

Provision of Companies Act 1985	Destination in Companies Act 2006
s.162A Treasury shares	
(1)	s.724(3)
(2)	s.724(4)
(3)	s.724(5)
s.162B Treasury shares: maximum holdings	
(1)	s.725(1)
(2)	s.725(2)
(3)	s.725(4)
s.162C Treasury shares: voting and other rights	
(1)	s.726(1)
(2) and (3)	s.726(2)
(4)	s.726(3)
(5)	s.726(4)
(6)	s.726(5)
s.162D Treasury shares: disposal and cancellation	
(1)	ss.727(1), 729(1)
(2)	s.727(2) (changed)
(3)	s.727(3)
(4)	s.729(4)
(5)	s.729(5)
s.162E Treasury shares: mandatory cancellation	
(1)	s.729(2)
(2)	s.729(3)
s.162F Treasury shares: proceeds of sale	
(1)	s.731(1)
(2)	s.731(2)
(3)	s.731(3)
(4) and (5)	s.731(4)
s.162G Treasury shares: penalty for contravention	
	s.732(1) and (2) (changed)
s.163 Definitions of "off-market" and "market" purchase	
(1)	s.693(2)
(2)	s.693(3)
(3)	s.693(4)
(4) and (5)	s.693(5)
s.164 Authority for off-market purchase	
(1)	ss.693(1), 694(1)
(2)	s.694(2) (changed)
(3)	ss.694(4), 697(3), 700(3)
(4)	ss.694(5), 697(4), 700(4)
(5)	ss.694(1), (3) and (4), 698(1), (3) and (4), 700(5)
(6)	ss.696(1) to (5), 699(1) to (6), 700(5) (changed)
(7)	ss.697(1) to (4), 698(1), (3) and (4), 699(1) to (6), 700(3) to (5)

Provision of Companies Act 1985	Destination in Companies Act 2006
s.165 Authority for contingent purchase contract	
(1)	s.694(3)
(2)	ss.694(2), (4) and (5), 695(1), (3) and (5), 696(1) to (5)
s.166 Authority for market purchase	
(1)	ss.693(1), 701(1)
(2)	s.701(2)
(3)	s.701(3) and (5)
(4)	s.701(4) and (5)
(5)	s.701(6)
(6)	s.701(7)
(7)	s.701(8)
s.167 Assignment or release of company's right to purchase own shares	
(1)	s.704
(2)	s.700(1) to (5)
s.168 Payments apart from purchase price to be made out of distributable profits	
(1)	s.705(1)
(2)	s.705(2)
s.169 Disclosure by company of purchase of own shares	
(1)	ss.707(1) to (3), 708(1) (changed)
(1A)	ss.707(1) to (3), 708(1) (changed)
(1B)	ss.707(1) to (3), 708(1) (changed)
(2)	s.707(4)
(3)	s.707(5)
(4)	s.702(1) to (4) (changed)
(5)	s.702(6)
(6)	ss.707(6) and (7), 708(4) and (5)
(7)	s.703(1) and (2) (changed)
(8)	s.703(3)
(9)	s.702(7)
s.169A Disclosure by company of cancellation or disposal of treasury shares	
(1)	ss.728(1), 730(1)
(2)	ss.728(2), 730(2)
(3)	ss.728(3), 730(3)
(4)	ss.728(4) and (5), 730(6) and (7)
s.170 The capital redemption reserve	
(1)	s.733(1), (2) and (4)
(2) and (3)	s.733(3)
(4)	s.733(5) and (6)
s.171 Power of private companies to redeem or purchase own shares out of capital	
(1)	s.709(1) (changed)
(2)	s.709(2)
(3)	s.710(1) and (2)
(4)	s.734(2)
(5)	s.734(3)
(6)	s.734(4)

Provision of Companies Act 1985	Destination in Companies Act 2006
s.172 Availability of profits for purposes of s.171	
(1)	s.711(1) and (2)
(2)	s.712(2)
(3)	s.712(6)
(4)	s.712(3)
(5)	s.712(4)
(6)	s.712(7)
s.173 Conditions for payment out of capital	
(1)	s.713(1) and (2)
(2)	s.716(1)
(3)	s.714(1) to (3)
(4)	s.714(4) (changed)
(5)	s.714(5) and (6) (changed)
(6)	s.715(1) and (2)
s.174 Procedure for special resolution under s.173	
(1)	ss.716(2), 723(1)
(2)	s.717(3)
(3)	s.717(4)
(4)	s.718(2) and (3) (changed)
(5)	s.717(5)
s.175 Publicity for proposed payment out of capital	
(1)	s.719(1)
(2)	s.719(2)
(3)	s.719(3)
(4)	ss.719(4), 720(1)
(5)	s.719(4)
(6)	s.720(1), (2) and (4) (changed)
(7)	s.720(5) and (6)
(8)	s.720(7)
s.176 Objections by company's members or creditors	
(1)	s.721(1) and (2)
(2)	s.721(2)
(3)	s.722(2) and (3)
(4)	s.722(4) and (5)
s.177 Powers of court on application under s.176	
(1)	s.721(3)
(2)	s.721(4) and (5)
(3)	s.721(6)
(4)	s.721(7)
s.178 Effect of company's failure to redeem or purchase	
(1)	s.735(1)
(2)	s.735(2)
(3)	s.735(2) and (3)
(4)	s.735(4)
(5)	s.735(5)
(6)	s.735(6)

Provision of Companies Act 1985	Destination in Companies Act 2006
s.181 Definitions for Chapter VII	s.736
s.182 Nature, transfer and numbering of shares	
(1)	ss.541, 544(1) and (2)
(2)	s.543(1) and (2)
s.183 Transfer and registration	
(1)	s.770(1)
(2)	s.770(2)
(3)	s.773
(4)	s.772
s.184 Certification of transfers	
(1)	s.775(1) and (2)
(2)	s.775(3)
(3)	s.775(4)
s.185 Duty of company as to issue of certificates	
(1)	ss.769(1) and (2), 776(1) and (3)
(2)	s.776(2)
(3)	s.777(1) and (2)
(4)	ss.769(2), 776(3), 778(1)
(4A)	s.778(1)
(4B) and (4C)	s.778(2)
(4D)	s.778(3)
(5)	ss.769(3) and (4), 776(5) and (6)
(6)	s.782(1)
(7)	s.782(2) and (3)
s.186 Certificate to be evidence of title	
(1)	s.768(1) and (2)
(2)	s.768(2)
s.187 Evidence of grant of probate or confirmation as executor	s.774
s.188 Issue and effect of share warrant to bearer	
(1)	s.779(1)
(2)	s.779(2)
(3)	s.779(3)
s.189 Offences in connections with share warrants (Scotland)	
(1)	s.781(1) and (3)
(2)	s.781(2) and (4)
s.190 Register of debenture holders	
(1)	s.743(6)
(5)	s.743(2) and (6) (changed)
(6)	s.743(3)
s.191 Right to inspect register	
(1)	s.744(1)
(2)	s.744(2)
(3)	s.749(1)
(4)	ss.746(1) and (2), 749(2) and (3)
(5)	ss.746(3), 749(4)

Provision of Companies Act 1985	Destination in Companies Act 2006
(6)	s.744(5)
(7)	s.748(1) and (2) (changed)
s.192 Liability of trustees of debentures	
(1)	s.750(1) and (3)
(2)	s.750(2)
(3)	s.751(1) and (2)
(4)	s.751(3) and (4)
s.193 Perpetual debentures	
	s.739(1) and (2)
s.194 Power to re-issue redeemed debentures	
(1)	s.752(1)
(2)	s.752(2)
(3)	s.753
(4)	s.752(3)
(5)	s.752(4)
s.195 Contract to subscribe for debentures	
	s.740
s.196 Payment of debts out of assets subject to floating charge (England and Wales)	
(1)	s.754(1)
(2)	s.754(2)
(3)	s.754(3)
(4)	s.754(4)
s.197 Debentures to bearer (Scotland)	
	s.742
s.198 Obligation of disclosure: the cases in which it may arise and "the relevant time"	
(2)	s.792(1) and (2) (changed)
s.203 Notification of family and corporate interests	
(1)	s.822(1) and (2)
(2)	s.823(1)
(3)	s.832(2)
(4)	s.823(3)
s.204 Agreement to acquire interests in a particular company	
(1)	s.824(1)
(2)	ss.824(1) and (2), 988(4)
(3)	ss.824(3), 988(6)
(4)	s.824(4)
(5)	ss.824(5), 988(7)
(6)	ss.824(6), 988(5)
s.205 Obligation of disclosure arising under s.204	
(1)	s.825(1)
(2)	s.825(2)
(3)	s.825(3)
(4)	s.825(4)
s.207 Interests in shares by attribution	
(1)	ss.783, 785(1)
(2)	s.785(2)

Provision of Companies Act 1985	Destination in Companies Act 2006
(3)	s.785(3)
(4)	s.785(4)
(5)	s.785(5)
(6)	s.785(6)
(7)	s.788
(9)	s.784(3)
(10)	s.783
s.208 Interests in shares which are to be notified	
(1)	s.820(1)
(2)	s.820(2)
(3)	s.820(3)
(4)	s.820(4)
(5)	s.820(6)
(6)	s.820(5)
(7)	s.820(7)
(8)	s.820(8)
s.210A Power to make further provision by regulations	
(1)	s.828(1) and (2)
(5)	s.828(3)
s.211 Register of interests in shares	
(3)	s.808(2)
(4)	s.808(7)
(5)	s.808(4)
(6)	s.810(1) to (3)
(7)	s.819(1)
(8)	ss.809(1), 810(4), 811(1) and (2), 813(1) to (3) (changed)
(9)	s.826(1)
(10)	ss.808(5) and (6), 819(2) and (3)
s.212 Company investigations	
(1)	s.793(1) and (2) (changed)
(2)	s.793(3), (4) and (6)
(3)	s.793(5)
(4)	s.793(7)
(5)	ss.820(1) to (8), 822(1) and (2), 823(1) to (3), 824(1) to (6), 825(1) to (4)
(6)	s.821(1) and (2)
s.213 Registration of interests disclosed under s.212	
(1)	s.808(1) to (3) (changed)
(3)	ss.808(2) and (4) to (7), 809(1), 810(1) to (4), 811(1) and (2), 813(1) to (3), 819(1) to (3), 826(1)
s.214 Company investigation on requisition by members	
(1)	s.803(1) and (2) (changed)
(2)	s.803(3) (changed)
(4)	s.804(1)
(5)	s.804(2) and (3) (changed)
s.215 Company report to members	
(1)	s.805(1)

Provision of Companies Act 1985	*Destination in Companies Act 2006*
(2)	s.805(2) and (3)
(3)	s.805(1) and (3)
(4)	s.826(1) and (2)
(5)	s.805(6)
(6)	s.805(7)
(7)	ss.805(4), 807(1) to (5)
(8)	s.806(3) and (4)
s.216 Penalty for failure to provide **information**	
(1)	s.794(1)
(1A)	s.794(3)
(1B)	s.794(2)
(3)	s.795(1) and (3)
(4)	s.795(2)
(5)	s.796(1) and (2)
s.217 Removal of entries from register	
(1)	s.816 (changed)
(2)	s.817(1) (changed)
(3)	s.817(2) and (3)
(4)	s.818(1) and (2)
(5)	ss.817(4), 818(3)
s.218 Otherwise, entries not to be removed	
(1)	s.815(1)
(2)	s.815(2)
(3)	s.815(3) and (4)
s.219 Inspection of register and reports	
(1)	ss.807(1), 811(1)
(2)	ss.807(2), 811(2)
(3)	ss.807(3) and (4), 813(1) and (2) (changed)
(4)	ss.807(5), 813(3)
s.220 Definitions for Part VI	
(2)	s.827
s.221 Duty to keep accounting records	
(1)	s.386(1) and (2)
(2) to (4)	s.386(3) to (5)
(5)	s.387(1) and (2)
(6)	s.387(3)
s.222 Where and for how long records **to be kept**	
(1) to (3)	s.388(1) to (3)
(4)	s.389(1), (2) and (4)
(5)	s.388(4) and (5)
(6) ·	s.389(3) and (4)
s.223 A company's financial year	
(1) to (5)	s.390(1) to (5)
s.224 Accounting reference periods and **accounting reference date**	
(1)	s.391(1)
(2) and (3)	s.391(2)
(3A)	s.391(4)
(4) to (6)	s.391(5) to (7)

Provision of Companies Act 1985	Destination in Companies Act 2006
s.225 Alteration of accounting reference date	
(1)	s.392(1)
(3) to (7)	s.392(2) to (6)
s.226 Duty to prepare individual accounts	
(1)	s.394
(2) to (6)	s.395(1) to (5)
s.226A Companies Act individual accounts	
(1) and (2)	s.396(1) and (2)
(3)	s 396(3) (changed)
(4)	s.396(4)
(5) and (6)	s.396(5)
s.226B IAS individual accounts	
	s.397
s.227 Duty to prepare group accounts	
(1)	s.399(2)
(2) to (7)	s.403(1) to (6)
(8)	s.399(2) and (3)
s.227A Companies Act group accounts	
(1) and (2)	s.404(1) and (2)
(3)	s.404(3) (changed)
(4)	s.404(4)
(5) and (6)	s.404(5)
s.227B IAS group accounts	
	s.406
s.227C Consistency of accounts	
(1) to (5)	s.407(1) to (5)
s.228 Exemption for parent companies included in accounts of larger group	
(1) and (2)	s.400(1) and (2)
(3)	s.400(4)
(4)	s.400(5)
(5)	s.400(3)
(6)	s.400(6)
s.228A Exemption for parent companies included in non-EEA group accounts	
(1) and (2)	s.401(1) and (2)
(3)	s.401(4)
(4)	s.401(5)
(5)	s.401(3)
(6)	s.401(6)
s.229 Subsidiary undertakings included in the consolidation	
(1) and (2)	s.405(1) and (2)
(3)	s.405(3) and (4)
(5)	s.402
s.230 Treatment of individual profit and loss account where group accounts prepared	
(1)	s.408(1) (changed)
(2)	s.408(2) (changed)
(3) and (4)	s.408(3) and (4)

Provision of Companies Act 1985	*Destination in Companies Act 2006*
s.231 Disclosure required in notes to accounts: related undertakings	
(1) and (2)	s.409(1) and (2) (changed)
(3)	s.409(3) and (4) (changed)
(4)	s.409(5)
(5)	s.410(1) and (2)
(6)	s.410(3)
(7)	s.410(4) and (5)
s.231A Disclosure required in notes to annual accounts: particulars of staff	
(1)	s.411(1)
(2) to (4)	s.411(3) to (5)
(5)	s.411(2)
(6)	s.411(7)
(7)	s.411(6)
s.232 Disclosure required in notes to accounts: emoluments and other benefits of directors and others	
(3)	s.412(5)
(4)	s.412(6)
s.233 Approval and signing of accounts	
(1) and (2)	ss.414(1) and (2), 450(1) and (2)
(3)	ss.433(1) to (3), 436(1) and (2)
(4)	ss.444(6), 445(5), 446(3), 447(3) (changed)
(5)	ss.414(4) and (5) (changed)
(6)(a)	s.433(4) and (5)
s.234 Duty to prepare directors' report	
(1)	ss.415(1), 417(1), 418(2)
(2) and (3)	s.415(2) and (3)
(5)	ss.415(4) and (5), 419(3) and (4)
s.234ZZA Directors' report: general requirements	
(1)	s.416(1) and (3)
(2)	s.416(2)
(3) and (4)	s.416(4) (changed)
s.234ZZB Directors' report: business review	
(1) and (2)	s.417(3) and (4)
(3)	s.417(6)
(4)	s.417(8)
(5)	s.417(6)
(6)	s.417(9)
s.234ZA Statement as to disclosure of information to auditors	
(1) to (4)	s.418(1) to (4)
(6)	s.418(5) and (6)
s.234A Approval and signing of directors' report	
(1)	s.419(1)
(2)	ss.433(1) to (3), 436(1) and (2)
(3)	ss.444(6), 445(5), 446(3), 447(3)
(4)	ss.419(3) and (4), 433(4) and (5)

Provision of Companies Act 1985	Destination in Companies Act 2006
s.234B Duty to prepare directors' remuneration report	
(1)	ss.420(1), 421(1) and (2)
(2)	s.421(1) and (2)
(3) and (4)	s.420(2) and (3)
(5) and (6)	s.421(3) and (4)
s.234C Approval and signing of directors' remuneration report	
(1)	s.422(1)
(2)	ss.433(1) to (3), 436(1) and (2)
(3)	s.447(3)
(4)	s.422(2) and (3)
s.235 Auditors' report	
(1)	ss.475(1), 495(1)
(1A)	s.495(2)
(1B) and (2)	s.495(3)
(2A)	s.495(4)
(3)	s.496
(4) and (5)	s.497(1) and (2)
s.236 Signature of auditors' report	
(1)	s.503(1) and (2)
(2)	s.505(1) and (2) (changed)
(3)	s.444(7) (changed)
(4)	s.505(3) and (4)
s.237 Duties of auditors	
(1) to (4)	s.498(1) to (4)
(4A)	s.498(5)
s.238 Persons entitled to receive copies of accounts and reports	
(1) and (1A)	ss.423(1), 424(1) to (3) (changed)
(3)	s.423(4)
(4)	s.424(4) (changed)
(5)	s.425(1) and (2)
(6)	s.423(5)
s.239 Right to demand copies of accounts and reports	
(1) and (2)	ss.431(1) and (2), 432(1) and (2)
(3)	ss.431(3) and (4), 432(3) and (4)
s.240 Requirements in connection with publication of accounts	
(1)	s.434(1) (changed)
(2)	s.434(2) (changed)
(3)	s.435(1) and (2) (changed)
(4)	s.436(1) and (2) (changed)
(5)	ss.434(3), 435(3) (changed)
(6)	s.435(5) and (6)
s.241 Accounts and reports to be laid before company in general meeting	
(1)	s.437(1) (changed)
(2)	ss.437(2), 438(1) and (4)
(3) and (4)	s.438(2) and (3)

Provision of Companies Act 1985	Destination in Companies Act 2006
s.241A Members' approval of directors' remuneration report	
(1) and (3)	s.439(1)
(4)	s.439(2)
(5)	s.439(3)
(6)	s.439(4)
(7)	s.439(3)
(8)	s.439(5)
(9)	s.440(1) and (4)
(10)	s.440(2) to (4)
(11)	s.440(2) and (3)
(12)	s.439(6)
s.242 Accounts and reports to be delivered to the registrar	
(1)	s.441(1), 444(1) and (2), 445(1) and (2), 446(1) and (2), 447(1) and (2) (changed)
(2)	s.451(1)
(3)	s.452(1) and (2)
(4) and (5)	s.451(2) and (3)
s.242A Civil penalty for failure to deliver accounts	
(1)	s.453(1)
(2)	s.453(2) (changed)
(3) and (4)	s.453(3) and (4)
s.242B Delivery and publication of accounts in ECUs	
(1) to (4)	s.469(1) to (4)
s.244 Period allowed for laying and delivering accounts and reports	
(1) and (2)	s.442(2) and (3) (changed)
(4) and (5)	s.442(4) and (5)
(6)	s.442(7)
s.245 Voluntary revision of annual accounts or directors' report	
(1) to (3)	s.454(1) to (3)
(4)	s.454(4) (changed)
(5)	s.454(5)
s.245A Secretary of State's notice in respect of annual accounts	
(1)	s.455(1) and (2)
(2) to (4)	s.455(3) to (5)
s.245B Application to court in respect of defective accounts	
(1) to (3)	s.456(1) to (3)
(3A)	s.456(4)
(4) to (7)	s.456(5) to (8)
s.245C Other persons authorised to apply to court	
(1)	s.457(1)
(1A)	s.457(5)
(2) and (3)	s.457(2) and (3)
(4)	s.457(7)

Provision of Companies Act 1985	Destination in Companies Act 2006
(4A)	s.457(5)
(4B)	s.457(4)
(5)	s.457(6)
s.245D Disclosure of information held by Inland Revenue to persons authorised to apply to court	
(1)	s.458(1)
(2)	s.458(2)
(3)	s.458(1)
s.245E Restriction on use and further disclosure of information disclosed under section 245D	
(1) and (2)	s.458(3)
(3)	s.458(4) and (5)
(4)	s.458(4) (changed)
(5)	ss.1126, 1130
s.245F Power of authorised persons to require documents, information and explanations	
(1) to (8)	s.459(1) to (8)
s.245G Restrictions on further disclosure of information obtained under section 245F	
(1) and (2)	s.460(1) and (2)
(3)	ss.460(3), 461(1) to (6)
(4) to (6)	s.462(1) to (3)
(7)	s.460(4) and (5)
(8)	s.460(4)
(9)	ss.1126, 1130
(10)	s.460(3)
(11)	s.461(7)
s.246 Special provisions for small companies	
(3)	s.411(1)
(4)	ss.416(3), 417(1)
(5)	s.444(1) and (3) (changed)
(6)	s.444(3) (changed)
(7)	ss.444(6), 450(1) and (2)
(8)	ss.414(3), 419(2), 444(5), 450(3)
s.246A Special provisions for medium-sized companies	
(1)	s.445(1)
(2)	s.445(3) (changed)
(2A)	s.417(7)
(3)	s.445(3) (changed)
(4)	s.450(3)
s.247 Qualification of company as small or medium-sized	
(1)(a)	ss.382(1), 465(1)
(1)(b) and (2)	ss.382(2), 465(2)
(3) and (4)	ss.382(3) and (4), 465(3) and (4)
(5)	ss.382(5), 465(5) (changed)
(6)	ss.382(6), 465(6)

Provision of Companies Act 1985	Destination in Companies Act 2006
s.247A Cases in which special provisions do not apply	
(1) to (1B)	ss.384(1), 467(1)
(2)	ss.384(2), 467(2) (changed)
(2A)	ss.384(3), 467(3)
(3)	ss.383(1), 466(1)
s.247 Special auditors' report	
(1)	s.449(1)
(2)	ss.444(4), 445(4), 449(2)
(3) to (5)	s.449(3) to (5)
s.248 Exemption for small and medium-sized groups	
(1) and (2)	ss.398, 399(1) and (2) (changed)
s.249 Qualification of group as small or medium-sized	
(1)(a)	s.466(2)
(1)(b) and (2)	s.466(3)
(3)	s.466(4)
(4)	s.466(5) and (6)
(5) and (6)	s.466(7)
s.249A Exemptions from audit	
(1)	s.477(1)
(3)	s.477(2) and (4)
(6)	s.477(3)
(7)	s.477(4)
s.249AA Dormant companies	
(1) and (2)	s.480(1) and (2)
(3)	s.481
(4)	s.1169(1)
(5) to (7)	s.1169(2) and (3)
s.249B Cases where exemptions not available	
(1)	ss.478, 479(1) to (3)
(1A)	s.479(3)
(1B)	s.479(1) to (3)
(1C)	s.479(2), (5) and (6)
(2) and (3)	s.476(1) to (3)
(4)	s.475(2) and (3)
(5)	s.475(4)
s.249E Effect of exemptions	
(1)(b)	ss.444(2), 445(2), 446(2) (changed)
s.251 Provision of summary financial statement to shareholders	
(1)	ss.426(1), 427(1)
(2)	s.426(2) and (3)
(3)	ss.427(2), 428(2)
(3A)	ss.427(3), 428(3)
(4)	ss.427(4), 428(4)
(5)	ss.427(6), 428(6)
(6)	s.429(1) and (2)
(7)	ss.434(6), 435(7)

Provision of Companies Act 1985	Destination in Companies Act 2006
s.254 Exemption from requirement to deliver accounts and reports	
(1) to (3)	s.448(1) to (3)
(4)	s.448(4)
s.255A Special provisions for banking and insurance groups	
(4)	s.1164(5)
(5)	s.1165(5)
(5A)	ss.1164(5), 1165(6)
s.255D Power to apply provisions to banking partnerships	
(1)	s.470(1)
(2) and (2A)	s.470(2)
(4)	s.470(4)
(5)	s.470(3)
s.256 Accounting standards	
(1) and (2)	s.464(1) and (2)
(4)	s.464(3)
s.257 Power of Secretary of State to alter accounting requirements	
(1)	s.484(1)
(2)	ss.473(1) to (4) (changed), 484(3)
(3)	s.484(4)
(4)(c)	s.484(2)
s.258 Parent and subsidiary undertakings	
(1) to (6)	s.1162(1) to (6)
s.259 Meaning of "undertaking" and related expressions	
(1)	ss.1161(1), 1173 "parent company"
(2) to (5)	s.1161(2) to (5)
s.261 Notes to the accounts	
(1) and (2)	s.472(1) and (2)
s.262 Minor definitions	
(1)	ss.474(1), 539, 835(6), 1173 "credit institution" (changed)
(2)	s.474(2)
(3)	s.853(4) and (5)
s.263 Certain distributions prohibited	
(1)	s.830(1)
(2)	s.829(1) and (2)
(3)	s.830(2) and (3)
(4)	s.849
(5)	s.850(1) to (3)
s.264 Restriction on distribution of assets	
(1)	s.831(1) and (6)
(2)	s.831(2) and (3)
(3)	s.831(4)
(4)	s.831(5)
s.265 Other distributions by investment companies	
(1)	s.832(1) to (3)
(2)	s.832(4)

Provision of Companies Act 1985	Destination in Companies Act 2006
(3)	s.832(7)
(4)	s.832(5)
(4A)	s.832(6)
(5)	s.832(6)
(6)	s.832(5)
s.266 Meaning of "investment company"	
(1)	s.833(1)
(2)	ss.833(2), 834(1)
(2A)	s.833(3)
(3)	s.833(4) and (5)
(4)	s.834(2) to (5)
s.267 Extension of ss.265, 266 to other companies	
(1)	s.835(1)
(2)	s.835(2)
s.268 Realised profits of insurance company with long term business	
(1)	s.843(1), (2), (4) and (5)
(2)	s.843(3) and (4)
(3)	s.843(6) and (7)
(4)	s.843(7)
s.269 Treatment of development costs	
(1)	s.844(1)
(2)	s.844(2) and (3)
s.270 Distribution to be justified by reference to company's accounts	
(1) and (2)	s.836(1)
(3)	ss.836(2), 837(1)
(4)	ss.836(2), 838(1), 839(1)
(5)	s.836(3) and (4)
s.271 Requirements for last annual accounts	
(2)	s.837(2)
(3)	s.837(3) and (4)
(4)	s.837(4)
(5)	s.837(5)
s.272 Requirements for interim accounts	
(1)	s.838(2)
(2)	s.838(3)
(3)	ss.838(4) and (5), 839(4)
(4) and (5)	s.838(6)
s.273 Requirements for initial accounts	
(1)	s.839(2)
(2)	s.839(3)
(3)	s.839(4)
(4)	s.839(5) and (6)
(5)	s.839(6)
(6) and (7)	s.839(7)
s.274 Method of applying s.270 to successive distributions	
(1)	s.840(1)
(2)	s.840(1) and (2)
(3)	s.840(3) to (5)

Provision of Companies Act 1985	Destination in Companies Act 2006
s.275 Treatment of assets in the relevant accounts	
(1)	s.841(1) and (2)
(1A)	s.841(3)
(2)	s.841(5)
(3)	s.842
(4) to (6)	s.841(4)
s.276 Distributions in kind	
	s.846(1) and (2) (changed)
s.277 Consequences of unlawful distribution	
(1)	s.847(1) and (2)
(2)	s.847(3) and (4)
s.278 Saving for provision in articles operative before Act of 1980	
	s.848(1) and (2)
s.280 Definitions for Part VIII	
(1)	s.853(1)
(2)	s.853(2)
(3)	s.853(3)
s.281 Saving for other restraints on distribution	
	ss.851, 852 (changed)
s.282 Directors	
(1)	s.154(2) (changed)
(3)	s.154(1)
s.283 Secretary	
(1)	s.271 (changed)
(3)	ss.270(3), 274 (changed)
s.284 Acts done by person in dual capacity	
	s.280
s.285 Validity of acts of directors	
	s.161(1) and (2) (changed)
s.286 Qualifications of company secretaries	
(1)	s.273(1) and (2) (changed)
(2)	s.273(3)
s.287 Registered office	
(1)	s.86
(3)	s.87(1)
(4)	s.87(2)
(5)	s.87(3)
(6)	s.87(4)
s.288 Register of directors and secretaries	
(1)	ss.162(1) to (3), 275(1) to (3) (changed)
(2)	ss.167(1) and (2), 276(1) and (2)
(3)	ss.162(5), 275(5)
(4)	ss.162(6) and (7), 167(4) and (5), 275(6) and (7), 276(3) and (4)
(5)	ss.162(8), 275(8)
(6)	ss.162(6), 167(4), 275(6), 276(3)

Provision of Companies Act 1985	Destination in Companies Act 2006
s.289 Particulars of directors to be registered under s.288	
(1)	ss.163(1), 164 (changed)
(2)	ss.163(2) and (4), 277(2) and (4) (changed)
s.290 Particulars of secretaries to be registered under s.288	
(1)	ss.277(1), 278(1) (changed)
(2)	s.278(2)
(3)	s.277(2) and (4)
s.292 Appointment of directors to be voted on individually	
(1)	s.160(1)
(2)	s.160(2)
(3)	s.160(3)
(4)	s.160(4)
s.303 Resolution to remove director	
(1)	s.168(1) (changed)
(2)	s.168(2)
(3)	s.168(3)
(4)	s.168(4)
(5)	s.168(5)
s.304 Director's right to protest removal	
(1)	s.169(1) and (2)
(2)	s.169(3)
(3)	s.169(4)
(4)	s.169(5)
(5)	s.169(6)
s.309 Directors to have regard to interests of employees	
(1)	s.172(1)
s.309A Provisions protecting directors from liability	
(1)	s.232(1) and (2)
(2)	s.232(1)
(3)	s.232(2)
(4)	s.234(1)
(5)	s.233
(6)	s.232(3)
s.309B Qualifying third party indemnity provisions	
(1) and (2)	s.234(2)
(3)	s.234(3)
(4)	s.234(3) and (6)
(5)	s.234(4)
(6) and (7)	s.234(5)
s.309C Disclosure of qualifying third party indemnity provisions	
(1)	s.236(1) (changed)
(2)	s.236(2) and (3)
(3)	s.236(4) and (5) (changed)
(4)	s.237(1)
(5)	ss.237(1) to (3) and (5) to (8), 238(1) and (3) to (5)

Provision of Companies Act 1985	Destination in Companies Act 2006
s.310 Provisions protecting auditors from liability	
(1)	s.532(1) and (3) (changed)
(2)	s.532(2)
(3)	s.533
s.312 Payment to directors for loss of office, etc	
	ss.215(1), 217(1) and (3) (changed)
s.313 Company approval for property transfer	
(1)	ss.215(1), 218(1) and (3) (changed)
(2)	s.222(2)
s.314 Director's duty of disclosure on takeover, etc	
(1)	ss.215(1), 219(1) (changed)
s.315 Consequences of non-compliance with s.314	
(1)	ss.219(1) and (2), 222(3) (changed)
(3)	s.219(5)
s.316 Provisions supplementing ss.312 to 315	
(1)	ss.218(5), 219(7)
(2)	s.216(1) and (2) (changed)
(3)	s.220(1)
s.317 Directors to disclose interest in contracts	
(1)	s.182(1) (changed)
(2)	s.182(2) (changed)
(3)	s.185(1) and (2) (changed)
(4)	s.185(4)
(5)	s.185(1) (changed)
(7)	s.183(1) and (2)
(8)	s.187(1) to (4)
s.318 Director's service contracts to be open to inspection	
(1)	ss.228(1), 237(2)
(2) and (3)	ss.228(2), 237(3) (changed)
(4)	ss.228(4), 237(5)
(6)	s.230
(7)	ss.229(1), 238(1)
(8)	ss.228(5) and (6), 229(3) and (4), 237(6) and (7), 238(3) and (4) (changed)
(9)	ss.229(5), 238(5) (changed)
(10)	ss.228(7), 237(8)
s.319 Director's contract of employment for more than 5 years	
(1)	s.188(1) and (3) (changed)
(2)	s.188(4) (changed)
(3)	s.188(2) (changed)
(4)	s.188(6)
(5)	s.188(5)
(6)	s.189
(7)	ss.188(7), 223(1)

Provision of Companies Act 1985	Destination in Companies Act 2006
s.320 Substantial property transactions involving directors, etc	
(1)	s.190(1) and (2) (changed)
(2)	s.191(1) to (5) (changed)
(3)	s.223(1)
s.321 Exceptions from s.320	
(1)	s.190(4)
(2)	ss.192, 193(1) and (2) (changed)
(3)	s.192
(4)	s.194(1) and (2)
s.322 Liabilities arising from contravention of s.320	
(1)	s.195(1) and (2)
(2)	ss.195(2) and 196
(3)	s.195(1), (3) and (4)
(4)	s.195(3), (5) and (8)
(5)	s.195(6)
(6)	s.195(7)
s.322A Invalidity of certain transactions involving directors, etc	
(1)	s.41(1) and (2)
(2)	s.41(2)
(3)	s.41(3)
(4)	s.41(1)
(5)	s.41(4)
(6)	s.41(5)
(7)	s.41(6)
(8)	s.41(7)
s.322B Contracts with sole members who are directors	
(1)	s.231(1) and (2) (changed)
(2)	s.231(1)
(3)	s.231(5)
(4)	s.231(3) and (4) (changed)
(5)	s.231(7)
(6)	s.231(6)
s.235 Register of directors' interests notified under s.324	
(5)	s.809(2) and (3)
s.330 General restriction on loans etc to directors and persons connected with them	
(2)	s.197(1) (changed)
(3)	ss.198(1) and (2) (changed), 200(1) and (2)
(4)	s.201(1) and (2) (changed)
(5)	s.223(1)
(6)	s.203(1) and (6) (changed)
(7)	s.203(1) (changed)
s.331 Definitions for ss.330 ff	
(3)	s.199(1)
(4)	s.199(2) and (3)
(6)	ss.198(1), 200(1), 201(1)
(7)	s.202(1)

Provision of Companies Act 1985	Destination in Companies Act 2006
(8)	s.202(3)
(9)	ss.202(2), 212
(10)	s.202(3)
s.333 Inter-company loans in same group	
	s.208(1) (changed)
s.334 Loans of small amounts	
	s.207(1) (changed)
s.335 Minor and business transactions	
(1)	s.207(2) (changed)
(2)	s.207(3)
s.336 Transactions at behest of holding company	
	208(1) and (2) (changed)
s.337 Funding of director's expenditure on duty to company	
(1) and (2)	s.204(1) (changed)
(3)	s.204(2) (changed)
s.337A Funding of director's expenditure on defending proceedings	
(1)	s.205(1) (changed)
(2)	s.205(5)
(3)	s.205(1) (changed)
(4)	s.205(2)
(5)	s.205(3)
(6)	s.205(4)
s.338 Loan or quasi-loan by money-lending company	
(1)	s.209(1)
(2)	s.209(2)
(3)	s.209(1)
(6)	s.209(3) and (4)
s.339 "Relevant amounts" for purposes of ss.334 ff	
(1)	ss.204(2), 207(1) and (2), 210(1)
(2)	ss.204(2), 207(1) and (2), 210(2) to (4)
(3)	s.210(3) and (4)
(5)	s.210(5)
(6)	s.211(1)
s.340 "Value" of transactions and arrangements	
(2)	s.211(2)
(3)	s.211(3)
(4)	s.211(5)
(5)	s.211(6)
(6)	s.211(4)
(7)	s.211(7) (changed)
s.341 Civil remedies for breach of s.330	
(1)	s.213(1) and (2)
(2)	s.213(3) and (4)
(3)	s.213(5) and (8)
(4)	s.213(6)
(5)	s.213(7)

Provision of Companies Act 1985	Destination in Companies Act 2006
s.345 Power to increase financial limits	
(1)	s.258(1)
(2)	s.258(2)
(3)	s.258(3)
s.346 "Connected persons", etc	
(1)	ss.252(1), 254(1), 255(1)
(2) and (3)	ss.252(2) and (3), 253(2) (changed)
(4)	s.254(2) and (5)
(5)	s.255(2) and (5)
(6)	ss.254(6), 255(6)
(7)	ss.254(3), 255(3)
(8)	ss.254(4), 255(4)
s.347 Transactions under foreign law	
	s.259
s.347A Introductory provisions	
(1)	s.362 (changed)
(3)	s.379(1)
(4)	s.364(2)
(5)	s.365(1) (changed)
(6)	s.363(1) and (2)
(7)	s.363(1) and (2) (changed)
(8)	s.379(1)
(9)	s.363(1)
(10)	ss.366(5), 379(2)
s.347B Exemptions	
(1)	s.375(1)
(2)	s.375(2) (changed)
(3)	s.376(1) and (2)
(4)	s.378(1) (changed)
(5)	s.378(3)
(6) and (7)	s.378(1) (changed)
(8)	s.377(1)
(9)	s.377(3)
(10)	s.377(2)
(11)	s.377(4)
s.347C Prohibition on donations and political expenditure by companies	
(1)	s.366(1), (2) and (5) (changed)
(2)	s.367(3) and (6) (changed)
(3)	s.368(1) and (2)
(4)	s.367(5)
(6)	s.366(6)
s.347D Special rules for subsidiaries	
(1)	s.366(2)
(2)	s.366(2) and (5) (changed)
(3)	s.366(2), (3) and (5) (changed)
(4)	s.367(3) and (6) (changed)
(5)	s.368(1) and (2)
(6)	s.367(5)
(9)	s.366(6)
s.347F Remedies for breach of probibitions on company donations etc	
(1)	s.369(1)
(2)	s.369(2) and (3) (changed)

Provision of Companies Act 1985	Destination in Companies Act 2006
(3)	s.369(2) and (5)
(4)	s.369(2)
(5)	s.369(6)
(6)	s.369(3) (changed)
s.347I Enforcement of directors' liabilities by shareholder action	
(1)	s.370(1) and (2) (changed)
(2)	s.370(3)
(3)	ss.370(4), 371(1)
(4) and (5)	s.371(2)
(6)	s.371(3)
(7)	s.371(4)
(8)	s.371(5)
s.347J Costs of shareholder action	
(1)	s.372(1)
(2)	s.372(2)
(3)	s.372(3)
(4) and (5)	s.372(4)
(6)	s.372(5)
s.347K Information for purposes of shareholder action	
(1)	s.373(1)
(2)	s.373(2)
s.348 Company name to appear outside place of business	
(1)	s.82(1) and (2)
(2)	s.84(1) and (2)
s.349 Company's name to appear in its correspondence, etc	
(1)	s.82(1) and (2)
(2) and (3)	s.84(1) and (2)
s.350 Company seal	
(1)	s.45(2) and (3) (changed)
(2)	s.45(4) and (5)
s.351 Particulars in correspondence etc	
(1) and (2)	s.82(1) and (2)
(5)	s.84(1) and (2)
s.352 Obligation to keep and enter up register	
(1)	s.113(1)
(2)	s.113(2)
(3)	s.113(3) and (4)
(4)	s.113(6)
(5)	s.113(7) and (8)
(6)	s.121 (changed)
(7)	s.128(1) and (2)
s.352A Statement that company has only one member	
(1)	s.123(2) (changed)
(2)	s.123(3) (changed)
(3)	s.123(4) and (5)
(3A)	s.124(1) and (2)

Provision of Companies Act 1985	Destination in Companies Act 2006
s.353 Location of register	
(1)	s.114(1) (changed)
(2)	s.114(2)
(3)	s.114(3) and (4)
(4)	s.114(5) and (6)
s.354 Index of members	
(1)	s.115(1) and (2)
(2)	s.115(3)
(3)	s.115(4) (changed)
(4)	s.115(5) and (6)
s.355 Entries in register in relation to share warrants	
(1)	s.122(1) (changed)
(2)	s.122(4)
(3)	s.122(5)
(4)	s.122(2) and (6)
(5)	s.122(3)
s.356 Inspection of register and index	
(1)	s.116(1) (changed)
(3)	s.116(2)
(5)	s.118(1) and (2) (changed)
(6)	s.118(3)
s.359 Power of court to rectify register	
(1)	s.125(1)
(2)	s.125(2)
(3)	s.125(3)
(4)	s.125(4)
s.360 Trusts not to be entered on register in England and Wales	
	s.126
s.361 Register to be evidence	
	s.127
s.362 Overseas branch registers	
(1)	s.129(1)
(2)	s.129(1) and (5)
(3)	ss.130(1) to (3), 131(1) and (4), 132(1) to (4), 133(1) to (3), 134(1) to (3), 135(1) to (5)
s.363 Duty to deliver annual returns	
(1)	s.854(1) and (2)
(2)	s.854(3) (changed)
(3)	s.858(1) to (3)
(4)	s.858(1), (2) and (4) (changed)
s.364 Contents of annual return: general	
(1)	s.855(1) (changed)
(2)	s.855(2)
(3)	s.855(3)
s.364A Contents of annual return: particulars of share capital and shareholders	
(1)	s.856(1)
(2)	s.856(2)

Provision of Companies Act 1985	Destination in Companies Act 2006
(3)	s.856(2) (changed)
(4)	s.856(3)
(5)	s.856(4)
(6)	s.856(5)
(8)	s.856(6)
s.365 Supplementary provisions: regulations and interpretation	
(1)	s.857(1) and (2)
(2)	s.857(3)
(3)	s.859
s.366 Annual general meeting	
(1)	ss.336(1), 337(1)
(4)	s.336(3) and (4)
s.368 Extraordinary general meeting on members' requisition	
(1)	s.303(1) and (2)
(2)	s.303(2) and (3) (changed)
(2A)	s.303(2)
(3)	s.303(4) and (6) (changed)
(4)	ss.304(1), 305(1) and (3)
(5)	s.305(4)
(6)	s.305(6) and (7)
(7)	s.304(4)
(8)	s.304(1)
s.369 Length of notice for calling meetings	
(1) and (2)	s.307(2) and (3) (changed)
(3)	ss.307(4), 337(2) (changed)
(4)	s.307(5) and (6) (changed)
(4A)	s.308 (changed)
(4B)	ss.308, 309(1) and (3) (changed)
(4C)	s.309(2)
s.370 General provisions as to meetings and votes	
(1)	ss.284(4), 310(4), 318(2), 319(2)
(2)	s.310(1)
(4)	s.318(2) (changed)
(5)	s.319(1)
(6)	s.284(1) and (3)
s.370A Quorum at meetings of the sole member	
	s.318(1) and (3) (changed)
s.371 Power of court to order meeting	
(1)	s.306(1) and (2)
(2)	s.306(3) and (4)
(3)	s.306(5)
s.372 Proxies	
(1)	s.324(1)
(2)	s.324(2) (changed)
(3)	s.325(1) (changed)
(4)	s.325(3) and (4)
(5)	s.327(1) and (2) (changed)
(6)	s.326(1) to (4) (changed)

Provision of Companies Act 1985	Destination in Companies Act 2006
s.373 Right to demand a poll	
(1)	s.321(1) and (2) (changed)
(2)	s.329(1) and (2) (changed)
s.374 Voting on a poll	
	s.322
s.375 Representation of corporations at meetings	
(1)	s.323(1)
(2)	s.323(2) and (3) (changed)
s.376 Circulation of members' resolutions	
(1)	ss.314(1) and (4), 315(2), 316(2), 338(1) and (4), 339(2), 340(2)
(2)	ss.314(2) and (3), 338(3)
(3)	ss.315(1), 339(1)
(5)	ss.315(1), 339(1)
(6)	s.339(3)
(7)	ss.315(3) and (4), 339(4) and (5)
s.377 In certain cases, compliance with s.376 not required	
(1)	ss.314(4), 316(2), 338(4), 340(2) (changed)
(3)	s.317(1) and (2) (changed)
s.378 Extraordinary and special resolutions	
(1)	s.283(1), (4) and (5) (changed)
(2)	s.283(1) and (4) to (6) (changed)
(4)	s.320(1) and (3)
(5)	s.283(5) (changed)
(6)	s.301 (changed)
s.379 Resolution requiring special notice	
(1)	s.312(1)
(2)	s.312(2) and (3) (changed)
(3)	s.312(4)
s.380 Registration, etc of resolutions and agreements	
(1)	s.30(1)
(2)	s.36(1) and (2) (changed)
(4)	s.29(1) (changed)
(4A)	s.29(2)
(5)	s.30(2) and (3)
(6)	s.36(3) and (4) (changed)
(7)	ss.30(4), 36(5)
s.381 Resolution passed at adjourned meeting	
	s.332
s.381A Written resolutions of private companies	
(1)	ss.288(1), 289(1) (changed)
(2)	s.296(1) (changed)
(4)	s.288(5)
(7)	s.288(2)
s.381C Written resolutions: supplementary provisions	
(1)	s.300

Provision of Companies Act 1985	Destination in Companies Act 2006
s.382 Minutes of meetings	
(1)	ss.248(1), 355(1)
(2)	ss.249(1), 356(4)
(4)	ss.249(2), 356(5)
(5)	ss.248(3) and (4), 355(3) and (4) (changed)
s.382A Recording of written resolutions	
(1)	s.355(1) (changed)
(2)	s.356(2) and (3)
s.382B Recording of decisions by the sole member	
(1)	s.357(1) and (2)
(2)	s.357(3) and (4)
(3)	s.357(5)
s.383 Inspection of minute books	
(1)	s.358(1) and (3) (changed)
(3)	s.358(4) (changed)
(4)	s.358(5) and (6) (changed)
(5)	s.358(7)
s.384 Duty to appoint auditors	
(1)	ss.485(1), 489(1) (changed)
(2)	s.489(2)
s.385 Appointment at general meeting at which accounts laid	
(2)	ss.489(2) and (4), 491(1) (changed)
(3)	s.489(3) (changed)
(4)	s.489(4) (changed)
s.387 Appointment by Secretary of State in default of appointment by company	
(1)	ss.486(1), 490(1)
(2)	ss.486(2) to (4), 490(2) to (4)
s.388 Filling of casual vacancies	
(1)	ss.489(3), 526
s.389A Rights to information	
(1)	s.499(1)
(2)	s.499(2)
(3)	s.500(1)
(4)	s.500(2)
(5)	s.500(3)
(6)	ss.499(3), 500(4)
(7)	ss.499(4), 500(5)
s.389B Offences relating to the provision of information to auditors	
(1)	s.501(1) and (2)
(2)	s.501(3)
(3)	s.501(3) (changed)
(4)	s.501(4) and (5)
(5)	s.501(6)
s.390 Right to attend company meetings, &c	
(1)	s.502(2)
(2)	s.502(1)
(3)	s.502(2)

Provision of Companies Act 1985	Destination in Companies Act 2006
s.390A Remuneration of auditors	
(1)	s.492(1)
(2)	s.492(2) and (3)
(4)	s.492(4)
(5)	s.492(5)
s.390B Disclosure of services provided by auditors or associates and related remuneration	
(1)	ss.494(1), 501(1) and (2)
(2)	s.494(2)
(3)	s.494(3)
(4)	s.494(4)
(5)	s.494(5)
(8)	s.494(1)
(9)	s.494(6)
s.391 Removal of auditors	
(1)	s.510(1) and (2)
(2)	s.512(1) to (3)
(3)	s.510(3)
(4)	s.513(1) and (2)
s.391A Rights of auditors who are removed or not re-appointed	
(1)	ss.511(1), 515(1) and (2) (changed)
(2)	ss.511(2), 515(3)
(3)	ss.511(3), 515(4)
(4)	ss.511(4), 515(5)
(5)	ss.511(5), 515(6)
(6)	ss.511(6), 515(7)
s.392 Resignation of auditors	
(1)	s.516(1) and (2)
(2)	s.516(3)
(3)	s.517(1) to (3)
s.392A Rights of resigning auditors	
(1)	s.518(1)
(2)	s.518(2)
(3)	s.518(3)
(4)	s.518(4)
(5)	s.518(5) to (7)
(6)	s.518(8)
(7)	s.518(9)
(8)	s.518(10)
s.394 Statement by person ceasing to hold office as auditor	
(1)	s.519(1) to (3) and (7) (changed)
(2)	s.519(4) (changed)
(3)	s.520(2)
(4)	s.520(3)
(5)	s.521(1)
(6)	s.520(4)
(7)	ss.520(5), 521(2) (changed)
s.394A Offences of failing to comply with s.394	
(1)	ss.519(5), 521(3) to (5)

Provision of Companies Act 1985	Destination in Companies Act 2006
(2)	ss.519(6), 521(4)
(4)	s.520(6) and (8) (changed)
s.395 Certain charges void if not registered	
(1)	ss.860(1), 861(5), 870(1), 874(1) and (2)
(2)	s.874(3)
s.396 Charges which have to be registered	
(1)	ss.860(7), 861(2)
(2)	s.861(3)
(3)	s.861(1)
(3A)	s.861(4)
(4)	s.861(5)
s.397 Formalities of registration (debentures)	
(1)	ss.863(1) to (4), 870(3)
(2)	s.864(1) and (3)
(3)	s.864(2)
s.398 Verification of charge on property outside United Kingdom	
(1)	s.866(1)
(2)	s.870(1)
(3)	s.866(2)
(4)	s.867(1) and (2)
s.399 Company's duty to register charges it creates	
(1)	ss.860(1) and (2), 863(5)
(2)	ss.860(3), 863(5)
(3)	ss.860(4) to (6), s.863(5)
s.400 Charges existing on property acquired	
(1)	ss.861(5), 862(1)
(2)	ss.862(2) and (3), 870(2)
(3)	s.870(2)
(4)	s.862(4) and (5) (changed)
s.401 Register of charges to be kept by registrar of companies	
(1)	s.869(1), (2) and (4)
(2)	s.869(5) and (6)
(3)	s.869(7)
s.402 Endorsement of certificate on debentures	
(1)	s.865(1)
(2)	s.865(2)
(3)	s.865(3) and (4)
s.403 Entries of satisfaction and release	
(1)	s.872(1) and (2) (changed)
(2)	s.872(3)
s.404 Rectification of register of charges	
(1)	s.873(1)
(2)	s.873(2)
s.405 Registration of enforcement of security	
(1)	s.871(1) and (3)

Provision of Companies Act 1985	Destination in Companies Act 2006
(2)	s.871(2) and (3)
(4)	s.871(4) and (5)
s.406 Companies to keep copies of instrument creating charges	
(1)	ss.875(1), 877(2) (changed)
(2)	s.875(2)
s.407 Company's register of charges	
(1)	ss.876(1), 877(2) (changed)
(2)	s.876(2)
(3)	s.876(3) and (4)
s.408 Right to inspect instruments which create charges, etc	
(1)	s.877(1), (2) and (4) (changed)
(2)	s.877(2) (changed)
(3)	s.877(5) and (6)
(4)	s.877(7)
s.410 Charges void unless registered	
(1)	s.878(1)
(2)	ss.886(1), 889(1)
(3)	s.889(2)
(4)	ss.878(7), 879(1) and (3)
(5)	s.879(5) and (6)
s.411 Charges on property outside United Kingdom	
(1)	s.886(1)
(2)	s.884
s.412 Negotiable instrument to secure book debts	
	s.879(4)
s.413 Charges associated with debentures	
(1)	s.879(2)
(2)	ss.882(1) to (4), 886(3)
(3)	s.883(1) to (3)
s.414 Charge by way of ex facie absolute disposition, etc	
(1)	s.881(1)
(2)	s.881(2) and (3)
s.415 Company's duty to register charges created by it	
(1)	ss.878(1) and (2), 882(5)
(2)	ss.878(3), 882(5)
(3)	ss.878(4) to (6), 882(5)
s.416 Duty to register charges existing on property acquired	
(1)	ss.880(1) and (2), 886(2)
(2)	s.886(2)
(3)	s.880(3) and (4) (changed)
s.417 Register of charges to be kept by registrar of companies	
(1)	s.885(1)
(2)	s.885(2)
(3)	s.885(3)
(4)	s.886(6)

Provision of Companies Act 1985	Destination in Companies Act 2006
s.418 Certificate of registration to be issued	
(1)	s.885(4)
(2)	s.885(4) and (5)
s.419 Entries of satisfaction and release	
(1)	s.887(1) and (3) (changed)
(1B)	s.887(2)
(2)	s.887(4)
(3)	s.887(2) (changed)
(4)	s.887(5)
s.420 Rectification of register	
	s.888(1) and (2)
s.421 Copies of instruments creating charges to be kept by company	
(1)	ss.890(1), 892(2) (changed)
(2)	s.890(2)
s.422 Company's register of charges	
(1)	ss.891(1), 892(2) (changed)
(2)	s.891(2)
(3)	s.891(3) and (4)
s.423 Right to inspect copies of instruments, and company's register	
(1)	s.892(1), (2) and (4) (changed)
(2)	s.892(4) (changed)
(3)	s.892(5) and (6)
(4)	s.892(7)
s.425 Power of company to compromise with creditors and members	
(1)	ss.895(1), 896(1) and (2)
(2)	ss.899(1) and (3), 907(1), 922(1)
(3)	ss.899(4), 901(3) and (4) (changed)
(4)	s.901(5) and (6)
(6)	s.895(2)
s.426 Information as to compromise to be circulated	
(1)	s.897(1)
(2)	s.897(1) and (2)
(3)	s.897(1)
(4)	s.897(3)
(5)	s.897(4)
(6)	ss.895(1), 897(5) to (8)
(7)	s.898(1) to (3)
s.427 Provisions for facilitating company reconstruction or amalgamation	
(1)	s.900(1)
(2)	s.900(1) and (2)
(3)	s.900(2)
(4)	s.900(3) and (4)
(5)	s.900(6) to (8)
(6)	ss.900(5), 941

Provision of Companies Act 1985	Destination in Companies Act 2006
s.427A Application of ss.425–427 to mergers and divisions of public companies	
(1)	ss.902(1), 903(1), 907(2), 922(2)
(2)	ss.904(1), 919(1)
(3)	s.938(1) and (2)
(4)	s.902(3)
(8)	s.941
s.428 Takeover offers	
(1)	s.974(1) to (3)
(2)	s.974(4) and (5)
(2A)	s.974(6)
(3)	s.976(1)
(4)	s.976(3)
(5)	s.975(1) and (2) (changed)
(6)	s.975(3) (changed)
(7)	s.974(7)
(8)	s.991(1)
s.429 Right of offeror to buy out minority shareholders	
(1)	s.979(1) and (2) (changed)
(2)	s.979(3) and (4) (changed)
(3)	s.980(2) (changed)
(4)	s.980(1) and (4)
(5)	s.980(5)
(6)	s.980(6) and (8)
(7)	s.980(7)
(8)	ss.977(1), 979(8) to (10) (changed)
s.430 Effect of notice under s.429	
(1)	s.981(1)
(2)	s.981(2)
(3)	s.981(3)
(4)	s.981(4) and (5) (changed)
(5)	s.981(6)
(6)	s.981(7)
(7)	s.981(8)
(8)	s.981(6)
(9)	s.981(9)
(10)	s.982(2) and (3)
(11)	s.982(4) and (5)
(12)	s.982(6)
(13)	s.982(7)
(14)	s.982(8)
(15)	s.982(9)
s.430A Right of minority shareholder to be bought out by offeror	
(1)	ss.983(1) to (3), 984(1)
(1A)	s.983(1)
(2)	s.983(4)
(2A)	s.983(5)
(3)	s.984(3)
(4)	s.984(2)
(5)	s.984(4)

Provision of Companies Act 1985	Destination in Companies Act 2006
(6)	s.984(5) and (7)
(7)	s.984(6)
s.430B Effect of requirement under s.430A	
(1)	s.985(1)
(2)	s.985(2)
(3)	s.985(3)
(4)	s.985(4) and (5) (changed)
s.430C Applications to the court	
(1)	s.986(1) and (2)
(2)	s.986(2)
(3)	s.986(3)
(4)	s.986(5)
(5)	s.986(9) and (10)
s.430D Joint offers	
(1)	s.987(1)
(2)	s.987(2) and (3) (changed)
(3)	s.987(5) and (6)
(4)	s.987(4) and (7)
(5)	s.987(8)
(6)	s.987(9)
(7)	s.987(10)
s.430E Associates	
(1)	ss.975(4), 977(2) (changed)
(2)	s.979(9)
(3)	s.983(8)
(4)	s.988(1) and (4)
(5)	s.988(2)
(6)	s.988(3)
(7)	s.988(3), (5) and (7)
(8)	s.988(1)
s.430F Convertible securities	
(1)	s.989(1)
(2)	s.989(2)
s.458 Punishment for fraudulent trading	
	s.993(1) to (3)
s.459 Order on application of company member	
(1)	s.994(1)
(2)	s.994(2)
(3)	s.994(3)
s.460 Order on application of Secretary of State	
(1)	s.995(2) and (3)
(1A)	s.995(1)
(2)	s.995(4)
s.461 Provisions as to petitions and orders under this Part	
(1)	s.996(1)
(2)	s.996(2)
(3)	s.996(2)
(5)	s.998(1) to (4)
(6)	s.997

Provision of Companies Act 1985	Destination in Companies Act 2006
s.652 Registrar may strike defunct company off register	
(1)	s.1000(1)
(2)	s.1000(2)
(3)	s.1000(3)
(4)	s.1001(1)
(5)	ss.1000(4) to (6), 1001(2) to (4)
(6)	ss.1000(7), 1001(5)
(7)	s.1002(1) to (3)
s.652A Registrar may strike private company off register on application	
(1)	s.1003(1) (changed)
(2)	s.1003(2) (changed)
(3)	s.1003(3)
(4)	s.1003(4)
(5)	s.1003(5)
(6)	s.1003(6)
(7)	s.1003(6)
s.652B Duties in connection with making application under section 652A	
(1)	s.1004(1)
(2)	s.1004(2)
(3)	s.1005(1)
(4)	s.1005(2)
(5)	s.1005(3)
(6)	s.1006(1)
(7)	s.1006(2)
(8)	s.1006(3)
(9)	s.1004(3)
s.652C Directors' duties following application under section 652A	
(1)	s.1007(1)
(2)	s.1007(2)
(3)	s.1007(3)
(4)	s.1009(1)
(5)	s.1009(2)
(6)	s.1009(4)
(7)	s.1009(3)
s.652D Sections 652B and 652C: supplementary provisions	
(1)	s.1008(1) and (2)
(2)	s.1008(3)
(3)	s.1008(3)
(4)	s.1008(4)
(5)(c)	ss.1004(4), 1006(1), 1007(2), 1009(4)
(6)	s.1010
(8)	s.1011
s.652E Sections 652B and 652C: enforcement	
(1)	ss.1004(5) and (7), 1005(4) and (6), 1006(4) and (6), 1007(4) and (6), 1009(5) and (7)
(2)	ss.1006(4) and (7), 1007(4) and (7)

Provision of Companies Act 1985	Destination in Companies Act 2006
(3)	ss.1004(6), 1005(5)
(4)	s.1006(5)
(5)	ss.1007(5), 1009(6)
s.654 Property of dissolved company to be bona vacantia	
(1)	s.1012(1)
(2)	s.1012(2)
s.655 Effect on s.654 of company's revival after dissolution	
(1)	s.1034(1)
(2)	s.1034(2)
(3)	s.1034(4)
(4)	s.1034(5)
s.656 Crown disclaimer of property vesting as bona vacantia	
(1)	s.1013(1)
(2)	s.1013(2) (changed)
(3)	s.1013(3) to (5) (changed)
(5)	s.1013(6) and (7)
(6)	s.1013(8)
s.657 Effect of Crown disclaimer under s.656	
(1)	s.1014(1)
(2)	ss.1015(1) and (2), 1016(1) and (2), 1017(1) to (5), 1018(1) to (5), 1019
(4)	s.1020(1) and (2)
(5)	s.1021(1) and (2)
(6)	s.1021(3)
s.658 Liability for rentcharge on company's land after dissolution	
(1)	s.1023(1) and (2)
(2)	s.1023(3)
s.680 Companies capable of being registered under this Chapter	
(1)(a) and (b)	s.1040(1)
(1) (closing words)	s.1040(2), (3) and (6)
(1A)	s.1040(1)
(2)	s.1040(1)
(3)	s.1040(4)
(4)	s.1040(4)
(5)	s.1040(5)
s.683 Definition of "joint stock company"	
(1)	s.1041(1)
(2)	s.1041(2)
s.694 Regulation of oversea companies in respect of their names	
(4)	s.1048(1) and (2) (changed)
(5)	s.1048(3) to (5)
s.695 Service of documents on oversea company	
(1) and (2)	s.1139(2) (changed)

Provision of Companies Act 1985	Destination in Companies Act 2006
s.695A Registrar to whom documents to be delivered: companies to which section 690A applies	
(4)	s.1059
s.699A Credit and financial institutions to which the Bank Branches Directive (89/117/EEC) applies	
(3) ("financial institution")	s.1173(1)
s.704 Registration offices	
(2)	s.1060(1) and (2)
(4)	s.1062 (changed)
(7) and (8)	s.1119(1) and (2)
s.705 Companies' registered numbers	
(1) to (3)	s.1066(1) to (3)
(4)	s.1066(4) and (5)
(5)(za)	s.1066(6)
s.705A Registration of branches of oversea companies	
(1)	s.1067(1) (changed)
(2)	s.1067(1)
(3)	s.1067(2)
(4)	s.1067(3)
(5)	s.1067(4) and (5)
s.707A The keeping of company records by the registrar	
(1)	s.1080(4)
(2)	s.1083(1) (changed)
(3)	s.1084(1) to (3) (changed) and (5)
(4)	s.1084(4)
s.708 Fees payable to registrar	
(1)	s.1063(1) to (3) (changed)
(2) and (3)	s.1063(4) (changed)
(4)	s.1063(6)
(5)	s.1063(5) (changed)
s.709 Inspection, &c. of records kept by the registrar	
(1) opening words	s.1085(1) and s.1100
(1)(a) and (b)	s.1086(1)
(2)	s.1085(2) (changed)
(3)	s.1091(3)
(4)	s.1091(5)
(5)	s.1092(1) and (2)
s.710 Certificate of incorporation	
	s.1065
s.710A Provision and authentication by registrar of documents in non-legible form	
(2)	s.1115(2)
s.710B Documents relating to Welsh companies	
(1) to (3)	s.1104(1) and (2)
(4)	s.1104(3)
(5)	s.1104(4)

Provision of Companies Act 1985	Destination in Companies Act 2006
s.711 Public notice by registrar of receipt and issue of certain documents	
(1)	ss.1064(1) to (3), 1077(1) to (3), 1078(2) and (3) (changed)
(2)	s.1079(4) (changed)
s.713 Enforcement of company's duty to make returns	
(1)	s.1113(1) to (3)
(2) and (3)	s.1113(4) and (5)
s.714 Registrar's index of company and corporate names	
(1)	s.1099(1) to (3) (changed)
(2)	s.1099(4) and (5)
s.715A Interpretation	
(1) ("document") and (2)	s.1114(1)
s.718 Unregistered companies	
(1)	s.1043(1), (3) and (5) (changed)
(2)	s.1043(1)
(3)	s.1043(2) and (5) (changed)
(5)	s.1043(4)
(6)	s.1043(6)
s.719 Power of company to provide for employees on cessation or transfer of business	
(1)	s.247(1)
(2)	s.247(2) (changed)
(3)	s.247(4) to (6) (changed)
(4)	s.247(7) (changed)
s.721 Production and inspection of books where offence suspected	
(1)	s.1132(1) and (2)
(2) to (4)	s.1132(3) to (5)
s.722 Form of company registers, etc	
(1)	ss.1134 and 1135(1) (changed)
(2)	s.1138(1)
(3)	s.1138(2) and (3)
s.723 Use of computers for company records	
(1)	s.1135(1) (changed)
(2)	s.1135(5)
s.723A Obligations of company as to inspections of registers, &c.	
(1)	s.1137(1) and (2)
(2)	s.1137(3)
(3)	s.1137(3)
(4)	s.1137(4)
(6) and (7)	s.1137(5) and (6)
s.725 Service of documents	
(1)	s.1139(1)
(2)	s.1139(4)
(3)	s.1139(4)

Provision of Companies Act 1985	Destination in Companies Act 2006
s.727 Power of court to grant relief in certain cases	
(1) to (3)	s.1157(1) to (3)
s.730 Punishment of offences	
(4)	s.1125(2)
(5)	ss.1121(1) and (3) (changed)
s.731 Summary proceedings	
(1)	s.1127(1) and (2)
(2)	s.1128(1)
(3)	s.1128(2)
(4)	s.1128(4)
s.732 Prosecution by public authorities	
(1)	s.1126(1)
(2)	s.1126(2) (changed)
(3)	s.1129 (changed)
s.734 Criminal proceedings against unincorporated bodies	
(1)	s.1130(1) and (2) (changed)
(2)	s.1130(3)
(3)	s.1130(2)
(4)	s.1130(2)
s.735 "Company", etc	
(1)(a) and (b)	s.1(1)
(1)(c)	s.1171 (changed)
(3)	s.1171
s.736 "Subsidiary"; "holding company" and "wholly-owned subsidiary"	
(1) and (2)	s.1159(1) and (2)
(3)	s.1159(4)
s.736A Provisions supplementing s.736	
(1) to (11)	s.1159(3), Sch.6
s.736B Power to amend ss.736 and 736A	
(1)	s.1160(1)
(3) to (5)	s.1160(2) to (4)
s.737 "Called-up share capital"	
(1) and (2)	s.547
s.738 "Allotment" and "paid up"	
(1)	s.558
(2)	s.583(2) to (3)(d)
(3)	s.583(5)
(4)	s.583(6)
s.739 "Non-cash asset"	
(1) and (2)	s.1163(1) and (2)
s.741 "Director" and "shadow director"	
(1)	s.250
(2)	s.251(1) and (2)
(3)	s.251(3)
s.742 Expressions used in connection with accounts	
(1) ("fixed assets")	s.853(6)
(1) ("parent company")	s.1173(1)
(2)	s.853(4) and (5)

Provision of Companies Act 1985	Destination in Companies Act 2006
s.742A Meaning of "offer to the public"	
(1)	s.756(1) and (2)
(2)	s.756(3)
(3)	s.756(4) and (5)(a) to (d) (changed)
(4)	s.756(4)
(5)	s.756(4)
(6)	s.756(5)(e) and (6)
s.742B Meaning of "banking company"	
(1) to (3)	s.1164(1) to (3)
s.742C Meaning of "insurance company" and "authorised insurance company"	
(1) to (4)	s.1165(2) to (4)
(5)	s.1165(8)
s.743 "Employees' share scheme"	
	s.1166
s.744 Expressions used generally in this Act	
"articles"	s.18(4)
"the Companies Acts"	s.2(1) and (2) (changed)
"the court"	s.1156(1) to (3) (changed)
"debenture"	s.738
"EEA State"	s.1170
"equity share capital"	s.548
"the Gazette"	s.1173(1)
"hire-purchase agreement"	s.1173(1)
"insurance market activity"	s.1165(7)
"officer"	ss.1121(2), 1173(1)
"oversea company"	s.1044 (changed)
"prescribed"	s.1167
"the registrar of companies" and "the registrar"	s.1060(3)
"regulated activity"	s.1173(1)
"share"	s.540(1) and (4)
s.744A Index of defined expressions	
	Sch.8
Sch.2 Interpretation of references to "beneficial interest"	
Part 1 References in sections 23, 145, 146 and 148	
para.1(1)	ss.139(1), 672(1)
para.1(2)	ss.139(2), 672(2)
para.1(3)	ss.139(3), 672(3)
para.1(4)	ss.139(4), 672(4)
para.2(3)	s.672(5)
para.2(4)	s.672(6)
para.3(1) and (2)	ss.140(1) and (2), 673(1) and (2)
para.4(1)	ss.138(1) and (2), 674
para.4(2)	s.138(1)
para.4(3)	s.674
para.5(1)	ss.675(1) and (2), 676
para.5(2)	ss.139(5) and (6), 140(3), 675(1) and (2)
para.5(3)	ss.139(6), 140(4), 676

Provision of Companies Act 1985	Destination in Companies Act 2006
Sch.4 Form and content of company accounts	
Part 3 Notes to the accounts	
para.56(2) and (3)	ss.382(6), 465(6)
Part 7 Interpretation of Schedule	
para.94(1) and (2)	s.411(6)
Sch.7B Specified persons, descriptions of disclosures etc for the purposes of section 245G	
Part 1 Specified persons	
	s.461(1)
Part 2 Specified descriptions of disclosures	
	s.461(4)
Part 3 Overseas regulatory bodies	
	s.461(5) and (6)
Sch.10A Parent and subsidiary undertakings: supplementary provisions	
para.1	Sch.7 para.1
para.2(1)	Sch.7 para.2(1)
para.2(2)	Sch.7 para.2(2)
para.3(1)	Sch.7 para.3(1)
para.3(2)	Sch.7 para.3(2)
para.3(2)	Sch.7 para.3(3)
para.4(1)	Sch.7 para.4(1)
para.4(2)	Sch.7 para.4(2)
para.4(3)	Sch.7 para.4(3)
para.5(1)	Sch.7 para.5(1)
para.5(2)	Sch.7 para.5(2)
para.6	Sch.7 para.6
para.7(1)	Sch.7 para.7(1)
para.7(2)	Sch.7 para.7(2)
para.8	Sch.7 para.8
para.9(1)	Sch.7 para.9(1)
para.9(2)	Sch.7 para.9(2)
para.9(3)	Sch.7 para.9(3)
para.10	Sch.7 para.10
para.11	Sch.7 para.11
Sch.13 Provisions supplementing and interpreting sections 324 to 328	
Part 4 Provisions with respect to register of directors' interests to be kept under section 325	
para.27	s.809(2) and (3)
Sch.14 Overseas branch registers	
Part 1 Countries and territories in which overseas branch register may be kept	
	s.129(2)
Part 2 General provisions with respect to overseas branch registers	
para.1(1) and (2)	ss.130(1), 135(3)
para.1(3)	ss.130(2) and (3), 135(4) and (5)
para.2(1)	s.131(1)
para.3(1)	s.134(1) and (2) (changed)

Provision of Companies Act 1985	Destination in Companies Act 2006
para.3(2)	s.134(3)
para.4(1)	s.132(1) and (2) (changed)
para.4(2)	s.132(3) and (4)
para.5	s.133(1) and (2)
para.6	s.135(1) and (2)
para.7	s.131(4)
Sch.15A Written resolutions of private companies	
Part 1 Exceptions	
para.1	s.288(2)
Part 2 Adaptation of procedural requirements	
para.3(1) and (2)	ss.571(7), 573(5)
para.5(1) and (2)	ss.695(2), 698(2)
para.5(3) and (4)	ss.696(2), 699(2)
para.6(1)	ss.717(2), 718(2)
para.6(2)	s.717(2)
para.6(3)	s.718(2)
para.7	s.188(5)
Sch.15B Provisions subject to which ss.425–427 have effect in their application to mergers and divisions of public companies	
para.1	ss.907(1) and (2), 922(1) and (2)
para.2(1)	ss.905(1), 906(1) to (3), 920(1), 921(1) to (4)
para.2(2)	ss.905(2) and (3), 920(2)
para.2(3)	s.920(3)
para.3	ss.908(1) and (3), 909(1) and (7), 911(1), (2) and (4), 912, 923(1) and (4), 924(1) and (7), 925(5), 926(1), (2) and (4), 927(1) to (3), 928
para.4(1)	ss.908(2), 923(2)
para.4(2)	s.923(3)
para.5(1)	ss.909(2) and (3), 924(2) and (3)
para.5(2)	ss.909(3), 924(3)
para.5(3)	ss.909(4), 924(4)
para.5(4)	s.935(1) (changed)
para.5(6)	s.935(2)
para.5(7)	ss.909(5), 924(5)
para.5(8)	ss.909(6), 924(6)
para.6(1)	ss.910(1), 911(3), 925(1), 926(3)
para.6(2)	ss.910(2), 925(2)
para.6(3)	ss.910(3), 925(3) (changed)
para.6(4)	ss.910(4), 925(4)
para.7	ss.914, 930
para.8(1)	ss.913(1), 929(1)
para.8(2)	ss.913(2), 929(2)
para.9(1)	s.939(1)
para.9(2)	s.939(1) and (2)
para.9(3)	s.939(3) and (4)
para.9(4)	s.939(5)
para.10(1)	ss.918(1), 932(1)

Provision of Companies Act 1985	Destination in Companies Act 2006
para.10(2)	ss.916(3) to (5), 918(2) to (4), 932(2) to (5)
para.11(1)	ss.933(1) to (3), 934(1)
para.11(2)	s.933(1) to (3)
para.11(3)	s.934(1)
para.11(4)	s.934(2) to (4)
para.12(1)	ss.915(1) and (6), 917(1) and (6)
para.12(2)	s.915(2)
para.12(3)	s.915(3) to (5)
para.12(4)	s.917(2)
para.12(5)	ss.917(3) to (5), 931(3) and (5)
para.13(1)	s.931(1)
para.13(2)	s.931(2)
para.13(3)	s.931(3), (4) and (6)
para.14(1)	s.916(1)
para.14(2)	s.916(2)
para.14(3)	s.916(3) to (5)
para.15(1)	s.940(1)
para.15(2)	s.940(2)
para.15(3)	s.940(3)
Sch.20 Vesting of disclaimed property; protection of third parties	
Part 2 Crown disclaimer under section 656 (Scotland only)	
para.5	s.1022(1)
para.6	s.1022(2)
para.7	s.1022(3)
para.8	s.1022(4) and (5)
para.9	s.1022(6)

COMPANIES ACT 1989

1. Section 130(6) of the Companies Act 1989 (power by regulations to apply provisions relating to company contracts and execution of documents by companies to overseas companies) is re-enacted in section 1045 of the Companies Act 2006.
2. Section 207 of the Companies Act 1989 (transfer of securities) is re-enacted in sections 783, 784(3), 785 and 788 of the Companies Act 2006.

INDEX